The premier law-enforcement academies in the United States (reading top to bottom): the J. Edgar Hoover FBI Building in Washington, D.C., which has its training academy in Quantico, Virginia; the Northwestern University Traffic Institute in Evanston, Illinois; and the Southern Police Institute in Louisville, Kentucky. Photographs courtesy of the institutions.

The Encyclopedia of Police Science
Second Edition

Editor
William G. Bailey

Editorial Board Members
Victor G. Strecher
Larry T. Hoover
Jerry L. Dowling

GARLAND PUBLISHING, INC.
New York & London
1995

Library of Congress Cataloging-in-Publication Data

The encyclopedia of police science / editor, William G. Bailey : editorial board
    members, Victor G. Strecher, Larry T. Hoover, Jerry L. Dowling. — 2nd ed.
        p.   cm. — (Garland reference library of the humanities ;
  vol. 1729)
    Includes bibliographical references and index.
    ISBN 0-8153-1331-4
    1. Police—United States—Encyclopedias.   I. Bailey, William G.,
  1947–   . II. Series.
    HV7901 .E53   1995
    363.2'03—dc20   94-46828
                                                  CIP

Printed on acid-free, 250-year-life paper
Manufactured in the United States of America

Contents

Editor's Note

The first edition of *The Encyclopedia of Police Science* was published in 1989 with one hundred forty-three entries written by some of the best police scholars and practitioners in the country. As a seminal effort the encyclopedia filled a void in the criminal justice literature by providing a ready reference to the little-known field of policing. Little known? Yes, because the daily news and our popular culture are the main conduits for knowledge and they are inadequate, if not misleading. On the news front one name has come to symbolize the worst in American policing, that of Rodney King. These days it is almost impossible to speak or write about police without his mention. There are nine references to, and one complete entry on, King in this encyclopedia.

Were the Los Angeles police officers who subdued Rodney King in such a graphic manner, as captured on video, right or wrong? The first trial cleared the officers of wrongdoing. Then after a terrible riot and federal intervention the second trial reversed the decision. Subsequently, Los Angeles Chief of Police Daryl Gates was forced to resign and Rodney King won a large settlement from the city. In the aftermath the public drew lessons from the King incident concerning police brutality, such as how the scales of justice tip, where America stands on racial equality, and other painful or reassuring lessons. But perhaps what was missing in the swirl of emotions was a look back at the riot itself. When all hell broke loose we got to see what life would be like *without* law enforcement. Of course one could say the *police* caused the riot, or LAPD procedures caused it, or a few rogue cops precipitated the violence. The other choices are that the police acted within bounds and the riot had been on near-boil for years. Whatever the cause or causes—not to forget that socio-economic pressures ranked high—any display of utter mayhem should remind us why we depend on police. They restored order in Los Angeles that day and police across the country continue to maintain order day in and day out around the clock. The public takes this for granted, yet thinks less of the police because of the King incident.

Novels, television, and films glamorize police beyond anything realistic, although lately the trend has been toward achieving more authenticity, which in effect raises our expectations. "You are there" ride-along cop shows play to large audiences and make police appear to be everywhere at once, screeching their patrol cars and then smashing in doors to raid drug dens. Not quite Robocop, whose invincibility outshines his metallic body, flesh-and-blood police also get the job done. Interestingly in light of the King incident, fictional law officers rough up suspects with impunity and even cheers. The public embraces all the Dirty Harrys and Harriets as long as they don't breathe real air. Fiction admits excess. Drama's the thing. On the contrary, those who actually ply the trade must live with routine and within regulations. On a daily basis police operations split about 80/20. Eighty percent of the time the work is mundane. The remaining twenty percent calls for the type of heroics portrayed in fiction, and then the heroics are not so dashing and final. Popular culture can also hold up a smoky mirror. At this writing police managers seek to return to the depiction of police as gentle guardians. The foot-weary but stalwart officers of yesteryear are the answer to today's mounting crime. Proponents of community policing believe implicitly in greater personal contact, and in the bargain the public will once again learn to trust the thin blue line.

For this edition seventy new entries expand the discussion of American police. More than one writer has contributed an entry on some topics, for example, citizen complaints, policing multi-ethnic communities, community-oriented policing, terrorism, and youth gangs. Four out of the five bring us back to Rodney King, as well they should. If by terrorism one includes riots, then all five pertain to King. Where required, entries from the first edition have been updated. More legal cases and statistical studies have been added. An international perspective, in particular British policing, Interpol, and cooperation in the war on drugs, has a voice. The bibliographies contain a flurry of recent references to augment the previous listings. Each new edition of an encyclopedia throws out the challenge to collect fresh information, to snare what might have been previously elusive, and to produce a work that encapsulates every aspect of the subject without being cursory. That was my goal. I reconvened the editorial board: Dr. Victor G. Strecher, Dr. Larry T. Hoover, and Jerry L. Dowling, J.D., all respected professors of criminal justice at Sam Houston State University. Together we compiled the list of new entries. As before, I sought writers both in and outside of academe, and ones who espoused a myriad of opinions. Several graduate students assisted, who by the time of publication will be full-fledged professionals. Any unsigned entries were written by the editor.

It has been my pleasure to communicate on the telephone or by letter to the new and former writers for this edition. I am doubly grateful because everyone I contacted had more work stacked in the "in" box than in the "out" box. The writers' willingness to contribute to the project along with their best wishes made it easier for me to get under way and to finish. At Garland Publishing, I thank Gary Kuris for saying, "It's time for a new edition," when I was dreaming of sweet escape. Production manager Helga McCue insisted on a clean text free of errors. She has my appreciation, as do Jane Kolleeny, who edited the entire manuscript for Garland, and Diane Ersepke, who proofread every word and made corrections. At a time when meticulous editing is supposedly on the wane these three professionals caught whatever was amiss. Computer-whiz Chuck Bartelt did a fine job of converting the original material to disk and of integrating it with the new for desktop publishing. Alexander Metro took over in the later stages and called me relentlessly to clarify my intentions and to wrap up the encyclopedia. Every editor who thinks he or she has sent in a splendid product should have such taskmasters. Everyone else at Garland even remotely connected with bringing out the second edition has my heartfelt thanks.

William G. Bailey

Contributors

Geoffrey P. Alpert, Professor, teaches in the College of Criminal Justice, University of South Carolina.

Austin A. Andersen is Chief of the Legal Research Unit, Legal Counsel Division, at FBI Headquarters.

Emilie Andersen Allan is a Professor of Behavorial Sciences, St. Francis College.

Malcolm Anderson is Provost of Law and Social Sciences and Dean of Social Sciences, the University of Edinburgh, Scotland.

Nancy C. Anson is Adjunct Professor of Sociology, Albany State College.

Richard H. Anson is a Professor of Criminal Justice, Albany State College.

David A. Armstrong is an Assistant Professor of Criminal Justice, McNeese State University. He consults in the fields of police training, administration, and management, and also serves as the Training Coordinator for the local Marshal's Office. He was a police officer for 15 years, holding ranks from patrolman to Police Chief.

Richard M. Ayers, former Chief of the Management Science Unit at the FBI Academy, is currently a management consultant in Fredericksburg, Virginia.

William G. Bailey, Associate Professor, is the Criminal Justice Bibliographer, Newton Gresham Library, Sam Houston State University.

David H. Bayley is a Professor of Criminal Justice, SUNY at Albany.

Donald C. Becker is an Associate Professor of Public Service Administration, University of Central Florida.

Joanne Belknap is a Professor of Criminal Justice, University of Cincinnati.

William H. Bieck is a Principal Associate with Public Administration Service, a consulting firm in McLean, Virginia.

Richard A. Blak is a police psychologist in Fresno, California.

Michael B. Blankenship, Associate Professor of Criminal Justice, Memphis State University, was formerly a police officer for 7 years in Asheville, North Carolina.

William P. Bloss is a doctoral candidate in the College of Criminal Justice, Sam Houston State University, and teaches at San Jacinto College North.

Mark Blumberg is a Professor of Criminal Justice, Central Missouri State University.

Diane C. Bordner is the Director of Professional Research Services, Inc., Atlanta, Georgia.

Thomas J. Bouquard, a veteran Captain with the Buffalo Fire Department, has also been a New York State Trooper.

Anthony V. Bouza, retired Chief of Police, Minneapolis Police Department, is now an author of repute. His latest books are *A Carpet of Blue: An Ex-Cop Takes a Tough Look at America's Drug Problem* and *How to Stop Crime.*

Dorothy H. Bracey, Professor, chairs the Department of Anthropology, John Jay College of Criminal Justice.

Steven G. Brandl, Professor, teaches in the Criminal Justice Program, University of Wisconsin, Milwaukee.

Michael F. Brown, Professor, teaches in the Criminal Justice Department, Southeast Missouri State University.

Joseph P. Buckley, III, is the President of John E. Reid and Associates, where he has conducted over 5,000 polygraph examinations.

Noel C. Bufe is the Director of the Northwestern University Traffic Institute, Evanston, Illinois.

John M. Burkoff is a Professor of Law, University of Pittsburgh School of Law.

James W. Burrows, an independent researcher, jointly prepared the original study from which this abridgment was made for the Criminal Conspiracies Division, Office of Criminal Justice Programs, Law Enforcement Assistance Administration.

Harry M. Caldwell is a Professor of Law, Pepperdine University.

William F. Carfield is Professor Emeritus, College of Law Enforcement, Eastern Kentucky University.

David L. Carter is a Professor of Criminal Justice at Michigan State University.

Jan and Marcia Chaiken conduct research for Abt Associates, Inc., Cambridge, Massachusetts.

Samuel G. Chapman retired as Professor in the Department of Political Science and Law Enforcement Administration, University of Oklahoma. Now in Nevada, he devotes his time to writing and research.

Peter W. Colby is a Professor in the Department of Public Services, Brevard Center, University of Central Florida.

John A. Conley, Professor, Criminal Justice Faculty, University of Wisconsin—Milwaukee, is a noted criminal justice historian.

Gary W. Cordner is Professor of Police Administration in the College of Law Enforcement, Eastern Kentucky University. He has worked as a police officer in Ocean City, Maryland; served as a consultant to the Pontiac, Michigan, and Baltimore County, Maryland Police Departments; and been police chief in St. Michaels, Maryland.

Catherine A. Cotter, an independent researcher, jointly prepared the original study from which this abridgment was made for the Criminal Conspiracies Division, Office of Criminal Justice Programs, Law Enforcement Assistance Administration.

Steven M. Cox, Professor, Department of Law Enforcement Administration, Western Illinois University, also serves as a consultant to numerous criminal justice agencies.

G. David Curry, Ph.D., teaches in the Department of Sociology/Anthropology, West Virginia University.

Phillip A. Davidson, Director, Tennessee Law Enforcement Training Academy, founded and trained the SWAT Team for the Nashville Police Department.

Michael Davis is Senior Research Associate in the Center for the Study of Ethics in the Professions, Illinois Institute of Technology.

Scott H. Decker is an Associate Professor and Chairperson for the Department of Administration of Justice, University of Missouri, St. Louis.

William DeJong conducts research for Abt Associates, Inc., Cambridge, Massachusetts.

Joseph C. DeLadurantey, Captain, is the Commanding Officer for the Scientific Investigation Division, Los Angeles Police Department.

Rolando V. del Carmen is a Professor of Criminal Justice, College of Criminal Justice, Sam Houston State University.

Ronald G. DeLord, J.D., is President of the Combined Law Enforcement Associations of Texas. He has served with both the Beaumont and Mesquite, Texas, Police Departments.

William Dienstein is a Professor Emeritus of Sociology and Criminology, California State University, Fresno.

Marion T. Doss, Jr., J.D., is an Associate Professor in the Department of Political Science, James Madison University. He served in the U.S. Navy from 1954 to 1980 as a midshipman, surface line officer, naval aviator, and intelligence officer.

Jerry L. Dowling, J.D., Professor, teaches in the College of Criminal Justice, Sam Houston State University. Formerly he was a Special Agent, Federal Bureau of Investigation, working in the Dallas–Fort Worth area.

Roger Dunham is a Professor of Sociology, University of Miami.

William G. Eckert is the Director of the Milton Helpern International Center for the Forensic Sciences, Wichita State University.

Steven A. Egger, Associate Professor, teaches Criminal Justice at Sangamon State University, Springfield, Illinois. Previously he was project director for the Homicide Assessment and Lead Tracking System, New York State Police, Albany.

Katherine W. Ellison, social psychologist, has worked for more than 20 years as a consultant and lecturer to law-enforcement agencies around the country. She is a Professor, Department of Psychology, Montclair State College.

David G. Epstein is with the Office of Counter-Terrorism, U.S. Department of State. Formerly he was Assistant Director for Faculty Management, Federal Law Enforcement Training Center, and Chief of Police in Savannah, Georgia.

Edna Erez, LL.B., Ph.D., is a Professor, Criminal Justice Studies, Kent State University.

Ronald W. Fagan, Professor of Sociology, teaches in Seaver College, Pepperdine University.

Randy Farrar, J.D., Ph.D., is Staff Attorney with the Federal Court, Eastern District of Texas, and Adjunct Professor of Criminal Justice, University of Texas at Tyler.

Edward A. Farris, Professor, teaches in the Department of Criminal Justice, New Mexico State University.

Michael Feldberg, Ph.D., teaches Criminal Justice at Metropolitan College, Boston University. In addition, he trains police in ethical behavior.

Ginny Field is a writing instructor at the FBI Academy, Quantico, Virginia.

Paul G. Flynn is a Professor of Law, Pepperdine University.

Vern L. Folley has served as a police Patrolman and Sergeant for the Tucson, Arizona Police Department, as Chief of Police for Albion, Washington, and Bismarck, North Dakota, as Chief of Nuclear Public Safety and Security for the Tennessee Valley Authority, as Director of the Southcentral Pennsylvania Criminal Justice Training Center, among other law-enforcement occupations.

Gail S. Funke conducts research for the Jefferson Institute, Washington, D.C.

James J. Fyfe is a Professor of Justice, American University, and a senior fellow of the Police Foundation. He was a member of the New York City Police Department for 16 years and left that agency with the rank of lieutenant.

Jennifer F. Gardner is completing her graduate work in psychology at the University of Alabama.

Jennifer M. Garrison is a research assistant to Dr. Rene J. Herrera, Department of Biological Sciences, Florida International University. Her special interest is in forensic science.

Bruce W. Gay, Assistant Professor, teaches Criminal Justice at Western Carolina University.

Vernon J. Geberth retired with over 20 years of service in the New York City Police Department. He was the Commanding Officer of the Bronx Homicide Task Force with a case load of some four hundred murders a year. Lieutenant Commander Geberth received over 60 medals for bravery and exceptional police work.

Gilbert Geis, Professor, teaches in the Program of Social Ecology, University of California, Irvine. He is former president of the American Society of Criminology and a winner of that group's Edwin H. Sutherland Award for outstanding research contributions to the field.

Stephen D. Gladis works as a Special Agent with the Office of Congressional and Public Affairs, Federal Bureau of Investigation.

Denis O. Gray, Ph.D., teaches in the Department of Psychology, North Carolina State University.

Edith Greene is an Assistant Professor of Psychology, University of Colorado in Colorado Springs.

Mary Jeanette Hageman worked with police and their families from 1971 to 1981. She has taught in six colleges and universities across the United States, most recently with Virginia Commonwealth University.

Richard N. Harris, Associate Professor of Sociology at St. John's University, is also a clinical social worker.

Armand P. Hernandez is an Associate Professor in the School of Justice Studies, Arizona State University, Tempe. He has been a police officer in Pusan, Korea, Newport News and Fort Eustis, Virginia, Cleveland, Ohio, and San Jose, California.

Rene J. Herrera is an Associate Professor of Biological Sciences, Florida International University.

Robert J. Homant is a Professor of Criminal Justice and program coordinator in Human Services and Corrections, University of De-

troit Mercy. He was a prison psychologist for 8 years and currently has a private practice in addition to his academic duties.

Larry T. Hoover is a Professor of Criminal Justice, Sam Houston State University. Previously he served with the Michigan Law Enforcement Officers Training Council and Lansing, Michigan, Police Department. Dr. Hoover is a past president of the Academy of Criminal Justice Sciences.

Frank Horvath is a Professor of Criminal Justice, School of Criminal Justice, Michigan State University. He is a frequent consultant on the use of polygraph testing and has testified before a number of state legislatures regarding the use of detection of deception procedures.

William Imfeld is the Assistant Special Agent in charge of the Albany, New York, FBI Field Office.

John K. Irwin is a Professor of Sociology and the Department Chair, San Francisco State University.

Leanor Boulin Johnson is an Associate Professor in the Department of Family Resources and Human Development, Arizona State University.

Stephen Jurovics, Ph.D., is a consultant with a private corporation in Raleigh, North Carolina.

Victor E. Kappeler, Associate Professor, College of Law Enforcement, Department of Police Studies, Eastern Kentucky University, served as a police officer and criminal investigator for the Commonwealth of Kentucky from 1978 to 1985.

Clifford Karchmer is a Senior Researcher with the Police Executive Research Forum.

Andra J. Katz is a doctoral candidate in the School of Criminal Justice at Michigan State University and is a colleague of David L. Carter.

Roger L. Kemp is the city manager of Placentia, California. He holds M.P.A., M.B.A., and Ph.D. degrees and is a graduate of the Program for Senior Executives in State and Local Government at Harvard University. Dr. Kemp is on the faculty at the Center for Public Policy, California State University, Long Beach, and at the Graduate School of Management, Golden Gate University, Los Angeles.

Kimberley L. Kempf is an Associate Professor, Department of Administration of Justice, University of Missouri, St. Louis.

Malcolm W. Klein is a Professor of Sociology and the Director of the Center for Research in Crime and Social Control at the University of Southern California.

Carl B. Klockars, Associate Professor of Criminal Justice, teaches in the Department of Sociology, University of Delaware.

Peter B. Kraska is an Assistant Professor, Department of Criminal Justice Studies, Kent State University.

Peter C. Kratcoski, Professor, is Chairman of Criminal Justice Studies, Kent State University.

David Lester, Professor, teaches in the Psychology Program, Stockton State College, New Jersey.

Michael J. Lieberman, J.D., is Associate Director of the Anti-Defamation League of B'nai B'rith in Washington, D.C.

John Light is a Training Specialist, Southern Illinois Criminal Justice Training, Mobile Team 15, Carbondale, Illinois.

Elizabeth F. Loftus is a Professor of Psychology and Adjunct Professor of Law at the University of Washington.

Lesli Kay Lord, Ph.D., is a veteran of the Field Operations unit, San Diego Police Department. She has worked in Patrol, Traffic Investigations, and as a training officer at the Police Academy. She teaches for the San Diego Community College District, San Diego State University, and Chapman College.

Vivian B. Lord, Ph.D., manages the Justice Services Department for the North Carolina Justice Academy in Salemburg.

Roy Lotz, Associate Professor, teaches in the Department of Sociology, John Jay College of Criminal Justice.

Paul Louis, Associate Professor of Criminal Justice, Memphis State Unversity, worked for 7$^1/_2$ years as a juvenile probation supervisor, juvenile and adult probation officer, alcoholism-risk assessment officer for DWI offenders, and family counselor in Texas.

Peter A. Lupsha is a Professor in the Department of Political Science, University of New Mexico.

Donal E.J. MacNamara is an Emeritus Professor of Criminal Justice, John Jay College of Criminal Justice.

R. Bruce McBride is the Director of University Public Safety for the State University of New York. In this capacity, he is responsible for coordinating law-enforcement activities on SUNY's 26 campuses. He became a faculty member at Utica College of Syracuse University in 1984.

William U. McCormack, J.D., is a legal instructor at the FBI Academy.

David McDowall, Professor, teaches in the Institute of Criminal Justice and Criminology, University of Maryland at College Park.

J. Thomas McEwen is a Senior Researcher at the Institute for Law and Justice, Alexandria, Virginia.

Marilyn D. McShane, is Associate Professor in the Department of Criminal Justice, California State University, San Bernardino.

Brendan Maguire is a Professor in the Department of Sociology, Anthropology, and Social Work, Western Illinois University.

George F. Maher, Chief of Operations for the Nassau County Police Department, started as a Patrolman in 1951. He organized and was former Team Leader for the Department's Hostage Negotiating Team, 1974–1979.

Peter K. Manning, Professor, teaches in the Departments of Sociology and Psychiatry,

Michigan State University, and at the Centre for Socio-Legal Studies, Wolfson College, Oxford.

Harry L. Marsh is an Associate Professor in the Department of Criminology, Indiana State University, Terre Haute. He spent 13 years of his 22-year Air Force career as a Special Agent with the Air Force Office of Special Investigations and the Department of Defense's Defense Investigative Service.

Stephen Mastrofski is an Associate Professor of Administration of Justice, Pennsylvania State University.

E.R. Menzel is the Director of the Center for Forensic Studies, Texas Tech University.

Greg Meyer is a police tactics consultant, trainer, and expert witness who specializes in nonlethal weapons. His consulting business is in Bellflower, California.

Joseph Missonellie is a detective with the Wyckoff, New Jersey, Police Department. He is a former employee of the N.J. Police Training Commission and has served as an instructor at the Bergen County Police Academy on the use of videotape.

Eric W. Moore, J.D., Ph.D., teaches Criminal Justice at Corpus Christi State University.

Frank Morn is a Professor of Criminal Justice Sciences, Illinois State University.

Stanley E. Morris is the Director of the United States Marshals Service.

Gregory B. Morrison is a Doctoral Candidate in Criminology, Law & Society at the University of California, Irvine. Before seeking the Ph.D, he spent time as a police officer and firearms instructor and most recently was the Operations Manager and a Senior Instructor for the American Pistol Institute at Gunsite Ranch, Arizona.

Bill Murphy is the Public Information Officer for the New York City Transit Police Department.

James J. Ness is Director of the Administration of Justice Programs, Barton County Community College, Great Bend, Kansas.

Robert S. Newsom retired from the San Diego County Sheriff's department after an active career (1947–1976). He was with the Fraud-Arson Unit for 10 of those years, Commander of the Detective Bureau for 4 years, and left as Chief of Administration.

Robert E. Nichols, Jr., is a training officer with the Wisconsin State Patrol Academy.

Elaine Niederhoffer teaches in the New York City Public School System. Married to the late Arthur Niederhoffer, she shared his interest in police, assisted him with his research, and today continues his work.

Gabriel E. Novick is a Ph.D. candidate in the Biological Sciences Department at Florida International University.

Carla M. Noziglia is the Director of the Crime Laboratory, Las Vegas Metropolitan Police, having learned the skills of her profession while working at various other crime laboratories and hospitals since 1963. She is past President of the American Society of Crime Laboratory Directors.

Michael O'Brien is an Assistant State Attorney and Chief of the Economic Crimes Unit in the Office of the State Attorney, Orlando, Florida.

Timothy N. Oettmeier, Ph.D., is a veteran of the Houston Police Department's Field Operations Command.

Lawrence R. O'Leary, Ph.D., is the Director of O'Leary, Brokaw & Associates, Inc., a St. Louis based consulting firm that specializes in the development and administration of assessment centers for law-enforcement agencies.

Elinor Ostrom is a Professor of Political Science, Indiana University at Bloomington.

Denny F. Pace, Professor and Department Head, Department of Public Services, Police, Fire, Human Services, and Public Administration Programs, Long Beach City College.

Roger B. Parks is an Associate Professor of Public Management and Public Policy, Indiana University at Bloomington.

Kenneth J. Peak is a Professor in the Department of Criminal Justice, University of Nevada, Reno.

Stephen L. Percy, Assistant Professor, teaches in the Department of Government and Foreign Affairs, University of Virginia.

David M. Petersen is a Professor, Department of Sociology, Georgia State University.

Joseph L. Peterson, Professor, teaches in the Department of Criminal Justice, University of Illinois, Chicago.

Erdwin H. Pfuhl, Jr., retired recently as a Professor, Department of Sociology, Arizona State University. He now lives in Montana.

Mark R. Pogrebin, Professor, teaches in the Graduate School of Public Affairs, University of Colorado at Denver.

James M. Poland is a Professor, School of Health and Human Services, Division of Criminal Justice, California State University, Sacramento.

Eric D. Poole is a Professor of Public Administration, University of Colorado at Denver.

Henry Poole serves as coordinator of the Murders Unsolved Team of the North Carolina Bureau of Investigation, Raleigh, North Carolina.

Frank R. Prassel, former investigating and prosecuting officer for the U.S. Army, earned J.D. and Ph.D. degrees from the University of Texas at Austin. Presently he is an attorney serving as Chairman of Criminal Justice Studies, University of Arkansas, Fayetteville.

Christine Rose Ramirez is studying law enforcement in the College of Criminal Justice, Sam Houston State University.

Richard A. Raub, formerly with the Illinois State Police, is President of Raub Associates, a management consulting firm.

Thomas F. Rich is a researcher with the ENFORTH Corporation, Cambridge, Massachusetts.

Malcolm Richards is Chief Superintendent, Gloucestershire Constabulary, and a Ph.D. candidate at the Centre for the Study of Public Order, University of Leicester, England.

James F. Richardson is a Professor of History, University of Akron, and a revered police historian.

Charles F. Rinkevich is Director of the Federal Law Enforcement Training Center, Glynco, Georgia. He has served with the U.S. Law Enforcement Assistance Administration as Regional Administrator in both Philadelphia and Atlanta, and as Executive Director of the Pennsylvania State Crime Commission, among other appointments.

Douglas Ruch is a researcher with the Police Executive Research Forum.

Harley M. Sagara is the Supervising Criminalist, Los Angeles County Sheriffs Department, Criminalistics Laboratory.

Ferdinand Schoeman is a Professor, Department of Philosophy, University of South Carolina.

Daniel L. Schofield is Chief of the Legal Instruction Unit at the FBI Academy, Quantico, Virginia.

Donald O. Schultz is the Coordinator of the Criminal Justice Program for Broward Community College, Pompano Beach, Florida. In addition, he teaches at the Broward County Police Academy.

Forrest R. Scogin is Associate Professor of Psychology, University of Alabama.

Joseph E. Scuro, Jr., is a police legal advisor and law-enforcement consultant in San Antonio, Texas.

Dale K. Sechrest is Associate Professor of Criminal Justice, California State University, San Bernardino.

Stan Shernock is Associate Professor and Chair of the Department of Justice Studies and Sociology at Norwich University in Northfield, Vermont.

Jerome H. Skolnick, J.D., teaches in the School of Law, University of California, Berkeley.

Sam S. Souryal, is a Professor of Police Science and Administration, College of Criminal Justice, Sam Houston State University. His professional experience includes 17 years of police service with the Cairo Metropolitan Police, Egypt.

Darrell J. Steffensmeier is Professor of Sociology, Pennsylvania State University.

Michael Steinman, Associate Professor, teaches in the Department of Political Science, University of Nebraska—Lincoln.

James W. Stevens is a Professor of Criminal Justice, University of Texas at Arlington.

B. Grant Stitt, Associate Professor, teaches in the Department of Criminal Justice, the University of Nevada, Reno.

Anthony V. Stone, Ph.D., M.P.H., has a psychology practice in Smyrna, Georgia.

Ezra Stotland is a Professor Emeritus of Psychology and former Director of Programs in Society and Justice, University of Washington.

John G. Stratton is a Clinician-Consultant with Psychological Services West, Hermosa Beach, California.

Victor G. Strecher, Professor, College of Criminal Justice, Sam Houston State University, was previously Dean of the same college and Director of the Texas Criminal Justice Center.

Richard J. Terrill is a Professor, Department of Criminal Justice, Georgia State University.

W. Clinton Terry, III, is a Professor, School of Public Affairs & Services, Criminal Justice Department, Florida International University.

Howard D. Teten, an investigative consultant living in Manassas, Virginia, was a police

officer in San Leandro, California, from 1958 to 1962 and a Special Agent with the Federal Bureau of Investigation from 1962 until his retirement in 1986. During his 17-year assignment as a Supervisor and Unit Chief in the FBI Training Division, he prepared more than 650 psychological criminal profiles and is considered the originator of the FBI's profiling program.

James M. Tien is a researcher with the ENFORTH Corporation, Cambridge, Massachusetts.

Donald A. Torres, Professor, John Jay College of Criminal Justice, was a Special Agent for the U.S. Secret Service and U.S. Army Intelligence and an inspector (criminal investigator) for the Inspection Services, Internal Revenue Service.

Harvey Treger, Professor of Social Work and Criminal Justice, University of Illinois, Chicago, is past President of the Police–Social Work Association.

Ralph F. Turner is a Professor Emeritus, School of Criminal Justice, Michigan State University.

Joseph B. Vaughn, Associate Professor, Department of Criminal Justice Administration, Central Missouri State University, was formerly Chief Deputy Sheriff of Camden County, Missouri, and adjunct faculty member at Drury College, Springfield, Missouri.

Michael S. Vaughn is an Assistant Professor, Department of Criminal Justice, Georgia State University.

Joseph J. Vince, Jr., is a Special Agent with the Bureau of Alcohol, Tobacco and Firearms, United States Treasury Department. He won Special Agent of the Year in 1976 and 1977.

John M. Violanti, Ph.D., works for the New York State Police and also teaches in the University of Buffalo School of Medicine, Social and Preventive Medicine Division. He was a police officer for 22 years.

Donald B. Walker is an Associate Professor, Criminal Justice Studies, Kent State University.

Samuel Walker is Professor of Criminal Justice, University of Nebraska at Omaha.

Richard H. Ward is a Professor of Criminology, University of Illinois, Chicago.

Steven M. Ward is the Chief of Security at the University of Southern California, Los Angeles. He is also past Director of the National Sheriffs' Institute.

Billy L. Wayson conducts research for the Jefferson Institute, Washington, D.C.

Donald J. Weisenhorn retired as Professor, College of Criminal Justice, Sam Houston State University. He continues to maintain a lively interest in the field.

Paul M. Whisenand is a Professor of Criminal Justice, California State University, Long Beach, and President of PMW Associates.

Gordon P. Whitaker is a Professor of Political Science and Faculty Research Associate in the Institute for Research in Social Science at the University of North Carolina, Chapel Hill.

Frank Williams is a Professor, Department of Criminal Justice, California State University, San Bernardino. His military service record includes a stint as Chief of Police, Chief of Law Enforcement, and Chief of Corrections at Chanute Air Force Base.

Donald C. Witham is Chief of the Management Science Unit at the FBI Academy, Quantico, Virginia.

Martin Wright is the Deputy Assistant Director, Office of Criminal Investigations, Environmental Protection Agency.

Dawn B. Young, Ed.S, is the Laboratory Director of Forensic Pathologists, Inc., Bossier City, Louisiana.

The Encyclopedia of Police Science

A

Accidental Death/Murder of Police Officers

By any yardstick, the men and women who work as law-enforcement officers in America are serving in a profession which is characterized by inordinate personal risk. These employees are aware from the start that their calling is no parlor game: They know that at any time, day or night, the unusual may happen and they may suffer an injury which could be fatal. For instance, in 1990 there were sixty-five police murdered and another 71,794 assaulted while going about their work.

While the prospect of being an assault victim looms large in officers' minds, they should be equally wary of being injured or killed by an accident as they go about their work. This aspect of law enforcement hardly receives the notice it deserves.

How large is the problem? While massive, no one can say just how widespread it is because there are no figures which set out the number of officers injured on duty each year. On the other hand, the number of personnel fatally injured in accidents has been reported by the FBI each year since 1960. The toll is shocking: In the thirty-one years 1960 through 1990, 1,600 police officers have been accidentally killed. The fatalities range from a low of twenty deaths reported in 1960 to seventy-nine in 1989. An average of almost fifty-two officers have succumbed to accidents each year in the thirty-one-year span.

Table 1 shows the circumstances unique to the accidental deaths of officers from 1973 through 1990. Motor car and motorcycle crashes took the lives of 530 of the 1,096 persons fatally injured during these eighteen years. Another 251 officers died accidentally while on

foot rendering assistance to stalled motorists, directing traffic, giving street directions, issuing traffic citations, etc., or while serving at road-block sites.

Accidents involving fixed-wing or rotor aircraft took the lives of 138 officers. These accidents had various causes ranging from weather conditions, to mechanical failures, to pilot error such as striking unseen obstructions like power-line cables or towers.

Table 1

Law Enforcement Officers Accidentally Killed, 1973–1990, Circumstances at Scene of Incident

Circumstances	Total	Percent
Automobile accidents	449	40.9
Motorcycle accidents	81	7.4
Aircraft accidents	138	12.6
Struck by vehicles (traffic stops, road blocks, etc.)	117	10.7
Struck by vehicles (directing traffic, assisting motorists, etc.)	134	12.2
Accidental shootings (crossfires, mistaken identities, firearm mishaps)	84	7.7
Accidental shootings (training sessions)	14	1.3
Accidental shootings (self-inflicted)	20	1.8
Other (falls, drownings, etc.)	59	5.4
Total Accidental Deaths:	1,096	100.0

Sources: *Law Enforcement Officers Killed and Assaulted—1982* and *1990*. (Washington, DC: U.S. Department of Justice, Federal Bureau of Investigation), p. 40.

No sharp or unusual trends surface when the data are analyzed year by year from 1973 through 1990. Nevertheless, the data prompt a few observations. For example, 63 of the 138 officers who succumbed to aircraft accidents died in the six years 1981 through 1986. These were the years when the air wings of many police forces were implemented. The toll may reflect the newness of many units during this period of dramatic expansion.

The fact that from 1986 through 1990 only one of twenty officers was killed accidentally while handling a firearm in other than combat circumstances may be a practical result of far greater and better training given personnel about police weaponry. That there was only one accidental death from shootings during training sessions from 1988 through 1990 is remarkable (and fortunate), since during these years thousands of forces changed from a six-shot standard .38 caliber revolver to a 9mm semiautomatic sidearm with much greater cartridge capacity. During these years many forces introduced a host of semiautomatic long guns into the array of police weaponry, too.

In conclusion, accidents are endemic to police work. Hence, there is always the prospect that a mishap may occur that will lead to injury or death. The challenge to police administrators is to take timely and realistic measures to reduce the prospect of mishaps. Casualty reduction programs, enhanced training of all sorts, better supervision and greater officer accountability are all geared toward making the worker and the work environment safer. Casualty and loss reduction programs are urgent and are also a good investment by management.

Murder of Police Officers

The number of police officers murdered has escalated sharply in recent years—from twenty-eight in 1960 to sixty-five in 1990, with ninety or more murdered in thirteen of the intervening years, as shown in Table 2. The high number of deaths contributes to the fear that police frequently express about the hazardous nature of their job.

Three studies on police casualties merit special consideration. The first, by Professor Mona Margarita (1980), studied police murders in New York City over the 133-year span from 1844 to 1978. The second, by Professor Samuel G. Chapman (1986), studied the deaths of all law-enforcement officers in Oklahoma

from 1950 through 1984 and contrasts these homicides with the 2,129 police murdered nationwide in the period from 1960 through 1984. The third, and most current, was done by the Uniform Crime Reports Section of the FBI (1972–1990). It assembled data on selected felonious killings of law-enforcement officers during the 1980s.

The Precipitating Incident

A pioneer study of police murders spanning the years 1961–1963 by Albert Cardarelli (1968) found that the leading cause of police murders in urban areas was related to the investigation of robbery incidents, followed by the investigation of suspicious persons. In less densely populated areas, Cardarelli found that making an arrest or transporting a prisoner were the primary causes of officer deaths.

Most police murders result from a police-initiated contact with the suspect. David Konstanin (1984), who studied police deaths from 1978 to 1980, found that police-initiated contact was the cause of 73.3 percent of all police deaths. He identified the largest single cause of police murders as the officers' investigation of suspicious persons.

Later studies appear to bear out Cardarelli's initial conclusions. Konstanin found that robbery accounted for 10.8 percent of all officer deaths nationally. Margarita's New York City study found that 28.5 percent of all officer deaths resulted from a robbery investigation. Chapman's Oklahoma study revealed that officers who were murdered were usually attempting arrests for crimes other than burglary or robbery. In contrast to national data, a significant number of the Oklahoma victims were killed while handling or transporting prisoners. The sprawling nature of the state and the relative isolation of its two major state prisons seem directly related to the increased danger officers face when transporting prisoners. Table 3 presents the circumstances at the scene of the incident when officers were murdered for the thirty-one-year span, 1960–1990.

Margarita's New York City analysis suggests that officer deaths are intrinsically linked to the crime that the officer is investigating. She believes that investigation of a serious crime, such as robbery, where a weapon is already present, leads the suspect to strike out with goal-directed behavior in an effort to avoid arrest. Margarita does not see such violence as an impulsive act, because the goal of the suspect is

Table 2

Distribution of Police Officers Assaulted and Murdered: 1960–1990

Year	Total Assaults	Rate per 100 Officers	Assaults with Injury	Rate per 100 Officers	Number of Officers Murdered
1960	9,621	6.3	NR*	NR	28
1961	13,190	8.3	NR	NR	37
1962	17,330	10.2	NR	NR	48
1963	16,793	11.0	NR	NR	55
1964	18,001	9.9	7,738	4.3	57
1965	20,523	10.8	6,836	3.6	53
1966	23,851	12.2	9,113	4.6	57
1967	26,755	13.5	10,770	5.4	76
1968	33,604	15.8	14,072	6.6	64
1969	35,202	16.9	11,949	5.7	86
1970	43,171	18.7	15,165	6.6	100
1971	49,768	18.7	17,631	6.6	126
1972	37,523	15.1	12,230	5.8	112
1973	32,535	15.0	12,880	5.9	127
1974	29,511	15.1	11,468	5.9	132
1975	44,867	15.4	18,974	6.5	129
1976	49,079	16.8	18,737	6.4	111
1977	49,156	15.3	17,663	5.5	93
1978	56,130	16.1	21,075	6.2	93
1979	59,031	17.3	21,764	6.4	106
1980	57,847	16.7	21,516	6.2	104
1981	57,116	17.2	20,272	6.1	91
1982	55,755	17.5	17,116	5.4	92
1983	62,324	16.5	20,807	5.5	80
1984	60,153	16.2	20,205	5.4	72
1985	61,724	15.8	20,817	5.3	78
1986	64,259	16.9	21,639	5.7	66
1987	63,842	16.8	21,273	5.6	74
1988	58,752	15.9	21,015	5.7	78
1989	62,172	16.7	21,893	5.8	66
1990	71,794	17.4	26,031	6.3	65

Source: Federal Bureau of Investigation, *Uniform Crime Reports* and *Law Enforcement Officers Killed and Assaulted* (Washington, DC: Government Printing Office). Data were extracted from each document for the years set out above.

*NR: Not reported in *Uniform Crime Reports* until 1964.

self-protection from injury or from being taken into custody.

Interestingly, the characteristics of officer murders in the relatively rural setting of Oklahoma would also fit within this New York City framework. As will be more fully explored later, most of the Oklahoma suspects had previous arrest records, thus providing additional incentive to avoid capture and another arrest. Several of the persons who murdered Oklahoma law officers were fugitives from justice; two others were AWOL from military units. This informa-

tion, coupled with the high death rate of officers transporting prisoners in Oklahoma, suggests that escape is a primary reason that persons attempted to murder police.

The Suspect

Most of the data reported on suspects stems from Chapman's Oklahoma study. The typical Oklahoma suspect was white and male. Persons in the twenty-to-twenty-four-year-old age group were most likely to murder officers: One of every three suspects fits this category. One in every five suspects was from age twenty-five to twenty-nine. Also, almost all of the Oklahoma suspects were under the influence of alcohol or other drugs at the time of the fatal attack. The New York City data are very similar, with one important difference: Almost one of every two New York City suspects was male in the eighteen-to-twenty-five-year-old age group. Another difference was that almost three of every four of the New York City suspects were of minority group status. Given that Oklahoma is far more racially homogeneous than New York City, this difference appears to be more a function of demographics than of criminal proclivities allegedly common to particular ethnic groups. Contrary to popular belief, most of the Oklahoma suspects did not have significant records of violent crime prior to the incident. Rather, most had criminal records for such nonviolent offenses as burglary, vagrancy/loitering, or common drunkenness. Only six had a history of violent crimes; another five were fugitives from justice. While only limited data are available on the New York City suspects, over 88 percent on which data were available had past criminal histories, but the nature of the charges was not specified.

It appears, then, that most people who murder police have had some form of contact with the criminal-justice system prior to the homicide. This probably accounts for the heavy motivation to "escape" to avoid a new encounter. Yet the Oklahoma study notes that there is no consistent pattern that would afford the potential victim cause to be wary. Professor Chapman characterized the police murderers as "people who had a bad day, got fogged up on drugs, and ended up murdering police."

Major's research (1991) shows that the 1,077 persons suspected of murdering police during the 1980s were demographically very close to the characteristics of offenders described above. In addition, she noted that 24 percent of those identified were on parole or probation at the time of the killings.

Data from the FBI study of selected felonious police killings are essentially similar to those reported above. In addition, the study probed extensively into the psychological makeup of persons who murdered police, concluding that "there is no single personality type that kills law enforcement officers."

Instances of police murder receive not only maximum media visibility, they are stridently investigated. Nationally, almost 94 percent of all police murders from 1960 through 1990 were solved. Oklahoma authorities have compiled a 100 percent clearance rate from 1949

TABLE 3

Circumstances at Scene of Incident for Law Enforcement Officers Killed: 1960–1990

Circumstances at Scene	1960–1964		1965–1990	
	Number	Percent	Number	Percent
Responding to disturbance calls				
(person with gun, family quarrels, etc.)	45	20.0	367	16.1
Burglaries in progress or pursuing burglary suspects	28	12.4	132	5.8
Robberies in progress or pursuing robbery suspects	51	22.7	382	16.9
Attempting all other arrests				
(excluding arrests for burglaries and robberies)	62	27.6	526	23.2
Civil disorders (mass disobedience, riot, etc.)	NG*	—	14	.6
Handling, transporting, custody of prisoners	NG	—	103	4.6
Investigating suspicious persons or circumstances	28	12.4	225	9.9
Ambush (entrapment and premeditation)	NG	—	107	4.7
Ambush (unprovoked attack)	NG	—	91	4.0
Mentally deranged	11	4.9	65	2.9
Traffic pursuits and stops	NG	—	255	11.3
Totals	225	100.0	2,267	100.0

Sources: Samuel G. Chapman, *Cops, Killers and Staying Alive* (Springfield, IL: Charles C. Thomas, 1986) p. 9; *Law Enforcement Officers Killed and Assaulted* and *Uniform Crime Reports*, 1960–1990 (U.S. Department of Justice, Federal Bureau of Investigation).

*NG: Not given.

through 1990. Conviction rates are also very high across the nation in cases where suspects have been taken to trial.

Facing a high prospect of arrest, are potential offenders deterred by the death penalty? Professor Cardarelli's data did not support such a notion. Neither did research conducted by Professor William Bailey (1982), who studied the relationship among police murders, the existence of the death penalty, and the execution of persons convicted of killing officers. Bailey found no difference in the number of police deaths in states that abolished the death penalty and in those that kept capital punishment. He also found no difference among states that had actually executed convicted offenders and states that had not.

From these data, it appears that murders of police officers are unpremeditated acts that are more a function of the unfortunate convergence of people, time, and place. Chapman's characterization of the offender would lead to this conclusion, too, as would Margarita's finding that the commission of murder is dependent first on an officer detecting another crime and then pressing the investigation.

The Officer

Data about murdered officers in both Oklahoma and New York City reveal that victims have been predominantly white, male, married, and between the ages of thirty-five and forty-five. Although a significant number of the murdered Oklahoma officers had served less than five years, the average length of service for the officers was 6.8 years. Most of the New York City officers had been in police work from two to ten years. In neither locale could the majority of the murdered officers be considered as rookies. Also, the probability of death declined as length of police service increased, which may be attributed to the fact that promotion may come with seniority along with less hazardous roles. Table 4 shows selected characteristics of officers murdered over the fifteen-year span 1976–1990. These data are essentially congruent with Margarita's and Chapman's findings and those reported by Ms. Major.

Race often appears to be connected to the murder. For example, in Oklahoma all of the minority officers were killed by persons of the same race—probably a function of assignments. Konstanin found that, nationally, black officers are murdered at a much higher rate than white officers, a conclusion substantiated by the New York City study when controlling for time. In the 1970s, 36 percent of the New York City officers killed were black. Nationally, Konstantin found that black officers, while constituting only 6 percent of the nation's police personnel, accounted for 10.7 percent of all officers murdered. Professor James Fyfe (1981), formerly a ranking New York City officer, explains the higher involvement of black officers in life-or-death situations as a function of assignment to hazardous duty in high crime, inner-city areas.

Beginning with the murder of District of Columbia Officer Gail Cobb in 1974, twenty-one women officers have been killed in the line of duty through 1990. Officer Cobb's death was the first time a woman police officer had been murdered on duty since the FBI began keeping records in 1960. As more women officers are assigned patrol and detective duty and roles in vice and narcotics enforcement, and as violence against officers in general remains at a high level, it may be anticipated that the deaths of women police will continue to occur and, perhaps, to increase. Professor Chapman asserts that the murder of female officers is a product of ". . . the *job* and its very nature, *not gender*."

TABLE 4

Selected Characteristics of Police Officers Killed: 1976–1990

Sex of Officers	Number	Percent
Male	1,249	98.3
Female	21	1.7
Race of Officers		
White	1,112	84.6
Black	145	11.0
Other	58	4.4
Age of Officers		
Under 25 years	124	9.8
25–30 years	329	25.9
31–40 years	467	36.8
Over 40 years	349	27.5
Length of Service		
Less than 1 year	57	4.5
1–4 years	385	30.5
5–10 years	415	32.9
Over 10 years	405	32.1

Source: *Law Enforcement Officers Killed and Assaulted, 1976–1990.* (Washington, DC: U.S. Department of Justice, Federal Bureau of Investigation).

Geography, Violence, and the Police

Beginning with Cardarelli's study in the 1960s, two significant trends surfaced with regard to the relationship between police murders and geography: (1) most police murders occur in urban areas; and (2) a disproportionate number of police murders occur in the populous southern United States. The southern factor is dramatically illustrated in the FBI figures below, which show officer deaths by region during the 15 years, 1976–1990.

Region	Number	Percent
Northeast	161	12.7
Midwest	222	17.5
South	601	47.3
West	220	17.3
U.S. Territories and Foreign	66	5.2

Professor David Lester (1978, 1982) has conducted two studies of characteristics of the cities in which police murders occur. Both studies confirm the finding that the most dangerous place to be a police officer is in the South. In addition, Lester has found that police murders are more likely to occur in cities that have a high number of police-caused homicides and high murder/manslaughter/assault rates. Lester's second study found that police murders are more likely to occur in cities with high rates of suicides/accidents with firearms and poverty within the population.

Authors studying the geographic relationship to police murders explain the relationship through use of the "subculture of violence" theory of criminologists Marvin Wolfgang and Lawrence Ferracuti. This theory posits that some geographic regions or social subgroups have both a tradition of violent behavior and a system of values that condones, rather than condemns, violence. Lester believes the high correlation of police murders with other violent activities in these urban areas lends support to the "subculture of violence" explanation of police murders. Simply stated, the southern factor may be a product of an inherited culture of violence, which puts a high premium on the protection of one's honor and property.

Commemorating Deceased Officers

Most states and many county and city police forces have in some fashion paid tribute to their fallen officers. These take such forms as monuments, plaques, or exhibits and are presented in good taste appropriate to the supreme sacrifice.

On October 15, 1991, President George Bush dedicated the National Law Enforcement Officers' Memorial in the District of Columbia, saying, "America will not forget those who died . . . and those who protect and serve every single day of the year." The memorial honored upwards of 13,000 police personnel who have died in public service throughout American history. The memorial rests on three acres of federal land called Judiciary Square. Routine maintenance of the memorial is provided by the National Park Service.

Another organization, the Law Enforcement Memorial Association, Inc., of Wheeling, Illinois, has documented the deaths of about 7,000 additional police. This organization reports the first police fatality in what has become the United States was in 1724. The extensive archives of this organization should prove of utility to scholars who seek to more clearly define what can be done to reduce police casualties.

Conclusion

Police will continue to be murdered as long as there is a need for police to answer routine calls or investigate suspicious behavior. As noted by Meyer and his associates (1986), there is little evidence that attacks on officers will decline in the near future. The best means of preventing police murders is by improving communication of relevant information to the officer, increasing an officer's awareness of situations in which attacks may occur, and by training officers to better understand the dynamics of attack situations. Unfortunately, the best that can be done is to increase an officer's ability to survive an attack, since it is difficult to reduce the possibility of it happening.

Samuel G. Chapman

Bibliography

Bailey, William C. "Capital Punishment and Lethal Assaults against Police." *Criminology* 19(4) (February 1982): 608–25.

Cardarelli, Albert. "An Analysis of Police Killed by Criminal Action: 1961–1963." *Journal of Criminal Law, Criminology and Police Science* 59 (1968): 447–53.

Chapman, Samuel G. *Cops, Killers and Staying Alive.* Springfield, IL: Charles C. Thomas, 1986.

Federal Bureau of Investigation. *Law Enforcement Officers Killed and Assaulted.* Washington, DC: Government Printing

Office, 1972–1990.

———. *Killed in the Line of Duty: A Study of Selected Felonious Killings of Law Enforcement Officers.* Washington, DC: Government Printing Office, 1992.

Fyfe, James J. "Who Shoots? A Look at Officer Race and Police Shooting." *Journal of Police Science and Administration* 9 (1981): 367–82.

Konstantin, David. "Law Enforcement Officers Feloniously Killed in the Line of Duty: An Exploratory Study." *Justice Quarterly* 1(1) (March 1984): 29–46.

Lester, David. "A Study of Civilian-Caused Murder of Police Officers." *International Journal of Criminology and Penology* 6 (1978): 373–78.

———. "Civilians Who Kill Police Officers and Police Officers Who Kill Civilians: A Comparison of American Cities." *Journal of Police Science and Administration* 10 (4) (1982): 384–87.

Major, Victoria L. "Law Enforcement Officers Killed 1980–1989." *FBI Law Enforcement Bulletin* 60 (May 1991): 2–5.

Margarita, Mona. *Criminal Violence against Police.* Ann Arbor, MI: University Microfilms International, 1980.

———. "Killing the Police: Myths and Motives." *Annals of the American Academy of Political and Social Sciences* 452 (November 1980): 63–71.

Meyer, C. Kenneth, et al. *Ambush-Related Assaults on Police: Violence at the Street Level.* Springfield, IL: Charles C. Thomas, 1986.

Witkin, Gordon, Ted Gest, and Dorian Friedman. "Cops under Fire." *U.S. News and World Report* 109 (December 3, 1990): 32–44.

Administration

Webster's dictionary defines *administration* as "performance of executive duties" and as "the execution of public affairs as distinguished from policy-making." The latter definition is based on the classic distinction between politics and administration. In our system of government, policy-making is primarily a function of the political process, while policy execution is the responsibility of administrative agencies.

Police administration, then, is concerned with the performance of executive duties within police departments and with the execution of certain government policies. Many of these policies relate to the problem of crime and include laws prohibiting various forms of behavior, procedures for dealing with law violations, general approaches to the crime problem (deterrence, incapacitation, rehabilitation), and expressions of public sentiment toward different types of crime. Of course, police departments are but one segment of a network of government agencies responsible for the administration of crime-related policies. This network is sometimes called the "criminal justice system" and includes police agencies, as well as prosecution, defense, court, prison, probation, parole, and a host of other administrative agencies.

The administration of crime-related policies accounts for only a portion of the policy-execution aspect of police administration. Police departments may also share responsibility for administering government policies pertaining to the welfare of children, regulation of traffic, proper care and control of pets, welfare of the homeless, and a tremendous variety of other social and public affairs. Moreover, in their administration of government policies related to crime and other problems, police departments are regulated by additional policies that convey the government's allegiance to equality, fairness, privacy, minimum use of force, and other principles.

Thinking of police administration in terms of the execution of police-related policies is quite useful. This broad definition encourages us to include everything from the police chief's leadership style to different methods of handling domestic disputes within the scope of police administration. There is one deceptive feature of this definition, however. Because police administrators and police officers have so much discretion in the performance of their duties, they do more than merely execute policy. When police officers, for example, decide to ignore (or to crack down on) public drunkenness in their patrol areas they are making policy as much as executing it. Modern public-administration theory recognizes that all administration involves a certain amount of policy-making; because police administration and police work are characterized by considerable discretion, they include an unusual degree of policy-making in their policy execution.

Before looking more closely at police executive duties and several major approaches to police administration, a brief historical overview is in order.

Development of Police Administration
We begin this brief overview of the history of police administration with the creation of the London Metropolitan Police in 1829 and then examine early American police administration, the professionalization movement, and recent developments.

Peelian Principles
While informal, voluntary, and private systems for providing police services existed before 1829, that year marked the creation of a paid, public, full-time police force in London and for all intents and purposes the inception of modern police administration. Faced with the task of establishing a 1,000-member police force from scratch, Sir Robert Peel relied on the following fundamental principles (Lee, 1901):

1. The police should be under government control.
2. The basic mission of the police is the prevention of crime and disorder.
3. Police success is dependent upon public approval.
4. The police should be organized along military lines.
5. Securing and training proper persons is essential.
6. Police should be hired on a probationary basis.
7. Police strength should be deployed by time and area.
8. Police should employ only the minimum force necessary.

Adherence to these principals served the early English police well. Although the creation of the London Metropolitan Police Force was extremely controversial and was initially met by considerable public opposition, within a few years grudging public respect had been won. The first commissioners, Rowan and Mayne, carefully executed Peel's principles. They took great care in hiring police officers and used the probationary period to weed out those who would not conform to strict rules of conduct. They kept all police officers uniformed and only minimally armed so as to emphasize prevention of crime, accountability to the public, and restraint in the use of force. They also took great pains to demonstrate that the police served all

the people and were not a tool of whichever political party happened to be in power.

Early American Police Administration
Large American cities, including Boston, Philadelphia, and New York, formed paid, full-time police forces within a decade or two of London, while smaller cities and towns (and states) followed suit later in the 1800s and early 1900s. Although the London Metropolitan Police Force served as the model for American police departments, several important differences developed. For example, American police at first resisted wearing uniforms and were soon carrying firearms among their equipment. In general, early American police were less successful than their English counterparts in gaining the respect and cooperation of the public and had to resort to force and weaponry more often to accomplish their aims.

In part, of course, this difference in relations with the public was due to the vastly greater ethnic and social diversity found in American communities and to the frontier character of much of early America. Police in London enjoyed far greater public consensus about proper behavior than did their colleagues in Boston, Philadelphia, and New York. And they certainly enjoyed a more orderly and controlled community than did police officers in such towns as Chicago, St. Louis, and Denver.

Perhaps the single most important feature of early American police administration was its close ties to partisan politics. Police departments clearly served the interests of the political party in power rather than the community as a whole. Police officers were hired on the basis of their political connections, not because they had passed a written test or possessed certain objectively-chosen credentials or traits. Police resources were allocated on the basis of political considerations, not on the basis of crime analysis or other objective criteria. Enforcement decisions, especially pertaining to vice control (gambling, prostitution, liquor laws), were made to benefit the political party in power and to damage the opposition party.

Professional Police Administration
In the late 1800s and early 1900s a reform movement swept through American government, including police administration (Fogelson, 1977). Central to the reforms was government by reason, by rational decision-making. Reformers sought to separate politics and

administration and to put administration in the hands of trained professionals. Civil service and merit systems were created to guarantee that personnel decisions were based on objective criteria, rather than political connections. Independent commissions were created to improve governments' efficiency. Many formerly elective offices were changed to appointive.

These reforms dramatically affected police administration. Police chiefs gained some independence from the political process. Hiring of officers became a matter of testing and background investigation and programs were established to train recruits. Police work became a genuine career rather than a temporary political reward, and police enforcement decisions depended less on political considerations. In general, police administration came to be seen as the science of police policy execution, and police chiefs more as administrators than as politicians.

Modern Problems
Professional police administration remains the standard today. Since the 1960s, however, some limitations have become apparent. In particular, some police departments have fallen out of touch with segments of their communities, often to the point of extreme hostility. In retrospect, this development can be attributed partially to the professional model itself, which, in seeking objectivity and independence, has divorced itself from politics and from other expressions of community preferences. Professional administrators have seen themselves as best qualified to decide what was best for the community. Also, in the name of efficiency professional administrators have adopted strategies (motorized patrol), tactics (aggressive patrol), and policies (frequent rotation of assignment) that have contributed to the estrangement of police and community.

Another shortcoming of the professional model has been its failure to achieve its stated primary objective of crime control. In the 1960s and 1970s, at the height of the professional movement and during a period of increased hiring, training, and education of police officers, crime increased dramatically. Many millions of dollars spent on police equipment, education, and programs failed to stem the tide. Professional police administration may have achieved some success in reducing two serious forms of police misconduct, corruption and brutality, but recent revelations demonstrate that even such flagrant abuses as these have not been eliminated entirely.

Some form of community-oriented policing seems most likely to displace or at least modify the professional model of police administration in the years to come. The community-oriented model emphasizes the need for the police to be responsive to community interests and, in fact, to engage the community in the task of controlling crime and disorder. In community-oriented policing, long-term effectiveness in solving neighborhood problems is emphasized, rather than the short-term efficiency of motorized random patrol and immediate response to every call for service. Professional police administration, when modified by this explicit community orientation, brings American policing closer in line with the principles laid down by Sir Robert Peel in 1829.

The Scope of Police Executive Duties
Police administrators must pay attention to multiple factors that include objectives, tasks, resources, structure, culture, management, and environment, which are outlined below (see Hoover, 1992).

Objectives
The primary objectives of a police department are protection of life and property and maintenance of public order. One of the administrator's basic responsibilities is to ensure that all activities contribute to the achievement of these objectives. This requires the administrator to instill the organization with a sense of purpose that is shared by all employees.

Tasks
The administrator must design and implement the specific tasks that will lead to attainment of the department's objectives. Traditionally, three categories of police tasks have been utilized–operations, administration, and services. Operations tasks, such as patrol, criminal investigation, and traffic, are performed in direct assistance to the public. Administration tasks, including training, personnel, and budgeting, are performed on a day-to-day basis within the police department. Service tasks, such as detention, communications, and alcohol-testing, are similarly performed within the department but are required on a more continuous basis than are administrative tasks. Administration and service tasks support operations tasks.

Resources

The police administrator must acquire and wisely utilize the resources needed to perform the tasks necessary for goal achievement. This requires him or her to participate in the government budget process that determines the police department's annual funding and then to use those funds skillfully. Most of the police department's funds are spent on salaries and benefits, and most of its resources are human. A major part of the police administrator's job, then, involves acquiring and utilizing human resources.

Structure

With personnel assigned to tasks that will contribute to the attainment of objectives, the organization next needs structure to guide task performance. Structure includes hierarchy, distribution of authority, job descriptions, policies, procedures, rules, and regulations. The police administrator must create a framework that lends structure and organization to the various tasks being performed and the many people working within the department.

Culture

Every organization develops a culture based on the norms and values that guide employee thinking and behavior. Police administrators must shape their organizations' cultures in order to encourage proper behavior and discourage improper behavior. Norms and values consistent with the organization's objectives and with democratic principles should be supported in every possible manner. The tendency of police organizations to develop deviant cultures or subcultures based on inappropriate norms and values must be vigorously resisted.

Management

The police administrator must also provide management within the organization. No matter how precise the structure, how supportive the culture, and how clear the objectives, problems and questions arise in task performance. Also, personnel vary in talents and commitment. Management is needed to solve problems, answer questions, supervise employees, and generally keep the department on track toward goal attainment.

Environment

A police department does not function in a vacuum but rather is affected by forces and developments originating beyond its boundaries. The department's objectives are determined in part by the community and the political process; its funding level is determined through the political process; employees are recruited from and live in the outside world; operations tasks are performed out in the community; some procedures and regulations are mandated by the courts and other agencies; and so on. Consequently, an important duty of the police administrator is management of the department's interaction with its environment. This can include representing the department, fighting for resources, fending off threats, and educating the community about police work and crime. This externally oriented aspect of police administration is crucial but often overlooked.

Major Approaches to Police Administration

Police administration textbooks and training programs have changed over the years, sometimes in response to police administrative practice and sometimes in advance of practice. Today, several approaches can be identified that differ primarily in the emphasis they give to the seven factors outlined above.

The Classical Approach

The classical approach to police administration dominated textbooks and training in the 1960s and probably still has more influence over practice than any other. This approach is best illustrated by the pioneering textbooks *Police Administration* (O.W. Wilson, 1950; later editions co-authored by Roy McLaren) and *Municipal Police Administration* (1938, edited under the direction of the International City Management Association; now retitled *Local Government Police Management* and edited most recently by William Geller). The classical approach emphasizes structure and management: organizational principles (unity of command, chain of command, delegation of authority); management functions (planning, directing, controlling); and functional components of policing (patrol administration, traffic supervision, jail management).

The classical approach remains popular and influential today for several reasons. It is at the heart of the law enforcement agency accreditation program now in its second decade of operation. It is the primary means of risk management for minimizing a police agency's civil liability exposure. It has been encouraged by developments in administrative law, which require more and more documentation in support of disciplinary actions. And it provides an appearance, at least, of close control over police power and discretion that is comforting to citizens and police administrators alike.

The Human-Relations Approach

The human-relations approach now seems to dominate police administration textbooks and training although its importance in practice is less certain. This approach emphasizes resources, culture, and management. The underlying rationale is that police productivity is strictly a function of people productivity and that police management is almost totally people management. This approach focuses on morale, communications, motivation, group dynamics, and leadership. Many of the police administration textbooks published since 1970 have substantial human-relations content or are clearly based on human-relations theories (see Gaines, Southerland, and Angell, 1991; Roberg and Kuykendall, 1990; and Sheehan and Cordner, 1989, for examples).

In recent years, police agencies have shown considerable interest in a variety of popular management techniques affiliated with the human-relations approach, including situational leadership, quality circles, principles of excellence, management by values, and total quality management. Some police executives have argued that police management must establish better human relations in its dealings with employees before it can reasonably expect those employees to treat the public with increased care and respect (Couper and Lobitz, 1991).

The Strategic Management Approach

The strategic management approach to police administration emphasizes objectives, tasks, and resources. Police administration is conceived primarily as a rational adaptation of means to ends, of planning and designing tasks that will lead to the achievement of organizational objectives. Police-related research, exemplified by the Kansas City Preventive Patrol Experiment, the Rand study of criminal investigations, and the PERF study of police response time, focused on police operational tasks and their effectiveness and gave rise to such programs as Managing Patrol Operations, Managing Criminal Investigations, and Differential Police Response Strategies. More recently, community policing and problem-oriented policing have emerged as leading new police strategies (see Cordner and Hale, 1992).

The strategic management approach has gained considerable stature over the last decade or two as resource constraints have forced police administrators to focus more and more on the efficiency and effectiveness of police programs and strategies. The "Perspectives on Policing" series prepared at Harvard University and distributed by the National Institute of Justice has been influential in popularizing this approach, as have the books *Beyond 911: A New Era for Policing* (Sparrow, Moore, and Kennedy, 1990) and *Beyond Command and Control: The Strategic Management of Police Departments* (Moore and Stephens, 1991). The heightened concern over efficiency and effectiveness has enhanced the role of policy analysis, program evaluation, and other analytical aspects of police administration.

The Institutional Approach

The institutional approach to police administration emphasizes the environment and policy execution instead of focusing so exclusively on internal management duties. The two books that best illustrate this approach are Herman Goldstein's *Policing a Free Society* (1977) and *Police Leadership in America* (1985), edited by William Geller. These books consider the police administrator's external relations with political leaders, city managers, the media, labor unions, and community groups. They also consider such matters as defining the police function, developing alternatives to formal legal processing, and structuring police discretion, all of which are extremely important in the big picture of executing government policy, but are likely to be overlooked when the focus is exclusively on the internal management of the police department.

Conclusion

The practice of police administration in America has become much more rational and efficient since the creation of the first organized police forces in the 1840s. Professional administration brought to policing great improvements in personnel, training, technology, and organization. Along the way, however, police departments became less responsive to the public, and citizens took less responsibility for crime control. These trends are only now being reversed.

The emphasis of police administration has also changed over the years. Initial reform efforts stressed professional administration and structure and control. In the 1960s, increasing attention was paid to improving police productivity through more inspired leadership and to serving employee needs. In recent years the emphasis has been on analysis and improvement of police tactics and strategies and on the police agency's relations with its environment. If these trends continue, the result should be an integration of approaches that will be a valuable guide to the successful practice of police administration.

Gary W. Cordner

Bibliography

Cordner, Gary W., and Donna C. Hale. *What Works in Policing? Operations and Administration Examined.* Cincinnati: Anderson, 1992.

Couper, David C., and Sabine H. Lobitz. *Quality Policing: The Madison Experience.* Washington, DC: Police Executive Research Forum, 1991.

Fogelson, Robert M. *Big-City Police.* Cambridge, MA: Harvard University Press, 1977.

Gaines, Larry K., Mittie D. Southerland, and John E. Angell. *Police Administration.* New York: McGraw-Hill, 1991.

Geller, William A., ed. *Police Leadership in America: Crisis and Opportunity.* New York: Praeger, 1985.

———, ed. *Local Government Police Management.* 3d ed. Washington, DC: International City Management Association, 1991.

Goldstein, Herman. *Policing a Free Society.* Cambridge, MA: Ballinger, 1977.

Hoover, Larry T., ed. *Police Management: Issues & Perspectives.* Washington, DC: Police Executive Research Forum, 1992.

Lee, W.L. Melville. *A History of Police in England.* London: Methuen, 1901.

Moore, Mark H., and Darrel W. Stephens. *Beyond Command and Control: The Strategic Management of Police Departments.* Washington, DC: Police Executive Research Forum, 1991.

Roberg, Roy R., and Jack Kuykendall. *Police Organization and Management.* Pacific Grove, CA: Brooks/Cole, 1990.

Sheehan, Robert, and Gary W. Cordner. *Introduction to Police Administration.* 2d ed. Cincinnati: Anderson, 1989.

Sparrow, Malcolm K., Mark H. Moore, and David M. Kennedy. *Beyond 911: A New Era for Policing.* New York: Basic Books, 1990.

Wilson, O.W., and Roy C. McLaren. *Police Administration.* 4th ed. New York: McGraw-Hill, 1977.

Age and Crime

The view that involvement in crime diminishes with age is one of the oldest and most widely accepted in criminology. For most forms of crime, but especially for what in most societies are designated "serious" crimes (murder, rape, assault, robbery), the proportion of the population involved in crime tends to peak in adolescence or early adulthood and then to decline with age.

This discussion of age and crime begins with a look at statistics for the country as a whole, focusing on the most common societal pattern, whereby conventional crimes are dominated by casual youth offenders. Factors associated with the early entrance and exit that mark the most common pattern are discussed next, followed by an examination of ways in which societal age-crime patterns vary by crime type, by race, and across cultures and over time. The issue of individual age-crime patterns is considered next, with a focus on the criminal career patterns of more serious offenders, factors associated with their longer persistence in crime and eventual exit, and patterns and trends in both offending and victimization among older age groups in the population. This is followed by a discussion of the impact of age structure and cohort size on societal crime rates. The final section provides a brief consideration of the interaction among age, gender, and crime.

Age-Crime Statistics for the Country as a Whole

The peak age (the age group with the highest age-specific arrest rate) is younger than twenty-five for all but one (gambling) of the nearly thirty different crimes reported in the FBI's *Uniform Crime Reports* (UCR) program, and rates begin to decline during the teenage years for more than half of the crime categories. In fact, even the median age (50 percent of all arrests occurring among younger persons) is younger than thirty for most crimes. In general, the "younger" age distributions (median ages in the teens or early twenties) are found for ordinary property crimes like burglary, larceny, arson, and vandalism, and for liquor and drug violations. Personal crimes like aggravated assault and homicide tend to have somewhat "older" age distributions (median ages in the late twenties); as do some of the public order offenses like public drunkenness and driving under the influence; and certain of the property crimes that juveniles have less opportunity to commit, like embezzlement, fraud, and gambling (median ages in late twenties or thirties).

Although young people obviously account for a disproportionate share of arrests, official statistics may not provide a completely accurate picture of the participation in crime by different age groups. Because a relatively small proportion of crimes result, in arrests, it is possible that arrest statistics either overrepresent the young (young offenders may be easier to apprehend), or underrepresent them (law enforcement may be more lenient in the handling of youths).

Nevertheless, other data sources tend to corroborate the age-crime distribution found in the FBI data. For example, Hindelang and McDermott (1981) examined the perceived age of offenders as reported by victims to the National Crime Survey for crimes in which the offender was seen (e.g., rape, robbery, assault, and purse snatching) for the years 1973–1977. They found the highest rates of offending were for those aged eighteen to twenty, followed by those aged twelve to seventeen. The lowest rates were for those over the age of twenty. Self-report studies of delinquency and of adult criminality also show a pattern of general decline in rates of offending following a peak in midadolescence to young adulthood, paralleling the distribution depicted by UCR data (Elliott et al., 1983; Rowe and Tittle, 1977).

Explaining the Youthful Peak in Offending
A variety of social, cognitive, and physical factors can help explain the rapid rise in age-specific rates of offending during early adolescence. This rise in offending rates coincides with a period of life in which youths find themselves on the one hand barred from integrating themselves into the world of adulthood, but faced on the other hand with major sources of reinforcement for offending: money, status, power, autonomy, identity claims; strong sensate experiences stemming from sex, natural adrenaline highs, or highs from illegal

substances; and peers who similarly value independence, or even defiance of conventional morality. Further, their dependent status as juveniles insulates teens from many of the social and legal costs of illegitimate activities, and their stage of cognitive development limits prudence concerning the consequences of their behavior. At the same time, they possess the physical prowess required to commit crimes. Finally, it should be remembered that a certain amount of misbehavior seems to be natural to youth; as Jolin and Gibbons (1987:238) point out, "much youthful lawbreaking is simply a stage of 'growing up.'"

Some writers attribute the rapid drop in rates of offending during late adolescence and early adulthood to a decline in physical abilities. But the research literature on biological aging shows that physical abilities (energy, strength, stamina, and the like) continue to increase long after the age at which societal rates of robbery or burglary have begun to decline sharply (around ages fifteen to seventeen). Furthermore, after peaking between ages twenty-five and thirty, physical abilities decline much more slowly than offending rates for physically demanding crimes (Shock et al., 1984).

Biological and physiological factors may contribute toward an understanding of the rapid increase in delinquent behavior during adolescence, but they do not help explain the abrupt decline in the age-crime curve following the peak age. Only in the sphere of social statuses and roles do changes of corresponding abruptness occur.

For those in late adolescence or early adulthood (roughly aged seventeen to twenty-two, the age group showing the sharpest decline in arrest rates for FBI Index crimes), important changes occur in at least five major spheres of life:

1. Strengthened social bonds and greater access to legitimate sources of material goods and excitement: jobs, credit, alcohol, sex, and so forth.
2. Age-graded norms: externally, increased expectation of maturity and responsibility; internally, anticipation of assuming adult roles, coupled with reduced subjective acceptance of deviant roles and the threat they pose to entering adult status.
3. Peer associations and lifestyle: reduced orientation to same-age/same-sex peers and increased orientation toward per-

sons of the opposite sex and/or persons who are older or more mature.

4. Increased legal and social costs for deviant behavior.

5. Patterns of illegitimate opportunities: Wth the assumption of adult roles, opportunities increase for crimes that are less risky, more lucrative, and/or less likely to be reflected in official statistics (for example, gambling, fraud, and employee theft).

As young people move into adulthood or anticipate entering it, most find their bonds to society strengthening, with expanded access to work or further education and increased interest in establishing permanent relationships and "settling down." Sampson and Laub (1990), using data collected by Sheldon and Eleanor Glueck, report that job stability and strong marital attachment have important social control effects in reducing adult criminal behavior on the part of both those with and those without official records of juvenile delinquency.

Late adolescence is a time when young people take significant charge of their lives and make choices (often stressful ones) that will to a large extent shape the rest of the life course. Leaving school, finding employment, going to college, enlisting in the military, and getting married not only increase social integration, informal social control, and social expectations oriented to the standards of conventional society, but also involve a change in peer associations and lifestyle routines that diminish the opportunities for committing these offenses.

With the accumulation of material goods and the taking on of social statuses that are dependent on favorable reactions from others, the potential costs of legal and social sanctions increase. In brief, the motives and opportunities for low-yield and/or exploratory types of crime decline with the movement (real or anticipated) out of adolescence.

Variations in the Age-Crime Curve
Although crime tends to decline with age, substantial variation can be found in the parameters of the age-crime curve (such as peak age, median age, and rate of decline from peak age) across the fifteen- to twenty-year age span between the early teens to roughly age thirty. For example, certain crimes have somewhat older peak ages, and a more gradual decline in rates for older age groups—particularly for a num-

ber of crime categories not included in the FBI Crime Index. Variations in the age-crime pattern are also found for different population groups, cultures, and historical periods.

To a large extent, variations in societal age-crime patterns reflect patterns of age-stratified inequality. Age is a potent mediator of inequality in both the legitimate and illegitimate opportunity structures of society. Just as the low-wage, deadend jobs of the legitimate economy are disproportionately held by the young, so too are high-risk, low-yield crimes committed disproportionately by the young. At the opposite end of the opportunity scale, because it is rare to find them in positions of power and influence in business or politics, young people are unlikely to score big in the world of white-collar crime or in the lucrative rackets of organized crime.

"Flatter" age curves (that is, those with an older peak age and/or a slower decline in offending rates among older age groups) are associated with several circumstances:

- Types of crime for which illegitimate opportunities change (perhaps even increase) rather than diminish with age;
- Population groups for whom legitimate opportunities do not markedly increase with age;
- Cultures and historical periods in which youth have greater access to legitimate opportunities.

Crime Types. Flatter age curves are found for a number of UCR crime categories, including some of the minor property crimes, violent crimes, and many of the public order offenses. For these categories, illegitimate opportunities change with age. For example, young people have certain opportunities for fraud, such as falsification of identification to purchase alcohol or gain entry to "adult" establishments; but, being too young to obtain credit, youths lack opportunities for other common frauds such as passing bad checks, defrauding an innkeeper, or credit card forgery. Similarly, young people have more opportunities than do older people for some kinds of violence (for example, playground fights or gang violence), but less opportunity for other kinds of violence that stem from primary group conflicts (for example, spousal violence).

Older people may shift to less visible criminal roles such as bookie or fence. Or, as a spinoff of legitimate roles, they may commit surreptitious crimes or crimes that, if discovered, are unlikely to be reported to the authorities, such as embezzlement, stock fraud, bribery, or price-fixing. The fragmentary evidence on persons involved in lucrative crimes (for which systematic official data are unavailable) suggests that they are likely to be middle aged or older (Shapiro, 1984).

For example, an analysis of the age distribution of persons identified as major gambling and loansharking racketeers in the state of Pennsylvania for the 1980–90 period shows most to be between their mid-forties and mid-sixties, with some continuing to practice their trade well into their seventies (Pennsylvania Crime Commission, 1991; Steffensmeier and Allan, 1993a). Similarly, most fences of stolen goods are typically middle aged or older (Steffensmeier, 1986).

Still less is known of the age distribution of "respectable" or "upperworld" offenders who commit lucrative business crimes such as securities fraud, price-fixing, bribery, and so forth. Of course, one would not expect youths to hold the types of legitimate positions that provide access to such criminal opportunities. An analysis of data extracted from *New York Times* articles on profitable business crimes (defined here as those involving gains of $25,000 or more) during the 1987–1990 period reveals a preponderance of middle-aged or older offenders, with a modal age between forty and fifty (Steffensmeier and Allan, 1993a).

Minority Differences. For black inner-city youths, the high level of youth inequality that characterizes modern societies is compounded by problems of racial discrimination that persist in our nation, and they are less able to leave behind the inequality of youth status. As blacks move into young adulthood they continue to experience limited access to the adult labor market. Adult offending levels among blacks therefore continue at higher levels than among whites, making for a flatter age-crime curve.

This is supported by a comparison of the adult percent of property crime arrests (controlling for differences in juvenile and adult populations) for blacks and whites (Steffensmeier and Allan, 1993a). Across all crime categories, the adult percent of arrests (APA) is greater for blacks than for whites, in some cases strongly so.

The greater probability of criminal careers continuing into adulthood for members of minorities is substantiated by Sullivan's (1989) case study research with New York street gangs in white, black, and Hispanic neighborhoods. He reports that in comparison to white gang members (who begin to drift away from the group and from delinquent activities during their late teens as they begin to move into jobs), black and Hispanic youth face a greater dearth of job opportunities and this delays desistance from delinquency.

Cross-Cultural and Historical Differences. The relationship between age-stratification and the steep rise and fall in the age-curve for ordinary property crime is also supported by the "flatter" curves found in societies and for historical periods in which the culture provides for a smoother transition between the periods of youth and adulthood.

For example, in small pre-industrial societies, the passage to adult status is relatively simple and continuous. Formal "rites of passage" at relatively early ages (compared to the modern United States) avoid much of the status ambiguity and role conflict that torment American adolescents. Youths often begin to assume responsible and economically productive roles well before they reach full physical maturity. It is not surprising, therefore, to find that such societies have significantly flatter and less skewed age-crime patterns (for a review, see Steffensmeier et al., 1989).

Much the same is true for earlier periods in the history of the United States and other industrial nations. During both agricultural and early industrial periods, children were expected to leave school at an early age and do their part in helping to support their families. The responsible roles assumed by many youths in earlier periods forestalled the feelings of rebellion seen among contemporary teens who are isolated from truly productive roles within their families.

Crime and delinquency among the young is heightened in modern societies that "lack institutional procedures for moving people smoothly from protected childhood to autonomous adulthood" (Nettler, 1978:241). This could account for the progressively "younger" and more sharply peaked age-crime curves found in recent decades, both in UCR arrest data for 1940, 1960, and 1980, and in the age breakdown of United States prisoner statistics for the years 1890–1980 (Steffensmeier et al., 1989). However, changes in the age-crime curve are gradual and can only be detected when a sufficiently large time frame is used.

Criminal Careers
The youthful peak and rapid drop-off in offending that constitutes the most common societal pattern for conventional crimes is but one of a number of patterns identified when criminal careers are tracked for individual offenders. With respect to individual lawbreakers, Jolin and Gibbons (1987) describe four different age-crime patterns:

1. Early entry into lawbreaking, followed usually (but not always) by desistance from crime at a relatively early age, the common pattern described above.
2. "Career criminality," characterized by entry into lawbreaking during the teens or early twenties, but with no withdrawal from crime until middle age.
3. "Career criminals," who also begin offending at an early age and continue during adulthood, but who continue offending after middle age.
4. "Old first timers," whose initial involvement in crime does not occur until middle age or later.

In large cities, as many as half of all males will experience police contacts for nontraffic offenses at some time during their lives. Although this is most likely to occur during adolescence, about half of all adult arrestees have had no juvenile arrests. Most individuals, particularly those with no juvenile police contacts, have very brief criminal "careers," with only one or two police contacts over the life span. On the other hand, a small proportion have numerous police contacts over an extended period of their lives.

These career delinquents and career criminals account for a large proportion of all serious crime, and their age patterns differ in important ways from the age distribution for criminal conduct in the population at large (Blumstein et al., 1986). Rather than a pattern of declining involvement following a high frequency of criminal acts in late adolescence and young adulthood, the career criminal has a relatively constant high rate of involvement from adolescence through adulthood, often not terminating until the late thirties or early forties, or even older.

Among the factors identified predictive of adult criminal careers are labor market difficulties (Allan and Steffensmeier, 1989; Sampson and Laub, 1990) and severity of juvenile disposition (Shannon, 1988). Legal stigma, educational deficits, poverty, and perhaps minority status, interact to multiply the difficulty in locating stable work that could strengthen social bonds or provide an alternative to illegitimate opportunities. Institutional confinement not only increases the stigma and the difficulty in finding a job, but it also may confirm a criminal self-concept and expand criminal opportunities in the form of skills and contacts that can be developed in such settings.

As individuals become more committed to a criminal lifestyle, legitimate attachments become more remote. Thus, the age-crime curves of individual career criminals are much flatter, with a fairly constant high rate of offending until much later in life.

Older Criminals
First, contrary to media concern about a "geriatric crime wave," there has been no increase in the frequency or severity of elderly crime *per capita* in recent decades (Steffensmeier, 1987). The proportionate involvement of the elderly in crime is about the same now as it was twenty-five to thirty years ago. When the elderly do break the law, moreover, their lawbreaking involves minor alcohol-related or theft offenses rather than serious crimes.

Although crime rates among older persons are relatively low, two patterns of offending can still be found: (1) those whose first criminal involvement occurs relatively late in life; and (2) those who started crime at an early age and continue their involvement beyond the forties and fifties. Interestingly, a fair number of previously law-abiding persons become involved in crime at an older age, particularly in shoplifting, homicide, and alcohol-related offenses. What evidence is available on first-time older offenders suggests that situational stress and lack of alternative opportunities play a primary role. The unanticipated loss of one's job or other disruptions of social ties can push some individuals into their first law violation at any age (Jolin and Gibbons, 1987).

Older offenders who persist in crime are more likely to belong to the criminal underworld. These are individuals who are relatively successful in their criminal activities or who are extensively integrated into subcultural or family criminal enterprises. They seem to receive relational and psychic rewards (for example, pride in their expertise), as well as monetary rewards from lawbreaking, and as a result see no need to withdraw from lawbreaking (Steffensmeier, 1986). But even they eventually slow down.

Retiring from a Life of Crime
What accounts for the fact that, ultimately, most persistent lawbreakers "burn out," often in spite of what correctional agencies do or do not do to them? Empirical research suggests that exiting from a criminal career requires the acquisition of meaningful bonds to conventional people or institutions, particularly a stable job and/or an enduring relationship to a spouse (Sampson and Laub, 1990). A good job shifts a criminal's attention from the present to the future, provides a solid basis for the construction of a noncriminal identity, and alters an individual's daily routine in ways that make crime less likely. Good personal relationships also create bonds to the social order that an individual wants to protect.

The development of social bonds may be coupled with cognitive factors that are triggered by a sort of "burnout" or belated deterrent effect as offenders grow tired of the "hassles" of repeated involvement with the criminal justice system. Still other offenders may quit or "slow down" as they find their abilities and efficiency declining with increasing age, loss of "nerve," or sustained narcotics or alcohol use.

The Effects of Age Structure on a Nation's Crime Rate
Because involvement in crime diminishes with age, it follows that fluctuations in the age composition of a population can have a significant impact on the crime rates of the population. For example, Steffensmeier and Harer (1991) report that both the dramatic increases in the overall crime rate during the 1960s and early 1970s and the decrease in the rate during the 1980s are linked, respectively, to the post–World War II "baby boom" and the post-1960s "baby bust." They note that virtually all of the reported decreases in the Index crime rate during the 1980s are attributable to the declining proportion of teenagers in the population—that is, to a "baby bust" effect. In fact, once age effects are purged, the UCR statistics actually show a 7 percent rise in the nation's crime rate during the years from 1980 to 1988.

Thus, a major share of crime rate trends is attributable to shifts in the age composition of the United States population. In fact, age composition effects can mask the "true" trends. Once age effects are purged, Steffensmeier and Harer report that the UCR violent crimes of homicide, forcible rape, aggravated assault, and robbery actually increased about 20 percent over the decade, in spite of a doubling in the nation's imprisonment rates during the 1980s, suggesting that the criminal justice system does not contain the solution to the nation's crime problem (Steffensmeier, 1992).

Effects of Cohort Size
A related issue concerns the effect of "cohort size" on a nation's crime rate. A cohort is a group of people born during the same period. For example, the "baby boom" cohort refers to the unusually large number of people born between the years 1945 and 1960. A number of demographers (Easterlin, 1978; Ryder, 1965) have proposed that large cohorts (like the post–World War II baby boom cohort) will have higher crime rates. They argue that in large cohorts, too many young people compete for jobs and education and the resulting dearth of opportunities will push a higher proportion toward illegitimate opportunities.

To test this intriguing hypothesis, some studies report "significant" cohort size effects (Maxim, 1985; Smith, 1986), while others find no such effects (Steffensmeier, Streifel, and Shihadeh, 1992). However, whether or not "significant" effects are reported, the more important finding is that all the studies are in agreement that cohort size accounts for very little of the variation in the nation's crime rate over an extended period of time.

Age-by-Gender Differences in Crime
In an investigation of the age-gender-crime relationship using UCR arrest data for three periods (1935, 1960, and 1985), Steffensmeier and Streifel (1991) report more similarities than differences. The single major difference in the age curves of males and females is for prostitution, with females having a much greater concentration of arrests among the young. Although this difference may be due in part to more stringent enforcement of prostitution statutes when young females are involved, the younger and more peaked female age curve is also a function of the extent to which opportu-

nity structures for sexual misbehaviors differ between males and females. Clearly, sexual attractiveness and the marketability of sexual services are strongly linked to both age and gender: Older women become less able to market sexual services, whereas older men can continue to purchase sexual services from young females or from young males (Steffensmeier and Streifel, 1991).

Conclusion

Age is one of the most powerful predictors of criminality. In comparison with adolescents, the decline of offending rates as adults age can be understood in terms of strengthened social bonds; increased access to legitimate sources of material goods and excitement; changes in patterns of peer associations, age-graded norms, and illegitimate opportunities; and increased legal and social costs for deviant behavior. Because of the strong relationship between age and crime, changes in the age-distribution of the population can have important effects on trends in crime over time.

Emilie Anderson Allan
Darrell J. Steffensmeier

Bibliography

Allan, Emilie A., and Darrell Steffensmeier. "Youth, Underemployment, and Property Crime." *American Sociological Review* 54 (1989): 107–23.

Blumstein, Albert, Jacqueline Cohen, Julius Roth, and Christy Visher, eds. *Criminal Careers and "Career Criminals."* Washington, DC: National Academy Press, 1986.

Easterlin, R. "What Will 1984 Be Like? Socio-Economic Implications of Recent Twists in Age Structure." *Demography* 15 (1978): 397–421.

Elliott, Delbert, Suzanne Ageton, D. Huizinga, B. Knowles, and R. Canter. *The Prevalence and Incidence of Delinquent Behavior: 1976–1980.* Boulder, CO: Behavioral Research Institute, 1983.

Hindelang, Michael, and M. McDermott. "Variations in Sex-Race-Age-Specific Incidence Rates of Offending." *American Sociological Review* 46 (1981): 461–74.

Jolin, Annette, and Don Gibbons. "Age Patterns in Criminal Involvement." *International Journal of Offender Therapy* 31 (1987): 237–60.

Maxim, P. "Cohort Size and Juvenile Delinquency: A Test of the Easterlin Hypothesis." *Social Forces* 63 (1985): 661–79.

Nettler, Gwynn. *Explaining Crime.* New York: McGraw-Hill, 1978.

Pennsylvania Crime Commission. *1990 Report—Organized Crime in Pennsylvania: A Decade of Change.* Philadelphia: Commonwealth of Pennsylvania, 1991.

Rowe, Allan, and Charles Tittle. "Life Cycle Changes and Criminal Propensity." *Sociological Quarterly* 18 (1977): 223–36.

Ryder, Norman. "The Cohort as a Concept in the Study of Social Change." *American Sociological Review* 47 (1965): 774–87.

Sampson, Robert J., and John H. Laub. "Crime and Deviance Over the Life Course: The Salience of Adult Social Bonds." *American Sociological Review* 55 (October 1990): 609–27.

Shannon, Lyle. *Criminal Career Continuity: Its Social Context.* New York: Human Sciences Press, 1988.

Shapiro, Susan. *Wayward Capitalists.* New Haven, CT: Yale University Press, 1984.

Shock, Nathan, et al. *Normal Aging: The Baltimore Longitudinal Study of Aging.* Washington, DC: Department of Health and Human Services, 1984.

Smith, M.D. "The Era of Increased Violence in the United States: Age, Period, or Cohort Effect?" *Sociological Quarterly* 27 (1986): 239–51.

Steffensmeier, Darrell. *The Fence: In the Shadow of Two Worlds.* Totowa, NJ: Rowman & Littlefield, 1986.

———. "Invention of the 'New' Senior Citizen Criminal." *Research on Aging* 9 (1987): 281–311.

———. "More Pennsylvania Prisons Did Not Reduce Violent Crime." *Overcrowded Times* 3(6) (1992): 1–7.

———, and Emilie Allan. "Age-Inequality and Property Crime." In *Age Stratification and Crime.* Eds. John Hagan and Ruth Peterson. Chicago, IL: University of Chicago Press, 1993a.

———, and Emilie Allan. "Gender and Age." *Criminology: A Contemporary Handbook.* 2d ed. Ed. Joseph F. Sheley. Belmont, CA: Wadsworth, 1993b, chapter 4.

———, Emilie Allan, Miles Harer, and Cathy Streifel. "Age and the Distribution of Crime: Variant or Invariant?" *American Journal of Sociology* 54 (1989): 107–23.

———, and Miles Harer. "Did Crime Rise or Fall During the Reagan Presidency? The Effects of an 'Aging' U.S. Population on the Nation's Crime Rate." *Journal of Research in Crime and Delinquency* 28 (1991): 330–59.

———, and Miles Harer. "Is the Crime Rate Really Falling? An Aging U.S. Population and Its Impact on the Nation's Crime Rate, 1980–1984." *Journal of Research in Crime and Delinquency* 24 (1987): 23–48.

———, and Cathy Streifel. "Age, Gender, and Crime Across Three Historical Periods: 1935, 1960, 1985." *Social Forces* 69 (1991): 869–94.

———, Cathy Streifel, and Edward Shihadeh. "Cohort Size and Arrest Rates Over the Life Course: The Easterlin Hypothesis Reconsidered." *American Sociological Review* 57 (1992): 306–14.

Sullivan, Mercer. *"Getting Paid": Youth Crime and Work in the Inner City.* Ithaca, NY: Cornell University Press, 1989.

Arrest

The word *arrest* is derived from the French *arrêter*, which means "to stop, to obtain, to hinder, to obstruct." In addition to being "an ordinary English word" (Lord Eilhorne in *Spicer v. Holt*, 1976:71), arrest has multiple meanings and measures for various criminal-justice agencies, the police in particular.

Arrest is legally defined as "the apprehending or restraining of one's person in order to be forthcoming to answer all alleged or suspected crimes" (Blackstone, 1979; Warner, 1983). Arrest occurs whenever the following elements are present: (a) a police officer has a reason to believe that a crime has been committed (probable cause); (b) the officer intends to take the suspect into custody; and (c) the person arrested experiences and feels loss of freedom and restriction of movement.

Legal determination of whether a given contact is an arrest can be difficult (Whitebread and Slobogin, 1986:79). This poses a daily practical problem for police. On the one hand, seizures accompanied by handcuffing, drawn guns, and the use of words to the effect that one is under arrest constitute arrest; on the other, brief questioning of a citizen on the street is generally not considered an arrest. Between the two extremes lie many types of police detentions, the legal nature of which has to be determined by the courts (Whitebread and Slobogin, 1986).

The meaning attached to "arrest" is largely dependent on the purpose and context of its use. The definition or determination of arrest is complex because of the ramification for the person arrested and the emotional context in which it often takes place.

The nature of the definitional problem associated with arrest was aptly observed and highlighted by one court (*United States v. Bonanno*, 1960:71):

> It is axiomatic that before a finding can be made that there has been an illegal arrest, a showing must be made that there has been an arrest. Thus, an immediate problem of definition arises. Joined to that problem, is the danger, that the defining process will cast an air of deceptive simplicity over the broader task actually faced by the Court. One must never forget that this is a decision on the rights of individuals and the duties of government and not an abstract exercise in definition. In dealing with words there is always a temptation to allow them to become separated from their objective correlatives in the everyday world, and to treat them as if they have, or ought to have, one single simple meaning, unaffected by the contexts in which they occur and divorced from the world of things and events that give them their context and justification.

"Arrest" is just such a word, not only because it is necessarily unspecific and descriptive of complex, often extended processes, but because in different contexts it describes different processes, each of which has built up, in both legal and common parlance, sharply divergent emotional connotations.

Probable Cause

The quantum of knowledge required to justify an arrest for probable cause has been defined by the Supreme Court as "whether at that moment [of arrest] the facts and circumstances within [the officers'] knowledge and of which they [have] reasonable trustworthy information [are] sufficient to warrant a prudent man in believing that the [suspect] had committed or was committing an offense" (*Beck v. Ohio*, 379 U.S. 89, 91 [1964]). When the arresting officer's own observations are the basis for the arrest, only indicators of criminality noted prior to the arrest or evidence obtained as a result of a legitimate patdown based on reasonable suspicion (*Terry v. Ohio*, 1968) may be used to develop probable cause. Mere failure to identify oneself, protest one's innocence, or distance oneself from criminal suspects is, by itself, not sufficient to constitute probable cause (Whitebread and Slobogin, 1986:103).

In addition to the officer's personal knowledge, other sources for probable cause are information from a third party such as credible informants whose input is reasonably corroborated, "respected citizens" or typical witnesses to or victims of crime, or reports from other police jurisdictions. Mere suspicion of criminal activity is not sufficient to justify arrest. Once the probable-cause requirement is met, subsequent discovery of information that casts doubt on whether probable cause existed at the time of the arrest will not invalidate the arrest (*Henry v. United States*, 1959).

Taking a Person into Custody

An arrest can be carried out with or without an arrest warrant. An arrest warrant is an order to arrest a specific individual that is signed by an impartial magistrate if the proof presented by the police or the district attorney constitutes probable cause in his or her mind. Since the Fourth Amendment prohibits arbitrary arrests, the probable-cause requirement applies to both warrant and warrantless arrests.

Whenever feasible, police should obtain a warrant before making an arrest. Warrantless arrests occur mostly in "emergency" situations and are often made by patrolmen. In these kinds of arrests either the suspect did not have time to leave the scene of the crime or is held by citizens for the patrolman to arrive.

The police can make an arrest in a number of ways. The officer may announce that a person is under arrest and tap the arrestee's shoulder to reinforce the verbal statement. This is considered a "mild" form of arrest. If the situation calls for it, the officer may use an appropriate amount of force to accomplish the arrest, ranging from physical subjugation to the use of deadly force. The degree of force considered appropriate is particularly dependent on the degree of resistance offered by the suspect.

The police must provide the arrestee with specific statutory and constitutional protections. For example, the Federal Rules of Criminal Procedure require that the arrested person be taken before the nearest available magistrate without any unnecessary delay, one purpose being to prevent possible abuses by police during interrogation. The person being arrested must also be given the Miranda warning. Miranda requires that the police inform the person they arrest of their Fifth Amendment right against self-incrimination, their right to be silent, and their Sixth Amendment right to be represented by counsel. While he or she is in their custody, the police are responsible for the physical well-being of the arrestee.

Arrest and Detention

Review of arrest and other types of contact between police and citizens indicates that restraint or restriction of a citizen's liberty may or may not amount to arrest. Police encounters with citizens range from contact in which there is no use of police authority and citizens are not compelled to respond to a stop (prompted by reasonable suspicion); detention short of arrest, and finally arrest; in which all powers of the police may be exercised (Creamer, 1980).

Although arrest involves taking a person into custody and restraining his or her movement, certain events that involve restrictions on one's liberty are not considered arrest. These include placing someone in custody for reasons related to their mental health, taking a child younger than eighteen under certain conditions to a police station, or placing intoxicated persons under protective custody (Gless, 1980:281).

A major definitional difficulty is the distinction between detention and arrest. The two concepts have certain elements in common: (1) the actual or constructive apprehension of an individual at a particular point in time; and (2) the continued retention of that person for a period of time to be determined (Telling, 1978:324). The concepts differ, however, in the degree that the police may intrude on individuals' rights and interests as protected by the Fourth, Fifth and Sixth Amendments. In analyzing detentions and determining whether they amount to an arrest, the courts have considered as key factors the purpose of the detention (e.g., fingerprinting versus questioning), its manner (police detention versus grand-jury subpoenas), location (stationhouse confrontations versus seizures in the "field" or at the border), and duration of detention. None of these factors, however, is determinative; rather, the "totality of circumstances" is the test of whether the detention amounted to an arrest (Whitebread and Slobogin, 1986).

Arrest and Police Practices
Because arrest has certain legal requirements (probable cause) and creates significant legal risks for the police (for example, they may be liable for false imprisonment or be subject to a civil suit for damages), officers may sometimes avoid arrest and use field interrogation powers and techniques (or detention) to accomplish their purposes (for examples and cases see Telling, 1978 and Zander, 1977). Detention for investigation describes a broad category of police activities, which range from stopping individuals on the street through holding persons for purposes of interrogation from a few minutes to a few hours (Abrams, 1967:1103–13). The detention of persons is often an established police practice. For instance, detention for interrogation (which may continue for several hours) is a prevalent practice (La Fave, 1965: ch. 16; Markowitz and Summerfield, 1952:1202, 4). One study indicated that "though it constitutes an arrest, persons detained are not booked . . . and no record is kept of such cases" (Markowitz and Summerfield, 1952:1204; see also Telling, 1978:321; La Fave, 1965: ch. 16). The legal classifications of such encounters do not arise unless the citizen is subsequently charged with an offense and the fruits of the detention are introduced against him or her at the trial—confessions, incidentally seized evidence, fingerprints, and such.

Behaviorally, arrest has been defined as the transporting of a suspect to a police station (Black, 1971; La Fave, 1965:3–4). Transportation of a suspect to the station is distinct from other preliminary investigative devices such as stopping and questioning, frisking, or other on-the-spot checks for a variety of reasons. The degree of interference is substantially greater when a suspect is actually taken to the station; whatever the purposes of the extended custody (for investigative or prosecution purposes or to realize other deterrent, rehabilitative, or punitive functions), the police view it differently from other types of contacts. The person being transported also views such extended custody as different from on-the-street investigation. The consequences of being taken to the police station may be more serious. For instance, an arrest record may be made, often including photographing and fingerprinting.

In practice, however, suspects are sometimes taken to the station for investigation under circumstances that do not constitute an arrest. One practice is to take the suspect in without telling him that he is arrested and without recording the detention as an arrest. Another is to "invite" the suspect to headquarters (La Fave, 1965:302). This method of acquiring information is justified as necessary for the prevention of crime. Some police officers believe that they have not "arrested" a suspect until they have formally booked him on the police blotter.

The definition of arrest and numerous court decisions (Cook, 1971:180) suggest that a critical factor in determining whether an arrest has occurred is the intent of the officer to take custody of the individual for the purpose of charging him with a crime. In practice, police often arrest citizens for other purposes. Arrest is used by police for harassing or getting offenders off the street (La Fave, 1965:150), as a device for peace-keeping in certain neighborhoods, as a means to enforce and legitimize their authority (Reiss, 1971), or for demonstrating to superiors or to the public that an efficient job is being done (Markowitz and Summerfield, 1952:1202). Furthermore, it has been observed that arrest has come to have meaning and importance as a form of immediate intervention independent of the criminal-justice system for dealing with various exigencies.

The understanding or belief of the person arrested is also an important legal element of arrest. Generally, an individual is not under arrest if he has no knowledge or reason to suspect that he has been arrested (Cook, 1971:177). The law recognizes the importance of the subjective element—that arrest is primarily a personal and subjective experience that must be felt by the individual to occur.

The understanding or belief of citizens concerning the nature of a confrontation with the police or their freedom to leave the place of the encounter has therefore often been the subject of criminal trials and legal discussions. For instance, it has been argued that a person detained for field interrogation "will undoubtedly not consider himself under arrest, and consequently can in all honesty answer in the negative if later asked whether he has been arrested" (La Fave, 1965:347).

Research has indicated, however, that citizens are unable to distinguish between arrest and other types of police contact and that they may interpret various contacts as arrests. Citizens often admit to having been arrested when they actually have no arrest record (Erez, 1984).

Arrest Records and Recording

Empirically, it has been demonstrated that ambiguity concerning the nature of various types of contacts between citizens and police also results in multiple definitions of arrest for purposes of data recording, reporting, and statistical tabulation. "Whether a youngster obtained an arrest record or not could be a function of different officers' conceptions of what constituted the meaning of arrest" (according to Klein, Rosenweig, and Bates, 1975: 83). These conceptions resulted in definitions that ranged from "booking" through "brought into the station," "any detention (or citation, too) at the station," and even "field contacts" (Klein et al., 1975:85–86). Other researchers (Sherman, 1980b:471) have documented similar variations in the definition of arrest:

> . . . in the San Jose, California department arrest was defined as charging, but in Denver . . . all persons brought to a station house were counted as arrested. Cincinnati was reported to make frequent use of investigative detention, in which suspects were kept in custody at a police station for up to twenty-four hours without being counted as having been arrested. In Detroit, arresting patrol officers turn everything over to detectives at the station house, where the detectives . . . released an estimated 50 percent of the persons arrested for major felony offenses because of weak evidence or other reasons; contrary to UCR instructions, the persons released were not counted as having been arrested.

Based on its research, the Police Foundation (Sherman, 1980a, 1980b) suggests that the counts of arrests in different cities may be based on as many as five different points of reference: contacting suspects on the street; transporting suspects to a police station; detaining a suspect at a police station; booking a suspect at a police station; or filing charges against a suspect with a prosecutor. In addition, "in most U.S. police departments one can distinguish between contacts (sometimes recorded, often not), arrests (custody or temporary detention), and bookings (permanent records, often with fingerprints and 'mugging')" (Klein, 1982).

The booking process, the external or formal proof of arrest, is usually a clerical activity performed soon after the suspect has been delivered to the precinct or district station. Booking results in an arrest record with a detrimental effect on the person booked. On the other hand, booking may constitute some check upon police abuse. Booking makes it possible for friends, counsel, and others to learn that the suspect has been arrested (La Fave, 1965:380). Important legal rights and privileges arise by the time of booking, for example, the right to counsel and the right against self-incrimination. Although the suspect has Fifth and Sixth Amendment protections at the time of arrest, police may delay the booking process in the hopes that such rights will not be demanded until booking occurs. In some cases the police may refrain from booking the suspect/arrestee in order to give him the opportunity to exculpate himself before his involvement is recorded and publicized.

Thus, although the distinctions among arrest, detention, or other types of contacts with the police are important and very consequential for the person involved, the behavioral difference among these categories is not always clear or verifiable by records. Many arrests are not labeled as such and therefore not recorded; or the record of contact that the police believe to constitute an arrest is avoided. The reasons are several. Police may avoid booking a person in order to spare him the detrimental effects of an arrest record, or may believe they have not "arrested" a person until he has been formally booked. Police may manipulate the formal safeguards of arrest, which is one way they deal with their dilemma of balancing the need for order with the rules of procedural law. The upshot is that many "informal" arrests do not appear in official arrest statistics. Arrest events, whether recorded or not, may be nonetheless experienced as such by the individuals involved and become an integral part of their biographies (Erez, 1984).

Factors Influencing Police Discretion to Make an Arrest

Police are vested with wide discretionary power in their decision to arrest. Conflicting organizational goals, the dependence of police on the communities they serve, and various situational factors make full enforcement of the law neither possible nor desirable. Extensive research has identified several legal and extralegal factors influencing discretionary arrest decisions. The primary legal factor is the seriousness of the offense (Terry, 1967: 179). The police are more likely to arrest both adults and juveniles when the offense is a felony rather than a misdemeanor (e.g., Black, 1971).

Situational factors influencing the decision to make an arrest include the demeanor of the suspect—antagonistic or hostile suspects run the risk of being arrested (Black, 1971; Reiss, 1971). The presence and action of a complainant will also influence police to make an arrest. A preexisting victim-suspect relationship will reduce the likelihood of arrest; police make arrests more often when the suspect is a stranger to the victim (Black, 1971; La Fave, 1965). The way the police enter the scene is a factor: In reactive encounters arrest is more likely than in proactive ones (Black, 1971; Reiss, 1971). Location of the encounter is another factor: In public places arrest is more likely than in private ones (Black, 1976).

The extralegal factors that influence the arrest decision include age—juveniles tend to be arrested more often than adults; sex (Visher, 1983)—males more than females; race—blacks more often than whites; and socioeconomic status (Smith et al., 1984)—the poor more than the wealthy. Many of these characteristics have been associated with the "symbolic assailant," who is viewed by police as criminogenic and potentially violent and is thus a threat to both the citizenry and police.

Other extralegal factors include the organizational structure of police departments. For instance, the presence of specialized units such as vice and juvenile squads and a department's "style" of policing will affect arrest rates. Departments that follow a "legalistic" style will produce more arrests than those that adopt a "service" style, while the departments that follow a "watchman" style will produce the fewest arrests.

Judicial Review of Arrest Practices and the Police

Police are empowered to arrest and to use force legitimately so as to maintain order and civility in a free and democratic society. Citizens grant this authority to police reluctantly because of fear that its abuse could lead to the erosion of freedom. Because citizens demand that police be efficient in combating crime but at the same time place restraints on their powers, a dilemma is posed for the police—how to balance demands for crime control with individuals' personal freedom and rights.

Police arrests are inevitably subject to judicial review. When the courts rule that the officers have violated procedural law, the police feel not only that their professional competence is questioned, but also that they are hamstrung because the guilty go free (Reiss, 1971). As the rules governing police work are in constant flux, the police continuously test the limits of their arrest authority in their daily efforts to control crime.

Edna Erez

Bibliography

Abrams, Gerald H. "Constitutional Limitations on detention for Investigation." *Iowa Law Review* 52 (1967): 1093–1119.

Black, Donald. "The Social Organization of Arrest." *Standard Law Review* 23 (1971): 1087–111.

———. *The Behavior of Law*. New York: Academic Press, 1976.

Blackstone, Sir William. *Commentaries on the Laws of England*. 4 vols. Chicago: University of Chicago Press, 1979.

Cook, Joseph G. "Subjective Attitudes of Arrestee and Arrestor as Affecting Occurrence of Arrest." *Kansas Law Review* 19 (1971): 173–83.

Creamer, J. Shane. *The Law of Arrest, Search and Seizure*. New York: Holt, Rinehart and Winston, 1980.

Erez, Edna. "On the 'Dark Figure' of Arrest." *Journal of Police Science and Administration* 12(4) (1984): 431–40.

Gless, Allan G. "Arrest and Citation: Definition and Analysis." *Nebraska Law Review* 26 (1980): 279–326.

Klein, Malcolm W. "Watch out for that Last Variable: A Paper Presented at the NATO Conference on the Biosocial Basis of Antisocial Behavior." Skiathos, Greece, September, 1982. (Unpublished paper presented at the NATO Conference.)

———, Susan Labin Rosenweig, and Ronald Bates. "The Ambiguous Arrest." *Criminology* 13(1) (1975): 78–89.

La Fave, Wayne R. *Arrest: The Decision to Take a Suspect into Custody*. Boston: Little, Brown, 1965.

Markowitz, Paula R., and Dr. Walter Summerfield. "Philadelphia Police Practice and the Law of Arrest." *University of Pennsylvania Law Review* 100 (1952): 1182–216.

Reiss, Albert J. *The Police and the Public.* New Haven, CT: Yale University Press, 1971.

Sherman, Lawrence. "Enforcement Workshop: Defining Arrests—The Practical Consequences of Agency Differences, Part I." *Criminal Law Bulletin* 16 (1980a): 376–80.

———. "Enforcement Workshop: Defining Arrests—The Practical Consequences of Agency Differences, Part II." *Criminal Law Bulletin* 16 (1980b): 468–71.

Smith, Douglas, C.A. Visher, and L.A. Davidson. "Equity and Discretionary Justice: The Influence of Race on Police Arrest Decision." *Journal of Criminal Law and Criminality* 75 (1984): 234–49.

Telling, David. "Arrest and Detention: the Conceptual Maze." *Criminal Law Review* (June 1978): 320–31.

Terry, Robert. "The Screening of Juvenile Offenders." *Journal of Criminal Law, Criminology and Police Science* (June 1967): 173–81.

Visher, Christy. "Gender, Police Arrest Decisions, and Notions of Chivalry." *Criminology* 21(1) (1983): 5–28.

Warner, Sam B. "The Uniform Arrest Act." *Virginia Law Review* 28 (1983): 315–47.

Whitebread, Charles H., and Christopher Slobogin. *Criminal Procedure.* New York: Foundation Press, 1986.

Zander, Michael. "When Is Arrest Not an Arrest?" *New Law Journal* 127 (1977): 352–54, 379–82.

Arson Investigation

Arson investigation determines the origins and causes of a fire, one that has been maliciously set to burn down the property of another or to incinerate one's own property for some illegal purpose. The investigator's charge is to gather all the facts and evidence at the fire scene, then to decide whether the fire was of incendiary, natural, or accidental origin.

Training

To become an expert in arson investigation a person must be trained in a curriculum that is all encompassing. The local police academy in conjunction with the fire academy should offer the following courses:

- Standard certified police academy courses
- Legal aspects
- Chemistry of fire
- Behavior of fire
- Building construction
- Fire-scene investigation
- Initial fire attack and suppression
- Interviews and interrogation
- Fire typology
- Courtroom testimony
- Motives of the arsonist

Those eligible for training should meet one or more of these criteria:

- Paid firefighter—five years' service
- Paid police officer—five years' service
- Paid firefighter on a standing promotional examination
- Paid lieutenant or captain (police or fire)
- Volunteer firefighter—ten years' service
- Volunteer firefighter—present or past chief officer
- Volunteer firefighter—qualified state instructor
- College degree in criminal justice or police science

The training program should be nationally certified. Certification ensures that graduates have been prepared adequately for the occupation of arson investigator. Some amount of legal training is important. It apprises the investigator of the various court decisions affecting arson investigation, civil rights, search and seizure, and so on. This knowledge must be updated constantly. In the same light, new chemical compounds found at fire scenes might confound the investigator, if he or she has not learned about them beforehand. A college degree in criminal justice or police science is, perhaps, the most important requirement because of the inclusive education gained. This fund of general knowledge has many applications in arson investigation.

The Criminal-Justice System

In the past, police and fire personnel have not always agreed on whose responsibility it was to investigate. Tension between them has reached the highest levels of authority, stifling attempts to form an ideal police-fire collaboration. What is presently needed is a system of education that will make police officers of firefighters and firefighters of police officers. Reluctance to adopt such a system has continued to stymie progress, created unhealthy competition, and deprived the antagonists of shared knowledge. The training curriculum outlined above corrects this unhappy situation by bringing together police and fire personnel in one educational setting for the purpose of sharing knowledge.

Step-by-Step Procedure

Firefighters say that each fire is different, but an arson investigator must devise and stay with a procedural plan for investigation that treats all fires the same. This carbon-copy approach is essential when presenting a case in court. Standardized reporting of evidence during arson prosecution helps the district attorney to win the case. An arson investigator who assembles the casework in a meticulous manner is way ahead of the one who turns in neglectful, slovenly work.

Step 1. The investigator begins a case-numbered notebook that serves as the total information source for the investigation. The basic notebook contains the case number; names and numbers of officers assigned to investigate; time and date of fire; fire dispatch incident number; time and date investigator reported at scene of fire; name and rank of fire officer requesting investigation; how alarm was received; and a statement of fire knowledge (type of fire, flame color, results of fire, etc.).

Step 2. The investigator ascertains the legal grounds for probing the fire scene; readies tools of the trade (rubber boots, coat, hard hat, flashlight, etc.); checks to see if the fire scene has been protected; and interviews the officer who requested the investigation.

Step 3. The two-person arson investigation team talks to the person who first reported the fire and to anyone else who has something to say about it. The team takes photographs of the fire scene, notes the burn pattern, collects evidence, and tries to visualize the scene before the fire. Then a systematic inspection of the entire structure's remains follows to determine the point of origin of the fire and to establish the cause of it beyond a reasonable doubt, i.e., accident, negligence, or incendiary.

Step 4. Both investigators compare notes and decide if further investigation is warranted. If arson is suspected, all physical evidence will go eventually to the crime lab and all written notes and interviews to the district attorney.

Step 5. The team locates the owner of the burned-out structure and interviews him or her as soon as arson is suspected. If possible, the interview is taped. The story given at this crucial point will prove useful later on if the owner is implicated in a case of arson.

Step 6. The team rechecks the evidence to make sure it is properly tagged, labeled, and locked up before starting a door-to-door canvass of the area. To produce a lead as to whom the arsonist might be, the investigators question everyone in the neighborhood of the fire.

Step 7. The team should never be in a hurry to leave the fire scene and its environs; often either a slow-to-respond witness will come forward or an additional bit of evidence will be found.

Step 8. The team reconvenes and reviews the facts one more time, so as to rule out any hastily made decisions.

Step 9. If the team is positive that arson was committed, the investigators seek interdepartmental cooperation; for example, to turn up pivotal information a check is run of the Property Insurance Loss Register (PILR) or the municipal license department to discover violations of health, electrical, and fire-prevention codes.

Step 10. The team confers with the district attorney to review the case for possible prosecution.

Step 11. The district attorney determines that there is a viable case and wants to pursue it with the arson investigation team.

Magnitude of the Problem

According to the 1991 *Uniform Crime Reports*, as compiled by the Federal Bureau of Investigation, 11,845 law-enforcement agencies reported 99,784 arson offenses. By property type, the number of structure arsons amounted to 46,478 offenses; mobile arsons were 23,595; and the "other" category totaled 16,074. Average damage per arson offense was $11,980. The national arson clearance rate for 1991 was 16 percent; agencies in cities with fewer than 10,000 inhabitants showed the highest rate, clearing 25 percent of the arson offenses brought to their attention; other, larger cities cleared only 15 percent for the low.

Thomas J. Bouquard

Bibliography

Battle, Brendan P., and Paul B. Weston. *Arson*. New York: Arco Publishing, 1975.

Boudreau, John F., et al. *Arson and Arson Investigation: Survey and Assessment*. Washington, DC: National Institute of Law Enforcement and Criminal Justice, LEAA, October 1977.

Bouquard, Thomas J. *Arson Investigation: The Step-by-Step Procedure*. Springfield, IL: Charles C. Thomas, 1983.

International Association of Arson Investigators. *Selected Articles for Fire and Arson Investigators*. Springfield, IL: IAAI Publishers, 1976.

Kirk, Paul L. *Fire Investigation*. New York: John Wiley and Sons, 1969.

Tuck, Charles A., Jr. *NFPA Inspection Manual*. 4th ed. Boston: National Fire Protection Association, 1976.

Artificial Intelligence

By the year 2000, artificial intelligence (AI) will make computers indispensable and the AI industry is expected to be worth as much as $1 trillion. There are many reasons why AI will have disproportionate influence in the future. Undoubtedly, a major factor was Japan's announcement in the fall of 1981 that it would build superspeed computers that would have AI capabilities, the so-called "fifth generation" of computers. In terms of police application, combining AI and parallel processing (the Japanese "fifth generation" computer) makes a national automated fingerprint system and crime analysis system very possible. Since that announcement, Japan declared in the spring of 1984 that a "sixth generation" computer project was to be launched. The United States responded to the challenge through the government (primarily Defense Department funding), corporations, nonprofit corporations (e.g., SRI and Rand), universities (Stanford, MIT, USC, Yale, Carnegie-Mellon, much of the University of California system, etc.), and a consortium known as the Microelectronics Computer Technology Corporation. Japan's research lead in nonsilicon electronics will provide further impetus to United States activities. Another factor is simply that most information processing involves reasoning, decision-making, problem-solving, creativity, language, and related areas, not calculating and data processing. Computers will still process data and perform all the activities they are expected to handle; however, new software and new computers will be available (Harmon and King, 1985:1).

Defining Artificial Intelligence

Definitions of AI vary because AI is an interdisciplinary science. Basically, AI is concerned with developing computer systems that generate the types of results normally associated with human intelligence; the goal of AI has always been to develop computer programs that could in some sense think; the model of AI has always been the human brain (Harmon and King, 1985).

AI research has focused on three areas: natural language processing (computer programs that read, speak, and understand language used in everyday conversation—these programs are known as "front end" packages, that is, they can be attached to a large database and queries can be made by simply asking questions in English); robotics (visual, tactile, and movement programs are currently available); and expert systems (computer programs that emulate the behavior of human experts). The remainder of this article will focus on expert systems since it is the most popular research/applications area and since it appears, at this time, that the impact of expert systems will be greater than other AI technologies.

Expert Systems (ES)

ES have generated the most interest in AI thus far, having attained a high degree of sophistication and experienced a measure of success in a number of fields (medical and science applications dominate). Currently, ES are emerging in the police field. At the local level, one is being utilized for case analysis in the Green River homicide investigation in the state of Washington; another is being utilized for residential burglaries in Baltimore County, Maryland (Ratledge and Jacoby, 1989); a third is a rapist profiling program (Cameron, 1990). At the state level, interest is being shown in developing automated fingerprint identification systems

(Cameron, 1990). At the federal level, a number of agencies are utilizing ES. For example, an ES is being used by the IRS Inspection Service in its anticorruption activities. It utilizes link analysis, has natural language aspects, and has an explanation/justification component (Coady, 1985). Another one is being developed as part of the Secret Service Master Central Index (MCI), which will also be able to correlate investigative information (Carlon and Vezeris, 1985:19). Other ES are being developed/used by the FBI. These ES will be utilized in supporting investigations of organized crime, narcotics, counterterrorism, and a name search program (Krause, 1986). The FBI has also developed ES in the areas of arson and violent crime (Ratledge and Jacoby, 1989).

An analysis of all ES development thus far reveals that most exhibit problem-solving behavior and are characterized primarily by a diagnosis/prescription paradigm. Other categories of ES applications are interpretation, design, planning, monitoring, debugging, control, repair, prediction (this will be an important aspect of the counterterrorism and arson ES being developed by the FBI), and instruction. The latter is often called intelligent computer assisted instruction (ICAI). ICAI is a knowledge-based system that utilizes tools and techniques of AI in order to make the system more flexible and responsive than other CAI approaches. It contains four components: an expertise module (the body of knowledge that is to be taught); a student/trainee module (this module displays the degree of understanding of the material taught—it can highlight errors, indicate why they are erroneous, and suggest corrections); a tutoring/teaching module (this module determines how materials should be presented by the system—it selects problems to be solved, monitors and criticizes performance, provides assistance, and selects materials); and an interface module, which conducts the training in natural language. There are very few true ICAI systems used in law enforcement, although a number of fairly sophisticated computer assisted instruction systems are available.

The following is an example of one U.S. Navy ICAI system that is primarily devoted to conceptual skill development. STEAMER is an ICAI system that instructs naval recruits in how to operate steam propulsion systems found on many naval ships. STEAMER handles a very difficult problem area and utilizes software techniques developed by AI engineers. This area was chosen for development because it is one of the greatest training problems faced by the navy. The navy needed a training system that would deal with the procedures involved in running the steam propulsion plant as well as the consequences of different procedures attempted during various contingencies. STEAMER utilizes two personal computers. One displays a steam plant diagram; the other displays information about the plant and provides a tutoring system that allows a student to interact with the program. All the major parts of the plant are displayed. Any subsystem can be accessed by pointing the giving and "expand" command. The trainee can go to whatever depth is desired, right down to the smallest part. The trainee then interacts with a highly effective, inspectable, simulation program (Harmon and King, 1985:239–40).

In the criminal justice system, ES are now utilized in "crime solving, decision making, training, and program planning and design. They contain the best knowledge available about law enforcement issues and practices and serve as consultants and advisers to law-enforcement officials" (Ratledge and Jacoby, 1989:1). Thus far, ES development has focused on crime-solving. Although emphasis on this particular role is appropriate at the federal level, it is not sufficient for local agencies since a considerable amount of time is expended in noncriminal activities. To date, very few ES applications have been developed in the noncriminal area. One can, however, imagine some useful applications in the areas of domestic disturbances and mental cases. If a fully developed and validated ES were available to advise on domestic disturbance decisions, for example, the quality of decisions made by officers (many of whom are not that experienced, motivated, or competent to give these activities the attention they deserve) might be improved. Needed expert use in the domestic area is often scarce and ES are excellent vehicles for capturing and distributing scarce expertise to less skilled or less experienced practitioners (Waterman, 1986). Officers would no longer intervene "blindly" in these situations; information would be available for assessment of risk of domestic violence based on all past interventions; advice on intervention strategies would guide officer intercession. The ES would also allow for monitoring and evaluation of intervention (which would also enhance research and theory development).

A

Characteristics of Expert Systems

Knowledge. The core of the ES is the corpus of knowledge that accumulates during system building (Waterman, 1986). For example, the FBI is currently extracting the expertise of its top agents and introducing that knowledge into the ES it is developing (Krause, 1986). The knowledge acquired must be associated with a well-defined, narrowly bounded knowledge domain (the FBI has identified four such knowledge domains thus far). Knowledge must be represented in a certain way (e.g., frames, rules, semantic nets) so that the problem can be easily solved. Both the FBI and IRS use the rule approach (the strategy is usually expressed as: if premise, then conclusion, or if condition, then action). Coady (1985:22–23) provides an example of this popular knowledge representation using a hypothetical IRS bribery investigation (for a more comprehensive view, see Waterman, 1986, or Harmon and King, 1985). Many of the rules in ES are heuristic; i.e., results and solutions are based on "rule of thumb" or intuition, if/then types of rules that help limit the search for solutions. Heuristics are used because most of the tasks undertaken are typically difficult and poorly understood; i.e., unstructured (this is one of the major differences between ES and conventional computer systems).

Inference. The second major structural characteristic of an ES is the "inference engine." This is the general problem-solving knowledge that draws inferences, adds facts/rules, and controls the order of reasoning. It cannot be ascertained from the literature what inference and control strategies are used by current police ES.

Metaknowledge Facility. The knowledge about knowledge facility means that ES can explain and justify what is done and why. This retrospective form of reasoning, is the most common of three approaches. The other two are hypothetical reasoning (where the system explains what would have happened differently if a particular fact or rule had been different), and counterfactual reasoning, where the ES explains why an expected conclusion was not reached (Waterman 1986: 91). The FBI has an explanation facility available on line so that rules that led to an ES prediction can be examined (Krause, 1986); the IRS system, similarly, can explain step-by-step how the conclusions were reached (Coady, 1985:23).

User Interface. ES can be run by non-computer personnel (natural language interface facilitates use of the system) in an interactive mode (although a dialogue exists between the system and the user, the former directs the user much of the time, which makes ES very user friendly).

Expandability. Updating and expanding the ES is relatively easy. The knowledge base is separate from the inference apparatus so that incremental performance improvement is possible. Some systems keep statistics that provide the basis for new rules; some expand and refine their knowledge bases automatically, which allows for "learning" to occur over time and experience.

Constructing Expert Systems

ES can be developed easily and quickly through system building tools (Gevarter, 1983; Harmon and King, 1985; Oxman, 1985; Waterman, 1986). These tools range from very high-level programming languages to low-level support facilities.

The programming languages used for ES are usually symbol-manipulation languages, e.g., LISP (manipulates symbols in the form of lists) and PROLOG (manipulates logical expressions). Although LISP (and its many variations) is the most widely used language in the United States, PROLOG is gaining in popularity. In fact, both the FBI and IRS have based their ES on this particular language. The more popular high-level languages, e.g., PASCAL, COBOL, FORTRAN, etc., are not generally utilized for noncomputational or symbolic tasks.

Programming environments or knowledge engineering languages are special packages of prewritten code (usually done in LISP and PROLOG) that can be quite sophisticated. These tools can greatly reduce ES development time and cost. They run on large computers, LISP machines, or PROLOG machines, and are designed to build ES that contain hundreds to thousands of rules. They are capable of utilizing a mix of consultation paradigms. Although not used in constructing law enforcement ES at this time, they will be in the future. An example may be warranted. ART is a general tool that can be applied to many programs. It contains features similar to other systems; however, the inference engine and a computational ability make ART different from other AI tools. The inference engine (called an applier and described as an opportunistic reasoner) moves opportunistically, i.e., it is not constrained to one control strategy (e.g., backward or forward chaining). ART has been used to design software programs for newspaper pages, space shuttle flights, and space stations; to diagnose digital circuits and satellite networks; plan financial assets, liability, and management profiles; and prepare flight schedules (information on ART obtained from the Arizona Meeting on AI).

Knowledge Engineering "Shells." Shells contain knowledge representation and inference strategies and a control component. By separating the inference engine from the ES knowledge base, AI researchers were able to derive "shells" that could then be attached to new knowledge bases. This became the conceptual breakthrough for rapid ES development and the catalyst to the current ES revolution. EMYCIN was the first ES shell (it was the inference engine from the medical ES called MYCIN). Today, EMYCIN and other types of "shells" are proliferating in the United States and the concept has recently become popular with the European computer community. These shells, like computers, vary greatly in cost and complexity. The FBI has been using "shells" of this type for ES development, but, as previously stated, it found the PROLOG language to be superior for its purposes. Consequently, the shell approach has been discarded by the FBI. Since "shells" will be used by many police agencies in the future (there are dramatic time/cost reductions and ES can be developed quite easily by nonprogrammers), a brief orientation follows.

There are two types of shells: rule-based and example-based. Rule-based systems, utilizing a deductive approach, are the more popular and versatile type of shells. They require the builder to represent knowledge through if/then rules. (The "if" part of a rule presents the situation; the "then" part is the response.) This knowledge representation process may be difficult for builders who have trouble articulating what is known. Example-based systems, utilizing an inductive approach, are very easy to build, but are not as versatile (instead of rules, these systems contain examples, e.g., a community that has substantial illegal gambling, drugs, prostitution, and corruption denotes the presence of organized crime). Generally, rule-based systems are more appropriate for broad problems where variables experience intermittent change; example-based systems are more appropriate for limited situations that are characterized by stability (Fersko-Weiss, 1985:105). Fortunately, most of these systems utilize natural language-type processes along with menus and other types of development aids.

Miscellaneous types of system building tools are aids (in designing and knowledge acquisition) and support facilities (the extra software packages that make the tool user-friendly and more efficient).

Future of Expert Systems
ES are currently being used in law enforcement to correlate investigative information, determine patterns of criminality or conspiracy, advise on aspects of an investigation, predict criminal activities, etc. The author is not aware of any ES solely devoted to law enforcement administration at this time, although applications could be developed quite quickly utilizing the "shell" approach. Nevertheless, in the near future, in addition to those ES already mentioned in this article, police applications could include a/an:

- *Personnel Knowledge System.* The PKS could aid managers in making personnel decisions (for example, a personnel problem could be entered into the system and, after a period of consultation, proposed course(s) of action would be prescribed).
- *Automated Procedures Manual.* The APM could assist employees in obtaining the information needed in dealing with procedural problems. This could decrease training costs—since less time would be devoted to instructing personnel in memorizing procedures and supervisors could spend less time advising employees—and should improve the quality of actions and decisions made by personnel.
- *Information Knowledge System.* The IKS would allow managers to remain current on more information in less time. The IKS would automatically set up files and indexing systems and would perform a wide range of analysis and abstracting activities related to correspondence, newspapers/magazines, and professional/technical publications. For example, a manager could query the IKS on some topic and find all correspondence, memos, reports, policies, articles, etc.,

related to the area of interest. Furthermore, the IKS would entertain questions covering any information in the database.

- *Training Knowledge System.* The TKS would not only involve the trainee with conventional drill and practice, but would allow for exact problem identification and provide the remediation necessary to correct the specific problem(s) encountered by the user. The TKS could also allow for conceptual instruction.
- *Job Analysis Knowledge System.* The JAKS could assist the manager in recruitment/selection and training.
- *Programming Knowledge System.* The PKS could reduce the time and effort programmers currently require to create and maintain programs. As programming becomes more automatic and user-friendliness increases, many programming functions will disappear and line personnel will be able to take a more active role in this area.

By the year 2000, the following are very possible:

- ES should be utilized by all levels of government policing (as the price/power of hardware improves, as software becomes more available, and as expertise develops, ES will be widely adopted by law enforcement). Currently, as can be seen from preceding examples, federal agencies have a virtual monopoly on ES because of expertise and cost requirements.
- The FBI will maintain a leadership position in ES development and use. The FBI will also maintain numerous national ES in administrative and operational areas.
- Law enforcement will continue to spearhead ES development and utilization within the criminal justice system. ES in the legal profession are emerging. Although the types of applications are small—document generation, interpretation/prediction, scheduling/monitoring, case management—and relatively unsophisticated, the potential is great. Neil Frude, in his book *The Intimate Machine*, gives an example of a police interrogation ES, a rather unusual application in this area.
- ES techniques (as well as other AI technologies) will greatly impact on all law-

enforcement software. The trend is clear. Currently, ES concepts are being used in decision support software; ES techniques are being used in database processing. Paradox, for example, utilizes the ES technique known as heuristic query optimization (goal-directed problem reduction). This technique optimizes the search procedure by finding the shortest and most rapid route to the information. ES are transforming data networks: diagnostic ES infer causes of irregular behavior and then coordinate work orders so that repairs can be made; control ES monitor and predict a network's workload in order to route calls efficiently; and interpretation ES review network operations and explain them by assigning meaning (Stach, 1985:246); ES techniques are also impacting on word/data processing programs.

- ES will routinely rely on the microcomputer as the major component of the system. The laptop computer could also be involved as its power increases.
- As computers become more "intelligent," the need for programming will decrease. (Chorafas, 1985, sees ES applications and development greatly enhanced through AI languages that will be fully initiated, projected, manipulated, and maintained by computers.)
- ES will allow police administrators to better manage, control, plan, schedule, monitor, evaluate, correlate, expedite, interpret, predict, diagnose, decide, design, repair, train, hypothesize, theorize, etc.
- ES will, in conjunction with parallel processing hardware, allow for instantaneous location and retrieval of any crime-related information; ES will surface uncorrelated facts/inferences, recognize patterns of criminality/conspiracy, advise on all legal matters relating to investigations, and predict criminality.
- There will be a decrease in ad hoc decision-making/problem-solving. The ES will obviate this type of activity in areas covered by the technology, although, due to a number of reasons, ad hoc decision-making and problem-solving will still occur. When it does, however, the ES could be consulted for a "second opinion." Decisions and solutions that dif-

fered significantly from those provided by ES would probably have to be justified. (Although ES will become common in police agencies, in most cases they will serve as "assistants" that support and enhance, not replace, work or professional workers.)

- ES advice will be available on a real-time basis; i.e., knowledge accessibility will be immediate and continuous. This will allow more attention to be focused on the more relevant decision/problem factors and should shorten decision-making and problem-solving time.
- Memorization of large amounts of information will be unnecessary with knowledge-based ES. In addition, ES will prove to be a useful medium for disseminating practice innovations.
- Inexperienced personnel will be taught the information that is considered important and the reasoning processes employed in problem-solving. This can be accomplished by consulting the ES, which would need an explanation component, or by creating an intelligent computer-assisted instruction system (ICAI).
- ES will allow police personnel to remain current on more information in less time (the "Connection Machine" can already scan 16,000 articles in 1/20 of a second) and provide a wide range of analysis and abstracting on selected topics.
- The ES–human relationship will be a symbiotic one. Sometime during the twenty-first century, however, the machines will surpass our ability to keep up with them.
- ES will assist in creating a collective intelligence capability for problem-solving, through teleconferencing and computer conferencing.

Current and Potential Uses
Artificial intelligence technologies (e.g., natural language processing, robotics, and expert systems) are emerging in the law enforcement field. By the year 2000 artificial intelligence will be widely used and should revolutionize the way police agencies function. This article looks at artificial intelligence with special emphasis on expert systems because these problem-solving programs are expected to have the most impact on administration and operations. The future of expert systems is then set out.

During the early 1960s, the computer became a useful tool for police administration and operations. Today, the computer is an essential device: It is used by police agencies at every level of government and applications cover a wide range of activities. According to one nationwide study, for example, police use of microcomputers was extensive at the municipal government level, surpassed only by the data processing department (Kraemer et al., 1985). In addition, computers are getting faster, smaller, more inexpensive, and "smarter." Consequently, the current trend is to put computer capabilities at the end user level; the central issue is related to control of the technology—who sets policy, who implements those policies, and how the policies are changed. The major concern is exploitation of the new technology; the dominant problem is matching the requirements and capabilities of computers to the requirements and capabilities of police personnel.

Armand P. Hernandez

Bibliography
Cameron, J. "Artificial Intelligence, Expert Systems, Microcomputers and Law Enforcement." *Police Chief* 57(3) (1990): 36–41.
Carlon, J., and J. Vezeris. "The Secret Service Master Central Index." *Police Chief* 52(11) (1985): 18–21.
Chorafas, D. *Management Workstations for Greater Productivity*. New York: McGraw-Hill, 1985.
Coady, W. "Automated Link Analysis: Artificial Intelligence-Based Tool for Investigators." *Police Chief* 52(9) (1985): 22–23.
Doherty, M. "Applying Parallel Processing Techniques to Automated Fingerprint Identification." *Police Chief* 53(5) (1986): 47–49.
Fersko-Weiss, H. "Expert System Decision-Making Power." *Personal Computing* (November 1985): 97–105.
Gevarter, W.B. "Expert Systems: Limited but Powerful." *IEEE Spectrum* (August 1983): 39–45.
Gold, J. "Not Too Soon It Got Smart." *Computer Decisions* 18(1) (1986): 46.
Harmon, P., and D. King. *Artificial Intelligence in Business*. New York: John Wiley and Sons, 1985.

Kraemer, K., J. King, D. Dunkle, J. Lane, and J. George. "Microcomputer Use and Policy." *Baseline Data Report* 17. Washington, DC: International City Management Association, 1985.

Krause, R. "The Best and the Brightest." *Law Enforcement Technology* (August/September 1986): 25–27.

Manuel, T. "Fifth Generation Computers May Soon Be Available in U.S." *Electronics* 58 (1985): 21.

Oxman, S.W. "Expert Systems Represent Ultimate Goal of Strategic Decision Making." *Data Management* 23 (1985): 36–38.

Ratledge, E., and J. Jacoby. *Handbook on Artificial Intelligence and Expert Systems in Law Enforcement.* New York: Greenwood Press, 1989.

Stach, J. "Expert Systems Find a New Place in Data Networks." *Data Communications* 14 (1985): 245–61.

Waterman, D. *A Guide to Expert Systems.* Menlo Park, CA: Addison-Wesley, 1986.

Whyte, C. "A Sense of Balance." *PC World* 3 (1985): 286–95.

Assaults on Police Officers

Attacks on the police have reached unconscionable levels. As reported to the Federal Bureau of Investigation, assaults rose from 9,621 in 1960 to 71,794 in 1990. Officers suffered an injury at a fairly consistent rate of fifteen to seventeen total assaults per one hundred personnel during the past twenty years. Table 1 shows the distribution of police officers assaulted and murdered for the thirty-one-year span 1960 through 1990. A total of 1,341,379 officers have been assaulted during these thirty-one years, or an average of 43,270 incidents each year.

The Assaultive Incident

The most striking fact about assaults on the police is that very few are premeditated. Rather, an attack typically results from an officer performing a routine police activity. Frequently, the officer was answering a disturbance call or trying to make an arrest for a crime other than burglary or robbery, according to the 1990 FBI report *Law Enforcement Officers Killed and Assaulted.* The Police Assaults Study, based on research conducted in 1972–1974 at the University of Oklahoma by Chapman (1974), found

that most assailants had either been drinking alcohol or were under its influence at the time of assault.

The act that specifically triggered the assault was the attempt to arrest a suspected perpetrator of the crime to which the officer had been summoned. However, the Police Assaults Study found that a substantial number of officers in the south-central region were assaulted while transporting or processing an offender. Another investigator, Mona Margarita (1980a), concluded that the offender's desire to avoid capture, arrest, or injury was a motive for the assault.

A nagging question remains unanswered: Why do some assaults cause only minor injury, while others seriously or fatally injure an officer? Margarita has suggested that one important factor is the seriousness of the event to which the officer responds. For example, injury resulting from routine traffic-law enforcement is generally less severe than that which occurs when an officer responds to a serious crime. Naturally, where a deadly weapon is used in the commission of a crime, there is an increased probability that the officer will sustain serious injury or be killed. Meyer et al. (1979), confirmed this in an analysis of robbery and robbery-related incidents. In the cases analyzed, the level of violence escalated to a point where the officer was either shot at but not hit, was wounded, or was killed. In contrast, a study by Chapman et al. (1974) of general municipal assaults found a far less intensive level of violence which featured, for the most part, a round of wrestling, pushing, shoving, or hitting of officers. If hurt at all, officers suffered no more than bruises and scratches. Table 2 sets out selected characteristics associated with the environment and dynamics of police assault incidents for a nine-year period.

Alarmingly, the 1980s have seen the urban phenomenon of street gangs and drug dealing impact on cop fighting. Drive-by shootings and territorial squabbles among gangs have made police patrol ever more hazardous, according to Witkin et al. (1990). So has the upsurge in drug dealing and use.

The Assaulted Officer

Officers who have been assaulted share few common characteristics. In fact, assaults are more a function of time and place than of an officer's personality or behavior. Data gathered by the Police Assaults Study suggest that most conventional wisdom on this matter is in error. One belief is that the shorter, more slightly built officer is more vulnerable to victimization or is more likely to be aggressive to counteract perceived vulnerability. Most assaulted officers, the study found, tended to be of average height (sixty-nine to seventy-two inches) and of medium build. Another erroneous perception is that assaulted officers lack either the experience or training to handle an explosive situation. On the contrary: The study showed that the typical assaulted officer had been with the force for over three and one-half years and had received

substantial specialized training in a variety of subjects, including public relations.

Some observers have suggested that officers from ethnic minorities are more likely to be given hazardous assignments than whites and, therefore, are more likely to be assaulted. The Police Assaults Study found that while minority officers accounted for 7 percent of the total police in the south-central region, they accounted for only 8 percent of the officers assaulted. In essence, minority officers seem neither more nor less likely to be assaulted than Caucasian officers. Another question concerns

TABLE 1

Distribution of Police Officers Assaulted and Murdered: 1960–1990

Year	Total Assaults	Rate per 100 Officers	Assaults with Injury	Rate per 100 Officers	Number of Officers Murdered
1960	9,621	6.3	NR*	NR	28
1961	13,190	8.3	NR	NR	37
1962	17,330	10.2	NR	NR	48
1963	16,793	11.0	NR	NR	55
1964	18,001	9.9	7,738	4.3	57
1965	20,523	10.8	6,836	3.6	53
1966	23,851	12.2	9,113	4.6	57
1967	26,755	13.5	10,770	5.4	76
1968	33,604	15.8	14,072	6.6	64
1969	35,202	16.9	11,949	5.7	86
1970	43,171	18.7	15,165	6.6	100
1971	49,768	18.7	17,631	6.6	126
1972	37,523	15.1	12,230	5.8	112
1973	32,535	15.0	12,880	5.9	127
1974	29,511	15.1	11,468	5.9	132
1975	44,867	15.4	18,974	6.5	129
1976	49,079	16.8	18,737	6.4	111
1977	49,156	15.3	17,663	5.5	93
1978	56,130	16.1	21,075	6.2	93
1979	59,031	17.3	21,764	6.4	106
1980	57,847	16.7	21,516	6.2	104
1981	57,116	17.2	20,272	6.1	91
1982	55,755	17.5	17,116	5.4	92
1983	62,324	16.5	20,807	5.5	80
1984	60,153	16.2	20,205	5.4	72
1985	61,724	15.8	20,817	5.3	78
1986	64,259	16.9	21,639	5.7	66
1987	63,842	16.8	21,273	5.6	74
1988	58,752	15.9	21,015	5.7	78
1989	62,172	16.7	21,893	5.8	66
1990	71,794	17.4	26,031	6.3	65

Source: Federal Bureau of Investigation, *Uniform Crime Reports* and *Law Enforcement Officers Killed and Assaulted* (Washington, DC: Government Printing Office). Data were extracted from each document for the years set out above.

*NR: Not reported in *Uniform Crime Reports* until 1964.

the relation of staffing patterns to assault. Both an analysis of assaults in Kansas City, Missouri, made by Decker and Wagner (1982) and the 1990 FBI report, *Law Enforcement Officers Killed and Assaulted*, indicate that, overall, there appears to be no significant difference in the level of assaults on officers working alone or with one or more others. The FBI data, however, reveal that officers working alone are more likely to be assaulted while responding to disturbance calls or attempting arrests for other than burglary or robbery or making traffic stops. Officers in two-person motor patrol units are more likely to be assaulted while engaged in the same kinds of events listed above as well as handling or transporting prisoners.

Sometimes an officer actually precipitates the attack on him or herself. Psychologist Hans Toch, in his studies *Violent Men* and *Agents of Change*, presents several case studies in which an officer provoked an assault by engaging in either overt or subtle action that fed the tension. *Agents of Change* was a study of violence in the Oakland, California, police department. In it, Toch and his associates worked with a small group of officers who displayed an inordinate pattern of involvement in violent encounters. Obviously, some officers fit this category, but it is unjustified to put all Oakland officers in it!

The Assailant

Data were collected nationally by the Police Assaults Study on assailants in robbery- and ambush-related assaults and in assaults that took place in selected municipalities in the seven-state south-central region. Assailants' characteristics and behaviors differed markedly with the type or seriousness of the crime. The typical municipal assailants were usually younger (eighteen to thirty-four years of age), male, white (although 42 percent of the incidents involved nonwhite assailants—a percentage which is disproportionately high given their distribution in the general population), with low occupational status (blue collar or unemployed), and had either been drinking or were under the influence of alcohol.

Interestingly, data from Albuquerque, New Mexico, revealed that, as a group, assailants maintained respect for law-enforcement officers even after assaulting them. This group, though, did see the assaulted officer as having invited attack by overstepping acceptable bounds of behavior. Assailants in robbery- and ambush-related incidents tended to be younger males (84 percent under thirty), black, and un-

TABLE 2

Selected Characteristics Associated with the Environment and Dynamics of Police Assault Incidents: 1982–1990

Region	Number of Officers	Percent
Northeast	139,950	25.0
Midwest	89,881	16.0
South	203,711	36.3
West	127,253	22.7
Total	560,795	100.0
Circumstances at scene of incident:		
Disturbance calls	182,769	32.8
Arrests other than robbery or burglary	113,908	20.3
Handling, transporting, custody of prisoners	69,104	12.3
Traffic pursuits and stops	54,746	9.7
Investigating suspicious persons or circumstances	47,263	8.4
Other	93,005	16.5
Total	560,795	100.0
Weapons used in assault incidents:		
Firearms	26,372	4.7
Knife or cutting instrument	14,220	2.5
Other dangerous weapons	50,964	9.1
Personal weapons	469,239	83.7
Total	560,795	100.0

Source: Federal Bureau of Investigation, *Law Enforcement Officers Killed and Assaulted* (1982–1990) inclusive (Washington, DC, Government Printing Office).

employed. Alcohol and drug use did not appear to be prominent factors in these assaults. Analysis of this type of assault indicates that the level of violence escalates dramatically when robbery is involved. In fact, robbery precipitates almost as many police murders as any other type of crime.

Social Causes of Assaults against Police

As a symbol of authority, an officer frequently is the target of hostility directed towards agents of the political and social system. The irony is that the officer has virtually no say in making the laws that must be enforced and is caught in the middle, a target of hostility over which he or she has no control.

Meyer et al. (1979) postulate that the typical assailant is frustrated. This person, and others similarly frustrated, belongs to a "subculture of violence" in which frustration is often manifested by a violent act. As the officer is the power symbol, striking out at this particular street-level bureaucrat enables the assailant to express frustration. This, in turn, provides status among peers.

Prevention of Assaults

The random nature of attacks on officers is such that police should learn to identify potentially life-threatening situations quickly and act to defuse them. Primary among preventive measures are programs that combat police complacency and enhance awareness of the factors inherent in assaultive situations. Behavioral simulation is likewise advantageous; it affords vicarious experience by introducing officers to typical situations. Also, communication and information technologies can more fully inform officers of danger before they enter into it. Among the root causes of assaults is a political and social system that endures poverty, illiteracy, racism, homelessness, unemployment, and the associated feelings of blocked opportunities and hopelessness. Further study of these conditions and of the psychological and sociological characteristics of police and their assailants is needed to provide a more definitive profile of the nature and causes of violence directed against police.

Samuel G. Chapman

Bibliography

Chapman, Samuel G. *Cops, Killers and Staying Alive.* Springfield, IL: Charles C. Thomas, 1986.
_____. *Perspectives on Police Assaults in the South Central United States.* Vols. 1–3. Norman, OK: Bureau of Government Research, 1974.
Decker, Scott H. and Allen Wagner. "The Impact of Patrol Staffing on Police-Citizen Injuries and Dispositions." *Journal of Criminal Justice* 10 (1982): 375–82.
Federal Bureau of Investigation. *Law Enforcement Officers Killed and Assaulted* (for calendar years 1972–1990 inclusive). Washington, DC: Government Printing Office.
Major, Victoria L. "Law Enforcement Officers Killed 1980–1989." *FBI Law Enforcement Bulletin* 60 (May 1991): 2–5.
Margarita, Mona. "Killing the Police: Myths and Motives." *Annals of the American Academy of Political and Social Sciences* 452 (November 1980a): 63–71.
_____ "Police as Victims of Violence." *Justice System Journal* 5(3) (1980b): 218–33.
Meyer, C. Kenneth, et al. "Violence and the Police: The Special Case of the Police Assailant." *Journal of Police Science and Administration* 7(2) (1979): 161–71.
Toch, Hans, et al. *Agents of Change: A Study in Police Reform.* Cambridge, MA: Schenkman Publishing, 1975.
Witkin, Gordon, Ted Gest, and Dorian Friedman. "Cops Under Fire." *U.S. News and World Report* 109 (December 3, 1990): 32–44.

Assessment Centers

Trained personnel in an assessment center employ techniques designed to generate job-related behavior in candidates for jobs and in employees being considered for promotion. Among the many users of assessment-center techniques are hundreds of law-enforcement agencies of varying size.

The Office of Strategic Services (OSS), predecessor of the Central Intelligence Agency (CIA), funded the first operational assessment center in the United States, using it to select spies in World War II. At about the same time, a member of the German military high command was testing similar methods in selection of officers for the Wehrmacht (Thornton and Byham, 1982).

Postwar applications of the process were very limited until 1956, when Dr. Douglas Bray, director of human resources research at American Telephone and Telegraph (AT&T), began studying an experimental version (Bray et al., 1974). More than 200 recently hired people were systematically processed and evaluations were locked away. Eight years later, researchers compared each employee's progress with predictions made by the assessment center. Results were interesting. Although the findings were slightly different for those who had graduated from college and those who had not, 74 percent of those who had been promoted to a supervisory position one level or higher had been identified by the assessment center as having good management skills. Even more impressive was the fact that 94 percent of those people who had not been promoted had been identified as not having management potential.

Why Do Police Departments Use Assessment Centers?

Until the 1970s many police departments promoted people because they had influential contacts, or did well in objective paper-and-pencil tests, or impressed a civil-service board or a board made up of a variety of people from law-enforcement personnel in neighboring departments, state highway patrol, private-sector managers, and perhaps representatives of the local department of human resources. Many such boards are less than effective. Interviewers rarely have an accurate, current picture of the duties and responsibilities that will be shouldered by the person who fills a post. Many interviewers are not trained. Not surprisingly, the interview as a predictive tool has proved to be only marginally effective (O'Leary, 1976, 1979). Paper-and-pencil tests also have turned out to be poor at predicting a person's management performance.

In contrast, research indicates that the assessment center predicts job performance and measures management skills with remarkable accuracy. Another important reason for police departments' increasing acceptance of assessment centers was passage of the 1964 Civil Rights Act as amended in 1972. This required police departments to prove the validity of their promotional process if it had an adverse impact (i.e., screened out) on blacks, Hispanics, and women as compared with white male candidates.

Applications and Logistics

Among the first law-enforcement agencies to use the assessment-center process were two quite different in duties and composition: the New York Police Department and the Mississippi Bureau of Narcotics. Both departments started using assessment centers in the early 1970s. The FBI has run a developmental and promotional assessment center in Quantico, Virginia, for a number of years, and the Equal Employment Opportunity Commission has used the process for the promotion of people within its own organization. (Note: The EEOC is the watchdog agency created by Title VII of the 1964 Civil Rights Act to enforce fair-employment guidelines.)

There are three fundamental phases in assessment: observation, scoring, and discussion. However, the first component, if the process is to be effective, is analysis of the target position. Unless the job is analyzed accurately the assess-ment center may measure competences that are not job-related.

During the first phase, observation, the candidate participates in a number of job simulations. Examples are in-basket, oral presentation, coaching, and counseling. The purpose of this phase is to allow trained assessors to observe the candidate's behavior systematically as he or she goes through the exercises, which last one or two days.

The assessors then score their notes and observations independently of one another. During this scoring phase each assessor reviews his or her observation of the candidate's behavior and slots it into the appropriate competence or job-related quality being measured. For example, an in-basket exercise would help to determine a candidate's decisiveness if he or she took action or committed himself in eighteen out of twenty items for which a decision could be made or failed to make decisions.

The final stage brings the assessors together for discussion, almost invariably monitored by an experienced administrator. The assessors—three to five for each candidate—must be able to justify their scores for the candidate with behavioral observations. Assessors challenge each other often; all are aware that their collective assessment will strongly influence the candidate's career. On one objective all agree: Their function is to give the most accurate picture possible of the candidate's management skills and potential.

Questions for Police Departments

Assessment centers are not cheap, costing between $500 and $3,000 for each candidate. However, a number of researchers have argued that the cost is recovered within a brief period. The alternative, hit-or-miss method is almost certainly more expensive in the long run, since it will promote a higher proportion of unsuitable candidates, thereby reducing a police department's cost-effectiveness.

The assessment-center process has been used on ranks from patrolmen and detective up to the chief's position. One of the most productive ranks on which to use the process is that of sergeant, because he or she has not until that point in a police career proved the ability to manage.

Criticisms of the method focus on its misapplication, particularly the use of poorly trained assessors and the processing of applicants too quickly. Other criticisms are aimed at overreliance on the results and consequent discounting of a candidate's performance on the job.

Current and Future Applications

Assessment centers may be used to pinpoint employees' specific management strengths and weaknesses. That use allows an organization to narrow the focus of its management-training programs, thereby making its existing managers even more competent. The FBI has used the method in this way.

Assessment centers' validity, legality, utility, and credibility seem certain to guarantee their increased use by police departments. Nor has the method's usefulness been exhausted. Some experts urge that it should be used to assist managers in their appraisal of subordinates' performance.

Lawrence R. O'Leary

Bibliography

Bray, D. W., et al. *Formative Years in Business: A Long Term AT&T Study of Managerial Lives*. New York: Wiley Interscience, 1974.

Cascio, W.F., and V. Silbey. "Utility of the Assessment Center as a Selection Device." *Journal of Applied Psychology* 64 (1979): 107–18.

Dunnette, M.D., and S.J. Motowidlo. *Police Selection and Career Assessment*. Washington, DC: National Institute for Law Enforcement and Criminal Justice, Law Enforcement Assistance Administration, U.S. Department of Justice, 1976.

MacKinnon, D.W. "An Overview of Assessment Centers." *CCL Technical Report #1*. Berkeley: University of California, Center of Creative Leadership, May, 1975.

Neidig, R.D., and P.J. Neidig. "Multiple Assessment Center Exercises and Job Relatedness." *Journal of Applied Psychology* 69(1984): 182–86.

O'Leary, L.R. "Fair Employment, Sound Psychometric Practice and Reality: A Dilemma and a Partial Solution." *American Psychologist* 28(2) (1973): 147–50.

———. "Objectivity and Job Relatedness, Can We Have Our Cake and Eat It Too?" *Public Personnel Management* 5(6) (November/December 1976): 423–33.

———. *Successful Police Officers: Their Selection and Promotion*. Springfield, IL: Charles C. Thomas Publishers, 1979.

Thornton, G.C., and W.C. Byham. *Assessment Centers and Managerial Performance*. New York: Academic Press, 1982.

A

B

Bertillon System

The Bertillon system was named after Alphonse Bertillon (1835–1914), a French criminologist often called the "Father of Scientific Detection." The system, also known as *bertillonage*, utilized anthropometry, "the study and technique of human body measurement for use in anthropological classification and comparison." Bertillon applied anthropometry to the identification of criminals; previously, police records had been inexact.

Bertillon argued that identification of a prisoner rested upon the following indications:

1. Length and width of the head
2. Length of the left, middle, and little finger
3. Length of the left foot
4. Length of the left forearm
5. Length of the right ear
6. Height of the figure
7. Measurement of the outstretched arms
8. Measurement of the trunk, i.e., measurement from bench to the top of the head of a person seated

Other identifying characteristics were noted such as scars, peculiar marks, color of eyes, hair, and beard, along with a description of the nose. Calipers, sliding compasses, and three graduated wall charts were the standard measuring equipment; precision was the objective. To analyze eye color Bertillon turned the subject's face toward the light. The examiner then observed the color of the inner circle of the iris to distinguish it from the outer circle. (Bertillon maintained that eye color was easily mistaken. A dark-blue eye looks black in low light and a gray eye "is generally nothing but a blue eye with a more or less yellowish tint, appearing gray on account of the shadow cast by the eyebrows." Ear identification was more complex. The focus was on eleven unique formations: lower rim, upper rim, front rim, tragus, lobe, antitragus, cavity of the shell, rim of the shell, furrow of the rim, navicular cavity, and starting point of rim. Whether the ear was indented, flattened, or showed bruises was also recorded.

For the correct recording of information, Bertillon insisted that the examiner and his assistant both independently perform the procedure as a double check for accuracy. Once a subject was minutely described, he (adult white males comprised Bertillon's records) could hardly be confused with another man. The Prefecture of Police in Paris inaugurated the system in 1882, and by 1883 had already positively identified 49 men as habitual criminals; the following year 241 more were identified, and in 1885, over 500.

Bertillon's classification scheme began simply by recognizing an individual's size: small, medium, or large, as noted on an index card. Later, the scheme underwent stages of subdivision until the individual was catalogued in every way. Each personal characteristic was filed in its proper place among thousands of index cards so that an investigator could retrieve any one characteristic to build a composite picture and thus reconstruct the individual.

Another prominent feature of *bertillonage* was photography. Each subject was photographed full-face and in profile with his register number "conspicuously fastened to his coat"; this was called a *portrait parle*.

Before fingerprints, Bertillon was emphatic about the uniqueness of ears and would discard photographs that did not capture them in sharpest outline. He also compiled photographic albums that exhibited the diversity of human appearance. Montages of foreheads, chins, lips, wrinkles, the eyeball and orbit, facial expressions, a synoptical table of the forms of the nose, etc., were his passion. For him, any written or verbal record depicting personal differences aided criminal identification.

Police departments throughout Europe and North America adopted the Bertillon system. It remained in vogue only until the late 1890s, when the fingerprint method of identification swept aside the tedious system. Bertillon was one of the first criminologists to embrace the fingerprint method, but he believed it to be no more than supplementary to his own. His *portrait parle* was retained and is still in use today. Anthropometry, misused by pseudo-anthropologists to proclaim one race's superiority over another, has fallen into disuse and ignominy.

Bertillonage furthered the emerging science of detection even though it was soon replaced by better methods. That surgery, disease, maiming, or accident could alter the human body weakened the system, whereas fingerprinting and now genetic coding provide nearly indelible indications of identity.

Bibliography

Bertillon, Alphonse. *Alphonse Bertillon's Instructions for Taking Descriptions for the Identification of Criminals and Others by the Means of Anthropometric Indication.* New York: AMS Press [1889] 1977.

———. *Signaletic Instructions, Including the Theory and Practice of Anthropometrical Identification.* New York: Werner, 1896.

Rhodes, Henry T.F. *Alphonse Bertillon, Father of Scientific Detection.* New York: Abelard-Schuman, 1956.

British Policing

Over the next several years, the police service in England and Wales is likely to experience the greatest change it has ever encountered. According to one author:

> The police institution is beset by innovation and undergoing changes which seem momentous since the establishment of the Metropolitan Police. The tacit contract between police and public, so delicately drawn between the 1850s and 1950s had begun to fray glaringly by 1981. The still open question is whether current efforts will suffice to repair it. (Reiner, 1985:62)

At the present time, various central government commissions are currently examining such diverse issues as:

- The practices and procedures to be adopted by the police in regard to the criminal justice process;
- The current and future structure of the service;
- The political and managerial control of forces.

These commissions have been created at least partially in response to serious difficulties which have faced the service since the 1980s including both external relations between police and public and internal revelations of scandal and wrongdoing.

The purpose of this paper is therefore, fourfold. First, to provide a brief historical description of the development of the police service in England and Wales since its inception in 1829. Second, to examine the current structure, including the political and managerial controls under which it operates. Third, to discuss some of the difficulties that the service has been experiencing over the past few years and, finally, to comment on three major initiatives that have been promulgated by central government to address those perceived problems.

The History and Development of British Police Forces

The first formal professional police force in England and Wales was the London Metropolitan Force, which was created following enactment of the Metropolitan Police Act in 1829. This act provided for a single force for the metropolis and ensured that policing would cover a radius of approximately seven miles from the city center.

In 1835, the Municipal Corporations Act required new towns and boroughs in England and Wales to establish police forces. This act applied to 178 corporate towns, although not all towns took advantage of the Act to establish police forces. The problem of rural police forces was addressed in the County Police Act of

1839, which was intended to permit regular police forces for the fifty-six existing counties in England and Wales. Since the Municipal Corporations Act gave virtual unlimited discretion to local authorities in setting standards of pay, recruitment, and service, the result was the creation of forces widely differing in quality. In order to avoid this result among counties, the County Police Act of 1839 retained significant powers given by central government, a condition which still exists today. The home secretary was empowered to regulate the conditions of pay and service of county forces and provided that the appointment of the chief constable of each force be approved by him. Again, since this act was "enabling" rather than "obligatory"—only twenty-eight counties created police forces under it.

By 1848, there were 182 police forces in Great Britain. However, over time, a number of smaller forces were amalgamated with either the county force in which they were situated or with larger city departments. According to Stead:

> The next principle measure was the County and Borough Police Act of 1856, known as the "Obligatory Act." This is the major landmark in the making of Britain's modern police system. . . . The Act of 1856 produced a model for the nationwide standardization of police that characterizes the British system today. (Stead, 1985:49)

This legislation placed on central government, for the first time, the responsibility of ensuring that a police force was established in every county and borough throughout the United Kingdom and to ensure that they were operating in an efficient manner. In addition to the home secretary's responsibilities, as stated earlier, a further important provision was that the central government undertook the obligation of providing a proportion of financing for those forces certified as efficient. As a result, central and local government became partners in providing police service in Britain—a model that continues to exist in contemporary policing. By 1939, 183 police forces were in existence in England and Wales.

The watershed for the development of the modern police service came with the Royal Commission on Police in 1962. The outcome of the commission's deliberations was the Police Act of 1964, which sets the structure of policing in England and Wales and is the basis upon which modern policing is formulated. Stead notes:

> The Police Act of 1964 marks a decisive stage in police development. It reaffirmed the principle of local participation in police governance. It gave Parliament a whole range of subjects on which it can question the Home Secretary and it makes possible the consolidations of the 1960s. (Stead, 1985:103)

Following the local government reorganization in 1974, the number of forces was reduced to forty-three. As of 1992 there were fifty-two police forces in the United Kingdom with 29,243 special constables to assist in law enforcement. These forces vary in size from 798 sworn officers (City of London Police) to over 28,000 (Metropolitan Police Force). These totals take no account of civilian staff whose numbers have swelled considerably over the past few years as forces have implemented extensive civilianization programs to ensure that police officers are not tied down with clerical and administrative tasks.

Although the geographic area which each force covers varies, the boundaries are coterminus with the principle local government areas. Each force has the total responsibility for policing policy and operations taking place within its area.

While this reorganization was hailed by many as promoting greater economy and efficiency through the elimination of many small forces, it was not without its critics. Stead indicates:

> Whether greater size really brought greater efficiency was doubted, when it kept the command too remote from the front line. One major disadvantage was felt in the most important sphere of all—that of the police's relationship to the public. . . . The change entailed some loss on the human side of policing and must be seen in the context of a wholesale reshuffling of local government structures, from which the country has yet to recover. (Stead, 1985:95)

In short, the readjustment of forces in 1974, while encouraging efficiency by creating larger forces resulting in greater economy, also created problems in service delivery. Larger police forces resulted in both greater separation between the administration and those at the sharp end of policing, and greater personal distance between the forces and the public which they served. The latter problem was no small issue for a police service that prided itself on service delivery and relied heavily on its personal relationship with the people it served. One of the commissions currently examining local government structure, which will be discussed at a later point, may well bring further consolidation producing even larger forces with greater geographic areas to police.

The Structure of Police Authority

The chief officer of each force (i.e., a chief constable in all forces except the Metropolitan and City of London forces, each of which is headed by a commissioner) is totally responsible for the operational policing in his area. However, in all forces except the two outlined above, the local authority has the responsibility under the Police Acts of 1964 and 1976 to maintain an adequate and efficient police force for its area. In this regard, they appoint a police committee composed of local politicians and magistrates to oversee policing issues. They also have the responsibility for appointing the chief constable and serve as his disciplinary authority.

On a national basis, the secretary of state for home affairs (the home secretary), who is a senior member of the government, has a direct responsibility for the police service. He exercises his control through the home office and his role is primarily to maintain a consistent national policy on policing. This responsibility is undertaken primarily through the medium of home office circulars, which do not have the force of law, but which provide chief officers with advice and guidance on a variety of policing issues. In addition, central government through the home office funds 51 percent of all policing costs and, as a result, maintains a considerable level of control. In effect, therefore, police forces are controlled by what is called a tripartite arrangement among:

- The home office, which maintains a consistent national policy;
- The local authority, which is responsible for maintaining an adequate and efficient police force for its area; and
- The chief constable, who is responsible for the operational efficiency and the day-to-day management of the force.

In summary, therefore, although the home secretary possesses administrative power and control over the police service, he tends to limit the use of such authority. Thus, the chief constables and the local authorities are afforded a good deal of discretion to operate their police force in a manner suitable to local needs and requirements.

While this system has withstood the test of time, questions are currently being raised as to whether the same arrangement should continue in the future. Vize (1992) indicates that the review of police organizations, which was commenced on the instructions of the home secretary in the summer of 1992 and which will be commented upon below, would include a detailed examination of the powers of police authorities, including their control of constabulary budgets. This review raises issues of principle, particularly that of the accountability of local forces and will no doubt be strongly resisted both within the service and by local politicians, since such a move hints at more central control of the police service by the home office.

Having commented on issues concerning the control of police forces, we now propose to look at the rank structure which is currently in operation. With the exception of the Metropolitan and City of London forces, the rank structure for sworn personnel, which is outlined below, is identical in all police forces in England and Wales:

- Chief Constable
- Deputy Chief Constable
- Assistant Chief Constable
- Chief Superintendent
- Superintendent
- Chief Inspector
- Inspector Sergeant Constable

It should be noted that there are a considerable number of layers of management in this structure which results in an average of one supervisor to every three constables. This ratio is very high when compared with management levels in commerce and industry and, therefore, raises the question as to whether there is scope for "flattening" the police management structure.

Contemporary Issues

At no other time since its inception has the police service in England and Wales come under greater scrutiny than it has over the past several years. Gone are the days when it enjoyed the support of virtually all the community, a fact evidenced by the results of the British Crime Surveys of 1983 and 1988. These surveys reveal that while there is continuing support for the police, it has been declining over time. This situation has been brought about, in part, by the adverse publicity the service has attracted due to malpractice on the part of some of its members. It is also a consequence of social, political, and economic changes experienced by British society over the past twenty years.

One of the most significant factors that contributed to the erosion of public support for the police service was the outbreak of serious urban disturbances across England in the 1980s. Just as the United States experienced rioting in a number of major cities in the 1960s, rioting in English cities broke out in the early 1980s. The first of these occurred in the St. Paul's District of Bristol in April 1980. Almost one year to the day later, serious disorders in Brixton resulted in widespread damage and injury to 279 police officers and 45 citizens (Benyon, 1984:3). Other cities that experienced rioting in 1981 included Birmingham, Sheffield, Leeds, Leicester, and Derby.

In response to the Brixton disturbances, Parliament appointed the Rt. Hon. Lord Scarman, OBE, a highly respected appeals court judge to head an inquiry into the causes of the disorders. The results of the investigation were released in November 1981. According to the Scarman Report:

> . . . a combination of a high incidence of deprived groups in the population, the difficulties of living in the inner cities, the economic, social, and political disadvantages of the ethnic minorities, and the latter's complete loss of confidence in the police . . . constituted a potential for collective violence. Scarman regarded "Operation Swamp" . . . a massive and visible police presence as the accelerator event which triggered actual political violence. (Benyon, 1984:28)

With respect to the role of the police:

> Lord Scarman came to the view that the "history of relations between the police and the people of Brixton during recent years has been a tale of failure." (Benyon, 1984:100)

Further disorders were experienced in 1982 and again in 1985. The most serious of these took place in London in October 1985:

> The rioting began at about 7 P.M. on Sunday 6 October 1985, and during a night of extraordinary violence PC Keith Blakelock was stabbed to death, 20 members of the public and 223 police officers were injured and 47 cars and some buildings were burned. (Benyon and Solomos, 1987:7)

Commenting on the observation that the 1981 and 1985 urban disturbances were fundamentally antipolice, David Smith notes:

> It does appear that racism and racial prejudice within the police, and the concentration of certain kinds of policing on young people generally and particularly young black people has brought forth a response both at the individual level and also at a more collective level. (Benyon and Solomos, 1987:72)

Certainly, just as the Scarman Report indicated, the cause of these riots, similar to those in the United States in the 1960s, goes much deeper than simply the attitudes of individual police officers and different styles of policing in predominately minority communities. Widespread discrimination, poverty, and high rates of unemployment in the inner cities were the locus of urban unrest while distrust and dissatisfaction with the police service provided the spark. Nevertheless, as a consequence, the spotlight was thrown on the British police service resulting in the most serious adverse publicity and strain with the public than it had experienced in many decades.

The public image of the police service was further eroded by violent confrontations between the police and picketers during a number of notorious industrial disputes, especially the Miner's Dispute in 1984–85. On April 15, 1989, a large and unruly crowd attending a soccer game at Hillsborough resulted in a disaster in which ninety-five persons lost their lives with many more injured. In this latter incident, the police were severely criticized for their crowd-control tactics and a lack of command control. The investigations that followed produced further negative publicity for the police service.

While all of these incidents (the riots, industrial disputes, and the soccer disaster) involved serious criticisms of the relationship between the police and the public in order maintenance functions, the integrity of the service was still widely acclaimed for its efficiency and dedication in fighting crime. Much of this confidence eroded as a consequence of two major scandals involving the police and the activities of the Irish Republican Army. In the early 1970s, a series of pub bombings resulted in the deaths of twenty-six persons in Guilford and Birmingham. Four persons were convicted in the Guilford incident and six in the Birmingham bombing. Following a series of inquiries and appeals, the Guilford Four were released in 1989 and the Birmingham Six in 1991 on the grounds of tainted evidence. In each case, the convicted individuals served over fourteen years in prison, based on evidence produced by alleged coerced confessions, uncorroborated testimony, and faulty scientific investigations. Once again, the public image of the police service was rocked, morale was seriously effected, and public inquiry into police behavior was initiated.

In sum, throughout the decade of the 1980s, the British police service faced greater adversity and met with more public criticism than it had faced in half a century. Public trust declined while the central government's interest in policing increased. Graef, who addressed many of these issues, concluded:

> Perhaps the management of Police Forces throughout the Western world was faltering, jaded, unimaginative, inert, and shy on accountability. (Graef, 1990:456)

Interest on the part of central government has been demonstrated by home office through home office circulars, the Audit Commission, the Home Affairs Select Committee, and the Police Complaints Authority. These bodies are demonstrating an ever-increasing interest in policing issues to ensure not only greater accountability but also that a more effective, efficient, and value for money service is provided. For example, the Home Affairs Select Committee (1989) commented that:

> The Police Service of England and Wales commands considerable public resources which demand exceptional management skills if Forces are to respond to the needs of the public. The fundamental questions which arose during our enquiry concern whether the current system of training and career development for police officers based on a 19th-Century system and constrained by the separate organisation of each is adequate for the Police Service as it approaches the 21st Century.

Clearly the concentration of interest in policing in the United Kingdom is more than just a passing phenomenon that is likely to disappear once the initial enthusiasm has worn off. It is symptomatic of a change in relationships among police, their masters, and their customers.

All these issues have necessitated a change in the role of police managers at all levels of the organization, and, in consequence, over the past few years emphasis has been placed on identifying the skills those officers require to undertake these new responsibilities. However, despite the efforts that have been made in this regard, there is considerable debate taking place within Parliament, the service, and the media on the quality of senior police managers. For example, Johnson (1990) indicated that recent events within the service have encouraged the ordinary public to think that the police are not really able to provide a professional service and that radical proposals are needed to improve police management. On the other hand, Robertson (1990) reported that it would be easy to conclude that police executives are either disinterested in pursuing efficiency and general excellence or that they are simply ill-equipped to administer large and complex organizations. To endorse either assumption would be patently unfair, for while particular chief officers may suffer lethargy in one direction or the other, such a rash generalization would be inaccurate.

Nevertheless, in a world where the theory and practice of business administration and human resource management is undergoing constant refinement, it is essential that today's police managers, particularly those at a senior and executive level, should be attuned to both private and public sector management developments to avoid accusations of inertia and stagnation.

It is against the background outlined above that central government has implemented three important reviews, which are likely to greatly affect the police service and the criminal-justice system. The first is the Royal Commission on Criminal Justice, which has the following extensive terms of reference:

> To review the effectiveness of the Criminal Justice System in England and Wales in securing the conviction of those guilty of criminal offences and the acquittal of those who are innocent, having regard to the efficient use of resources.

In particular, they were asked to consider whether changes were needed regarding:

- The conduct of police investigations and their supervision by senior police officers;
- The role of the prosecutor in supervising the gathering of evidence and deciding whether a case should proceed;
- The right of silence for the accused;
- The powers of the courts to direct proceedings;
- The role of the Court of Appeal in considering new evidence on appeal; and
- The arrangements for considering and investigating allegations of miscarriages of justice when appeal rights have been exhausted.

During the course of its work, the commission is examining many aspects of the criminal-justice system and in that regard has received submissions from many interested individuals and bodies including the police service. While its deliberations are not yet complete, there is no doubt that their recommendations are likely to have significant implications for the practices and procedures of the police.

The second is the review currently being undertaken by the local government commission into the future of local government. Its terms of reference are to examine all relevant issues and make recommendations concerning the future structure, boundaries, and electoral changes to particular local government areas. The review will take the form of a rolling program and, in consequence, it will take some time to cover the whole of the country. However, the results could have major implications for the police service. For example, if local authority boundary changes take place, it could result in the demise of many of the smaller forces, the amalgamation of others, and even the breaking up of some of the larger forces.

The possibility of such changes is a fact recognized by current Chief Constable O'Dowd in a speech at a recent international police conference in London on the future of the police service in England and Wales. He concluded that there would be fewer police forces within three years. Many people believe that the restructuring of forces is high on the hidden political agenda.

The final review and probably the most important as far as the police service is concerned is that which the home secretary established in May 1992, under the chairmanship of Sir Patrick Sheey, to review police responsibilities and rewards. The inquiry team, which must report by May 1993, comprises management consultants, academics, and industrialists who will address a variety of policing issues including:

- The structure of forces to insure that they meet the management needs of today's police service;
- The roles and responsibilities of the various ranks within the service;
- The salaries of police officers to insure the salary reflects the responsibilities of the particular individuals;
- Rewards and sanctions for good and bad performance; and
- The conditions of service, work practices, and the improvement of professional standards.

This review is quite clearly very wide in its scope and will affect every officer in the country in one way or another. While many are awaiting the results with considerable apprehension, others recognize that change is inevitable and welcome the opportunities that will no doubt occur as a consequence of these reviews.

Summary and Conclusions

While the results of these three major commissions will produce significant changes in policing in England and Wales, the changes that occur must preserve both the traditional relationship between the British police service and its public and the internal morale and cohesion of the forces. As Reiner notes:

> An adequate approach to police reform must be grounded in an understanding of police culture and practices, not a simplistic view that if only the right

authorities were in charge all would be well. (Reiner, 1985:198)

Two particular areas of concern that are likely to arise as a consequence of these commissions are the reduction in the number of forces, which would produce larger forces, and the "flattening" of the rank structure through the elimination of some current ranks. The former change is a likely outgrowth of the Local Government Commission and the latter from the deliberations of the Sheehy Commission.

Changes in the size of forces, which may alter the relationship between police and community, appear especially critical. Wells clearly anticipates these problems:

If the police organisation is, or appears to be, a centrally imposed anonymous body, as in many states of Europe and elsewhere, there will be little sense of the "familia": rather than intimate and integrated, the police will seem remote and out of sympathy with local needs. (Benyon, 1987:81)

Further he notes:

Force policy and philosophy should be aimed at making ranks from commissioner to constable more obviously tied to community structures. . . . Any move which makes the police appear as impersonal, external to the community and, accordingly anonymous must be resisted. (Benyon, 1987:79)

Clearly, any forthcoming recommendations from the Local Government Commission, which would create larger forces responsible for wider geographic areas and containing greater population heterogeneity, must address these concerns.

Another set of concerns involving the internal cohesion of the forces is likely to emerge from the Sheehy Commission. One recommendation that is nearly certain to be made is the elimination of certain current ranks thus collapsing the rank structure. While one possible result of this change could produce a closer integration of command and line officers, thus improving communication in both directions, it will also raise issues of professional development and promotional opportunities that could affect the morale of younger officers. A recent article, which appeared in one of Great Britain's national newspapers, has taken note of this concern:

The ranks of chief inspector, chief superintendent, deputy chief constable and possibly commander seem certain to disappear and the status of constables, sergeants and inspectors enhanced. . . . . Abolition of chief inspectors and chief superintendent posts would seriously diminish promotion prospects for thousands of officers and create career bottlenecks. Existing chief inspectors and chief superintendents are also worried about what would happen to them. (Darbyshire, 1993:1)

Another controversial recommendation which is certainly likely to occur is "performance based pay increments." While the concept of reward for those officers who are effective in carrying out their duties and no reward for those who demonstrate subpar performance is attractive in theory, there are serious questions regarding the translation of theory into practice. What criteria are to be used to measure performance? What norm will be established for satisfactory performance so that those who fall above and below that norm can be recognized? Clearly these are crucial questions that beg easy answers. These questions are imbedded in the much larger question of the functions of policing, which has been the center of controversy since the establishment of professional police forces. A related issue is the fact that policing produces a qualitative product rather than one which is quantitative in nature. The president of the Association of Chief Police Officers, Mr. John Burrow, is quoted as saying:

We agree in principle with the concept, but our dilemma is that there are many aspects to performance-related pay. It clearly can't be based on the number of arrests or traffic summonses issued. That would do more damage to public relations than the improvement in police performance it would achieve. (Darbyshire, 1993:1)

In conclusion, therefore, it is apparent that the police service in England and Wales is entering a period of great uncertainty that will only be resolved once the decisions from the various inquiries are known. There is no doubt that changes will be extensive and wide-ranging and will result in considerable conflict, particularly in respect to local accountability vis-à-vis centralized control; a change in the traditional relationship between the police and the communities which they serve; and changes in police practices and procedures brought about as a result of the changes in the criminal justice process as a whole.

Such conflict will hopefully be the catalyst to reorganize the service to meet the changing circumstances and the ever-increasing demands that are likely to be placed upon it. Many managers at all levels will no doubt have difficulty in coming to terms with the changes and will fall by the wayside, but for those willing to accept the challenge that will be forthcoming, the future should be very interesting and exciting.

Donald B. Walker
Malcolm Richards

Notes

1. In the Metropolitan Police the rank structure above chief superintendent is commander, deputy assistant commissioner, assistant commissioner, deputy commissioner, and commissioner. In the city of London, it is assistant commissioner, deputy commissioner, and commissioner.

Bibliography

Benyon, John. "The Riots, Lord Scarman and the Political Agenda." In *Scarman and After*. Ed. John Benyon. New York: Pergamon Press, 1984. 3–19.

Benyon, John, and John Solomos. "British Urban Unrest in the 1980's." In *The Roots of Urban Unrest*. Eds. John Benyon and John Solomos. New York: Pergamon Press, 1987. 3–21.

Darbyshire, Nell. "Merit Only Pay Plan for the Police." In *Daily Telegraph*. (January 22, 1993): 1.

Graef, R. *Talking Blues*. London: Fontana/ Collins, 1990.

Home Affairs Select Committee. *Higher Police Training and the Police Staff College*. London: H.M.S.O., 1989.

Hough, M., and P. Mayhew. *The British Crime Survey: First Reports*. London: H.M.S.O., 1983.

Johnson, P. "Change or Be Changed." *Police Review* (August 10, 1990).

Mayhew, P., D. Elliott, and L. Dowds. *The British Crime Survey*. London: H.M.S.O., 1988.

Reiner, Robert. *The Politics of the Police*. New York: St. Martin's Press, 1985.

Robertson, W.W. "Your Money and Your Life." Unpublished paper. Bramshill, England: Police Staff College, 1990.

Smith, David. "Policing and Urban Unrest." In *The Roots of Urban Unrest*. Eds. John Benyon and John Solomos. New York: Pergamon Press, 1987. 69–74.

Stead, Philip. *The Police of Britain*. New York: Macmillan, 1985.

Taylor, Stan. "The Scarman Report and Explanations of Riots." In *Scarman and After*. Ed. John Benyon. New York: Pergamon Press, 1984. 20–34.

Vize, R. "Fears Grow for Survival of Police Authorities." *Local Government Chronicle*. (October 23, 1992).

Wells, Richard. "The Will and the Way to Move Forward in Policing." *The Roots of Urban Unrest*. Eds. John Benyon and John Solomos. New York: Pergamon Press, 1987. 75–89.

William John Burns

William John Burns (1861–1932), founder of the Burns International Detective Agency and chief of the Federal Bureau of Investigation, was born in Baltimore, Maryland, son of an Irish merchant tailor who became police commissioner of Columbus, Ohio. The son, gifted with an incisive mind and talent for ratiocination, helped his father to solve crimes. Young Burns came to prominence after the 1885 state election. Officials suspected tally-sheet forgery, and Burns both pinpointed the degree of fraud and identified those responsible for it. Just twenty-four years old and by all reckoning a novice, Burns was besieged with job offers. In 1889 he joined the U.S. Secret Service in St. Louis, moving to Washington, D.C., five years later. The variety and volume of federal investigations stimulated him and each case honed his already considerable natural skills. Those years saw him graduate from apprentice to master detective. His successes were many and well publicized. In the Brockway case (1894) Burns put behind bars a counterfeiter who had eluded conviction for twenty-five years. In 1896 Costa Rican revolutionaries began counterfeiting U.S. currency to support their cause; Burns stepped in and linked the leaders to the crime. In 1897 five prisoners were lynched in Versailles, Indiana, by a masked mob; Burns posed as an insurance agent and learned their names.

In 1903 Burns quit the Secret Service to join the Department of the Interior. One of his early successes there was to bring to justice top-level public officials guilty of land frauds in several western states. Case closed, he next went to San Francisco where "Boss" Abe Ruef ruled the city and ran a web of corruption. Burns took an unusual three years to put Ruef and his henchmen in the penitentiary.

In 1909 he and William P. Sheridan formed the Burns and Sheridan Detective Agency, headquartered in Chicago, soon contracting with the American Bankers Association to provide its 11,000 member banks with protection.

News of the bank deal spawned a similar agreement with the National Retail Dry Goods Association and with various hotel chains. Because of the extra work, he had to act quickly to increase his staff. Boarding trains at all hours, he went in search of worthy employees. The pace of expansion became too much for Sheridan who sold his interest in the business to Burns. On March 11, 1910, the William J. Burns National Detective Agency was born—"national" because he had already established a network of regional offices in less than a year.

Also in 1910 dynamiters blew up the building of the *Los Angeles Times.* Twenty-one people died. After a thorough investigation Burns presented indisputable evidence that the McNamara brothers and Ortie McManigal of the International Association of Bridge and Structural Iron Workers were responsible. Burns had connected threads of proof that no one else had noticed, and the three confessed to the crime.

Burns and his agency were now most assuredly far-famed, if not legendary. A newspaper photograph taken of Sir Arthur Conan Doyle and Burns together suggested that Doyle's Sherlock Holmes and the real-life detective Burns were one and the same.

Burns continued to solve sensational cases. In 1914 a Jew, Leo Frank, was charged with the murder of a young girl in antisemitic Georgia. Burns produced telling evidence to show that another man had committed the crime. A mob in Marietta, blinded by prejudice and deaf to the truth, rushed Burns and almost took his life.

Frank was not so lucky; another vigilante group dragged him from a prison farm and lynched him. In 1921 Harry M. Daugherty, President Harding's attorney general, appointed Burns chief of the Federal Bureau of Investigation. During his tenure there his most striking foray involved an inquiry into the activities of the Ku Klux Klan. He retired in 1925.

Critics of Burns point out that he invaded privacy at will, used strong-arm tactics, and circumvented the law whenever it pleased him. He flippantly dismissed his accusers as did others in authority on the grounds that he was such an asset to law enforcement. He once paid a small fine for breaking and entering; another time he evaded serving a fifteen-day jail sentence for contempt of court. A pragmatic man, he shrugged off his image of godlike prowess:

> Sherlock Holmes was a very interesting character, but in all my years as a detective I never had occasion to learn to play the violin, to study tobacco ashes or to use a magnifying glass. Plain common sense is all I ever had any use for.

Somehow between cases Burns found time to write magazine articles and books. *The Masked War* (1913) capitalized on the McNamara affair; *The Argyle Case* (1913) and *The Crevice* (1915) dramatized other actual investigations. What he did not write about himself others did. *McClure's* alone ran more than fifteen stories recounting his deeds. *True, Ladies' Home Journal,* and *The Nation* were among other magazines that delighted in telling the world about "America's Front-Page Detective."

Burns was married in 1880 to Annie M. Ressler and they had six children. He died from a heart attack in Sarasota, Florida, his winter vacation home.

Bibliography

Caesar, Gene. *Incredible Detective: The Biography of William J. Burns.* Englewood Cliffs, NJ: Prentice-Hall, 1968.

Harlow, Alvin F. "William John Burns." *Dictionary of American Biography.* Vol. II, sup. 1. New York: Charles Scribner's Sons, 1944, 134–35.

National Cyclopaedia of American Biography 24:209–10.

New York Times (April 15, 1932): 19:1.

Campus Police

Campus police departments provide specialized protection and law enforcement in a style determined by college and university administrators. Ideally, the campus police should complement rather than compete with county, municipal, and state law enforcement agencies.

The sheer size of the higher-education system helps to explain why specialized policing is necessary. As of 1990, there were 3,559 colleges, universities, and branch campuses, educating some 13.7 million students. The current fund expenditures for the system were $146 billion, much of which in the form of property, facilities, and equipment required protection (National Center for Educational Statistics, 1991).

Many campuses are as big as medium-sized towns and, like their municipal counterparts, must cope with traffic and parking problems and with rising crime. However, campuses differ markedly from municipalities in a key demographic sense: Their populations are not cross-sections of society as a whole, but consist mainly of people brought together for a limited time for the purpose of continuing their education. College policing therefore requires styles and emphases different from those of law-enforcement agencies in the outside world.

Origins and Changing Needs

Yale University started the first generally recognized campus police department in 1894, when it employed two full-time commissioned New Haven officers. Not until the 1920s, however, did the campus watchman or guard become a familiar figure in educational institutions. These watchmen, usually retired men employed only at night and on week-

ends, were given no training as law-enforcement officers and were not expected to perform as such. Their chief duties were to secure buildings at night and on weekends (e.g., closing windows, locking and unlocking doors, and other property protection duties) and to patrol the campus so as to detect fire hazards, check boilers, detect leaky pipes, and otherwise perform preventive maintenance duties. After the repeal of prohibition in the early 1930s, the watchmen-guards gradually began to enforce rules and regulations governing students' conduct. They became responsible, for example, for detecting curfew violaters and reporting infractions of the ban on drinking on campus.

Watchman-type operations predominated until the 1950s. During that decade, university administrators began to recognize that a more organized protective force was needed on campus to deal with problems caused by increases in enrollment: behavioral incidents, expansion of the physical plant, and traffic and parking. Consequently, retired police officers were hired as upper-level administrators. They tended to establish campus police departments after the model most familiar to them—urban police departments. Despite structural reorganization, switches in titles from watchmen to security officers, and increases in department size, most campus enforcement organizations remained little more than the guard-type operations that had preceded them. Like their watchman predecessors, most line security officers were older men, poorly educated, poorly paid, and untrained; they continued to perform the same security-type functions (i.e., protection of university property and equipment, and preventive maintenance). Generally lacking in police authority, campus officers had little more power to control the behavior of others than the ordinary citizen. Consequently, when detecting crime, the security officer's major responsibilities were to protect evidence, detain the suspect (if known), and notify the local police. Moreover, like their predecessors, campus officers continued to operate under the doctrine of in loco parentis; this, in effect, limited their enforcement powers by establishing a double standard on campus, which called for the detention of "outsiders" for arrest but referred student lawbreakers to the dean's office for internal discipline. Additionally, officers were often expected to turn a blind eye when faculty, staff, and other employees were guilty of minor infractions of the law.

Campus Unrest

The transition from the "silent" generation of the 1950s to the active generation of the 1960s and early 1970s left many colleges and universities totally unprepared for what was to follow (Powell, 1981; President's Commission on Campus Unrest, 1971). With the advent of campus protests, disruptive student activities, violence, and increases in reported crime and fear of crime, an increasing number of educational institutions began replacing their line security officers with better-educated and trained officers with police powers to arrest and to enforce state statutes on campus. The decision to upgrade and professionalize campus police was in part a direct result of the negative experience of outside police intervention (e.g., Kent State) during the student dissent era, and in part a growing realization that if the university did not govern itself it would be governed by others who were less responsive to its needs. Thus, professional police departments began to emerge on campus during the 1960s and early 1970s.

Policy Parameters

At present, there is a tremendous diversity in university and college police forces. At one extreme are watchmen or guards who typically are untrained; their chief duties are to unlock doors, detect vandalism, and deal with maintenance problems. In the middle of the spectrum are modern security forces that continue to have watchman functions but also play a pseudo police role, including some degree of regulation of student's conduct. At the other end of the spectrum are sophisticated police forces, often headed by former police officers and organized like municipal departments. These officers have full peace-officer authority, project a strong police image in their uniforms and equipment, and are concerned with straightforward applications of the law in the academic community. Among these three points lies a wide variety of campus forces (Gelber, 1972; Neil, 1980; Powell, 1981).

Even though the student protests and unrest of the 1960s and early 1970s spawned a plethora of studies of campus disorder, little serious attention was directed to the nature of campus police work. There has been only a limited number of scholarly investigations of campus police and, as a consequence, a solid overview of the organization, administration, and operations of campus policing does not exist. In the few studies conducted, the predominant emphasis has been on departmental structure and functions. We find that campus police departments vary in size, organizational structure, and range of function due to type of institutional control (public or private), type of institution (university or college), source of authority (legislation, deputization, contract guard), size of enrollment, location (urban, rural, suburban), and academic level (junior, senior, graduate). More specifically, public institutions tend to have larger police agencies than private ones: Most American universities with an enrollment of 10,000 or more tend to operate police departments with broad responsibility for the entire range of police services. Those with fewer students tend to operate a night watchman or guard system that is responsible only for the physical plant and university facilities (Bartram and Smith, 1969; Nielsen, 1971). Larger departments are more likely to investigate crimes (Scott, 1976). Although most agencies require entry-level training for officers, large urban schools tend to place more emphasis upon specially trained, experienced, and fully qualified officers (Adams and Rogers, 1971; Bartram and Smith, 1969; Scott, 1976). There has been a dramatic increase in employment of women in recent years, especially in large urban public schools. Most campus police departments have a proprietary rather than contractual relationship with the institution in which they are located; the likelihood of a contractual relation with a private security agency increases if the institution is a private, small college.

Only one investigation has examined the organization and everyday activity of campus policing and contrasted it with municipal police work (Bordner and Petersen, 1983). This study described what officers at an urban university did, how they were organized, their attitudes and values, and the nature of their work. Numerous similarities with and differences between campus policing and municipal policing are identified. Campus police share many problems with municipal police (e.g., crime); however, campus police typically deal with issues not high on the priority list of municipal departments (e.g., parking). Nonetheless, both campus and municipal police are responsible for the enforcement of laws and apprehension of violators, maintenance of order, preservation of human life, protection of property, and provision of services to the community they serve. Moreover, the procedures and operations of both municipal and campus police are essentially similar. Both types of police work shifts and irregular hours and are on call for emergencies; patrol districts answer calls for assistance, investigate vehicle accidents, write traffic citations, make arrests, and take other actions when necessary.

However, two unique qualities make campus policing appreciably different from its municipal counterpart. Campus police serve a clientele that is demographically different from the general populace served by urban police. University police function in an artificial and highly structured environment that brings together a particular group of people to work or study in a geographically limited area for a short period of time. In their daily work, campus police are confronted with educated and professional people, not law violators. This constituent group bears little resemblance to the cross-section of society to which the local police officer is responsible. In short, unlike their municipal counterparts campus police do not deal with a multitude of different publics; rather they serve a select clientele. A second unique quality of campus policing is philosophical. The emphasis within the educational community is not on arrest but on prevention and service. The university campus is composed of unique people requiring an atypical approach in comparison to the usual municipality. These facts call for a nonrepressive approach to policing— that is, characterized by common sense, circumspection, gentleness, compassion, and understanding. An action-oriented approach is seen as having no place on the college campus. Campus police instead place heavy emphasis upon the temperance of authority in the performance of their everyday duties. Thus, campus police are more concerned with the maintenance of an atmosphere conducive to learning and the protection of the academic community from hazards (criminal and noncriminal) than with controlling or policing the community per se.

David M. Petersen
Diane C. Bordner

Bibliography

Adams, G.B., and P.G. Rogers. *Campus Policing: The State of the Art.* Los Angeles: University of Southern California, Center for Justice Administration, 1971.

Bartram, J.L., and L.E. Smith. "A Survey of Campus Police Forces." *Journal of the College and University Personnel Association* 21 (1969): 34–42.

Bordner, D.C., and D.M. Petersen. *Campus Policing: The Nature of University Police Work.* Lanham, MD: University Press of America, 1983.

Gelber, S. *The Role of Campus Security in the College Setting.* Washington, DC: Government Printing Office, 1972.

Neil, R. E. "A History of Campus Security: Early Origins." *Campus Law Enforcement Journal* 10 (1980): 28–30.

Nielsen, S.C. *General Organizational & Administrative Concepts for University Police.* Springfield, IL: Charles C. Thomas, 1971.

Powell, J.W. *Campus Security and Law Enforcement.* Boston: Butterworth, 1981.

President's Commission on Campus Unrest. *The Report of the Commission on Campus Unrest.* Washington, DC: Government Printing Office, 1971.

Sims, O.S., ed. *The Challenge of New Directions in Campus Law Enforcement.* Athens: University of Georgia Center for Continuing Education, 1972.

Canine Unit

Law-enforcement agencies use trained handler-dog teams (or a canine unit) for a variety of reasons: to search large areas when suspects have eluded police; to track down criminals or find lost persons; to control unruly crowds or mobs; to detect illicit drugs or concealed explosives; to defend their handlers and others against attack; to assist in routine patrols; to guard suspects and police property; and to strike fear into criminals. Yet, in spite of their beneficial uses, police dogs have not been totally accepted as a standard adjunct on every American police force. At issue are the cost-effectiveness of maintaining expensive animals, the constant training and retraining requirements, the dogs' true ability to carry out their duties, their interference with regular police duties, and certain legal-liability concerns.

Roles Dogs May Play

Police service dogs fall into one of two fundamental categories: 1) all-purpose; or 2) specialist. A dog trained for an all-purpose police role must be amply endowed with multiple abilities and be a very robust, intelligent animal. A specialist dog must possess especially well developed and discriminating scenting powers. All-purpose dogs are generalists in terms of the police roles they play; those animals whose mission is exclusively sniffing for narcotics, explosives, corpses, and for traces of petroleum-based substances are considered specialists in terms of their roles.

History of Dogs in Police Work

Accounts of dogs protecting their masters and also engaging in detective work can be found in ancient texts. But it was not until the early 1300s in Saint-Malo, France, that the first organized force of dogs patrolled the streets for civic protection. These dogs served valiantly until 1770 when some attacked and fatally injured a young naval officer who had broken curfew. The entire dog force was then disbanded. Also in France, on Mont-Saint-Michel, a great rock just off the Normandy coast, the abbey and town once kept dogs to ward off strangers.

The first city to establish a police-dog training school was Ghent, Belgium, in 1899. In that year, the Ghent population was a closely packed 175,000 for which thirty-seven dogs padded through the streets between 10 P.M. and 6 A.M., under the care and guidance of ten police constables. German and French experimental schools predated the Ghent program by a few years, but did not achieve the same notable success.

By 1906, Ghent's canine force had increased to more than 50 animals and the number of handlers to 120. The authorities, obviously pleased with their four-footed police,

claimed that night crimes had all but disappeared. No longer as an experiment, other European cities began to follow Ghent's lead, and by 1910 in Germany alone more than 600 towns had canine patrols.

In 1910 the British police started using dogs on a small scale, mainly as companions for patrol constables. No formal training programs existed and any breed was thought suitable for the task. Only after thirty-six years and several home office reports on their efficacy were police dogs granted a semblance of permanent status.

The Lancashire Constabulary was foremost in England in developing a progressive dog-training program. Before 1951, it had used four bloodhounds for tracking and ten Labradors for patrol, but then switched over to Doberman pinschers and German shepherd dogs. Once the British police concluded that dogs were invaluable, they took to them readily. For example, on January 1, 1992, there were 2,749 animals in service with forces in England, Wales, Scotland, and Northern Ireland. Of these, 1,736 were general purpose dogs; 465 were specialists; and 137 were dual-purpose animals.

Meanwhile, the first American police department to initiate a dog program was that of South Orange, New Jersey, in March 1907. Seven months later, New York City started a program when a police lieutenant brought five German shepherds from Belgium for evaluation. Soon other American cities did the same, including New Haven, Connecticut; Glen Ridge, Englewood, and Ridgewood, New Jersey; Baltimore, Maryland; Detroit, Michigan; Muncie, Indiana; Berkeley, California; Babylon Town, New York; and the Pennsylvania and Connecticut State Police forces.

The South Orange and New York City canine programs were not really the first ones in America. Rather, an unusual program had served security needs at the U.S. mint in Philadelphia since just after the Revolutionary War. This program began on January 7, 1793, when $3.00 were appropriated for the purchase of a dog named Nero, reputed to be a savage brute. Nero and successor dogs over the next twenty-five years patrolled the enclosed yard overnight along with a night watchman armed with a short sword and loaded pistol. Nero is reported to have assumed full responsibility for the mint's night security if the watchman was absent.

In 1935, the Royal Canadian Mounted Police implemented Canada's first canine program. It has been operational since then and is the longest running program in North America. In 1990, there were about 325 patrol dog-handler teams in about fifty different Canadian forces, including ones in eight of the ten provinces; Newfoundland and Prince Edward Island are the exceptions. In addition, some 100 specialist dogs are used across Canada for important olfactory work.

The Best Breeds
Several breeds of working dogs have been or are presently being used for police patrol by forces across the world. These include:

Airedales	Giant schnauzers
Akitas	Labradors
Alaskan malamutes	Mastiffs
Belgian Malonois	Newfoundlands
Bloodhounds	Poodles
Bouvier des Flandres	Retrievers
Doberman pinschers	Rottweilers
German shepherds	Spaniels

There are some other breeds as well. However, of all, the German shepherd is the most commonly used breed and has been for years. It is a breed which has been widely heralded in the literature time and again as ideally suited for police work, especially all-purpose roles.

Establishing a Police-Dog Program
As time passed, some forces declared that dogs were worth their weight in gold; others indicated that dogs impeded a larger range of police work. The American public had a say: Some citizens felt safer with dogs around, others felt intimidated.

Once a police force reaches a decision to implement a canine unit, there are several things to be done. Perhaps the hardest step is selling the idea to the community. Dogs are expensive and the community often doesn't welcome the cost. Legal counsel must address the legal and liability issues to be certain the jurisdiction is protected from civil litigation. Handlers must be selected and be made competent to work with top-quality dogs. Kenneling arrangements must be made along with modifying vehicles for the transport of dogs. Veterinary care and nutritional patterns must be worked out since the dogs must be kept in top health for their demanding roles. Precise records must be kept on

every aspect of the program. Finally, a successful canine program requires good public relations, including demonstrations given before various bodies and clubs to show what animal–handler teams can accomplish in the way of protecting the public. Of course, interspersed among all these requirements is the importance of the teams' initial training and their regular, intensive retraining so that proficiency levels remain high, hence acceptable for work on the streets.

Dogs and handlers cannot be allowed to rest on their laurels. Basic training involves obedience, agitation and attack, recall, and tracking and scent recognition. Beyond the importance of training and retraining, there are four elements critical to a successful canine unit: (1) there must be policies and procedures in place which are appropriate to the canine unit; (2) handlers should be held responsible for the dogs' actions; (3) both handlers and service dogs should be trained in accordance with the unit's policies; and (4) every team must be supervised and held accountable for performance in accordance with departmental policies.

Hallmarks of Successful Programs
Many American police service dog programs have been very successful and have been made integral units in the war on crime. Several common characteristics are found in exemplary programs. Among these are that the dogs and handlers are carefully selected, fully trained and are regularly retrained. In addition, policies and procedures appropriate to the canine unit are in place and are regularly reviewed for their timeliness. Also, these units are well administered and comprehensive records of the units' performance are kept which document almost every facet of training, assignments, activities, arrests, and so forth. And, importantly, every handler-dog team is certified to a mandated standard of performance and is recertified at least annually. Teams that are not certified are not allowed to work until they have been brought up to standard.

Reasons Why Programs Fail
Not every police canine program proves a success. Research reveals that there are usually multiple reasons for terminating a program. Among the termination factors are that handlers left the force and other officers chose not to replace them; the unit became ensnared in local politics, sometimes of substantial emotion;

the program was insufficiently funded; training and retraining proved inadequate; there were consequences from unwarranted dog bites; the dog(s) was slain, injured, or retired; and a new police administration lacked commitment to the program.

Current Debates

Why don't more jurisdictions use police service dogs? The expense and time-consuming nature of the activity are prominent drawbacks, but Knutson and Revering (1983) point out that there is also "a completely illogical prejudice against police dogs." For example, some citizens protest against their use—as if police clubs, mace, and large-caliber weapons were less a threat than an animal one-half to one-third the size of a human.

Some persons allege that police dogs constitute deadly force, like a firearm. Without question, a trained dog may inflict injury in the course of helping to make an apprehension. But it is very rare that injuries prove fatal; in fact, there may be no trauma at all other than some localized bruising. The key issue is that dogs must be trained to be completely responsive to the handlers' commands, including to immediately come off a chase if so commanded. Trained police service dogs are regarded as an intermediate range of force between an officer's hands and fists and the consequences of a projectile sent by a firearm.

Another issue that surfaces on occasion is whether the use of police dogs to detect illicit drugs is legal. As it now stands, the judge presiding over a drug confiscation case determines the admissibility of evidence and must rule on proper or improper search and seizure procedures. Defendants contesting the right of police dogs to invade their privacy are on the increase. Thus far, the courts have upheld the use of police dogs for detecting drugs by means of their extraordinary olfactory senses, but there always seems to be a challenge to such seizures pending.

Summary

In early 1993, there were some 3,000 American police forces using some 14,000 trained handler-dog teams for law enforcement. About 7,000 of the teams are on patrol, serving in all-purpose roles. The others fill specialist roles where the dogs' keen olfactory senses may detect contraband substances, help locate human remains, and assist in arson investigations.

Trained handler-dog teams have proven their value to the public's safety. We may expect to see more four-footed police on duty in years to come.

Samuel G. Chapman

Bibliography

Chapman, Samuel G. *Police Dogs in North America*. Springfield, IL: Charles C. Thomas, 1990.

del Carmen, Rolando V., and Regina Saucier. "Of Sniffs and Bites: Legal Issues in Police Dog Use." *Police Chief* 52 (August 1985): 50–53.

Kingston, Kimberly A. "Hounding Drug Traffickers: The Use of Drug Detection Dogs." *FBI Law Enforcement Bulletin* 58 (August 1989): 26–32.

Knutson, James T., and Andrew C. Revering. "Police Dogs: Their Use as Reasonable Force." *FBI Law Enforcement Bulletin* 50 (May 1983): 60–64.

McKown, Mike. "Why the 'Find & Bite' Will Be History: An Interview With Chicago's Sgt. Ken Burger, Ret." *Dog Sports Magazine* 14 (March 1992): 11–13.

Skousen, W. Cleon. "Do's and Don'ts for a K-9 Corps." *Law and Order* 21 (May 1973): 82–89.

Capital Punishment

Legal and Ethical Issues

The issue of capital punishment has generated much debate by proponents and opponents on various moral, economic, ethical, philosophical, sociological, psychological, and legal grounds. Historically, the United States Supreme Court's rulings on capital punishment have been grounded in the Eighth and Fourteenth Amendments' prohibition against infliction of "cruel and unusual punishment." The amendments' ban was not on the death penalty as such but most likely on other extreme forms of punishment (Bedeau, 1982).

The U.S. Supreme Court held in a 5–4 decision in *Furman v. Georgia* in 1971 that the death-penalty statutes under review were unconstitutional because they were too arbitrary, capricious, and discriminatory in their application (408 U.S. 238 [1972]). As a result of the Furman decision, 35 states (and California by referendum) passed new capital-punishment statutes. In *Gregg v. Georgia* (428 U.S. 153 [1976]), the Supreme Court upheld the constitutionality of capital punishment. On January 17, 1977, Gary Gilmore was executed in Utah, the first person executed in ten years.

Harris (1986) identifies five principal arguments that support capital punishment: the death penalty is a traditional punishment, the authors of the Constitution accepted its use, a clear majority of the states responded to Furman by writing new death-penalty statutes, it is believed by most of the public to be an appropriate penalty for many murderers, and many people feel it can be justified on the basis of retribution and deterrence.

Public Opinion
In the numerous Supreme Court decisions on capital punishment, the justices have referred to public opinion, but there has been disagreement on how to assess and interpret it. Over the years, opinion-polling organizations have surveyed the public's views. According to Gallup polls, public support for the death penalty seesawed until about 1966, from 61 percent in 1936, to 68 percent in 1953, to 42 percent in 1966 (Erskine, 1970). Since 1966, there has been a generally upward trend in support, to the point at which about three-fourths of the American public supports the use of capital punishment, at least for certain kinds of murder. But there is some indication that the public's support is not as deep as it is broad: support tends to decrease when people are asked whether they favor the death penalty for specific crimes (Harris, 1986; Sarat and Vidmar, 1976).

People who support capital punishment tend to be older, less educated, male, white, and wealthier than the average. There is more support among Catholics than Protestants, Republicans than Democrats and Independents, white-collar workers, manual laborers, and farmers than professionals and businesspersons. Supporters of capital punishment tend to have authoritarian, dogmatic, discriminatory, and retributive values.

People support capital punishment for a complex mixture of motives. Some argue that capital punishment is a utilitarian response to a growing fear of criminal victimization and that its use deters crime (Thomas and Foster, 1975). Others support the death penalty because it satisfies their desire for retribution or revenge and because they feel it is an appropriate response to crime (Kohlberg and Elfenbein, 1975; Sarat and Vidmar, 1976). Some people argue for the death penalty because it ensures that offenders cannot repeat their crime (Harris, 1986).

Police Attitudes
Few empirical studies have systematically surveyed police views on punishment and the death penalty. In general, studies report that the police are more supportive than the general public of punishment as an appropriate response to some types of criminal behavior. In addition, they tend to support harsher penalties. Watson and Sterling (1969) found that two out of three (65 percent) police officers in their survey believed that punishment is effective in limiting or preventing crime. Eight out of ten (82 percent) police officers believed that criminals should be punished more severely. Carlson and Associates (1971) found that more police officers (from what they identified as traditional and innovative departments) than college students favored punishment in the treatment of criminals. Fagan (1986) found that more than eight out of ten (84 percent) of a group of Northwest police officers (as compared to seven out of ten [72 percent] of a public sample) felt that "for a terrible crime there should be a terrible penalty." He also found that the police tended generally to support severe penalties for various types of crime (but generally, not significantly more severe than the public).

A clear majority of police officers support the use of capital punishment as a response to certain crimes and criminals. Crawford and Crawford (1983) found that fewer than 10 percent of police officers in a large West Coast city opposed the death penalty (as compared to 26 percent of the firefighters and 56 percent of the students in their sample). Fagan (1986) found that almost nine out of ten (85 percent) police officers (as compared to about one-half [46 percent] of the public sample) in a northwestern state "strongly favored" the state's capital punishment statute. He also found that the police officers expressed strong belief in the death penalty as an appropriate response to a perceived crime problem and as a deterrent. But the police were not confident that there is evidence supporting its deterrent effect on criminals. In addition, there was not strong agreement (fewer than two out of five) that "some persons cannot be rehabilitated but should be executed." Fagan found that officers who were pro-capital punishment tended to be male, married, live in smaller cites, feel religion is important, have less education and income than average, be concerned about crime, and rate themselves as politically conservative. The best predictor of police support for capital punishment was anti-court sentiment: belief that the courts impose too many restrictions on police investigative practices and that there are too many ineffective and uncooperative court administrative policies.

It is significant that one of the reasons given by many members of the public for favoring capital punishment is that it supports and protects the police. A 1973 Harris poll found that about one-half (54 percent) of the public respondents agreed that "we need capital punishment to help protect the police." The same survey found that about 40 percent of the public felt that all persons who kill a policeman or prison guard should receive the death penalty, while about the same percentage said it should depend on the circumstances of the case and characteristics of the person. About three-fourths (77 percent) of the proponents of capital punishment in a northern California survey said they felt it was necessary to support and protect the police (versus only 5 percent of the opponents to capital punishment) (Ellsworth and Ross 1983).

Police Personality

The reasons for police and public support for capital punishment are not significantly different. A number of studies have tried to identify a model "police personality." The typical police personality is thought to include such characteristics as authoritarianism, suspicion, racism, hostility, insecurity, conservatism, and cynicism. Because of the nature of their work, the police tend to be isolated from, and suspicious of, the public, creating what Westley (1970) calls the "blue curtain." Skolnick (1975) talks about the policeman's "working personality" as being shaped by his constant exposure to potential danger, the worst elements in society, and the need to use force and the authority of his badge. Regoli and Poole (1979) found that a police officer's cynical feelings intensify his need to exert authority over others.

Niederhoffer and Blumberg (1976) identify seven different traits that characterize the police culture, among them the belief that one cause of crime is widespread permissiveness. Miller (1973) describes the majority of police officers as subscribing to the ideological premise of what he calls the "rightist." The "rightest" ad-vocate strict punishment because it deters potential criminals: "Dangerous or habitual criminals should be subject to genuine punishment of maximum severity, including capital punishment where called for . . ." (31).

There are two general modes of police personality development. The predispositional model posits that the police personality is a product of the traits that the individual brings to the position. The socialization model posits that the police personality is a product of the formal and informal demands of the police profession. Though there is evidence to support both models, most support the socialization model. Most of the data do not indicate that there is a unique police personality; if it does differ, it is in an exclusively neutral way.

Crime and Punishment

Research indicates that police views on punishment and capital punishment do not differ significantly from those of the public. More of the police support strong punishments, including the death penalty. Police officers' support for capital punishment should be seen in the larger context of their crime-fighting functions and their general dissatisfaction with court policies and practices. Police feel that the courts generally sentence too leniently, that there are too many delays and procedural restrictions in judicial processing, and that there is too much plea negotiation (Crawford and Crawford, 1983; Fagan, 1986).

Police and courts often have different role expectations and operate under different societal pressures and restrictions. There is a conflict between the police as crime-control administrators stressing social order, initiative, and efficiency on the one hand, and on the other a set of forces that is adversarial and regulates the conduct of police and other legal agents charged with the detecting, processing, trying, and sentencing of people accused of committing crimes. As Westley (1970) notes, the police tend to lose faith in the courts. "He may feel that the only way in which the guilty are going to be punished is by the police" (82). Confronted with crime every day, and with a court system that they feel is too lenient and burdened by procedural regulations, the police see capital punishment as a meaningful response to crime and criminals, though they believe that it should be used with discretion.

Ronald W. Fagan

Bibliography

Bedau, Hugo A., ed. *The Death Penalty in America.* 3d ed. New York: Aldine, 1982.

Carlson, H., et al. "Social Attitudes and Personality Differences Among Members of the Two Kinds of Police Departments (Innovative and Traditional) and Students." *Journal of Criminal Law, Criminology, and Police Science* 62 (1971): 564–67.

Crawford, P., and T. Crawford. "Police Attitudes Toward the Judicial System." *Journal of Police Science and Administration* 11 (1983): 290–95.

Ellsworth, P., and L. Ross. "Public Opinion and Capital Punishment." A Close Examination of the Views of Abolitionists and Retentionists." *Crime and Delinquency* 1 (1983): 116–69.

Erskine, H. "The Polls: Capital Punishment." *Public Opinion Quarterly* 34 (1970): 290–307.

Fagan, R. "Police Attitudes Toward Capital Punishment." *Journal of Police Science and Administration* 14 (1986): 193–201.

Harris, P. "Over-Simplification and Error in Public Opinion Surveys on Capital Punishment." *Justice Quarterly* 3 (1986): 429–55.

Kohlberg, L., and D. Elfenbein. "The Development of Moral Judgments Concerning Capital Punishment." *American Journal of Orthopsychiatry* 45 (1975): 614–21.

Lefkowitz, J. "Psychological Attributes of Policemen: A Review of Research and Opinion." *Journal of Social Issues* 31 (1975): 3–26.

Miller, Frank W., et al., *The Police Function.* Mineola, NY: Foundation Press, 1973.

Neiderhoffer, Arthur, and Abraham S. Blumberg, eds. *The Ambivalent Force: Perspectives on the Police.* New York: Dryden Press, 1976.

Regoli, Robert M., and Eric D. Poole. "Measurement of Police Cynicism: A Factor Scaling Approach.." *Journal of Criminal Justice* 7(1)(1979): 37–51.

Rokeach, M., M. Miller, and J. Snyder. "The Value Gap Between the Police and the Policed." *Journal of Social Issues* 27 (1971) 155–71.

Sarat, A., and N. Vidmar. "Public Opinion, the Death Penalty, and the Eighth Amendment: Testing the Marshall Hypothesis." *Wisconsin Law Review* 1 (1976): 171–97.

Skolnick, Jerome H. *Justice without Trial: Law Enforcement in Democratic Society.* New York: Wiley, 1975.

Thomas, C., and S. Foster. "A Sociological Perspective on Public Support for Capital Punishment." *American Journal of Orthopsychiatry* 45 (1975) 641–57.

Watson, N., and J. Sterling. *Police and Their Opinions.* Washington, DC: International Police Association, 1969.

Westley, W. *Violence and the Police.* Cambridge, MA: MIT Press, 1970.

Case Management

A key ingredient in successful criminal investigations is use of an effective case-management system. This has been important since the 1950s, largely as the result of work by O.W. Wilson. However, it was only after the Rand Corporation published *The Criminal Investigation Process: A Summary Report* in 1976 that police administrators gave serious consideration to a scientific approach. One of the earliest innovators was the Rochester (New York) Police Department, which pioneered use of "weighted" scales to identify cases with the highest probability of solution.

A series of studies in the 1970s was aimed at refining management of criminal investigations. Some of the more important research focused on investigation of specific crimes, particularly burglary, robbery, and rape.

Despite breakthroughs which have shown that systematic case management can be both efficient and effective, many police departments still use "hit or miss" methods.

Simply put, case management is a planned, coordinated, and tested way of maximizing both efficiency and productivity in the reporting and investigation of crime. Good case management starts when a police department or other investigative agency first becomes aware of a crime. Research supports the theory that design of forms, preliminary investigation, and case screening will enhance investigative outcomes.

The *Managing Criminal Investigations* manual, developed as part of the executive training program of the National Institute of Justice, lists six areas of criminal investigation.

These are: (1) the investigative roles of patrol; (2) case screening; (3) management of the continuing investigation; (4) police–prosecutor relations; (5) the monitoring system; and (6) organization and allocation of resources. More recent research, conducted through the Integrated Criminal Apprehension Program (ICAP), stresses the importance of data collection, analysis, planning, and service delivery.

Case management emphasizes allocation of resources to cases that have a high probability of solution. Undoubtedly some crimes, such as murder, will be investigated regardless of probability; but even in those cases with a high priority, management must allocate resources and decide when further investigation would be futile. Nevertheless, research supports the notion that certain criteria increase or decrease the probability of success. Thus management of an investigator's caseload, as well as individual case management, is deemed important.

Despite intensive research and the expenditure of federal dollars to improve the understanding and investigation of crime, a great many questions remain unanswered. Among them are the optimum size of an investigative unit, the size of individual caseloads for specific crimes, and the choice of investigation versus patrol as an effective means of crime control. Further, most of the research done in the 1970s and early 1980s failed to consider in any meaningful way application of the computer to case management and analysis of crime patterns in the investigation.

Research also supports the notion that examination of physical evidence, while less significant as a means of solving most crimes, does increase the probability of conviction. Development of single-digit computerized systems will also influence case management in the next decade.

Many police departments continue to employ old methods and antiquated procedures, with inadequate equipment and sloppy techniques. Lack of managerial control over investigations leads to such shortcomings as inequitable caseloads, improper assignment of cases, incorrect priority decisions, lateness of investigator response, and lack of investigative continuity. Unquestionably, the absence of managerial direction has contributed to the poor results of crime investigations in most police departments.

Ideally, the investigative unit will be equipped with one or more personal computers, with access to the department's mainframe. Some police departments provide dictating equipment to investigators, whose reports are transcribed by a secretarial pool. The proper use of technology in case management combines efficiency with effectiveness. Another area of debate and discussion centers on the use of generalist versus specialist investigators. The type of organization will have an impact on case management.

Case management is perhaps best explained using a decision-tree model, which provides a set of options on decision points that must be considered.

Before a case is assigned to an investigator, management must examine individual caseloads. Management must keep track of active cases, review inactive cases, and oversee investigators.

Many researchers have tried to measure productivity and performance, but very few guidelines are purely objective. Subjective analysis of performance is a supervisory responsibility and is important to case management. A combination of objective statistics and subjective review should be utilized. This is also true with regard to the assignment of cases, because investigators differ in experience, knowledge, and temperament. Serious or "hot" cases are usually assigned to experienced investigators or those who may possess specific skills.

Once a case has been assigned, its basic handling or management generally falls to the investigator. Each investigator should maintain a list of active cases, recording their states of development and other relevant information. The investigator should also prepare an investigative program that will include a list of results he or she plans to achieve in order to investigate the case, the strategy to be followed, and a time sequence. This may seem complicated, but it is in fact relatively simple, and the use of a computerized database format or a planning form will enhance the effort. The time sequence should include opportunities for management review and discussion.

The *Managing Criminal Investigation* manual offers a number of worthwhile examples for forms development. It also lists the "Typical Activities Associated with Case Investigations," which include:

- Develop an investigative plan.
  — Analyze the case and available information.

— Determine which investigative steps are of highest priority.
— Define the steps to be taken to best approach the crime.
— Assess the potential information sources.

- Confer with superiors concerning the plan.
- Discuss the case with other specialists and appropriate uniformed officers.
- Telephone the victim (and make an appointment, where appropriate).
- Interview the victim, witnesses, and potential witnesses (e.g., neighbors).
- Make other telephone contacts.
- Conduct a records search.
- Transmit official APBs, etc.
- Conduct required surveillance.
- Prepare required reports and records on case progress.
- Contact other governmental agencies.
- Travel in connection with investigative effort.
- Interrogate suspects or prisoners in custody.
- Arrest and process the prisoner.
- Confer with the prosecutor.
- Appear in court after the arrest.
- Other.

The list is not all-inclusive but serves as a starting point for the development of more comprehensive checklists. Some checklists will be directed at specific types of investigations. Virtually all management texts extol the virtue of checklists when there are a great many tasks to be performed. Despite this, few investigators use them, relying mostly on experience and memory.

Because most investigators are handling more than one case at a time, it is also worthwhile to develop a daily plan of activities. This will save time and serve as a daily case review. By reviewing daily activities with the supervisor, it may also be possible to save considerable time by reassigning certain activities, such as picking up records. The amount of time wasted in most investigative units is unacceptable by almost any management practice, yet it continues to be commonplace for investigators to work in teams when not necessary, to duplicate efforts, and despite this, to fail to coordinate and communicate activities with colleagues.

In the end, case management is nothing more than a means to enhance performance,

and good case management will also include measures of performance. Performance in criminal investigations can be measured in several ways; e.g., arrest, clearance, conviction; but it is important that all of those involved, from top administration to the line operation, be familiar with and knowledgeable about management-agreed measures of performance. The success of case management is directly related to the stated, and sometimes unstated, goals of the organization.

Richard H. Ward

Bibliography

Cawley, Donald F., et al. *Managing Criminal Investigations Manual.* National Institute of Justice. Washington, DC: Government Printing Office, 1977.

Greenberg, I., and R. Wasserman. *Managing Criminal Investigations.* U.S. Department of Justice National Institute of Law Enforcement and Criminal Justice Office of Developing and Testing. Washington, DC: U.S. Department of Justice, 1979.

Hastings, T.F. *Managing Criminal Investigations.* (Rochester, New York, Police Department, Final Executive Summary Report). LEAA, Rochester, NY: Rochester Police Department. (PDTE: Unknown)

Johnston, H. *Managing Criminal Investigations—Field Test: An Evaluation.* (Santa Monica, California, Police Department). Washington, DC: Government Printing Office. U.S. Department of Justice, LEAA, 1978.

North, K.E. "Management Control of Investigations." *Prosecutor* 14(3) (January/February 1979): 189–92.

Rand Corporation. *The Criminal Investigation Process: A Summary Report.* Santa Monica, CA: Rand Corporation, 1976.

Stewart, J.K. "Management Plan: Effective Criminal Investigation," *Police Chief* 47(8) (August 1980): 71–76.

U.S. Department of Justice. *Integrated Criminal Apprehension Program.* Bureau of Justice Assistance. Washington, DC: Government Printing Office, 1985.

Ward, Richard. *Introduction to Criminal Investigation.* Reading, MA: Addison-Wesley, 1975.

Wilson, O.W., and Roy C. McLaren. *Police Administration.* 4th ed. New York: McGraw-Hill, 1977.

Case-Processing Costs

Criminal justice analysts grapple with case-processing costs to determine the price of justice. How much does it cost to arrest, try, and convict an offender? What criminal justice components are involved? What do we have to know about the system to estimate costs? And, finally, can costs be controlled? Declining revenues and taxpayer concern about waste in government have given rise to increased scrutiny of proposed and existing programs that in a more beneficent past might have gone unnoticed. Thus a primary issue is the economic performance of a program, or of operations, throughout the criminal justice system.

Key concepts in cost analysis are as follows. The "case-processing approach" adds an essential dimension to setting crime-control policy because it recognizes the interrelationship of criminal justice agencies and focuses on people moving through the system. Public agency budgets have traditionally been the platforms on which policy debates are staged, but one inescapable insight from analyzing case-processing costs is that the budget is a woefully inadequate instrument for setting crime-control policy. Health, public assistance, education, waste management, and other policy areas are concentrated administratively and politically. Criminal justice, however, is diffused between levels and branches of government, between elected and appointed officials, between agencies. It serves diverse, sometimes opposing, constituencies. Therefore, attempts to "get tough" or "be more humane" by adding money here or eliminating a budget item there are repeatedly thwarted by value differences, parochial interests, and conflicting incentives. Granted, the police, jail, judge, and prosecutor depend on each other to process a case: Delays at booking keep officers from the street; court congestion increases police overtime expenditures; last minute plea agreements destroy court calendars. Dependent as they are, these same agencies are independent when it comes to budgeting. Probably the most that policymakers can hope to achieve by resource allocation alone is some productivity improvement in specific agencies or their subunits.

Another key concept in cost analysis is "cost objective"—any activity for which a separate measurement of cost is derived. The case-processing flow looks like this:

Response to citizen complaint	Preliminary hearing
Onview arrest	Indictment
Booking	Motions
Bail/bond decision	Plea
Appointment of counsel	Bench trial
Jail commitment	Jury trial
Investigation	Appeals
Case screening and charging	Presentence investigation
Prisoner transport to court	Probation supervision
Court lockup	Jail incarceration
First appearance	Prison incarceration

Cost objectives can be precise or general as the analysis requires. The application of analysis to these types of cost objectives does not limit the information to a single agency, and clarifies the many interdependencies among criminal justice organizations. It can help agency managers identify the services they provide to others and the proportion of their budget that is in some way beyond their control.

A third key concept is "loaded resource unit"—the dollar amount of all direct and indirect costs associated with a measure of resource use. For example, an hour (the measure) of a circuit (felony) court judge's time (the resource) is valued at $473.43 in one jurisdiction. The hourly rate breaks down to include:

Salary	Supplies
Fringe benefits	Rent
Court clerk expenses	Equipment
Clerical support	Judicial administration
Witness fees	City administration
Translators	State administration
Travel	

A loaded resource unit summarizes all costs associated with the use of a resource and thereby provides a convenient measure of criminal-justice-processing costs.

Fourth, "cost allocation" is the process of distributing an aggregate dollar amount to cost objectives, agency functions, or any other subdivisions of interest to the study, using measures of resource use such as time, square footage, and miles traveled.

And finally, "indirect costs" are incurred for a common or joint purpose because they cannot be allocated to direct operations (as a direct cost would be), or the effort to do so would be disproportionate to the advantage of separating out the information. Examples of indirect costs are for training, planning and research, fiscal man-agement, public relations, and information systems.

One Case

Abstractions are best understood when tested in life. The case of John, a property offender, will demonstrate the foregoing key concepts and present a comprehensive picture of cost analysis in action. John is arrested and booked at a cost of $287.64, inclusive of patrol and detective resources. These officers cannot work alone, so their hourly rate ($33.60 and $54.00, respectively) includes:

Salaries	Automobiles
Fringe benefits	Equipment
Property and records	City administration
Evidence technicians	Police administration
Regional forensics	Division-level administration
Clerical support	Supplies

John arrives at the jail where a magistrate sets bail in 0.5 minutes ($7.80), and John returns home to explain his long absence. First appearance is held in district court the next day to determine if counsel is available and to set a date for the preliminary or probable cause hearing. Being indigent, John is assigned counsel at an average cost of $63.57 per appearance. The taxpayers are billed $156.74 for John's first appearance—$22.31 for the judge, $7.96 for the bailiff, and $62.90 for the prosecutor, plus assigned counsel. Loaded onto the judge's hourly rate are:

State administration	Rent
City administration	Supplies
Judicial administraion	Equipment
Court clerk	

This brings the loaded hourly rate to $85.80. The first appearance takes fifteen minutes. Processing costs to this point are $452.18.

A preliminary hearing is held in three weeks using $287.74 worth of resources. John is bound over to the grand jury, which indicts him for shoplifting at the Quik Stop at a cost of $267.11. About a thousand dollars has been spent so far. Several weeks later the circuit court holds a hearing to affirm availability of counsel and set times for pretrial motions and a trial

date. Since the defendant is still out on bail, the cost is only $197.20. However, the judge's loaded hourly rate comes to $437.43. Fortunately, the plea on a property felony takes about thirty-eight minutes and costs the taxpayers only $275.58.

A total of $484.23 is needed to cover the costs of judge, bailiff, defense counsel, and prosecutor when the plea is heard. The bailiff's hourly salary and fringe rate loaded is $30.60. Sentencing is delayed until next month. At that time, John accepts a penalty of private counseling and twelve months' probation ($416.40) at the sentencing hearing, which costs $354.77. These final steps bring the cost of the case to $2,459.63. A presentence investigation and time in court by a probation officer would have added $487.60. In tabular fashion these are the costs for John's case:

Cost Objective	Cost	Cost Contributor
Arrest	$287.64	Police
Booking/bail	7.80	Magistrate
First appearance	22.31	District judge
	7.96	Bailiff
	62.90	Prosecutor
	63.57	Assigned counsel
Preliminary	69.50	District judge
hearing	24.79	Bailiff
	108.64	Prosecutor
	63.57	Assigned counsel
	5.04	Patrol
	16.20	Detective
Grand jury	267.11	Grand jury
Circuit court	87.48	Circuit judge
hearing	6.12	Bailiff
	40.03	Prosecutor
	63.57	Assigned counsel
Plea	257.58	Circuit judge
	19.28	Bailiff
	143.80	Prosecutor
	63.57	Assigned counsel
Sentencing	218.72	G-J judge
	15.30	Bailiff
	57.18	
Prosecutor	63.57	Assigned counsel
Supervision	416.40	Probation
Total	$2,459.63	

Keep in mind John was free on bail, not held in pretrial detention; had appointed counsel; foreswore pretrial motions; did not demand a jury trial but pled guilty; and received a probation sentence with counseling service paid from his health plan.

Conclusion

An analysis of case-processing costs dramatically illustrates the formidable task facing officials responsible for shaping crime-control policy. There is no single cost or resource "faucet" one can turn on or off at will, or even a single decisionmaker who can create and implement policy. John's case demonstrates how separate levels of government, different agencies, and each individual who makes a case decision can independently affect demands for criminal justice resources. Implementation of well-intentioned crime-control policy affects demands in a similarly fragmented, uncoordinated fashion. Interestingly, this fragmentation is a result of the constitutional requirement of "separation of powers" and "all powers not expressly granted." Therefore, it should not be unexpected that case-processing costs accumulate at a rapid and often seemingly random rate—one branch of government makes decisions that affect costs in another branch.

Billy L. Wayson
Gail S. Funke

Bibliography

Bennett, L.A., et al. "Focus on Police Operations." *Police Chief* 53 (October 1986): 66–91.

Chabotar, Kent J. *Measuring the Costs of Police Service.* Washington, DC: U.S. Department of Justice, National Institute of Justice, 1982.

Harris, J.S. *Public Costs of Driving under the Influence Processing: A Study in the California Municipal Courts.* Oakland: California Office of Court Services, 1990.

Kelley, J.T. *Costing Government Services: A Guide for Decision Making.* Washington, DC: Government Finance Officers Association, 1984.

Litan, R.E. "Speeding Up Civil Justice." *Judicature* 73 (October–November 1989): 162–67.

Schmidt, Peter, and Anne D. Witte. *An Economic Analysis of Crime and Justice: Theory, Methods, and Applications.* Orlando, FL: Academic Press, 1984.

Wayson, Billy L., et al. *Users Manual for Estimating Standards Compliance Costs.* Washington, DC: U.S. Department of Justice, LEAA, 1981.

———, and Gail S. Funke. *What Price Justice? A Handbook for the Analysis of Criminal Justice Costs.* Washington, DC: U.S. Department of Justice, National Institute of Justice, 1989.

C

Child Abuse Investigation

Child abuse is a pervasive problem that includes physical, sexual, and emotional misconduct. People may consider child abuse to be anything from failing to pay child support to murder. However, certain types of conduct regarding adult–child relations are more likely to come to the attention of police than others. When adult behavior towards a child constitutes an obvious crime, then police will likely be called first. In addition, laws continually change regarding what actions are considered in the best interest of the child. For example, most states now have laws that make it a crime not to place a young child in a safety seat while traveling in an automobile.

In the past, fear, ignorance, or embarrassment kept many people from informing authorities about possible cases of child abuse. Between 1963 and 1967 every state passed laws requiring that professionals such as teachers, doctors, and police officers report suspected cases of child abuse. Now, law-enforcement officials regularly respond to calls about child maltreatment or what may at first appear to be "accidental" injuries or deaths. Reports of other less obvious forms of abuse, such as sexual molestation and incest, are also increasing. This increase may not mean that the number of cases is growing, but simply that people now report a higher percentage of incidents. Nevertheless, estimates are that less than one-half of all acts of family violence are reported to police. This is understandable when small children are involved, since they do not know how to report abuse to the police or welfare officials.

Operational Definitions

Because the concept of child abuse covers so many areas, operational definitions are needed. First, it is necessary to differentiate between abuse and neglect. Abuse usually refers to acts of commission; neglect may represent acts of omission. The first category includes physical abuse, sexual abuse, and inadequate sheltering and protection. Acts of omission cover emotional neglect or parental acts that are not directed at children but have the effect of encouraging delinquency, such as illicit sexual activity and drug or alcohol abuse. Broader concepts of abuse and neglect include conditions that result in children running away or being designated as "missing." Legal definitions vary from state to state and in various agencies within states. There is also great difficulty in determining which acts are crimes and when and where formal intervention is indicated.

Causative Factors

Child abuse has been attributed to a number of factors. Current research points to the psychopathology of parents, including immaturity, alcoholism, drug addiction, and social isolation. One national victimization survey reported that children are often the catalysts of arguments that spur domestic violence. In many cases, children become victims in disputes over discipline and custody arrangements. Additionally, children will often try to attract fighting parents' attention in the hope that they will unite over the "new problem." Unfortunately, by interfering in a volatile situation, youngsters may find themselves the target of built-up anger and frustration.

A recent trend has developed in American jurisprudence allowing children to initiate court proceedings against their parents for child abuse, including suits to terminate the parent-child relationship. Historically, the judiciary acted with the presumption that parents know what is best for their children. But now that the country has developed an awareness of the phenomenon of child abuse, lawyers have been able to win cases affirming the constitutional rights of children. This development, however, has been controversial and the subject of criticism, particularly by conservative segments of society.

Changes in family and employment patterns in society have increased the amount of time children spend with step-relatives, baby-sitters, and day-care centers as primary caregivers. Some experts believe this may expose the child to more opportunities for possible victimization. High risk situations may be created when there is little regulation or supervision of careproviders.

The underlying basis for most explanations is that child abuse is a learned behavior. This means that many people who abuse children were themselves abused as children. People who have been convicted of child sexual abuse often admit to having been sexually abused as children themselves. Moreover, their first sexual encounters were with either their parents or other relatives. These offenders have indicated that they learned a lifestyle wherein child sex abuse was common, if not "normal."

Child abuse has been attributed also to inadequate parenting skills. Abusive parents are unequipped and unprepared to raise children. Many parents have poor parenting skills because their parents were poor role models. In cyclical fashion, immaturity on the part of young teenage parents can perpetuate what is often referred to as the problem of children having children.

Child abuse may also be the result of impulsive behavior. Without thinking, a parent will react violently to a set of circumstances. Reports have indicated that levels of child abuse tend to increase when parents are under stress. Child abuse is often a problem in families where the primary wage earner has been laid off.

Emotional abuse may be less obvious than other forms of child abuse, but its impact can be just as severe. Children who receive inadequate nurturing from their parents and other adults suffer scars that may affect them throughout their lives. These scars may be just as hideous as are the scars associated with physical abuse. Teachers and others in contact with an abused child may notice fearfulness around adults, discipline problems, or antisocial behavior as symptoms of emotional trauma. Emotionally abused children often develop a poor self-image, which can lead to depression, anxiety, sleep disorders, drug and alcohol abuse, compulsive gambling, sexual disorders, and even suicide.

Patterns of abuse may start innocently enough but later develop into more serious problems. Parents who have been abusive since a child was very young may continue the pattern of abuse with episodes of violence throughout the child's teenage years. Physical punishments may also increase in quality and quantity during adolescence with fault often being projected onto the child. In some cases, the child is blamed and punished for behavioral changes normally associated with adolescence.

State Involvement

Child abuse is of concern to the state and the criminal justice system for two reasons. The state's concern originated with a general humanitarian perspective of helping children who have been victimized. Starting in the 1800s, church groups attempted to provide for children who had been neglected and/or brutalized. Since that time, the state has become increasingly involved in protecting children. The legal basis for the state's actions on behalf of children is the principle of *parens patriae*. Assuming the role of the ultimate parent, the state protects and looks after the best interests of the child. Under this doctrine, the state has the power to remove a child from an abusive environment and place him or her in a family shelter or foster home.

Along with the idea of protecting the child is the notion of dealing with the offender. In cases where child abuse is primarily in the form of parental neglect, the state will try counseling in an effort to reform or rehabilitate the offender. In more extreme circumstances, legal action may be taken. In most states, physical or sexual assaults on children can lead to punishments ranging up to life imprisonment. In some states that recognize the death penalty, physical assaults resulting in the death of a child can subject an offender to capital punishment.

A second factor motivating the state to become involved is the desire to protect society from the subsequent problems caused by child abuse. Research has shown that many battered children suffer neurological disorders, retardation, or impairment of intelligence development. Many children will learn patterns of abuse, incorporate these behavioral patterns into their own lifestyle, and subsequently abuse others. Research studies also show that many juveniles who have committed a violent act, including murder, come from family environments in which child abuse, aggression, constant arguing and physical fighting among parents, and heavy use of alcohol are common. Furthermore, there also appears to be a link between child abuse and subsequent delinquent behavior. In other words, victimized children are more likely to participate in criminal behavior than nonvictimized children.

The thrust of the states' actions has been on detecting and correcting the problem of child abuse. In order for the state to break the cycle of learned child abuse, detection is critical. However, legal, ethical, and moral problems exist in detecting and uncovering child abuse. The Constitution provides people with a basic right to privacy. People have a right to be left alone at home, and the state cannot arbitrarily intrude into the affairs of a family. Being real-istic, the criminal justice system is somewhat dependent upon the efforts of society in general to detect specific cases of child abuse.

Recognizing Abuse
Law-enforcement and child-welfare officials need training in order to recognize the signs of child abuse. Some studies indicate that abusive parents are more likely to use punitive disciplinary practices as opposed to reasoning and simple commands. Abusive parents tend to be angry and disgusted after disciplinary interventions with children. They are generally hostile when police are called in response to family violence. Through proper training, police officers should be better equipped to intervene and defuse family violence. Training should include learning to recognize the symptoms of abuse, becoming familiar with recent statutes and case law, and understanding the role and function of social-service agencies, medical authorities, and the courts. Most agencies now provide police recruits with such training, although many still do not have written policies on the handling of such cases.

In responding to suspected cases of child abuse police officers should search for any physical evidence that might be used in subsequent cases. Oddsized/shaped bruises or wraparound injuries may mean that cords, straps, belts, bats, or other items may have been used to brutalize a child. Burns, scars, or injuries on unusual places on a child's body may also be warning signs. New computer technology has made it possible for investigators to digitally enhance the photos of young missing children so that their age progression will not hinder a search. In cases involving child pornography, police officers will look for pictures, cameras, and pornographic literature on the premises of the assailant. Officers and/or social workers also need to observe the behavior and attitudes of everyone involved in order to develop a more accurate picture of a child's environment. A child should be placed in emergency protective custody if a determination is made that a child's home is an unfit place for him or her to live by reason of neglect, cruelty, or physical abuse.

In addition to possible immediate medical attention for injuries, social workers will have to determine if any other types of treatment may be necessary. Children and parents may need counseling. Social workers need to be prepared to explain or justify why they believe treatment is necessary.

Any action taken by employees of the state on behalf of a child is subject to question. Consequently, police officers and/or social workers must carefully document their findings in the event court proceedings are initiated. In felony cases, prosecutors will need substantiated facts and evidence to obtain a conviction or, when appropriate, terminate the parental rights of the abuser. Moreover, attorneys *ad litem* (attorneys appointed by courts to represent children in family law matters) rely on reports from state employees in determining what type of action would be in the best interest of the children. Similarly, courts need concrete evidence in order to make decisions regarding the future of a child.

Investigating Cases and Interviewing Children

One of the principal tasks of law-enforcement personnel is the investigation of reports of child abuse. Most departments have specially assigned investigators for child abuse cases and these persons are either on duty or on call twenty-four hours a day. Police officers generally become aware of child abuse cases only after a complaint has been filed or a report of a possible offense has been received. Officers, along with social workers, then have the responsibility of investigating the facts and circumstances of the allegations to determine whether a child needs protective custody and if charges should be filed against any adult who may be involved.

Police officers and/or social workers normally interview anyone who can provide worthwhile information relative to a case, particularly family members and complainants. New techniques have been developed to make interview sessions with police and prosecutors less traumatic for children. Some departments use "children friendly" rooms decorated with bright colors, cartoon paintings, teddy bears, toys, and small furniture. Investigators wear plain clothes and use puppets and dolls to ease the child into conversation about events that occurred. In cases of child sexual abuse, the gradual introduction of anatomically correct dolls allows the child to point out places on the body that were touched without the confusion created by different levels of language skills.

Another way to reduce stress on children being interviewed is to combine all interviewing needs into the fewest number of sessions possible. This means that police officers, pros-

ecutors, psychologists, and child-welfare workers should coordinate their questions in advance and borrow information from the same interviews to avoid having the child repeat similar testimony.

Summary

A concern for law enforcement is that there are too many reported cases of child abuse for the number of people employed by state and local officials to handle them. A single caseworker may receive between twenty and twenty-five new cases to investigate each month and carry a total caseload of seventy children. Consequently, the caseworker will not have much time to focus on any particular incident.

The shortage of referral agencies or relief organizations to help abusive families continues to be a dilemma for the police. The absence of resources to help the victims of battering leaves police with the sole responsibility of resolving incidences of family violence. Police must resort to either arrests or removals in order to address the problem of abuse, which unfortunately often constitutes only a temporary and inadequate solution.

A final concern regarding child abuse is how the state should deal with the offender. One of the problems associated with child abuse is the repetition of similar offenses after an offender has been convicted of child abuse. Often, child sex abusers have had previous convictions for sex crimes. One study found that child molesters had on the average three times as many victims as rapists of adult women. One would conclude that child sex abusers need relatively high levels of attention from the criminal justice system, whether it be from counseling or longer periods of incarceration.

Marilyn D. McShane
Randy Farrar

Bibliography

American Humane Association. *Highlights of Official Aggregate Child Neglect and Abuse Reporting—1987.* Denver, CO: American Humane Association, 1989.

Bonheur, H., and R. Rosner. "Sex Offenders: A Descriptive Analysis of Cases Studied at a Forensic Psychiatric Clinic." *Journal of Forensic Sciences* 25(1)(1980): 3–14.

Finkelhor, D., L. Williams, and N. Burns. *Nursery Crimes: Sexual Abuse in Day Care.* Beverly Hills, CA: Sage, 1988.

Freeman, Kenneth, and Terry Estrada-

Mullaney. "Using Dolls to Interview Child Victims: Legal Concerns and Interview Procedures." *Research in Action, NIJ Reports* 207 (January/February 1988): 2–6.

Martin, Susan, and Douglas Besharov. *Police and Child Abuse: New Policies for Expanded Responsibilities.* Washington, DC: U.S. National Institute of Justice, 1991.

———, and E.J. Hamilton. "Police Handling of Child Abuse Cases: Policies, Procedures and Issues." *American Journal of Policing* 9(2)(1990).

Sgroi, S. *Handbook of Clinical Intervention in Child Sex Abuse.* Lexington, MA: Lexington Books, 1982.

Tower, Cynthia Crosson. *Understanding Child Abuse and Neglect.* 2d ed. Needham Heights, MA: Allyn and Bacon, 1993.

Willis, C., and R.H. Wells. "The Police and Child Abuse: An Analysis of Police Decisions to Report Illegal Behavior." *Criminology* 26 (1988): 695–715.

Wingert, Pat, and Eloise Salholz. "Irreconcilable Differences." *Newsweek* (September 21 1992): 84–90.

U.S. Department of Health and Human Services. Children's Bureau. *Adolescent Abuse and Neglect: Intervention Strategies.* Washington, DC: U.S. Department of Health, 1983.

Citizen Attitudes and Complaints

Studies of police community relations have shown that public perceptions of the police differ widely. This article reviews public attitudes toward and complaints about the police, summarizes the main findings that have emerged from research, and suggests subjects for further study.

Background

In the late 1960s significant attention began to be focused on police–community relations. A key document was the report in 1967 of the President's Commission on Law Enforcement and Administration of Justice, *The Challenge of Crime in a Free Society.* This viewed tensions between police and community as contributing to rising crime. With even more urgency the 1968 *Kerner Report*, put forth by the National Advisory Commission on Civil Disorders, detailed blacks' widespread dissatisfaction with and anger toward police, and concluded that these had been important factors in the urban riots that began in 1964.

Concerns over police–community relations had somewhat conflicting connotations that depended on their source. Liberals' concerns were related to the civil rights movement and stressed the need for more principled treatment of citizens at all stages of criminal-justice processing. This required, among other things, more controls over police behavior. Conservatives, on the other hand, wanted to strengthen police operations in order to combat rising crime rates and stressed the need for greater economic and moral support for "your local police."

From either point of view, however, the citizenry's attitude toward the police (ATP) became important. From the liberal viewpoint, a positive ATP, especially among ethnic minorities, was a goal insofar as it was an indicator of improved police behavior. From the conservative point of view, a positive ATP could be seen as helpful in a number of ways: more cooperation with police in terms of reporting crimes and giving information; support for higher levels of funding; support for a variety of modifications of liberal Supreme Court decisions; and simply better morale for police officers, who were coming to see themselves as surrounded by a hostile citizenry.

The Nature of Attitudes

Few studies of ATP have been grounded in any particular theory of attitudes. Furthermore, within social psychology, where most of the theoretical research has been done over the past half century, there is no generally agreed-upon theory, or even definition, of attitude. With that caveat, a particular theory of attitude formation and change, based more or less loosely on the work of Milton Rokeach, will be adopted for this essay.

An attitude will be defined here as the set of all those evaluative beliefs and other relevant cognitions that an individual holds toward some object or situation. According to this definition, a belief about the courteousness of "the local police" reflects or is part of an attitude, presuming the individual cares whether police are courteous; a belief about how tall the average police officer is would not be relevant to one's attitude—unless one had a preference for tall authority figures.

Because attitudes are primarily evaluative—they place something on a subjective good-bad continuum—they are generally presumed to affect an individual's behavior. Since the very beginning of attitude research, however, it has been difficult to demonstrate any strong link between attitudes and behavior. A number of factors make the link between attitudes and behavior problematic. First, individuals may hold beliefs that are conflicting or even logically contradictory—being for law enforcement but against crackdowns on drunk driving, for example. Individuals may or may not be aware of the conflicting nature of their beliefs; a particular belief may be totally unconscious or it may be compartmentalized (kept psychologically separate from other beliefs about the same object). Second, individuals may be motivated to misrepresent their beliefs to a researcher—either to maintain social desirability or to "vote" for a particular side of an issue. Finally, even if respondents do accurately reflect all their relevant beliefs toward some object, their behavior in a particular situation may still be unpredictable, since a minimum of two attitudes (toward the object and the situation) will always be relevant. In addition, the relevance of the behavior to one's attitude or values—the perceived instrumentality—may not be so evident to the individual as to the researcher. It need not be surprising, then, that individuals who are apparently strongly propolice may not support more police power, or more taxes to hire more police, or stricter enforcement of traffic regulations. In general, the simpler the context and the more precisely an attitude is defined and measured, the stronger the relationship will be between attitudes and behavior.

Any attitude, then, may be seen as existing within a larger complex of other attitudes and values, and performing a number of functions. Attitudes help individuals determine how to attend to, retain, and organize the welter of information to which they are exposed. They provide a basic view of the world, a sense of meaning and connectedness. They provide handy scripts for behavior. They help express and actualize values and ideology. Finally, they help defend one's ego, for better or worse, against threatening information and experiences.

Because of the complexity of the cognitive system of which attitudes are a part, and because of the multiple functions that they perform, it should not be surprising that meaningful and enduring change in significant attitudes does not come easily. One approach to attitude change is through a process of clarification or consistency, in which an individual's attention is focused on already existing values, beliefs, memories, etc., so that their salience or relevance to a particular attitude is increased, thus altering the cognitive balance of forces. The other main approach to attitude change is through new information or experiences. Thus, a story in the newspapers, an anecdote told by a friend (or enemy), a television drama, and an anonymous telephone call selling booster tickets are all potential modifiers of one's ATP.

Attitudes toward Police
Overview
Many factors (independent variables) interact to determine ATP. These factors can be roughly subdivided into demographic, personality, and experiential variables. The main demographic variables for ATP include race or ethnic group, age, gender, socioeconomic status, education, and a variety of geographic concepts (urban-rural, population density, city, neighborhood, local crime rates, etc.). Of course, a demographic variable, such as being black, does not cause attitude formation per se. However, such a variable is sociological shorthand for a wide variety of experiences that individuals are more likely to have because of such a characteristic. Because demographic variables are much easier to measure, they are much more widely studied than are personal experiences, which are presumed to be direct determinants of attitudes. Personality variables include a person's values and other attitudes, political ideology, and character traits, such as dogmatism or authoritarianism. Experiential variables include victimization, positive and negative encounters with police officers in a variety of roles (victim, suspect, offender, vehicle operator, personal acquaintance, and consumer of a variety of police services), vicarious experiences (especially of family and friends), exposure to police in a variety of entertainment and news media, and knowing or unknowing participation in a variety of police-sponsored programs, such as neighborhood foot-patrol, operation identification, neighborhood watch, etc.

ATP's effects have been studied less than its causes. Behavioral effects include willingness to report a crime, demand for other police services, cooperation with various police-sponsored programs (participation in neighborhood watch, adoption of recommended security measures, etc.), and support for police-related ballot issues (e.g., a bond issue for a new police station).

One behavioral effect that has received a fair amount of attention is citizen complaint. There is no statistical correlation between ATP and filing a complaint. In fact, someone with a very propolice attitude might be more motivated to complain about police behavior than a person with a negative ATP who encounters a similar incident. The first person may want to maintain high police standards; the second may believe that bad police behavior is so typical that it hardly warrants comment, or that an official complaint would be useless. Generally, however, filing of a complaint is seen as a negative indicator, and on a community-wide level the number of complaints is thought to reflect the attitudes of a significant part of the community. Presumably, a successful program aimed at improving police–community relations would result in both a higher-than-average ATP and a lowered number of formal complaints. Besides their role as an indicator of ATP, formal complaints are also significant for the number of emotionally charged issues that they raise about police practices. For this reason research and theorizing on complaints will be treated in a separate section below.

Measurement Issues
Before looking at some specific research finding, we need to examine certain measurement problems. First, it is not entirely clear what ATP means. ATP can refer to beliefs in the importance of law enforcement, to beliefs about how well a given city or area is policed, to beliefs about the job-related behavior of the average policeman. A typical question is: "Has the performance of the local police been very satisfactory, satisfactory, mixed, etc.?" Answers are often difficult to interpret. An "unsatisfactory" rating may reflect hostility toward existing police or a perceived need for more police. The belief that there should be more citizen control over police operations may reflect a negative ATP, as is generally assumed, or it may reflect a more positive desire to broaden the scope of police operations. Another complication is that statements reflecting generally positive sentiments toward police often mask significant areas of dissatisfaction that are revealed by more specific questions. Finally, it is also difficult to known how to characterize a given level of re-

sponse. For example, if 75 percent of a community "agree slightly" that "the local police are doing an adequate job," is this a generally positive response that police administrators should be happy about, or does this indicate a significant amount of dissatisfaction? The percentage of a sample found to have a favorable ATP varies greatly because of the wording and content of the items making up the attitude scale.

Although the usual method for measuring ATP is through subjects' response to one or more simple statements, a semantic differential, an adjective checklist, or a more open-ended question may also be used. Although each method has its advantages and disadvantages, the various approaches to measuring ATP all seem to correlate reasonably well, and as long as a given measuring instrument is used in the same manner throughout a study, meaningful comparisons between groups can be made.

Empirical Findings: General
The most representative data on ATP come from a series of national surveys conducted between 1967 and 1982 and reported in the U.S. Department of Justice's *Sourcebook of Criminal Justice Statistics*. In a 1981 national survey, in response to the question, "How would you rate the job done by law enforcement officials on the local level," 65 percent of the white sample responded "excellent" or "pretty good," as did 52 percent of the black sample. This finding sets the tone for a wide variety of surveys using a variety of techniques: generally positive evaluations of the police, with blacks being noticeably lower in their ratings, though still usually positive. This trend seems to have been reasonably stable since 1967, although there was a slight decline in ATP from 1970 to 1977, followed by a slight upward trend from 1978 to 1982.

Race and ATP
Given the fact that the concern over ATP first began with the civil rights movement and the urban riots of the 1960s, and given the general finding that blacks show a lower ATP on virtually every survey, it is not surprising that more attention has been paid to race than any other variable (although a few surveys report Hispanics separately, the literature is largely limited to black-white differences).

It should be noted, however, that blacks' lower ATP depends partly on the nature of the question being asked. For example, although blacks generally indicate a somewhat higher concern over crime than do whites, they are less likely than whites to attribute crime increases to inadequate police (6 percent versus 11 percent in a 1981 survey). Blacks are also much more likely than whites to support the right to strike for police: 42 percent versus 25 percent in a 1981 survey. In a series of surveys from 1973 to 1982, blacks were slightly more inclined than whites to feel that not enough money was being spent to fight crime (71 percent versus 66 percent in 1980; 72 percent versus 71 percent in 1982).

One of the largest black-white differences in national surveys came in response to the question of whether there were situations in which "you would approve of a policeman striking an adult male citizen." While 76 percent of whites responded yes, only 45 percent of blacks did so. This sort of finding has tended to support the idea that blacks' lower ATP was a result of the "quality" of their personal contacts with police.

There appears to be no clear answer to whether or not blacks currently receive poorer treatment from police. Many "ride-along" studies, for example, have failed to find any difference in police behavior in encounters with black citizens. Although several studies have found that blacks are more likely to report slower police response time or to have received an unnecessary personal search ("stop and frisk"), the difference in blacks' and whites' perceptions of police treatment are not large, especially when white and black samples are matched on geographic location. It should also be pointed out that blacks (as well as whites) express less satisfaction with state and federal than with local law enforcement. This finding strongly suggests that factors other than direct experience determine ATP. In any event, most of the differences in ATP between blacks and whites remain when various experiential variables are taken into account.

Other explanations for blacks' lower ATP, while reasonable, are based more on speculation than data. Some authors feel that blacks have higher expectations of police service—either because their inner-city location requires more reliance on police for a variety of services, or because they possess a greater sense of "distributive injustice": a feeling that society and its institutions ought to compensate for the effects of racial discrimination. These expectations of service may also clash with police expectations

that citizens will show deference to lawful authority; these police expectations may, in turn, be misperceived by blacks as a racially motivated put-down.

These (possible) differences in black expectations and perceptions need to be understood in terms of cultural and neighborhood history. On a historical level, police mistreatment of blacks is well documented and a certain suspiciousness of police intentions is clearly understandable. Thus, it is not unlikely that positive interactions with police would be met with skepticism, while negative encounters (either personally or vicariously experienced) would be taken as confirming blacks' image of the police as representative of white oppression.

The above generalizations about the causes of blacks' lower ATP need to be highly qualified. Besides the fact that blacks' general ATP can be characterized as positive, Wesley Skogan (1979) found that there were large differences from city to city. In surveys conducted in 1975, for example, it was found that only 14 percent of Chicago's blacks gave their police a "good" rating, compared to 50 percent of blacks in Denver. More important, the difference between blacks and whites in their rating of police varied greatly from city to city: Blacks' ATP was only 5 percent below whites in Denver and only 9 percent below whites in Atlanta, compared to 30 percent below or more in Chicago, Los Angeles, St. Louis, and Philadelphia. The gap between blacks and whites was largely unrelated to the general ATP in a city. These data suggest that blacks' lower ATP is to be accounted for more by local history or "neighborhood culture" than generalizations about "the black experience" as such.

Police departments have differed, of course, in the extent to which they have tried to improve relations with the blacks. Although the evidence is not strong, it does seem that a combination of such factors as increasing the percentage of black police, civilization of police, and some degree of citizen involvement in complaint boards raises blacks' ATP slightly. Given that police departments are attempting to overcome the effects of some one hundred-plus years of negative treatment of blacks, meager findings in this area need not be discouraging.

Other Demographic Variables
The only other demographic variable that has consistently been found to correlate with ATP is age: People below the age of about thirty gener-

ally show lower ATP; among those over thirty, ATP rises very slightly with age. Some studies find that lower socioeconomic status (including less education or income) is associated with lower ATP, but when race and neighborhood are controlled this variable becomes insignificant.

The effects of age are generally attributed to the greater frequency of involuntary police contacts (arrests and potential arrests) that occur during the crime-prone years. This explanation is somewhat complicated by the fact that gender is seldom found to be related to ATP. That is, women, who account for only about 15 percent of arrests, do not have a higher ATP than men. One would have to hypothesize, therefore, that younger women acquire their more negative ATP from their participation in a youth culture—a plausible but so far untested assumption.

Personality Variables

A more favorable ATP is often associated with a more conservative political stance and with relatively favorable attitudes toward public officials and the court system. Authoritarian attitudes, however, have been found to be associated more with support for increased police power than with satisfaction with the quality of policing.

Research by Milton Rokeach, Martin Miller, and John Snyder found that a sample of white male police officers had a common value system that distinguished them from several other identifiable groups. The difference between the police and a national sample of blacks was striking, especially in terms of police officers' much lower evaluation of "equality." Although ATP was not measured, this finding suggests the possibility that perceived value differences may play a part in lower ATP.

In general, then, little is known about the role of personality variables in ATP or concerning the functions that one's ATP might play in one's broader value-attitude system or personality make-up.

Effects of Personal Experiences

Studies of the effects on ATP of personal experience with police may be subdivided into a number of categories. These include the impact of crime victimization and the police response, the impact of various police programs designed to improve ATP, and a variety of miscellaneous contacts—from asking for directions to being arrested.

Subjects' evaluation of their recent experiences with police officers generally correlate closely with ATP. Such a finding is open to several interpretations, however. It may be that citizens with a favorable ATP are more likely to: (a) remember favorable experiences, (b) evaluate any given experience as favorable, and (c) induce courteous behavior from police. Thus, there is no strong evidence that increasing police officer courtesy, or "professionalism," will improve a negative ATP. The evidence is somewhat stronger that negative experiences with police lower ATP. This includes being arrested, being frisked, or observing police misconduct.

Victimization and the Police Response

Police have often been criticized for the insensitivity of their response to crime victims, especially battered women and rape victims. Although there is not much evidence that being a crime victim per se lowers ATP, there is ample evidence that the nature of the police response does matter.

Much attention has been given to the variable "response time," since this is a fairly easy-to-measure and objective indicator of police service to crime victims. What seems to matter, however, is not the rapidity of the police response but the extent to which the caller's expectations are met. Within limits a slow response, if anticipated, does not lower ATP.

A police response that demonstrates some level of concern, such as a thorough crime-scene investigation, a telephone follow-up, or conducting a crime-prevention survey, has also been found to improve victims' ATP. Although the exact nature of the desired response will vary with the type of crime and personality of the victim, three basic factors can be identified in an effective response. These factors involve thoroughness (taking control of the situation), information (letting the victim know what is to happen, giving advice), and support (listening to the victim, expressing concern). While such a response may improve victims' general evaluation of the police—as courteous, responsible, well-intentioned, etc.—it may also decrease the perception of police effectiveness as crime fighters. As long as such a change in perception is realistic, however, the trade-off would seem to be well worth it.

Police Programs and ATP

A combination of minority recruitment and civilian involvement in complaint review may improve blacks' ATP slightly. A third type of program, police–community relations training, is designed to improve police behavior, presumably resulting in improved ATP in the community, which in turn should lead to more police-community cooperation and eventually to crime reduction. The most positive evidence in support of this theory comes from a study by Nicholas Lovrich, which compared crime trends in 161 cities that were subdivided according to whether they were high or low in their commitment to police–community relations (PCR) training. Despite showing a very slightly higher crime rate prior to 1969, when funding for such training began, the high-PCR cities eventually showed a modestly lower rate of crime increase. This study is admittedly inconclusive for a number of reasons, but especially because it is probably that high-PCR cities have also adopted a variety of other proactive strategies. Furthermore, ATP was not measured, so there is no direct evidence that it was affected by the PCR programs, or that it played a part in lowering crime rates relative to other cities. One finding, however, does lend some support to the theory that PCR training lowered crime rates by improving ATP. Based on victimization surveys in a subsample of the cities, it was found that 67.5 percent of robberies were reported in high-PCR cities compared to 52.5 percent in low-PCR cities. This higher reporting rate not only makes the lower official crime rate in the high-PCR cities more impressive, but also suggests that a higher level of citizen cooperation was achieved.

ATP and Behavior
The most neglected area of ATP research concerns how it affects citizens' behavior. A 1982 national survey found that blacks were somewhat less likely than whites to have called the police during the previous year (31 percent versus 35 percent), despite their somewhat higher victimization rate. But there is no direct evidence that within the black community a person's ATP affected his or her tendency to request police services.

Based on self-report, there is some evidence that belief in police effectiveness correlates with reporting crime, and belief in police fairness correlates with level of cooperation. Some studies, however, have failed to find a relationship between crime reporting and ATP, even when measured in terms of police effectiveness. Clearly more research would be useful in this area.

Complaints
Frequency and Nature
Citizens' complaints about police behavior are relatively infrequent. In a classic observational study of police behavior in the mid-1960s, excessive use of force was found in about three out of a thousand encounters; some evidence of incivility was observed in about 13 percent of all encounters. Because of differences in recording procedures from city to city, it is very difficult to generalize about the frequency of formal complaints about such behavior. Furthermore, the frequency of complaints has been found to vary tremendously with the institution of new complaint-review procedures. Nevertheless, a reasonable estimate would be that a typical large city generates about one official complaint annually for every thousand residents.

The nature of recorded complaints seems to vary with the extent to which citizens are encouraged to make their complaints known. If the complaint procedure is difficult and/or the review process is seen as unfair to the citizen, relatively few complaints will be generated and they will involve a fairly high level of physical-abuse charges. If the level of complaints increases because new procedures are instituted, charges of verbal abuse tend to predominate. There is some evidence that blacks are more likely to allege verbal abuse and harassment (unnecessary stops, searches, orders to move along), while whites are more likely to allege procedure and service problems.

Relation to ATP
With the exception of research by Scott Decker and Allen Wagner (1982), the literature on complaints is not well integrated with the ATP literature. When population demographics were taken into account, Decker and Wagner found that a complainant was four times more likely to be male and/or young (aged fifteen to twenty-four), and three times more likely to be black. The unmarried, the unemployed, students, and blue-collar workers were also overrepresented in the complainant population. Noting the overrepresentation of youth and blacks, as well as the fact that only about 4 percent of all complaints were sustained in that city, the authors theorized that negative police encounters coupled with inadequate complaint investigation procedures contributed importantly to low ATP.

Although Decker and Wagner's theory seems reasonable, Alpert and Dunham (1988) suggest that complaints may not be a significant factor in citizens' ATP. Alpert and Dunham compared five Dade County (Miami-area) neighborhoods in terms of how important they felt twenty factors were in evaluating a police officer. In none of the five neighborhoods were citizen complaints against an officer ranked higher than twelfth. Courtesy and human-relations skills were rated highly, except in a low-income black neighborhood, where they were ranked sixteenth and seventeenth. This neighborhood placed much more value on such order-maintenance functions as appearance, taking appropriate action, initiative, arrests, and forcefulness.

Disposition

The vast majority of police departments have some sort of formal procedure for handling citizens' complaints. Typically, this involves an investigation by an internal affairs division, resulting in the complaints either being sustained, not sustained (not enough evidence to make a determination), exonerated (the alleged actions occurred but were reasonable), or unfounded (the alleged actions did not occur). The "sustained" category is sometimes subdivided into "improper conduct" (officer at fault) or "policy failure" (officer followed procedure but the citizen was unfairly harmed). The "not sustained" and "unfounded" categories generally account for most dispositions, since meaningful physical evidence or an unbiased witness is usually lacking. The "sustained" category generally accounts for the fewest dispositions, perhaps 5 percent or less in most cities. When a complaint is sustained the penalty, imposed by the department, may be anything from a verbal reprimand to firing, with the possibility of a recommendation for criminal prosecution.

Civilian Review

The central issue with citizen complaints concerns the most appropriate method for handling them. Because a strictly internal review often gives the appearance of being biased against the citizen, various experiments with civilian involvement in the complaint review process have been tried. The first major city to establish a civilian review board was Washington, D.C., in 1948, followed by Philadelphia in 1958. The issue of civilian review of police became highly politicized in the 1960s, however. After only four months of operation, a New York City civilian review board was ended by a police-sponsored referendum in 1966. The Philadelphia board was effectively ended in 1967 because of police opposition. Opponents of civilian review generally argued that civilians could not appreciate the complex nature of police work and that police would close ranks in noncooperation.

Nevertheless, efforts continued to involve civilians in the complaint-review process and a variety of different approaches emerged, notably in Detroit, Chicago, Kansas City (Missouri), Oakland, Berkeley, Miami, Baltimore, and Portland (Oregon), along with a few other cities. With the exception of Berkeley, all of the processes retain a high level of police input. Lack of data, complicated variations in the process, and differences in local conditions make generalizations about civilian review difficult. A few general findings have emerged, however.

First, civilian involvement is able to resolve a higher percentage of complaints, often through a "conciliation" process. The percentage of sustained complaints also increases, reaching 15 percent in Detroit, for example. Second, this increased resolution occurs in spite of the fact that the procedure usually involved more due process for the accused officer. Some studies have shown that because of this increased protection, officers would rather face civilian review than an internal affairs board. Third, at least in the short run, a civilian complaint board can increase the number of complaints filed—by as much as 500 percent in New York and Detroit; this may have more to do with the publicity attendant to the new process than to any deep-seated confidence in the process by the new complainants. Fourth, whether an individual complainant sees the process as more fair depends largely on the outcome of his or her particular complaint.

David Bayley has aptly made the point that no data exist, or are likely to be obtained, that would indicate which method of complaint handling will result in the most appropriate control of police. Because of the need to encourage citizen confidence by maintaining the appearance of objectivity, however, most commentators seem to favor some level of civilian involvement, usually for appellate review or for overseeing the basic complaint review process of a police department's internal affairs division. It also needs to be kept in mind that the complaint review process is only one of many methods of control, departmental accreditation, internal affairs investigations, media attention, and city government control of police management.

Conclusion

By the late 1980s there seemed to be a general consensus that citizens' ATP was no longer a major problem. Although black citizens' ATP remained stubbornly below that of their white counterparts, the recruitment of women and minorities into policing, along with increased commitment by administrators to community relations issues, had served to improve the general image of the police. To be sure, there was a lack of evidence that this improved image was paying off in improved law enforcement; nevertheless, a measure of the effects on citizen attitudes has become a fairly routine aspect in evaluating any new approach to policing—such as various community policing programs.

Then on March 3, 1991, an amateur videotape captured several Los Angeles police officers beating Rodney King after a police pursuit. Although insiders claimed not to be surprised, the fact remains that the LAPD had a reputation for effective police selection and training. There was some fear, therefore, that this incident would set back the whole area of police–community relations. When serious rioting broke out one year later, in the aftermath of the officers' acquittal, these fears seemed justified.

Surveys conducted both after the Rodney King incident and after the acquittals, however, show relatively few effects on general ATP. In a national survey conducted a few weeks after the original incident, for example, 60 percent of the respondents indicated a great deal of respect for their local police, with only 7 percent indicating "hardly any." When the results were subdivided by race, blacks' ATP was found to be less favorable by a margin of 11 percent—a fairly standard finding in such surveys. Yet even for this relatively less satisfied group, 51 percent indicated a great deal of respect and an additional 32 percent indicated "some" respect.

Perhaps even more indicative of the general citizenry's ATP was a June 1992 Gallup survey in which the "honesty and ethical standards" of police was compared with that of twenty-four other occupational groups. Police were rated seventh, just behind dentists and engineers and ahead of such occupations as journalists, bankers, business executives, and congressmen. Overall, 42 percent of the sample gave police high marks, 42 percent thought the police were average, and only 14 percent rated police standards as low. It should be noted that these marks were a few percentage points lower than the typical survey conducted between 1981 and 1990, but this decline was also evident for the vast majority of the occupational groups. Once again, blacks' ratings were noticeably lower: The percentage of blacks giving police low marks increased from 22 percent in 1985 to 37 percent in 1992. While there is no direct evidence linking this falloff in blacks' ATP to the Rodney King incident, such a link would certainly be a reasonable hypothesis.

In November 1992 a fatal police beating in Detroit also raised accusations of widespread police racism and brutality, even in Detroit's well-integrated department. Newspaper reports have suggested that the process for investigating citizen complaints against the police had grown ineffective during the previous ten or so years. It seems likely that the various complaint review processes around the country are in need of continuing reform and renewal.

Undoubtedly concern over ATP and the handling of citizen complaints will continue for some time, especially with respect to minority communities. This concern will manifest itself especially in training police for better community relations, in policy setting, and in program evaluation in such areas as police use of force, high-speed pursuit, and community and problem-oriented policing.

Robert J. Homant

Bibliography

Albrecht, Stan L., and Miles Green. "Attitudes Toward the Police and the Larger Attitude Complex." *Criminology* 15 (1977): 67–86.

Alpert, Geoffrey, and Roger Dunham. *Policing Multi-Ethnic Neighborhoods.* Westport, CT: Greenwood Press, 1988.

Bordua, David J., and Larry L. Tifft. "Citizen Interviews, Organizational Feedback, and Police-Community Relations Decisions." *Law and Society Review* 6 (1971): 155–82.

Cordner, Gary W. "Fear of Crime and the Police: An Evaluation of a Fear Reduction Strategy." *Journal of Police Science and Administration* 14 (1986): 223–33.

Decker, Scott H., and Allen E. Wagner. "Race and Citizen Complaints against the Police: An Analysis of Their Interaction." In *Managing Police Work: Issues and*

Analysis. Ed. Jack R. Greene. Beverly Hills, CA: Sage, 1982. 107–22.

Homant, Robert J. "The Image of the Police: A Survey of Detroit-Area Residents." *American Journal of Police* 1 (1982): 150–77.

———, Daniel B. Kennedy, and Roger M. Fleming. "The Effect of Victimization and the Police Response on Citizens' Attitudes Toward Police." *Journal of Police Science and Administration* 12 (1984): 323–32.

Skogan, Wesley G. "Citizen Satisfaction with Police Services." In *Evaluating Alternative Law Enforcement Policies*. Lexington, MA: D.C. Heath. Eds. Ralph Baker and Fred A. Meyer, Jr. 1979. 29–42.

Taylor, Robert W. "Historical Developments and Contemporary Concepts in Police–Community Relations." *American Journal of Police* 3 (1984): 145–67.

Tyler, Tom R. "The Influence of Citizen Satisfaction with Police Behavior upon Public Sector Support for Increases in Police Authority." *Law & Policy* 6 (1984): 329–38.

U.S. Civil Rights Commission. *Who Is Guarding the Guardians?* Washington, DC: Government Printing Office, 1981.

Citizen Complaints in the New Police Order

A dynamic tension exists in the role of government in a society that aspires to be democratic. On the one hand government is created to provide citizens with safety, security, and service, while on the other it serves as an instrument that organizes many aspects of social life bringing a sense of order, stability, and conformity to social interactions. The tension between service and control has been dramatized in the writing of political philosophers. Political philosophers expressed this tension in terms of a "social contract," attempting to present the proper balance between government as "service provider" and as "citizen controller." By entering into the social contract, citizens are thought to surrender certain natural rights and vest government with the power to maintain social stability and to ensure citizen interests. In exchange for relinquishing the right to use physical force, for instance, citizens expect government to provide effective systems for regulating conduct and forums for resolving social conflict.

The police institution is the most visible of all government's formal social control creations. The tension between the dual roles of government is no better portrayed than in the actions of social control agents, who continually struggle with the conflict that arises when balancing their governmental role as service provider and citizen controller. Historically, police have provided little in terms of social service and much in state sanctioned social control. Yet, if the contemporary rhetoric of leading police administrators, the printed words of scholars, and the remarks of politicians are to be believed, the role police play in society is changing. Spokespersons from both policing and academe are addressing citizens and their colleagues on an emerging philosophy of policing. This new philosophy and its operationalization are usually spoken of as "community" and "problem-solving" policing. While these role strategies differ in implementation, they are driven by reconceptualizing police as service providers rather than citizen controllers. While many scholars question the viability of instituting such a reconceptualization (Strecher, 1991; Williams and Wagoner, 1992), the rhetoric from the trenches is certainly permeated with expressions of a shift in police role strategy.

As with any significant philosophical or political change, this reform movement has been accompanied by a new language. Police chiefs are now referred to as "executives"; citizens are referred to as "clients" or "consumers"; and the control that police provide is shrouded in the jargon of "service." Remarks of Los Angeles Chief Willie Williams capture the essence of the role strategy: "I liken the L.A. police to a business. . . . We have $3\frac{1}{2}$ million customers . . ." (Wickerham, 1993:13A). In like fashion, the actions of the New York City Police Department in placing a twelve-page guide on how to use departmental services in a local news source reflects attempts to transform rhetoric into reality ("Across the Nation," 1993). As these examples show, police are invoking the language of business and capitalism (Manning, 1992). Perhaps because they are relinquishing their "monopoly on legitimate violence," they are embracing "the language of economics and management . . . to reconceptualize the police mandate" (Manning, 1992:1). This fundamental shift in philosophy and its attendant rhetoric, if accompanied by operational change, promises to have profound consequences on virtually every aspect of policing.

One aspect of policing that provides insight into the integration of the "new" service rhetoric and the "old" control reality is how police respond to citizen complaints. Few other aspects of policing provide a more direct and empirical link between the emerging language of service and actual practices than does the police response to citizen complaints. Within this context, this article explores citizen complaints against police. Highlighted first are some assumptions that drove the development of the current citizen complaint system. Second, the nature of citizen complaints levied against the police are reviewed and assessment is made of the responsiveness of the police institution to these challenges to their control authority. By examining police responses to citizen complaints, an assessment can be made of the division between the emerging rhetoric of service and the reality of citizen control. Finally, the article explores the possible transformations that citizen complaint systems might find if the new police role strategy is institutionalized.

Traditional Views and Responses to Citizen Complaints

The history of citizen complaints against police has been a quest to develop a system of ensuring accountability to the citizenry that empowers it. Fundamental in establishing police accountability was the creation of a system from which assessments could be made as to whether police abused their powers and authorities as citizen controllers. The desire to develop a system of accountability for police deviations in control practices is best expressed in this report: "In 1903, a New York City police commissioner turned judge noted that his court had seen numerous citizens with injuries received when the police effected their arrest. He felt that many of them had done nothing to deserve an arrest but most of them made no complaint" (Wagner and Decker, 1993:276). Implicit in this judicial observation is that there existed no effective mechanism for citizens to levy complaints against police or even a desire by police officials to encourage citizen complaints. What transpired in the ninety-some years since this observation was the development of a police-controlled citizen complaint system in every major law enforcement organization.

With an overriding concern with police abuse, the emerging system focused on technical rule violations by police—especially physical abuse. To assure police accountability the resulting system had to allow agencies to document and investigate citizen complaints so that some assessment of performance could be obtained to demonstrate that police are accountable to and controlled by government and citizen. Unfortunately, like many aspects of modern policing, the citizen complaint system was born of two fundamental legalistic precepts—accountability and control. The current citizen complaint system was modeled after, and founded upon, assumptions that permeate the larger legal system. Because it stressed localized accountability and patterned itself after other legal forums, the citizen complaint system became legalistic in form and adversarial in nature, therefore mirroring the criminal justice system. With an emphasis on accountability and control, a focus on legally and organizationally defined abuse, and driven by the assumptions that underpin an adversarial model of justice, the citizen complaint system became a quasijudicial forum. From its inception, then, the process pitted police against public in a quasilegal forum that focused not on the adequacy of police as service providers but on technical violations of legal and organizational rules.

Given a legalistic framework, the system's twin focal concerns became the establishment of the validity of citizen allegations and the disposal of complaints in finite fashion. The system was constructed with all the safeguards of a due process model of justice, but failed to benefit from its neutrality. Police agencies adopting citizen complaint systems provided an array of shields similar to those offered defendants in criminal trials, thus insulating themselves from sanction by housing investigative and adjudicative functions in station houses. Approximately 84 percent of the nation's largest police departments use a complaint system that relies exclusively on internal investigation and adjudication (West, 1988). The system allowed law enforcement to control the types of citizen complaints it accepted; the extent to which police investigated complaints; the weight given to evidence uncovered by police investigations; the burden of proof required for adjudication; and ultimately the disposition of citizen complaints.

In developing the system, police have erected formidable barriers to citizen complaints. Suffice it to mention just a few obstacles police have used to bar the flow of citizen complaints. First, there are inherent deterrents to citizen complaints against police. These include a lack of citizen knowledge that they can and should complain; a lack of citizen knowledge concerning actionable police conducts; the time and energy needed to complain; and a fatalistic citizen attitude concerning the effectiveness of complaining. While these barriers are inherent in any system of accountability, historically police have done little to remove these obstructions. Second, police have employed a deterrent "strategy" to reduce the number of citizen complaints. While differences in complaint systems abound many police departments have adopted tactics that effectively block a large proportion of potential citizen complaints. These tactics have generally included requiring citizens to file complaints in person rather than anonymously; requiring citizens to file complaints at station houses; restricting access to the complaint system (either through location or language barriers); requiring citizens to sign written formal statements (often accompanied by warnings of criminal prosecution for falsely reporting); requiring citizens to take polygraph tests before beginning an investigation; and limiting complaints to only those behaviors recognized by police as falling within their self-defined areas of accountability. Finally, and hopefully to a lesser extent, police have used some draconian measures to prevent citizen complaints. Some of these measures have included making citizens wait at station houses for hours (hoping they will forego complaining); threatening minority citizens with notification of the immigration and naturalization service; making it known that police will run warrant checks on anyone filing a complaint; and threatening citizens with defamation lawsuits (see generally Christopher, 1991; Kolts, 1992; Mayor's Citizen Commission, 1991). In short, police have not only availed themselves of the protections of a legalistic system of citizen complaints, but they have used many tactics to discourage challenges to their control authority. Many of these tactics undermine the integrity of the citizen complaints system.

Those citizen complaints that reach disposition are classified according to a typology developed by police officials. This classification functions to sustain police concern with reducing the volume of viable complaints that enter the system and limits the effectiveness of the system as a mechanism of accountability and control. Most police organizations classify the citizen complaints they decide to investigate in one of the following fashions:

1. *Unfounded*—the act complained of did not occur. This classification results when the investigators find non-involved citizens or police witnesses who contradict the allegations of the complainant.
2. *Not Sustained*—the evidence is insufficient to clearly prove or disprove the allegations made. This classification almost always results when the only witnesses to the allegations were the accused officer and the complainant, or witnesses in some way affiliated with the complainant, such as the complainant's family or friends.
3. *Exonerated*—the event of alleged conduct occurred but it was justified, lawful, and proper.
4. *Sustained*—the police officer engaged in the alleged conduct and the conduct was out of policy. Excessive force and improper tactics complaints are rarely sustained unless there are noninvolved, independent witnesses who corroborate the complainant's version of the facts (Christopher, 1991:155).

Inherent in this classification, as with the entire complaint process, is the assumption that citizens bring improper or false complaints against police. While false complaints do occur, the existing classification weights more heavily the desire to determine whether a citizen complaint is valid than it does understanding the reason for the complaint. A second intent reflected in the current classification is the desire to dispose of complaints in finite fashion with the least disruption to the institution. This means that complaints must be disposed of with a designation that generally vindicates police conduct to avoid other legal entanglements. Vindication can take the form of an "exoneration" of the conduct as proper, it can call into question the validity of the citizen's complaint by labeling it "unfounded," or it can fail to sustain the complaint by challenging the sufficiency of misconduct evidence. The vast majority of complaints lodged against police are disposed of through this vindication process. A national self-report survey of the largest police agencies found that on average only 11 percent of citizen complaints are classified as sustained (West, 1988).

The police have generally failed to established either accountability or control of abuse of authority under the present system. Nor does the present system seem able to handle the bulk of concerns citizens have with the police institution. The manner in which citizen complaints are disposed of reflects these shortcomings. Consider how few citizen complaints are sustained by select law-enforcement agencies in various cities.

Table 1 indicates that only a very small percentage of all complaints filed against the police are sustained. The research demonstrates that of all types of citizen claims, physical abuse claims are sustained at the lowest rates (see footnotes below) whereas complaints of rudeness, verbal abuse, or improper attitude are sustained at higher rates (Kappeler, Carter, and Sapp, 1992). There are several ironies in this finding. First, a system designed to provide accountability and control of physical abuse has been shown to be the least effective in dealing with this area of police conduct. Second, the system seems most conducive to controlling nonphysical abuse when one would suspect that these forms of abuse would produce the least credible evidence of police misconduct. Finally, of all the sustained complaints reported in Table 1, relatively few officers every received the sanction of suspension, demotion, or termination from duty (see original sources of data). It is hard not to conclude that the citizen complaint system, as employed by many police organizations, has failed to establish either accountability to the citizenry or governmental control of the police.

Citizen Complaints in the New Police Order
If police adopt a service orientation to citizen complaints, one that fashions its approach upon the rhetoric of the business community, police may find that the general assumptions that underpin the existing system will have to be altered. First, a system built around an ethos of service would require police to accept more citizen complaints. Not only would po-

TABLE 1

Police Response to Citizen Complaints in Select Agencies

Jurisdiction	Year(s)	Total	Sustained	Source of Data
Columbia, MO	1985–90	413	92 (22%)	Kappeler, Sapp and Carter, 1992[1]
Los Angeles, CA (PD)	1986–90	3,419	171 (5%)	Independent CA Commission on LAPD, 1991[2]
Los Angeles, CA (SD)	1990–92	514	27 (6%)	Special Counsel on LASD, 1992[3]
Metro City	1971	304	16 (5%)	Wagner, 1980[4]
	1972–73	280	32 (11%)	
Milwaukee, WI	1985–90	206	1 (.05%)	Mayor's Citizens Comm., 1991[5]
Omaha, NE	1989	255	26 (10%)	Walker, 1992[6]
Philadelphia, PA	1959–68	868	145 (17%)	Hudson, 1972
St. Louis, MO	1980–90	2,218	202 (9%)	Official Records[7]
Truck Stop City	1971	253	40 (16%)	Culver, 1975
	1973	279	13 (5%)	

1 Includes complaints initiated by police officials which inflates the percentage of sustained complaints.

2 Includes only allegations of excessive force and improper tactics. LAPD sustained only 2 percent of its citizen complaints for excessive force but since the Commission report contains conflicting percentages the most conservative figure is reported.

3 Includes only citizen complaints of excessive use of force.

4 Only 2 percent of citizen complaints for physical abuse were sustained.

5 Includes four complaints against the city fire department.

6 Sustained rate was derived from disciplinary actions taken and may be an underestimate.

7 The official reports claim a much higher rate of sustained complaints due to the inclusion of complaints brought against civilian employees and excluding unfounded, exonerated, and withdrawn complaints from analysis. The authors' independent analysis of the official data, however, indicates only 9 percent of citizen complaints are sustained. In 1990, 12.6 percent of physical abuse complaints were sustained whereas 36 percent of improper attitude complaints were sustained.

lice be obliged to accept complaints in greater volume, they would be required to accept a greater variety of complaints including those that challenge the quality of service and the adequacy of police as service providers. The police would also have to be concerned with the outcome of complaints not as possible disruptive forces to the integrity of the institution, but, rather, as measures of the effectiveness of police in providing service to a consumer population that could go elsewhere for service. Additionally, the process by which police handle citizen complaints would have to be altered under the new police order. The investigation of citizen complaints against police could no longer focus on establishing the validity of the citizen's complaint, but rather on the underlying concern the citizen had with the police. Police departments might find themselves adopting the business adage that the "citizen is always right" rather than requiring citizen complaints to meet the current police-imposed burden of proof, as under the existing system. Finally, police would have to abandon the vision of the complaint system as an adjudicative process in favor of negotiation or mediation processes designed to satisfy its "customers." Such outcomes if followed by "imposed service improvements" rather than "departmental sanctions" could alter both police and public perception of the citizen complaint system.

The likelihood of such a transformation is open to debate. It is questionable whether one can expect substantive changes in the police handling of citizen complaints, given the increasing litigious environment in which they operate and the protective nature of police subcultures. The more important question, therefore, is what consequences can we expect from police attempts to tailor the citizen complaint system to the new police order.

Such an attempt to transform the citizen complaint system has both possibilities and perils. Developing a consumer approach, for example, has the definite possibility of opening up the institution of policing to greater and more detailed public scrutiny and control, an appealing possibility for those who value a government guided by democratic principles and a service orientation. By expanding what constitutes a recognizable citizen complaint, investigating complaints based on responding to "consumer" needs, and by processing cases in a mediation format, the citizen complaint system could become a critical component in promoting the new police order.

A realistic peril of this new order and its attendant role strategy is that reform may only appear to seriously address citizen complaints by spotlighting those that coincide with the police definition of service provider. While the police institution focuses the community's attention on their "new" role, the handling of complaints associated with the pervious role of police as citizen controllers may remain unchanged. This situation is evidenced by some police departments' attempts to integrate community police with drug enforcement efforts in hopes of generating more intelligence information. As with attempts to reform other organizational practices that threaten members' security, the envisioned complaint processing practices may end up being only superficially service driven and sustaining instead of challenging the original problem of police abuses as citizen controllers. Another peril lies in how police might define "service" and "customer." One can envision police definitions that exclude certain segments of society from the distinction of "customer." Such a system might develop "preferred" customers who receive preferential treatment based on their ability to differentially influence the type, quality, and distribution of police services. Whatever the possibility and perils, clearly the citizen complaint system will play a dominant and strategic role in the new police order.

Victor E. Kappeler
Peter B. Kraska

Bibliography

"Across the Nation." *USA Today* (April 2, 1993): 7A.

Christopher, W. *Report of the Independent Commission on the Los Angeles Police Department.* Los Angeles, CA: Author, 1991.

Culver, J.H. "Policing the Police: Problems and Perspectives." *Journal of Police Science and Administration* 3(2) (1975): 125–35.

Dugan, J.R., and D.R. Breda. "Complaints About Police Officers: A Comparison Among Types and Agencies." *Journal of Criminal Justice* 19 (1991): 156–71.

Hudson, J.R. "Organizational Aspects of Internal and External Review of the

Police." *Journal of Criminal Law, Criminology, and Police Science* 63 (1972): 427–33.

Kappeler, V.E., D. Carter, and A. Sapp. "Police Officer Higher Education, Citizen Complaints and Departmental Rule Violation." *American Journal of Police* 11(2) (1992): 37–54.

Kolts, J.G. *The Los Angeles County Sheriff's Department: A Report by Special Counsel.* Los Angeles, CA: Author, 1992.

Manning, P.K. "Economic Rhetoric and Policing Reform." *Criminal Justice Research Bulletin* 7(4) (1992): 1–8.

Mayor's Citizen Commission. *A Report to Mayor John Norquist and the Board of Fire and Police Commissioners.* Milwaukee, WI: Authors, 1991.

Strecher, V.G. "Histories and Futures of Policing: Readings and Misreadings of a Pivotal Present." *Police Forum* 1(1) (1991): 1–9.

Wagner, A. "Citizen Complaints Against the Police: The Complainant." *Journal of Police Science and Administration* 8(3) (1980): 247–52.

Wagner, A.E., and S.H. Decker. "Evaluating Citizen Complaints Against the Police." In *Critical Issues in Policing: Contemporary Readings.* Eds. R. Dunham, and G. Alpert. Prospect Heights, IL: Waveland Press, 1993. 275–89.

Walker, S. *The Police in America*, 2d ed. New York: McGraw-Hill, 1992.

West, P. "Investigation of Complaints Against the Police: Summary of a National Survey." *American Journal of Police* 7(2) (1988): 101–22.

Wickerham, D. "L.A. Police Chief: Treat People Like Customers." *USA Today* (March 29, 1993): 13A.

Williams, F.P., and C.P. Wagoner. "Making the Police Proactive: An Impossible Task for Improbable Reasons." *Police Forum* 2(2) (1992): 1–5.

Civilian Review Boards

During the 1970s, civilian review boards (CRBs) were thought to provide a better means to control police misconduct. In effect CRBs permitted an appointed group of outsiders (nonpolice) to judge—exonerate or condemn—officers suspected of wrongdoing. The public credo was that police would not police themselves. Therefore, an autonomous body of adjudicators given the power to decide misconduct cases appeared to be the answer. More and Wegener (1990) state that the CRB concept began to flourish in the late 1950s. Most likely, the concept of citizen or civilian review of police antedated that time period. The reason for assigning an earlier date is because the impetus for CRBs is usually a flagrant, or even a shocking, instance of police misconduct. Long before the 1950s victimized and/or enraged citizens would have demanded a say in police matters and exerted pressure in some way.

If a police officer issues such orders to a percolating crowd as "Move on" or "Break it up," citizens complain. If a police officer is not completely respectful of everyone involved, citizens complain. And the most universal, if a police officer appears to engage in discriminatory enforcement of minor laws and ordinances—the "Why me?" syndrome—citizens complain. Since these examples are perceived as abuses of power and in that light daily occurrences, any CRB would have its hands full hearing all the complaints. For that matter, any police internal affairs department would be so handcuffed by the same looping complaints as to be ineffective. More officers would sit in line for review than there would be out on the streets to protect the public from itself. For a CRB to be responsible, it would have to concentrate on real wrongdoers, what used to be called "crooked cops." Even that is dubious because an officer suspected of committing a felony should go to regular court, not to citizens' review.

In the mid-1970s a survey conducted by the National Opinion Research Center found that 45 percent of the respondents favored CRBs, 35 percent opposed them, and the remaining 20 percent were undecided. The less-than-half in favor is perplexing. During the late 1960s and into the early 1970s police seemed to be barbarians. The televised mayhem in Chicago at the 1968 Democratic Convention and the Kent State killings did not uplift law enforcement. If at any point in recent history CRBs could have gained a foothold, the mid-1970s should have been optimal. Unified police resistance to CRBs and a good deal of persuasive talk curtailed the movement. In an article written for *Police Chief* (1977), Gary F. Stowell posed the critical question:

Reaction to a CRB in police circles is clear: Almost any decision made by a police officer in a crisis situation could conceivably leave him open to charges before a CRB. How could a civilian sit in judgment on a police officer's actions any more than he could sit in judgment on a doctor's actions in an operating room?

New York Police Commissioner Vincent Brodrick added another dimension: "It is vital that when a police officer's action is reviewed, it be reviewed by one who has the capacity to evaluate the propriety of the action, but also to its complement, the propriety in the same situation with the officer having failed to take the action." FBI Director J. Edgar Hoover had long before made his opinion known. CRBs "undermine the morale and sap the efficiency of the police. They deter officers in the proper performance of their duties for fear of having charges placed against them, which will be judged by individuals wholly unfamiliar with police work." Also a decade earlier, Chief O.W. Wilson had warned, "A review board in this city would destroy discipline in the Chicago Police Department. If we would have a civilian review board, it would create a situation where I, as the head of the police department, would be confronted by an adversary group, which the entire department would tend to unite against." On-and-off the record most police alluded to CRBs as witch hunts of benefit to no one.

The Hartford Study
The Hartford Institute of Criminal and Social Justice published an influential study in 1980 entitled, "Civilian Review of the Police—The Experiences of American Cities." The Institute prepared the study in response to a proposal by the Hartford, Connecticut, City Council to establish a civilian review board. A shocking incident confirmed the Council's resolve. In February of 1980 the Council endorsed the concept of a CRB. But in March after Guy Brown, who turned out to be innocent, was shot by a Hartford police officer, public outcry forced the Council to act on its endorsement. On October 17 the Council passed an amendment calling for the immediate creation of a permanent civilian review board. To advise the Council of what to do next, the Institute surveyed literature on the topic and conducted interviews to determine

how other municipalities set up their CRBs, and with what success.

In all, the Institute was able to collect information in detail from seven cities and on a limited basis from several more. The cities surveyed, the type of review board, and the date established were as follows:

1. Chicago, IL. Office of Professional Standards; physically within the police department but separate from the Internal Affairs Division; operated by three civilian administrators appointed by the Superintendent of Police; one black, one white, one Hispanic—all lawyers. 1974–.
2. Detroit, MI. Board of Police Commissioners; administered by the Office of the Chief Investigator; composed of five civilians appointed by the Mayor with the approval of the City Council; minority representation, including one woman. 1974–.
3. Kansas City, MO. Office of Citizen Complaints; five-person civilian staff appointed by the Board of Police Commissioners. 1970–.
4. Memphis, TN. Police Advisory Commission; composed of no more than eighteen and no less than ten civilian members; appointed annually by the Director of Police and the Mayor from a list of candidates provided by the Commission; Commission members represented both extremes, for and against police. 1977–.
5. New York, NY. Civilian Complaint Review Board; located within the police department with seven members: three police appointed by the Police Commissioner and four community representatives assigned by the Mayor; ethnic mixture. 1953 forward—police members only; after 1966—addition of civilians.
6. Oakland, CA. Citizens Complaint Board; Mayor appoints seven citizens to one-year terms subject to approval by the City Council; cross-section of the community. 1980–.
7. Philadelphia, PA. Police Advisory Board; five, then eight civilian members appointed by the Mayor with no fixed length of term; cross-section of the community with two retired police officers to add balance. 1958–1969.
8. Baltimore, MD. Complaint Evaluation Board; unstated membership, all were

government employees or elected officials with one active police officer as member. c. 1965–.

9. Miami, FL. Office of Professional Compliance; four members with a Director appointed by the City Manager and the Police Chief. 1980–.

10. Minneapolis, MN. Minneapolis Civil Rights Commission; unstated membership staffed by the City Council; short-lived due in part to the Commission subpoenaing the president of the City Council. 1965.

11. Rochester, NY. Civilian Review Board; nine members appointed by the City Manager; disbanded when no longer funded. 1963–1971.

12. Washington, DC. Civilian Review Board; seven members including two attorneys, how appointed not stated. 1948–1965; in 1965 completely restructured, then oddly disbanded the same year; reproposed in 1980.

13. York, PA. Police Review Board; City Council appointed five York residents to act as a board and also to advise the Mayor and other officials about police "oppressiveness." 1960–1962.

(Note: Where a single year is given with a dash after it, the CRB continued until at least 1980 when the Institute conducted its study.)

The civilian review boards also differed in the amount of authority granted them. Some of the boards had investigatory power and could issue subpoenas, while others subsisted as advisory only. Another prominent fact from the Institute's study is that either the boards were adversarial beyond normal expectations, or suspiciously agreed in nearly every instance with the police review. In conclusion, the Institute listed arguments for and against CRBs.

In Favor:

- CRBs are a means to gain more effective relationships with the public.
- Courts cannot handle every legitimate complaint leveled at police.
- Civilians are traditionally less strict in reviewing police misconduct.
- An officer exonerated by a CRB is less likely thought of having been whitewashed.
- CRBs are useful as public relations vehicles.

- Police have too much discretion in carrying out their duties and must be watched.
- CRBs are a safety valve for both police and citizens to get at the facts.
- CRBs increase respect for the law when reviews are handled promptly.
- CRBs increase public confidence in police departments by demonstrating police agreement to undergo civilian review.
- CRBs often aid in dispelling the belief that police are brutal and arbitrary.
- Police appear less isolated and more accountable.
- CRBs deter misconduct before it happens because police fear public review.
- Citizens want some form of settlement (an apology) even if the complaint does not merit court action.
- Police cannot deal fairly with complaints against their fellow officers.

Against:

- Only police know their business.
- Internal, not external, review places the responsibility for handling misconduct with those who best know how to cure it.
- CRBs destroy morale.
- CRBs are redundant to police review.
- Other adequate means are available to citizens with legitimate complaints, e.g., the courts.
- Every profession should have the right to discipline itself.
- Criminals or anyone can harass police to get them in trouble.
- CRBs are unlawful; the police powers of a city cannot be delegated.
- CRBs fail to provide for procedural safeguards, e.g., rules of evidence, protection against double jeopardy, etc.
- CRBs entertain minor to frivolous complaints.
- CRBs by their very existence continue to polarize police and citizens.
- The history of CRBs is lackluster.
- Emotional catharsis takes place more often than dispassionate inquiry.
- Police job security hangs in the balance.
- Police are less efficient, knowing the CRB can call them in for anything.

Of the reasons for and against, the third "for" reason—Civilians are traditionally less strict in reviewing police misconduct—stands out. If true, logic dictates the reason should be in the against list. The whole rationale behind civilian review is to convene a group of citizens who will do a better job of reviewing police misconduct (more punitive) than the supposed buddy system does in the department. If police are harder on themselves than the public would be, then why involve citizens at all? This reason alone does much to defeat the CRB concept.

Current Accountability
Even though civilian review boards have not worked out well, the need for greater accountability external to police control is still a burning issue. The Rodney King incident in Los Angeles has fueled the debate more than any single event in recent memory. Other King-type cases occur with regularity, whether the police are at fault or not. Any show of force by police usually guarantees citizen backlash and a cry for investigation—if not the head(s) of the officer(s) involved. Because an alert citizen videotaped Rodney King being beaten or subdued, depending on individual perception, no one could deny it happened exactly as filmed. The shock value of the incident and the lawless aftermath has reinvigorated discussion of civilian review boards and other accountability mechanisms. The ombudsman or "citizen advocate" is one such control. As a government official, the ombudsman investigates abuse and/or misconduct in the police department and elsewhere throughout city government. He or she is a grievance commissioner that chooses which complaints to investigate. With such a broad jurisdiction the ombudsman oversees a general complaint office, not focusing on any single department. Therefore police do not feel they are the only ones under scrutiny. The Hartford study credited a number of cities with adopting the ombudsman concept, though it could not obtain enough information from those cities to clarify types of operation.

A second external control combines the civilian review board with the office of ombudsman. Independent review panels, as they are called, investigate public complaints directed at any city department and/or employee. Thus all city employees, not just police, are held accountable for their actions. Naturally, many police officers and public employee unions dislike the panels and will resist them. Until one or both of these controls achieves success or a better concept arises, internal discipline administered by police to police will continue to suffice.

Bibliography
Barton, Peter G. "Civilian Review Boards and the Handling of Complaints Against the Police." *University of Toronto Law Journal* 20 (1970): 448–69.
Brent, David J. "Redress of Alleged Police Misconduct: A New Approach to Citizen Complaints and Police Disciplinary Procedures." *University of San Francisco Law Review* 11 (Summer 1977): 587–621.
Broadaway, Fred M. "Police Misconduct: Positive Alternatives." *Journal of Police Science and Administration* 2 (June 1974): 210–18.
Carrow, Milton M. "Mechanisms for the Redress of Grievances Against the Government." *Administrative Law Review* 22 (1969): 1–37.
The Hartford Institute of Criminal and Social Justice. "Civilian Review of the Police— The Experiences of American Cities." Hartford, CT: The Institute, 1980.
Hudson, James R. "Police Review Boards and Police Accountability." *Law and Contemporary Problems* 36 (Fall 1971): 515–38.
Lenzi, Margaret A. "Reviewing Civilian Complaints of Police Misconduct—Some Answers and More Questions." *Temple Law Quarterly* 48 (Fall 1974): 89–125.
More, Harry W., and W. Fred Wegener. *Effective Police Supervision*. Cincinnati: Anderson, 1990.
Olson, Robert W. "Grievance Response Mechanisms for Police Misconduct." *Virginia Law Review* 55 (June 1969): 909–51.
Stowell, Gary F. "Civilian Review Boards." *Police Chief* 44 (April 1977): 63–65.
Yeager, Matthew G., and William P. Brown. "Police Professionalism and Corruption Control." *Journal of Police Science and Administration* 6 (September 1978): 273–82.

Code of Ethics
In 1957, the International Association of Chiefs of Police (IACP) adopted a document entitled "Law Enforcement Code of Ethics." Except for

the 1956 California code on which it was modeled, the IACP document seems to have been the first "code of ethics" for police. Behind this code lay a century-and-a-half of "rules and regulations," "oaths," "pledges," "prayers," "guiding principles," and other documents containing similar provisions (Kleinig and Zhang, 1992). Yet this code was understood as a contribution to making policing a "profession" (Johnson and Copus, 1981). What does a code of ethics have to do with creating a profession? Why might earlier substantively similar documents not be able to do the same thing? Indeed, what is a code of ethics? What is it not?

Code in Morality, Law, and Ethics
A code is a formal statement of a practice—whether a description of existing practice (like a dictionary's definitions) or a formula creating the practice (like a definition in a contract). A code need not be written; an oral formulation will do. But, in any society where writing is common, most codes will sooner or later be put in writing for the same reason most other guides to action are. Writing makes them easier for individuals to remember and teach, easier to change by express agreement, and so on.

A code of *ethics* is a formal statement of a certain kind of practice. What kind of practice? To answer that question, we must distinguish ethics from both morality and law.

Morality. For our purposes, morality may be divided into three standards of conduct: rules, principles, and ideals. Other aspects of morality may be defined in terms of these standards. For example, a certain moral virtue—say, justice—would be a settled disposition to deliberate in accordance with the principles of justice; good character, a complex of moral (and certain nonmoral) virtues; and so on.

Rules, principles, and ideals all guide the choice of action, can be codified, and (codified or not) can provide a basis for justifying or evaluating what we do (just as nonmoral rules, principles, and ideals do). They differ from one another only in how they guide conduct.

Moral rules are those standards of conduct each of us (rational persons) wants every other to follow even if everyone else's following them means we must do the same. Moral rules are requirements (or prohibitions) one is supposed to obey all the time (unless the conduct in question is justified under an exception). Among moral rules relevant to police work are: "Don't

kill"; "Don't deprive of liberty"; "Don't cause pain"; "Don't steal"; and "Keep your promises." Moral rules can also be stated with "shall" (for example, "You shall not kill").

Moral rules generally have exceptions. The exceptions resemble the rules in at least two ways. First, exceptions are as rule-like as the rules themselves. For example, among the exceptions to "Don't kill" are "except in self-defense" and "except in defense of an innocent person." Second, exceptions are justified in much the way that rules are. A would-be exception is actually an exception only if people are willing to allow others the same freedom from the rule as they want for themselves. Exceptions provide terms of justification for what would otherwise be morally unjustified (a simple violation of a moral rule). So, for example, self-defense is an exception to "Don't kill" (in part at least), because each of us wants to be able to repel unjustified attacks even if our being able to do that means being repelled in turn should we unjustifiably attack another. Having "Don't kill" with that exception, we are safer than we would be without it. We can control whom we unjustifiably attack but not who unjustifiably attacks us. We are therefore less likely to be attacked (unless we attack others), since we are more likely to kill an attacker than we would be if use of deadly force in self-defense were not justifiable.

If we don't do as a moral rule requires and have no justification, our conduct is morally wrong; if we don't even have a good excuse for our conduct, we deserve blame and perhaps punishment.

Moral *principles* differ from moral rules in having the dimension of weight. While rules require (or forbid) acts, principles do not. They merely state considerations that should have a certain weight in choice of action (what is good to do or bad to omit doing). While moral rules can be rewritten using "shall" without significant change of meaning, moral principles cannot. They naturally take "should" rather than "shall."

Consider the moral principle, "Help the needy." Though grammatically similar to "Keep your promises," "Help the needy" requires no act. Though Alex is now playing poker with friends rather than helping the needy (when he could be doing that instead), he is not necessarily doing anything wrong (as he would be if he were sitting there when he had a promise to keep). Though Alex should always help the needy and even now could do something for them (for example, by writing a check), Alex's conduct satisfies the *principle* "Help the needy" if their needs weigh in his deliberations enough to outweigh certain otherwise decisive considerations (and he acts accordingly).

Normally, giving due weight to the needs of the needy will mean helping the needy now and then. Moral principles are morally important because, in morally decent people, they create tendencies to act which, being realized in action often enough, maintain (more or less) a state of affairs all rational people want (for example, a system of charity). Indeed, moral principles may be defined as those tendencies to act, which everyone wants everyone else to have, even if that means having them too.

Why both moral principles and moral rules? We prefer moral principles to moral rules when we do not want the relatively determinate conduct a rule imposes or cannot agree on what the rule should be. Principles allow more flexibility in choice of acts than rules do. But they do that by allowing others to be less predictable than they would be if subject to rule. Moral principles work best for conduct where predictability is less important, for example, because what is involved is doing good or the harm to be prevented is relatively minor.

Since moral principles do not (directly) require conduct, conduct cannot (as such) violate a principle; and since no conduct can violate a principle, we cannot blame people for conduct because it violates a principle. We can, however, still blame people for not giving a principle due weight in deliberations. For example, if Belle's acts, words, or some combination of these show a tendency to discount the principle "Help the needy," we can say that she is stingy or uncharitable (that is, that she lacks the disposition to give due weight to the needs of the needy). To say that is to blame her for *how* she decides to act rather than for *what* she decides. The way she decided is crucial. Had Belle made the right donation only because she routinely (but ignorantly) made a mistake in calculation, she would still be stingy or uncharitable—though she would as well deserve (nonmoral) blame for her mathematical ignorance.

While moral principles provide grounds for moral blame, they do not do the same for moral praise. In this, they resemble moral rules. Like rules, principles help to define minimal decency. A minimally decent (or upright) person merely obeys the moral rules and gives moral principles the weight due them. Her conduct is merely satisfactory. To say of someone, for example, that she is "merely upright" is "to damn with faint praise." We expect more of people than that. Though we do not require more, we withhold praise until we get it. We do not, for example, describe a merely decent person as "virtuous," "just," or "good." For such terms to apply, a person must do more than merely obey the moral rules and give moral principles their due.

That is where ideals come in. Moral ideals take us beyond mere decency. They are ways of acting everyone wants everyone else to support even if that means supporting them too (so long as such support is consistent with obeying moral rules and giving due weight to moral principles). We support conduct by encouraging it with compliments or donations, by removing obstacles such as taxes or zoning laws, or by excusing from otherwise deserved punishment. Ideals are easy to recognize. Consider the golden rule:

While we are willing to have others praise, reward, and otherwise encourage people to treat each other as they themselves would like to be treated (and, indeed, to give such moral support ourselves), we are not willing to *require* people to do what the golden rule says. We do not want that much regimentation. The golden rule cannot be rewritten with "shall" without changing its meaning. It is not a moral *rule* (in our sense). This is as much a fact about us as about the "rule" itself.

For similar reasons, the golden rule cannot be a moral principle. The corresponding moral principle would require us, in all deliberations, to give the interests of others at least as much weight as our own. Few of us are willing to be so benevolent (except in such special circumstances as administering a public charity). Though the golden rule can be written with "should," the "should" has a different sense than it has in a moral principle. The golden rule is an ideal.

Ideals are to principles much as principles are to rules. Because they ask more, we allow more freedom in the way people respond to them. One can fall far short of an ideal without necessarily deserving blame. Indeed, one can fall far short and still deserve praise—for coming closer than other people normally do. One can be a saint even if far from perfect.

These distinctions do not constitute an exact description of actual usage (though they do catch something important in actual usage, especially the usage of careful speakers). They are offered here as a useful way to discipline ordinary language. So, for example, though we often speak of conduct as being "ethical" or "highly ethical" when we wish to praise it for coming unusually close to a moral ideal, the analysis of morality presented here recommends that, instead, we describe such conduct as "morally good," saving "ethical" for morally good conduct of a special sort.

Ethics and Law. As used here, "ethics" means moral standards applying to all members of a group simply because they are members of that group. "Standard" means a rule, principle, or ideal. Ethics differs from group to group. Legal ethics applies to lawyers, not to police or politicians; Hopi ethics, to Hopis; business ethics, to people in business. Different groups can, of course, have equivalent standards, standards beyond those of ordinary morality (which everyone shares), but they will nonetheless not have the same ethics. For example, suppose both Hopis and Catholics have a rule forbidding remarriage after divorce. A divorced Catholic can remarry in violation of the Catholic rule but not in violation of the Hopi rule (unless she is also a Hopi). She must be a Hopi to come under the Hopi rule. A group is defined by a single practice in which all (and only) its members participate.

Ethics therefore resembles law in applying to persons only insofar as they belong to a group (rather than insofar as they are rational persons as such). Ethics also resembles law in not being entirely deducible from ordinary morality (even in combination with situational factors). Like law, ethics is made, not merely found, and is therefore capable of being made in more than one way. Morality constrains what can be ethics without totally determining it.

Ethics differs from law in being (by definition) part of morality (though distinct from ordinary morality). Ethics differs from ordinary morality only in adding rules, principles, or ideals, for example, by turning a moral ideal into an ethical principle or rule. Ethics is "morality plus. . . ." How ethics can be both part of morality and yet more than ordinary morality will be explained below.

Because ethical standards are, by definition, moral standards (in at least the minimal sense of being morally permissible), "Nazi ethics," "criminal ethics," and the like can be ethics only in the degenerate sense in which counterfeit money is still money. Ethics has no more to do with ethic or ethos than morality does with morale or mores.

This use of "ethics" differs from two other common uses. "Ethics" is often a mere synonym for "morality." "Ethics," as used here, is not. Instead, it names a special domain of morality, one with its own rules, principles, or ideals (in addition to and consistent with those of ordinary morality).

"Ethics," as used here, also differs from what philosophers generally mean by it. As used here "ethics" does not name the study of morality, the theory of the good, the attempt to describe an ideal or rationally defensible morality, or even the successful outcome of such an attempt. Like "morality," "ethics" here names a practice that is not merely intellectual.

Why adopt this use of "ethics" rather than one of the others? There are at least two reasons. First, this use generally corresponds to what professionals mean when they talk about *their* professional ethics. Second, thinking about ethics this way is more helpful in discussions of professional ethics than thinking about ethics in other ways.

Codes of Ethics and the Police

A code of ethics is a formal statement of a group's ethics. We may distinguish three distinct kinds of code: statements of ideal ("credos" or "aspirations"); statements of principle ("guidelines" or "ethical considerations"); and statements of requirement ("codes of conduct," "mandatory rules," or simply "duties"). There are also mixed forms. In some of these, statements of ideal, principle, and rule are clearly distinguished; in others, statements of one kind sit next to statements of other kinds without any suggestion of difference. Unfortunately, most codes of police ethics are of this last kind.

Consider, for example, the IACP's "Law Enforcement Code of Ethics" (as revised in 1991; Kleinig and Zhang, 1992:92–96). It is divided into two parts: (a) an untitled statement in the first person (six unnumbered paragraphs); and (b) "Canons of Police Ethics" (eleven numbered and titled "Articles," without subdivisions) stated in the third person. There is no explanation of the connection between the two parts.

Both parts seem to state ideals (that is, standards few humans would want to be held to). Yet, the ideals are stated in ways suggesting mandatory rules. For example, the first paragraph of the first part begins: "As a law enforcement officer, my fundamental duty is to serve the community. . . ." The next two paragraphs, while dropping "duty," replace it with the equally mandatory language of oath or promise: For example, "I will keep my private life unsullied. . . ." The second part, in contrast, tends to mix the language of description with that of duty. For example, Article 1 says (in part): "The law enforcement officer always represents the whole community . . . ," while Article 2 begins: "The first duty of the law enforcement officer, as upholder of the law, is to know its bounds upon him in enforcing it."

Any officers who take this code's language literally will quickly learn that they cannot do what the code seems to require. They will then either have to quit the force or learn to take the code "with a grain of salt." That cannot be good for the officers or the force.

The IACP's code, though perhaps the most confused of the major police codes, is far from being the only police code showing such confusion. Even the best, the United Nations' "Code of Conduct for Law Enforcement Officials" (1979) is not above such confusion (Davis, 1991:18–19). Yet, though common in police codes, such confusion is not nearly so common in the codes of ethics of lawyers, engineers, nurses, or the like. Why that should be so is hard to say. One likely explanation is that police, unlike these other occupations, are not yet clear about what a code of ethics is supposed to be or, at least, about how a profession is supposed to create one. We must now consider that question.

Writing a Practical Code of Ethics

A code of ethics sets standards for some domain of conduct. What that domain is is relevant to how the code should be written. The more important the conduct governed is to the lives of those affected, the more reason there is for the code to state requirements; the less important the conduct, the more reason for it to state principles or ideals. Use of unnecessary force, for example, seems something police should be required to avoid. Avoiding unnecessary force should, then, not be stated as a mere ideal or principle in police decisions. In contrast, avoiding dishonesty "in thought and deed" seems too

much to require of police. How many of us, police or not, are willing to accept as a *requirement* no dishonest thoughts, no white lies? Any code concerned with reducing dishonesty should therefore include honesty as a principle or ideal (or demand certain sorts of honesty by rules much more narrowly drawn).

In general, a code of rules will be substantially longer than a code of principles or ideals. In part, that is because rules should be stated with their exceptions. (Consider, for example, the American Bar Association's *Model Rules of Professional Conduct*, Gorlin, 1990:335–85.) But, in part too, codes of rules tend to be longer because a standard bearing directly on conduct in the way rules do invites more specificity than standards that bear less directly in the way principles or ideals do. Because (all else equal) the violation of a rule is much easier to recognize than is discounting a principle or ignoring an ideal, and so much easier to condemn or punish, we generally insist on much more detail in rules. We want the boundaries of conduct as clearly defined as possible.

Suppose that we are trying to draft a code of police ethics. For any proposed provision the first question should be: "Does this state the minimum below which no officer dare fall [except]?" If the answer is yes, the provision is a *possible* mandatory rule (that is, a plausible candidate for such a rule). Otherwise, the provision can only be a principle or ideal (assuming it belongs in the code at all). To decide which it is, principle or ideal (or not code material at all), we must answer two more questions.

One is: "Can an officer make good police decisions without giving some weight to this consideration?" If the answer is no, the consideration is a possible principle. If, however, the answer is yes, we must ask one more question: "Would it still be good for an officer to do as this provision says?" If the answer is yes, the standard is a possible ideal. Otherwise, it is not. So, for example, "honesty in thought and deed" seems a possible principle. An officer who gave no weight to honesty would be a perpetual embarrassment to the force, dangerous to his partners, and useless to the courts.

On the other hand, "honesty in thought and deed" probably cannot be an ideal for police. "Going undercover," though a practice about which many have grave doubts, is at once common, ancient, and central to the way police themselves conceive their work. If (as it seems) gathering intelligence by going undercover is part of the normal police function, police cannot commit themselves to complete honesty even as an ideal. Lying, falsification, and dissembling may be part of good police work. Honesty thus differs from, for example, "being constantly mindful of the welfare of others," a stated good for police to achieve, however hard in practice.

That honesty can be a principle but not an ideal of police ethics suggests the complex relationship between principles and ideals. Principles are not simply standards meant to bring about conduct inherently easier to achieve than that which ideals ask. Principles and ideals differ in the way they obtain conduct. Ideals identify a state of affairs to be aimed at—and, if possible, achieved. Nothing can be our ideal if we do not want to achieve it. In this respect, ideals are more like rules, which also identify a desired state of affairs (though one mandated rather than merely urged). Principles, in contrast, do not identify a state of affairs to aim at or achieve, only considerations to be taken into account. There need be no ideal corresponding to a principle (except an "ideal of deliberation"). We can want some matter always considered (and given a certain weight)—for example, honesty—even if we never want our conduct determined solely by that consideration. In this respect, principles bear less directly on conduct than do ideals. That is why honesty can be a principle of police work even if it cannot be a rule or ideal.

We have so far spoken only of "possible" rules, principles, or ideals of police ethics. What distinguishes possible from actual? Answering that question will take us to the most important part of understanding codes of ethics, understanding how to put them into practice.

Putting a Code of Ethics into Practice
A code of ethics must set a standard beyond ordinary morality if it is to be a code of ethics at all. It must require something more than ordinary morality requires, lay down a principle ordinary morality does not, or set an ideal ordinary morality does not. Otherwise, the document in question could (at best) be a code of (ordinary) morality. That follows from our definition of ethics. Yet, if a code is to be realized in practice, it cannot be very "high minded." It cannot set standards too high, that is, higher than most of those subject to it are willing to go. A code must "buy" obedience. The more a code

demands of those subject to it, the more it must "pay" them to obey. How can a code of ethics get those subject to it to obey? We may distinguish four ways: command, reward, oath, and convention.

"Command" obtains obedience by stating what is wanted and attaching bad consequences to failure to comply. The bad consequences might include undesirable assignment, fine, suspension, or imprisonment. Command (in this sense) does not presuppose good motives on the part of those subject to it. The command might be an alien imposition made potent by strict surveillance and swift response to each individual's disobedience. Command pays for obedience in goods external to morality. Command is the characteristic means by which law, especially criminal law, is enforced. Command works better with rules than with principles or ideals (because obedience to rules is easier to detect than fidelity to principles or ideals).

"Reward" obtains obedience by stating what is wanted and attaching *good* consequences to compliance. The good consequences may be money, honor, better assignments, promotion, or the like. Like command, reward does not presuppose good motives on the part of those rewarded. Like command, reward must rely on a capacity to detect obedience and disobedience and to respond accordingly. Reward differs from command only in the consequences those imposing the standard attach (good consequences for obedience rather than bad consequences for disobedience). If command is characteristic of the way the law secures obedience, reward is characteristic of the way a market secures it.

"Oath" is a means of taking on a moral obligation more or less independent of the content. "Oath" includes swearing, pledging, vowing, promising, and any other formal undertaking. Oath, unlike command or reward, does presuppose some good motive in those from whom it is to be exacted. Oath-takers must be relatively decent people, that is, beings who respect an oath. Otherwise, there is no point to administering the oath.

This connection with morality limits what can be done by oath. While law or market can obtain even immoral conduct (for example, by threatening to punish one who does not do as told or by offering a large reward to those who do), oath cannot (except through misunderstanding). An oath ordinarily motivates only insofar as it seems morally obliging and can morally oblige only insofar as what it requires is morally permissible.

Ethics by oath is therefore internal to morality in a way ethics by command and ethics by reward are not. Ethics by oath makes direct appeal to conscience. So, ethics by oath can secure obedience in circumstances where difficulties of supervision mean that (mere) command and reward cannot. Ethics by oath fits principles and ideals better than ethics by command or reward does.

Oaths, though internal to morality, are still external to ethics (in our sense); they have no necessary connection with groups. A particular oath can bind but one individual. Nothing in an oath as such requires oath-takers to work together, even if the oath binds more than one. The obligations of each oath-taker may endure whatever other oath-takers do (just as your mortgage obliges you even if all others default on theirs).

Oaths are external to ethics in another way. An oath is usually a condition of taking an office (or other responsible position). For example, a police officer is supposed to be sworn in before he or she can exercise the police power. This use of oath at least suggests that the officer cannot be trusted with that power until formally swearing to what the oath prescribes. The obligations of office are treated (in large part at least) as morally independent of occupying the office. Even if regularly re-administered, an oath treats the office as if it did not itself impose obligations on its occupants (or, at least, as if it did not impose enough obligation). Convention, the last means of obtaining obedience to a code of ethics, is not like that.

A "convention" is a practice in which the participation of each is valuable only insofar as others participate as well. Many games are conventions in this sense. Stud poker, for example, requires at least two players (and is best with five to eight). Conventions are cooperative undertakings. Each participant benefits from what others do while helping to make possible similar benefits for the others by doing as they do. These benefits are (in part at least) what make participation worth the trouble.

Conventions can create moral obligations. When each voluntarily participates in a morally permissible practice to obtain the benefits that the practice creates, each has a moral obligation not to disobey the rules generating those benefits. Disobeying the rules of such a practice is cheating. Cheating is (ordinarily) morally wrong. So,

for example, cheating at stud poker is (ordinarily) morally wrong. Anyone who voluntarily sits down to play poker is morally obliged to play by the rules. That obligation continues until one gets up from the table, informs the other players that one no longer intends to play by the rules, or otherwise quits the game.

Conventions can also create moral responsibilities (in the sense of that term in which one's responsibilities are something more than the sum of one's duties or obligations). So, for example, while the rules of stud poker do not require a player to try to win, a player would (ordinarily) be acting irresponsibly if he did not try to win. Not only would the player probably disappoint the other players, but he or she would also not be playing properly.

The player would be ignoring a principle of the game. While "obligation" and "duty" seem to be terms corresponding to "rule," "responsibility" seems to correspond to "principle." Principles state our responsibilities, just as rules state our obligations or duties. (We do not seem to have a similar term corresponding to "ideal.")

Treating a code of ethics as a convention (in this sense) means treating ethics as a practice in which the reasons for obedience must be internal to the practice itself. Ethics by convention will differ sharply from ethics by command, reward, or oath. Since police voluntarily join the force and can quit at will (though, as with other employments, not without financial costs such as loss of pension), police ethics can be treated as convention. If police ethics can be treated as convention, the question becomes, should it be?

Codes of Ethics and Professions

Command or reward can put almost any standard into practice (including many that are morally impermissible). Fear and greed are powerful incentives. Those employing such incentives need only concern themselves with how closely the conduct in question can be supervised and how much enforcement will cost.

What is true of standards in general is true of codes of ethics in particular (except that, strictly speaking, no morally impermissible standard can be part of a code of ethics). Those putting a code of ethics into practice by command or reward will not necessarily be able to trust those subject to it any farther than they can see. Command and reward presuppose close supervision.

Unlike ethics by command or reward, ethics by oath does not presuppose close supervision. Conscience can serve instead (assuming the subject is a morally decent person). Ethics by oath nonetheless resembles ethics by command and reward in being largely independent of what the code actually says. Virtually any morally permissible oath is (morally) binding, however arduous or unsatisfying the conduct it commits one to. The oath need only be taken voluntarily. Those willing to pay morally decent people a lot to take the oath (for example, by making the oath a condition of otherwise attractive employment) will have little trouble finding such oath-takers.

The same is not true of ethics by convention. While ethics by convention, like ethics by oath, depends on conscience, it differs from ethics by oath in the way conscience is brought in. Conscience will make no claim unless the convention in question itself generates enough in benefits to make voluntary participation attractive. The code is therefore subject to constraints on content that ethics by command, reward, or oath is not. We cannot set standards very high without making participation too burdensome. We also cannot set standards very low. Standards must produce enough (morally permissible) benefits to make participants want the practice. A code of ethics cannot do that without a standard significantly higher (that is, morally better) than would otherwise prevail.

What internal benefits can make obedience to a code of *police* ethics attractive? The answer depends both on what police want out of their work and on what they are willing to pay to get it. The answer may vary from department to department. If, for example, police merely want to make an honest living, caring little about what others think of them, probably no code of ethics can provide internal benefits sufficient to make participation attractive. If such police are to have a code of ethics, the legislature, city council, or police commission will probably have to rely on some combination of command, reward, and oath to motivate them to obey. The code will, in effect, be indistinguishable from other regulations governing the police. Talk of "ethics" will be uninformative (though not inaccurate).

This, of course, has been the pattern to date. Model codes of police ethics like the IACP's have generally been the work of administrators or academics, not of ordinary police. When jurisdictions have adopted a code, it has

been with little or no consultation with officers on patrol or even with their associations. This perhaps explains the unrealistic standards these codes routinely set. This also probably explains much of their impotence. But that is not the only scenario.

Imagine, instead, a department consisting largely of police who want to serve their fellow citizens by helping to maintain good order, who want their uniform to bring special respect, or who otherwise see police work as more than just another way to earn a living. The benefits each individual seeks (service, respect, and so on) will depend (in part at least) on what others in the department do. For example, no police officer can maintain good order alone or alone assure respect for the uniform. Such achievements require the cooperation of other officers (as well as the appropriate response of public and officials). Such achievements require police to work together as voluntary participants in a common enterprise the primary purpose of which goes beyond what law, market, and ordinary morality exact. In other words, such achievements require police to think of themselves as sharing a common profession. Insofar as they think of themselves in that way, they will probably be able to write a code generating enough internal benefits to make participation attractive in the profession that the code defines.

Among police, the term "profession" has two (related) senses. The more common sense contrasts "professional" with "unskilled." We increase the professionalism of a police force by requiring more education to join, by improving training, and by otherwise raising technical standards. In this sense, a profession is simply a highly skilled occupation; there is no connection between profession and ethics.

In the other sense of "profession," the sense used earlier, there is such a connection. In this sense, a profession is a voluntary cooperative undertaking the (primary) purpose of which is public service. Such an undertaking imposes (moral) obligations defined (in part at least) by the profession's code of ethics. Professionals differ from other people in having (by convention) obligations others do not. In this sense, being a professional means belonging to a profession (a group organized around a code of ethics).

The contrast between these two senses of profession is important. Police sometimes justify having a code of ethics as a way to get privileges, status, or income comparable to that of lawyers, physicians, or other "true professionals." Police tend to think of professional status as something *society* grants in the way the state grants a license to practice medicine or law. That is a mistake. Some professions have relatively low income, low status, and few privileges. Think, for example, of priests, teachers, or nurses. And many people with relatively high income, high status, and great privilege are not professionals. Think, for example, of movie stars, "professional athletes," or stock arbitrageur. Police do not have high income, high status, or great privilege in any free society. They probably never will, code of ethics or not.

But they can be professionals in a free society, something not so easy in (what we somewhat misleadingly call) "a police state," that is, a country where the government maintains power by force rather than by consent. Under such a government, the police are often required to torture, execute without trial, or otherwise engage in morally impermissible conduct. They cannot be professionals in the morally worthy sense, however they long to be, however much technical skill they develop, and however many privileges an oppressive government accords them as a means of remaining in office.

In a free society, the police have little control over how society will treat them. What they have instead is the ability to conduct themselves in ways everyone should recognize as morally good. They can conduct themselves by a code setting standards beyond what is merely morally decent. They can work in the company of people who (generally) maintain those standards. They can develop the basis for justified self-respect and professional pride, whatever the larger society knows or thinks.

The police are not, of course, even potentially, a "free profession" in the sense law and medicine are (or at least were until recently). Like engineers and teachers, military officers and clergy, the police belong to a "captive profession," a profession in which the members must work within institutions over which they have only limited control. Those in charge (senior officers, a police chief, or police commissioner) will be chosen by those above, not by those below. That makes achieving ethics by convention harder—but not impossible.

Police, like engineers and teachers, have in fact been able to maintain significant freedom of action despite departmental regulations and elaborate systems of inspection, investigation, and recording. They have that freedom for much the same reason engineers and teachers do. Their superiors require their judgment, judgment that cannot be reduced to rules or exercised from above. Few departments can afford the supervision necessary to assure that the ordinary officer obeys regulations. Probably no department would in fact want to pay the cost, whether in efficiency or morale, of such supervision. So almost everyone in a police department, or served by it, is likely (in the long run at least) to benefit from a department in which ordinary officers generally consider their (workable) code of ethics a standard each should follow in part because the others are doing the same. That, in turn, means everyone has an interest in having the police adopt a code that can work (in part at least) as a convention. That interest is, however, not the only interest involved. Other interests weigh against ethics by convention, especially the interests of police.

The "Higher Standard" for Police

If a code of ethics must set a standard of conduct higher than law, market, and ordinary morality do (just to be a code of *ethics*), most codes of police ethics do not seem to be codes of ethics at all. Consider, for example, provisions concerning the unnecessary use of force in the UN's "Code of Conduct for Law Enforcement Officials": Article 3 forbids police the "use of more force than necessary in the performance of their duty"; and Article 4 does the same for "inflicting, instigating, or tolerating any act of torture or other cruel, inhuman, or degrading treatment or punishment" (Kleinig and Zhang, 1992:98–99). These provisions (except perhaps for "tolerating") do not seem to go significantly beyond law and ordinary morality. Beating a prisoner where there is no need is both illegal and immoral, UN Code or no. The police do not need a code of ethics to make such acts wrong. What then do they need a provision like this for?

The question is clearest for the unnecessary use of force, but it is a question that can be asked of most provisions of most codes of police ethics (except those that set unrealistically high standards). Consider one more example: Among the standards of the IACP's "Law Enforcement Code of Ethics" (1991) was "honest in thought and deed in both my personal and official life" (Kleinig and Zhang, 1992:92). We noted earlier that this seems to be a principle rather than an ideal or rule. Yet, if a principle, it is a principle all morally decent people share, not a higher standard. We should all be honest in thought and deed (though not "too honest").

If codes of police ethics do not in fact state a standard of conduct higher than ordinary morality, they differ in an important way from those of most other professions. Virtually all professional codes include some provisions restating ordinary morality. Such provisions seem designed to counteract the special temptations or pressures to ignore moral standards characteristic of the profession's work. But most codes of ethics include much that goes beyond ordinary morality (and thereby become codes of ethics, strictly speaking). So, for example, the Code of Ethics of the National Society of Professional Engineers specifically requires an employed engineer to notify his/her employer before accepting a second job (III.1.c) and forbids engineers who employ others to accept payment from either an employee or an employment agency for giving employment ([III.6.a]) Gorlin, 1990:72).

Why do police codes characteristically fail to set a standard higher than ordinary morality? No doubt one reason is the very language in which police codes have been written. The confusion among ideals, principles, and rules makes it hard to tell whether a higher standard has been set. But there seems to be at least one more reason that police codes generally fail to set a higher standard: Police find it harder than most of us to maintain even the minimum standard of decency. That is not because they were "criminal types" before they joined the force. Police work itself seems to have a strong tendency to corruption. Police see much more of the underside of life than most of us, not only the worst people but even good people at their worst. Police are far more likely to be offered a substantial bribe than most of us, to be threatened with death or wounds, and to hear of other people's wrongs. Their sense of what is normal must suffer in consequence. They are also much more likely than most of us to feel like failures. Most people the police see much of end up dead, in jail, on the run, or just down and out. "Bitterness" seems as much an occupational disease of police as brutality, suspicion, cynicism, and petty theft (Johnson and Copus, 1981:39–83; Payton, 1967:6–22).

For the police, then, the object of ethics must be somewhat different from that of most other professions. The police will do well to remain decent human beings; the problem of

police ethics, and of police administration too, then, is to help them do that. A code can help police to maintain ordinary moral decency in at least three ways. First, a code can simply serve to remind police of what is (and therefore of what is not) expected of them. Second, it can provide a common vocabulary for discussion of hard cases. Was this use of force unnecessary? Third, the emotional language so common in police codes might also help to inspire an officer to do more than he/she would otherwise do.

Whether police codes in fact *significantly* support minimally decent conduct in any of these ways is, of course, an empirical question, one about which social scientists should tell us more. We might guess, though, that while reading a stirring code may do as much good as listening to a rousing Sunday sermon or making a New Year's resolution, it is unlikely to do more. If that were all police codes were good for, they would not be good for much.

More important here, if police codes only restated ordinary morality—moral ideals as police ideals, moral principles as police principles, and moral rules as police rules—they would not be codes of *ethics* (in our sense). They would not set a higher standard. What then do "police ethics" have to do with ethics? Article 8 of the UN's Code suggests an answer but one that will probably make most police uncomfortable. That article not only redundantly requires law enforcement officials to "refrain from" conduct violating the code, but it also requires them to "prevent and rigorously oppose all violations of this code." Once a violation has occurred (or can be expected), a law enforcement officer "should report the matter within the chain of command, or take such other actions as are lawfully open . . . , including, when necessary, the reporting to any agency with reviewing or remedial power."

Article 8 seems to be the only explicit "whistleblowing" provision in any code of police ethics to date. But, given the realities of police work, such a provision is probably necessary to any police code that is to be more than a mere restatement of what law, market, and ordinary morality exact. Part of the specifically professional responsibility of police, probably the crucial one, is helping other police do the right thing. That may on occasion mean breaking "the code of silence," the rule that helps police to protect themselves from outside interference and so to preserve enough autonomy to make professional judgment possible.

While police certainly should look for ways to preserve autonomy less likely than the code of silence to shield corruption, that is beside the point here. Police can do much to help each other maintain minimum standards of moral decency without breaching the code of silence. Putting a fellow officer "on report" is not the only way, or even the best way, to maintain professional standards. Consider, for example, what might happen if, when one officer loses his head and begins beating a prisoner, another officer interrupts with such words as these: "Did we join the force to beat up this helpless man? Isn't our job to protect everyone from the monsters of this world, not to become monsters ourselves?" Such comments in the heat of action can do much to make whistleblowing unnecessary, provided they remind the officer of earlier substantial discussions of police ethics and of commitments the officer actually has.

Conclusions

Publishing a code forbidding police to do what is morally wrong, code or not, will probably add nothing to an officers' moral knowledge. Nor will it add to their moral duties. Even requiring officers to swear an oath to obey such a code will not change the substance of those duties. Closer supervision, harsher discipline, less pressure from above for "results," or alternative methods for handling the problems that now lead police to do what they should not, seem more likely to reduce wrongdoing than any code or other regulation that simply restates ordinary morality (in whole or in part).

A code of police *ethics* (that is, a code that goes beyond ordinary morality) can help prevent undesirable conduct only insofar as the police can be kept morally decent people (people over whom conscience exercises considerable authority). Because some police work seems to be inherently corrupting, police departments need to be more careful than they are about the work they make police do. For example, they probably need to take on less undercover work than they now do. They also need to be more careful about making officers work such long or irregular hours that the officers lose touch with the world beyond police work. Departments may even want to require "sabbatical leaves" every few years.

A code of ethics can help prevent undesirable conduct in a way ordinary regulations cannot only if police think of themselves as professionals in the morally interesting sense. Insofar as police think of themselves as mere individual employees, a "code of ethics," whatever its substance, will be no more than another departmental regulation. Its moral foundation will be the employment contract (whether supplemented or not by a special oath). Calling it a "code of ethics" will not make it a more useful document.

Because what distinguishes a code of ethics from other regulations governing police conduct is its connection with policing as a profession; giving police a living code of ethics means something more than issuing another regulation, making police swear an oath as a condition of employment, or even regularly informing them of their duties. Giving police a living code means choosing its terms so that police benefit enough from having it in force that it becomes reasonable for them to help enforce it. That, in turn, probably means giving ordinary police officers a central part in writing, interpreting, and enforcing the code. Codes that seem to come from above generally do not touch the world below. So police departments need to think about ways to combine their quasimilitary organization with the decentralized controls characteristic not only of free professions like law and medicine but of the captive professions like the professorate and engineering. Decentralized control or autonomy is part of what makes a profession possible.

The primary standards of a police code probably cannot in practice demand much more of police than ordinary morality does. So the important part of a code of ethics for police will not be the primary standards (for example, those forbidding unnecessary brutality or urging honesty in thought and deed), but the secondary standards (for example, those making the conduct of each police officer the professional responsibility of every other). While few police codes include such secondary standards, all should. Otherwise, a police officer reading the code could properly conclude that he/she is responsible only for his/her own conduct. So long as the primary standards are satisfied, he/she has done all that he/she should; he/she is a true professional.

The teaching of police ethics probably needs to be changed accordingly. Right now the emphasis seems to be on the individual police officer doing his or her duty and "keeping his or her nose clean." Little, if anything, is said about an officer's responsibility for helping fellow officers do the right thing. There is little or no training in how to carry on a practical discussion of ethics with fellow officers. Yet in police work, as in other professions, moral support is an important part of maintaining standards. Police clearly have a support system in place, "the code of silence." The problem is to turn it into a system of *moral* support. Doing that means among other things teaching police how to talk to one another about their profession's ethics. They should begin by considering whether they want a code of ethics at all.

Michael Davis

Bibliography

Davis, M. "The Ethics Boom: What and Why? *Centennial Review* 34 (1990): 163–86. Helps put recent interest in codes of ethics in historical perspective.

———. "Do Cops Really Need a Code of Ethics?" *Criminal Justice Ethics* 10 (Summer/Fall 1991): 14–28.

Felkenes, G. "Attitudes of Police Officers Toward Their Professional Ethics." *Journal of Criminal Justice* 12 (May/June 1984): 211–20.

Gorlin, R.A. *Codes of Professional Responsibility* 2d ed. Edison, NJ: ENA Books, 1990. A collection of important contemporary codes of ethics outside law enforcement, useful for comparison.

Hansen, D. *Police Ethics*. Springfield, IL: Charles C. Thomas, 1973. See Chap. 1 ("Codes of Ethics") and Chap. 2 ("Practicality Versus the Code of Ethics").

Johnson, C., and G. Copus. "Law Enforcement Ethics: A Theoretical Analysis." In *The Social Basis of Criminal Justice: Ethical Issues for the 1980's.* Eds. F. Schmalleger and G. Gustafson. Washington, DC: University Press of America. 1981. 39–83.

Kleinig, J., and Y. Zhang. *Professional Law Enforcement Codes: A Documentary Collection.* Westport, CT: Greenwood Press, 1992. Includes a large number of law enforcement codes, both American and foreign, going back to early in the last century. Good introductory essay and bibliography. A "must" for anyone working in this field.

Kultgen, J. *Ethics and Professionalism.* Philadelphia, PA: University of Pennsylvania Press, 1988. Chap. 10 ("Professional Codes"). Presents an analysis of codes somewhat different from that presented here.

Ladd, J. "The Quest for a Code of Professional Ethics: An Intellectual and Moral Confusion." In *Professional Ethics Project: Professional Ethics Activities in the Scientific and Engineering Societies.* Eds. Rosemary Chalk, Mark S. Frankel, and Sallie B. Chafer. Washington, DC: American Association for the Advancement of Science, 1980. 154–59. Best case against professional ethics as distinct from morality. But see criticism of this paper in Davis (1990).

Payton, G.T. *Patrol Procedure and Enforcement Concepts.* 3d ed. Los Angeles: Legal Book, 1967. Chap. 1. Sobering description of police work and attitudes.

Community-Oriented Policing: COP and POP

Community policing (often referred to as community-oriented policing) has been given a variety of titles and definitions. Some police professionals and policy-makers distinguish Community-Oriented Policing (COP) from Problem-Oriented Policing (POP), while others consider the terms to be interchangeable. Trojanowicz and Bucqueroux (1989:3) described community policing in the following manner:

> Community Policing is the first major reform in policing since departments embraced scientific management principles more than half a century ago. It is a dramatic change in the way police departments interact with the public, a new philosophy that broadens the police mission from a narrow focus on crime to a mandate that encourages the police to explore creative solutions for a host of community concerns, including crime, fear of disorder, and neighborhood decay.

> Community policing rests on the belief that only by working together will people and the police be able to improve the quality of life in the community, with the police not only as enforcers, but also as advisors, facilitators, and supporters of new, community-based, police supervised initiatives.

For some, the definition of community policing includes an orientation that permeates all facets of police work and emphasizes police accountability to the community and the organization, management based on stated values, decentralized structure, shared decision-making with the community, and officers being empowered to solve problems (Michaelson, Kelling, and Wasserman, 1988).

Thus, community policing is characterized by organizational values that stress community involvement and embraces key concepts such as decentralization (neighborhood police having responsibility for handling problems in the neighborhoods), problem-solving, and respect for the community being policed (Hartman, Brown, and Stephens, 1988). The goals of community policing are generally characterized as controlling crime, reducing the fear of crime, maintaining order, and improving the quality of life in neighborhoods. Although the programs differ in structure and may include such features as foot patrol, neighborhood-based stations, and specialized crime control units, they share many of the following operational and organizational principles:

1. Permanently assigning officers to specific neighborhoods or beats.
2. Developing a knowledge base about problems, characteristics, and resources in the neighborhood.
3. Outreaching to businesses and residents, making the police more visible in the neighborhoods.
4. Involving the community in the identifying, understanding, and prioritizing of local problems, and in developing and implementing plans to solve them.
5. Delegating responsibility to community police for creating solutions to crime and order maintenance problems.
6. Providing information to the community on local crime problems and police efforts to solve them.
7. Opening the flow of information from the community to the police to assist with making arrests and developing intelligence on unlawful activities in the community. (McElroy, Cosgrove, and Sadd, 1990).

The theory underlying community policing is well expressed in Wilson and Kelling's article, "Broken Windows" (1982:36). In this work, the authors emphasize that the police have a responsibility to protect the community as a whole, as well as individuals residing in that community. Thus police must take care of order-maintenance problems such as disorderly conduct, vagrancy, drunkenness, youth rowdiness, and vandalism, and they must also work to improve the quality of life for the residents of the community. Police are responsible for reducing crime, since its existence leads citizens to avoid the streets and each other and thus weakens the social controls in a community.

Greene and Taylor (1988) suggest that community officers can be more effective in fulfilling the order-maintenance function than regular motorized patrol officers because "these community based officers are said to be more familiar with local rules and community regulars, have a better idea of what response may be desired because they have spent more time in the community contact, and are better able to distinguish between regulars and strangers. This enhanced community sensitivity makes a successful resolution of incidents more likely (200)." Community policing also should lower citizens' fear because the daily presence of the officer in the community makes people feel safer.

The Difference Between COP and POP
Problem-Oriented Policing (POP) has been viewed by some as an alternative to Community-Oriented Policing (COP) (Eck and Spelman, 1987; Goldstein, 1987) and by others as a component of COP (Rosen, 1992; Trojanowicz and Bucqueroux, 1989). Moore (1992) views POP and COP as overlapping concepts with a distinctive thrust differentiating them. He describes POP as a situational approach and COP as fostering a working partnership between the police and the community.

A Problem-Oriented Policing approach grounded in the directives of the National Institute of Justice requires that the problem-solving system follow five basic principles:

1. Officers of all ranks and from all units should be able to use the system as part of their daily routine.
2. The system must encourage the use of a broad range of information, including but not limited to conventional police data.
3. The system should encourage a broad range of solutions, including but not limited to the criminal justice process.

4. The system should require no additional resources and no special units.
5. Finally, any large police agency must be able to apply it.

The problem-solving process adopted in Newport News, Virginia, included four stages:

1. Scanning—identifying an issue and determining if it is a problem.
2. Analysis—collecting information on the problem from all available sources.
3. Response—using the information to develop and implement solutions to the problem.
4. Assessment—determining if the response to the problem was effective. (Eck and Spelman, 1987: xix–xx)

One might argue that this is an approach that has always been used in police work and thus does not represent anything new. Others, however, argue that the systematic approach to solving problems has not always been that apparent in police work, particularly when the department is highly centralized, specialized, and reactive. Certainly POP and COP are compatible. As Cordner and Hale (1992:14) concluded recently, the combination of COP/POP offers "one of our brightest prospects for improved police effectiveness."

Emergence of Policing
Kelling and Moore (1988) have shown that the police establishment, like all other institutions, is subject to change, with the changes often resulting from the reaction of the citizenry to occurrences in the community, which they find to be intolerable.

In the United States, when police departments were established as public organizations during the 1840s, the police were closely tied to political entities. The police establishment of the "political era" had many of the characteristics of community policing, such as a decentralized neighborhood-based structure with close personal relationships with the citizens. Programs and techniques were grounded in foot patrol, call boxes, and police performing a variety of functions including patrol, investigations, and order-maintenance and service-type activities. Keeping the prominent citizens and politicians satisfied was a major goal of the police.

A reform era emerged during the 1930s, but in succeeding decades there was still consid-

erable involvement of the police in politics. By the 1960s, police work was grounded on the professional model with a highly centralized, organizational design calling for specialization of labor, a bureaucratic structure, and a detached, somewhat formal, form of communications between the police and citizenry. The programs and technologies included auto patrol and sophisticated communication systems. Outcome was measured in terms of crime control, with increases and decreases in the crime rates used as measurements of success or failure. The community-policing, problem-solving approach, which gained some support in the 1970s and gained much more attention during the late 1980s, is the result of many factors, including the knowledge that the professional, centralized police organization model did not lead to the reduction of crime expected.

Thus, the movement toward community policing was stimulated by the realization that various segments of the community, in particular youth, poor persons, and minority group members, were dissatisfied with the performance of the police and the services they provided, and by the realization that the traditional approaches of dealing with crime, in particular street crimes, were not too successful. For example, the *Uniform Crime Reports* (UCR) show that in any given year less than one-fourth of reported burglaries, robberies, auto thefts, or larceny-theft crimes are cleared by arrest (*Uniform Crime Reports,* 1992:202).

Extent of Community Policing
In a survey of large city police departments conducted by Cardarelli (1993), it was found that of the twenty-five large city departments that indicated they had a community policing program, twenty-four were started in the past three to five years; the newness of these programs was reflected in the confusion of law enforcement administrators on the meaning of community policing. Some equated community policing with foot patrols and periodic meetings with community residents, others with community relations. Only a small number stated that community policing must involve the residents in the decision-making process related to policing policies. Greene and Taylor (1988:7) reported that 35 percent of the 202 police agencies in Florida listed in the "Directory of Florida Chiefs of Police" had some form of community-oriented policing. They found that many police departments mentioned utilizing such ap-

proaches as neighborhood crime watch, team policing, citizen advisory boards, and bicycle and foot patrol—approaches to police work falling into the scope of community policing, but they did not interpret these activities as being a form of community policing.

Skolnick and Bayley (1986) have identified a number of obstacles to the introduction of community policing into a police department. These include resistance from police administrators, police unions, and patrol officers, and the prevailing culture of policing. The resistance of the administration may stem in part from the fact that with community policing, officers have autonomy and have the authority to make decisions. In some cities the rank and file patrol officers have reacted against the media attention given to community-policing programs by exhibiting a lack of willingness to cooperate or to acknowledge the importance of the COP program. In other cases, not fully understanding the essence of community policing, police administrators and patrol officers have characterized COP as a community-relations program and have not regarded it as within the realm of "real police" work. This attitude is reenforced by the "police culture," which mistakenly equates "real police" work exclusively with law-enforcement activity. While voicing full support for community policing when speaking to the public or the political establishment, the actions of police administrators may differ when resources become scarce and a decision must be made on what programs to delete.

Some writers perceive community policing as a philosophical approach to police work, which must prevail throughout the entire department if it is to be effective. For example, Trojanowicz and Bucqueroux (1989:20) state that community policing is not something to be used periodically; instead it is a permanent commitment to new community problem-solving.

Albritton (1993:13) noted that "police organizations have often transformed reform proposal and experiments to fit their own agenda and priorities; rarely have they adopted these proposals in all their theoretical 'purity.'" He attributes this phenomenon to that fact that in the final analysis police administrators still believe that the most efficient way to achieve the demands for effective crime-fighting approaches is through the traditional centralized, highly mechanized, organizational structure employed by most large city police departments. He states: "Pursuing the traditional crime fight-

ing mandate seems to be the 'one efficient way' for policing to justify its operations and maintain a relative degree of police credibility and support in society" (14). Cordner and Hale (1992:12) concede that "in most departments community policing is not intended to completely substitute for motor patrol but rather to supplement and complement motor patrol's reactive efforts."

Effectiveness of Community-Oriented Policing

Goldstein (1987:8) noted the many perceived benefits of community policing, "e.g., decreased tensions between the police and the community, more effective use of police resources on increased quality of police service, increased effectiveness in dealing with the community problems, increased job satisfaction for the police participating in the programs and increased accountability to the community."

In order to implement and assess the effects of community policing, one must establish a framework that considers both the external environment and the internal environment of the police agency in which community policing is employed. External environmental factors such as the socioeconomic conditions of the community (large cities have undergone significant changes in their racial and ethnic make up as well as a decline of population); legislative mandates and court orders (rights of victims in domestic cases, rights of homeless people); budgetary constraints (budget reductions); and the community dynamics (residents requesting some control over the decision-making process on matters affecting their quality of life) all affect the type of policing employed.

Internal environmental factors to consider in implementing community policing include the predominate style of policing endorsed by the organizational norms of the department. For example, since community policing requires considerable cooperation between the police and the citizenry in crime prevention and control activities, an administrative philosophy that stresses the service element of community policing is required. The political environment of a department must be considered. For example, are the political leaders interested in portraying an image of being tough on crime or are they really interested in improving the quality of life in their city? The matter of whether or not the upper administrators of the department are willing to decentralize and share decision-making with lower-level administrators is also of considerable importance in determining if community policing can be implemented.

Most of the research on community policing has focused on changes in citizens' fear of crime, satisfaction with the police, reduction of crime, and the organizational problems created when trying to incorporate new programs into an existing structure. To date, most of the findings are inconclusive.

Many of the administrative concerns, such as appropriate training for community policing and developing an equitable method to reward community policing officers, are now being debated.

Peter C. Kratcoski

Bibliography

Albritton, J.S. "The Technique of Community-Oriented Policing: An Alternative Interpretation." Unpublished manuscript, 1993.

Cardarelli, Albert P., and Jack McDevitte. "Toward a Conceptual Framework for Evaluating Community Policing." In *Issues in Community Policing*. Eds. P.C. Kratcoski and Duane Dukes. Cincinnati: Anderson, 1995.

Cordner, Gary W., and Donna C. Hale. *What Works in Policing: Operations and Administration Examined*. Cincinnati: Anderson, 1992.

Crime in the U.S. Washington, DC: Government Printing Office, 1992.

Eck, John E., and William Spelman. *Problem-Solving: Problem-Oriented Policing in Newport News*. Washington, DC: Police Executive Research Forum, 1987.

Goldstein, Herman. "Toward Community-Oriented Policing: Potential, Basic Requirements, and Threshold Questions." *Crime and Delinquency* 33(1)(1987): 6–30.

Greene, H.T. "Community-Oriented Policing in Florida." Unpublished manuscript, 1993.

Greene, J. R., and R. B. Taylor. "Community-Based Policing and Foot Patrol: Issues of Theory and Evaluation." In *Community Policing: Rhetoric or Reality*. Eds. Jack R. Greene and Steven D. Mastrofski. New York: Praeger, 1988.

Hartman, F., L. Brown, and D. Stephens. *Community Policing: Would you Know It If You Saw It?* East Lansing, MI: Neighborhood Foot Patrol Center, 1988.

Kelling, George L., and Mark H. Moore. "The Evolving Strategy of Policing." Washington, DC: National Institute of Justice, 1988.

McElroy, J., C.A. Cosgrove, and S. Sadd. *CPOP: The Research*. New York: Vera Institute of Justice, 1990.

Michaelson, S., G. Kelling, and R. Wasserman. "Toward a Working Definition of Community Policing." Unpublished paper for Programming in Criminal Justice Policy and Management, John F. Kennedy School of Government, Harvard University, 1988.

Moore, H.M. "Problem-solving and Community Policing." In *Modern Policing*. Eds. M. Tonry and N. Morris. Chicago, IL: University of Chicago Press, 1992.

Rosen, M. "An Interview With Commissioner Lee P. Brown of New York." *Law Enforcement News* (May 15, 1992) 18, no. 358: 11.

Skolnick, Jerome H., and David H. Bayley. *The New Blue Line: Police Innovation in Six American Cities*. New York: Free Press, 1986.

Spelman, William, and John E. Eck. "Problem-Oriented Policing." *Research in Brief*. Washington, DC: National Institute of Justice, 1987.

Trojanowicz, Robert, and Bonnie Bucqueroux. *Community Policing: A Contemporary Perspective*. Cincinnati: Anderson, 1989.

Wilson, James Q., and George L. Kelling. "Broken Windows: The Police and Neighborhood Safety." *Atlantic Monthly* 249 (March 1982): 29–38.

Community-Oriented Policing: International

In the United States, community policing is more often aspiration than implementation. Although notable initiatives are succeeding against great odds in Detroit, Houston, Santa Ana, Newport News, and Baltimore County, most municipal police forces are using community policing to embellish rather than transform standard operating procedures. At the same time, small-scale experimentation is common and there are many test cases from which interested police executives can learn.

In reviewing international experience, there is a close connection between substantiality of community policing from place to place and the reasons police leaders find it attractive. It is not by accident that the more ambitious experiments have taken place where there was a sense of strategic need. Great Britain's recent controversial but wide-ranging innovations under the rubric of community policing derive from the racial turmoil of the late 1970s and 1980s. Singapore uses community policing to build the nation, in the belief that a neighborhood police presence helps draw together diverse ethnic groups into genuine communities.

The central premise of community policing is that the public should play a more active and coordinated part in enhancing safety. The police cannot bear the responsibility alone, nor can the criminal justice system. In an apt phrase, the public should be seen as "coproducers" with the police of safety and order. Community policing thus imposes a new responsibility on the police, namely, to devise appropriate ways of associating the public with law enforcement and the maintenance of order. Hard-bitten older officers recognize full well their job is made easier if the public cooperates and supports the police. They have spent their professional lives asking for assistance from the public. Therefore, if community policing is to mean something distinctive, it must refer to programs that change the customary interaction between police and public. In this substantial sense community policing is very much alive around the world and appears to be growing rapidly. A full-fledged program incorporates: (1) community-based crime prevention; (2) a reorientation of patrol activities to emphasize nonemergency servicing; (3) increased accountability to local communities; and (4) decentralized command.

Community-Based Crime Prevention
Although Neighborhood Watch is an American invention of the early 1970s, it varies considerably throughout the world and sometimes even within the same country. The London Metropolitan Police defines Neighborhood Watch as involving three elements: public surveillance—people act as the eyes and ears of the police; property marking—residents mark their property with the post code, house or flat number, and their initials; and home security—police visit any household and make recommendations for improving home security. Above all, Neighborhood Watch tries to inculcate a feeling of identity and social responsibility. Throughout Great Britain the program has been advanced by the police and by government as

its most important crime prevention strategy. Figures given by Her Majesty's Inspectors of Constabulary indicate that as of 1988, 9,242 schemes were in operation or 18.1 percent of the total police force in England and Wales (Bennett and Lupton, 1992). They are established either through a police initiative or as a result of local interest expressed to the police.

A number of criticisms have been leveled in Britain at both Neighborhood Watch and the more expansive vision. A careful, but admittedly tentative, evaluation of two Neighborhood Watch areas conducted by the Institute of Criminology at the University of Cambridge suggests there is not much reason to believe the program is very effective. There are also criticisms that while Neighborhood Watch may be helpful to middle-class families that own homes, the type of advice the police are prepared to offer is of little practical value to individuals whose income and standard of living are too low for them to be able to afford improvements. Finally, multiagency policing has been criticized as an overreaching by police into aspects of citizens' lives in which police have no business.

The most ambitious and extensive neighborhood crime prevention program is in Japan, though it is not called Neighborhood Watch and does not owe its inspiration to the United States. From time immemorial Japanese neighborhoods have had the rudiments of informal government, the creation of custom rather than statute. Membership has been automatic and participation compelled by social pressure. Its leaders mediated disputes, lobbied for municipal services, organized neighborhood improvement campaigns, communicated information about local concerns, and sponsored festivals. As an outgrowth of this tradition, most Japanese neighborhoods now have crime-prevention associations that distribute information, sell security hardware, publish newsletters, maintain close liaison with local police, and occasionally patrol the streets. All neighborhood organizations belong to provincial and national crime prevention associations.

In Australia Neighborhood Watch is relatively new, beginning in Victoria State in the early 1980s. Although police officials studied the American experience systematically before formulating their own program, the "Victoria Model" made some important modifications. For example, the basic unit is not a block but an area containing approximately 400 to 600 residences, or about 2,000 people. As in Britain, the police work closely with residents to identify people who would make responsible leaders and then sound them out for election. In order to remain a certified Neighborhood Watch group, meetings must be held at least once a month. Newsletters containing crime information and crime-prevention tips are standard. The program is not free in Australia. Members are expected to make a small yearly contribution for ongoing expenses. Australian Neighborhood Watch groups are not left on their own, but belong to larger associations which support and coordinate their work. There are successively zonal, city, and state associations, containing representatives from the levels below.

Police around the world have also developed extensive education programs designed to help targeted groups protect themselves more successfully. Police departments now produce a vast literature in many languages offering crime prevention advice to the elderly, school children, working women, vacationers, and other groups. In addition to writing and publishing brochures and leaflets, specialists in police agencies, usually based in headquarters' crime prevention units, give lectures, organize meetings, conduct classes, and coordinate media campaigns. There are now national and even international networks of crime prevention personnel that trade material, exchange experts, and generally encourage one another to bear up against the skepticism of their colleagues in the police.

Reorientation of Patrol Activities
Buttressed by research that has shown that random motorized patrolling and rapid response may not effectively deter crime or lead to the more certain apprehension of criminals, community-police reformers contend that patrol operations should encourage a deeper involvement with the community, an involvement not instigated predominately by emergency calls for service. The most dramatic change is the redeployment of patrol officers from motor vehicles into small, decentralized police posts. They are called shopfronts in Australia, Neighborhood Police Posts (NPPs) in Singapore, and "koban" in Japan. The Japanese and Singaporean posts are miniature police stations, responsible for all aspects of policing except criminal investigation, whereas Australia's Broadmeadows shopfront does not do general police work, but is responsible solely for community crime prevention. Physi-

cally, the multifunctional Japan "koban" and Singaporean NPPs consist of a reception room with a low counter or desk, telephone, radio, and wall maps; a resting room for personnel, often with a television set; a small kitchen or at least a hot plate and refrigerator; an interview room; a storeroom; and a toilet. Japanese "koban" have been built wherever space was available—in bus and railway stations, among rows of shops, at intersections of busy roads, on residential lots, and even on the grounds of temples. Because land prices have skyrocketed in Toyko recently, the cost of building new "koban" has become a significant drain on police resources. Some land owners, moreover, would like the "koban" to move so they can resell the land. Singapore's NPPs, by contrast, are much newer and well-equipped, having been built to order since 1983. Most are located on the ground floor of the large multi-storied public-housing estates where approximately 84 percent of the population now lives.

An intensive form of community involvement is house visits, where officers go door-to-door asking about security problems, offering services, soliciting suggestions about police activity, and sometimes collecting information about residents. "Koban" and NPP officers are expected to call at every residence and business in their beats at least once a year. House visits in Singapore demand daunting linguistic skill. Singapore has four official languages—English, Mandarin, Malay, and Tamil. To complicate matters, Chinese families may speak in different dialects—Cantonese, Hakka, or Hokkien. NPP officers knock at barred gates that provide security while letting in fresh air in the tropical climate. Conversations are almost always conducted through the bars. Foot patrols and horse patrols—traditional strategies of policing—are coming back everywhere. In Japan and Singapore, foot patrols are the mainstay of deployment. Singapore stresses vertical patrols, where officers walk through the open-air corridors of high-rise housing blocks, beginning at the top floor and working their way down. Singapore patrol officers are still a visible presence, therefore, from building to building as well as within them. In most countries, however, foot patrols are used selectively, mostly in areas of high-pedestrian traffic like shopping centers, entertainment strips, and public transportation facilities.

A particular kind of reoriented patrolling frequently identified with community policing is order maintenance. In this connection it refers to the suppression of disorderly or uncivil behavior by individuals in public places, rather than control after the fact. The main purpose of order maintenance is to reduce anxiety thereby encouraging people to use public places more freely, and to prevent the decay of urban neighborhoods. From the police point of view the trick of order maintenance is to read correctly the behavior code considered appropriate for each area by its respectable inhabitants. If police can do this, they demonstrate that criminal elements are not in charge.

Increased Police Accountability

Police forces are establishing an array of liaison officers and councils with groups whose relations with the police have been troubled, such as Aborigines in Australia, Koreans in Japan, Indians and Afro-Caribbeans in Britain, and gays in many places. Melbourne, Australia, even has a liaison committee with lawyers. Naturally enough, liaison officers spend much of their time fending off potential crises—the uprush of anger, confusion, and violence sometimes generated by police encounters with these groups. They also try to cultivate contacts in those communities and develop programs to meet special needs. And they are frequently asked to create educational programs that will increase the knowledge and sensitivity of their colleagues in dealing with nonmainstream groups.

Police are also trying to cooperate more closely with established groups and institutions that have a working interest in crime and order. Even more far-reaching, police are creating new formal committees and councils to advise them about security needs and operations. In Britain, for example, despite the fact that each police force is responsible to a Police Authority whose membership is one-third judicial magistrates and two-thirds elected local council politicians, the police in various cities have recently set up special Consultative Committees at police-station level. Their purpose is to mobilize public participation, assess consumer opinion about police services, and communicate information that will help the police carry out their duties more effectively. Striking at a sometimes even more sensitive nerve, efforts are expanding to allow civilians to observe police operations in order to ensure they are conducted fairly and legally. Britain now allows "lay visitors" to inspect police stations, with particular attention paid to the holding cells. So too does Sweden. Police complaint tribunals have recently been established in all Australian states, contrary to the most sanguine predictions even eight years ago. In short, community policing embraces the expansion of civilian input into policing. Reciprocity of communication is not only accepted but encouraged. Under community policing, the public is allowed to speak and to be informed about strategic priorities, tactical approaches, and even the behavior of individual officers.

Decentralization of Command

A key assumption of community policing is that communities have different policing priorities and problems. Policing must be adaptable. To accomplish this, subordinate commanders must be given the freedom to act according to their own reading of local conditions. Redrawing the boundaries of command, which goes on constantly in world policing, may or may not involve the devolution of authority upon local commanders. This critical element depends on the scale of command as well as the commitment of senior police managers. Command decentralization is more than a mapmaking exercise. On the whole, then, community policing implies that smaller and more local is better.

The enhancement of decision-making responsibility under community policing extends beyond subordinate commanders. It also involves the rank-and-file. In addition to their traditional duties, community police constables and patrol officers must be able to organize community groups, suggest solutions to neighborhood problems, listen unflappably to critical comment, enlist the cooperation of people who are fearful and resentful, participate intelligently in command conferences, and speak with poise before public audiences. Such duties require new aptitudes. Officers must be able to think on their feet and be able to translate general mandates into appropriate words and actions. A new breed of police officer is needed, as well as a new command ethos. International community policing transforms the responsibilities of all ranks—subordinate ranks to become more self-directing; and senior ranks to encourage disciplined initiative while developing coherent plans responsive to local conditions.

Potential Obstacles

Students of police have frequently noted the machismo qualities in the world of policing. Those who are attracted to the occupation are often very young in chronological age and in maturity of temperament and judgment. England sets nineteen as the age of entry. Recruits typically have athletic backgrounds, are sports minded, and are trained in self-defense. It is not uncommon for trainees to bulk the upper body—like football players, through weight lifting—so as to present a more formidable appearance in street encounters. They are also trained to handle a variety of offensive weapons, including deadly weapons. They are taught how to disable and kill people with their bare hands. No matter how many warnings may be offered by superiors about limitations on use of force, its possible use is a central feature of the police role and of policemen's perceptions of themselves.

The training and permission to use force combined with the youth of police can well inhibit the capacity of a police officer to empathize with the situation of those being policed in ethnically diverse and low-income neighborhoods. Senior officers are not only less likely to be macho, but also are more likely to feel comfortable in the problem-solving, almost parental role associated with community policing. The "street-wise" cop is another glaring obstacle. Street-wise officers are likely to be cynical, tough, and skeptical of innovation. Conversely, management cops are less obstinate. They tend to be legalistic, rule oriented, and rational, and are thus more likely to be at least initially interested in the idea of community policing. The management cop is not necessarily more accepting of the idea of policing as a broader social issue, but is likelier to be receptive to a more expansive vision of the police role. By contrast, the self-conception of the traditional street cop remains firmly rooted in early training experiences.

Other obstacles not based on police subculture but equally difficult to surmount are:

- Many police executives now regard the emergency response system they have created in the name of community policing as a monster that consumes the operational guts of the department. Calling the emergency number is so easy that police could spend all their time speeding in patrol cars to anonymously placed calls, often handling trivial matters that may not even involve law violations.
- Community policing cannot develop without expanding the dimensions of an already sizeable bureaucracy.
- Police unions internationally see community policing as a threat to professionalism. Police are the designated and appropriately trained personnel to handle crime, whether through prevention or apprehension. Citizens are neither needed nor wanted. Moreover, community policing implies a degree of police accountability to citizens, yet another hazard to police unions. And perhaps most important, unions fear loss of jobs and benefits.
- The insistence on two officers per patrol car to avert danger hampers increased use of foot patrol and ministations. (Indeed, the two-officer car may prove to be the largest constraint upon the development of community policing.)
- Decentralization of command may not easily be adapted to police departments with a strong centralized orientation. The more hierarchical the accountability system, the more difficult it will be to introduce community policing.
- Evaluation of the community-oriented police officer whose dual task is crime prevention and apprehension is not easy. A dedicated officer will slowly initiate subtle changes in community behavior and attitudes—changes nearly impossible to measure. Because police forces have not learned how to reward "crime prevention" performance, they find it hard to encourage rank-and-file officers to dedicate themselves to it.
- Some citizens may come to believe that community policing actually interferes with standard crime fighting and demand a return to more traditional modes of policing.
- Community policing can fail to integrate crime prevention with crime investigation. Often "lesser" officers are assigned to foot patrol and ministations, leaving the better officers to solve crimes.
- Community is an inherently ambiguous, almost elusive idea. It implies a commonality of interest, values, identities, demands, and expectations. Police-community reciprocity can be achieved only where there is a genuine bonding of interests between the police and the served citizenry, on the one hand, and among definable sections of the public, on the other.

Even given the above obstacles, if police forces encourage community-based crime prevention, emphasize nonemergency interaction with the public, increase public input into policy-making, and decentralize command, substantial benefits can accrue both to the community and to the police.

Jerome H. Skolnick
David H. Bayley

Bibliography

Bayley, David H. *Community Policing in Australia: An Appraisal.* Adelaide, S. Australia: National Police Research Unit, 1986.

———, and Walter L. Ames. *The Police and Community in Japan.* Berkeley: University of California Press, 1981.

Bennett, Trevor. "An Evaluation of Two Neighborhood Watch Schemes in London." Cambridge, England: Institute of Criminology, Cambridge University, 1987.

———, and Ruth Lupton. "A Survey of the Allocation and Use of Community Constables in England and Wales." *British Journal of Criminology* 32 (Spring 1992): 167–82.

Fielding, Nigel. *The Police and Social Conflict: Rhetoric and Reality.* Atlantic Highlands, NJ: Athlone Press, 1991.

Friedmann, Robert R. *Community Policing: Comparative Perspectives and Prospects.* New York: St. Martin's Press, 1992.

Hazelhurst, K.M. *Crime Prevention for Aboriginal Communities.* Canberra: Australian Institute of Criminology, 1990.

Hope, T., and M. Shaw, eds. *Communities and Crime Reduction.* Proceedings of an International Conference. London: Home Office Research and Planning Unit, 1988.

Jackson, G. "Reform of Policing in New South Wales." *Anglo-American Law Review* 20 (1991): 15–26.

Jon, S.T., and Stella Quah. *Neighborhood Policing in Singapore.* Singapore: Oxford University Press, 1987.

Mather, P. "An Investigation of the Relationship between the Style of Police Foot Patrol and Fear of Crime within Communities." Master's thesis, Philosophy in Social Policy. University of Newcastle-upon-Tyne, 1990.

Mawby, R.I. "Community Involvement in Policing: A Comparative Analysis." In *Comparative Policing Issues: The British* *and American Experience in International Perspective.* London: Unwin Hyman, 1990.

Morgan, Rod, and Christopher Maggs. *Setting the P.A.C.E.: Police Consultation Arrangements in England and Wales.* Bath, England: Center for Analysis of Social Policy, University of Bath, 1985.

Rizkalla, S., et al. "Community Crime Prevention—An Innovative Program." *Canadian Journal of Criminology* 33 (1991): 421–34.

Torstensson, M. "The Work of Police in the Urban Environment." in *Crime and Measures against Crime in the City.* Ed. P. Wikstrom. Stockholm: National Council for Crime Prevention, 1990.

Wadman, Robert C., and Sir Stanley E. Bailey. *Community Policing and Crime Prevention in America and England.* Chicago: Office of International Criminal Justice, University of Illinois, 1993.

Walker, C.R., and S.G. Walker. "The Citizen and the Police: A Partnership in Crime Prevention." *Canadian Journal of Criminology* 32 (1990): 125–35.

Community-Oriented Policing: Rationale

In a sense community-oriented policing is not something new in the history of law enforcement. What is new is the nature of the communities that officers are required to police. In years gone by the nature of American society was quite different. Society was smaller, less complex, and considerably more homogeneous. Many of the problems that present-day police, as formal agents of social control, are required to handle used to be dealt with by citizens in an informal manner. Previous generations saw neighborhoods, even in large urban environments, where a true sense of community flourished. This sense of community, identification with one's neighbors, and the closer and more intimate nature of relationships acted to facilitate social control on a neighborhood basis. Thus informal social controls operated so that disputes were settled without police intervention, juvenile problems were dealt with by and between families, and neighborhood safety and security was everyone's business. People knew when they saw a stranger walking down the street because everyone was familiar with their neighbors and often they interacted much like a large extended family.

Today the nature of society is vastly different. Mobility has created a situation where people no longer have roots which foster the development of community in the traditional sense. It is quite rare that individuals grow up in the same neighborhood that their parent did. People move quite often and many do not even know who their neighbors are, nor do they care. They feel that they should not invest their time in getting to know and care about others when either they or the others will be moving along to another place soon. Another barrier to the close interpersonal relationships that make for a strong sense of community is heterogeneity. It is virtually a law of human interpersonal relations that likes attract. Due to many sources of dissimilarity, such as ethnicity, race, background, and geographic origins, people lack the prerequisites of a common sense of identity, which can allow them to easily communicate with one another and thus develop significant interpersonal bonds. Thus, in many areas of our society people are precluded from forming bonds with their neighbors, bonds necessary for a sense of community to develop. As a result people do not look out for each other's property or concern themselves with what is happening next door. They do not choose to get involved in the community or any of its problems. If any type of problem arises people simply call the police. The police are the interveners and arbitrators whose job it is to fix things, to restore order, and protect individuals from each other. Further, people do not want to help the police or be involved in any way. After all, the police are *paid* to deal with problems, so why should citizens feel any obligation to get implicated?

In this cold and impersonal environment the task of policing becomes extremely difficult. The reason is that police can only be as effective and efficient as the citizens will help them to be. Getting citizen cooperation and support where there is very little sense of community is extremely important. As a result what has evolved is a new orientation to policing that is called community-oriented policing. In this approach the police are put into the position of having to create or at least facilitate a sense of community where there is little or none.

Although it is evident from the foregoing that today's society has rapidly changed, in many ways *policing* has not. The patrol officer on the beat remains largely unchanged, dealing with problems of all kinds in much the same way as he or she has done since policing was established in the mid-1800s.

However, many police administrators and academicians view this as a new era in policing. The now much maligned professional method of policing (which placed high priority on such factors as arrest rates, response times, and officer mobility) has come under serious challenge. As a result, "community policing" has evolved, attempting to improve crime control through a working partnership with the community.

The traditional style of policing is reactive, incident-driven, and focuses upon response rates and retrospective investigation. Several studies point to the need for a mode of policing oriented towards order-maintenance rather than enforcement. Data from cities of all sizes consistently establish that patrol officers spend from 70 to 85 percent of their time dealing with noncriminal matters. Studies have also found that the typical tour of duty for a police officer does not involve a single arrest. In short, much of what police already do on duty is unrelated to conventional law-enforcement activities. It involves other kinds of service activity.

Although the term "community policing" is of recent origin, surfacing only in the past decade, the development of a cooperative, police/community effort for the identification and solution of community problems is not of recent origin. It is probably akin to the policing style envisioned by Sir Robert Peel, organizer of the first professional police force in London in 1829. Peel envisioned the officers assigned to footbeats in the neighborhoods, enabling them to interact with the citizenry, and, as minions of the law, maintaining order. Today's complex society, however, has eschewed the Peelian style of policing rendering it a luxury in an era of mechanized saturation of beats. But more and more police agencies are undertaking a return to these earliest police methods.

Here, community institutions such as families, schools, and neighborhood and merchants associations are seen as key partners with the police in the creation of safe, secure communities. The community's views have greater status under community policing. It is basically a "return to the basics," deploying patrol officers in much the same way as Peel deployed them approximately 150 years ago.

The theory behind community policing is that the effectiveness of existing police tactics can be enhanced if the police increase the quantity and quality of citizen contacts and utilize thoughtful analyses of the precipitating causes of the offense. Professional and bureaucratic authority is lessened as citizens contribute more to definitions of problems and identification of solutions. The basic practices of traditional policing methods are supplemented, under community policing, with problem solving, information gathering, specialized forms of patrol, community input and organization, citizen education, foot patrol, and victim counseling.

Community policing is a philosophy and not just a specific tactic; it is proactive, decentralized, and designed to reduce crime and the fear of crime. Police officers are, under this philosophy, once again closely involved with the community. However, no single plan of implementation exemplifies community policing. It has been applied in various forms by police agencies in the United States and abroad, depending on the needs of the community and political and operational resources available to the police. The promotion of community, trust, and cooperation establishes the cornerstone of goals in community policing. Regardless of the approach, each program carries common benefits, including improved delivery of police services, improved police–community relations, and mutual resolutions to identifiable concerns.

In the decentralized community strategy, the patrol officers create for themselves the best responses to problems and, as generalists, become intimately involved with citizens. Studies show one clear implication of both foot patrol and fear reduction experiments: This closer contact reduces citizens' fear of crime. Controlling the fear of crime is also an important element of community-oriented policing. Immersing officers into the community is one of many strategies for controlling fear; studies now show that increased foot patrol reduces citizens' fears.

In the past decade a large number of communities have implemented the community-policing concept, with several of them carefully monitoring and documenting the effects. Following are some examples. Flint, Michigan, began its foot patrol experiment in 1979. The project dealt with the problems the community identified, and the patrol officer developed into a neighborhood problem-solver. Officers were encouraged to work problems through from beginning to end. Newport News, Virginia, entered community-oriented policing in 1983,

establishing that management and line officers can be successfully engaged in the process, with impressive results and with a more positive, productive atmosphere in the agency.

Since New York City began its Community Patrol Officer Program (CPOP) in 1984, it has been expanded to cover all of the city's seventy-five precincts. Designated Community Patrol Officers (CPOs) provide a full range of services within beats and work with residents to identify and hopefully solve local problems. Houston began the concept in 1982, including the commitment to fashion a partnership with each neighborhood (with changes in beats so as to conform more closely to "natural neighborhoods"), opening storefronts, and conducting an experiment in citizen fear reduction. Finally, community surveys in Reno, Nevada, and crime analyses in Seattle demonstrated that the program results in community perceptions improving and crime rates declining, respectively. Other programs, such as Neighborhood Watch, are related to community policing and have achieved a high degree of symbiosis with it.

With all of these benefits and the continued diversification of American society, it would appear that community-oriented policing in both theory and practice will be with us for quite a while.

Kenneth J. Peak
B. Grant Stitt

Bibliography

Johnson, T.A., G.E. Misner, and L.P. Brown. *The Police and Society: An Environment for Collaboration and Cooperation.* Englewood Cliffs, NJ: Prentice-Hall, 1981.

Kelling, G.L. "Perspectives on Policing." Monograph no. 1. *Police and Communities: The Quiet Revolution.* Washington, DC: National Institute of Justice, U.S. Department of Justice, 1988.

———, and M.H. Moore. "Perspectives on Policing." Monograph no. 4. *The Evolving Strategy of Policing.* Washington, DC: National Institute of Justice, U.S. Department of Justice, 1988.

———, R. Wasserman, and H. Williams. "Perspectives on Policing." Monograph no. 7. *Police Accountability and Community Policing.* Washington, DC: National Institute of Justice, U.S. Department of Justice, 1988.

Sparrow, M.K. "Perspectives on Policing." Monograph no. 9. *Implementing Community Policing*. Washington, DC: National Institute of Justice, U.S. Department of Justice, 1988.

Trojanowicz, R., and B. Bucqueroux. *Community Policing: A Contemporary Perspective*. Cincinnati: Anderson, 1990.

____, and D. Carter. *The Philosophy and Role of Community Policing*. East Lansing: Michigan State University, 1988.

Weatheritt, M. "Community Policing: Rhetoric or Reality?" In *Community Policing: Rhetoric or Reality?* Eds. J.D. Green and S.D. Mastrofski. New York: Praeger, 1988. 153–75.

Computer Crimes

Definitions of computer crime continue to change as the uses and misuses of computers expand into new areas. When computers were first introduced, computer crime was defined simply as a form of white-collar crime committed inside a computer system. As computer applications broadened—particularly into telecommunications—computer crimes likewise amplified and began to include offenses in which computers were either directly or indirectly involved in committing crimes. The most appropriate definition for computer crime today is any illegal act for which knowledge of computer technology is used to commit the offense. Thefts of hardware and software, manipulation of data, illegally accessing computer systems by telephone, and altering programs all fit under this definition. Another feature of this definition is that a computer can be either actively or passively involved in an offense. Illegally changing data in a database, destroying files, and using a hacking program to gain access into a system are examples of active involvement of a computer. By contrast, passive involvement means the computer is a tool in the offense, but computer crime charges may not be relevant.

Types of Computer Crime

As listed in Table 1, internal computer crimes are alterations to programs that result in the performance of unauthorized functions within a computer system. These offenses, usually committed by computer programmers, require an extensive amount of computer knowledge. A programmer may, for example, change an existing program so that it appears to operate normally but in fact performs unwanted functions whenever certain logical conditions are satisfied. Under these conditions, the programmer may erase files, change data, or cause the system to crash. Because these crimes have been around for years, they have been given names, such as Trojan horses, logic bombs, and trap doors, to indicate different programming techniques for performing the unauthorized functions. Viruses, the most recent type of internal computer crime, are sets of instructions that not only perform unauthorized functions, but also secretly attach themselves to other programs. With this self-propagating process, viruses spread through a system to other systems when the infected program is copied or transmitted.

Telecommunications crimes involve the illegal access or use of computer systems over telephone lines. A hacking program tries to find

---

TABLE 1

Categories of Computer Crimes

Internal Computer Crimes	*Support of Criminal Enterprises*	
Trojan horses	Databases to support drug distributions	
Logic bombs	Databases to record client information	
Trap doors		
Viruses		

Telecommunications Crimes	*Hardware/Software Thefts*	*Computer Manipulation Crimes*
Phreaking	Software piracy	Embezzlements
Hacking	Thefts of computers	Frauds
Illegal bulletin boards	Thefts of microcomputer chips	
Misuses of telephone systems	Thefts of trade secrets	

valid access codes for a computer system by continually calling the system with randomly generated codes. With a valid code found in this manner, the system can be accessed and costs diverted to an innocent customer. Phone phreaking is telephone fraud carried out by electronic devices that emit tones signaling normal long-distance transactions to the telephone system. These illegal devices trick the telephone system into believing that long-distance charges are being legitimately processed.

Computer manipulation crimes involve the changing of data or creation of records in a system for the specific advancement of another crime. Virtually all embezzlements in financial institutions require the creation of false accounts or modifications of data in existing accounts in order to perform the embezzlements.

Databases developed by illegal drug operators for tracking distribution fall into the category of support for criminal enterprises. Drug arrests have been made in which computerized information played an essential role in the conviction of the offenders. All too often, however, local police departments do not have the capabilities to analyze computer crime, or do not believe the information will be of particular value. Computer bulletin boards are another source of information to support illegal activities. Bulletin boards allow for the storing of information to be retrieved by someone dialing into the system. While storing information on bulletin boards may not by itself be illegal, the use of bulletin boards has certainly advanced many illegal activities.

A common offense is software piracy—defined as the unauthorized copying of a proprietary package. The most blatant form of piracy occurs when someone purchases a proprietary program, makes copies, and sells the copies for profit. Stealing trade secrets about products under development is another type of theft. In areas of the United States where there is a concentration of research and development, thefts of hardware from microcomputer chips to large mainframes are not uncommon. While hardware and software thefts may be dismissed as merely thefts on a grander scale, they are computer crimes because the computers are the target of an illegal activity. Income lost due to computer crime is difficult to assess. Accounting firms such as Ernst and Whinney in Cleveland estimate that high-tech thieves steal $3 to $5 billion annually in the United States alone.

Law Enforcement Response

Federal agencies have traditionally had more involvement with computer crimes than agencies at the state and local level. Legislative authority comes specifically from Section 1029 ("Fraud and Related Activity in Connection with Access Devices") and Section 1030 ("Fraud and Related Activity in Connection with Computers") of Title 18 of the United States Code. The Federal Bureau of Investigation, the Internal Revenue Service, and the United States Secret Service are the primary federal agencies that have trained investigators for tracking computer crime.

In 1979 only six states had computer crime statutes. The recent increase in the number of states having computer crime laws is indicative of legislative concern. A few state agencies have become active in computer crime investigation, notably the Illinois State Police and the Arizona State Attorney General's Office. Responses by local police departments and prosecutors' offices to computer crimes have been mixed. While some state agencies have provided training to detectives on how to detect and investigate computer crimes, most agencies have not. However, in the 1986 National Assessment Program survey, conducted by the Institute for Law and Justice, 75 percent of police chiefs and 63 percent of sheriffs rated computer crime investigation as a potentially significant cause of future workload in their departments. In large jurisdictions (over 500,000 population) the responses were even higher at 84 percent for police chiefs and 75 percent for sheriffs.

Alameda County, California

Because Alameda County (Silicon Valley) has long been one of the centers for hardware and software development, the District Attorney's Office has been involved in computer crime investigation for years. One attorney in the office is a nationally recognized expert who prosecuted his first computer crime case in 1974. He has also been instrumental in developing legislation in California on computer crimes. Microcomputers appear in the majority of cases handled by the office. As a consequence, there is a greater need for law enforcement agencies and attorneys in the county to understand "data preservation" for evidentiary purposes. As the office becomes more proficient more cases will go to trial and more attorney time will be required for prosecution. In 1987 the office filed thirty specific computer crime charges against alleged offenders. An investigator in the office (not an attorney) handles approximately thirty-five computer crime cases annually, involving embezzlement, frauds, hacking, and misuse of telephone systems. Through a search warrant a computer system is brought into the office if it is believed to be an "instrument to the crime." The investigator checks the system and determines what information can be obtained from it. In addition, the investigator serves as an important resource for law-enforcement agencies in the county that do not have the necessary expertise to pursue computer crime.

Baltimore County, Maryland, Police Department

The Economic/Computer Crime Unit here was established in March 1986 with the assignment of two investigators. The unit had been three years in the planning process, starting in July 1983 with a department committee formed to assess the impact of computer crime on the community. Two investigators were appointed to the unit after an extensive selection process. One investigator had been with the police department for over fifteen years and had specialized in the investigation of white-collar crimes, particularly embezzlements. This investigator had no computer background prior to the assignment. The other investigator, formerly with the Narcotics Unit of the department, had become personally interested in microcomputers as a hobby. The training received by these two investigators consisted of a three-month internship with the county's data-processing section, approximately two weeks spent with the data-processing section of the Baltimore Gas and Electric Company, and the introductory course on computer crime investigations offered by FLETC (Federal Law Enforcement Training Center). During the first year of operation, the unit members spent half their time on advertising their presence both internally to the department and externally to businesses. For officers in the department, a training bulletin was written describing the legal provisions of computer crimes in the state statutes and giving a procedure for officers to report computer crimes. The unit coordinates its cases with a prosecutor in the State Attorney's Office of the county. The standard operating procedure is to have the attorney involved in a case from the start to assist with search warrants, arrests, and case disposition. Over a two-year period

the unit handled forty-one computer cases including embezzlements, software piracies, bulletin board, and Trojan horse offenses. Thirty-five persons were arrested, all of whom pled guilty but in many instances the computer crime charges were dropped or reduced as part of the plea-bargaining process.

Dimensions of Computer Crime

Computer crime can occur anywhere in the country. With the proliferation of microcomputers for personal and business use, the opportunities for criminal activity have increased tremendously. A major problem, of course, is that these crimes are not being reported to the police, especially in those jurisdictions that do not have special investigative units. The characteristics of the persons committing the offenses depend on the type of computer crime. Hacking and phreaking are generally committed by juveniles and young adults. These individuals are usually males who are bored by school work, not socially outgoing, and have few outside activities. They frequently view their actions as a game and see no harm in beating a large comapny. As one prosecutor put it, they do not know the difference between "Pacman and Pac Bell." Disgruntled employees commit many internal computer crimes and thefts. These employees may have no other distinguishing features than overtly displaying their displeasure with the company. They often destroy files with their motive being revenge rather than financial gain. A third type of offender is the person with prior convictions for fraud who merely applies his or her experience and skill to perpetrate more fraud with the help of computers. Conversely, opportunists take advantage of their positions of trust and authority to commit embezzlement. These individuals rarely have arrest records and are not hardened criminals. When confronted by police the opportunists quickly admit their offenses.

The caseloads of computer crime units are lower than other investigative units. In the foregoing examples of Alameda County and Baltimore County, both areas where computer crime logically should thrive, the caseloads were indeed low. The primary reason for low caseloads is the inordinate amount of time required to develop a case. Telecommunications crimes are particularly complex. These cases may extend into several jurisdictions and even into other states. They always involve common carriers and local telephone companies that must be individually contacted for assistance. Investigators find that assistance is not always easy to obtain since the company may not be the actual victim and the request may be time consuming to fulfill. Internal computer crime cases are likewise tedious to substantiate.

The difficult issues in computer crime cases are twofold: (1) How does the officer applying for the warrant describe what he or she is looking for? (2) What are the limits upon what a searching officer can seize? The answer to the first question rests mostly in the description of the suspected crime. If the crime is adequately described, the application for a warrant can reasonably use generic descriptions of the instruments, fruits, and evidence of the crime likely to be found in the place to be searched. The application can state that the search is for computers and related equipment, supporting documentation, printouts, code books, and the like without specifying manufacturer, models, specific programs and the like. The limits on the scope of a seizure are more problematic. Computer disks and diskettes have such large storage capacities they can easily contain a great deal of information that has nothing to do with the subject matter of the investigation. A troublesome example is the storage of the suspect data in a computer system belonging to someone who has no connection with the crime being investigated, such as an accounting firm that keeps records for the suspect on a hard disk with the records of hundreds of other persons. Further complications arise when suspects have taken security measures designed not simply to protect the contents of their files, but to destroy them when an unauthorized user tries to access them.

Depending on the type of case, computer crime charges may or may not be the primary prosecutorial focus. With internal computer crimes it is the main charge without question. However, even with embezzlements, computer crime charges should be placed against the suspected offender when there is reasonable belief that such crime has been committed. There are several reasons for including computer crime charges with other offenses. First, the investigative unit should receive credit in these arrests for having sufficient evidence to include the charges. Second, the prosecutor may be able to make good use of the charges in the plea-bargaining process. Finally, computer crime charges will create judicial awareness of the significance of the offense.

J. Thomas McEwen

Bibliography

Arkin, Stanley S., ed. *Prevention and Prosecution of Computer and High Technology Crime.* Oakland, CA: Matthew Bender, 1988.

Bequai, August. *Technocrimes.* Lexington, MA: D.C. Heath, 1987.

Combating Computer Crime: Prevention, Detection, Investigation. New York: Chantico, 1992.

Conly, Catherine H. *Organizing for Computer Crime Investigation and Prosecution.* Washington, DC: U.S. Department of Justice, National Institute of Justice, 1989.

McEwen, J. Thomas. *Dedicated Computer Crime Units.* Washington, DC: U.S. Department of Justice, National Institute of Justice, 1989.

Nicholson, C.K., and R. Cunningham. "Computer Crime." *American Criminal Law Review* 28 (1991): 393–405.

Parker, Donn B. *Computer Crime: Criminal Justice Resource Manual.* Menlo Park, CA: SRI International, 1989.

———. *Computer Crime: Investigation and Prosecution.* Menlo Park, CA: Stanford Research Institute, 1989.

Sterling, Bruce. *The Hacker Crackdown: Law and Disorder on the Electronic Frontier.* New York: Bantam Books, 1992.

Computer Technology

The use of computers in law enforcement has been quite extensive during the last two decades. In 1967 the FBI first implemented the well-known National Crime Information Center (NCIC), which has served as the basis for development of national files on wanted persons, stolen vehicles, stolen weapons, and other valuable items.

Since that early beginning United States law enforcement agencies at all levels have sought to expand applications of computer technology in order to: (1) serve appropriate police functions; (2) improve the efficiency of current operations; and (3) allow the realization of new opportunities for service with the emerging technology. As the sophistication of computers and related equipment has advanced and the cost has decreased, police departments have benefited from already developed and tested automated processes.

Since the first edition of this volume was published in 1989, many new applications of computers in policing have evolved and some exciting directions for the future have unfolded. For instance, multijurisdictional Automated Fingerprint Identification Systems (AFIS) have been developed; numerous interfunctional and regional general purpose criminal justice information systems have been designed and implemented; and several state and one national database dealing with violent criminals and serial killers have been put in place.

Additionally, the Federal Bureau of Investigation's recent decision to redesign the Uniform Crime Reports is based on the assumption that police departments with modern computer-based information systems can provide the more extensive and complex crime data specified by the National Incident-Based Reporting System (NIBRS). The experiences over the past ten to fifteen years have led the FBI to conclude that computer readable data from all police agencies can be expected at a level of detail and at a quality level sufficient for the newly designed system.

In reviewing the systems previously designed and implemented by law enforcement agencies and to provide a framework for understanding these new types of systems, it is convenient to analyze such systems according to the following framework: Administrative systems; Data retrieval systems; Analytical systems; Process control systems.

Administrative Systems

As in most large organizations, police departments have found that computers can be very effective in handling administrative functions and relieving employees of routine and boring clerical tasks. Computers have been used in personnel records handling, budgeting activities, payroll processing, and a variety of other administrative duties.

The recent development of word-processing systems and the reduction in costs for processing equipment and information storage have created additional opportunities for administrative applications. In the future it will be commonplace for all large- and medium-sized police departments to have word-processing systems available for supporting all administrative tasks as well as clerical activities in individual bureaus and units that require comprehensive report preparation.

Data Retrieval Systems

Data retrieval systems include the widely recognized NCIC system noted above. These have as their primary function the provision of individual records or items of data for immediate use in departmental operations. Patrol officers may use these systems to provide suspect, victim, or witness identification, or other police personnel may employ such systems in administrative support activities.

For instance, when a police officer stops a vehicle, it is often desirable or necessary to check the vehicle registration and the driver's history to determine whether the person is dangerous and/or whether current arrest warrants in other cities and states require his detention. Additionally, the computer may provide information listing the vehicle as stolen or other data of importance in evaluating the current situation.

This entire process may include an inquiry made through the NCIC, a state data bank, and a regional or local data-processing system. Basically, the NCIC provides information on (1) stolen property; (2) wanted persons; (3) missing persons; (4) federal and state criminal history; (5) information from the Criminalistics Laboratory Information System; and (6) information from the Canadian Warrant File. State and local data-processing systems may provide information on a wide variety of additional subjects which are not included in NCIC.

Information may be provided to the officer in several ways. First, the officer may request information on vehicles and/or drivers over the police radio system. The dispatcher or other officers located in the communications center receives the request from the officer and makes an inquiry by terminal to the NCIC. Information is then relayed back to the officer by radio when responses from the different levels of the system are received.

A second method for initiating an inquiry is through a mobile digital terminal (MDT) located in the police vehicle. Through an MDT officers can enter inquiries directly and receive responses on the terminal without communicating with the dispatching center. While mobile digital terminals have been experimental during the past several years, they are becoming more common and probably will be universally implemented in patrol vehicles before the year 2000.

The inquiry made by the officer, or by the information clerk, will normally be routed through a regional "message switching" system to a state information center, which also contains "message switching" equipment for routing the inquiry to the NCIC. An NCIC response will then be routed back to the inquiring department along with any other information requested and available from the state databases.

This latter category of data sources may include files of warrants from throughout the state that are not allowed in the NCIC, driver's history, criminal history, or other data. A wide range of files may be provided by the state system based on policies in each state to supplement databases maintained at the national level.

The NCIC is currently accessed by all states through terminals linked to the NCIC directly or through the state message-switching systems. The approach used during the last decade has been to utilize message-switching networks in each state for channeling requests for information from local police departments to the FBI and for routing responses back to the local police agency. This procedure has eased the burden on the overworked national system by consolidating information requests for processing through high-speed lines and microwave transmission.

Likewise, at the local level "regional" or "local" message-switching systems exist to consolidate calls for routing to state data banks. These systems not only provide a routing of data between state agencies and local departments, but may be used to route requests to search other local databases. For instance, a county government may maintain a listing of persons on probation for access by police agencies while a municipality may maintain a file on habitual criminals or repeat offenders. An effective data-retrieval system would provide immediate data on all criminal activities by accessing appropriate databases in the overall network.

Additional data files included under data-retrieval systems are pawn-shop tickets, field-interrogation reports, traffic tickets, and specific files on police reports such as offense reports, arrest reports, and incident reports. Depending on the sophistication and design of the system, these unique databases may be automatically cross-referenced to determine overlap and other patterns.

More recently developed systems have emphasized the creation of specialized files for such purposes as tracking drug dealers and drug operations, identifying figures associated with organized crime groups, identifying and tracking members of youth street gangs, and the matching of fingerprints on a multijurisdictional basis. Many of these systems have simply evolved as the need for dealing with specific problems has confronted police departments.

Analytical Systems

Computerized systems designed to perform analytical functions usually evolve from operations data collected through the normal course of organizational activity (for instance, from dispatching or regular police reports). Additionally, some analytical and research-oriented programs may be separately designed and operated (for instance, through collection of survey data or occasional one-shot data collection efforts). The most efficient and up-to-date systems utilize information gathered through the normal course of departmental operations.

Examples of functions served by these analytical systems are criminal investigation, crime analysis, research and planning, management analysis and evaluation, manpower allocation, budgetary analysis and auditing, and other systems or programs aimed at providing summary data for review and evaluation purposes.

Analytical systems emphasize general information, summary data, and statistical analysis. As contrasted with data-retrieval programs, which emphasize retrieval of a single record from very large databases, the analytical systems are intended to provide a basis for general decision-making, management evaluation, exception reporting, and overall departmental planning. Planning and crime analysis supported by these methods may be either short range or long range and may concern individual departmental functions or total departmental operations.

The analytical functions in police operations, including the investigation function, have benefited from the development and utilization of microcomputers. Personal computers may be used for the immediate development and analysis of small or large databases. These operations can be completed in a manner that ensures the security of police records and limits access to those with a need for specific information.

Process Control Systems

During the past decade many police agencies have implemented a variety of systems to support and control police operations. Beginning in the late 1960s, the larger police departments began using computers to aid in dispatching, manpower allocation, crime analysis, and a variety of other operations on a real-time basis. Some of these activities were routine for police departments while others supported decision-making on a unique or nonroutine basis.

The following description of computer-assisted dispatching, commonly termed "CAD" systems, provides a basic overview of the programs being implemented in police departments today and the command and control approaches that will be of primary interest to systems developers during the 1990s. Most systems use the basic design outlined below with some exceptions for local conditions. For instance, some CAD systems may not have geographic base files and others lack support files that save considerable dispatcher time and effort.

The basic flow of activities in command and control systems is quite similar in all departments. This process might be described as follows:

1. The police department (command and control center or dispatching center) receives a call for service from a citizen. This call will normally be handled by a civilian or sworn officer.
2. After preliminary evaluation of the call, the complaint taker types complaint information into a computer terminal for processing by the system and for routing to a dispatcher.
3. The file on the complaint is then routed to the computer for certain types of information and processing activities. For instance, when the system is equipped with a geographic base file, it can locate an address within certain police geographic areas for assignment purposes. The computer attaches information regarding the geographic areas to the basic record before routing the complaint record to the dispatcher.
4. Based on the geographic location of the incident and the geographic codes assigned by the computer, the system will then conduct an analysis of the officer availability file to determine recommended assignments. Should the officer assigned to the particular area identified by the system be unavailable for service, the computer will identify the officer assigned to the closest beat and recommend this officer as a substitute.

5. The program may also identify back-up officers in the same manner as described above. Some systems are programmed to recommend at least six officers to respond to an incident with the extra officers available for back-up service if necessary.
6. Some computer programs may also provide additional support at this point. For instance, they may make automatic searches of regional, state, or national databases to determine whether persons or objects involved in the incident are listed and the reason for their inclusion. This is especially valuable in situations where vehicles are reported stolen or involved in criminal offenses and identifying information can be immediately provided to the complaint taker by the reporting citizen.
7. The computer may also use the geographic base file to identify other information about the area that may be useful to the officer servicing the incident. For instance, the identification of hazardous materials within the area or within a particular structure can be of value to an officer. Registration of weapons, previous offenses of occupants, or threats against officers from occupants of specific residences may be provided to the officer through automatic search of local files available in the computer system.

After the computer has completed its tasks in preparing the incident record for handling by the dispatcher, the system routes the information to the communications center. In most applications the incident routing would be to a specific dispatcher who has responsibility for the area of the city identified by the geographic base file system.

Upon receiving the record, the dispatcher uses the information provided by the system to decide on a police unit for handling the incident. This may be the unit suggested by the computer, or it may be another unit that, for some other reason, is selected by the dispatcher. In most systems the dispatcher is not bound by the recommendation of the computer but is required to consider the suggestions before making modifications. After making an assignment, the dispatcher will then enter information to update files on officer availability and on the specific incident being handled.

After the dispatcher has entered information to update unit availability files, the system logs the call into its history file with the precise time that each event occurred for later management analysis. When the assigned police officer has completed the call, the dispatcher will again add information to update the unit availability file as well as other files supporting the master record started by the initial call entry. The master record should then indicate that a written report will later be required of the officer and it should indicate what disposition will be made of the record in this particular incident.

The following advantages of computer-assisted dispatching systems have been demonstrated over the past several years:

1. Automatic logging of messages received by the communications center and full documentation of all transactions that occur.
2. Automatic routing of messages to dispatchers from complaint takers when these two functions are separate (as is the case in most systems).
3. Identification of "hazardous addresses" or "common places" when files on these subjects are available within the computerized system.
4. Automatic prioritization of calls for service based on criteria set by the department.
5. Identification by the computer of duplicate requests for service by comparison of location of the call and the type of call.
6. Maintenance of information on the status of all patrol units and their location when assigned to a call by the communications center.
7. Automatic coding of addresses according to police geographic areas and other geo-codes required in servicing incidents.
8. Accurate time stamping of all activities for use in operations analysis and manpower planning.
9. Immediate availability of information on all incidents previously handled by officers or currently being processed by officers either in the communications center or in the field.
10. A general reduction in clerical work within the communications center thus allowing dispatcher concentration on more important and pressing activities.

CAD systems extend more authority to field units since they can be provided with access to information on the operation of their units at all times and can better plan for future events. Commanders in substations may influence the decisions of communications center personnel since they are supplied with information on a continuous basis.

Some cities have successfully linked a "direct field entry reporting system" into computer-assisted dispatching. Using this approach, the patrol officer telephones the incident report to an information center after completing the assignment. The police report is then directly and immediately entered into the computer system and linked to the original call for service record. The officer's report—after analysis for completeness and accuracy by a reviewing officer—is immediately printed out on terminals in sections of the department that have a need for the report.

Some cities have also experimented with what are termed "automatic vehicle location" systems (AVL). These systems seek to provide immediate and precise information on the location of a patrol vehicle through use of a computer terminal and a map overlay. A variety of systems have been tested over the last two decades, but they are still considered to be experimental. Many cities have abandoned earlier efforts to fully implement such systems due to cost and technological problems.

Current and Future Developments
Computer technology will undoubtedly impact police service during the next several decades. Some specific expectations for future systems applications include:

1. further development of large national data banks on homicides that might be part of serial killings;
2. use of mini or personal computers for processing local investigative data;
3. expanded use of word processing systems for report writing, administration, and analysis;
4. further development of regional and state files on habitual offenders and career criminals to enhance surveillance and apprehension;
5. increased use of mobile digital terminals (MDT) in patrol units and other police vehicles;

6. expanded use of direct field entry reporting systems for completing police reports and for speeding information transfer into the police communications process; and

7. further development and improvement in fingerprint matching and retrieval systems.

James W. Stevens

Bibliography

Archambeault, Williams G., and Betty J. Archambeault. *Computers in Criminal Justice Administration and Management.* Cincinnati: Anderson, 1984.

Burns, Scott. "EDS Helps Effort to Take Byte out of Crime." *Dallas Morning News* (May 11, 1993).

Clede, Bill. "Micro-Computers on Patrol." *Law and Order* (September 1986): 36–42.

Federal Bureau of Investigation. *FBI Law Enforcement Bulletin* 52 (March 1983). Issue devoted to criminal justice information systems.

Howlett, James B., Kenneth A. Hanfland, and Robert K. Ressler, "The Violent Criminal Apprehension Program." *FBI Law Enforcement Bulletin* 55 (December 1986): 14–22.

International Association of Chiefs of Police. *The Police Chief* 53 (May 1986). Series of articles in this issue on police information systems.

Kraemer, Kenneth L., and John Leslie King, eds. *Computers in Local Government: Police and Fire.* Pennsauken, NJ: Auerbach, 1981.

Neudorfer, Charles D. "Fingerprint Automation: Progress in the FBI's Identification Division," *FBI Law Enforcement Bulletin* 55 (March 1986): 3–8.

Stevens, James W. "Computer Assisted Dispatching." *Proceedings of the Sixth Annual Law Enforcement Data Processing Symposium.* IACP. 1982: 101–25.

———. "Identification and Processing of Career Criminals: The Police Role." *Computers, Environment, and Urban Systems* 8 (2)(1983): 63–70.

———. "Computerization in Law Enforcement." *Police Studies* 7 (1984): 209–18.

Stratton, Neil R.M. "Birth of an Information Network." *FBI Law Enforcement Bulletin* 62 (February 1993): 19–22.

U.S. Bureau of Justice Statistics. *The 1986 Directory of Automated Criminal Justice Information Systems.* Rockville, MD: Justice Statistics Clearinghouse/NCJRS, 1986.

Waldron, Joseph, et al. *Computers in Criminal Justice: An Introduction to Small Computers.* Cincinnati: Anderson, 1983.

———. *Microcomputers in Criminal Justice: Current Issues and Applications.* Cincinnati: Anderson, 1987.

Constable

In many respects constables perform duties similar to sheriffs. They serve criminal and civil legal papers, transport prisoners, collect back taxes and debts owed the government, and provide emergency assistance when needed. Different from sheriffs, constables no longer retain the peace-keeping or criminal investigatory powers they once had. Thirty-seven states mandate the office of constable; nine states never recognized the office; and the remaining states employed constables at one time, but no longer. In some states the office is elective, in others, appointive. Constables serve in both urban and rural areas and like sheriffs have the power to deputize.

History

The word constable comes from the Latin, "*comes stabuli,*" meaning "head of the stables." In ancient Rome the first men to perform the role of constable were trustworthy servants who guarded the royal stable and armaments. The French introduced the position of constable into British common law, following the Norman invasion of the British Isles in A.D. 1066. With more expansive duties than stable groom, the transported constables kept the militia and the king's armaments in a state of readiness to defend village communities throughout England. Before long the Lord High Constable emerged to represent the king in all military affairs and wield considerable power. In France the same elevated personage enjoyed even greater authority. The French constable stood next in line to the king on matters of state. On a lower level English constables, public civil officers as opposed to military, acted as a legion of enforcers for the Lord High Constable. The Blackstone Commentaries on the Common Law provided for a broad range of constable duties and powers. Constables were entrusted with collecting taxes, arresting lawbreakers, conducting searches, transporting prisoners, and serving all criminal and civil papers. Even the local apothecary had to open his books and records to the constable.

In the American colonies the constable was the first law-enforcement officer. His duties varied from place to place according to the particular needs of the people he served. Usually, the constable sealed weights and measures, surveyed land, announced marriages, and executed all warrants. Additionally, he meted out physical punishment and kept the peace. The first constable on record was Joshua Pratt of Plymouth colony (1634). His primary responsibility was to maintain vigilance against disorder by overseeing the Watch and Ward, the Ward during the day and the Watch at night. Curiously, New England settlers went so far as to appoint Indian constables who supervised Indian deputies under their command. In populated cities like New York a large contingent of constables went about their duties. The indomitable Jacob Hays served as high constable in New York for over forty years and built a reputation for stringent law enforcement. Farther west in youthful cities like St. Louis, the constabulary was the precursor of regular police forces. Being the first law enforcement officers in the colonies did not guarantee job security. As with sheriffs, the rise of centralized police departments by the mid-1800s appeared to diminish the need for their services. Nevertheless, constables have survived another 150 years.

Lack of Cohesion
The National Constables Association (NCA) was founded in 1973 in New Jersey as the National Police Constables Association (NPCA). Little came of the NPCA, so in 1976 several dedicated members moved the association to Pennsylvania where it was incorporated as the NCA. Dropping "Police" from the title was a show of independence that may have estranged cordial relations. Seemingly, police, sheriffs, and constables cannot get along with one another. If government funding is low, police believe they should get the lion's share. Not only money but authority and jurisdiction are at stake. Some police see sheriffs as too power-hungry and constables as taking bread from their mouths, while sheriffs and constables remind police of their rich heritages and cannot understand why their brethren are so monopolistically bent. Speaking on behalf of the NCA, Pennsylvania representative Peter H. Kostmayer underscored the value of constables to the nation:

> More and more local municipalities are finding it increasingly difficult to pay for the salary and benefits of new patrolmen. Constables are legally self-employed contractors who provide their own liability insurance, health insurance, the use of their own emergency vehicles, and their own uniform and radio communications equipment. . . .In all cases, the constable can be paid for services on a salaried basis, an hourly basis, or on a fee plus mileage basis at almost no cost to the taxpayer.

Since constables are sanctioned by law to carry out noncrime prevention duties under the direction of the chief of police, to serve courts papers, and to perform a myriad of other duties for the county commissioners and local municipalities, they should be in great demand. Those are jobs regular police disdain and should not have to do anyway given their main charge of crime prevention. However, sporadic friction continues to separate constables, police, and sheriffs. The national census of constables and deputy-constables is unknown. Estimates for Pennsylvania, the home state of the National Constables Association, run as high as 5,000 professionals. The NCA has proposed to President Bill Clinton that constable positions be made part of a jobs package to stimulate the economy (1993). The proposal asks for 3 million new positions that would ensure the continuance of constables and in the bargain be cost effective to government. If today the United States still adhered to the English model, constables would be full-fledged police as they once were. Throughout Great Britain police forces are called constabularies and the highest ranking officer is the chief constable. The exception is the London Metropolitan Police Force, New Scotland Yard, administered by a commissioner, his deputies and assistants, along with a group of commanders.

Information provided by
the National Constables Association.

Constitutional Right to Privacy
The Supreme Court has established that the Constitution provides all Americans a right to privacy. The courts, however, have held that

public servants have a lesser expectation of privacy from government intrusion than does the ordinary citizen. In balancing the privacy rights of police officers with the needs of law-enforcement agencies, the courts have allowed law-enforcement agencies much greater discretion to regulate areas where Americans typically have a high expectation of privacy.

Up through the 1950s, the Supreme Court applied the privilege doctrine, which gave public employers broad authority to regulate the on-the-job and off-the-job conduct of public employees, to the public employment relationship. For example, most public agencies prohibited employees from publicly criticizing the management of their agencies. Other public employers prohibited their employees from engaging in either private or public conduct which violated commonly accepted moral standards. Law-enforcement agencies, not surprisingly, required employees to adhere to particularly strict standard of conduct rules.

The Supreme Court, through a series of landmark cases decided during the 1960s and 1970s, transformed the constitutional relationship between public employers and their employees. The Court issued rules that prohibited public employers from arbitrarily restricting the exercise of constitutional rights by public employees either on or off the job. The First Amendment, according to the Court, gave public employees the right to speak out on matters of public interest and to join organizations of their choice. The Fourth Amendment restricted unreasonable searches and seizures of public employees. The Fifth and Fifteenth Amendments guaranteed some public employees procedural due process in personnel actions.

Throughout the period of judicial expansion of the constitutional rights of public employees, the Supreme Court recognized that public employers continued to have authority to limit the exercise of fundamental constitutional rights by public employees, if the need to protect the public interest outweighed the right of public employees to exercise their rights.

The Privacy Rights Revolution

Besides recognition of the right of public employees to exercise traditional constitutional rights, the constitutional rights revolution led to judicial recognition of the privacy rights of public servants. However, public employers still have considerable discretion: (1) to investigate the backgrounds of applicants for public positions; (2) to establish rules of conduct regulating the on- and off-the-job conduct of public employees; and (3) to conduct searches of public employees and equipment used by public employees for evidence of misconduct and poor job performance.

Judicial recognition of privacy rights began with the decision in *Griswold v. Connecticut* (1965), when the Supreme Court ruled that the constitutional right to personal privacy prohibited states from restricting access to contraceptives by married individuals. According to Justice Douglas, who wrote the opinion, the right is not explicit, but rather is to be found in various penumbras and emanations from the Bill of Rights and the First, Fourth, Fifth, Ninth, and Fourteenth (concept of personal liberty) Amendments.

The Supreme Court, since the *Griswold* decision, has extended the right to privacy to prohibit unreasonable governmental interference with marriage, procreation, abortion, contraception outside the marriage relationship, family relationships, and child rearing and education (*Dronenburg v. Zech* [1984]).

The privacy rights revolution, however, did not absolutely prohibit the states from using their respective police powers to regulate the sexual conduct of married and unmarried individuals. In 1986, the Supreme Court ruled in *Bowers v. Hardwick* that enforcement of Georgia's sodomy law did not violate the constitutional right to privacy. On the other hand, a number of lower federal courts have required public employers to demonstrate a link between the personal information collected from job applicants and the position being filled.

In determining whether a public employer has violated the privacy rights of a prospective or actual employee, the courts consider two basic issues. First, does the employee have an expectation of privacy in the area subject to regulation. Second, does the need for greater governmental efficiency, improved public safety, and the importance of protecting public confidence in government outweigh governmental interference with an established privacy right.

The list of privacy issues involving public employees includes: (1) prohibitions on conduct to the prejudice of good order and discipline; (2) requests for personal information related to pre-employment screening or promotions; (3) physical searches for evidence of work-related materials; and (4) mandatory production of bodily fluids.

Despite the privacy rights revolution, law-enforcement agencies continue to argue that they have a well-recognized interest in the performance and reputation of police officers. Consequently, most law-enforcement agencies set high standards of personal integrity for new agents or officers. The objective of having law-enforcement personnel serve as community role models often comes into conflict with the desire of law-enforcement personnel to have the same freedoms as other citizens.

Law Enforcement, Public Trust, and the Privacy Paradox

Because law-enforcement agencies at all levels of government enforce policies denying public employment for conduct which is illegal, immoral, or unbecoming an officer, they have faced strong criticism for violating the privacy rights of their employees. Consequently, a disproportionate percentage of public employee privacy rights cases have involved law-enforcement agencies.

Sexual Histories and Law Enforcement Personnel

The process of hiring law-enforcement personnel and the enforcement of departmental codes of conduct most often present sexual privacy issues for law-enforcement managers.

Law-enforcement agencies frequently ask applicants for sworn positions whether they ever participated in illegal sexual activity. Many police departments disqualify individuals who admit to illegal sexual acts from becoming sworn officers. An often cited rationale is that applicants who commit illegal acts before becoming a law-enforcement officer are much more likely to become blackmail targets and, in any event, have demonstrated disrespect for the rule of law. In *Wells v. City of Petersburg* (1990), the Fourth Circuit held that a police department may ask applicants questions about prior homosexual activity.

In other words, law-enforcement agencies continue to inquire into the private sexual activities of applicants and employees as part of the process of screening out those individuals who have committed illegal acts. Supporters of the illegal-acts disqualification rule argue that individuals who commit illegal acts have no right or moral authority to enforce laws by controlling the conduct of others. According to

this line of reasoning, illegal sexual acts should be treated like any other type of illegal conduct. As a result, state and federal courts have shown extreme reluctance to limit the right of law-enforcement agencies to deny individuals law-enforcement positions because of prior illegal sexual acts.

Federal courts, however, look much more carefully at law-enforcement agencies that request job applicants to provide general personal sexual information as part of the application process. In *Thorne v. City of El Segundo* (1983), the Ninth Circuit ruled that a police department violated the constitutional privacy rights of an applicant when an interviewer asked her questions with respect to her sexual history.

Judicial interpretations of the constitutional right to privacy sharply restrict the type of information law-enforcement agencies may collect with respect to the sexual histories of both job applicants and employees. Consequently, law-enforcement agencies may only request sexual history information relating to illegal sexual acts or other job related standards of conduct.

Sexual Codes of Conduct and Law-Enforcement Personnel

The revolution in public employee constitutional rights led the vast majority of public organizations to cease regulation of the off-the-job sexual conduct of their employees. Prior to the revolution, many public employers had enforced strict moral turpitude clauses. In contrast, many law-enforcement agencies continue to enforce codes of conduct which include prohibitions on certain types of off-duty sexual activities. Federal and state courts, as a general rule, still permit law-enforcement agencies to deny employment to individuals who have engaged in illegal sexual conduct.

First, many law-enforcement agencies prohibit the employment of homosexuals. The Supreme Court in *Bowers v. Hardwick* (1986) held that the Constitution did not prohibit states from enforcing sodomy prohibitions. Law-enforcement agencies operating in states that make sodomy illegal typically prohibit the employment of individuals who admit to being homosexual. Although a number of states and local governments have enacted laws prohibiting private and public employers from discriminating against job applicants on the basis of sexual preference, the Supreme Court has refused to find that the Constitution prohibits public employers from discriminating against individuals on the basis of sexual preference.

Second, many law-enforcement agencies prohibit employees from engaging in illegal sexual activities. The United States Court of Appeals for the Ninth Circuit, in *Fleisher v. City of Signal Hill* (1987), upheld the dismissal of a probationary police officer for having had sexual relations with a minor prior to being hired as a police officer, even though the officer had disclosed the relationship to the police officer who had conducted his employment interview.

In *Fugate v. Phoenix Civil Service Board* (1986), the Ninth Circuit upheld the dismissal of an officer for having had sexual relations with a prostitute. The illegality of prostitution played a major role in the decision of the federal court.

The Virginia State Police fired a state trooper for maintaining an adulterous relationship with a neighbor (*Suddarth v. Slane* 1982). Although adultery is a crime under Virginia law, local prosecutors generally refuse to prosecute individuals for adulterous conduct. In *Fabio v. Civil Service Commission of City of Philadelphia* (1980), a Pennsylvania court upheld the firing of a Pennsylvania officer for adultery. Even though Pennsylvania law no longer makes adultery a crime, it is still considered an immoral act (Annotation 1981/1988). Moreover, the Pennsylvania courts do not seem to distinguish between public and private immorality in cases in which the private misconduct leads to public disgrace (*Faust v. Police Civil Service Commission* [1975]; *Richter v. Civil Service Commission* [1978]).

Federal courts have found it much more difficult to resolve the question of whether law-enforcement agencies could constitutionally prohibit cohabitation between police officers. Many law-enforcement agencies prohibit fraternization between supervisors and their subordinate officers. In support of this position, these law-enforcement agencies argue that fraternization policies prevent the development of a conflict of interest between the responsibilities of a supervisor and any personal relationships that might have developed between the supervisor and a subordinate. Other supporters of fraternization policies argue that these policies help to protect subordinate employees from being harassed for sexual favors by their supervisors.

In *Shawgo v. Spradlin* (1983), the Fifth Circuit Court of Appeals upheld the firing of a police officer for living with a policewoman. The Sixth Circuit, on the other hand, held in *City of North Muskegon v. Briggs* (1984) that a police department violated the privacy rights of an officer when it fired a married police officer for living with another woman. The Supreme Court, in both cases, refused to overturn the decisions.

A review of cases dealing with the sexual privacy rights of law-enforcement personnel indicates that, unless state or local law preempts regulation, law-enforcement agencies have considerable discretion to enforce prohibitions against law-enforcement personnel committing illegal or immoral sexual acts. Moreover, law-enforcement agencies may also prohibit supervisors from having sexual relations with those individuals whom they supervise.

Personal Information and the Right to Privacy

The Supreme Court, as noted, has held that public employers may not place unreasonable restrictions on the exercise of First Amendment rights by public employees. Specifically, public employers must respect the freedom of speech and association rights of their personnel.

Besides prohibiting public employers from punishing public employees for the exercise of their First Amendment rights, the First Amendment also places restrictions on the type of information public employers can constitutionally require job applicants to provide. In addition, the Constitution requires public employers to protect the confidentiality of job related personal information.

In determining whether requests for personal information violate the privacy rights of public employees or prospective employees, the federal courts historically have applied a test which balances the public interest in requiring the disclosure against the potential injury to the individual caused by the disclosure with due consideration of the adequacy of agency safeguards to prevent unauthorized disclosure.

In *Fraternal Order of Police, Lodge No. 5 v. City of Philadelphia* (1987), the Court of Appeals for the Third Circuit held that the police department could require applicants for the police department's special investigation unit to provide information regarding their physical and mental condition as well as personal financial data. The court, however, blocked the use of the questionnaire until the police department established adequate safeguards to prevent unauthorized disclosure of the personal information.

The *Fraternal Order of Police* decision makes clear that the courts will not grant public employers, including law-enforcement agencies, unlimited discretion to collect personal information from prospective job applicants and employees seeking promotions. Consequently, law-enforcement agencies must take great care in gathering personal information with respect to job applicants.

The Fourth Amendment and the Public Employee

The Fourth Amendment provides public employees the greatest privacy rights protection. It protects both private citizens and public employees from unreasonable searches and seizures by public actors. Mandatory drug testing and searches of the property of public employees present the most frequent Fourth Amendment issues faced by public employers.

Work Place Searches

Public employers, increasingly, face the problem of determining the scope of work place searches associated with investigations of misconduct or poor performance. The Supreme Court in the 1985 case of *O'Connor v. Ortega* ruled that public employees do have an expectation of privacy in work place areas used by employees. However, the Court held that public employers also have a legitimate interest to conduct investigations of work-related misconduct.

A plurality of the Court in *O'Connor* ruled that the courts must determine on a case-by-case basis the expectation of privacy the public employee has in different areas of a public work place. The majority in the *O'Connor* decision held that public employees do not have a high expectation of privacy in desk drawers and file cabinets because employees understood or should have understood that their employers might need to search desks and file cabinets for work related materials. Therefore, the employers had the authority to conduct a warrantless search of the desk drawers and file cabinet of the plaintiff employee as long as the search was reasonable under the circumstances.

In the aftermath of the *O'Connor* decision, challenges to public work place searches have increased. Lower federal courts, however, have generally upheld the constitutionality of work place searches by public employers searching for evidence of work-related misconduct. The

Sixth Circuit Court of Appeals, in *American Postal Workers Union, Columbus Area Local AFL-CIO v. United States Postal Service* (1989), upheld warrantless searches of the lockers of Postal Service employees largely because the Postal Service previously notified their employees that they retained the right to search the lockers.

Drug Testing and the Fourth Amendment

The Supreme Court in *National Treasury Employees Union v. Von Rabb* (1989) issued new mandatory drug testing guidelines for public employers. Prior to the *National Treasury Employees Union* decision, the courts had required public employers to have, at a minimum, individualized reasonable suspicion of illegal substance use before requiring an employee to take a drug test.

The war on drugs and increased concern by employers over liability for actions taken by employees using drugs led to an explosion in private and public sector drug testing during the 1980s. Public and private sector employers faced significantly different legal environments in implementing mandatory drug testing. Public employers, in contrast to their private sector counterparts, faced the major problem of overcoming the Fourth Amendment and its ban against unreasonable searches and seizures.

The federal courts, through the mid-1980s, ruled that the Fourth Amendment prohibited random drug testing of most public employees. With the exception of public employees employed by public transportation agencies, the courts ruled that public employers must have, at a minimum, individualized reasonable suspicion of drug use before requiring an employee to take a drug test. This requirement made it next to impossible for public employers to implement random drug-testing programs.

The majority of the high court, in *National Treasury Employees Union v. Von Rabb*, accepted the argument of the Customs Service that employees applying for positions requiring them to carry firearms, make use of classified material, and be involved with drug interdiction should be subject to random drug tests.

The *National Treasury Employees Union* decision represented a partial victory for advocates of public sector random drug testing. The decision, however, did reaffirm a previous holding that public employers do have an expectation of privacy in their persons while on the job and that public employers must have a compelling reason to expect the courts to permit searches of public employees without reasonable suspicion.

Conclusion

The constitutional rights revolution forced public and private employers to revise their personnel policies and practices with respect to the right of their employees to exercise their established constitutional rights. Despite the constitutional rights revolution, public agencies face the problem of maintaining public confidence in the integrity of their organizations.

Federal and state courts have failed to come up with a simple solution of how to balance the need to maintain public confidence in government without interfering with the exercise of legitimate constitutional rights by public employees. Nevertheless, most police departments impose relatively strict standards of moral conduct on their officers and expect to be supported by the courts.

Marion T. Doss, Jr.

Bibliography

Annotation. "Sexual Misconduct or Irregularity as Amounting to 'Conduct Unbecoming an Officer,' Justifying Officer's Demotion or Removal or Suspension From Duty." 9 A.L.R. 4th 614 (1981) and 9 A.L.R. 4th 41 (Supp. 1988).

"Developments—Public Employment." *Harvard Law Review* 97 (Summer 1984): 1738–56.

Doss, Marion T., Jr. "Police Management: Sexual Misconduct and the Right to Privacy" *Journal of Police Science and Administration* 17(3) (September 1990): 194–204.

Mosher, Frederick. *Democracy and Public Service.* New York: Oxford University Press, 1968.

Roberts, Robert N., and Marion T. Doss, Jr. "The Constitutional Privacy Rights of Public Employees." *International Journal of Public Administration* 14(3) (1991): 315–56.

Rosenbloom, David H. *Democracy and Public Service.* Ithaca, NY: Cornell University Press, 1971.

Shafritz, Jay M., Albert C. Hyde, and David H. Rosenbloom. *Personnel Management in Government.* New York: Marcel Dekker, 1986.

Cases

American Postal Workers Union, Columbus Area Local AFL-CIO v. United States Postal Service, 871 F.2d 556 (6th Cir. 1989).

Bowers v. Hardwick, 478 U.S. 186, 106 S.Ct. 2841, 92 L.Ed.2d 140, *reh. denied* 107 S.Ct. 29, 92 L.Ed.2d 779 (1986).

Briggs v. North Muskegon Police Department, 563 F.Supp. 585 (W.D.Mich. 1983, aff'd mem., 746 F.2d 1475 (6th Cir. 1984), *cert. denied sub nom. City of North Muskegon v. Briggs,* 473 U.S. 909, 87 L.Ed.2d 659 (1985).

Dronenburg v. Zech, 741 F.2d 1388 (D.C.Cir. 1984).

Fabio v. Civil Service Commission of City of Philadelphia, 414 A.2d 82, 9 A.L.R.4th 600 (Pa. 1980).

Faust v. Police Civil Service Commission, 347 A.2d 765 (Pa. Commw. 1978).

Fleisher v. City of Signal Hill, 829 F.2d 1491 (9th Cir. 1987).

Fraternal Order of Police, Lodge No. 5 v. City of Philadelphia, 812 F.2d 105 (3rd Cir. 1987).

Fugate v. Phoenix Civil Service Board, 791 F.2d 736 (9th Cir. 1986).

Griswold v. Connecticut, 381 U.S. 479, 14 L.Ed.2d 510 (1965).

National Treasury Union Employees v. Von Rabb, U.S. , 109 S.Ct. 1384, 103 L.Ed.2d 685 (1989).

O'Connor v. Ortega, 480 U.S. 709, 94 L.Ed.2d 714 (1987).

Richter v. Civil Service Commission, 387 A.2d 131 (Pa.Commw 1978).

Shawgo v. Spradlin, 701 F.2d 470 (5th Cir.), cert denied sub nom. Whisenhunt v. Spradlin, 464 U.S. 965, 78 L.Ed.2d 345 (1983).

Suddarth v. Slane, 539 F.Supp. 612 (W.D.Va. 1982).

Thorne v. City of El Segundo, 726 F.2d 459 (9th Cir. 1983).

Wells v. City of Petersburg, 895 F.2d 188 (4th Cir. 1990).

Contract Police

Until recently, contracting has not been considered a desirable means of providing public services, especially in law-enforcement and related areas. Today, however, interest is growing. The use of contracting in criminal justice has attracted particular attention in the field of corrections.

Still, it is often noted that the police department is the fundamental city agency, representing the most basic power of government. Therefore, many people are surprised to learn that many local governments contract some or all aspects of policing. For instance, Robert Poole cites numerous examples of private and intergovernmental contracting to provide better police services. A 1984 comprehensive study by the International City Management Association gives a good indication of the scope of such innovative strategies. For example, in the area of crime prevention and patrol, only 74 percent of the 1,660 cities and counties in the survey provided this service solely by themselves. A full 5 percent (eighty-three communities) utilized intergovernmental contracts, 3 percent contracted with the private sector, and 2 percent contracted with nonprofit organizations, usually neighborhood associations. Support services like training and laboratory work are contracted out even more often.

Why Contract?
When a local government establishes its own police force, its size and jurisdiction are largely determined by the population and boundaries of the municipality. Little if any consideration is given to such questions as: Is the community too small to afford an appropriately trained and equipped department? Is the community too large to meet the diverse needs of its citizens with just one method and style of policing? and, Do the city limits "contain" law-enforcement problems, or do crime and traffic spill over from and to neighboring communities?

Large police agencies are able to afford training, equipment, and specialization that small forces can only dream about, but it is also true that police officials are nearly unanimous in emphasizing the fact that community cooperation and assistance are absolutely essential for effective law enforcement. Big-city departments seem incapable of achieving the close personal relations with citizens that small suburban forces do, or that decentralized big-city departments might. Law enforcement seems caught in a dilemma, needing to seek the advantages of bigness and smallness simultaneously.

Contracting offers a way out of this dilemma, offering the advantages of both small-scale community control and large-scale specialized production. It is based on the simple idea that a local government can offer a service to its citizens without actually producing the service itself. A contractual arrangement exists when one unit of government pays another unit of government or a private producer to provide a public service for its citizens. Contracting separates the governmental unit that determines the type and level of service desired from the actual provider of the service.

Contracting may improve public services for two major reasons. First, separation of demand and financing from provision permits each function to be performed more effectively. Division of demand and provision allows communities to achieve the advantages of both largeness and smallness. Under such a system, the local government retains authority to specify the kind, amount, and cost of services in negotiation with one or more potential providers of the service. Thus community control is retained. At the same time, one provider, such as the county government, may serve many communities and thus achieve economies of scale in production, offer specialized services, and supply coordination for cross-jurisdictional problem-solving. Each community can receive the services it desires, rather than being forced to compromise its values with those of other communities. Citizens are more likely to receive the kind of services they want at a price they are willing to pay. City officials, freed from the responsibility of supervising (and defending) provision of a service, become spokespersons for their citizens in dealing with the contractor.

The second advantage of contracting is that it introduces competition into the provision of public services. At the very least, the local government has the option of providing a service itself rather than contracting. Frequently, it may also have the option of contracting with a number of private producers, larger governmental units, or other local governments. Competition through contracting may ease the difficulties caused by the fact that most local government services are now provided by municipal bureaus that are, in effect, monopolies. Competitive pressures should force contract producers, whether public or private, to study their techniques more closely in order to justify their costs to consumer municipalities and to discover lower-cost methods of provision, or risk losing their customers.

Two Examples
The best-known example of intergovernmental contracting is the Contractual Services Plan of Los Angeles County, usually called the

Lakewood Plan. The plan had its origins in 1953, when Lakewood incorporated to avoid annexation by Long Beach. Lakewood citizens had considerable doubts concerning their ability to finance their own local government services, and thus entered into contractual agreements with Los Angeles County for a wide range of services, including law enforcement. Thirty cities now receive police services from the Los Angeles County Sheriff's Department under the Lakewood Plan. These cities represent about 10 percent of the county's residents, and their contract payments represent roughly 17 percent of the LASD budget. John J. Kirlin categorized the relationship between the contract cities and the LASD as one of mutual dependence, in which the cities have great control over the quantity of service that they purchase, but relatively little over the style—the LASD is a professionalized, legalistic department. He further suggested that the contract cities may be organizing points for citizens to influence LASD policies through city officials, and concluded that the arrangement is preferable to a large, consolidated department.

Another study of a police contract in Burbank, Illinois, concluded that the Chicago suburb received police services from the County Sheriff at a much lower cost than similar-sized suburbs, yet obtained comparable performance as measured by crime, arrest, and clearance statistics, as well as citizen surveys and traffic-fine revenues. Competitive pressures were present in the relationship as a result of the short terms of the specific contracts, and the continuing efforts of Burbank officials to explore the establishment of their own police department. Since Burbank provides the equivalent of 7–8 percent of the sheriff's total budget in exchange for services, presumably it was a valued "customer." Where these conditions are achieved, contracting should be successful.

Later, however, Burbank terminated the agreement and established its own police department. The underlying reason seemed to be that the prospects of competition (possibly losing the contract) eventually made the County Sheriff's Department less responsive to Burbank's increasing demands for "municipal-style" policing. The fundamental difference between a Los Angeles County Sheriff with thirty to forty customer communities and a Cook County Sheriff with just one or two ultimately undermined the quasimarket-like relationship in Burbank, Illinois.

Conclusion

Given the financial pressures on local governments and the generally sympathetic environment for privatization at present, we may expect to see more contract police arrangements, particularly in the South and West, where growth often overwhelms the forces of tradition that restrict change elsewhere.

Peter W. Colby

Bibliography

Bish, R., and V. Ostrom. *Understanding Urban Government.* Washington, DC: American Enterprise Institute, 1973.

Colby, P. "Intergovernmental Contracting for Police Services." *Journal of Police Science and Administration* 10 (March 1982): 34–42.

———. "The Pros and Cons of an Intergovernmental Contract for Policing: Lessons from the Burbank Experience." *Institute for Public Policy and Administration Research Report.* University Park, IL: Governors State University, 1986.

Kirlin, J. "The Impact of Contract Services Arrangements on the Los Angeles Sheriff's Department and Law Enforcement Services in Los Angeles County." *Public Policy* (Fall 1973): 553–83.

Poole, R. *Cutting Back City Hall.* New York: Universe, 1980.

Valente, C., and L. Manchester. "Rethinking Local Services." Washington, DC: International City Management Association, 1984.

Warren, R. "A Municipal Services Market Model of Metropolitan Organization." *Journal of the American Institute of Planners* 30 (August 1964): 193–204.

Courtroom Testimony

Solution of a crime has its final test in a court of law. A careful police investigation will have gathered these elements of casework beforehand: knowledge or proof that a crime has been committed; the existence of a victim(s)—unless it was a victimless crime; an approved report of the investigation answering the questions of who, what, where, when, why, and how; and evidence that has been identified and preserved for the prosecutor. With these prior requirements met, the next task for the police officer is to assist the prosecutor or district attorney in his or her case presentation.

Deposition

In a deposition the police officer states the facts of the case while under oath with an attorney(s) present. A stenographer produces a typed transcript of what the officer saw and did, which becomes a legal instrument. Whether the officer is a defendant, an investigator, or a witness, he or she prepares for the deposition in a prescribed way for self-protection or to aid a conviction. The first step is for the officer to review the police department's policy for giving a deposition and to notify his or her department supervisor that a deposition will be forthcoming. Second, the officer reviews all of his or her own written reports concerning the incident and those of other officers to avoid conflicting statements; the idea is to be consistent throughout the deposition. The officer should not contact other officers or witnesses to ask them about discrepancies in their statements; the defense attorney will use this extra questioning to discredit the police. Third, the officer examines all the physical evidence in the case; usually the officer has already spent considerable time doing this and needs only to revivify his or her memory. Fourth, the officer practices for the deposition and tries to anticipate surprise questions. Fifth, the officer meets with an attorney to clarify all recollections and statements. Sixth, the officer at the deposition tells the truth in every instance; if in doubt, an "I do not remember" or "I do not know" answer is the correct one, but neither answer should be repeated too often if credibility is not to be lost. Also, the officer does not "volunteer" information. Seventh and last, the officer who is adept at giving a deposition educates his or her fellow officers in the art.

Court Manners

Before appearing in court, the officer meets with the prosecutor to discuss the information the officer will present. Then, with both parties apprised of what will be said in court, all that is left is for the officer to observe a certain decorum:

- Arrive in court early.
- Maintain a dignified and attentive bearing. Wear modest clothing to suggest an image of honesty.
- Do not whisper or talk unnecessarily to others nearby.
- Do not approach the court clerk or prosecutor unless there is business to conduct which is pertinent to the case.
- Stay in the courtroom during the calling of the trial calendar. Continual coming and going will tend to disrupt court proceedings.
- Walk erect with a military bearing. Do not swagger or act overly confident.
- Do not smile at the jury or at court personnel. Maintain a businesslike manner.
- Do not gather in the hallways, etc., to visit and talk with fellow police officers.
- If, for some reason, the officer cannot be in court at the specified time, the proper court official should be notified.
- Speak distinctly and clearly. Use good English and avoid the use of slang (unless the officer quotes someone else exactly).
- Do not rush the testimony and think before speaking. Slight hesitation signifies thought.
- Avoid vulgarity (again, unless quoting exactly).
- Ask to have a question repeated if not heard clearly.
- Answer as briefly as possible.
- Avoid yes-or-no questions. If additional comment must be made to explain the question, request to be able to answer fully.
- If there is an opportunity to say something favorable on behalf of the defendant, do so. This will demonstrate lack of bias or prejudice.
- Do not hesitate to correct mistakes or errors.
- Do not appear to want to convict the defendant.
- Notes should not be taken to the stand unless needed to remember the information. In this case the defense attorney should have the opportunity to examine them.
- Do not answer until the entire question has been asked, and do not anticipate what the question will be.
- If there is an objection to a question, wait for the court's ruling before answering.
- Do not show personal feelings when testifying. Do not be sarcastic or facetious.
- Do not leave the witness chair too hastily. Wait for permission to leave and do so in an unrushed manner.
- Unless excused from further testimony, do not leave the courtroom.
- Always address the judge as "Your Honor." Use "Counselor," when answer-

C

ing the prosecutor and defense attorney, and refer to other persons as Mr., Mrs., Ms., or other officers by rank.

The Rule

In the great majority of criminal cases and civil actions, "the rule" will be invoked. Basically, this means that all witnesses in the case must leave the courtroom while the trial is in progress. The judge will order all witnesses not only to be removed but also not to discuss the case with anyone. Because of "the rule," of course, officers cannot listen to the testimony of other witnesses, especially police witnesses. In a properly prepared case "the rule" should not affect an officer's testimony if he or she has reviewed personal reports, all follow–up supplemental reports by other law-enforcement personnel, and depositions important to the case, and has had at least one pretrial conference with the prosecutor or district attorney.

During civil litigation, when an officer is being sued by a citizen, the officer is allowed to remain in the courtroom. As a defendant, he or she has the right to hear all the testimony, especially from the accusers.

Donald O. Schultz

Bibliography

Pantaleoni, C.A. *Handbook of Courtroom Demeanor and Testimony.* Englewood Cliffs, NJ: Prentice-Hall, 1971.

Rutledge, Devallis. *Courtroom Survival: The Officer's Guide to Better Testimony.* Costa Mesa, CA: Custom, 1984.

Schultz, Donald O. *The Police as the Defendant.* Springfield, IL: Charles C. Thomas, 1984.

Tierney, Kevin. *Courtroom Testimony: A Policeman's Guide.* New York: Funk and Wagnalls, 1970.

Courts

Courts both symbolize justice and administer it. Courthouse architecture—often classic, stately, imposing—is meant to inspire awe and reverence among those who pass and enter the building. Judges, too, are symbols of the law's majesty, sitting on an elevated bench, wearing black robes, wielding a gavel, and being addressed as "Your Honor." The formal language of the law, with its frequent use of Latin, reinforces the pomp and solemnity.

Only in court are the aura and mystique of the law made manifest, expressing the collective mores and will of society. Not surprisingly, judges rank high in studies of prestige, with justices of the U.S. Supreme Court standing first among all occupations. High prestige implies high expectations; many people criticize judges for not living up to them. Critics include the press, defendants, lawyers, police—even other judges. A common criticism is that judges are too lenient with offenders; dismissing cases for legal, technical reasons; reducing felony charges to misdemeanors; and letting convicted offenders go free or nearly free with fines, short jail terms, and probation.

The public generally rates judicial performance low and police performance high. Police gain notoriety by being overly assertive: arresting the innocent, abusing suspects, plating evidence, and entrapping. People who think judges too soft with criminals are likely to applaud, if only tacitly, police who err in the opposite direction.

Judicial leniency is publicized; police leniency is not (Wheeler et al., 1968). The police often have probable cause for making an arrest but choose not to use it. On the other hand, more judges are prosecution- than defense-minded in their leanings and decisions (Wice, 1985). For example, in *voir dire* (examination of potential jurors before trial), judges sometimes make only the most perfunctory attempts to determine whether veniremen are prejudiced against the defendant (Kairys et al., 1975).

Prosecution

Much lay criticism of judges is based on misunderstanding. The general public holds judges responsible for dismissing charges; in fact, the prosecutor is responsible for more dismissals. One study showed that the prosecutor typically rejected twenty out of one hundred felony arrests after initial screening. Thirty more were dismissed later by the prosecutor or judge (Boland et al., 1982). Of the remaining fifty, forty-five offenders pleaded guilty while only five went to trial. Prosecutors thus play a pivotal part in the determination of a case.

Prosecutors bargain for guilty pleas in many cases. Hence, they do not usually go to trial or push for the maximum sentence. Several reasons have been offered for this unwillingness to push for severity: (1) prosecutors do not want to risk losing a case at trial, (2) prosecutors face a large backlog of cases, (3) some suspects are initially overcharged, (4) some cases are routine and easily disposed, of, and (5) some cases are too weak to pursue very far. Weaknesses may be due to various factors. Problems with witnesses or victims are particularly common. Either their stories are implausible or they keep changing them, or they are unwilling to testify—perhaps because they fear reprisal or perhaps they know the offenders personally (such offenders are of course easiest to identify and therefore to find and arrest).

Police and prosecutors are often assumed to be like-minded and to have the same goals. But this is true only in the most exiguous sense. Often their relations are tense, sometimes breaking into overt conflict. Police think that their arrests should be prosecuted vigorously and result in conviction and punishment. Law enforcement for them is both a career and a moral commitment; hence they accept the idea that they are the "thin blue line." No one imputes such qualities to assistant prosecutors, who typically are recent law-school graduates who plan to leave the job in a few years for more lucrative fields. Controlling offenders is neither their career nor their passion. They want a reputation for achievement, which in the prosecutor's office means handling a large number of cases expeditiously, securing guilty pleas, and not losing cases at trial. Prosecutors have limited resources, so they pursue cases only if the evidence appears strong enough to produce convictions were the cases to go to trial. In addition, prosecutors face pressures not only from police, but also countervailing ones from defense attorneys and judges.

Complaints about courts' dismissing so many cases filter up to the state legislatures, which assume that judges are at fault—hence the new laws mandating determinate sentencing. When such laws are combined with the many guilty pleas and the prosecution-minded juries, they result in a population explosion in American prisons. Even before the wave of laws on determinate sentencing, American laws were tougher than those in Western Europe. Perhaps this is because legislators pass these laws with the most serious career criminals in mind.

Defense

Defense attorneys are important members of the judicial process, but have far less power than prosecutors or judges. Defense attorneys may be hired by defendants or appointed by the judge when defendants are indigent. In some urban courts, as many as 90 percent of defendants are considered indigent by the judge. Therefore the case is turned over to the public defender or assigned counsel. Public defenders predominate in urban courts, assigned counsel in rural ones.

Studies indicate that on the whole public defenders are consistently adequate or capable. Private defense attorneys hired by the defendants are much more variable, ranging from the brilliant to the ineffective. The public, long nurtured on Perry Mason television reruns or headline exploits of F. Lee Bailey, Edward Bennett Williams, and Melvin Belli, continues to believe in the myth of brilliant, vigorous defense advocates. Few lawyers live up to this standard, however, perhaps because the pay is uncertain and the status low compared with that of other lawyers.

The life of a public defender is frustrating: (1) Few cases can be won at trial, so success in the conventional sense is elusive, and (2) clients are notoriously unsupportive. Like the general public, clients entertain the idea that defense attorneys should fit the Clarence Darrow or F. Lee Bailey mold. Defendants rarely cooperate with public defenders by telling them the truth, and defendants refuse to believe that public defenders are bona fide defense lawyers. This is because public defenders spend so little time counseling them, because there is a different public defender at each stage of the court process, and because public defenders are paid by the state and function as part of the same work group with judges and prosecutors every day. Resentful clients and poor pay make the life of public defenders unattractive; many leave after a few years on the job.

Most people arrested for felonies are poor, so they tend to be powerless. In the cities, many of them are young and either black, Hispanic, or members of some other minority. Thus they have little in common with judges, who are usually white, non-Hispanic, middle class, and older; but most researchers find that such extralegal factors are relatively unimportant in sentencing decisions (Hagan, 1974; Kleck, 1981; Lotz and Hewitt, 1977). Seriousness of offense and past record are the factors that matter most.

Juries

Finally, there are the jurors. Trials are costly, time consuming, and unpredictable—three reasons why few cases go to a jury and many are instead disposed of via dismissals and guilty pleas. But the United States holds more trials by jury than any other nation, indeed more than all others combined. And what transpires in these trials forms a baseline for the rest of the cases: Defense attorneys and prosecutors first try to anticipate how a jury would react to their case, then they decide what kind of plea bargain to make. Three kinds of cases are more likely than others to result in a trial: First, very serious crime (murder, kidnapping, and forcible rape), which would be likely to draw a stiff penalty even if there were a plea bargain. Second, those cases where the defense attorney thinks there is a good prospect of gaining an acquittal. Third, those cases where the defendant ignores the public defender's advice and stubbornly insists on a trial.

Over the centuries juries have been both praised and castigated, called the palladium of liberty, and damned as the apotheosis of amateurs selected for their lack of ability. Such rave and critical reviews abound, but juries were little understood because for a long time researchers ignored them. In 1966 Kalven and Zeisel brought forth a compendium of findings: *The American Jury*. They discovered among other things that (1) in about 80 percent of the cases where juries are not hung, they reach the same verdict as judges (to convict or acquit); (2) juries apparently understand the facts of a case, because their verdicts are no more likely to disagree with the judges' in difficult-to-understand cases than in easy ones; (3) many of the judge-jury disagreements are due to jury values—jurors go outside the law sometimes in search of equity; and (4) very rarely does a minority persuade the majority to switch its votes in jury deliberations.

Pretrial Publicity

The same year *The American Jury* was published, the United States Supreme Court took up the issue of fair trail versus free press and overturned the conviction of Dr. Sam Sheppard for murder. It said that his trial had been marred by pretrial publicity, and that during the trial the press had been allowed to dominate the courtroom. Subsequently, commentators have consistently maintained that pretrial publicity affects jurors in a minuscule fraction of cases, if ever. Researchers, however, have discovered that (1) a majority of crime stories in the press violate fair trial standards (mentioning, for example, that the defendant has a prior record or

has made a confession) and (2) jurors exposed to prejudicial publicity are more likely to vote for conviction (Padawer-Singer and Barton, 1975; Tankard et al., 1979). The more informed people are about a case, the more likely they are to regard the suspect as guilty—and such information usually comes from the media.

Some jury trials are big events, attended by the national media and followed closely by a large number of citizens. They help to put the courts in the best light, by showing the due process model at work. The lawyers are in their attacking mode, the judge is dignified as he or she rules on points of law, and the jury makes the final decision (democracy in action). But while all of this press attention may promote interest in the law and support for the adversary process, it may be carried too far if the police and prosecutor feed the media damaging information about the defendant, diminishing his or her chance of getting a fair trial.

Roy Lotz

Bibliography

Boland, Barbara, et al. *The Prosecution of Felony Arrests.* Washington, DC: Institute for Law and Social Research, 1982.

Hagan, John. "Extra-legal Attributes and Criminal Sentencing." *Law and Society Review* 8 (Spring 1974): 357–83.

Kairys, David, et al. *The Jury System.* Cambridge, MA: National Jury Project and National Lawyers Guild, 1975.

Kalven, Harry, Jr., and Hans Zeisel. *The American Jury.* Boston: Little Brown, 1966.

Kleck, Gary. "Racial Discrimination in Criminal Sentencing." *American Sociological Review* 46 (December 1981): 783–805.

Lotz, Roy. *Public Attitudes Toward Crime and its Control.* Pullman: Washington State University, 1976.

———, and John Hewitt. "The Influence of Legally Irrelevant Factors on Felony Sentencing." *Sociological Inquiry* 47 (January 1977): 39–48.

Padawer-Singer, Alice M., and Allen H. Barton. "The Impact of Pretrial Publicity on Jurors' Verdicts." In *The Jury System in America.* Ed. Rita James Simon. Beverly Hills, CA: Sage, 1975. 123–39.

Tankard, James W., et al. "Compliance with American Bar Association Fair Trial-Free

Press Guidelines." *Journalism Quarterly* 56 (Autumn 1979): 464–68.

Wheeler, Stanton, et al. "Agents of Delinquency Control." In *Controlling Delinquents*. Ed. Stanton Wheeler. New York: John Wiley and Sons, 1968. 31–60.

Wice, Paul B. *Chaos in the Courtroom*. New York: Praeger, 1985.

Crime Analysis

Various types of crime analysis are performed in response to a multiplicity of police functions. In general, crime analysis provides information to help manage patrol operations and, to a lesser extent, criminal investigations. More specifically, crime analysis includes identifying the temporal and geographic parameters of crime, providing investigative leads to help solve crimes, identifying both infrequent and habitual offenders, and promoting intelligence gathering. An informal cliché suggests that "police officers are only as good as their information."

Types of Analysis

Tactical crime analysis, the most prevalent type of crime analysis, consists of a set of techniques and procedures used to identify existing and emergent crime patterns. This involves a systematic process for collecting, collating, analyzing, and disseminating timely, relevant, and accurate information about crime patterns, crime trends, and information on persons suspected of committing crimes.

In their simplest form, crime patterns are multiple crimes in a series—at least two and usually many more, i.e., from five to perhaps over twenty or thirty incidents. These patterns develop because they are frequently committed by the same individual, the same group (perhaps a gang), or a group in which individual composition is periodically subject to change. Though the criminal antics of people like John Dillinger or Bonnie and Clyde were historically reported as "crime sprees," today they would most likely be called crime patterns or "serial crimes."

The primary purpose of identifying crime patterns is to enhance police capabilities to interdict suspects who are engaged in criminal activity thereby suppressing ongoing criminality. The identification of crime patterns is perhaps second in importance only to learning the names of perpetrators engaged in criminal activity. Not infrequently, analysis of crime patterns themselves reveals the names of likely suspects, because of the distinctive modi operandi used by the culprits in the commission of types of crimes they are accustomed to committing.

While the term "crime pattern" is used widely among crime analysts, it lacks precise definition. Most analysts would agree that a single individual or group of individuals involved in committing specific types of crimes, e.g., theft of auto parts and accessories, bank robbery, etc., would indeed constitute a crime pattern. But consensus is evasive when other issues are addressed. For example, what about a particular convenience store that has been robbed again and again by more than one person? Would this series of crimes constitute a pattern? Or what about a group, cluster, or constellation of residences that have been burglarized in a particular area of a city? Does this "cluster" or "constellation" of crime define a pattern, even if it is suspected that more then one person is independently involved in burglarizing these homes?

As a matter of fact, different agencies define crime patterns differently. For example, crime analysts working for the New York City Transit Police limit a crime pattern to specific individuals or groups of individuals engaged in criminality. Crimes that repeatedly occur at a particular location or are concentrated around a "segment of [rail] line," where it is known that the perpetrators are acting independently, are referred to as "chronic conditions."

On the other hand, crime analysts working for the San Diego (California) Police Department, an agency that pioneered many innovative analytical techniques during the mid-1970s, would call a cluster or constellation of crimes a crime pattern. This is not to say that a particular agency is either right or wrong in its definition of a crime pattern. It simply illustrates that more work is needed in honing standard operational definitions of terms used by crime analysts.

Aside from analysts working in municipal police departments and in county sheriffs' offices, there are two federal agencies involved in crime analysis. One is the National Center for Missing and Exploited Children, located in Arlington, Virginia. This agency collects and disseminates data from all over the country to help locate and recover children, including infants, who have disappeared or who have been involved in parental or stranger abductions. In processing literally thousands of leads for specific cases, the National Center for Missing and Exploited Children has achieved considerable success in helping law enforcement in the recovery of missing and exploited children and in reuniting youngsters with their legal guardians.

The other agency is the Federal Bureau of Investigation's National Center for the Analysis of Violent Crime, located in Quantico, Virginia. Although the Federal Bureau of Investigation can legally enter certain types of crimes involving children, most of the work at the National Center for the Analysis of Violent Crime has primarily dealt with adult offenders. It uses data received from various law-enforcement jurisdictions, such as autopsy, forensic, and investigative reports, to determine if a series of crimes, either located in a particular area of the country or possibly spread across the entire country, were committed by a serial killer such as Ted Bundy; Gerald Eugene Stano; John Wayne Gacy, Jr.; Albert DeSalvo, the Boston Strangler; Richard Ramirez, the Night Stalker; Henry Lee Lucas; Kenneth Bianchi, the Hillside Strangler; David Berkowitz, the so-called Son of Sam; San Francisco's Zodiac Killer; Wayne Williams; or, more recently, the likes of Jeffrey Dahmer. Unlike a mass murderer, who guns down dozens of people in the course of a single, wild-eyed incident, serial killers seem to methodically strike repeatedly over the course of many months or even years.

Whereas tactical crime analysis monitors crime daily, trend analysis is used to identify seasonal or cyclical variations in crime rates. Such analysis is used to document and subsequently project seasonal fluctuations for certain types of crime. An increase in armed (i.e., aggravated), commercial robberies before Christmas and the theft of patio furniture in early spring are examples of crime trends that generally can be predicted in most large cities. But there are other long-term vagaries that surpass seasonal variations in crime trends. When the sale of citizens' band radios became popular, so too did the theft of these products. This was also true for thefts of ten-speed bicycles, "spoker" hubcaps, and certain types of sports car seats. Trend analysis can also serve to signal and thus direct important crime prevention work.

A more recent addition to analytical techniques involves link analysis, used primarily to establish and verify interaction networks among individuals. For example, covert activities such as authorized wiretaps can reveal linkages between underworld figures engaged in racketeering and reputed pillars of the community. This type of analysis can produce convincing evidence to support cross-examinations in criminal prosecutions. Link analysis has also been used successfully in the Serious Habitual Offender Comprehensive Action Program (SHOCAP), a national initiative sponsored by the U.S. Department of Justice's Office of Juvenile Justice and Delinquency Prevention (OJJDP). Participating agencies use link analysis to identify serious, habitual juvenile offenders and to determine the composition of gangs, including gang leaders and the gang's "pecking order."

Another type of crime analysis, taxonomical analysis, can be used to detect similarities in modi operandi for unsolved homicides, stranger-initiated aggravated assaults (i.e., unsuccessful homicides), and certain types of sexual assaults. Because of their relative infrequency, isolated incidents of homicide do not generally lend themselves to tactical analysis at the local level. Analysts doing this kind of work examine uncleared cases that were closed because statutes of limitation had expired (except for homicide, for which there is no statute of limitation in most, if not all, states) or inactivated because investigative leads had been exhausted. Taxonomical analysis is intended to complement tactical analysis by identifying previous, undetected patterns that might surface again or be related to other ongoing crimes occurring in another jurisdiction. The irruption of a pattern detected through tactical crime analysis can sometimes be linked to similar incidents that occurred in the past. An analysis of previous cases may result in the identification of persons who were recently paroled or escaped from correctional institutions.

Associated Tasks

A variety of other tasks are also performed by crime analysis. These include having crime analysis develop written replies to all types of information requests from citizens, preparing monthly and year-to-date frequency distributions of *Uniform Crime Reports* (UCR) data, analyzing dispatch data to develop patrol deployment schedules, etc. Ironically, many crime analysts find little time to perform crime analysis because they are busy with other assignments (Bellmio [1983] notes one study that found only about 20 percent of crime analysts' time was actually spent in conducting crime analysis).

The variety of tasks performed by crime analysts is indicated in guidelines initially developed in the early 1980s by the Commission on Accreditation for Law Enforcement Agencies. These state: "Although the title of this chapter is Crime Analysis, the intent is to include all activity in the analysis function." Given the concept's lack of precise definition, it could be argued that more disagreement than consensus exists regarding the role of crime analysis in policing. It must be remembered, however, that crime analysis is a relatively recent concept. The term was first mentioned by O.W. Wilson in the second edition of his book *Police Administration* (1963), but little effort was made to establish formal crime-analysis procedures until well into the mid-1970s. Then rapid development was sparked because of emphasis placed on crime-analysis development through the Law Enforcement Assistance Administration and, in particular, one person within that agency, Robert O. Heck, who possessed an uncanny ability to operationalize research findings into meaningful management constructs.

Historical Development
The roots of crime analysis are as historically diverse as modern-day analysts' activities. Long before the formation of the London Metropolitan Police, Henry Fielding, noted author and playwright and Chief Magistrate of Westminster Court, began collecting and analyzing data on thefts and individuals believed to be involved in these crimes. In 1752, he began publishing a periodical entitled "The Covent Garden Journal" as a means of circulating descriptions of wanted persons and information about recovered stolen property, thereby perhaps developing the prototype of today's "crime bulletin."

Overlooking, if not outright ignoring, the early contributions of Sir Henry Fielding, some researchers contend that the genesis of contemporary crime analysis work was done in England (i.e., Scotland Yard) after the turn of the century. This work involved classifying various types of criminal modi operandi, and knowledge of this work was eventually introduced in the United States by August Vollmer. Others credit techniques developed to analyze traffic incidents at the Northwestern Traffic Institute in the late 1930s as contributing to the development of crime analysis. And still others maintain that crime analysis gradually evolved from the introduction of modern records management systems devised by Vollmer in the early part of this century. Vollmer was apparently the first police administrator to realize the benefits of aggregating dispatch data to establish beat structures for deployment of patrol officers. He also suggested that police records could be used for strategic planning and introduced the idea of "spot maps" to identify potential danger locations in a city.

Vollmer envisioned the need for crime analysis to support more effective management of patrol operations; Wilson refined the concept and was instrumental in popularizing its use. In the first edition of *Police Administration* (1950), Wilson discussed the analysis of police records to identify changes in criminal activities that might prompt police attention. In his second edition (1963), Wilson describes crime analysis as a means of determining "the locations, time, special characteristics, similarities to other criminal attacks, and various significant facts that may help to identify either a criminal or the existence of a pattern of criminal activity." And in the third edition (1972) Wilson addressed organizational issues for incorporating crime analysis into law-enforcement agencies, and he gave examples of duties to be performed by crime analysts. He also devoted a full page to displaying what a crime analysis bulletin should look like.

Between publication of the second and third editions of Wilson's book, President Lyndon B. Johnson established a Commission on Law Enforcement and Administration of Justice (1965). Comprehensive in scope, this commission studied the impact of crime on society, the courts, corrections, the police, juvenile delinquency, organized crime, etc. The final report, published in 1967, consisted of a series of task-force reports that addressed the issues examined.

In tracing the historicity of crime analysis, it is instructive to find the term crime analysis used in the section of the commission's report that dealt with the police. Contextually, the commission suggested the use of "detailed crime analysis and planning studies" to assist departments in "deploying their forces more effectively." But in another section of the commission's report (i.e., Task Force Report: Science and Technology), which specifically dealt with criminal justice information systems, crime analysis was not mentioned. Paradoxically, this section begins with the following statement: "The importance of having complete and timely information about crime and offenders available at the right place and the right time has been demonstrated throughout this . . . report." It thus appears that the commission's conceptual treatment of crime analysis was rather nebulous and failed to build upon Wilson's discussion of the concept in the second edition of his book.

In contrast, the National Advisory Commission on Criminal Justice Standards and Goals (1973) clearly encouraged police departments to improve their crime-analysis capa-bilities. To cite just a few examples, this commission suggested that departments use information from filed interrogation (i.e., interview) and arrest reports, crime and miscellaneous incident reports, and data from moving citations and accident reports (for vehicle registration information) to help them to combat crime.

Recommendations by Wilson and others, and those contained in the two commission reports, along with a study published by the American Bar Association that examined *The Urban Police Function* (1972), provided credence to the use of crime analysis in municipal policing. Although rudimentary, a conceptual foundation for crime analysis had thus been formed by the early 1970s. A few police departments, Sacramento and Kansas City (Missouri), for example, had already experimented in developing crime-analysis techniques by as early as 1972, and the Dallas Police Department had established an intelligence analysis unit by 1971.

Impetus for accelerated development of crime analysis came from the federal government. The Omnibus Crime Control and Safe Streets Act of 1968 was designed to assist police departments in suppressing crime. This legislation led to creation of the Law Enforcement Assistance Administration and its research arm, the National Institute of Law Enforcement and Criminal Justice (now called the National Institute of Justice).

Toward the mid-1970s, these agencies expanded crime analysis, helped by the availability of federal funds appropriated for programmatic initiatives to fight crime. Helpful also were the funding stipulations, including evaluation criteria that required police departments to submit detailed plans for award consideration. This meant that police departments had to justify their proposed activities and project anticipated, measurable results to be eligible for funds; a step that usually required departments to establish some, albeit elementary, sort of crime analysis capability. Finally, and of no small consequence, were findings that emerged from major research projects started during the early 1970s.

The Kansas City Studies

Of particular importance were preliminary results of studies done in Kansas City, Missouri: The Police Foundation's Kansas City Preventive Patrol Experiment and the Kansas City (Missouri) Police Department's Response Time Analysis Study. These two studies challenged the most basic of time-hardened assumptions influencing the traditional rationale for managing patrol operations. The preliminary findings demanded a radical rethinking of the patrol function. This rethinking reiterated the concerns expressed earlier by Vollmer and Wilson that information available within police departments was not being used to its fullest potential. Even before final reports from these studies were published, preliminary results were incorporated into other proposals that would eventually shape the direction of a plethora of research emanating out of the 1970s that primarily addressed the patrol function and, to a lesser extent, dispatch operations and criminal investigations.

The notion to assess the value of random, preventive patrol came from within the Kansas City (Missouri) Police Department in 1971. Officers who had volunteered to serve on the South Central Patrol task force were asked to identify strategies to lessen crime in their division. After debating alternative strategies, the officers submitted to the command staff a position paper questioning the effectiveness of preventive patrol. Management then sought funds and technical assistance from the Police Foundation to design a series of methodologies to evaluate the effectiveness of preventive patrol.

To test the deterrent effects police visibility had in preventing crime, the Police Foundation's evaluation team randomly divided the fifteen beats that comprised the South Central Patrol Division into three equal groups; proactive, reactive, and control. Officers assigned to reactive beats were not permitted to enter their beats unless officially dispatched to handle a call (or in hot pursuit of another vehicle), although they were encouraged to enter the proactive areas. Conversely, officers assigned to the proactive beats were expected to be aggressive by making increased car checks and "ped" checks (i.e., pedestrian stops). It was the intention of the methodological design to have two to three times the amount of police visibility in the proactive areas. Finally, officers assigned to the control beats were expected to conduct business as usual, i.e., to drive systematically/unsystematically throughout their beats until interrupted by a dispatched call for service. Once calls were serviced, officers returned to performing routine, preventive patrol.

Analysis of this data revealed that there were no statistically significant differences in crime rates among the three patrol areas examined. The study therefore concluded that random patrol was not an effective deterrent of crime.

As if the Kansas City (Missouri) Police Department didn't arouse enough national attention among police administrators by questioning the sanctity of preventive patrol, another research effort initiated by this agency sought to assess the value of rapid police response. Since the advent of the radio patrol car, rapidity of police response had become a conventional measure of police effectiveness. The perceived need to reduce response time had served as justification to increase officer strength and expend large sums of money for additional police cars and telecommunications equipment. While it was not unreasonable to assume that rapid police response would produce more arrests, little empirical data existed to support such a proposition. Sponsored by the National Institute of Law Enforcement and Criminal Justice, the Response Time Analysis Study was primarily designed to examine relationships between police response time and the probability of achieving on-scene criminal apprehensions.

Surprising to many, results from this study failed to support any direct correlation between rapid police response and increased felony arrests. Analysis of data revealed that almost two-thirds of most serious crime is discovered after it occurs (i.e., "cold crimes"). Except for a few particularly heinous crimes in which an expeditious response is required to preserve physical evidence, the need for rapid police response is generally diminished by the proportion of serious crimes detected after they have occurred. For the remaining one-third of serious crime that is observed by witnesses or in which victims are directly involved with one or more perpetrators during the commission of an of-

fense, the study found that extensive delays in citizen reporting tended to negate the effect rapid police response had in achieving the desired outcomes, i.e., witness availability and on-scene arrests.

Results of the response-time study and the preventive patrol experiment annoyed traditional patrol practitioners. A major but unpopular conclusion from the response-time study indicated that additional patrol officers needed to reduce police response time in order to increase on-scene arrests would have negligible impact. The preventive patrol experiment indicated that preventive patrol did not prevent crime, or, put another way, random patrol produced random results.

Directed Patrol Project
Following the collection and a cursory, initial analysis of data from the preventive patrol experiment, police administrators with the Kansas City (Missouri) Police Department were at a loss to suggest an immediate alternative to preventive patrol. But analysis of data had also disclosed a substantial amount of uncommitted patrol time—the residual of patrol time not required to handle dispatched calls for service. This finding led to the design of a program that sought to structure, i.e., direct, uncommitted patrol time. The Directed Patrol Project proposal was submitted to the Law Enforcement Assistance Administration's Patrol Emphasis Program (PEP), and was awarded funding in 1975. Influenced by material contained in this and a similar proposal submitted from the Norfolk (Virginia) Police Department, discretionary grant guidelines for PEP specifically required prospective applicants to have an established crime-analysis capability, although, parenthetically, these same guidelines also indicated that funding for "supplemental assistance for a crime analysis unit" would be provided. In all, seven cities were selected to participate in this program. A year later, the Directed Patrol Project was melded with the Law Enforcement Assistance Administration's Patrol Emphasis Program (PEP) and, in many ways, facilitated its development.

Integrated Criminal Apprehension Program
The following year PEP evolved into the Integrated Criminal Apprehension Program (ICAP), a national initiative that, before the demise of the Law Enforcement Assistance Administration in 1982, would provide funding support

for almost seventy agencies across the country. Explicit objectives included increased criminal apprehensions and increased identification and arrest of career criminals. Building upon what had been learned from PEP, random, preventive patrol was to be replaced increasingly by directed patrol activities. Given these expectations, it is not surprising that the role of crime analysis in helping departments to achieve these results became a central concern.

As with its forerunner, ICAP sought to expand the role of patrol officers by having them undertake tasks that, traditionally, had been reserved for detectives. These tasks included tactical operations, such as stakeouts and electronic and physical surveillance. It was also expected that these officers would become more proficient in performing comprehensive preliminary investigations (e.g., photographing crime scenes, collecting physical evidence, conducting neighborhood canvasses to locate and interview witnesses and to interrogate suspects, etc.) and, for some types of crime, conducting follow-up investigations.

In another departure from tradition, this new role demanded information that previously had been unnecessary for officers conditioned to suppress crime through random patrol. ICAP developed the prototype model for crime analysis to provide the types of information needed to help manage and therefore direct patrol operations. Still in use today, this model indicates five basic components: (1) data collections; (2) data collation; (3) data analysis; (4) product development and dissemination; and (5) feedback on data utilization to evaluate patrol tactics and strategies.

Offense Report
While none of the above components is more important than another, both the quantity and quality of information available for collection constitutes a critical first step in the crime analysis process. The primary source for crime analysis data usually comes from a department's offense report. Ideally, this report should indicate the most serious offense committed, including additional, less serious offenses; the names of suspects, along with their clothing and physical descriptions (including physical oddities) and any unusual behavioral mannerisms, weapons, and tools used during the commission of the crime; vehicle description and license plate data; and the names, phone numbers, and addresses of victims and witnesses. The report

should differentiate locations where crimes occurred (if known) from locations where crimes were reported. If known, the time or approximate time of the crime should be recorded. If this time is not known, a time interval should be constructed that reveals, for example, the time when victims of a residential burglary left their apartment and the time they returned to discover that a crime had occurred. This report should also contain a detailed chronology of investigative activities conducted by responding officers together with statements made by victims and witnesses and, if they can be recalled accurately, verbatim remarks made by suspects.

Many departments that have implemented crime analysis have had to eventually revise their offense reports to capture additional types of pertinent data needed to facilitate crime analysis. Particularly for large departments that annually experience a considerable amount of crime, more information may be required for analysis. Consider, for example, auto thefts. Could the owner of the vehicle produce a title or sales receipt? Was the car insured and, if so, by whom? If financed, who holds the lien? What was the condition of the vehicle when recovered, e.g., "stripped," "chopped," burned?

Examination of an offense report from the Houston (Texas) Police Department (HPD), for example, suggests that considerable attention is paid to weapon information, suspects' physical descriptions, their actions, and demeanor. This report provides information on both where victims were and how vulnerable they were before being attacked, e.g., alone, handicapped, hitchhiking, and intoxicated. It also lists forty premise codes to categorize crime locations. Additionally, HPD's automated mode for analysis of robbery incidents includes nine premise codes to distinguish among different types of parking lots.

Criminal Intelligence
While a well-thought-out and well-designed offense report is necessary to perform crime analysis, the information it contains may not be enough to cover the intelligence aspects. Criminal intelligence has two objectives. One is to associate the names of persons perpetrating crimes with their offenses. The other is to identify individuals conspiring to perpetrate crime. The former objective is contained in the description of tactical crime analysis presented at the outset of this article.

More often than not, it will be almost impossible for officers to list suspects when completing offense reports, because, as already mentioned, most serious crime is discovered after it occurs. Unless the victim saw the offender or witnesses can be located, no suspects will be described. Hence, other sources of data must be obtained to help identify possible suspects:

- Field interview reports contain the names and physical descriptions of persons questioned because of suspicious circumstance. These reports also capture vehicle information.
- Dispatch records can document call activities in a particular area such as "prowlers," suspicious persons, speeding cars, and alarms.
- Reports prepared by evidence technicians describe the types of physical evidence collected, e.g., latent fingerprints, etc.
- Follow-up investigation reports may provide information from witnesses not contacted during the preliminary investigation or additional information not mentioned by witnesses when initially interviewed.
- Booking slips might suggest possible suspects, because they reveal the names of persons arrested, possibly on other charges, in close proximity to where a particular crime occurred.
- Accident reports and traffic citations issued also list the names of persons contacted by the police in the vicinity of where a crime occurred.
- Pawnshop tickets and records from automobile salvage yards disclose the names of persons who have sold property possibly taken unlawfully.
- Known offender and modus operandi files contain the names of persons with extensive criminal histories.

Aside from these internal sources of information, some external sources of data may also be important. Among these are reports taken by other agencies, such as the transit, port, and airport authorities; park police; high-school, university, and hospital security groups; adjacent municipalities; and the military police. A listing of persons wanted on felony and misdemeanor warrants, including fugitive warrants, should be maintained. Information about persons, both juveniles and adults, paroled from prison and on probation needs to be collected. Data regarding these individuals should include any distinctive modus operandi, their addresses and, if employed, place of work together with the names and phone numbers of their parole and probation officers. Finally, although often overlooked, there is information from bailbond firms regarding previous arrests of certain individuals, along with the names of their associates.

Once information has been collected it must be collated. This not only involves reproducing, sorting, and aggregating data in preparation for analysis, but also establishing file systems, either automated or manual, so information can be found easily and retrieved quickly. The importance of developing logical file systems cannot be exaggerated. Cursory attention can result in a cumbersome "system" that impedes achievement of the very objectives for which the function was intended.

The next step is analysis. The ability to identify existing and emergent crime patterns is directly dependent on the previous steps. The analyst must be able to expeditiously access timely and accurate information, which is essential in crime analysis. Officers who use crime analysis to design directed patrol operations need to know "what's happening" now, and not what "went down" a month ago. In general, crime patterns usually only last a few weeks. If this type of information cannot be produced, the credibility of analysts suffers, and the need to sustain the crime-analysis function will eventually succumb to alternative sources of data or disappear altogether.

The Crime Analyst
Although some courses in crime analysis are offered, genuine learning comes primarily from on-the-job training. Unfortunately for those who either volunteer for or are assigned to crime analysis, there are no magic formulas— no eloquent equations to assist them in their work. While crime analysis is not a science, many of the same qualities that make for a good scientist are found also in the crime analyst. These include effective organizational skills, tenacity, imagination, insight, and intuition. Of no less importance, because of the need to work with other people and to finesse ways to acquire additional information, strong interpersonal skills can be a valuable asset.

Many police departments, if not most, utilize police officers rather than civilians to staff crime analysis. Departments that employ civilians or use civilian volunteers do so primarily for budgetary reasons. There is no empirical evidence to suggest that certified police officers are more effective than civilians in performing crime analysis and vice versa. But a few of the departments that use police officers as crime analysts also allow them to use their own information to "set up on" locations that exhibit a higher than average probability of being "hit."

The practice of permitting police officers assigned to crime analysis to use their own information for tactical operations is generally discouraged. The disadvantages are obvious. It has a negative effect on officers assigned to patrol, who perceive the crime analysts as elite specialists. Hence, it can and probably will alienate those for whom the system was supposedly designed. Moreover, if officers assigned to crime analysis are allowed to pick and choose the "sexy crimes," who wants to take care of the other, more mundane stuff that is left over? It also disrupts the continuity required to perform crime analysis systematically. If all the analysts are out "on the street," who is left to do the analysis?

Of course, most police officers, particularly the younger ones, like to "work hot crimes." This may be what attracts officers to work in crime analysis to begin with. But, given the disadvantages described above, alternative arrangements need to be explored. One option is to have officers periodically rotate through crime analysis. This has several advantages. Through learning about the information needed to identify crime patterns and possible suspects, officers usually become better investigators. They also become more adept in writing offense reports, and they are generally more willing to share information with crime analysts and other officers.

Irrespective of whether the analysis is done by civilian employees or certified officers, once pertinent information has been developed it must be distributed promptly. Comprising the fourth step in the crime analysis process are several methods used to disseminate crime analysis information. Crime analysts should periodically attend roll calls to deliver personal briefings about criminal events. For large departments consisting of five or more precincts spread over several hundred square miles, closed-circuit television can be used. But the most common method used to distribute and display crime analysis information is through bulletins. Because these often contain confidential information, it is not uncommon for police departments to have a written policy governing their distribution.

Department Bulletins

Many mid-sized agencies produce a daily bulletin, sometimes called the "hot sheet." This lists the more serious offenses reported during the previous twenty-four hours. It may also include the names of persons arrested on felony charges during this time frame along with descriptions of suspects, vehicles used in the commission of crimes, and stolen vehicles. Because of the relative infrequency of serious crime, small departments have no need to prepare this type of bulletin. Very large departments, on the other hand, might be so overwhelmed with serious crime that this type of bulletin would serve little purpose.

Another type of report produced regularly is the crime analysis information bulletin. Although larger departments usually restrict use of this bulletin to listing or displaying similar crime types that were reported in certain areas of patrol districts or beats, e.g., auto thefts, residential burglaries, etc., it can, as the name implies, contain almost any type of information. Examples include safety tips to alert officers of a type of lipstick tube that has been modified to fire bullets, the names of persons recently paroled, forthcoming special events, unique property recovered in another city, and information about suspects believed to be en route to a particular locale. Some agencies use special bulletins or the daily bulletin to convey information contained in these examples.

A crime pattern alert bulletin describes a series of crimes, listing the days and times of occurrence. Incident locations are usually shown on a map in the bulletin or attached to it. There is generally enough information in this bulletin to generate some type of tactical action (i.e., directed patrol) to interdict the series. It is often accompanied by a tactical action plan (TAP) attached to the bulletin. The tactical action plan, originally developed by the San Diego (California) Police Department, summarizes the crime problem and provides space for persons assigned responsibility to describe their proposed response. It should include the names of officers involved, results expected, time required for implementation, and any special equipment needed, such as unmarked vehicles, surveillance equipment, special weapons, and protective gear. Additionally, in the event that no action is planned, this form should explain the lack of proposed activity, e.g., unavailability of personnel, equipment, etc.

Crime analysis intelligence bulletins provide the names of persons suspected or known to be implicated in perpetrating crime. As with crime pattern alert bulletins, they may also include photographs of suspects and list the names of their friends and companions, relatives, vehicle information, and places where they are known to frequent or stay.

Wanted person(s) bulletins present information about persons for whom an arrest warrant or capias has been issued. This bulletin usually displays a picture of the wanted person and provides a physical description along with any monikers and aliases. It is always a good idea to reproduce a copy of the warrant or capias on the reverse of this bulletin. And it is important to provide a phone number that officers can call to verify if the person named in the warrant or capias is still wanted.

Other types of information that might be distributed by crime analysts include monthly summaries of individuals who were "field interviewed" along with the location of where these stops were made. This type of data allows patrol officers to monitor the mobility of persons likely to be involved in perpetrating crime. And given the closer relationship many departments have established with the public during recent years, some departments develop neighborhood or community "alert bulletins" for housing and apartment associations and "block-watcher" groups.

Development of formats to display crime analysis information has almost become an art form. Care must be taken to construct a bulletin that is "user friendly," providing the reader (i.e., scanner) with quick access to pertinent information. Frequently, different types of bulletins are color coded, implying that information contained in some types of bulletins is more important than that contained in others. It is always a good idea to involve patrol officers, the potential users of information produced, to assist in the design of these bulletin formats.

Evaluation of Crime Data

The final component in the crime analysis process involves establishing procedures to obtain feedback not only about the quality of the data

produced but also for results achieved in utilizing information. Several approaches have been used to evaluate data quality. One approach is to have officers complete brief questionnaires about information received. For example, was the information presented easy to understand? Was enough information provided? Was the information developed too old to be used?

Another approach is to establish a "user's group" to monitor the quality of information disseminated. Some departments have even resorted to conducting "trashcan surveys" to see if information forwarded has even been picked up or discarded.

As mentioned earlier, tactical action plans can be analyzed to assess the effectiveness of various types of directed patrol activities used to suppress crime. Over time, valuable information can be obtained by comparing results achieved in implementing various tactical actions. This helps in the development of long-term strategies for more effective crime control and in identifying training issues needed to support tactical operations.

Efficacy of Crime Analysis

Having described each of the steps in the crime analysis process, one may wonder whether this model is amenable to analyzing all types of crime. Before concluding, brief mention should be made of criteria governing the selection of crimes to be analyzed. There are three criteria. In order of priority, the first deals with the frequency or extent of crime. How often do these crimes occur? Is there a sufficient number of crimes to justify creating a crime analysis capability?

The second criterion deals with resources. Can the department afford to staff and equip a crime analysis unit? If so, does the department have available patrol or investigative resources to utilize information produced? Can patrolling be managed more effectively so as to increase the time dedicated to crime prevention and directed patrol activities?

The last consideration, perhaps a bit more abstract, assesses whether certain crimes are susceptible to police intervention. Can these crimes be impacted through crime prevention or directed patrol activities? Can suspects be identified and, if so, apprehended through conventional means? Or are unconventional means required to impact the crime problems? Can members of the community be encouraged to work with the police in combating crime? If so, what can they do? Are there any legal implications that need to be explored in soliciting their support?

Given traditional alternatives, crime analysis can be an effective tool in combating crime, but it is by no means a panacea for a community's crime problems. A study published in 1976, for example, found little conclusive evidence to substantiate the value of crime analysis. And a more recent evaluation could not demonstrate any direct relationship between crime analysis and criminal apprehension.

But the findings from these studies have been seriously challenged. One researcher, for example, questioned results from the most recent evaluation, cited above, stating that ". . . while the researchers made a valiant effort to provide a rationale for their approach, the conclusions are tenuous. The evaluators did not find that crime analysis did not work; what they found was no strong evidence that it did work."

Mixed reviews regarding the significance of crime analysis are not surprising, given the function's relatively short life. Based on the state of developmental sophistication, crime analysis is best described as an emerging specialty. This description does not excuse the need for periodic and critical examination of the process. Quite the contrary, it encourages it.

As indicated at the outset of this article, crime analysts analyze all types of information. Perhaps this is where the problem lies. An analysis of traffic accidents to pinpoint locations of dangerous intersections is not crime analysis. Unless a vehicle was used intentionally to damage or destroy property (i.e., malicious destruction of property) or cause serious bodily injury (i.e., aggravated assault), the accident is not a crime, although vehicle (not penal) codes have probably been violated.

Police administrators need to distinguish conceptually among the various types of analysis performed in relationship to the types of information needed to facilitate management decisions. For example, operations analysis, of tantamount importance to crime analysis in providing informational support, involves traffic analysis, producing "exception reports" (i.e., identifying monthly or twenty-eight-day fluctuations in crime rates among beats), and analyzing calls for service data to reconfigure beats and deploy officers across shifts and by day of the week.

Unlike crime analysis, which is more interested in determining whether two or more crimes comprise a pattern, strategic analysis seeks to identify factors that contribute to crime and noncrime problems. This type of analysis, yet to be demonstrated by most police departments, attempts to identify and, hopefully, reduce or eliminate factors that contribute to crime causation and other problems that require persistent police attention. Almost every large city, for example, must deal with "street people," transient persons who walk the streets and live under bridges and in vacant buildings. Sometimes these people are the victims of crime, while a few may perpetrate crime. Some have been released from mental-health institutions to be "mainstreamed" back into society. Regardless of personal backgrounds or individual predilections, they cause an incessant flow of complaints to the police. This is a complex issue that not only requires input from individuals affiliated with the police, the courts, and corrections, but also from the clergy, the business community, educators, and officials from health care and other service organizations. While the crime analysis and operations analysis functions may help by providing information to examine this issue, they are not equipped to resolve it. Solutions to these types of problems require in-depth research and a collective response from the entire community.

Perhaps the most interesting and certainly the most ambitious crime analysis project currently underway is being developed by the Hillsborough County (Florida) Sheriff's Office in conjunction with training and technical assistance provided through the Missing and Exploited Comprehensive Action Program (M/CAP). While the focus of crime analysis attention has traditionally been on adult offenders, more recent emphasis, primarily because of the U.S. Department of Justice's Office of Juvenile Justice and Delinquency Prevention's Serious Habitual Offender Comprehensive Action Program (SHOCAP), has been placed on serious juvenile offenders. Now the Hillsborough County Sheriff's Office is developing data collection procedures, not dissimilar to those used in strategic analysis, to identify children who have been victims of crime or are at risk of becoming victims of crime. Moreover, these analytical procedures will provide health and human care practitioners working with police, with accurate information that can be used for timely and effective intervention to protect children that stand in harm's way.

Analytical techniques will also be developed that address children who are reported missing, children who are either victims of stranger or parental abductions, and children who are being exploited. Children who voluntarily or involuntarily leave home will be identified. And data on those that turn to crime to survive "the streets" will be collected and analyzed. Not without notice is the development of information and intelligence sources to identify individuals that, for one reason or another, are predisposed to harm children. Unlike more conventional crime analysis entities, this innovative work combines a balanced emphasis on both preventing harm to children and on identifying and apprehending those who put children in peril through criminal victimization.

As for the future, crime analysis will incorporate increased use of automation. This is inevitable, although previous applications have not been entirely successful. Experimentation in developing neural networks and artificial intelligence to identify crime patterns is already underway and promises to expedite a good deal of the manual work now performed by crime analysts.

Crime analysis will experience accelerated transfer of applications and techniques to private enterprise in the years to come. This has already begun in the insurance industry, where insurance companies and consortia have employed persons with crime analysis backgrounds to identify insurance frauds. Given the continued expansion of crime analysis in policing and in the private sector, more jobs can be expected for crime analysts. This may focus more attention on training needs and curriculum development. Unless police departments can keep abreast of automation technologies and sustain the continuity required to produce timely and accurate crime analysis information, there is a distinct possibility that by the year 2000 private firms will be performing this service for law enforcement agencies. Law enforcement agencies have already come under increasing pressure to respond to more and more calls for service while financial support dwindles. This begets political pressure for chiefs of police to put more and more officers on the street, "where they belong," thus stripping important administrative, training, and operations support functions needed to sustain day-to-day work.

Admittedly, the salaries of sworn officers are more costly than are those for civilians. And certified officers are perhaps more prone to be transferred than civilians or lost through attrition and promotion. A few communities in the United States have recently opted to hire private security guards to patrol their streets, having disbanded their own police force. The decade of the 1990s will certainly prove instructive as to how law enforcement agencies will be able to provide the informational management infrastructure to support effective patrol and investigative operations needed to address increasing work loads and crime calls, the latter of which appear to be escalating into more and more violence, particularly among youth.

William H. Bieck

Bibliography

American Association of Retired Persons. *Simplified Crime Analysis Techniques.* Washington, DC: The Association, 1984.

Bellmio, Peter. "Ongoing Development of Crime Analysis Units." *FBI Law Enforcement Bulletin* 52(10) (October 1983): 8–14.

———. "Overview of Crime Analysis." *Loss Control and Security Handbook*. Ed. Lawrence J. Fennelly. Boston: Butterworth, 1987.

Bennett, Lawrence A. "Crime Analysis: A Management Challenge." *The Police Chief*. Gaithersburg, MD: International Association of Chiefs of Police, October 1986.

Bieck, William H. "Plan of Action for City Wide Implementation of a Centralized/Decentralized Crime Analysis System." Houston (Texas) Police Department, December 1984.

Bieck, William H., et al. "The Patrol Function." *Local Government Police Management*. Ed. William A. Geller. 3d ed. Washington, DC: International City Management Association, 1991.

Board of Police Commissioners. Kansas City, Missouri, Police Department. *Response Time Analysis Study: Executive Summary*. Washington, DC: Government Printing Office, 1977.

Buck, George, et al. *Police Crime Analysis Unite Handbook*. Washington, DC: Government Printing Office, 1973.

Crowe, Timothy D. *Crime Prevention Through Environmental Design: National Crime Prevention Institute, Louisville, Kentucky*. Boston: Butterworth-

Heinemann, 1991.

Gay, William G., et al. "A Four-Sight Assessment of the Integrated Criminal Apprehension Program." Washington, DC: University City Science Center, 1984.

Grassie, Richard P., et al. *Crime Analysis Executive Manual*. Washington, DC: Government Printing Office, 1977.

Heck, Robert O. *A Collection of Various Commentaries and "Talking Papers" on Crime Analysis*. Washington, DC: U.S. Department of Justice, Office of Juvenile Justice and Delinquency Prevention, 1980.

Kelling, George L., et al. *The Kansas City Preventive Patrol Experiment: Executive Summary*. Washington, DC: Police Foundation, 1974.

Meredith, Nikki. "The Murder Epidemic." *Science* (December 1984).

Miron, H. Jerome, et al. *Improving Police Management*. Washington, DC: Police Management Association, 1987.

National Advisory Commission on Criminal Justice Standards and Goals. *Police*. Washington, DC: Government Printing Office, 1973.

Oettmier, Timothy N., et al. "Integrating Investigative Operations." *Executive Session Series*. Houston (Texas) Police Department, 1989.

Reinier, G. Hobart, et al. *Crime Analysis in Support of Patrol*. Washington, DC: U.S. Government Printing Office, 1976.

Spelman, William. "Crime Analysis: A Review and Assessment." Washington, DC: Police Executive Research Forum, 1987.

Sullivan, George P., et al. "A Summary of Primary Crime Analysis Functions." San Diego: San Diego (California) Police Department, December 1981.

———. "Crime Analysis in Support of Decision Making." Carlsbad, CA: Police Management Advisors, January 1984.

Crime Laboratory

Police rely heavily on the positive identification of evidence in a case and its link to the suspect in solving a crime. In fact, this identification alone often secures a conviction. The police department crime laboratory is, therefore, of singular importance and houses a necessary array of highly trained individuals and technology.

Forensic science is the application of science to the law. It is in the crime laboratory that the forensic scientist plies his or her craft. The field of forensic science is new and hence is constantly growing and changing. In today's crime laboratory there are many specialists. This was not so just a few years ago. In the early days of forensic science, a few scientists had to wear many hats and examine a variety of evidence types. Whereas before one scientist might have tested controlled substances, analyzed blood alcohols and bloodstains, and compared hairs and fibers, now there are specialists especially in the areas of serology—the study of body fluids—and toxicology—the study of toxic substances (usually drugs) in body fluids. Specialization has come about because of the vast store of knowledge needed to interpret myriad evidence resulting in a final answer.

Lab Requirements

The basic equipment and supplies needed for a crime laboratory vary with the types of analyses performed. Before equipment is purchased, some considerations and a commitment must be made. Qualified forensic scientists are hired, with degrees in chemistry, biology, or one of the related sciences. Support personnel are also hired to type affidavit reports, file, etc. An area for the laboratory, which is safe for the storage of hazardous chemicals, well ventilated, and secured by alarms, with entry allowed only to the forensic scientists, must be designated. A separate area is set aside with its own alarm and lock for the securing of evidence and controlled substances.

The funding agency for the laboratory should underwrite any ongoing training expenses. Approximate cost for this additional training is $3,000 per person per year. At no cost to the agency, though, are training seminars given at the FBI Academy in Quantico, Virginia; the seminars cover a multitude of forensic subjects. One training course that does have a fee, but is invaluable, is the Forensic Chemist's Seminar at the Drug Enforcement Administration Training Center in McLean, Virginia; this excellent course deals with controlled-substance identification methodologies. Since forensic science is currently evolving at a fast pace, membership in forensic societies is essential to keep abreast of new developments. Two such societies are the American Academy of Forensic Sciences and the American Society of Crime Laboratory Directors. Besides the national ones, regional forensic societies offer many learning opportunities.

A Drug Enforcement Administration (DEA) license is needed to purchase, handle, use, and store controlled substances, as is a state license. General laboratory supplies cost approximately $20,000. In a typical police crime lab a visitor sees lab coats, test tubes, racks, microscope slides, spot plates, scissors, weighing papers, spatulas, tweezers, gloves, chemicals, a safety shower and eyewash, spill pillows, safety blankets, safety goggles, a refrigerator/freezer, a burn station, a first-aid kit, a flammable storage cabinet, an acid storage cabinet, and fire extinguishers. The controlled substances acquired are for use as primary and secondary standards. The equipment and supplies listed below pertain to specific types of examination:

Marijuana identification. Stereo microscope, reagents, thin-layer chromatography tanks, sprayers, silica gel plates.
Blood alcohol analyses. Blood-alcohol kits, gas chromatograph, column, compressed gases, recorder, miscellaneous supplies (an automated headspace gas chromatograph is expensive, but the best).
Controlled substance analysis. Physicians' Desk Reference, analytical balance, ultraviolet viewer, microscope, fume hoods, infrared spectrometer, compilation of known spectra, pellet maker.
Firearms. Comparison microscope with fiber optics, workstation complete with tools and supplies, shooting tank (horizontal), reference collection of firearms for parts, subscriptions to firearms journals/magazines, membership in Association of Firearm and Toolmark Examiners.
Library. Forensic texts, catalogues from laboratory supply companies.

Evidence Submission Procedure
The police crime lab devises and enforces a procedure so that evidence is always submitted in the same manner and to the same place. Evidence envelopes and seals are provided to the submitter for packaging the evidence. Evidence envelopes contain the following information: suspect's name, report number, incident, date of incident, submitting officer's name, date of submission, and completed chain of custody. After the evidence is packaged, it is sealed with an evidence seal, on which are placed the sealer's initials, service number, and date. The chain of custody is a most important step in the process. Depending on the laws of evidence endorsed by courts in the area, it might be required that every person who has custody of the evidence—no matter for how brief a time—must sign the chain of custody. An alternative might be that every person who opens the evidence must sign the chain. The officer who collects the evidence at the scene of the crime is the first name on the chain, and next to his or her name is the date. On the next line is the name of the second person to receive the envelope, and so on. Defense attorneys look for a broken chain of custody or a shoddily done envelope to discredit the evidence.

Evidence must also be packaged properly, so that no part of it is damaged or lost. Controlled substances must be tightly sealed to avoid leakage, arson evidence put in cans to avoid evaporation, blood tubes protected from breakage, and wet evidence completely dried before packaging. Evidence of any type is never packaged in plastic because it promotes mold formation; paper is used. An Evidence Analysis Request form should clearly state what analysis the forensic scientist is to perform. The properly filled-out request accompanies the evidence, is logged in the master log book, stamped with the date, and placed in the evidence vault for safekeeping. Cases are then assigned for evidence analysis on a first-come, first-served basis, unless a certain urgency exists. The evidence stays in the evidence vault until called for by the examiner, who opens the package without damaging the collecting officer's seal, if at all possible. After analysis, another seal is affixed by the examiner, with his or her initials, service number, and date. The evidence is then returned to the vault, awaiting either pickup by the law-enforcement agency or destruction.

In any case where source is to be determined, such as blood or semen, known samples must be submitted. This requirement is critical in homicides and sexual assaults. Known blood and semen must be collected from both victim and suspect for proper identification of origin.

Court Testimony
By the very nature of their work, forensic scientists are expert witnesses in court. They possess knowledge and skill outside of the range of the average person when it comes to identi-

fication of evidence. But to be a good expert witness requires skill of a different sort—a skill in communication. Complex chemical and biological reactions must be explained to a jury of "peers," who might possess knowledge of varying degrees, from that of a high-school dropout to that of a nuclear scientist. So it is imperative that the forensic scientist in the role of expert witness make eye contact with the jury and communicate his or her laboratory findings plainly, accurately, and unequivocally.

Carla M. Noziglia

Bibliography

Maehly, Andreas C., and Lars Stromberg. *Chemical Criminalistics.* New York: Springer-Verlag, 1981.

Osterburg, James W. *The Crime Laboratory: Case Studies of Scientific Criminal Investigation.* 2d ed. New York: Boardman, 1982.

Peterson, Joseph L., et al. *Crime Laboratory Proficiency Testing Research Program.* Washington, DC: National Institute of Law Enforcement and Criminal Justice, LEAA, 1978.

Steinberg, Harold L. *Standard Reference Collections of Forensic Science Materials: Status and Needs.* Washington, DC: National Institute of Law Enforcement and Criminal Justice, LEAA, 1977.

U.S. Federal Bureau of Investigation. *Handbook of Forensic Science.* Washington, DC: Government Printing Office, 1975.

Crime Scene Search

When investigating a crime, the law enforcement officer must be concerned with two important issues: the people involved in the crime and the tangible items that remain at the scene. These issues parallel the two major types of evidence, which are testimonial evidence and real evidence. Testimonial evidence is information obtained through oral statements of victims, witnesses, and suspects. Physical evidence pertains to the broad category of material objects through which the crime was committed; be it in an active role, such as a firearm, or in a passive role, such as a hair transferred onto the victim's clothing. The crime-scene search deals primarily with the recognition, documentation, and legal collection of physical evidence.

Physical evidence is always present at crime scenes, but unfortunately many investiga-

tors have failed to recognize the enormous potential for information it holds. This is particularly true of very small items, generally known as trace evidence. The origin and the transfer of trace evidence was postulated in the early 1900s by Dr. Edmond Locard of the University of Lyon in France. Locard's "principle of exchange" stated that when an individual enters a scene he leaves traces of himself behind and also takes traces from the scene when he leaves. Locard's principle pertains not only to commonplace exchanges such as fingerprints and bloodstains, but also to minute evidence such as fibers, hairs, and soil.

Preliminary Observations

Much of the success of the total investigation will depend upon the conduct and observation of the officer(s) first at the scene. Because every crime scene is unique, it is not possible to provide a step-by-step procedure of what the first officer should or should not do. Briefly, the first officer should render aid to the injured; ascertain if the victim is dead; remove suspects, witnesses, and extraneous police officers; make initial observations of the physical condition of the scene, such as the position of doors, lighting, odors, or signs of activity; and should disturb the scene as little as possible.

Whether the investigator is a uniformed policeman, detective, crime-scene technician, or criminalist, he or she is faced with an environment that contains items of evidence that are very fragile and easily lost. One normally receives only a single chance to conduct a search of a scene properly, so hasty decisions and quick actions may destroy potential physical evidence. The popular portrayal in the entertainment media of a detective who meanders about the scene while picking up items at random is a classic example of the wrong method by which to process a crime scene. A crime-scene investigation is first and foremost governed by a plan of action that has been well thought out.

Upon arrival at the scene, the investigator should choose as his or her "command post" a secured spot away from the areas to be searched. This command post can serve as a message and information center, storage place for unused equipment, rest area, and garbage dump for the trash produced during the processing of the scene. Contamination of the scene can be minimized by the use of such an area simply because it reduces the traffic in the crime-scene proper. The investigator must next obtain all the information available about the crime, the victims, and the critical areas of the scene from statements and observations by the first officer, other police personnel, and any witnesses. After a thorough briefing, the investigator should start a preliminary survey of the scene, preferably without entering the most critical areas. If they must be entered, the investigator should step carefully and disturb nothing.

This investigatory phase is for careful observation of the condition and location of evidence, points of entry and exit, and other areas of criminal activity, including the route and direction of travel of the perpetrator. Particular care should be taken to preserve shoeprints and other transfer-trace evidence.

Photographs may be taken after crime-scene locations have been subjected to preliminary survey. A running narrative, either tape-recorded, written, or both, should describe everything that is observed. After completing the preliminary survey, the investigator should return to his or her command post to process mentally all that has transpired.

The investigator uses experience, intuition, and understanding of the complexities of crime scenes in formulating a systematic plan for a search. The investigator must consider all the "who, why, and how" questions to be answered in postulating a scenario to explain what has taken place at the location. The investigator should step into "the shoes of the suspect" in an attempt to reconstruct motives, actions, sequence of activity, and direction of travel the suspect may have taken. This type of thought process can serve as an initial outline for the search, and to target certain areas for more detailed examinations. Every item in the scene that appears to be out of place must be noted and evaluated, even if it appears to be totally unrelated to the present scenario. The investigator must keep an open mind, for the scenario may have to be amended or even completely changed as new information comes to light. In summary, the general approach to any crime-scene investigation at this stage is one of alertness for every detail, coupled with flexibility, a system, and thoroughness.

Personnel

Although the crime-scene investigator is personally responsible for all that happens at the location, he or she should not try to perform all the tasks that must be done. Division of labor for specific tasks and working within a team concept, with the investigator as the quarterback, appears to be the most effective use of personnel and material resources. In some jurisdictions, crime-scene searches are directed by a pair of investigators, who share the responsibilities and decision-making. The old adage of "two heads are better than one" best describes this situation. Theories can be discussed, labor divided, and time used more efficiently. Also, in smaller jurisdictions, the investigative pair may be the only people at the scene to perform all the necessary tasks. Today, many police departments use both patrol officers and detectives to process crime scenes, and some civilian personnel are trained to collect physical evidence. These individuals normally photograph the scene, dust for latent fingerprints, and collect certain items of physical evidence.

In large police agencies, specific crime-scene tasks are performed by specialists. Identification officers are qualified to take routine photographic records of the scene and detailed photographs of individual items of evidence. These officers are also expert in the collection and comparison of fingerprint evidence. Techniques for the chemical processing of fingerprints and their visualization by video enhancement instruments and laser technology are performed by these individuals. Staff artists sketch and make accurate measurements of all items in the crime scene, which can later be used to produce architectural-quality representations of the scene in either two- or three-dimensional formats. Photographers respond to scenes for very specialized types of photography such as infrared, aerial infrared, and low-light situations involving the recording of chemical luminescence. Personnel equipped with video recording gear are sometimes used to record the step-by-step processing of the scene. Computer enhancement and optical manipulations of photographic materials can also be done by these individuals. Criminalist personnel are scientists trained in the recognition, collection, and analysis of physical evidence. These criminalists are of great help in the evaluation and collection of fragile and complex types of evidence, such as physiological fluids, trace evidence, and hazardous chemicals. In homicide cases, the medical examiner–coroner's office will be present to take control of the deceased for identification and to investigate the cause of death. At major crime scenes, an information officer serves as a liaison between the investigative team and members of the press. In some instances, a representative from the prosecutor's office may ask to be present at a scene, especially during service of search warrants or court orders to obtain forensic samples from suspects.

Documentation and Collection
After the briefing of specialized personnel, the actual search should begin with documentation and collection of fragile items that are in danger of being lost or destroyed by continued exposure to traffic or to the weather. Documentation means that an item of evidence is photographed in detail, with scales included, as it was found, and then notes, sketches, and measurements are made so that the exact location of the item is recorded in relationship to all others. The collection step includes examination of the item for trace evidence and fingerprints before carefully marking the item or its container so that it can be identified and the chain of custody initiated. Collection also entails the gathering of control and standard samples for comparison or elimination purposes, should a suspect be later apprehended. For example, a portion of carpeting from the scene is needed to serve as a standard sample should trace amounts of carpet fibers be recovered from the clothing or shoes of a suspect. Proper packaging is essential to minimize the likelihood that the evidence will be altered or degraded after collection. Trace evidence should be packaged in small, carefully marked paper bundles or envelopes to prevent loss or cross-contamination. Physiological stains must be air-dried and then individually packaged in paper containers so that the stains can "breathe," thus reducing bacterial decay. Volatile arson evidence must be kept in airtight containers to prevent evaporation of any flammable fluids that may be present. These packaging practices are essentially a matter of common sense and are covered more completely in other references.

After the documentation and collection of these emergency items have been completed, the critical "action" areas where criminal activity has occurred are next in priority. Obviously, the location of a homicide victim would be considered an action area, but the investigator should not start with a detailed examination of the body. Instead, the area around the body should be examined meticulously for any trace evidence or anything that looks out of place. Start the search with the floor around the body and then progress along the possible paths of entry or exit. The word "thorough" must be emphasized: Search everywhere, including the walls, ceiling, and behind and underneath large objects. The body should not be ignored completely, but at this point examined only to determine a probable cause of death. This cursory examination will indicate what types of evidence to be alert for during the investigation, such as blood or sharp implements if the victim appears to have suffered stab wounds. A detailed examination of the body can be performed later by a pathologist, with the investigators in attendance. Contamination or loss of evidence that may be present around the body will be prevented by not examining or removing the body initially.

After each action area has been processed, outlying areas that will release guard personnel should be searched next, and then all adjoining areas should be searched to insure that nothing is overlooked. Indoor scenes in residences can usually be completely searched and examined for fingerprints by a blanket method. However, large indoor or outdoor scenes may require other systematic methods of search. Examples of such methods are the zone, strip, spiral, wheel, and grid methods. The grid and zone methods are especially effective in the investigation of bombings, where evidence from explosive devices is dispersed over a wide area. In some outdoor scenes, where fixed objects are scarce, measurements for location purposes must be taken by using triangulation and compass readings. Outdoor crime scenes at night present difficult situations at best, and detailed investigation should usually be postponed until daylight hours, instead of attempting a search with artificial lighting and portable generators. Vehicles have the limited boundaries of the interior, exterior, and undercarriage, which can be searched utilizing a blanket method.

As the crime-scene search nears conclusion, the scenario that the investigator postulated initially may be substantiated by the evidence, or may be revised, or totally rejected. Whatever the case, the total crime-scene search process has enabled the investigator to properly document and collect items of physical evidence that are important to the case. Also, another significant aspect of the investigation has been achieved—reconstruction of the events of the crime. By evaluating all the information and evidence observed, the investigator can put together a series of events that could have resulted in the situation present at the scene when he or she arrived. This reconstruction, combined with further laboratory analyses by forensic experts of physical evidence collected, can provide a powerful witness to the elements of the crime, the progression of events, and the people responsible.

Harley M. Sagara

Bibliography

Davies Geoffrey, ed. *Forensic Science.* 2d ed. Washington, DC: American Chemical Society, 1986.

DeForest, Peter R., R.E. Gaensslen, and Henry C. Lee. *Forensic Science: An Introduction to Criminalistics.* New York: McGraw-Hill, 1983.

Goddard, Kenneth W. *Crime Scene Investigation.* Reston, VA: Reston, 1977.

Saferstein, Richard. *Criminalistics: An Introduction to Forensic Science.* 2d ed. Englewood Cliffs, NJ: Prentice-Hall, 1981.

Schultz, Donald O. *Crime Scene Investigation.* Englewood Cliffs, NJ: Prentice Hall, 1977.

——. *Criminal Investigation Techniques.* Houston, TX: Gulf, 1978.

Svensson, Arne, Otto Wendel, and Barry A.J. Fisher. *Techniques of Crime Scene Investigation.* 3d ed. New York: Elsevier, 1981.

U.S. Department of Justice. Federal Bureau of Investigation. *Handbook of Forensic Science.* Washington, DC: Government Printing Office, 1981.

Crimestoppers

The Program

The Crimestoppers program[1] encourages citizens to engage in *anonymous* informing in order to assist police in solving felony crimes.[2] Though information has been published concerning the origin, characteristics, and effectiveness of this program (e.g., Rosenbaum et al., 1987, 1989), other relevant matters concerning its character deserve consideration, including how this activity differs from whistle-blowing and from the customary expectation that citizens will report crime information to the police. Though each type of informing involves revealing otherwise secret information and possibly a violation of trust, several differences exist.

First, the Crimestoppers program involves organized interests actively promoting anonymous informing. Whistle-blowing, however, characteristically lacks organizationally based support and frequently faces energetic organizational opposition (Nader et al., 1972).[3]

Second, because of the public nature of their activity and a general lack of organizational support, whistle-blowers often receive little or no protection against reprisals. Consequently, despite efforts to provide statutory protection, many (if not most) whistle-blowers have suffered severe penalties including firing from jobs and being subjected to long-term stigmatization (Glazer and Glazer, 1989:133ff.; Proxmire, 1972:14; Westin, 1981:1). The anonymity of Crimestoppers is intended to minimize these problems.

Third, Crimestoppers promotes anonymous informing by means of monetary rewards, whereas traditional reporting by citizens and whistle-blowing have ideally been viewed as ethical matters involving moral and civic responsibility.[4] For example, Glazer and Glazer (1989:4) describe the whistle-blowers they studied as "men and women of conscience" acting "in accordance with their ethical principles against the explicit instructions of management."

Fourth, whistle-blowers have less concern than anonymous informers for keeping their identity secret. Indeed, their efforts often necessitate widespread publicity in order to generate the public support and corrective action they seek.

Finally, and in a related vein, covert informers convey information exclusively to officials or to those in authority, whereas whistle-blowing or "leaking" most often seems to be directed first to an intermediary, then to public officials, and then to the general public (Bok, 1983:216).

Additionally, the anonymous informing promoted by Crimestoppers differs in several ways from the traditional practice of citizens reporting crime-related information to police. First, Crimestoppers encourages citizens to exchange information for untaxed cash rewards, the amount of which may vary with the informer's "level of performance" (Rosenbaum et al., 1987:14–16). Thus, rather than merely informing, people are expected to provide "good" information (i.e., information clear enough and specific enough to lead to an arrest or indictment) before a reward is paid.[5] Names of suspects, addresses, license-plate numbers, automobile makes and models, serial numbers, descriptions of stolen items, and so on must be provided to give police some direct course to follow.[6] Hearsay, rumor, or idle gossip is ignored and/or discarded. It would appear, then, that the ideal of citizens being motivated by a sense of community spirit and civic responsibility has been supplemented if not supplanted by material considerations.

Second, unlike the customary "snitch system" of police using known, paid informers, Crimestoppers relies on informer anonymity, an important difference. Characteristically, police–informer relations have been tenuous because the snitch was often involved in crime as deeply as those on whom he or she informed, and gave information to police in exchange for leniency (Sanders, 1977). Because informer's anonymity helps to preclude such relationships, the Crimestoppers program seems to be an attractive substitute for the traditional "snitch system."[7] Thus, at the time of their initial call to Crimestoppers, anonymous informers are assigned a case-specific number or other unique code. Rewards are paid in cash to avoid record-keeping. Contacts with police, including arranging for payment of a reward, must be initiated by the caller using the assigned number or code. As a result, no face-to-face contact between informer and police need ever occur. This may pose problems for police because if additional information is required or if the anonymous informer is needed as a witness, the police have no way to identify or contact the person. Yet because police believe that assured anonymity encourages people to inform, these difficulties are accepted.[8]

Third, Crimestoppers relies on the media to promote the general visibility of the program and to elicit citizens' input in specific cases (Lavrakas et al., 1990). The print and electronic media are especially important in promoting general public awareness, and for broadcasting accounts of crimes under investigation for which police need information. On television these accounts often include a simulation of the crime, along with whatever information police see fit to release.[9] Nationally and locally, police give "average" to "very high" ratings to the media for their cooperation in keeping Crimestoppers highly visible (Rosenbaum et al., 1987:23–26). In some cities police are especially pleased with the ethnic media response because they believe that input from members of these

communities is needed in the fight against crime. More extensive consideration of the role of the media follows shortly.

Finally, although Crimestoppers programs in the United States are endorsed by federal, state, and local governments, presently they are privately funded and limited to the municipal and county levels. Programs investigated by the author were initiated by citizens' groups (albeit, at the behest of police), and are controlled by civilian directors with police advisors. Operating capital, especially for paying rewards (the greatest expense), is derived almost entirely from private sources through cash contributions, public auctions of donated items, proceeds from sporting events, and similar means. Public funds pay only the salaries of the few police officers who monitor citizens' calls. In this regard, Crimestoppers seems to parallel vigilantism because one attraction of the latter was that it reduced the cost of local government (R. M. Brown, 1976, 1983).[10]

Crimestoppers and Changing Moral Meaning
The Crimestoppers program is consistent with the emphasis Anglo-Saxon law enforcement has traditionally assigned to localism and the expectation that citizens should raise a "hue and cry" and assist police in maintaining or restoring public order (Critchley, 1970:35). However, even while the need for citizen aid is acknowledged, both police and citizens' attitudes toward informing and informers have been ambivalent (Marx and Archer, 1976:156). The morality of informing in our society is especially questionable when it is done anonymously. Despite its acknowledged utility (leading, no doubt, to its persistence), anonymous informing, i.e., snitching, is recognized as "morally repulsive" (Agrell and Huldt, 1983:5), satisfies the definition of "dirty work" (Hughes, 1962), and leads to several questions regarding its place in a democratic society (Marx, 1987; 1989:514–17; Rosenbaum and Lurigio, 1985). The repugnance of anonymous informing is shared by police who acknowledge its utility but generally hold informers in low esteem (M. F. Brown, 1989; Harney and Cross, 1968; Klockars, 1985:66–68; Skolnick, 1975:141–42; Wilson, 1970:301).

This negativism is expressed in everyday speech where morally loaded labels such as "rat," "squealer," "fink," "snitch," "stoolie," "tattler," and "gossip" are given to those who inform anonymously or otherwise disclose secret information about others. Countless generations have been taught a seemingly absolute rule—"Don't squeal."[11] Stereotypically, squealing is the act of "low-life" types and reflects their "morally defective character." Informing, especially under conditions of anonymity, is simply wrong; when directed against members of one's ingroup (family, friends, coworkers, neighbors), it amounts to betrayal and treachery (Akerstrom, 1989:25; Marx, 1987). In short, in American society the social reality of informing is multiple rather than singular, and in any specific situation its meaning is problematic. While we publicly acknowledge and defend the need for citizen informing, in private we reject informing and informers, especially those who operate in secrecy. Why is that the case?

The negative moral meaning of informing likely derives from the importance and the positive valuation of trust and secrecy as means of maintaining group solidarity and identity (Westley, 1970:129) and reflects the condemnation of betrayal, its opposite. Simmel reminds us that in everyday life, knowledge (or information) is often treated as property, the value of which may be enhanced by its exclusiveness, i.e., its secrecy (Wolff, 1950:330–34). Indeed, the value of some knowledge is more a consequence of its secrecy or exclusiveness than of its content. In turn, the significance of secrecy resides in its capacity to enhance or enrich life by creating a "world apart" from that which is public and evident. Though its utility in this regard is not limited to such instances, the ability of secrecy to create a "world apart" is especially significant when used to mask "evil." The attractiveness and the logic of secrecy, then, give rise to the negative moral meaning of its opposite, betrayal and informing. Again, this phenomenon is noticeable in everyday language. "Rats" and "squealers" betray confidences; "stool pigeons," "snitches," and "finks" violate secrecy and/or trust by stealth. In short, the immorality of informing and betrayal derives from and resides in the social significance of secrecy and trust.

In view of the strongly negative moral meaning of anonymous informing and of informers or snitchers, how has that role come to be normalized and legitimated on the grassroots level and even identified as an expression of civic duty? Several factors have led to this change in meaning.

Fear and the "War on Crime"

The legitimation of previously morally problematic activities (such as anonymous informing) often is preceded by "pessimized" conditions that people in general define as troubling, possibly intolerable, and for which they feel corrective action is needed (Pfuhl, 1986:72–73; Rubington and Weinberg, 1987:24). As revealed in public opinion polls covering the period from the 1960s onward (during which Crimestoppers developed), crime is such a "pessimized" condition (Flanagan and McGarrell, 1989:144; Jamieson and Flanagan, 1989: 183).

During that period the public mood was marked by a pervasive fear of criminal victimization (DuBow et al., 1979; Skogan and Maxfield, 1981). As noted in *The Figgie Report* (1980:8), "Crime and the fear of crime have, like a dark dye, permeated the fabric of American life"; the *fear of crime* was regarded as a problem equal to the crime problem itself (Gordon and Heath, 1981:229). So contagious and so pervasive was this fear that some observers coined the category "the not-yet victimized" (Moore and Trojanowicz, 1988:1) to draw attention to the anticipatory nature of people's concern and to emphasize that people's fear of crime seemed to have exceeded the probability of victimization (Gordon and Heath, 1981: 228–29; Pepinsky and Jesilow, 1984: 21ff.). Thus, regardless of their actual condition, millions of Americans viewed crime as a pervasive and immediate threat to their well-being, which called for drastic action and certainly for priority treatment by police. People felt compelled to take their communities back from drug dealers, prostitutes, and thieves. This pessimistic view of crime and the desire for corrective action was (and remains) very much a part of the American consciousness and, I suggest, was a necessary precondition for the legitimation and popularization of previously objectionable tactics. After all, "extreme conditions call for extreme methods."

Supplementing this widespread public pessimism over the crime issue were three other elements vital to the legitimation process: (1) the development of victimization surveys revealing that over half of serious victimizations are never reported to police; (2) the belief that this situation reduces the effectiveness of reactive policing (Kelling et al., 1974); and (3) growing support for citizens' involvement in crime control. Together, these four elements—widespread public fear regarding crime and seemingly random violence, documentation of undisclosed public knowledge regarding criminality, broad-based demands for corrective action, and an acknowledgment of the need for a reversion to the tradition of citizen involvement in crime fighting (because the prevailing reactive policing methods were insufficient to curb crime)—set the stage for the emergence of the "community policing" effort (Kelling, 1988:2), including the role of "anonymous citizen informer."

Changing Moral Meanings and Values

Though necessary, widespread pessimism was not sufficient to bring about the legitimation of snitching and the Crimestoppers program. It was also necessary to construct a social reality concerning anonymous informing that would make it compatible with public moral meanings and values. Such a reality had to (1) reverse the prior negative moral meaning of informing, (2) incorporate informing into the public's sense of the proper relationship between itself and police, and (3) define informing as a suitable way to deal with the threat of crime and criminals.

A value base for this reality was readily available. First, American culture is filled with myths and stereotypes concerning crime and criminals, including the belief that good and evil are objectively discrete categories, that the population is divisible into the "dangerous classes" and the "good people" (Veysey, 1970: 289), that "most crime is committed by the poor," and that "some groups are more law-abiding than others" (Pepinsky and Jesilow, 1984:47ff.). In general, people tend to equate the "crime problem" with street crime and to locate criminals in the lower reaches of "moral space" (R.M. Brown, 1976:88).

When coupled with a growing sense of danger and concern about crime, this division of the population into "dangerous classes" and "good people" could have been expected to help people resolve doubts concerning the morality of informing and to free them from restrictions posed by norms against snitching. Out of self interest, "right-minded" citizens (i.e., those opposed to crime) are encouraged, if not obliged, to pass relevant information to police. The call for citizen aid in dealing with crime needed no independent justification. Public values are largely anticriminal. The Crimestoppers program rests on those values.

Second, the Crimestoppers program has continuity with the instrumental character of traditional vigilantism (R.M. Brown, 1976:109; DuBow and Emmons, 1981). Historically the police have shown opposition (though variable) to extralegal involvement by citizens in the criminal-justice process (Marx and Archer, 1976). Nonetheless, this type of "vigilantism" could well appeal to many people: those who are concerned about the crime problem, those who feel that their interests have been addressed inadequately by formal authority, and those who believe in localism and self-reliance or self-help.[12] Accordingly a call for participation in a police-related program, even one that requires anonymous informing, could be expected to elicit a positive response.

Comments made by citizen informers interviewed by the author were consistent with the preceding analysis. Reflecting the moral division of the population, one interviewee stated, "I work for my stuff and no one has a right to take it away. I want their kind off the street." Another said, "I've got kids that need to be protected. And citizens need to get involved; we have an obligation to [help] one another." Other interviewees explained and justified their behavior on the basis of their distress about what they regarded as the immediacy of the threat posed by the crime situation and their sense that "something has to be done."

Third, the values of localism and the Crimestoppers program have been endorsed by several "respectables," thus increasing their legitimacy. Among these "respectables" are former FBI Director William Webster (Hartman, 1986) and former President Ronald Reagan (Jones, 1985:9). Given the role of endorsement in the legitimation process (Pfuhl, 1986:77–78), testimonials from such notables could only promote acceptance by citizens while quieting opposition.

Fourth, the Crimestopper program gained support and legitimacy on the basis of its alleged pragmatic character, a value that Americans have long embraced (Williams, 1960:428–31). When its alleged pragmatism was linked with two other values, localism and voluntarism, the predicted positive consequence of anonymous citizen informers in the "war against crime" appeared to be incontestable. This predicted effect is expressed in the slogan "It only works when you watch," which reinforces in turn the idea that voluntarism and individual action can affect crime. This pragmatism is reinforced by occasional official comments focusing on the value of information provided by citizens leading to the arrest of serious, sometimes violent offenders (*C.J. International*, 1990).

The Role of the Media

In order to achieve public acceptance and legitimation, the Crimestoppers program and anonymous informing had to be portrayed so as to fit what citizens probably would define as a proper relationship among themselves, the police, and their contribution to crime control. This task—a matter of moral entrepreneurship—fell to the mass media and to the police.

The print media have contributed considerably toward this end. Between 1971 and 1973 *Reader's Digest* published several stories describing various "secret witness" programs that allowed citizens to name names while remaining anonymous (Armbrister, 1972, 1973; Stewart-Gordon, 1971). These articles explained the operation of the programs and characterized them as "ingenious," "economical," "popular," and "successful," as well as "a remarkable public service." Anonymous informing was being endorsed. These stories extolled the virtues of citizens' participation in the fight against crime, complete with anecdotes with which readers could identify. In its "Local Self-Reliance" section, for example, one magazine praised community-based crime control programs in several cities and provided addresses and phone numbers that readers could use to secure more information (*Mother Earth News*, 1981:166). Similar articles were carried in *McCalls* (July 1981:37), *The Futurist* (April 1982:84), *Teen* (July 1984:47), and *Glamour* (November 1984:68). Each article pointed up the "increasing popularity" of citizens' involvement in the crime-control effort and reported on its efficacy and safety. In this way, the print media helped to construct a social reality that linked Crimestoppers with prevailing values and defined the role of "citizen as anonymous informer" in a morally acceptable way.

Normalization and legitimation of anonymous informing have also been affected by the close working relationship between the electronic media and the police. The media rely almost exclusively on the police for producing most of their crime stories (Fishman, 1978:542, 1980:8; Gordon and Heath, 1981:230ff.). In view of this relationship, it is not surprising that media officials define their contribution to Crimestoppers as part of their "objective" reporting function, and as consistent with their traditional moral "gatekeeping" role in the community. An executive in charge of news production at one TV station stated that broadcasting Crimestoppers advertisements is merely a "form of reporting that adds a request for public input." Participation in Crimestoppers is also regarded as a community service. One media official in charge of producing Crimestoppers advertisements suggested that these broadcasts are modern "wanted posters" that reach large audiences and that promote community safety and well-being.

In addition, in an effort to protect the image of the media as an autonomous or "free" and objective entity, media officials seek to fend off potential criticism and to preclude the idea that police may be exerting undue influence over them. One media interviewee stated,

> The media role is not dictated by police. It is not the police being totalitarian or anything. We feel, even though police select the cases to be broadcast, that this is a problem we handle jointly. It serves to promote an awareness in the community that would not be there otherwise. The risk [of police influence over the media] seems to be a price worth paying for the "product." Doing Crimestoppers is a voluntary thing on our part. It's done in a spirit of community service. If TV can help inform the community of police needs and help police better serve the community, then it's all to the good.

In short, media personnel justify their contribution to Crimestoppers by defining it as a highly utilitarian and legitimate extension of their ordinary role of presenting news and serving the community. From this definition, it is only a short step to the public legitimation of anonymous informing.

The electronic media also encourage citizens to accept and approve of the Crimestoppers program by superimposing an entertainment format on a news/documentary format in their advertisements. That is, reenactments of the offenses are followed by requests for information. Like the news, Crimestoppers segments have become entertainment and reflect an understanding in the media business: Dramatized news "entertains, is popular, and maximizes audiences" (Altheide and Snow, 1979:75–81; Ericson, Baranek, and Chan, 1987:51).

The use of an entertainment format is acknowledged by media officials in the following excerpt from an interview:

Q: What are your thoughts—pro or con—about putting crime control efforts into an entertainment format?

A: Doing that makes the program "sell" better. It promotes and holds audience attention. Other formats may not do as well.

Q: Would "other formats" be a "talking head" type or an educational format?

A: Yes. The other basic thing is that an entertainment format allows for greater freedom of presentation. We try to remain factual, but the entertainment format generates a greater degree of emotional reaction. These broadcasts "touch" people in ways educational stuff wouldn't. Descriptive stuff gets sterile and boring. We can avoid that with dramatization. That lets us present the condition or experience of the victim in a way the audience can identify with.

Although Crimestoppers ads are a part of the general news effort, they depart from a standard news format in their method of presenting crime information. Ordinarily, news is proffered from the perspective of observers such as police, prosecutors, reporters, or witnesses who provide "cleaned up" second- or third-hand descriptions and interpretations of events and conditions. In contrast, Crimestopper's dramatizations present information from the perspective of the victim, that is, first hand. These presentations are more immediate and "audience relevant" than standard news presentation (Altheide, 1985:9, 1989:68). On that basis they may be expected to generate greater audience identification than ordinary news broadcasts.[13] As Meyrowitz notes, such televised reenactments of crimes tend to involve us in issues we once thought were not our business, to thrust us within a few inches of faces of murderers and Presidents, and to make physical barriers and passageways relatively meaningless in terms of patterns of access to social information (1985:308).

As a result, the viewing audience is involved more immediately in the dramatized crimes. The line between viewer and victim becomes obscured, while identification of audience members with victims may be increased. That identification assists in legitimating anonymous informing.

In following an entertainment format, Crimestoppers advertisements resemble dramatic TV crime shows: Both portray situations as simple conflicts and seek to heighten their dramatic element (Snow, 1983:23ff.). Other format characteristics include mood music, the voice-over, and camera and editing techniques designed to develop a rhythm and tempo that normally are associated with dramatic TV crime fiction. The careful use of light and shadow in simulations of offenses also heightens the sense of drama in the action between victims and perpetrators. In addition, most of the cases used in dramatizations are alleged to have occurred at night.

Crimestoppers ads also strongly resemble the classic horror film (Snow, 1983:198ff.). Both types of production capitalize on people's fears; in the case of Crimestoppers it is the fear of victimization, while in the horror film it is fear of being terrorized by inhabitants of a "nightmare" world. In some horror films, however, the source of evil remains ambiguous and the victim's fate uncertain, whereas the actuality of real ("innocent") people being victimized by criminals is a certainty in the Crimestoppers spots. In both cases, the elements of fear and the "irrational" serve to attract.

Despite parallels, differences exist between Crimestoppers ads and fictional crime shows. For example, horror films frequently call for extraordinary methods of solution (e.g., exorcism), whereas Crimestoppers ads call for no more than that the public come to its own defense using simple methods and aided by "trusted public servants." Unlike fictional presentations, then, the Crimestoppers' ads tell viewers that there is a rational and logical way to deal with crime. This message seems to be well suited to appeal to the modern consciousness, which is shaped by the bureaucratic logic that proposes the greatest and most immediate payoff for the least cost (Weigert, 1981:9).

Added to this is the "plain folks" element of Crimestoppers ads which promotes audience identification with victims (Snow, 1983:22). In one city, the victims portrayed in the Crimestoppers reenactments included a shopkeeper trying to make a living, a person spending a quiet evening at home alone with a book, people engaged in an evening of shopping, children playing in front of or near their home, a real-estate agent preparing to receive clients at a vacant house, and travelers stopping to help a seemingly stranded motorist. In short, the cases selected for broadcast by police apparently are designed to promote viewers' identification with victims.

When the audience's identification with victims is coupled with the element of anonymity, citizens' attribution of legitimacy to Crimestoppers and their willingness to participate in the program (i.e., to inform) may be expected to increase. Not only are people "drawn into" these scenarios; the promise of anonymity as well as autonomy also permits them to participate without interrupting or jeopardizing their ordinary roles and status. The decision to participate, the degree of participation, and when or whether to withdraw remain under the actor's control; autonomy need never be relinquished. With the exception of some concern that their identity might become known to the perpetrator and that they or members of their family might be endangered, none of the citizen informers interviewed by the authors experienced any disruption of their personal affairs as a result of contacting Crimestoppers.

The viewers' identification with victims and their tendency to perceive crimes in personalized ways are also linked to the variety of emotions generated by the Crimestoppers ads (Snow, 1983:23). Interviews disclosed that several people who had informed identified with victims and had experienced rather vivid emotional reactions, including being "very upset," experiencing "all emotions," being "anxious" but "very confident," and feeling "great relief." Informants also noted that by informing, they felt they were acting (indirectly) in their own defense. This point suggests that audiences may become "victims" of their own emotions, the emotions that help them define Crimestoppers and anonymous informing as proper and effective means of combating crime. Essentially they have overcome moral and ethical objections to anonymous informing.

The Role of the Police
Police have also played an important role in this matter. From their perspective, the legitimacy of the Crimestoppers program and its televised ads rests largely on their perceived utility for resolving "dead-end" cases, those in which leads have

been exhausted and new ones are needed (Rosenbaum et al., 1989:411). In keeping with that perception, several police interviewees suggested that the media role is nothing more than an extension of the customary police investigation and of the propriety of citizens giving information to police. If there is anything unique about Crimestoppers, however, police suggest it is the means rather than the end. As one police interviewee stated, "The real payoff of media clips is getting citizens accustomed to and comfortable with the idea of Crimestoppers and giving information to the police." In the police view, then, Crimestoppers' legitimacy is reflected in being regarded as a case of "what is, is right."

Police also seek to legitimate and make acceptable the role of anonymous citizen informer by the cases they select for broadcast. In keeping with information reported by Carriere and Ericson (1989:53), a substantial proportion of the cases advertised by the police departments that I studied involved violent crimes against persons, especially employees of business places (e.g., the assault or killing of convenience market clerks).[14] These cases are presented *not* because leads have been exhausted, said one police interviewee, but "because they are likely to arouse considerable [audience] emotion. It seems person cases get more emotional response and the public is more moved than in property cases." This police representative, a strong advocate of Crimestoppers, felt that the images portrayed in the media were vital in arousing public concern and generating a bond between police and citizens. He believed that legitimation would follow. Hence, not only do police release information selectively to the media; in addition their goals dovetail with and are promoted by media presentation of material in the most attractive (i.e., entertaining) format. Thereby the desired image is cultivated and legitimation is promoted.

Finally, although the media and the police pay lip-service to one another, each group clearly operates according to its own agenda. For example, media officials know very well how Crimestoppers' ads might influence viewing behavior, rating, and station income, as well as how they satisfy FCC licensing regulations regarding public service.

For their part, the police seem sincerely to appreciate the media role, but nonetheless view the media as a means to an end. They seek to cultivate and maintain cooperative relations with the media. Nonetheless, by manipulating information and distributing it selectively to the media, police are consciously building up a backlog of "IOU's" among media personnel, on which they will draw when necessary. As an example of this instrumental view of the media, one police official gave camera operators differential access to crime scenes, thereby placing them under obligation, as he did other media personnel. Thus, although both agencies contribute to the legitimacy of Crimestoppers, each seems also to be consciously engaged in a narrower, self-serving function.

Conclusion

The significance of Crimestoppers and the legitimation of the anonymous citizen informer may well be variable, and the consequences may be mixed. Some people regard it as a welcome and overdue return to a time when citizens took an active role in law enforcement. As noted, the solution of crimes requires input from citizens. This input has long been thwarted by citizens' reluctance to become involved, to be publicly identified and required to testify against accused persons, and possibly to endanger themselves and/or others (Manning, 1977:363–54). Anonymity is regarded as at least a partial solution for the problems of citizens as well as police.

The sociological importance of Crimestoppers, however, is not limited to its impact on clearance rates or on the dollar value of recovered stolen property. More important perhaps is that Crimestoppers marks a critical shift in the publicly approved role of the state in combating crime. In relation to its potential for the further elaboration of police surveillance (Marx, 1988) and the broader issue of the invasion of privacy (Lacayo, 1991), the legitimation of anonymous informing takes on added social psychological and socio-political importance.

As Goffman (1963:41ff.) noted, the management of information about one's self—especially one's failings—involves managing stigma. An interest in the management of stigma leads in turn to a heightening of the value of privacy and secrecy as tools with which to protect one's "self." Earlier comments herein on the value of secrecy pertain and lead to this question: What are the implications of legitimating procedures that have the potential to obscure, if not to eradicate, the distinction between private and public roles (Bensman and Lilienfeld, 1979)? Will the proclaimed virtue of informing in the "war on crime" be offset by its potential for generating personal and social distress due to the erosion of privacy (Kiefer, 1992)? Because *anything can be criminalized* and *everyone has something to hide*, and because mutual trust is the foundation of primary relationships, this matter deserves more extensive examination. As interests of moral entrepreneurs shift and as the influence of their supporters ebbs and flows, who will be reporting to whom about what? With what result? At present the long-range, unintended consequences of this matter are open to debate (Marx, 1989).

In addition, legitimating anonymous informing carries potentially serious sociopolitical consequences. Ours has been an "open" society where personal freedoms have lodged in the interstices between elements of the institutional order. Crimestoppers appears to raise serious questions about our ability to maintain those spaces and, accordingly, our individual freedoms. Will the normalization of snitching as a method of domestic social control erode the ground between public and private space (Reiss, 1987)? Almost certainly, by legitimating snitching and by encouraging the general public to report private information to public authorities, the "eyes and ears" (and hence the power) of those authorities have been extended to an inestimable degree, allowing them to penetrate and observe the most private arenas of human interaction. Moreover, having accomplished this intrusion without a noticeable outlay of public funds, public authorities may act without accountability. What, then, might be the effect on interpersonal trust and the social bond? Might the legitimation and institutionalization of anonymous informing pose an even greater threat than the criminality it was intended to combat?

Erdwin H. Pfuhl, Jr.

Notes

1. Similar efforts include, among others, programs encouraging citizens to anonymously report persons who drive "erratically" (suggesting drunkenness), who poach wild game, who litter or commit other environmental offenses, who display expired vehicle license plates, and single occupant vehicles/drivers who travel in freeway lanes officially reserved for car pool vehicles (See Marx, 1989:515; Rosenbaum et al., 1987 and 1989).

2. Police department personnel interviewed for this study indicate Crimestoppers seeks only nondrug-related felony crime information. However, misdemeanor and drug-related information is accepted and routed to the appropriate detail, depending on the department definition of how particular offenses are to be worked.

3. A possible exception is the October 1990 congressional legislation authorizing payment of rewards of up to $50,000 to whistle-blowers "for information leading to prosecution of S&L crooks" (*Tempe Daily News/Tribune*, 1990). Use of the term "whistle-blower" in this press release, however, suggests that it was being used as a synonym for "informer."

4. This distinction is far from perfect. First, some whistle-blowers are likely motivated by rewards, as suggested by the False Claims Act Amendments of 1986. This act guarantees rewards of 15 to 30 percent of the amount recovered by the U.S. government in cases brought against private corporations accused of fraud (*Business Week*, 1988). Similarly, the Internal Revenue Service rewards people (up to 10 percent of the amount recovered) for turning in tax cheats. The IRS, however, is said to pay out an average of only $1,000 per case (Saunders, 1987). Second, by no means are all anonymous informers motivated only by monetary reward. Many act out of their sense of good citizenship and social responsibility.

5. The precise criteria used to determine whether a reward will be paid vary from one organization to another and are established by its directors.

6. Incidental to securing such information, police are "training" willing citizens in the proper manner of informing. Apparently not all informers need such training, however, because approximately two-thirds of those calling Crimestoppers are alleged to be offenders or "fringe players." (see Rosenbaum et al., 1989:412–13).

7. Not all such relationships and problems have been eliminated by Crimestoppers. Police interviews reveal that a significant, though variable, proportion of Crimestoppers calls comes from persons who probably would have operated as paid police informers in an earlier day. More-over, some paid informers (i.e., snitches) allegedly have been encouraged by police contacts to use the Crimestoppers program in order to secure rewards paid from "private" funds. In addition, in one instance that I studied, videotapes of Crimestoppers announcements were played over closed-circuit TV in a county jail so the inmates could see them. Those having information about the reported crimes were encouraged by the financial reward system to report anonymously. If this information led to a reward, the money was placed in a special account for the inmate and was given to him or her as a "stake" at the time of release. In either case the element of anonymity is lost, and traditional problems are likely to persist.

8. It is not assumed that citizens who call Crimestoppers, especially the "repeats," always remain unknown to the police. In fact, interviews with police department personnel revealed that just the opposite occurs. Thus, in the practice of "funneling" regular snitches are directed to contact Crimestoppers so they may be "paid" without further reduction of an already thin snitch fund. The practice is defended on the grounds that informers are reluctant to cooperate without a guaranteed reward and the assurance of anonymity or confidentiality. Nonetheless, the effort to provide anonymity, and the degree to which anonymity is supposedly maintained, suggests Crimestoppers differs qualitatively from the traditional police–informer arrangement.

9. This point applies to local TV presentations as well as to "Crime 800," the national Crimestoppers television broadcast.

10. These methods of funding Crimestoppers reveal another dimension of the increasing privatization of law enforcement in the United States (see Matthews, 1989).

11. What child attending Sunday school has not heard of Judas Iscariot's condemnation for having betrayed Jesus for thirty pieces of silver? Despite the historic debate about his motives, in everyday language Judas's name symbolizes the act of betrayal (Navasky, 1980).

12. In fact, the initial reaction of many police officials to Crimestoppers (as well as

to other programs) was quite negative precisely because they believed it smacked of vigilantism, a condition inconsistent with police interests. To some extent such opposition has been overcome because Crimestoppers permits citizens to contribute to crime control without being part of an organization that could threaten police hegemony or other interests.

13. It is seldom acknowledged that Crimestopper stories often are written and produced by police from their own perspectives and with their own interests in mind. Just as a story concerning events in Moscow but datelined Washington reflects the United States' perspective, a story of crime "datelined" by a municipal police department reflects its perspective. Nonetheless, in Crimestoppers' ads that perspective is presented to the viewing audience as a first-person experience.

14. One police department noted that crimes against persons, especially violent crimes, accounted for about 80 percent of the advertised cases.

Bibliography

Agrell, W. and B. Huldt, eds. *Clio Goes Spying: Eight Essays on the History of Intelligence*. Malmo, Sweden: Scandinavian University Books, 1983.

Akerstrom, M. 1989. "Snitches on Snitching." *Society* 26:22–26.

Altheide, D.L. *Media Power*. Beverly Hills, CA: Sage, 1985.

———. "The Culture of Electronic Communication." *Cultural Dynamics* 2(1989): 62–78.

Altheide, D.L., and R.P. Snow. *Media Logic*. Beverly Hills, CA: Sage, 1979.

Armbrister, T. "TIP is Turning In Pushers." *Reader's Digest* (October 1972): 265–72.

———. "Join the War Against Crime and Drug Pushers." *Reader's Digest* (September 1973): 103–06.

Bensman, J., and R. Lilienfeld. *Between Public and Private: Lost Boundaries of the Self*. New York: Free Press, 1979.

Bok, S. *Secrets: On the Ethics of Concealment and Revelation*. New York: Random House (Vintage), 1983.

Brown, M.F. "Criminal Informants." In *The Encyclopedia of Police Science*. Ed. William G. Bailey. New York: Garland, 1989. 108–11.

Brown, R.M. "The History of Vigilantism in America." In *Vigilante Politics: An Absorbing Story of a Dangerous Shortcut: Order Without Law*. Ed. H. Jon Rosenbaum. Philadelphia: University of Pennsylvania Press, 1976. 79–109.

———. "Vigilante Policing." In *Thinking About Police: Contemporary Readings*. Ed. Carl B. Klockars. New York: McGraw-Hill, 1983. 57–71.

Business Week. "Squealing for Dollars." (July 25, 1988): 38.

C.J. International. "Crimestoppers Helps" 6 (September–October 1990): 5.

Carriere, K.D., and R.V. Ericson. *Crime Stoppers: A Study in the Organization of Community Policing*. Toronto: University of Toronto Centre of Criminology, 1989.

Critchley, T.A. *The Conquest of Violence*. New York: Schocken Books, 1970.

DuBow, F., and D. Emmons. "The Community Hypothesis." In *Reactions to Crime*. Ed. Dan A. Lewis. Beverly Hills, CA: Sage, 1981. 167–81.

DuBow, F., E. McCabe, and G. Kaplan. *Reactions to Crime: A Review of the Literature*. U. S. Department of Justice. Washington, DC: Government Printing Office, 1979.

Ericson, R.V., P.M. Baranek, and J.B.L. Chan. *Visualizing Deviance*. Toronto: University of Toronto Press, 1987.

The Figgie Report on Fear of Crime: America Afraid. "Part I: The General Public." Willoughby, OH: A-T-O, 1980.

Fishman, M. "Crime Waves as Ideology." *Social Problems* 25 (June 1978): 531–43.

———. 1980. *Manufacturing the News*. Austin: University of Texas Press, 1980.

Flanagan, T.J., and E.F. McGarrell, eds. *Sourcebook of Criminal Justice Statistics—1988*. U. S. Department of Justice, Bureau of Justice Statistics. Washington DC: Government Printing Office, 1989.

The Futurist. "Crime Stoppers: Putting the Brakes on Felons." (April 1982): 84.

Glamour. 1984. "Help Catch A." (November 1984): 68.

Glazer, M.P., and P.M. Glazer. *The Whistleblowers: Exposing Corruption in Government and Industry*. New York: Basic Books, 1989.

Goffman, E. *Stigma: Notes on the Management of Spoiled Identity*. Englewood

Cliffs, NJ: Prentice-Hall, 1963.

Gordon, M.T., and L. Heath. "The News Business: Crime and Fear." *Reactions to Crime*. Ed. Dan A. Lewis. Beverly Hills, CA: Sage, 1981. 227–50.

Harney, M.I., and J.C. Cross. *The Informer in Law Enforcement*. 2d ed. Springfield, IL: Charles C. Thomas, 1968.

Hartman, T.L. "Crime Stoppers: An Effective Law Enforcement Tool." *The Police Chief* (July 1986): 66–67.

Hughes, E.C. "Good People and Dirty Work." *Social Problems* 10 (Summer 1962): 3–11.

Jamieson, K.M., and T.J. Flanagan, eds. *Sourcebook of Criminal Justice Statistics—1988*. U. S. Department of Justice, Bureau of Justice Statistics, Washington, DC: Government Printing Office, 1989.

Jones, A. "How Crime Stoppers Stop Crime." *Readers' Digest* (January 1985): 7–9.

Kelling, G. L. "Police and Communities: The Quiet Revolution." *Perspectives on Policing* 1 (June 1988). Washington DC: Department of Justice, National Institute of Justice.

———, T. Pate, D. Dieckman, and C.E. Brown. *The Kansas City Preventive Patrol Experiment: A Summary Report*. Washington, DC: Police Foundation, 1974.

Kiefer, Francine S. "Stasi Files Expose Past Injustices." *Christian Science Monitor* (January 6, 1992): 3.

Klockars, C.B. *The Idea of Police*. Beverly Hills, CA: Sage, 1985.

Lacayo, R. "Nowhere To Hide." *Time* (November 11, 1991): 34–40.

Lavrakas, P.J., D.P. Rosenbaum, and A.J. Lurigio. "Media Cooperation with Police: The Case of Crime Stoppers." In *The Media and Criminal Justice Policy*. Ed. Ray Surette. Springfield, IL: Charles C. Thomas, 1990. 225–41.

Manning, P.K. *Police Work: The Social Organization of Policing*. Cambridge, MA: MIT Press, 1977.

Marx, G. 1987. "Pro Se." *Student Lawyer* 15(1987)(6): 8–10.

———. *Under Surveillance, Police Surveillance in America*. Berkeley, CA: University of California Press, 1988.

———. "Commentary: Some Trends and Issues in Citizen Involvement in the Law Enforcement Process." *Crime and Delin-quency* 35(1989)(3): 500–19.

———., and D. Archer. "Community Police Patrols and Vigilantism." In *Vigilante Politics: An Absorbing Story of a Dangerous Shortcut: Order Without Law*. Eds. Jon Rosenbaum and Peter C. Sederberg. Philadelphia: University of Pennsylvania Press, 1976. 129–57.

McCalls. "When It's Nice to Have Nosy Neighbors." 37 (July 1981).

Matthews, R., ed. *Privatizing Criminal Justice*. Newbury Park, CA: Sage, 1989.

Meyrowitz, J. *No Sense of Place: The Impact of Electronic Media on Social Behavior*. New York: Oxford University Press, 1985.

Moore, M.H., and R.C. Trojanowicz. "Policing and Fear of Crime." *Perspectives on Policing* 3 (June 1988). Washington, DC: Department of Justice, National Institute of Justice.

Mother Earth News. "Local Self-Reliance." 166 (March/April 1981).

Nader, R., P.J. Petkas, and K. Blackwell, eds. *Whistle Blowing: The Report of the Conference on Professional Responsibility*. New York: Grossman, 1972.

Navasky, V.S. *Naming Names*. New York: Viking Press, 1980.

Pepinsky, H.E., and P. Jesilow. *Myths That Cause Crime*. Cabin John, MD: Seven Locks Press, 1984.

Pfuhl, E.H., Jr. *The Deviance Process*. 2d ed. Belmont, CA: Wadsworth, 1986.

Proxmire, W. "The Whistle Blower as Civil Servant." In *Whistle Blowing: The Report of the Conference on Professional Responsibility*. R. Nader et al. New York: Grossman, 1972. 12–19.

Reiss, A.J. "The Legitimacy of Intrusion into Private Space." In *Private Policing*. Eds. C.D. Shearing and P.C. Stenning. Beverly Hills, CA: Sage, 1987. 19–44.

Rosenbaum, D.P., and A.J. Lurigio. "Crime Stoppers: Paying the Price." *Psychology Today* 19 (June 1985): 56–61.

Rosenbaum, D.P., A.J. Lurigio, and P.J. Lavrakas. *Crime Stoppers: A National Evaluation of Program Operations and Effects*. Washington, DC: U.S. Department of Justice, NIJ, January 1987.

———. "Enhancing Citizen Participation and Solving Serious Crime: A National Evaluation of Crime Stoppers Programs." *Crime and Delinquency* 35 (July 1989): 401–20.

C

Rubington, E., and M.S. Weinberg. *Deviance: The Interactionist Perspective*. 5th ed. New York: Macmillan, 1987.

Sanders, W. B. *Detective Work*. New York: Free Press, 1977.

Saunders, L. "Squeal." *Forbes Magazine* 4 (May 1987): 62–63.

Skogan, W.G., and M. Maxfield. *Coping with Crime: Victimization, Fear and Reactions to Crime*. Beverly Hills, CA: Sage, 1981.

Skolnick, J.H. *Justice Without Trial: Law Enforcement in Democratic Society*. 2d ed. New York: John Wiley and Sons, 1975.

Snow, R.P. *Creating Media Culture*. Beverly Hills, CA: Sage, 1983.

Stewart-Gordon, J. "Secret Witness: New Weapon Against Crime." *Reader's Digest* (November 1971): 190–198.

Teen. "The News." (July 1984): 47.

Tempe Daily News/Tribune (Tempe, AZ). 1990. "Whistleblowers Offered Rewards for Tips on Fraud." (October 30, 1990): A–3.

Veysey, L., ed. *Law and Resistance: American Attitudes Toward Authority*. New York: Harper & Row, 1970.

Weigert, A.J. *Sociology of Everyday Life*. New York: Longman, 1981.

Westin, A.F., ed. *Whistle Blowing: Loyalty and Dissent in the Corporation*. New York: McGraw-Hill, 1981.

Westley, W.A. "Secrecy and the Police." In *The Ambivalent Force: Perspectives on the Police*. Eds. A. Niederhoffer and A.S. Blumberg. Waltham, MA: Ginn and Company, 1970. 129–32.

Williams, R.M., Jr. *American Society: A Sociological Interpretation*. 2d rev. ed. New York: Alfred A. Knopf, 1960.

Wilson, J.Q. "Police and Their Problems: A Theory." In *The Ambivalent Force: Perspectives on the Police*. Eds. A. Niederhoffer and A.S. Blumberg. Waltham, MA: Ginn and Company, 1970. 293–307.

Wolff, K.H. *The Sociology of Georg Simmel*. New York: Free Press, 1950.

Criminal History Information

Police, prosecutors, judges, and correctional officials must be able to determine accurately and in a timely manner not only whether particular individuals have prior criminal records, but also the extent and nature of criminal involvement. The information needed includes such matters as whether arrested individuals were charged, prosecuted, and convicted for an earlier offense(s); what the conviction offense was; whether it was a felony; whether it involved violence or the use of a weapon; whether the individual was on bail, probation, or parole at the time of the offense or has a history of violation of release conditions; whether a sentence of imprisonment was imposed and served; and whether the individual remained free of criminal involvement for specified periods of time between offenses. Having current and accurate information is vital to criminal justice functioning. Without such information the whole criminal-justice system suffers and could literally fall apart.

The State Survey
In 1989 the Bureau of Justice Statistics commissioned the SEARCH Group in Sacramento, California, to conduct a survey of state criminal history record repositories. On completion the survey would offer a comprehensive review of the nation's criminal history systems and establish a baseline against which future advances could be measured. The SEARCH Group commenced its work with all fifty states and the District of Columbia participating. Among the findings reported in 1990 were these highlights:

- Forty-seven states and the District of Columbia have automated some records in either the criminal history record file or the master name index.
- Ten states (Colorado, Georgia, Hawaii, Idaho, Michigan, Montana, Nevada, Oregon, Rhode Island, Washington) have fully automated both the criminal history record file and the master name index.
- Three states (Maine, Mississippi, West Virginia) have no automated criminal history information.
- Twenty-three states report that 70 percent or more arrests within the past five years in the criminal history database have final dispositions recorded.
- Thirteen states currently flag some or all felony convictions in their criminal history databases.
- Over 45.6 million individual offenders were in the criminal history files of the

states' criminal history repositories on December 31, 1989.

- Most states have experienced a growth in the size of their criminal history files since 1984; five states have smaller criminal history files than they did in 1984.
- Over 3.5 million final dispositions were reported in 1989 to the thirty-four state criminal history repositories.
- Thirty-two states and the District of Columbia require prosecutors to report to state criminal history repositories their decisions to decline prosecution in criminal cases.
- Forty-one states and the District of Columbia require felony courts to report the dispositions of felony cases to the state repository.
- Twenty-four states require law-enforcement agencies to notify the state repository when an arrested person is released without formal charging but after the fingerprints have been obtained and submitted.
- Twenty-four states and the District of Columbia have statutes that provide for the expungement of felony convictions. In nine states the record is destroyed by the state repository; in sixteen, the record is retained with the action noted.
- Forty-seven states have statutes that provide for the awarding of a pardon. In forty of these states, the criminal history record will be retained with the action noted.
- Thirty-five states have legal provisions for the restoration of a convicted felon's civil rights. In thirty of those states, the record is retained with the action noted.
- The average number of days between arrest and receipt of arrest data and fingerprints by the state criminal history repositories is eleven, ranging from less than one day in the District of Columbia up to forty-two days in Washington State.
- The average number of days between receipt of fingerprints by the state criminal history repository and entry into the master name index is twenty-nine, ranging from less than one day in North Dakota to 365 days in Louisiana.
- The average number of days between receipt of final trial court depositions by the state criminal history repository and

entry into the criminal history databases is seventy-nine, ranging from less than one day in North Dakota to 952 days in Georgia.

- Twenty states and the District of Columbia report that they currently conduct record checks of their state criminal history repository in connection with the sale of firearms.

The term "disposition" means information disclosing the final outcome of a "reportable event." The following are reportable events:

- An arrest.
- The release of a person after arrest without the filing of a charge.
- A decision by a prosecutor not to commence criminal proceedings or to defer or indefinitely postpone prosecution.
- A decision by a prosecutor to drop charges forwarded by the arresting agency or to add charges to those forwarded by the arresting agency.
- The presentment of an indictment or the filing of criminal information or other statement of charges.
- A release on bail or other conditions pending trial or appeal.
- A commitment to, or release from, a place of pretrial confinement.
- Failure of a person to appear in court as ordered.
- The dismissal of an indictment or criminal information or any of the charges set out in such indictment or criminal information.
- An acquittal, conviction or other court disposition at or following trial, including dispositions resulting from pleas.
- The imposition of a sentence.
- Failure to pay a fine.
- A commitment to, release from, or escape from a state or local correctional facility, including commitment to or release from a parole or probation agency.
- A commitment to or release from a hospital or other facility as not criminally responsible or as incompetent to stand trial.
- The entry of an appeal to an appellate court.
- A judgment of an appellate court.
- A pardon, reprieve, commutation of sentence, or other change in sentence

length, including a change ordered by the court.

- A revocation of probation or parole or other change in probation or parole status.
- Any other event arising out of or occurring during the course of criminal proceedings declared to be reportable by regulations issued by the Secretary of Public Safety.

For any or all of this information that comprises a criminal history record to be either difficult to determine or missing debilitates the criminal-justice system.

National Task Force
In direct response to the state study, SEARCH, the National Consortium for Justice Information and Statistics, the National Center for State Courts, and the Bureau of Justice Statistics established a National Task Force that same year. It was clear that criminal history record information was inadequate on a statewide basis and even more lacking nationwide. The Task Force's job was to review disposition reporting problems and make recommendations for improving the reporting to state central repositories. In all, nineteen findings confirmed the state study and pointed out glaring defects in the criminal-justice system:

1. There is a high incidence of recidivism, and many recidivists have active criminal careers involving multiple arrests and convictions.
2. Because recidivism is common, and because many recidivists have active criminal careers, appropriate decisions made about these individuals by both criminal justice and noncriminal justice decision-makers must take into account the recidivists' criminal history records.

Accurate and complete criminal history record information:

3. assists law-enforcement personnel to identify individuals for investigative purposes;
4. is necessary for prosecutors to make charging and plea bargaining decisions;
5. is necessary for courts to make appropriate pretrial release decisions;

6. is necessary for prosecutors and courts to make effective case management decisions;
7. is necessary for courts to make appropriate disposition decisions;
8. is critical for correctional and parole agencies to make appropriate and fair decisions;
9. is critical to make appropriate and reliable security clearance and other national security determinations;
10. is critical to make appropriate and reliable determinations of eligibility to purchase and/or carry a firearm;
11. is critical to make appropriate and reliable noncriminal justice licensing and eligibility determinations;
12. is critical to make governmental and private-sector employment decisions involving positions of trust, such as working with children or the elderly, or having the responsibility for significant financial or other assets;
13. is critical for public policy and research; and
14. is critical to assure that record subjects are treated in a fair and equitable manner.
15. Research indicates that, despite significant recent progress, the dispositions on criminal history records maintained by state central repositories are often missing, incomplete, or posted late.
16. Research indicates that disposition reporting rates vary significantly among state central repositories, with some repositories showing disposition reporting rates of 50 percent or less, and some showing 70 percent or more.
17. Research indicates that the causes for inadequate disposition reporting are many and varied and cannot be attributed to any one component of the criminal-justice system.
18. Information and telecommunication technologies exist to facilitate the reporting of disposition and other data to state central repositories.
19. The criminal-justice system needs to develop a reliable, high-quality criminal history record information product that takes into account the heterogeneity of needs and that is readily accessible; available on a timely basis; readable; and

customized to be of maximum utility to legitimate users.

Strategies for Improvement

The Task Force devised a number of strategies to correct the lamentable lack of criminal history record information. All of the strategies focused on statewide reform and, in particular, on initiatives by state central repositories and offices of court administration. A key recommendation was to establish state task forces to carry out the strategies of the national task force, without which status quo would continue to reign. Each state task force should include representatives from all components of the criminal-justice system within the state. All legitimate users of criminal history record information should be identified. Each state should adopt a plan to create a statewide, comprehensive criminal history record system that links databases. The databases should contain the most current information possible. Each database site should establish uniform, automated reporting procedures for the repository and the courts. Existing statutory and other reporting requirements should be amended to expedite electronic delivery of information.

The remaining strategies for the states to act on concerned missing information. Procedures for monitoring missing arrests and dispositions came first. Fingerprints obtained in all reportable cases must be submitted to the central repository in each state. Furthermore, to ensure accurate linkage of entries a fingerprint-supported number—a unique tracking number—should be assigned to each case upon initiation of case processing. For the type of meticulous work involved with maintaining the repositories, each state should establish professional training programs. Also concerning maintenance, each state should perform routine, external audits based on uniform guidelines to measure the reliability and completeness of criminal history record information in the central repository. And finally, apportionment of funding among the components of the criminal-justice system should be made according to existing resources and the level of responsibility for each component.

The American criminal-justice system is considered one of, if not *the*, best system in the world. Yet full reporting of criminal history information to state central repositories that then could link nationally has not been achieved. Of all the needs to share information throughout the spectrum of human endeavor, accurate and timely reporting of criminal history records should be a high priority.

Bibliography

Assessing Completeness and Accuracy of Criminal History Record Systems: Audit Guide. Washington, DC: U.S. Department of Justice, Office of Justice Programs, 1992.

Guidance for the Improvement of Criminal Justice Records. Washington, DC: U.S. Department of Justice, Bureau of Justice Assistance, 1991.

Report of the National Task Force on Criminal History Record Disposition Reporting. Washington, DC: U.S. Department of Justice, Office of Justice Programs, 1992.

Statutes Requiring the Use of Criminal History Record Information. Washington, DC: U.S. Department of Justice, Office of Justice Programs, 1991.

Survey of Criminal History Information Systems. Washington, DC: U.S. Department of Justice, Office of Justice Programs, 1991.

Criminal Informants

The acquisition and organization of legally reliable evidence is the essence of the criminal-investigation process. Evidence is usually obtained through the use of one or more of the three I's of investigation: interviewing, instrumentation, and information. Information provides direction to investigation. Information about a crime may be obtained from many sources. However, people motivated by the desire to improve the community usually have only limited knowledge of crime. Investigators must often turn to another, more questionable source of information: the criminal informant.

American law-enforcement agencies have long made use of informants. In the nineteenth and early twentieth centuries, detectives concentrated on identifying suspects and set about building a case from testimony of witnesses and confessions, or from actually catching offenders in the act (Lane, 1967; Richardson, 1970).

In time, investigators began to concentrate less on suspects and more on crimes. The shift away from suspects came because investigators began to view the collection of physical evidence as the most essential part of their job. Recently, however, an interest in the use of informants has reemerged. A major conclusion from a recent study of investigation suggested a need for both patrol officers and investigators to make greater use of informants (Eck, 1983).

Using an Informant's Information
The concept of probable cause is at the heart of American law enforcement. Of particular importance is the hearsay method for establishing probable cause most commonly used by officers relying on informants.

In *Aguilar v. Texas*, the Supreme Court created what became known as the two-pronged test for establishing probable cause on hearsay evidence. This test required that two things be done: (1) that the credibility of the informant be established, and (2) the reliability of the informant's information also be established.

The first prong of the test was usually satisfied in one of two ways. First, if the informant made statements which led to prosecution this was generally considered proof of an informant's reliability. This technique is particularly valuable when using informants for the first time.

Multiple use of an informant establishes a "track record," the second means used to demonstrate an informant's credibility. A police officer preparing an affidavit for a warrant can cite the track record as proof that the informant has provided accurate information leading to a specified number of arrests and convictions. Demonstrating the reliability of an informant's information, the second prong of the test, is most commonly accomplished by stating the informant's direct knowledge of the facts.

In *Spinelli v. United States*, the Supreme Court approved the technique of corroboration as a means to establish probable cause. Under this concept, the Court suggested that facts, when combined in sufficient number, could establish probable cause. Thus, traditional investigative techniques such as surveillance, record checks, and neighborhood canvasses could be of value in obtaining warrants.

In 1983, the Supreme Court handed down a decision that impacted the use of informants. In *Illinois v. Gates*, the Court established a totality of the circumstances test to determine the existence of probable cause. In *Gates*, a police officer received an anonymous letter so detailed that a judge felt the information contained in the letter was adequate to establish probable cause and issued a search warrant. At no point in the letter did the informant identify himself or provide information as to his credibility, from the perspective of *Aguilar*. The judge inferred the informant's credibility from the detailed information provided in the letter. The Court had eliminated the "first prong" of the two-pronged test, that of establishing credibility of the informant. Presently, the techniques set forth in *Aguilar*, *Spinelli*, and *Gates* affect use of an informant's information.

Protecting an Informant's Identity
Investigators must make every effort to protect informants. The reasons are obvious: No one can be expected to provide information if it leads to his or her injury, death, or ostracism. Two cases have established principles that determine circumstances under which courts can compel disclosure of an informant's identity. In a 1957 case, *Roviaro v. United States*, the Supreme Court held that when an informant is a material witness in a case, such as a participant, his/her identity must be revealed to the defendant. This requirement stems from the Sixth Amendment, the right of a criminal defendant to confront his accusers. Thus, if an informant is actually making drug buys, for example, this activity must be undertaken with the informant aware that he/she might have to testify in court. In a later decision, however, the Supreme Court held that where an informant, whose reliability has already been established, only provides information which establishes probable cause, the informant's identity need not be disclosed (*McCray v. Illinois*).

In some states, the identity of an informant may be protected as a privileged communication between police officer and informant. Where that privilege exists, a police officer may refuse to disclose the identity of an informant who has only provided information leading to probable cause. In those states where privilege does not exist, an informant's identity may be treated as a matter of relevancy. A prosecutor may argue that as long as the informant is not a material witness, revealing his or her identity is not relevant. The trial judge will then make an *in camera* determination on the need to reveal the informant's identity.

Problems Related to the Use of Informants
By its very nature, the use of informants requires secrecy. The potential for abuse is there-

fore enormous. One of the most complex problems concerns to whom informants should provide information. Should they provide it only to specified police officers who will then have exclusive use of the information or should the informants' names and their information be maintained in a master informant file?

Proponents of individual control argue that informants are developed on a personal basis. A working relationship, based upon a degree of trust, facilitates the flow of information. Once the relationship has been altered by inclusion of the informant's name in a master file, the informant's fear of exposure may hinder the acquisition of any further information. Another argument is that once the informant's identity is known to others it may become impossible to protect his or her identity, despite the most stringent security measures.

Arguments in support of centralized control hold that centralization lessens the potential for corruption either by police or informants. Administrative review may serve as a check on police officers engaging in corrupt and illegal acts. Centralization also makes an informant's information available to other investigators.

Use of informants also presents problems vis-à-vis the system as a whole. The American criminal-justice system is rooted in the concepts of accountability and punishment; that is, persons are to receive their just desserts for violating the law.

The "buy-bust-flip" procedure by which informants are developed reduces the certainty of being held accountable for violating the law. The "buy-bust-flip" technique of developing informants is well documented (Jacobson 1981; Wilson 1978). In its simplest form, the technique involves hand-to-hand purchases of drugs: the buy, which results in an immediate arrest, is the bust. The arrestee is then given an unpleasant choice: going to prison or becoming an informant (the flip). While it could be argued that being compelled to perform in the sometimes risky role of informant is a form of punishment, it is equally likely that the person will feel it to be the more attractive option. But the threat of punishment cannot be effective as a deterrent unless it is certain. As long as law violators believe that an avenue of escape as an informant exists, there can be no certainty of punishment.

Another problem of informant use relates to the selection of a target. Investigations tend to focus on individuals and activities already known to the informant, not necessarily on the most serious offenders. Allocation of resources should be made only after careful sifting of all available information, rather than on only the idiosyncratic knowledge of an informant. The decision to investigate someone is also tied to the amount of "buy money" available. For example, if an agency's resources are limited, purchases will be small. The larger the budget, the larger the prize. Eventually, however, the prize becomes too expensive and the person making the last transaction becomes the target. Thus, money, not criminal activity, determines who is prosecuted.

Informant Control

The Commission on Accreditation for Law Enforcement Agencies requires that agencies seeking accreditation establish policies governing the use of informants. While it is unrealistic to expect law-enforcement agencies to develop an all-encompassing policy, it is necessary to promulgate a series of workable guidelines. The policy statement should begin with a frank declaration that informants are a valuable resource to be used. Information provided by informants will be kept in a master file, but access must be tightly controlled. The policy must state that neither the agency's administration nor its individual members will allow informants to commit crimes, and those who do will be prosecuted. Officers must be prohibited from offering immunity without review by the prosecuting attorney. Informants must be briefed on entrapment laws and warned that they cannot present themselves as sworn or nonsworn employees of the agency. Finally, the commission emphasizes the need for special efforts to protect juvenile informants.

Conclusion

The use of criminal informants is an essential aspect of criminal investigations. It is also an area in which the potential for abuse is enormous. An understanding of the issues associated with informant use and a policy regulating the use of informants can reduce the possibility of informant misuse. The solution, however, lies not in the creation of rigid policies, but in the continual reevaluation of the goals of the police and the extent to which those goals are appropriate in a democratic society.

Michael F. Brown

Bibliography

Brown, Michael F. "Criminal Informants: Some Observations on Use, Abuse, and Control." *Journal of Police Science and Administration* 13(3) (September 1985): 251–56.

Eck, John E. *Solving Crimes: The Investigation of Burglary and Robbery.* Washington, DC: Police Executive Research Forum, 1983.

Jacobson, Ben. "Informants and the Public Police." In *Criminal and Civil Investigations Handbook.* Ed. Joseph J. Graw. New York: McGraw-Hill, 1981.

Kleinman, David Marc. "Out of the Shadows and into the Files: Who Should Control Informants?" *Police* 13(6) (1980): 36–44.

Lane, Roger. *Policing the City: Boston, 1822–1908.* Cambridge, MA: Harvard University Press, 1967.

Morris, Jack. *Police Informant Management.* Orangevale, CA: Palmer Enterprises, 1983.

Richardson, James. *New York Police: Colonial Times to 1901.* New York: Oxford University Press, 1970.

Wilson, James Q. *The Investigators.* New York: Basic Books, 1978.

Wilson, O.W. *Police Administration.* New York: McGraw-Hill, 1972.

Van den Haag, Ernest. "The Criminal Law as a Threat System." *Journal of Criminal Law and Criminology* 73 (1982): 709–85.

Criminal Investigation

Criminal investigation is the process of gathering facts. Just as one assembles pieces of a jigsaw puzzle to form a pattern or picture, so the investigator gathers facts and materials to form a coherent picture of an offense. The allegation that a certain person (or persons) has committed a specific violation of the criminal code must be proved beyond a reasonable doubt in a court of law. The proof is obtained by investigation.

The function of the investigator is to supply answers to the questions: *who? what? when? where? how?* and, sometimes, *why?* The adequacy of the investigation and the skill of the investigator can result in a successful prosecution and conviction of the offender or the exoneration of a person unjustly accused. An inadequate investigation can result in a failure of the prosecution or the conviction of the wrong person.

Investigation is a difficult task. It can be monotonous, unrewarding, dangerous, political, and filled with confrontations that challenge mental well-being. The investigator must be able to function in a complex environment where influences unrelated to the job of investigation can interfere with its progress. The education of an investigator, therefore, does not end with formal schooling. The investigator must always be aware of what is going on in the community as well as in the state, the nation, and the world.

Requisites for an Investigator

The investigator must ascertain whether or not an offense was committed; how it was committed; when it was committed, where it was committed; who committed the offense; and in certain cases, why it was committed. In order to do this, the investigator must possess (1) the intellectual ability to learn; (2) perseverance in the face of obstacles; (3) personal integrity that can withstand physical, emotional, and material temptations; (4) an understanding of people, their mental processes, their culture, their customs, and their environments; (5) knowledge of available scientific aids and a willingness to use them; (6) ability to reach conclusions based on evidence; (7) knowledge of self; (8) ability to withstand prejudice; (9) patience to await judgment until evidence is available; and (10) knowledge of the techniques and procedures required in a criminal investigation.

Tools for an Investigation

Observation. The investigator must be able to see accurately all there is to see, use language to convey to others what he or she has seen, and describe accurately what has been seen. No detail can be overlooked or brushed aside as being insignificant. The trained observer not only sees the object but also locates it in relation to the situation. The situation is composed of numerous details, all of which must be included in an accurate description. Photographs of the scene constitute a record that can be used as an aid in observation, but a photograph is not an observation. Observation gives meaning to what is seen; it is a mental impression.

Description is essential to communicate the observation. The use of appropriate words, oral or written, in communication requires a knowledge of vocabulary and composition.

Emotional states, ailments, disabilities, prejudices, and legends can limit the accuracy of the observations of witnesses, and even that of the investigator. Many factors can contribute to inaccurate observation and faulty description in addition to the factors listed above. Witnesses will describe scenes that upon checking prove to be impossible because the witness could not observe what he/she described from the place from which the witness claims to have made the observation. The description may be a total fabrication by a witness seeking recognition.

Use of Records. Records, public and private, are often essential to an investigation. Much information is required to build a case. Knowledge about the many records and the information they contain is necessary. The investigator must know who controls the desired records and how to approach these sources. The amount of information recorded about individuals borders on the incredible. The sources range from the easily available, such as telephone directories, city directories, and the like, to less available information maintained by private, semipublic, and government agencies.

Interviewing and Interrogation. The investigator must possess the ability to interview and gather information from a variety of people in all walks of life—children, bartenders, cab drivers, delivery persons, prostitutes, doormen, clerks, beauticians, and so on. Knowledge about who may know what develops with experience.

Interrogation is a function of investigation. The purpose of interrogation is to get information about the offense under investigation and about the perpetrator. All categories of people can be interrogated: witnesses, subjects, employers, coworkers, friends, relatives, etc. Interrogation is not a substitute for investigation; it is an aid to investigation. There are legal requirements surrounding interrogation with which the investigator must be familiar. Failure to observe these requirements will negate the use of the information obtained as evidence.

Confidential informants can provide the investigator with useful information, otherwise unavailable, about a crime or the planning of a crime. In a sense, these informants are civilian undercover agents. Their identity is not disclosed. The informant usually is involved with offenders. His or her value lies in the information he can gather through his close association with offenders. Contacts with the informant must be arranged so that his identity will not be compromised.

Confidential informants act from a variety of motives. Whatever the motive may be, the investigator must double check every bit of information given by the informant before any action is taken.

Modi Operandi. The methods of operation of offenders, knowledge of the way in which an offense is committed, enables the investigator to identify an offense as being committed by a known offender or as one of a series of offenses committed by a certain person as yet not identified. It also enables the investigator to use the modi operandi (MO) files maintained by other enforcement agencies. MO files are based on the premise that people tend to do things in a manner unique to the individual. Aspects of such behavior tend to be repetitive. The manner in which an offense has been committed may often identify the perpetrator. The behavior is characteristic of the person.

Surveillance. Surveillance is the process of keeping persons, premises, and vehicles under observation without being discovered. The purpose of surveillance is to learn as much as possible about the activities of the subject, where he goes, with whom he comes in contact, and what objects and persons attract his attention. The investigator endeavors to remain unobserved. Surveillance can be conducted on foot, by vehicle, by air, or from a fixed position.

Undercover Work. Undercover agents can be a source of information. Such agents may be members of a law-enforcement agency. The agent, acting under cover, must drop his or her own identity and assume that of another in keeping with the situation he is exploring. The change of identity requires the agent to be a very capable actor, often to preserve life and limb.

Experts. The investigator must gather and apply the knowledge of experts to the case; and must be aware of the many fields in which experts can examine evidence and supply information otherwise unobtainable. Some of the familiar fields are forensic chemists, documents examiners, ballistic experts, fingerprint experts, pathologists, and medical examiners. It is necessary for the investigator to furnish the expert with the materials gathered during the course of the investigation. In so doing, the investigator must know how to protect and preserve the evidence transmitted to the expert. The investigator must know what to expect of the expert and what not to expect. If the case comes to trial, the expert will testify in court as to his findings.

Report Writing. The report of the investigation, relating in detail what was done, how it was done, and what was discovered, is the official statement of the investigation and becomes the basis of the case in the trial of the subject. The report enables the prosecuting attorney to decide if there is sufficient evidence to warrant prosecution. The person under investigation should be referred to in the report as the subject. Labeling the person a suspect can be considered making a judgment, which may be used to charge the investigator with bias.

Court Testimony. The investigator must develop the ability to testify in court in an impartial, objective, and unbiased manner. Personal demeanor on the witness stand will affect the outcome of the case. The investigator must avoid the appearance of "getting" the defendant, of any display of zealousness, or demonstration of special interest in securing a conviction. The investigator must narrate the facts obtained during the investigation; and must keep in mind that he or she is limited to testifying to the facts within the scope of personal knowledge. The investigator cannot offer opinions or testify as to the finding of the experts.

Legal Limitations. The investigator must comply with the legal limitations in arrest, search, and seizure. Failure to follow the legal requirements results in rejection of evidence obtained and subsequent loss of the basis for conviction. Respect for law enforcement depends to a large degree on observance of the citizen's right to be secure in his or her person, house, papers, and effects against illegal arrest, search, and seizure.

Conclusion
Criminal investigation is an integral part of law enforcement. It is the search for facts which lead to the discovery of the person or persons who have committed an act declared illegal by the laws of the society. The facts to support a criminal case are supplied through investigation. If the facts are deemed sufficient by the prosecuting agency, a case is developed that becomes the

basis for a trial. The trial may result in a conviction, a dismissal of the charges because of insufficient evidence, or exoneration because the investigation did not provide the facts necessary for conviction.

William Dienstein

Bibliography
Bennett, Wayne W., and Karen M. Hess. *Criminal Investigation*. St. Paul, MN: West Publishing, 1981.
Bozza, Charles M. *Criminal Investigation*. Chicago: Nelson-Hall, 1978.
DeLadurantey, Joseph C., and Daniel R. Sullivan. *Criminal Investigation Standards*. New York: Harper & Row, 1980.
Dienstein, William. *Techniques for the Crime Investigator*. 2d ed. Springfield, IL: Charles C. Thomas, 1974.
Gilbert, James N. *Criminal Investigation*. Columbus, OH: Merrill, 1980.
Mulvaney, Robert E. *Techniques of Criminal Investigation*. Santa Cruz, CA: Davis, 1976.

Criminal Investigation: Outcomes
The police organization provides three valued outputs—service, order maintenance, and law enforcement. These outputs also comprise the major work activities within the police organization. "Service" refers to the provision of assistance to the public in regard to noncrime-related matters. "Order maintenance" involves activities oriented around maintaining the public peace. "Law enforcement" involves intervening in situations where a law has been violated and the perpetrator needs to be identified and apprehended. Conceptually, the criminal-investigation process is located within the law-enforcement component of the police mission.

Criminal investigation, defined here as the process of collecting crime-related information after a criminal incident has come to the attention of the police, is an important aspect of the police mission. Although research has shown that relatively little police time is spent on crime-related activities (e.g., Greene and Klockars, 1991), the police claim these activities as their own and, therefore, it is this aspect of the police mission that gives legitimacy to the police organization (Manning, 1977).

The investigation of crime is also a critical aspect of the criminal-justice system. One of the primary goals of the criminal-justice system is to control crime. It is through the activities performed by the components of the justice system that efforts are made to attain this goal. For example, with long prison sentences imposed by the courts, offenders may be deterred (or incapacitated) from engaging in sanctioned behaviors. However, if the police are unable to identify and apprehend offenders, then the activities of the other components cannot be performed. Therefore, to the extent that the police are unable to identify and apprehend criminals, the ability of the entire criminal-justice system to control crime diminishes.

Given the importance of investigative activities, it is worthwhile to examine the effectiveness of the process. To establish, and perhaps subsequently improve, the effectiveness of the criminal-investigation process, it is necessary to first measure the extent to which the outcomes associated with the process are being attained and then identify the factors that facilitate or constrain the attainment of these outcomes. Not surprisingly, most studies which have examined the effectiveness of the criminal-investigation process have used "crime-solving" as the criterion on which to make performance judgments (e.g., Eck, 1983; Greenwood, Chaiken, and Petersilia, 1977). However, other important outcomes have also been associated with the process—specifically, convicting suspects (e.g., Garofalo, 1991; Petersilia, Abrahamse, and Wilson, 1987) and satisfying crime victims (e.g., Brandl and Horvath, 1991).

The purpose here is to discuss the effectiveness of the criminal-investigation process vis-à-vis solving crimes, convicting suspects, and satisfying victims. The problems associated with the measurement of each outcome are identified, the appropriateness of each outcome as an indicator of "investigative success" is considered, and the empirical research which has examined the effectiveness of the process in relation to each outcome is discussed. In doing so, the complexities of measuring the effectiveness of the criminal-investigation process are better appreciated and a more complete understanding of the capabilities of the process is attained.

Solving Crimes
Clearance and arrest data are typically used to measure the performance of the police in solving crimes. The police can clear a crime "when at least one person is arrested, charged with the commission of the offense, and turned over to the court for prosecution" or "by exceptional means when some element beyond law enforcement control precludes the placing of formal charges against the offender" (Federal Bureau of Investigation, 1992:202). On the basis of clearance data, the clearance rate can be calculated. The clearance rate refers to the number of FBI Part I, or Index, crimes (murder, rape, robbery, aggravated assault, burglary, larceny theft, and motor vehicle theft [arson has been added but reporting is not complete]), which are cleared in a given period of time divided by the number of crimes known to the police in that same period. The arrest rate is similar to the clearance rate except that only crimes in which a suspect is taken "into custody" are included.[1]

The limitations and criticisms of these measures are many. For instance, in regard to clearance data, police practices of "unfounding" crimes (i.e., determining that a reported crime did not actually occur) and attributing numerous crimes to a suspect in custody (often based on modus operandi alone) may systematically and unjustifiably distort the data. A crime can also be cleared when the victim refuses to cooperate with the police in the investigation or prosecution, although this does not indicate that a crime is "solved." With arrest statistics, there is definitional variance across departments on what actually constitutes "in custody," or an arrest. For example, according to Sherman and Glick (1984), 11 percent of agencies surveyed counted an arrest whenever a suspect was brought to the station even if the suspect was later freed, 16 percent counted an arrest whenever a restraint was used on a suspect, and 29 percent counted an arrest when a suspect was detained at the police station for questioning, even if never formally charged. As a result, different rates of arrest could be obtained by departments that simply use different definitions of "arrest."

Although clearance and arrest data are imprecise measures of the crime-solving outcome, the appropriateness of the crime-solving outcome itself remains largely uncontested. It is, after all, a necessary condition for future criminal-justice system processing. However, it is not a *sufficient* condition for future processing; the police may be able to make a substantial number of arrests, or a dramatic increase in arrests, but that, by itself, is little guarantee of future processing.[2] It is the processing after an arrest that may lead to the attainment of other elusive outcomes like deterrence or incapacitation. In essence, the crime-solving outcome, at least as measured by clearance and arrest data, does not provide any indication of the *quality* of arrests or clearances.

Depending on the nature and type of crime, the police have varying success in "solving" crimes. In 1991, approximately 21 percent of UCR Index crimes were "cleared." [3] Generally, the police are more successful in solving personal crimes than property crimes: Specifically, 67 percent of murders, 57 percent of aggravated assaults, 52 percent of forcible rapes, 24 percent of robberies, 20 percent of larceny thefts, 14 percent of motor-vehicle thefts, and 13 percent of burglaries were cleared by an arrest or other means in 1991 (Federal Bureau of Investigation, 1992).

What determines whether or not a crime is solved? Some analysts have come to the conclusion that the *circumstances* that surround the incident (e.g., the culprit can be named by witnesses) largely determine the case outcome, while others argue that the *efforts* of investigators are equally important in determining the outcome. If circumstances are most influential, then the police have only limited control over the crime-solving outcome. However, if investigative effort is most influential, then crime solvability is within control of the police. A review of several pertinent studies helps inform this debate.

Spelman and Brown (1991) analyzed the role of police response time in making on-scene arrests by interviewing over 4,000 victims, witnesses, and bystanders in 3,300 serious crimes (i.e., Part I crimes not including homicide or arson), which occurred in four cities (Jacksonville, FL; Peoria,IL; Rochester, NY; and San Diego, CA). Overall, they found that only about 3 percent of all serious crimes reported to the police resulted in a response-related arrest. Since about 75 percent of all crimes do not involve contact between the victim/witness and the offender (i.e., they are "discovery crimes"), often an extended period of time elapses between when the crime occurs and when the crime is discovered and reported. This, in turn, allows the offender to flee the scene of the crime and prohibits a fast police response leading to an arrest. The remaining 25 percent of crimes (i.e., "involvement crimes") actually involve a confrontation between the victim/witness and the offender. However, delays of reporting the crime to the police, even of a few minutes, often allow the suspect to flee the scene of the crime before the police arrive.[4] Only when citizens do not hesitate in calling the police to report "involvement" crimes can police response time make a difference. In short, police ability to make *on-scene* arrests is determined largely by circumstances (i.e., type of crime, citizen reporting time) outside of their immediate control.

Other studies have focused directly on the role of information in solving crimes. Isaacs (1967) analyzed data on 1,905 crimes reported to two of fifteen Los Angeles Police Department field divisions in January 1966. Isaacs found that of the 1,905 crimes, 336 (18 percent) resulted in an arrest while 146 (8 percent) resulted in "other clearances" (e.g., victim refused to prosecute, unfounded). Of the 336 cases that resulted in an arrest, 309 (92 percent) were made by patrol officers during the initial investigation, while the remaining twenty-seven (8 percent) were made by detectives. Based on limited statistical analyses performed on the data, the author concluded that "[o]ne of the most significant characteristics of a case, affecting its chances of being cleared, is whether the suspect was named in the crime report by the victim" (96). For example, of the 1,905 crimes, 1,556 (82 percent) involved suspects who were *not* named in the crime report. Of these 1,556 cases, 1,375 (88 percent) were *not* cleared. Conversely, of the 1,905 crimes, 349 (18 percent) involved suspects who *were* named in the crime report. Of these cases, only forty-eight (14 percent) were *not* cleared.

In an analysis of burglary, robbery, and grand larceny crimes which were reported to the New York City Police Department during the first six months of 1967, Greenwood (1970) found that when a suspect could be named by the victim, the chances of an arrest were substantially greater than when only a description was provided, or other evidence was available. For example, the analyses showed that approximately 9 percent of reported robberies resulted in an on-scene arrest while the remaining 91 percent were initially unsolved. Of the unsolved cases, the victim could name a suspect in about 2 percent and could describe the suspect in 67 percent. For those cases with a named suspect, 46 percent resulted in an arrest, while only 2 percent of the cases with a description resulted in an arrest. Once again, circumstances—namely, the victim providing the suspect's name—were found to largely determine the outcome of the case.

A study conducted by Greenwood, Chaiken, and Petersilia of the RAND Corporation in 1977 supported, and elaborated on, the conclusions of Isaacs (1967) and Greenwood (1970). Their results, based primarily on an analysis of the computer readable case assignment file maintained by the Kansas City (MO) Police Department,[5] showed that 30 percent of cleared crimes[6] resulted from an arrest by a patrol officer at the scene of the crime. In approximately 50 percent of the cleared crimes, the perpetrator was "known" when the crime report was first taken and, as described by the researchers, the detective's task was to simply locate the perpetrator, take him/her into custody, and assist in preparing the case for court. An additional 20 percent of all cleared crimes could be attributed to detective work but most of these cases were actually solved because of information provided to detectives by patrol officers or the public, or because of "routine investigative practices" (i.e., fingerprint searches, informant tips, mugshot show-ups). Only about 3 percent of clearances could be attributed to special investigative action.

While the presence of suspect information was found to be important, Greenwood, Chaiken, and Petersilia (1977) found that the presence of physical evidence, fingerprints in particular, had little impact on whether a crime was solved. Based on data collected from three departments (Long Beach, CA, Berkeley, CA, and Richmond, VA), it was determined that only 1–2 percent of all burglary cases were cleared as a result of recovered fingerprints although fingerprints were recovered in 30–61 percent of such cases (see also Bloch and Bell, 1976:45).

Accordingly, like Isaacs (1967) and Greenwood (1970), Greenwood, Chaiken, and Petersilia (1977) explain that the great majority of cleared crimes are solved because of arrests by patrol officers or because the identity of the perpetrator is known when the crime report reached the detective. "If information that uniquely identifies the perpetrator is not presented at the time the crime is reported, the perpetrator, by and large, will not be subsequently identified" (Greenwood, Chaiken, and Petersilia, 1976:65).

If it is true that the great majority of crimes are not solved unless the identity of the perpetrator becomes known during the initial investigation, it helps explain why the police have more success in solving personal crimes than property crimes. Personal crimes, by definition, involve contact between the victim and the offender *and* they also often involve offenders who are known to their victims. Accordingly, favorable circumstances (victim–offender contact and victim–offender relationship) exist for personal crimes to be solved.

Eck (1983) provides contrast with Isaacs (1967), Greenwood (1970), and Greenwood, Chaiken, and Petersilia (1977) by emphasizing, or at least not minimizing, the importance of investigative effort in solving crimes. Using data collected from three police departments (DeKalb Co., GA; St. Petersburg, FL; and Wichita, KS), he examined activities performed by patrol officers and detectives to produce crime and/or suspect information, and the relationship between this information and a suspect being arrested. The study focused on burglaries and robberies. According to Eck, cases can be grouped into three categories depending on the strength of the evidence associated with the case. First, those cases with weak evidence will rarely conclude with an arrest, regardless of investigative effort. Second, those cases with moderate evidence will often result in an arrest but only if effort is allocated to them. Third, cases with strong evidence will usually result in an arrest, even with only minimal investigative effort. As such, circumstances determine the outcome of the cases in the first and third group, but effort determines the outcome of the cases in the second group.

In addition, Eck found that some investigative activities, and/or the information produced by those activities, were significant contributors to arrest, others were not. For example, victims were interviewed in almost every case; however, victims were one of the least likely sources to provide information leading to the arrest of a suspect—a small percentage of victim interviews produced information which could lead to an arrest. On the other hand, witnesses, informants, other members of the department, and departmental records were more likely to provide the necessary information for an arrest. The problem, however, is that these sources of information are not entirely within the control of the police—witnesses and informants may simply not be available (even if they are searched for) and/or there may not be enough leads to indicate what departmental records to check. On the face of it, these findings highlight the importance of performing certain investigative activities; however, certain circumstances must still exist for these activities to be productive.

C

In sum, the general conclusion drawn from Spelman and Brown (1991), Isaacs (1967), Greenwood (1970), and Greenwood, Chaiken, and Petersilia (1977) is that the circumstances associated with the criminal incident largely determine whether or not the case is solved. According to Eck (1983), circumstances determine the case outcome in many instances, but in some cases, investigative effort determines the disposition if favorable circumstances exist.

Convicting Suspects

Another standard on which to judge the performance of the police in investigating crimes is "convicting suspects." This criterion is most often measured by the percentage of all arrests for which a conviction is eventually obtained (Petersilia, Abrahamse, and Wilson, 1990). Other related measures have also been used: the percent of all cases which the police send forward to the prosecutor, the percent of all arrests accepted by the prosecutor for purposes of filing a complaint, or the percentage of all arrests for which an incarceration sentence is obtained. Because these measures are most often based on arrest data, they are subject to the same limitation of "arrest rates" discussed above—that the definition of arrest essentially determines the summary statistic.

Those who advocate the use of "convicting suspects" as an appropriate investigative outcome argue that the quantity of crimes solved is essentially meaningless if other outcomes (like punishment, deterrence, etc.) are not achieved (Skogan and Antunes, 1979). These outcomes can only be attained if those who are responsible for crimes are convicted. Moreover, it is argued that the police have a direct bearing on how far a case is processed and what the disposition will be. As explained by Forst, Lucianovic, and Cox (1977:49), "[t]here can be no doubt that the police do make a difference—they determine largely what happens after arrest."

Several arguments have also been offered against the use of "convicting suspects" as a measure of investigative success. First, in direct contrast to the argument offered above, it is suggested that the police have only minimal control over what happens during the adjudication process—other actors within the process control charging and conviction decisions (e.g., prosecutor, judge, jury). Therefore, the police should not be evaluated on the abilities, prac-

tices, or policies of these other criminal-justice actors.

Second, the use of convictions as a measure of investigative effectiveness assumes that the police make arrests for the sole purpose of convicting suspects. The conviction criterion does not allow for consideration of the arrest as a situational tool of the police—a means by which to induce information (i.e., develop an informant) or restore order (Petersilia, Abrahamse, and Wilson 1990).

Third, use of the conviction measure also assumes that the only purpose of submitting cases to the prosecutor is to bring charges against the suspect. It ignores other purposes such as reducing public pressure on the police or simply documenting the criminal behavior of a suspect, even though it is recognized by the police that there is too little evidence for charges to be filed (Petersilia, Abrahamse, and Wilson, 1990). To the extent that these arguments are true, the use of convictions as a measure of investigative success is inappropriate.

Research has shown that a substantial proportion of arrests do not result in charges being filed by the prosecutor or in convictions being obtained. In other words, there is substantial case attrition. As determined by Boland, Mahanna, and Sones (1992), on average, of one hundred felony arrests brought by the police to the prosecutor, six are diverted, eighteen are rejected by the prosecutor, and another twenty-one are dismissed in court. Of the fifty-five cases carried forward, fifty-two are disposed of by guilty pleas while three are by trial (one acquittal).

Several studies have examined the causes of case attrition. At the most simplistic level, cases are most often rejected and dismissed because it is perceived by the prosecutor (or judge) that a conviction is not likely or even possible. Research has found, not surprisingly, that the most important factor that contributes to this perception is the strength and quality of the evidence associated with the case. In essence, there is an evidentiary gap between what constitutes "probable cause" for an arrest and "beyond a reasonable doubt" for a conviction.

Forst, Lucianovic, and Cox (1977) analyzed PROMIS[7] data on 14,865 adult arrests made by the Washington, D.C. Police Department and presented for prosecution to the Superior Court Division of the U.S. Attorney's Office. The researchers found that when physical evidence (e.g., fingerprints) was recovered, the probability of a conviction was substantially greater than when it was not recovered. In addition, when there were cooperative victims available, convictions were more likely. Finally, when police made an arrest soon after the offense occurred, physical evidence was more often recovered and, thus, a conviction was more likely.

Forst et al. (1982) provided a multijurisdictional comparison of conviction rates using 1977–1978 PROMIS data. This study supports the findings offered by Forst, Lucianovic, and Cox (1977). Across the eight jurisdictions, the percentage of cases rejected at the initial screening by the prosecutor ranged from 16 to 46 percent. Despite this variance, the most commonly cited reasons for the rejections were "evidence problems" and "witness problems." Although these problems are never explicitly defined by the authors, they once again explain that cases with physical evidence were more likely to result in convictions than those cases without, and cases with at least two (cooperative) witnesses were significantly more likely to conclude with a conviction than cases with fewer than two witnesses. Like the earlier study, the researchers found that the time which elapsed between the offense and the arrest was related to the probability of securing physical evidence and multiple witnesses, and thus, of obtaining a conviction.

Chen (1991) analyzed PROMIS data from the Los Angeles Prosecutor's Office and offers additional support for some of the earlier findings. Specifically, he found that strength of the evidence associated with the case—namely, number of police officer witnesses, along with number of experts, eyewitnesses, other lay witnesses, and victims—exerts positive effects on the acceptance of cases for preliminary hearing and arraignment (analysis of initial screening decision not provided).

Given the general conclusion that lack of evidence leads to the rejection and dismissal of cases, an important question becomes: "Why isn't the evidence to support a conviction present in any given case?" It is with this question that there is disagreement. One argument suggests that evidence (broadly defined) is not recognized because police are uncertain as to what they are looking for or evidence is lost because of other inadequate police practices. For instance, witnesses are not available because the police are unable to locate them or witnesses do not wish to cooperate because of

the officers' actions toward them (Forst et al., 1982). Police officers may not collect (or recognize) physical evidence, at least in part, because of lack of feedback from prosecutors on the necessity of such evidence in obtaining convictions (McDonald, Rossman, and Cramer, 1982). Research that has examined the effectiveness of programs designed to increase communication between the police and the prosecutor has found that such efforts do little in reducing the amount of case attrition (e.g., Garofalo, 1991). Accordingly, at least some of this argument has not been able to withstand empirical scrutiny.

The opposing argument suggests that the evidence needed to secure a conviction is often just simply not available. Factors inherent within the offense, and beyond the control of the police, largely determine the amount and nature of the evidence available. Research has consistently shown, for example, that a prior relationship between the victim and defendant is strongly related to lower conviction rates. According to Forst et al. (1982), offenses in which the victim and defendant were friends, acquaintances, or relatives result in 50 to 60 percent fewer convictions than offenses which involve strangers. The primary reason for this is that victims in such cases are often uncooperative in the prosecution process, if they wish to pursue the case at all. Another reason is that crimes which occur between friends, etc., may be viewed by the prosecutor (and the police) as not being as serious as crimes which occur between strangers; when there is a relationship between the parties, the crime may be viewed more as a private matter than a criminal matter. It follows then that, completely independent of police action, some crimes (like personal crimes which often occur between friends, acquaintances, or relatives) are inherently more difficult to convict than others. It is interesting to note that personal crimes are more likely to be solved than property crimes, but are less likely to result in a conviction.

Research has also shown that other factors which are completely outside the control of the police (e.g., offender's use of a weapon in the commission of the offense, offender's previous arrest record, amount of harm done to the victim) also affect case rejection and dismissal decisions (see Chen, 1991; Garofalo, 1991; Schmidt and Steury, 1989). With an empirically informed understanding of the factors that influence case rejection and dismissal decisions, it appears that obtaining convictions, like solving crimes, is more a function of circumstances outside the immediate control of the police than of investigative capabilities and practices.

Satisfying Crime Victims
The use of victim satisfaction as a standard on which to judge the effectiveness of the criminal-investigation process is a relatively new concept. The satisfaction outcome emerged from the citizen attitudes studies conducted since the turbulent 1960s and has taken on new importance in the last decade with the movement toward community policing. The satisfaction outcome is essentially an extension of the consumer perspective into the public sector where the traditional market mechanism of willingness to pay is absent.

Typically, through interviews or self-administered questionnaires, crime victims who recently reported their victimization to the police department are asked about their degree of satisfaction with the police response and/or certain aspects of it. For example, Brandl and Horvath (1991) asked a sample of crime victims to describe specific aspects of the police response (expectations of response time, officer demeanor, officer's crime-scene activities, and existence of recontacts) and to express their overall satisfaction with the police in regard to the specific incident. This type of data not only provides insight into the effectiveness of the process vis-à-vis victim satisfaction but also provides a means to identify policies and practices which need adjustment or change.

Because victim satisfaction data are collected via survey research methods, the validity and reliability of the data are subject to all the threats inherent in survey research. Of particular concern in this regard are sample selection bias, response rate bias, and errors that result from question wording (see Babbie, 1990). In addition, there is concern about the extent to which victims can accurately perceive (and recall) police activities, and thus, the extent to which victims' judgments produce valid data (see Parks, 1984; Schneider et al., 1978; Stipak, 1979).

Several arguments can be offered in support of victim satisfaction as a standard on which to judge the effectiveness of the criminal-investigation process. First, and most basically, satisfying victims (or citizens more generally) is thought to represent a legitimate goal in itself, a "good" end to be pursued for its own sake.

This reasoning is congruent with the recent trend toward "community policing," of providing more responsive and "humane" police services (Goldstein, 1987).

A second argument in support of victim satisfaction as an investigative outcome, although yet to be tested empirically (cf. Frank, 1992), is that victim satisfaction is a prerequisite for victim *cooperation* with the police — a means by which victims/citizens and the police can become "co-producers" of crime prevention — again, a cornerstone of the community policing concept (Goldstein, 1987). In this light, insuring satisfaction may be of utmost importance because, as discussed earlier, the police are dependent on victims to report incidents and to provide information necessary to identify, apprehend, and convict offenders.

One frequently offered argument against the use of the victim satisfaction standard is that it distracts from efforts at attaining more important outcomes like solving crimes. Significant resources can be applied toward satisfying victims but, as the argument goes, they are essentially wasted resources because they often have little to do with solving crimes (e.g., dusting for fingerprints).

Also potentially problematic is that using victim satisfaction as an indicator of investigative effectiveness assumes that the performance of the police can substantially affect victims' degree of satisfaction. If other factors such as prior experiences with the police and background characteristics (i.e., race, age, income) exert a substantial independent impact on satisfaction, the use of satisfaction as an indicator of investigative effectiveness would be inappropriate.

Previous research has documented varying levels of victim satisfaction. Shapland (1983), in interviews with 287 crime victims in England, found that over 70 percent were satisfied with how the police handled the incident. Percy's (1980) analyses, based on interviews with victims in several jurisdictions, showed that 62 percent of the respondents were satisfied with what the police did. Poister and McDavid (1978) conducted interviews of 111 crime victims in Harrisburg (PA) and found 46 percent to be satisfied with the police response to the victimization. According to Brandl and Horvath (1991), approximately 62 percent of the 436 surveyed victims from a medium-sized midwestern city were satisfied with how the police handled the incident.

These studies, along with a few others, have documented some of the factors related to victim satisfaction with police performance. Specifically, previous research indicates that the demeanor of the patrol officer during the initial investigation is one of the most important factors. According to Shapland (1983:253), "the major determinant of satisfaction was . . . [the police officer's] attitude toward the victim. Those police officers who appeared to be interested in what the victim said, took the time to listen to them and seemed to take them seriously, promoted feelings of satisfaction in the victims." Similar results were found by Brandl and Horvath (1991). In this research, we found that victims who perceived officers to exhibit a more "professional" demeanor [8] were significantly more likely to be satisfied than those who did not. In fact, the officer's demeanor was the most powerful predictor of satisfaction. The importance of the officer's demeanor was also highlighted by some of the comments provided by victims on the returned questionnaires. For example:

> "The police officers who came to the scene were unfriendly, rude, and very uncaring. They treated me like I was the criminal. I would never call them for help again."

> "I felt that the officers had a poor attitude . . ."

> "I felt as if the officer didn't believe me, because of the way he was talking to the other officer who showed up."

> "The officer had a very bored attitude. It seemed that he felt dissatisfied by having to 'stoop' so low as to write down anything about a 'minor burglary.'"

Investigative activities performed by the patrol officer during the initial investigation have also been found to be strongly related to victim satisfaction (Brandl and Horvath, 1991; Percy, 1980; Poister and McDavid, 1978). For example, Percy (1980) found that when the officer made an arrest, comforted someone, or provided crime prevention information, victims were more likely to be satisfied. Poister and McDavid (1978) found that there was a tendency for respondents to express satisfaction when the police conducted a general investiga-

tion as opposed to just talking with victims or asking questions. According to Brandl and Horvath (1991), the investigative effort [9] of the patrol officer was positively related to victim satisfaction in property crimes but not personal crimes. In particular, the importance of looking for fingerprints was evident by the frequency of related comments provided on the returned questionnaires. A few quotes from dissatisfied victims are illustrative:

> "They could have taken fingerprints but did not until two days later and only because I complained to the department."

> "My children asked why the police didn't take fingerprints . . . I explained to them that we were not important enough."

> "I felt that a more thorough investigation including taking fingerprints would possibly have helped solve the crime."

> "The police officer who responded to the call was very nice and courteous. However, when asked if they could take fingerprints, I was told no."

> "I figured the window used to gain entry should have been dusted for fingerprints."

> "There were fingerprints all over the dashboard and nothing was done about that either."

Response time is another dimension of the police response which has been found to affect victim satisfaction. Poister and McDavid (1978) found that victims who perceived the police to take more time to respond (in minutes) were more likely to be dissatisfied. According to Percy (1980), victim *expectation* of police response time was a better predictor of satisfaction than actual response time. Victims who perceived the police to respond faster than expected were more likely to be satisfied than victims who perceived the police to respond slower than expected. Brandl and Horvath (1991) found the same general relationship but that expectation of response time was more important in determining the satisfaction of personal crime victims than property crime victims.

Finally, the existence of victim recontacts has sometimes been shown to affect satisfaction, other times not. Shapland (1983) found that the receipt of feedback on the status of the case had a positive impact on satisfaction. According to Brandl and Horvath (1991), a recontact with the status of the investigation only affected the level of satisfaction expressed by serious property (burglary and auto theft) crime victims (also see Greenwood, Chaiken, and Petersilia, 1977; Skogan and Wycoff, 1987). Neither Brandl and Horvath (1991) nor Poister and McDavid (1978) found that a recontact to ask additional questions of the victim influenced satisfaction.

In regard to the influence of victim characteristics on victim satisfaction, the findings of previous research indicate that they have inconsistent and relatively weak effects compared to the police response variables. Accordingly, one can infer that the police, by exhibiting certain behaviors and performing certain activities, can substantially affect the level of satisfaction expressed by crime victims.

Conclusion

On the basis of this discussion, several conclusions concerning the effectiveness of the criminal-investigation process can be offered. First, it is apparent that none of the investigative outcomes discussed here—solving crimes, convicting suspects, or satisfying victims—are immune from measurement problems. Our understanding of the true capabilities and limitations of the criminal-investigation process is thus limited in this respect.

Second, none of the investigative outcomes is within complete control of the police, although it appears that the actions of the police can influence victim satisfaction more than the other two outcomes. Therefore, since circumstances outside the control of the police exert a substantial effect on the probability of a conviction being obtained or a crime being solved, structural changes in the investigative process will likely have little or no *direct* affect on apprehension or conviction success. As explained by Greenwood, Chaiken, and Petersilia (1976), "the method by which police investigators are organized (i.e., team policing, specialist vs. generalist, patrolmen-investigators) cannot be related to variations in crime, arrest, and clearance rates" (64). They continue "differences in investigative training, staffing, workload, and procedures appear to have no appreciable effect on crime, arrest, or clearance rates" (64).[10]

However, the police may be able to substantially and directly affect victim satisfaction through procedural changes. For example, given the importance of expectations of response time in satisfying victims, police telephone operators could, as a matter of policy, provide crime victims with an estimate of police arrival time (Percy, 1980) and thus, make expectations congruent with the services actually received. In regard to officer demeanor, it does not seem unreasonable, at the very least, to stress among officers the importance of sensitivity in interpersonal interaction with victims. As for investigative effort, at a minimum, victims could be made aware of the tasks that were, or will be, performed in the investigation.[11] With the understanding that the police have different amounts of control over the investigative outcomes comes a more realistic understanding of the capabilities of the criminal-investigation process.

Third, to establish the utility of certain investigative practices, it is necessary that the three outcomes be considered simultaneously because what is important for achieving one outcome may not be important in achieving another. For instance, research has shown that fingerprints are not very useful in solving crimes (but see note 10). On this basis, one might conclude that obtaining fingerprints is not an important aspect of investigative operations. However, it has also been shown that victims (especially victims of serious property crimes) often expect the police to exert effort investigating the crime, including "dusting for prints," and are dissatisfied if they do not.[12] Moreover, research also indicates that the presence of physical evidence—especially fingerprints—substantially improves the probability of obtaining convictions. Given this broader perspective, it would be an error to conclude that obtaining or looking for fingerprints is an insignificant aspect of investigative operations.

Police response time provides another illustration of this same point. Fast response of the police may do little in leading to the on-scene apprehension of offenders, but it may contribute to the successful collection of evidence useful in obtaining convictions. In addition, victim expectations of response time is important in satisfying victims. Therefore, police response time is a critical aspect of investigative operations. With these illustrations in mind, it would seem appropriate to broaden the conceptualization of the desired outcomes of the criminal-investigation process when judging the effectiveness of the process. This conclusion is even more significant if the three outcomes are related. If, say, victim satisfaction is related to solving crimes or convicting suspects (e.g., satisfied victims are more likely to become "coproducers"), then the police can *in*directly affect these outcomes by directly affecting victim satisfaction.

Finally, there is a need for additional research to examine the relationships between the investigative outcomes, and the impact of various investigative practices and policies on these outcomes. With such efforts, we may become more knowledgeable about the limitations and capabilities of the criminal-investigation process, and the criminal-justice system more generally.

Steven G. Brandl

Notes

1. The difference between the number of clearances and the number of arrests can be substantial. For example, Eck (1983) found in one agency that only 58 percent of cleared burglary cases resulted from an arrest. In another site, 100 percent of cleared cases resulted from an arrest. Greenwood (1970) found that of the burglary crimes that were cleared, only 26 percent were by an actual arrest. Of the robberies that were cleared, 60 percent were as a result of an arrest.

2. As an example, Bloch and Bell (1976) found that patrol-detective teams working in low income, minority neighborhoods produced higher "on-scene" arrest rates than nonteams; however, they were less successful than nonteams in obtaining prosecution of suspects. The researchers offer several reasons for the teams' higher arrest rates, all of which relate to the investigative procedures used by the teams (e.g., more intensive use of photographs of criminal suspects). An alternative, and perhaps more likely, explanation is that the patrol-detective teams made more legally unjustified arrests in these low-income neighborhoods. As a result, more of these arrests were not supportable in court.

3. Aggregate clearance rates are quite stable over time. For the past decade, the clearance rate has averaged approximately 20 percent with a range of 19 to 21 percent.

4. Spelman and Brown (1991) found that of all involvement crimes reported while still in progress, 35 percent resulted in a response-related arrest. Of those reported a few seconds after the crime was committed, 18 percent resulted in a response related arrest; if reported sixty seconds after the crime, the chances were about 10 percent. Of those crimes reported between one and five minutes after the crime was committed, only 7 percent resulted in a response-related arrest. Most involvement crimes were reported between one and five minutes after the crime was committed.

5. The study also involved a national survey of the nation's three hundred largest police departments and site visits to twenty-nine of these departments.

6. Included crimes consisted of homicide, aggravated assault, felony morals, robbery, burglary, theft, auto theft, and forgery/fraud. Their analyses were based exclusively on cases that were cleared. Therefore, reported percentages are based only on cleared crimes and thus, are not equatable with percentage figures presented earlier.

7. PROMIS, Prosecutor's Management Information System, is a management tool that enhances the prosecutor's ability to allocate resources in an efficient and effective manner. The system can store and recall information on pending cases. For research purposes, it contains a wealth of information on the processing of cases within the judicial system.

8. This variable was measured with an index that included whether the officer was perceived to be "courteous," "understanding," "concerned," and "competent."

9. "Investigative effort" was also measured with an index that included whether or not the patrol officer was known to have searched the crime scene, examined evidence, attempted to locate or question witnesses, or made out a crime report.

10. It is likely however that other types of changes, especially those technological in nature, will have a significant and direct impact on apprehension and conviction success. For example, AFIS (i.e., Automated Fingerprint Identification System) technology may enhance the usefulness

of fingerprints in identifying suspects. DNA profiling, or genetic fingerprinting, provides a positive link between certain body cells and a particular identified individual and, thus, can greatly enhance the usefulness of such physical evidence in obtaining convictions.

11. In the data collected by Brandl and Horvath (1991), it was seen that approximately 20 percent of victims were not even aware of the fact that the patrol officer completed a report in regard to the incident.

12. Whether the police should routinely collect fingerprints to promote feelings of satisfaction is debatable. On one hand, this activity appears to influence victim satisfaction, which is arguably an important outcome of the investigative process. On the other hand, such an activity may unjustifiably support and promote the media-like image of the police and, as a consequence, create unrealistic expectations that the police should be able to solve the crime if fingerprints are recovered. The solution appears to be one of balancing efficiency with education and satisfaction.

Bibliography

Babbie, Earl. *Survey Research Methods.* Belmont, CA: Wadsworth, 1990.

Bloch, Peter B., and James Bell. *Managing Investigations: The Rochester System.* Washington, DC: Police Foundation, 1976.

Boland, Barbara, Paul Mahanna, and Ronald Sones. *The Prosecution of Felony Arrests, 1988.* Washington, DC: National Institute of Justice, 1992.

Brandl, Steven G., and Frank Horvath. "Crime Victim Evaluation of Police Investigative Performance." *Journal of Criminal Justice* 19 (1991): 293–305.

Chen, Huey-tsyh. "Dropping in and Dropping Out: Judicial Decisionmaking in the Disposition of Felony Arrests." *Journal of Criminal Justice* 19 (1991): 1–17.

Eck, John E. *Solving Crimes: The Investigation of Burglary and Robbery.* Washington, DC: Police Executive Research Forum, 1983.

———. *Criminal Investigation.* In *What Works in Policing?* Eds. Gary W. Cordner and Dona C. Hale. Cincinnati: Anderson, 1992. 19–34.

Federal Bureau of Investigation. *Crime in the United States, 1991.* Washington, DC: Government Printing Office, 1992.

Forst, Brian, Judith Lucianovic, and Sarah J. Cox. *What Happens After Arrest?* Washington, DC: Institute for Law and Social Research, 1977.

Forst, Brian, Frank J. Leahy, Jr., Jean Shirhall, Herbert L. Tyson, and John Bartolomeo. *Arrest Convictability as a Measure of Police Performance.* Washington DC: National Institute of Justice, 1982.

Frank, James. "The Consequences of Citizens' Attitudes Toward Police." A paper presented at the Academy of Criminal Justice Sciences meeting, Pittsburgh, PA, 1992.

Garofalo, James. "Police, Prosecutors, and Felony Case Attrition." *Journal of Criminal Justice* 1(1991): 439–49.

Goldstein, Herman. "Toward Community-Oriented Policing: Potential, Basic Requirements, and Threshold Questions." *Crime and Delinquency* 33(1987): 6–30.

Greene, Jack R., and Carl B. Klockars. "What Police Do." In *Thinking About Police: Contemporary Readings.* Eds. Carl B. Klockars and Stephen D. Mastrofski. New York: McGraw-Hill, 1991. 273–84.

Greenwood, Peter W. *An Analysis of the Apprehension Activities of the New York City Police Department.* New York: Rand Corporation, 1970.

———, Jan M. Chaiken, and Joan Petersilia. "Response To: An Evaluation of the Rand Corporation's Analysis of the Criminal Investigation Process." *Police Chief* 12(1976): 62–71.

———. *The Criminal Investigation Process.* Lexington, MA: D.C. Heath, 1977.

Isaacs, Herbert H. "Police Operations—The Apprehension Process." In *The President's Commission on Law Enforcement and Administration of Justice. Task Force Report: Science and Technology.* Washington, DC: Government Printing Office, 1967. Chap. 2.

McDonald, W.F., H.H. Rossman, and J.A. Cramer. *Police-Prosecutor Relations in the United States.* Washington, DC: U.S. Department of Justice, 1982.

Manning, Peter K. *Police Work: The Social Organization of Policing.* Cambridge,

MA: MIT Press, 1977.

Parks, Roger B. "Comparing Citizen and Observer Perceptions of Police-Citizen Encounters." In *Understanding Police Agency Performance*. Ed. Gordon P. Whitaker. Washington DC: U.S. Department of Justice, 1984. 121–35.

Percy, Stephen L. "Response Time and Citizen Evaluation of the Police." *Journal of Police Science and Administration* 8(1980): 75–86.

Petersilia, Joan, Allan Abrahamse, and James Q. Wilson. *Police Performance and Case Attrition*. Santa Monica, CA: Rand Corporation, 1987.

———. "The Relationship Between Police Practice, Community Characteristics, and Case Attrition." *Policing and Society* 1(1990): 23–38.

Poister, Theodore H., and James C. McDavid. "Victims' Evaluation of Police Performance. *Journal of Criminal Justice* 6(1978): 133–49.

Schmidt, Janell, and Ellen Hochstedler Steury. "Prosecutorial Discretion in Filing Charges in Domestic Violence Cases." *Criminology* 27(1989): 487–510.

Schneider, Anne L., William R. Griffith, David H. Sumi, and Jamie M. Burcart. *Portland Forward Records Check of Crime Victims*. Washington DC: U.S. Department of Justice, 1978.

Shapland, Joanna. "Victim-Witness Services and Needs of the Victim." *Victimology* 8(1983): 233–37.

Sherman, Lawrence W., and Barry D. Glick. *The Quality of Police Arrest Statistics*. Washington, DC: Police Foundation, 1984.

Skogan, Wesley G., and George E. Antunes. "Information, Apprehension, and Deterrence: Exploring the Limits of Police Productivity." *Journal of Criminal Justice* 7(1979): 217–41.

Skogan, Wesley G., and Mary Ann Wycoff. "Some Unexpected Effects of a Police Service for Victims." *Crime and Delinquency* 33(1987): 490–501.

Spelman, William, and Dale K. Brown. "Response Time." In *Thinking About Police: Contemporary Readings*. Eds. Carl B. Klockars and Stephen D. Mastrofski. New York: McGraw Hill, 1991. 163–69.

Stipak, Brian "Citizen Satisfaction with Urban Services: Potential Misuse as a Performance Indicator." *Public Administration Review* 39(1979): 46–52.

Criminal Justice Plans

Each United States president through the Office of the Attorney General makes recommendations on how to combat violent crime. The intent of the federal government is to influence state criminal-justice systems to adopt at least part, if not all, of its recommendations. Coordinated efforts to stem violent crime are the impetus behind such plans. Yet consensus on how to achieve the goal of coordination is not easy to arrive at. The federal government is careful to state its recommendations in nonobligatory but resolute terms. It is then incumbent on the states to debate the federal recommendations according to local needs, obstacles, and public demands to form their own plans. Naturally, federal and state criminal-justice plans affect law enforcement. The plans direct police in their daily duties, making their jobs easier or more difficult depending on administrative vision.

Violent crime in America is primarily the work of the repeat, violent offender. In other words, a small segment of the population commits a large share of the worst crime. Attorney General William P. Barr, under President George Bush, had this to say about lax treatment of violent offenders:

> Common sense tells us that incapacitating these chronic offenders will reduce the level of violence in society. . . . Moreover, the experience of the past thirty years supports the common sense notion that tough law enforcement works. The permissiveness of the 1960s and early 1970s resulted in skyrocketing crime rates. As incarceration rates fell, violent crimes soared, nearly quadrupling from 1960 to 1980. The tougher approach of the 1980s turned this around—dramatically slowing the increase in crime and even bringing about some decreases, notwithstanding the wave of violence associated with drug trafficking during this period. (Office of the Attorney General, 1992)

With tougher law enforcement as the banner of the Bush administration, Attorney General Barr promulgated a no-nonsense list of twenty-four recommendations to strengthen criminal justice. Barr's recommendations varied from previous plans not only in intensity but also in nature, due to society's outrage at mounting crime. Each presidential administration proceeds differently on the crime issue as do the states under gubernatorial leadership. An interesting area for research is to determine the fallout from either a get-tough-on-crime or a lax administration. Whereas Attorney General Barr criticized the 1960s and early 1970s for permissiveness, critics of the Bush administration insist that getting tough on crime led to civil rights and privacy infringements (1988–1992). Furthermore under Bush, federal and state police netted more bit players than kingpins, and drug-trafficking continued unabated.

Federal Recommendations
The following twenty-four recommendations to strengthen criminal justice are those set forth by the Office of Attorney General from William P. Barr to President George Bush, dated July 28,1992.

1. Provide statutory and, if necessary, State constitutional authority for pretrial detention of dangerous defendants.

    Commentary: Every state should authorize its judges to order the detention, without bail, of defendants who are a proven danger to witnesses, victims, or the community at large. States should also provide that convicted violent offenders will be detained during their appeals absent special circumstances.

2. Adopt truth in sentencing by restricting parole practices and increasing time actually served by violent offenders.

    Commentary: The fact that sentences imposed by many State systems bear almost no resemblance to time actually served breeds disrespect for the criminal justice system on the part of criminals, the public, juries, and the victims of crime.

3. Adopt mandatory minimum penalties for gun offenders, armed career criminals, and habitual violent offenders.

    Commentary: Every State should have a statute similar to the Federal armed career criminal law [18 U.S.C. 924(e)]. The statute provides that any person who has been convicted of three violent felonies or drug offenses shall be sentenced to at least 15 years imprison-

ment without possibility of parole. A graduated punishment scheme would impose minimums of 5, 10, and 15 years for armed felons with one, two, or three or more prior convictions, respectively.

4. Provide sufficient prison and detention capacity to support the criminal justice system.

    Commentary: Any criminal justice system that absolves prisoners of their sentences because of lack of space, or makes lack of space a factor in sentencing or parole, is cheating its citizens.

5. Provide an effective death penalty for the most heinous crimes.

    Commentary: The death penalty serves to permanently incapacitate extremely violent offenders who cannot be controlled even in an institutional setting. Finally, the death penalty serves the important societal goal of just retribution.

6. Require able-bodied prisoners to work or to engage in public service to offset the costs of their imprisonment.

    Commentary: Law-abiding citizens have a right to expect that those who have violated the law will not lead a life of leisure in prison.

7. Adopt drug testing throughout the criminal justice process.

    Commentary: States should consider drug testing of at least certain felony arrestees to allow judges to make more informed decisions about conditions for pretrial release and sentencing after conviction. Random drug testing of those in prison would help ensure that drugs are not being smuggled into the institution.

8. Utilize asset forfeiture to fight crime and to supplement law enforcement resources.

    Commentary: States are encouraged to utilize this sanction as a complement to criminal prosecution in drug trafficking and appropriate violent crime cases. States should review their asset forfeiture laws to ensure they do not contain loopholes such as that in the California statute, which makes forfeiture of land used to grow marijuana difficult.

9. Establish a range of tough juvenile sanctions that emphasize discipline and responsibility to deter nonviolent first-time offenders from further crimes.

Commentary: One promising possibly is boot camps. Another is mandatory, highly-structured community service or public works programs. A sentence to a boot camp or a public works program, rather than probation, could change a first-time offender's attitude toward himself and society, thereby preventing the commission of further crimes.

10. Increase the ability of the juvenile justice system to treat the small group of chronic violent juvenile offenders as adults.

Commentary: Every experienced law enforcement officer has encountered 15- and 16-year-olds who are as mature and as criminally hardened as any adult offender. One approach is to create a legislative presumption that any juvenile age 14 or older who commits an enumerated crime of violence (murder, rape, kidnapping, or armed robbery) will be tried as an adult.

11. Provide for use of juvenile offense records in adult sentencing.

Commentary: Many apparent first-time offenders in this country have in fact committed numerous serious crimes as juveniles, yet evidence of these crimes may not be available or, by law, may be considered legally irrelevant to sentencing for adult offenses. While the desire to forgive a youthful indiscretion and not saddle an otherwise law-abiding adult with a criminal record is commendable, that rationale simply does not apply to a juvenile offender who continues a life of crime in adulthood.

12. Enact and enforce realistic speedy trial provisions.

Commentary: Many State laws set extremely lax standards for a speedy trial—up to 1 year from the date of arrest. Delays in bringing criminals to trial benefit no one except the guilty, and delays particularly hurt victims, who suffer prolonged anguish while awaiting the trial.

13. Reform evidentiary rules to enhance the truth-seeking function of the criminal trial.

Commentary: One approach is to provide by statute that whenever police officers act in good faith, but commit a technical error of law or fact, evidence should nevertheless be admitted in court. States are urged to adopt the traditional impeachment rule by providing for the admission of all felony convictions and convictions of crimes involving dishonesty against all witnesses, including a defendant. Many State evidence codes are also unduly restrictive and unnecessarily frustrate the search for truth through limitations on the use of past criminal conduct of the defendant as evidence of guilt.

14. Reform State habeas corpus procedures to put an end to repetitive challenges by convicted offenders.

Commentary: Traditionally, habeas corpus was a remedy for detention without trial, an important protection against government overreaching. In recent years, the writ of habeas corpus has been converted from a bulwark of individual liberty into a device employed by prisoners to endlessly reexamine issues decided at trial and on appeal.

15. Invest in quality law enforcement personnel and coordinate the uses of social welfare resources with law enforcement resources.

Commentary: Police work involves substantial risk, long hours and much personal sacrifice. Prosecutors make substantial economic sacrifices by foregoing often lucrative private practices for government service. Judges work long hours and often risk retaliation from criminal defendants. Correctional officers put their lives on the line in a hostile environment every day. The public has a substantial interest in retaining the services of seasoned professionals in each of these critical areas, and compensation for law enforcement personnel at all levels should be sufficient to recruit and retain such professionals.

16. Maintain computerized criminal history data that are reliable, accurate, and timely.

Commentary: A history of violence or failures to appear is often the key to convincing a judge to detain a defendant before trial. The inability to provide detailed criminal histories at a first appearance can result in the release of a dangerous defendant. A criminal history database can also form the basis for a point of sale check prior to the purchase of a firearm.

17. Provide statutory authority for prosecutors to grant "use" and "transactional" immunity.

    Commentary: Selective grants of immunity are the prosecutor's method of lifting the veil of secrecy from drug enterprises, violent gangs, and organized crime associations. Accomplices are often the only witnesses to suspected criminal acts. At present, State laws are a patchwork on the subject of immunity.

18. Provide statutory authority for electronic surveillance, pen registers, and trap-and-trace devices.

    Commentary: Use of electronic surveillance can build an extremely effective case based on the wrongdoer's own words, while avoiding the risks of using undercover agents or informants. A pen register records the numbers dialed from a telephone by monitoring the electrical impulses caused by dialing. A trap-and-trace device reveals the telephone number of the source of all incoming calls to a particular number. State law on the employment of these devices is presently a hodgepodge of obstacles.

19. Provide for hearing and considering the victims' perspective at sentencing and at any early release proceedings.

    Commentary: In most States, the defendant has the right to address the tribunal after conviction and before sentencing. States should also provide for the use of victim-impact evidence in capital cases, and when survivors desire it, the State should compile and present evidence from survivors detailing the loss suffered by the victim's family and friends.

20. Provide victim-witness coordinators.

    Commentary: The coordinators keep victims and survivors apprised of the status of proceedings, as well as whether or not the defendant has been released on bail before trial. They can also make victims aware of restitution or other remedies available to them, among other services.

21. Provide for victim restitution and for adequate compensation and assistance for victims and witnesses.

    Commentary: While all 50 States have some form of victim restitution law, in many cases these laws are not adequately enforced. Mechanisms must exist for monetary fines and restitution payments to be collected during imprisonment and after release.

22. Adopt evidentiary rules to protect victim-witnesses from courtroom intimidation and harassment.

    Commentary: Every State should have two evidentiary protections for complaining witnesses. The first is a rape-shield law. Evidence of reputation and past sexual conduct of the victim generally has no place in the trial for a sexual offense. Second, child witnesses, where necessary, should be protected from traumatic confrontations with their alleged abusers.

23. Permit victims to require HIV testing before trial of persons charged with sex offenses.

    Commentary: The latest medical evidence indicates that early testing and treatment can delay the onset of AIDS in those who test HIV-positive and prolong survival of those with AIDS. Offender test results should be provided to the victim and the court. Moreover, at the request of the victim, the defendant should be tested again periodically, for example, after 6 months and 12 months given the latency period of the virus.

24. Notify the victim of the status of criminal justice proceedings and of the release status of the offender.

    Commentary: Victims of crime should be apprised of any change in a convicted offender's status, such as entrance into work release, weekend furlough, or community incarceration. States should also ensure that adequate protection measures are taken before release, where objective facts create a legitimate fear of further victimization.

These recommendations have been given in full for several reasons. They point out deficiences in the American criminal-justice system, as perceived by the federal government at what was to be the end of the Bush administration. They attempt to reverse the trend that Attorney General Barr considered too lenient in the 1960s and 1970s by restoring just retribution. And they underscore why police are often at odds with the criminal-justice system that seemingly does not aid police with swift justice.

State Action Plans

Attorney General Barr's twenty-four recommendations add muscle to criminal justice—if and when enacted at the state level. Many of the federal recommendations call for statutory creation or revision, which cannot be accomplished quickly even to meet imperative demands. Each state with its multitude of interest groups, citizen rights committees, legal watchdogs, and other influential parties is often handcuffed when it comes to following federal guidelines. Scaling down to the personal level, for example, not everyone reviewing the twenty-four recommendations would embrace them wholeheartedly. Put in simplistic terms, the recommendations might appear too tough to a civil libertarian or too weak to a law-and-order advocate. Recommendation five alone, concerning the death penalty, is perhaps just a step below the abortion issue in strident public debate. Having the paternal federal government place state government on its knee for a heart-to-heart talk is ironic. Both should share the same goals. However, at times state sovereignty makes for wayward offspring.

For example, the Criminal Justice Plan for Texas 1993 reflects some of the twenty-four federal recommendations, excluding the evidentiary revisions to speed up court proceedings. The plan put words into action by funding state grants in over thirty program areas. Texas Governor Ann W. Richards prefaced the plan with these remarks:

> We have finally begun to attack the root causes of criminal behavior. At least 8 out of every 10 people in our prison system committed crimes related to or stemming from abuse of drugs or alcohol. Our rates of recidivism are far too high because our system of criminal justice has failed to adequately treat substance abuse. As a result of House Bill 93, passed during the second called session of the 72nd Legislature, the Texas prison system will have 12,000 cells available for substance-abuse felons. We will deal with the root cause of criminal behavior while we have a "captive audience" (Office of the Governor, 1992).

In Texas expansion of prisons is top priority, which appears as federal recommendation four. This fact illustrates how state and federal criminal-justice plans necessarily converge. It also exhibits divergence in that the federal recommendation ignores treatment. Get-tough directives usually fail to voice anything more than retribution. Cell blocks dedicated to treating prisoners with drug-abuse problems is a goal worthy of inclusion in any criminal-justice plan. And more important, get-tough directives fill American prisons like nothing else, requiring the Texas solution.

The thought might occur: Since the Texas plan was written in 1992 it could not have incorporated the federal recommendations released the same year. While this is true, the federal recommendations were not devised out of thin air, nor were they presented as entirely new. All twenty-four had somewhat lengthy histories and were enumerated again to refresh state memory. Some of the specifrc federal recommendations found their way into the Texas plan through a general statement:

> Developing programs to aid the prosecution of dangerous criminals is also crucial. Fair and speedy movement through the criminal justice system will demonstrate to violent offenders that we [Texas law-makers] are serious about cracking down. Programs that provide prosecution and defense attorney training can be implemented to enhance counsel's ability to maneuver through the complex legal system. Specialized information systems can expedite incident mapping or trial court case management.

Indeed general, the statement lacks the immediacy and impact of the federal mandates couched in advisory terms. Whereas the federal government says, "Here's a blueprint for waging war on crime," Texas state government replies, "We hear you, but the subject needs more study." Other Texas priorities for 1993 involved reducing gang-related and drug-related crime, and seeking better victim services. Relatively new to Texas, gang crimes filled the newspapers and kept urban police dispatching special juvenile units. Federal recommendations nine through eleven insist on treating violent juveniles as adults, especially in sentencing. Texas may or may not heed the advice. Because experience with gang crime is short in the state, adopting a tougher stance remains to be seen. Coming at the end, federal recommendations nineteen through twenty-four on victims' rights are nevertheless essential to the whole structure of reform. In the Texas plan victims' rights materialized in the form of assistance programs such as crisis intervention, advocacy counseling, and emergency shelter projects. Victim-witness counselors (stronger than advocacy counseling), victim restitution, HIV testing, and the other federal directives were not spelled out as such. Again, general statements failed to incorporate specific actions.

The other forty-nine states have devised criminal-justice plans similar and dissimilar to that for Texas. The federal government through the Attorney General's Office can promulgate directives much more easily than the states. The directives come from the president and one office working together. Even with congressional gridlock for other types of legislation, the process of passing new criminal law is simpler at the federal than the state level. For better or worse, state legislatures are more cautious about granting their criminal-justice systems additional power. Federal and state criminal-justice plans will continue to agree on some points and disagree on others. The process is necessary and American police, who carry out the plans, may wonder at times why all criminal-justice systems do not operate as one.

Bibliography

Dunworth, T., and A.J. Saiger. *State Strategic Planning under the Drug Formula Grant Program*. Santa Monica, CA: Rand Corporation, 1992.

Office of the Attorney General. *Combating Violent Crime: 24 Recommendation to Strengthen Criminal Justice*. Washington, DC: U.S. Department of Justice, Office of the Attorney General, 1992.

Office of the Governor. *The 1993 Criminal Justice Plan for Texas*. Austin: Office of the Governor, Criminal Justice Division, 1992.

Skolnick, Jerome H. "Critical Look at the National Drug Control Strategy." *Yale Law and Policy Review* 8 (1990): 75–116.

"Symposium: Making Sense of the Federal Sentencing Guidelines." *U.C. Davis Law Review* 25 (Spring 1992): 563–771.

"Symposium: Punishment. Federal Sentencing in the Wake of Guidelines." *Yale Law Journal* 101 (June 1992): 1681–2075.

"Victims' Rights Symposium." *Pacific Law Journal* 23 (April 1992): 815–1316.

Criminology

Definition

The study of crime and criminals is the province of the field of criminology. As the late Edwin Sutherland wrote in his classic work *Principles of Criminology* (1939:1):"Criminology is the body of knowledge regarding crime as a social phenomenon. It includes within its scope the processes of making laws, of breaking laws, and of reacting toward the breaking of laws." While Sutherland's definition of criminology is commonly accepted and widely quoted, it is not quite accurate because it declares that the study of crime is solely focused on *social* factors. In fact, the study of crime by criminologists has encompassed several fields of knowledge which are not primarily social in nature.

It is also necessary to add that criminology has been generally defined as the *scientific* study of crime and criminals. Thus, not all those who comment on crime and criminals (such as forensic experts, lawyers, judges, and those who work in the criminal justice system) are criminologists. This distinction of a scientific approach to the subject is, however, not as simple as it seems. There are scholars who consider themselves criminologists and yet do not embrace the scientific method. While these scholars are often Marxist or radical in their orientation, the key element is their denial of objectivity and quantification in research. Instead, they generally practice a methodology that studies crime and criminals from a dynamic, historical perspective. Further, these scholars usually focus on the "making of laws" and "reaction to the breaking of laws" rather than on the actual behavior of the law-breaker. A few scholars, known as phenomenologists, study the meaning of behavior, rather than the categories above.

As a final note on the definition of criminology, the terms "crime" and "criminal" are not as clear as they might seem. There has been much debate about what constitutes crime and criminals. Some have argued that the definition of crime is fully a legal matter; that is, if something is prohibited by law it is then and only then a crime. Others answer that since the laws are not really concerned with behavior itself, a legal definition does not provide a clear-cut focus for behavioral distinctions. The act of taking a life, for example, is not necessarily murder because states perform executions and nations go to war. They suggest that a *social* definition more tuned to deviance, in all of its forms, is a better approach. Yet other scholars point out that if a crime or deviant act is not noticed, then for all intents and purposes the act might as well not have occurred and the individual involved is not deemed criminal or deviant. Thus, the legal or social definitions of crime and criminals capture only those acts and persons to whom we react. This problem makes it quite difficult to talk of criminals and "noncriminals" and obscures the subject matter of the field.

Disciplinary Focus

Criminology is generally understood to be an offspring of the discipline of sociology. While this is arguably the case, such a statement slights both the history of criminology and the various disciplines that comprise the breadth of the field. At one time or another, the disciplines of philosophy, history, anthropology, psychology, psychiatry, medicine, biology, genetics, endocrinology, neurochemistry, political science, economics, social work, jurisprudence, geography, urban planning, architecture, and statistics have all played prominent roles in the development of criminological theory and research. Since the 1930s, however, sociology has been the primary source of academic training for most criminologists. There have been very few academic departments of criminology in the United States and most of the scholarly preparation of criminologists has taken place in sociology departments. Nevertheless, in spite of this sociological focus, it should be recognized that criminology is characterized by a relative integration of materials from several disciplines. The advent and rise, through the last three decades, of the multidisciplinary field of criminal justice has challenged sociology as the training ground for criminology, and many criminologists are now either working in or receiving their academic training from criminal-justice departments. This movement promises to more directly integrate sociological criminology with other disciplines.

Within the general discipline of criminology lie several interest areas. In their more general forms they are allied with such fields as philosophy of law, sociology of law, sociology of deviance, penology/corrections, police science, administration, and demography. It is possible, then, to identify oneself as a criminologist and yet spend an entire career working within a relatively small area of the field, such as policing.

Criminology in Academia

Since the discipline is so closely allied with sociology, there were very few criminology departments in the colleges and universities of America through the end of the 1960s. In fact the most common way to enter the criminological field was to take a degree in sociology with a specialization in criminology. Until approximately 1970, only three major schools, University of California at Berkeley, Florida State University, and University of Maryland, had doctoral programs in criminology (the oldest related program, Michigan State University, was chiefly a police administration program). The count of schools offering criminology doctorates stands today at four. The program at Berkeley has been lost, having been phased out in the mid-1970s. Two new programs expressly titled as criminology degrees are now at the University of Delaware and Indiana University of Pennsylvania. The current approach seems to be the creation of doctoral programs in criminal justice, and there are now some dozen or so of those programs. In truth, there is now little distinction between criminology and criminal-justice doctoral programs.

The Development of Criminology

Criminology, as a generic form of study relating to crime and criminals, can be traced far back into history. It is only recently, however, that a systematic study developed. Perhaps the best estimate of the "birth" of criminology lies with the rise of the European Classical Period in the eighteenth century. The real thrust of the period was not so much the study of the criminal, but the system of justice itself. With relatively capricious and arbitrary law in effect, the writers of the day (Montesquieu, Voltaire, Beccaria, Bentham) criticized the system of justice and proposed massive reform. Referred to as the Classical School of criminology, the ideas of these reformers became the basis for today's criminal law and justice systems, and originated the modern concept of deterrence.

In the nineteenth century the study of crime and criminals began in earnest. Quetelet in France, Guerry in Belgium, and Mayhew in England were studying and mapping the distribution of crimes in what were the first real studies using so-called social statistics. Another group of people, under the leadership of Gall and Spurzheim, were engaged in the study of phrenology (the relationship of skull configuration—as a proxy for brain structure—to behavior) and produced some of the first scientific studies of criminals. The generally accepted beginning of scientific criminology, however, occurred in the 1870s with the work of an Italian physician, Cesare Lombroso.

Drawing on the positive science methods of the day (thus the generic name "the Positive School"), Lombroso's work on the relationship between physical features, personality, and criminals led to theories of a "born" criminal and spurred both genetic and hereditary studies. It was during this period that the term criminology itself came into popular usage. Followed by two other Italians, Ferri and Garofalo, Lombroso's work was extended into the arena of social and environmental factors. With the rise of sociology as a discipline in the 1890s, scientific criminology expanded under a number of fronts.

The first two decades of the twentieth century saw an assortment of criminological explanations rise, most notably the social varieties, the emotional/psychoanalytic, and the combined product of then new intelligence testing and heredity research. By the 1920s, sociological studies were in full swing and the Sociology Department of the University of Chicago began to dominate criminology. The major explanations of criminality became tied to the transmission of values from one person to another, especially in areas that were culturally different and socially disorganized. In addition, statistical studies that placed crime and delinquency in particular areas of the city became popular.

By the 1940s criminology had become concerned with the effect of social conditions on people in general and began an examination of the relationship among social structure, social class, and crime. Commonly known as "structural functionalist" theories, their focus was on differing rates of criminality or delinquency among groups of people in society. This approach held sway until the 1960s, when criminology, along with the rest of society, became concerned with civil rights and liberal political issues. The dominant theme of this period was quite reminiscent of a return to the old Classical School with its emphasis on justice and equality before law. Concerns shifted away from the criminal and toward the way in which the criminal-justice system reacted to and processed people.

Following the federal government's crusade and "war" against crime during the late 1960s and early 1970s, which culminated with the creation of the Law Enforcement Assistance Administration (now the National Institute of Justice), criminology became much more concerned with studying the criminal justice system itself. Under the aegis of LEAA funding, criminologists examined the operation of the police, the courts, and correctional systems with an eye to evaluating their effectiveness. Also of concern was the treatment of victims and the measurement of crime, both of which were blended into a new area of interest known as victimology. Since the discipline of criminal justice was also coming into its own during this period, the two fields began a merger, if not in fact, then in substance. The discipline of criminology is today quite difficult to distinguish from that of criminal justice.

Major Forms of Criminology

While it is difficult to categorize criminology, one method is that of distinguishing among the study of the causes of criminality, the study of rates of criminality, and the study of the criminal-justice system as it operates. The first, with its focus on explaining behavior, is referred to as etiology. The study of rates focuses on the prevalence and incidence of criminality and is called epidemiology. The third area of interest is more divergent than the other two and is composed of such aspects as punishment philosophies, penology, and policing.

Etiological criminology has contributed to an understanding of both criminal behavior (and of deviance in general) and the presence of crime in society. Explanations have been generally of two types: processual and structural. The processual variety of theories attempts to explain how people *become* criminals and/or come to commit criminal acts. These theories are most often psychological or social psychological in orientation and usually deal with individual motivation and behavior. Because of the complexity of individual events, processual theories are sometimes only applicable to specific types of crime. Structural theories, on the other hand, are those that focus on the effect of society (and its institutions) on people in the aggregate and explain why different groups have different crime rates. As a result, structural theories are usually sociological in tone. It is theories of this type that have been the most successful in making sense out of crime in society, but they do not tell us which *individuals* will commit crimes.

Epidemiological criminology has given us an understanding of how (and sometimes why) rates of crime vary across classes of people or across time and space. We have learned, for example, that certain classes of people are more likely to be arrested for crimes (that is, they have higher crime rates). Further, we know that rates of crime vary with particular environmental conditions and geographic areas. Epidemiology also entails the study of the incidence of crime under various conditions, be they economic, social, or political. Criminologists have tracked the amount of crime across different types of political structures, in different economic times, and are currently much concerned with the amount of victimization and fear of crime in society.

Criminology that studies the criminal-justice system provides us with information on the way the system works, how closely reality matches our ideals, and alternatives which might reconcile the two. This type of criminology is perhaps best referred to as the study of the "system in action." This form of studying the various components of the criminal-justice system is in contrast to examinations of formal structure and is characterized by a study of the informal. In short, it focuses on the way things really work, not the way they are supposed to work. Thus, criminologists working in this area have studied the operation of police departments, the relationships between police and citizens, bail systems, plea bargaining, and the social structure of prisons, to name but a few of the areas of interest. Finally, for lack of a better classification, we can also place those criminologists who are interested in punishment theories within this category. Some current issues in this area are the death penalty, selective incapacitation, career criminals, and the construction of sentencing guidelines.

Relationship Between Criminology and Police Science

Along with the rise of academic criminology in the United States came the field of police science. Actually, police science departments preceded criminology departments in the colleges and universities. While often difficult to distinguish from each other, police science departments usually focus more on the technical aspects of policing: administration, management, crime analysis, and the "doing" of law enforcement. Criminology, when it deals with the police province, more often uses the "system in action" focus. Thus, criminological approaches to the problem of policing are apt to be sociological in nature and to focus on informal structures and relationships.

Contributions of Criminology to Police Work

Since it is difficult to separate early criminology from early police science, one may argue that some of the first scientific contributions may have come from either source. Nonetheless, a review of the first three decades of the *Journal of Criminal Law and Criminology* suggests that much of contemporary policing was developed on research from the early twentieth century. Articles include training, personnel selection, psychological testing, the use of technology, fingerprinting, and so forth. Obviously, too, the various techniques of crime analysis have their origins in early work on crime statistics.

On a more contemporary front, the criminological work of Egon Bittner, Albert Reiss, Jerome Skolnick, and Peter Manning has found its way into police training and community relations work. Similarly, the work of political scientist James Q. Wilson, who some view as a criminologist, has also had an effect on police administration practices. The products of civil disobedience research and victimization studies have changed police selection processes and created an emphasis on education. More recent work by criminologists has led many police departments to rethink several of their basic conceptions. Kelling's Kansas City Preventive Patrol Experiment caused police departments nationwide to rethink their patrol procedures. Several response time studies suggested that immediate response to all citizen calls was not necessary and that response time was not as critical to making an arrest as was thought. Sherman and Berk's research on response to spousal assault calls led to changes in response and arrest policies for disturbance calls. Studies by Rand Corporation and the Police Executive Research Foundation on detective work and crime-solving resulted in patrol officers being given more responsibility in the investigative process and in new ways to screen cases. A criminological theory, routine activities, has precipitated a new analytical approach to locating crime, known as "hot spots." And, finally,

Herman Goldstein's work, particularly his book *Problem-Oriented Policing*, influenced many police departments to give up traditional policing for variations on community policing.

In short, criminology is not focused on the police by any means but it has had a profound effect, which ranges from the Classical School's reform of criminal-justice operation and philosophy to the techniques in use by police departments today. With the current emphasis on system examination and efficiency research, it is only reasonable to assume that police and criminologists will continue to build on their relationship. Indeed, among the components of today's criminal-justice system, it is the police who are relying most heavily on criminological research to make substantial changes in basic structure and methods of operating.

Frank Williams

Bibliography

Beccaria, Cesare. *On Crimes and Punishments*. Trans. H. Paolucci. Indianapolis: Bobbs-Merrill, [1764] 1963.

Bentham, Jeremy. *An Introduction to the Principles of Morals and Legislation*. New York: Kegan Paul, [1789] 1948.

Bittner, Egon. *The Functions of the Police in Modern Society*. Washington, DC: Government Printing Office, 1970.

Bordua, David J. *The Police: Six Sociological Essays*. New York: John Wiley and Sons, 1966.

Carte, Gene E., and Elaine H. Carte. *Police Reform in the United States: The Era of August Vollmer (1905–1932)*. Berkeley, CA: University of California Press, 1975.

Ferri, Enrico. *Criminal Sociology*. Trans. J. Killey and J. Lisle. Boston: Little, Brown, [1881] 1917.

Garofalo, Raffaele. *Criminology*. Trans. R. W. Millar. Boston: Little, Brown, [1885] 1914.

Goldstein, Herman. *Policing a Free Society*. Cambridge, MA: Ballinger, 1977.

———. *Problem-Oriented Policing*. Philadelphia: Temple University Press, 1990.

Greenwood, Peter, Joan Petersilia, and Jan Chaiken. *The Criminal Investigation Process*. Lexington, MA: D.C. Heath, 1977

Guerry, Andre M. *Essai Sur la Statistique Morale*. Paris: Crochard, 1883.

Kelling, George L., Tony Pate, Duane Dieckman, and Charles E. Brown. *The Kansas City Preventive Patrol Experiment: A Summary Report*. Washington, DC: The Police Foundation, 1974.

Lombroso, Cesare. *L'Uomo Delinquente (The Criminal Man)*. Milano: Hoepli, 1876.

Manning, Peter K. *Police Work: The Social Organization of Policing*. Cambridge, MA: MIT Press, 1977.

Martin, Susan E., and Lawrence W. Sherman. *Catching Career Criminals: The Washington, D.C. Repeat Offender Project*. Washington, DC: The Police Foundation, 1986.

Neiderhoffer, Arthur. *Behind the Shield: The Police in Urban Society*. New York: Doubleday, 1967.

Pate, Tony, Amy Ferrara, Robert Bowers, and Jon Lorence. *Police Response Time: Its Determinants and Effects*. Washington, DC: The Police Foundation, 1976.

O'Rourke, L.S. "The Use of Scientific Tests in the Selection and Promotion of the Police." *Annals of the American Academy of Political and Social Sciences* 146 (1929): 147–59.

President's Commission on Law Enforcement and Administration of Justice. *Task Force Report: The Police*. Washington, DC: Government Printing Office, 1976.

Quetelet, Adolphe. *Research on the Propensity for Crime at Different Ages*. Trans. S. F. Sylvester. Cincinnati: Anderson, [1831] 1984.

Reiss, Albert J., Jr. *The Police and the Public*. New Haven, CT: Yale University Press, 1971.

———. *Policing a City's Central District: The Oakland Story*. Washington, DC: Government Printing Office, 1985.

Sherman, Lawrence. *Police Corruption: A Sociological Perspective*. New York: Doubleday Anchor Books, 1974.

———. *The Quality of Police Education*. San Francisco: Jossey-Bass, 1978.

———, and Richard Berk. *The Minneapolis Domestic Violence Experiment*. Washington, DC: The Police Foundation, 1984.

Skolnick, Jerome. *Justice Without Trial: Law Enforcement in a Democratic Society*. New York: John Wiley and Sons, 1966.

Spellman, William, and Dale K. Brown. *Calling the Police*. Washington, DC: Police Executive Research Forum, 1982.

Staufenberger, R. A. *Progress in Policing:*

Essays on Change. Cambridge, MA: Ballinger, 1980.

Sutherland, Edwin H. *Principles of Criminology.* Philadelphia: Lippincott, 1939.

Vollmer, August. "Police Progress in the Past Twenty-Five Years." *Journal of Criminal Law and Criminology* 24 (1933): 161–75.

———. *The Criminal.* Brooklyn: Foundation Press, 1949.

Wilson, James Q. *Varieties of Police Behavior: The Management of Law and Order in Eight Communities.* Cambridge, MA: Harvard University Press, 1968.

Critical Incidents

It is generally accepted that law-enforcement personnel, fire fighters, paramedics, etc., expose themselves to stressful events to a higher degree than most other professions. The negative effects of stress are well known, if not on a cognitive level, certainly on an experiential level. Intense or acute stress reactions often follow a critical incident. In defining critical incident, Mitchell (Mitchell and Resnick, 1981) has focused on the response side of human functioning: "A critical incident is any situation faced by emergency personnel that causes them to experience strong emotional reactions which have the potential to interfere with their ability to function either at the scene or later." It would appear that certain tragic events are so dramatic, shocking, or disturbing to our collective psyches that we agree they are stressful and therefore critical incidents. Those, of course, include natural disasters, multiple fatalities and/or injuries, shootings or near shootings, prolonged search and rescue operations, and death or serious injury to a fellow officer.

Observation of Vietnam era veterans who suffered from what became known as Post-Traumatic Stress Disorder (PTSD) made a significant contribution to the study of critical incidents. Not only did we as a nation learn how we had scarred ourselves physically and emotionally, we learned more about the dramatic cumulative effects of stress. In general, we learned that the more frequently an individual experienced threat to his physical and psychological integrity, the more likely he would be injured and damaged psychologically. While it is estimated that only 4 to 10 percent of those who experience a critical incident develop full-fledged PTSD, as high as 90 percent of law-enforcement officers exposed to critical incidents experience some emotional, physical, or psychological reaction to the exposure.

Treatment

Critical incident stress debriefing (CISD) is conducted as a prophylactic, i.e., to minimize the damaging effects of the stressful event on an officer. Through CISD the officer comes to see his or her reactions to the critical incident as a normal response to an abnormal situation. Traditionally, officers have been taught to stuff their feelings and deny the hurt. CISD allows the affected officer to recognize and cope more effectively with his or her reactions. Furthermore, CISD establishes departmental policy in an effort to avoid liability issues. Sending an officer back to work after experiencing a critical incident when he or she is not psychologically fit to perform well is reason enough to complete CISD. Certain stressful events form CISD criteria. They are:

1. Violent death of a fellow worker in the line of duty.*
2. Taking a life in the line of duty.*
3. Suicide of a fellow worker.*
4. Shooting someone in the line of duty (not resulting in death).
5. Violent or traumatic injury to a fellow worker.
6. Responding to and/or handling of infant mortality.
7. Responding to and/or handling multiple fatalities.
8. Responding to and/or handling a prolonged rescue operation in which victims expire.
9. Responding to and/or handling a barricaded suspect.
10. Responding to and/or handling a hostage-taking and negotiation.
11. A SWAT or tactical units operation where danger is present.
12. Observing an act of corruption, bribery, or other illegal activity by a fellow worker.
13. Suspension and/or threat of dismissal.
14. Structural flashover (electrical danger) and shelter deployment.

---

*Indicates high priority for removing personnel from the scene.

Virtually all involved personnel should take part in CISD, particularly if the magnitude of the critical incident dictates a major event for the agency. Peripheral and support personnel—particularly dispatchers—are often deeply affected by the critical incident, as well as those in the thick of action. Representatives from the command level should attend CISD to demonstrate their sensitivities to the pain and anguish of their officers.

The Process
Although CISDs flow through stages their demarcation is flexible. Once again, Dr. Jeffrey Mitchell provides an analytical footing by defining the stages. Initial defusing is performed shortly after the critical incident with a spontaneous sharing of feelings, support, and ventilation. Initial defusing is not part of the formal CISD. In the introductory phase a mental-health professional explains his or her role, sets the ground rules, addresses the issue of confidentiality, and prohibits critiquing the incident from a functional point of view. Next, the fact phase elicits information about the personnel involved and the nature of the call for police help. The feeling phase uncovers any emotional reactions associated with the critical incident and related experience. The symptom phase enumerates the participants' emotional, physical, and cognitive reactions. The teaching phase explores the stress response syndrome in all of its manifestations. The reentry phase readies an officer and other participants to return to duty when fit. And finally, the follow-up phase is conducted several weeks or months after the critical incident to ascertain mental well-being.

Dr. Mitchell's model identifies the important components of a CISD. Another approach is to facilitate the telling of one's story, i.e., the participants all experienced the critical incident differently. There is no right version or one way to tell the story. At times, misperceptions or events perceived out of chronological or temporal order will be more accurately placed within the cognitive framework of the personnel involved. Ideally the assembled participants as a group should have the answers to most factual questions. Under stress incoming data are typically subjected to partial or distracted attention and therefore are prone to distortion. In addition, those who experience strong emotion during the critical incident will have experienced it through a particular set of filters.

Often the critical incident will evoke previously repressed or suppressed feelings or conflicts that may be related or unrelated to the job.

It is not unusual that the sights, smells, and sounds of a current incident will take individuals back to earlier memories of violence, death, and destruction. For example, the sound of a helicopter often resensitizes an officer to his experience in Vietnam; having to use deadly force will certainly remind an officer of any previous similar episodes; and investigating violent injuries to a child most undoubtedly impacts the officer who has children of his or her own. It is important that participants of the CISD come to know the authenticity of their emotional reactions. The group dynamics grant permission for members to voice their own inner experiences without embarrassment or fear of ridicule.

During the process of CISD a number of common issues emerge as the affected officers tell their stories:

- distress regarding vulnerability and relative powerlessness
- distress regarding threatened loss of control (leads to isolation)
- distress regarding feelings of responsibility (leads to guilt)
- fear of repetition (leads to hypervigilance)
- depression and reaction to loss (leads to numbness)
- distress regarding aggressive impulses (particularly in shootings)
- emotional liability (may include startle response)
- anger or even rage toward victims, onlookers, media, administration, etc.
- questioning of career choice and professional identification
- reaffirmation of one's professional and individual efficacy and competence

It is recommended that the affected officer upon returning to duty physically place himself or herself at the scene of the critical incident. The rationale for this is twofold. First, it allows the officer to reinforce his or her mastery of the emotional reaction to the critical incident. Contraindicators include an intense phobic reaction as part of the clinical picture. In almost every case of a post-traumatic reaction, the affected officer has feared "it would happen again" in some form. Second, some officers unconsciously avoid the critical incident scene, which interferes with their performance of duties. Based on state-dependent learning theory, rearousal of strong emotions often elicits the stereotypic behaviors involved in the highly charged critical incident. An example of rearousal occurred when a California highway patrol officer involved in a nonfatal shooting set out three weeks later in high-speed pursuit of a suspect. The pursuit ended when the suspect's car engine burnt out. As the suspect lowered the tinted window, the officer, who had his service weapon ready, "flashed back" to the face of the earlier shooting victim and came close to "dropping the hammer."

Closure

Depending on the magnitude of the critical incident and the number of personnel involved, the official CISD will typically run two to five hours. As the stories are told and the feelings disclosed, the facilitator (mental-health professional) should note which participants have chosen not to share with the group. An invitation or gentle encouragement to do so usually elicits verbalizations from those who have hesitated. If an individual strenuously objects to sharing, he or she should be treated as someone who has the right to private reactions and adaptations. Formal closure of the session begins with this message: "There is no right way to close this session, but this feels like the time. If anyone has anything they want to put out there, this is the time to do so." Typically there are further "letting go" responses. At this point the facilitator should also share personal reactions to the session. Unlike individual psychotherapy, it is appropriate for the facilitator not only to provide feedback to the group but also to show some emotion. The facilitator should remain at the CISD site to consult with any officers who wish to explore individual issues they believe require a one-on-one dialogue. Transference (a shift of feelings for an admired/loved/respected person from that person to the facilitator) and countertransference (indifference to the facilitator), which are problematic for the psychotherapist, rarely occur during CISD. Closure is important in the sense that it allows personnel to return to service knowing the healing process has begun, and they are ready for the next set of challenges.

If the number of involved personnel exceeds twelve and other debriefers are available, the larger group is split into smaller groups of six to twelve officers, where further processing of feelings occur. Depending on the magnitude of the critical incident, those spin-off groups may be comprised of naturally defined entities. For example, major critical incidents often involve multiple agencies so that EMTs may comprise one component, SWAT personnel another, dispatchers another, perimeter personnel another, coroner's office personnel another, and so on. Sometimes it might be advisable to combine groups, depending on the issues that arose during the critical incident in regard to mutual aid and coordination of efforts, etc. These issues may, in fact, be a major source of stress that prevents groups from working well together. This aspect of conducting CISDs is certainly more art than science and requires adroit handling.

Refinement of critical incident stress debriefing comes with experience. After a mental-health professional has completed a hundred or so sessions, he or she finally begins to appreciate what the work is about. Networking with other professionals who have had this unique and specialized training and/or served as facilitators will enhance the therapy offered.

Richard A. Blak

C

Bibliography

Blak, Richard A. "Critical Incident Debriefing for Law Enforcement Personnel: A Model." *Critical Incidents in Policing.* Washington, DC: U.S. Department of Justice, Federal Bureau of Investigation, 1991.

Conroy, R.J. "Critical Incident Stress Debriefing." *FBI Law Enforcement Bulletin 59* (February 1990): 20–22.

International Association of Chiefs of Police. *Fear: It Kills; A Collection of Papers for Law Enforcement Survival.* Washington, DC: U.S. Department of Justice, Bureau of Justice Assistance, 1990.

Kirschman, E. "Critical Incident Stress." *Law Enforcement Technology 19* (March 1992): 22–27.

Mitchell, Jeffrey T., and H.L.T. Resnick. *Emergency Response to a Crisis Intervention Guide P.O.S.T. for Emergency Service Personnel.* Bowie, MD: Robert J. Brady, 1981.

Reese, J.T., and H.A. Goldstein, eds. *Psychological Services for Law Enforcement.* Washington, DC: Government Printing Office, 1986.

Solomon, R.M. *Dynamics of Fear in Critical Incidents.* Arlington, VA: International Association of Chiefs of Police, 1989.

Crowd/Riot Control

People gather together in large and small groups in a variety of settings for a variety of reasons and with very different consequences. Most of these gatherings have no immediate implications for the police, some create minor problems, and some lead to confrontation between the police and members of the assembly.

Civil Unrest

Historically, civil unrest in a variety of forms has occurred throughout the United States. Sit-ins, nonviolent protests, demonstrations, and strikes that typically begin peacefully, but may end in violence, have confronted the police with problems that severely test their ability to maintain order and to protect lives and property. Such confrontations are difficult to predict and, given a particular combination of factors, may occur virtually anywhere at any time when large numbers of people are present. Although the role of the police in dealing with crowds has been much discussed, the actual occurrence of violent crowds often catches the police largely unaware and their reaction is often less than ideal. By helping the police to identify different types of crowds, and to recognize different types of warning signals, it may be possible to improve police performance in this area.

Types of Crowds

As Figure 1 indicates, it is possible to distinguish a number of different types of crowds based upon action orientation, stability, group consciousness, emotional intensity, duration, and the likelihood of creating difficulties for the police. Those crowds which are most often problematic for the police may be characterized as "acting crowds," or crowds in which: (1) the participants perceive themselves as members of the collectivity; (2) participants are in immediate proximity; (3) the attention of the participants is focused on a particular object or issue; (4) participants are pursuing some goal or purpose as a group; and (5) emotional tension among participants is quite high. Riots, protests, and demonstrations are familiar examples of acting crowds.

Based on a review of existing research, it appears that acting crowds are most likely to emerge under certain social conditions as indicated in Figure 2.

Further, certain types of events appear to precipitate the development of acting crowds.

FIGURE 1

Characteristics of Different Types of Crowds

Types of Collectivity	Action Orientation	Stability of Membership	Self-consciousness of Participants as Members of a Group	Emotional Intensity	Duration of Assembly	Difficulty for the Police
Casual Crowd	very low	low to none	very low	very little	short	rarely
Conventionalized Crowd	moderate to high	moderate to very high	high	moderate to high	long	sometimes
Acting Crowds						
a. mobs, riots	very high	moderate to high	very high	very high	short to long	almost always
b. celebrational assemblies	moderate to low	low to moderate	moderate to high	moderate to very high	short to long	sometimes
c. civil disobedience	high	very high	very high	high to very high	long	sometimes
d. demonstrations or protest marches	high	high	very high	moderate to very high	long	sometimes

Source: Cox and Fitzgerald, 1983.

FIGURE 2

Predisposing Social Conditions:

a. Social or cultural differences especially in relative wealth or power or rates of social mobility
b. The definition of the differences as unacceptable or intolerable by at least one segment of the community
c. Well-established networks of interaction and communication
d. A social structure conducive to group formation and mobilization (e.g., leadership structure, cultural or ethnic uniformity, etc.

Source: Cox and Fitzgerald, 1983.

A physical encounter between demonstrators and onlookers, an arrest by the police, or any other event that attracts and holds the attention of potential crowd members may lead to a "milling" process characterized by the intensifying of emotions and increasingly high levels of excitement. The emotions and excitement, sometimes carefully planned and orchestrated, are contagious and spread rapidly through the crowd, which begins to focus on a common target, objective, or purpose. In some instances the target will be defined by a leader, in others the more or less spontaneous hostile behavior (throwing a rock or bottle at a police car) of one or more individuals in the crowd is imitated by others. The acting crowd is now oriented toward a particular target and loss of life and damage to property are very real threats, particularly when the crowd becomes a mob.

A mob consists of a large group of densely packed individuals who have submerged their own identities in the crowd, who respond almost exclusively to what is happening in their immediate environs, and among whom the emotions of anger and hate are highly aroused. Such mobs may engage in rioting characterized by violence and destruction. The stages in the development of acting crowds are depicted in Figure 3.

Acting Crowds and the Police
The best strategy available to the police is undoubtedly to prevent formation of crowds that appear to have a high potential for violent behavior. In our society, however, citizens have the right to assemble peacefully, and unless there is very strong evidence to indicate that they are likely to become violent, such gatherings cannot generally be prohibited. Requiring permits for large demonstrations is generally acceptable, however, and this may provide the police with prior knowledge that may help them in preventing such crowds from becoming unruly or in dealing with them if they do become dangerous.

Whenever the police are alerted to the fact that a large gathering is planned, they should assess the potential for violence and prepare contingency plans for different eventualities. Such plans should include a survey of the site where the crowd is to assemble, arrangements for a communications center/command post, detailing a sufficient number of officers to the scene (including plain-clothes officers who may circulate through the crowd), and, where appropriate, development of mutual-aid pacts with other law-enforcement agencies. In addition, all police departments should ensure that officers have received training in crowd control and dispersal tactics and that such training is repeated periodically throughout their employment. Such training should focus on using minimum force and on circumstances that warrant the use of force, e.g., self-defense or defense of others, and should include a discussion of the various formations available for use in containing and dispersing crowds. Information concerning the nature and stages of crowds should also be provided to all officers so that they recognize quickly when a crowd enters the various stages. Specific departmental policies for dealing with serious offenses committed by individuals in the crowd should be detailed, explained, and practiced prior to use. Where feasible, the leaders of the demonstration and other concerned parties should be identified and contacted prior to the event for the purposes of ensuring that their constitutional rights, as well as those of bystanders and property owners,

FIGURE 3

Major Stages in the Life History of the Acting Crowd:

a. Gathering of people
b. Milling and social contagion
c. Emergence of leaders
d. Identification of the target or focus
e. Attempted action against the target
f. Dissolution of the crowd

Source: Cox and Fitzgerald, 1983.

will be protected and that they understand that it is in their best interests to keep the demonstration/gathering peaceful.

Prevention of crowd violence depends upon regular collection and analysis of accurate intelligence concerning the social conditions outlined in Figure 2. Among the warning signs that might indicate dangerous conditions are the following: (1) an increase in rumors, pamphlets, ridicule, or slogans of a sensational nature, particularly when such rumors relate to unfair treatment of disadvantaged persons by representatives of the establishment; (2) an increase in the number of violent incidents or threats of violence between two competing groups or between the police and a particular group; (3) similar types of disturbances at scattered locations, which may serve to test police resources and patience; (4) an increase in the number of attacks on specific types of private property (e.g., buildings owned by members of one racial/ethnic group in a neighborhood populated by members of a different racial/ethnic group); (5) an increase in the number of public displays of disrespect for authority, the establishment, and the police. Such warning signals should alert the police to the fact that there are possibly violent undercurrents flowing in the community, which may erupt when a precipitating incident occurs. Under these circumstances, all large public gatherings should be closely monitored and contingency plans should be prepared in the event that such gatherings become violent. Among other things, public gatherings might be limited to carefully chosen locations bordered by natural or physical barriers (either already existing or constructed purposely), which may help to contain the crowd and thus restrict any damage to a particular geographic area. Police lines may be of some value, but once a large mob is on the move, such lines will seldom suffice to halt it. If containment is successful, the crowd (mob) will eventually exhaust its energies without doing widespread damage to the community.

Simultaneous with containment, law-enforcement officers should attempt to disperse the crowd. Dispersal is usually accomplished by announcing calmly that the gathering is no longer lawful and that participants are ordered to leave the area. Members of the crowd should then be given a realistic amount of time to leave and avenues for their exit must be provided. Those who do attempt to leave should be allowed to do so and if arrests of those leaving are

warranted, such arrests should be made later. Further, once members of the crowd have left the area, they should not be allowed to reenter, for obvious reasons. Arrest of instigators is another fairly effective dispersal technique provided such instigators can be identified, arrested, and removed from the scene very quickly.

In spite of the best plans, spontaneous, unapproved, and unplanned demonstrations will sometimes occur and may turn into riots. Though good intelligence and planning should minimize the number of such occurrences, some simply cannot be predicted. To deal with such situations, police administrators should have contingency plans, which will allow them to rapidly deploy personnel prepared to take appropriate action on very short notice. Where human lives are being threatened in a riot situation, a show of well-planned, organized force is likely to be the only alternative. Under such circumstances, mutual-aid pacts become extremely important and the ability to move rapidly while maintaining channels of communication is crucial. Here, too, containment and dispersal are the goals.

The media often play an important role in shaping public attitudes and images of the police. Heavy media coverage may transform a localized disturbance into a city-wide or even national phenomenon, since the media are the principal source of news about what is happening in a particular community, and since what they present may or may not be in context. The media have the responsibility of reporting what is happening as objectively as possible, and this includes presenting the police view of the events being covered. Thus, a departmental spokesperson should be available to the media to furnish information about the role, obligations, and conduct of the police in riots, protests, or demonstrations. Such information is necessary to counteract the impact of groups who "stage" events for the explicit purpose of obtaining media coverage.

Conclusion

Conflict in human communities is a universal, and some would maintain, necessary phenomenon. Whenever such conflict develops to the extent that police intervention is required, the police are in the spotlight. The extent to which they deal efficiently and effectively with such conflict depends upon their maximizing civility and minimizing force. When the police are successful, such conflict is either contained, preventing widespread damage to society, or dealt with in such a way that the conflict is channeled into arenas in which it may be resolved in a more peaceful fashion.

Steven M. Cox

Bibliography

Cox, Steven M., and Jack D. Fitzgerald. *Police in Community Relations: Critical Issues*. Dubuque, IA: William C. Brown, 1983.

Das, Dilip K. "Handling Urban Disorders: Are the Lessons Learned from Past Police Practices Incorporated in State-Mandated Recruit Training?" *Police Studies 7* (3): 175–184.

Evans, Robert, ed. *Readings in Collective Behavior*. Chicago: Rand McNally, 1975.

Federal Bureau of Investigation. "Prevention and Control of Mobs and Riots." Washington, DC: Government Printing Office, 1965.

Janowitz, Morris. *Social Control of Escalated Riots*. Chicago: University of Chicago Center for Policy Studies, 1968.

LeGrande, J.L. "Nonviolent Civil Disobedience and Police Enforcement Policy." *Journal of Criminal Law, Criminology, and Police Science* 58(3) (1967): 393–404.

McKenzie, Ian K. "Unlawful Assembly: Riot, Rout: The Mechanics of the Mob." *Police Studies* 5(1) (1982): 40–46.

Momboisse, Raymond M. *Crowd Control and Riot Prevention*. Sacramento, CA: State Printing Office, 1964.

———. *Industrial Security for Strikes, Riots, and Disasters*. Springfield, IL: Charles C. Thomas, 1968.

National Commission on the Causes and Prevention of Violence. *To Establish Justice, To Ensure Domestic Tranquility*. Washington, DC: Government Printing Office, 1969.

Swan, L. Alex. *The Politics of Riot Behavior*. Washington, DC: UP of America, 1980.

Edwin Upton Curtis

Edwin Upton Curtis (1861–1922), mayor and police commissioner of Boston, was born in Roxbury, Massachusetts, son of a lumber merchant. After attending the grammar and Latin schools in Roxbury, Curtis went to the little Blue Family School for Boys in Farmington, Maine. In 1882 he graduated from Bowdoin College, then studied law at Boston University Law School, and was admitted to the Suffolk County bar in 1885. An early interest in Republican Party politics resulted in his election as Boston city clerk. Two years later he resumed his law practice but continued to express concern for civic reform and in 1894 was elected mayor of Boston. He soon changed the municipal structure by appointing a board of commissioners to oversee elections, revising the system of financing public schools, and placing each city department under a commissioner.

His tenure as mayor over, he took up law again, but did not turn his back on public service, and in 1918 was appointed police commissioner. He took the job at a time when low salaries disgruntled rank-and-file police. Mayor Andrew J. Peters would not approve a pay increase; in response the passed-over officers organized a local union affiliated with the American Federation of Labor. Curtis immediately suspended union members from duty, whereupon three-fourths of the force went on strike (September 9, 1919). Curtis then announced that no strikers would be reinstated. Suddenly, all the heat was on Curtis for his too regal display of power. Newly elected Massachusetts Governor Calvin Coolidge went to his aid, telling the press, "Mr. Curtis is the police commissioner of Boston . . . I have no intention of removing him as long as he is commissioner and am going to support him."

The need for that support became clear all too soon, as the low-life of Boston seized the moment. Crapshooting in public, harassment of strollers, tripped fire alarms, and much aimless wandering by young rowdies were the first signs of lawlessness. Then prankster behavior turned to vandalism and looting. The sound of shattering glass filled the air, as did hoots, cries, and pistol shots. Small bands of nonstriking police tried to stop the pilferage but instead encountered death threats. Anarchy reigned for several days until the loyal police, the Massachusetts State Guard, and citizen volunteers formed an emergency militia directed by Curtis. Together they quelled the rioting. In all eight persons died, one of them a patrolman, twenty-one were wounded, and at least fifty were injured. Property damage ran to a third of a million dollars.

Mayor Peters blamed Curtis for the havoc and, contradicting fact, credited himself with restoration of order. Undaunted, the "obstructive" Curtis got busy creating a new police force, but as scapegoat he received little backing from city politicians and organized labor detested him. Nevertheless, he succeeded in blocking reentry of the strikers and in recruiting obedient men. For him, police waived the right to strike from induction day onward; they were unlike most other workers in that they pledged to keep the peace, a fragile commodity as the strike had shown. To labor sympathizers Curtis, of course, was a tyrant; to the public he was a savior.

Hard work in rebuilding the police force exhausted Curtis; by 1921 his health was failing. Friends urged him to retire, but he could not. What he drilled into recruits—that the entire lot of police was faithful and diligent service—continued to sap his own strength. The strike of 1919 had to be rectified, and he toiled to the end to vindicate the department and himself, dying in office. The Boston press carried lengthy obituary notices in appreciation of the much maligned Edwin Upton Curtis. He had expended himself for an altruistic cause.

Bibliography

The Boston Police Strike: Two Reports. New York: Arno Press and *The New York Times,* [1919, 1920] 1971.

Dictionary of American Biography. Vol. II. New York: Charles Scribners and Sons, 1928: 612.

Russell, Francis. *A City in Terror: 1919, The Boston Police Strike.* New York: Viking Press, 1975.

D

Dallas Police Department

In 1841, when John Neely Bryan carved out enough space to build a cabin on the banks of the Trinity River, Dallas was born. Within five years the rudiments of a law-enforcement agency were established in the form of a vigilance committee to protect the growing number of settlers from marauding Indians. By 1856 Bryan's lone cabin had grown to an incorporated town one-half mile square. One year later, Andrew M. Moore was elected town marshal by popular vote. Subsequent marshals and their deputies guarded Dallas until 1881, when J.C. Arnold was elected the first chief of police.

By this time Dallas had already enjoyed a lot of history. The city seceded from the Union in January 1861 and aligned with the Confederacy. Occupied by federal troops, the military governor and carpetbaggers appointed the city marshals until 1871, when the elections reverted to Dallas citizens. In 1899 the city adopted a new charter and placed the police department under the control of the governor of Texas. The governor appointed a police commissioner who served with other city commissioners to appoint a police chief.

Police uniforms came to Dallas in 1881. They were heavy blue trousers with the familiar gold stripe on the legs, a heavy blue shirt, cap, and a double-breasted blue wool coat. The outfit was a little on the warm side but wore like iron. More important, Dallas got its first telephone that year. By the next year mounted police officers were based at the calaboose on Houston Street for the sole purpose of answering telephone calls to the police. This astonishing means of communication was probably the most important innovation to that point in police history. Newspaper accounts of the era

list an abundance of burglars, safe-cracking experts, prowlers, drunks, and other assorted bad men. The department itself was understaffed, overworked, and low on necessary equipment. In short, there was too much of the bad and not enough of the good.

The Twentieth Century

By 1903, when it brought Oak Cliff into its fold, the city had already annexed East Dallas. Dallas now covered fifteen square miles with a population of 45,000. Forty-seven patrolmen dressed in military-type blouses and London-style helmets patrolled the streets of this bustling metropolis, mostly on foot. In 1907 the department acquired an automobile and two motorcycles. There was even a substation at Beckly and Jefferson in Oak Cliff, manned by three patrolmen. The turn of the century also produced vacations; each Dallas policeman was allowed one day off a month.

Communications took a leap forward in 1908, with the introduction of the Gamewell system. Each hour the officers would call the station to get assignments and report their activity. Soon a light was added to the boxes so that an officer could be notified of a call from the station sergeant. By 1911 a riot car replaced the old horse-drawn wagon. It worked the same way, by picking up officers on the way to the scene. A year later the first squad car took to the street and the mounted officer gradually began to take his place in history.

The Dallas Police Department was trying desperately to match its growth with that of the city's. It boasted fifty-nine officers: forty-two patrolmen, eleven mounted officers, four motorcycle officers, two patrol wagon drivers, and three foot patrolmen at the Oak Cliff substation. In 1917 patrolmen went to an eight-hour shift; they had worked twelve hours a day for sixty years.

The 1920s
The 1920s hit Dallas with a bang. The city had grown to 23.54 square miles and a population of 158,926. Registered vehicles numbered 27,248. The 130-man police department was mobile by now and so were the crooks. By 1921 ninety-five officers and their "police reserve," forty volunteer firemen, blanketed Dallas at night in a scramble to reduce the rising crime rate. As soon as the crime uprising had been curbed, thirty officers were dropped from the payroll. It was a temporary truce. Murders and burglaries were skyrocketing again by the end of the decade.

The 1920s were a bellwether period for the department. Although no police academy was available to new officers until October of 1945, classes were in session by 1925 to teach officers the city ordinances and laws of evidence. In 1920 Henry Garrett installed a twenty-watt radio transmitter in the central fire station to dispatch fire calls to radio-equipped fire chiefs' cars. In between fire calls, he broadcast phonograph records "just to keep the station on the air." By 1925 he had moved the operation to Fair Park with a 500-watt transmitter to become WRR radio. It was the first municipally owned radio station in the nation.

The explosion of criminal violence led to an enlarged detective section, and in 1921 a special section was formed to deal specifically with the growing trend—auto theft. Rudiments of the traffic division were visible in 1901, two years after the first wheezing, clattering, smelly automobile drove into town. But by 1920 something more was needed. That year saw twenty-four persons killed in traffic accidents, with over 27,000 motor vehicles on the city streets. In 1921 officers were issued raincoats and made to remain at their intersection even when it was raining. In 1922 Dallas was the very first city to install traffic lights. A tower was erected in the triangle at Elm and Ervay streets, where the officer could see traffic in all directions. He manually operated the traffic lights to meet the traffic needs as he saw them.

With the slap of the 1920s the police department awoke to the hard realities of urbanized lawlessness and was brought fully to its feet with continuing technological breakthroughs. Who before had heard of radio, flying police-men, traffic lights, specialized detective squads, and one-way streets?

The 1930s
Economic depression, prohibition, and violence typified the 1930s. Two hundred sixty-five Dallas police officers rode herd on 260,000 citizens. Police department policy for liquor raids was shoot first and ask questions later. Newspaper articles were filled with banner headlines and stories detailing lurid kidnappings and murders. A certain feeling of helplessness prevailed. Criminals vowed they'd never be taken alive, that no jail could hold them.

In October 1931 Dallas became the Southwest's first city to install radio receivers in squad cars. They could receive messages but they could not answer the dispatcher or communicate with other patrol cars. Two years later police cars were answering 37,685 calls. By 1939 two-way radios had been installed in all patrol cars.

Police training made some strides during the thirties. Classroom instruction on city ordinances and laws of evidence initiated a decade earlier constituted the training school. But training primarily was military drill. Officers had to attend the school forty hours a year in their off-duty time and received no compensation. A full-time instructor was added in 1933. However, recruits were still just given a badge, a gun, and a uniform and pushed into the streets to fight crime, for the most part.

In 1932 the Texas Department of Public Safety was created in Austin, allowing a quicker system for the exchange of fingerprints and information to Texas cities. Binders were still being used in Dallas for wanted circulars, all circulars going into the binders in alphabetical order. The identification workload raised manpower to four detectives and one supervisor. But 1933 brought an improvement in the filing system. "Jackets" for each criminal replaced the loose binders. In 1934 technology called again, and Dallas joined New Orleans as the only two departments in the Middle South boasting a comparison microscope for ballistics. The "rogues gallery" file was replaced with a more complicated modus operandi file in 1935. By this time the jail office and the records bureau were under the Superintendent of Identification, and the identification process was called the Bureau of Identification and Records.

The detective section was revamped in the early 1930s. A burglary and theft bureau was established in 1933 to join the auto theft bureau. At that time the detective section consisted of an inspector, three lieutenants, one desk sergeant, and nineteen detectives. A homicide and robbery bureau consisting of four men and one supervisor was added. Even the warrant office specialized during the 1930s, having until then only a small administrative staff. Beat patrolmen served the majority of warrants; however, in 1932 Chief C.W. Trammel ordered the warrant office quartered in the records bureau, which took over its supervision, and warrant officers in "scout cars" began to serve the bulk of the warrants.

The 1940s

After Pearl Harbor in 1941, 130 officers traded in their police uniforms for military ones, leaving Dallas—a city of 300,000 people and over 47 square miles—with a police department of 145 men. For most citizens the war effort was "total," but criminals saw it as a time to ply their trade with increasing vigor. The fact that the guardians had been halved set the odds in their favor. To fill the gap, temporary officers were hired to serve until men in the service were back home. Once World War II was over formal police training came into its own. A new school was created and from 1945 to 1950 fifty classes were held. All phases of police training were included in the curriculum to give the recruit a working knowledge of Texas law and police procedure before going into the field. One of the few good breaks the police department got during the war years was temporary relief from traffic problems.

The 1950s

Corruption has sickened most police departments at one time or another. The Dallas Police Department can be proud to note that research has illuminated only two incidents in 128 years of law enforcement. Back in the mid-1920s two officers were robbing people parked at night in "Lovers' Lane" locations. They were subsequently identified, arrested, tried, and jailed. Then in 1953 seven officers were released from service for being implicated in a "police burglary ring." A detective lieutenant was sentenced to the state penitentiary.

Traffic was promoted to a division in November of 1951. A deputy chief was placed in command of 100 men whose primary jobs were traffic related. In 1952, 104 men in the traffic division handled several effective programs related to traffic duty. Programs for bicycle licenses, school patrol, juvenile traffic school, safety films, and effective communication via television and radio helped to educate young citizens and promote traffic safety.

In 1952 the department got its first polygraph unit. In February a Meritorious Conduct Board was created to honor officers for outstanding performance and the police reserve unit was established. The records bureau was fully mechanized by 1952 and the daily "Hot Sheet" was introduced. The list of stolen car license numbers apparently worked. By 1958 the records bureau had assumed responsibility for keeping all departmental records. That year the jail section processed more than 90,000 prisoners, the identification bureau fingerprinted more than 19,000 people, and the property section impounded nearly 17,000 motor vehicles.

Dallas and the Dallas Police Department wound up the 1950s on a familiar note: Everything was bigger. Chief Hanson commanded 966 sworn police officers and 175 civilians; Dallas now measured 277.07 square miles and the population stood at 691,680.

The 1960s

One event in the 1960s will forever stigmatize Dallas and its police force: President John F. Kennedy was assassinated as his entourage drove west on Elm Street leaving the downtown area. Energetic, handsome, and beloved by many Americans, his untimely death blackened Dallas's reputation. Security preparations for the president's visit were extensive: four hundred Dallas officers were assigned to security, crowd, and traffic control. But, nevertheless, Lee Harvey Oswald found his mark. He also wounded Texas Governor John Connally, riding in the motorcade, and later, while fleeing, shot Officer J.D. Tippit four times, killing him on the spot. Shock turned to outrage when nightclub owner Jack Ruby shot and killed Oswald in the basement of city hall as officers were transferring him to the county jail. It would take years before Dallas could once again believe in itself.

Meanwhile, the police had to combat domestic crime. Around Oakland Street and Second Avenue, an area notorious for burglaries, robberies, and assaults, two officers armed with riotguns patrolled on foot. They received special permission to substitute gym shoes for their heavier footwear and were as likely to be found patrolling from rooftops as on the ground. Saturation patrol of other selected high offense areas and "shotgun squads" placed inside selected business houses were the "get-tough" responses.

The canine corps was introduced in 1961, consisting of three German shepherds and their handlers. Work was completed on the Dallas Police Academy in 1962. The city began reimbursing college tuition to officers with acceptable grades. Educational incentive pay was introduced in 1968, with a maximum of $80. Two years later this amount was doubled to $160 a month. More than half of the police department was enrolled in college. With the Academy bustling and more officers earning higher-education degrees, police professionalism was on the rise.

In 1967 the freeway patrol started operating. Specially equipped radar cars worked exclusively on the freeway system within the city limits. Implementing recommendations from a study by the International Association of Chiefs of Police, the police department was completely reorganized in 1968. A new tactical squad, trained in riot control and other emergency procedures, emerged. And community service centers were established to present the police to citizens in nonstress situations. A year later, more hurdles were built to hamper the criminal element. The fourth ward was inaugurated to place more officers on the street during peak crime hours, and the patrol helicopter section became operational. The computerized National Crime Information Center was introduced in Dallas and wanted persons were seconds away from identification and arrest.

Present Day
The City of Dallas has been in the unenviable position of holding the number one spot in the nation on the total crime index. In 1991 there were 500 murders in Dallas, up from 322 in 1987. Clearance rate for murder was 70 percent, slightly higher than the national clearance rate of 67 percent. In 1991 there were 1,208 rapes, which had dropped from a high of 1,344 in 1990. Aggravated assaults numbered 13,450. There were 8,760 robberies of individuals, 2,493 business robberies, 9,646 business burglaries, and 21,867 residential burglaries. Clearance rates were 22.1 percent, 30.9 percent, 15.4 percent, and 25 percent, respectively. Except for robbery of individuals, the other clearance rates were higher than the national average for each. Auto theft accounted for 25,085 stolen vehicles, for a clearance rate of only 11 percent, lower than the national rate of 15 percent. In the larceny category, 71,920 offenses kept police busy.

Two things are certain: Dallas will not lose population and its crime problem will not vanish. As police innovations come about, they will be employed to add stature to today's officers in carrying on the tradition of Andrew M. Moore, the first elected town marshal in 1857.

Abridged from the official history provided by the Dallas Police Department.

Deadly Force
Although police techniques such as neck-restraint holds have occasionally proven fatal, the use of deadly force by police in the United States most often occurs when officers discharge their firearms at other human beings. In some such cases, deaths result but, in others, officers miss or merely wound their targets. The number of deaths caused by police firearms, therefore, measures only some percentage of police deadly force by shooting and, to count accurately—or to define—police deadly force by firearms, it is necessary to include all instances in which officers shoot at other human beings, regardless of whether deaths result. Because *deadly force is force capable of killing or likely to kill*, it is the *decision* to shoot rather than the *consequences* of the shooting that define it.

Frequency of Police Deadly Force
Information about police use of deadly force is sketchy. No central authority collects systematic data on its use from America's approximately 20,000 police departments, and even attempts to collect information about deaths at the hands of the police are highly unreliable. For many years, National Center for Health Statistics (NCHS) data were regarded as the most accurate source of information on "deaths by legal intervention of the police." These data, compiled from the reports of local coroners and medical examiners, generally indicate that approximately 250–350 people suffer such deaths annually. In their comparison of NCHS data with figures obtained directly from the police departments of several major cities, however, Sherman and Langworthy (1979) concluded that, largely because of coroners' misclassifications, NCHS data were underreported by as much as half.

The findings of Sherman and Langworthy are supported by International Association of Chiefs of Police (IACP) studies (Matulia, 1985). IACP data on justifiable homicides by police in the nation's fifty-seven largest cities, which employ about one-quarter of all American police personnel, are presented in Table 1.

TABLE 1

Justifiable Homicides by the Police in Fifty-Seven Cities with Populations over 250,000, 1970–1983

Year	Number
1970	291
1971	388
1972	314
1973	317
1974	356
1975	360
1976	268
1977	262
1978	249
1979	291
1980	251
1981	217
1982	211
1983	229
Total	4,004
Annual mean	286

Source: Matulia, 1985:A-3–A-5.

Police Authority to Use Deadly Force
The generally downward trend in justifiable homicide by police shown in Table 1 is probably attributable to several factors. Increasingly sophisticated police training and tactics (e.g., as in the proliferation of crisis-intervention and hostage-negotiation programs) have helped officers to defuse potentially violent situations and to structure confrontations in ways that do not leave them with no choice but to shoot in order to survive. Perhaps the most important explanation of this decrease in killings by police has been the recent adoption of laws and police regulations prohibiting use of deadly force in situations not involving dangerous offenders or imminent threats to the lives of officers or others.

Police have generally been authorized to employ deadly force in two circumstances. The *defense of life* rule, found in the criminal statutes or case law of all American states, permits police to use deadly force to defend themselves or others against unavoidable and imminent threats to their lives and safety. The *fleeing felon* rule authorizes the police to employ deadly force to apprehend fleeing felony suspects when no other means of doing so are available.

The fleeing felon rule has long caused controversy. The rule originated in the English common law when, because the police as we know them did not exist, "deadly force" usually meant hand-to-hand combat between suspects and the unarmed and untrained private citizens who were legally responsible for apprehending them. Further, during that period, virtually all felonies were punishable by execution. Thus, from the perspective of the citizen attempting to apprehend a suspect who knew that he would almost certainly be executed if brought to justice, there was little distinction between the defense of life and fleeing felon rules. Both involved what, to his quarry and, consequently, to him, were life-and-death situations.

By the 1930s, critics argued that there was an inconsistency between the great limitations on the criminal-justice system's authority to execute those *convicted beyond a reasonable doubt* of the most serious crimes and the broad police discretion to employ deadly force to apprehend those *suspected* of such lesser crimes as larceny and auto theft (American Law Institute, 1931). In 1967, the President's Commission on Law Enforcement and Administration of Justice observed that several of the urban riots of the 1960s had been triggered by police use of deadly force, and suggested that the prevalent, and nearly unbridled, police discretion in this critical area was damaging to police–community relations. The Commission recommended that "all [police] departments formulate written firearms policies which clearly limit their use to situations of strong and compelling need (President's Commission, 1967:189).

By that time, several of the states had limited the fleeing felon rule to situations involving *armed* fleeing suspects, or persons believed by police to have committed *violent* felonies. Even in states where laws authorized police to use deadly force to apprehend suspects of nonviolent felonies, many police departments responded to the Commission's recommendation by adopting internal departmental regulations prohibiting such actions. As research showed that such regulations reduced police use of deadly force, had no adverse effects on crime rates or the safety of the public or police, and that they probably improved police–community relations, the adoption of such regulations increased (Fyfe, 1979).

More recently, in 1985, the United States Supreme Court heard the case of *Tennessee v. Garner* (105 S.Ct. 1694), which involved the fatal police shooting of an unarmed fifteen-year-old boy who was fleeing from an unoccupied house in which he had apparently stolen a wallet containing ten dollars. In its decision, the Court ruled that laws authorizing police use of deadly force as a means of apprehending unarmed and nonviolent felony suspects violate the Fourth Amendment's guarantees against unreasonable seizure. With that ruling, the Court found unconstitutional the deadly force laws of thirty-one states, and presumably imposed upon them and their police departments the responsibility to abolish the rule authorizing police deadly force to apprehend nonviolent fleeing felony suspects.

Race and Police Use of Deadly Force
Questions about race are inextricably woven into any discussion of American justice, and police deadly force is no exception. Every study has found that minorities, especially blacks, are victims of deadly force far disproportionate to their representation in the general population (Blumberg, 1981; Fyfe, 1981, 1982; Geller and Karales, 1981). Two explanations for this phenomenon have been offered. The first holds that blacks are over-represented among deadly force victims because they are disproportionally involved in crime and other activities likely to lead to violent interaction with police. The second holds that police employ deadly force in a discriminatory fashion and that, all other things being equal, officers are far more likely to shoot blacks than whites. With one exception (Fyfe, 1982), the research suggests that black involvement as victims of deadly force closely parallels their involvement as victims and perpetrators of violent crime and that the first explanation is generally valid.

A second question related to race and deadly force involves officers rather than the people they shoot. American policing has traditionally been an undertaking of white males, and it has suggested that such officers are overly inclined to use deadly force against minorities (Jenkins and Faison, 1974). The research suggests that this assertion also is ill-founded. Fyfe found that black New York City officers were more likely to use firearms, especially against blacks, than were white officers. He also reported, however, that racial differences in use of deadly force were generally attributable to disproportionate assignment of black officers to New York's most dangerous duties and areas (Fyfe, 1981a). Still, despite similar findings in Kansas City (Blumberg, 1983) and Chicago (Geller and Karales, 1981), it is probable that isolated incidents of discriminatory deadly force do occur and are not captured in statistical studies.

Deadly Force: A Prognosis
The primary duty of the police is to protect life. Thus, virtually any means of reducing the loss of life associated with police work is desirable. Recent changes in law and police policy have limited officers' discretion in the use of deadly force, reduced the opportunity for arbitrariness and discrimination, and have inflicted no measurable damage on any area of police operations. Sophistication in police training and tactics continues to increase, and several attempts to develop viable nonlethal alternatives to deadly force have begun. It is also probable that the increasing presence of minority officers in police ranks has helped to ease race related police–community tensions and mutual mistrust.

Thus, we are likely to witness future decreases in the use of police deadly force. But, for as long as our streets are so violent, and for so long as there remain social inequities over which police exercise no control, it is also likely that police will continue to kill, that minorities will continue to bear the heaviest cost of deadly force, and that individual deadly force incidents will continue to cause controversy.

James J. Fyfe

Bibliography
American Law Institute, *Proceedings* 9 (1931): 195–334.
Blumberg, Mark. "Race and Police Shootings: An Analysis in Two Cities." In *Contemporary Issues in Law Enforcement*. Ed. James J. Fyfe. Beverly Hills, CA: Sage, 1981. 152–66.
———. "The Use of Firearms by Police Officers: The Impact of Individuals, Communities and Race." Ph.D. diss., SUNY, Albany, NY, 1983.
Fyfe, James J. "Shots Fired: An Examination of New York City Firearms Discharges."

Ph.D. diss., SUNY, Albany, NY, 1978.

———. "Administrative Interventions on Police Shooting Discretion: An Empirical Examination." *Journal of Criminal Justice* 7 (Winter 1979): 309–24.

———. "Race and Extreme Police-Citizen Violence." In *Race, Crime, and Criminal Justice*. Eds. R.L. McNeely and Carl E. Pope. Beverly Hills, CA: Sage, 1981. 89–108.

———. "Who Shoots? A Look at Officer Race and Police Shooting." *Journal of Police Science and Administration* 9 (December 1981a): 367–82.

———. "Blind Justice: Police Shootings in Memphis." *Journal of Criminal Law and Criminology* 73 (Summer 1982): 702–22.

Geller, William A., and Kevin J. Karales. *Split-Second Decisions: Shootings of and by Chicago Police*. Chicago: Chicago Law Enforcement Study Group, 1981.

Jenkins, Betty, and Adrienne Faison. *An Analysis of 248 Persons Killed by New York City Policemen*. New York: Metropolitan Applied Research Center, 1974.

Matulia, Kenneth J. *A Balance of Forces*. 2d ed. Gaithersburg, MD: International Association of Chiefs of Police, 1985.

President's Commission on Law Enforcement and Administration of Justice. *Task Force Report: The Police*. Washington, DC: Government Printing Office, 1967.

Sherman, Lawrence W., and Robert H. Langworthy. "Measuring Homicide by Police Officers." *Journal of Criminal Law and Criminology* 70 (December 1979): 546–60.

Deadly Force: Fleeing-Felon Doctrine

Capital punishment is quite controversial because many people question whether or not the state should be allowed to take a citizen's life. For this reason, scholars have devoted a considerable amount of time researching this question and courts have been required to undertake a lengthy review process before a criminal may be put to death. On the other hand, police use of firearms has historically received relatively little attention despite the fact that more citizens die as a result of police bullets than are executed after trial. In addition, circumstances dictate that police use deadly force (i.e, force that is likely to kill or cause serious bodily injury) without any opportunity for a judicial determination that the citizen has engaged in improper conduct.

Beginning in the late 1960s, public concern regarding the misuse of police firearms began to increase. Many of the urban disorders of that decade had been precipitated by police shootings that some perceived as unjustifiable. As a consequence, state legislatures and police administrators in a number of jurisdictions initiated action to address this problem. Eventually, concern over police use of deadly force culminated in an important U.S. Supreme Court decision limiting the circumstances under which law enforcement officers could fire their weapons at citizens (Blumberg, 1993).

The Fleeing-Felon Doctrine

Police officers have the right to use deadly force in situations where they face the threat of death or serious injury. In addition, deadly force may be used to protect citizens from death or serious injury. However, until recent years, law-enforcement personnel in the United States could also fire their weapons for the purpose of apprehending a fleeing felony suspect, regardless of the nature of the offense.

The "fleeing-felon" doctrine evolved in England during the Middle Ages and was brought over to the thirteen colonies where it became law in every American jurisdiction. Despite the fact that society had changed in a number of important ways, the "fleeing-felon" doctrine was still widely followed as late as the 1960s. However, a variety of criticisms were beginning to be raised with respect to these statutes (Blumberg, 1993).

For one thing, all felonies were punishable by death at the time this common-law doctrine developed. Therefore, it did not matter whether deadly force was used to apprehend a fleeing felon because he/she would be executed anyway. In modern times, this is no longer the case. Only a tiny fraction of convicted felons receive the death penalty. For this reason, critics questioned the wisdom of a policy that permits a police officer to use lethal force for the purpose of apprehending a suspect who most likely would receive a prison sentence upon conviction, or even probation.

Second, opponents of the "fleeing-felon" doctrine note that the number of felonies has expanded greatly since the Middle Ages. During that period, only the most serious crimes were classified as felonies. However, the list has

D

grown over the centuries to include many types of offenses that pose little physical danger to the public. Consequently, the use of deadly force is no longer directed only at persons who pose a significant threat. The police can also fire their weapons to apprehend unarmed persons who have committed such nonviolent crimes as burglary or car theft.

Third, critics of this doctrine point out that in common-law times, there was no communication among law-enforcement agencies. Suspects who were able to evade capture stood an excellent chance of escaping justice. Today, this is no longer the case. Police departments are able to utilize very sophisticated computer technology including the FBI's National Crime Information Center (NCIC) to alert other agencies that a particular suspect is at-large. Therefore, the choices are no longer limited to the use of deadly force or allowing the felon to permanently escape. Nowadays, the option is either to shoot/kill the offender or to allow this individual to escape and hope that he/she will be captured later.

Finally, opponents are disturbed that the power granted the state under this doctrine has increased due to changes in technology. When the rule first evolved, its practical meaning was that the constable and/or his deputies could use weapons such as swords, knives, or farm implements in hand-to-hand combat designed to apprehend felons who wished to evade capture. However, with the invention of handguns and the creation of modern municipal police departments, the impact of this doctrine was no longer limited to hand-to-hand combat. Instead, officers could fire their weapons at fleeing suspects over a greater distance.

Reform of Deadly Force Policy and Law

Beginning in the 1960s, some state legislatures began to modify their statutes. The most common change was either to prohibit the use of firearms for the purpose of apprehending a suspect who had not committed a violent felony or to prohibit officers from firing at a felon who had not used or threatened to use deadly force in the commission of a crime. In other jurisdictions, even though state law remained unchanged, police agencies issued administrative guidelines that achieved the same result through departmental policy (Fyfe, 1979).

Initially, these steps were quite controversial. Police administrators who imposed stricter guidelines were accused of placing their officers in greater jeopardy. Some argued that a restrictive firearms policy was yet another way of "handcuffing the police." However, these reforms became more acceptable as officers were trained to operate under the new policy and recognized that it did not place them in greater danger or hinder their ability to fight violent crime.

By the mid-1980s, restrictive firearms policies had become the norm in large and medium-sized departments in the United States (Fyfe and Blumberg, 1985). The "fleeing-felon" doctrine was still official policy in many smaller agencies located in states that had not changed their statute. However, the U.S. Supreme Court dealt a death blow to the common-law approach in *Tennessee v. Garner* (1985) when it ruled that the fleeing-felon doctrine violated the Fourth Amendment to the U.S. Constitution, which requires that seizures be reasonable. In effect, the Court held that the use of deadly force to stop a fleeing suspect is not reasonable unless the officer has probable cause to believe that this individual poses a danger either to the police or the community (Alpert and Fridell, 1992).

The Frequency of Police Shootings

There are no published data regarding the number of persons who are shot and/or killed by the police each year in the United States. The most comprehensive attempt to assess the extent of this phenomenon was undertaken by the Crime Control Institute. Relying on data supplied by agencies in fifty of the largest U.S. cities, the study concluded that 172 persons were killed by the police in these cities in 1984, a drop of one-half from 1971 when the total was 353 (Sherman and Cohn, 1986:1). Much of this decline was due to the fact that fewer blacks were being killed. The report notes that the decrease is not attributable to either a decline in the civilian homicide rate or the general level of violence within these communities.

There are several factors that have contributed to a decrease in the number of citizen fatalities at the hands of the police. For one thing, as already noted, the overwhelming majority of large- and medium-sized police departments instituted restrictive firearms policies even prior to the 1985 ruling by the U.S. Supreme Court in *Tennessee v. Garner*.

Second, police training has improved dramatically. Law-enforcement officers have generally received extensive training on how to shoot. Unfortunately, there has not always been proper training on when it is proper to shoot. As late as 1968, the only instructions one agency gave its members regarding firearms was "never take me out in anger, never put me back in disgrace" (Milton et al., 1977:47). Clearly, much has changed. Many departments now spend a considerable amount of time discussing not only when the law allows officers to use their weapons, but also how the police can deal with various situations in ways that reduce the likelihood an incident will escalate to the point that deadly force is required.

Third, civil lawsuits have become much more common. Police shootings that do not meet the increasingly stringent requirements set down by the courts can result in large damage awards against the department. Ultimately, the municipality or its insurance carrier must absorb the cost of the judgment. For this reason, police administrators and municipal officials have a strong financial incentive to implement and enforce policies that minimize this risk.

Finally, one must recognize the impact of police shootings on police–community relations. In many cities, shootings of minority citizens have exacerbated racial and ethnic tensions between police and the community. Not surprisingly, a restrictive firearms policy is often a high priority item for African-American and Hispanic political leaders. Because questionable police shootings frequently lead to civil unrest, a strong consensus has developed that the police must use deadly force only when absolutely necessary to protect life or to apprehend a dangerous criminal.

Research on Police Shootings
Since the early 1970s, there have been a large number of studies examining various aspects of police firearms usage (Alpert and Fridell, 1992). Although these analyses utilized different methodologies and were conducted by different researchers in a variety of locations, there is some consensus among scholars regarding certain aspects of this problem.

For one thing, shootings are a rare event in the career of a police officer. Although there are enormous differences among departments with respect to the rate at which officers use deadly force (Sherman and Cohn, 1986), the majority of law-enforcement personnel spend their entire career without ever firing at a citizen. Not surprisingly, officers who are assigned to the SWAT team or other "high-risk" units have a some-

what greater likelihood of becoming involved in a shooting incident (Fyfe, 1978).

Second, the large differences in shooting rates among communities are not explained by the crime rate, the population density or the number of officers employed in a particular jurisdiction (Milton et al., 1977). Researchers have concluded that departmental policy is the most critical factor in determining the level of police firearms usage. Departments that have permissive policies or do not hold officers accountable for policy violations are likely to have higher rates of police shootings than agencies that make a greater effort to control police use of deadly force.

Finally, there is no aspect of police activity that has generated more controversy than the relationship between police shootings and race. All research studies agree that African-Americans are shot/killed by the police in numbers that are disproportionate to their representation in the general population (Blumberg, 1993). However, there is considerable disagreement regarding why this is the case. Many critics of the police charge that the disparity results from racial discrimination and that law enforcement officers are more likely to shoot minority citizens than whites under similar circumstances. Defenders of the police counter that this is not true. Instead, they assert that the disparity is due to the disproportionate involvement of minorities in the types of criminal activity that are likely to result in a violent confrontation with the police. In effect, they are making the claim that the same socioeconomic factors that contribute to the overrepresentation of African Americans in arrest statistics and the prison population also contribute to a higher likelihood of minority citizens becoming shooting victims.

It is not an easy task to resolve this controversy. For one thing, researchers must wrestle with a number of difficult methodological concerns (Blumberg, 1981). Second, police work is very decentralized in the United States, and policies and practices often vary widely among departments. For this reason, the factors that explain a high number of minority shootings in one jurisdiction may not be present in another (Fyfe, 1988). Nonetheless, researchers have not found evidence in most of the departments that have been studied to support the view that the disproportionate number of minority shooting victims is the result of racial discrimination on the part of individual police officers.

Conclusion

The trend in the last two decades is toward greater restrictions on the use of police firearms. State legislatures, police administrators, and the Supreme Court have all played a role in limiting the circumstances under which the police can employ deadly force against a citizen. It should be noted that these restrictions have in no way made the life of a police officer more dangerous. Between the early 1970s and the latter part of the 1980s, the annual number of law-enforcement personnel killed by citizens decreased substantially. This is not surprising because despite various restrictions which have been placed on police firearms, the right of officers to use deadly force in self-defense has not been compromised.

Mark Blumberg

Bibliography

Alpert, Geoffrey P., and Lorie A. Fridell. *Police Vehicles and Firearms: Instruments of Deadly Force.* Prospect Heights, IL: Waveland Press, 1992.

Blumberg, Mark. "Race and Police Shootings: Analysis in Two Cities." In *Contemporary Issues in Law Enforcement.* Ed. James J. Fyfe. Beverly Hills, CA: Sage, 1981.

———. "Controlling Police Use of Deadly Force: Assessing Two Decades of Progress." In *Critical Issues in Policing: Contemporary Readings.* 2d ed. Eds. Roger G. Dunham and Geoffrey P. Alpert. Prospect Heights, IL: Waveland Press, 1993.

Fyfe, James J. "Shots Fired: Examination of New York City Police Firearms Discharges." Ph.D. Diss., State University of New York, Albany, 1978.

———. "Administrative Interventions on Police Shooting Discretion: An Empirical Examination." *Journal of Criminal Justice* 7 (Winter 1979): 309–24.

———. "Observations on Police Use of Deadly Force." *Crime and Delinquency* 27/3 (1981): (376–89).

———. "Blind Justice: Police Shootings in Memphis." *Journal of Criminal Law and Criminology* 73 (Summer 1982): 702–22.

———. "Police Use of Deadly Force: Research and Reform." *Justice Quarterly* 5/2 (1988): (165–205).

———, and Mark Blumberg. "Response to Griswold: A More Valid Test of the Justifiability of Police Actions." *American Journal of Police* (1985).

Milton, Catherine H., Jeanne W. Halleck, James Lardner, and Gary L. Abrecht. *Police Use of Deadly Force.* Washington, DC: The Police Foundation, 1977.

Sherman, Lawrence W., and Ellen G. Cohn (with Patrick R. Gartin, Edwin E. Hamilton, and Dennis P. Rogan). *Citizens Killed by Big City Police, 1970–1984.* Washington, DC: Crime Control Institute, 1986.

Denver Police Department

In the early days Denver was a wild and rowdy place, breeding violence and ruffians. Before December 19, 1859, when voters chose John C. Moore as mayor and William E. "Bill" Sisty as their first marshal, constables had tried to keep the peace. But the "ravenous human bloodhounds" had subdued them, "desperate and lawless characters having no fear of god or man." Even Horace Greeley took time to write about Denver during his overland trip in 1859: "I apprehend that there have been more brawls, more fights, more pistol shots in this log city . . . than in any community of no greater numbers on earth." Yet after Sisty's election violence persisted. Whether it was apathy among the citizenry, the lack of a jail or deputies, or perhaps fear for his life in a town full of desperadoes, Sisty resigned five months later. With the loss of their first marshal, the problem of law and order became the responsibility of the people themselves, and so a "police corps" was formed in hopes of dealing with the criminal element. They existed, it is believed, until about October 1860. At about that time, a People's Court and Vigilante Committee were formed to curb lawlessness. Punishment for breaking the law was often severe—death with no appeal.

A second elected marshal quit after only a month in office and by acclamation of city council William F. Shaffer was named to fill out the term. In those days, marshals were required to post a $10,000 bond to "insure that they would carry out their duties satisfactorily," but in return for the appointment (or elected position) they received $25.00 per month and fees ranging from $.50 for each incarceration to $2.00 for a court appearance. In addition, there were fees for serving subpoenas, serving an order or notice, and discharging prisoners from jail. Under Shaffer, the city acquired its first jail at 1437 Blake Street, a building that once housed the *Rocky Mountain News*. It was both jail and headquarters until fire destroyed it on April 9, 1863, along with seventy other buildings. Two more men headed law enforcement before a new territorial legislature officially consolidated the towns of Auraria, Highland, and Denver City into the City of Denver. With a new charter the mayor had supreme control over the marshal, whose officers were selected by the police commission and the city council. The spoils system became entrenched and political affiliation the determining factor for employment.

On January 23, 1862, the Denver City Council created the position of chief of police with George E. Thornton the first to bear the title. Although not clear, it does appear that the chief became head of the department, while the marshal was relegated to the position of assistant. Oddly, just six months later the chief's position was abolished and Thornton demoted. Even odder yet, he was allowed to act as chief of police but authority shifted and he answered to the marshal. This confusion was quickly forgotten in light of the Great Flood of West Denver, which struck May 18, 1864. While the local Indians, who had warned the white man about impending doom, watched from dry ground the high waters washed away City Hall, Police Headquarters, and numerous other buildings. Another significant event at this time was the establishment of the United States Mint at 16th and Holladay (later Market) streets. A year later the first in a series of mint robberies occurred.

On July 18, 1864, council reestablished the position of chief of police, naming William N. Keith a formal marshal, but the position was again abolished on August 24, 1864, then revived in December with Arlington O. Ashley serving. Council continued its on-again, off-again policy by abolishing the position in mid-1865. It was officially restored in 1873, but until that time it would be the duty of marshals to enforce law and order in Denver. For the remainder of the nineteenth century, the Denver Police Department claimed an array of chiefs from all walks of life, some from the ranks, others from without. Ranging from one who served four separate appointments to another who resigned the position he never really held, most served faithfully, gaining great respect for their years of service, while others shamed their sworn duty by allowing themselves to be caught up in political scandal.

With the elections of 1877, a man named Baxter Stiles, a Republican, was elected mayor and, as was his prerogative, chose to go outside the department in selecting a new chief. Robert Y. Force was his choice, but not the council's, who refused to confirm him. The council got even by reducing the number of police officers to a dangerous low of two men (Officers Howe and Sherman were to split patrol of the city—one by day and one by night). At this time Denver's population was 25,000, and it was easily recognized that two men could not possibly enforce the laws. So Chief Force resigned for the good of the department. A weak individual followed him and was blamed for the lynching of a Chinese worker, Sing Lee, during a nasty riot. Several other chiefs made some notable improvements before Austin W. Hogel stepped forward, later to be known as the best man ever to hold the office. As chief he initiated a stringent set of rules and regulations for every officer to follow, military-type police procedures, and the granting of more power to the Police Board, a recent development whose influence was so limited that it existed in name only. He also obtained a patrol wagon, telephone, and signal system; began a rogue's gallery; and reestablished three eight-hour shifts. The final legal hanging was likewise another landmark during Hogel's tenure.

Henry Brady took over from Hogel on July 29, 1887, after a blatant political maneuver. Mayor William S. Lee, elected three months earlier, wanted his own man in the position and gave notice that any officer who supported Hogel in his quest for nomination of sheriff (a second job Hogel sought, perfectly legal then) risked dismissal. There was no other choice but for Hogel to resign. Lee and Brady then had a free hand to debase government as they pleased. The corruption of this administration reached its peak during the elections of 1889. With the consent and knowledge of the mayor and aided and encouraged by the police chief, repeated and fraudulent voting was conducted in precincts throughout the city. But a week later their game was over. A new mayor, Wolfe Londoner, refused to reappoint Brady, who simply yawned and submitted his resignation. Brady was indicted by a grand jury on charges that he accepted a bribe while serving as chief. He was tried in district court but found not guilty.

The next chief, John Farley, was a highly efficient administrator who immediately restored control over the department. He did an exceptional job, considering that the State Legislature passed an act creating the Fire and Police Board, which diluted his authority. No agency in the history of the city was vested with as much power as the board. Not only did it virtually control the members of the Police Department, but also its arm extended to such areas as issuing business and automobile licenses, zoning laws, controlling liquor establishments, and strange as it seems, regulating when women were allowed to frequent restaurants and saloons. The "City Hall War" tested the governor of Colorado, who after firing two corrupt board commissioners, learned that they would not vacate their positions. The dispute festered until the Supreme Court ruled that the governor did indeed have authority to remove the commissioners. With a new board, Farley and two other men walked away from a political situation not to their liking. Their resignations resulted in the board's hiring outside of the department. Confirmed as the new chief of police, Hamilton Armstrong served longer in point of time than any other chief, not only in Denver, but at the time, anywhere in the United States. Iron-fisted, in one day he closed all public gambling dens and confiscated all their equipment. He did much the same for prostitution, both illegal activities having been tolerated by past administrations. His four intermittent terms of office (1894–1921) ended with his death and realization that the public was apathetic toward vice, rendering his efforts in vain.

The Home Rule Era
Early in the new century John A. Rush, a Democratic state senator, envisioned freedom from political deception in government and introduced a bill that came to be known as "The Rush Home Rule Bill." It created the City and County of Denver and provided Home Rule without interference or political pressure from state government. It placed appointment of the Fire and Police Board in the hands of the mayor and sanctioned a civil service system. Popular vote ratified the bill on November 4, 1902, although it was not until March 29, 1904, that the city adopted the system and became incorporated as the City and County of Denver. After legal hassling, it was finally confirmed by the Supreme Court in June 1919.

The charter retained the Fire and Police Board, whose members would be chosen by the mayor. They in turn appointed a chief of police who would serve for four years, but could be removed at their discretion without reason or cause. The Civil Service Commission's authority would include classification of positions, competitive examinations, creation of an eligibility list, a probation period, and promotions based on merit. A minimum of 125 officers, but no more than one per thousand population, would be the new standard. Salaries would range from $250 per month for the chief to $85 for patrolmen. A pension system dawned with the establishment of a relief fund to be administered by the Fire and Police Board for the aged or disabled who had been on the force for twenty years.

The first chief of police under Home Rule was Michael A. Delaney. He advocated the "third degree" method in dealing with criminals; consequently he battled lawsuits almost daily and received numerous letters threatening his life. There were constant charges of brutality within the Police Department, brutality at City Jail, and brutality against newspaper reporters. Yet Delaney persevered and gained the reputation of an expert in handling criminals the "stern, old reliable way." In 1910 the first traffic squad was formed, consisting of the largest men in the department. Eight in all, they weighed a combined 1,766 pounds, or an average of 220 pounds each. The idea was to employ men who could be seen without the danger of them being struck down in the middle of an intersection by a motor car burning up the street at fifteen miles an hour. On the other hand, those assigned to the motorcycles were the smallest men in both stature and weight.

An interesting experiment occurred in 1912 when a new chief, Felix O'Neill, ordered his men to "turn in their clubs." They would no longer be used and furthermore, "any officer who beats or mistreats a prisoner must be prepared to show justification for his actions under penalty of discharge." His men, in a quandary after "third degree" Delaney, were displeased with their new pacifist role and thought O'Neill too soft. Curiously, the public, which had demanded a cessation of brutality a few months before, now complained of "laxity in law enforcement." Later, demonstrating more uncertainty of command, Glenn S. Duffield, was appointed chief, a man who had long been associated with gambling and was a frequent patron of the City Park race track.

The tramway strike of 1920 caught the Police Department completely unaware. A pay increase was rescinded, causing the strike, and the strike-breakers brought in to work for the disgruntled tramway employees precipitated a full-scale riot. Two trollies were burned, two people died, and $25,000 worth of equipment was destroyed. The police appeared helpless as the rioting continued, so that mayor called in troops from Fort Logan and Denver became subject to military law. After almost a month of unrest, seven people had died, fifty had been injured, and material damage was too high to estimate. Some good did come out of this tragedy, though. The city fathers acknowledged that the department was ill-staffed and by the following year an additional hundred men had been hired.

New Leadership and Professional Growth
Herbert S. "Rugg" Williams was appointed to the office of chief of police on February 1, 1921. In all, his police career would span sixty-two years, longer than any other officer on any metropolitan police force in the United States. The 1922 Mint robbery focused national attention on Denver; after $200,000 in five-dollar bills had been stolen Chief Williams and a guard, Charles T. Linton, were shot and killed. FBI agents and the local authorities took until 1934 to resolve the case; even then some questions were still unanswered. Only $80,000 of the original amount was recovered, and the perpetrators at that late date had either died or were serving time for other crimes.

During the years between 1924 and 1938 there were as many as five chiefs of police. In 1930 officers flew airplanes for the first time with a squad of seventeen men. Later disbanded, the squad was reorganized in 1939, this time with only four men. Again it was disbanded and remained so until August 15, 1968, when it was reorganized as the first helicopter unit. Police radios were installed for the first time in 1932 in ten patrol cars. The same year, KGPX, the Denver Police Radio Station, began broadcasting with 150 watts of power. Other innovations marked this period of gradual enhancement of police service.

On January 1, 1938, August Hanebuth became chief and would hold the office until May 29, 1947. He held to the philosophy that the patrolman's job was out on the street and that's where they should be assigned. He also believed that "there were too many records to keep." Police work is for officers he observed, so let somebody else keep the records. Chief Hanebuth handled the manpower loss caused by World War II by stating that if a man volunteered for the service, he was gone and his job would not be there when he returned. But the Civil Service overruled him and did grant military leave to members of the Police Department, thereby guaranteeing their jobs when the war was over. John F. O'Donnell followed Hanebuth as chief; during his term the department revamped its procedures to conform with FBI standards, and in addition, a modern crime laboratory was installed. He established a training school for all officers and proposed giving all plainclothes officers the rank of detective. Herbert E. Forsythe became the next chief and at forty-four was the youngest man ever to hold the office. He began replacing officers with civilians in many positions (desk officers) and returning them to active duty. He also reestablished the rank of lieutenant in 1953 and instituted the controversial practice of the one-man patrol car. Soon the mayor cited him for modernizing the department, improving the city's traffic safety, and lowering the crime rate.

Walter "Bud" Johnson served as chief for five years and is credited with initiating the motorcycle night squad and consolidating the morals, narcotics, and intelligence bureaus. James E. Childers lasted for only two years in office after Johnson, due primarily to a police burglary scandal which he could not clear up. Two more chiefs tried to wash away the stain of the scandal—on "Black Saturday" charges had been filed against many officers for theft and the public outcry had been intense—but time to forget and a new chief were what it would take to restore police credibility. July 1, 1972, was the appointment date of Arthur G. Dill, whose continuous service as chief was longer than that of any other man in the position, ten years and eleven months. Chief Dill witnessed the opening of new headquarters at 1331 Cherokee Street, a modern six-story building adjacent to the new detention facility, which was occupied the same year. Also at this time street officers began carrying portable radios for communication while at a distance from their patrol units. To curtail the ever rising burglary rate, the SCAT Unit was created; and another innovation, the Escort Unit, was

D

formed to counteract the crime rate in certain residential areas.

After a slight three months in office, Robert B. Shaughnessy relinquished his authority as chief to Thomas E. Coogan, who was appointed on August 26, 1983. Now in the 1990s David L. Michaud is the chief of police, administering a department comprised of 1,364 sworn officers and 257 civilian members. The number of sworn officers per 1,000 population in 1992 was 2.96 at a per capita cost for police services of $185.20. Chief Michaud allocates his officers thusly: 53% to patrol, 19% to criminal investigation, 12% to traffic, 6% to staff services, 7% to community services, and 3% to his support staff. Denver's crime index is typical in that burglary and auto theft account for the highest number of reported offenses. In 1992 there were 93 murders, up 4.5% from 1991, with a clearance rate of 41.9%. The department's highest clearance rates were for aggravated assault (58%) and for drug abuse cases (95%).

Abridged from the official history provided by the Denver Police Department

Detectives

One of the most important functions of law-enforcement agencies is criminal investigation. This is largely carried out by detectives, and everyone knows what a detective is—someone who looks like McGarrett, talks like Kojak, processes crime scenes like Sherlock Holmes, has the "street savvy" of Charlie Chan, leads an exciting life like James Bond, cracks one tough case after another like Mike Hammer, is legally knowledgeable and technically proficient like Joe Friday, and is as tough as Dirty Harry or Philip Marlowe. Usually this detective works alone or has the services of the ever-present, obedient companion who handles all the menial tasks. The real hero of police work, then is the detective; that is, the fictionalized version of the detective. The fictionalized detective symbolizes the ultimate status, success, and achievement of police work: He is the epitome of intelligence and logic, a clever, almost flawless specialist in his field who is admired for his integrity, dedication, and tough-guy image. This representation of detective work greatly exaggerates reality rather than portrays it. The detective novel and the Hollywood image have glamorized the detective function while ignoring the facts (McCullough, 1984).

So what is a realistic image of detective work and the investigative process? Crimes are solved because almost every individual in the police agency contributes something. Often patrol and detective divisions work together to solve crimes. While it may commonly be assumed that the investigation of crimes is the sole responsibility of detectives, the reality is that few aspects of contemporary police investigative work do not involve other police specialists. Indeed, criminal investigation is a highly professional and specialized activity, but detectives are not the only police officers who possess the skills and talent needed to solve crimes. In fact, a Rand study reported that detectives spend only approximately 7 percent of their time on activities that actually lead to solving a crime. Solutions to criminal events reflect activities of patrol officers, public cooperation, and routine processing of information rather than the clever application of investigative strategies by detectives.

Typically, detective work varies from agency to agency, according to size, resources, and location. Smaller police agencies may require detectives to perform all phases of the investigative function and all types of criminal investigations. In large metropolitan police agencies the detective division is a highly specialized unit separated from the larger patrol division. Detectives concentrate on the investigation of specific crimes such as homicide, narcotics, vice, burglary, arson, and robbery.

No matter what type of criminal offense occurs, the police must take some action. In the case of a major crime, such as homicide, detectives will become involved in various stages of the investigation. For example, the crime scene must be searched, relevant evidence collected, witnesses interviewed, suspects interrogated, and the prosecuting attorney consulted. But, above all, numerous meticulous reports must be filed. The preparation of initial and follow-up reports is the most important aspect of the investigative process. Comprehensive and accurate reports reflect the details of the investigation that may later lead to the successful prosecution of the offender.

An illustrative criminal case describes the tasks of the detective. "Mike O'Kelly" is a veteran homicide detective working for a large metropolitan police agency. When investigating sudden, violent deaths, O'Kelly will be required to perform a wide range of functions. Helped by the preliminary crime report prepared by a patrol officer, O'Kelly will begin to reconstruct events that took place at the crime scene. Reconstruction is accomplished by carefully searching the scene, noting where each item of evidence is located. Bloodstains, weapons, position of the victim, and other items of physical evidence are carefully noted in a detailed sketch of the crime scene. The crime scene is photographed and other specialists—fingerprinter, criminalist, or coroner—are called to assist in the search for evidence.

Witnesses are located and interviewed for additional information. Police records, crime index files, MO or "modus operandi" files, and other computer files are searched to assist the detective in developing a "suspect set"—people known to the police. The competent detective knows that the smaller the suspect set the greater the likelihood the offender will be apprehended (Ericson, 1981).

Supplemental reports are then completed and presented to the prosecuting attorney for review and judgment. If a suspect has been located, arrest and search warrants are obtained (if necessary) and the suspect is advised of his or her rights and formally charged with the crime. At this point it would appear that O'Kelly's investigation has ended, but the contrary is true. Unlike the fictionalized detective, O'Kelly may be just beginning his work. Additional reports must be written, physical evidence linked to the crime scene, and the suspect interrogated in the hope of obtaining an admission or confession of guilt. All investigative leads are followed no matter how insignificant. After the case goes to trial, O'Kelly once again works closely with the prosecuting attorney in preparing his trial testimony. If O'Kelly has successfully accomplished all phases of the investigative process, the suspected offender may be found guilty. Most important, O'Kelly must work within the framework of established legal precedents and guidelines. Where the fictionalized detective will do almost anything to circumvent the law, à la Dirty Harry, O'Kelly must rigorously follow court decisions; if he does not he certainly will lose the case. Finally O'Kelly will consult with a probation officer to determine an appropriate sentence for recommendation to the judge.

In sum, the exaggerated images and unrealistic expectations of fictionalized detectives differ widely from the reality of detective work. Nevertheless, what it takes to solve a criminal case and to discover and verify a response to the central question of all detective work, i.e., "whodunit?" is basically the same. Detective fiction and "real" detective work involve the solution to a puzzle. However, O'Kelly must work extremely diligently to find that solution. Unlike the fictionalized detective who solves every case, the real-life detective actually "solves" few criminal cases. For example, 63 percent of homicide cases are "cleared" by an arrest made at the scene of the crime or later identification of suspects by witnesses. The most important piece of information in locating offenders is the name of the suspect. Only 11 percent of homicides are cleared by linking evidence to suspects. Even though detective work appears burdensome and time consuming, with few crimes solved, the glamour of detective work is quite infectious. Most of the mystery and romance of policing surrounds the job of investigating crimes and catching crooks (Ericson, 1981).

Nearly all patrol officers at some time desire a promotion to the detective division. The patrol division is the incubator for the detective division. Wilson (1978) argues that police administrators should select detectives from the patrol force. The many hours of routine patrol service, with its variegated problems and experience in preliminary criminal investigations, provide substantial training for future detectives. The qualities of a good detective are difficult to define but one thing seems certain. Several years of patrol experience provide the potential detective with the opportunity to improve report-writing skills, verbal ability, observational techniques, and analytical abilities. In fact, one of the most famous metropolitan police detectives rose from the ranks of the patrol force and eventually became chief of detectives in New York City in the late nineteenth century. Inspector Thomas Byrnes was an innovative, keen-minded person who selected the best patrol officers for detective assignments. Byrnes specifically trained his detectives in recognizing individual criminal techniques. Later, this method of recognition became known as modus operandi or method of operation, an essential investigative tool to this day. The modus operandi is the signature of the criminal.

However, no discussion of the historical contribution to the work of detectives could be complete without mention of America's foremost private detective, Allan Pinkerton. The Pinkerton detective agency was opened in the early 1850s and provided investigative services to both private and governmental clients. By the end of the Civil War, Pinkerton's fame as an innovative detective was widespread. Among the numerous investigative tools originated by Pinkerton were the art of surveillance or "shadowing," working as an undercover operative or "assuming the role," and the police lineup of known criminals. Pinkerton is also credited with promoting the centralization of criminal identification records, advocating the acceptance in court of handwriting examination, and advancing the cause of international police cooperation. The early success of the Pinkerton detective agency was emulated by newly formed municipal state and federal police agencies (Pinkerton, 1973).

Unquestionably, the best-known federal investigative agency is the Federal Bureau of Investigation. The FBI is responsible for detecting and investigating violations of a variety of federal criminal codes. A major contribution of the FBI is the refinement of Pinkerton's identification system. The creation of a nationwide identification file consolidated the records of thousands of local police agencies, making it much easier for detectives to exchange criminal information. The FBI also publishes the *Uniform Crime Reports Bulletin*, which has become the most reliable gauge for measuring the level of serious crime in the United States. The detection of crime has been enhanced further by the creation of the largest crime laboratory in the world, processing a wide range of evidence daily to assist detectives. Perhaps the greatest contribution to the investigative process has been the public image of the FBI. By maintaining a reputation for investigative competence, unquestionable integrity and incorruptibility, the FBI has been essential in improving the status of all police investigators (Wilson, 1978).

What has been acknowledged by the FBI as well as detectives across the country is that the detection of crime and the apprehension of offenders must involve the cooperation of the community. Detectives are only as good as the information supplied by members of the public. An informant can be anyone who has information to share with the police investigator. Thus, a public image that stresses police/citizen involvement can be instrumental in locating wanted offenders.

In sum, contemporary detective work involves four specific objectives. First, to establish the fact that a criminal offense has occurred; second, to identify the elements of the offense; third, to detect and apprehend the offender; and fourth, to present relevant evidence in court.

Undoubtedly the fictionalized detective will continue to be a constant reminder of the unrealistic expectations of the community to "solve the crime" quickly. The community is often baffled by the detective/investigator's inability to round up suspects and quickly resolve the "case" like the movie detective. Detective work is truly the ultimate in status and success in the difficult world of policing contemporary society, whether fictionalized or "real."

James M. Poland

Bibliography

Chaiken, Jan, Peter Greenwood, and Joan Petersilia. "The Rand Study of Detectives." In *Thinking About Police*. Ed. Carl B. Klockars. New York: McGraw-Hill, 1983.

DeLadurantey, Joseph, and Daniel Sullivan. *Criminal Investigation Standards*. New York: Harper & Row, 1980.

Ericson, Richard V. *Making Crime: A Study of Detective Work*. Toronto: Butterworths, 1981.

Leonard, V.A. *The Police Detective Function*. Springfield, IL: Charles C. Thomas, 1970.

McCullough, David W. *Great Detectives: A Century of the Best Mysteries from England to America*. New York: Pantheon, 1984.

Pinkerton, Allan. *Professional Thieves and the Detective*. New York: Carleton, 1973.

Powers, Richard G. *G Men: Hoover's FBI in America*. Carbondale: Southern Illinois University Press, 1983.

Waegel, William B. "Patterns of Police Investigation of Urban Crimes." *Journal of Police Science and Administration* 10(4) (December 1982): 452–65.

Wilson, James Q. *The Investigators: Managing FBI and Narcotics Agents*. New York: Basic Books, 1978.

Discretion

Police discretion may be defined as the capacity of police officers to select from among a number of legal and illegal courses of action or inaction while performing their duties (Davis, 1969). Discretion allows an officer to choose among different objectives (e.g., peacekeeping, maintaining public safety, enforcing the law), tactics (e.g., choosing to enforce traffic laws by patrolling or sitting at a stop sign), and outcomes (e.g., choosing to warn rather than cite a traffic violator) in the performance of his or her work. While officers have discretion in a wide range of incidents from crime calls to disturbances to the handling of mentally ill individuals, most scholarly literature on discretion focuses on the selective enforcement of law, that is, factors affecting officer decisions to arrest or not arrest violators.

Officer discretion is sometimes confused with two related concepts: selective enforcement and directed patrol. Selective enforcement is a form of administrative discretion in which police policy-makers or managers identify departmental priorities for units of officers. An example of selective enforcement would be a chief's decision to enforce gaming laws against street dice games, but to overlook their violation at church bingo games.

Directed patrol is an example of supervisory discretion in which a field supervisor commands his or her subordinates to pay short-term, intense attention to a specified area, or to particular forms of behavior within an area. For example, in response to resident complaints, a sergeant might direct a beat officer to remove loitering teenagers from a specific street corner, or to ticket cars double-parked in front of a specific retail store.

Discretion versus Full Enforcement

The use of discretion by police officers has only recently been recognized as a proper aspect of their authority. Formerly, the public and police administrators shared the assumption that police officers and agencies were bound to enforce all laws against every violator, and that failure to do so was itself illegal. A minority of legislators, prosecutors, and judges still hold to this view. Police administrators have been reluctant to admit that individual officers use discretion when enforcing laws, or that they have quietly promulgated less than full-enforcement policies in regard to minor crimes or violations of municipal ordinances. They fear a public outcry that the laws are being enforced unequally, or liability, should official permission not to enforce the laws against, say, speeding or drunk driving lead to the injury or death of a violator or third party.

Williams (1984), H. Goldstein (1977), and Davis (1969, 1975) have documented the inaccuracy of the belief that legislatures intended all laws to be fully enforced in all circumstances. Davis cites state and federal regulatory agency rule-making as a precedent justifying selective enforcement decisions by police administrators, while Williams and Goldstein cite legislative history, case law, and inadequate levels of fiscal appropriations to police agencies to refute the idea that legislatures truly intend all laws to be enforced at all times. Thus, an officer's decision not to arrest a violator in particular circumstances cannot be criticized on the grounds that such inaction is unauthorized by law. However, an officer's poor use of discretion may be criticized on other grounds.

The Necessity for Officer Discretion

Discretion is not only proper, but it is a necessary part of police work. First, statutes by their nature must be written in language too general to provide enforcement guidelines for every circumstance in which they might be broken. The example of a driver violating the speed limit to rush an injured party to a hospital is one of literally countless cases in which a law is broken but should probably not be enforced. Second, many officers see criminal statutes as a means for doing justice and maintaining the good order of society, not simply as ends in themselves. The documented refusal of many police officers to arrest in spousal assault cases in which the victim refuses to file a complaint against his or her assailant is based in part on the officers' assessment that their mission is to restore order in disturbances, and that arrest is a tool to this end. Thus, the few arrests that are made in spousal assault cases usually occur when the party causing the disturbance will not comply with an officer's commands.

Finally, there is the problem of resource allocation: If an officer arrests an individual for an outstanding traffic warrant or transports a mentally ill person to a hospital, the officer is unavailable (possibly for several hours) to perform other, potentially more critical tasks, i.e., respond to a robbery in progress, intervene in a family disturbance, or direct traffic at a fire or accident scene. In this sense, allowing an officer discretion to allocate his or her time is a way for police organizations to recognize that police service is a finite resource. In deciding which problems to attend to and how to resolve them, police policy-makers and individual officers distribute police resources on an "as-needed" basis.

Factors Influencing the Use of Discretion
Researchers have identified numerous factors that influence how a police officer makes discretionary decisions. In regard to arrest (the most frequently studied aspect of discretion), Black (1980), LaFave (1965), and Reiss (1971) have noted that an offender's age, race, and sex affect an officer's decision to arrest or release. Other studies have shown that situational and interactive factors may play an even greater role in shaping the officer's actions: Is the victim/complainant present and is he or she willing to press charges? Do the victim and offender have a previous relationship and did the victim provoke the offender's actions? Is there a witness present? Is the offense the result of a chronic behavior pattern between the victim and violator and is arrest likely to influence the offender to change his or her behavior? Is the offender's attitude toward the officer respectful or uncivil?

In a study of enforcement of Maine's drunk-driving statutes, Meyers et al. (1987) discovered that approximately one-third of police officers in the state had, at least once in the twelve months prior to the study, chosen not to stop a vehicle even though the officers had probable cause to believe that the vehicle was being operated by a driver under the influence of drugs or alcohol. Approximately one-quarter of the officers used their discretion not to arrest a driver they had probable cause to believe was drunk after they had stopped him. The factors associated with the Maine officers' use of discretion to overlook potential or actual offenses were length of police service; rank or level of command; the officers' general opinion of support for DUI enforcement in other sectors of the criminal-justice system; and levels of frustration with delays and low conviction rates in the system. Thus systemic concerns as well as the nature of the offense and the offender also shape officer use of discretion.

Problems Associated with Officer Discretion
J. Goldstein (1960) notes that police discretion leads to countless numbers of "low visibility decisions" by individual officers. His phrase has two connotations: First, that the existence and breadth of officer discretion are not widely appreciated or understood by the public because they are rarely acknowledged by police administrators or elected officials; and second, that the use of discretion by officers is not usually scrutinized by the public, elected officials, the courts, police administrators, or supervisors.

Patrol officers and detectives work alone or with a loyal, trusted partner. Many policing situations involve a sole complainant or offender, or those who are not motivated to bring their contact with the police to light. Especially where an arrest is not made or a formal report not filed by the officer (circumstances that characterize the great majority of police–citizen encounters), the officer's use of discretion cannot be reviewed. Because discretionary decisions by individual officers are both sub rosa and unregulated, they have the potential to become problematic.

Inconsistency is one problem associated with discretion. On its face, discretion allows officers to give differential treatment to individuals. Some critics of the police observe that differential treatment often turns out to be discriminatory, for example, that blacks get stopped on suspicion more frequently than whites in similar circumstances, or that men get arrested for assaulting an officer more frequently than women, even when the women's assaultive behavior is virtually identical to that of men. American society proclaims its citizens equal before the law, but discretion may give rise to situations in which, it appears, some individuals have less to fear from the law than others.

Unpredictability is another problem associated with discretion. For citizens trying to conform their behavior to the dictates of law, variations in officer behavior may create confusion. Consider the commuter who drives to work each weekday on a stretch of highway with a fifty-five-mile-per-hour speed limit. The motorist usually travels at sixty-five miles per hour, and the officer normally assigned to the morning shift tolerates speeds up to sixty-eight miles per hour. During the officer's vacation period, however, another officer with a different standard for speeding—sixty-three miles per hour—issues the commuter a citation for speeding. In a formal sense, the commuter is being penalized for exceeding the legal speed limit but in reality is being punished because the substitute officer has a different personal standard for speeding than the one the commuter had been meeting.

Discriminatory or inconsistent use of discretion may be criticized on the grounds that it results in unfairness to individuals. The ideal of equality under the law implies that all citizens should receive relatively similar treatment when they perform relatively similar acts. Cohen (1985), however, observes that fairness can have a second meaning: just deserts. The just-deserts principle argues that, to be treated fairly, each person should receive the treatment he or she deserves, regardless of whether this treatment is equal to that of others. Officers can use their discretion to give individuals their just deserts in particular cases. Thus, Cohen argues, "The problem of discretion is the problem of good judgment."

To assess the quality of an officer's judgment, one should consider whether it would be fair to cite the motorist (referred to earlier) speeding an injured victim to a hospital. While it might be consistent for an officer to cite the motorist for driving at the same speed as others the officer had cited, the motorist might not deserve to be treated the same as those who were simply contemptuous of the law, or who had no defensible reason for speeding. For police officers, then, the problem of discretion is knowing which behaviors and individuals to treat in relatively similar ways, and which to treat as exceptions.

Lack of accountability has also been cited as a problem associated with officer discretion. Because some officers assume that they have virtually unlimited discretion in performing their duties, supervisors and administrators express concern that they cannot predict or control how their officers will behave when not receiving direct oversight, or that officers will use illegal or unauthorized means to achieve the ends of police work. Brown (1981) has observed that police departments present extreme cases of organizations in which line workers (patrol officers and detectives) have, in some respects, more autonomy in decision-making than supervisors, managers, or executives, whose work is closely scrutinized by those who outrank them.

Officer autonomy stems from many factors. The great bulk of patrol work cannot be planned with great efficiency; most patrol officers are given their daily workload by a dispatcher, one incident at a time, in response to citizen requests for service. This makes the individual patrol officer's workload seem unpredictable and, by implication, unmanageable. Few departments plan a patrol officer's daily tasks, and only occasionally do sergeants have time for direct supervision of individual patrol

units. Detectives working in plainclothes are even less visible to supervisors or the public than uniformed patrol officers and are thus even less accountable for their use of time or effort. Consequently, some administrators and observers fear that officer discretion is primarily invoked as an excuse for low productivity. They also fear that discretion linked with haphazard supervision and little accountability will tempt officers into selling nonenforcement to violators of laws or ordinances. In this regard, Sherman (1978) has identified excessive officer discretion as a potential source of corruption.

Positive Aspects of Discretion
While discretion has its potential pitfalls, it can also have its benefits. Muir (1977) sees the choice-making and inventiveness involved in using discretion as a means by which officers can undergo moral development. Muir observes that a patrol officer's experience of decision-making with a variety of situations, settings, and clienteles can expand the officer's intellectual horizons and prepare him or her to govern others with a sense of fairness, rather than with arbitrariness or excessive zeal. When allowed to choose from among a wide range of objectives, tactics, and outcomes to critical and threatening situations, officers can develop a sense of their personal courage and official powers, both what their authority and charisma can accomplish and what are their limits. In Muir's estimate, discretionary exercise of power and authority has the potential to morally "ennoble" police officers. Abusing or failing to use the gift of discretion well, on the other hand, can "corrupt" an officer.

Attempts to Limit or Regulate Discretion
Having come to acknowledge the reality of officer discretion and their incapacity to eliminate it, many police administrators now believe they must "structure" discretion; that is, regulate it so that its negative effects are minimized. One means of shaping discretion is administrative rulemaking or the enunciation of policies and standard operating procedures. For example, most major urban departments now have a restrictive policy on the use of deadly force based on the defense-of-life doctrine. This standard is often stricter than that imposed by many of the states (thirty-seven states still permit the shooting of an unarmed fleeing felon). Under the defense-of-life standard, an officer is permitted to fire a gun only to preserve his or her life or

that of another in imminent danger, and only if innocent bystanders will not be endangered by the shot. Implementing this standard has had the effect of reducing the range of situations in which officers may use their weapons and accordingly has lowered the number of gunshots fired by officers in departments that have adopted the policy.

A second method of structuring discretion is legislative action mandating stereotyped officer responses to well-defined situations. Several states have adopted laws in the area of domestic violence, for example, that require an officer at the request of a victim to arrest or remove the offender from the scene; others have required officers to report all cases of suspected child or elder abuse.

Department-wide training is another method that is thought effective in restricting discretion insofar as it exposes all officers to standard procedures for the handling of typical incidents. When offered in conjunction with standard operating procedure manuals and increased supervisory accountability, training can create common expectations of acceptable behavior. Finally, internal investigations and field inspections are reasonable means for assuring consistency of officer behavior in the treatment of citizens.

Future Trends in Police Discretion
Discretion is likely to become a source of increasing conflict between police officers and police administrations. The efflorescence of civil liability litigation, pressures for equal treatment by minority groups, the desire by management to increase officer productivity, and the tracking capacities of advanced communications and data-processing technology are a few of the forces that are likely to impel police administrators to seek additional methods for structuring (i.e., limiting) individual officer discretion.

Conversely, discretion is for many officers the most interesting—if confusing and at times anxiety provoking—aspect of their work. Using discretion wisely is ethically challenging; using it well allows an officer to invoke sanctions against those he or she thinks deserve punishment and to forgo them for those who do not. The use of discretion is the inventive cutting edge of daily police work. By using it, officers express their autonomy and individuality in people management and problem-solving. It also can become the license behind which some officers shield their lack of knowledge of rules

and procedures, or their willingness to cut corners in the performance of their work.

Advocates of higher education for the police have argued that a compelling reason for police officers to obtain a liberal education is to broaden their approach to dealing with a diverse public, that is, to use their discretion with good judgment and sensitivity. Many assume that well-educated officers will demonstrate superior wisdom and complexity of judgment in deciding which forms of behavior are acceptable and which individuals deserve action by the police. Others argue that "common sense" and "street smarts" are more important than formal education for the wise exercise of discretion.

Since the 1960s, police officers have found themselves under pressure to improve their productivity and broaden their knowledge base to cope with a wider variety of social problems. Many current proposals to reform policing in the 1990s will involve line-level patrol officers and detectives using broader discretion in the course of their work. The widely admired "problem-solving" approach (H. Goldstein, 1977) begins by acknowledging that the great majority of calls for police service are for repetitive incidents, and that a reactive patrol response to dispatch after dispatch is ineffective for eliminating the cause of the call-generating problem. Problem-solving policing calls on individual officers to innovate new strategies and tactics for eliminating the sources of repeat calls. Officers will be expected to employ wide discretion to invent permanent solutions to these repetitive problems, particularly those that do not necessarily require a law-enforcement response.

Neighborhood-responsive policing, pioneered in Boston and Houston, encourages police planning and the delivery of services on the basis of community input into police operations. Line officers as well as supervisory and administrative personnel meet regularly with community groups to set enforcement priorities for neighborhoods. In a sense, such programs invite communities to set the limits of officer discretion in treating problems identified by the community groups participating in the programs.

Police administrations must learn to balance their efforts to limit discretion within the bounds of acceptable behavior (i.e., assuring that officers do not blatantly discriminate nor act overly tolerantly toward violations of the law) with efforts to encourage creative use of discretion to solve chronic police problems, do justice to individuals, and meet community standards of public order.

Michael Feldberg

Bibliography

Bittner, Egon. "The Police on Skid Row: A Study of Peacekeeping." *American Sociological Review* 32 (1967): 699–715.

Black, Donald J. *The Manners and Customs of the Police.* New York: Academic Press, 1980.

Brown, Michael K. *Working the Street: Police Discretion and the Dilemmas of Reform.* New York: Russell Sage, 1981.

Cohen, Howard. "Authority: Limits of Discretion." In *Moral Issues in Police Work.* Eds. Frederick Elliston and Michael Feldberg. Totowa, NJ: Rowman and Allanheld, 1985. 27–41.

Davis, Kenneth Culp. *Discretionary Justice: A Preliminary Inquiry.* Baton Rouge: Louisiana State University Press, 1969.

———. *Police Discretion.* St. Paul, MN: West Publishing, 1975.

Goldstein, Herman. "Police Discretion: The Ideal *vs.* The Real." *Public Administration Review* 23 (1963): 140–48.

———. *Policing a Free Society.* Cambridge, MA: Ballinger, 1977.

———. "Improving Policing: A Problem-Oriented Approach." *Crime and Delinquency* 25 (1979): 236–38.

Goldstein, Joseph. "Police Discretion Not to Invoke the Criminal Justice Process: Low-Visibility Decisions in the Administration of Justice." *Yale Law Journal* 69 (1960): 543–89.

Houston Police Department. "Developing a Policing Style for Neighborhood-Oriented Policing: Executive Session 1." Houston: Houston Police Department, n.d.

LaFave, Wayne R. *Arrest: The Decision to Take a Suspect into Custody.* Boston: Little, Brown, 1965.

Meyers, Allen R., Timothy Heere, David Kovenock, and Ralph Hingson. "Cops and Drivers: Police Discretion in the Enforcement of Maine's 1981 OUI Law." *Journal of Criminal Justice* 15(5) (1987): 361–68.

Muir, William Ker, Jr. *Police: Streetcorner Politicians.* Chicago: University of Chicago Press, 1977.

Reiss, Albert J. *The Police and the Public.* New Haven, CT: Yale University Press, 1971.

Sherman, Lawrence W. *Scandal and Reform: Controlling Police Corruption.* Berkeley: California University Press, 1978.

Williams, Gregory Howard. *The Law and Politics of Police Discretion.* Westport, CT: Greenwood Press, 1984.

Wilson, James Q. *Varieties of Police Behavior: The Management of Law and Order in Eight Communities.* Cambridge, MA: Harvard University Press, 1968.

Discretion: Two Models

That there are similarities between law enforcement and the military, such as uniforms, rank structures, and insignias, is an obvious fact. Perhaps the most important similarity, however, is their authority to employ force to maintain order. In emergencies, both require near-automatic and unquestioned acceptance of authority by their members. This kind of discipline is crucial to success in a situation that demands the use of deadly force by a police officer or a concerted attack on an enemy stronghold. As a result, law enforcement has traditionally been founded on this "military model of authority."

Yet in reality, while disciplined performance is always required in emergency law-enforcement situations, such circumstances make up a very small percentage of normal policing time. Studies have shown most police officers spend the majority of their time on rather routine, administrative, and nonlaw-enforcement duties. Therefore the question arises: Should officers base their routine activities on the old military model?

The Military Model

Perception of the traditional American police-authority model as a military one evolved from several influences. First, the American model grew out of the nineteenth-century English authority-based system that was imported into the United States in 1844. In 1829, Sir Robert Peel instituted in London a police force based in part on a military model of internal discipline to respond to the failure of an undisciplined and ineffective citizen/watchman system and the violent overreaction of the military to public disorder. Impressed with Peel's success, a New York delegation recommended that his concepts be replicated in New York City. This was the birth of the military model in the United States.

Second, the responsibility for deadly force that has been entrusted to the police absolutely requires strict discipline in its exercise. The strict military discipline necessarily associated with the use of firearms reinforces the military model as officers strap on their guns each day.

Third, the organization and rank structure of most traditional police departments mirror closely the military model. Departments are divided into squads and platoons and led by sergeants and lieutenants, not organized into groups and departments and headed by supervisors and managers. Further, police uniforms, ceremonies, and training all project a military model.

Fourth, men and women drawn to the profession hold authority-based values, giving it a military look, philosophy, and atmosphere. In sum, the military model places a high premium on discipline and discourages the exercise of discretion. A necessary model in time of potential conflict, and especially when the use of deadly force might be involved, it is deliberately taught to all recruits. As a consequence of this history, tradition, and training, many of today's officers tend to use a heavy authority-based (military) model for all circumstances in all situations, regardless of its suitability.

The Discretionary Model
Black's law dictionary offers the following definition of discretion:

> When applied to public functionaries, discretion means a power of right conferred upon them by law of acting officially in certain circumstances, according to the dictates of their own judgment and conscience of others.

While most types of organizations increase discretionary power with rank, law enforcement allocates such power at all levels. Low-ranking police officers routinely exercise an enormous amount of discretion in the normal course of their duties. Traffic officers can choose to issue a citation to a citizen exceeding the speed limit, arrest him or her, provide a warning, or ignore the situation entirely. Similarly, a patrol officer can follow several courses of action when responding to a family dispute. Virtually all routine calls can potentially be handled in a variety of ways—at the discretion of the individual officer. At higher levels in the police organization, a number of officials routinely exercise administrative discretion. In public-administration literature, administrative discretion has become synonymous with the political activity of appointed officials, and the administrative discretion of police managers is quite comparable to the discretion exercised by public officials.

The general policy of discretion rests on the belief that the individual official at a scene is best able to decide how to resolve the situation. The professionalism of any discipline is conventionally measured by the autonomy it allows its members over certain tasks and the discretion it grants them to ensure that performance is within the limits of appropriate laws or regulations.

Comparisons of the Two Models
In the discretionary model success is defined as the minimum intrusion and use of coercion by the police. By way of contrast, performance within a military model is measured by ascertaining how closely the relevant rules and policy were followed. This letter-of-the-law mentality can lead to an overreliance on rules and may serve to negate any skills, talent, or experience that an officer brings to the scene. The rules can take on an infallible quality often misused by many. Worst of all, following the rules can become the desired end, not resolving potentially threatening situations with a minimum of violence or injury.

Then again, some situations require that all parties closely follow the appropriate rules. In law enforcement, rules must be followed exactly during the use of deadly force, the pursuit of a fleeing felon, or when coordinated action is taken by several officials. Freelancing in these matters would be inappropriate and potentially dangerous. Thus departments must recognize that most of their sworn officers require two different sets of guidelines to discharge their duties. Whenever society becomes disenchanted with the manner in which officials exercise their discretion, it acts to remove the privilege. For example, mandatory sentencing of certain types of offenders was brought about by citizens who perceived that a number of judges were "too soft" on criminals. If discretionary powers are taken away, officials have fewer options available to them and also have their professional status lowered.

Training in Discretion

Several teaching methodologies can be employed to present key discretion concepts. Case studies that describe actual situations, in which officers relied on their experience and judgment to resolve potentially explosive situations, are excellent teaching aids. Ideally, the officer involved in the incident would participate with the training staff and class. In addition, case studies could be developed to highlight specific policy points regarding acceptable practices.

One of the most important training goals should be to provide officers with a clear notion of when and where to apply discretionary behavior. Guidelines and checklists can assist officers with these critical questions. Also, by specifying clearly the types of situations in which discretion would be unacceptable or perhaps illegal, departments can demonstrate the bounds of acceptable behavior.

Role playing provides an excellent technique to frame problems of discretion. Elements of realism and immediacy can be injected into many role-playing scenarios. Videotaping these scenarios has the added benefit of enabling officers to criticize their own actions. In the field of management and leadership training, a variety of situational and contingency models can be employed. All in all, the methods by which departments discuss and teach discretion are not nearly as important as the fact that the topic is formally presented. Training programs must begin to discuss the locker-room folk wisdom and common sense that officers pick up after months, even years, of experience. Methods to record and to institutionalize this human knowledge must be found, and ways to communicate the resulting techniques to the officers must be developed.

Donald C. Witham
Stephen D. Gladis

Bibliography

Aaronson, David E. et al. *Public Policy and Police Discretion*. New York: Clark Boardman, 1984.

Elliott, J.R., and Mitchell H. States. "The Concept of Power and the Police." *Journal of Police Science and Administration* 8(1) (1980): 87–93.

Goldstein, Herman. *Policing a Free Society*. Cambridge, MA: Ballinger, 1977.

Klockars, Carl B. "The Dirty Harry Problem." *American Academy of Political and Social Science Annals* 452 (November 1980): 33–47.

Witham, Donald C., and Stephen D. Gladis. "The Nature of Police Authority." *FBI Law Enforcement Bulletin* 55(11) (1986): 16–20.

D

Discrimination

Traditional views of discrimination by social scientists are presented in terms of acts with harmful effects that are precipitated by prejudice or concern for the prejudice of others. However, since the 1960s three other applications of discrimination have emerged: interest theory, internal colonialism, and institutional discrimination.

Interest theory suggests that the main force behind discrimination is the protection of the privileges and power of nonminorities. In essence, prejudicial discrimination becomes supplanted by gain-motivated or vested-interest discrimination. A closely related perspective is internal colonialism, in which colonizers use technology, especially military firepower, to maintain control of the social, economic, and political life of a society. This kind of discrimination becomes a social process to ensure racial stratification and combination. An offshoot of this theory is institutional discrimination, in which privilege becomes embedded in the norms and roles of social, economic, and political organizations. Prejudice, or the irrational and negative attitudes directed toward outgroups because of real or alleged cultural differences, is not necessarily an ingredient. Discriminatory behavior has both effects and mechanisms; effects refer to the negative impact on behavior, while mechanisms refer to the modes of operation leading to the harmful effects. Unlike traditional models of discrimination, institutional discrimination can be either overt or covert, and becomes embedded in organizational processes both intentionally and unintentionally.

The institutional definition of discrimination has been incorporated in public policy in many areas of American life, including employment and service by public agencies. For example, in the statutory language of the 1964 Civil Rights Act related to employment, "discrimination" is defined in the following manner:

It shall be an unlawful employment practice for an employer—

(1) to fail or refuse to hire or to discharge any individual with respect to his compensation, terms, conditions, or privileges of employment, because of such individual's race, color, religion, sex, or national origin;

(2) to limit, segregate, or classify his employees or applicants for employment in any way which would deprive or tend to deprive an individual of employment opportunities or otherwise adversely affect his status as an employee, because of such individual's race, color, religion, sex, or national origin. (Civil Rights Act 1964, Public Law 92–261 Section 703[a][1][2])

These and other statutes refer to intentional discrimination against an individual's race, color, religion, or national origin, and to that caused by behavior and practices that appear to be applied to everyone equally but, in reality, deny certain individuals and groups employment opportunity. While the institutional viewpoint provides a good operational framework for this project, one cannot entirely discount the role of prejudice, especially when it is found to be a part of the occupational subculture, as is the case in American policing.

Police Subculture and Discrimination

An occupational subculture consists of a group of specialists recognized by society and themselves as having an identifiable complex of common culture, values, communication symbols, techniques, and appropriate behavior patterns. Police forces form a distinctive occupational subculture through habits their members acquire in their occupation. Studies show that they have a common argot, use esoteric knowledge, utilize internal sanctions on peers, have a strong sense of unity, and often exercise professional courtesy. Additionally, early studies have shown that they feel a sense of social isolation from the rest of the society. Often, in either one-on-one or group encounters, certain "outgroups" are viewed as inferior and dangerous.

Various studies lead to the inescapable conclusion that nonwhite citizens are often perceived in this manner. Nonwhites, especially blacks, were less likely to receive efficient police services, were often arrested and beaten during the process, and were perceived as what one study described as "symbolic assailants."

Events in this decade have exemplified these notions. In Miami, Los Angeles, and New Orleans there have been riots over police maltreatment of suspects; in these cases, the suspects, though unarmed, were often beaten, and the suspect officers were often found not guilty in subsequent judicial proceedings. In many of these case studies, rioting occurred as the result of nonprosecution of suspected officers. What these incidents and studies conclude is that nonwhites often do not receive the same level of courtesy and respect shown to white citizens, that they are more likely to be involved in violent confrontations with police over even routine arrests and complaints, and that the delivery of services to the community is comparatively low in terms of efficiency. It is not surprising, then, that many white officers give little encouragement to nonwhite police recruitment.

While social and political dynamics have provided some jobs for nonwhites and others in police organizations, Rafky (1975) shows that intentional and unintentional barriers contribute to the problem of discrimination. He has labeled these as individual, organizational, and societal. Individual barriers for nonwhite candidates include lack of interest in a police career due to negative perceptions and past encounters with police, or the notion that one can do better than becoming a police officer in terms of pay and status. As Cooper (1980) suggests, becoming a cop is often described in the ghetto terms of "Uncle Tom" and "black judas goat" by nonwhite citizens.

Unintentional barriers on the individual level include inadequate educational, character, or physical qualifications. According to a civil-service director in central New York: "There are thousands of blacks and Hispanics who sign up to take our tests, but after review we find that they don't have the educational qualifications for the job."

On the organizational level, the police department may intentionally exclude or dissuade nonwhites from employment through deliberate exclusionary policies and work procedures. Civil tort actions by individuals and groups against police personnel selection and retention are based on these intentional barriers. The first barriers can occur during the selection process. Before the 1964 Civil Rights Act it was easy to get rid of undesirable candidates through a process termed "sophisticated patronage." Biases in written tests and subjective decisions on the results of oral interviews and background investigations made it possible for police agencies to prevent nonwhites from completing the selection process successfully. For those candidates who were hired, there were intentional practices that occurred during academy training. In one lawsuit filed by nonwhite candidates who left a training academy, it was alleged that the staff and white recruits systematically harassed the nonwhite recruits. Examples cited included the use of racial slurs during class lectures, disproportionate "work details" resulting from academy rules violations, and failure of the academy staff to address the situation during the training program (*United States v. State of New York*, 593 F. Supp 1216 [1984]).

The police organization can make life difficult for nonwhite officers working in the field by indirectly telling them they are not wanted. Such practices may include nonassignment to special training school or details, using racial slurs during roll call and radio transmissions, poor performance evaluations, and assignment to patrol duties that are very dangerous, e.g., vice in a ghetto neighborhood.

Departmental procedures and policies may unintentionally limit nonwhite recruitment. Very often, announcement of the civil-service test is limited to certain bulletin boards; therefore, the test dates are only known to a few. The long, drawn-out process from test-taking to hiring may in itself force many candidates, regardless of race, to accept jobs that are readily available instead of scarcer ones to which they aspire.

On the societal level, racist attitudes by influential individuals or policy-making boards can prohibit or discourage nonwhite recruitment.

Quotas and Reverse Discrimination

As Glazer (1975) and others discuss, the statutory language and political intent of initial Title VII legislation did not include preferential treatment for nonwhites and women over white male candidates. Since 1964, however, federal and state case law, Equal Opportunity Employment Commission (EEOC) administrative rulings, and organizational employment practices have determined that statistical imbalances between the number of nonwhites represented in an organization and the determined labor pool constitutes prima facie discrimination. Remedies for imbalances have included quota systems and preferential treat-

ment for nonwhites and women in employee selection and layoff. Despite strong political and legal opposition by private and public-sector labor unions and aggrieved individuals, these remedies have been found constitutional. For example, in 1979 the Supreme Court upheld the use of a voluntary quota system for selecting black candidates for a training program over the objections of an unsuccessful white applicant who claimed that he had been the victim of discrimination (*United Steel Workers v. Weber*, 443 U.S. 193). In his majority opinion, Justice Brennan wrote that the intent of Title VII was to improve the economic plight of nonwhites through the use of preferred selection systems.

Before Weber, the use of quotas and preferential treatment had received judicial approval through a number of Supreme Court cases and EEOC rulings under the aegis of "disparate impact" theory. In 1971, in *Griggs v. Duke Power Company* (401 U.S. 424), the Court ruled that employment tests and practices that exclude a disproportionate number of nonwhites and women may be discriminatory, regardless of whether there was intent by an employer to discriminate. If disparate impact exists, the employer must demonstrate that such tests and practices related to business necessity and the demands of the position.

Disparate impact was applied to police departments in their failure to recruit nonwhites and women in comparison to statistical representation of these minorities in designated labor forces. Disparate impact formed the basis for court orders and consent decrees by which police agencies had to remedy the historical effects of discrimination through review of hiring and testing procedures and the use of goals and quotas. In the case of consent decrees between employers and a federal or state agency or court, there was no admittance of intentional discrimination on the part of the employer agency.

Quotas and preferred hiring plans to address racial imbalances remain in effect for most major municipal police departments in New York State, including Buffalo, Rochester, Syracuse, Onondaga County Sheriff's Department, Albany, Newburgh, and New York City. In Rochester, two nonwhite officers must be hired for every three white officers hired, until the agency achieves 25 percent minority representation (*Howard et al. v. Freedman*, 74 Civ. 234 [1975]). The New York State police entered a consent decree with the Department of Justice in 1979, which specifies that each academy class be composed of 40 percent black and Hispanic troopers, 10 percent women, and 50 percent white males (*United States v. State of New York et al.*, 593 F. Supp. 1216 [1984]).

When minority representation in a police agency matches minority representation in a defined community labor pool, affirmative action is said to be successful. Quotas and preferred hiring, on the other hand, have had a backlash effect because many qualified white candidates have complained that they were not considered for employment simply because of race. In police circles, this practice is known as "dipping"; in public policy discussion regarding quotas it is referred to as "reverse discrimination." No substantial body of literature addresses the topic of reverse discrimination. The term is subject to a number of difficult legal and moral dimensions involving judicially mandated quotas prescribed at the end of a lawsuit or the outcome of a voluntary affirmative action program. The authors use, instead, the term "affirmative discrimination," borrowed from Glazer's (1975) discussion of the development of quotas and preferential treatment since the enactment of Title VII legislation. Affirmative or reverse discrimination denotes three areas of action, in which: (1) racial preferences are used to prescribe the selection of candidates who otherwise appear less qualified than rival candidates; (2) the use of preferences for minority candidates who have not proven that they were the victims of past discrimination; and (3) the use of targets and goals to determine the number of minority candidates to be hired on the basis of race.

Reverse discrimination related to employment continues to be the basis of many lawsuits and public-policy debates with regard to voluntary and court-mandated affirmative action plans and consent decrees. Federal government policy on the use of quotas and preferential treatment to address racial imbalances has been altered considerably since 1981, because the Reagan administration did not consider these measures proper remedies for the effects of employment discrimination. According to the then assistant attorney general, William B. Reynolds, as reported in the *New York Times*, April 30, 1985, "affirmative action needlessly creates a caste system in which an individual is unfairly disadvantaged for each person who is preferred."

Although individuals and nonwhite policy groups have continued to press for quotas, and there have been no substantial changes in the laws, a recent court ruling has been viewed as chipping away the basis of affirmative action. In the case of *Firefighters Local Union No. 1784 v. Stotts et al.* (467 U.S. 561), the Supreme Court ruled that a bona fide seniority system's layoff provisions could not be altered by court order to protect the gains of minorities. The suit was filed by Stotts, a Memphis, Tennessee, firefighter, who opposed that city's plan to lay off black firefighters because of a fiscal problem. The city's plan to use the "last hired, first fired" seniority rule would have had an adverse effect on black personnel who had been hired under the terms of a 1980 consent decree, which was the result of a suit also filed by Stotts, charging that Memphis's hiring and promotion practices were discriminatory. The Court's decision overturned the decision of the district court and appeals court that the "last hired, first fired" rule was discriminatory.

While the immediate issue questioned whether the district court had exceeded its powers in entering an injunction requiring the layoff of white employees, the Department of Justice has taken the position that the Stotts ruling forbids preferential hiring or promotions for nonvictims of discrimination, and that public policy should no longer include judicial or administratively imposed quotas to achieve racial balance in the workforce (Fallon and Weiler, 1985). Thus the decision has been hailed by many antiaffirmative action groups and individuals as "the nail in the coffin of affirmative action."

Stotts represents the clash between the jurisprudence models of individual and group justice. Historically, the model of individual justice recognizes that when a wrong has been done, the wrongdoer must correct it and compensate the victim. What Title VII legislation and subsequent court cases have done is to challenge this long-standing tradition with the concept of group justice, whereby compensation is granted to entire groups of racial classes. This group justice model remains the cornerstone of all civil-rights legislation in protecting and advancing the interests of disadvantaged groups.

Despite the Stotts ruling, preferred hiring of nonwhites and women in the public sector is still practiced. The main issues in police hiring involve civil-service requirements. According to Thibault, Lynch, and McBride (1985), the present civil-service system for police and other public services, which was developed in the early twentieth century, has not changed substantially. Employment requirements and testing practices are outmoded and discriminatory, as exemplified by the high number of successful lawsuits challenging such standards as height and weight, written and physical agility tests, and other requirements. Some commentators contend that these requirements represent the racist thinking of the past and measure neither ability nor potential for doing a job.

R. Bruce McBride

Bibliography

Alex, N. Black in Blue: A Study of the Negro Policeman. New York: Appleton, Century Crofts, 1969.

Cooper, J.L. The Police and the Ghetto. Port Washington, NY: Kennikat Press, 1980.

Fallon, R.H., and P.C. Weiler. "Firefighters v. Stotts: Conflicting Models of Racial Justice." Supreme Court Review. Chicago: University of Chicago, 1985.

Glazer, N. Affirmative Discrimination: Ethnic Inequality and Public Policy. New York: Basic Books, 1975.

McBride, R.B., E.A. Thibault, and L.A. Lynch. Informal Group Structure in Police Organizations. Paper presented at the annual meeting of the New York Sociological Association, October 9, 1981.

Manning, P.K. "Socialization for Police." In Policing: A View from the Street, Eds. P.K. Manning and J. Van Maanen. Santa Monica, CA: Goodyear, 1978.

Rafky, D.M. "Racial Discrimination in Urban Police Departments." Crime and Delinquency (July 1975): 233–42.

Regoli, R.M., and D.F. Jerome. "The Recruitment and Promotion of a Minority Group into an Established Institution: The Police." The Journal of Police Science and Administration 3 (December 1975): 410–16.

Remmington, P.W. Policing: The Occupation and the Introduction of Female Officers. New York: University Press, 1981.

Thibault, E.A., L.A. Lynch, and R.B. McBride. Proactive Management for the Community Police. Englewood Cliffs, NJ: Prentice-Hall, 1985.

DNA Fingerprinting

In order to fully understand the potential of DNA fingerprinting and the impact it has brought to the field of police investigation, it must be recognized that the key lies in the capability to positively identify individuals and populations (Herrera and Tracey, 1992). With the exception of identical twins, humans are genetically distinct from one another (Kirby, 1990). Even identical twins exhibit variations due to mutations during development and environmental effects. This genetic uniqueness is of prime significance in understanding the power of DNA fingerprinting. Although the DNA from any one individual is indistinguishable in appearance when it is extracted, at the molecular level it is different. Except for somatic mutations and rearrangements which take place subsequent to fertilization in all body tissues, the DNA in your hair is the same DNA that is in your white blood cells. This means that for the most part, with the exception of red blood cells which lack DNA, and sperms and eggs which have half the amount of DNA compared to other tissues, the DNA in all our cells is quantitatively and qualitatively identical.

The essence of DNA fingerprinting is the identification of one or more particular or distinctive features of an individual's genetic makeup (Kirby, 1990). These peculiarities in human DNA are referred to as genetic markers because they allow scientists to identify the genetic material of organisms even as it is inherited from generation to generation. Before the advent of DNA profiling, typing with genetic markers was limited. The main types of genetic typing were blood group analyses and soluble polymorphic proteins in the form of allozymes and isozymes. These systems are limited because they represent few markers, and separation of fluids and analyses are complex, expensive, and time consuming (for example, in rape cases, a vaginal swab contains fluids from both the victim and the rapist, making analysis and interpretation cumbersome). With the creation and evolution of new methods to extract DNA from almost all samples, such as blood, teeth, bones, and even fossils, DNA profiling can be applied to a multitude of identification problems.

A notable advancement related to the identification of individuals and populations was restriction fragment length polymorphism (RFLP) analysis. This technique, based on locating and identifying unique areas within each individual's genome, is extremely powerful in its ability to discriminate among individuals. Yet RFLP is restricted by the abundance and quality of DNA required for reliable results. RFLP analysis is also a very time-consuming method, taking several weeks for completion. Variable number tandem repeats (VNTRs) are repetitive DNA sequences that are hypervar-iable among individuals and are therefore also useful for DNA typing.

A technique with the potential to revolutionize the realm of DNA fingerprinting is known as the polymerase chain reaction (PCR). PCR is not only fast (a few hours), but also sensitive enough to amplify minute amounts of DNA. With this procedure investigators are less restricted by the quality and quantity of DNA available (Reynolds et al., 1991). After DNA amplification, scientists can analyze large quantities of the genetic material in a variety of ways, and always keep a stock that can be reamplified as needed. PCR has influenced practically all areas of biology. In addition to forensic science, PCR has had an impact in paternity, immigration disputes, population genetics, and evolution. In a current study undertaken at Florida International University, PCR is employed to provide information on the genetic relationships between different human populations (Batzer et al., 1991 for methodology).

Restriction Fragment Length Polymorphism
Present at a particular murder scene are several spatters of blood. Does this blood belong to the victim, to the murderer, or perhaps a mixture of both? These questions may not be as difficult to answer now as they once were. Only recently have there been advances that let us examine the DNA, deoxyribonucleic acid, present in these blood spatters. DNA is the genetic material in living things. The sequence of nucleotides (the building blocks of the genetic material) in your DNA and the environment to which you are exposed determine, for example, how tall you will be or when you will go gray.

Nucleotides are composed of a nitrogen base, a sugar, and a phosphate group. There are four different types of nitrogen bases: adenine, guanine, cytosine, and thymine, denoted as A, G, C, T, respectively. Nucleotides bind to each other forming strands. DNA is made up of two nucleotide strands in which the As associate chemically with the Ts and the Gs with the Cs to form a structure reminiscent of a twisted ladder (see figure 1a). These four bases are present in every living creature. It is a misconception that everyone has genetic sequences that are *entirely* different. In fact, 99 percent of the nucleotide sequences totaling 3 billion base pairs in human DNA are identical in all individuals (Neufeld and Coleman, 1990). What is important and provides for individual uniqueness are those relatively rare regions that contain variability. This variability in people's DNA takes the form of additions, deletions, and substitutions of nucleotides. Sometimes one or a few nucleotides are affected while often hundreds or more are involved. These are the differences that make organisms, including humans, unique in terms of eye color, hair texture, personality, etc. For identification purposes, it is best to have these areas of variability being polymorphic. Polymorphic means there are several different forms of the same basic structure (Kirby, 1990). For example, eye color is a polymorphic trait. People can have green, blue, brown, gray, or hazel eyes. They all have eyes, just in different colors. At the level of a DNA sequence or gene, this means nucleotide differences among individuals at a given DNA site.

Therein lies the key to one of the main techniques in DNA fingerprinting: RFLP analysis. The detection and typing of polymorphic areas in the DNA or genome is the goal of RFLP analyses. Because a chain of DNA, on the average, is about six-feet long (humans have forty-six chains of DNA, one in each chromosome), it needs to be cut in order to be worked with. Biological catalysts, known as restriction enzymes, cut the DNA into fragments (see figure 1b). Restriction enzymes recognize specific nucleotide sequences (usually four to six nucleotides long) and cut the DNA wherever it detects that sequence. These fragments are then segregated by size on an agarose or acrylamide gel using the procedure known as electrophoresis (see figure 1c). The gel is the medium in which the DNA is separated. The DNA is placed in the gel which is submerged in a buffer solution (to keep a constant pH) and electricity is applied at low voltage. Because DNA is negatively charged, the pieces of DNA will migrate across the gel to the positively charged end. Different-sized fragments will migrate at different speeds, thus separating the DNA pieces according to their size. The DNA is then transferred onto a nylon membrane by capillary action or absorption in a procedure known as southern blotting (see figure 1d). A series of radioactive probes in the solution is then added

FIGURE 1: RFLP ANALYSIS

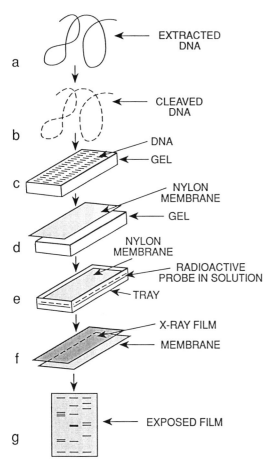

a ← EXTRACTED DNA

b ← CLEAVED DNA

c ← DNA
← GEL

d NYLON MEMBRANE
← GEL
NYLON MEMBRANE

e ← RADIOACTIVE PROBE IN SOLUTION
← TRAY

f ← X-RAY FILM
← MEMBRANE

g ← EXPOSED FILM

RFLP analysis: **a** Large molecules of DNA, approximately 50,000 base pairs in length, are extracted from the sample. This can be from evidence left at the crime scene or blood extracted from a suspect. **b** Biological catalysts known as restriction enzymes cut the large DNA double helixes into fragments by recognizing sequences that are generally four to six nucleotides long. **c** The fragments of DNA are then separated according to size by means of electricity on an agarose or acrylamide gel. **d** The DNA is then transferred onto a nylon membrane using a procedure called southern blotting, which is explained in detail in the text. **e** The nylon membrane is then soaked in a solution containing radioactive probes. These probes will bind to their complementary base pairs on the DNA attached to the membrane. **f** After washing the excess probe off the membrane, it is exposed to x-ray film. This will signal wherever the radioactive probe bound to the DNA. **g** The x-ray film is then developed and visualized. The banding patterns are then compared to determine whether or not there is a match.

to the DNA previously fixed onto the nylon membrane (see figure 1e). The probes are pieces of DNA of a certain nucleotide sequence that will bind to their complementary sequence on the previously cut and transferred DNA. These probes will bind to the sequences the same way the two strands of DNA bind to each other. This is possible because the probe and the DNA on the nylon membrane are single stranded and complementary to each other. The radioactivity that is emanating from the probe serves to mark the fragment of DNA to which it binds. The next step is to expose the radioactively labeled membrane to x-ray film (see figure 1f). The radioactivity will expose the film wherever it is present, leaving "bands" or "fragments" wherever the probe is attached to the DNA. These bands are what is actually analyzed to determine the DNA fingerprint (see figure 1g).

In summary, RFLP analysis uses a probe directed to a particular DNA location. Within that region, restriction enzymes will differentially cut depending upon the number and the location of the restriction sites that they recognize. That is the key to the variability observed. It is important to note that each individual inherits a different set of restriction enzyme sites from each parent. The position of the restriction enzyme site, in turn, determines the sizes of the fragments produced. After electrophoresis the size of the DNA fragments is determined using DNA fragments of known sizes. Frequencies are then assigned; such as one in one thousand people exhibit this pattern of fragments. The frequency of positions of fragments is calculated by a procedure from population genetics. An example of this procedure is the counting method (Risch and Devlin, 1992): Two hundred people are typed using this process, two out of those two hundred have a fragment in a certain position. Therefore it is said that the chance of an individual possessing that fragment is one in one hundred, or 0.01. Since each individual contains at least two fragments, one from each parent, the frequency of the other fragment needs to be ascertained. If six out of the two hundred contained that particular fragment then its frequency is 0.03. These two frequencies are multiplied together to give an overall frequency of 0.0003, or one in three thousand people, who share this pattern. Frequencies for additional bands are treated in the same manner by multiplying all individual frequencies to obtain the probability for the pattern.

The frequencies for the positioning of each fragment are population-specific since different ethnic groups are genetically different. In other words, different populations have different frequencies for specific DNA fragments. For example, blacks and Caucasians do not share the same frequencies of patterns. Current research is being performed to determine which human populations need to have separate sets of frequency databases. When determining how frequent a particular DNA fragment pattern is for paternity, maternity, or forensic purposes, it is important to calculate probabilities in relation to the population that the individual in question belongs to; otherwise the values may be inaccurate. Although scientifically sound, this approach is not problem free. For example, in the American judicial system a suspect is considered innocent until proven guilty. Yet, when the suspect's DNA patterns and the crime scene DNA profiles are compared to suspect-specific frequency databases, it is assumed that the defendant is in fact the criminal. In addition, the concept of ethnically pure populations or individuals is not realistic. This can introduce inaccuracy to the probability calculations.

Whenever you hear about DNA fingerprinting, the numbers are usually a staggering 1 in 10 million or so. How do these numbers come about? In the previous example only one probe was utilized. In practice a few probes, recognizing a few different sequences, are employed. The frequencies of each probe are all determined and the numbers are multiplied together, usually yielding those very high probabilities. Therefore, the blood at the murder scene can be typed along with the blood of any suspect. If the results match, that could be the key to bringing the killer to justice.

Variable Number Tandem Repeats
One of the most common procedures used in forensic DNA fingerprinting is one that examines repeated regions in the genome. These repeated regions are referred to as variable number tandem repeats (VNTRs) (Jeffreys et al., 1985) and like RFLPs are a form of polymorphism. Individuals usually differ in the number of repeated units in their chromosomes. It is believed that these repeats may be caused by unequal exchange of genetic material between chromosomes during mitotic or meiotic division or by DNA slippage during replication (Jeffreys et al., 1985). The procedure used is very similar to RFLP analysis, the fundamental difference

being that the probe is directed to tandemly repeated sequences located on the DNA and the restriction enzymes cut on the outside of these repetitive sequences, thus creating bands of different sizes depending on the number of repeats at that loci or site (Neufeld and Coleman, 1990). VNTRs can be related to the cars of a train, one right after the other in tandem. A train can have two cars or twenty cars. The number of these repeated sequences is variable in humans. Each individual inherits a repeated section of DNA from each parent. Therefore, there will be two fragments that will contain this repeated sequence in each individual. Since these reiterated elements are very susceptible to mutations, which change the number of repeated units, each of the two fragments will in all probability be different in size. The positioning of these fragments, which is due to the number of repeated sequences present, is analyzed as in RFLP analysis by electrophoresis, southern transfer, and x-ray exposure (see above).

Polymerase Chain Reaction
The grandparents of a little boy report him missing. Foul play is suspected but no murder can be proven without a body. Two years later a skull is found within a mile of the family's home. A few years ago, the answer to whether or not this is the little boy's skull would probably have remained unknown. But with the arrival of new technology, this question and others like it can be answered. Although RFLP and VNTR typing procedures are very useful forms of identification, they share two problems. RFLP and VNTR typing require fairly fresh DNA in relatively large quantities. This is where one of the newest techniques for DNA fingerprinting is of most use. This method is known as the polymerase chain reaction (PCR) and is ideally suited for forensic analysis of DNA. It is known as "polymerase" because of the use of an enzyme known by that name, and "chain" because the reaction exponentially amplifies one DNA molecule into two, then four, then eight, and so forth. The procedure is much more sensitive than RFLP and VNTR analysis and it is less limited by the quality of DNA available (Reynolds et al., 1991). With PCR partially degraded, DNA can be amplified to some degree, usually enough to allow typing and identification. Therefore, skeletal remains, such as the skull mentioned above, although weathered for even two years, can provide enough DNA to be typed using PCR

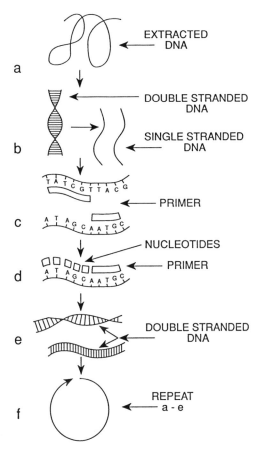

a — EXTRACTED DNA

b — DOUBLE STRANDED DNA — SINGLE STRANDED DNA

c — PRIMER

d — NUCLEOTIDES — PRIMER

e — DOUBLE STRANDED DNA

f — REPEAT a - e

PCR is a procedure capable of amplifying DNA. This is accomplished by using an enzyme that has the ability to copy the single-stranded DNA and produce a double-stranded molecule at high temperatures. In practice the reaction takes place at different temperatures, which are repeated in each cycle. **a** As in RFLPs, the initial step is to extract the DNA from the sample. **b** The first temperature acts to denature the DNA. This separates the double-stranded DNA molecules into single-stranded molecules. **c** The second temperature in the cycle anneals the primers to the single-stranded DNA at their complementary sequences. **d** The final step in the cycle is the elongation in which individual nucleotides are added to the single-stranded DNA starting from where the primer is and extending to the other end. **e** The procedure started with one double helix of DNA and ended with two. **f** The cycle is repeated and for each time the number of DNA molecules grows exponentially.

(Hochmeister, 1978). PCR is also quicker, easier, and does not require radioactivity as do the RFLP and VNTR methods.

The power of PCR lays in its capacity to manufacture large quantities of DNA from minute amounts of partially purified DNA (Herrera and Tracey, 1992). This method is so powerful when applied to forensic science that it has been described as *evidence amplification*. The essence of the PCR reaction is the repeated replication of a specific area of DNA throughout various temperature cycles to produce millions of copies of that particular sequence. The reaction is set up into cycles of three temperatures that each serves a purpose. The reaction contains DNA, the four nucleotides, a buffer to control pH, a polymerase enzyme that links nucleotides together, magnesium, and the primers specific for the region of DNA to be amplified. The first step in the process is the denaturing of the double-stranded DNA into its single strands of nucleotides, usually by heating the DNA solution at 96 degrees centigrade for ten minutes (see figure 2b). The second temperature provides the annealing conditions for the primers, which varies but is usually 72 degrees centigrade for one-and-a-half minutes (see figure 2c). Primers, which are portions of manufactured DNA with specific sequences of nucleotides, bind to their complementary bases on the single-stranded DNA template. The third temperature is for the elongation of the nascent nucleotide chain and takes place usually at 58 degrees centigrade for two minutes (see figure 2d). This is where the nucleotides (A, C, G, and T) bind to the DNA, like building blocks. The polymerase enzyme brings the individual nucleotides to the DNA attaching them one by one to the primer and in doing so building up a new DNA strand according to the original complementary sequence. The replicated DNA segment is delineated by the binding sites of the two primers on the original DNA molecule. The further away the primers are located from each other, the larger the piece of DNA amplified. In this process one double-stranded DNA molecule yields two double-stranded portions of DNA (see figure 2e). This temperature cycle is repeated and each time the number of double-stranded DNA increases exponentially. The advantages of this method are many. Since this technique is capable of amplifying minute amounts of DNA, perhaps as little as one cell equivalent (Reynolds et al., 1991), it is expected that this methodology will have a strong impact on forensic science. The technology has been perfected to the point that DNA from single cells can be amplified and studied. In forensic laboratories, DNA can be extracted and amplified from single hairs, small amounts of blood, semen, saliva (perhaps even chewing gum), bone, teeth, and cigarette butts (Reynolds et al., 1991). The possibilities are endless.

FIGURE 3: TYPICAL PCR AMPLIFICATION OF AN ALU INSERTION SITE

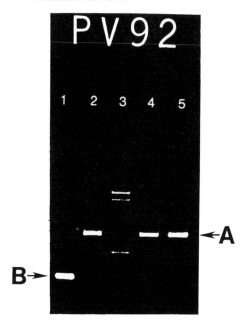

A typical agarose gel containing the PCR amplification products from a region of the apolipoprotein gene. Band A is the DNA fragment containing an Alu repetitive element. Band B is the DNA fragment without the Alu insertion. Lane one represents an individual that is homozygous for the lack of insertion, which means that both DNA sites, the one coming from the mother and the one coming from the father, do not contain the insertion. Lanes two, four, and five contain amplified DNA from individuals who are homozygous for the insertion, meaning they have the insertion in both DNA sites. Lane three contains marker DNA (Hae III digested phi X 174) with fragments of known sizes. These marker bands allow for size determination of the insertion and lack of insertion PCR products. A heterozygous individual, not shown in this figure, would exhibit both bands, one representing the insertion (about 400 base pairs) and the other representing the absence of it (about 120 base pairs).

As much as this technique should prove to be a revolution to forensic science, it has been slow in its application. There is currently only one PCR system that has been used for forensic DNA typing in the United States. That system is the DQ alpha. Currently, commercially sold as a kit, DQ alpha is a PCR system with primers specific for a region of DNA flanking the DNA coding for the DQ protein. This protein is highly polymorphic with six different versions or variants known as alleles. The same basic procedure as described above is used to type these variations. VNTRs can also be detected using PCR. The length of the amplified fragment (determined by its position on the gel) reflects the number of tandem repeats (Higuchi, 1987). The greater the number of repeats, the larger the size of the fragment and the slower its migration in the gel during electrophoresis.

An Alternative Typing Method
Alternative typing methods do exist, although acceptance into the criminal-justice system is a long process. The risks of convicting an innocent person or setting a criminal free on the basis of a new and untested scientific method are too great. One DNA typing method that employs PCR is currently being examined in the laboratory at Florida International University. This procedure involves the detection of Alu elements. Alu is the largest family of repetitive elements (Singer, 1982). Each element is about 300 nucleotides long and more than 500,000 copies are found in the genome of primates, including humans (for review see Deininger, 1989). Alu members, as well as other repetitive elements, seem to originate from a master gene or Alu source that is still undergoing amplification by insertion into other parts of the genome. Mutations in that master gene may result in the formation of a new subfamily within the Alu family. One recently formed subfamily was found to be human specific (HS) (Batzer et al., 1990, Batzer et al., 1991). As these HS Alu insertions were inserted recently in human evolution, not all individuals will contain the insertion in both copies of their genetic material.

Alu PCR is somewhat different from other currently used procedures mentioned above because recent HS Alu insertions behave as dimorphic DNA markers, meaning they can take on two different forms. For example, an individual could have an Alu insertion in a specific DNA site or not. Since humans have two copies of the genetic material, any given individual can have the Alu insertion in both copies of the genetic material. This person would be homozygous for the insertion. It is also possible for an individual to lack the Alu insertion in both copies of the genetic material. This is referred to as homozygous for the lack of insertion. Another possibility is that an individual can have the insertion of an Alu element in one copy of their genetic material and lack it in the other. This individual would be heterozygous. The insertion and lack of insertion are the two forms that make Alu PCR dimorphic. The fact that these Alu insertions are very stable over time and that they are randomly inserted makes Alu elements a valuable marker to study populations. Our studies on Amerindian groups using HS Alu PCR yielded important information on the populations' genetic constitutions. The results from these studies also indicate the necessity for separate DNA databases for some populations. This study further emphasizes the need for the criminal-justice system to recognize more individualized databases than the ones already employed. In turn, more accurate databases allow for more reliable frequency calculations of suspects' DNA fingerprints. This further reduces the chance of a false conviction or the release of a criminal back to the streets.

Jennifer M. Garrison
Gabriel E. Novick
Rene J. Herrera

Bibliography

Batzer, M.A., V.A. Gudi, J.C. Mena, D.W. Foltz, R.W. Herrera, and P.L. Deininger. "Amplification Dynamics of Human-Specific (HS) Alu Family Members." *Nucleic Acids Research* 19(1991): 3619–23.

Batzer, M.A., G.E. Kilroy, P.E. Richard, T.H. Shaikh, T.D.Desselle, C.L. Hoppens, and P.L. Deininger. "Structure and Variability of Recently Inserted Alu Members." *Nucleic Acids Research* 18 (17)(1990): 6793–98.

Deininger, P.L. "SINEs: Short Interspersed Repeated DNA Elements in Higher Eukaryotes." In *Mobile DNA*. Eds. M. Howe, and D. Berg. Washington DC: AMS Press, 1989. 619–36.

Herrera, R.J., and M.L. Tracey. "DNA Fingerprinting: Basic Techniques, Problems, and Solutions." *Journal of Criminal Justice* 20 (1992): 237–48.

Higuchi, R. "PCR and Forensic DNA Typing." In *Advances in Forensic Haemogenetics* 2 (August 26–29, 1987): 73–89. Ed. W.R. Mayr. Vienna: 12th Congress of the Society for Forensic Haemogenetics.

Hochmeister, M. "Forensic Applications of PCR-Based Typing of DNA." In *Advances in Forensic Haemogenetics* 2 (August 26-29, 1987): 63-71. Ed. W.R. Mayr. Vienna: 12th Congress of the Society for Forensic Haemogenetics.

Horn, G.T., B. Richards, and K.W. Klinger. "Amplification of a Highly Polymorphic VNTR Segment by the Polymerase Chain Reaction." *Nucleic Acids Research* 17(5) 1989: 2140.

Jeffreys, A.J., V. Wilson, and S.L. Thein. "Hypervariable 'minisatellite' regions in human DNA." *Nature* 314(1985): 67–73.

Kasai, K., Y. Nakamura, and R. White. "Amplification of a Variable Number of Tandem Repeats (VNTR) Locus (pMCT118) by the Polymerase Chain Reaction (PCR) and its Application to Forensic Science." *Journal of Forensic Sciences* 35(5)(1990): 1196–200.

Kirby, L.T. *DNA Fingerprinting: An Introduction*. New York: Stockton Press, 1990.

Neufeld, P.J. and N. Coleman. "When Science Takes the Witness Stand." *Scientific American* 262(5)(1990): 46–53.

Reynolds, R., G. Sensabaugh, and E. Blake. "Analysis of Genetic Markers in Forensic DNA Samples Using the Polymerase Chain Reaction." *Analytical Chemistry* 63(1991): 2.

Risch, N.J. and B. Devlin. "On the Probability of Matching DNA Fingerprints." *Science* 255(1992): 717–20.

Singer, M.F. "SINEs and LINEs: Highly Repeated Short and Long Interspersed Sequences in Mammalian Genomes." *Cell* 28(1982): 433–34.

Thorton, J.I. 1989. "DNA Profiling: New Tool Links Evidence to Suspects with High Certainty." *C&EN* (November 20, 1989): 18–30.

Domestic Violence

Domestic violence, in particular spouse abuse, was not recognized as a special problem until the 1970s. During the last two decades family violence has been transformed from a private matter to public concern, suitable for the intervention of the criminal-justice system. Societal acceptance of domestic violence as a criminal matter has made demands on the police to change their traditional ways and practices of handling spouse-abuse victims and offenders.

This entry first provides a definition of domestic (spousal) abuse and describes its magnitude. It then reviews the historical roots of the problem and the traditional police handling of spousal abuse. It also describes the changes in societal attitudes toward domestic violence and evolving legal rulings that led to a transformation in the way police respond to it. The impact of criminological research on the manner in which police handle domestic violence is discussed, including the findings and policy implications. The entry concludes with a discussion of the remaining concerns in the policing of domestic violence.

Definition and Extent of Domestic (Spousal) Violence

Domestic violence includes the physical, sexual, and psychological abuse of a family member, most commonly a spouse, and the destruction of her property (Tong, 1984). Physical abuse is not just slapping or shoving; it includes punching with fists, choking, kicking, knifing, slamming the victim against the wall, throwing her to the floor, or shoving her down the stairs. Spousal abuse also commonly includes rape or sexual assaults on the victim (Browne, 1987). While the impact of psychological abuse is often minimized, many domestic violence victims view it as the most devastating type of battering. In addition to demeaning comments made to the victim, the offender often makes threats to the spouse regarding her welfare and the welfare of the children. Acts such as punching holes in the wall, breaking down the door, and wielding a gun against the victim or her children can be as frightening and devastating as a physical attack. Finally, abuse often includes the destruction of the victim's property, including the killing or harming of pets. An offender can commit one or a combination of these four categories of abuse.

While the labels "domestic violence" and "spouse abuse" are often used to describe these behaviors, it is important to note two important facts. First, research has consistently found that 90 to 95 percent of the victims are women. Efforts to portray partners in battering relation-

ships as "mutually combative" have been criticized, as the measures used were seriously flawed (Dobash et al., 1992). Thus the vast majority of domestic violence is committed by men against their intimate female partners. The historical status of women in society, discussed in the next section, explains this gender difference in victimization and offending.

A second important fact is that research has found a substantial amount of abuse in unmarried relationships, such as in cohabitating or dating couples (Erez, 1986; Makepeace, 1981) and from ex-husbands or ex-cohabitants (Erez, 1986). Further, some experts have noted what Mahoney (1991) has defined as *separation assault*—violence that often begins or escalates when a woman attempts to leave a relationship through divorce or through a breakup.

The first psychologist to study battered women, Lenore E. Walker (1979) identified a "cycle of violence" that appears to occur in most violent domestic relationships. The cycle begins with the *tension-building phase*, followed by the actual *battering incident*, and finally the *conciliation phase*. During the conciliation phase, the offender attempts to convince the victim that he regrets the abuse and often promises that it will never happen again. The abuser may genuinely be sorry and believe he will never harm her again. However, experts have found that as time goes on in most battering relationships, the length of the cycle decreases, the level of injury during the battering incident increases, and the conciliation phase decreases, or in some cases, becomes nonexistent (Dobash and Dobash, 1979). Thus, once the cycle of violence has occurred a number of times, the victim is usually so afraid of the offender that he does not need to "win her back" with charm; he relies on her fear of abuse if she leaves him.

Accurate incidence and prevalence data remain beyond reach, but several sources, such as calls to the police or self-report data, provide rough estimates of the magnitude of the problem. Estimates of family violence vary greatly: In terms of absolute numbers, they range from 2.1 million (Langan and Innes, 1986) to more than 8 million (Straus, 1989). It has been estimated that violence occurs in one in six relationships (Straus, 1980). Others suggest that about half of all married women will be beaten by their husbands at least once, and many of them are beaten as frequently as once a week or even daily (Langley and Levy, 1977:12). Probability estimates suggest that 25 to 30 percent of couples will experience a violent incident (Gelles and Straus, 1988; Straus, 1980). The variation in the estimates is due to definitional differences in the meaning of abuse, differences in the data sources, variation in the time frame for the estimates, or in the estimates of the extent of underreporting of abuse in official statistics (Hirschel et al., 1992). The severity of the injuries and the danger facing the victims of abuse are often high. Weapons are used in 30 percent of all domestic violence incidents (Claus and Ranel, 1984). Almost one-third (31 percent) of all women murdered in the United States are killed by their husbands, ex-husbands, or lovers (Rose and Goss, 1989). The U.S. Surgeon General has stated that spousal abuse is the "single largest cause of injury to women in the U.S." (Hightower and McManus, 1989).

Historical Background
Domestic violence appears to be a cultural universal, its historical roots are ancient and deep. The emergence of monogamous pairing relationships—designed to provide women protection from violation by men other than their spouses and guarantee husbands their identities and rights as fathers—resulted in a dependency status of wives in a familial setting regarded as private (Martin, 1976). The monogamous marriage has been characterized by differential power between the partners. The woman was essentially defined as her husband's property; her sole purpose to satisfy his needs—bearing his children and tending to his household (Martin, 1976). In medieval times, husbands had the power of life and death over their dependents and the right to unrestrained physical chastisement of the wife and other family members (Pleck, 1987). Physical cruelty, including murder of the wife or a serf, was allowed as long as it was inflicted for disciplinary purposes (Davis, 1971). Women were killed by their husbands for reasons such as talking back, scolding and nagging, miscarrying, or sodomy (Martin, 1976).

The English common law, in the name of the protection of the family, provided husbands the right to chastise their wives only "moderately"; it excluded death (Blackstone, 1987:177). The English law, which was brought to the American colonies, allowed husbands to retain their right to physically chastise their wives, as long as they did not use a stick larger than their thumb (the origin of the expression "rule of thumb"). In 1824, in *Bradley v. State*, the Mississippi State Supreme Court held that "the husband be permitted to exercise the right of moderate chastisement." The court stated that family arguments were best left inside the walls of the home and were not proper matters into which the court should intervene. This position was reinforced by cases which held that the court could not invade the domestic domain unless some lasting injury was inflicted, or the excessive violence was exercised only to gratify "bad passions" (*State v. Black,* 1864). The courts thus recognized the husband's right to use the necessary degree of force to make the wife "behave" and "know her place" (*Joyner v. Joyner,* 1862).

The subjection of the wife to the husband's authority was reflected in the marriage contract. Through marriage, the woman had to give up her name, move to her husband's home, and become his dependent. The husband was designated as the head of the household, and the marriage vow required the wive to "love, honor, and obey" him. The various restrictions imposed on the wife through the marriage contract (such as to own or manage their property, enter into contracts, or sue) made the wife economically dependent on the husband. This legal and economical dependency has been "justified" by the state's overriding interest in keeping the family intact.

The protection of the family was also the major reason for a de facto decriminalization of wife abuse. The sanctity of the family home and the charge that "a man's home is his castle" led to treating spouse abuse differently than assaults between persons who were not intimate. Because the wife was viewed as belonging to her husband, what happened between them was regarded as a private matter and was not a concern to the criminal-justice system (Dobash and Dobash, 1979).

The major change in the legal rights of married women occurred at the end of the nineteenth century. Many of the legal restrictions on them were lifted, and the right of the husband to chastise his wife was abolished. Yet, in spousal relationships, the belief that physical abuse does not constitute a crime continued to guide the police in their response to domestic violence cases until the 1970s. At this time, the women's movement began to address the problem, and women's groups and advocates initiated actions designed to bring about a change in the police handling of domestic violence cases.

Police Attitudes and Changing Practices concerning Domestic Violence

Like most crimes, the first contact the victim and offender have with the criminal-justice system is likely to be the police. This initial contact was found to be particularly important with domestic violence victims—if the police response is considered "inadequate," it negatively affects the victims' self-esteem and makes them less likely to turn to the criminal-justice system in the future (Brown, 1984).

Until recently, the appropriate police response to domestic violence was not a concern to either practitioners or academics (Finesmith, 1983). Throughout the 1970s police officers treated domestic violence as a private matter, unsuitable for the intervention of the criminal-justice system. Arrest in misdemeanor domestic violence cases was rarely performed. Police attached low priority to domestic violence. In the police culture, intervention in domestic situations was not viewed as "real" police work; spousal abuse was perceived as unglamorous as well as unrewarding (Straus, 1980). Further, until recently, police frequently ignored such calls or purposely delayed responding to them for several hours (Buzawa and Buzawa, 1990). Research shows that the average response time for domestic violence cases in 1977 was 4.65 minutes, compared to 3.86 for nondisturbance calls (Oppenlander, 1982). When the police eventually arrived they rarely did anything about domestic violence incidents and some even laughed at the woman (Martin, 1976). Police reluctance to respond to domestic violence cases was attributed to a hope that the problem would be resolved before they arrived or that the disputant would be gone (Oppenlander, 1982).

Although a pattern of underenforcement of domestic violence calls was discerned (e.g., Erez, 1986; Oppenlander, 1982), it has been argued that it is not clear whether domestic violence was more underenforced than offenses in general, and violent interpersonal incidents in particular (Sherman, 1992a:11). The low level of enforcement of domestic violence incidents was primarily attributed to legal requirements that the offense be committed in the presence of an officer, which technically barred officers in many states from making warrantless arrests unless they witnessed the abuse. Other possible explanations include the erroneous police perception that domestic violence incidents are very dangerous situations for the police, victim preferences against arrest, and possible police officers' support or sympathy for the abusive male partner (Sherman, 1992a, 1992b). This attitude was reinforced by the long-held belief that violence within the family is a private matter and that taking action against abusers will hurt their families, particularly if they are economically dependent on the abuser. Female complainants were also viewed as uncooperative. This perception rendered arrest and prosecution in the eyes of the police as a waste of time (Parnas, 1967).

The policy of avoiding arrest in domestic violence cases received some professional attention in the 1960s. Social scientists and psychologists began to advocate mediation in "family disturbance" incidents (Bard, 1970). Mediation and crisis intervention were promoted as the appropriate measures to handle domestic violence. The idea that police be engaged in conflict mediation and attempt to counsel disputants rather than arrest them was accepted by many police departments across the country. Police officers received training in mediation and many police departments established family crisis intervention units (Bard, 1970, 1975). Some departments even established police crisis teams that included social workers (Burnett et al., 1976). This approach resulted in a further decrease in arrests in cities in which crisis intervention was practiced. In fact, it has been reported that mediation training teaches officers that it is better to side with batterers than it is to side with victims (Oppenlander, 1982; Tong, 1984), and how victims might have "caused" the offenders' behavior (Rowe, 1985; Zoomer, 1989). Since police officers frequently arrive during Walker's (1979) "conciliation phase," such strategies fit in well with the idea of mediation; the offender usually wants the incident settled in a nonformal manner. It became apparent that mediation resulted in keeping domestic violence out of the criminal-justice system (Rowe, 1985).

Mediation was soon rejected by both the police and women's groups. For police officers, mediation seemed more like social work than activities suitable to be considered police work. Some researchers also noted that the police were ill-prepared to perform crisis intervention (e.g., Langley and Levy 1977, 1978).

Further, no evidence was produced to substantiate that mediation was useful in the long run (Sherman, 1992a:14). Women's groups objected to this approach because it ignored or underplayed the danger to women in abusive relationships. Mediation was also regarded by women's advocates as fundamentally flawed, because mediation assumes equality of culpability between the parties to a dispute and fails to hold the offender accountable for his actions (Rowe, 1985). It was argued that a mediation policy in domestic violence, therefore, inadvertently contributed to a dangerous escalation of the violence.

In some jurisdictions women's groups began to file suits against police departments on behalf of abused women whom the police failed to protect by arresting the abuser. In Oakland, California, *Scott v. Hart* (1976) was filed as a class action suit on behalf of women in general, and black women in particular, who were victims of domestic violence. In New York, in *Bruno v. Codd*, several battered women sued the police for failure to arrest their abusive husbands. These two cases were eventually settled with the police. In *Thurman v. City of Torrington, CT*, the plaintiff and her son were awarded $2.3 million dollars because the police were negligent in protecting them from the abusive husband/father.

Following this litigation the pressure on the police to adopt a full enforcement policy in domestic violence increased substantially. Arrest was now advocated because domestic violence began to be perceived as a criminal act, to be treated no differently than assaults among nonfamily members. "This legal response to family violence must be guided primarily by the nature of the abusive act, not the relationship between the victim and the abuser" (Claus and Ranel, 1984:4). The pressure by litigation alone, however, could not resolve the problem of the "in presence" requirement for warrantless misdemeanor arrests. Legislative action was necessary to provide officers with the power to arrest in misdemeanor domestic violence cases (Sherman, 1992a, 1992b).

The advocated preferred (or presumptive) arrest policy slowly began to be transformed into laws in several jurisdictions and states. By 1984 the number of police departments that adopted such policies had increased fourfold (Sherman and Cohn, 1989). Nonetheless, the actual implementation of this policy remained problematic.

Deterrent Effect of Arrest on Repeated Domestic Violence

The position which advocates full enforcement of the police arrest powers in domestic violence cases implicitly assumes that the arrest of abusers will help reduce repeat incidents. Despite the fact that the deterrent effect of arrest has never been necessary to justify arrest in other criminal offenses, deterrence via arrest has become a central issue in attempts to convince policymakers to change the traditional way of handling domestic violence cases by the police. This situation called for a scientific study of the effect on domestic violence recidivism rates.

To provide clear and compelling evidence for the superiority of arrest compared to the traditional response of the police (separation of the parties or mediation), a controlled experiment was deemed necessary and justified under the Federal Judicial Center guidelines of 1982 (Sherman, 1992a, 1992b). In Minneapolis in 1980, a newly appointed police chief, Anthony V. Bouza, was willing to have his police force participate in such a study. Thus the first controlled experiment on the deterrent effect of arrest in domestic violence cases was initiated and has since been referred to as the "Minneapolis experiment." Sherman and Berk conducted the Minneapolis experiment in 1981 and 1982, by randomly assigning cases to three types of treatment: separation of the parties, mediation or advising, and arrest. Analysis of the data collected through this experiment showed that arrest was more effective than the other two responses in deterring repeat abuse. The findings from the Minneapolis experiment were confirmed in replication studies in Southern California (Berk and Newton, 1985) and Ontario, Canada (Jaffe et al., 1986). Although researchers Sherman and Berk (1984a, 1984b) and Lempert (1989) have identified several methodological problems with this experimental design that may question the validity of some of the results, the Minneapolis experiment received national attention and was highly instrumental in promoting arrest as the preferred response to domestic violence cases across the country.

By 1989 about 76 percent of the large city police departments adopted a mandatory arrest policy, and over 80 percent a preferred arrest policy (Hirschel and Hutchinson, 1991). Predictably, the national arrest rate for misdemeanor domestic violence rose by 70 percent from 1985 to 1989 (Sherman, 1992a). However, this did not amount to a full compliance with pro-arrest policies. Research shows that despite official pro-arrest policies by many police departments, the arrest rate continues to be low (e.g., Buzawa, 1988; Ferraro, 1989a; Lawrenz, Lembo, and Schade, 1988).

Several factors may account for this low compliance: persistent negative attitudes of the police concerning the seriousness of the abuse (Belknap, 1992) or the appropriateness of intervention in family matters; identification with the abuser; and fear of being sued in civil court for wrongful arrest (Hirschel et al., 1992). In addition, the erroneous perception that such intervention is highly dangerous to the police also persisted. The perception that responding to domestic violence involves higher probability of injury or death to the officers has been a part of the police folklore for a long time (Konstantin, 1984). It was often promoted in crisis intervention training to attract the attention of recruits reluctant to adopt the mediation approach (Fyfe and Flavin, 1991). This perception was also supported by misinterpretation of "disturbance calls" data, which grouped family violence with all other types of disturbances, such as fights in bars (Garner and Clemmer, 1986). While an in-depth analysis of police injury and death rate has raised serious doubts about the danger to police in domestic violence incidents, some studies continue to suggest that in some locations domestic calls may still constitute the most dangerous category for police, both in assault and injury (Hirschel et al., 1992).

To overcome remaining resistance to the preferred arrest policy by some police officers and departments, and to provide further evidence of the superiority of the arrest response, replications of the Minneapolis experiment were funded by the National Institute of Justice in six different locations around the country: Omaha, Charlotte, Milwaukee, Colorado Springs, Dade County (Florida), and Atlanta (the last study is still incomplete). These studies also employed an experimental design, but there were some variations among them (for a summary of these experiments, see Sherman, 1992a).

The result of the studies completed so far (see Hirschel et al., 1992; Symposium on Domestic Violence, 1992) question the overall deterrent effect of arrest in misdemeanor domestic violence cases. Specifically, the results in three cities (including Minneapolis) show some evidence of a deterrent effect, while in three other cities evidence of increased violence following an arrest has been discovered. The results also indicate that arrests have different effects on different kinds of people, with a consistent variation dependent on the employment status of the suspect. Arrest has the effect of crime reduction on employed suspects as compared to unemployed ones. But arrest is likely to backfire by increasing the violence of suspects with low social bonds—those who are unmarried or with criminal records (Sherman, 1992a; 1992b). This finding is contrary to earlier research (Jaffe et al., 1986), which, while not controlling for social bonds, found that victims' expectations concerning increased violence following the arrest of their batterers did not materialize.

The attention to arrest as a means of reducing domestic violence and the interpretation of the results of the Minneapolis experiment and its replications have been criticized by legal experts, feminist scholars, social activists, and researchers. Practitioners and women's advocates argue that to conclude that the repeat violence following an arrest is a "backfire" for the arrest is erroneous. Rather, they argue that arrest alone is ineffective in halting the long-term expected progression of violence by socially marginal offenders. Research has documented that domestic violence escalates in spousal relationships, whether or not the abuser is arrested (Frisch, 1992). Social activists argue that the heavy emphasis on arrest as a panacea for domestic violence detracts from the role of community attitudes and practices in determining the scope and nature of the problem. Further, the preoccupation with pro-arrest policies results in focusing on the individual, rather than acknowledging societal factors that perpetuate the dependency of women on batterers (Ferraro, 1989b). Some have criticized the lack of coordination among the police, the judiciary, and social services in responding to domestic violence (Gamache, Edleson, and Schock, 1988). The inadequate resources allocated to pursuing the cases through the legal system are also ignored (Lerman, 1992). The low probability of prosecution in spousal abuse cases, and the fact that arrest is only a minor nuisance to the abuser, who is usually out of jail within a few hours following the arrest, also explain the lack of any deterrent effect of arrest (Hirschel et al., 1992; Lerman 1992).

Feminists have argued that the experiment effects were interpreted only from the viewpoint of the abuser and ignored the perspective of the battered woman. For instance, the supposed deterrent effect of arrest on employed middle-class men could be attributed to the fact that middle-class women would not want to jeopardize their comfortable lifestyle by having their provider arrested. Furthermore, Sherman's (1992a, 1992b) belief that the employment status of the offender is important ignores the importance of the employment status of victims. One study found that women who are employed are more able to successfully leave battering relationships than their unemployed counterparts (Strube and Barbour, 1984). Another possibility is that the poor inner-city woman continues to be victimized by repeated abuse because, unlike her middle-class wealthier counterparts, she cannot easily find alternate living arrangements and social services for herself and her children. Thus she has no alternative but "to remain in her place as a sitting duck for the abuser when he returns" (Bowman, 1992).

One result of the attention given to the Minneapolis experiment and its replications is that the issue of addressing domestic violence has become two-fold. First, the focus on police response to domestic violence has been evaluated almost exclusively in terms of the arrest versus mediation decision. Clearly, there are other actions police take, in addition to arresting batterers, when responding to domestic violence calls. For instance, the use of referrals by the police seems crucial in informing battered victims and their offenders of programs, shelters, and rights. Too little attention has been paid to this important function of the police in domestic violence. Second, the research agenda focusing on the deterrent effect of pro-arrest policies has limited the definition of "success" to include only whether arresting batterers affects their recidivism rates. This ignores other influences that arrest might have, such as providing victims and their children an opportunity to escape, as well as communicating to victims and their children that the batterers' behavior is reprehensible. It was reported that the rate of domestic violence homicides decreased following the implementation of Oregon's pro-arrest policy for domestic violence in 1977, while the rate of nondomestic homicides increased (Jolin, 1983). Shelter workers and some individual police departments have also noted a decrease in the number of women killed by their intimate male partners following the implementation of pro-arrest policies.

Conclusion

The gradual changes in societal attitudes toward spousal abuse and the evolving recognition of its criminal nature have led to a reevaluation of state law concerning domestic violence and police response to it. Following the Minneapolis experiment, which cautiously suggested that arrest may deter repeat violence, the arrest powers of the police in misdemeanor domestic violence cases were strengthened. Most police departments throughout the country adopted either preferred or mandatory arrest policies. Yet, the police reluctance to apply the arrest option still persists. The result of the replication studies of the Minneapolis experiment may provide some grounds for this reluctance: These studies suggested no overall deterrent effect of the arrest in misdemeanor domestic violence cases. The police response to domestic violence and the amount of discretion they may or should use in making arrests in misdemeanor incidents remains an open question, if the only justification for arrest is its deterrent effect. The magnitude of the problem and the persistent police reluctance to respond to domestic violence as they do to other criminal matters may convince policy-makers that arrest alone may not be panacea and that other avenues need to be explored to handle this social problem.

Edna Erez
Joanne Belknap

Bibliography

Balos, Beverly, and Katie Trotzky. "Enforcement of the Domestic Abuse Act in Minnesota: A Preliminary Study." *Law and Inequality* 6 (1988): 83–125.

Bard, Morton. "Training Crisis Intervention: From Concept to Implementation." Washington, DC: U.S. Department of Justice, 1970.

———. "Role of Law Enforcement in the Helping System." In *Criminal Justice as a System: Readings*. Eds. Alan R. Coffey and Vernon E. Renner. Englewood Cliffs, NJ: Prentice-Hall, 1975. 56–66.

Belknap, Joanne. "Perceptions of Woman Battering." In *The Changing Roles of Women in the Criminal Justice System*. Ed. Imogene L. Moyer. Prospect Heights, IL: Waveland, 1992. 181–201.

Berk, Richard A., and Phyllis J. Newton. "Does Arrest Really Deter Wife Battery? An Effort to Replicate the Findings of the Minneapolis Spouse Abuse Experiment." *American Sociological Review* 50 (1985): 253–62.

Blackstone, William. *Commentaries on the Laws of England.* Ed. W. Hardcastle Brown. St. Paul, MN: West, 1987.

Bowman, Cynthia Grant. "The Arrest Experiments: A Feminist Critique." *Journal of Criminal Law and Criminology* 83 (1992): 201–08.

Brown, Stephen E. "Police Responses to Wife Beating: Neglect of a Crime of Violence." *Journal of Criminal Justice* 12 (1984): 277–88.

Browne, Angela. *When Battered Women Kill.* New York: Free Press, 1987.

Burnett, Bruce B., John J. Carr, John Sinapi, and Roy Taylor. "Police and Social Workers in a Community Outreach Program." *Social Casework* 57 (1976): 41–49.

Buzawa, Eve S. "Explaining Variations in Police Response to Domestic Violence: A Case Study in Detroit and New England." In *Coping with Family Violence.* Eds. Gerald T. Hotaling, David Finkelhor, John T. Kirkpatrick, and Murray A. Straus. Newbury Park, CA: Sage, 1988. 169–82.

———, and Carl G. Buzawa. *Domestic Violence: The Criminal Justice Response.* Newbury Park, CA: Sage, 1990.

Claus, Patsy, and Michael Ranel. "Family Violence." U.S. Department of Justice, Bureau of Justice Statistics, Special Report, 1984.

Davis, E.G. *The First Sex.* New York: Putnam, 1971.

Dobash, R. Emerson, and Russell Dobash. *Violence Against Wives.* New York: Free Press, 1979.

Dobash, Russell P., R. Emerson Dobash, Margo Wilson, and Martin Daly. "The Myth of Sexual Symmetry in Marital Violence." *Social Problems* 39 (1992): 71–91.

Erez, Edna. "Intimacy, Violence and the Police." *Human Relations* 39 (1986): 265–81.

Ferraro, Kathleen J. "Policing Woman Battering." *Social Problems* 36 (1989a): 61–74.

———. "The Legal Response to Woman Battering in the United States." In *Women,*
Policing, and Male Violence: International Perspectives. Eds. Jalna Hanmer, Jill Radford, and Elizabeth A. Stanko. London: Routledge and Kegan Paul, 1989b. 155–84.

Finesmith, Barbara K. "Police Responses to Battered Women: A Critique and Proposals for Reform." *Seton Hall Law Review* 14 (1983): 74–109.

Frisch, Lisa A. "Research that Succeeds, Policing that Fails." *Journal of Criminal Law and Criminology* 83 (1992): 209–16.

Fyfe, James J., and Jeanne Flavin. "Differential Police Processing of Domestic Assault Complaints." Paper presented at the Annual Meeting of the Academy of Criminal Justice Sciences, Nashville, TN, 1991.

Gamache, D.J., J.L. Edleson, and M.D. Schock. "Coordinated Police, Judicial, and Social Service Response to Woman Battering." In *Coping with Family Violence.* Eds. Gerald T. Hotaling, David Finkelhor, John T. Kirkpatrick, and Murray A. Straus. Newbury Park, CA: Sage, 1988. 193–209.

Garner, Joel, and Elizabeth Clemmer. *Danger to Police in Domestic Disturbance: A New Look.* Washington, DC: U.S. Department of Justice, 1986.

Gelles, Richard J., and Murray A. Straus. *Intimate Violence.* New York: Simon and Schuster, 1988.

Hightower, Nikki R., and Susan A. McManus. "Limits of State Constitutional Guarantees: Lessons from Efforts to Implement Domestic Violence Policies." *Public Administration Review* 49 (1989): 269–84.

Hirschel, J. David, and Ira W. Hutchinson. "Police Preferred Arrest Policies." In *Wife Battering: Policy Responses.* Ed. Michael Steinman. Cincinnati, OH: Anderson, 1991. 49–72.

———, Ira W. Hutchison, Charles W. Dean, and Ann Marie Mills. "Review Essay on the Law Enforcement Response to Spouse Abuse: Past, Present, and Future." *Justice Quarterly* 9 (1992): 247–83.

Jaffe, Peter, David A. Wolfe, Anne Telford, and Gary Austin. "The Impact of Police Charges in Incidents of Wife Abuse." *Journal of Family Violence* 1 (1986): 37–49.

Jolin, Annette. "Domestic Violence Legislation: An Impact Assessment." *Journal of Police Science and Administration* 11 (1983): 451–56.

Konstantin, David N. "Homicides of American Law Enforcement Officers: 1978–80." *Justice Quarterly* 1 (1984): 29–45.

Langan, Patrick A., and Christopher A. Innes. "Preventing Domestic Violence Against Women." Washington, DC: U.S. Department of Justice, 1986.

Langley, Roger, and Richard C. Levy. *Wife Beating: The Silent Crisis.* New York: Dutton, 1977.

———. "Wife Abuse and the Police Response." *F.B.I. Law Enforcement Bulletin* 47 (May 1978).

Lawrenz, Frances, James F. Lembo, and Thomas Schade. "Time Series Analysis of the Effect of a Domestic Violence Directive on the Number of Arrests Per Day." *Journal of Criminal Justice* 16 (1988): 493–98.

Lempert, Richard. "Humility is a Virtue: On the Publicization of Policy Relevant Research." *Law and Society Review* 23 (1989): 145–61.

Lerman, Lisa G. "The Decontextualization of Domestic Violence." *Journal of Criminal Law and Criminology* 83 (1992): 217–40.

Mahoney, Martha R. "Legal Images of Battered Women: Redefining the Issue of Separation." *Michigan Law Review* 90 (1991): 2–94.

Makepeace, James K. "Courtship Violence among College Students." *Family Relations* 30 (1981): 97–102.

Martin, Del. *Battered Wives.* San Francisco: Glide, 1976.

———. "Battered Women: Society's Problem." In *The Victimization of Women.* Eds. J.R. Chapman and M. Gates. Beverly Hills: Sage, 1978.

Oppenlander, Nan. "Coping or Copping Out?" *Criminology* 20 (1982): 449–65.

Parnas, Raymond I. "The Police Response to the Domestic Disturbance." *Wisconsin Law Review* (Fall 1967): 914–60.

Pleck, Elizabeth. *Domestic Tyranny: The Making of Social Policy against Family Violence from Colonial Times to the Present.* New York: Oxford University Press, 1987.

Rose, K., and J. Goss. *Domestic Violence Statistics.* Bureau of Justice Statistics, National Criminal Justice Reference Service, 1989.

Rowe, Kelly. "The Limits of the Neighborhood Justice Center: Why Domestic Violence Cases Should Not Be Mediated." *Emory Law Journal* 34 (1985): 855–910.

Sherman, Lawrence. "The Influence of Criminology on Criminal Law: Evaluating Arrests for Misdemeanor Domestic Violence." *Journal of Criminal Law and Criminology* 83 (1992a): 1–45.

———. *Policing Domestic Violence.* New York: MacMillan, 1992b.

Sherman, Lawrence W., and Richard A. Berk. *The Minneapolis Domestic Violence Experiment.* Washington, DC: Police Foundation, 1984a.

———. "The Specific Deterrent Effects of Arrest for Domestic Assault." *American Sociological Review* 49 (1984b): 261–72.

Sherman, Lawrence W., and Ellen G. Cohn. "The Impact of Research on Legal Policy: The Minneapolis Domestic Violence Experiment." *Law and Society Review* 23 (1989): 117–44.

Straus, Murray A. *Behind Closed Doors: Violence in the American Family.* Garden City, NY: Anchor, 1980.

———. "Assaults by Wives on Husbands: Implications for Primary Prevention of Marital Violence." Paper presented at the Annual Meeting of the American Society of Criminology, Reno, NV, 1989.

Strube, M.J., and Barbour, L.S. "Factors Related to the Decision to Leave an Abusive Relationship." *Journal of Marriage and Family* (November 1984): 837–44.

Symposium on Domestic Violence. *Journal of Criminal Law and Criminology* 83 (1)(1992).

Tong, Rosemarie. *Women, Sex, and the Saw.* Totowa, NJ: Rowman and Allanheld, 1984.

Walker, Lenore E. *The Battered Woman.* New York: Harper & Row, 1979.

Zoomer, Olga J. "Policing Woman Beating in the Netherlands." In *Women, Policing, and Male Violence: International Perspectives.* Eds. Jalna Hanmer, Jill Radford, and Elizabeth A. Stanko. London: Routledge and Kegan Paul, 1989. 125–54.

D

Drug Abuse Prevention Education

During adolescence many young people—despite warnings from parents, the schools, and the media—begin experimentation and use of a variety of harmful or potentially harmful substances, including tobacco, alcohol, and drugs. Two of the better-known studies of adolescent substance use were initiated in the early 1970s: the Monitoring the Future Project, which surveys high-school seniors; and the National Household Survey, which includes a sample of adolescents aged twelve to seventeen years. Both studies monitor trends in the prevalence of drug use by means of repeated surveys conducted at regular time intervals. Recent results from these studies reveal the continued wide-

TOBACCO, ALCOHOL, AND DRUG USE AMONG HIGH SCHOOL SENIORS, BY SUBSTANCE AND FREQUENCY OF USE: 1975 TO 1989

Substance and Frequency of Use	Class of 1975	Class of 1980	Class of 1983	Class of 1984	Class of 1985	Class of 1986	Class of 1987	Class of 1988	Class of 1989
Percentage Reporting Having Ever Used Drugs									
Cigarettes	73.6	71.0	70.6	69.7	68.8	67.6	67.2	66.4	65.7
Alcohol	90.4	93.2	92.6	92.6	92.2	91.3	92.2	92.0	90.7
Any illicit drug	55.2	65.4	62.9	61.6	60.6	57.6	56.6	53.9	50.9
Marijuana only	19.0	26.7	22.5	21.3	20.9	19.9	20.8	21.4	19.5
Any illicit drug other than marijuana*	36.2	38.7	40.4	40.3	39.7	37.7	35.8	32.5	31.4
Selected illicit drugs:									
Cocaine	9.0	15.7	16.2	16.1	17.3	16.9	15.2	12.1	10.3
Heroin	2.2	1.1	1.2	1.3	1.2	1.1	1.2	1.1	1.3
LSD	11.3	9.3	8.9	8.0	7.5	7.2	8.4	7.7	8.3
Marijuana/hashish	47.3	60.3	57.0	54.9	54.2	50.9	50.2	47.2	43.7
PCP	—	9.6	5.6	5.0	4.9	4.8	3.0	2.9	3.9
Percentage Reporting Use of Drugs in the Previous Thirty Days									
Cigarettes	36.7	30.5	30.3	29.3	30.1	29.6	29.4	28.7	28.6
Alcohol	68.2	72.0	69.4	67.2	65.9	65.3	66.4	63.9	60.0
Any illicit drug abuse	30.7	37.2	30.5	29.2	29.7	27.1	24.7	21.3	19.7
Marijuana only	15.3	18.8	15.1	14.1	14.8	13.9	13.1	11.3	10.6
Any illicit drug other than marijuana*	15.4	18.4	15.4	15.1	14.9	13.2	11.6	10.0	9.1
Selected illicit drugs:									
Cocaine	1.9	5.2	4.9	5.8	6.7	6.2	4.3	3.4	2.8
Heroin	0.4	0.2	0.2	0.3	0.3	0.2	0.2	0.2	0.3
LSD	2.3	2.3	1.9	1.5	1.6	1.7	1.8	1.8	1.8
Marijuana/hashish	27.1	33.7	27.0	25.2	25.7	23.4	21.0	18.0	16.7
PCP	—	1.4	1.3	1.0	1.6	1.3	0.6	0.3	1.4

— Data not available.

* Other illicit drugs include hallucinogens, cocaine, and heroin, or any other opiates, stimulants, sedatives, or tranquilizers not prescribed by a doctor.

Note: A revised questionnaire was used in 1982 and later years to reduce the inappropriate reporting of non-prescription stimulants. This slightly reduced the positive responses for some types of drug use.

Source: U.S. Department of Health and Human Services, Alcohol, Drug Abuse, and Mental Health Administration, *National Trends in Drug Use and Related Factors Among American High School Students, 1975-1986;* and University of Michigan, Institute for Social Research, *Monitoring the Future,* various years.

spread abuse of a variety of illicit substances by adolescents and young adults. The U.S. Department of Education publishes Youth Indicators on an annual basis, which tabulates data and charts trends, as shown in the preceding illustration.

Although the rates of adolescent substance abuse have leveled off since the dramatic increases seen in the 1960s and 1970s, the percentage of young people who experiment with and use drugs remains intolerably high. Sadly, the United States has the highest level of teenage drug use of any industrial nation in the world.

Projects DARE and SPECDA

Project DARE (Drug Abuse Resistance Education) began in Los Angeles when Chief of Police Daryl Gates approached Superintendent of Schools, Dr. Harry Handler, in January 1983 to explore how they could collaborate to deal more effectively with the problem of drug and alcohol use among adolescents. Law-enforcement efforts to control the distribution and sale of illicit drugs on school campuses in Los Angeles, primarily through undercover work and periodic drug busts, had made little impact and had alienated students and school personnel from police. Chief Gates viewed project DARE as a priority and offered to reassign officers to the program. After examining current drug abuse education and prevention programs, a joint police/school task force made its recommendations. First, the program would address the broad spectrum of substance abuse, including drugs, alcohol, and tobacco. Second, the program would extend from kindergarten through high school. Third, veteran police officers, recognized by the students as experts in the field of substance abuse, would serve as full-time instructors. And fourth, emphasis would be placed on teaching the skills and developing the strength of character that enables students to make responsible decisions regarding substance use.

By July 1983 ten police officers had been selected and trained to teach the DARE curriculum. During the 1983–1984 school year, 189 fifth- and sixth-grade students were taught the core curriculum. In addition, approximately 79,000 other students were taught the K-4 curriculum or received a one-day assembly program. By degrees the program moved toward full implementation. During the 1986–1987 school year every elementary school under the Los Angeles Police Department's jurisdiction had a DARE officer assigned to teach the core curriculum; approximately 258,000 students from 347 elementary schools received their DARE graduation diploma. The junior high school curriculum reached approximately 91,000 seventh-graders in 58 middle schools. In total, Chief Gates committed 53 line officers to serve as DARE instructors, plus supervisory and clerical staff.

Project SPECDA (School Program to Educate and Control Drug Abuse) evolved shortly after DARE. In September 1984 Nathan Quinones, the chancellor of the New York City Board of Education, and Benjamin Ward, commissioner of the New York Police Department, held a press conference to announce the formation of a planning committee to develop a new drug prevention education program. After a draft curriculum took shape, a pilot project in two of the Board of Education's thirty-two school districts, one in the Bronx and one in the Bedford-Stuyvesant section of Brooklyn, was initiated in February 1985. Students participated in an eight-week program with weekly presentations given by a uniformed police officer in partnership with a Board of Education drug counselor. Assembly programs for elementary, junior high, and high school students were also given.

This initial effort involved twenty-seven police officers (selected from one hundred and fifty applicants) and fifty drug counselors. The Criminal Justice Center of John Jay College evaluated the pilot project and deemed it a success. In September 1985 the program expanded to seven districts, one in each of the police department's patrol boroughs. By January 1987, the program expanded further into twenty-eight of the city's thirty-two school districts. Meanwhile, the police department's commitment of resources was enormous. In 1987 SPECDA's education unit involved one hundred and two instructors, fifteen sergeant field supervisors, two lieutenant field supervisors, four command staff (including a captain), and six administrative aides. In addition, a coordina-tor's office in charge of program planning and public relations contributed a deputy inspector, a lieutenant, a sergeant, a line officer, and one civilian employee. SPECDA's goals were the same as DARE's, with perhaps a bit more attention devoted to forming a bond of trust between young people and police officers.

Project DARE's core curriculum for fifth- and sixth-grade students was adapted by Dr. Ruth Rich, a curriculum specialist with the Los Angeles Unified School District, from a curriculum for Project SMART (Self-Management and Resistance Training) designed by the Health Behavior Research Institute of the University of Southern California. While there is an abbreviated curriculum for younger children and junior high school students, the heart of the DARE program addresses fifth- and sixth-grade children. Through DARE students learn that real friends will not push them into trying alcohol and drugs and that being grown up means making their own decisions and coping with problems in a positive way. Most important, students learn and practice specific strategies for responding to peers who offer them substances. Several features of the DARE curriculum deserve special mention:

1. Students are given a DARE notebook that includes all of the worksheets and handouts they need for their lessons.

2. The first item in the notebook is a DARE word list (e.g., drug, peer pressure, risk) that provides space for students to write in definitions.

3. An early lesson is on general personal safety, as that is the traditional focus of police officer presentations in the schools. With this lesson the instructor can ease more gradually into the anti-drug lessons.

4. Each classroom has a question box in which students can anonymously deposit written questions about police work, drugs, or any other relevant topic. During each class the DARE officer answers some of the questions.

5. While Project DARE's administrators expect the instructors to follow the curriculum outline, innovation occurs. For example, an officer might bring a stuffed bear to class dressed in a policeman's uniform; the "DARE Bear" is placed on the desk of the student who answers the officer's first question correctly.

6. While participation of the regular classroom teachers is not necessary, in some cases, teachers take an active role—helping pass out materials, answering students' questions as they complete in-class assignments, and participating in discussions at critical points.

Project SPECDA's core curriculum has sixteen lessons divided evenly between fifth and sixth grade. Each lesson offers a menu of related activities from which the SPECDA team can choose depending on students' ability level, interests, and reactions to earlier sessions. It is up to the police officer/drug counselor teams to select activities and to decide how to present the lesson, who will take the lead for each part, and so on. For example, in the first lesson for grade five, the activity "Try on a Police Officer's Badge" is structured as a written homework exercise. One team adapted it to create a role-play with a student selected to play the part of a police officer and allowed to wear the SPECDA officer's hat and badge. An important feature of the curriculum is the presession lesson taught by the regular classroom teacher to prepare students for meeting the SPECDA team. With this lesson they learn that drug abuse is a major problem in American society, that it presents a serious danger to young people, and that there are programs such as SPECDA to help combat it. The teacher next reads a fictitious letter to an imaginary action reporter from "A Worried Parent," which describes how her ten-year old son took some pills that an older boy offered him. Imagining themselves as the action reporter the students write reponses to the letter to share with the class. After a discussion of the role that police and drug counselors can play in teaching children about drugs and how to say no, the teacher announces the SPECDA team will be coming and asks the students, as a homework assignment, to prepare questions they want to ask.

Obstacles to Program Success
DARE, SPECDA, and other "Just Say No" programs are a legitimate police initiative, similar in intent to neighborhood watch, Officer Friendly, and other crime-prevention efforts. Yet, the reassignment of officers from patrol and other essential law-enforcement work to teach in classrooms is a profound step. Every veteran officer is an important weapon in the fight against crime, whose training represents a significant financial investment. In communities where public concerns about crime are especially great, it may be politically impossible for the police department to staff a drug-prevention program. Ultimately, of course, the wisdom of

redeploying officers must emerge from evaluation data.

While redeployment is one obstacle, distrust between police and schools is another. At first, many skeptics expected police and school cultures to clash. The police effort to stem the drug trade sometimes appears in conflict with the school's interest in disciplining its students without outside interference. Police and schools have different administrative styles. Police, as paramilitary organizations, have a firm, hierarchical command. Schools are usually more flexible, less stringent in their demands on staff, and more often committed to a participatory decision-making process. Many police officers and teachers hold certain stereotypes about one another. The "macho," "dumb," "right-wing" cop is matched by the "wimpy," "idealistic," "left-wing" teacher. A claim that the worlds of education and law enforcement are mutually incompatible is sometimes used as an argument for rejecting a police/school prevention program.

Some police officers reject a school assignment as not "real police work." For example, this notion surfaces in relation to bearing arms. In New York City, SPECDA officers remain armed as administrators believe their uniformed officers must be protected at all times while on duty. In Los Angeles, on the other hand, the officers are unarmed as administrators are concerned that the gun distracts students and can create an unwanted barrier between students and officers. "Not real police work" finds its counterpart in the educator's concern that police "don't know how to teach." Another factor is that with both DARE and SPECDA, police officers are reminded they are visitors in the classroom; they must respect the regular teacher's authority and accede to his or her classroom rules.

Competing programs also affect the implementation of DARE and SPECDA models. In Massachusetts the Governor's Alliance Against Drugs encourages local schools to adopt any of several commercially available, comprehensive, and developmentally based K-12 curricula that can be taught by specially trained classroom teachers. At first, when a group approached the state about implementing Project DARE some officials worried the DARE curriculum with its focus on fifth- and sixth-grade students would let the schools "off the hook" in terms of implementing the comprehensive curriculum. Reassured that DARE would not supplant the state's

program, but could be a vital part of it, most state officials eventually came to see DARE as a good option for local communities to consider.

Yet another obstacle is mounting program expenditures. Extra costs include those for training, teaching materials, equipment, promotional materials, and travel. Selling the prevention program may be more difficult if the schools are expected to cover some of the expenses. Alternatively, corporations, foundations, or civic organizations may be willing to pay costs for certain components of the program.

Assessment

To measure the effectiveness of a police/school drug prevention education program, funders, senior administrators, or government officials may require a rigorous evaluation, one that involves control groups and the collection of follow-up data for several years. Setting up such a study is complex, depending a great deal on the extent of program implementation, the presence of other antisubstance-abuse programs, recordkeeping procedures, the ease of data access, and financial resources. There are three principal sources of data that program administrators can routinely use: (1) surveys and interviews with students, teachers, and others; (2) school-based data on students' school performance; and (3) self-report questionnaires completed by the students. Mainly, assessors look for change in student knowledge and attitudes in critical areas: the power of peer influence, the acceptability of drug/alcohol use, the consequences of drug/alcohol use, attitudes toward police, and seeking adult consultation about drug/alcohol use.

William DeJong

Bibliography

Barrett, A.C., and D.A. White. "How John Henry Effects Confound the Measurement of Self Esteem in Primary Prevention Programs for Drug Abuse in Middle Schools." *Journal of Alcohol and Drug Education* 36 (Spring 1991): 87–102.

DeJong, William. *Arresting the Demand for Drugs: Police and School Partnerships to Prevent Drug Abuse.* Washington, DC: U.S. Department of Justice, National Institute of Justice, 1987.

Drug Abuse Resistance Education (DARE). *Drug Abuse Resistance Education (DARE) Training Center Policies and Procedures.* Washington, DC: U. S. Department of Justice, National Institute of Justice, 1991.

Gocek, M.A. *Youth and Drugs in the Community*. Monroe, NY: Library Associates, 1989.

Jacobs, N., et al. *A School Program to Educate and Control Drug Abuse: Pilot Program Evaluation*. New York: Criminal Justice Center, John Jay College of Criminal Justice, 1985.

Pellow, R.A., and J.L. Jengeleski. "Survey of Current Research Studies on Drug Education Programs in America. *Journal of Drug Education* 21 (1991): 203–10.

Police Department Annual Reports. If the department has DARE or a DARE-type program the activity will show up in the annual report.

Drug Enforcement

Street crime in America has risen inexorably over the past thirty years to appallingly high levels. The terrifying explosion of murders, rapes, assaults, robberies, burglaries, thefts, and auto larcenies has been abetted and accelerated by a unique proliferation of firearms, but the underlying fuel for such carnage has been drugs.

The War on Drugs

Studies in major cities consistently reveal a wide, deep, and truly surprising link between drug use and crime. While estimates and analyses vary, there is little doubt that drug abuse is intimately tied to between 60 and 90 percent of street crime in America.

Every census of America's recidivists reveals widespread patterns of addiction to alcohol and hard drugs, in addition to the usual indices of race, poverty, exclusion, and the other characteristics that are emblematic of membership in the underclass.

Any phenomenon as complex as criminal behavior is going to demand thorough research and is likely to produce complicated, multifaceted causal factors, but the connection between drugs and crime is both obvious and inescapable.

The disintegration of the American family, flight from the cities, enormous disparities between the over and underclasses, and the problem of racism constitute the social and economic forces spawning crime. Drugs become the vehicles of escape from these conditions and guns become the tools used to facilitate this flight.

America's unwillingness to recognize the complex social and economic forces at work has led to a simplistic reliance on draconian measures that, after twenty years of devoted pursuit, have at least provided the undeniable benefit of proving that they cannot and will not, by themselves, resolve the problems of drug abuse and criminality.

Just as one cannot step into the same river twice, the drug problem in America shifts under our feet, even as we attempt to freeze-frame its aspects in order to study it more confidently.

Two decades of heavy-duty enforcement have filled our prisons with low-level users and dealers, resulted in huge seizures, and produced daily spectacles on our nightly news broadcasts. Yet they failed to stem supply or produce anything remotely resembling a shortage—or even a local panic—and consequently the prices have moved inexorably downward. A crack snort was going for as little as $.75 on the streets of New York in 1992. If all of this proved nothing else, it demonstrated the iron laws of supply and demand and the distributive genius of capitalism in a lucrative field.

Anecdotes and Statistics

The statistics demonstrate the risks—but they are faceless and, ultimately, unterrifying abstractions. Data represent events that happen to others. Thus the tripling of the murder rate, from 1960 to 1991, and the to-be-expected mirroring in all other categories of street crime doesn't prove very scary, even when we consider that we murder as many Americans, currently, every twenty-nine months, as were killed or missing in battle during the 144 months of the Vietnam War—about 58,000 total casualties.

So we have to put a face on the numbers with which we can identify. Anecdotes about the fates overtaking recognizable victims at least have the power to move us, through the terrors they produce. When the viewer can relate to a victim, with the observation that "there, but for the grace of God, go I," the numbers can be felt, feared and, perhaps, receive a sensible response. The latter has not yet occurred.

Drugs and Street Crime

Americans have been notoriously unwilling to recognize that they've created the conditions of poverty, homelessness, ghettoization, and exclusion that create the monsters they love to hate. Thus we focus on the Willie Hortons—and the need to destroy them without a scintilla of effort to understand them and thereby, perhaps, consider adopting the social and economic policies that might reverse their proliferating numbers.

Street criminals strike because they need funds to buy drugs, because of the erratic behaviors induced by the use of drugs, as a result of their traffic in drugs and the competitions it produces, as well as to subsidize their lifestyles.

An enormously high percentage of prison inmates report heavy use of hard drugs in the weeks before their crimes and during the commission of the offenses for which they've been incarcerated. The very heavy involvement of alcohol proves a needed reminder that, although legal, this is the most widely abused drug in our culture, having created at least 10 million addicts and millions more problem drinkers.

Stepping-Stones
While tobacco seems to be a tangential and accompanying drug, alcohol and marijuana should be labeled "stepping-stone drugs" in that their use very frequently predates graduation into the hard drugs of cocaine (crack); heroin; the psychedelics LSD or PCP; or amphetamines, barbiturates, and other such exotics as Methaqualone and designer (laboratory-manufactured) drugs.

The characteristic addict emerges from an abusing environment, has frequently been given amounts of beer or wine as early as the sixth, seventh, or eighth years of life, and use escalates in dosages and the intensity and variety of drugs over the years. By their teens many addicts are thoroughly hooked for life. Even the few sober ones who have been "saved" face a daily struggle against inner impulses that will haunt them all their lives. There is no "cure" but there is recovery and a continuing battle.

The Addict as Predator and Victim
The addict then becomes at once predator-menace-victim as he/she deals, steals, mugs, exploits, and gets exploited. Over a typically short career an enormous number of crimes occur. Studies generally estimate the true recidivist's activity at about fifty robberies (muggings, hold-ups) or two hundred burglaries (break-ins) a year, for a career that usually starts at about fifteen and that ends around thirty. That street crime is the province of the male members of the underclass hardly needs iteration. The return of the incarcerated addict to the environment that prompted escape into drugs ensures the cyclical inevitability of a return to drug use, crime, and prison.

Recent Trends
Although the most recent epidemic—mostly featuring cocaine and its crack derivative—appears to have peaked in 1985, the numbers of arrests increased exponentially beyond that year, reaching over a million in 1990. At the same time spooked legislatures were stiffening penalties with mandated sentences and longer terms. The result was the imprisonment of more and more low-level addicts and sellers for longer and longer periods. It was the heralded War on Drugs that mostly crammed our prisons to bursting. There was never much thought of using these penalties to coerce users into abstinence and treatment.

Draco's Approach
For a country that genuinely believes itself to be notably tolerant of wrongdoers, the facts provide a sobering rebuttal. The number of admissions to local jails reached over 10 million in 1991 and the number of prisoners incarcerated for serious crimes rose to over 800,000 in that year.

The rate of incarcerations per crime has risen steadily and the percentage of commitments to state prisons for drug offenses has risen from 13.2 percent in 1985 to 29.5 percent in 1989, while the percentage of those committed for other serious offenses declined, from 54.9 percent in 1985 to 39.4 percent in 1989. It is easy to see how our War on Drugs was faring against the serious offenders who were not charged with drug violations—they were receiving increasingly lenient treatment to make room for the addicts.

Crime Trends and Riots
Meanwhile a survey of American households showed that nearly 23 million were victimized by some crime in 1991, and this is presumably a low total. The enormous and inexorable rise in murders, however, hints strongly that the true levels of violence are both largely unreported and increasing in their numbers.

Occasional eruptions, such as the Los Angeles riots in the spring of 1992, reflect the permanent existence of a disaffected and large ghetto underclass that only awaits the spark that ignites it to revolt. It might even be said that alcohol and drugs serve as the opiates that keep this potentially restive population pacified. There is little doubt that their occasional eruptions prove every urban police chief's worst nightmares.

Drugs—America's Number One Domestic Problem

On September 5, 1989, President George Bush called drugs America's number one domestic problem. He dedicated billions of dollars to sweeps, roundups, and constitutionally suspect enforcement strategies aimed at the highly visible street dealers and users. Little was spent on research, study, the adoption of a multidisciplinary approach, prevention, education, or treatment. Even in the popular enforcement area the "Mr. Bigs" got scant notice as the emphasis focused on the irritating and highly visible street junkies and dealers, a great many of whom were, of course, members of the underclass.

A much-ballyhooed creation—a drug czar and a national office to lead the War on Drugs—became a repository for political debt payments and for the employment of friends and supporters. While huge sums were allocated for enforcement, not a cent was applied to the creation of a President's Commission on Crime and Drugs that might have helped develop a national strategy toward violence and the guns and drugs that make it so much more widespread and lethal.

The organizational confusion at the national level was eloquently illustrated by the tangled missions of the FBI and the Drug Enforcement Agency—neither of which was offered the lead role in what clearly should have been a mandate for the DEA to take charge. The military was pressed into unpracticed service, along with a potpourri of other federal, state, and local agencies, in a hysterical attempt to at least seem to be doing something. Thus was the semblance of action created that fed us the nightly images on the ten o'clock news.

Decriminalization

Decriminalization of hard drugs—a bad idea that would produce hugely greater numbers of users and which would fray our already tattered moral fabric—was seized upon as the panacea by the intellectual elitists who can produce impressive sound bytes and who seem to dominate the nascent industry of television punditry. They've turned the talking head into the latter-day equivalent of the Sophists, entertaining us with their glibness, wit, and intelligence, without bringing insight, wisdom, or experience to bear on a problem that irresistibly tempts them to pontifications. Their facileness serves as testimony of our hunger for simple, clever answers to immensely difficult problems.

The analogy to alcohol is inescapable yet its legalization and accessibility have created huge problems.

It ought not to be forgotten that raising the legal drinking age to twenty-one actually reduces alcohol consumption by the young, even as the prohibition is often widely flouted. We tend to focus on the failures but the fact is that Prohibition was not, as the War on Poverty was not, an unmitigated disaster. Both had their victories and both deserve a better fate than cavalier dismissal. We can learn from the successes and failures contained in both those social experiments, even as we can admit that they were, indeed, largely failed enterprises.

Today, there is a growing movement for the adoption of a warning label that alerts users to the addictive and harmful properties of alcohol, in the same way that tobacco products have been labeled since 1969. Such educational initiatives have the power to alter social conventions, such as heavy-duty smoking in public places, which once seemed intractable. The reachable and educable segments of our population can and have been reached by the hortatory methods employed. The alienated and excluded present a much more difficult problem. They have a lot less to lose from the harmful and addictive properties of alcohol, tobacco, or drugs.

It must be added that many attempts at tolerations that bordered on decriminalization foundered on the shoals of bitter experience.

Britain's famous doctor-monitored, prescription-of-heroin program collapsed under a welter of abuses. Switzerland set aside a public park for the use of addicts and had to abandon the effort as crimes, deaths, appalling conditions, and the attraction of addicts from the corners of Europe turned the park into a dangerous and unusable cesspool of violence and death. The Netherlands' policy of mostly tolerating low-level usage in its coffee shops has fared better, even while investing its cities with an unwelcome notoriety for what some labeled libertinage.

The one thing on which all three major presidential candidates agreed in their 1992 debates was that decriminalizing hard drugs was a bad idea. In this view they were virtually unanimously joined by the entire law-enforcement establishment of the United States as reflected in the myriad resolutions passed by the different segments of the criminal-justice system at their meetings.

The inescapable fact is that, despite some undeniable benefits deriving from decriminalizing hard drugs, to do so would be to place the imprimatur of government approval over the use of drugs.

Early History

There was a time when all drugs were legal and maiden aunts got hooked on cough syrup. Having a nip for "medicinal purposes" became the bywords of not-so-innocent citizens who would have been horrified at being labeled "junkies."

Alarm over spreading addiction and its consequences led to an international conference in The Hague in 1912, which resulted in laws making hard drugs mostly illicit. America adopted this view in the landmark Harrison Act of 1914 that became the nation's new policy statement banning hard drugs. That law became the embodiment of the policy of prohibition followed to the present day. It must be said that the world's nations follow this policy with rare exceptions—and those have more to do with tacit tolerance of low-level use of some drugs than they do with the adoption of explicit laws that contradict ours.

The Numbers

Every statistic in the slippery and ever-changing field of drug use ought to be greeted skeptically and offered humbly. It is wisest to refer to estimates and to carefully label assertions and their sources.

The federal government, for example, estimated that there were 8.2 million casual users of cocaine in 1988, that this number declined to 6.2 million in 1990, and increased to 6.4 million in 1991. The number of heavy drug users of all types was estimated at 5.8 million in 1992.

Although the use of cocaine appeared to peak in 1985, the use among the harder-to-count ghetto residents, as reluctantly acknowledged by both the Secretary of Health, Education and Welfare and the drug czar, appeared to be rising in 1992. Emergency treatment for cocaine rose 12 percent for the first quarter of 1992, as 30,103 persons sought medical attention. There was a 15 percent increase in heroin abuse, foreshadowing a comeback for this once preeminent drug.

Enforcement

It is clear that America has relied on enforcement for the past 20 years. This is the one area of police operations where aggressiveness is encouraged, frequently to the exclusion of constitutional niceties. Legislative halls crawl with "good faith" exceptions to the Fourth Amendment's protections against unreasonable searches and seizures—as if all that were needed to legitimize a constitutional breach would be the assertions of good faith by the breacher of those rights.

While we bridle at the use of decoys, stings, stake-out units, and other similar aggressive enforcement tactics in most aspects of street crime, drug enforcement remains the one area in which such approaches are de rigeur.

The War on Drugs was the one domestic program for which the Bush administration never said "the money's not there."

By 1993 federal expenditures alone neared $13 billion; we had succumbed to "czarism"; penalties had been increased and mandated defoliations had been pursued; Panama had been invaded in 1989's largest drug bust; and lip-service had been paid to such programs as "weed and seed," in which unemployed ghetto blacks were the weeds and nonexistent capitalists willing to invest in the ghetto were the seed.

No elected official dares vote against appropriations for more sweeps and roundups or against unworkable draconianisms that are manifestly ineffective.

Since everyone agrees that America is losing its War on Drugs should the effort be abandoned? Should the focus be changed? In short, what needs to be done?

Toward a National Effort

The War on Drugs will have to be prosecuted on many fronts, and it will take coordination and cooperation among many disparate groups and persons.

Local Action

Within our communities we ought to undertake programs that focus on strengthening family ties and the forces at work in that vital unit of social organization. The war starts there and the weapons are structure, discipline, affection, stability, support, sobriety, interest, and all the other factors describing a functional family.

Friends and peers form important influences on our young and these should be monitored for wholesome values. Lonely, desperate children frequently gravitate to the most harmful circles. Studies show that the greatest risk to a girl is to date a boy who uses drugs.

Schools are important centers of activity in a child's life and should be seen as resources contributing to children's health. Parents have to be engaged in partnerships with teachers and participate in the life of these institutions.

Television can be an influence that leads to hedonism, passivity, ignorance, or worse. Its cultural influence needs to be monitored and controlled. It needs to be shaped into a force that provides more positives (learning, useful lessons, sound values) and fewer negatives (inuring viewers to violence; inculcating materialistic, consumerist, sybaritic instincts).

The community must think of the influence of churches (by which is meant all religious institutions such as mosques, synagogues, etc.) and of their importance in shaping members.

There must be concern with educational, employment, and recreational amenities—such as alcohol-free social clubs, athletic facilities, summer job programs, dropout preventions, and such.

Recent surveys show increased use of tobacco, alcohol, and drugs by students in the sixth through eighth grades. It is obvious that communities and parents are losing their War on Drugs in the critical areas of family stability, friendships, schools, television, and other aspects of community life.

A National Strategy

The development of an approach that would produce a national plan for our War on Drugs needs to consider a number of stark realities:

- Abolish the office of the drug czar and help restore Americans' faith that governmental barnacles will be removed.
- Create a President's Commission on Crime and Drugs that brings a multidisciplinary approach to the problem of violence. Organizations like the Drug Policy Foundation could serve as invaluable resources in marshalling the various disciplines and in insuring a comprehensive approach.
- Reduce federal spending on drugs by at least half—from over $12 billion to around $6 billion—and concentrate the expenditures on prevention; education (Drug Abuse Resistance Education; programs by the Partnership for a Drug Free America, and such); treatment; and an enforcement program that targets the bigger predators using the smaller fish as bait—and that channels, through the coercive power of the threat of prison, low-level users into treatment and abstention.
- Make the Drug Enforcement Agency the lead organization in the effort.
- Encourage local efforts through grants such as community policing and other grassroots initiatives.

Americans characteristically scorn thought and love motion. We like to say "the thing has been studied to death, let's get some action!" Yet our government functions on the basis of much committee study and deliberation (when it functions at its best) preceding the adoption of action programs. The drug problem has not been studied to death—or anything close to extremes. Our War on Drugs is a Tower of Babel of confused and contradictory voices crying for a national plan.

International Action

Drugs constitute an enormous problem of supply and demand, in which the suppliers blame the users for creating a market, and the users decry the existence of a supply that seems to beg for more users. In between lie the true profiteers of all this misery.

The complexity of the problem must be acknowledged. The Andean farmer grows the coca leaf—as the Afghanistan farmer grows the poppy—for logical and compelling economic reasons that cannot be ignored. That this agriculture gets tangled with revolutions, insurrections, or civil wars only heightens the complexity.

The user seeks the relief drugs supply because of social, cultural, and economic conditions that dictate a need to escape the awful realities of daily life.

Between the user and grower lies a cadre of traffickers, suppliers, bankers, manufacturers, chemists, politicians, and other entrepreneurs who gravitate toward the gold.

Reducing the need to escape into drugs and providing an attractive alternative to the drug grower will require the development of difficult policies. No peace treaty or trade agreement conjures up the complexities of undertaking a comprehensive assault on the world's drug problem, yet nothing like the resources lavished on those enterprises has ever been even considered for use in the War on Drugs.

The War on Drugs must be fought, but it needs a battle plan that encompasses its many fronts. The current approach is doomed to continue to fail, but its failure should not blind us to the possibilities of victory inherent in the adoption of a more thoughtful approach.

Anthony V. Bouza

Note

The material for this entry was drawn from two recent works by the author; *A Carpet of Blue: An Ex-Cop Takes a Tough Look at America's Drug Problem* (Minneapolis; Deaconess Press, 1992) and *How To Stop Crime* (New York; Plenum Publishing, 1993).

Drug Enforcement Administration

The Drug Enforcement Administration (DEA) enforces the law and regulations relating to narcotic drugs, marijuana, depressants, stimulants, and the hallucinogenic drugs. Its objectives are to reach all levels of source of supply and to interdict illegal drugs before they reach the user. To achieve its mission, the Administration has stationed highly trained agents along the many and varied routes of illicit traffic, both in the United States and in foreign countries. DEA's enforcement program is aimed at disruption of the highest echelons of the traffic in the priority drugs of abuse. Drug enforcement action by state and local agencies is also an essential part of the national drug-enforcement strategy.

Inception

The earliest federal drug enforcement efforts can be traced organizationally to the Internal Revenue Service. In 1915, 162 collectors and agents placed in the IRS Miscellaneous Division were assigned responsibility under the Harrison Narcotics Act for "restricting the sale of opium." Over the years a number of agencies became involved in federal drug law enforcement. In 1973 the U.S. attorney general was given overall federal responsibility for drug law enforcement. DEA was established July 1, 1973, by Presidential Reorganization Plan No. 2. It resulted from the merger of the Bureau of Narcotics and Dangerous Drugs, the Office for Drug Abuse Law Enforcement, the Office of National Narcotics Intelligence, those elements of the Bureau of Customs that had drug investigative responsibilities, and those functions of the Office of Science and Technology that were related to drug enforcement. Clearly, reorganization was needed. On January 21, 1982, the attorney general gave the Federal Bureau of Investigation concurrent jurisdiction with DEA over drug offenses. DEA's administrator now reports to the director of the FBI, who was given general supervision of the drug-enforcement effort. DEA agents work side by side with FBI agents throughout the country in major drug cases—a significant change in narcotics law enforcement.

Mission

Enforcement of drug laws by DEA emphasizes the reduction of available cocaine, PCP, illicit and legally produced but diverted stimulants such as amphetamines and methamphetamines, as well as barbiturates and other depressants and sedative-hypnotics. Trafficking in multiton quantities of marijuana and other types of cannabis such as hashish and "hash oil" receives similar enforcement attention. DEA's response to the varying patterns, methods, and international routes of the traffic in illicit drugs must be flexible and timely. After the "French connection" for heroin from Marseilles was cut off in 1973, Mexican brown heroin began to replace it. To counter the new threat, DEA's interdiction and eradication programs moved into place, resulting in a reduction of both opium production and level of purity of heroin on the streets of the United States. In anticipation of possible smuggling from Southeast Asia, measures to slow its progress were undertaken immediately. Cocaine, imported illegally from South America, is an increasing problem now receiving special attention through programs designed to reduce the illicit traffic and the cultivation of coca leaf, from which cocaine is derived.

DEA never lacks for business, whether it has to identify type and variety of drug or plan some new way of seizing the contraband. The animal tranquilizer and hallucinogen, phencyclidine (PCP), has replaced other hallucinogens such as LSD as the most abused of this type of drug. Because of the serious psychological effects of using PCP, including violent and irrational behavior, clandestine manufacturing and trafficking in PCP have become an important target of DEA's enforcement operations. PCP laboratories, difficult to detect but easily set up, have been discovered and dismantled in increasing numbers.

Compliance and Regulatory Affairs
The DEA is also responsible for regulating the legal distribution of narcotics and dangerous drugs. This includes monitoring all imports and exports of controlled substances and establishing manufacturing quotas for all Schedule I and II controlled substances. All individuals handling controlled substances are required to register with DEA and are periodically investigated by DEA compliance investigators, who ensure that record keeping and security safeguards of all controlled substances comply with existing federal regulations. Other responsibilities of DEA's regulatory program include monitoring various drug-abuse patterns and determining whether or not a drug should be controlled, based on its abuse potential.

Training
The DEA's National Training Institute conducts intensive training in narcotics and dangerous drug law enforcement for law-enforcement officers from agencies throughout the United States and the world. Ten-week schools allow police officers to receive training similar to that which DEA special agents receive. In addition, they are introduced to management concepts that will enable them to develop and lead drug investigative units and organize drug traffic prevention programs in their own communities. Specialized two-week schools offer eighty hours of instruction to state, county, and city officers in the basic techniques of narcotics and dangerous drugs investigation. These schools are held at DEA's National Training Institute in Washington, D.C., and at field locations across the United States. The programs conducted in foreign countries range from two or three days to three weeks and are presented in the native languages.

Interagency Cooperation
DEA's global agents provide intelligence information to Bureau of Customs agents and the Border Patrol so they can intercept illegal drugs and traffickers at entry points into the United States. DEA also coordinates EPIC (the El Paso Intelligence Center), the first joint fact-finding operation in the annals of federal law enforcement. This interagency group, located in the southwestern border area, receives and disseminates information on drug trafficking and illegal alien activity along the southern border. DEA Mobile Task Forces (MTF), another cooperative effort, have been successful in removing illicit drugs from the streets through coactive planning tailored to the specific assignment. DEA State and Local Task Forces (SLTF) assure that drug-enforcement ventures do not stagnate, and act as an impetus for nonfederal law-enforcement assaults on drug trafficking. The administration regularly responds to requests for investigative assistance from state and local authorities, and through its six regional laboratories provides analyses of drug evidence and also supplies related expert testimony. More recently DEA/FBI task forces have been established to identify potential organized crime narcotics activities.

Achievements mid-1980s
Acting Administrator John C. Lawn, appearing before a House Subcommittee on Crime, May 1, 1985, reported the following notable achievements of DEA:

> The DEA rate of arrests has gone from less than 1,000 per month in FY 1980 to nearly 1,100 per month in FY 1984. Arrests in those cases targeted at the top echelon, or Class I cases, have increased approximately 40 percent. Convictions are up from about four hundred per month in FY 1980 to more than nine hundred per month in FY 1984.
>
> Cocaine removals were up 380 percent and totaled 11.7 metric tons in FY 1984. Marijuana seizures increased 270 percent and heroin seizures increased 80 percent.
>
> During FY 1984, DEA investigations also accounted for the seizure of 190 clandestine laboratories, including 120 methamphetamine, 18 PCP, and 17 cocaine laboratories.

Other impressive figures accrued for task-force operations, the cannabis eradication program, EPIC, and international control of illicit drugs. For example, based on DEA information, the Colombian government seized seven cocaine laboratory complexes and ten tons of cocaine, later described as the "largest drug raid ever in the world." DEA's budget and employee request for FY 1986 was for a total of $345,671,000 and 4,564 permanent positions. That represented a net increase of 134 positions and $15,683,000 above the 1985 enacted level.

Total Federal Effort

The DEA has primary responsibility for enforcing federal drug laws and policies, but it does not and can not carry the entire burden for enforcement. A number of other federal departments assist in the effort. The Federal Bureau of Investigation has concurrent jurisdiction with DEA over federal drug laws focusing on complex conspiracy investigations. The 93 U.S. attorneys are the chief federal law-enforcement officers in their districts; they are responsible for investigating and prosecuting federal drug offenses and are often involved in drug task forces and asset forfeiture cases. The Immigration and Naturalization Service performs interdiction duties through its Border Patrol and is responsible for deporting aliens convicted of drug crimes. The U.S. Marshals Service manages the Department of Justice Asset Forfeiture Fund, serves warrants on federal drug suspects and fugitives, and escorts them when in custody. The U.S. Customs Service interdicts and seizes contraband, including illegal drugs that are smuggled into the United States. The Internal Revenue Service assists with the financial aspects of drug investigations, particularly money laundering. The Bureau of Alcohol, Tobacco and Firearms investigates federal drug offenses that involve weapons. The U.S. Coast Guard enforces federal laws on the high seas and waters subject to U.S. jurisdiction, and is involved with the interdiction of drugs smuggled via water into the United States. The Federal Aviation Administration's radar system detects suspected air smugglers. The U.S. Department of Defense detects and monitors aerial and maritime transit of illegal drugs into the United States. The U.S. State Department formulates international antidrug policy and coordinates drug control efforts with foreign governments. The Postal Inspection Service of the U.S. Postal Service enforces laws against the use of the mails in transporting illegal drugs and drug paraphernalia.

International Narcotics Control

The DEA has more than 343 employees in 50 countries throughout the world. Under the policy direction of the secretary of state and the U.S. ambassadors, the DEA provides consultation, technical assistance, and training to drug law-enforcement officials in those countries. The DEA also collects and shares international drug data and assists in drug control activities and investigations where authorized. The United States encourages foreign governments to control cultivation and production of illegal drugs. So far success has been modest but promising; the following figures are for 1990. In Bolivia an estimated 8,100 hectares of coca were eradicated, representing 14% of coca cultivation. In Mexico and Guatemala about half the opium poppy crop was destroyed. Eradication of opiates is more difficult in other areas of the world due to the lack of government support for such efforts. In Belize 84% of the estimated marijuana crop was destroyed, 46% in Jamaica, 25% in Colombia, and 16% in Mexico. Colombian authorities seized 50 metric tons of cocaine and destroyed more than 300 processing labs. They also arrested 7,000 traffickers and extradited fourteen drug suspects to the United States for prosecution. Mexico seized 46.5 metric tons of cocaine and destroyed twelve heroin labs. Bolivia destroyed 33 cocaine hydrochloride labs and 1,446 maceration pits that produce cocaine paste. India seized twelve heroin labs, and Turkey seven labs.

The War on Drugs

The combined federal effort and the promise of greater international cooperation continue to bolster the DEA in its pursuit of the seemingly impossible. Drug control figures are always disappointing to cite. Domestically, no matter how large a confiscation/bust might be it is a mere token of what is left out on the street. The modest international figures for 1990 are for that year only and do not carry over. Drug crops destroyed one year can return even twofold the next year. Current political and law-enforcement thinking believes that since supply cannot be cut off, much more effort should go into stemming demand. Given that new emphasis, the DEA will still conduct business as usual, although there was some worry in 1993. The Clinton administration, wanting to streamline the federal bureaucracy, considered merging the DEA and FBI. Furthermore, it was argued that such a merger would eliminate disputes that hindered both agencies in their ability to combat and prosecute drug traffickers. FBI Director Louis J. Freeh favored the merger, which also included placing the Bureau of Alcohol, Tobacco and Firearms under FBI control. Naturally, the DEA and BATF put up strong resistance. On October 21, 1993, Attorney General Janet Reno announced that the Clinton administration would abandon its proposal. The FBI would not become the sole federal law-enforcement agency for the United States.

Bibliography

Drug Enforcement Administration: A Profile. Washington, DC: U.S. Department of Justice, DEA, Office of Planning and Evaluation, 1981.

Drug Enforcement Administration Reauthorization for Fiscal Year 1986. Hearing Before the Subcommittee on Crime, House of Representatives. Washington, DC: Government Printing Office, 1986.

Efficacy of the Federal Drug Abuse Control Strategy—State and Local Perspectives. A Report of the House Select Committee on Narcotics Abuse and Control. Washington, DC: Government Printing Office, 1984.

Federal Drug Law Enforcement Coordination. Hearing Before the House Select Committee on Narcotics Abuse and Control. Washington, DC: Government Printing Office, 1982.

International Narcotics Trafficking. Hearings Before the Senate Permanent Subcommittee on Investigations, November 10, 12, 13, 17, and 18, 1981. Washington, DC: Government Printing Office, 1981.

Rachal, P. *Federal Narcotics Enforcement: Reorganization and Reform.* Boston: Auburn House, 1982.

Wilson, James Q. *The Investigators: Managing FBI and Narcotics Agents.* New York: Basic Books, 1978.

E

Education

The first police education programs were created in the 1930s at San Jose State University and Michigan State University. Sociological programs that offered course sequences in criminology date back even further. Gradual growth in independent, identifiable criminal-justice programs occurred throughout the 1940s and 1950s but at an uneven rate across the country. A substantial number of programs were created in the California system while only a scattered few were added east of the Rocky Mountains. By the early 1960s approximately sixty programs existed nationally. The confluence of several conditions in the mid-1960s contributed to a higher-education growth rate that was probably the most rapid in any professional field.

First, an aroused awareness of civil constitutional rights followed the initiation of the civil rights movement in the early 1960s. Concern with the quality of the administration of justice was a natural outgrowth of this awareness. Second, the justice system found itself in the front lines of political confrontation as a result of both the civil rights protests and the political turmoil surrounding the Vietnam conflict. Television beamed physical encounters between police and protesters into most homes in the country. Third, crime began increasing dramatically in the early 1960s. There is considerable debate in criminology circles as to why this occurred, but it is clear that most of the increase was real and not merely an artifact of better reporting. Study commissions convened in response to these problems have unanimously recognized inadequate preparation of police personnel as contributing significantly to inappropriate system reaction.

Development of Academic Programs

The need for educational standards for police personnel was first documented in the Wickersham Commission Report in 1931. That recommendation has been reiterated by the President's Commission on Law Enforcement and the Administration of Justice in 1967, the National Advisory Commission on Civil Disorders in 1968, the Commission on the Causes and Prevention of Violence in 1969, the American Bar Association Project on Standards for Criminal Justice in 1972, the National Advisory Commission on Criminal Justice, Standards and Goals in 1973, and the Police Foundation's Advisory Commission on Higher Education for Police Officers in 1978.

Pressures for improving justice-system personnel resulted in a massive infusion of federal funds for student stipends in 1968. The Law Enforcement Education Program (LEEP) distributed more than $300 million over the following twelve years (Sherman, 1978). The consequent growth in the number of academic programs was phenomenal.

However, neither pressures for educational upgrading nor the LEEP program would have resulted in such rapid expansion had it not been for parallel development of the community college and its unique educational philosophy. These provided a conducive environment for the expansion of this nontraditional, interdisciplinary applied field of study. Such occupations were traditionally viewed by liberal arts institutions as too vocational to be the concern of higher education. The community colleges' initiation of one-year certificate and two-year associate programs at acceptable academic levels helped attract students who previously would have had to make a quantum leap from a high school to a baccalaureate degree to obtain credentials. Likewise, the community college open-door philosophy made it possible to initiate programs drawing on police practitioners who otherwise could not have gained employment at the university level. The community college's unique incorporation of all these principles, and its concomitant institutional growth, was the primary cause of expansion in criminal-justice programs from approximately fifty programs in 1960 to 750 in 1977.

Critics of the quality of police education often blame the community-college philosophy for excessive provincialism and vocationalism (Sherman, 1978). Much of the criticism is justified. However, such criticism should not blind us to the fact that the mere existence of this academic institution has accomplished more for educational upgrading than all the rhetoric of the past forty years. Even in the most vocational programs, a significant amount of curricular content is philosophically reflective and intellectually critical of the administration of justice. And in a great number of community-college programs, the curriculum is as analytic as that in any senior institution. Certainly there is room for vast improvement in quality. But the contribution of the community college to police education merits recognition. Criminal-justice education has developed in a time of continuing search in higher education for balance between traditional liberal arts baccalaureate preparation and the growth of vocational preparation as a primary mission. This issue of role and mission as it translates into specific curricular requirements is far from settled.

Criminal-justice education is not easily categorized. Some aspects of criminal-justice curricula are drawn from traditional disciplines, other aspects from professional schools, and a limited body of knowledge is truly unique to the field. The term *focused area of study* has been coined in an attempt to describe accurately the nature of criminal-justice education. Criminal justice exemplifies the need to mold general and professional education in new configurations. Realignment of higher education structures is not easy. Thus, although the growth of criminal-justice education in the last decade has been phenomenal, it has also been tumultuous.

For a number of years, institutions of higher education developed dual programming to attempt to cope with the need to maintain traditional liberal arts requirements against pressures for specific vocational preparations—

thus, the distinction between bachelor of arts and bachelor of science degrees and between transfer and terminal associate degree programs. In the last thirty years, however, a number of social/technological professions have developed with considerable curricular variability accompanied by heated debate over what is the appropriate mix of educational experience. The criminal-justice field, along with nursing, social work, and teacher education, is such a profession.

Criminal-justice academic programs differ from the others in two respects. First, criminal justice is not an identifiable profession but rather a complex of professions all working with the same societal problem—criminal offenders. Second, the need for higher education standards was recognized for the other social/technological professions far earlier than for criminal justice. Hence, current debate is not primarily over whether schoolteachers need a baccalaureate degree but over the nature of that preparation. In police education, the debate concerns not only the nature of higher education preparation, but also whether there is any need for higher education at all.

The Rationale for Collegiate Standards

It is more difficult than one might realize initially to define how college education is expected to improve police performance. For instance, in a police department with extremely low productivity in terms of arrest rates, clearance rates, and the like, one might well expect that obtaining more officers with a college background would lead to increased productivity in these areas. If this were one of the goals of recruiting college-educated officers, and the behavior of the officers was directed toward these ends, then certainly higher arrest and clearance rates would indicate the success of the imposition of higher educational requirements.

On the other hand, arrest and clearance rates are often highly inflated and, in fact, counterproductive; that is, arrests are made with insufficient evidence, or crimes are cleared on dubious criteria. If this is true, and it often can be, then the hiring of college-educated officers might cause the reduction of arrest and clearance rates, even though reductions in these rates are usually thought to indicate poorer performance. Similarly, one might expect the crime rate to go up or down, depending on the ability of officers to establish rapport with a community.

In short, determining the success of any police program, including higher personnel standards, is an extremely complex task. The appropriateness of a particular productivity measure depends on the individual agency and situational characteristics. Hence, efforts to establish the validity of higher educational standards for police are plagued by an inability to define appropriate variables to differentiate "good" from "bad" performances.

There are several rationales for educationally upgrading America's police. One relates to improving the effectiveness of police performance because of the ever-expanding expectations and definitions of performance variables. The second relates to the effectiveness with which the police are able to perform their "order maintenance" or conflict-resolution function through more balanced use of social counseling and law-enforcement techniques. Another relates to ensuring proper exercise of police discretionary power (Hoover, 1975).

It should be pointed out that these rationales, although distinctive, are not mutually exclusive. One is certainly justified in positing that better use of social counseling will ultimately mean less crime or that maintenance of democratic values in the American police service is ultimately related to its ability to control crime. Similarly, if the police are unable to control crime, it is highly unlikely that they can be expected to perform their social-service role adequately, and perhaps even less likely that they will maintain a democratic value system. The interrelatedness of the three issues strengthens even further the argument for higher educational standards.

Developing an Analytic Perspective

Recognition that critical analysis should form the foundation of basic criminal-justice academic programming is gaining increasing acceptance. In 1973 the Criminal Justice System Task Force of the National Advisory Commission on Criminal Justice Standards and Goals stipulated: "Care should be taken to separate the academic nature of the curricula from training content and functions best performed by police, courts, and corrections agencies."

The police role is not merely a technical function requiring knowledge of certain procedures and regulations. Rather, the role is imbued with great responsibility requiring insight and understanding of the social sciences. A liberal arts education based in the social sciences will best provide the kind of critical thinking and discriminating decision-making that policing demands.

Education for the performance of the police role thus exceeds a mere traineeship, as important as certain kinds of training might be. Education is designed to prepare professionals who are to exercise a great amount of discretion in the social judgments they will face. Education in this sense translates into the development of an understanding and appreciation of theory relating to the control of criminal behavior by structured societal response to such behavior.

Attitudes and perspectives result not from prescriptive training but from analysis of social structures. The attitudes that education for policing should foster are democratic ones: fundamental support of due process, compassion, humanism, a desire to effect constructive social change, and a self-concept congruent with the community-service ideal.

The administration of justice is the most visible and direct application of the principles and ideals of democratic government in the United States. As such, it is essential that balanced judgment flowing from inculcated democratic values characterize those who daily perform the roles of the criminal-justice system. The last decade has brought acknowledgment that wide discretion exists in all components of the criminal-justice system. The only guarantee that the administration of justice is truly democratic from initiation to conclusion is that the value systems of those who administer such justice are indeed democratic. The most effective means ever found to ensure the inculcation of such a value system is analytic education.

Analytic education also engenders the ability to generalize, to base responses in a given situation on an understanding of the broader context of an individual's role. The development of this ability is what educational institutions can do best. Its development follows from critical analysis of the criminal-justice system through face-to-face interaction with faculty. Teaching the "why" of criminal-justice processes is the primary function of basic academic programming. This is not to say that the importance of teaching students the "how" of various processes can be ignored. Educational institutions most certainly have a role to play in this regard, but regular academic courses should offer coursework consisting of critical analysis of the system.

Developing a Systematic Perspective

An issue that academics face in preparing students to fulfill criminal-justice roles is meeting both common and distinct preparation needs. The preparation needs are common enough that it makes little sense to establish separate and indistinguishable programs to prepare, for instance, police officers and parole officers. Both are basically human interaction occupations. At the same time, however, there are very distinct preparatory needs unique to a given role. Typically, a criminal-justice program prepares students for the following occupations:

> Police officer
> Probation officer
> Correctional counselor
> Parole officer
> Correctional officer
> Evidence technician
> Juvenile counselor
> Legal aide
> Court administrator
> Security manager
> Criminalist
> Forensic scientist

All of these roles demand some level of training and human interaction skills. All of them demand some knowledge of the law, but with different emphases. Knowledge of management and administration is often deemed appropriate, depending on the particular student's career objectives. Finally, there is the need to understand the entire justice process.

Traditionally, educational institutions have played a significant role in inculcating a sense of congruent goals and objectives in members of related professions. Hence, whenever such professionals interact with one another in the "real world," a total system perspective influences the nature of decisions made.

Curricular Recommendations

The first widely circulated guidelines recommending a model curriculum appeared in 1968 under joint sponsorship of the American Association of Community and Junior Colleges and the International Association of Chiefs of Police, entitled *Guidelines for Law Enforcement Education Programs in Community and Junior Colleges*, by Thompson Crockett and James Stinchcomb. Under sponsorship of Law Enforcement Assistant Administration's (LEAA's) National Institute of Law Enforce-

ment and Criminal Justice (NILE-CJ), two monographs were prepared in the early 1970s, the first by Peter Lejins, entitled *Introducing a Law Enforcement Curriculum at a State University*, and the second by Charles W. Tenney, Jr., entitled *Higher Education Programs in Law Enforcement and Criminal Justice*. In 1976 NILE-CJ released a monograph by Larry T. Hoover entitled *Police Educational Characteristics and Curricula*, which includes guidelines for a recommended professional course of study for a criminal-justice baccalaureate curriculum. A 1977 publication of the American Association of Community and Junior Colleges, entitled *Guidelines for Criminal Justice Programs in Community and Junior Colleges*, recommended core courses entitled Introduction to Criminal Justice, Introduction to Criminology, Concepts of Criminal Law—Legal Process, and Social Values and the Criminal Justice Process. The police option courses include Concepts of Police Operations, Police Organization Theory, Criminal Investigation, Criminal Justice Internship, and Dynamics of Substance Abuse.

There persists considerable program variability across the field as a result of the breadth of material related to the study of the structured societal response to crime. There is a general distinction between programs that focus on the study of etiology and demography of crime (i.e., traditional criminology) and those that focus on the processes involved in the administration of justice (i.e., criminal justice or administration of justice).

Larry T. Hoover

Bibliography

Berkley, George. *The Democratic Policeman.* Boston, MA: Beacon Press, 1969.

Hoover, Larry T. *Police Educational Characteristics and Curricula.* Washington, DC: Government Printing Office, 1975.

———, and Dennis W. Lund. *Guidelines for Criminal Justice Programs in Community and Junior Colleges.* Washington, DC: American Association of Community and Junior Colleges, 1977.

National Advisory Commission on Criminal Justice Standards and Goals. *A National Strategy to Reduce Crime.* Washington, DC: Government Printing Office, 1973a.

———. *Police.* Washington, DC: Government Printing Office, 1973b.

President's Commission on Law Enforcement and the Administration of Justice. *Task Force Report on Police.* Washington, DC: Government Printing Office, 1967.

Sherman, Lawrence W. *The Quality of Police Education.* San Francisco: Jossey-Bass, 1978.

Smith, D.C. *Empirical Studies of Higher Education and Police Performance.* Washington, DC: Police Foundation, 1978.

Strecher, Victor G. *The Environment of Law Enforcement.* Englewood Cliffs, NJ: Prentice-Hall, 1971.

Webb, Vincent, and Richard Ward. *Quest for Quality.* New York: University Publications, 1984.

Emergency Management

There are many types of emergencies and disasters—both natural and man-made. Natural ones include floods, hurricanes, earthquakes, tidal waves, tornadoes, volcanic eruptions, landslides, avalanches, blizzards, forest fires, wind damage, resource shortages, and drought. Those man-made typically encompass power outages, explosions, civil disorders, work stoppages, biological attack, industrial and transportation accidents, hazardous-material spills, water contamination, radiological and arson incidents, and chemical, nuclear, and terrorist attacks.

Police officials will be blamed if they are not prepared to respond properly to emergencies and disasters—natural or man-made. Court decisions have already established legal precedents in both these important areas of the law. Failure to initiate emergency management often results not only in expensive and time-consuming litigation but also in additional loss of life and property.

Public Expectations

The potential for some type of natural or man-made disaster exists in all communities. Under normal circumstances, few police agencies place a high priority on emergency management. Citizens, however, expect their local law-enforcement agencies to be able to manage a disaster effectively. Most citizens routinely expect their local police departments to:

- Alert citizens in advance of a disaster.
- Quickly and accurately assess the magnitude of an emergency.
- Keep citizens properly informed of the situation.
- Safely evacuate dangerous areas.
- Move citizens to a safe place.
- Provide for a rapid restoration of services.
- Give assistance in the form of recovery services.
- Mitigate the impact of future emergencies.
- Be able to adequately protect life and property.

Not many police departments, though, are actually prepared for emergencies. Many local emergency plans are merely appendages of their local-government structure and normal operations. Many chiefs of police, faced with the pressures of their daily workload, either ignore or delegate responsibility for emergency management to a lower-level coordinator. The results of a survey conducted by the International City Management Association in 1983 are highlighted below:

- Few communities seem to be prepared properly for a crisis or disaster.
- Local governments report over $16 billion in property losses, 2,490 deaths, and 9,161 injuries from disasters since 1970.
- Most local governments (83 percent of cities and 90 percent of counties) have a formal emergency management plan. The rest have no formal response plan. Communication and coordination problems were reported as the major difficulty during the last disaster.
- Only 81 percent of cities and 73 percent of counties consider their technology to be sufficient when responding to emergencies.
- City and county managers have, in recent years, become more aware of the need to adequately prepare for emergencies.
- The threat of a major disaster striking an American city today is greater than ever before in our history.
- Cities and counties with professional administrators had a noticeably higher rate of response than did those with other forms of government.

Emergency Management Guidelines

When incorporated into local governments' response plans, these guidelines will help law-enforcement personnel to limit the loss of life and property in times of a disaster or emergency:

- Public officials should be reminded that they may be held liable if they are not thoroughly competent in their emergency-management responsibilities.
- Known hazards should be accounted for in the emergency-management plan.
- Most of the emergency responsibility should be placed on employees who live in or near the city.
- Only current job titles and organization structures should be used in the plan to avoid ambiguity and confusion.
- Up-to-date telephone numbers for emergency-response team members should be listed in the plan. Backup personnel should also be identified.
- Most plans list functional responsibilities rather than the actual tasks to be performed. Many plans use such phrases as "conduct a reconnaissance" and "evacuate the area" without setting forth what steps should be taken.
- Detailed tasks should be identified for all functional responsibilities. Nothing should be left to the imagination.
- Emergency-management responsibilities are frequently not centralized, making it difficult to determine precise roles and duties.
- All responsibilities should be centralized and clearly specified—both at the top management and department levels.
- All plans should list community resources that could be used in a disaster. The names and locations of hospitals, social service agencies, doctors, nurses, and equipment should be known in advance.
- Most local governments have mutual-aid agreements for police and fire services only. These pacts should be expanded to ensure the availability of a wide variety of resources and services.
- Don't test the city's plan in an actual emergency. Conduct simulated disaster exercises beforehand. Work out all the "bugs" in advance.
- The Emergency Operations Center (EOC) is the pulse of any government's response to a disaster. Its functions, delegation of authority, and individual du-

ties should be specified clearly in the plan.
- Most emergency management plans are formulated and implemented from the top down. Plans should be drawn up or revised by an "emergency-management committee" to elicit the cooperation of those people involved in the plan's implementation.
- A provision to waive building codes and zoning laws temporarily should be included in the plan. This will allow for the use of temporary housing or mobile homes on residential sites once they have been cleared for use.
- Since the appointed manager is usually held responsible, he or she should not delegate the total administration of the plan to others.

Of course the local police department alone cannot assume all these responsibilities but must coordinate its emergency management with that of other local-government departments, hospitals, social organizations, and other groups. Full integration of duties among all those concerned with public welfare is the key.

Roger L. Kemp

Bibliography
Drabek, Thomas E. *A Study of Managerial Strategies in Local Emergency Preparedness Agencies.* Denver, CO: University of Denver, 1983.
Federal Emergency Management Agency. *The "Body of Knowledge" in Emergency Management.* Washington, DC: FEMA, June 1983.
Guffrida, Louis O., Director, FEMA. *The Integrated Emergency Management System.* Washington, DC: FEMA, May 20, 1983.
ICMA and FEMA Joint Report. *How Prepared Is Your Community for its Next Emergency? A Manager's Checklist.* Local Government Emergency Management Handbook Series No. 2. Washington, DC: ICMA-FEMA, 1983.
Kemp, Roger L. "The Role of Emergency Management in America's Local Governments." *Hazard Monthly* 11(11) (1982).
———. "Preparedness vs. Liability." *Response* 5(6) (1986).
———. "The Public Official and Emergency

Management." *Journal of Civil Defense* 19(2) (1986).

Emotion Management

The expression of emotions in the United States has been described as the gradual domestication of impulsive behavior. According to Elias (1982), there has been an increasing tendency to self-consciously modify our expressive behavior to that of perceived group standards. Liljestrom (1983) goes so far as to suggest that our culture emphasizes rationality and, as a result, lacks respect for feelings. This tends to inhibit individuals from taking their own emotions seriously and often prevents them from analyzing their responses to emotional situations. Similarly, individuals find it difficult to distinguish manipulations and false pretensions from truthful and spontaneous emotions.

Emotions can be experienced at both the surface and the deep levels (Denzin, 1985; Gorden, 1981). Surface emotions are easily known to observers through physical and verbal expressions (Goffman, 1961). Deep emotions, on the other hand, are rarely visible, being studiously held in check by the individual (Sommers, 1984). We learn to control our emotional responses through what Hochschild (1983) terms "emotion norms." These are subjective experiences that are to be expected and accepted in particular situations. However, there are those situations in which individuals are unsure whether the intensity of the emotions is appropriate. In such instances they may define their emotional responses by comparing situations (Schachter, 1959). In short, the individual utilizes similarly situated others as a reference group for determining the intensity and quality of contextual emotional expression. Nowhere is this more consciously acted upon than in the situational interactions between professionals and clients in maintaining social distance.

One element of professional socialization is the process of learning to develop appropriately controlled affect when interacting with clients (Kadushin, 1962). Professionals are expected to act "personably" but not "personally" in their relations with those they serve (Smith and Kleinman, 1989); that is, professionals should maintain polite and courteous relations without revealing their own personal feelings. The preservation of social distance is critical.

According to Shibutani (1961:383, 385), social distance is maximized in situations in which each person maintains his or her personal reserve. As long as one is self-conscious and confines oneself to playing conventional roles, expectations of professional–client relations are reinforced:

> There are cultural prescriptions as to the appropriate sentiments to be developed toward each of the other participants in standardized activities. . . . Attempts to control sentiments usually consist of social distance. An effort is made to minimize the possibility of sympathetic identification. The greater the social distance, the longer the behavior is likely to remain subject to social control. When people get to know one another too intimately, personal claims develop, and allowances are made which interfere with strict adherence to conventional norms. But for the effective performance of any of their duties, all parties must deny sentimental consideration.

Shibutani further claims that sentiments are directly associated with empathy in that they embody personalized meanings acquired through identification with others, whereby specific emotional reactions are evoked and understood in specific situational contexts. Empathy is inversely related to social distance and thus permits unacquainted persons to be perceived as objects.

Professionals are expected to refrain from personal involvement with clients; consequently, they must maintain a detached and dispassionate demeanor in their professional encounters. Such a professional orientation among police is intended to avert identification in citizen interactions and to ensure objective and consistent law-enforcement actions. For police, social distance functions to inhibit affected responses in emotionally charged situations, allowing them to maintain a professional persona of being calm and in control, which is what the public expects. We explore the emotion management strategies employed by police officers, examining how they account for their handling of emotions in dealing with tragic events.

Police Culture and Emotional Control

As professionals trained to serve and protect, police officers are expected to maintain a poised presence, even under the most tragic circumstances. Their authority and effectiveness in handling such events would be compromised if officers could not control their emotions. In the face of human tragedy (e.g., victims of homicide, suicide, auto accidents, child abuse), officers must maintain their composure, distancing themselves from intense emotional reactions evoked in such encounters (Pogrebin and Poole, 1988). Police generally believe that the public expects them to be fearless and calm, able to handle critical situations in an objective manner. The standards that police place upon themselves for managing emotions are often severe and uncompromising.

Stratton (1984) notes that from the beginning of their law-enforcement careers, officers are socialized to repress their emotions on the job in order to maintain a professional image in the eyes of both the public and their fellow officers. Police come to view their own emotions as an occupational weakness or hazard, potentially impairing their ability to perform their duties effectively. Thus officers have difficulty dealing with the normal emotions that individuals are expected to experience in the face of tragic events. In denying their own latent emotions, police develop a shared misunderstanding of the feelings of their fellow officers.

Stratton (1984) observes that this stoic stance can also adversely impact one's primary relations off the job. Over time any display of emotion may become uncomfortable; consequently, feelings are routinely suppressed. The process of hiding one's feelings when emotional reactions are considered natural and expected becomes problematic in managing interpersonal relationships. Even among those officers who have experienced tragic events in their personal lives, emotions remain closely guarded.

Officers seldom express their personal feelings about tragic incidents because they do not feel comfortable revealing their latent concerns. The mere talking about one's pain, guilt, or fear is considered taboo. For if one must talk about personal feelings, one is seen as not really being able to handle them, i.e., not being fully in control of one's emotional responses. Smith and Kleinman (1989) report that among medical students the expression of emotions in their interaction with patients is perceived as an indication of incompetence. Emotional conflicts or dilemmas experienced in their work are rarely discussed, preventing medical students from perceiving their problems as collective ones. As a result of this professional norm, in-

terpersonal barriers for seeking common solutions are created and maintained. The police find themselves in an analogous situation where they are unable to reveal their feelings to fellow officers, let alone to discuss them, for fear of being viewed as inadequate—as not having what it takes to be a solid, dependable police officer.

As officers confront the emotional demands of tragic situations, they become increasingly cognizant of the negative label they may acquire if they are unable to control their personal feelings. Being perceived as emotionally predisposed, whether it be an expression of anger or one of sympathy, can lead to suspicions and concerns for the officer's ability to withstand the pressures of police work. For example, officers do not want a partner or backup who cannot be implicitly trusted to act decisively in any situation, for their lives may depend upon it. An officer's perceived emotional makeup is thus critical to his or her acceptance as a "regular cop." As Hochschild (1979) notes, individuals can influence the way they are perceived by others by manipulating their emotional expressions. The police often attempt to manage their displays of emotion by adopting a detached or aloof demeanor. Many police are also reluctant to express their emotions because they see such exposure as a character flaw (Maslach and Jackson, 1979). This reluctance may be attributed in part to socialization within the police culture that embraces a "toughness" ethic.

Finally, the police culture views emotional responses toward either suspects or victims as potentially status-threatening (Hunt, 1984; Manning, 1980). Sympathetic or nurturing behavior, for example, is regarded as professionally demeaning. Such behavior falls outside the realm of real police work. Following this work ethic, officers must remain free of the emotional ties that could undermine the professional–client status hierarchy or, as seen in the traditional police culture, that could compromise the integrity of the "us-versus-them" dichotomy.

Emotion Management Strategies

Emotion measures the impression of self created by a particular situation and relates how that impression compares to the sentiment of a person's identity (Averett and Heise, 1987). A vocabulary of sentiments embodies shared experiences, perceptions, and definitions of situations. It provides meaning for group activity, promotes group distinctiveness, and ensures group solidarity (Whorf, 1956). For police, sentiments appear to be couched and constrained within narrow occupational prescriptions. The police cultural norms of emotional control become the dominant individual responses, supported by a collective group consciousness. As Stryker and Serpe (1981) claim, the more important an identity is to an individual, the more often he or she will choose to act in ways which express that identity. Also, the greater the dependence of interpersonal relationships on the maintenance of consistent identities, the more committed individuals are to playing their respective roles.

One's perception of self influences his or her choice of behavioral alternatives. Individuals are motivated to act in ways that will confirm and reinforce those identities with which they have aligned themselves (Burke and Reitzes, 1981). Among police the normative expectations incumbent in a professional role identity provide the motivational basis for emotional control:

> The extent to which behavior can be organized in terms of group norms is revealed by the manner in which manifestations of emotional dispositions, generally thought to be quite spontaneous, are circumscribed in these standardized situations in which there are understandings as to how participants are supposed to feel and react (Shibutani 1961:42).

One's conception of this role behavior necessitates an organization of appropriate narrative accounts for his or her emotional responses. These accounting techniques in turn serve to inhibit both role behavior and emotional responses outside acceptable group standards. Group norms are thus reinforced, group solidarity is enhanced, and group identity is confirmed.

While a professional role identity serves to minimize the differences in behavior and emotional response among individual police officers, how their work and attendant emotions are perceived varies according to their position in the police organization. Differences in perspectives of police work are particularly evident between line officers (who deal directly with suspects and victims, up close, and personal) and command staff (who manage and administer the organization, far removed from street work). It is not surprising then that street cops and management cops do not always share similar sentiments for tragic situations.

According to Coutu (1951), professional training and socialization are designed to prevent role-taking (e.g., empathy or identification with a client) and to ensure professional role-playing. For police, the implication is that if an officer in dealing with a suspect "took the role of the other," he or she might not be able to exercise discretion fairly and uniformly. Yet judicious role-taking may be useful in performing certain law-enforcement tasks and achieving specific law-enforcement objectives.

Poole and Pogrebin (1989) note that a lack of role-taking ability may foster negative consequences. Failing to show an understanding or concern for a victim or suspect's situation could inhibit cooperation and communication, thus limiting the officer's investigative effectiveness. There are those occasions when role-taking encounters with victims or suspects are thus deemed situationally acceptable, or even desirable, in carrying out police duties.

Emotion Work

Police officers are not directly taught to control their emotions in any formal context, such as at the police academy; rather, they learn appropriate emotional responses incrementally through on-the-job training experiences. This initial socialization period is particularly intense for police recruits during their probationary period; consequently, they come to depend on their field training officers as their primary role models and significant others in acclimating themselves to the police culture. Part of this occupational socialization process is what Shields and Koster (1989:44) refer to as "emotion culture, . . . a group's set of beliefs, vocabulary, regulative norms, and other relational resources pertaining to emotion." Emotion culture informs the individual of shared group norms regarding expectations of appropriate emotional responses and also sets the stage for the emotion set the individual internalizes and comes to rely upon as nature.

To Hochschild (1979) "emotion work" involves attempts to change the intensity or quality of one's feelings in order to bring them into line with situational emotional demands. She points out that emotion work is necessary when individuals perceive that they are in violation of prevailing feeling rules. These rules dictate what individuals with particular identities ought to feel in any given situation. The professionalization of private emotions helps to routinize occupational encounters, thus increasing the predictability of social interaction (Hochschild, 1983). But it is also likely that professional desensitization can be generalized beyond the confines of occupational experiences, negatively affecting one's entire emotional response set (see Violanti and Marshall, 1983).

Emotion work serves to modify one's genuine feelings. When individuals encounter emotions inconsistent with their committed identities, they seek to manipulate the outward expression of their emotions for others, keeping their underlying personal feelings private (Gorden, 1981). This is a common strategy utilized by officers when they are witness to the types of tragedies endemic to police work. Suppressing true feelings often leads to a protracted emotional state that ultimately needs to be resolved in order for police themselves to make sense of their world.

Impression management is guided by conscious strategies to convey a particular self-image to a social audience (Goffman, 1959) and by an adherence to cultural norms of expression management in particular situations (Ekman and Friesen, 1975). Yet the stoic posture for many officers results in an internal burden that is never satisfactorily dealt with.

Humor and Diffusion of Tragedy
Displays of emotion, although quite understandable in tragic encounters, may be perceived as an indication of vulnerability. To avoid this impression, officers often couch their feelings in humor. In this way officers are able to lessen the harshness of the tragic experience and vent their emotions in an acceptable, indirect manner. Joking relations concerning tragic events provide a way for officers to express their emotions without damaging their professional image as confident and fearless (Pogrebin and Poole, 1988). It is through humor that police can collectively empathize with each other's feelings. As Fine (1983:175) argues, such humor fosters "a source of control for the participant on how to deal with threatening or embarrassing topics."

Management of emotional expressions enhances group functioning by maintaining collective action (Gorden, 1981). Emotional anxieties and tensions are thus neutralized and normalized via collective coping strategies that reinforce group solidarity. What officers fail to comprehend is that when they rationalize tragic events through humor, they may be manifesting a need to share emotional experiences (Alpert and Dunham, 1988).

However, there are those tragedies where humor would be considered untoward and exceeding respectable bounds. Some tragic occurrences are so emotionally charged that humor is considered taboo; these feelings are implicitly understood and guarded. More so than in any other police–citizen encounter, emotion management is universally somber when tragedy involves children (e.g., child abuse, accidents, and crib deaths). Stenross and Kleinman (1989) claim that the tragic consequences of crimes place a great emotional burden on police to make sense of these outcomes; that is, tragic events are often more difficult to manage without some meaningful assessment of their impact on victims. When children are affected by crime, making sense of tragic consequences is particularly problematic.

Conclusion

The expression of personal feelings is severely limited within the police culture. Professional conduct norms dictate that officers must remain calm and in control, constantly guarding their emotions. They learn that emotions such as anger, disgust, and sadness must not be displayed in order to maintain a professional image for the public and their fellow officers. Their ability to deal directly with emotional stress, strain, and anxiety is, therefore, highly constrained. Officers are likely to experience difficulty accepting their lack of control or understanding of the tragic situations they encounter.

While emotional suppression may serve to achieve occupationally functional objectives (e.g., in-group solidarity and professional demeanor), over time such latent feelings may take their toll on the quality or effectiveness of police performance. For example, prolonged suppression of emotions may adversely affect police–citizen encounters. Hardening of emotions may cause officers to be less understanding and responsive to the problems of citizens with whom they interact. Protecting oneself from emotional penetration while on duty can be perceived by citizens as callousness and insensitivity, a perception that does not lend itself to citizen confidence in or support for their police. Ultimately, tragic events may help to shape an officer's view of the police role or even to define his or her style of policing.

Mark R. Pogrebin
Eric D. Poole

Bibliography

Alpert, G.P., and R.G. Dunham. *Policing Urban America.* Prospect Heights, IL: Waveland Press, 1988

Averett, C., and D.R. Heise. "Modifying Social Identities: Amalgamation, Attributions and Emotions." *Journal of Mathematical Sociology* 13 (1987): 103–32.

Burke, P.J., and D.C. Reitzes. "The Link Between Identity and Role Performance." *Social Psychology Quarterly* 44 (1981): 83–92.

Coutu, W. "Role Playing Versus Role Taking: An Appeal for Clarification." *American Sociological Review* 16 (1951): 180–84.

Denzin, N.K. "Emotion and Lived Experience." *Symbolic Interaction* 8 (1985): 223–40.

Ekman, P., and W.V. Friesen. *Unmasking the Face: A Guide to Recognizing Emotions from Facial Clues.* Englewood Cliffs, NJ: Prentice-Hall, 1975.

Elias, N. *The Civilizing Process.* Trans. E. Jephcott. New York: Pantheon Books, 1982.

Fine, G.A. "Sociological Approaches to the Study of Humor." In *Handbook of Humor Research.* Vol. 1. Eds. P.E. McGhee and J.H. Goldstein. New York: Springer-Verlag, 1983.

Goffman, E. *The Presentation of Self in Everyday Life.* Garden City, NY: Doubleday, 1959.

———. *Encounters: Two Studies in the Sociology of Interaction.* Indianapolis: Bobbs-Merrill, 1961.

Gorden, S. "The Sociology of Sentiments and Emotion." In *Social Psychology: Sociological Perspectives.* Eds. M. Rosenburg and R.H. Turner. New York: Basic Books, 1981.

Hochschild, A.R. "Emotion Work, Feeling Rules and Social Structure." *American Journal of Sociology* 85 (1979): 551–75.

———. *The Managed Heart: Commercialization of Human Feeling.* Berkeley: University of California Press, 1983.

Hunt, J. "The Development of Rapport Through the Negotiation of Gender in Field Work among Police." *Human Organization* 43 (1984): 283–96.

Kadushin, C. "Social Distance Between Client and Professional." *American Journal of Sociology* 67 (1962): 517–31.

Liljestrom, R. "The Public Child, the Commercial Child and Our Child." In *The Child and Other Cultural Inventions.* Eds. F.S. Kessel and A.W. Siegel. New York: Praeger, 1983.

Manning, P.K. "Organization and Environment: Influences on Police Work." In *The Effectiveness of Policing.* Eds. R.V.G. Clark and J.M. Hough. Farnborough, England: Gower, 1980.

Maslach, C., and S.E. Jackson. "Burned-out Cops and Their Families." *Psychology Today* 12 (May 1979): 59–62.

Pogrebin, M.R., and E.D. Poole. "Humor in the Briefing Room: A Study of the Strategic Uses of Humor among Police." *Journal of Contemporary Ethnography* 17 (1988): 182–210.

Poole, E.D., and M.R. Pogrebin. "Attribution and Empathy: Interaction Between Detectives and Suspects Under Arrest." *Police Studies* 12 (1989): 132–40.

Schachter, S. *The Psychology of Affiliation.* Palo Alto, CA: Stanford University Press, 1959.

Shibutani, T. *Society and Personality. An Interaction Approach to Social Psychology.* Englewood Cliffs, NJ: Prentice-Hall, 1961.

Shields, S.A., and B.A. Koster. "Emotional Stereotyping in Child Rearing Manuals, 1915–1980." *Social Psychology Quarterly* 52 (1989): 44–55.

Smith, A.C., and S. Kleinman. "Managing Emotions in Medical Schools: Students' Contacts with the Living and the Dead." *Social Psychology Quarterly* 52 (1989): 56–69.

Sommers, S. "Reported Emotions and Conventions of Emotionality among College Students." *Journal of Personality and Social Psychology* 46 (1984): 207–15.

Stenross, B., and S. Kleinman. "The Highs and Lows of Emotional Labor: Detectives' Encounters with Criminals and Victims," *Journal of Contemporary Ethnography* 17 (1989): 435–52.

Stratton, J.G. *Police Passages.* Manhattan Beach, CA: Glennon, 1984.

Stryker, S., and R. Serpe. "Commitment, Identity, Salience and Role Behavior." In

Personality, Roles and Social Behaviour.
Eds. W. Ickes and E.S. Knowles. New
York: Springer-Verlag, 1981.

Violanti, J.M., and J.R. Marshall. "The Police Stress Process." *Journal of Police Science and Administration* 13 (1983): 106–10.

Whorf, B.L. *Language, Thought and Reality: Selected Writings of Benjamin Lee Whorf.* Ed. J.B. Carroll. Cambridge, MA: MIT Press, 1956.

Richard Edward Enright

Richard Edward Enright (1871–1953), police commissioner of New York City, was born in Campbell, New York. Before becoming a policeman at the age of twenty-five, he worked as a telegrapher in Elmira and Queens. Twenty-two years later he became the first commissioner to have risen from the ranks. A mere lieutenant at the time, he had been passed over three times for promotion to captain, having angered his superiors by championing rank-and-file police once too often while president of the Police Lieutenants' Benevolent Association. But a new mayor, John F. Hylan, respected Enright, elevated him, and together they confronted turbulent New York City during World War I and into Prohibition.

In his first year as commissioner, 1918, Enright set about changing things. One of his campaigns concerned money donations to assist beginning police. A rookie, paid only $1,200 a year, had to buy his own uniforms and equipment, costing about $284.00. Those necessities did not last long and had to be renewed frequently. Enright asked for public contributions to a loan account instead of government funds because he thought if those were granted, every city employee would demand a paraphernalia allowance. Another hurdle to be dealt with was World War I; police made ideal soldiers and he did not want to be left without a force to combat domestic enemies. So he went to Washington, D.C., to plead draft exemption for his police. When suffragettes exhorted him to employ more women, his response was to hire a few, but he shrank from committing himself fully to their cause. When routine disappearances of people plagued the city, his answer was to increase the hours of operation of the Missing Persons Bureau to twenty-four a day. He discredited the old method of catching lax or dishonest policemen through the use of spies ("shooflies"), substituting for it an honor system, which worked for a time. Previously, for a policeman to earn merit his arrest record had to be high; Enright revised the policy to rule out any harassment of citizens by an officer zealous for promotion. Yet, somewhat in contradiction, because of the war he ordered his men to arrest "slackers" evading conscription and to roundup known "enemy aliens" for safekeeping.

War transgressors in hand, he ordered his vice squad to close every illegal gambling resort in the city; he simply would not pay homage to smug politicians or diamond-bedecked gangsters. But his most controversial move came when he abolished the Crime Prevention Bureau and the Social Service Squad. Those two revered agencies had become staples of the department and their demise shocked police and citizens alike. The Crime Prevention Bureau (262 officers) acted as a second detective force in plainclothes. The Social Service Squad (80 officers), also in plainclothes, went into the community to reclaim wayward youth from a life of crime. Friction had sparked between the uniformed and plainclothes police because of divergent management styles and the greater freedom enjoyed by those out of uniform. Enright settled the issue by returning the "privileged ones" to uniform. There was no room in the department for warring factions. It had been quite a first year of change for this man of purpose.

Enright endured harsh criticism for cutting out dead wood. He transferred, demoted, or forced into retirement men he considered expendable or counterproductive to his aims, at the same time begging the mayor for new recruits. He wanted young stalwarts molded by him, not hangers-on counting their days until pension time. But he erred badly when he evicted "Honest Dan" Costigan, celebrated for his vice investigations; that action injured his credibility and it would take many good deeds later to right the wrong. Next in his trial by fire came Prohibition and with it defiant crime. Only a few years before he had purified the city, but in 1922 he had to stand up to charges of graft and corruption in his own department. Wheeling back momentarily, he straightened himself and brought libel suits against his detractors. Neither side won a clear victory. Then, in 1924, he was forced to prefer charges against some of his men, thirteen inspectors and many more deputy inspectors and captains, for "failure to prevent violation of the Prohibition laws." An odious task, the two series of suits conflicted with each other. The first proclaimed police innocence, the second guilt. Prohibition was to blame more than Enright; it was too difficult to keep everyone law-abiding, even the police, especially given that many people viewed Prohibition as an ill-conceived stricture.

Enright won the confidence of his officers anew by allowing them more days off, by enlarging the police relief fund, by improving the pension system, and by establishing a convalescent camp near Tannersville, New York, for ill or wounded members of the force. For all police he developed the International Police Conference to promote worldwide interaction and cooperation. An occasional writer, he urged that everyone be fingerprinted not just for police but for universal registration, the purpose being to resolve any type of identity question; and he insisted that every criminal should have to pay damages to both victim and police with money earned while in prison.

One year before he retired as commissioner (December 30, 1925), Brentano's published his first novel *Vultures of the Dark*. The plot pitted a shrewd detective against a master crook whose daughter he had fallen in love with. Reviewers praised Enright for his gripping account of detection methods but dismissed his overlay of romance. Encouraged by the attention he dashed off a second novel, *The Borrowed Shield* (G. Howard Watt, 1925), which few people noticed and his career as a novelist ended. Also that same year he completed the writing of *Syllabus and Instruction Guide of the Police Academy*, a 148-page manual.

After retirement he published a pulp magazine with little success. Then he ventured into an automatic alarm signal business, which did make him some money. Later he initiated a law-enforcement service for the National Recovery Administration (a New Deal emergency measure to reduce unemployment [1933]). At his death he was director of the United States Detective Bureau. His hobbies were memorizing poetry, reading history and philosophy, and mulling over Napoleon's triumphs and failures. A serious injury to his spinal cord took his life.

Bibliography

Enright, Richard E. "Everybody Should Be Fingerprinted." *Scientific American* 133 (October 1925): 224–25.

———. "Our Biggest Business—Crime." *North American Review* 228(4) (October 1929): 385–91.

Moore, H.H. "A Plan to Help Policemen Out of Tight Places." *The Outlook* 120 (September 25, 1918): 126–127.

New York Times 5 (February 10, 1918): 1; 15 (September 5, 1953): 1.

Entrapment

Of all of the terms that are employed in discussing police operations perhaps the most misunderstood is that of *entrapment*. A police officer is disguised as an elderly bag lady walking the streets of a run-down neighborhood and is accosted by a young thug. Immediately surveillance team members rush the scene and arrest him. He screams, "Entrapment!" A young female officer dressed like a hooker is leaning on a lamp post and a passing motorist solicits her for an act of prostitution and he is arrested. He claims he was entrapped. The police set up a storefront sting operation where they act as fences and buy stolen merchandise. Individuals caught in the sting complain that they were entrapped.

Are the above instances cases of entrapment? Probably not. In these three instances the police are merely creating a situation in which an individual who is disposed or inclined to commit a criminal act has the opportunity to do so. He or she committed the illegal act and was arrested. These procedures are similar to the police setting traps to apprehend individuals who are actively engaged in committing ongoing criminal activities, such as speed traps using radar, one-way mirrors to observe thefts, or staking out liquor or convenience stores to nab armed robbers. Such situations do not amount to entrapment as it is usually defined.

Entrapment is defined as a law-enforcement practice where the police plan, suggest, encourage, or aid in the commission of a particular crime that would not otherwise have occurred in order to make an arrest. Thus, entrapment can occur only if the idea for the crime originates with law-enforcement officials or someone working on their behalf.

The utilization of police procedures that can be construed as fitting within the definition of entrapment seems to be growing. The reason for this is threefold. First, the police are under a great deal of pressure to reduce crime and often the police perceive that the courts have restricted many of the traditional enforcement practices, especially in the area of search and seizure. The second reason for the increased prevalence of these practices is related to the nature of the laws police are called upon to enforce, specifically white-collar and victimless crime laws. These offenses are extremely difficult to detect and most often do not have complainants; thus the police must resort to proactive, covert enforcement strategies. The third, more cynical reason is that specialized police units are under enormous political, both internal and external, pressure to make significant numbers of arrests, which can induce officers to literally create crimes in order to meet quotas.

The most notorious entrapment case of modern times involved the internationally renowned millionaire automaker, John De Lorean. On October 19, 1982, a multimillion dollar cocaine deal was concluded in a Los Angeles hotel room as the profiteer, John De Lorean, toasted the success of this clandestine operation. Moments later De Lorean found out that the two individuals playing the roles of "financier" and "distributor" were FBI special agents and the "dealer" a paid government informer. The entire meeting had been videotaped and De Lorean was under arrest for conspiracy to traffic fifty-five pounds of cocaine. De Lorean was ultimately acquitted on all eight counts of conspiring to smuggle $24 million worth of cocaine on the basis of the entrapment defense.

Entrapment and the Entrapment Defense
There is another source of confusion that arises when one attempts to distinguish between entrapment as a police procedure and the entrapment defense as it is applied by the courts. The entrapment defense, it should be pointed out, allows the defendant who admits factual guilt to be excused from criminal liability and punishment because the police have in essence abused their power. In order to comprehend the distinction between the police practice and the defense it is necessary to examine some cases where the issue of entrapment has been addressed by the courts. To date only five entrapment cases have been heard by the United States Supreme Court. In the first, *Sorrells v. United States* (1932), a federal agent posing as a tourist made numerous requests for Sorrels to sell him liquor in violation of prohibition status. Sorrells finally relented and obtained some from

another person and was arrested when he sold it to the agent. In *Sherman v. United States* (1958), Sherman, a drug addict undergoing treatment, met a government informer at his doctor's office who also claimed to be undergoing treatment and who repeatedly pleaded with Sherman to get drugs for him. Ultimately, Sherman consented and was arrested when he sold the drugs to him. In *United States v. Russell* (1973), government agents provided an essential, difficult to obtain, ingredient for the manufacture of a drug; then purchased the drug from the defendant, who had manufactured it and arrested him. In the next case, *Hampton v. United States* (1976), a government agent provided Hampton with an illegal drug another agent had promised to buy at a high price. Hampton was arrested when he made the sale. In the last case, *Jacobson v. United States* (1992), two agents of the U.S. Postal Service sent solicitations through five fictitious organizations and a bogus pen pal, to explore Jacobson's willingness to order pieces of child pornography by mail. They had obtained his name and address from a bookstore list indicating that Jacobson had previously ordered two *Bare Boys* magazines containing photographs of nude preteen and teenage boys. At the time Jacobson had ordered these magazines federal law permitted the distribution of this kind of material. After two years Jacobson responded to the repeated solicitations, out of curiosity, and was arrested after a controlled delivery of a photocopy of a pornographic magazine.

The primary criterion that the Supreme Court has used in deciding guilt or innocence in cases where the defendant pleads "not guilty by reason of entrapment" is whether the defendant was predisposed to commit crimes of the type charged. If defendants have been found ready and willing to commit the type of crime charged, they have been found guilty despite the fact that the police instigated the commission of the crime in question. The Court ruled that the defendants in Sorrells, Sherman, and Jacobson were not predisposed and thus reversed their convictions. In Russell and Hampton, however, the Court found that the defendants were predisposed and upheld their convictions.

The application of the criterion of predisposition as the requirement for conviction of an individual who claims he/she was entrapped has been defined as the "subjective test" of entrapment. The conduct of the police in enticing or otherwise getting the individual to commit the crime is not called into question, however outrageous that conduct might be. An "objective test," which has received only minority support of the Court, would consider police conduct, not predisposition of the defendant, to be the dispositive factor in determining legal guilt. As Justice Frankfurter stated in *Sherman:* "No matter what the defendant's past record and present inclinations to criminality, or the depths to which he has sunk in the estimation of society, certain police conduct to ensnare him into further crime is not to be tolerated." This objective criteria brings into question what the nature of police conduct in a free society should be. This issue is basic to concerns for the ethical responsibility of law enforcement as it continues to strive to be a truly recognized and accepted profession by the American public.

Given the definition of entrapment proposed above, it should be apparent that police conduct, and not the legal determination of entrapment, must be the criterion used to label police behavior. The legal distinction made by the courts is a separate issue.

B. Grant Stitt

Bibliography

Final Report of the Select Committee to Study Undercover Activities of Components of the Department of Justice. Washington, DC: Government Printing Office, 1983.

Greaney, G.M. "Crossing the Constitutional Line: Due Process and the Law Enforcement Justification." *Notre Dame Law Review* 67 (1992): 745–97.

Goldsmith, M. *Entrapment Defense in Narcotics Cases: Guidelines for Law Enforcement.* Washington, DC: U.S. Department of Justice, Bureau of Justice Assistance, 1990.

Jacobson v. United States 112 S.Ct. 1535 (1992).

Marx, Gary T. *Undercover: Police Surveillance in America.* Berkeley and Los Angeles: University of California Press, 1988.

Miller, Frank W., et al. "Undercover Investigations." In *Police Function.* Eds. F.W. Miller et al. Westbury, NY: Foundation Press, 1991.

O'Neill, Kevin H. "Entrapment, De Lorean and the Undercover Operation: A Constitutional Connection." *John Marshall Law Review* 18 (1985): 342–405.

Sale, J.A., and B.P. Kuehne. "Law of Entrapment and Governmental Overreaching." In *White-Collar Crime: Business and Regulatory Offenses.* Eds. Otto G. Obermaier and Robert G. Morvillo. New York: Seminar Press, 1990.

Skolnick, Jerome H. "Risks of Covert Facilitation." *Journal of Social Issues* 43 (1987): 79–85.

Stitt, B. Grant, and Gene G. James. "Entrapment: An Ethical Analysis." In *Moral Issues in Police Work.* Eds. Frederick A. Elliston and Michael Feldberg. Totowa, NJ: Rowman & Allenheld, 1985.

Stotland, Ezra. "Taking the Crime out of Covert Facilitation." *Journal of Social Issues* 43 (1987): 95–100.

Whelan, M.F.J. "Lead Us Not Into (Unwarranted) Temptation: A Proposal to Replace the Entrapment Defense with a Reasonable-Suspicion Requirement." *University of Pennsylvania Law Review* 133 (June 1985): 1193–230.

E

Environmental Crimes

Chemical wastes have been dumped into America's environment for over 350 years, dating back to Pilgrim settlements in Massachusetts and the manufacture of saltpeter and alum. By the late 1930s, the chemical industry in the United States was producing over 170 million pounds of synthetic-organic chemicals annually. This figure skyrocketed to an estimated 2 trillion pounds annually by the late 1980s, a direct result of the "chemical revolution" that has transformed America since World War II. While the chemical revolution benefits the public by creating new products to enhance living standards, it also has a significant downside. The chemical revolution has produced millions of pounds of hazardous waste, and alarmingly, if early 1980s estimates of only 10 percent proper disposal are accurate, America faces an enormous silent enemy.

Pollution laws existed at both the state and federal levels by 1899; however, more than sixty years passed before there were criminal sanctions for illegal disposal of hazardous wastes. In the late 1970s and early 1980s, the Resource Conservation and Recovery Act (RCRA) and "superfund" legislation finally allowed prosecutors to seek stiff criminal sanctions for the illegal disposal of hazardous wastes. As a result tremendous progress has been made in the effort to enforce environmental laws. Approximately 614 indictments or informations have been filed, over $31 million in criminal fines have been imposed, and 474 corporations or individuals have been convicted.

Investigative Plan
A typical environmental crime investigation may begin with a complaint from a former disgruntled employee, who says that a certain company, in order to avoid the high costs of legal disposal, buried over three hundred 55-gallon drums of hazardous waste in the back part of the company's property. If the allegation is determined to be credible, several critical steps are taken. The hazardous wastes involved are identified, the party responsible for dumping the wastes is identified, and the investigation is documented in order to prove criminal intent. As soon as a case is opened, investigators learn as much as possible about the suspect company—what the company is authorized and not authorized to do. Investigators also determine what documentation the company is required to maintain so they will know what should be reviewed or inspected when confronting the company. Much of the information that investigators need is available from state, local, and regulatory agencies. For example, states maintain lists of authorized hazardous waste generators and transporters, as well as treatment and storage/disposal facilities. Fire departments sometimes have information concerning on-site inspections or unusual occurrences at the company's facilities. Health departments may have complaints of contamination in nearby areas. In addition, licensing agencies have information about business operations, company officers and owners, and annual reports. And reports filed with the Securities and Exchange Commission may reveal principal products, legal proceedings, financial data, and other significant information.

There are several effective techniques to use during hazardous-waste investigations:

- Stationary, moving, and aerial surveillance to document ongoing criminal activity;
- Long-range photography and closed-circuit television to document probable cause;
- Tracing the origins of drum and barrel markings to manufacturers and purchasers;
- Remote monitoring devices to gather evidence;
- Consensual monitoring of information and cooperating witnesses to obtain first-hand incriminating statements; and
- Grand juries, which may result in unexpected evidence through compelled cooperation.

Since exposure to hazardous materials causes physiological symptoms, investigators should let their senses help them in the investigation. It is also a good idea for investigators to take photographs to provide clear evidence of what they see. It is important to note any precautions the company has taken to prevent waste from escaping, such as fences, settling ponds, warning signs, and monitoring devices. If the company uses these precautions as a defense during prosecution, investigators should be ready to explain why they did not work.

An investigative support team should be put together to ensure proper preparation and execution of a site sampling plan; proper evidence collection and chain of custody; and proper analyses, storage, and disposal of samples. A prosecutor should be available not only to recognize and interpret legal nuances but also to evaluate the potential for prosecution. Other support team members include technical specialists (engineers, chemists, geologists); equipment operators for detecting and unearthing buried evidence; health and safety specialists who know the dangers of exposing hazardous substances; regulatory-agency personnel who evaluate public health risks; and photographers, sketch artists, legal clerks, and the like to substantiate evidence. During on-site excavation, regular police assist with crowd control. Fire departments and emergency medical personnel are on hand in case of accidents. And HAZMAT (hazardous material) personnel assist with decontamination and confinement procedures.

The next step is for investigators to obtain a search warrant. Before a search warrant can be issued, probable cause that a crime has been committed and that evidence exists in the place to be searched must be shown. Furthermore, no search warrant should be issued until there is a health and safety plan that is understood by all search participants. No samples of hazardous or potentially hazardous substances should be taken by other than properly trained and environmentally protected personnel. Prior to serving the warrant, each person on the investigative team should read the search warrant and affidavit. Team members must understand where to search and what is to be seized. The team should be able to locate and secure the necessary evidence in an efficient and effective manner that is safe to all concerned.

Environmental Protection Forum

Environmental crime has no jurisdictional boundaries. It can occur anywhere, at any given time. Therefore, a broad spectrum of participants from law enforcement and other public-service departments is needed for any program designed to combat the environmental criminal. The Office of the State Attorney for the Ninth Judicial Circuit in the State of Florida organized the Central Florida Environmental Protection Forum. Previous efforts against environmental violators involving the office had been fragmented, and cooperative efforts between law enforcement and regulatory agencies were infrequent. By establishing the forum, organizers hoped to identify problems encountered in detecting, investigating, and prosecuting the environmental offender. They also wanted the forum to serve as a means for participants to gain an understanding of the different perspectives and capabilities of the agencies involved in the fight against environmental crime.

The forum serves primarily as an information exchange. A thorough knowledge of state and federal environmental laws is critical. Environmental crimes are complex, technical, and differ in significant ways from other types of crime. Environmental statutes, amendments, relevant definitions, defenses, and exceptions may be spread over several volumes. And while normally no individual obtains permission to commit an offense, it is quite possible that a suspected environmental violator may claim an exception under a particular statute in order to be issued a permit from an environmental-regulatory agency. For example, a local township may be dumping raw sewage into a nearby lake, but if a permit to do so has been issued by a regulatory agency, criminal prosecution probably will not be initiated. Simulated environmental crime scenes provide additional information to participants. The shift of command can pose problems as control at the scene is passed from the fire department and its containment activities to the police department for investigation, and finally to the regulatory agency for cleanup.

Establishing an environmental forum produces immediate benefits. Perhaps the most important benefit of environmental training is that it gets the various agencies to work together. No longer are agencies faceless entities, but people trying to do their jobs professionally. Police officers may learn that the best place to send environmental crime evidence is not to a crime laboratory but to a regulatory-agency's laboratory. Fire departments and regulatory agencies do not want their personnel "turned into cops." Their concern is to avoid possible claims by future defendants that all forum members are agents of law enforcement. As necessary as it is for successful prosecution of environmental crimes, cooperation will not occur spontaneously but must be fostered through the exchange of information.

The Environmental Crimes Act of 1992

On September 9, 1992, the U.S. Committee on Energy and Commerce heard numerous complaints filed against corporations for environmental crimes and personal injury or death. Six main cases occupied the committee. In May 1987 the PureGro Company dumped about 3,500 gallons of liquid waste containing Telone—a listed hazardous waste—and other chemical compounds including pesticides, insecticides, herbicides, and fertilizers on the corner of a field near Pasco, Washington. Toxic fumes from this material severely affected a nearby farm couple and caused over twenty other people in the area to become ill. The husband of the farm couple died a year later.

Weyerhaeuser Forest Products near Aberdeen, Washington, dumped oil-based paint waste including commercial grade solvent—a hazardous waste—into a storm-drain system. The drain emptied into a slough, which fed into the Chehalis River. Later, after a warning, EPA agents caught Weyerhaeuser dumping into a second drain that led to the sanitary sewer system of the City of Aberdeen.

Thermex, a Dallas-based company, abandoned a facility near Casper, Wyoming, leaving behind twenty-seven drums of chemicals and about 13,000 gallons of wastewater, both of which were hazardous wastes.

ChemWaste covered up the fact that a rogue employee stored fourteen drums of exceptionally dangerous dioxin-contaminated material in a miniwarehouse. The warehouse was located in a residential neighborhood of Baton Rouge.

Hawaiian Western Steel was caught dumping dust from their metal melting operation and told to dispose of it properly within ninety days. The company responded by allowing the waste to sit "unlabeled" on the mill grounds for several years and added more dust to it.

A Mr. Van Leuzen who lived on prime wetlands in the Bolivar Peninsula near Galveston, Texas, used hazardous waste for landfill to build up his receding property. When warned to cease and desist, Van Leuzen emphatically refused to comply.

All six cases required extensive EPA action and litigation, even though the defendants were caught red-handed and should have been punished immediately. These types of cases, all too common, prompted Representative Charles E. Schumer to remark before the U.S. Committee on the Judiciary:

> Currently, of all our environmental laws, few criminal penalties exist for creating an environmental hazard that can kill or injure. Only three—the Clean Water Act, the Clean Air Act, and RCRA, the hazardous waste law, carry the threat of jail time for knowing endangerment. This sends a message to corporate polluters that says, "Go ahead, rape and torture the land, and we'll look the other way."

Following his tirade, Representative Schumer introduced H.R. 5305, the Environmental Crimes Act of 1992. The bill imposed a maximum fifteen-year prison term for a first offense, a fine, or both. The penalty would be doubled for a second conviction. Corporations convicted would pay fines of up to $1 million. The bill did not pass and had not been reintroduced in 1993.

Martin Wright
William Imfeld
Michael O'Brien

Bibliography

Cohen, M.A. "Environmental Crime and Punishment: Legal/Economic Theory and Empirical Evidence of Enforcement of Federal Environmental Statutes." *Journal of Criminal Law and Criminology* 82 (Winter 1992): 1054–108.

Harris, Christopher, et al. *Hazardous Waste, Confronting the Challenge.* Westport, CT: Quorum Books, 1987.

Harris, K.C. "Hazards of Environmental Crime." *Security Management* (February 1992): 27–32.

Matulewich, V.A. "Environmental Crimes Prosecution: A Law Enforcement Partnership." *FBI Law Enforcement Bulletin* 60 (April 1991): 20–25.

O'Brien, Michael. "The Environmental Protection Forum." *FBI Law Enforcement Bulletin* 60 (April 1991): 9–12.

"Symposium: Environmental Crime." *George Washington Law Review* 59 (April 1991).

U.S. Committee on Energy and Commerce. *EPA's Criminal Enforcement Program.* Washington, DC: Government Printing Office, 1992.

U.S. Committee on the Judiciary. *Environmental Crimes Act of 1992.* Washington, DC: Government Printing Office, 1992.

Wright, Martin, and William Imfeld. "Environmental Crimes: Investigative Basics." *FBI Law Enforcement Bulletin* 60 (April 1991): 2–5.

Exclusionary Rules

"Exclusionary rules" operate to suppress evidence at criminal trials obtained as a result of unconstitutional activity by police officers. The drastic rules are designed to deter them from violating constitutional restrictions on unreasonable searches and seizures and unlawful interrogations.

Where Did the Exclusionary Rule Come From?
The Supreme Court first used an exclusionary rule in *Weeks v. United States* (232 U.S. 383 [1914]). Police officers had searched Weeks' room, seizing papers and possessions to use against him in a criminal trial. Since the search was undertaken without a search warrant or any other legal justification and thus was unconstitutional, the Supreme Court ruled that the evidence seized could not be admitted at trial:

> The tendency of those who execute the criminal laws of the country to obtain conviction by means of unlawful seizures and enforced confessions . . . should find no sanction in the judgment of the courts which are charged at all times with the support of the Constitution and to which people of all conditions have a right to appeal for the maintenance of such fundamental rights. (*Weeks,* 392)

The *Weeks* decision established an exclusionary rule in federal courts. An exclusionary rule was applied to state court proceedings in the landmark decision of *Mapp v. Ohio* (367 U.S. 643 [1961]).

The facts in *Mapp* graphically illustrate why the Supreme Court concluded that an exclusionary rule was necessary. Three Cleveland police officers attempted to gain entrance to Mapp's house, claiming to have obtained information from an unnamed source that she was concealing a fugitive and evidence of illegal gambling. After being refused entrance, they forced their way in by breaking down the back door. The police denied Mapp's attorney admission when he arrived. When Mapp demanded to see a search warrant, one of the officers flourished a piece of paper which she grabbed and placed inside her dress. During a struggle the officers recovered the paper (no warrant was ever offered in evidence and probably never existed) and handcuffed her. She was then forced to accompany the officers as they searched her house from top to bottom, purportedly looking for the fugitive and evidence of gambling materials, neither of which was ever found. The police did, however, eventually find "obscene materials" and Mapp was convicted in the Ohio courts for possessing them.

As the Supreme Court explained in *Mapp*, it really had no choice but to impose an exclusionary rule in these circumstances:

> Were it otherwise, then just as without the *Weeks* rule the assurance against unreasonable federal searches and seizures would be a "form of words," valueless and undeserving of mention in a perpetual character of inestimable human liberties, so too, without that rule the freedom from state invasions of privacy would be so ephemeral and so neatly severed from its conceptual nexus with the freedom from all brutish means of coercing evidence as not to merit this Court's high regard as a freedom "implicit in the concept of ordered liberty." (655)

Five years later, in *Miranda v. Arizona* (384 U.S. 436 [1966]) the Supreme Court also applied an exclusionary rule to protect Fifth Amendment rights when an individual is interrogated in police custody without having first received proper warnings about his or her constitutional rights.

State Exclusionary Rules

Many states adopted their own exclusionary rules prior to the *Mapp* decision. Since *Mapp*, most other states have concluded that an exclusionary rule is required. As a result, even if the Supreme Court were to overrule *Mapp* (which appears highly unlikely at present) most if not all states would still have an exclusionary rule in force under state law.

Limits on Federal Exclusionary Rule

The federal exclusionary rule applies only in limited settings.

Unconstitutional Acts by the Government. The exclusionary rule applies *only* to evidence acquired through unconstitutional acts by government employees, usually, but not exclusively, police officers. The rule also applies, for example, to public-school teachers and administrators. If the person who committed the unconstitutional act was an "agent" of a government employee, the exclusionary rule applies. Similarly, if the police make an unconstitutional search jointly with private citizens, the exclusionary rule applies, no matter who actually seized the evidence in question.

The exclusionary rule also applies *only* if the conduct in question was unconstitutional, not simply unlawful. Some acts are constitutionally permissible but nonetheless are prohibited by statute or administrative regulation (for example, executing a search warrant at night without special judicial approval).

Criminal Proceedings. The exclusionary rule applies primarily in criminal proceedings, since they are one of "those areas where its remedial objectives are thought most efficaciously served" (*United States v. Calandra*, 414 U.S. 338, 348 [1974]). In *Calandra*, the Supreme Court ruled that someone called to testify before a grand jury, for example, has no right to refuse questioning on the basis of unconstitutionally seized evidence because "[w]hatever deterrence of police misconduct may result from the exclusion of illegally seized evidence from criminal trials, it is unrealistic to assume that application of the rule to grand jury proceedings would significantly further that goal" (351).

The Supreme Court has also held the exclusionary rule inapplicable on this basis to civil deportation proceedings (*I.N.S. v. Lopez-Mendoza*, 468 U.S. 1032 [1984]) and to claimed search and seizure violations made in federal habeus corpus proceedings (*Stone v. Powell*, 428 U.S. 465 [1976]). Similarly, in *United States v. Janis* (428 U.S. 433 [1976]), the Court permitted evidence seized illegally by the Los Angeles police to be used in a federal civil proceeding for back taxes brought by the Internal Revenue Service. The Court reasoned that use of the exclusionary rule in such cases does not provide "a sufficient likelihood of deterring the conduct of the state police so that it outweighs the societal costs imposed by the exclusion" (454).

A few noncriminal areas remain in which the exclusionary rule is still applied. In *One 1958 Plymouth Sedan v. Pennsylvania* (380 U.S. 693 [1965]), for example, the Supreme Court permitted use of the exclusionary rule in a "quasicriminal" proceeding for forfeiture of a car used in violation of criminal laws.

Standing. To be entitled to use the exclusionary rule, a criminal defendant must possess "standing," which exists only where the defendant claims a violation of his or her personal rights. A defendant's personal constitutional rights are violated if the constitutional harm was done to that defendant personally, or at a place (for example, his or her home) or to something (for example, his or her briefcase) where he or she possessed a "legitimate expectation of privacy" (*Rakas v. Illinois*, 439 U.S. 128 [1978]).

Fruits. Evidence derived from unconstitutional acts is inadmissible even when it has been obtained as an *indirect* result of the constitutional breach. For example, if the police search someone's home unconstitutionally and seize papers or materials, thereby obtaining information that leads them to search someone else's home, whatever evidence they find at the second home is "derivative" of the initial illegality and is, in former Justice Felix Frankfurter's words, "fruit of the poisonous tree." Such "fruits" are inadmissible to a criminal trial under the exclusionary rule against a defendant who has standing to raise the issue.

There are exceptions to this rule. The Supreme Court held in *Wong Sun v. United States* (371 U.S. 471, 488 [1963]) that, to decide when the fruits doctrine applies, the "question . . . is 'whether, granting establishment of the primary illegality, the evidence to which instant objection is made has been come at by exploitation of that illegality or instead by means sufficiently distinguishable to be purged of the primary taint." In *Wong Sun*, the Court held that an illegally arrested defendant's statement was *not* subject to the exclusionary rule because the defendant had been released for several days before he voluntarily returned to the police station to talk. This statement was not the "fruit" of the earlier illegal arrest since, in the Supreme Court's view, "the connection between the arrest and the statement had 'become so attenuated as to dissipate the taint' " (491). (See also *New York v. Harris*, 495 U.S. 14 [1990].)

The Supreme Court has been careful, however, not to apply the attenuation exception too generously. For example, the Court has concluded that when police officers give an illegally arrested defendant *Miranda* warnings these are not sufficient in and of themselves to "attenuate" the prior police misconduct. Accordingly, a statement made under such circumstances may be suppressed (*Taylor v. Alabama*, 457 U.S. 687 [1982]; *Brown v. Illinois*, 422 U.S. 590 [1975]).

Impeachment with Illegally Seized Evidence. Statements made by a defendant may be suppressed at trial because they were obtained illegally for failure to give *Miranda* warnings. The statement may become admissible, however, if the defendant takes the stand and testifies in a way that contradicts those excluded statements. This is called "impeachment" as the purpose of allowing the statements in evidence is to impeach the defendant's credibility; the statements are not permitted to be part of the prosecution's direct proof of the defendant's guilt (its so-called case in chief).

The Supreme Court has also allowed impeachment based on physical evidence obtained illegally under the Fourth Amendment. In *United States v. Havens* (446 U.S. 620 [1980]), the defendant testified that he did not own certain incriminating items of clothing. The Supreme Court ruled that this testimony was properly impeached by the prosecution through admission of illegally seized clothing to contradict the defendant's testimony.

Inevitable Discovery. The Supreme Court will also permit the introduction of evidence at trial otherwise subject to suppression under the exclusionary rule, where the government can prove by a preponderance of the evidence that it would have discovered the evidence inevitably, without regard to the law-enforcement officers' otherwise unconstitutional acts (*Nix v. Williams*, 467 U.S. 431 [1984]).

Criticisms of the Exclusionary Rule

General. The exclusionary rule is a frequent target of criticism. The most frequently repeated complaint is some variation of former Justice (then New York Court of Appeals Chief Judge) Benjamin Cardozo's comment: "The criminal is to go free because the constable has blundered" (*People v. Defore*, 242 N.Y. 13, 21, 150 N.W. 585, 587 [1926]). Four Supreme Court justices (not a majority) expanded upon this criticism in 1954: "Rejection of the evidence does nothing to punish the wrong-doing official, while it may, and likely will, release the wrong-doing defendant. It deprives society of its remedy against one lawbreaker because he has been pursued by another" (*Irvine v. California*, 347 U.S. 128, 136 [1954]).

One of the most vocal critics of the exclusionary rule has been former Chief Justice Warren Burger. In 1971, he commented:

I do not question the need for some remedy to give meaning and teeth to the constitutional guarantees against unlawful conduct by government officials. . . . But the hope that this objective could be accomplished by the exclusion of reliable evidence from criminal trials was hardly more than a wistful dream. Although I would hesitate to abandon it until some meaningful substitute is developed, the history of the suppression doctrine demonstrates that it is both conceptually sterile and practically ineffective in accomplishing its stated objective. (*Bivens v. Six Unknown Named Agents of Federal Bureau of Narcotics*, 403 U.S. 388, 415 [1971] [Chief Justice Burger dissenting])

Other Supreme Court justices vigorously defend the rule. Former Justice William Brennan, Jr., for example, argued:

It is . . . imperative to have a practical procedure by which courts can review alleged violations of constitutional rights and articulate the meaning of those

rights. The advantage of the exclusionary rule—entirely apart from any direct deterrent effect—is that it provides an occasion for judicial review, and it gives credibility to the constitutional guarantees. By demonstrating that society will attach serious consequences to the violation of constitutional rights, the exclusionary rule invokes and magnifies the moral and educative force of the law. (*United States v. Peltier*, 422 U.S. 531, 554 [1975] [Justice Brennan dissenting])

Deterrence of Police Misconduct. Beginning in the 1970s, the Supreme Court repeatedly made the point that deterrence is the primary justification for utilizing the exclusionary rule. As the Supreme Court held in 1974, the "rule's prime purpose is to deter future unlawful police conduct and thereby effectuate the guarantee of the Fourth Amendment against unreasonable search and seizure" (*Calandra*, 347).

The question has often been raised, however, of whether the exclusionary rule in practice has any significant deterrent effect on police misconduct. Former Chief Justice Burger argued: "Whatever educational effect the rule conceivably might have in theory is greatly diminished in fact by the realities of law enforcement work. Policemen do not have the time, inclination, or training to read and grasp the nuances of the appellate opinions that ultimately define the standards of conduct they are to follow" (*Bivens*, 417).

Chief Justice Burger's implication that police officers lack the ability and inclination to learn and follow the law may be viewed as somewhat condescending. Most scholars simply cannot establish the extent to which the rule deters any significant amount of misconduct. The Supreme Court has reached a similar "nonconclusion": "Although scholars have attempted to determine whether the exclusionary rule in fact does have deterrent effect, each [study] appears to be flawed" (*Janis*, 449–450).

Alternative Remedies as a Substitute for the Rule

The Supreme Court in *Mapp* concluded that an exclusionary rule was necessary because "the obvious futility of relegating the Fourth Amendment to the protection of other remedies. . . . [T]hat such other remedies have been worthless and futile is buttressed by . . . experience" (652).

Civil suits for damages against police officers who violate the Constitution, for example, are not much help. The Supreme Court has ruled that police officers do not have complete immunity from such complaints (*Anderson v. Creighton*, 483 U.S. 635 [1987]; *Malley v. Briggs*, 475 U.S. 335 [1986]). However, these lawsuits are difficult to pursue since the police officer's reasonable "good faith" in undertaking the conduct in question is a defense, even though the officer's actions may have been unconstitutional.

Increased and more effective use of police disciplinary proceedings might also be seen as a viable deterrent to police misconduct. Experience has shown, however, that such proceedings do not, and perhaps cannot, be expected to operate effectively and systematically to discipline police officers for unconstitutional activity.

The potential substitute for the exclusionary rule that has received the greatest amount of scholarly attention is some sort of administrative proceeding created specifically to handle complaints about police misconduct and to afford compensation to people whose rights have been violated. This approach has never been adopted, largely for political reasons, and has been criticized in any event as impractical and unworkable.

Judicial Integrity. Some critics have argued that the Supreme Court has relied too much on the rationale of deterrence of the police and not enough on the rationale of judicial integrity in justifying the federal exclusionary rule. The Court in *Mapp* clearly acknowledged that: "'There is another consideration [in deciding to apply the exclusionary rule]—the imperative of judicial integrity.' . . . The criminal goes free, if he must, but it is the law that sets him free. Nothing can destroy a government more quickly than its failure to observe its own laws, or worse, its disregard of the charter of its own existence" (659; quoting *Elkins v. United States*, 364 U.S. 206, 222 [1960]). However, the Supreme Court in the 1970s and 1980s has often stated that deterrence is the primary rationale for the exclusionary rule, and that judicial integrity is, if anything, merely a "subordinate factor" (*Calandra*, 348).

This controversy is more than semantic; it affects the scope of the exclusionary rule's application. If deterrence of police misconduct is the *only* rationale for the rule, then, as the Supreme Court majority concluded in the 1970s and 1980s, the rule should be applied only where deterrence of police misconduct is significantly furthered. If, however, judicial integrity is also an independent reason for the rule's existence, the rule should be applied more often since the integrity of the judicial process is compromised whenever illegally seized evidence is admitted.

Reasonable Good-Faith Exception. In 1984, the Supreme Court adopted a "reasonable good-faith exception" to the exclusionary rule where illegally seized evidence is acquired pursuant to a constitutionally defective search warrant (*United States v. Leon*, 468 U.S. 897 [1984]). The Supreme Court adopted this exception because it concluded that police officers cannot be deterred from obtaining or executing an unconstitutional search warrant when they do not realize they are doing anything wrong.

Evidence seized pursuant to a defective search warrant can still be suppressed under the exclusionary rule, however, when a defendant can establish that "the magistrate abandoned his detached and neutral role" or where "the [police] officers were dishonest or reckless in preparing their affidavit or could not have harbored an objectively reasonable belief in the existence of probable cause" (*Leon*, 926). In both situations, the Supreme Court concluded, police officers cannot be deemed to be acting in reasonable good faith and, hence, the exclusionary rule applies.

It is important to note that the Supreme Court adopted a "*reasonable* good-faith exception" and not just a "good-faith exception." This means that police officers' mere good faith in obtaining or executing a search warrant is *not* sufficient, standing alone, to excuse application of the exclusionary rule. "Reasonableness" is evaluated by asking, on the basis of the particular warrant and affidavits in question, whether "no reasonably well-trained police officer could have believed that there existed probable cause to search" (*Leon*, 926). When that is the case, despite the reasonable good-faith exception, the exclusionary rule still applies.

John M. Burkoff

Bibliography

Alschuler, Albert. "'Close Enough for Government Work': The Exclusionary Rule after *Leon.*" *Supreme Court Review* (1984): 309–58.

Amsterdam, Anthony G. "Perspectives on the Fourth Amendment." *Minnesota Law Review* 58 (1974): 349–477.

Burkoff, John M. "The Court that Devoured the Fourth Amendment: The Triumph of an Inconsistent Exclusionary Doctrine." *Oregon Law Review* 58 (1979): 151–92.

Canon, Bradley C. "The Exclusionary Rule: Have Critics Proven that It Doesn't Deter Police?" *Judicature* 62 (1979): 398–409.

Dripps Donald. "Living with *Leon.*" *Yale Law Journal* 95 (1986): 906–48.

Kamisar, Yale. "The Exclusionary Rule in Historical Perspective: The Struggle to Make the Fourth Amendment More Than 'An Empty Blessing.'" *Judicature* 62 (1979): 336–50.

———. "Does (Did) (Should) the Exclusionary Rule Rest on a 'Principled Basis' Rather than an Empirical Proposition?" *Creighton Law Review* 16 (1983): 565–667.

LaFave, Wayne R. "The Fourth Amendment in an Imperfect World: On Drawing 'Bright Lines' and 'Good Faith.' " *University of Pittsburgh Law Review* 43 (1982): 307–61.

———. "Controlling Discretion by Administrative Regulations: The Use, Misuse, and Nonuse of Police Rules and Policies in Fourth Amendment Adjudication." *Michigan Law Review* 89 (1990): 442–519.

Nardulli, Vincent. "The Societal Costs of the Exclusionary Rule Revisited." *University of Illinois Law Review* (1987): 223–39.

Orfield, Myron W. "The Exclusionary Rule in Chicago." *Search and Seizure Law Report* 19 (1992): 81–88.

Schlesinger, Steven R. *Exclusionary Injustice: The Problem of Illegally Obtained Evidence.* New York: Dekker, 1977.

Stewart, Potter. "The Road to *Mapp v. Ohio* and Beyond: The Origins, Development and Future of the Exclusionary Rule in Search-and-Seizure Cases." *Columbia Law Review* 83 (1983): 1365–404.

Wasserstrom, Silas, and William J. Mertens. "The Exclusionary Rule on the Scaffold: But Was It a Fair Trial?" *American Criminal Law Review* 22 (1984): 85–179.

Wilkey, Malcolm R. "The Exclusionary Rule: Why Suppress Valid Evidence?" *Judicature* 62 (1978): 214–32.

E

Eyewitness Identification

Eyewitness identification plays a crucial role in a large number of criminal cases. Identification of a suspect by an eyewitness often provides the only information on which a prosecution is based. Unfortunately, there is considerable room for error in an eyewitness account of the incident and identification of the suspect. Research studies have demonstrated that the initial observation of an assailant by a witness or victim is often quite brief and may be colored by poor observation conditions and the victim's alarm or fear. Further, suggestive questioning at a pretrial identification proceeding can also distort a witness's or victim's identification of the suspect (Loftus, 1979; Wells and Loftus, 1984).

Accounts of wrongful convictions resulting from mistaken identifications are numerous, and the dangers that such misidentification pose to the judicial system have long been recognized. Indeed, the Supreme Court has acknowledged the inherent unreliability of eyewitness identification. "The vagaries of eyewitness identification are well known; the annals of criminal law are rife with instances of mistaken identification" (*United States v. Wade* [1967]).

Three factors contribute to the problematic nature of eyewitness identification. First is the inherent unreliability of human perception and memory. As research in the field of experimental psychology has shown, a person's perceptual and memory systems do not passively record and store information from the environment. Rather, the process of acquiring information is constructive; people attend selectively to certain features of their environment and later add to or alter the representation of the event as it resides in memory. This implies that vagaries in a witness's report can result from factors operating at the very moment the crime was committed and observed.

A second factor that contributes to unreliable eyewitness testimony is human susceptibility to suggestion. This may be of two sorts: susceptibility either to unintentional, and often very subtle suggestive influences; or to intentional, and often quite blatant persuasive forces. Both these influences could operate in the same identification. Regardless of the source of susceptibility, it means that the unreliability of perception and memory may be compounded by suggestive influences that occur prior to the actual identification of a criminal defendant.

The third factor that may distort an eyewitness report has more to do with the person hearing this evidence than with forces that directly affect the witness. Laypersons and even some judges are unaware of the potential unreliability of eyewitness identifications. As a result, they may give more weight to such testimony than it deserves. Identification of a defendant by a victim or witness often provides the most persuasive evidence at trial.

The potential unreliability of an eyewitness report results, then, from factors operating at the time the crime occurred; in the interval between the incident and a subsequent trial; and during trial, when the judge or jurors are unduly impressed by a witness's identification.

Recent research into eyewitness identification has focused on the ways that questioning of witnesses can affect their testimony, on the effectiveness of various investigative tools, and on the use of hypnosis to refresh eyewitnesses' memories.

1. Question Wording. Studies have shown that the form in which a question is asked can determine the accuracy of its answer. For example, Marquis, Marshall, and Oskamp (1972) showed that compared to other forms, narrative reports unprompted by questions include fewer errors but also tend to be less complete. On the other hand, interrogatory or structured questions result in more complete but less accurate responses. Psychologists have devoted a great deal of attention to this dilemma and now generally agree that a reliable way to elicit information is to first allow a person to give a narrative report, unprompted by questions, and then to ask specific, structured questions.

Loftus and Palmer (1974) showed that the precise wording of a question can influence the answer that is given. For example, if people watch a film of an automobile accident and are asked to estimate the speed of moving vehicles when prompted either by the question "How fast were the cars going when they smashed into each other?" or "How fast were the cars going when they contacted each other?" the former group will respond with an estimate that is considerably greater than that of the latter. One implication of this research is that a law enforcement or courtroom official could subtly affect a witness's answers by asking questions

that either inadvertently, or sometimes deliberately, elicit a certain response.

2. Interviewing Strategies. Geiselman et al. (1985) evaluated the effectiveness of different interview strategies for optimizing eyewitness memory performance. Subjects in their study viewed police training films of simulated violent crimes and were questioned individually by experienced law-enforcement personnel forty-eight hours later. Subjects who were given specific instruction to try to recreate in their minds the context surrounding the incident, to report everything they remembered, and to recall the events in different orders and from different perspectives (a "guided memory interview") were able to recall more information about the crimes than were subjects who gave an open-ended report and then were asked specific questions about the film.

After a crime has occurred, the victim or witness may be requested to view photographs for a potential identification or to observe a lineup and decide if anyone in it looks familiar. When a witness is asked to view a photospread, the police probably will not have a suspect in mind. In the actual lineup, however, police almost always have a suspect. If the witness selects someone from the lineup, he or she will be asked to testify to this at any subsequent trial. Several factors can influence the degree to which a lineup is free of suggestive influences.

1. Lineup Instructions. Instructions given to a witness prior to observing the lineup can influence the accuracy of an identification. In one experiment during a class demonstration, a male confederate of the experimenters approached the professor, became interested in the electronics apparatus being used in the demonstration, pushed the equipment onto the floor, and then fled out of a rear door. After some time, the instructor informed subjects that the event had been staged, and asked them to view a lineup. The researchers manipulated lineup instructions by giving one group of witnesses an instruction indicating that the offender was present in the lineup and by failing to provide a place on the response form for witnesses to indicate that the offender was absent. The other group of subjects was told that the offender might not be in the lineup and was given the option of indicating this response. Witnesses in the first group were more likely to choose someone from the lineup and also made more false identifications than witnesses who were told that the suspect "may or may not be" in the lineup.

2. Lineup Composition. The composition of a lineup can also influence accuracy. What the people look like, how they are dressed, and how their voices sound are all significant factors. Obviously, persons other than the suspect should be as similar in these respects to the subject as possible. Otherwise, the distractors (nonsuspects) can be rejected immediately as implausible and the true suspect picked by default.

Wells, Leippe, and Ostrom (1979) developed a procedure to determine whether a lineup is composed of people who fit some minimal description of the defendant. Say the lineup has six people, including the defendant. If the lineup is fair, a person who did not witness the crime, but was given a brief description of the culprit's appearance, should have one chance in six of selecting the actual defendant from the lineup. Wells et al. have tested the fairness of a lineup by reading people a description of the suspect, showing them a photograph of a lineup, and asking them to select the person they think committed the crime. If the defendant is chosen more than one-sixth of the time the lineup is biased.

3. Photo-Based Lineups. After a witness attempts to identify the perpetrator from an array of photographs, an in-person lineup will often follow. Almost invariably, only one person is shown in both contexts. If a witness selects someone from the photo array, it is possible that he or she will choose the same person from the lineup because that person seems familiar, even though the familiarity came from exposure to the photospread and not from exposure at the time of the crime. These lineups are "photo-biased."

A number of studies have suggested that hypnosis can provide reliable memory prompts to a witness who, due to trauma, lack of attention, or the passage of time, may have repressed or forgotten vital evidentiary information. These reports have been largely anecdotal, describing a number of seemingly unsolvable cases that were resolved only through the use of hypnosis. Enhanced memory has occasionally been demonstrated under controlled laboratory conditions. But the more typical finding from laboratory studies of hypnotically refreshed memory is that hypnotized witnesses are not more accurate than nonhypnotized subjects, and in some instances, are more susceptible to leading questions. Putnam (1979) showed subjects a film of a car–bicycle accident and questioned them either in the waking state or while hypnotized.

There were no differences between groups on objective questions, and hypnotized subjects made significantly more errors on leading questions.

Other researchers had subjects watch a stress-provoking film of several workshop accidents. Afterward, subjects were asked both leading and nonleading questions, either while under hypnosis or in the normal, waking state. As in Putnam's study, subjects in the waking state were more accurate on leading questions, and there was no difference in recall on nonleading questions (Sheehan, Grigg, and McCann, 1984).

These conflicting findings suggest that early anecdotal reports showing that memory is enhanced by hypnosis should be scrutinized very carefully. More sophisticated experimental designs fail, with some exceptions, to confirm those reports. The studies suggest that more attention needs to be focused on alternatives to the hypnosis interview. The use of a guided memory technique is one alternative worthy of further research.

Elizabeth F. Loftus
Edith Greene

Bibliography

Geiselman, R.E., R.P. Fisher, D.P. MacKinnon, and H.L. Holland. "Eyewitness Memory Enhancement in the Police Interview: Cognitive Retrieval Mnemonics Versus Hypnosis." *Journal of Applied Psychology* 70 (1985): 401–12.

Loftus, E.F. *Eyewitness Testimony*. Cambridge, MA: Harvard University Press, 1979.

———, and J. Palmer. "Reconstruction of Automobile Destruction: An Example of the Interaction Between Language and Memory." *Journal of Verbal Learning and Verbal Behavior* 13 (1974): 585–89.

Marquis, K.H., J. Marshall, and S. Oskamp. "Testimony Validity as a Function of Question Form, Atmosphere and Item Difficulty." *Journal of Applied Social Psychology* 2 (1972): 167–86.

Putnam, W.H. "Hypnosis and Distortions in Eyewitness Memory." *International Journal of Clinical and Experimental Hypnosis* 27 (1979): 437–48.

Sheehan, P.W., L. Grigg, and T. McCann. "Memory Distortion Following Exposure to False Information in Hypnosis." *Journal of Abnormal Psychology* 93 (1984): 259–65.

E

Wells, G.L., M.R. Leippe, and T.M. Ostrom. "Guidelines for Empirically Assessing the Fairness of a Lineup." *Law and Human Behavior* 3 (1979): 285–93.

Wells, G.L., and E.F. Lotfus. *Eyewitness Testimony: Psychological Perspectives.* Cambridge, England: Cambridge University Press, 1984.

F

Family Life

The family is an institution that has been legally structured and created to meet and perform certain needs and roles. Because so many of our biological, psychological, and sociological needs are fulfilled in families, most people marry. Police officers are no different, even given the fact that theirs is a stress-filled and dangerous occupation. In addition, there has always been administrative pressure for officers to be not only role models in the community, but also in their private lives. For example, in some police departments officers living out of wedlock can be fired, or at least seriously reprimanded, because they do not "respect" moral and social norms.

Many officers have married and remained so regardless of personal happiness and/or satisfaction. But in the 1970s, as society began to experience higher divorce rates, so did police. Whereas the family was generally seen to be a stress reducer for other occupations, the police family was observed to be a producer of stress itself. In one study (Ward, 1979), a survey of police divorce rates revealed rates ranging from 17 percent in Baltimore, Maryland, to 27 percent in Santa Ana, California, to 33 percent in Chicago. Researchers have identified factors that make it difficult for police families to function effectively. The irregular work hours, the loss of nonpolice friends, the missed holidays, and the emotional drain due to having to deal with stressful situations and danger are among these factors. At home, instead of the spouse's acting as a buffer against stress for the officer, the opposite usually occurred—the spouse became one of the stressors.

The Ward study showed that police administrations had done little to alleviate the obvious strains of police work. Within three to five years of joining the force many officers were divorced. Some officers not only divorced the spouse, but also later quit the force. Of course, the loss of trained employees in any profession is costly to the organization. Moreover, stress and its byproducts began to be defined as "management problems as well as personal problems, for they affected the efficiency and effectiveness of the force itself" (Bracey, 1979).

Role Theory

Role is defined as a set of obligations and rights that accompany a specific status or position in society. Early sociological writers viewed roles as links between individual behavior and social structure. The implication that positions and their attendant roles were elements of society pushed investigators into all kinds of occupational study—including the closed fraternity of the "Blue Society," as police organizations were sometimes called. Their research demonstrated that the acquisition of a role through the socialization process meant that individuals learned patterns of response from the behavior of others. The Niederhoffers, in 1978, used the word "cynical" to describe the police officer as he or she reacted to other people in relationships which focused around the job of policing.

Many officers are secretive about their occupation. Secrecy and protectiveness also surround police family life. All this secrecy has resulted in a dearth of empirical data, even though a literature rich in personal testimony exists. Another obstacle to research is the 1972 amendment to the 1964 Civil Rights Act, which protects the classification of marital status. Police departments no longer had to keep formal statistics on officers' marital status, so today these figures are not readily available. Not until the early 1970s did female activists who were also police spouses turn their attention to police family research.

Police Spouses

The movement to upgrade orientation programs for spouses was influenced by several factors, including pressure from police wives. Those police organizations that sponsored a tea-and-cookie type of orientation, during which benefits, including death benefits, were explained to the trainees' spouses, were asked to provide more realistic and comprehensive seminars. Wives knew only too well how devastating the police occupation was on marriage. Some women, such as Barbara E. Webber, became more involved; she edited the small *Handbook for Law Enforcement Wives* (1974). Claudia Baker and Peggy Rhodes of Seattle, Washington, created a seminar for new officers' wives, to be conducted along with the regular police academy training for the entire state of Washington. They developed a ten-week, four-hour-session workshop that soon became a prototype and inspiration for kindred programs on the West Coast, the East Coast, and finally throughout the United States. The national television networks broadcast three of the Washington sessions.

At about the same time, Arthur Niederhoffer, a former New York police officer, joined by his wife, started to collect empirical data on the East Coast, primarily in New York City. The work of the Niederhoffers and of Mary J. Hageman in Washington State are the earliest and most extensive empirical evidence of police family stress.

In their book *The Police Family* (1978) the Niederhoffers called the police occupation a "jealous mistress." They viewed the pressures of departmental expectations, the push for a college degree, and other striving after greater professionalism as detrimental to family life. They also discovered that divorce among police was no higher than the average level of divorce in the United States; police families seem to follow the divorce trends around them. Hageman's study revealed more of a dilemma. Police officers questioned about their family life usually denied that there had been any changes in their emotional relationship with their spouses and reported they were happily married. Veteran and rookie officers responded similarly. Asked the same probing questions, spouses answered

in ways that supported the existence of stress as theorized by psychologists and other experts. Rookies' wives reported that their spouses rarely detached themselves from their feelings, whereas the wives of veterans felt that their spouses did quite often. Thus, the statistical findings were significant for both questions of emotional detachment and repression of feelings, with a high measure of association.

From those responses it could be argued that police officers were learning to cope with occupational stress by emotional detachment and uninvolvement. As the length of service increased, the denial style became more than a "working personality"; it affected a marriage. Spouses would say that their officer mates did not act like human beings until they had been on vacation for two weeks. Answers to questions about marital happiness were too global; everyone was statistically happy. Yet, when more behavioral questions were asked, such as, "How much do you argue?" marital strife came out. Revelations of this type did not predict divorce, but did indicate that the police occupation was more at fault in the marriage than the basic personality of the officer spouse.

An evaluation of the spouse orientation program in Washington State disclosed two powerful, mitigating factors. First, preventive education with an emphasis on communication skills assisted both partners in the marriage. Second, police administration views were all important:

> A real paradox seems to exist in the police department which honors the value of having men with a stable family situation but is perceived as not encouraging marriage and family for its officers. (Maynard and Maynard, 1982)

In other supportive studies, Lester and Guerin (1982) found statistical significance in relating higher satisfaction with marriage to the officer's perception of his mate's satisfaction with his police career. Also, men who had been officers first and then had married seemed to enjoy more satisfactory marriages (Cherry and Lester, 1979).

Current Programs

John G. Stratton, director of Psychological Services for the Los Angeles County Sheriff's Department, evaluated its program begun in 1975:

too many lawsuits were being filed in the United States. They concluded that this feeling may be self-perpetuating; that is, the perception that increasing numbers of people are involved in litigation gives rise to the belief that lawsuits are an inevitable fact of life, which may result in feelings of vulnerability. This vulnerability may serve as a form of self-justification for suing others. Indeed, it seems that the law-enforcement trainees exhibited such vulnerability since they felt that fear of litigation was an unavoidable consequence of their jobs (Brodsky and Gianesello, 1992; Scogin and Brodsky, 1991).

This idea that law-enforcement officers' increased feelings of vulnerability may serve as a form of self-justification for suing others moves the fear of litigation from outside of the department into the department. The police department administration itself may have cause for a unique fear of litigation, which is intradepartmental. Indeed, Bale (1990) has examined stress litigation stemming from police work.

He looked at the connection among work, stress, and emotional distress and their role in extensive litigation in the workers' compensation system. Terry (1985) reported that police work has been viewed as either the most stressful or among the most stressful of all occupatons and that perceived stresses and strains of police work are thought to cause certain physiological ailments among police officers, as well as the presence of high divorce and suicide rates. Likewise, Bale (1990:413) stated:

> Police officers perform stressful and dangerous work that is highly visible to the public, both in the community and in its many media representations. Police officers are often covered by disability schemes that allow them generous presumptions of compensability for heart attacks. These provisions, reflecting a widely held view, expressed by some courts, that police work is inherently more stressful than most occupations, can directly aid police officers bringing claims that work stress helped induce other medical conditions, such as a peptic ulcer or a mental illness.

Bale (1990) goes on to state numerous cases in which police officers have been successful in workers' compensation claims that involved stress on the job. Some of the cited litigation addresses claims concerning harassment and abuse of authority; physical intimidation and other forms of threat; adverse personnel decisions; excessive demands; whistle-blowing; and internal investigations into alleged illegal activity. As Bale (1990) notes, a growing set of legal remedies are transforming distressing workplace situations into forms of money, medical care, and justice.

This growing area of stress litigation within law enforcement suggests that future studies on the fear of litigation in police officers need also address the differences in the fears of officers who are in contact with the public and those officers involved in administrative and organizational tasks. Furthermore, it may be useful to examine if officers who feel that fear of litigation is an unavoidable consequence of their job indeed feel more vulnerable. If so, would they then feel more justified in bringing a stress-related lawsuit against their own department?

Although this concept of police fear of litigation is relatively abstract at present, numerous implications from the limited available research are relevant. First, Scogin and Brodsky (1991) suggested that preservice and in-service training on liability and the process of litigation is highly desirable. They also concluded that the impact of the concerns about litigation on work and personal functioning is not known. They proposed that fear of litigation may be adaptive in that it discourages questionable activities. On the other hand, it might be detrimental in that officers may become overly conservative and engage in avoidant law-enforcement behavior. Their recommendation for further research was to contrast the litigation fears of veteran officers, as well as those who have undergone litigation preservice and in-service training, to recruits or those who have not received such training.

Scogin and Brodsky (1991) also commented that because law enforcement is inherently stressful, moderate levels of worry about lawsuits adds to the emotional wear and tear of the job. This point of view directly ties into the question about the self-perpetuating concept of the fear of litigation in police officers. Is there some point at which the stress induced by fear of litigation from outside the department becomes a contributor to increased stress litigation within the department? To better answer this question, future research should examine this issue to more fully understand the entire range of effects of fear of litigation in police officers.

Jennifer F. Gardner
Forrest R. Scogin

Bibliography

Bale, A. "Medicolegal Stress at Work." *Behavioral Sciences and the Law* 8 (1990): 399–420.

Breslin, F.A., K.R. Taylor, and S.L. Brodsky. "Development of a Litigaphobia Scale: Measurement of Excessive Fear of Litigation." *Psychological Reports* 58 (1986): 547–550.

Brodsky, S.L. "Speaking Out: A Litigaphobic Release from Involuntary Commitment." *Public Service Psychology* 2(3) (1983): 11.

———. "Fear of Litigation in Mental Health Professionals." *Criminal Justice and Behavior* 15 (1988): 492–500.

———, and W.F. Gianesello. "Worrying about Litigation: A Normative Study of College Students and the General Public." *Law and Psychology Review* 16 (1992): 1–12.

———, and J.E. Schumacher. "The Impact of Litigation on Psychotherapy Practice: Litigation Fears and Litigaphobia." Ed. E.A. Margenau. *The Encyclopedic Handbook of Private Practice.* New York: Gardner Press, 1990. 674–76.

Scogin, F., and S.L. Brodsky. "Fear of Litigation among Law Enforcement Officers." *American Journal of Police.* 10(1)(1991): 41–45.

Terry, W.C. "Police Stress as a Professional Self-Image." *Journal of Criminal Justice* 13 (1985): 501–12.

Wilbert, J.R., and S.M. Fulero. "Impact of Malpractice Litigation on Professional Psychology: Survey of Practitioners." *Professional Psychology: Research and Practice* 19 (1988): 379–82.

Federal Bureau of Investigation

The FBI is the principal investigative arm of the U.S. Department of Justice. It is charged with gathering and reporting facts, locating witnesses, and compiling evidence in cases involving federal jurisdiction. The FBI investigates all violations of federal law except those that have been assigned by legislative enactment or otherwise to another federal agency. The FBI's jurisdiction includes a wide range of responsibilities in the criminal, civil, and security fields. Priority has been assigned to the four areas that affect society the most: organized crime, drug trafficking, terrorism, and white-collar crime. The FBI also offers cooperative services such as fingerprint identification, laboratory examination, police training, and the National Crime Information Center to duly authorized law-enforcement agencies. FBI headquarters in Washington, D.C., consists of ten separate divisions, three executive-assistant directors, an office of congressional and public affairs, and a director's staff. The FBI's investigations are conducted through fifty-nine field offices. Most of its personnel are trained at the FBI Academy in Quantico, Virginia.

Origins

The FBI was organized in 1908, when Attorney General Charles Bonaparte directed that Department of Justice investigations be handled by a small group of special investigators. In the following year the name Bureau of Investigation was given to the group. The organization grew gradually during the succeeding years. The World War I Selective Service Act and espionage laws brought new duties. Then the National Motor Vehicle Theft Act was passed in 1919 to curb the transportation of stolen automobiles from state to state, challenging FBI agents directly after the war. In 1924 Attorney General Harlan F. Stone, who later became chief justice of the United States, appointed twenty-nine-year-old J. Edgar Hoover as director of the bureau, not knowing at the time that Hoover and the FBI would become synonymous.

Young Hoover accepted the appointment with the understanding that the bureau was to be a career service in which ability and good character were to be the requirements for admission, and performance and achievement the sole bases for promotion. It was apparent that it would take time to build the FBI into a streamlined, investigative machine to fight crime. New requirements for special-agent appointments were set up, providing for college graduates trained in law and accounting. Each applicant was thoroughly investigated before appointment. Training schools were started in Washington, D.C., to equip special agents with modern crime-detection methods. The trainees received instruction in the use of firearms, defensive tactics, legal matters, arrest problems, first aid, the art of interviewing, investigative techniques, laboratory matters, fingerprint work, moot court, and a detailed study of violations of federal law over which the FBI has jurisdiction. This training was not designed to satisfy the beginner's needs only, but was implemented periodically to retrain agents throughout their career.

As the FBI grew, its records and files expanded and with each passing year its tremendous wealth of criminal information became more and more valuable. In 1924 Congress approved the transfer of fingerprint records at Leavenworth Federal Prison and the criminal records maintained by the International Association of Chiefs of Police to the FBI. These numbered 810,188 and formed the nucleus of the FBI identification division. Today, thanks to the cooperation of national and international law-enforcement organizations, the division has the world's largest collection of fingerprints. To provide scientific aid in criminal investigations, the FBI laboratory was established in 1932. Since then, the laboratory has conducted several million examinations of evidence. Because the FBI is a fact-finding and fact-gathering agency, its investigations are as important in clearing the innocent as in convicting the guilty. In many instances where circumstantial evidence has pointed to innocent persons, scientific findings of the FBI have cleared them. The laboratory is now the largest criminal laboratory in the world.

In July 1935 the first session of the FBI National Academy convened in Washington, D.C., with representation from local, county, and state law-enforcement agencies. This academy was created in view of a pressing need for qualified instructors and administrators in law-enforcement techniques. Since its founding, thousands of officers from the United States and several foreign countries have graduated. A new academy facility opened in 1972 on the Marine Corps Base at Quantico, Virginia. Its complex of buildings presents a college-like atmosphere, including classrooms, library, dormitories, gymnasium, and other ancillary services.

The FBI's National Crime Information Center (NCIC), a nation-wide computerized index and communications hookup that includes Canada, is a remarkable achievement in the fight against crime. This computerized index stores information relating to the following: stolen, missing or recovered guns, stolen articles, wanted persons, stolen/wanted vehicles, stolen license plates, and stolen/embezzled/missing securities. NCIC is one of the greatest innovations law enforcement has seen in decades, mainly because it assists law-enforcement officers in the discharge of responsibilities with dispatch and thoroughness, resulting in a higher risk of detection for the criminal. The FBI's "Ten Most Wanted Fugitives" program was inaugurated to enlist public support in identifying fugitives from the law. This service, made possible by the cooperation of the country's newspapers, magazines, and radio and television stations, has been an effective and potent weapon in ascertaining the whereabouts of badly wanted individuals.

Each year the FBI conducts a series of conferences on a national basis for law-enforcement administrators and command personnel in a subject matter of current interest. Conferences have dealt with such matters as bombing and bomb threats and extremist groups and violence. Thousands of police participants have attended these useful meetings. On January 21, 1982, the attorney general gave the FBI concurrent jurisdiction with the Drug Enforcement Administration (DEA) over drug offenses. The DEA's administrator now reports to the director of the FBI, who was given general supervision of the drug-enforcement effort. DEA agents work side by side with FBI agents throughout the country in major drug cases—a significant change in narcotics law enforcement.

Criticisms

An agency as powerful and pervasive as the FBI must have its critics. On one side, J. Edgar Hoover, its long-time director, sought to create a positive and near mythical image of the FBI. His "G-Men" were invincible and America owed him its praise for capturing some of the most notorious criminals. To read Andrew Tully's book, *The FBI's Most Famous Cases*, is to thrill to the scent of the chase. But other books, such as Sanford J. Ungar's *FBI: An Uncensored Look Behind the Walls*, challenge the FBI's official line. Both types of studies need to be read for a better understanding of this vital and versatile law-enforcement agency.

Bibliography

Collins, Frederick L. *The FBI in Peace and War*. New York: G.P. Putnam's Sons, 1962.

Cook, Fred J. *The FBI Nobody Knows*. New York: Macmillan, 1964.

F

Felt, W. Mark. *The FBI Pyramid from the Inside*. New York: G.P. Putnam's Sons, 1979.

Overstreet, Harry A., and Bonaro Overstreet. *The FBI in Our Open Society*. New York: W.W. Norton, 1969.

The Story of the Federal Bureau of Investigation. Washington, DC: U.S. Department of Justice, Federal Bureau of Investigation, 1974.

Tully, Andrew. *The FBI's Most Famous Cases*. New York: William Morrow, 1965.

Ungar, Sanford J. *FBI: An Uncensored Look Behind the Walls*. Boston: Little, Brown, 1976.

Federal Commissions and Enactments

One reason for the growth in popularity of crime commissions and crime surveys in the early twentieth century was the widespread belief that prohibition had fueled organized crime and that well-publicized violence and lawlessness represented a "crime wave." Another reason was the increase in robberies and burglaries and resulting high insurance premiums. In Chicago, for example, the Association for Commerce, alarmed over a series of bank hold-ups and payroll robberies, established the Chicago Crime Commission in 1919. Such groups often concluded that crime could be reduced by catching more criminals, which many felt required a speedier law-enforcement response.

Between 1964 and 1968 liberal Supreme Court decisions appeared to limit police authority as racial violence erupted throughout the United States. In the wake of riots and assassinations the police became targets of intense criticism and debate in four major national crime-commission reports. Recommendations were based on the belief that police needed to be better educated, trained, equipped, and managed. The commissions also felt that a wide variety of social-service and economic-aid programs could do much to reduce crime.

By the end of the 1960s crime became a critical domestic issue for polls and political platforms. Legislation inspired by the varied commissions attempted to make strengthening of the criminal-justice system a national effort. While the commissions and enactments of the 1980s echo many of the concerns of two decades ago, public attitudes and court decisions reflect a strict "crime control" philosophy. Technological resources and "get tough" laws appear to be tailored to making the job of the police easier and the "fight" against crime more productive.

National Commission on Law Observance and Enforcement

Some critical sociologists working in the 1920s and 1930s blamed police problems on the United States' socioeconomic structure and its laws. Perhaps to counteract this, President Herbert Hoover empowered the National Commission on Law Observance and Enforcement to look only superficially at the top layer of police and, hopefully, find the problems there. Though the commission pointed out the problems of fast-growing cities, the increasing number of aliens, and pervasive political corruption, it did find many faults in law-enforcement operations. Poor education, officers' low intelligence, overwork, corruption, brutality, the lack of specialized assignments, poorly trained and politically entangled management were cited as difficulties plaguing the police.

Established in 1929 and directed by former U.S. Attorney General George Wickersham, the commission released its fourteen-volume report in 1931. Volume 11 (*Lawlessness in Law Enforcement*) outlines a study of "the third degree." The report criticized the employment of police tactics that inflicted suffering or physical/mental pain in order to extract confessions or information about crimes. Numerous cases were documented where the third degree had been used. The authors also surveyed fifteen cities with laws against the third degree. Police who used violence and strong-arm tactics were condemned as criminals themselves.

Volume 14 (*Report on Police*) was written almost entirely by two research assistants of noted police scholar August Vollmer and is said to represent much of his view. The widespread use of police brutality throughout the 1920s (especially in Buffalo, Cleveland, and Chicago) was attributed to departments with ingrained corruption and political interference. However, the report argued that the single biggest drawback to good morale and the effective functioning of the police was the short and uncertain tenure of the chief. The chief administrator, it was recommended, should be a professional (not a civilian) who knew his city and his men well. In addition, the recommendations included better quality personnel, more modern equipment, autonomy of operations from political influence, administrative reorganization, and better professional leadership.

The 1965 Law Enforcement Assistance Act
The Law Enforcement Assistance Act was a research and development grant program of $20.6 million awarded to 359 separate projects during the act's three years. Though only $4.4 million was used to support training programs and $1.4 million for college-level education, the grant was considered a decisive factor in the expansion of professional training for police.

The 1967 President's Commission on Law Enforcement and the Administration of Justice
The final report of the President's Commission was titled *The Challenge of Crime in a Free Society.* Its recommendations led to the construction of the Omnibus Crime Control and Safe Streets Act of 1968 and the subsequent development of the Law Enforcement Assistance Administration. One of the most important contributions of the Commission report was the development of what was believed to be a more accurate method for measuring the incidence of crime—the victimization report. Using this technique, the panel found that fewer than one-half of all crimes are reported to police. Though police–community relations were a popular topic at this time, the report did not dwell on it, instead emphasizing broader police administration issues.

Nine task-force studies accompanied the final report, as well as interviews with fifty professional criminals in four cities. The writers lamented the lack of research on the deterrent effects of various patrol techniques and advocated team policing. Along with more than 200 other recommendations, the report also proposed that police develop strong internal controls to prevent employee misconduct. This idea of "repressive patrolling by internal discipline investigators" was later criticized by the 1973 Standards and Goals Commission as "objectionable, expensive and demoralizing."

The 1968 Omnibus Crime Control and Safe Streets Act
The Omnibus Crime Control and Safe Streets Act (OCC&SS) was a series of measures designed to reduce crime and increase the effectiveness of state and local law enforcement. The act provided for state councils to dispense funds for crime-prevention programs and the education of law-enforcement personnel through a specially designed umbrella agency, the Law Enforcement Assistance Administration (LEAA).

One of LEAA's major contributions was the underwriting of academic financial assistance in the Law Enforcement Education Program (LEEP). While LEAA sponsored the production of crime-related educational programs, LEEP channeled money directly to students through forgivable loans that covered tuition and books. In retrospect LEEP funding went predominantly to married (72 percent), white (84 percent), males (90 percent). Over 50 percent were military veterans, meaning that they were receiving both VA and LEEP benefits.

Criticisms of LEAA funding were that too much money was being spent on extensive-police hardware and not enough on reducing or preventing crime. The mayor of New York joined leaders of nine other large cities in petitioning the federal government for a more equitable distribution of funds. Officials claimed that big cities had bigger crime problems and deserved a larger proportion of the funds and that city government should be allowed to decide how to spend the money. In addition, a 1976 National Urban League report complained that of the 184 professional level LEAA employees, only nine were black and no blacks worked in the Office of Management and Planning, where decisions on grant priorities and policies were made.

The OCC&SS Act made substantial changes in criminal procedure ensuring the likelihood of convictions. Guidelines for the admissibility of confessions were relaxed to include any voluntary submissions or eyewitness testimony, thereby reducing their inadmissibility caused by delays in federal processing. Also included were less stringent standardized procedures for the procurement of wiretaps. Tapping and bugging were to be permitted if a crime had been, was being, or was to be committed, providing evidence could not be readily produced by alternative methods.

A major portion of the act was devoted to a strict rewriting of firearms policy referred to as the Gun Control Act. Violent outbreaks of protest during the turbulent 1960s inspired this legislation, which was aimed at regulating the firearms industry and enforcement of gun law violations. Provisions included the restriction of interstate firearms traffic and denial of firearms to minors, drug abusers, convicted felons, the mentally ill, and fugitives from justice. However, facing the weaknesses of this bill, the International Association of Chiefs of Police admitted that private transfer and residential thefts were the major source of guns used by criminals. Police have therefore developed firearm owners' security and public-awareness programs to encourage citizens to protect firearms carefully and to report thefts promptly to police.

The Omnibus Crime Control and Safe Streets Act was amended and extended for another three years in 1970. Clarification was added to the grants and planning aspects of LEAA, and five additional bills, including the Drug Control Act and the Organized Crime Act, were adopted to form what President Richard Nixon boasted was a major crime-fighting package.

The 1968 National Advisory Commission on Civil Disorders (the Kerner Commission)

The Kerner Commission was formed to provide insight into the major civil disturbances of the 1960s. Its report combined three major studies by research groups at the University of Michigan and Johns Hopkins and Columbia universities. The work provided an in-depth analysis of who participated in riots during 1967 and an overview of racial attitudes in major American cities. The message of the commission was clear: all just and necessary means should be taken to ensure the peace and safety of the public. Even so, the writers realized that the lack of common opportunities for all within society and lack of a diligent national effort to achieve equality were much to blame for civil disobedience.

The significance of this particular report was perhaps overshadowed by the various local commissions formulated in response to specific incidences of rioting or violent protest. Also, more directly relevant to criminal justice, the National Commission on the Causes and Prevention of Violence was formed during this same year.

The 1969 National Commission on the Causes and Prevention of Violence

Established by President Lyndon Johnson in 1968, this commission delivered a fifteen-volume report, including seven task-force reports, after eighteen months of intensive work. Convinced that most violence could be prevented, the researchers recommended that the nation double its investment in crime prevention and the administration of justice. Specifically, the authors emphasized the need for increased police/community activities in the ghettos. Indicating that racial prejudice compromised police performance, the commission noted that police often ignored crimes committed in the ghettos and treated ghetto residents roughly. The commission went on to criticize internal review boards as not only potentially biased but also not credible with the public. Though it was realized that police resent external review boards, the suggestion was still made that an independent civilian grievance agency review citizen complaints against the police.

Because it was believed that the Gun Control Act would not reduce the number of guns or curtail street sales, the commission pressed for research to design devices to assist law enforcement agencies in detecting concealed firearms on a person. The writers also advocated the construction of a prototype police auto to replace the modified stock sedans and the equipping of vehicles with photographic, dictation, and sound-recording equipment.

The commission lamented the lack of good police administration and the limited training of current management. It proposed the establishment of free social-service academies for police and other civil-service workers; completion of courses would result in advanced entry-level jobs. It was recommended that the traffic function be lifted from police to lessen overwork and increase efficiency. Also, according to the report, police who were moving to other departments should not start at the bottom again, but be allowed lateral entry. Finally, it was suggested that a criminal-justice administrative assistant to mayors or county executives be utilized to help promote crime control measures, budget items, develop standards, and mediate among police, courts, and correction institutions.

The 1970 Comprehensive Drug Abuse Prevention and Control Act (Controlled Substances Act)

Title II of the act pertained to law enforcement and served as a model for a uniform categorization of substances to be controlled by the federal government. Schedule I drugs—those with a high potential for abuse and no currently accepted medical use (heroin, marijuana, LSD)—were strictly regulated. Schedule II drugs also had a high potential for abuse though some accepted medical use (opium, morphine, cocaine). Severe punishments were set for trafficking in or illegal possession of controlled substances. Most states followed with similar or even harsher penalties for violations.

The most controversial aspect of the legislation was the provision for unannounced forcible entry pursuant to the execution of a warrant. This "no-knock" clause applied to offenses involving controlled substances for which the penalty was imprisonment for more than one year. Though the constitutionality of this allowance was continually upheld in courts, public and media opposition was so intense that the provision was repealed four years later. In retrospect, its demise can most likely be attributed to abuse by overzealous federal agents. Although some states have retained "no-knock" laws, even in areas outside drug investigation many require the specification of a "no-knock" intention at the time the warrant is obtained.

The 1970 Organized Crime Control Act
Organized crime has always been a particularly sensitive area for police because gambling and racketeering were perceived as major sources of police corruption. Under the Organized Crime Control Act it became illegal to use money from organized crime to do legitimate business in interstate commerce. Provisions also included stronger gambling laws, increased sentences for dangerous "special" offenders, and establishment of federal control over interstate and foreign commerce in explosives.

The 1973 National Advisory Commission on Criminal Justice Standards and Goals
In 1971 LEAA Administrator Jerris Leonard appointed this commission to formulate, for the first time, national criminal-justice standards and goals for crime reduction and prevention at state and local levels. Two years later, six reports were issued, one devoted entirely to police.

The report emphasized the police chief's responsibility for identifying priorities and allocating resources to them. Pointing out that previous commissions had criticized the lack of community contact between police and citizens, the writers added, "police don't like to get out of their cars." The commission advised that community accountability meant keeping track of praise and complaints and suggested that policies be written, widely disseminated, and based on law.

Though the seven goals outlined in the volume were vague and the standards beyond number, many special needs were addressed. Areas with significant minority populations should develop the means to ensure effective communications, including bilingual employees to interact with people who did not speak English. Agencies with more than 400 employees should utilize a special public-relations unit. Their duties would include presentations within the public schools. The use of neighborhood watch groups was also encouraged. Though the implementation of tactical forces equipped with the necessary specialized devices for "special crime problems" could mean trained crisis-intervention personnel for rape and domestic assault cases, it has most often been interpreted as the need for SWAT teams and riot squads.

The commission recognized that team policing was a popular form of police reorganization at a time when administration and personnel, as well as the public, were reform oriented. Broadly, the report advocated "geographic policing" for better community relations (meaning that the public would know their officers), and team policing for larger departments. They realized, however, that more study of team policing was necessary to determine overall effectiveness. Programs used in Tucson, Arizona; Syracuse, New York; Holyoke, Massachusetts; and Dayton, Ohio, could be examined and evaluated. It was also explained that combining into teams patrol with higher-paid investigation personnel could cause friction.

Finally, the commission wrote that the police chief might use the help of employee-relations specialists, particularly in collective negotiations. The chief should also recognize the right of the officer to join or not to join "employee organizations" (unions).

The 1978 National Advisory Commission on Higher Education for Police Officers (the Sherman Report)
Sponsored by the Police Foundation and under the direction of Lawrence Sherman, the Commission on Higher Education for Police Officers published its findings as *The Quality of Police Education* in 1978. The members viewed curriculum reform as education reform, and thus police reform. The report criticized most recently established programs that placed emphasis on the technical/vocational aspects of policing and those that employed former police rather than full-time academic scholars. The

commission advocated a well-rounded liberal-arts program with criminal-justice courses not to exceed one-quarter of the total taken. The criminal-justice courses they recommended were law and ethics, with less concern for management and supervision. Colleges, the commission felt, should employ full-time Ph.D. faculty, discourage off-campus teaching, and grant no academic credit for completion of police academies. Administrators were warned to guard the integrity of their programs against outside political pressure. Community colleges should phase out two-year terminal degrees and prepare students to transfer to four-year programs.

The report urged Congress to continue funding the Law Enforcement Education Program (LEEP) at current levels. It also advised police to be more concerned with recruiting the educated than attempting to educate the recruited. Educated personnel could be better utilized, particularly in experimenting with new organizational designs. A time was predicted when, hopefully, all new personnel would have baccalaureate degrees and leaves of absence for educational purposes would be granted and encouraged. Most of all, the commission hoped that higher education would be viewed by management as a resource and not a threat.

The 1984 Comprehensive Crime Control Act

President Ronald Reagan's 1984 crime fighting package allocated $69 million for programs that provided management training and technical assistance for police. Chapter 6, the Justice Assistance Act, provided federal money and discretionary grants for state and local criminal-justice agency programming. Funds were to support the implementation of methods that would improve the operational effectiveness of law enforcement particularly in rural areas. Objectives included sting-type operations that would disrupt illicit commerce, means for combating arson, and more sophisticated crime-analysis techniques for the patrol or field unit.

The Comprehensive Crime Control Act created new laws to assist authorities in the seizure of evidence. It became a felony to destroy or remove property to prevent seizure and also to warn another that his property is about to be the subject of a search. Changes in the law made it easier to use wiretaps by broadening the definition of emergencies not requiring a court order; by including all situations posing threat of danger; and expanding the list of crimes for which wiretaps may be used. The legislation also increased death benefits for dependents of public-safety officers.

The Crime Control Act of 1990

The Crime Control Act of 1990 provided funds to improve the quality of records and data sharing among the various law-enforcement agencies. First, the act designated that funding go to upgrade the National Crime Information Center, which links more than 16,000 federal, state, and local law-enforcement agencies. The act also required that states receiving certain federal funds must upgrade their criminal-justice records particularly those files that track felony dispositions. Criminal histories and fingerprints were also slated for automation improvements. In addition, the act called for better reporting to the FBI.

Other funds appropriated by the legislation were directed toward fighting the nation's "War on Drugs." The FBI and the DEA received money to support intensive investigations of drug trafficking organizations.

The National Commission to Support Law Enforcement (Title 34: 42 USC 3721)

This commission was established by law on November 29, 1990, to study the conditions of law-enforcement employment. Other areas of focus included the effectiveness of information-sharing systems and intelligence among federal, state, and local law-enforcement agencies, the adequacy of equipment, physical and human resources, and the quality of research, education, and training. The commission was made up of law-enforcement officers as well as managers, academics specializing in law-enforcement, and members of both the House, Senate, Department of Treasury, and the Department of Justice.

Summary

When citizens and the media react to crime rates and the need to apprehend criminals, attention always seems to focus on police performance. Over the years politicians and the public have turned to commissions to provide answers to the question "What are we doing wrong?" The brutish and corrupt police practices of the 1920s, riotous clashes of the 1960s, and citizen dissatisfaction of the 1990s have pointed out identical needs: improve management and training, increase resources, and better community relationships. Recommendations have also remained consistent: reorganization, education, and technology, or variations on the theme.

Since the Wickersham Commission report in 1931, there has been an increasing tendency to view elements of the criminal-justice system not just as independent isolated functions, but as a multifaceted and interactive system. We recognize that police function in an environment filled with social, psychological, and economic conflicts more complex than any job description could reflect. Whether it is masses of immigrants, industrialization, or racial tension and unemployment, the rhetoric of police-community relations has symbolized an even greater urban crisis. Though debate will continue on the practical or theoretical value of any particular report or act, the pictures they paint of the events and ideology of their day are important lessons in the history of American police.

Marilyn D. McShane

Bibliography

National Commission on the Causes and Prevention of Violence. *Violence in America* (Final Report, December 1969). Reprint. New York: Confucian Press, 1981.

National Commission on Law Observance and Enforcement. *Lawlessness in Law Enforcement.* Vol. 11. Reprint. Montclair, NJ: Patterson Smith, 1968.

———. *Report on Police.* Vol. 14. Reprint. Montclair, NJ: Patterson Smith, 1968.

National Urban League. "A Review of the Law Enforcement Assistance Administration's Relationship to the Black Community." New York: National Urban League, 1976.

Omnibus Crime Control and Safe Streets Act of 1968. Public Law 90–351. 90th Congress, H.R. 5037, June 19, 1968. Reprint. Traffic Institute of Northwestern University.

Platt, A. *The Politics of Riot Commissions.* New York: Macmillan, 1971.

President's Commission on Law Enforcement and Administration of Justice. *The Challenge of Crime in a Free Society.* Washington, DC: Government Printing Office, 1967.

———. *Task Force Report: The Police.* Washington, DC: Government Printing Office, 1967.

Walker, S. "Reexamining the President's Crime Commission." *Crime and Delinquency* 24(1) (1978): 1–12.

Washington Post. October 27, 1990. B1:6.

Weissman, J. *Drug Abuse: The Law and Treatment Alternatives.* Denver, CO: Anderson, 1978.

Federal Law Enforcement Training Center (FLETC)

All major federal law-enforcement personnel except the FBI are trained at the Federal Law Enforcement Training Center (FLETC) near Brunswick, Georgia. Established in 1970, this bureau within the Department of the Treasury is an interagency training facility for the nation's federal criminal investigators and uniformed police officers. Approximately 16,000 students from all fifty states and U.S. territories graduate each year from the FLETC's 1,500-acre Glynco facility and its smaller Marana, Arizona, facility.

History

The need for consolidated training for federal law-enforcement officers became apparent as a direct result of two studies. The first, conducted in 1967 by the Bureau of the Budget (now Office of Management and Budget), concluded that comprehensive training was not available to most federal officers because of inadequate facilities.

The second analysis, made in 1968 by an interagency task force representing ten federal executive departments and independent agencies, specifically identified the type of facility that was needed. The recruit training requirements for both criminal investigators and police officers were also specified, as well as advanced training requirements for law-enforcement officers of all the participating organizations. In May 1969 Congress appropriated funds for planning and building the Center.

The Department of the Treasury was selected as the FLETC's parent agency because it had the largest number of personnel to be trained and had been conducting cross-agency training in its own Law Enforcement Officers School. Training operations began in 1970.

Mission

The FLETC's mission is to serve as the focal point for the bulk of the federal government's law-enforcement training effort. Its specific responsibilities are to:

- Provide the facilities, equipment, and support services necessary for law-enforcement training;
- Conduct common recruit and advanced training for the personnel of the participating law-enforcement organizations;
- Provide facilities and student support services necessary for participating organizations to conduct their own advanced or specialized training;
- Conduct research in law-enforcement training methods and curriculum content in order to improve training programs;
- Conduct specialized programs for state and local law-enforcement personnel; and
- Upon request, advise and assist participating organizations concerning their law-enforcement training needs.

Organization

The FLETC is part of Treasury's Office of Enforcement, along with the Bureau of Alcohol, Tobacco, and Firearms; U.S. Customs Service; and the U.S. Secret Service. Glynco's training policy, programs, and standards, however, are established by an interagency, eight-member board of directors. They occupy positions at the assistant secretary or equivalent level and represent the major agencies which have organizations participating in the FLETC's programs. The FLETC director serves under the authority of the Treasury Office's assistant secretary for enforcement and also is the executive secretary for the board of directors. Assisting him in the management of the FLETC are a deputy director and six assistant directors. They, along with the legal counsel and chief of staff operations, constitute the executive staff.

Operations

While Glynco is the headquarters for the FLETC and is primarily designed for residential training operations, limited training is conducted at other locations. This option is exercised when the programs being conducted do not require specialized facilities, and when regional geographical concentrations of personnel can be most economically trained at locations other than Glynco.

Establishment of the Marana facility, about thirty miles northwest of Tucson, resulted from a request in 1984 from the Bureau of Indian Affairs (BIA) for the FLETC to assume

responsibility for the BIA Indian Police Academy. In addition to that training, the Marana facility is presently being used by the FLETC and participating agencies as a site for short-term, advanced training of personnel located in the western United States.

Facilities

Major facilities at Glynco consist of two classroom buildings, each equipped with the latest audiovisual equipment; specialized areas such as interviewing complexes and criminalistics labs; indoor and outdoor firing ranges, with approximately 100 points each; a physical-training complex equipped with matted training rooms, cardiopulmonary resuscitation classrooms, and a weight-training room; and a large driver-training complex where six separate courses of instruction in handling vehicles can be conducted simultaneously. These are complemented by dormitories and support facilities.

Staff

The FLETC instructor staff consists of experienced professionals who have a minimum of five years of law-enforcement work. Some of the instructors are federal officers and investigators on assignment to the center from their parent organizations. This mix of permanent and temporary instructors creates a desirable balance of experience, fresh insight from the field, and a blend of diverse backgrounds.

Students

Before going to Glynco, students have already been hired as federal criminal investigators (also known as special agents) or police officers of one of the participating organizations: The U.S. Secret Service; U.S. Marshals Service; U.S. Customs Service; Immigration and Naturalization Service; Bureau of Alcohol, Tobacco, and Firearms; U.S. Border Patrol; Internal Revenue Service; National Park Service; and the various Inspectors General are some of the almost sixty federal organizations that train at Glynco.

Basic Programs

Most of the training at Glynco is of a basic nature for newly hired, entry-level personnel. Students attend one of twelve basic programs, which range in length from five to seventeen weeks, depending on their specialty area of law enforcement. All programs are presented through a combination of instructional methodologies, including conferences, lectures, demonstrations, discussions, and practical exercises that often use role players. These role players, drawn from the local community, act as victims, witnesses, and suspects.

Advanced Programs

Glynco also provides advanced and specialized training in subjects that are common to two or more of the participating organizations. Offered are approximately thirty programs in skills ranging from using a microcomputer as an investigative tool to investigating the theft of archaeological resources; from marine law enforcement to advanced law-enforcement photography; and from basic instructor training to computer fraud and data-processing investigations. Agencies also conduct advanced and specialized programs at Glynco to meet their own unique training needs. The FLETC logistically supports this training by feeding, housing, and transporting all students, and by maintaining and scheduling the training facilities.

State and Local Programs

In 1982, another facet of training was added: Glynco began training personnel from state and local enforcement agencies in specialized programs geared toward specific concerns of those agencies. This initiative resulted from recommendations in the Attorney General's Task Force on Violent Crime, which suggested that the unique federal expertise and facilities at Glynco be shared with state and local law-enforcement personnel. Course developers and instructors from numerous federal as well as state and local law-enforcement agencies are used in this cooperative effort. Examples of programs include fraud and financial operations, cargo theft, advanced arson for profit, and undercover investigative techniques. Also included are seminars on law enforcement matters and justice as they affect juveniles.

Charles F. Rinkevich

Bibliography

Goodroe, Charles. "Federal Training for State and Local Police Agencies." *Law and Order* (March 1985): 22–24.

Kuntz, Gregory F. "Development and Implementation of Glynco's Physical Assessment Test." *Police Chief* (November 1985): 22, 24–28, 30.

"More Than a Decade of Expansion at Federal Training Center." *Federal Criminal Investigator* (Summer 1986).

Phillips, Peter W. *The Organizational Development of the Federal Law Enforcement Training Center from 1967–1979: A Case Study*. Gaithersburg, MD: National Criminal Justice Reference Service, 1983.

Rinkevich, Charles F., and Patricia H. Hudson. "Juvenile Justice Training at Glynco." *Police Chief* (February 1984): 52–53.

Thirtieth Report by the Committee on Government Operations. *Unmet Training Needs of the Federal Investigator and the Consolidated Federal Law Enforcement Training Center*, 91st Congress, 2d Session, House Report No. 91-1429. August 14, 1970. Washington, DC: Government Printing Office.

Federal Police and Investigative Agencies

Since the earliest days of the Republic, Congress has chosen to spread responsibility for the enforcement of federal laws and regulations among many agencies rather than to concentrate them in one, all-encompassing police or investigative force. The result is a diversity of agencies with police or quasi-police powers.

Some agencies employ both plainclothes and uniformed personnel; others have powers of investigation, but their officers do not carry firearms or have powers of arrest; other officers are uniformed and armed, but do more investigative than general, police-related duties; and still others concentrate on policing designated geographical areas. All agencies' tasks are specified in federal statutes, treaties, and signed agreements, and are subject to the federal administrative code.

Not all agencies have their own investigative force and may indeed lack investigative authority. However, all federal agencies have access to the Department of Justice, which has the Federal Bureau of Investigation (FBI) as its investigative arm, with jurisdiction over more than 200 offenses. Other agencies rely on an investigative arm under an umbrella agency such as the Department of the Treasury. Even so, no fewer than sixty-three federal agencies have police, investigative, enforcement, or arrest powers. Many other agencies conduct investigations of one kind or another.

The Office of Personnel Management, which investigates personnel and job applicants for many agencies, defines the duties of a general investigator, General Service GS-1810, and criminal investigator, GS-1811. The GS-1810 position requires investigators to plan and conduct investigations into administration of and compliance with federal laws and regulations. Investigators do not carry firearms, conduct search and seizure duties, or make arrests. The GS-1811 position requires investigators to plan and conduct investigations of alleged or suspected violations of federal law; they may carry firearms, (subject to agency and congressional authority), make arrests, conduct searches, seize evidence, and perform undercover duties.

Uniformed federal police officers protect life, property, and the rights of individual citizens; enforce federal, state, county, and municipal statues; preserve the peace; prevent, detect, and investigate accidents and crimes; arrest violators; and aid in emergencies. Many, but not all, uniformed federal officers have no authority to carry firearms while off duty or when not on federal property. By specific agreement, state or other peace officers assist the federal force by performing law-enforcement and public-safety duties on federal property, including forests and lands.

A checklist follows of the more prominent federal police and investigative branches. Bracketed dates are for the units' founding, though most were preceded by earlier bodies with similar functions:

The Department of Defense (DOD) probably employs the most police, security, and criminal investigative personnel, although they are limited in jurisdiction over civilians. Two DOD agencies are primarily staffed by civilians: the Defense Criminal Investigative Service, also known as the DOD-Office of Inspector General (1972); and the Naval Investigative Service (1915). The rest of the DOD agencies generally utilize military, with some civilian, investigators. These are the Defense Investigative Service (1972), which undertakes all military and civilian DOD personnel background investigations, regardless of agency; the Army Intelligence and Security Command (1917), which employs plainclothes security investigators; the Military Police (1776); the Criminal Investigative Command (1915); the Air Force Office of Special Investigations (1943); the Office of Security Police (1948); and the Defense Intelligence Agency (comparable to the Central Intelligence Agency). It is impossible to determine how many agents, uniformed security, or investiga-tive personnel are employed in this field because some figures are classified.

The Department of Justice (DOJ) was established in 1870 as successor to earlier agencies, the first attorney general having been appointed in 1789, as were the first thirteen presidentially appointed U.S. marshals (presently there are ninety-four, one for each federal judicial district and a force of 1,706 civil-service deputy marshals). The other law-enforcement agencies under the DOJ are the Immigration and Naturalization Service (1940), which has over 4,000 investigators, inspectors, and border patrol agents; the FBI (1908), which has over 9,000 special agents (over 450 women); the Bureau of Prisons (1930); the Division of Probation (1940), whose 1,800 probation officers perform both probation and parole investigator duties; and the Drug Enforcement Agency (1973), which has over 2,000 agents.

The Department of the Treasury (1789) has wide responsibilities. The U.S. Customs Service, with 4,500 inspectors, 600 special agents, and 1,300 investigators, is under its jurisdiction. So is the Internal Revenue Service, with 2,400 special agents under the criminal-investigation division and 400 criminal-investigator inspectors under the inspection service. The Alcohol Tax Unit (1862) was renamed the Bureau of Alcohol, Tobacco, and Firearms in 1972 and has about 2,400 special agents; and the U.S. Secret Service, which has about 1,600 special agents, 1,200 uniformed officers, and fifty-eight officers under the Treasury police force, was established in 1865. Other agencies under Treasury with police or law-enforcement personnel include the Office of Inspector General (OIG) and the Bureau of Printing and Engraving. The U.S. Mints have guard forces, but investigations of stolen gold or background investigations are conducted by other Treasury agencies. The Federal Reserve Banks act as agents for the Treasury by issuing Federal Reserve notes and securities and have individual guard forces for the protection of premises.

The Department of Interior (1849) has five agencies with law-enforcement powers: the Division of Law Enforcement Services under the Bureau of Indian Affairs (1756), with some 1,100 police and investigative personnel; the Division of Ranger Activities (1974) has approximately 1,700 full-time rangers plus part-time ranger personnel; the Fish and Wildlife Service (1940) has some 950 enforcement personnel (including 190 special agents); the Park

Police (1919) is under the National Park Service and has about 600 uniformed and investigative personnel; and the OIG (1978) has approximately forty criminal investigators.

The Department of Transportation (DOT) has four basic components with federal law-enforcement powers. They include the entire Coast Guard, which has approximately 37,000 enlisted and officer personnel; the U.S. Coast Guard Intelligence and Law Enforcement Branch (1915), with approximately ninety plainclothes special agents; the OIG-DOT (1978) has about sixty-five criminal investigators; and the Federal Aviation Administration Police, which has 145 uniformed officers and investigators. The Coast Guard, which has wide search and seizure jurisdiction and authority to board marine vessels to check papers and licenses, constitutes a reservoir of law-enforcement personnel who carry weapons on duty, but generally, except for the personnel in the Intelligence and Law Enforcement Branch, do not have this authority off duty. Even though under a civilian agency, Coast Guard personnel are subject to the Uniform Code of Military Justice.

The Department of Agriculture (1862) has many agencies with inspection or investigative duties; not all have arrest powers. The Forest Service (1945) has approximately 4,000 forest rangers, 700 law-enforcement specialists, and 100 special agents (county or state law-enforcement officers often provide police coverage on forest lands by contract); and the OIG (1962) has fifty-five investigators who perform criminal investigative or personnel integrity inquiry duties.

The Postal Inspection Service is one of the oldest federal law-enforcement agencies in the United States, tracing its origins to about 1737. The postal system is protected by federal legislation and postal inspectors who are authorized to investigate mail depredation and crimes associated with the Postal Service; they do not investigate crimes by private postal carriers. This agency has some 4,150 law-enforcement employees, including 1,900 postal inspectors and 2,200 uniformed security personnel.

The General Services Administration, or GSA (1949), is composed of many varied sections and divisions which provide services, office space, and other facilities for all federal departments, including law-enforcement agencies. The backbone of the GSA component that provides protection to federal buildings and property is the GSA police, which has approximately 2,250 officers and investigators; there are also about 110 criminal investigators in the OIG. GSA law-enforcement personnel investigate criminal violations committed against federal agencies or personnel on federal property, but the FBI has primary jurisdiction over crimes committed on federal property, lands, or reservations, even though it may waive or defer this jurisdiction to the GSA or other federal agencies. In many federal buildings the GSA police have agreements with the U.S. Marshal's Service on areas of jurisdiction, since the Marshals provide protection to federal judges, juries, and others while they are on federal property (federal courts are housed in federal buildings protected by GSA personnel).

The Office of Personnel Management (OPM) is primarily in charge of civil-service matters for the government and often provides personnel examinations and interacts with federal agencies to determine and ensure proper hiring qualifications for government positions, including federal police or enforcement personnel. It also conducts personnel security investigations for federal agencies that do not have a force conducting such inquiries. There are over 460 investigators in the Office of Compliance and Investigations (GS-1810 investigators) and three criminal investigators in the OIG (who investigate integrity or corruption cases within the OPM).

The Department of State (1789) relies on its Office of Security (1917) to bring cohesion to its intelligence and investigative operations. The Office of Security, with approximately 475 special agents, investigates passport fraud violations, protects official visitors to the United States (except heads of state, who are protected by the Secret Service), and provides security officers at U.S. embassies.

A variety of agencies with criminal investigators (GS-1811) work in various federal department OIG offices, such as the Environmental Protection Agency (1970), which has approximately twenty-five investigators (there is also an Office of Legal Enforcement Counsel with twenty-five investigators); the OIG of the Health and Human Services, with over 400 investigators; the OIG of the Housing and Urban Development with approximately seventy-five criminal investigators; the Department of Labor (1976) divides its OIG operation into an Office of Investigations for general criminal investigations and the Office of Labor Racketeering,

F

which investigates corrupt union and organized crime activities; the OIG of the National Aeronautic Services Administration (1978) has approximately fourteen special agents; the Government Printing Office (1861) started the OIG office in 1978 (about fifteen investigators and 110 uniformed officers); and the Veterans' Administration (1930) has approximately sixty-five special agents in the OIG and 1,850 investigators and uniformed personnel in the VA Security Service who patrol and investigate offenses on VA grounds and property.

The Department of Commerce (1789) has about sixty-five special agents and intelligence personnel under the International Trade Administration; ninety-three special agents in the National Marine Fisheries Service, which comes under the National Oceanic Atmospheric Administration (1970); and criminal investigators assigned to the OIG office.

The Metropolitan Police Department (MPD) of the District of Columbia is a federal police department under Home Rule. Because Washington is a federal district encompassing ten square miles, every offense committed there is a federal crime prosecuted in federal courts. A multitude of federal agencies have arrest or criminal investigative authority in the DC depending on geographical location. For example, the White House grounds, the Executive Office Building adjacent to the White House, and the Blair House, which is the official guest house (across from the White House on Pennsylvania Avenue), are under the jurisdiction of the Secret Service, both special agents and the uniformed division (formerly the White House Police). Crimes committed on Pennsylvania Avenue are under the jurisdiction of the MPD; and violations that occur in Lafayette Park adjacent to the Blair House and across from the White House are under the jurisdiction of the Park Police (National Park Service, Department of the Interior). The MPD, which has approximately 3,900 officers and detectives, polices the District of Columbia, although other federal agencies have jurisdiction in specific buildings and property under their control.

The U.S. Capitol Police (1801) has about 1,250 uniformed officers and investigators, who provide police and investigative services on Capitol grounds, in annex buildings, and the Capitol Power Plant. They also provide protective services to members of Congress anywhere in the United States.

The U.S. Supreme Court Police (1939) have jurisdiction in the Supreme Court Building and adjacent grounds. One of the smallest uniformed agencies with the DC area is the National Zoological Park Police (1890), with approximately forty full-time and part-time officers. This force is under the Smithsonian Institution and provides police services to the National Zoological Park which covers 165 acres of property.

More than half a dozen regulatory agencies employ criminal or general investigators, or personnel who conduct field inquiries and determine violations. They are the Federal Communications Commission (1934), which has jurisdiction over radio and television transmissions and some other forms of communication; the Federal Maritime Commission (1914), which has general responsibility for regulating common carriers by water and in foreign commerce, issues licenses to operate in American waters, and maintains jurisdiction in other such areas; the Federal Trade Commission (1914) investigates false advertising and unsafe products; the Food and Drug Administration (1927) has jurisdiction over the purity and safe packaging of medicines and food; the Interstate Commerce Commission (1887) regulates and sets rates for interstate carriers; and the Security Exchange Commission (1934) regulates, investigates, and corrects problems in securities, stocks, and bonds offered to the public. Other smaller agencies also have investigative powers.

The Tennessee Valley Authority (TVA) is a self-financed, government-owned corporation protected by federal law; it was created in 1933. It has approximately 850 law-enforcement personnel to protect facilities on TVA lands, but primary investigative jurisdiction lies with the FBI.

Donald A. Torres

Bibliography

Cummings, Homer, and Carl McFarland. *The History of Justice and the Federal Executive.* New York: Da Capo Press, 1970.

Felt, Mark W. *The FBI Pyramid from the Inside.* New York: G.P. Putnam's Sons, 1979.

Hall, John P. *Peacekeeping in America: A Developmental Study of American Law Enforcement.* Dubuque, IA: Kendall Hunt Publications, 1975.

Kaiser, F.M. *Law Enforcement Reorganization at the Federal Level.* Washington,

DC: Library of Congress Congressional Research Service, Major Issues, 1980.

Millsbaugh, Arthur C. *Crime Control by the National Government*. Washington, DC: The Brookings Institute, 1937.

Rektor, Bela. *Federal Law Enforcement Agencies*. Astor, FL: Danubian Press, 1975.

Torres, Donald A. *Handbook of Federal Police and Investigative Agencies*. Westport, CT: Greenwood Press, 1985.

Fencing Stolen Property

"Fencing"—the crime of buying and reselling stolen merchandise—is one of the links that binds theft to the larger social system. Without someone to dispose of stolen property, thieves would have to rely on their own connections, and both the costs and the risks of crime would increase substantially. For the rest of society, the fence provides an opportunity for interested people to buy something at less than market price.

The central role of the fence in property crime was recognized in the late eighteenth century by Patrick Colquhoun in his book, *A Treatise on the Police of the Metropolis* (1796). He wrote:

> Nothing can be more just than the old observation, "that if there were no Receivers there would be no Thieves." Deprive a thief of a sale and ready market for his goods and he is undone.

Fencing remains a rather poorly researched area in criminology for several reasons. First, it often wears the cloak of legitimate business and is carried out in a rational, businesslike manner, so that it has few of the qualities traditionally associated with crime. Second, because fencing is a crime with low visibility and is conducted in secrecy, researchers have directed their attention to more visible crimes such as theft, or to violent crimes against persons for which statistics are available. Third, the cloak of secrecy and the maintenance of a legitimate "front" make detailed investigation difficult.

The legal requirements for demonstrating that fencing has occurred are complex. In America, as in England, there are three elements to the crime: (1) The property must have been stolen; (2) the property must have been received or concealed (though the fence may not have actually seen or touched it); (3) the receiver must have accepted it with knowledge that it was stolen.

Case Studies of Fences

Much of what is known about fencing today comes from two in-depth studies of individual fences, one being Carl Klockars' work, *The Professional Fence* (1974), and the other by Darrell Steffensmeier, *The Fence: In the Shadow of Two Worlds* (1986). Klockars interviewed "Vincent Swaggi" (not his real name), a well-known fence in his city, while Steffensmeier interviewed "Sam Goodman" (also an alias), a well-known fence in the fictitious "American City." Steffensmeier also interviewed thieves and customers who had contact with Sam, several other fences, and law-enforcement officials to authenticate Sam's account of events.

Both works portray the fence as an "entrepreneur" and describe fencing as an enterprise requiring resourcefulness, charisma, ingenuity, and a good grasp of market practices and the rules of economic competition. Pricing norms and prevailing market conditions are used to determine what is "fair," and a sense of justice is developed based on the risks borne both by the thief and by the fence. Fences must pay a fair price so that thieves will come back to them again with stolen goods. However, because of their greater experience and knowledge, fences tend to dominate thieves in the pricing of stolen goods. The thieves often need money quickly, have few options other than to agree to the fence's offer, and are under pressure to get rid of the stolen merchandise. Professional thieves who steal high-priced items are usually given the highest amounts—about 40 to 50 percent of the wholesale price. The amateur or drug addict thief who is not in a good bargaining position will receive the smallest amounts—often only ten to twenty cents on the dollar. Klockars and Steffensmeier also point out that fences are not above chicanery and take advantage of any opportunity to pad their profits. Both Vincent and Sam were proud of the tricks they sometimes played with quality, quantity, and price to dupe thieves, especially small-time thieves.

The studies of fencing by Klockars and Steffensmeier detail the networks in which the fence is embedded, and the way the fence interacts with thieves, criminal-justice officials, antiques dealers and collectors, truckers, dockworkers, competing fences, and many other people. Both studies look at the rewards of fencing, including money, reputation in the criminal community, excitement, and a sense of mastery over one's life. Vincent and Sam justified their fencing involvement by claiming that the fence is not the same as a thief, does little harm to the victims of theft, does not differ much from legitimate businesspeople, is able to operate only with the support of legitimate people (including the police), breaks no more rules than most people, and does a lot of good for others.

Networking connections are vital to the fence whose business is essentially word-of-mouth. The importance of networking was first established by Marilyn Walsh (1977). She identified three types of networks: (1) play networks, groups of seasoned burglars and fences who meet socially and exchange information; (2) work-a-day networks, often based on employer-employee relations, as when a fence with a legitimate business receives stolen merchandise from an employee; (3) and kinship networks, dominated by family ties, often with young members stealing and older members selling. Steffensmeier shows that Sam's networking was extensive, developed through word-of-mouth, referrals, and sponsorship by underworld figures. As characterizes many fences, Sam played an active role in cultivating contacts with employee thieves, in coaching thieves on techniques of theft and product identification, and in developing long-term relationships with buyers.

To be successful, a fence must meet the following conditions:

1. Keep upfront cash—most deals are cash transactions, so an adequate supply of ready cash must always be on hand.
2. Display knowledge of dealing—learning the ropes—the fence must be schooled in the knowledge of the trade; developing a "larceny sense"; learning to "buy right" at acceptable prices; being able to "cover one's back" and not get caught; finding out how to make the right contacts; knowing how to "wheel and deal" and create opportunities for profit.
3. Maintain connections with suppliers of stolen goods—this will depend on the kind of fence one is, but many fences will purchase goods from a wide variety of thieves and suppliers, including burglars, drug addicts, shoplifters, dockworkers,

and truck drivers. Especially valuable are long-term relationships with suppliers of high-value stolen goods who are relatively free of police interference. The warehouse worker who pilfers is a better supplier than the narcotics addict who is more likely to be apprehended and talk to the police.
4. Maintain connections with buyers—the successful fence must have continuing access to buyers of stolen merchandise who are inaccessible to the common thief.
5. Seek complicity with law enforcers—the successful fence must work out a relationship with law-enforcement officials who invariably find out about the fence's operations.

Steffensmeier (see also Klockars) found that to stay in business, the fence must either bribe officials with good deals on merchandise or act as an informer who helps police recover particularly important merchandise and arrest thieves.

Lay and Professional Fences

The studies by Klockars and Steffensmeier concentrate on the activities of large-scale dealers or "professional" fences. Jerome Hall (1952) distinguished professional dealers from other criminal receivers (e.g., "occasional" and "lay") by the intent to resell the stolen property and by the regularity or persistence with which they purchased stolen goods. Klockars elaborated on Hall's definition by delineating three criteria that help to differentiate the professional fence from other receivers of stolen property. The professional fence (a) has direct contact with the thief, (b) buys and sells regularly and profitably, and (c) is a "public" figure who has acquired a reputation among lawbreakers, law enforcers, and others in the criminal community.

There is very little information on the extent of fencing activities by nonprofessional receivers of stolen property, although several studies have recognized the importance of amateur classes of criminal receiver and their importance to the initiation and continuing support of property crime. Henry (1978) and Cromwell et al. (1990) report that a significant proportion of property, whether stolen by ordinary people in legitimate jobs or by burglars, is sold directly to the public—purchased for personal consumption or for resale. Steffensmeier concluded there is no way of knowing at present what proportion of stolen goods passes through "professional" fences. Thieves may sell stolen property on street corners, in bars, or at flea markets, or to part-time receivers whose primary business activity is something other than buying and selling stolen property. They may sell the stolen merchandise to friends, neighbors, coworkers, and schoolmates. Some thieves keep the goods or trade them for drugs. McIntosh (1976) described the practice of selling directly to the consumer as "self-fencing." She concluded that many thieves sell or pawn their goods to lay receivers, acquaintances, police officers, shopkeepers, and other thieves.

Professional fences get their share of minor thefts and employee pilferage, but for the most part they receive property stolen by career-oriented thieves; that is, they are the major outlets for thefts involving moderate to large quantities of merchandise and they also handle a sizable proportion of high value, but small quantity, thefts.

Types of Fences
Already by the late eighteenth and early nineteenth century, with the growth of fencing operations accompanying industrialization, it was commonplace for students of fencing to distinguish among receivers according to scale of operations and criminal intent. Colquhoun, who provided the outstanding interpretation of the trade in stolen goods at the beginning of the nineteenth century, divided receivers into twelve different classes.

1.	Opulent Receivers who trade on a large scale	20
2.	Interior Receivers who deal with Lumpers , & c.	25
3.	Copeman in connection with Revenue Officers	20
4.	Dealers in Old Iron, and Old Ships' Stores, & c.	55
5.	Small Grocers and Chandlers	55
6.	Publicans	35
7.	Twine and Rope Spinners	20
8.	Female Receivers	50
9.	Covetous Receivers	60
10.	Careless Receivers	150
11.	Receivers on the Banks of the Thames	40
12.	Jew Receivers and others who travel with Carts	20
	Total	550

Colquhoun observed the individuals of the first class, though small in number, are the most important traders in stolen goods:

> Of all others, [they] are the most noxious and destructive to Commercial property ... These availing themselves of the pecuniary resources they possess, give existence and vigor to depredation, upon a large scale, by solicitations and facilities, without which they could not have been committed; and when under the embarrassment of detection, avail themselves of pecuniary resources, in calling forth the talents of Counsel and the whole chicane of the law, to enable them to elude the punishment due to their crimes; in which the friends of Morality and Justice have to lament that they are too often successful, producing thereby incalculable injuries to the Community at large.

After Colquhoun other commentators also distinguished between the "lesser" or "occasional receivers" and what were increasingly being designated as the "professional receiver," or the "fence-master," who is at "the top of the guilty profession." The trend toward distinguishing "lesser" from the "more important" receivers culminated in the publication of *Theft, Law, and Society* (first edition, 1935), in which Jerome Hall developed a simple typology, distinguishing his "professional receiver" dealer from both the "lay receiver," who knowingly bought stolen property for his own consumption, and the "occasional receiver," who bought stolen property for resale but only infrequently.

Recently, Cromwell et al. (1990) proposed that criminal receivers of stolen property can be distinguished along several dimensions:

1. the frequency with which they purchase stolen property
2. the scale or volume of purchases of stolen property
3. the purpose of purchase (for personal consumption or for resale)
4. the level of commitment to purchasing stolen property

Building on Hall's typology, Cromwell et al. delineate three levels of receiver:

1. Professional receivers—their principal enterprise is the purchase and redistribu-

tion of stolen property. The professional receiver generally makes purchases directly from the thief and almost exclusively for resale. These receivers are proactive in operation, establishing a reliable and persistent flow of merchandise, buying continuously and on a large scale, and providing strategic aid as well as organization for the thief's illicit activities.

2. Avocational receivers—they purchase stolen property primarily for resale, but do not rely on buying and selling stolen property as a main source of livelihood. Fencing is a part-time enterprise, secondary to, but often associated with, their primary business activity (which may be legal or illegal).

3. Amateur or "citizen" receivers—otherwise honest citizens who buy stolen property on a relatively small scale, primarily, but not exclusively, for personal consumption. Crime is peripheral, rather than central, to their lives. Amateur fences typically are initially solicited as customers and buy merchandise that is seldom represented as stolen, although they may know or suspect that the property was not obtained legally by the seller.

Fences can be distinguished along other dimensions relative to the kind of cover used to conceal their fencing trade, to the scale of their fencing operation, and to their relationship to the larger criminal community. First, all fences are by definition businesspeople: They are middlemen in illegitimate commerce, providing goods and services to others, regardless of whether they operate from a legitimate business or rely solely on individual resources. Although a few operate independently of any business "front," most fences are simultaneously proprietors or operators of a legitimate business, which provides a cover or front for the fencing. Businesses most often favored are those having a large cash flow (e.g., coin and gem shop, second-hand store, auction house, and restaurant) and the flexibility to set one's own hours (salvage yard, bail-bonding).

Second, fences can be distinguished by how closely the stolen property corresponds to the legitimate goods sold—that is, whether the trade in stolen goods is fully covered, partly covered, or uncovered by the fence's legitimate

business identity. Fencing through noncovered fronts—where illicit lines of goods are distinct from the legitimate commerce—tends to be small in scale. Typically these kinds of fences are owners or operators of bars, restaurants, and similar businesses where knowledgeable contact with thieves may occur and where contacts with would-be customers and certain types of business arrangements are possible. The stolen goods may be disposed of by selling them to a patron or business associate who is a proprietor of an unrelated business, or they may be peddled to a larger fence.

Third, fences also vary in terms of "product specialization"—the kinds of stolen goods they handle. At one pole is the generalist, a fence who will buy and sell virtually anything a thief offers. At the other pole is the specialist, who handles only certain kinds of goods such as auto parts or jewelry. Most fences are specialists in that they handle only one or a few product lines.

Finally, fences can be distinguished in terms of the "respectability" of their legitimate operations and their "affinity" with the criminal community. On the one hand, some fences operate establishments that are perceived by the community-at-large as strictly clean (e.g., restaurants, appliance stores); some fences operate businesses that are perceived as clean but somewhat suspect (e.g., taverns, auto parts shops, antique shops, and jewelry stores); and other fences operate what are viewed as quasi-legitimate businesses (e.g., pawnshops, coin and gem shops, second-hand discount stores, salvage companies, auction houses, and bail-bonding). On the other hand, some fences are more disreputable than others in that they come from thief or hustler backgrounds or have a fairly extensive affinity with the criminal underworld.

Although some commentators (e.g., Walsh, 1977) have described the typical fence as essentially a "respectable businessman," what evidence is available strongly suggests otherwise. The typical fence is characterized by one or more of the following: prior criminal contact or background in criminal or quasilegal activities, such as theft, hustling, or the rackets in general; operation of a quasi-legitimate business such as a second-hand discount store, salvage yard, an auction house, a foundry, or a bail-bonding business; and affinity with the underworld, such as ongoing business and leisure associations with established members of the underworld. It is hardly surprising that many organized crime members and associates are involved in the fencing of stolen property (Pennsylvania Crime Commission, 1991).

That the fence is not your average businessman does not overlook the greed of many legitimate merchants. One of the major outlets, after all, for stolen goods handled by fences is that of legitimate businessmen who are willing to buy suspect merchandise if it assures them of a higher profit. But running a fencing business is another matter. The chances of an everyday merchant becoming a dealer in stolen goods, should he so desire, may be as remote as are the chances of the typical ex-con becoming a legitimate businessman.

The Fence's Relationship to Theft Reconsidered

The fence does play a primary role in the marketing of stolen property, but that role is often hyped by commentators and law-enforcement officials as bigger and more important than it ought to be, and also ignores the involvement of other participants in an illegal trade. The old saying "if no fences no thieves" assumes that thieves are not autonomous or "free" in their stealing behaviors, and that the police and the public have little or nothing to do with the maintenance of a criminal system. But, while the thief is supposed to be dependent on the fence, he is, at the same time, assumed to engage in his theft activity independently of him, so that an inherent paradox exists. If the thief is independently motivated to theft, then he will steal irrespectively of whether or not fences exist. Furthermore, emphasizing that the thief depends on and could not exist without the fence ignores the fact that the fence is in precisely the same position as the thief; he is dependent on outlets or a market for stolen property. Frequently, this problem is resolved by the involvement of merchants who are tempted to purchase stolen goods at cheap prices in order that they may sell at a higher profit. Public demand for stolen goods also helps maintain the fence. Budget-conscious consumers are often willing to buy stolen goods, "no questions asked," and need little encouragement. In addition, when they are victims of theft, ordinary citizens are frequently willing to forego prosecution once their stolen goods have been restored to them or they have received compensation. In a similar way, insurance companies and private detective agencies protect the fence from public or legal reaction to the theft, either by diluting the rightful owner's desire to pursue those responsible by providing compensation, or by cooperating with him for the return of stolen property.

Finally, the saying "if no fences no thieves" ignores that official complicity of some kind is often required if the prospective fence hopes to buy and sell stolen goods regularly and over a period of time. Sometimes the official protection a fence enjoys is an outgrowth of the corruption of law enforcement on a large scale. Present-day fences connected to Mafia or localized syndicates, for example, may benefit from the corruption of legal authorities achieved by way of general racketeering activities. Other times, the basis of the police-fence stems from the operating reality that both have access to resources desired by the other:

> The fence is able to give information about thefts, for he knows who commits them; he can also set up a thief, arranging for the police to be present; he is often able to secure the return of stolen goods as a result of his knowledge and contacts; and finally, he is able to offer the police "bargains" or gifts of stolen goods. . . . In return for all this, police can warn the fence of impending investigations or the danger of purchasing certain goods. They can provide protection by not pursuing their enquiries should their investigations lead to him. (Henry, 1977:124)

The sociolegal writings on the traffic in stolen property have addressed two complicated issues. One is the fence's role in the overall flow of stolen property from thieves to eventual consumers. The other issue is whether or not enforcement efforts should be more rationally directed at the fence than at other agents in the traffic in stolen property—thieves, occasional receivers, those to whom the fence sells, or complicitous authorities.

Darrell J. Steffensmeier

Bibliography
Colquhoun, P.A. *A Treatise on the Police of the Metropolis*. London: Printed by H. Fry for C. Dilly in the Poultry, 1796.

F

——. *A Treatise on the Commerce and Police of the River Thames*. London: Printed for Joseph Mawman, 1800.

Crapsey, Edward. *The Nether Side of New York*. New York: Sheldon, 1872.

Cromwell, Paul, James Olson, and D'Aunn Avary. *Breaking and Entering: An Ethnographic Analysis of Burglary*. Newbury Park, CA: Sage, 1990.

Hall, Jerome. *Theft, Law, and Society*. 2d ed. Indianapolis: Bobbs-Merrill, 1952.

Henry, Stuart. "On the Fence." *British Journal of Law and Society* 4 (1977): 124–33.

——. *The Hidden Economy*. London: Martin Robertson, 1978.

Klockars, Carl. *The Professional Fence*. New York: Free Press, 1974.

McIntosh, Mary. "Thieves, and Fences: Markets and Power in Professional Crime." *British Journal of Criminology* 16 (1976): 257–66.

Roselius, Ted, and Douglas Denton. "Marketing Theory and the Fencing of Stolen Goods." *Denver Law Journal* 50 (1973): 177–205.

Steffensmeier, Darrell. *The Fence: In the Shadow of Two Worlds*. Totowa, NJ: Rowman & Littlefield Publishers, 1986.

——, Project Director/Principal Writer. *Organized Crime in Pennsylvania—A Decade of Change: The 1990 Report*. Pennsylvania Crime Commission, 1991.

Walsh, Marilyn E. *The Fence: A New Look at the World of Property Theft*. Westport, CT: Greenwood Press, 1977.

Field Training and Evaluation Program

Program Overview

One of the first formal field training and evaluation programs (FTEPs) was developed in 1972 by the San Jose (California) Police Department. The purpose was to provide graduating academy recruits with structured training administered by field training officers (FTOs) specializing in the instruction and evaluation of recruit performance in job-related tasks. The goal of the program was to help the recruit to develop academy-learned knowledge and skills and to perform tasks in response to the needs of community residents.

Most FTEPs modeled after the San Jose program are administered in phases of three weeks. The program can last anywhere from six weeks to twenty-four weeks, the length being determined by departmental resources. FTEPs provide the recruit with training in a broad range of job-performance categories. To ensure program validity, the categories should be directly related to a detailed job-task analysis of the position of police officer within the respective agency.

Any number of job-related categories can be used within the program to measure recruit performances. A sample of the categories includes: officer safety, field performance under stressful conditions, driving skills, control of conflict, report writing, use of the radio, self-initiated field activities, knowledge of policies, procedures, traffic laws, penal code, managing calls for service, and relationships with officers, supervisors, and citizens. These basic categories represent the foundation of the FTEP. Recruits are shown how to apply what they have learned from their academy training. Additionally, these categories serve as the basis from which the recruits expand their abilities as they encounter and cope with new, daily experiences.

The program therefore requires the FTO to perform a multiple role. First and foremost, each FTO is a police officer dedicated to delivering a multitude of different services to the public. Second, the FTO is a trainer responsible for exposing, instructing, and developing the knowledge and skills of the recruit. Lastly, the FTO is an evaluator responsible for assessing the performance of the recruit in association with standardized program evaluation guidelines.

Program Format
Instruction Phases

The recruit will attend a brief orientation session before being assigned to an FTO. Initially, the recruit will complete a series of instructional phases (usually three phases, each three weeks in duration). Time spent in each of the instructional phases corresponds to the recruit's shift assignment. As an example, the recruit could complete the first instructional phase on the day shift. The second instructional phase could be spent on the night shift, with the remaining phase completed during the evening shift. Continuity usually exists within departments relative to these assignments; however, each department may vary the phase assignments.

The FTO will provide detailed instructions designed to guide and improve the recruit's performance. At the end of each training day, detailed documentation of the recruit's performance is recorded by the FTO on a daily activity report.

As recruits progress through the instruction phases, they are expected to perform a number of predefined tasks. These number as many as two or three hundred of the separate responsibilities that a police officer could encounter at any time during a tour of duty. The tasks are administered from a checklist within the recruit's training manual, which each FTO uses as a guide to document the recruit's accomplishments. The checklist also serves as a historical reference that communicates to each ensuing FTO which activities the recruit has or has not performed. Concomitantly, as the recruit completes each instructional phase and performs different tasks the recruit assumes more and more responsibility for his or her own actions. The nature and degree of difficulty of tasks on the checklist also increases as the recruit moves toward the end of each instruction phase. Associated with this shift in responsibilities is a change in expectations by the FTO and recruits.

Recruits must demonstrate their ability to perform the job of a police officer. Technically, by the end of the last instructional phase, recruits should be able to discharge their responsibilities in accordance with program standards. The FTO determines whether the recruits are capable of doing their job independently. As this becomes more evident, the FTO begins to allow recruits more flexibility in the performance of their duties throughout their tours of duty.

Part of each day is set aside for the FTO and the recruit to discuss daily performance. At the end of each week, the recruit, FTO, and supervisor will meet to discuss the recruit's weekly progress. Meetings are also held at the end of each instruction and evaluation phase. The purpose of these meetings is to provide recruits with an opportunity to discuss any problems, strengths, and weaknesses they may be experiencing. Meetings also provide an avenue to check the administrative performance of the FTO so as to ensure that program standards are being observed.

Evaluation Phases

Once the recruits complete the instructional phases, the evaluation process begins, providing them with an opportunity to demonstrate their level of proficiency in each of the previously referenced performance categories. This phase usually lasts from two to three weeks. During this phase, the recruits are expected to demonstrate a degree of independence in the performance of their duties. Again, the recruit's performance is assessed in accordance with the same daily categories utilized during the instructional phases. Successful completion of the evaluation phase is based upon demonstrated ability judged to be acceptable by the FTO when compared against standardized evaluation guidelines. Upon graduation from the program, recruits will finish the remainder of their probationary period before becoming fully fledged police officers.

Should a recruit fail to successfully complete the evaluation phase, choices are available to department personnel. First, the recruit may be dismissed, as would happen during any other portion of the selection process if performance fell below minimum standards. A second more viable option is to recycle the recruit through a "remedial training" phase. Upon completion of the remedial training phase of two to three weeks, the recruit enters a final evaluation phase, also lasting two to three weeks. If the recruit fails to complete this phase successfully, he or she is terminated. Successful completion allows the recruit to complete the remaining probationary period.

Program Considerations

Despite the similarities of the various FTEPs implemented within different agencies, a number of variations have enhanced administration of programs as well as improving their validity and reliability.

FTO Role Modification

So as to lighten the burden on FTOs innovative departments have separated instructional and evaluational responsibilities. As recruits progress through the instructional phases, their performance is monitored and documented by field training instructors (FTIs). Documentation focuses upon identifying the level of additional training needed to complete tasks on the training checklist. When the recruit enters the evaluation phase, a field training evaluator (FTE) assesses performance. This is measured against standardized evaluation guidelines developed for each of the job-related performance categories used within the department's program. This separation of roles removes the difficulty of having the FTOs simultaneously function as both supporters and critics of a recruit's performance.

Standardized Evaluation Guidelines

Another significant program consideration focuses on the need to use standardized evaluation guidelines. FTEP administrators have generally chosen to use a "graphic scaling technique" to document performance measurements. This utilizes a sliding numeric scale, usually beginning with the number 1, designating unacceptable performance, and ending with the number 7, designating an outstanding performance.

To ensure a reasonable degree of reliability, program administrators use anchor points on the graphic rating scales. An anchor point specifically describes the level of performance for each particular number. On a seven-point graphic rating scale, numbers 1, 4, and 7 are designated as anchor points. Since performance standards are specifically described for each of the anchor points, FTOs are more easily able to match observed performances with the remaining scale points.

Additional documentation is required if the performance is unacceptable or outstanding. Some departments require documentation for all observed performances, regardless of the grade awarded. Although administration of the FTEP is perceived by the department to be a fair and impartial way to screen prospective police officers, recruits will sometimes challenge recommendations for dismissal or termination. Since the chief of police is usually the only person authorized to dismiss a recruit, he or she will rely heavily on documentation generated by FTOs to discount any allegations of favoritism, bias, or prejudice lodged against the department by the recruit.

Termination Review Committees

To assist the chief of police further in making such a decision, termination review committees (TRCs) have been established. These are independent department personnel assembled to review the recruit's file. The material reviewed generally consists of documentation associated with the recruit's performance while progressing through the instruction and evaluation phases. The committee's review is specifically designed to determine whether inadequacies or unfair practices adversely affected the recruit's standing within the FTEP. This procedure strengthens the checks and balances within the program and assures the recruit of all possible advantages in the search to verify the validity of a recommendation for dismissal.

Standard Operating Procedures

A final significant program consideration centers upon the development of standardized operating procedures (SOPs). SOPs are designed to describe in detail how the FTEP operates. Guidelines governing program personnel, organizational structure, administrative reporting procedures, training and evaluation requirements, and program separation procedures are developed with the specific intent of establishing program continuity and consistency. This is especially important since the administration of the FTEP requires the participation of personnel from different shifts. This is further exacerbated when the program is administered across different precincts by different commanders.

Conclusion

In large departments, additional improvements beyond the implementation of SOPs have been developed. The most popular change has been the designation of centralized program administrators whose sole responsibility is to monitor, guide, and direct the administration of the FTEP within the department. Through this role, administrators achieve standardization of program application throughout the department. This assists the department in maintaining the continuity of the program, thereby easing the burden on the field commanders by removing from them direct responsibility for administering the program.

Although the concept of field training is relatively new to policing, significant strides have been made with the FTEP since its formal inception in 1972. A recent nationwide study conducted by Michael McCampbell (sponsored under a grant from the National Institute of Justice) is the most extensive assessment of FTEPs published to date. Numerous recommendations are suggested to guide and direct the efforts of administrators as they seek to improve and implement the program in their agencies.

Another recent endeavor centers upon the creation and national distribution of the *Field Training Quarterly* (FTQ). The FTQ discusses such issues as formalized training curriculums for certifying FTOs, incentive criteria to reward FTO excellence, and selection criteria for FTOs, all of which affect FTEPs across the country. A communication conduit among departments throughout the nation, the FTQ is expected to foster additional improvements within the FTEP.

Timothy N. Oettmeier

Bibliography

Eisenberg, Terry. "Six Potential Hazards Inherent in Developing and Implementing Field Training Officer (FTO) Programs." *Police Chief Magazine* (July 1981): 50–51.

Fagan, M. Michael. "How Police Officers Perceive Their Field Training Officer." *Journal of Police Science and Administration* 13 (July 1985): 138–52.

Hendrix, B.G., and F.M. Webb. *The Field Training Quarterly* 1(1)(January 1987). Houston Police Department.

Houston Police Department. *Field Training and Performance Evaluation Program: Standard Operating Procedures Manual.* Houston: Field Training and Administration Office, 1985.

———. *Field Training and Performance Evaluation Program: Termination Review Committee Standard Operating Procedures Manual.* Houston: Field Training and Administration Office, 1986.

Kaminsky, Glenn, and Michael Roberts. *A Model Manual for the Training and Development of Field Training and Evaluation Program Concept.* Jacksonville: University of North Florida, Institute of Police Technology and Management, 1985.

McCampbell, Michael S. *Field Training for Police Officers: The State of the Art.* Washington DC: National Institute of Justice, U.S. Department of Justice, Grant No. 85-IJ-CX-0039, June 1986.

Molden, Jack. "Houston is New FTO Resource." *Law and Order Magazine* 35(3)(March 1987): 12.

Oettmeier, Timothy N. "Justifying FTO Terminations." *Journal of Police Science and Administration* 10 (March 1982): 64–73.

Pogrebin, Mark R., Eric D. Poole, Robert M. Regole, and Jeanne D. Zimmerman. "A Look at Police Agency Retention and Resignation: An Assessment of a Field Training Officer Program." *Police Science Abstracts* 12 (January–February 1984): i–iv.

"Fighting Words" Doctrine

Fifty years ago, the U.S. Supreme Court in *Chaplinsky v. New Hampshire* (315 U.S. 568 [1942]) defined "fighting words" as "those words which by their very utterance inflict injury or tend to incite an immediate breach of peace." The Court held that such words are not protected by the First Amendment and can be the basis for criminal prosecution. More recent court decisions delineate the parameters of the "fighting words" exception to First Amendment protection.

In *Houston v. Hill* (482 U.S. 451 [1987]), Raymond Hill observed his friend Charles Hill intentionally stopping traffic on a busy street, evidently to enable a vehicle to enter traffic. Two Houston police officers approached Charles Hill and began speaking with him. Raymond Hill, in an admitted attempt to divert the officers' attention from his friend Charles, began shouting at the officers, "Why don't you pick on somebody your own size?" After one of the officers responded, "Are you interrupting me in my official capacity as a Houston police officer?" Hill shouted, "Yes, why don't you pick on somebody my size?" Raymond Hill was then arrested and convicted under a city ordinance for "wilfully or intentionally interrupting a city policeman . . . by verbal challenge during an investigation." The Supreme Court ruled Hill's conviction violated the First Amendment. The Court reaffirmed that "the First Amendment protects a significant amount of verbal criticism and challenge directed at police officers" and that an ordinance punishing spoken words directed to a police officer is constitutional only if "limited in scope to fighting words that by their very utterance inflict injury or tend to incite an immediate breach of the peace." The Court also suggested that the "fighting words" exception requires "a narrower application in cases involving words addressed to a police officer, because a properly trained officer may reasonably be expected to exercise a higher degree of restraint than the average citizen and thus be less likely to respond belligerently to fighting words. The Houston ordinance unconstitutionally criminalized speech directed to an officer because it broadly authorized police to arrest a person who in any manner verbally interrupts an officer.

Working Principles

Other recent federal and state court decisions have established four generally accepted principles that assist officers in deciding whether to arrest for speech directed at them. The first principle is direct threats to officer safety. The Supreme Court of North Dakota held that direct threats to officers were unprotected "fighting words." In *City of Bismarck v. Nassif* (449 N.W.2d 789 [1989]) three police officers were sent to Nassif's residence after he called police to complain they were not doing anything about his earlier complaint regarding vandalism to his car. He also threatened to take the law into his own hands and told police he had a gun. When officers arrived, Nassif exited his house appearing upset, shouting loudly, and acting aggressively. After attempting to reason with him, one officer told Nassif they were leaving. Nassif then said, "You fucking son of a bitch, I'm going to go back into the house and get my shotgun and blow you bastards away." Based on this threat to their safety, the officers arrested Nassif for disorderly conduct.

The court concluded that Nassif's statement, along with the circumstances of this encounter with police, constituted language that falls within the meaning of "fighting words" unprotected by the First Amendment. The court relied on language from a U.S. Supreme Court opinion in which Justice William O. Douglas wrote that the First Amendment protects a significant amount of verbal criticism and challenge directed at police officers unless the language is "shown likely to produce a clear and present danger of a serious substantive evil that rises far above public inconvenience, annoyance, or unrest"—*Terminiello v. Chicago* (337 U.S. 1 [1949]). The court found Nassif's threat to get his shotgun and shoot the officers sufficient to produce a clear and present danger of a serious substantive evil. See also *Brown v. State* (576 N.E.2d 605 [1991]).

The second principle is speech that disrupts performance of duty. Following the *Houston v. Hill* precedent in *Wilkerson v. State* (556 So.2d 453 [1990]) the defendant started yelling and cursing officers who had just arrested some drug dealers. An officer told her, at least two times, to leave the area because she was interfering with their efforts to make the arrests, but she refused to leave and continued cursing and yelling at them. After other bystanders began yelling at and cursing the officers and the defendant again refused to leave the area, she was arrested on a charge of obstructing an officer in the performance of his duties. The court found that Wilkerson was not arrested for merely yelling at and cursing the officers, but rather for refusing to leave the area where the officers were attempting to make arrests because her physical presence was obstructing their performance of duty. In that regard, the court noted that "officers may lawfully demand that citizens move on and away from the area of a crime without impermissibly infringing upon the citizen's First Amendment rights."

A higher standard of composure applied to police is the third principle. In *Buffkins v. City of Omaha* (922 F.2d 465 [1990]) the U.S. Court of Appeals for the Eighth Circuit found as a matter of law that officers could not have reasonably concluded they had probable cause to arrest Buffkins for disorderly conduct for using "fighting words" when she called the officers "asshole." Buffkins was suspected of being a drug courier and was detained at the airport. She protested that the officers' conduct was racist and unconstitutional and she became increasingly loud during the period of detention and questioning. The officers eventually informed Buffkins that she was free to go and told her to "have a nice day," to which she replied "asshole system" or "I will have a nice day, asshole." The officers then decided to arrest Buffkins for disorderly conduct. Buffkins subsequently filed a civil lawsuit against the officers claiming her arrest for disorderly conduct was unconstitutional. The court concluded that Buffkins' speech was not an incitement to immediate lawless action for the following reasons:

1. Neither arresting officer contended that Buffkins became violent or threatened violence.
2. Both officers admitted that nobody outside the interview room heard Buffkins' comments.
3. Buffkins's use of the expletive in referring to the officers could not reasonably have prompted a violent response from trained officers who are expected to exercise greater restraint in their response than the average citizen.

The fourth principle concerns the use of profanity, name-calling, and obscene gestures. In *Duran v. City of Douglas* (904 F.2d 1372 ([1990]), the U.S. Court of Appeals for the Ninth Circuit ruled that the First Amendment protected profanities and an obscene gesture directed toward a police officer and that the officer's subsequent detention and arrest of Duran for disorderly conduct was unconstitutional. After arriving at a downtown hotel in response to a bartender's complaints about an unruly patron, officers found Duran intoxicated and threatening the bartender. One officer and Duran exchanged a few heated words, after which Duran was escorted out of the bar by the officer. Duran then left in an automobile driven by his wife. Soon thereafter while on patrol, the officer observed Duran directing an obscene gesture toward him through an open window, and the officer began following the car. As the officer followed the car down a rural highway, Duran began yelling profanities in Spanish and continued to make obscene gestures. The officer followed the car to Duran's residence in a mobile home park, at which time he initiated a traffic stop by turning on his emergency lights. The officer ordered Duran to step away from the car, to which Duran replied, "I don't have to." The officer told Duran that the reason for the traffic stop was to find out why he had yelled profanities and made an obscene gesture toward him. Duran responded with further profanities in both Spanish and English and was then arrested for disorderly conduct. The court recognized that Duran's conduct toward the officer was "boorish, crass, and, initially at least, unjustified . . . hard-working law enforcement officers surely deserve better treatment from members of the public. But disgraceful as Duran's behavior may have been, it was not illegal; criticism of the police is not a crime." The court also noted there was no evidence that Duran's conduct constituted a disturbing of the peace, since the car was traveling late at night on a deserted road on the outskirts of town. Moreover, the court cautioned that the officer's stopping of the car "at least partly in retaliation for the insult he received from Duran . . . would constitute a serious First Amendment violation."

The First Amendment protects a significant amount of speech directed to law-enforcement officers, including some distasteful name calling and profanity. Words addressed to officers are not protected by the First Amendment if they constitute either direct threats to officer safety or actually obstruct officers in the performance of their duty. To ensure the constitutionality of arrests, legal training for law-enforcement officers should include a review of First Amendment rights in relation to the "fighting words" doctrine.

Daniel L. Schofield

Table of Additional Cases

City of Bismarck v. Schoppert (469 N.W.2d 808 [1991]).
Elbrader v. Blevins (757 F.Supp. 1174 [1991]).
Enlow v. Tishomingo County, Miss. (962 F.2d 501 [1992]).
Foster v. Metropolitan Airports Commission. (914 F.2d 1076 [1990]).
Gamble v. State (591 N.E.2d 142 [1992]).
Nationalist Movement v. City of Cumming, Forsyth County, Ga. (934 F.2d 1482 [1991]).
Person v. State (425 S.E.2d 371 [1992]).
Price v. State (600 N.E.2d 103 [1992]).
R.A.V. v. City of St. Paul (112 S.Ct. 2538 [1992]).
Robinson v. State (588 N.E.2d 533 [1992]).

Fingerprint

The soles of the feet and palms of the hands are covered with a special type of skin which has complex patterns of ridges. These papillary ridges, or friction ridges (so named in keeping with their function), originate from minute elevations, papillae, found on the inner dermis. Friction skin contains no sebaceous, or oil, glands, but a high concentration of sweat glands. This affects the composition of palmar perspiration, a factor important to the forensic examiner concerned with techniques for detection of fingerprints.

The impression left on an article when the friction skin of a finger or thumb is pressed against it constitutes a fingerprint. Inked impressions on fingerprint cards are produced by deliberately depositing ink on the friction skin of the fingers and thumbs. Scene-of-crime impressions are made via perspiration or contaminants. They are usually invisible to the naked eye and are thus called latent prints. Fingerprints constitute the most definitive means of identification because of three features:

1. Fingerprints are unique. The probability that two identical fingerprint patterns in the world's population exist, including different fingers of an individual's hands and even corresponding fingers of identical twins, is infinitesimally small. This uniqueness is supported by the comparison of millions of fingerprints over the past eighty years, and statistical calculations.

2. Fingerprints are invariant. Except for size change with growth, the details of ridge patterns remain unchanged during an individual's lifetime. An injury only produces permanent scarring if it penetrates to the dermis. Permanent scars can themselves be utilized for identification. The ridge patterns on the palms of the hands and soles of the feet can also serve for identification.

3. General pattern types enable fingerprints to be classified systematically. Thus it becomes possible to establish files that can be searched to effect identifications.

Fingerprint Identification and Classification

The friction ridges of fingers form patterns that can be grouped into arches, loops, and whorls. These patterns are not used for identification, except in the sense of immediate elimination if the developed latent print differs in pattern type from that of the suspect. Fingerprint identification relies instead on individual ridge characteristics (minutiae), their relative locations, and whether dissimilar features can be explained. The most common ridge characteristics are ridge endings and bifurcations (a ridge divides into two, much like a river dividing into two forks). Other common characteristics are short ridges, enclosures (or islands), and dots.

Fingerprint patterns are divided into arches, loops and whorls, depending on whether they contain none, one, or two deltas, respectively, provided that the delta does not amalgamate (merge together) with the core of the fingerprint. A delta is either a bifurcation in which the two forking ridges diverge rather than run parallel, or a pair of adjacent ridges that diverge. A loop has one or more ridges that recurve back, i.e., the incoming and exiting ridge portions are roughly parallel. An arch has no recurving ridges. The flow of ridges appears wave-like. Arches are subdivided into plain and tented arches. Plain whorls have at least one ridge that forms a complete spiral-like circuit or at least one ridge that marks a complete oval or other variant of a circle. Additional patterns that are classified as whorls are the double loop whorl, the central pocket loop whorl, and the accidental whorl.

Fingerprint classification systems are generally extensions of a system devised by Sir Edward Richard Henry and first adopted by Scotland Yard in London in 1901. Classifica-tion schemes are quite complex. A glimpse of this complexity can be gleaned from the primary classification, which is just a part of the original Henry System. That system, in turn, has been expanded to accommodate today's very large fingerprint files. In the primary classification, the fingers are paired and then summed in the form of a ratio,

$$\frac{\text{r. index + r. ring + l. thumb + l. middle + l. little}}{\text{r. thumb + r. middle + r. little + l. index + l. ring}}$$

The only important fingerprint pattern at this stage is the whorl type. It is assigned a numerical value of 16 if found on a finger of the leftmost pair in the above ratio (r. index, r. thumb), 8 if on a finger of the next pair, 4 for a finger of the third pair, 2 for a finger on the fourth pair, and 1 for a finger on the last (l. little, l. ring) pair. All other fingerprint patterns are assigned a value of 0. To the sums thus obtained, 1 is added in both the numerator and denominator of the above ratio. The obtained numerical fraction is the primary classification. For instance, if both thumbs contain whorls and all other fingers arches or loops, the primary classification is $F(5/17)$. According to the primary classification, the possible pattern combinations of the ten fingers of the hands form 1,024 classes. Further classifications are therefore needed.

Latent Fingerprint Development

The detection of latent fingerprints on articles of evidence is one of the most important facets of criminal identification because it is generally the strongest physical evidence one can introduce in court. This detection of latent fingerprints generally relies on the preferential adherence of substances to the latent fingerprint (sweat) deposit or on the reaction of chemicals with latent fingerprint residue. A typical fingerprint deposit is comprised of 98–99 percent water, which soon evaporates to leave behind roughly 10^{-6} g. of residue about equally composed of inorganic (e.g., salt) and organic (e.g., amino acid) components. What makes the detection of this residue a particularly challenging problem is its chemical complexity, coupled with the extraordinary variety in texture and composition of the surfaces on which one needs to detect latent prints.

Of the many chemical and physical treatments for fingerprint development, only dusting (physical adherence of fine powder to fingerprint residue) and ninhydrin treatment (reaction of ninhydrin with amino acid of fingerprint residue to form a purple-blue product) are routinely used today. Other procedures, such as fuming with iodine vapor or silver nitrate treatment, are used in special situations only. More exotic methods, such as tagging with radioactive material, and more instrumentally oriented methods, such as metal film deposition in vacuum, autoradiography (an X-ray method), and neutron activation, have been explored. These methods are not routinely used in police work because of restricted applicability, expense, and complexity. A procedure developed in Japan in the late 1970s utilizes the vapors of methyl- or ethyl-cyanoacrylate ester. The compound polymerizes on latent fingerprint residue to form a white product. This procedure is now widely used for fingerprint development on smooth surfaces.

In 1976, it was discovered that lasers could be utilized for detection of latent fingerprints. This general method is revolutionary in concept, since it makes use of a different physical principle (fluorescence) than the conventional methods to yield superior sensitivity. To elucidate this, consider a latent print on a white surface developed strongly by black powder. Ambient light is scattered from the surface around the ridges to reach the eye or photographic camera, but not from the ridges themselves because the powder absorbs the light. Absorption/reflectance thus is the essence of conventional fingerprint development. If the print were only weakly developed, the fingerprint ridge sites would reflect only slightly less than the surroundings. The detection of a weak print therefore amounts to the sensing of a small difference between two large signals, originating from reflected ambient light, and this is an inherently insensitive detection mode. In the opposite situation, in which only light from ridge sites reaches the camera or eye, the detection of a weak fingerprint amounts to the sensing of a small signal. That this is an intrinsically more sensitive detection mode is clearly demonstrated by the eye: one does not see stars in daylight (small difference between large signals), but easily at night (small signal). Fingerprint detection via fluorescence originating from the latent fingerprint, the essence of the laser method, corresponds to this second mode of signal detection. The laser method involves a variety of procedures among which the ninhydrin/$ZnCl_2$ and cyanoacrylate ester/dye staining treatments are particularly successful because of sensitivity, ease of use, wide applicability, and, very importantly, compatibility with conventional routine procedures. The laser method is routinely used by a growing number of law-enforcement agencies.

Digital Fingerprint Processing
Fingerprint card files are very cumbersome to search. Moreover, it is impossible to search such files to match a latent fingerprint developed on an article of evidence unless a suspect has been identified. In recent years, computers have found increasing use for fingerprint filing and searching purposes. Fingerprints are entered into the computer in digital form. To do so, one cannot simply measure distances and angles between ridge characteristics. This is because the pressure conditions under which rolled (inked) prints and crime scene prints are deposited differ substantially, leading to different distortions. Thus more elaborate approaches need to be taken to digitize fingerprints. For instance, the location of a minutia and the approximate direction of the associated ridge flow are combined with the number of intervening ridges between this minutia and neighboring minutiae, together with approximate directions of these neighbors with respect to the central minutia. Fingerprints are digitized automatically by reading with electronic scanners. With the advent of fingerprint computers, cold searching, i.e., the identification of a developed crime scene print without the presence of a suspect on hand, became a reality.

An important area of future fingerprint processing deals with electronic image recording (by TV camera for instance) coupled with computer image enhancement techniques, such as false coloring, contrast manipulation, and edge enhancement. These procedures are designed to increase the contrast between the fingerprint ridge detail and the often quite nonuniform background. Furthermore, researchers are studying the differences found between fingerprint and background fluorescence lifetimes. This will provide another means to enhance contrast electronically for an exact identification.

E.R. Menzel

Bibliography
Knowles, A.M. "Aspects of Physicochemical Methods for the Detection of Latent Fingerprints." *Journal of Physics E: Scientific Instruments* 11 (1978): 713–21.

Menzel, E.R. *Fingerprint Detection with Lasers*. New York: Dekker, 1980.

—————. "Pretreatment of Latent Prints for Laser Development." *CRC Critical Reviews in Forensic Sciences*: in preparation.

Moenssens, A.A. *Fingerprint Techniques*. Philadelphia: Chilton, 1971.

Olsen, R.D., Sr. *Scott's Fingerprint Mechanics*. Springfield, MA: Charles C. Thomas, 1978.

Thomas, G.L. "The Physics of Fingerprints and Their Detection." *Journal of Physics E: Scientific Instruments* 11 (1978): 722–31.

Firearm Availability and Homicide Rates

Whether firearm availability helps cause homicides is a matter of controversy. This is not surprising, because the question is central to the wisdom of gun control. If widespread firearm ownership increases lethal violence, restricting access to guns may lead to lower rates of murder. If levels of gun ownership do not influence homicides, these restrictions will be of only symbolic value.

There is no doubt that many murderers use firearms—most often handguns—to commit their crimes. Currently, guns are the instrument of death in about 60 percent of homicides in the United States. In 1990 this amounted to almost 15,000 killings, 11,000 of them due to handguns (Federal Bureau of Investigation, 1991a).

Homicides of police officers are even more likely to involve firearms than is true for other citizens. Between 1981 and 1990, for example, gunshot wounds claimed the lives of 90 percent of all law-enforcement officers murdered in the line of duty (Federal Bureau of Investigation, 1991b). Lester (1987) shows that the risk of firearm murder for a city police officer rises with the gun murder rate in the city at large.

Despite these figures, it is not necessarily true that reduced firearm ownership would decrease the rate of homicidal violence. Homicide rates may depend only on the number of persons who wish to kill. If guns were not handy, murderers might simply switch to other weapons.

Two issues have received heavy attention in studies of the influence of gun availability on murder. The first of these is a theory to explain how rising levels of availability might increase homicide rates. The second is the empirical association between the two variables.

Weapon Choice Theory

The mechanism most often used to link firearm ownership to homicide rates is the weapon choice theory of Zimring (1968) and Cook (1991). This theory rests on the idea that many murderers do not set out with a desire to kill. A robber meets resistance, for example, or two strangers argue in a bar. The offender attacks the victim with whatever weapon is at hand, ending the assault after inflicting injury. The fate of the victim then depends heavily on the weapon used in the assault. If the weapon is highly lethal, it is more likely that the victim will die.

According to the weapon choice theory, firearms are more deadly than are most other means of attack. If fewer guns were available, the offender would not be as likely to have one. A less effective weapon would be used, lowering the risk of death.

The theory assumes that people bent on violence can find a gun if they make enough effort. However, more effort should be required when firearms are less widely available, and fewer offenders will have a gun nearby if general levels of ownership are low.

The weapon choice theory implies that lower levels of firearm ownership will not change the total amount of violent crime. Violent persons can, and will, use other weapons. Yet if these weapons are not as dangerous as guns, assaults will not be as likely to end in death.

Evaluation of the Weapon Choice Theory

The weapon choice theory asserts that guns are highly lethal weapons and that homicides are often unintentional. There is little question about the first point. In Zimring's (1968) study, for example, the death rate was five times higher for persons attacked with guns than for persons attacked with knives.

It is not as easy to estimate how many murderers lack a firm wish to kill. This point depends on motivations, and motivations are difficult to study. Scattered evidence suggests that criminal shootings are often a matter of chance. For example, Wright and Rossi (1986) surveyed a sample of felons about their use of weapons. In this sample, 76 percent of the offenders who had fired a gun during a crime reported that they did not begin with a plan to do so.

Yet these and other data measure motivations only indirectly, and this part of the theory probably will remain arguable (Wright, Rossi, and Daly, 1983). As a result, the effect of firearm ownership on homicides must be found empirically.

Evidence on the Relationship between Firearm Availability and Homicides

Figure 1 is a plot of homicides and new handguns produced per 100,000 residents of the United States. The data are annual, between 1950 and 1989. The two variables follow very similar time paths, with increases in the homicide rate closely mirroring those in handgun production.

FIGURE 1

Homicides and New Handguns per 100,000 United States, 1950–1989

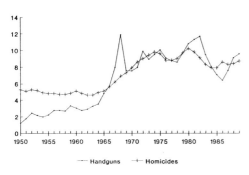

This comparison suggests that the influence of firearm ownership on homicides is worth study. By itself, however, it does not show that rising levels of gun ownership cause increases in murder. This is so for three reasons.

First, the number of firearms in private hands is not accurately counted. Estimates of the stock of guns in the United States vary widely, and useful figures do not exist for areas smaller than the entire nation. Figure 1 uses *new* handguns, and homicides also may be committed with firearms obtained in earlier years. Yet guns wear out over time and no one knows how many older weapons remain in service.

Second, firearm ownership may depend on the same social and demographic factors that influence homicide rates. For example, changes in attitudes favorable to violence may lead to higher levels of both firearm access and murder. Gun ownership and homicides thus may be related only because they share common causes.

Finally, some firearm ownership may be a *response* to crime. That is, people may buy guns to protect themselves as homicide rates rise. Then the two variables will be correlated because homicides help cause the demand for guns.

Many studies attempt to deal with one or more of these problems. No study has satisfied all critics, but this research presents a largely consistent picture.

Studies of the Entire United States

Several studies examine the association between the stock of firearms and homicide rates over time in the United States. As in Figure 1, they measure gun availability using annual data on firearm production.

Examples of this approach include Kleck (1979; 1984), Magaddino and Medoff (1984), and Philips, Votey, and Howell (1976). Each study held constant several common causes of gun availability and homicides, and Kleck's two studies also considered if murder rates affect ownership levels. Except Kleck (1984), these researchers all found that increases in the stock of firearms resulted in higher rates of homicidal violence.

In using production data to measure firearm access, these studies must estimate the average lifetime of a gun. Any such estimate is no more than a guess, and errors here may influence the results. Further, murder rates in the United States have increased most in large cities, while gun ownership has increased most in rural areas (Wright, Rossi, and Daly, 1983). It is thus possible that the national findings are due to unrelated trends.

Studies of Cities within the United States

A second set of studies considers the influence of firearms on the homicide rates of cities in the United States. There are no counts of gun owners for these areas, and the city studies gauge availability with indicators of firearm *use*. Common indicators include the fraction of robberies committed with guns and the fraction of suicides committed with guns. The values of these indicators presumably increase with levels of ownership.

Research using this approach includes Cook (1979), Kleck (1991), and McDowall (1991). All three studies controlled for common

F

causes of firearm ownership and homicide rates, and Kleck and McDowall allowed for a mutual relationship between the two variables. Cook discovered that city robbery murder rates rose with levels of gun availability, while McDowall found that availability strongly influenced annual homicide rates in Detroit. In contrast, Kleck concluded that firearm access did not affect the murder rates of the cities that he examined.

These studies assume that firearm ownership in a city varies with gun use. Yet most indicators of use involve violent acts, and they may tend to exclude responsible owners. To the degree this is so, the indicators will be poor general measures of availability.

International Studies

A third approach compares murder rates in nations that differ in ease of access to guns. In one study of this type, Killias (1990) used survey data to estimate gun ownership in eleven nations. Levels of ownership ranged from very high (the United States and Switzerland) to very low (England and Wales). Killias found that gun homicide rates increased with the ownership levels of these nations.

In another international study, Sloane et al. (1988) compared murder rates in Seattle, Washington, with those in Vancouver, British Columbia. The two cities are only 140 miles apart and they have similar demographic compositions and patterns of crime. They differ in that Vancouver has stricter handgun regulations. Sloane et al. found that Seattle's gun homicide rate was five times higher than Vancouver's, while the rate of other homicides was identical in both cities.

Cultural differences among nations are a problem for these studies. It is likely that both gun ownership and homicide rates are due in part to factors unique to a nation. Such factors are hard to measure, and the small number of countries for which data are available limit efforts to control them.

Magnitude of the Relationships

Although current research is not beyond question, studies using different methods largely agree that homicide rates rise with firearm availability. Still, the size of the relationship is often modest. McDowall (1991) estimated that Detroit's 1986 homicide rate would have been 4 percent lower if access to firearms had been at 1980 levels. Yet even then the city's 1986

homicide rate would have been a 45 percent increase over 1980. Similarly, Cook's (1979) results show that a 10 percent decrease in a city's level of ownership would reduce the rate of robbery murder by only 4 percent. Limiting access to firearms thus may not cut murder rates as much as hoped for by advocates of gun control.

David McDowall

Bibliography

Cook, Philip J. "The Effect of Gun Availability on Robbery and Robbery Murder: A Cross Section Study of Fifty Cities." In *Policy Studies Review Annual*. Vol. 3. Eds. Robert H. Haveman and B. Bruce Zellner. Beverly Hills, CA: Sage, 1979. 743–81.

———. "The Technology of Personal Violence." In *Crime and Justice: A Review of Research*. Vol. 14. Ed. Michael Tonry. Chicago: University of Chicago Press, 1991. 1–71.

Federal Bureau of Investigation. *Crime in the United States*. Washington, DC: Government Printing Office, 1991a.

———. *Law Enforcement Officers Killed and Assaulted*. Washington, DC: Government Printing Office, 1991b.

Killias, Martin. "Gun Ownership and Violent Crime: The Swiss Experience in International Perspective." *Security Journal* 1 (1990): 169–74.

Kleck, Gary. "Capital Punishment, Gun Ownership, and Homicide." *American Journal of Sociology* 84 (1979): 882–910.

———. "The Relationship Between Gun Ownership Levels and Rates of Violence in the United States." *In Firearms and Violence: Issues of Public Policy*. Ed. Don B. Kates. Cambridge, MA: Ballinger, 1984. 99–135.

———. *Point Blank: Guns and Violence in America*. New York: Aldine de Gruyter, 1991.

Lester, David. "The Police as Victims: The Role of Guns in the Murder of Police." *Psychological Reports* 60 (1987): 366.

McDowall, David. "Firearm Availability and Homicide Rates in Detroit, 1951-1986." *Social Forces* 69 (1991): 1085–101.

Magaddino, Joseph P., and Marshall H. Medoff. "An Empirical Analysis of Federal and State Firearm Control Laws." In

Firearms and Violence: Issues of Public Policy. Ed. Don B. Kates. Cambridge, MA: Ballinger, 1984. 225–58.

Phillips, Llad, Harold L. Votey, Jr., and John Howell. "Handguns and Homicide: Minimizing Losses and the Costs of Control." *Journal of Legal Studies* 5 (1976): 463–78.

Sloane, John Henry, Arthur L. Kellermann, Donald T. Reay, James A. Ferris, Thomas Koepsell, Frederick P. Rivara, Charles Rice, Laurel Gray, and James LoGerfo. "Handgun Regulations, Crime, Assaults, and Homicide: A Tale of Two Cities." *New England Journal of Medicine* 319 (1988): 1256–62.

Wright, James D., and Peter H. Rossi. *Armed and Considered Dangerous: A Survey of Felons and Their Firearms.* New York: Aldine de Gruyter, 1986.

———, Peter H. Rossi, and Kathleen Daly. *Under the Gun: Weapons, Crime, and Violence in America.* Hawthorne, NY: Aldine, 1983.

Zimring, Franklin E. "Is Gun Control Likely to Reduce Violent Killings?" *University of Chicago Law Review* 35 (1968): 721–37.

Firearms: History

Contemporary American law-enforcement officers carry handguns for self-defense and to seize the fleeing felon. Though difficult to imagine police officers without their prominently displayed sidearms, early law-enforcement officers did not routinely carry firearms. Seeing a mid-nineteenth-century municipal policeman's firearm was unusual, for if he carried one, he almost surely kept it concealed. That practice was to change. From the 1830s—when growing civil disorder led municipalities to establish coordinated police services—to the outbreak of the Civil War, many law-enforcement officers wore civilian dress, concealed their badges, and received no formal training. Even during riots, the early law-enforcement officers were often armed only with clubs.

The Revolver

Samuel Colt introduced his revolving multishot pistol in the 1830s. Not until the 1850s, however, would his firm's commercial success begin transforming the nature of personal armed defense. The Colt revolver was an early applica-

tion of mass production technology, and this made his handguns relatively inexpensive and widely available. The effect was immediate. In the quasi-military context, for example, the revolver allowed the Texas Rangers to revolutionize mounted combat. With five or six shots immediately available instead of the single-shot pistol's one, the Rangers pursued their foes on horseback and engaged them at close range, rather than the time-honored tactic of dismounting and using rifles from long range. The revolving handgun was also taken up by the police officer and the private citizen, for Colt's initial success with large, heavy-duty military revolvers was soon followed by scaled-down versions more suitable for daily urban carry.

Firearms and the Nineteenth-Century Policeman

Riots were the driving force behind municipal policing's inception. A more effective force than the mere combination of the nightwatch, constables, and city militia was needed, and the military's response to disorder often proved too harsh. Riots alone, however, do not explain the police practice of routinely carrying handguns. Riots were infrequent, and large-scale riots were not experienced even yearly in the large cities. Besides, firearms could have been stored at armories and distributed to the police in the event of a riot. One must look elsewhere for the principal reason for police interest in handguns.

Daily officer–citizen contacts have always carried the potential for violence and at times this violence turns lethal. The police "crime-fighting" role increased police–citizen contact, and the unpredictable nature of routine policing activities, investigations of suspicious circumstances, and making arrests fueled the growing perception that an armed police was necessary. Many politicians, prominent citizens, and newspaper editors supported the move toward an officially armed police since lawbreakers often carried concealed firearms and seemed less inhibited toward using them against the police. Though nineteenth-century officers were feloniously slain through beatings and knifings, most died from gunshot wounds—just as they do today. Officers typically worked alone and without effective communication with fellow officers, supervisors, the precinct station, or headquarters. Arrested persons usually had to be escorted to jail on foot. Thus the patrolman was isolated from those who would otherwise assist him, his field contact with suspects was lengthy, and public assistance could not be counted upon in the event of trouble. Although police and community leaders were often ambivalent about the growing practice of patrolmen carrying concealed handguns, they reluctantly saw it as the only reasonable alternative to an increasingly violent policing environment.

The arming process differed among jurisdictions, and even among precincts, in the largest departments. For instance, an 1857 political struggle in New York City over police control led to the municipal police being replaced by the state-controlled "metropolitans." The new force was officially armed only with a billy club, but following a series of attacks on lone policemen, the police commission quietly agreed to allow officers to carry handguns. Not all of this era's supervisors approved of their patrolmen being armed. One New York City police commander held that an officer who found it necessary to use his handgun was "unfit" for duty.

Boston police officers were also at first officially armed only with an eighteen-inch billy club, though one report notes that they used guns in an armed confrontation with harbor thieves during this same period. By 1865 Detroit officers were allowed to carry handguns but not on the day shift. That practice persisted well into the 1880s. The city did not supply the weapons and the decision to go armed—as well as the decision to employ its deadly force—rested with the officer.

Police supervisors were divided in their opinions on armed police officers. Many of these commanders performed their duties while unarmed and frowned upon their subordinates doing otherwise. Others took the opposite position and encouraged their officers to carry revolvers. These personal opinions, combined with formal authority and the force of personality, commonly substituted for official policy, despite the potentially serious consequences of deadly force for police officers and the public.

Firearm Standardization

The developing police service gave little thought to the issue of armed officers and their use of deadly force. Few standards existed, and the policeman's handgun was usually self-procured, went without inspection, and was carried in a coat or pants pocket. Training was at first ignored, but the approaching century brought "progressivism" to policing. The growing scrutiny of policing and a move toward professional status led to an emphasis on "efficiency." This influenced policing in many ways, including the carry and use of firearms.

In 1884 the Boston Police Commission formally armed every member of the patrol force with Smith & Wesson .38 caliber revolvers. As early as 1886 Cincinnati policemen were not "fully equipped" for duty unless they had their revolvers and spare ammunition. The New York City Police Commission, under the influence of Theodore Roosevelt from 1895 to 1897, standardized on the Colt .32 revolver—although the men could continue to use previously owned revolvers that were still in proper working order. The commission did not underwrite the new revolvers' expense, but it did arrange for a substantially discounted price.

By 1900 armed police officers were the norm. Many large departments were standardizing on specific handgun makes and models, and the traditional pocket carry was giving way to the belt holster. The revolver worn on the outside of the uniform and thus plainly visible to all unmistakably marked the American police as a revolver-armed force.

Prohibition marked the beginning of a particularly lawless period in American history, and it led some law enforcement agencies to reconsider weaponry. Though a few new sidearms drew interest—principally for their higher velocity to penetrate automobile sheet metal and the "bullet-proof" vests sometimes used by criminals—the .38 caliber revolver remained the mainstay. The .357 Magnum revolver represented one "high-velocity" alternative to the traditional .38 Special. While it used the same diameter bullets as the .38, it launched them at higher velocity. This also added recoil, but the general operating and handling characteristics were comparable. Useful increases in effective range or power, however, are not accomplished by switching handgun *cartridges*. Increased firearm effectiveness for unusual circumstances was better served by augmenting sidearms with rifles, shotguns, or—in some cases—machine guns. Even the powerful handguns are inferior to these classes of weapons.

Until well into the 1960s the American policeman's prototypical sidearm remained the six-shot Colt or Smith & Wesson double-action revolver. Plainclothes officers often opted for the concealability offered by smaller versions; for instance, those with a shorter barrel and/or with a five-shot cylinder. But a major change was in the making, even though its full impact would not be felt for twenty years.

Semi-Automatic Pistols

In 1966 the El Monte, California, police department adopted the Colt .45 ACP semi-automatic pistol as its service sidearm. This pistol had been used by the United States Armed Forces since 1911, and its basic design dated to the late 1890s. It is a rugged, reliable, large-caliber pistol well-suited to personal armed combat. Nevertheless, the police community waited for the *double-action* semi-automatic pistol's introduction before beginning to retire the long-serving revolver. Semi-automatic or "self-loading" pistols use part of the energy generated by the burning powder to cycle the weapon. This function ejects the spent cartridge, recocks the firing mechanism, and chambers a cartridge from the magazine. At the instant that the shooter realizes the pistol has fired, it has already sent the bullet on its way and reset itself for the next shot. The double-action pistol's first shot is much like trigger-cocking[1] the double-action revolver, for it is accomplished with a long continuous pull on the trigger. Subsequent shots are fired from the slide-cocked hammer position. The double-action semi-automatic pistol design therefore demands proficiency in at least *two* firing modes—trigger- and slide-cocked. Under some conditions (e.g., the need for a very accurate first shot), officers may find it desirable to thumb-cock the double-action pistol for the first shot. This contrasts with the double-action revolver, which can be exclusively trigger-cocked if so desired, and the single-action semi-automatic pistol, which requires competency with only the slide-cocked shot.

In 1967 the Illinois State Police adopted a Smith & Wesson double-action pistol chambered for the 9 mm Parabellum cartridge. Characteristics common to many semi-automatic handguns swayed the decision: (1) a more compact shape, (2) more cartridges when fully loaded, (3) increased mechanical safety, and (4) faster ammunition replenishment, since a full magazine can be exchanged for the one in the pistol that is nearly spent or empty. Though the direct effects of these characteristics on officer safety and gunfighting remain moot, the semi-automatic pistol was destined to eventually replace the revolver if for no other reason than that it became standard technology. The 9 mm cartridge was the early favorite among the police—the .45 ACP being the only other choice at the time—and it remains the most popular choice for police service. The 9 mm's basic ballistic profile[2] is similar to the .38 Special's, but the cartridge's overall size enabled manufacturers to produce weapons that used magazines with a capacity of a dozen or more cartridges. A more recently introduced cartridge is the 10 mm ".40 Smith & Wesson," which attempts a compromise of sorts between the 9 mm Para-bellum and the .45 ACP (11 mm, approximately). The .40 Smith & Wesson cartridge provides a larger diameter bullet than the pistols chambered for the 9 mm Parabellum (though not as large as the .45 ACP), and an increased magazine capacity greater than virtually all .45 ACP pistols (though not as large as the 9 mm).

In 1983 the Connecticut State Police selected the Beretta M92 adopted by the U.S. military as its official sidearm. This began a decade of change and police departments across the country began switching to the semi-automatic handgun. At least 115 agencies adopted the Beretta pistol by 1986, and by 1992 that number rose to over 800. Wider model choice among the manufacturers continued to feed the change as did increasingly favorable perceptions of the semi-automatic pistol's reliability. Semi-automatic pistols are somewhat sensitive to ammunition anomalies and magazine damage, but revolvers, too, are susceptible to malfunctions. Operator error is perhaps more a factor with the pistol since it requires somewhat more manipulative competence than its revolving predecessor, but neither requires exceptional dexterity.

Training

While firearms training may have been provided by a few police agencies before the turn of the century, it was neither structured nor systematic. The New York City Police Department, under Commissioner Theodore Roosevelt's leadership, changed that in 1895. While the training was rudimentary it was a step in the right direction. The Los Angeles Police Department built its firearms training facility and instituted periodic firearms training in the 1930s. Nevertheless, police firearms training cannot be thought to have been systematically conducted in the large cities on a national basis until after World War II. Even a city the size of Boston had to forego training from 1936 until 1946 due to manpower shortages.

The National Rifle Association (NRA) became interested in police firearms training and use in the 1920s, and it began to include the police in its competitive handgun events. The NRA also held special practical matches utilizing "disappearing man" targets and false storefronts. Known generally as a "Hogan's Alley," this practical exercise was a predecessor to contemporary tactical training. The NRA sponsored police-only matches beginning in the 1960s, and its firearms training programs continue to be conducted nationally.

In 1934 the Federal Bureau of Investigation's agents were authorized by Congress to be routinely armed. J. Edgar Hoover established the National Academy for police training the following year and firearms instruction was offered. FBI agents also provided training in firearms use to local police firearms instructors through the firearms instructor programs. Over the years the NRA and the FBI have been the only two widely recognized sources for instructor development.

There has been an increased interest in police firearms training field since the 1970s. Over the years, civilian and military influences on police training have been considerable, with the former providing many of the innovations now taken as standard procedure in progressive departmental training. More attention is now paid to both safety and confrontational-based gun handling, as well as to more realistic marksmanship instruction. The decision to employ deadly force can be practiced through a variety of approaches, including interactive computer simulators and role-playing exercises. Tactical considerations—procedural methods in their most basic sense—have also received greater attention. The International Association of Law Enforcement Firearms Instructors (IALEFI) was established in the mid-1980s, and it provides a professional forum for trainers to evolve doctrine and technique.

The Present Day
Some commentators opine that the best police weapon would be lightweight, always hit the target, and instantly incapacitate the target without causing any permanent damage. The future may indeed hold such technological promise, but at present the semi-automatic pistol has clearly become the sidearm of choice within America's law-enforcement community.

New cartridge and bullet designs have been introduced since 1980 and firing mechanisms have undergone revision as well. The Glock pistol, for instance, presents the police with a handgun using a single-firing mechanism—something featured on many earlier semi-automatic pistols.[3] Some manufacturers produce pistols that can only be trigger-cocked, though the "double-action only" label given to these pistols is a misnomer since they have only *one* firing mechanism. Nevertheless, since this pistol returns some degree of simplicity to a class of handguns, it seems to be a wise decision.

Many people assume that the police officer armed with a semi-automatic pistol is better equipped than his or her revolver-carrying counterpart. Police deaths have been dropping since the early and mid-1980s, but the downward trend began in the mid-1970s. Soft body armor and greater attention to field procedures surely deserve some credit for the decline in deaths. A police department's sidearm choice may only marginally influence the national police mortality and morbidity rate. Some commentators view the change to semi-automatic pistols as a fashion statement or logical technological upgrade. Others hope for improved effectiveness but can provide only limited evidence, and still others offer that the change will not solve the problems to which their proponents lay claim. And it hardly matters what equipment one uses if *missing* with one's shots remains the typical shooting incident outcome. The vast majority of police shots do not connect, though it has been suggested that hit rates have increased with the change from revolvers to pistols. Precisely what accounts for such an increase, however, may be difficult to establish.

As is so often the case the person using the tool makes a real difference. To paraphrase some trainers: A properly trained officer's performance with only slightly inferior equipment will surpass that of the inadequately prepared officer perhaps sporting technologically superior equipment. Therefore, the properly trained revolver shooter will best his or her minimally trained counterpart armed with the latest equipment. The perception that the police are "outgunned" by the criminal element seems widely held, and this has been partly responsible for the recent changes in police weaponry.

Footnotes
1. While there are differences between handguns, generally speaking there are but a few manners in which to cock the hammer prior to firing. The hammer

may be manually *thumb-cocked* (such as on single-action "western" revolvers) and then the trigger pressed, or it can be *trigger-cocked* by a relatively long pull on the trigger (such as on modern revolvers), which cams the hammer rearward and then releases it to fire the handgun. Most semi-automatic pistols *slide-cock* their firing mechanism as part of their normal firing operation, i.e., the slide's rearward travel during cycling cocks the hammer.

2. The .38 Special revolver cartridge and the 9 mm pistol cartridge operate within similar bullet weight/velocity limitations.

3. Despite what one often hears or reads about the Glock pistol, it is not a double-action handgun in any conventional sense.

Gregory B. Morrison
David A. Armstrong

Bibliography

Ayoob, Massad. "Service Weapons: A Management Analysis." *Police Product News* 11 (August 1986): 50.

Berman, Jay Stuart. *Police Administration and Progressive Reform: Theodore Roosevelt as Police Commissioner of New York.* Westport, CT: Greenwood Press, 1987.

Bowman, John. "A Practical Look at Changing to the Auto-Loader." *Law and Order* 33 (October 1985): 46.

Carte, Gene E., and Elaine H. Carte. *Police Reform in the United States.* Berkeley: University of California Press, 1975.

Chandler, George Fletcher. *The Policeman's Art.* New York: AMS Press, [1922] 1974.

Fairburn, Richard. "Biretta Model 92SB-F, New World Standard?" *Police Product News* 11 (February 1986): 20.

Gammage, Allen Z. *Police Training in the United States.* Springfield, IL: Charles C. Thomas, 1963.

Kennett, Lee, and James Laverne Anderson. *The Gun in America: The Origins of a National Dilemma.* Westport, CT: Greenwood Press, 1975.

Lane, Roger. *Policing the City: Boston, 1822–1885.* Cambridge, MA: Harvard University Press, 1967.

Miller, Wilbur R. *Cops and Bobbies: Police Authority in New York and London, 1830–1870.* Chicago, IL: University of Chicago Press, 1973.

Morrison, Greg. "The Service Sidearm: A Critique of Selection Criteria." *Police* 14 (May 1989): 20.

Morrison, Gregory Boyce. *The Modern Technique of the Pistol.* Paulden, AZ: Gunsite Press, 1991.

Parulski, George R., Jr. "Smith and Wesson Model 39 and 59." *Police Product News* 5 (January 1980): 18.

Richardson, John C. *The New York Police: Colonial Times to 1901.* NY: Oxford University Press, 1970.

Schneider, John C. *Detroit and the Problem of Order, 1830–1880: A Geography of Crime, Riot, and Policing.* Lincoln: University of Nebraska Press, 1980.

Sprogle, Howard O. *The Philadelphia Police, Past and Present.* New York: Arno Press [*New York Times* self-published original, 1887], 1971.

Steele, David E. "Pros and Cons of the Police Auto Pistol." *Handguns* (April 1990): 31.

Firearms Tracing

At 6:04 A.M., a handgun abandoned on top of a garbage can is found by Detroit cruiser officers;

Following an armed robbery at 12:43 P.M., a Miami detective locates a semi-automatic pistol in a rape victim's vehicle, inadvertently left behind by her assailant;

At 5:25 P.M., Los Angeles County sheriff's deputies recover the only clue at the scene of an armored car robbery, a discarded 9 mm pistol; and

At 10:05 P.M. Chicago narcotics officers, executing a search warrant at the residence of a major dope dealer, find a large cache of weapons.

Law-enforcement officials are faced every day with the challenge of crimes involving firearms and receive valuable assistance from firearms tracing.

Tracing is the systematic tracking of firearms from manufacturer to purchaser (and/or possessor). Since 1972 the Treasury Department's Bureau of Alcohol, Tobacco and Firearms (ATF) has provided firearms tracing free of charge to all federal, state, local, and foreign law-enforcement agencies. In countless instances, firearms trace information provided by ATF's National Firearms Tracing Center has been a decisive factor in the successful conclusion of criminal investigations throughout the nation and in a multitude of foreign countries.

The roots of firearm tracing are found in the Gun Control Act of 1968. This law was enacted by Congress with the intent "to provide support to Federal, State, and local law enforcement officials in their fight against crime and violence." The act required that federally licensed firearms dealers keep exact records of sales, thereby giving law-enforcement agencies an opportunity to trace firearms back to the criminal. In this manner, records maintained by reputable citizens in the course of their business could be presented as evidence in court proceedings.

Firearms tracing is possible because of the support and cooperation of more than 250,000 federal firearm licensees. Firearms manufacturers, importers, wholesalers, and retailers in the United States and foreign countries cooperate in tracing by furnishing specific information on request from records of manufacture, import, or sale.

As well as assisting law enforcement, the National Firearms Tracing Center provides the firearms industry with a secure and cost-efficient method of transmitting trace data. This center has achieved, for the firearms industry and for law enforcement, a single, centralized point for the proficient research of firearm movements and purchasers.

From the inception of this concept to the present, ATF has traced more than half a million firearms, both domestically and from fourteen foreign countries. In the calendar year 1985 alone, more than 45,000 trace requests were received at the center.

In order to determine the extent of usefulness of firearm tracing to enforcement of the law, a random sampling of 24,852 successful traces was evaluated. The survey found that 81 percent was of some law-enforcement value. Even more significantly, 54 percent aided in solving a crime and/or assisting in an apprehension or indictment. The crimes in which the traced weapons were involved include murder, assault, terrorist acts, robbery, burglary, and narcotics, as well as illicit firearms trafficking.

Tracing Assists Citizens

Many firearm purchasers fail to record the description and serial numbers of their weapons. When these firearms are lost or stolen, the owners are unable to convey this crucial information to the proper authorities, thereby significantly reducing the chances of recovering their property. Firearms traces have proved to be a reliable alternative method of establishing property ownership and have assisted in the return of many firearms to their rightful owners. Thousands of firearms have been returned to victims of residential and commercial burglaries, thefts, and simple loss. Insurance companies have benefited as well from this unique method of determining property status, allowing them to reduce theft and loss claims by reclaiming otherwise lost property.

Firearms trace data have also been instrumental in determining the identity of fatal victims of crimes, accidents, and suicide. These traces have been particularly significant in the absence of traditional methods of establishing identity, such as personal documents, fingerprints, and dental charts.

Tracing Procedures

Requests to trace firearms may be submitted to the National Firearms Tracing Center by any federal, state, county, local, or foreign law-enforcement agency. Requests may be relayed through a local ATF office or sent directly to the center by means of NLETS (National Law Enforcement Telecommunication System), the mail, telex, telephone, or code-a-phone system. The center will conduct a trace to the individual purchaser; to a licensee in the originating state; to a government or law-enforcement office; or to a point where all possibility for a successful trace has been exhausted, whichever comes first.

Requests for firearm trace forms (ATF F 7520.5) should be used as a format for trace requests. Forms may be obtained from any ATF office or from the center directly.

When submitting a trace request, note first any special instructions in the box provided. For example, if the requesting agency wishes the trace to be stopped at the wholesaler, or if the trace is only needed to prove interstate movement, this should be stated. The requester must list his/her name, title, and full departmental address and telephone number, including zip and area codes. The name of the county in which the department is located is also necessary, since the center employs the National Criminal Information Center (NCIC) coding system to indicate police departments for computer and security purposes. Trace requests are handled in the following manner, according to the specified standards:

Priority I—Urgent. Firearm was used in a crime of violence and/or information is essential to apprehend or hold suspect. A reason for urgency must accompany this category or this priority will not be initiated. The Tracing Center will attempt to complete all urgent traces in eight working hours or one working day, unless a weekend intervenes.

Priority II—Expedite. Time factor is essential for completing investigation. Attempts will be made to complete all Priority II trace requests within three to five working days.

Priority III—Routine. A firearm trace is needed to complete investigation (e.g., establish interstate nexus). Priority III requests will be completed within five to seven working days or fewer.

NLETS Request

A firearms trace can be requested through NLETS by most law-enforcement agencies, by using the NCIC code for ATF Headquarters (DCATF0000). When sending a request by NLETS, the format prescribed by ATF F 7520.5 should be followed. Example of NLETS message:

From: Los Angeles, California, Police
    Department
To: ATF National Firearms Tracing Center
Subject: Request for Firearms Trace
    Priority I—Urgent
(Murder suspect apprehended; trace information to be used at time of hearing.)
Please trace the following firearm.
1. Rohm. 2. Revolver. 3. RG-38. 4. .38 caliber. 5. six-shot. 6. 4 inches. 7. Blue 8. Serial Number 163802. 9. Germany. 10. RG Industries, Miami, FL. 11. Outlaw motorcycle org.—Hell's Angels. 12. Homicide investigation. Firearm found at scene. If additional information is needed, or when returning trace results, forward to Detective Smith, Precinct No. 1, Telephone (213) 555-5555 ext. 44.

Telex Request

Foreign law-enforcement agencies may also ask that a firearm be traced. They should use an international telex communications system. The ATF telex number is (00255) 710-822-9229. When sending a request by telex, again follow the format prescribed by ATF F 7520.5. Example of telex message:

To: ATF, National Firearms Tracing Center
From: Name of Agency, Complete
    address, and telex number
Subject: Request for Firearm Trace
    Priority III—Routine
Please trace the following firearm.
1. Rohm. 2. Revolver. 3. RG-38.
4. .38 caliber. 5. six-shot. 6. 4 inches.
7. Blue. 8. Serial number 163802.
9. Germany. 10. RG Industries, Miami, FL. 11. Outlaw motorcycle org.—Hell's Angels. 12. Homicide Investigation. Firearm found at scene. If additional information is needed or when returning trace results, forward to Detective Smith, Precinct No. 1, Telephone (213) 555-5555 ext. 44.

Telephone Code-a-Phone System

The Tracing Center's code-a-phone system can be reached by calling (202) 566-7074. A recorded message will ask the caller to state the request. It is very important that the caller speak loudly, slowly, and clearly. When placing a message, follow the format on ATF F 7520.5. The caller will be asked to spell his/her last name and any other items he/she thinks may be misunderstood when the trace is being written up. He/she should use the phonetic alphabet when referring to a serial number that contains three letters.

The caller should provide all information prescribed by ATF F 7520.5. If the requester wishes to communicate directly with a member of the Tracing Center staff, he/she may telephone (800) 424-5057. Those requesters in doubt as to the description or type of firearm they want traced, should contact the Tracing Center for assistance. A requester should *never hesitate* to ask that a firearm be traced, regardless of the description available. Special requests or problems should be directed to the special agent in charge, Firearms Tracing Branch, at (202) 566-7162.

Largely because of the success of the center in providing crucial information, many departments, large and small alike, now regard firearms tracing as a routine investigative technique that is both informative and reliable. Varied applications of tracing have been used by police agencies to determine the supplier of weapons to criminals, patterns of burglaries, and illegal out-of-state shippers of firearms.

Today's criminals are employing an array of methods to commit crimes. To meet this challenge, law officers have had to develop and implement a variety of techniques. Firearms tracing, although not new, has supplied law enforcement officers with an additional functional investigative tool.

Joseph J. Vince, Jr.

Bibliography

Firearms and Explosives Tracing. Washington, DC: Department of the Treasury, Bureau of Alcohol, Tobacco and Firearms, 1983.

Project Identification: A Study of Handguns Used in Crime. Washington, DC: Department of the Treasury, Bureau of Alcohol, Tobacco and Firearms, 1983.

State Laws and Published Ordinances (Firearms). Washington, DC: Department of the Treasury, Bureau of Alcohol, Tobacco and Firearms, 1984.

Survey. Value of Firearm Traces. Washington, DC: Department of the Treasury, Bureau of Alcohol, Tobacco and Firearms, 1982.

Forensic Evidence

Police agencies place considerable reliance on forensic (scientific) evidence in the solution of crimes and the arrest and prosecution of suspected offenders. The ultimate use and worth of scientific evidence depends, however, upon a series of scientific, investigative, and managerial decisions by various police and laboratory personnel: crime-scene technicians, detectives, crime laboratory supervisors, and "bench" scientists (criminalists). Essential aspects of the collaboration are first, factors employed by scientific personnel affecting the acceptance, examination, and reporting of evidence within the context of a police investigation; and second, via a statistical analysis of police and laboratory case files, a discussion of the effects of scientifically analyzed evidence on the solution of serious crimes, and the prosecution of suspected offenders.

Submission of Physical Evidence

Physical evidence collected from the crime scene, hospital, or morgue is usually hand carried to the investigating agency's property storage area or the crime laboratory. Evidence may remain in the property room for days, weeks, or months if standards (or knowns) are unavailable, suspects have not been identified, or if the investigation lacks leads and is likely to be suspended or terminated. Because space in the laboratory is usually scarce, such evidence is usually stored in an external location.

Maintenance of the chain of custody is of foremost concern to the police personnel and the laboratory because a break in the chain may result in the evidence being ruled inadmissible in court. Consequently, detailed reporting procedures are used to document the storage and exchange of evidence.

The laboratory may occasionally refuse to accept the evidence, contending that it has been contaminated or compromised in some way. A good example would be packing in the same sack clothing from a homicide victim and from the suspect. Other perishable evidence, if not stored properly, may rot or otherwise be rendered useless. For the laboratory's own protection and reputation, examiners are careful to evaluate incoming evidence and to note any irregularities so that, subsequently, they will not be charged with carelessness or mishandling of the evidence.

Firearms, fingerprints, blood and bloodstains, hair, and semen are the primary categories of evidence (excluding controlled substances) received and examined by most crime laboratories. Biological fluids (mostly blood and seminal stains) and firearms dominate as evidence submitted to laboratories in the investigation of crimes of violence. Fingerprints, trace evidence, and tool marks dominate as the evidence submitted in property-crime cases. Only a fraction of the evidence submitted to crime laboratories is actually examined and reported. This is the result of many factors, including the high volume of crime and the abundance of physical evidence recovered from crime scenes and forensic laboratories' limited resources.

Most crime laboratories use their own judgment when deciding whether to examine an item of evidence, their decision resting heavily upon their scientific assessment of its potential value. Laboratories may defer the examination of evidence until a suspect has been located and standards taken. Frequently, laboratories will not analyze bloodstains unless a suspect is in custody from whom a comparative blood sample can be drawn. The laboratory's argument is that such an examination, without the known blood sample, is pointless and of virtually no benefit to the detective searching for a suspect. Evidence can be refrigerated to preserve the bloodstain until such time as a suspect is found.

Few laboratories use formal, written priority systems to determine the order in which evidence will be examined; such systems develop usually on an ad hoc basis. All other factors being the same, evidence is usually examined in an order which roughly coincides with that in which it has been submitted. This is especially true within major categories of evidence or within classifications of crimes. For example, suspected drugs and narcotics are normally placed in their own queue as they are submitted. Similarly, if one section of the laboratory, such as arson analysis, handles one class of crime exclusively, that kind of case is placed in a separate waiting line. If several different samples of a particular evidence type can be examined simultaneously, such as bloodstains, testing may be deferred until a sufficient number of samples has been received.

Crime laboratories have had to deal with more work in recent years because of an increase in evidence submissions; there has been no commensurate increase in staffing and physical resources. Backlogged evidence is stored in an evidence vault until it can be examined. Within a laboratory, however, one section may be able to provide results within days, while other sections may be weeks or months behind. Five basic considerations help laboratory supervisors to set priorities: perishability of the evidence, seriousness of the offense, presence of a suspect, pressure applied by attorneys or other officers of the court, and the scientist's personal appraisal of the evidence.

Emergency Cases. Biological fluids are examples of an evidence category given automatic higher priority because of their perishable nature. A second example of an emergency case is when a suspect is in custody and an analysis of suspected drugs is required if he or she is to be held beyond a certain time limit. Finally, the prosecuting attorney may require an immediate analysis if the case is ready for trial.

Seriousness of the Offense. Cases of an extraordinary nature not only receive a higher priority from police investigators, but also from the crime laboratory. Generally speaking, crimes against persons take priority over crimes against property and cases that receive extensive coverage in the media will be given a higher priority by the laboratory.

Suspects. The "absence" of a suspect may result in a much lower priority being given to the evidence or may mean that the evidence will not be examined at all. While some detectives are critical of the laboratory's invoking such a priority system, laboratory supervisors are forced to employ some system, and the presence or absence of suspects is commonly one of the systems used.

Prosecutor and Judicial Requests. The more overwhelmed laboratories become, the greater the likelihood that the decision to examine evidence is a direct result of a request from the prosecutor. Laboratories particularly strapped for resources will defer examinations until they are needed for court.

Scientific Evaluation of Evidence. A final basis for assigning priorities to evidence rests with the scientists themselves. Cases are usually given a cursory review upon submission. If this review is undertaken by a scientist who has a particular interest in this type of evidence or is intrigued from a personal or research standpoint, he or she may choose to forsake other considerations and examine the material. However, such a personal assessment is not common in the laboratories, where the bench worker rarely views the evidence until a supervisor has already decided to proceed with the examination.

The Results of Laboratory Testing

Tests may enable the examiner to identify a substance, for instance that a stain is blood or white powder is cocaine. Tests also enable the examiner to put material into a more restricted class by determining, for example, that a stain is human blood of Type A origin. Other examples include classification of a bullet as having been shot from a firearm of a certain caliber or a fiber as being of a particular type of synthetic. The identification/classification process may be just the first in a series of tests.

"Common origin" refers to a conclusion by the examiner concerning the origin or source of two or more items of evidence. In other words, the examiner concludes that the evidence—an item of heretofore undetermined origin—and a standard—an item of known source—once shared a common origin. By so doing, the laboratory is able to associate persons, instruments of the crime, and physical environments. The strength of this association varies from conclusive to one of probable or possible common origin. While it is primarily fingerprints, handwriting, and imprint or striation evidence (firearms and tool marks) that can yield findings of conclusive common origin, blood, hair, and other trace evidence may enable the examiner to state that the two items "probably" or "possibly" shared a common origin.

Examination of the evidence may help the investigator to determine how a crime has been committed. Such evaluations may indicate the movement and interactions of suspects and victims that corroborate or refute statements by witnesses, suspects, or victims. When a laboratory examination determines that evidence is not of the same origin as a standard taken from a known source, persons, objects, and locations tend to be disassociated. Negative identifications determine that a substance is not what an investigator suspects it to be. For instance, a suspected drug is shown not to be a controlled substance. The inconclusive category includes results that do not enable the laboratory to arrive at a firm conclusion.

Value of Scientific Results
An immediate, verbal report is sometimes made to the investigator in charge of a case. The examiner may or may not make a record of this communication, either in the form of a notation in the case file or in a more formal memorandum or report; different laboratories have different policies. These range from those that encourage communications with investigative staff to those that are more bureaucratic and require that all such communications be in writing and approved beforehand by a supervisor. A verbal report may also be an opportunity for an examiner to request that the investigator search for other types of evidence or collect other standards or knowns.

The formal laboratory report is customarily directed to the detective in charge of the investigation. This report usually expresses results in layman's terms and rarely contains much detail about the scientific examinations conducted. Such detail is reserved for the examiner's workbook and for the laboratory file. If the case goes to trial it is not uncommon for attorneys to accept the report as evidence in lieu of an appearance by the examiner. In cases that are disposed of by a plea, this written report usually provides scientific results to prosecutors and defense attorneys. Testimony in court is the other primary means by which laboratories convey their findings to judges, juries, and legal counsel.

Researchers at the Center for Research in Law and Justice at the University of Illinois–Chicago spent three years trying to determine the effects of scientific evidence on criminal investigations. About 1,600 investigations were randomly selected in which physical evidence had been collected and examined, and 1,100 cases in which physical evidence was not used. Empirical data were collected in four jurisdictions: Peoria and Chicago, Illinois; Kansas City, Missouri; and Oakland, California. These jurisdictions were selected on the basis of size and geographical distribution, their different approaches to evidence retrieval and analysis, and their interest in exploring the research questions posed at the beginning of the project.

The data were collected from case files maintained by the respective police agencies, crime laboratories, prosecutors, and court offices. Data collection focused on the five principal investigative stages of serious crime: the crime report, the preliminary investigation, the follow-up investigation, the collection and analysis of physical evidence, and the judicial outcome of the case.

The major findings were instructive. The rate of clearance for robberies and burglaries was significantly higher in investigations for which physical evidence had been collected and examined than in cases for which it had not. Forensic evidence had its greatest effect in cases which, traditionally, have the lowest solution rates—those with suspects neither in custody nor identified at the preliminary investigation stage. Moreover, significantly more persons arrested for the crimes of burglary and robbery were convicted in cases with analyzed forensic evidence. Rape prosecution also resulted in higher rates of conviction when semen was identified or when other physical evidence linked the defendant with the victim. Conviction rates in two of the jurisdictions studied were significantly higher in homicide cases when physical evidence linked the offender with the crime. The effect of evidence on the clearance and prosecution of aggravated assault cases was less pronounced and, in many situations, not significantly different from cases in which scientific evidence was not used.

That forensic science and crime laboratories are of some intrinsic value to the police has never been questioned. An explanation of their value, however, is usually anecdotal in nature. Over the years, the worth of a crime laboratory to a police agency has hinged primarily upon its performance in a handful of celebrated cases. On the other hand, forensic scientists believe their profession to have practically unlimited potential to aid criminal investigators. The fact remains, though, that most investigators do not look to the laboratory for help in developing leads or the generating of new suspects. Rather, they seek with fingerprints or some other type of associative evidence corroboration of a suspect's involvement.

Policy Recommendations

First, the crime laboratory must inform patrol officers, evidence technicians, and investigators about the analyses they can perform on various types of evidence. Similarly, they must acknowledge resource limitations so that false expectations are not planted in the minds of investigators. Second, laboratories must provide feedback on all examinations they perform to submitting technicians. Copies of laboratory reports should be routed to the submitting technician as well as to the case detective. Third, the laboratory, in conjunction with the detective division, should develop and disseminate criteria for the conditions under which they will examine submitted evidence. These criteria should be clearly stated and communicated to all personnel in the department. Fourth, the examination of evidence should be coordinated with the detective in charge of the particular investigation. Laboratories must strive to examine evidence in cases that are currently under investigation. Fifth, laboratory administrators must do their best to balance the demands of processing the volume of cases flowing into their operations with the need to examine individual cases in sufficient depth to extract the maximum information from the evidence. Crime laboratories must attempt to avoid an assembly-line approach to evidence evaluations, where analyzing many cases takes precedence over analyzing fewer cases well. Sixth, labora-

tories must recognize the need to put into practice an adequate management reporting system to permit an ongoing evaluation of the effectiveness of its examinations in clearing cases and prosecuting offenders. Seventh and last, laboratories must develop innovative means for managing their drug caseloads. Several laboratories have been successful in reducing their drug caseload volume by deferring examinations of some samples, marijuana for example, until it is clear the defendant will contest the charge of possession.

Joseph L. Peterson

Bibliography

Greenwood, Peter W., et al. *The Criminal Investigation Process, Volume III: Observations and Analysis.* Santa Monica, CA: Rand Corporation, 1975.

National Institute of Law Enforcement and Criminal Justice. *Forensic Science Services and the Administration of Justice.* Washington, DC, 1979.

Parker, Brian, and Joseph L. Peterson. *Physical Evidence Utilization in the Administration of Criminal Justice.* Washington, DC: Government Printing Office, 1972.

Peterson, Joseph L. *Utilization of Criminalistics Services by the Police.* Washington, DC: Government Printing Office, 1974.

———, ed. *Forensic Science: Scientific Investigation in Criminal Justice.* New York: AMS Press, 1975.

———, et al. *Forensic Evidence and the Police: The Effects of Scientific Evidence on Criminal Investigations.* Washington, DC: Department of Justice, NIJ, 1984.

President's Commission on Law Enforcement and Administration of Justice. *Task Force Report: Science and Technology.* Washington, DC: Government Printing Office, 1967.

Forensic Medicine

Forensic medicine deals with the medical investigation of living as well as deceased persons to produce evidence for use in criminal or civil trials. To begin with, an examination is made by a physician who has trained initially as a pathologist, become certified, taken a year of additional training in a center of medicolegal investigation, and become familiar with the various aspects of trauma and injury and their complications, including death. The practitioner of forensic medicine may thus examine deaths or injuries resulting from criminal activities. The examination includes documentation by photograph, diagram, transcription, radiography, or x ray. This information is then assembled and reported and when the case reaches the court or hearing stage the forensic medical practitioner must appear to give the required testimony as asked for by the prosecutor or plaintiff's attorney, and be prepared for cross-examination by the defense attorney.

Within the realm of forensic medicine are several fields of specialization. They are clinical forensic medicine, forensic pathology, forensic psychiatry, legal medicine, and serology and immunology.

Medicolegal Investigation: Colonial Period
It was clear to early American colonists that investigation of certain questionable, suspicious, and violent deaths had to be carried out following the coroner system to which they had been accustomed in their native England. In 1647 autopsies were already carried out in Massachusetts, when the colony's general court showed concern for the teaching of medical students by authorizing that "an autopsy should be made on the body of a criminal once in four years." In 1666 coroners in Maryland were appointed by county. Early records mention the dissection of bodies by physicians and regulation of the practice of medicine in the colonies. In the colonial period dissection was often carried out by anatomists; the discipline of pathology developed later. There is no recorded teaching of medical jurisprudence in the eighteenth century, although Dr. Benjamin Rush of Philadelphia did practice during this period and wrote up his lectures on the subject for his medical students. During the pre-colonial period postmortem examinations were described in the journals of Jacques Carter and Samuel de Champlain on cases of scurvy in an effort to learn the mysteries of this incapacitating malady.

In the eighteenth century, autopsies became more frequent and were more informative. Dr. Cadwallader Colden of Philadelphia urged legislation for universal postmortem examinations that would include complete examination of all organs; he advised that an effort be made to correlate anatomic findings with the clinical findings about the deceased patient. Philadelphia became the major center of medical learning in colonial America with the first medical school being developed at the University of Pennsylvania. Colonial physicians were often trained in London, Edinburgh, and Leyden.

The Republic
The first major change in medicolegal investigation in America occurred in Massachusetts in 1877, when that state became the first in the country to come to grips with the inherent deficiencies of the coroner system. This system allowed an untrained person, serving simply by political appointment, to decide the cause of unnatural death on the basis of whatever evidence he could obtain without physician certification. Massachusetts abolished the office of coroner and replaced it with that of medical examiner, who was a qualified physician. The first medical examiner of Boston was Dr. Frank W. Draper, professor of legal medicine at Harvard University, who wrote a textbook on legal medicine in 1905. The work was based on his experience in the handling of more than 8,000 cases during his twenty-eight years of practice. Development of the Massachusetts system meant there was a need for communication among the medical examiners of the state. This was accomplished by the creation of the Massachusetts Medicolegal Society. Its purposes were to elevate the status of the medical examiner's office, to assist him in the discharge of his duties, to collect and utilize such facts as had medicolegal value, to excite a general interest in the subject of forensic medicine, and to promote its successful cultivation. Every member was required to forward to the corresponding secretary a full and complete report of each case. In reviewing these transactions, covering the period from 1878 to 1936, we can gain insight into many of the problems that confront us today.

The Twentieth Century
In 1915 the medicolegal investigations in New York City changed from a coroner system to the medical-examiner system. This came about after the Wallstein Commission reported many serious defects in the coroner system. Dr. Charles Norris was thereupon appointed chief medical examiner and given the authority to order an autopsy when, in his judgment, it was necessary. Appointment of the medical examiner by the mayor from a civil service list provided the first civil-service appointment in the annals of American medicolegal investigation.

The New York medical examiner's office was the American birthplace of the discipline of toxicology, with the establishment of a toxicology laboratory under the direction of Dr. Alexander Gettler. Supporting Dr. Norris were Dr. Thomas A. Gonzalez, later to succeed Dr. Norris as chief medical examiner; Dr. Manuel E. Marten; and Dr. B.M. Vance. Following Dr. Gonzalez as chief medical examiner was Dr. Milton Helpern. In 1937 Gonzalez, Vance, and Helpern published a major work in forensic medicine entitled *Legal Medicine and Toxicology*. This was the most important text in this field in America during the first half of the twentieth century. The second edition appeared in 1954.

In Chicago, the mass gangland killing known as the St. Valentine's Day massacre led to the development of the first crime laboratory in America under Calvin Goddard. Also of note in the Deep South, the office of the coroner has held a high place in the government of each parish in Louisiana since the early days of colonization. Today, each parish has a physician coroner and an active state coroner's association providing cohesiveness and effective communication among coroners. New Orleans, in Orleans Parish, has a coroner system whose records antedate the Civil War. Early handwritten French records offer an interesting view of the activities of this office.

The history of medicolegal investigative systems has largely been the story of strong, dedicated individuals working to expand the profession and at the same time to become more professional themselves. At present many urban areas in America have an established forensic medicine program or center, and statewide medicolegal investigative systems exist in a number of states. A general analysis of requirements for the profession was set forth in 1967 in a report by the American Medical Association's Committee on Medicolegal Problems. This committee calculated that for each 100,000 inhabitants in a given geographic area, 250 of a total 1,250 deaths each year should be investigated.

Clinical Forensic Medicine

In general, this specialty consists of the examination or management of living cases posing a broad spectrum of problems. Acute cases include overdose or poisoning, alleged police brutality or torture, evaluation of severity of injuries in transport accidents, questions of psychiatric patient commitment, investigation of drunk driving, blood testing of amnesia victims after accident, investigation of sexual assault/rape victims, and brutality to animals. The chronic or less hurried examinations include paternity studies, questions of incest, evaluation of disability and compensation of victims of accidents or assaults, occupational hazards, product liability or therapeutic misadventures and malpractice, identification of immigrants, and poisons in food or drugs. Psychological or psychiatric work includes the psychological evaluation of a specific criminal act so as to determine whether the accused was insane at the time; or if the assailant has not been apprehended, evaluation of the crime from the standpoint of what kind of person could have done the deed. This provides very helpful support to police investigation of an unsolved crime. There may also be an evaluation of a person who is suspected of self injury or mutilation as well as a malingerer or insurance fraud case.

Forensic Pathology

Pathology is the study of disease and injury from the causative aspect, as distinct from those branches of medicine that are concerned with the diagnosis and treatment of disease. Pathology, therefore, is the study of the reasons why people become ill or are injured and provides descriptions of the bodily dysfunctions resulting from these illnesses or injuries. Within pathology are numerous subspecialties such as hematology (the study of blood), microbiology (the study of bacteria and other microorganisms), clinical biochemistry, and histopathology. The latter is the most closely allied to forensic problems in that histopathology is the study of cellular diseases and abnormalities both by microscopic examination and by gross inspection of diseased organs, which is then more accurately termed "morbid anatomy."

Although most pathologists are concerned with the morphology and causation of disease, a much smaller subgroup of this discipline is "forensic pathologists" or practitioners of legal pathology. The major function of the forensic pathologist is the investigation of sudden, unexpected, suspicious, or frankly criminal deaths. The major areas of forensic pathology are mechanical trauma, either with criminal connotations as in homicide by shooting, stabbing, or punching; or in civil matters such as road, rail, and air accidents; and the suicide, who falls into neither of these groups. Many natural deaths, accidents, and suicides may not look suspicious to a police officer, but the forensic pathologist, due to his or her familiarity with a much wider range of unusual circumstances, may well rapidly perceive the true nature of the death. The advantage of having a pathologist visit the scene of a homicide, for instance, is that he or she can get a total picture of the circumstances that no written description or even photographs can recapture at a later date. The position of the body, the position of a weapon present, the distribution of blood splashes, and many other factors assist the pathologist to build up a mental picture that will help in correlating and interpreting later autopsy findings. Many of the most notorious criminal cases in medicolegal history have started as "just another death," and it is frequently in the first few hours or even minutes of an investigation that errors are made that echo through the courts for years.

Forensic Psychiatry
Forensic psychiatrists may be called upon to help evaluate a defendant whose competence to handle personal affairs, such as the ability to enter into a contract or to execute legal documents, is in question. They may be asked to testify for the prosecution in a criminal case or the plaintiff in a civil suit. Occasionally, in unusual and complicated deaths, psychiatrists play a significant role before the trial begins or before the defendant is actually apprehended. Such an instance occurred in Los Angeles, California, when the manner of a prominent movie star's death came into question. During the investigation to determine whether the death was an accident or a suicide, the psychiatrist, pathologist, social worker, friends of the family, and the police acted in concert to determine the most likely cause. This technique, referred to as a "psychological autopsy," was developed in the 1950s through the efforts of Dr. Theodore J. Curphey and other physicians involved in suicide studies in Los Angeles.

The psychiatrist may be called upon during a criminal investigation if there is a question concerning the psychiatric nature of the assailant(s) that may have contributed to such a crime. In cases of multiple murders with peculiar sexual activities before or after the victims' deaths or of bizarre mass murders, such as the Tate–LaBianca case, psychiatrists can offer important knowledge concerning the murderer's behavior. After a case is reviewed for the type of personality, psychiatric problems,

and other peculiarities that the killer may have, a reasonable conclusion regarding the type of behavioral characteristics can be presented. This approach is valuable in the support of criminal and civil investigation.

Psychiatric evidence in a courtroom is preceded by a thorough examination of an individual to evaluate his or her mental status and to determine if the state of mind at the time of the offense conforms to the definition of insanity used in the jurisdiction where the crime occurred. Psychiatrists can determine the competency of the accused and his ability to stand trial. Psychiatric testimony may also be used to counter the opposition witnesses in a case involving a psychiatric problem. The psychiatric testimony may be supported by the results of psychological testing. Neurologic examination for organic dysfunction of the brain or psychomotor epilepsy may also be applied to support the psychiatric examination in assessing insanity and competency.

Legal Medicine
A practitioner of legal medicine can expect exposure to a wide range of delicate as well as scientific issues. Some of the most explosive and important issues of our times are abortion, birth control, artificial insemination, sterilization, defining death, euthanasia, medical malpractice, health-care delivery programs, public health and preventive medicine, industrial hazards, mental health, and drug abuse. These problems require a cross-fertilization of ideas, programs, and solutions from the more traditional academic disciplines and professions with which the medicolegal practitioner is familiar. In addition, these problems demand a synthesis of opinions from the general community in order to promulgate solutions that deal with numerous social, moral, ethical, and religious aspects. The medicolegal expert possesses the unique training, expertise, and position to best coordinate the attack on these problems.

Serology and Immunology
The study of blood and other body fluids has an important role in forensic science, a role that is expanding rapidly with advances in technology and genetics. Indeed, with the possible exception of toxicology (the study of the nature, effects, and detection of poisons and the treatment of poisoning), immunology (the study of immunity, i.e., an inherited, acquired, or in-

duced condition to a specific pathogen) is the most explosively developing subject in forensic science. The aspects of blood and body fluid examination fall into several major groups:

- Examination of blood stains to determine their origin;
- Examination of other stains such as saliva, semen, hair, and skin fragments to determine their origin; and
- Immunologic identification of individuals to determine or exclude their identity.

Both in civil and criminal fields the investigation of blood and other biologic fluids may be vital and, indeed, form the major part of the scientific evidence.

Other Forensic Experts
A forensic anthropologist attempts to determine biologic and physical information about a deceased person such as age, sex, stature, race, and even culture. The sources of such information are usually complete or fragmented skeletal remains, but may also include burned bodies and semiskeletal remains. Skilled forensic anthropologists can differentiate between postmortem changes in a body and those that occurred prior to death.

Forensic odontologists compare antemortem dental records to present observations of dental characteristics in a body. The major significance of these studies lies in identifying an otherwise unrecognizable body. Forensic odontology takes the general identification made by the forensic anthropologist and specifies exactly whose the body was. This specialty comes into play primarily with burn and other victims whose physical characteristics have been significantly altered.

Forensic toxicology deals with the detection and interpretation of organic and inorganic toxic materials. A forensic toxicologist works in concert with physicians, pathologists, and police in the investigation of suspicious deaths. New and rapidly growing areas of investigation are environmental pollution, industrial toxins, chemical and radiologic hazards, and drug and alcohol abuse.

To date, of all the forensic specialties, only forensic pathology and forensic psychiatry are consistently and uniformly accorded professional recognition by the courts.

William G. Eckert

Bibliography
Curran, William J., et al. *Modern Legal Medicine, Psychiatry & Forensic Science.* Philadelphia: Davis, 1980.
East, William N. *Medical Aspects of Crime.* New York: Gordon Press, 1980.
Eckert, William G. *Introduction to Forensic Sciences.* St. Louis, MO: Mosby, 1980.
Gordon, Isidor, and H.A. Shapiro. *Forensic Medicine: A Guide to Principles.* 2d ed. New York: Churchill Livingstone, 1982.
Tedeschi, G. Cesare, et al. *Forensic Medicine.* 3 vols. Philadelphia: Saunders, 1977.
Thorwald, Jurgen. *The Century of the Detective.* New York: Harcourt, Brace and World, 1964.
———. *Crime and Science: The New Frontier in Criminology.* New York: Harcourt, Brace and World, 1967.

F

Forensic Science

The application of scientific principles and procedures to the resolution of problems of law is known as forensic science. "Forensic" can describe a considerable number of scientific disciplines, among them chemistry, toxicology, psychiatry, pathology, biology, and engineering. It is therefore reasonable to think of forensic science in terms of the natural, physical, and social sciences, major groupings of accumulated and systematized bodies of knowledge wherein truths and laws have been observed and recorded. When used in the solution of legal problems, the many subgroups become specialties known as forensic pharmacology, forensic psychology, and so on. Indeed, any scientific subspecialty could be used in the solution of a legal problem.

Scientific Method and Law
In order to determine the historic beginnings of forensic science one must consider the evolution of legal processes in Europe, particularly England. The determination of guilt or innocence in criminal offenses evolved from primitive trials by ordeal, to the inquisitorial process, to the ultimate basic tenets of modern jurisprudence, namely, the presumption of innocence under Anglo-Saxon law and the presumption of guilt under Napoleonic Code. The scientific method or rational inquiry became part of the judicial process in the nineteenth century and the forensic sciences expanded steadily during the twen-

tieth. Advances in technology continue to fuel this growth.

Examples of early use of scientific knowledge to resolve problems of criminal conduct were probably afforded most by chemists and medical doctors. The notorious Jack the Ripper murders in London in 1888 provided an opportunity for medical examination of the victims and a possible interpretation of wound patterns. In May 1899, the case of James Maybrick, a Liverpool cotton broker, focused on the role of arsenic as the cause of death, the Marsh test for arsenic having been first used in 1839 in France. Photography is reported to have been used to record criminal portraits in Brussels around 1840, and in 1879 Alphonse Bertillon began developing a method of identification by means of a series of anthropometric measurements. These data, consisting of eleven to fourteen measurements of physical characteristics, skull axes, length of forearm, standing height, and so on, formed the basis of a collection of measurements cards recording statistics on known criminals, information which could be used for personal identification at a later date. The system of Bertillon measurements was eventually adopted by many European, American, and other police agencies. However, the difficulty of taking precise measurements limited the method's usefulness and sometimes resulted in miscarriages of justice.

At about the same time, two men working in widely separated countries, William Herschel in India in 1877 and Dr. Henry Faulds in Tokyo in 1880, laid the groundwork for the science of personal identification by means of fingerprints. Francis Galton published his book *Fingerprints* in 1892, while in 1896 Edward Henry, also working in India, developed a practical system for classifying and filing large numbers of fingerprints, a methodology that had eluded Galton. The Henry system of classification was subsequently adopted in all British colonies and was introduced to the United States in 1904 at the World's Fair in St. Louis, Missouri. Other systems of classification were developed and used in France, Indo-China, and South America. However, the Henry system, with some modifications as the files grow larger each year, is the system most widely used internationally.

Not until the close of the nineteenth century were the various techniques and practices of scientific criminal investigation brought to the attention of the general body of practitioners, police administrators, and scientists. An important contributor to the widespread dissemination of this information was Arthur Conan Doyle, trained in medicine and exceptionally observant and imaginative. Another was Hans Gross, an examining magistrate in Graz, Austria, intensely practical, thorough, and wide-ranging in his interests. Doyle's Sherlock Holmes stories, written between 1887 and 1917, sparked the imagination of investigators and undoubtedly contributed to improvement in the existing quality of criminal investigations. However, it was Hans Gross who collected in two volumes the available knowledge of the time that could actually be applied to criminal investigation and the administration of justice. His *Handbuch für Untersuchungsrichter* (*A Manual for Examining Magistrates*), published in 1893, may well be the benchmark for the beginning of contemporary forensic science. In the third edition (1898) "System der Kriminalistick" was added to the original title. The Madras English translation (*Criminal Investigation*), by John Adam and Collyer Adam, appeared in 1907. Subsequent editions appeared as recently as 1962, bearing fitting testimony to the worth of this basic treatise.

The addition of scientific techniques to the armaments of crime investigation advanced steadily during the twentieth century. Some highlights of this advance include benzidine and hemin tests for blood, Uhlenhuth's test for human blood, Landsteiner's ABO blood grouping system, and Alexander Weiner's identification of the Rhesus factor. The Stielow case made a significant impact on firearms identification, while the contributions of Charles Waite, Phillip O. Gravelle, Max Poser, and Calvin Goddard were of importance in the field of forensic ballistics, the last-named bringing forensic science to the forefront as a result of his work in solving the St. Valentine's Day gangland massacre, which took place in Chicago, Illinois, in 1929.

Early Centers of Learning
Establishment of the Scientific Crime Detection Laboratory at Northwestern University Law School in Chicago was a notable first effort to bring together a group of forensic scientists from varied disciplines to devote their talents to the investigation of crime and the administration of justice. A number of private examiners in different parts of the country were also doing pioneering work in questioned document

examination, fingerprint identification, firearms examination, microscopy, and forensic serology.

Much if not all of the work done in forensic science laboratories deals with physical evidence collected from crime scenes, victims, or those suspected of criminal behavior. The office of coroner, inherited from Anglo-Saxon legal tradition, functioned with varying degrees of sophistication and success in most jurisdictions. In 1877 in the Commonwealth of Massachusetts, the first office of medical examiner was established. Thirty-odd years later, New York City followed suit by opening the Office of Chief Medical Examiner, which served as the model for the subsequent establishment of many local, county, and state offices. Police laboratories were developed in cities throughout the nation. Interestingly, the size of a metropolitan area was not necessarily a criterion, for laboratories were established in cities of such differing populations as Detroit (1929), Buffalo (1935), Kansas City, Missouri (1937), and New York City (1934). Forensic science, with its early roots in Europe, was thus introduced to the United States in piecemeal fashion, with fingerprint and firearms identification playing a significant role. In general, the application of scientific procedures to the resolution of problems of law became a part of the fabric of the criminal-justice system during the first four decades of the twentieth century.

Early practitioners of forensic science were largely self-taught or had transferred formal training in well-established disciplines to the police, investigative, and legal areas. There were no programs of study in which forensic science students could enroll. However, the Institute of Applied Science in Chicago provided an excellent home study course in fingerprint identification, and other subjects dealing with criminal investigation and physical evidence were later added to its program.

August Vollmer, pioneering police administrator in Berkeley, California, was influential in developing university courses dealing with police matters, among them forensic science. At the outset these programs were offered in the criminology context, with the University of California, Berkeley, offering a curriculum in criminology as early as 1933. Dr. Paul Kirk subsequently developed the program in criminalistics at Berkeley, while at Michigan State University, which approved the BS degree program in Police Administration in 1935, Ralph Turner organized a four-year program in criminalistics in 1947. Other college programs were later developed at San Jose State University, Indiana University, and Washington State University, to name a few. World War II interrupted the establishment of additional programs, but the concept of college programs to train students for careers in forensic science was now firmly established. Additional programs were developed after the war, but the most rapid growth in this area of education did not occur until the 1960s, when the federal government created the office of Law Enforcement Assistance Administration. For a number of years following the establishment of this agency, practitioners of forensic science benefited from a windfall of grants for equipment, training, and research. While the bulk of the government's largesse fell to the police, courts, and corrections programs, some money was used to develop various education and training programs in forensic science. Research projects were funded as well, and scientific equipment was upgraded in nearly every forensics laboratory in the nation.

Formal training in the multiple disciplines of forensic science was virtually nonexistent in the early twentieth century. Only in the late 1940s was the Department of Legal Medicine created at Harvard University, with Dr. Alan Moritz as its first chairman. Here an opportunity was provided for medical doctors with a specialty in pathology to receive intensive training in the skills of forensic pathology. The doctors trained in this program later became established in various state and local government units and set sorely needed standards for medical examiners or coroners.

Education and training for criminalistics continued a slow but steady growth after World War II, moving forward at an unprecedented rate after 1968 with the infusion of federal funds. Specialized training in forensic toxicology never emerged as a separate discipline, but a few universities did offer short programs focusing on this discipline. Such programs were generally open only to well-trained analytical chemists, a shortcoming remedied in the 1960s and 1970s, when the nation became concerned with drug abuse and chemical dependency problems. University programs rapidly responded to the demand for additional forensic toxicologists. As a result, it is now possible to obtain superb training and education in the combined areas of analytical chemistry, pharmacology, physiology, toxicology, and clinical chemistry, all of them essential components of forensic toxicological expertise.

Academy of Forensic Sciences

In 1948 the first meeting of the American Academy of Forensic Sciences (AAFS) was held in St. Louis, Missouri. Approximately thirty-five scientific papers were presented to a small but interested audience, an audience and membership which have increased steadily in the ensuing years. At the 1987 meeting in San Diego, California, over 1,400 persons registered, marking the largest attendance in the academy's history. The organizational meeting of AAFS, held at Northwestern University Law School in 1950, approved seven sections, including immunology, pathology, toxicology, psychiatry, police science (later changed to "criminalistics"), jurisprudence, and questioned documents. By 1987 some sections had been combined, and engineering, odontology, physical anthropology and a general section had been added. The academy has been instrumental in encouraging the creation of specialty boards of certification in forensic pathology, forensic toxicology, and forensic psychiatry. It has also done much through its affiliate, the Forensic Science Foundation, to develop standards for the examination of physical evidence and for proficiency testing within laboratories. Following the publication of two volumes of Proceedings from early meetings of the academy, AAFS sponsored the publication of the Journal of Forensic Sciences (1950), which today is the major publication in its field.

In addition to the parent national organization, six regional groups have been established. These sponsor at least one annual meeting, publish newsletters, and arrange for "hands-on" workshops that are always well attended. Whereas prior to 1948 there were but few quality forensic science meetings to enrich the practitioner and neophyte, the discipline is now so well established that national and regional forums abound for exchange of scientific information and highly regarded journals are readily available.

The Fabric of Criminal Investigation

To put the discipline of forensic science in perspective from several viewpoints, one might ask how the basic concepts of criminal investigation have changed over the years. This question presupposes acceptance of the basic tenet of criminal investigation: the recognition and interpretation of evidence that proves or disproves whether an event has occurred. One would also need to know to what extent the body of knowledge dealing with the interpretation of evidence has grown. The first question can be answered by glancing at what constituted physical evidence at the time of Hans Gross, in contrast to what constitutes physical evidence today. Gross listed forty-plus topics that he considered useful and important in the investigation of criminal matters; A. Lucas, in *Forensic Chemistry and Scientific Investigation* in 1921, listed at least thirty topics relevant to the work of the forensic scientist. O'Hara and Osterburg in their book, *Introduction to Criminalistics* (1949), have some forty chapters that deal with physical evidence. The second edition of *Forensic Science*, edited by Geoffrey Davies (1968), lists several hundred topics and techniques that are used routinely by the forensic scientist.

However, if one looks carefully at the information provided by these and many other authors, it becomes apparent that the fabric of a criminal investigation has not really changed dramatically over the years. Latent fingerprints have existed since the time of the first recorded crime: only the surfaces on which they are deposited change with technology. Basic causes of death remain the same, e.g., damage to the heart, damage to the brain, or exclusion of air. Only the instruments of death change with advancing technology. Trace evidence continues to be trace evidence, but our ability to recognize its value changes with improved technology, such as electron microscopy, neutron activation analysis, gas chromatography, etc.

If the fabric of a scientific criminal investigation has remained basically unchanged, the amount of scientific knowledge that is available to identify these basic components has experienced unprecedented growth. One simple example may suffice. At one time a disputed paternity case might have been resolved by testimony of the mother and information about the period of gestation and the whereabouts of the putative father at the time of conception. Today the number of genetic markers that can be used to resolve such questions is impressive. Laboratories using the sixteen or seventeen testing systems currently available report exclusion results with 99 percent accuracy and inclusion results with 97 percent reliability. With the accelerating development of new analytical techniques and instrumentation, the knowledge and techniques available to the forensic scientist are unprecedented.

Herein, however, lies a dilemma. How is this increasing volume of information being interpreted, and how wisely is it being used in the administration of justice? On one hand, the steady advancement in understanding of the role of genetic markers in distinguishing among blood samples provides the technician with remarkable potential for accuracy in analysis. However, equally impressive advancement in the sensitivity and specificity of instruments used to determine blood-alcohol levels by analysis of breath has not contributed comparably to resolving civil dramshop cases. Being able to report blood-alcohol levels to the second decimal place (some instruments report to three places) does not appreciably improve the ability of the technician to determine if a suspect is "grossly intoxicated," "visibly intoxicated," or merely "under the influence" of alcohol. This discrepancy between advances in forensic science technology and its ultimate enhancement of the judicial process is apparent in many areas of current forensic science. Nonetheless, it is incumbent upon the forensic scientist to continue the search for techniques or procedures that may eventually enable him or her to attain the goal of establishment of proof beyond a reasonable doubt in as many instances as possible.

A second question about the use of forensic science in the administration of justice arises as we measure the many subspecialties on a scale of decreasing scientific objectivity or increasing subjectivity. For example, some kinds of chemical analyses, both quantitative and qualitative, are reproducible by analytical chemists in virtually all laboratories around the world; e.g., $AgNO_3 + NaCl = AgCl + NaNO_3$, a very objective identification of the flocculent white precipitate, silver chloride. Yet in the trial of Dr. Carl Coppolino (an anesthesiologist who in the 1960s was charged with murdering his wife and his lover's husband by injecting them with succinylcholine chloride—a drug commonly used in operations to prevent muscles from trembling, although when administered in excess can paralyze the muscles of the lungs, causing death), evidence relating to the isolation of endogenous succinic acid was highly debatable. While the objectivity of tests to determine the presence and nature of genetic markers is legitimate, precautions in testing must be observed to guard against false positive or negative reactions. Fingerprint identification can be

uniformly objective if all prints submitted for examination are clear, clean, and complete; but when a limited number of points for comparison are available, the interpretation may become subjective. The same can be said for firearms identification, in determining whether two bullets were fired from the same gun barrel. Moreover, as the techniques used in microscopy continued to advance, the examination of hairs and fibers becomes less subjective. Similarly, apart from chemical analysis of inks and paper, handwriting identification also contains elements of subjectivity. It is, however, reassuring to note that when a committee of well-trained and experienced document examiners is presented with a collection of forged and known handwriting specimens, members will almost invariably substantiate their colleagues' conclusions through independent examinations, e.g., as in the cases of the forged Howard Hughes manuscripts and the Mormon will. The same can be said of polygraph examinations. Forensic psychiatric opinion, however, still generates public skepticism because of the often diametrically opposed opinions that are proffered by its practitioners in the courtroom.

Courtroom Application

Thus, while a particular scientific discipline may legitimately be placed in the forensic category, it does not automatically have a high probative value in the courtroom. Its ultimate value must be assessed in terms of its objectivity versus subjectivity and whether its specificity and sensitivity are useful and meaningful. In other words, does the scientific testimony clarify the areas of dispute or does it simply confuse the issue to the benefit of one of the parties in the litigation? (sadly, a tactic deliberately used on occasion by trial lawyers).

A final point that bears scrutiny is how uniformly the discipline is used in the judicial process. There is no question that the skills of the forensic scientist are being used with considerable success in the investigation of crime, with investigative agencies utilizing new techniques in ever-increasing numbers. Tests that began as laboratory experiments have found their way into everyday use once their worth was established, as in the case of the dermal nitrate test for powder residue, introduced around 1930 and refined and improved to the point that today it is used routinely (when circumstances warrant) in the investigation of shooting cases. The forensic scientist also plays an increasingly important role in the investigation and litigation of civil cases.

However, in the courtroom we find an area of alarming disparity, particularly in criminal cases, between the forensic "fire-power," so to speak, of the prosecution and that of the defense, with by far the greater preponderance being in the arsenal of the prosecution. The defendant, unless he or she has considerable wealth or a court-appointed expert, usually has little or no forensic expertise in his or her defense. If the defendant is indigent, the chances of benefiting from forensic science testimony are practically negligible. This is not to say that there should be equal forensic science representation in all cases on both sides of an issue, or to imply that the government's use of forensic science is excessive. Occasionally the government's forensic-science evidence is so excessive that it can be misleading, with an over-zealous prosecutor attributing greater significance to scientific testimony than the evidence warrants. In such situations the defendant ought rightly to have ready access to testimony of equally competent expert witnesses, a situation seldom observed in practice for obvious reasons. The number of forensic-science professionals in private practice is minuscule. With the exception of a few scattered locations in California and in a few large urban centers in other parts of the country, it is difficult for private forensic scientists (document examiners, polygraph consultants, and forensic pathologists excepted) to maintain a viable practice. However, as the practitioners within the criminal-justice system become more attuned to the usefulness of scientific expertise in trial strategy, this imbalance should correct itself. In the meantime, the creation of a forensic-science facility that is not the exclusive property of either the government or the private sector might provide more equitable access for defendants. Such a laboratory could be supported jointly by all parties using its facilities, with users of its services having to review their preconceptions of the values of the adversary system and having to accommodate their trial strategies more precisely to, among other things, the attempt to discover rational and reasonable explanations of the events in question. Provisions would necessarily be made, of course, to retain the philosophy of the adversary system in such a way that responsible challenges and second opinions could be brought to the attention of judge or jury.

Whereas forensic science as utilized in the United States legal system has not achieved the same respect afforded it in many European courtrooms, it has nevertheless established a remarkable degree of acceptance since its inception at the close of the nineteenth century. It has evolved into a discipline; it has generated a body of knowledge; it is in the process of developing a philosophy and code of ethical conduct. One hopes that in the twenty-first century forensic science will be applied in an increasingly even-handed manner, commensurate with its technological advance, throughout the legal system.

Ralph F. Turner

Bibliography

Curran, Wm. J., Louis A. McGarry, and Charles Petty. *Modern Legal Medicine Psychiatry and Forensic Science*. Philadelphia: F.A. Davis, 1980.

Gerber, Samuel M. Ed. *Chemistry and Crime*. Washington, DC: American Chemical Society, 1983.

Gonzales, T.A., M. Vance, and M. Kelpern. *Legal Medicine and Toxicology*. New York: D. Appleton, Century, 1937.

Gross, Hans. *Criminal Investigations: A Practical Handbook for Magistrates, Police Officers and Lawyers*. Trans. John Adam and J. Collyer Adam. London: The Specialist Press, 1907.

Holmes, Paul. *The Trials of Dr. Coppolino*. New York: New American Library, 1968.

Saferstein, Richard. *Criminalistics: An Introduction to Forensic Science*. 3d ed. Englewood Cliffs, NJ: Prentice-Hall, 1986.

Turner, Ralph F. *Forensic Science and Laboratory Techniques*. Springfield, IL: Charles C. Thomas, 1949.

Wilton, George W. *Fingerprints: History, Law and Romance*. London: William Hodge, 1938.

Raymond Blaine Fosdick

Raymond Blaine Fosdick (1883–1972), lawyer, public servant, and author, was born in Buffalo, New York, son of a high-school principal. Of Puritan descent, Fosdick began his higher education at Colgate College but transferred to Princeton, where one of his intellectual idols, Woodrow Wilson, was president. Fosdick received his B.A. in 1905 and his M.A. in 1906 and was elected to Phi Beta Kappa. New York Law School granted him the LL.B. degree in 1908, after which he went to work for New York City Mayor George B. McClellan. At first assistant corporation counsel, Fosdick two years later became commissioner of accounts.

The next notable event in his life came when John D. Rockefeller, Jr., on behalf of the Rockefeller Bureau of Social Hygiene, asked him to make a broad study of police organizations in Europe. On the basis of a few previous meetings, two connected with an investigation of the white-slave traffic in prostitutes and one with a Bible class, Rockefeller had singled out Fosdick, a green attorney, for a demanding project. Fosdick immersed himself in the task and in 1915 *European Police Systems* was published. From his autobiography, *Chronicle of a Generation*:

> My itinerary took me to practically every large city in Europe except those in Russia. . . . In every city I visited I tried to see the police in actual operation. . . . The outstanding impression I received from my study in Europe was that police administration there was a distinct career which attracted the best brains obtainable. . . . Its elaborate training schools for recruits had no counterpart in the United States.

Fosdick's compliments continued to flow and American police appeared amateurish in comparison. Naturally, the book stirred immediate interest at home but gathered an even larger audience in Europe. An acute observer and fluent writer, Fosdick had proved his worth to such an extent that Rockefeller asked him to write a companion volume, *American Police Systems*, published in 1920. This time Fosdick visited seventy-two cities and, with what must have seemed a poison pen to the American police, indicted the whole system of law enforcement in this country:

> In America the student of police travels from one political squabble to another, too often from one scandal to another. He finds a shifting leadership of mediocre calibre . . . there is little conception of policing as a profession or as a science to be matured and developed.

Hardly finished yet, Fosdick continued:

Every police department is a graveyard of projects and improvements which, had they been developed to maturity, would have reconstructed the police work of the city. . . . We have, indeed, little to be proud of.

He did explain, however, that in European cities the volume of crime was much less and therefore more manageable. European populations were more homogeneous and less inclined to crime caused by assimilation barriers. With less crime to combat and people tied through kinship, European police could achieve a higher standard of professionalism. No matter, the word was out that, according to Fosdick, American police were decidedly inferior to European.

Criminal Justice in Cleveland, published in 1922, did not soften the blows dealt by the earlier books. Fosdick had joined ten other writers, such as Felix Frankfurter and Roscoe Pound, to conduct a "scientific study" of criminal justice in that city. Fosdick had, if anything, sharpened his criticism:

> Lack of intelligence and imagination in Cleveland's police work is shown in the ragged character of the internal arrangements of the department. . . . Inadequate equipment adds to this appearance of raggedness. . . . Official lethargy lies behind much that is distressing in this picture.

Cleveland and other American police departments (guilty in absentia) bristled at his denunciations, but the glaring public attention was impetus enough for most police departments to start on the uphill road to improvement.

Once again Rockefeller convinced Fosdick to take on a challenging project. He was to make a thorough study of how various countries of the world handled the sale of alcohol. In collaboration with Albert L. Scott, Fosdick wrote *Toward Liquor Control*, published in 1933. It presented the arguments for and against selling liquor through regulation by license or through a state authority system (preferred by Fosdick and Scott), though they admitted that no system was "final." Rockefeller's specific request for studies of the liquor business in Canada and certain European countries filled the appendices. Repeal of the Eighteenth

F

Amendment in 1933, and this book written in anticipation of repeal, relieved much of the workload police had shouldered during the thirteen years of Prohibition.

Fosdick's substantial contributions to policing were only one side of his career. He lived a long life full of other accomplishments and honors. In 1916 he rode with "Black Jack" Pershing in Mexico against Pancho Villa. In 1917 he observed military training methods in Canada, England, and France. What he learned went into *Keeping Our Fighters Fit* (1918), written with E.F. Allen, a book made necessary because America had not fought in a full-scale conflict since the Civil War. After World War I President Wilson chose him to represent the United States at the League of Nations; Fosdick resigned when the Senate failed to ratify the Covenant (1920). By 1930 he had been elected trustee of seven prestigious public service organizations: the Rockefeller Foundation, the Rockefeller Institute for Medical Research, the Rockefeller General Education Board, the International Education Board, the Spelman Fund, the Brookings Institution, and the National Institute of Public Administration. In 1936 he became president of the Rockefeller Foundation and the General Education Board. Entrusted with nearly two hundred million dollars, he administered the money prudently, much of it going for educational grants and disease-prevention research.

The author of fourteen books, Fosdick struck people as "a good conversationalist, genial, witty, and generous." Of course, his having been at the center of so much turbulent history enhanced his storytelling. Recipient of the Distinguished Service Medal and two doctorates, accorded the rank of commander of the French Legion of Honor, elected as a fellow of the American Academy of Arts and Sciences, and as a member of the American Philosophical Society, he had much to be proud of. Tragedy befell him in 1932 when his first wife shot and killed their two children before taking her own life. At the apogee of his public career in 1936 he married a second time, to Elizabeth Miner.

Bibliography

Current Biography. February 1945: 18–20.
Fosdick, Raymond B. *Chronicle of a Generation: An Autobiography*. New York: Harper and Brothers, 1958.
———. *American Police Systems*. Montclair, NJ: Patterson Smith, [1920] 1969.
———. *European Police Systems*. Montclair, NJ: Patterson Smith, [1915] 1969.
———, and Albert L. Scott. *Toward Liquor Control*. New York: Harper and Brothers, 1933.
———, et al. *Criminal Justice in Cleveland*. Montclair, NJ: Patterson Smith, 1968 (Reprint of 1922 ed.).
New York Times 41(July 19, 1972): 3.

Fraud Investigation

Throughout history some people have always cheated and tricked others. Since the fourteenth century such dishonesty and deceit has been known generically as fraud, a word that has far older etymological roots. Yet, oddly to our eyes, English law failed for many centuries to grapple effectively with fraud. Not until 1677 did the Statute of Frauds become law, requiring wills to be written, signed and witnessed, and deeds to be provided for the creation and assignment of all trusts. Victims of fraud could in principle find relief in equity, provided their own unbusinesslike behavior had not been a contributory factor. The English judiciary was uneasy about laying down rules for the definition of various types of fraud. Lord Nottingham, the lord chancellor, said that such rules "would be perpetually eluded by new schemes which the fertility of men's invention would contrive."

There was a widespread feeling in the eighteenth century, and even into our own times, that a person defrauded deserved to lose. As an English jurist asked rhetorically in the eighteenth century, "Shall we indict a man for making a fool of another?" A legal maxim summed up the attitude of many jurists and of the public at large: *caveat emptor*, or "let the buyer beware." Such hard-headed advice ignored the fact that many of the people defrauded were ignorant and gullible; that others, however prudent, had been cheated by master confidence tricksters; and that some offenses, such as the willful misrepresentation of goods or real estate, could be detected only by experts or after the fraudulent transaction had taken place. To be sure, many victims of fraudsters are trapped by their own greed, but to argue that they do not deserve redress is to shift the blame from where it really lies.

In the past decade or so legal and popular attitudes have undergone a dynamic metamorphosis in the United States, with *caveat venditor* ("let the seller beware") replacing *caveat emptor*. There has also been a marked change in the attitude of police administrators. Until recently many saw investigation of fraud as too time-consuming and difficult, with a relatively low probability of successful prosecution and adequate sentencing. Fraud investigation therefore took a back seat to the more emotive crimes of violence, burglary and automobile theft, and drug-related offenses. Now there is growing recognition that the losses caused by fraud are often more traumatic, and have longer-term effects, than the quick and sudden violence of the average street offense or burglary.

Nature of Fraud

The "trilogy of fraud" describes the three basic forms of theft: false pretenses, trick and device, and embezzlement. All three are statutory offenses. Effective investigation requires fundamental knowledge of each type of fraud.

False Pretenses

The requisites are (a) *specific intent to defraud*, a frame of mind on the part of the thief; (b) *misrepresentations* by the thief of a material fact, which can be in any form of communication, expressed or implied; (c) *reliance* by the victim on the representation, inducing him or her to release property to the thief and; (d) *actual loss*, this being satisfied if the victim in fact did not receive what he or she bargained for.

The intent of the *victim* is also material. It has to be the victim's intent that title should accompany the transfer of property to the thief. The victim's intent is essential as it differentiates between the elements of false pretenses and theft by trick and device.

False pretenses thefts present an added requisite, *corroboration*. This is usually demonstrated by the "false token" or writing subscribed to by the accused, or the testimony of two witnesses and corroborating circumstances. This is a precaution against perjury by an ostensible victim. Frequently, allegations of false pretenses are based upon contractual arrangements. This brings into play the parole evidence rule, which precludes any evidence of prior or contemporaneous verbal agreements that would alter the provisions of a written contract. However, in a criminal action based upon the same facts, the parole evidence rule is generally held to be operative only between the original parties to the contract, and in a criminal prosecution the state may go outside the provisions of the contract to establish the accused's real intent and the truth of representations made during negotiations.

Trick and Device

In this form of theft the basic elements of specific intent, misrepresentation, and reliance and loss are the same as those required in prosecution of theft by false pretenses. However, trick and device is distinguished by the intent of the victim, who does not intend to relinquish title to the property, only its possession to the accused. The victim expects that it (money, etc.) will be used only for a specific purpose, such as a loan, investment, or purchases. The accused, however, has no intention of putting it to such use, specifically intending from the outset to divert it to his or her own use. There is no requirement here for the "corroboration" demanded in false pretenses prosecutions. This form of theft is the basis for the prosaic street-cons or bunco games. It is a fast-moving, high-mobility operation, usually with smaller losses involved (although this is relative to those victimized) and a higher frequency rate. The "street-con" involves "The Three G's" (greed, gullibility, and goodness). One or all can be present. Whether it is the victim's avarice, naiveté, stupidity, or misunderstanding, the con-artist works to create a feeling of rapport and "confidence." The term "street-con" relates primarily to the "switch" scams, the "bank examiner," and similar approaches. However, this form of theft is not limited to the "short" or "street" buncos. The legal format (elements) has application to long-term, major frauds also, such as those in the securities-investment field, fraudulent loans and real estate scams.

Embezzlement

This form of theft is extremely difficult to prevent in spite of enforced basic accounting procedures and internal control methods utilized by the victim or his company. It is a crime of opportunity, frequently remains undiscovered for long periods, and is usually repetitive, not an isolated act. The embezzler, like the check writer, is the classic recidivist. The elements of the offense require that (a) there is a fiduciary relationship between the victim and the accused, a form of trust whereby the victim entrusts property to the accused (employee usually); (b) the property must come into the hand (dominion, control, possession) of the agent-servant-employee, as the property of the victim, the title remains with him or her at all times; (c) the employee-agent receives the property in the course of employment (some exceptions exist such as obtaining from a constructive trust), it must be lawfully in his or her hands, his or her receiving it properly in the scope of employment; (d) the agent-employee forms the intent to *take* the property for his or her own use or some use not contemplated within the trust and deprives the owner of it, this intent forming *after* possession is acquired legally; (e) the agent-employee takes control-possession of the property; and (f) the victim never intends the agent-employee to use the property for any purpose other than that specified or agreed upon. The rule of corroboration as in theft by false pretenses is not required here.

Motive is important to establish in examining the embezzlement. The crucial question is why does a certain suspect need the money? The need does not always have to be rooted in an antisocial behavior. It can represent perfectly legitimate problems, such as house payments, medical bills, or automobile expenses and costs.

Check Offenses
Although most jurisdictions have specific sections of the criminal codes that relate to the "paper" offenses—forgery, nonsufficient funds, checks, fictitious checks, etc.—the crimes are still essentially false pretenses. The technical areas include handwriting identification, document examination, paper type, and check classification systems, but the fundamental principles still remain: deceit and trust. The act of forgery occurs when a person, with intent to defraud, signs the name of another person (or a fictitious person) without authority to do so, or falsely makes, alters, or forges an instrument (checks, notes, bills, contracts, etc.) and tenders, utters, or passes it.

Nonsufficient funds (NSF) checks probably are the most prevalent offenses. When a person with the intent to defraud makes a check, knowing *at the time* there are insufficient monies on hand or credit with the bank to pay in full the amount on the face of the check, and presents, utters, or passes the instrument, he or she has committed the offense. The amounts required to differentiate between a felony and misdemeanor vary by jurisdiction. Because of the multiplicity of NSF check cases, many police agencies are forced to set an arbitrary minimum limit on the amounts involved.

This administrative device does not satisfy the victim, but budgetary and personnel demands prevail.

The Investigative Process
With a few exceptions, most major frauds are legislatively mandated to federal and state agencies. That still leaves the police with more than enough offenses to consume the time and other resources they have available.

A police agency that investigates fraud must adhere to the basic rule applicable to any specialized area of inquiry: placing someone in control who has the needed training and knowledge. Just as an efficient homicide investigator must have some understanding of physiology, biology, and psychology, so must the fraud investigator be acquainted with the applicable law, business practices, accounting principles, modern data-processing, and psychology. He or she must have this requisite array of knowledge, perhaps not to the level of the professional in these varied fields, but at least to the degree that enables the investigator to recognize the significance of the information developed and the need for specialized help. Consequently, in this era of specialization, the general-assignment investigator is losing ground in the larger and more progressive police agencies to specialized investigators.

Any investigation of a protracted nature requires the formulation of a plan which outlines definitively the areas of concern. One form that has proved its efficacy for countless years is a variation of the standard military operational order, or Five Paragraph Field Order: (1) the situation or assessment, (2) the mission, (3) the execution, (4) logistics, and (5) command.

(1) SITUATION ASSESSMENT. What allegedly occurred? Is the initial information received from a victim, or informants, or the ensuing investigation? Victims, through embarrassment and confusion, frequently furnish erroneous facts. This requires a logical assessment of the victim's motivation and emotional and mental state, his or her ability to relate accurately the representation being made, its falsity, his or her degree of reliance, and the actual property loss.

(2) MISSION. This segment relates the strategy to be used in a given case/situation. A case cannot be based solely upon the unsupported allegations of the victim. The legal requirements of the crimes have to be met. Investigative efforts will be directed to documentation, witness testimony, and instruments, all needed to prove

or disprove that a crime in fact has been committed. This is the who, what, when, and where of an investigation.

(3) EXECUTION. What tactically is to be done to carry out the mission? To do this, consideration has to be given to the documentation to be developed, the witnesses to be identified and interviewed, the corroboration to be established, and the suspects to be identified and researched, including their net worth and the source and application of their funds, and the similar acts and transactions to be analyzed to establish the plan, scheme, design, and intent of the suspects and victim. Intent is a subjective thing; a frame of mind that is extremely difficult to establish and prove.

(4) LOGISTICS (SUPPORT). Consideration is given here to the probable technical and expert assistance, which will be needed to support the investigators. It may be available within the police agency or it may have to be obtained from outside. Examples of such outside experts range from accountants and security analysts to plumbers and tile setters, can require any type of help that is needed to effectively carry out a successful inquiry. No approach is too ethereal or too prosaic.

(5) COMMAND. A fundamental principle applicable to all forms of police investigation concerns the director of operations. There can be *only one* person who has the responsibility, authority, and final overall accountability. These charges cannot be delegated or handled by a committee. A bifurcated approach, with its resulting duplication and conflicts of direction, hampers the effectiveness of any investigation, thereby reducing its chances of being successful.

Robert S. Newsom

Bibliography

Bailey, F. Lee, and Henry B. Rothblatt. *Defending Business and White Collar Crime.* Rochester, NY: Lawyers Cooperative Publishing, 1969.

Edelhertz, Herbert, et al. *Investigation of White Collar Crime.* Washington, DC: Department of Justice, LEAA, 1977.

Geis, Gilbert. *White Collar Criminal.* New York: Atherton Press, 1968.

Glick, Rush G., and Robert S. Newsom. *Fraud Investigation: Fundamentals for Police.* Springfield, IL: Charles C. Thomas, 1974.

Soble, Ronald L., and Robert E. Dallos. *The Impossible Dream.* New York:

New American Library, 1975.

Sutherland, Edwin H. *White Collar Crime.* New York: Holt, Rinehart and Winston, 1967.

F

Leonard Felix Fuld

Leonhard Felix Fuld (1883–1965), lawyer, economist, police expert, and philanthropist, was born in New York City, son of a wholesale merchant. After graduation from Horace Mann High School he entered Columbia University and within seven years (1902–1909) earned five degrees. His doctoral dissertation, "Police Administration: A Critical Study of Police Organizations in the United States and Abroad," was published by G.P. Putnam's Sons. Fuld stated in his preface, "It is believed that this is the first attempt to present a logical exposition of the principles of police administration." A notable event, the book was reviewed by most opinion-making journals and received uniform praise. In *The Annals of the American Academy of Political and Social Science* (January–June 1910) a critic remarked, "The detailed research necessary for such a work is still only too often discounted as 'academic.'" What Fuld had done was to write a readable book, 551 pages long, that made a mundane subject interesting. Not only was it written by a young man of obvious talent who had amassed a startling academic record, but also it covered the subject as never before.

Two of Fuld's degrees were in law, and he drew from that training to incorporate legal aspects of police administration into his master work. He traveled throughout Europe and the United States to see for himself how police departments functioned. He always reacted like a true social scientist engrossed in research, writing down everything. Back home in New York City he haunted police precinct stationhouses in an effort to catalogue every hourly motion. He assimilated police selection techniques, pored over duty descriptions, reviewed discipline procedures, checked-out equipment and examined it piece by piece, rummaged through records, and pondered crime control problems. Any single chapter of his book would have been subject enough for a dissertation, but Fuld chose to attempt an omniscient text. His was a commendable effort that succeeded in landing him a just reward. Fresh out of Columbia, he became a civil-service examiner for New York City.

Fuld's book was all the more remarkable because he was an outsider with no previous experience of police and was young and decidedly scholastic. In theory he should not have been able to create such an exemplary study; nevertheless he succeeded by uncovering and addressing the most important police questions of the day. Though he did not completely resolve them, he did articulate them well enough for others to visualize. For instance, he sided with municipal versus state policing, a much debated topic then:

> No English-speaking people has ever had a State constabulary—a police force appointed and controlled by the central authorities and operating as the sole police force throughout the entire State—and the establishment of such a State constabulary could be justified only on the ground that American cities have shown an utter incapacity for self-government in the department of police administration.

That passage and its elaboration in effect reinforced the objective of municipal policing to serve its people on a local level and to remain free of political taint. Another of Fuld's concerns was the criteria for the appointment of officers. Hiring abuses fouled the scene and displeased him intensely:

> Most police commissioners in the United States belong to that class which we have designated the "weak." It is a characteristic of the weak executive in any office to spend most of his time in attending to routine matters which by statute or custom require his personal attention and to look to his private secretary for information and advice.

So the police commissioner signed documents all day, while his private secretary sized up eligible applicants and arbitrarily winnowed them out. The professional blackmailer also had a hand in the selection process:

> He informs the applicant for appointment or promotion that if he will pay him a given sum of money he will get a certain political district leader to exert his influence to secure his appointment. . . . If the applicant refuses to pay

the sum demanded of him, it is comparatively easy for the blackmailer to gain the ear of the weak commissioner's private secretary and by narrating to that official some scandal in the life of the applicant for appointment defeat his chances of appointment.

Fuld stressed that once an applicant had passed the civil-service exam nothing should prevent his eventual employment. Any errors in the test design went against the examinee, so that a passing mark was harder to achieve. Thus it was blatant malfeasance to subject an exam survivor to a cursory interview or blackmail, as was common practice.

Efficient patrolling to halt crime was another sensitive area for Fuld:

> The new recruits of the force quickly imitate the veterans, and if the spirit of loafing dominates the police force the mere addition of more recruits will not prove to be a satisfactory remedy. . . . If you hold each officer personally responsible for crimes on his beat it is quite likely that he will attend strictly to his duties in order to prevent the commission of crimes on his beat.

Fuld added that an undermanned beat or frequent officer transfer subverted his simple solution. He despised, though, the use of spies or "shoo-flies" to tattle on napping police:

> It injures the morale of the police force when favored patrolmen are sent out in citizen's clothes to spy upon other patrolmen of the force. It is doubtful whether it is good policy to permit superior officers to spy upon the subordinates of the force. It is undoubtedly bad policy to encourage citizens to spy upon the police.

After publication of *Police Administration* Fuld divided his time between public service and making millions of dollars. His only subsequent involvements with police came when he assisted in the planning of the New York Police Academy and, two years before his death, when he set up a fund for advanced training of officers at the New Jersey State Police Academy. Fuld never married, living with his sister, Florentine, in one of his tenement buildings, where he, a wealthy man, had often been seen performing janitorial services. His sister died nine years before he did.

Fuld's friends ascribed his financial success to a job on Wall Street he had held early in his career. The president of Cities Service had employed Fuld to establish a school for security salesmen and from that episode he had emerged his own best student. He never allowed anyone else to manage his money but himself, and he wrote all his correspondence in longhand (5,000 letters a year). At his death he left $25 million in a perpetual trust fund to be adminis-tered by the Helene Fuld Foundation (named for his mother). The foundation was to promote the health of student nurses; he had already given away millions of dollars to hospitals for the benefit of their nurses.

F

Bibliography

Fuld, Leonhard Felix. *Police Administration: A Critical Study of Police Organizations in the United States and Abroad.* Montclair, NJ: Patterson Smith, [1909] 1971.

New York Times 37(September 1, 1965): 1.

G

Gender and Crime

Sex is the best single predictor of whether an individual will violate the law—men commit much more crime than women. This is true for every society, for every historical period, for every group, and for nearly every category of crime for which data are available. Together with hormonal differences that make men more aggressive than women, gender differences—in goals and norms, in socialization, in social control, and in criminal opportunities—result in gender differences in behavior that create much lower rates of crime among women than among men. This discussion of gender and crime begins with an examination of male and female differences in offending rates and patterns and then looks at explanations for these differences. This is followed by a consideration of trends in female arrests over the last three decades, along with explanations for the generally modest increases in female crime relative to male crime.

Male and Female Differences in Offending

Table 1 displays patterns and trends in male and female arrests as reflected in data from the *Uniform Crime Reports* (UCR) of the FBI for the years 1960, 1975, and 1990 for all arrest categories except rape (a nearly exclusively male crime) and the juvenile categories of runaway and curfew violation. Three types of information are provided: male and female arrest rates for 1960, 1975, and 1990 (columns 1–6); the female percent of arrests for each crime for the same years (columns 7–9); and the male and female offending profiles for 1960 and 1990 (columns 10–13). The focus of discussion in this section is on the most contemporary (1990) data, while trends over time are discussed in greater detail in a later section.

Male and Female Arrest Rates (Table 1, Columns 1–6)
The single most important difference to note between the female and male arrest rates per 100,000 population is that for a given crime, for a particular year, the female rate is always lower than the male rate—with the sole exception of prostitution. Similarities outnumber the differences, however. For example, crime categories for which males have high rates of arrest (relative to male rates for other crime categories), females also have high arrest rates (relative to female rates for other crime categories). For example, both males and females have relatively high arrest rates for several of the minor property crimes (especially larceny) and public order offense categories (especially driving under the influence—DUI). Patterns of change over time are also parallel for males and females (see discussion in later section).

Percent Female Arrests (Table 1, Columns 7–9)
The percentage of female arrests (PFA) is the percent of all arrests for each crime category accounted for by women, after adjusting for the sex composition of the population. If men and women are equally represented in arrests for a given crime, the PFA would be fifty. Looking at the 1990 data, with the exception of prostitution (the only category for which more women are arrested than men), the female percentage of arrests is highest for the minor property crimes (about 35 percent) and lowest for "masculine" crimes like robbery and burglary (about 8 percent each).

Arrest Profiles (Table 1, Columns 10–13)
The arrest profile percents are calculated separately for males and females. The number for

TABLE 1 Male and Female Arrest Rates/100,000, Female Percentage of Arrests, and Male and Female Arrest Profiles. (1960–1990, FBI Uniform Crime Reports)

Offenses	Male Rates			Female Rates			Female Percentage (of arrests)			Offender-Profile Percentage			
										Males		Females	
	1960 (1)	1975 (2)	1990 (3)	1960 (4)	1975 (5)	1990 (6)	1960 (7)	1975 (8)	1990 (9)	1960 (10)	1990 (11)	1960 (12)	1990 (13)
Against Persons													
Homicide	9	16	16	2	3	2	17	14	11	.1	.2	.2	.1
Aggravated Assault	101	200	317	16	28	50	14	13	13	1	3	2	2
Weapons	69	137	165	4	11	14	4	8	7	1	2	.5	.7
Simple Assault	265	354	662	29	54	129	10	13	15	4	6	4	5
Major Property													
Robbery	65	131	124	4	10	12	5	7	8	1	1	.5	.5
Burglary	274	477	319	9	27	32	3	5	8	4	3	1	1
Stolen Property	21	103	121	2	12	17	8	10	11	.3	1	.2	.5
Minor Property													
Larceny-Theft	391	749	859	74	321	402	17	30	30	6	10	9	20
Fraud	70	114	157	12	59	133	15	34	43	1	2	2	7
Forgery	44	46	51	8	18	28	16	28	34	.5	.5	1	1
Embezzlement	—	7	8	—	3	5	—	28	37	—	.2	—	.1
Malicious Mischief													
Auto Theft	121	128	158	5	9	18	4	7	9	2	1	1	1
Vandalism	—	187	224	—	16	28	—	8	10	—	2	—	1
Arson	—	15	13	—	2	2	—	11	14	—	.3	—	.1
Drinking/Drugs													
Public Drunkenness	2,573	1,201	624	212	87	71	8	7	9	36	8	25	4
DUI	344	971	1,193	21	81	176	6	5	11	5	15	3	9
Liquor Laws	183	276	428	28	43	102	13	14	17	3	5	4	5
Drug Abuse	49	523	815	8	79	166	15	13	14	1	7	1	6
Sex/Sex Related													
Prostitution	15	18	30	37	45	62	73	73	65	.2	.4	4	3
Sex Offenses	81	55	78	17	5	7	17	8	8	1	1	2	.3
Disorderly Conduct	749	597	499	115	116	119	13	17	18	11	5	14	6
Vagrancy	265	45	26	23	7	4	8	14	12	4	.3	3	.2
Suspicion	222	31	13	28	5	3	11	13	15	3	.1	3	.1
Miscellaneous													
Against Family	90	57	51	8	7	12	8	10	16	1	.5	1	.5
Gambling	202	60	14	19	6	2	8	9	15	3	.2	2	.2
Other Exc. Traffic	871	1,139	2,109	150	197	430	15	15	15	13	23	19	20
Total	7,070	7,850	9,211	831	1,383	2,122	11	15	19				

each crime represents the male and female arrests for that crime as a percent of all male arrests and all female arrests, respectively. (The homicide figures of .2 for men in 1990 and .1 for women mean, respectively, that only two-tenths of 1 percent of all male arrests were for homicide, and only one-tenth of 1 percent of all female arrests were for homicide.) For both males and females, the three most common arrest categories in 1990 are DUI, larceny-theft, and "other except traffic"—a residual category that includes mostly criminal mischief, public disorder, local ordinance violations, and assorted minor crimes. Similarly, arrests for murder, arson, and embezzlement are relatively rare for males and females alike.

The most important gender differences in arrest profiles involve the proportionately greater involvement of women in minor property crimes, such as larceny and fraud (about 28 percent of all female arrests versus 12 percent of male arrests) and in prostitution-type offenses, and the relatively greater involvement of males in crimes against persons and major property crimes (17 percent of all male arrests versus 11 percent of all female arrests).

The patterns found in the UCR data are corroborated by victimization data from the National Crime Survey (NCS), in which victims are asked the sex of offenders for those crimes where the offender is seen. The NCS numbers turn out to be very close to those of the UCR for robbery (7 percent), aggravated assaults (8 percent), simple assaults (15 percent), burglary (5 percent), and motor vehicle theft (5 percent). Self-report studies also confirm the UCR patterns of relatively low female involvement in serious offenses and greater involvement in the less serious categories (Elliott, Ageton, and Huizinga, 1987).

From these and other data sources, it is clear that in comparison to male offenders, females are far less likely to be involved in serious offenses, and the monetary value of female thefts, property damage, drugs, and injuries is typically smaller than that for similar offenses committed by males. Females are also less likely than males to be involved in group criminal endeavors. When female offenders are involved with others, particularly in more lucrative thefts or other criminal enterprises, they typically act as accomplices to males who both organize the crime and are the central figures in its execution. Perhaps the most significant gender difference is the overwhelming dominance of males

in more organized and highly lucrative crimes, whether based in the underworld or the "upperworld."

Explaining Female Crime

Why female rates are everywhere lower than male rates is a more important theoretical issue than explaining variability in female rates. This is because research indicates that the factors contributing to criminality are generally the same for females as for males. Like male offenders, female offenders (especially the more serious ones) are typically of low socioeconomic status, poorly educated, under- or unemployed, and disproportionately from minority groups. Female offenders, however, are more likely than male offenders to have dependent children. The fact that male offending rates are good predictors of female offending rates provides further evidence that female rates respond to the same societal conditions that influence male rates. This suggests that any conditions unique to women have less influence on female crime rates than societal conditions that have similar effects on both male and female rates.

However, to understand the lower rates of offending among females in relation to males, gender-specific factors become quite important. The remainder of this section focuses on factors that affect men and women differentially in terms of willingness and ability to commit crime—especially gender differences in socialization and norms, in social control, in criminal opportunities, in physical strength and aggression (real or perceived), and in the handling of criminal suspects.

Socialization and Norms

In comparison to males, females during their formative years are socialized to emphasize different behavioral goals and personal attributes. As males are being socialized to strive for money, careers, and success, females are being socialized to focus on their future roles as wives/sex objects and mothers/caregivers. As males are socialized to cultivate assertiveness, aggression, strength, and physical prowess, females are socialized to cultivate deference, supportiveness, warmth, and beauty. The dividing line between what is masculine and what is criminal is often thin and blurred; while the distinction between what is feminine and what is criminal is acute and difficult to breach.

Gender-specific norms serve both to inhibit and to channel female criminal involvement in a number of ways. Male norms of sexual aggression, together with female fears of sexual victimization, constrain women's mobility and limit their criminal opportunity by keeping them away from nighttime streets, rough bars, and other crime-likely situations. Female norms of deference, supportiveness, and caregiving strengthen internal controls so that females are less willing to engage in behavior that could jeopardize their children or relationships that are important to them. Child care responsibilities also place practical constraints on female time and mobility that would handicap a prospective criminal career.

Norms of female beauty and sexuality subject females to greater surveillance by parents and/or husbands or lovers (see Social Control, below), and also shape societal definitions of female deviance and the kinds of deviant roles most available to women. Ironically, when female offenders exploit male stereotypes by using their attractiveness or sexuality as a means of entry into criminal organizations, they are likely to find their crime roles organized around female attributes that limit the range of opportunities.

Social Control

The concept of social control cuts across the issue of women's relative willingness and ability to commit crime. To the extent that females are more subject to parental supervision and control, they have less objective freedom to engage in delinquent behavior and are less prone to risk-taking behavior such as delinquency. In contrast, flirting with or flounting the boundaries of acceptable behavior is not only expected but often is valued when it does occur—for males. Name-calling, such as "wimp" and "pussy," may even be targeted at males whose behavior is seen as controlled. Greater supervision and control also lead to greater female attachment to parents, teachers, and conventional friends, which in turn reduces the likelihood of influence by delinquent peers. Further, because they find themselves encapsulated within the family and the private sphere, even adult women continue to experience less freedom than do men to explore and cope with the temptations and tensions of the world beyond the family boundaries.

Access to Criminal Opportunity

Female criminal opportunities are limited not only by the greater external and internal controls already mentioned, but also by the same sorts of obstacles women experience in the realm of legitimate opportunities. Occupational segregation of females, for example, means that they are less likely to hold jobs (such as truck driver, dockworker, or carpenter) that would provide opportunities for theft, drug dealing, fencing, and other illegitimate activities.

Potential female offenders are also at a clear disadvantage in selection and recruitment into criminal groups, in the range of career paths and access to them, and in opportunities for tutelage, increased skills, and rewards. Thus the dominance of males (and the relative absence of females) is especially evident when we look at more organized and more lucrative kinds of criminal enterprise, from burglary rings, gambling operations, and drug cartels, to arson for profit mobs, fencing networks, racketeering, pornography, and black-market smuggling of weapons, liquor, and cigarettes. Incidentally, women also participate very little in more organized and lucrative kinds of corporate and "upperworld" crimes (Pennsylvania Crime Commission, 1991; Steffensmeier, 1983).

Physical Strength and Aggression

Real or perceived female weakness and lack of aggressiveness and risk-taking in comparison to males serve to limit female ability to engage in certain types of criminal behavior, particularly with respect to access to criminal subcultures, which place a premium on physical prowess for protection, enforcing contracts, and recruiting and managing reliable associates. Research indicates that aggressiveness has been found to covary consistently with male crime, and this trait is stronger among males than among females for reasons that are not altogether explained by culture.

Gender and the Handling of Criminal Suspects

Greater "leniency" toward females may explain a portion of the lower official offending rates of women in comparison to men. For example, in comparison to boys, girls who commit criminal acts (as opposed to juvenile status offenses like running away) are somewhat less likely to be arrested (Chesney-Lind, 1986). On the other hand, there appear to be few, if any, differences between adult men and women in arrest, prosecution, plea-bargaining, and conviction. But women defendants do appear to have a lower probability of being jailed or imprisoned. This

G

may be related in part to limitations in physical space available for women but may also be related to factors such as pregnancy or responsibilities for small children. Women are also more likely to demonstrate remorse, and they are viewed as less dangerous and more amenable to rehabilitation.

Explaining Patterns of Female Criminality
The factors just discussed help to explain *patterns* of female criminality by crime type. Namely, female participation is highest for those crimes most consistent with traditional norms and for which females have the most opportunity, and lowest for those crimes that diverge the most from traditional gender norms and for which females have little opportunity.

In the area of property crime, the percentage of female arrests is highest for minor property larceny (comprising the largest volume of female arrests), fraud, and forgery, which involve behaviors like shoplifting (larceny), "bad checks" (forgery), and welfare and credit fraud—all compatible with traditional female consumer/domestic roles. The lowest percentage of female involvement is found for serious property crimes like burglary and robbery, offense categories that are very much at odds with traditional feminine stereotypes, and to which women have very limited access. Even when women are involved in robbery, they are likely to be acting as accomplices to males (Miller, 1986; Steffensmeier and Terry, 1986), or as solo perpetrators (e.g., prostitutes or addicts) committing "wallet-sized" thefts.

Even female violence is more closely tied to the traditional female role than might seem immediately apparent. The female's victim tends to be a male intimate (husband or lover) or a child, the offense generally takes place within the home, the victim frequently is drunk, and self-defense often is a motive. For women to kill, they generally must see their situation as life-threatening, as affecting the physical or emotional well-being of themselves or their children.

The linkage between female criminality and gender stereotyping is probably most evident in the case of certain public order offenses for which the percentage of female involvement is high, particularly prostitution. The high percentage of female arrests for prostitution reflects both gender differences in marketability of sexual services and the sexual double standard. Although customers obviously must out-

number prostitutes, they are less likely to be sanctioned. Although often thought of as a female crime, prostitution is essentially a male-dominated criminal enterprise. The prostitute's working conditions are virtually all controlled by males such as pimps, clients, police, and businessmen who employ prostitutes.

High female involvement in substance abuse is also linked to the traditional role. Female initiation into the use of alcohol and other drugs often occurs in a dating context, and women are generally introduced to hard drugs (heroin, cocaine) by the man in their life, although hard-core addiction is less common among women. Unlike male addicts, other criminal involvements of female addicts are likely to follow rather than precede their addiction and are more likely to end when drug use ceases.

International data also depict patterns of female offending that are consistent with traditional female roles. Both developed and developing nations have a very low female percentage of involvement in major property crimes like robbery and burglary. A higher female percentage of arrests is found for minor property crimes among developed nations.

Female Arrest Trends
Since gender differences in factors like socialization, social control, and criminal opportunity help to explain the generally lower rates of female offending, there is a certain intuitive appeal to the notion that the women's movement might be expected to bring about a convergence in male and female rates of offending. The lively debate of recent decades makes it worthwhile to explore changes (if any) in patterns of female offending relative to male offending, and the reasons for such changes.

Table 1 (columns 1–6) reveals that since 1960 both male and female arrest rates have increased for a number of crimes, especially for larceny, fraud, DUI, and drugs. Decreases occurred for both males and females in a few categories like gambling, public drunkenness, and vagrancy. The arrest profiles of males and females (columns 10–13) reveal little change over this period.

The most dramatic increases in the female percentage of arrests (PFA—columns 7–9) since 1960 have been for the minor property offenses of larceny, fraud, and forgery, for which the female percentage of arrests ranges from 30 to 40 percent, as compared to only about 15 percent in 1960. As already noted, such offenses are consistent with the traditional female consumer role.

In contrast, much more modest increases in the female percentage of arrests have occurred for the major property crimes, averaging about 3 to 4 percent. For robbery, the PFA increased from 5 to 8 percent; for burglary, from 3 to 8; for stolen property, from 8 to 11. Among violent crimes, the PFA increased from 10 to 16 percent for simple assault, but held relatively steady for aggravated assault. For homicide, the PFA declined from 17 to 11 percent.

Other data sources reveal relative stability in female-to-male offending patterns. For example, National Youth Survey data from the mid-1960s to the 1980s show "no significant declines in the [male-to-female] sex ratios on eight specific offenses (Elliott, Ageton, and Huizinga, 1987)." Similarly, state and federal prison data show little change in the percent of female prisoners, averaging about 5 percent in the 1920s, 3 percent in the 1960s, and 6 percent today.

Finally, female involvement in professional and organized crime appears to remain very low. For example, in the Pennsylvania Crime Commission's (1991) *1990 Report* on organized crime in Pennsylvania during the 1980s, only a handful of women are identified as major players in large-scale gambling and racketeering. And even these few gained their position through association with a male (e.g., a husband or lover, father, son, or brother who had established the operation).

Explaining Female Arrest Trends
Researchers have developed at least six plausible explanations of female arrest trends, especially for the increase in female arrests for property crimes. These explanations include greater formalization of law-enforcement procedures, increased gender equality, increased economic insecurity for women, expanded opportunities for "female-type" crimes, changes in the criminal underworld, and increased female drug dependency.

Formalization of Law Enforcement
It is possible that some of the apparent increases in the female percent of arrests has been an artifact of changes in the law, in policing, and in record-keeping. Court decisions in recent decades have reduced some aspects of police discretion, and this has coincided with increased

bureaucratization of policing to establish more universalistic standards of decision-making, thus reducing the effects of gender on probability of arrest. Computerization and other improvements in record-keeping have reduced inaccuracies such as records in which sex is "unknown," which in the past used to be routinely added to the male arrest totals. Such factors would increase the apparent female offending rate by improving the accuracy with which official agencies process and record such offending.

Greater Gender Equality
Some have argued that female gains in the labor force can account for the large increases in PFA for the minor property crimes of larceny, fraud, and forgery. However, most such arrests are related to consumer roles rather than to occupations (e.g., shoplifting, bad checks, welfare, and credit card fraud). Very likely the increased number of women in the paid work force has resulted in higher levels of employee theft by women, but such trends cannot be determined from UCR arrest statistics. The typical arrestee has committed nonoccupational theft or fraud such as shoplifting or check forgery.

Expansion of female roles and activities can illuminate certain aspects of female crime trends. For example, the rise in the female percentage of arrests for DUI can be attributed, in part, both to women's greater participation in the public sphere (e.g., going to college, working, traveling) and to more women driving automobiles. However, it is debatable whether the expanding use of the automobile by women is better explained as a fundamental role change or as a societal-wide diffusion of a technological necessity (i.e., a required mode of transportation).

It is equally plausible to argue that greater equality or liberation for women will serve to reduce female crime. Greater female social participation may reduce stress, increase self-esteem, and in other ways positively affect what are often described in the criminological literature as the "causes" of crime.

Moreover, the liberation thesis is inconsistent with much of what is known both about female crime and contemporary gender roles:

(1) Increases in the female percentage of arrests that followed the beginning of the women's movement around 1970 are no

greater than during the 1960s, prior to the movement.

(2) The typical female offender bears no resemblance to the "liberated women," but rather comes from a background of poverty, unemployment or underemployment, and/or minority status.

(3) Feminism probably inhibits criminal motives, and feminists have a low probability of arrest.

Increased Economic Insecurity

Workplace gains for some women have been offset by the increased rates of poverty among women and children. Rising rates of divorce, illegitimacy, and female-headed households, coupled with continued segregation of women in low-paying occupations, have aggravated the economic pressures on women. Such economic insecurity increases the pressures to commit the very sorts of consumer-based crimes that have seen substantial increases in PFA: shoplifting, credit and welfare fraud, bad checks, and theft of services. Recent time-series and cross-sectional analyses confirm that higher female-to-male arrest levels are linked to structural conditions in which women face adverse rather than favorable economic circumstances (Steffensmeier and Streifel, 1992; Streifel, 1990).

Expanded Opportunities for Traditional Female Crimes

Like male offenders, female offenders gravitate toward activities that suit their interests and skills. Recent decades have witnessed expanding opportunities for minor thefts, frauds, and other activities that favor female involvement. These expanded opportunities have been fueled by changing economic patterns in at least five areas:

(1) Changes in the production, merchandising, and marketing of goods has made shoplifting easier through the proliferation of self-service marketing, shopping malls, and small, portable consumer goods.

(2) The growth of a credit economy has vastly expanded the opportunities for credit fraud theft of services, coupon fraud, and bad checks.

(3) The welfare state and its multiple services have also expanded the opportunities for female fraud, especially since

women with children constitute the largest segment of welfare recipients.

(4) Increased societal reliance on credentials provides both opportunities and "pressures to inflate the credentials, or to make them up when they do not exist."

(5) The emphasis of advertisers and the media on consumption and consumerism encourages shoplifting and other forms of theft and chiseling to stretch the paycheck or upgrade one's car, home, appearance, or lifestyle.

Changes in the Criminal Underworld

Changes in underworld patterns of crime may also have contributed to higher rates of female offending. In the circles of professional and organized crime, female participation is largely contingent on whether male criminals have a use for such participation. For example, with the emergence of drug trafficking as the dominant criminal market, women have been recruited to serve as mules or other subordinate workers where they are valued because they are likely to have clean records and to excite less law-enforcement suspicion. Female crime has also been enhanced by the increased involvement in drug trafficking of black and Hispanic organized crime groups, which have traditionally had higher levels of female involvement (especially among family members). At the same time, there has been a decline in certain forms of professional crime (e.g., safe cracking) that have traditionally been almost exclusively male. Finally, the large decline in the female percent of arrests for homicide may be seen as a consequence of the increased underworld use of instrumental violence (e.g., in drug trafficking), which is committed almost exclusively by males.

Increased Female Drug Dependency

Rising levels of illicit drug use by females over the past two or three decades may also help account for female crime trends. Drug addiction amplifies the income-generating crime of both sexes but more so for female than male crime (Inciardi, Lockwood, and Pottieger, 1993). Drug use often serves to initiate females into the underworld and criminal subcultures and to connect them to drug-dependent males who utilize them as crime accomplices or exploit them as "old ladies" to support "the man's" addiction (Covington, 1985; Miller, 1986; Steffensmeier and Terry, 1986).

Sex and Victimization

Victimization surveys find that men are much more likely than women to be the victims of violent crimes (e.g., homicide, robbery, and assault), and are equally likely to be victims of theft. Women are much more likely to be victims of sexual assault, particularly forcible rape—a crime that is often defined to include only female victims. The National Crime [Victimization] Survey does not collect data on homicide, but UCR data show that men are about three times more likely to be victims of homicide than women. The victimization data also show that women experience a greater fear of crime than men, and that the lives of women are much more affected by concerns of being victims of sexual assault or physical violence.

Conclusion

Criminologists have long recognized that gender is a very robust predictor of crime. The lower rates of females can be seen as consequences of gender differences in goals and the means to achieve them, in social control, in socialization, in access to criminal opportunities, and of hormonal differences that contribute to gender differences in aggression and physical strength.

Darrell J. Steffensmeier
Emilie Anderson Allan

Bibliography

Chesney-Lind, Meda. "Women and Crime: The Female Offender." *Signs* 12 (1986): 78–96.

Covington, Jeanette. "Gender Differences in Criminality among Heroin Users." *Journal of Research in Crime and Delinquency* 22 (1985): 329–53.

Elliott, Delbert, Suzanne Ageton, and David Huizinga. "Social Correlates of Delinquent Behavior." Unpublished paper, 1987.

Giordano, Peggy, Sandra Kerbel, and Sandra Dudley. "The Economics of Female Criminality: An Analysis of Police Blotters, 1890–1976." In *Women and Crime in America*. Ed. Lee H. Bowker. New York: MacMillan, 1981. 65–81.

Inciardi, James, Dorothy Lockwood, and Anne Pottieger. *Women and Crack-Cocaine*. New York: MacMillan, 1993.

James, Jennifer, Cathleen Gosho, and Robbin Watson Wohl. "The Relationship Between Female Criminality and Drug Use." *International Journal of the Addictions* 14 (1979): 215–29.

Miller, Eleanor. *Street Women*. Philadelphia: Temple University Press, 1986.

Pennsylvania Crime Commission. *1990 Report—Organized Crime in Pennsylvania: A Decade of Change*. Philadelphia: Commonwealth of Pennsylvania, 1991.

Steffensmeier, Darrell. "Assessing the Impact of the Women's Movement on Sex-Based Differences in the Handling of Adult Criminal Defendants." *Crime and Delinquency* 23 (1980): 344–56.

———. "Organization Properties and Sex Segregation in the Underworld: Building a Sociological Theory of Sex Differences in Crime." *Social Forces* 61 (1983): 1010–32.

———. "National Trends in Female Arrests, 1960–1990: Assessment and Recommendations for Research." *Journal of Quantitative Criminology* (1993).

———. "Sex Disparities in Arrests by Residence, Race, and Age: An Assessment of the Gender Convergence/Crime Hypothesis." *Justice Quarterly* 5 (1988): 53–80.

———, and Emilie Allan. "Gender, Age, and Crime. In *Handbook of Contemporary Criminology*. Ed. Joseph Sheley. New York: MacMillan, 1990.

———, and Cathy Streifel. "Time-Series Analysis of the Female Percentage of Arrests for Property Crimes, 1960–85: A Test of Alternative Explanations." *Justice Quarterly* 9 (1992): 77–103.

———, and Robert M. Terry. "Institutional Sexism in the Underworld: A View from the Inside." *Sociological Inquiry* 56 (1986): 304–23.

———, Emilie Allan, and Cathy Streifel. "Development and Female Crime: A Cross-National Test of Alternative Explanations." *Social Forces* 68 (1989): 263–83.

Streifel, Cathy. "Cross-Sectional Analysis of the Female Percentage of Arrests." Ph.D. diss. University Park: Pennsylvania State University, 1990.

G

Gun Control

The use of guns in crime is a major problem in the United States. Cook (1982) counted 682,000 violent crimes in 1977 in which a gun had been used, including 11,300 homicides, 367,000 assaults, 15,000 rapes, and 289,000 burglaries. Guns have several features that make them more dangerous than other weapons. They can be used by weak and unskilled assailants, they kill impersonally at a distance and quickly, and sometimes merely the display of a gun can immobilize the victim.

Guns are also responsible for a large number of deaths each year. From 1979 to 1987, there was an average of 32,639 deaths from firearms each year (encompassing suicides, homicides, and accidental deaths). The average overall death rate from firearms ranged from 4.6 per 100,000 per year in Massachusetts to 26.4 in Alaska (Centers for Disease Control, n.d.).

Focusing upon the use of guns in crime and death leads to strong support for gun control. However, guns are also owned by many Americans who have not committed and will not commit a crime. Guns are used for sport and competition and to give the owner a sense of security against enemies. Many gun owners (about 3 million) belong to the National Rifle Association (NRA), which has become a powerful lobby against any restrictions on the purchase and ownership of guns. Recently, however, organizations in favor of gun control, such as Handgun Control, have become more effective as lobbyists though the membership of Handgun Control is only about 200,000.

In fact, polls conducted for the NRA and the Center for the Study and Prevention of Handgun Violence have produced similar results, although their sponsors differed in their views on the issue (Wright, 1981). The majority in both polls (whether they owned a gun or not) favored registration of handguns, but there was little support for an outright ban on handguns, except for cheap small handguns ("Saturday Night Specials"). The majority in both polls felt that the right to own guns was a constitutional right, but that registration of guns would not violate that right. The majority also favored strict mandatory sentences for crimes committed with a gun, and many states have now introduced such laws. Other proposed gun-control measures have included prohibiting certain individuals from owning guns (such as criminals and those psychiatrically disturbed) and prohibiting the ownership of particular types of guns (such as cheap handguns and semi-automatic and automatic assault weapons). Others have suggested using product liability laws to force manufacturers to limit the kinds of weapons they sell.

Police are among those supporting stricter gun-control laws. In a study conducted by Lester (1984), both state and municipal police favored stricter handgun laws, bans on the manufacture of Saturday Night Specials and on forbidding citizens from carrying guns in cars, mandatory sentences for crimes committed with a gun, stricter requirements for commercial gun dealers, and longer waiting periods between obtaining a permit and taking ownership of a gun in order to permit a more thorough search of the buyer's background. Though many police officers are members of the National Rifle Association, the opposition of the Association even to restrictions on armor-piercing ("cop-killer") ammunition has increased police support for stricter gun-control laws.

Schuman and Presser (1981) discovered that opponents of stricter gun-control laws are more active in their opposition than proponents. For example, they donate more money and write more letters. Hence, stricter gun-control laws are difficult to pass.

The Use of Guns in Crime

Wright and Rosi (1986) surveyed felons in prison and found that half had used guns in their crimes. Of the gun-using criminals, 28 percent had used a gun once, 28 percent had used guns sporadically, and 44 percent had used them regularly. Of these regular users, handguns were over three times as common as shoulder weapons for the weapon of choice. The gun-using felons had committed every type of crime more frequently, and though representing only about 22 percent of the total sample they accounted for nearly one-half of the violent crimes.

The most common sources of handguns for these felons were friends (40 percent), the street (14 percent), and gun shops (11 percent). The most common sources for shoulder weapons were friends (33 percent), family (22 percent), gun shops (17 percent), and hardware/department stores (11 percent). Thirty-two percent of the handguns and 23 percent of the shoulder weapons were stolen.

Guns in the United States and the Netherlands

It is revealing to compare data on guns in the United States with data from a country where gun ownership is rare. Colijn, Lester, and

Slothouwer (1985) estimated that there were approximately 300 guns per 1,000 people in the United States as compared to 9 per 1,000 in the Netherlands. The rate of robbery with violence in 1980 in the Netherlands was 37 per 100,000 adults as compared to 303 in the United States, and the percentage of guns used in crimes is also lower in the Netherlands. For example, 13 percent of the crimes of robbery with violence in the Netherlands involved guns as compared to 45 percent in the United States.

Do Stricter Handgun Control Laws Prevent Crime?

The issue of gun control in America arouses powerful emotions on both sides of the issue. The National Rifle Association lobbies against any strengthening of gun-control laws, appearing to believe that allowing any change in the laws governing the purchasing or ownership of guns would lead inexorably to the banning of all gun ownership. Proponents of stricter gun control, led by Sarah Brady, are often represented in public by her disabled husband, James Brady, who was seriously wounded in the assassination attempt on President Reagan.

The strong opinions involved in this issue render evaluations of the research on the effectiveness of gun control on firearm deaths suspect. Kleck (1991) did not think that research had demonstrated that stricter gun control prevents firearm deaths. Lester (1984, 1993) reviewed the same research and concluded that strict gun control had prevented suicide and that even stricter gun control would prevent murder. It is difficult, therefore, to draw unambiguous conclusions from past research.

Although two of the three studies from the 1960s and 1970s argued that stricter gun-control laws did reduce the homicide rate, they can be criticized on methodological grounds. Lester and Murrell (1982) found that states with the stricter handgun-control laws in the 1960s did not have lower homicide rates in 1960 or 1970 or less of an increase in the homicide rate from 1960 to 1970. (They did, however, have a smaller proportion of homicides committed with guns.)

On the other hand, Lester and Murrell found that states with the stricter handgun-control laws did have lower suicide rates, both by gun and overall. They concluded that stricter handgun-control laws may prevent suicide, possibly by restricting the means available for committing suicide. Restrictions on the buying and selling of handguns were the critical variables here, while restrictions on the carrying of guns were not. Lester (1993) concluded that more recent research conducted in the 1980s and 1990s supported the conclusion that restricting gun availability would reduce the use of firearms for suicide and possibly for murder. Lester has urged that researchers move on to the study of why (and under what circumstances) some individuals would switch to a different weapon for suicide, murder, or criminal acts while others would not.

The apparently weak (or possibly nonexistent) effect of strict gun-control laws on the prevention of crime is understandable given the relatively weak controls even in those states with the strictest gun-control laws. Gun-control laws in the United States are much weaker than corresponding laws in Europe, for example. Thus, it is not surprising that these laws have not been conclusively shown to have any impact on the use of guns in crimes. Furthermore, even when stricter gun controls are passed, compliance with and enforcement of those laws is often lax.

David Lester

Bibliography

Centers for Disease Control. *Injury Mortality Atlas*. Atlanta, GA: Centers for Disease Control, n.d.

Colijn, G.G., D. Lester, and A. Slothouwer. "Firearms and Crime in the Netherlands." *International Journal of Comparative and Applied Criminal Justice* 9 (1985): 49–55.

Kleck, G. *Point Blank*. New York: Aldine de Gruyter, 1991.

Lester, David. *Gun Control: Issues and Answers*. Springfield, IL: Charles C. Thomas, 1984.

———. "Controlling Crime Facilitators." *Crime Prevention Studies*. Ed. R. V. Clarke. Monsey, NY: Criminal Justice Press, 1993.

———, and M.E. Murrell "The Preventive Effect of Strict Gun Control Laws on Suicide and Homicide." *Suicide and Life-Threatening Behavior* 12 (1982): 131–40.

Schuman, H., and S. Presser. "The Attitude-Action Connection and the Issue of Gun Control." *Annals of the American Academy of Political and Social Science* 455 (1981): 40–47.

Wolfgang, M., and N.A. Weiner, eds. *Criminal Violence*. Beverly Hills, CA: Sage, 1982.

Wright, J.D. "Public Opinion and Gun Control." *Annals of the American Academy of Political and Social Science* 455 (1981): 24–39.

Wright, J.D., and P.H. Rossi. *Armed and Considered Dangerous*. New York: Aldine de Gruyter, 1986.

Gun Control: Verification System

There are between 100 and 200 million firearms in the United States, with approximately 7.5 million new and used firearms sold each year through some 270,000 federally licensed firearms dealers. The Gun Control Act of 1968 (18 U.S.C. 922[g]) states that "it shall be unlawful for any person:

1. who has been convicted in any court of a crime punishable by imprisonment for a term exceeding one year;
2. who is a fugitive from justice;
3. [who] is an unlawful user of or addicted to any controlled substance (as defined in Section 102 of the Controlled Substances Act [21 U.S.C. 802]);
4. who has been ajudicated as a mental defective or who has been committed to a mental institution;
5. who, being an alien, is illegally or unlawfully in the United States;
6. who has been discharged from the Armed Forces under dishonorable conditions; or
7. who, having been a citizen of the United States, has renounced his citizenship, to ship or transport in interstate or foreign commerce, or possess in or affecting commerce, any firearm or ammunition; or to receive any firearm or ammunition which has been shipped or transported in interstate or foreign commerce."

The Bureau of Alcohol, Tobacco, and Firearms (BATF), the agency charged with administering federal firearm regulations, is responsible for implementing this act. In essence the BATF requires that all persons purchasing a firearm complete its BATF Form 4473. There are actually three versions of BATF Form 4473 for (1) over-the-counter, (2) low volume over-the-counter (where the licensed dealer sells no more than fifty firearms in a year), and (3) non over-the-counter purchases. All three versions require the prospective firearm purchaser to certify that he/she does not belong to any of the above seven disability categories before the firearm dealer can sell him/her a firearm. Completion of the form is the sole federal requirement for a firearm purchase. The prospective purchaser's responses on the form are not verified; indeed, the form does not contain a statement by the applicant that would authorize the release of information for such verification purposes. While local law-enforcement agencies in many states do attempt to verify that a prospective firearm purchaser does not belong to a disability category, firearms are still being obtained and used by ex-felons, unlawful controlled substance users, and mental defectives for commiting heinous firearms-related crimes.

BATF Activities

The federal government has the authority to regulate the sale of firearms because of its constitutional authority over interstate commerce. Primarily utilizing the provisions of the Gun Control Act of 1968, the BATF has promulgated a series of firearm regulations contained in Parts 47, 178, and 179 of Title 27 of the Code of Federal Regulations. The BATF exerts control by licensing firearm dealers and recording firearm sales. Potential firearm dealers are investigated by the BATF to determine if the applicant is eligible to sell firearms. A license is denied if, for example, the applicant has previously violated any firearm laws or is in one of the seven firearm disability categories. Returning to the purchaser applicant, he/she must provide full name, sex, height, weight, race, residence, date of birth, and place of birth, before indicating whether he/she is in any of the seven firearm disability categories. The firearm dealer then acknowledges on the form that the applicant is a personal acquaintance, or that the applicant has provided satisfactory identification. Typically, a driver's license is used for this purpose. After the applicant has been identified, the dealer records on the form the type, model, caliber or gauge, serial number, and manufacturer of each firearm sold. There is now a federally mandated waiting period between the time when BATF Form 4473 is completed and the sale is allowed. [A Republican filibuster killed a Democratic crime bill (1991) that included a five-day waiting period for the purchase of a firearm. In retaliation Democrats blocked a similar GOP bill backed by President George Bush. Then another version of the Democratic bill died in the Senate October 2, 1992. Known as the Brady bill—for James S. Brady, who was shot and left brain-damaged in an attempted attack on the life of President Ronald Reagan—the bill finally became law November 30, 1993.]

After the sale the completed BATF Form 4473 must be kept on the dealer's premises for twenty years. The form is not, however, forwarded to the BATF. Because of this tracing a firearm used in a serious crime to its owner is a time-consuming process. Once the BATF obtains the description of a firearm, including its serial number, they trace it to the firearm manufacturer, who in turn directs the BATF to the dealer to whom they sold the firearm. The BATF can then search, subject to strict laws and regulations, the dealer's 4473 forms to determine the owner of the firearm. Persons ineligible to purchase firearms under the Gun Control Act can have their disability waived by applying to the BATF "for relief" on BATF Form 3210. According to the BATF, about 2,000 persons per year apply for relief, virtually all of whom are convicted felons. About 50 percent of the applicants are granted relief. Although the number of persons granted relief each year is small (1,000), the number is nevertheless larger than the combined number of persons receiving dishonorable discharges and formally renouncing their citizenship. It is therefore obvious that persons granted relief must be accounted for in any national firearm eligibil-

ity verification system. It is not obvious that it is necessary to check the remote relief database for each firearm purchase.

An Integrated System

In configuring an integrated national firearm eligibility verification system, a number of primary considerations must be taken into account. Do potential data sources exist? At what governmental level is the data found? How accurate and complete are the data? Is the database manual or automated? Are there privacy and confidentiality issues involved in accessing the data? The following table summarizes data availability and coverage for disability categories 3–7 of the Gun Control Act. Categories 1 (felons) and 2 (fugitives) are omitted since they are obvious inclusions in a national verification system.

As can be seen the coverage problem is greatest for the category estimated to have the most members (i.e., unlawful users of controlled substances); it is least for the category with the fewest members, renunciates. Even when appropriate records exist there may be legal prohibitions on accessing and sharing the information. For the unlawful users of controlled substances category, federal regulations (42 CFR Part 2) now prohibit drug treatment programs receiving federal funds from disclosing patient records. In addition many states have their own laws requiring confidentiality of drug treatment records. For the mental defective category, every state has mental-health record confidentiality laws, although some states explicitly allow release of such information for the purposes of determining firearm eligibility.

| | | Number of Persons | | | |
| | | For Whom Records Exist | | With Automated Records | |
	In Disability Category (Est.)	Total	% of All in Category	Total	% of All in Category
Unlawful users of controlled substances	14,500,000	470,800	3	247,000	2
Mental defectives	2,700,000	2,700,000	100	800,000	30
Illegal aliens	2,300,000	550,000	24	550,000	24
Dishonorably discharged	20,000	20,000	100	7,200	36
Renunciates	9,800	9,800	100	9,800	100

Note: These columns should not be added since there may be substantial overlap across the disability categories, particularly unlawful users of controlled substances and those known to be convicted felons.

For both the dishonorably discharged and re-nunciate categories, the Defense and State Departments indicate that the Privacy Act (5 U.S.C. 552a[b]) prohibits routine dissemination of data about individuals in these categories. Thus, it appears that only the category of illegal aliens is currently free from legal restrictions on access.

Integrating the individual databases into a single system would have to overcome many obstacles. Such a system would require that drug-treatment centers; courts, authorities, commissions, and boards with mental-health jurisdiction; the Immigration and Naturalization Service; the Defense Manpower Data Center; and the Passport Services Office share relevant records on either a centralized or decentralized (i.e., distributed) basis. It would entail significant start-up and operating costs for both the integrated system and the literally thousands of local, state, and federal agencies that must either share or access the data. It would also require removing the current legal impediments for sharing or accessing the required data, as well as establishing new regulations and procedures for ensuring appropriate privacy and confidentiality protections. For three of the disability categories the data's accuracy, completeness, and validity would be good. The exceptions would be the unlawful users of controlled substances and illegal alien categories, both of which would have poor data validity. The system would have to provide for timely verification, since it is based on a point-of-sale verification approach. Obtaining the cooperation of thousands of data repositories to share their data, even if legal impediments were overcome, would be very time consuming, not to mention difficult to attain. Identification accuracy would also be poor since other than for the felon category there are no fingerprints or other biometric identifiers available to verify the identity of the firearm purchaser. Indeed, there would be no way to prove positively that a firearm purchaser is the person whose records can be assessed through the integrated system.

Technical and Policy Issues

In assessing the feasibility of a system to prevent firearm sales to ineligible persons other than felons, a variety of technical and policy issues must be considered. Specifically, the issues focus on:

Data Quality:

- Whether the level of data quality and coverage in existing databases is adequate to ensure that presale checks are accurate as required by statute;
- The extent to which current or anticipated levels of automation permit data to be accessed in sufficient time for immediate presale checks as required by statute;
- Whether the identification data included in the relevant databases is sufficient to prevent an unacceptable level of false positives (i.e., erroneous identification of eligible persons);

System Configuration:

- Whether the final system configuration should require that data currently maintained by different agencies be included in a single database, linked through a system, or maintained in decentralized databases;
- Whether the administration and policy control over operation of the system should be assigned to the federal government, a consortium of states, or some combination of the two;
- The extent to which the nonfelon checks should be coordinated with the felon identification database checks;

Legal Questions:

- Whether commingling of criminal and noncriminal records (including drug and mental-health records) in a single system presents problems;
- The extent to which legislation or regulations are needed to protect the confidentiality of data and to prevent unauthorized access to systems holding both criminal and noncriminal justice data;
- The need for legal and administrative procedures to ensure that persons prohibited from purchasing a firearm are permitted to review and challenge the data upon which the denial was based;
- The extent to which current federal and/or state legislation that prevents the release of data necessary to implement the record checks can be amended to facilitate implementation of appropriate record checks;
- Whether the definitions as set out in Section 922 of the Gun Control Act create

major impediments to data collection, and, if so, whether such definitions should be modified.

Policy Options

What can be done regarding firearm eligibility verification in the interim period prior to the adoption of a national verification system, should policy makers decide to approve one? First, the disability categories in the Gun Control Act should be reassessed in light of definitional problems. For example, rather than "persons who are unlawful users of or who are addicted to controlled substances," the category could be "persons who are in treatment or are under arrest for a drug-related offense." The mental defective category should also be reassessed. Some states indicate they allow mental patients to switch from involuntary to voluntary status at any time. Both John Hinckley (who shot President Reagan) and Jack Tilford (who shot to death seven persons in Kentucky) legally purchased their weapons, since both voluntarily committed themselves to mental institutions. Thus, while public concern is rising over the availability of firearms to the Hinckleys and Tilfords, it appears the Gun Control Act does not apply to such persons.

Second, the identification of illegal aliens could be improved by integrating a form similar to the INS's Employment Eligibility Verification (I-9) form into the BATF Form 4473. While still subject to fraudulent documents, this local verification method for identifying illegal aliens would be more effective than using the current BATF Form 4473 alone. Third, programs aimed at improving the quality of the databases described could be initiated. Just as the attorney general called for initiatives to improve the accuracy and completeness of criminal-history databases, a similar initiative for the nonfelon databases would facilitate the eventual implementation of a national firearm eligibility verification system. And fourth, the federal government, perhaps by developing and promulgating model legislation, could encourage the states to adopt consistent firearm-related statutes and maybe even similar verification procedures.

James M. Tien
Thomas F. Rich

Bibliography

National Institute on Drug Abuse. *Data from the Drug Abuse Warning Network.* Annual Publication. Washington, DC: National Institute on Drug Abuse, 1982–.

Orsagh, Thomas. *Estimates of Start-Up and Operational Costs of Systems for Identifying Felons Who Attempt to Purchase Firearms.* Fisher-Orsagh Associates, 1989.

Tien, James, and Thomas F. Rich. *Identifying Persons, Other Than Felons, Ineligible to Purchase Firearms: A Feasibility Study.* Washington, DC: U.S. Department of Justice, Bureau of Justice Statistics, 1990.

U.S. Congress, House. *Criminal Aliens: Hearings Before the Subcommittee on Immigration, Refugees, and International Law of the Committee on the Judiciary, House of Representatives.* Washington, DC: Government Printing Office, 1989.

U.S. Department of Justice. *Systems for Identifying Felons Who Attempt to Purchase Firearms.* Washington, DC: U.S. Department of Justice, Task Force on Felon Identification in Firearm Sales, 1989.

Wright, James D. *Armed in America: A Survey of Incarcerated Felons.* Washington, DC: U.S. Department of Justice, National Institute of Justice, 1985.

G

H

George W. Hale

George W. Hale (1855–?) compiled the pioneering *Police and Prison Cyclopaedia* published in its second edition by W.L. Richardson Company, Boston, in 1893. Born and educated in Lawrence, Massachusetts, Hale was a dashing adventurer in his youth. According to a biographical sketch in the *Cyclopaedia* written by William T. Sellers, editor of the *Lawrence Evening Tribune*, Hale worked on steamboats on the Mississippi and Arkansas rivers before going farther west to help an uncle rear sheep and Angora goats in California.

After the uncle died, Hale freighted supplies to the Resting Springs Mines in the Mojave Desert, returning with silver bullion. He then started his own teamster business, but a broken wagon wheel sent him plummeting headlong down a canyon. Once out of the hospital, Hale enlisted April 3, 1879, in Troop H, Sixth U.S. Cavalry, then stationed at Fort Verde, Arizona Territory. As a courier, he escaped with his life time after time in encounters with hostile Indians before being assigned to a clerical job in 1881. The following year, Hale applied for a discharge, received it, and went to work for the chief quartermaster. The call of the wild remained strong, however, and in 1883 Hale joined General George Crook's expedition against the Chiricahua Apaches in Mexico, who were led by Geronimo. Hale survived to return to Arizona Territory to work first on a hay ranch and then as timekeeper for a construction crew.

Presumably homesick after an absence of nine years, Hale then returned east, enlisting in Battery H, Fourth Heavy Artillery, stationed at Fort Warren, Boston Harbor. Although in the seemingly safe job of post schoolteacher, Hale was almost blown to smithereens by the premature discharge of a cannon. After leaving the army in 1887, Hale worked briefly in a Lawrence hardware store before achieving a perfect score on the civil-service examination for policemen. Appointed to the Lawrence force in May 1888, Hale had outstanding credentials for a patrolman. He had been considered one of the best riders in the Sixth U.S. Calvary—"a regiment noted for its good riders at that time," and firing a regulation Springfield rifle, he had hit his mark at 1,000 yards with 81 percent accuracy. At the same time, because of his military background and fluency in Spanish, high military and civic dignitaries recommended him for a position in the consular service in either Mexico, Central America, or South America. But he declined—his future was with the police department.

Hale's *Cyclopaedia* gained him international recognition as an authority on police work and as a meticulous scholar. The 1893 edition was not meant to be the last, but was for reasons unknown. As stated in his preface, Hale's ambitious plan was to update the *Cyclopaedia* annually. Also unknown is what prompted him to undertake such an arduous chore in the first place and what happened to him after 1893. No death date can be discovered. Hale was certainly an enigmatic character, and what we know about him, as repeated here, comes from the editor William T. Sellers and might be nothing more than literary gloss. What we can ascertain from reading the historically important *Cyclopaedia* is that it was compiled by a man who delighted in collecting all manner of facts about what we call today the criminal-justice system.

victims to both report hate crimes and assist in the accompanying investigation and prosecution.

- Judges should then be under scrutiny to provide substantial deterrent sentences after convictions.

3. Hate Crime Statutes: A Message to Victims and Perpetrators. In 1981, in response to dramatically increasing numbers of anti-Semitic incidents reported to its regional offices across the country, lawyers for the Anti-Defamation League drafted model hate crimes legislation for introduction into state legislatures. The model bill was intended to complement other ADL counteraction measures that focused on media exposure of extremists, prejudice reduction programs and diversity training, and more effective law enforcement.

ADL's model legislation increases the criminal penalties for vandalism aimed at houses of worship, cemeteries, schools, and community centers. The bill also provides for stepped-up criminal penalties for criminal acts when persons or groups are targeted "by reason of" their actual or perceived race, color, religion, national origin, or sexual orientation. The close nexus required by the language "by reason of" is designed to ensure that a hate-crime violation is charged only when the bias factor has played a causal role in the commission of the offense. A crime involving only an incidental or immaterial racial or religious slur is not a bias crime—and should not be charged as such.

In this manner, no one is punished merely for bigoted thoughts, ideology, or speech under a penalty-enhancement statute. But when prejudice prompts an individual to *act* on these beliefs and engage in criminal conduct, a prosecutor may seek a severer sentence. Increasing the penalties for these crimes has a deterrent impact—by demonstrating that they will be dealt with severely—and also reassures targeted groups that law-enforcement officers treat these matters seriously.

The core of the ADL hate crime statute is the "penalty enhancement" concept well known to criminal law. Penalty enhancements are very frequently authorized in line with the character of the crime (such as when the offender conceals his identity or uses a deadly weapon), as well as when the victim is targeted because of special status (elderly, very young, or disabled), or vocation (police officer, president of the United States). Many state hate-crime statutes also include provisions authorizing civil suits for damages and injunctive relief by victims, as well as parental liability for minor children's actions.

Legislation patterned on the ADL model, like the Wisconsin statute recently approved by the Supreme Court, is on the books in some two dozen states. A similar federal hate crime measure, the Hate Crime Sentencing Enhancement Act, sponsored by Representatives Charles Schumer (D-NY) and James Sensenbrenner (R-WI), is now pending before Congress and is likely to be enacted into law.

Legal Challenges to Hate Crime Statutes

Over the past five years, hate-crime laws in a number of states have been challenged by individuals convicted under them. These suits have generally been based on claims that the laws are vague and overbroad and impermissively infringe on First Amendment freedom of expression. In the past two terms, the U.S. Supreme Court has reviewed the constitutionality of two different hate-crime laws. The different results in these cases are instructive both for the drafting of future statutes and for enforcement of current laws.

R.A.V. v. St. Paul: A Flawed Approach to Hate Violence. The first hate crime case to reach the Supreme Court involved a challenge to a St. Paul, Minnesota, ordinance that stated: "Whoever places on public or private property a symbol, object, appellation, characterization or graffiti, including, but not limited to, a burning cross or Nazi swastika, which one knows or has reasonable grounds to know arouses anger, alarm or resentment in others on the basis of race, color, creed, religion or gender commits disorderly conduct and shall be guilty of a misdemeanor."

Prosecutors charged a teenager with violating this ordinance after he burned a cross in the yard of a black family in the middle of the night. The defendant challenged the ordinance, asserting that it was overbroad and violative of the First Amendment. The trial court ruled in favor of the defendant's motion, but the Minnesota Supreme Court reversed. The former court narrowly construed the ordinance, interpreting it to prohibit only "fighting words"—which, by their very nature, incite imminent lawless action. "Fighting words" had long been held to be without First Amendment protection.

On June 22, 1992, the U.S. Supreme Court unanimously struck down the St. Paul ordinance as an unconstitutional infringement on protected speech, but the justices were divided as to why. Justice Scalia's five-member majority opinion held that the ordinance was invalid because it constituted "content discrimination." Four other justices concurred in the result, but made clear they would have held the St. Paul ordinance unconstitutional because it could be applied to punish protected expression as well as criminal conduct.

Wisconsin v. Mitchell: *The Penalty Enhancement Approach.* The Court was silent in *R.A.V.* on the question of whether penalty-enhancement laws, like the ADL model bill, are constitutional. The Court took up this question in the last term.

The facts in *Mitchell* are not in dispute. On October 7, 1989, a group of ten young black men and boys gathered at an apartment complex in Kenosha, Wisconsin. Members of the group had watched the movie *Mississippi Burning*, and they were discussing a disturbing scene in which a white man beats a young black boy who was praying. Todd Mitchell exhorted the group to take action against whites. A short time later, a fourteen-year-old white male walked by the complex and Mitchell said, "There goes a white boy, go get him." Mitchell's group beat the youth severely, resulting in possible permanent brain damage.

After a jury trial, Mitchell was convicted of aggravated battery, which carries a maximum sentence of two years' imprisonment. But because the jury also found that Mitchell had intentionally selected the victim because of his race, the maximum sentence was increased to seven years. The Wisconsin hate-crime statute authorizes enhanced sentences when the defendant "[i]ntentionally selects the person against whom the crime . . . is committed . . . because of the race, religion, color, disability, sexual orientation, national origin, or ancestry of that person. . . ."

The trial court rejected Mitchell's contention that the statute was unconstitutional and sentenced him to four years' imprisonment. An appellate court affirmed the conviction, but the Wisconsin Supreme Court reversed, holding that the statute violates the First Amendment by punishing "offensive thought" and by "chilling free speech." That court held that because the statute required no additional act beyond that

needed to make out a conviction on the underlying statute, the additional penalty was actually punishment for bad motives.

A particularly impressive group of government officials, and human rights, police, and civil liberties organizations—headed by the United States government and the forty-nine other attorneys general—filed *amicus* briefs urging the Supreme Court to distinguish laws that restrict speech from laws, like Wisconsin's, that more severely punish bias-motivated conduct. Supporters of the Wisconsin statute asserted that the law is consistent with the First Amendment because it proscribes conduct, not speech, expression, or thought. The ADL's brief in support of the Wisconsin statute included fifteen national organizations, including the IACP, People for the American Way, NOBLE, the Southern Poverty Law Center, the National Gay and Lesbian Task Force, and the Fraternal Order of Police. Other briefs urging the Court to uphold the statute were filed by the American Civil Liberties Union, the National Conference of State Legislatures, the U. S. Conference of Mayors, and the National Governors Association.

On June 11, 1993, a unanimous Supreme Court dismissed Mitchell's free speech arguments, holding that Mitchell's actions constituted "conduct unprotected by the First Amendment." The Court ruled that while "a defendant's abstract beliefs, however obnoxious to most people, may not be taken into consideration by a sentencing judge," legislatures may determine to more severely penalize these crimes because "bias-motivated crimes are more likely to provoke retaliatory crimes, inflict distinct emotional harm on their victims, and incite community unrest."

The Court recognized that these laws do not suppress free expression, since they do not affect the rights of anyone to hold or promote any viewpoint, publicly or privately. It is only when prejudice prompts an individual to *act* on his or her beliefs and engage in criminal activity that a prosecutor may seek a severer sentence. Then, to be subjected to additional penalties under a hate-crime statute, the prosecution must prove, beyond reasonable doubt, that the victim of a crime was selected because of his/her actual or perceived race, religion, sexual orientation, or ethnicity.

The Court compared these hate-crime laws to federal and state antidiscrimination laws, the constitutionality of which have been repeatedly upheld. Federal and state civil-rights statutes make it unlawful to discriminate in employment, housing, and public accommodations by reason of race, religion, or national origin. Employers and property owners may well harbor hatred or contempt for members of other groups, but if they fire or fail to promote someone on that basis or deny someone housing on these invidious grounds, they break the law. Proof of such unlawful intent will often reside in the words they utter at or near the time of their discriminatory acts, yet using these expressions as evidence of the violation does not impermissibly "chill" protected speech.

Finally, the Court distinguished its holding in *R.A.V.*, stating: "The First Amendment, moreover, does not prohibit the evidentiary use of speech to establish the elements of a crime or to prove motive or intent." In fact, in criminal law, the words of an offender are often introduced at trial to prove intent. Consider, for example, a traffic fatality that the driver claims was an accident—he swears he looked away at the wrong moment. At trial, however, an eyewitness testifies that the driver said, within moments of impact, "I hate that S.O.B! I've waited years to get this chance!" The prosecutor will no doubt introduce the defendant driver's *words* to prove that he intended to kill—and therefore should be subject to punishment severer than someone who kills by accident. If the driver is convicted of first-degree murder, it should be clear that he is not being punished for his "beliefs" or "ideas." He is being punished—indeed, more severely punished—because he *acted criminally* on the basis of his belief, with a specific intent—an intent proven by his words.

Responding to Hate Violence: An Action Agenda

Along with human-rights groups like the Anti-Defamation League, the law-enforcement community has actively supported hate crime penalty-enhancement legislation and data-collection initiatives. With many indications that hate violence is on the rise, and with questions concerning the constitutionality of penalty-enhancement laws apparently resolved, attention has turned to education and outreach as appropriate steps to assist bias crime victims and to apprehend perpetrators:

- Departments should take steps to ensure comprehensive local implementation of the HCSA. Because the accuracy and uniformity of the data collected will only be as good as the reporters, every law-enforcement agency should train its officials in how to identify, report, and respond to hate violence.

- The establishment of specifically focused departmental policies and procedures for addressing hate violence is a proactive step that will send a strong message to victims and would-be perpetrators that hate crimes are not pranks and that police officials take them seriously. Every department should adopt a written policy, signed by its chief, to effectively respond to hate violence in a priority manner.

- Municipalities should establish an integrated hate-crime response network, including liaisons to local prosecutors, city or county human-rights commissions, and private victim advocacy organizations. Local human relations groups, like ADL, can be helpful in a number of ways. In addition to urging constituents to report hate crimes and assist at the investigation and prosecution stages, these organizations can assist in analyzing the hate-crime data for both their own constituents and for the media. This context can be especially useful in the case of aggressive, diligent police agencies that are called upon to explain why their hate-crime numbers are higher than neighboring, less attentive departments. Community groups will know which agencies have made serious efforts to confront hate violence.

- To ensure that hate-crime data are not collected in a vacuum, statewide tracking and trend analysis centers, such as the Bias Crime and Community Relations Office in New Jersey and the Maryland Racial, Religious, and Ethnic Intimidation Advisory Committee, should be established across the country.

Excellent resources have been developed to help municipalities establish hate-crime response procedures. Besides the FBI's very useful HCSA training guidelines and the IACP's Model Policy and Concepts and Issues Paper "Hate Crimes" cited above, hate-crime response experts from around the country—including ADL representatives—are developing a model curriculum for use by the Federal Law Enforcement Training

Centers (FLETC) for federal, state, and local police officials. A listing of these materials, along with a listing of other selected resources on hate-violence counteraction, follows this entry.

All Americans have a stake in effective response to violent bigotry. The fundamental cause of hate violence in the United States is the persistence of racism, bigotry, and anti-Semitism. Unfortunately, there is no quick, complete solution to these problems—legislative or otherwise. The long-term response is education and experience, leading to better understanding and acceptance of different cultures and diversity in our society.

While bigotry cannot be outlawed, hate-crime statutes demonstrate an important commitment to confront criminal activity motivated by prejudice. Effective response by public officials and law-enforcement authorities to hate crimes can play an essential role in deterring and preventing them. The success of hate-crime laws and data-collection efforts will be determined at the local level—and measured by the response of civic leaders and police officials to each criminal act motivated by prejudice.

Michael J. Lieberman

Bibliography

Addressing Racial and Ethnic Tensions: Combatting Hate Crimes in America's Cities. Washington, DC: Anti-Defamation League and the United States Conference of Mayors, June 1992.

1992 Audit of Anti-Semitic Incidents. Washington, DC: Anti-Defamation League, January 1993.

Anti-Gay Violence, Victimization and Defamation in 1992. Washington, DC: National Gay and Lesbian Task Force, 1993.

Bias Crime: America's Law Enforcement and Legal Response. Chicago: University of Illinois Office of International Criminal Justice, 1993.

"CQ Researcher: Are Longer Sentences for Hate Crimes Constitutional?" *Congressional Quarterly* (January 8, 1993).

Hate Crime: A Training Video for Police Officers. Washington, DC: Anti-Defamation League, 1990. Seventeen-minute training video and 24-page discussion manual.

Hate Crime Data Collection Guidelines. Washington, DC: Uniform Crime Reporting Program, U.S. Department of Justice/FBI, 1992.

Hate Crime: Policies and Procedures for Law Enforcement Agencies. Washington, DC: Anti-Defamation League, 1988.

Hate Crime Sentencing Enhancement Act of 1992. Hearings. U.S. Congress. House Judiciary Subcommittee on Crime and Criminal Justice, July 29, 1992.

Hate Crimes: Model Policy, accompanied by *Hate Crimes: Concepts and Issues Paper.* Arlington, VA 22201: International Association of Chiefs of Police, National Law Enforcement Policy Center, 1100 North Glebe Road, Suite 200, August 1, 1991.

Hate Crimes Statutes: A 1991 Status Report. Washington, DC: Anti-Defamation League. Spring/Summer 1988 and 1990 Supplement.

Hate Groups in America: A Record of Bigotry and Violence. Washington, DC: Anti-Defamation League, 1988.

Herek, Gregory M., and Kevin T. Berrill. *Hate Crimes, Confronting Violence Against Lesbians and Gay Men.* Newbury Park, CA: Sage, 1992.

Intimidation and Violence: Racial and Religious Bigotry in America. Washington, DC: United States Commission on Civil Rights, September 1990.

Investigating Hate Crimes: Training Key 409. Arlington, VA: International Association of Chiefs of Police, 1991.

Law Enforcement Bulletin. Washington, DC: Anti-Defamation League, periodic publication.

The Policy and Procedures for the Handling of Racial, Religious and Ethnic Incidents. Baltimore, MD: Baltimore County Police Department.

Racial and Religious Violence: A Law Enforcement Guidebook. Landover, MD: National Organization of Black Law Enforcement Executives (NOBLE), March 1986.

Racial and Religious Violence: A Model Law Enforcement Response. Landover, MD: National Organization of Black Law Enforcement Executives (NOBLE), September 1985.

The Response of the Criminal Justice System to Bias Crime: An Exploratory Review. Cambridge, MA: Abt. Associates, Inc., Finn and McNeil, 1987. Submitted to the National Institute of Justice.

Striking Back at Bigotry: Remedies Under

Federal and State Law for Violence Motivated by Racial, Religious, and Ethnic Prejudice. Baltimore, MD: National Institute Against Prejudice and Violence. May 1986; 1988 Supplement.

Training Guide for Hate Crime Data Collection. Washington, DC: Uniform Crime Reporting Program, U.S. Department of Justice/FBI.

Walk with Pride: Taking Steps to Address Anti-Asian Violence. San Francisco, CA: Japanese American Citizens League, August 1991.

Jacob Hays

Jacob Hays (1772–1850), high constable, New York City, was born in Bedford Village, Westchester County, New York, of Jewish parents. His father, a merchant, served under George Washington during the Revolutionary War. Jacob completed a common school education and at twenty-six, unhappily working in the family business, was ripe for almost any other career. So on behalf of his wayward son Hays senior spoke to Aaron Burr, later vice president of the United States, about Jacob's future. That talk resulted in Mayor Varick's appointing Jacob one of his "Mayor's Marshals" for the city of New York in 1798. In 1801 Mayor Edward Livingston promoted him to head the constabulary force. Hays held that position until his death, one year shy of a half-century, and came to be known admiringly as "Old Hays," a "terror to evil-doers."

In the early 1800s the annual budget for New York City's police protection was a mere $25,000 and each constable had to be assertive, resilient, and cover a lot of ground to make do. Hays personified such an individual and it was not long before the press mythicized him. Most of the stories about his exploits were based on fact, but it was the way they were told that created the legend. As late as 1937 the *New York World Telegram* boosted his reputation in a six-part series, "Old Hays—There Was a Cop!" This re-creation of a gang fight is typical of the admiring tone:

Old Hays trudged placidly toward the fray. Almost apologetically he made a passage through a tight fringe of onlookers, which gave way to him respectfully, and reaching at last the zone of combat, unlimbered his only weapon, the baton of the High Constable. "Swish" went the baton and the battered top-piece of a high plug-ugly tumbled into the mire. Plug-ugly bent instinctively to retrieve it, and the High Constable, dextrous as a ballet dancer for all his close-coupled bulk, gave him a boot that sent him sprawling. Again the gold-headed staff described a gleaming arc, and again.

Of course, this smacks of police brutality today, but back then in a boisterous society such an action was commendable. More stuff of legends occurred when the murder of a shipmaster sent Hays scouring through derelict neighborhoods. He questioned everyone who might provide a clue to the identity of the murderer, finally latching onto a likely suspect. The man, Johnson, pleaded innocence so convincingly that he might have been released if it had not been for the High Constable's ingenuity. With much drama Hays uncovered the nude body of the shipmaster, forced Johnson to look at it, and interrogated him at the side of the corpse. Johnson succumbed to the duress, admitted guilt, and was given the gallows. But once Hays was out of the picture Johnson reverted to proclaiming his innocence. Even as he stood on the scaffold in front of a sympathetic crowd his tearful pleas about dying a wronged man were plainly heard. Then Hays walked up and fixed his stare on the condemned party. The crowd hushed but soon gasped to hear Johnson tell the executioner, "Get on with it. I killed him, right enough. I can't lie while that man Hays has his eye on me."

By the 1830s his fame had extended to Europe and beyond. One story had it that an American and an Englishman were watching a street riot in London, when the American said, "Where I come from one man would have put down this disturbance." The Englishman replied, "You must then, Sir, come from New York in the United States, since that is the only place in which there lives such a man." Other talk about Hays dwelt on his uncanny ability for remembering faces and on his foolhardiness. He carried in his memory a mental rogues' gallery and would often be seen arresting a fugitive who thought himself anonymous. The dullard might be anywhere when a meaty hand would descend on his shoulder and take him away. Hays was not one to sit in his office and wait for his men to nab felons. Instead he roamed the city, in particular the docks, visually noting people, places, and events. Little escaped his notice and just the sight of him sniffing around sent criminals packing. Upon entering a den of thieves the only weapon he brandished was his gold-headed baton. A dignified accessory, no doubt, but not one to afford much protection against a knife or a pistol. It is hard to believe that an unarmed law-enforcement officer, brazen to a fault, captured violent men by hand, his eye freezing them on the spot. Yet Hays served for over fifty years on the force, made countless arrests, and did not suffer any serious injury.

Not above subterfuge, Hays used every method at his disposal to trap a criminal. He would plant an informer in quod (prison) to ply information. If that failed he would position himself with another official near a conduit pipe, which ran through the cell-block, for the purpose of eavesdropping. Whatever it took to get at the truth he tried. Only once was he removed from office, that of captain of the Third Watch District, by a negative caucus.

In 1844 the police force was reorganized and the office of High Constable dispensed with. So technically Hays was out of a job, but because of his high repute he was allowed to retain the title and emoluments until his death. When Charles Dickens visited New York City Hays escorted him through the tougher districts. The world-famous author was appalled at the degradation he saw and wrote an account of the tour which, due to its graphic details, enshrined Hays all the more. Dickens implied that if a single man of the law could prevail under such loathsome conditions, then he was clearly superior to other men. There must have been a good deal of veracity in the stories celebrating Hays for him to have been called "the first of the modern detectives, and indubitably a great man," by the press. Even a simple innovation of his—having constables work in pairs for protection and to keep each other honest—had not been thought of before. The fact that mothers warned their unruly children, "You be good, or Old Hays will get you!" increased his mythic stature.

After his death the New York City police force underwent further reorganization to align itself with municipal expansion and to prepare itself to fight ever-increasing crime. With the passing of Old Hays also went a time when one man in authority could tumble a plug-ugly into the mire and step away unscathed. Sheer dominance of personality could not suffice today, but when Old Hays was around he was a colossus in the city.

Bibliography

Denlinger, Sutherland. "Old Hays—There Was a Cop!" *New York World Telegram* (March 1–6, 1937).

National Cyclopaedia of American Biography 12:354.

Homicide Investigation

Practical homicide investigation is simply an emphasis on the basics, as well as the traditional methodologies, which law-enforcement personnel have used successfully for many years. In addition, it requires the detective to develop skills that transcend normal police operations. Each case should serve as a form of continuing education in building experience and detectives must be constantly alert to new developments within their profession.

In order to be successful, the homicide detective and/or commander must have above-average intelligence so as to absorb the many details that arise during a murder investigation. They must possess an in-depth knowledge of the law and legal systems within their jurisdictional purview in order to provide a prosecutable case. They must be aware of the medicolegal requirements in a death investigation, as well as the forensic considerations of evidence and how these relate to each specific case.

The homicide investigator should have a working knowledge of the disciplines that relate to psychology and human behavior; and, more importantly, be able to relate these principles and personal experience to the "real world" and the people he or she encounters during a murder investigation.

These are the true prerequisites of practical homicide investigation.

Problems Confronting the Homicide Investigator

Identifying and apprehending criminals has never been easy, and in homicide cases the task is further complicated by the fact that the complainant, the main witness, is deceased and therefore will never be able to "point the finger" at the accused. Instead, the investigator will have to rely not only upon eyewitnesses or circumstantial evidence, but often must try to elicit from the suspect what actually took place and then decide whether this account is consistent with the other facts he or she has accumulated. This can be a very frustrating experience, especially when you consider the following factors:

Higher Crime Rates. Higher crime rates and an increase of violence strain police resources and capabilities and tend to create public apathy or indifference; oftentimes persons will not want to "get involved" with the police, especially in a murder investigation.

More Intelligent Criminals. Many criminals today are more sophisticated and frequently are "graduates of the penal system," who have been duly schooled by "jailhouse lawyers" on how to "beat" the system. Additionally, television and the other media create technically correct scenarios that educate the lawbreaker.

Restrictive Court Decisions. These have an extremely negative impact on the investigative process. In fact, some state supreme courts are even more restrictive than the U.S. Supreme Court in their interpretations of the law. It should be noted that the Constitution exists to protect individual human rights. However, society also has a *right* and *duty* to protect its citizens from lawbreakers who offend society by disregarding the rights of others.

Human Nature and Criminal Behavior. "Things are not always as they appear to be." Homicide investigation is a tricky and devious business. It is not uncommon for the perpetrator to mislead the police purposely or "stage" a crime scene. A prudent attitude is, "Every time you think you've seen it all, along comes some two-legged deviate who'll surprise you with some new form of perversity."

Organizational Policies. Many times the investigator finds him or herself at odds with their own department's policies or procedures. These guidelines must be reviewed with an eye toward facilitating the goals. It is the responsibility of command to meet this need.

Interagency Relationships. The investigation of violent and sudden death is hard enough without the additional burden of jurisdictional disputes. These problems must be resolved in an intelligent and unbiased manner, so as to allow the full resources of law enforcement to accomplish their mission.

Composition of Practical Homicide Investigation
A formula for practical investigation includes the following ingredients:

Teamwork
    Documentation
    Preservation
    Common sense
    Flexibility

Teamwork. Homicides are not solved because the people wearing the suits are smarter than the men and women in uniform. In fact, the patrol officer represents the eyes and ears of the police organization. Teamwork is the essence of successful homicide investigation: It begins with the first officer on the scene. The detective and commander set the tone for this teamwork approach by past and present performance. Remember: The case may be assigned to one particular investigator, but the investigation is the responsibility of the entire police organization. One person is assigned but a number of persons are working on the case. There is enough glory in a successful case for the entire organization. The lead investigator should act as a coordinator, and the commander should assure that all resources are fully utilized.

Documentation. The documentation of events in a homicide investigation is paramount to the case. It all begins with chronological note-taking, and it starts with the *time* of notification. Develop a system that flows. Use the checklist approach. Documentation is accomplished through note-taking, photographs, sketches, and report writing. *Remember: Observe, Describe, Record.*

Preservation. The preservation of evidence begins with the preservation of the homicide crime scene. This preservation is accomplished through documentation. The homicide crime scene is without doubt the most important crime scene to which a police officer or investigator will be called upon to respond. Because of the nature of the crime, death by violence, the answer to what has occurred can be determined only after a careful and intelligent examination of the scene and professional evaluation of the various bits and pieces of evidence. The progression of command starts with the first officer and follows a logical path up the chain of command. All members have a responsibility to preserve the crime scene and must keep in mind the "theory of transfer and exchange." This theory is based on the following facts: (1) the perpetrator will take away traces of the victim and the scene; (2) the victim will retain traces of the perpetrator and may leave traces of the victim's self on the perpetrator; and (3) the perpetrator will leave behind traces of himself at the scene. Use of a crime-scene sign-in sheet will limit the number of police personnel entering the area. Responding police officers should set up two perimeters: one for the "official guests" and the other inside a secured location, which can be protected from all unauthorized personnel. Keep in mind the multiple crime-scene theory. The primary scene is where the body is discovered. However, additional scenes may contain evidence and/or weapons that must also be protected. "Everything and anything" is evidence; and until proven otherwise should be handled as such. This is one of the most important aspects of the homicide investigation. Often the corroborative information necessary for a prosecution exists in some item which was originally retrieved from the scene.

Common Sense. This vital quality does not necessarily prevail at the homicide crime scene. However, once you have established a routine with an organizational objective in mind, common sense will have a chance to surface. For example:

"Sometimes the solution is right before your eyes."
"Do not discount hunches."
"Do not become shortsighted."

Once someone has assumed control and command over the investigation, a very logical and systematic process can be undertaken. This is where a checklist approach can be of value in keeping the investigation on track.

Common sense versus rules of discovery: Do not prematurely designate suspects or submit official reports for the major case file until you look at the whole picture. Be constantly aware of the future impact of your decisions in a murder case and maintain your flexibility.

Flexibility. Flexibility allows for the unforeseen and the unpredictable. These elements often present themselves during a homicide investigation. The ability to make a 180-degree turn mid-stream in an investigation is the true test of flexibility. The homicide investigator must learn to "go with the flow" and follow his or her instincts.

Response to the Homicide Crime Scene
The Patrol Officer
The patrol officer confronted with a homicide investigation should take five basic steps to initiate a proper and professional inquiry. Since the homicide crime scene is not an everyday occurrence, the officer must be able to adapt to the circumstances. The following acronym of ADAPT will stay in the memory:

A   Apprehend the perpetrator if possible. Note I did not say arrest. In homicide investigations, the arrest is usually made by a detective. However, the apprehension is merely the taking into custody of someone.
D   Detain everyone present. It is imperative that witnesses and/or suspects be detained by the patrol officer and held at the scene for follow-up investigators.
A   Assess the crime scene. Make a quick visual inspection of the location with an eye toward determining boundaries.
P   Protect the scene. This generally means preserving the scene from further contamination by additional police personnel.
T   Take notes. This is the most important contribution an officer can make to the homicide investigation.

Preliminary Investigation at the Scene:
The Detectives
Investigation of a homicide starts with the notification to detectives. Methodical and routine procedure should initiate the case, as follows:

- Date and time of notification
- Method of transmission; i.e., telephone, radio, in person, etc.
- Name, rank, shield number, and other data identifying the person making the notification.
- Complete details.

Additional information is noted upon arrival at the scene. Investigators should take Polaroid or Instamatic photos of the scene immediately without disturbing anything, so as to "capture" the scene intact. These photos can be utilized later on in determining the positions of things before the crime-scene process began. Also, they can be reviewed by investigators arriving at the scene, without any further crime-scene contamination.

Procedures

Preliminary Interview of the First Officer. Detectives begin their investigation at the scene by interviewing the first officer for details of the event: (a) detailed account of any actions they took; (b) summary of events; (c) chain of custody; (d) any evidence retrieved by uniformed officers.

Complete Description of the Crime Scene and Body. A complete description of the dead body and surrounding area should be entered in the investigative notebook, as well as a complete description of the clothing worn by the deceased.

Implement Crime Scene Procedures. The detective implements crime-scene procedures by acting as the coordinator for a number of different units and/or agencies. During this phase of the investigation, the objective is simply crime-scene protection and coordination of efforts.

The Investigative Canvass. This is simply a survey or door-to-door inquiry by investigators to obtain information. It can best be described as a filtering process, whereby information can be analyzed and reviewed for follow-up investigation.

Preliminary Medical Examination at the Crime Scene. If the medical examiner or coroner is responding to the scene, the body should be left in its original position for proper review. Medical inquiry at the scene may disclose the circumstances and cause of death; that the death was caused in a certain manner. The condition of the body must be consistent with the cause. Ideally, the medical examiner and the homicide detective work as a team.

Interview of Ambulance Personnel. Many times, emergency personnel arrive at the scene before the police. These people should be interviewed by detectives in order to get their views of the scene and body prior to the arrival of the police.

Handling Witnesses at the Scene. Efforts should be made to have these persons separated as soon as possible and obtain a quick preliminary statement before they change their minds or are influenced by others at the scene. The formal interview can be conducted later on at the station house, but a quick summary of what was seen should be obtained by investigators at the scene out of earshot of the press, crowd, other witnesses, or the subject.

Crime-Scene Photographs. Photos are important because they are a permanent record, providing visible evidence that helps to re-create the original event. Both color and black and white photos should be taken. The crime scene should also be videotaped. However, videotape is not a replacement for still photographs. Instead, it should be used to enhance the documentation. At this stage of the investigation it is impossible to determine all the factors that will become important. Therefore, photos should be taken of the entire scene and surrounding areas. There should be close-up shots of the actual body and any item considered to be evidentiary in nature. They should be related to the overall scene. There shouldn't be any chalk lines or other indicators in the photos before the long and detailed shots are taken. Later on, markers can be added to accent certain close-up photos. As each photo is taken, an accurate record must be made of the exact time, exact location, detail being photographed, compass direction, focus distance, and identity of the photographer.

Required Photographs in Homicide Investigation

1. Front entrance to building or access to crime scene.
2. Entrance to the house, apartment, or room in which deceased was discovered.
3. Two full body views (one from each side). If the body has been moved, the original body location should be photographed.
4. Two photographs relating body location area to its general surroundings from opposite or diagonal directions.
5. Possible entrance and/or escape routes of the perpetrator to and from the crime scene.
6. Areas where force was used for entry or exit.

7. Area photograph of evidence in situ and a close-up photograph of the specific evidence.
8. Identification photographs of the deceased taken at the morgue.

The Crime-Scene Sketch. A good crime-scene sketch is nothing more than a simple line drawing indicating the position of the body in relation to fixed and/or significant objects in the scene. The investigator who prepares a crime-scene sketch should add a "legend" for clarity and as a guide to information contained therein.

The Homicide Crime-Scene Search. The scope of the search is determined by the reconstruction of events based upon the initial observations of the crime scene, position of the body, the boundaries of the scene, and an assumption of how and why the homicide occurred. Investigators must keep in mind that this preliminary theory is only provisional. If new evidence emerges that suggests a different series of events, they must be willing to reassess and modify their original theory as the new facts dictate. This is where flexibility becomes important.

Before any search is conducted, the scene should first be processed for "latent-print" evidence. The search can then concentrate on items found therein and upon the body of the deceased.

Crimes of violence, such as homicide, usually involve a struggle, a break, use of weapons, use of physical force, or other contact between the perpetrator and the victim. Therefore, it is a good possibility that trace evidence will be found and recovered. Remember the theory of transfer and exchange. The ability to recognize and discover evidence at the homicide crime scene is a prerequisite of successful search. The expertise of the homicide investigator and commander, acquired by training and experience, will probably determine what evidence is found, keeping in mind that "anything and everything" could be evidence.

Practically speaking, only one officer should be obtaining the evidence. This will keep the chain of custody tight and provide for a more accurate and uniform recording of evidence. Other investigators can assist in locating evidence, but should not handle anything. Instead, the finder can alert the searching officer, who will actually take it into custody. All of this information should be entered in the investigative notebook and additionally a reference should be made on the crime-scene sketch.

Collection of Evidence. The proper collection and disposition of evidence will be accomplished if the following guidelines are adhered to:

1. Each piece of evidence should be marked (on the container or item as applicable) to show its original position and location. This information should also be recorded in the investigative notebook.
2. Each article should be marked distinctively by the searching officer to identify the person who found the particular piece of evidence. Small or fluid specimens should be marked on their containers.
3. Each item should be described exactly and completely with the corresponding case numbers and the date and time of collection indicated.
4. Each item should be packed in a separate, clean, and proper-sized container to prevent cross-contamination or damage.
5. Each package should be sealed to retain evidence and prevent any unauthorized handling.
6. Each piece of evidence should show proper disposition:
   (a) Police department laboratory
   (b) Property clerk's office
   (c) FBI laboratory
7. Records for each piece of evidence should show the chain of custody. These records should reflect any movement of the evidence from the point of origin to its final disposition.

Remember, each item should be photographed before it is collected.

Release of the Crime Scene. The decision to release the crime scene should be carefully considered. Obviously, if the scene is released prematurely information may come forth that requires additional process or search. Accordingly, the crime scene should be held at least through the preliminary investigation, which is about seventy-two hours. This provides for completion of the initial canvass, preliminary interviews, the medicolegal autopsy, and follow-up visit to the scene by next of kin and others who may have knowledge of the location. In addition, homicide investigators should remember that any good defense attorney will visit the scene at first opportunity in an attempt to gauge the nature, character, and extent of the police investigation. Practically speaking, anything the police took to the scene should be removed. A proper receptacle should be placed at the crime scene for disposal of materials used in the examination and processing of evidence. When this has been completed, the receptacle can be removed from the crime scene.

Conclusion

In practical homicide investigation "knowledge is power." Knowledge that has been enhanced by experience, flexibility, and common sense provides the professional investigator with the means to utilize tactics, procedures, and forensic techniques to his or her advantage. Each case is unique but may involve similar and repetitive factors, which can be taken into account as the investigator plans for the specific case. It all starts with the crime scene and the preservation of evidence.

It continues with the diligent pursuit of each piece of information discovered throughout the investigation: Homicide investigators are obsessed with information-seeking. They obtain information from the crime-scene search, interrogation of suspects and witnesses; in-depth canvasses of areas and neighborhoods; police interviews of next-of-kin, associates, and friends of the deceased; evaluation of evidence by the laboratory; searches of public records, files, and intelligence sources; and confidential informants. They may seek the services of pathologists, serologists, entomologists, odontologists, anthropologists, and psychologists. However, these experts will be of little value unless the investigator has developed suspects and/or information that provide a basis for comparison.

The principle in practical homicide investigation is: Do it right the first time, for you get only one chance.

Vernon J. Geberth

Bibliography

DiMaio, Vincent J.M. *Gunshot Wounds: Practical Aspects of Firearms Ballistics and Forensic Techniques.* New York: Elsevier Science, 1985.

Geberth, Vernon. "The Investigation of Autoerotic Deaths." *Law and Order Magazine* 31(1) (1983): 20–24.

———. *Practical Homicide Investigation: Tactics, Procedures, and Forensic Techniques.* New York: Elsevier Science, 1983.

———. "The Investigation of Sex Related Homicides." *Law and Order Magazine* 34(7) (1986): 40–48.

———. "Mass, Serial, and Sensational Homicides: The Investigative Perspective." *Bulletin of the New York Academy of Medicine* 62(5) (1986): 492–96.

Harris, Raymond I. *Outline of Death Investigation.* Springfield, IL: Charles C. Thomas, 1962.

Hazelwood, Robert R., Park Elliot Dietz, and Ann Wolbert Burgess. *Autoerotic Fatalities.* Lexington, MA: D.C. Heath, 1983.

Snyder, LeMoyne. *Homicide Investigation,* 3d. ed. Springfield, IL: Charles C. Thomas, 1974.

Spitz, Werner U., and Russell S. Fisher. *Medicolegal Investigation of Death: Guidelines for the Application of Pathology to Crime Investigation.* Springfield, IL: Charles C. Thomas, 1973.

Svensson, Arne, Otto Wendel, and Barry A.J. Fisher. *Techniques of Crime Scene Investigation.* 4th ed. New York: Elsevier Science, 1987.

Homicides: Unsolved

With the rising murder rate in the United States, homicide investigators find their workloads increasing with each passing month, creating a backlog of murders that remain unsolved. The caseload of most detectives today prevents them from focusing on specific cases and following these cases through to a solution. In response the North Carolina State Bureau of Investigation established the Murders Unsolved Team (MUST) in 1986 to deal with the pervasive problem. After the formation of MUST local law-enforcement agencies in North Carolina could request assistance in the investigation of unsolved homicide cases. A primary benefit is that MUST agents are assigned only one case at a time and continue to concentrate their efforts on solving the case when local investigators move on to more pressing matters.

Organization

The State Bureau of Investigation (SBI) divides North Carolina into eight geographical districts with a MUST agent assigned to each district and one unit supervisor who oversees all MUST investigations. The agents—who generally have from five to seven years of field experience—report operationally to a unit supervisor who, in turn, reports administratively to the SBI district supervisor. When a local agency asks for help in a particular case, the MUST supervisor reviews the case to determine whether previous investigators followed all likely leads and whether they interviewed all possible witnesses and suspects. If not, and the case appears to hold some promise for solution, the supervisor accepts the case.

The supervisor then assigns the case to two MUST agents—one from the requesting agency's geographical district and one from a neighboring district—who then begin their investigation by reading the files on the case. If all agents already have cases assigned to them, the case is put on hold until agents become available. Next, the district SBI agent, the newly assigned MUST agents, and investigators from local law-enforcement agencies previously involved in the case meet to review all aspects of the case. When investigators exhaust all possible leads, the unit supervisor decides whether to place the case in an inactive status. Unit personnel never close files. Instead, the cases remain inactive until new leads develop, at which time the unit coordinator reactivates the case. MUST agents use a database to help manage complex cases that involve multiple agencies. Agents record who covers certain leads, what information they acquire, the results of the lead, and the date the lead is completed.

Cooperative Efforts

In 1988 the SBI solved a homicide through the cooperative efforts of the SBI, a physics professor, and the FBI. The case, which occurred in 1985, involved a man who died in his home from a twelve-gauge shotgun wound. Only his wife and three-year-old son were home at the time, and his distraught wife described to investigators how her young son pulled the shotgun from the closet, dragged it down the hall to the living room, and while sitting on her lap, accidently discharged the weapon, fatally wounding his father. The investigating team took detailed photographs of the entire crime scene that evening but limited their questioning to the wife, at her request. The following day the wife refused to take a polygraph test and referred detectives to her attorney. Shortly thereafter, she burned the couch because of the extensive blood damage and discarded other potential evidence in the house.

The investigation eventually came to a standstill and the wife moved to another state. However, relatives of the deceased wrote the state attorney general, urging that the investigation be resumed. In 1988, after reviewing the file, the state attorney general requested that the SBI undertake the case. SBI officials assigned the case to MUST. To begin, MUST investigators focused on the wife's story that the three-year-old child fired the twelve-gauge shotgun, especially since the child did not complain of any recoil injury or ear discomfort from the noise of the blast. They enlisted the aid of a physics professor at a local university to determine the precise force caused by the firing of a twelve-gauge shotgun. Using detailed information about the gun and shells, the professor calculated that the force of the blast would definitely injure a three year old. In addition, the SBI laboratory determined that the gun was fired from a distance of ten to twelve feet, not at close range as the wife described. Investigators contacted the FBI laboratory, which used the original 1985 photographs to reconstruct the crime scene. A comparison of the reconstruction, the wife's story, and laboratory analysis of the shell's trajectory revealed a damaging inconsistency. In order for the story to be accurate, the husband would have had to be sitting on a couch that was six feet in the air.

Finally, extensive interviews with friends and neighbors of the deceased revealed that he never took a loaded weapon into his house. Moreover, he kept all shells for the weapon on a high shelf in the hall closet so that his child could not reach them. The cooperative investigation took approximately eight months. In 1989 the wife was charged and convicted of her husband's murder—a murder that would have most likely remained unsolved had it not been for the efforts of MUST personnel. A simple—almost transparent—case such as this makes the original investigation appear slipshod. It should not be thought so. The MUST investigators focused exclusively on the case, while investigators from the local police department could provide only minimal attention because of their need to attend to other cases. The real problem was not poor investigative skills on the part of local law enforcement but the rising number of homicides in and out of big cities.

Track Record

MUST has an enviable record of successful investigations. Forty-six percent of assigned cases have been solved (1993). Plans call for doubling the number of MUST agents in each district. MUST methodology has proven effective and local agencies now tend to solicit assistance earlier in their investigations. North Carolina's State Bureau of Investigation through its creation of the Murders Unsolved Team provides a model for other states to follow.

Henry Poole
Stephen Jurovics

Honolulu Police Department

The years 1845, 1846, and 1847 were significant for the enforcement of law in Hawaii. During these years Kamehameha III, acting on the advice of the attorney general, John Ricord (the first lawyer to arrive in the kingdom in 1844), and with legislative approval, signed into law three organic acts, later to be termed the "Acts of Kamehameha III." Title II, Section 1, Chapter 1 of the Act of 1846 provided in part that the attorney general was to recommend a person to the king for appointment as marshal. The marshal, in turn, was to recommend to the attorney general for his approval the names of sheriffs of the major islands. Sheriffs were to select their own deputies, subject to the approval of the marshal.

The marshal and the sheriffs were "to keep the public peace; have charge of all jails; keep all prisoners safely; execute criminal sentences, civil judgments, decrees of the court; carry out executive mandates of the king, the governors, and heads of the executive departments; command the civil posse; detect crimes and apprehend criminals; enforce the revenue laws; and guard the public domain, public rights of piscary [fishing], and other public property from trespass and spoilation." On May 8, 1847, Henry Sea was appointed marshal of the Kingdom of Hawaii, but resigned in September to be replaced by Theophilus Metcalf. He held the office until 1850, when the forceful William Cooper Parke succeeded him. Parke made a survey of the police on Oahu and found that law enforcement was loosely controlled and vested in a group of one hundred Hawaiian men, who were stationed at the Old Fort, which was used as a jail and insane asylum. Thirty of these men were paid some sort of a wage, while the other seventy were compensated with 50 percent of any fine levied against a lawbreaker they had arrested and brought before the court. Members of the so-called police force could be identified as officers only if they wore a red band around their hats; most wore whatever clothing they had been able to obtain from visiting seamen. Parke took immediate measures to correct abuses on Oahu. He caused each man to wear a leather band on his hat, on which appeared "Police" together with a number, thereby doing away with the red band previously worn. He next divided the force into watches, each headed by a captain. Headquarters was relocated in a building at the foot of Nuuanu Avenue, in the area that housed the harbormaster and master pilot. He later published the first rules and regulations governing the conduct, behavior, and duty requirements for police officers. Twelve foreigners (*haoles*) were added to the police force to assist the Hawaiian officers in making arrests of other foreigners. Boisterous sailors on shore leave had little respect for the pure-blooded islanders, ran wild, and jeered at the law. Most were treated leniently because they spent money lavishly and the police were not able to handle major disciplinary problems. In 1852 a jailer killed an intractable sailor, causing a riot involving an estimated three thousand sailors, Parke's policemen, the Hawaiian militia, and some two hundred *haoles*. Two hundred sailors were arrested and confined to the fort; the jailer served five years for manslaughter.

A legislative act in 1859 passed control of the marshal from the attorney general to the minister of the interior. It also reduced the number of police officers on all islands. Then, in 1860, an immense tragedy struck. Just how leprosy was introduced to Hawaii was never determined, but it was out of control by 1860, and in 1865 the legislature ordered the Board of Health to round up all victims of the disease and send them to an isolated area, Kalawao, on the island of Molokai. The police on all islands were among those responsible for rounding up people who would become residents of the isolated peninsula from which there was no return.

The nadir of Marshal Parke's tenure was in 1872, when he was severely criticized for not suppressing an election riot. Supporters of the Dowager Queen Emma wreaked havoc in Honolulu in response to her loss of the throne to David Kalakaua. Zealots attacked a special committee on its way to congratulate Kalakaua, then invaded the courthouse and thrashed members of the Legislative Assembly. Some of the police, equally enraged over the election results joined the mob, leaving Parke and a few loyal men to defend themselves and others as best they could. The courthouse suffered considerable damage, and only a combined force of United States and British Royal Marines, coming ashore at the request of high government officials, quelled the riot. History later proved that the choice of Kalakaua had been a bad one. The new king was extravagant, building a lavish palace and indulging himself in an endless round of balls and parties. Even worse was his political tie to Claus Spreckles, the so-called "Sugar Baron," to whom he was financially indebted. Kalakaua's manipulation of laws and people, and his own manipulation by wealthy *haoles*, made a mockery of law and order.

On January 20, 1891, Kalakaua died in San Francisco and his sister, Princess Liliuokalani, was declared queen. She appointed as marshal of the kingdom Charles B. Wilson of Tahitian-English descent. In the next year Wilson was accused of allowing gambling, opium-dealing, and other forms of lawbreaking to flourish unchecked. The queen defended him, and they both stayed in power until January 17, 1893, the day the Hawaiian monarchy fell.

New Government and the Police
These were sensitive times, charged with high emotion and unsuccessful efforts to restore Liliuokalani to the throne. The Committee of Safety of the new government appointed E.G. Hitchcock, formerly sheriff of the island of Hawaii, as marshal. He is credited with having rounded up some 400 lepers in Kona for transfer to Molokai. His quick and efficient methods of dealing with criminals and lawbreakers obtained for him the sobriquet of "Holy Terror." During the Rebellion of 1895 he organized a mounted patrol as a branch of the police force. A very effective lawman, Hitchcock left office in 1895.

The United States annexed Hawaii on August 12, 1898, and in June 1900 the islands gained territorial status. Under the terms of the Organic Act by which Hawaii was granted its new status, the Office of Marshal of the Kingdom was replaced by the Office of the Territorial High Sheriff. The duties, responsibilities, and powers of the high sheriff were the same as those of the marshal. From 1905 until 1924 police performance was more or less satisfactory, depending on how one viewed it, although none could say that it was modern and progressive. Politicians were in control, and political demands and favors were part of the police sys-

tem. But the people of Honolulu knew all too well that the police force and its services were deteriorating. Street-corner and neighborhood gangs of hoodlums began operating almost without fear of the police. By early 1930, public demands that something be done about crime and the police forced Governor Lawrence M. Judd to appoint a commission to study the problem. Some laws were passed in 1931, on the commission's recommendation, but they had little effect on crime.

On the night of September 12, 1931, Mrs. Thalia Massie, wife of Lieutenant Thomas Massie, U.S.N., and daughter of a socially prominent southern white family, was allegedly abducted by five local males, taken to a desolate locality, and there beaten and raped. The case drew national attention, much of it adverse for Hawaii, because the "local" versus "*haole*" difference was emphasized. A bad situation grew worse when the trial of the locals ended in a hung jury, followed by a vigilante interrogation of one of the accused rapists, who then was shot and killed. The escape of two prisoners from Oahu prison during this period added more fuel to an already large fire; while they were free one of them burglarized the home of a business executive in one of the more prestigious residential sections of the city and raped his wife. Continued national exposure of Hawaii's law-enforcement problems set in motion a federal inquiry. Assistant U.S. Attorney Seth Richardson, Department of Justice, went to the islands early in 1932 to conduct an in-depth survey of conditions there. His findings, printed in the local newspapers, gave Hawaii a nearly clean bill of health. He found no organized crime, no present racial prejudices, and only moderate crime rates, including sexual kinds; but he did discover "ample evidence of extreme laxity in the administration of law-enforcement agencies."

The Richardson report made its desired impact, and in special session the territorial legislature passed an act creating in and for the City and County of Honolulu a completely new police organization. The Police Act (as it soon became known) established for the first time in Hawaiian history a five-member Police Commission, empowered to enact rules and regulations for the conduct of the department and its business. The commission had full authority to hire and fire a chief of police. The chief of police was authorized to hire officers and employees, who were to be held strictly accountable for their individual conduct and behavior, and for violating any of the commission's rules and regulations. The Police Act authorized the commission to establish a system of training and promotion, the latter based on merit. One of the most stringent provisions of the act prohibited any police officer from advocating the election or defeat of any candidate for public office. The rationale for this provision was clear: Get politics out of the police department and get police officers out of politics.

Charles F. Weeber, a man of impeccable reputation with a military background, was the commission's unanimous choice as the first chief of police. Chief Weeber proceeded to reorganize the department with the help of experts in police matters, until at long last a "new look" was achieved. He set many new policies, such as requiring officers to have a high-school education or its equivalent and to pass an entrance exam. Even those who made the grade could be terminated at any time within the first year for an infraction, which could not be appealed. One of Weeber's imports, William A. Gabrielson from Berkeley, California, became the next chief of police, serving from 1932 to 1946. Chief Gabrielson pushed forward with the reorganization, recruiting more officers for the department, dividing the city into beats, modernizing patrol with cars equipped with two-way radios, implementing polygraph testing, and so on. By 1940 the department enjoyed public respect, but was to undergo drastic change in a few short months.

Honolulu Police and World War II

At 3:30 P.M. on December 7, 1941, Governor Joseph B. Poindexter signed a proclamation that turned the government of the territory of Hawaii over to the military. For police officers, military control was a strange aspect of law enforcement. All criminal trials were conducted by a military judge in Provost Court, and officers found themselves enforcing not the familiar criminal laws of Hawaii but instead a completely new code known as the Orders of the Military Governor. Nevertheless, from the time of the Japanese attack on Pearl Harbor until the end of the war in 1945, Honolulu's police force managed very well. Plans for operating under extreme emergency conditions were immediately implemented, and all regular and special emergency stations and posts were manned. Reserves reported for duty and from mid-1942 until the end of the war the unit functioned as a separate patrol force.

In 1945 a protection racket involving police officers and professional gamblers surfaced, and it looked as if guilt ran deep in the department. A police sergeant, under grant of complete immunity from prosecution, confessed to being a middle-man for payoffs and identified other officers who were on the take. A number of them were indicted, and both the federal Internal Revenue Service and the Hawaii Taxation Department took an interest in the trials, alleging that money paid as graft was taxable income. Only one of the officers was convicted and after petitioning for reinstatement those found not guilty were returned to duty without loss of pay and benefits.

On June 1, 1946, the Police Commission named William Hoopai as the new chief of police, hoping that he could restore public confidence in the department in the wake of the payoff scandal. Hoopai was a "local boy," the first to take the position. One of the more serious problems during the postwar period was drug trafficking, because drugs brought an increase in other crimes, among them, prostitution and thefts. In addition, there was an influx of a new criminal element, the professional vice offender. Chief Hoopai responded by forming a new unit, the Metropolitan Squad. This was a five-man unit headed by a sergeant, with authority to function in a specialized area— hoodlumism and gang activities. A fast, hard-hitting, mobile strike-force, it roamed the island seeking out pockets of vice.

Manpower, a consistent source of irritation and frustration for any police chief, was a serious concern of Chief Hoopai's. He lacked personnel and money, not to mention that he himself was overworked. To give him someone to whom he could delegate, the Police Commission created the new position of deputy chief of police.

The Modern Era

Daniel S.C. Liu followed Hoopai as chief of police, inheriting from him the undermanned, underpaid department. But other worries absorbed his time. Confidence tricksters had moved into Honolulu in force, and police officers had to learn about their tricks. Juvenile crime necessitated organization of the Police Activities League, its mission being to start youth clubs with attractive programs that would keep youngsters off the street. Narcotics offenses were on the increase and the syndicates controlling this vice tried to corrupt police officers. Chief Liu dampened the drug barons' efforts somewhat with the arrest and conviction of two principal vice lords, together with a police officer caught while carrying narcotics from a merchant ship. Another of Chief Liu's campaigns was to promote community relations by insisting that his officers exercise the utmost courtesy when dealing with the public. His aim was to change the notion that policemen were all-brawn-and-no-brain toughs sent out to crack heads. He also saw the need for better-educated officers and asked for and received funds that enabled him to send qualified officers to the FBI National Academy, the Northwestern Traffic Institute, and to seminars, conventions, and other sessions in which the latest in police techniques were taught. His initial dilemma was lessened by the passage of legislative bills favorable to police in Hawaii, which provided for salary increases, uniform allowances, improved vacation allowances, and a modernized pension plan.

A special committee of local administrative and line officers convened in 1959 to consider every phase of city and county operations. Out of this study came a recommendation that police services needed to expand in every way if the department were to keep pace with growing Hawaii. So in the next few years the department officially became responsible for the management of the City and County Jail, moved into larger headquarters on South Beretania Street, opened new substations, and experienced other welcome changes. After thirty-seven years of continuous service, nearly twenty-one of them as chief of police, Liu announced his intention to retire on July 1, 1969. Before he did, however, he reiterated his dream of one day seeing a police academy open. Liu achieved national recognition for the department, upgraded standards and values, encouraged higher education, and implemented technological advances.

Francis Keala, graduate of the University of Hawaii and the FBI National Academy, took the oath of office on December 24, 1969, and as the new chief encountered civil unrest over the Vietnam War, a surge in drug importation, more "street people" to contend with, and disrespect for police. A revision in the City Charter did brighten matters considerably by clarifying once and for all the separation of authority of the Police Commission and the chief of police. It held that the chief of police is charged with responsibility for the administration of the department, and the Commission, "except for purpose of inquiry, or as otherwise provided in this Charter, shall not interfere in any way with the administrative affairs of the Department."

Chief Keala, no less than Liu, continued to restructure his organization to align with the pressing demands of a metropolis vulnerable to crime. He sought greater professionalism, hired qualified women, enlarged the crime laboratory, boosted morale by awarding certificates of merit or department medals of valor, introduced computer technology, and made a host of other changes. The development of a labor union, the State of Hawaii Organization of Police Officers, created quite a stir. For the first time in its long history, the department and its top-echelon administrators found they had to become thoroughly familiar with labor-management relationship and problems and with the skills needed to negotiate a labor contract.

Present Day
More people are killed on Oahu roadways each year than are murdered; more money is spent on personal injuries and motor vehicle repairs due to traffic collisions than is lost as the result of burglaries. With that in mind, the Honolulu Police Department set as its top priority for 1991 the reduction of traffic injuries and deaths. Chief Michael Nakamura began a safe speed campaign with several new tactics. First, he had the flashing blue light on top of some patrol cars removed from the roof and placed on the front dashboard and rear deck. More warnings and citations were issued in speeding- and accident-prone areas. Speed monitoring machines operating in clear sight of oncoming motorists displayed large digital numbers to show rate of speed. DUI roadblocks were increased to cover the next weekend after a holiday weekend, because statistics showed that a substantial number of drunk-driver incidents occurred at such times. Happily, owing to these tactics, the traffic fatality rate in 1991 was the lowest in more than thirty years.

Abridged from the official history provided by the Honolulu Police Department

J. Edgar Hoover

J. Edgar Hoover (1895–1972), director of the Federal Bureau of Investigation, was born in

Washington, D.C., son of a career government employee who rose to become superintendent of engraving and printing in the Coast and Geodetic Survey. Young Hoover's mother taught her children the tenets of Calvinism and would not let them forget the sinfulness of human ways. Because of her and the example of a Presbyterian preacher whom he admired excessively, J. Edgar wanted to be a minister. He graduated from high school as valedictorian of the class of 1913 and began law school at night, working days in the Library of Congress as a messenger. Exactly why he turned from the ministry to law is not known, but during this time he still continued to participate in Bible classes and to preach moral values to anyone within earshot. Those who knew him in youth remembered that he loved sports, was a loner, and was humorless. In 1916 George Washington University awarded him the LL.B. degree and the following year the LL.M. degree.

His first law job was with the Department of Justice as a file reviewer. He enjoyed the detail work that others disliked and pleased his superiors with his diligence and organizational skills. In 1919 Attorney General A. Mitchell Palmer chose Hoover to help with prosecution of alien agitators, deportation of every "red" being the goal. Hoover wrote a report on the "communist conspiracy" and prepared numerous legal briefs sanctioning government raids of suspected "red" hideouts. The raids terrorized hundreds of innocent aliens, though in a major legal action Hoover and other Department of Justice lawyers won the deportation of anarchists Emma Goldman and Alexander Berkman. Hoover was later to regret his role in the mostly unwarranted persecution.

Favorable political winds blew his way on August 22, 1921. President Warren G. Harding's attorney general, Harry Daugherty, had fired William J. Flynn, chief of the Bureau of Investigation and replaced him with William J. Burns, the celebrated detective. On that date the highly visible Hoover was named assistant director. The Bureau's sphere of activity before World War I had encompassed investigating violations of neutrality, bankruptcy, antitrust laws, and white-slave trafficking. During the war it had focused on sabotage, espionage, and other subversive activities. Vice President Calvin Coolidge fired Harry Daugherty and gave the job of attorney general to Harlan Fiske Stone. When Burns announced that he planned to retire soon, Stone and Secretary of Commerce Herbert Hoover (no relation) jointly recommended promotion of the assistant director. So on May 10, 1924, J. Edgar Hoover took control of the Bureau of Investigation (at first as acting director; full confirmation came seven months later). Hoover would not relinquish that control for the next forty-eight years.

Hoover's early changes in the Bureau's functioning included the hiring of lawyers and public accountants as special agents, expansion of the central fingerprint bureau, and introduction of the latest scientific methods of detection. On June 11, 1930, a congressional act authorized the compiling of crime statistics gathered from police agencies throughout the nation. Hoover, the premier detail man, delighted in this task. To this day the FBI *Uniform Crime Reports* is the standard work by which the incidence of American crime is measured.

Federal legislation such as the National Kidnapping Act, the National Extortion Act, and the Bank Robbery Act gave FBI agents more leverage in the fight against crime and also more crime to contend with. "Public enemies" fled from state to state, posing a difficult problem for local authorities who could not easily cross jurisdictional lines. But FBI agents could and because they were Hoover's men, bent on subduing gangsterism, they often conducted their business ruthlessly. Hoover wanted quick results once he had committed his "G-Men"— so called by the press and popularized in the movies—to running down a public enemy. His methods of ensuring capture garnered criticism, since at times he appeared to flaunt the law. However, faultfinding by the legal and law-enforcement establishments did not diminish the fact that the FBI was very effective in apprehending the foremost criminals of the day.

In 1935 the Bureau of Investigation officially became the Federal Bureau of Investigation, and in that same year the FBI Academy at Quantico, Virginia, opened. The academy's purpose was to train "selected police officers from every State in the Union and many foreign countries" in state-of-the-art law enforcement techniques. Inception of the academy may have been the single most important event in Hoover's tenure in office. But no matter what the event he was swift to publicize it. Hoover knew that the press created public opinion and he wanted the best press possible for his FBI. So while G-men risked their lives in volatile confrontations, he spoke at public gatherings of their exploits, and before long the FBI assumed a legendary status. To acquaint America further with the Bureau he wrote *Persons in Hiding* (1938), which was filled with thrilling accounts of criminal cases. The book added considerable luster to the federal arm of the law and told Americans who had not yet heard of J. Edgar Hoover just who he was.

As World War II dawned President Franklin Roosevelt directed Hoover to engage in the same activities as he had in World War I, namely, stamping out subversion at home. Hoover already had a list of enemy aliens, so within twenty-four hours of the attack on Pearl Harbor 1,771 of them were in custody. The usual number of FBI agents, 600, was increased to a wartime peak of 5,000. This build-up successfully prevented any major instance of "foreign-directed sabotage." Hoover was rewarded with the Medal for Merit, the United States Selective Service Medal, and the Order of Honor and Merit of the Cuban Red Cross for his domestic peacekeeping efforts. The war over, the FBI undertook a prodigious assignment: to test the loyalty of more than 2.8 million federal employees. In addition, it was to investigate all violations of the Atomic Energy Act of 1946. Hoover made the transition from war to peace easily, and with his customary zeal for any assignment soon asserted publicly that the FBI had matters in hand.

On May 10, 1949, the twenty-fifth anniversary of his appointment as director, Hoover could justifiably take pride in his accomplishments. Due to his leadership, about 4,000 agents enforced some 120 major federal laws with a conviction rate of 97.2 percent—the envy of the law-enforcement world. That was surely his high point. By the late 1950s he was talked about in a much different way. Prolific wiretapping and McCarthyism fueled the debate over his unchecked power. He listened in on private conversations of whomever he desired, and not necessarily of those who threatened the country. He assisted Senator Joseph McCarthy's purge of communists, even though the memory of his earlier red-baiting still haunted him. Yet he continued to direct his men to ferret out communists and in 1958 promulgated his fear in *Masters of Deceit: The Story of Communism in America and How to Fight It*, a book that sold two and a half million copies. Sharp criticism of Hoover did not prevent President John F. Kennedy from reappointing him as director in 1960. Attorney General Robert Kennedy, though, did not get along with the feisty director and broke with him completely after his brother's assassination. Hoover disliked taking orders from the attorney general when before he had always gone straight to the head man. Besides, Robert Kennedy demanded that he assign more agents to civil rights and organized-crime cases, which he had neglected to do. Networking the country with wiretaps and hunting communists had been Hoover's priorities for too long.

Presidents Lyndon B. Johnson and Richard M. Nixon also reappointed the indomitable Hoover, waiving the mandatory retirement age of seventy. Hoover was at his imperial best in the latter stage of his career. He told off the Warren Commission, investigating President Kennedy's assassination, when he was accused of not sharing FBI intelligence with it; and he called the Reverend Dr. Martin Luther King, Jr., "the most notorious liar in the country," when the civil rights leader had said that the FBI cared little or nothing about protecting blacks. In his final years and particularly after his death Hoover attracted many written appraisals of his character and influence. The tendency has been to expose the roots of his power. The jurist, the politician, the psychiatrist, and the law-enforcement officer can all find much to ponder in his life; but none should forget that J. Edgar Hoover turned a politically subservient Bureau into a globally recognized force, suppressed kidnapping and gangsterism during the 1930s, stopped the infiltration of spies during World War II, and muffled the voice of communism in the postwar period.

His honorary academic degrees filled a wall as did his awards for good citizenship. Never married, he died alone in his bedroom after having worked a full day in his office. High blood pressure had overtaxed his heart.

Bibliography

Messick, Hank. *J. Edgar Hoover: A Critical Examination of the Director and of the Continuing Alliance Between Crime, Business, and Politics*. New York: David McKay, 1972.

Nash, Jay Robert. *Citizen Hoover: A Critical Study of the Life and Times of J. Edgar Hoover and His FBI*. Chicago: Nelson-Hall, 1972.

New York Times 52 (May 3, 1972): 1.

O'Reilly, Kenneth. *Hoover and the Un-Americans: The FBI, HUAC and the Red*

Menace. Philadelphia: Temple University Press, 1983.

Powers, Richard G. *Secrecy and Power: The Life of J. Edgar Hoover.* New York: Free Press, 1986.

Welch, Neil J., and David W. Marston. *Inside Hoover's FBI: The Top Field Chief Reports.* New York: Doubleday, 1984.

Horse-Mounted Police

Horse-mounted police are special units within police departments or public safety organizations that use horses either for patrol activities or for special operations. Sometimes the horse is used primarily for transportation to facilitate and inspire personal interaction among officers and citizenry. During special operations the height and bulk of the horse enhance the mounted officer's command presence and authority.

History

Modern law-enforcement organizations evolved from military antecedents; the horse, since the invention of the saddle, the stirrup, and the horse collar, has been the driving force in many military campaigns and police actions. Such uses of the horse can be traced from antiquity to the present. England provided the seminal roots for the American system. In 1629 King Charles I published "Articles of War," in which he ordered that the provost be allowed a horse, "for he must be riding from one garrison to another correcting many, lest the soldiers scathe the country and frighten the people." These articles spawned the first purely peacekeeping assignment of a mounted person.

A little over a century later magistrate Sir Henry Fielding requested that a light-horse regiment be assigned to his "Bow Street Runners" to patrol turnpikes and rural areas adjacent to London. Instead he was given six mounted men to join two others called "pursuers." Despite the dramatic success of this small unit, it was maintained for only two years, and not until about forty years later was a permanent mounted unit established.

During that forty-year hiatus (1762–1805) gangs and highwaymen assaulted, robbed, and plundered travelers and countrymen at will. That pestiferous turn of events ushered in the revival of mounted police as we recognize them today in Anglo-American settings. Fifty-two former cavalry men, under governmental control, were armed with pistols, sabres, truncheons, and handcuffs to confront that threatening juggernaut of vandals and scofflaws. Dressed in red waistcoats, these valiant men on sturdy horses soon were known affectionately as "Robin Red Breasts" by those who sought safety behind their ranks. Because of their undisputed effectiveness, the number of police horses was dramatically increased. Even now, 210 men and 176 horses are active with the London Metropolitan Police.

Sprouting from those seeds sown in England, many American municipalities adopted formalized mounted units. New York was first in 1871. Paradoxically, the main purpose of that unit was to regulate traffic where people were threatened and frightened by speeders and reckless drivers. By 1900 New York had more than 200 mounted men patrolling on a regular basis. That number reached a peak of 700 before it started its decline, but today there are still more than 100 horses employed there. Three years later San Francisco followed suit, and in 1883 Boston became the third municipality to provide for a permanent unit. Recorded history of mounted units is scant, but by the best reckoning available, it can be said that nearly every police department at one time or another used horses either under saddle or in harness.

With the popularization of the automobile during the 1920s the number of mounted units began to wane. No doubt the new conveyance was an attractive shift from foot and horseback since two officers could ride together and carry more supplies, accoutrements, and arms while being protected from the elements. Perhaps these very attractive features led to the two-man patrol which proved to be ineffective and wasteful, an adversity that plagued police departments well into the 1950s. Under those circumstances the only asset offered by the automobile was to answer calls rapidly over long distances; the automobile never proved to be very suitable for community relations or crowd control. Because the national guard and cavalry could be relied on to use their horses in major civil disturbances, the number of mounted units had diminished to about forty at the beginning of World War II.

Fortunately, from the end of World War I to the end of World War II relatively few uprisings required large formations of troops. One example was the so-called Bonus Army of 1932, when 15,000 veterans marched on Washington, D.C., and were unceremoniously dispatched from their camps by General Douglas MacArthur and his mounted soldiers. In 1946 the last army cavalry unit was deactivated and many municipalities had discontinued the use of horses. Thus mounted men as a last resort were no longer available, and yet to come were the riots of the 1960s and 1970s. The many controversies over tactics and use of force in these emergencies turned thoughts back to mounted units. Old retired units were resurrected and new units were created. Some units had been maintained over a long period of time without interruption, including New York (1871), San Francisco (1874), Boston (1883), Baltimore (1890), Cleveland (1906), and New Orleans (1920). On the other hand, some cities had discontinued their units for a spell. Included in these were Detroit, deactivated 1870, reactivated 1893; Richmond, Virginia, discontinued 1925, revived 1941; Wilmington, Delaware, abolished in 1928, resurrected 1980; Chicago, dormant from 1945 until 1974; and St. Louis, Missouri, which was latent from 1948 to 1971. In contrast to the life, demise, and resurrection of the foregoing units, some units were created recently: Rutgers University (1972); San Jose, California (1973); Charleston, South Carolina (1978); Providence, Rhode Island (1979); and Lancaster, Pennsylvania (1980).

Added to the foregoing list are a host of other units in one category or another. Among them is the National Park Service with headquarters in Washington, D.C. This unit at last count was the largest, and by some claims the oldest. Whether the oldest or the largest, it is one of the most professional and seasoned units in this country and continues to be a model for other units, offering consultation and training for them.

The number of mounted units in the United States varies according to which persons or departments respond to surveys. But based on data collected and some judicial interpolation, the number of units lies between 100 and 120.

Justification

Perhaps the number of mounted units is not as important as the reasons for their existence. The reasons cited most often, listed in descending order, are: riot and crowd control, community relations, crime repression (visibility), general law enforcement, park patrol, noncriminal services, demands of the public, and traffic. Significantly, parades, funerals, and pageantry are hardly mentioned. Most units are placed within the patrol function followed by special operations and traffic. Units are placed so that they can maximize their unique capabilities. It is generally agreed that one person on horseback is equal to ten people on foot in riot and crowd control; moreover, there is no more effective and efficient way for the officer to interact with the people on the street in a favorable way. On horseback the officer is conspicuously present and stands ready to provide information and help on a one-to-one basis. Most people are attracted to horses, which is a source of pride to the officer.

Advantages and Disadvantages

Advantages in descending order are: the rider clear view, his or her visibility to the public, rapport with citizens, the ability to operate in close places, the facility of being able to perform most duties from the saddle, and contributions to clean air and fuel economy. Expressed disadvantages are exposure to inclement weather, lack of speed over long distances, limited carrying capacity, flesh-and-blood vulnerability, and street litter. With respect to weather, rain and snow are not considered impediments; however, sleet is thought to be a small problem. The horse and rider are able to withstand a wide range of temperatures from minus 20 degrees to 106 degrees Fahrenheit, but most units set the tolerance between 12 degrees and 100 degrees. It is agreed that horse manure is biodegradable, and that which falls upon the streets is soon dissipated by the wheels of automobiles. In residential areas, some of the residents eagerly collect it for gardening and horticulture. There are few incidents of intentional injury to the horse.

Selection of the Horse

Horses of all breeds are found within units, with the grade horse being used by most. A grade horse is of uncertain pedigree and can be of any mixture. Geldings are used almost exclusively, but one finds an occasional mare and a rare stallion. The horse should stand from fifteen hands (seventy inches) to seventeen hands (sixty-eight inches) and weigh from 1,000 to 1,300 pounds. At the time of acquisition, the horse will be between two and twenty years of age, with most between ten and twelve years old, and can be expected to serve from nine to thirteen years. The oldest horse in service is twenty-nine, but the mean age is fourteen years.

When no longer suitable for service, the horse is retired, given away, sold, traded, or removed by euthanasia. Most horses are donated to the department, some are owned by individual policemen, and others are purchased at a price between $1,000 and $1,500. If a horse does not prove dependable within thirty days he is usually disposed of in accordance with departmental policy. Most training of horse and rider is carried on by the local department, but there are prominent training centers that will lend a hand in Chicago, St. Louis, and Detroit, and under the auspices of the National Park Service.

Tack and Attire

All kinds of saddles are used, including forward seats, McClellans, and western-stock. Bridles include the bitless type to the full double bridle. At an expenditure of $500 to $900 adequate tack can be purchased. The rider usually wears either English or western-style clothing, depending on the local trend.

Selection of the Rider

Most riders must have an umblemished record of good and prudent behavior and an engaging personality in order to further community relations while enforcing the law. The mean age is twenty-three years and height ranges from 5 feet 6 inches to 6 feet 5 inches with the median about 5 feet 9 inches; weight might lie between 140 and 225 pounds with about 180 preferred as the maximum. With the acceptance of women riders, these guidelines are changing. Specialized training is required and the rider will carry a flashlight, radio, handgun, and baton. In crowd control situations, some seasoned commanders dispense with the baton and use chemicals. The gas mask has proved to be an encumbrance; few riders don them and tear gas will not affect the horse.

Deployment of Units

There are no geographical or climatic conditions that preclude the prudent use of horses. Moreover, all social, economic, and demographic conditions can accommodate them. All political entities from federal to village governments can and do use horses; so do private security organizations. Mounted units are effective and efficient in shopping, industrial, and commercial areas, ghettos, recreation areas, and along national borders. Productivity of these units is hard to measure, but there is a consensus that they are a valuable adjunct in almost every way. There is one caveat to would-be organizers of new units. If they are to be used for public relations and pageantry with little regard for enforcement, these units will be weighed in the balance and their demise can be anticipated. Mounted units are expected to pull their weight in the general scope of law enforcement. Therefore, the future of the police horse lies with the attitude and horse sense of police administrators and government officials who look beyond hardware and "high tech" for methods to cope with human behavior. Well-managed and appropriately deployed new units will be welcomed and praised by the people.

William F. Carfield

Bibliography

Campbell, Judith. *Police Horses*. New York: A.S. Barnes, 1967.

Carfield, William E. *Comparative Analysis of Twenty-Five Horse Mounted Police Units in the United States*. Richmond: Eastern Kentucky University, 1982.

Gourley, Douglas C. *Patrol Administration*. 2d ed. Springfield, IL: Charles C. Thomas, 1974.

Leinwand, Gerald, ed. *Riots*. New York: Washington Square Press, 1970.

Hostage Negotiations

Little has changed in the police methods of handling hostage situations since the terminology, and recognition of the problem, became common back in the mid-1970s. The New York City Police Department perfected a standardization of the common sense approach to dynamic, emotionally charged incidents and instituted a negotiator-team concept. The neighboring Nassau County Police Department was quick to realize the value of the idea and, aided by New York City, started its own hostage negotiating team in 1974. Police administrators nationwide began to realize that there was really no mystique in dealing with hostage, barricade, or suicide-attempt situations—all that was really needed was some in-depth training of qualified officers, an overall department policy, and a list of guidelines that would fit various types of incidents. Police negotiation teams were formed, trained, and became operational throughout the country. Not surprisingly, many high-anxiety situations were defused, lives were saved, and the accepted policy of talking people out of their dramatic intentions rather than a reliance on firepower became part of police methodology.

Since the early 1970s much has been said and some opinions have been written by professionals, particularly in the field of mental health, attempting to look into the field of negotiation and institute high standards for all to follow. These standards are acceptable as long as it is realized that almost every situation is as different as the emotional makeup of the subjects involved. There is nothing wrong with institutionalizing and allocating fancy titles for procedures, as long as the basic, simple concept of police "street psychology" is not forgotten. For the benefit of the officer who has to deal with the hostage holder, the emotionally disturbed, armed, and barricaded subject, or the person who is threatening to commit suicide, we should review the basic concepts.

First it has to be recognized that the life of the subject or subjects involved, whether they be hostages, hostage holders, barricaded subjects, or a person attempting suicide, is of foremost concern. For example, the apprehension of a perpetrator who uses a hostage to further his escape has to be secondary to the life and safety of the hostage. This concept has to be recognized and instilled in the mind of each police officer who may be used as a negotiator.

If a scene has been secured and there is no immediate danger to the public or police, there is no reason why a barricaded subject cannot be talked out or waited out, rather than blown out of his location. A would-be suicide should be recognized as a human being in a high-anxiety situation and all steps should be taken to lower the tension and wait out the period of time it takes to do so, if the public is not in jeopardy.

An assault or an attempt to neutralize the subject can always be tried, but a serious attempt should be made to end the incident without injury or loss of life. The situation can easily be escalated if necessary, but seldom deescalated easily.

The police approach to a hostage situation often depends on the type of subject being dealt with. A taker of hostages usually fits into one of four categories:

1. The criminal. This role is typified by the armed offender who is caught in the act by quick police response and takes a hostage in order to facilitate escape. The hostage-taker can predict with some accuracy how far the police can go and knows what to expect from them during the incident and after capture. Most of the time the hostage-taker will understand what the effect will be to his or her status if the hostage is killed or injured. Usually the negotiating team can convince the hostage-taker that the best course of action is to give up.

2. The mentally disturbed person. If the holder of a hostage, the barricaded subject, or the person on the ledge is calm, cool and collected, seems to be enjoying him- or herself and is much less excited than the situation demands, be careful. This is the type of person who will probably kill or jump and may be extremely difficult or impossible to deal with.

3. The unorganized group. This type of incident, usually the result of a spontaneous riot, or jail break, where hostages are seized can be very difficult to deal with unless rapid action is taken. Once the group is cohesive and a leader or leaders are chosen it becomes more of a problem. Most jails limit concessions and have policies that will not allow a prisoner to escape because he or she is holding a jail employee as a hostage. Ordinarily police will not negotiate with jail inmates but there are enough police-detention facilities to justify a hostage policy in the law-enforcement agency involved. Many times escape is not the prime demand but improvement in conditions in the facility is the foremost subject for negotiation. The agency that controls those conditions should be prepared to do the negotiations.

4. The terrorist group. Dealing with an organized terrorist group by local police agencies without outside assistance would be extremely difficult. Many of the concessions demanded would not fall within the scope of police responsibilities and the terrorists know it. The confrontation could have been months in the planning and all of the alternatives and arguments put forth by the negotiators will have been considered already by the group. Also the terrorists may be willing to die to further their cause and take any and all hostages with them. For the most part the terrorist does not want to deal with police and would want higher-level government officials and/or the media

involved in the negotiation sessions. However, the initial contact and the "feeling out" of the terrorists' plan and demands may be the responsibility of the first responder, the police officer. He or she can provide the valuable service of buying time for plans to be made and providing the hostage holders with a distracting focal point.

Now that we have identified with whom we are dealing, there is a list of basic, specific guidelines that have proved their value not only in the United States, but also in many countries that recognize the value of negotiation rather than immediate assault. Some of these guidelines can be valuable not only in dealing with the hostage holder, but also the barricaded subject and the person planning suicide.

Slow Everything Down. This is the number-one rule applying to all high-anxiety situations. Stalling for time works to the benefit of all involved:

- It provides time to contain and isolate the scene.
- The initial state of high emotion is given time to subside and rational thinking to return.
- As time passes the lives of hostages become more secure as the holder realizes the value of their continued safety and is subjected to increasing awareness of them as persons and not pawns.
- A long-range benefit is that fatigue will set in and alertness will fade. (This will also affect negotiators, requiring the need for knowledgeable relief personnel.)

Weapons Are Not Negotiable. This is an obvious rule, yet it must be stressed. The only loaded, functional weapon may be the one given to the hostage holder as a result of negotiations. This may be the weapon used to kill the hostage or police. Anyone who surrenders a weapon is taking the chance of being killed with it.

Negotiators Should Not Substitute for Hostages. This is also considered to be a cardinal rule of successful negotiations. Negotiators should ask themselves the reason for substitution. If the hostage holder is attempting to replace a hostage with a police officer, it may be that he or she feels more comfortable or justified in killing the replacement officer rather than the original hostage.

Avoid Lying. Obvious lies that can be easily controverted especially should be avoided. The credibility of the negotiator in the eyes of the subject can be completely destroyed by being caught in a single lie. No one can support a rule for *never* lying during negotiations, but the negotiator has to be extremely careful for the sake of continued effectiveness. If the subject has access to the media through radio or television, it is extremely dangerous to speak of things that will be negated by a news broadcast. Negotiations should be handled as sincere attempts to bargain, with lies told only when absolutely necessary.

Do Not Allow Relatives, Friends, Neighbors, Etc., to Negotiate. No one should be allowed to negotiate unless a full investigation proves that the relationship existing between the subject and proposed negotiator is positive and acceptable by the subject. The subject may have a profound fear, dislike, contempt, or distrust of the proposed negotiator, which would cause an opposite reaction to the one sought. This type of investigation is part of the all-important intelligence-gathering function of the team effort.

Things to Avoid. Do not use deadlines and discourage the subject from issuing one. *Do not grant outrageous demands*, but consider, or appear to be considering, all demands, even if extreme. *Do not converse with hostages.* Keep the holder on center stage and don't increase the importance of the hostage in his or her mind.

Command of the Scene. The senior officer (not the negotiator) should command the scene and continually evaluate the progress of the negotiations, deal with the media, control the actions of the assault team, and be the ultimate decision-maker with the input of those dealing with the subject. The safety of the public, security of the scene, perimeter control, traffic, media liaison, etc., have to be outside the negotiation process.

Intelligence Gathering. The key to the successful conclusion of many an incident is the availability of information for the negotiator regarding the reason for the subject's action, his emotional makeup and past history. It is extremely difficult to negotiate in the blind and the more known about the subject, the more the negotiator can evaluate what is being said. All revelations by the subject should be thoroughly checked. Intelligence gathering does not stop with information about the hostage holder. The background of each hostage, the logistics of the facility, and the gathering of evidence for future prosecution should also be the function of the negotiating team.

Negotiation Process. Ideally, the negotiations would be in person, with the negotiator and the subject able to see each other and converse in a normal manner. They can better relate to one another and the subject can be put more at ease. The sought-after transference of empathy can best take place between two people facing one another rather than with the utilization of the bull horn or a telephone. However, face-to-face negotiation is dangerous and the decision to do it is a step that should not be taken lightly.

Hostage negotiation, that is, the art of actually negotiating with the holder of a hostage for the final release of the hostage(s), talking a barricaded subject out of his predicament, or having the would-be suicide voluntarily surrender to the police, can be personally rewarding to each member of the negotiating team. The dialogue that convinces the subject to give up his intentions is worthy of remembrance, for it may be used again with variations to fit the incident. Each incident should be objectively critiqued by the entire team and the "bugs" worked out. As the experience of the team increases, their value to the agency and the community will increase at a rapid pace. But even if the negotiators are never used, the comparatively small amount of time invested in the project cannot help but bear some fruit. Administrators of agencies will be pleasantly surprised at the positive reaction of the media and the public to the idea of negotiation.

George F. Maher

Bibliography

Jacobs, J. *SWAT Tactics: The Tactical Handling of Barricaded Suspects, Snipers and Hostage-Takers.* New York: Gordon Press, 1986.

Maher, George F. *Hostage: A Police Approach to a Contemporary Crisis.* Springfield, IL: Charles C. Thomas, 1977.

Miller, Abraham H. *Terrorism and Hostage Negotiations.* Boulder, CO: Westview Press, 1980.

Miron, Murray S., and Arnold P. Goldstein. *Hostage.* New York: Pergamon Press, 1979.

Houston Police Department

The first law-enforcement efforts in the Houston area were made as early as 1832 under the Mexican government. John W. Moore, an Anglo settler, was appointed *alcalde* (mayor) of the Eastern Province. The *alcalde*'s duties included those of sheriff. Moore's appointment lasted only three years, for in 1835 Andrew Briscoe and DeWitt Clinton Harris went to the Mexican garrison at the Port of Anajuac to protest a duty being charged for ships entering and leaving the port. That and other actions precipitated war with Mexico, from which the Republic of Texas was born.

Barely four months after Sam Houston had routed the Mexican army at the Battle of San Jacinto, the Allen brothers from New York bought land nearby. In August, the hottest and most miserable month of the year, they founded the city of Houston, named for the victorious Texas general. In the fall of 1836 John W. Moore came into prominence again when he was elected the first sheriff of Harrisburg County. Law enforcement as a city venture began on June 22, 1837, with the appointment of a committee of civic leaders who were "to form the citizens into a patrol for procuring order." Later, because of the danger posed by "persons of a low type character," the mayor and city council authorized a committee to form a "secret police . . . to be at all times prepared to assist the officers of the city in quelling riots and disturbances and maintaining the peace and quiet of the same." Until after the Civil War there was little patrolling of the city, with no protection at night except that offered by the private guards, hired by local businessmen to protect their establishments, or volunteers.

Law enforcement began to be taken more seriously following the Civil War, and in 1865 the marshal was authorized by the city council to increase the police force to a number he deemed necessary to protect the city, but not to exceed forty men. Police salaries averaged $60 per month for patrolmen, which compared favorably with the wages of Houston laborers of that time. Police salaries were frequently paid irregularly or in scrip (paper money issued for temporary, emergency use) which was discounted at the expense of the officers. In 1866 Houston businessmen, dissatisfied with the protection afforded by the city marshal, petitioned the city council for permission to create a "merchants' police force for the more efficient protection of personal property and for the preservation of good order." The city council granted the petition with the stipulation that any special police assigned to duty would be paid for by the citizens and not from the treasury. Control of the police was given to the city marshal. This was the first use of special police in the conventional mode of law enforcement.

Authority of the police changed repeatedly from 1871 to 1897, and it is unclear just how control was divided among city officials. The mayor was in control at one point and had the power to appoint officers, yet a few months later the city council was empowered to vote on all nominations presented by the mayor. R.V. Patton was marshal until 1875 and during his term the first black police officers were hired. Few served as regular police officers, but several served as special officers. While black officers were only used in black neighborhoods of the city, they performed their duties with the same authority as the white officers. The lack of definition of the legal functions of regular and special police seems to have eliminated racial problems within the department, and blacks who served as special officers received the same legal prerogatives.

The economic depression of the 1870s worsened conditions for policemen. In December 1872 the department listed twenty-four officers, but by May 1978 their number was reduced to ten. At one point officers received no salaries for four months and were forced to appeal to the city council for immediate relief. The telegraph was introduced in Houston about this time, enabling the department to contact other police forces when cooperation was required to capture a criminal. On November 1, 1885, two officers referred to as "Cow Catchers" were mentioned for the first time in department records. These men were mounted on horses and were responsible for capturing the stray livestock found wandering on the city streets and placing the animals in the city pound. These officers were later to become the department's mounted traffic officers. In 1891 the City of Houston provided police officers with their first official uniform. It consisted of

a navy-blue high-crown hat with the word "policeman" affixed to it. The uniform itself was a navy-blue suit of trousers, with a white cord down the outside leg seam, a vest, and a coat complete with brass City of Houston buttons. Shortly before the turn of the century a detective unit was formed and a patrol wagon constructed at a cost of $450. The police force was composed of twenty-four men, and its modest size precluded organizational innovations that characterized other metropolitan police departments.

The Twentieth Century
When J.G. Blackburn took office in 1898, he represented the transition from a substandard police force to an emerging one. He was the last city marshal and the first official chief of police. Popular with the officers he led, he believed in systematic procedures to guide officers in the line of duty and spoke out against political favoritism. Promotion was based on merit. He appreciated the hazards and responsibilities of police work and instituted a patrol plan that divided the city into twelve beats, to be walked by pairs of officers. With his approval, Alderman Frank Rowe, an amateur criminologist, purchased some Bertillon measurement instruments and photographic equipment in the first attempt at establishing an identification program. 1902 was Blackburn's last year as chief, but in a short four years he had galvanized the force, instilled greater confidence in his men, and won for them a new respect.

The first female employee in the department came about due to the insistence of the Houston chapter of the Temperance Union. Termed a matron, she was placed in charge of the female annex of the police station. Another indication of social reform efforts included a grievance board for the department composed of four police commissioners. According to the Houston Police Department 1901 yearbook, "Its main scope of jurisdiction is in the matter of expulsion of members of the force." It also heard grievances and had the power to reinstate or oust members as it saw fit. Lack of any training programs reflected the belief that policing required only brawn and a minimum of intelligence. The following anecdote illustrates the limited education of some policemen at that time: The story goes that a patrolman, upon finding a dead mule in Congress Street near San Jacinto, began to write a report. Attempting to spell San Jacinto and failing, he grabbed the beast by the tail and dragged it down Congress to Main, where he proceeded to record this as the cross street.

The low status of policing expressed by inadequate salaries, an eighty-four-hour work week, the lack of a pension plan, and other compensation contributed to the drive for reform that pervaded this period. In one instance, a request by an officer for payment of three days lost because of a job-related illness was rejected, as was a petition submitted by an officer for reimbursement for work time lost because of injuries received during a streetcar strike.

In 1907 the City Council passed an ordinance that required registration of vehicles, lights for night-time driving, and the observation of an eight-mile-per-hour speed limit in the downtown area. A fifteen-mile-per-hour speed limit would be observed in surrounding areas. All automobiles were always required to yield the right of way to horses. To keep up with this dizzy traffic, the department acquired several Harley-Davidson motorcycles.

On the evening of April 1, 1910, Deputy Chief of Police William E. Murphy was shot to death while taking a break in the Acme Restaurant. His assassin, Earl McFarland, pleaded self-defense, and the jury believed him, owing to McFarland's previous employment as a police officer. Murphy became the highest-ranking officer ever to be killed in the line of duty. His lurid death demoralized the department for some time, and McFarland's acquittal stirred public controversy. Less sensational in that year the department obtained its first police car.

In 1912 B.S. Davidson was appointed chief of police. He worked several small wonders in changing the twelve-hour shift to an eight-hour day, and in establishing a humane department as part of the police that investigated assignments such as cruelty to children and animals. The following year saw the appointment of the first juvenile officer after fifty break-ins and burglaries were reported to be caused by juveniles. Another prime mover of the day was W.R. Ellis. Considered to be one of the greatest identification experts at the time, Ellis proceeded to overhaul the meager identification department, install personal indexes, and bring it up to modern police standards. He was one of the first in the country to establish extradition agreements. The addition of photographic records, properly filed and indexed, provided the Houston Police Department with an ID system unsurpassed in the country.

In the latter part of 1917, Eva J. Bracher was the first woman to be hired by the department as a police officer. Several years later she was to become the first female detective. But 1917 was to live on in memory more for a major riot that occurred. It seems the police raided a crap game and arrested a black woman and a partially drunk soldier. A black military policeman spoke to the arresting officers and hot words were exchanged. With increased bad feelings, a false rumor spread that the police had killed a black soldier. A riot ensued and at the end of it sixteen whites, including five police officers, were dead, along with soldiers, four black, two white, and one Hispanic. Acting mayor D.M. Moody requested martial law and incoming troops ended the mutiny. Subsequently, in one of the largest military court-martials in history, the army gave twenty-nine soldiers the death sentence, though only thirteen were hung in 1918, and fifty-three men received sentences of two to fifteen years.

The department acquired its first car radio in 1927. A portable radio was placed in the rear seat of a patrol car and tuned to the only radio station in Houston at that time: KPRC. The station would interrupt regular programming to broadcast police calls. Prior to 1929 it had been against a city ordinance for officers to carry a firearm where it could be seen. A gun was worn under the coat of the uniform, and in an emergency the officer had to fumble under his coat for his weapon. This law was a reflection of the military regulation the civil law copied. Sixty-five Gamewell boxes had been distributed throughout the city and were centrally controlled through a switchboard in the city electrician's office, police stations, and fire stations. Members of the force had keys to these boxes and had to ring in each hour, with a report taken down on a department form for every call.

The 1930s and 1940s

On June 1, 1930, the records division was created and began to use tabulating machines to record statistics on crime. The "Uniform Crime Detecting System" was started the following month. An in-service school for detectives soon began. The class covered subjects such as report writing and lectures were given by the district attorney and members of the city legal department. On May 1, 1933, the police department's name was changed to the Department of Public Safety, and George E. Woods was appointed director. The new agency included the police as well as the fire division; the mayor could then control both departments through the public safety director.

The year 1936 became a landmark when Robert E. Franklin, the department's communications supervisor, installed a radio in committeeman Raymond Pearson's airplane and the first aircraft patrolled the highway between Harrisburg and the San Jacinto battleground. Chester A. Williams became the chief of police on January 2, 1937, and created the accident investigation division. Lawrence C. Brown took over as chief two years later and organized the first police training school.

The Houston Police Officers' Association (HPOA) was formed in 1945. Initially organized to combat low morale among police, it was meant also to counteract the unfavorable publicity received by the department. Lack of training, the practice of employing political hirelings, and promotion of unqualified men to ranking positions had done much to discredit the department. Men organizing the group had to "slip around" and meetings were often secret. The struggle to improve conditions within the department was bitter. Additional reform followed in 1948 when a state referendum of voters gave aggrieved police officers immediate access to the courts, which in turn gave them protection from arbitrary demotion by unregulated political powers.

Sixty-One Riesner Street

The police headquarters building at 61 Riesner Street, the most modern police facility in the south, was opened in 1950. At a time when the first television sets were coming into use, the station had state-of-the-art surveillance cameras and TV monitors. In keeping with social change, women were hired in generous numbers, though they were limited to clerical duties and dispatching. In October 1964 Herman B. Short was appointed chief of police and did not step down until December 31, 1973. At last a man had been found who could endure the pressures of the job. Chief Short created the helicopter division, obtained new cars and modern equipment for the department, and made serious efforts to expand services. The police academy also began running overlapping classes of cadets.

History repeated itself in 1965 with another race riot. This time 400 students at Texas Southern University protested the Vietnam War by hurling rocks, beer cans, and vegetables at police. Four arrests were made. Then in May 1967 leftover ill-will prompted further student assault on police. The Vietnam War was still the irritant, but on this occasion the disturbance ended tragically. Police officer Louis Kuba was killed, a number of people were wounded, and 488 students were arrested. A third racial incident happened when in 1970 the Black Panthers dared any Houston Police Department unit to drive on Dowling Street (their headquarters were located on Dowling at Tuam). Chief Short declared that the citizens of Houston, especially police officers, would not be denied access to any public street, and the department moved in. Panther leader Carl Hampton was killed in the ensuing gun battle, but things settled down after this confrontation.

October 23, 1975, was the day that the communications and dispatch divisions moved into a new wing of the headquarters at 61 Riesner Street. One of the most up-to-date facilities, the division increased its radio channels from eight to sixteen. Each dispatcher had a computer-connected CRT screen, which could access information about stolen vehicles and pick-ups from other divisions, National Crime Information Center data, as well as a criminal's history. Each dispatcher also had the beat, number, and master district of every street in the city on microfiche, and the office also had a twelve-by-twenty-foot screen designed to indicate the location of units and whether they were in service. For emergency purposes, the screen could be used to project slides of maps of sections of the city. Incoming telephone lines were increased from ten to twenty for a faster response time.

At a cost of $5.2 million a new municipal court building was built. Located next to the main police station, it had eight courtrooms equipped with a computer-connected CRT to allow judges to check the criminal records of defendants. The Harris County district attorney's intake section was in the same building, a tunnel connecting it to the booking office of the city jail. There were twenty holding cells in the court building.

In 1982 Dr. Lee P. Brown announced that under his direction the Houston Police Department would become the showcase police department of the nation. With over 560 square miles to cover, a larger area than New York City and Chicago combined, Houston presented a formidable law-enforcement problem.

In 1983 the Houston Police Department began experimenting with a community policing program touted to reduce the fear of crime and boost residents' trust in police. The plan involved opening "storefront" stations in neighborhoods. Twenty-seven storefronts opened over the next nine years. Community policing also required police and residents to develop several levels of partnerships to prevent and solve crimes unique to each neighborhood. Plummeting oil prices financially strapped Houston in the mid-1980s, and the Houston Police Department Academy was closed to new cadets as a cost-saving measure. A hiring freeze instituted in the department lasted until 1989. Many officers in administrative positions were replaced by civilians to increase the number of officers on the street. Chief Brown left Houston to become police commissioner for New York City. His promise to make Houston the showcase police department of the nation was left unrealized.

In January 1990 the Houston Police Department became the talk of the nation for another reason. A woman, Elizabeth M. Watson, was named police chief. Watson broke ground earlier in her career as the first woman to attain the Houston Police Department rank of captain and then deputy chief. The year 1991 marked the Houston Police Department's 150th anniversary, a time for celebration. But after a rash of violent crimes, a new mayor was elected in November and change was bound to come. Bob Lanier won the election on the platform of putting more police on the streets. Using overtime strategies Mayor Lanier increased the patrol and investigative force by the equivalent of 655 officers. The extra officers eased residents' fear of crime and better pay boosted department morale. Mayor Lanier was not through yet. He appointed a new police chief, Sam Nuchia, a twenty-year Houston Police Department veteran turned federal prosecutor, to oversee the changes in a department that now had approximately 4,200 sworn officers, 1,600 civilians, and a budget exceeding $300 million for fiscal year 1992. Houston led the nation's fifty largest cities in crime reduction, experiencing an amazing 18 percent drop in overall crime by the end of 1992. The dramatic drop underscored the wisdom of putting more police on the streets. The goal now is to have at least 5,000 sworn officers on the force by mid-1994.

Abridged from the official history provided by the Houston Police Department

I

Inspection

Police departments serve several purposes. These are to protect life and property; prevent crime; detect and arrest offenders; preserve the peace and enforce the laws. Every function of the agency should be aimed at one or another of these objectives. Deviations are dysfunctional. In order to achieve these objectives the agency must compartmentalize itself into the box and function model that typifies the organizational structure. These organizational boxes are created to achieve the aims, after these have been prioritized.

Functions

Most municipal police agencies basically approach their tasks from a three-pronged perspective:

1. Attack street crime. This means organizing the agency to detect and arrest criminals, as well as make it more difficult to commit crimes.
2. Better service. The great majority of police work involves responding to emergencies, accidents, illnesses, and mishaps. The response mechanism involves such questions as 911; single-person patrols; prioritizing calls; and other factors focusing on improving the speed and efficiency of the response.
3. Traffic safety. Promoting the safe, speedy flow of traffic requires concentration on engineering, education, and enforcement—the three E's of traffic policy.

A well-organized police department has recognized its mission, prioritized its approach, and organized itself in the most relevant and cost-effective manner. The result should be an organization that understands its objectives and is moving effectively toward their realization. With the mission defined and the objectives established, the question for the chief must be How well are we doing? This is where inspection comes in.

Management

Despite the complaints of many executives there seems little doubt that the true problem in government is not money but management. Under the widening pressures of budgetary constraints, police managers have learned how to get more bang for the taxpayer's buck through inventive cutback management techniques. In a very real sense the budget crises that attended much of municipal life in the 1970s and 1980s proved a boon to executives who were forced to manage, as opposed to being mere caretakers of, police enterprises.

Management implies making maximum use of the resources available to achieve the organizational aims. The final responsibility for the results lies with the chief. Removed as he or she is from the daily functionings of the agency, how can he or she establish that subordinates adhere to policy faithfully? Tools have to be devised to enable verification that the operating levels are conforming to the program. The size and complexity of the models used to inspect the processes will, of course, depend on the size and complexity of the organization being examined.

Information becomes central to effective functioning. The accuracy of the information is critical to the outcome. Subordinates will be inventive in finding ways to report faithful conformity with procedures.

Control is central to the chief executive's direction of his or her agency and it will not be effective without essential pieces of information about the actual performance of the organization's members.

Inspection can serve as the helm that steers the vessel through uncharted seas. It enables the captain to make the necessary adjustments.

Inspection will not only establish whether there is compliance and conformity but will also reveal needs and deficiencies that need to be addressed, as well as whether programs that are being faithfully implemented actually work. Thus it is a very broad management strategy, which goes beyond mere verification and assessment of stewardship, important as these factors are.

Control

One of the constants of police administration is nasty surprises. How many chiefs and mayors have awakened to such scandals as narcotics evidence missing from police custody; some egregious brutality complaint that clearly reflects loss of control; collections or other corrupt practices that indicate a climate of wideopen practices; or any of a hundred other problems that communicate a sense of total loss of control over a police agency? Inspections will serve to restrict acts of non-, mal-, and misfeasance to the occasional, specific, and individual—as opposed to the tolerated, systemic, and clearly widespread.

Inspection

Inspection is an examination of persons, places, or things intended to establish whether they are contributing to the achievement of organizational objectives. Performance is evaluated, deficiencies discovered, needs are identified, and corrections suggested. It is a method for monitoring and controlling organizational behavior. It may be defined as an auditor verification.

Procedures

Inspection procedures can be reactive or proactive. The former involves after-the-fact inquiries, examinations, or investigations to establish the when, where, why, how, what, and who of an event, action, program, incident, or procedure. The latter involves cover testing of the process, frequently through replicating situations to establish whether abuses really are occurring.

Inspection is primarily aimed at determining the quality of a commander's stewardship, as opposed to specific inquiries into individual wrongdoing that characterizes the work of internal affairs units (IAU). It is important that the distinction be understood if organizational confusion is to be avoided. A police officer is accused of police brutality and an investigation is launched. This is typically the work of internal affairs. A command is accused of widespread and systemic use of brutality as an instrument of policy, which is at least tolerated—and perhaps even encouraged—by the commander. This requires an inspection. An officer is charged with a dishonest act and is investigated by internal affairs. Citizens complain of shakedowns, thefts, or extortions by the police, with the commander doing nothing. This falls within the province of inspections.

A precinct commander is accused of falsifying crime statistics to make his or her unit look good. This would fall within the purview of the IAU, but charges that the data are being fudged widely would be examined by inspections. The distinction centers on whether we are examining a specific, individual act or assessing the pervasiveness of a negative condition.

Inspection then becomes the verifying, auditing, and examining arm of the chief executive. It establishes the degree of compliance, detects deviations from policies, and informs the chief as to the operational realities, as opposed to the upbeat reports he or she is certain to be receiving from those charged with the responsibility for carrying out the chief's program.

An inspections unit will determine what the agency's priorities and policies are and then undertake examinations to establish how faithfully they are kept. It will do so through examination of records, the monitoring of performance, the observation of managerial competence, and the verification of findings through such independent means as polling, replications, and the use of undercover operatives.

Stewardship

Since the function centers on the commander's stewardship, and since modern theories emphasize the importance of managerial autonomy, in order to allow the development of the individual's talent, it becomes more important than ever that a chief executive officer have the tools necessary for the evaluation of progress made by his or her subordinates toward organizational goals. This, of course, makes the clear and explicit enunciation of those goals essential.

A police chief, for example, will typically require that any citizen, appearing at a police installation to report an act of police wrongdoing, be treated courteously and that the complaint be recorded and forwarded for investigation. This is the policy. If the chief asks for a report on the degree of compliance, he or she will inevitably receive a glowing account of how faithfully the requirement is observed. Executives who rely on such indices are in for rude surprises.

A proactive approach will involve the chief executive's replicating the situations he or she wants to verify. Are the troops complying with requirements? Send an agent, posing as an irate citizen, into a police station to ask how to report an incident of police brutality. The treatment of that agent will establish, more accurately than the report, the reality complaining citizens encounter.

Integrity tests might involve turning valuable property over to a cop on the street to see how he or she handles it. An errant motorist might explore a cop's honesty by hinting at a payoff. The law cannot be broken by those seeking to enforce it. The point is to replicate the circumstances pinpointed as possible sources of problems to establish the true state of things.

Overt and Covert

A solid inspection will operate on two levels, overt and covert. The overt function involves interviews, examination of records, physical inventories, random sampling, polling, and related techniques intended to elicit facts. Covert operations will involve the use of police informers within the ranks to report on actual conditions, as well as self-initiated and proactive integrity tests or checking on adherence to procedures. It might involve as simple a process as making a number of phone calls to establish a commander's accessibility to the public, or willingness to be the target of police shakedowns in order to test the suspicion, which under such controlled conditions would enable the inspectors to verify and record the activities.

A sound organization understands its mission and develops strong programs and sound policies to achieve its goals. It cannot then rest on its laurels and hope all will be faithfully performed. Systems of verification have to be established to ensure adherence to policy, at the street level.

Goals of Inspection

A sound inspection program will identify the effective leaders as well as those who must be weeded out. It will promote the organization's progress by identifying the high performers and pointing them toward higher responsibilities. It will also enable the agency to pinpoint those paying little more than lip service to organizational policies and goals. The importance of this latter point is frequently ignored, because of the desire to avoid negative connotations. The fact is that identifying the losers and winners becomes one of the key features of any system attempting to enhance organizational effectiveness.

A comprehensive inspection program will provide the chief executive with a report that completely describes the operations of the unit examined, thereby enabling the chief to make informed judgments on the levels of performance and to take corrective action or otherwise respond to positive findings. Such an inspection program will also promote organizational introspection—forcing commanders to focus on policy and then to verify how faithfully it is carried out. No commander would want to risk the chief's discovering the problems first.

Conclusion

An organization exists for a purpose. In order to achieve that purpose it must organize itself into boxes, assign tasks, and prioritize functions. Once it sets out to produce results the administration needs to verify how well it is doing. Inspection is the key to this process. The key ingredient of any such process of monitoring and control is the commitment of the chief to the task; the chief executive must believe in the process or it will fail.

Anthony V. Bouza

Intelligence

"Intelligence" is knowledge of past, present, and proposed community conditions, potential problems, and criminal activity. Intelligence may be nothing more than information that is credible and warns of potential danger; it is also the product of a complex process involving an informed judgment, a state of affairs, or a single fact. The "intelligence process" describes the handling of information and its conversion into material that is useful for law enforcement.

What Is "Useful Intelligence for Law Enforcement?"

When presented in terms of political intrigue and the sensational world of Hollywood melodramas, law enforcement may seem to be an endless "fishing expedition," the compilation of personal data that routinely infringes upon citizens' rights to privacy. Proper deployment of intelligence personnel, in contrast, protects people from organized criminal elements. Operations may focus on groups that tend to be violent or engage in activity that unlawfully disrupts citizens' lives.

In its "Report on Police" the National Advisory Commission on Criminal Justice Standards and Goals stated that

> because of the nature of organized criminal activity and the problems involving civil disorder, every police agency should develop and maintain the capability to gather and evaluate information and to disseminate intelligence to the proper sources. Organized criminal activity and civil disorder are not restricted to limited geographic areas but are widespread and highly mobile. Statewise systems must be able to interact with each other as well as with the national law enforcement intelligence unit. Wherever possible, intelligence operations directed toward organized crime and civil disorder should be separate, corroborating but never merging. . . .

Traditionally, the concept of civil disorder in this country has focused on racial unrest, student uprisings, and labor-union strikes. The comforting belief that "terrorism" happens elsewhere is no longer tenable. International terrorism hits Americans abroad and at various targets within the United States. Terrorism is a clandestine network of related events, whether loosely or closely organized. By studying who and what has been attacked, law-enforcement offices can deduce likely future targets, their locations, and the most effective precautionary measures. Thus the need exists to collect and analyze information.

The intelligence function of a police agency gathers information about activities of individuals or groups engaged in crime. The process that turns this basic intelligence into usable data involves evaluation, analysis, and then dissemination of the resulting material to key units within the law-enforcement agency. Those units may then use the information for reference, as a warning of things to come, or as an indication of criminal activities in the developmental stage.

Categories of Intelligence

There are two broad and sometimes overlapping categories of intelligence: tactical and strategic. *Tactical intelligence* contributes directly to achievement of a specific law-enforcement objective. It may be the receipt of a lead by an investigator, compilation of a list of potential surveillance subjects, or recording the activities of a loan shark. It may be as simple as passing a fact from one police intelligence unit to another. For example, an officer from one unit may pass along information on subject X and indicate that X is an associate of subject Y. Simple information becomes tactical intelligence if the requesting unit is assembling a file on a particular subject with a view to apprehending a suspect or suspects.

Strategic intelligence differs from tactical intelligence in that it deals with larger issues that concern top decision-makers of the law-enforcement agency, rather than the "nuts and bolts" of intelligence support that the investigator or patrol officer on the street needs to do his or her job. An example of strategic intelligence would be a report on the growth of organized crime that gave senior law-enforcement officials a complete picture of the strength, influence, and effectiveness of organized criminal activity within their own and neighboring jurisdictions.

"Organized crime" may be defined as criminal activity conducted by two or more persons, members of either a conglomerate arrangement, or a monolithic system. Organized crime has also been defined as a self-perpetuating conspiracy designed to wring exorbitant profits from society by any means. Organized crime is not restricted to a few selected crimes committed by a particular group of individuals; no type of crime is excluded from the workings of organized crime.

Inherent in the basic responsibilities of all law-enforcement agencies is the maintenance of public order, which includes both law enforcement and peacekeeping functions. Public disorder may include ideologically motivated illegal acts that cause bodily injury or property damage, interfere with the operations of government agencies or the lawful activities of organizations or individuals, or threaten the security of public buildings, the public's access to public facilities, or public security. Intelligence functions used to identify individuals or organizations advocating or fomenting public disorder are designed to protect citizens against unlawful acts.

Structure of the Intelligence Function
The intelligence function is traditionally structured as follows:

- Federal system—the Justice Department.
- State systems—independent state intelligence agencies.
- Regional systems—based on territorial need.
- Local systems—on a countrywide or citywide basis.

The Federal System. Divisions and bureaus within the Department of Justice are involved in a coordinated national intelligence-gathering effort. Federal agencies generally use the task- or strike-force concept to combat organized crime and public disorder. Basically, this concept calls for the use of several departments within the department to conduct follow-up investigations, develop intelligence, and, where required, prosecute in courts of law.

The State System. State systems gather, analyze, store, and disseminate intelligence. State intelligence systems vary in structure and authority. For example, Florida's Bureau of Law Enforcement is a statewide agency that engages in extensive intelligence activity. The Organized Crime Intelligence Branch of the Division of Law Enforcement of the California Department of Justice also provides excellent support and intelligence at the state level. Another example is the Michigan Intelligence Network (MIN), established by the Michigan Association of Chiefs of Police, Michigan Sheriffs' Association, and the Michigan State Police.

Regional Systems. A multistate or multi-jurisdictional system of intelligence gathering may provide unique advantages based on such factors as topography, cultural similarities, and cost-sharing. Consequently, some regional systems have been formed on both a formal and an informal basis to provide a means of exchange intelligence.

Local Systems. As a general guideline, every local law-enforcement agency with more than seventy-five employees has a full-time intelligence capability. In agencies with fewer than seventy-five members, designation of an officer to seek intelligence assistance from regional or state resources and encourage intelligence efforts within the agency is the alternative to a formal unit.

Intelligence operations are usually centralized. Decentralization requires more manpower; surveillance capabilities decrease; efforts become fragmented because of the wide distribution of manpower; and effective communication of criminal activities is hampered.

Placement of the Intelligence Function and Planning
Quality of intelligence depends on a number of factors. Perhaps the most important of these is separation of the intelligence function from operations. In most agencies, the intelligence unit reports directly to the police chief, eliminating the possibility of intelligence data being altered or lost as it filters through various command levels. As a staff organization, the intelligence unit is a part of the process of strategy formation, but not a proponent of a particular approach.

The management, personnel, records, and operations of the organized crime-intelligence unit are generally separate from those of the public disorder intelligence operation. Administration of the intelligence function requires sound planning, staffing, directing, and controlling. A system is generally developed for the accurate collection of information from non-intelligence units, other intelligence units, and sources outside law-enforcement agencies. Specific criteria are also developed for the selection of officers assigned to the intelligence unit.

Administration of the intelligence function requires proper controls to be established for the purpose of sensing deviations from agency policy. A mandatory requirement is that information be arranged so as to allow rapid and effective access and analysis. Files should be thoroughly cross-referenced and organized functionally as well as biographically.

File categories include organized crime, corruption, firearms violations, gambling, hijacking, labor, legitimate business (fronting for organized crime), loan-sharking, Mafia/Cosa Nostra/Syndicate, murder, narcotics, pornography, and prostitution. Separate files are maintained on persons and organizations relating to public disorder and terrorism. Files may also be kept on dates that have been or may become an occasion for disorder and on potential victims who have been or are likely to become targets for attacks.

Analysis of Intelligence Information

Incoming information is analyzed to indicate patterns, networks, connections, or new areas of criminal activity. Without proper analysis, information cannot contribute effectively to the strategic purposes of the law-enforcement agency. Minus an analytical capability, much of the incoming raw information will remain just that; moreover, a great deal of information will be lost in the filing system.

Collection is divided into two general categories, overt and covert. Overt collection includes information received from intelligence investigators, nonintelligence units within law enforcement, and other sources. This may also include information obtained via complaints by persons whose status or position places them in a position to see and hear important facts concerning criminal activity. Covert collection, on the other hand, is acquisition of information from a subject who is unaware that he or she is being observed or overheard. Covert collection involves physical surveillance of suspected members of the criminal community without their knowledge, as well as electronic surveillance and use of informers and undercover investigators.

Hypothesis is an effective and important intelligence tool. Basically, the analyst studies available information, tries to assemble it into a logical pattern, and develops tentative statements that appear to describe the operation under review. If the information is limited and poorly related, several possible hypotheses may be developed. Efforts are then made to test the reliability of information on which the hypotheses are based. Effectiveness depends upon there being a formal, permanent arrangement for the flow of raw information to reach the intelligence unit from all possible sources. These sources include intelligence officers, technical collection devices, other reporting elements within or outside law-enforcement agencies, public and official records, and information from the private sector.

Field reports from investigators of other officers cannot be thought of as "intelligence" until they have been evaluated, compared with

data on file, and possibly combined with other information. Documentation of this input is designed to solicit the type and nature of information required by the unit for meaningful evaluation.

In most law-enforcement agencies with an intelligence function, continual review of the successes, failures, and general operation of the unit is necessary to ensure conformity with department goals and objectives. The necessity of ensuring that the intelligence function serves the needs of the entire agency, and the community that agency seeks to serve, imposes special burdens on those who are responsible for organization and planning.

Joseph C. DeLadurantey

Bibliography

Bouza, Anthony V. *Police Intelligence: The Operating of an Investigative Unit.* New York: AMS Press, 1976.

DeLadurantey, Joseph C., and Daniel R. Sullivan. *Criminal Investigation Standards.* New York: Harper & Row, 1980.

Schultz, Donald O., and Loran A. Norton. *Police Operational Intelligence.* Springfield, IL: Charles C. Thomas, 1973.

U.S. Congress. Senate. Committee on the Judiciary. Subcommittee on Criminal Laws and Procedures. *The Erosion of Law Enforcement Intelligence and Its Impact on the Public Safety.* Washington, DC: Government Printing Office, 1978.

International Police Cooperation

The intensity of international law-enforcement cooperation has greatly accelerated in recent years, although some forms of police cooperation among independent states are as old as professional police forces. Throughout modern European history, there have been contacts among police authorities across international frontiers. In the mid-eighteenth century the legendary lieutenant-general of the Paris police, Sartine, the Comte d'Alby, was consulted by the pope. The police of the emperors of Austria police under Chancellor Metternich (1814–1848) had an elaborate network of agents, especially in the German states and in Switzerland. The czarist secret police, the Okhrana, had a much feared international organization until about the time of World War I. Although these contacts and networks were essentially concerned with "high policing"—in other words, state security—they and other liaisons dealt with "low policing" as well, mainly the fugitive and itinerant criminal, pirates, bandits, and smugglers.

Since the seventeenth century, there has been a process of differentiation and specialization of police functions in Europe. Distinctions have been made between internal and external security; the police have been separated from military forces (although not fully in countries with gendarmeries); and specialized corps for criminal investigation, public order, and other forms of policing have been established. This process has spread through much of the world, spurred on by the social changes generated by industrialization and economic modernization resulting in different patterns of policing in different countries. This has complicated the business of international police cooperation. But the need felt by police authorities for this cooperation has greatly increased with economic and social change. Indeed, virtually all the factors which, in the nineteenth and twentieth centuries, have been associated with the growing prosperity of the highly developed countries—urbanization, rapid mass transportation systems, almost instantaneous communications, the development and integration of international markets in commodities, manufacturing and financial institutions—have contributed to the growth of international criminality, both petty and sophisticated. These factors have assisted the mobility of criminals, the transportation of illegal substances, the organization of complex conspiracies, and provided new opportunities for theft, fraud, and the disposal of the profits of crime. Certain conditions also allow the growth of international criminality, such as the lack of stable political authority and social dislocation, which presently prevails in parts of the former Soviet Union and Eastern Europe. Measures to repress new forms of crime have always lagged behind the activities of criminals, and this has particularly been the case in crime with an international dimension.

The types of cooperation introduced to combat the increasing problems posed by transfrontier or international criminality can be classified as bilateral, global, and regional. The modes of cooperation are formalized liaison, coordination institutions, and probate or unofficial investigation. The obstacles to cooperation are the diversity of police systems, the diversity of criminal jurisdictions and legal systems, the doctrine of sovereignty, deeply held feelings and beliefs about political independence and the sacredness of state territory, and the divergence of interests and policy of the states participating in the international system.

Bilateral Cooperation
This is the oldest and remains, in many respects, the most important type of police cooperation. It has frequently been based on informal understandings among police forces in neighboring countries. The texts of bilateral police treaties, which first appeared in the nineteenth century and have become increasingly common in the last twenty-five years, seldom give an accurate impression of the significance and the value of this cooperation. The scope of the agreements, as the model agreement prepared by Interpol in 1975 illustrates, is potentially very wide. They can cover the exchange of general police information concerning matters such as traffic accidents, missing or stolen property; the exchange of crime prevention information about the operating methods of criminals; the movements of people who are suspected of crimes or who are in need of protection; the surveillance of suspected persons or vehicles; and the reporting of the transport of dangerous substances. Cooperation in criminal investigations can consist in the exchange of information or providing evidence to establish proof of an offense; exchanging police investigation records; police officers advising or participating in an enquiry in the cooperating country; and arrangements for the hot pursuit of offenders across international boundaries. Agreements can include the naming of police authorities competent to engage in transfrontier cooperation, the arrangements for cooperation such as the location and frequency of meetings, the methods of communication between the cooperating police forces, the role of the National Central Bureaus of Interpol, the form of the request to enter the territory of another state, the regulations concerning the use of vehicles and the carrying of firearms, the civil liabilities of police in foreign countries, and many other details.

In practice, police treaties or agreements usually include some, but never all, these items. The agreements may not have the solemnity of international treaties but can take the form of semiconfidential protocols or the exchange of letters of understanding. They sometimes appear to be drafted with a view to restricting the scope of contacts rather than facilitating cooperation between police forces—an example is the 1977 Franco-German police agreement. On occasion agreements about police cooperation, such as the 1964 German Federal Republic-Tunisia agreement and the 1972 Swiss-Austrian Treaty, have been attached as codicils to treaties concerned mainly with extradition or mutual legal assistance in criminal matters and, in these cases, contain very little substance about the form of police cooperation. On other occasions, agreements are limited to a specific form of criminal activity—most frequently arrangements for the suppression of drug trafficking. One type of agreement is virtually universal among neighboring friendly countries—the arrangements for policing land frontiers. In all cases, bilateral international agreements may be abrogated by one of the partners on the grounds that national interests are at stake.

One form of police cooperation which has been increasing in importance in recent years is the exchange or the unilateral posting of police liaison officers for extended tours of duty in foreign countries. In the wake of World War II, the United States pioneered the practice of having law-enforcement officers (as distinct from intelligence agents, state security officers, and embassy security personnel) as attachés. The large number of law-enforcement agencies at the federal level in the United States led to a proliferation of police officers on overseas postings—the FBI, the DEA, U.S. Customs, the Internal Revenue Service, the Secret Service, the Immigration and Naturalization Service (all with police powers and powers of arrest in the United States)—can be found in some large embassies. This large law-enforcement presence is sometimes a sensitive political matter in host countries; the entrepreneurial style of activities of some United States law-enforcement officials (the DEA in particular) can be viewed as constituting an infringement of sovereignty.

The FBI, under J. Edgar Hoover, was the first in the field of establishing overseas representation in the aftermath of World War II, partly for counterintelligence purposes and partly to combat organized crime. It continues to maintain contact with foreign police forces through Legats (legal attachés) in major embassies. In the annual Justice Department submission to Congress arguments defending the FBI budget state that the Legats play crucial roles in counterintelligence and in the fight against international organized crime. The number of FBI agents overseas is dwarfed by those of the DEA, which maintains over sixty permanent offices in forty-three countries. The DEA and its supporters believe that intelligence-gathering in source and transit countries reduces the importation of drugs into the United States. Its critics maintain that the supply of drugs to the U.S. market has not been significantly reduced, despite the large DEA effort (supplemented by U.S. Customs, the Border Patrol, state and local police forces, as well as by the CIA and U.S. Armed Forces (the two latter called in by President Reagan to help in the "war against drugs"). The more flamboyant Latin American operations of the DEA which, inter alia, have included the kidnapping of drug traffickers in foreign jurisdictions and bringing them to the United States for trial, and the joint operations with police and military in Latin American countries to destroy drug crops, have not always been well-regarded by other members of the law-enforcement community. In Europe, the use of paid informers, involvement through intermediaries in transactions concerning drugs, and the technique of controlled delivery have been regarded as being in the gray area between legality and illegality or sometimes being in direct contravention of the law. United States pressure and the 1988 Vienna Convention on drugs have, however, been modifying European attitudes and legislation in this regard.

The other two federal agencies prominently involved in international affairs have less extensive overseas representation—U.S. Customs in recent years has had about seventy officials in twelve embassies, and the Secret Service has only one large overseas office in Paris (with subordinate officers in Rome and London), which covers ninety countries in Europe, America, and the Middle East. The U.S. Customs Department has criminal law-enforcement responsibilities in areas such as drugs, child pornography, cargo theft, insurance fraud, and until the end of the Cold War, in the export of "critical technology" (advanced technology with important military applications) to the Soviet bloc countries. It was the most influential agency in COCOM (Coordinating Committee for Export Controls), which is based in Paris and coordinated multilateral action on this effort. It has also been increasingly involved in the Brussels-based Customs Cooperation Council. However, the failure of all but a few countries to ratify the 1977 Nairobi Convention on Mutual Administrative Assistance for Customs

Offenses reduces the quality of cooperation in this area.

The practice of police liaison officers in foreign postings has spread from the United States to countries as far apart as Canada, Japan, and Israel. It was relatively slow to develop in Europe where some foreign ministries took a negative view. The French Technical Service for International Police Cooperation (the SCTIP) has, since the 1960s, developed an impressive international network for advising on police techniques, equipment, and training. In 1971 France and the United States reached agreement on arrangements to combat the so-called French connection (the flow of mainly Turkish opium, which is refined into heroin in the Marseilles area for onward shipment to the United States); this agreement allowed for the exchange of liaison officers, and in 1986 it was extended to include Canada and Italy. In the 1980s drug liaison officers were also sent out from various European countries to Bolivia, Pakistan, Thailand, Cyprus, and the Netherlands, but they were fewer in number and had a lower profile than the DEA. In the mid-1980s, liaison officers specializing in terrorism were exchanged among France, Italy, and Germany. Since then the number of liaison officers has grown quickly, and increasingly they have become generalists rather than specialists. One of the objectives of intergovernmental cooperation in the European Community (EC), expressed particularly in the 1990 Trevi Action Program, is to both encourage and bring some order into the liaison officer system.

The liaison officer system has advantages because it allows direct personal contact among law-enforcement officers in different countries. This can expedite investigations, particularly by putting investigating officers in touch with the right authorities in the cooperating country. The good liaison officer can be a valuable resource in helping to clear up misunderstandings, and provide information about a foreign jurisdiction and its crime investigation and control policies. Sending police officers on temporary mission for the purposes of particular enquiries is not usually regarded as an adequate substitute for liaison officers, because often they cannot acquire sufficient information about the country to which they are visiting in the time available. The main way in which things go wrong is when liaison officers pursue enquiries in a foreign jurisdiction on their own initiative.

Global Cooperation

Multilateral global law enforcement is primarily coordinated by Interpol, but the United Nations and the Customs Cooperation Council also play a role. Interpol is the only global organization with an operational role; it provides a system of multilateral communication of police information when the secretary general initiates an inquiry; it does not, of course, have any executive police powers in any of the member states.

The origins of Interpol immediately predate World War I and may be traced to the international police conference held in 1914 under the patronage of Prince Albert of Monaco. The participants were drawn from a wide range of relevant professional groups—judges, magistrates, criminologists, civil servants, and members of parliaments with police officers in a small minority. The conference did not have immediate outcomes because of the outbreak of the war, but a second conference, dominated this time by police officers, was called in Vienna in 1923, which led to the setting up of the International Criminal Police Commission (ICPC) with its headquarters in the Austrian capital. The ICPC was taken over by the Nazis in 1938, but it was revived at a conference held in Brussels in 1946 because of the urgent need for communication among police forces in different countries in the disturbed conditions of postwar Europe. Fourteen of the seventeen participating nations in the 1946 conference were European and the revived ICPC was dominated by its European founders, especially by France, where the headquarters were established, long after the nations of other continents became a majority of the membership.

For more than a quarter of a century after it was revived in 1946, the ICPC had very modest resources. But it acquired new statutes in 1956 and with the statutes its present title—the International Criminal Police Organization (ICPO)—Interpol. It took possession of a purpose-built headquarters building in Saint Cloud in 1967, although it moved from there to a much more secure and imposing building in Lyons in 1989. A headquarters agreement was negotiated in 1972 and, when this proved inadequate, another was negotiated in 1982, which came into force in 1984, granting important legal immunities in France. Interpol gradually came to be recognized as a public international organization. This came as a result of participation of the general secretariat in the United

Nations, its mention in a number of international treaties concerning mutual legal assistance, its recognition as an international organization in the United States by presidential order in 1983, and other, less important, legal instruments of national and international law. Although the rights of individuals are secured by the 1984 headquarters agreement with France—a supervisory board can check on the data in the Interpol files and investigate complaints that Interpol may have communicated false information about them—some observers consider the lack of a treaty basis for the organization detracts from its authority and legitimacy.

Athough the organization is almost universally accepted as an intergovernmental organization, the lack of an international treaty or convention means that there is very little involvement of the political or ministerial level of government in its affairs. Delegates to the annual General Assembly are either serving police officers or officials in the relevant ministries. The organization is subject to relatively little political interference but lacks the political influence that ministerial involvement would give. There is also an ever-present possibility that governments will establish overlapping or competing organizations. Additionally, there is no solemn undertaking on the part of states to pay subscriptions or to cooperate in the communication of information about crime and criminals. There are skeptics who doubt whether an international treaty would bring benefits in terms of practical cooperation or increased resources to the organization. There has been no genuine lack of funds in recent years, particularly since the revival of United States interest in the organization, which coincided with President Reagan's term of office and increased with the election of John Simpson, chief of the U.S. Secret Service, to the presidency of Interpol in 1985. Political attacks on the organization have diminished in recent years—criticism made by members of or sympathizers to the Ron L. Hubbard's Church of Scientology, subsequently the Church of the New Comprehension, declined in virulence and frequency through the 1980s. Criticism within the law-enforcement community, with the exception of the American Association of Chiefs of Police, has been less frequent since Raymond Kendall assumed office as secretary general in 1985. Interpol has radically upgraded its computer and communications equipment, become more open with the media, dropped its practice of noninvolvement in terrorist cases, and has generally become more adaptable in the face of changing patterns of international crime.

The United Nations plays an essential supportive role in international law enforcement. It provides an important forum in which international treaties can be negotiated, it serves as a repository for statistical and legal information about criminal matters, and it provides a modest flow of aid to improve the capacity for criminal law enforcement in less developed countries. Through the U.N. Crime and Criminal Justice Program, congresses are held in which expertise can be shared. The United Nations has played an important role in promoting conventions on subjects such as trafficking in people, treatment of prisoners, crime prevention, and human rights. Undoubtedly, its biggest influence on practical law enforcement has been in the field of drug trafficking. The work of the United Nations' Division of Narcotic Drugs, established shortly after the founding of the UN, has since January 1992 amalgamated with other antidrug activities of the UN International Drug Control Program (UNIDCP) and promoted three basic conventions—the 1961 Convention on Narcotic Drugs, the 1971 Convention on Psychotropic Drugs, and culminating in the 1988 Vienna Convention. The last was mainly concerned with law-enforcement measures and has been leading to a considerable degree efforts to harmonize legislation to this goal, especially in the wealthier countries. This has been supported by the action of the Group of Seven (G7–periodic meetings of the seven most highly developed countries), which has supported measures against money laundering, including the setting up of a Financial Action Task Force in the Organization for Economic Cooperation and Development (OECD). This organization has done much to help break the barriers of commercial and banking secrecy to police investigations. In normal circumstances the direct contact between operational police officers and these global organizations is infrequent and of a modest nature. An example is the work of the UN Fund for Drug Abuse Control (UNFDAC—now also amalgamated in the UNIDCP), which in the late 1980s provided $600,000 in cooperation with Interpol for a Caribbean telecommunications network to combat the transit of drugs through the area. The work of these global organizations is of paramount importance to international police cooperation because disparity of legal systems and lack of effective legal instruments are often the reasons for the ineffectiveness or weakness of this cooperation.

Regional Cooperation

In the Americas there is much law-enforcement interaction on a multilateral basis through the regional meetings of Interpol, the International Drug Enforcement Conference, the Organization of American States, and other fora, but very little of this involves police operations. Operational cooperation is, at present, almost entirely on a bilateral basis, and most of it is initiated by the United States. The inauguration of the North American Free Trade Agreement may, in the longer term, result in systematic multilateral cooperation, but there are many obstacles in its path. Apart from interesting developments within the Association of South East Asian National, this applies also to other continents. The exception is Western Europe, where there have been moves toward institutionalized forms of law-enforcement cooperation over the last two decades.

Although it is now undergoing a review, the cornerstone of European police cooperation has been the Trevi Group—the regular meeting of the Ministers of Justice and the Interior of the EC countries originally set up in 1975 to coordinate measures against terrorism. Within the Trevi system four committees were established: Trevi 1 manages the secure communications link for passing sensitive terrorist-related intelligence among the twelve member countries; Trevi 2 exchanges information about police techniques, training, and equipment; Trevi 3 is a forum for discussing serious crime other than terrorism; and Trevi 4 is the "1992" committee concerned with coordinating the measures made necessary by the proposed abolition of frontier controls. An important landmark in the history of Trevi was the 1990 Action Program, which contained an impressive list of forms of cooperation in combating drug trafficking. Included among these is cooperation in controlled delivery, the use of joint investigating teams, and training and research programs; the problem of transfrontier and serious crime is addressed in Article 4 of the program; and the system of exchange of liaison officers among member countries is outlined in some detail in Article 9.

The Trevi form of cooperation did not go far enough for some governments, notably the German government. The idea of Europol (originally characterized as a European FBI) was championed by Chancellor Kohl of Germany. He argued that systematic operational cooperation among police forces was a necessary concommittant of the dismantling of frontier controls and the establishment of a closer European union. A ministerial meeting of Trevi in December 1991 decided to set up a European Drugs Unit with a wider remit than envisaged in the 1990 Action Program. In the same month the text of the Maastricht Treaty was approved by the governments of the twelve EC member states. Article 8A of this treaty explicitly acknowledges the German lead in the field of police cooperation by confirming the proposals made by Germany earlier in the year; endorsing developments in the fields of coordination of investigation and search procedures; the creation of databases; the analysis of criminal intelligence on a Europe-wide basis; joint crime prevention strategies; and measures relating to further training, research, forensic matters, and criminal records departments. In Strasbourg the twelve countries set up a "Europol Project Team" in September 1992 to work out a system of general police coordination and cooperation before the treaty was ratified. The setting up of Europol is (at the time of this writing) delayed because the meeting of EC heads of state and government has not yet agreed on the location of the organization.

The present position of operational police cooperation within the EC is complicated by the decision in 1985 by five of the original members to sign the Schengen Agreement, which has set up policing measures in light of dismantling frontier controls on goods and persons envisaged in the Single European Act of the same year. A second Schengen Agreement was signed in 1990 spelling out more operational details. Eventually, nine out of the twelve members of the EC joined the Schengen system—the three who exclude themselves are Britain, Ireland, and Denmark. Essentially, the Schengen system provides the instruments that allow the external frontiers (i.e., frontiers with non-EC countries) to be policed effectively and to allow quick responses to any urgent law-enforcement problem that might arise involving member countries with open borders (these are now described as internal borders). The first objective is to be achieved mainly by means of an online database, the Schengen Information System (SIS), established in Strasbourg and containing information such as wanted persons or persons in need of protection, prohibited immigrants, and stolen or suspected vehicles. The second objective is sought through an emergency operations system called the Sirène, which will consist of national offices receiving calls for immediate operational action in all member countries, staffed by police officers and by lawyers, who will check on the legality of the action requested.

The Schengen Agreements have been the target of some criticism by civil liberties groups, members of national parliament, and the European parliament, at least in part because of the allegedly secret way in which the agreements had been negotiated. The main questions are how the SIS will relate to Europol and, with the European Information System, which is being developed in the Trevi Group, how the nonmember countries—Britain, Denmark, and Ireland—will be associated with Schengen. The relationship between Interpol and the new multilateral systems of cooperation also presents some difficulties. In order to gain credibility with the law-enforcement community Europol will have to demonstrate that it can provide services that Interpol cannot. The present situation is one of transition, and there is no certainty about how the outstanding questions will be resolved. Few, however, doubt that the European Community will develop closer and more integrated operational police cooperation in order to confront shared law-enforcement problems.

Problems and Prospects of Cooperation
Specific problems vary according to the mode of cooperation, but there are general difficulties that confront all forms of cooperation. Formalized liaisons, such as the bilateral exchange of liaison officers or the multilateral committee of the Trevi Group, are useful, but their effectiveness depends on political willingness to cooperate and release information. They have no direct role in police operations and are not backed by legal instruments that are enforceable in the courts. The institutional form of cooperation can have an operational role, and in the case of Interpol this is the invaluable communications network. Institutions can be endowed with legal powers, but in sovereign states there has been and remains a reluctance to hand over police powers (defined as the power to investigate crimes and arrest of criminals) to international institutions. International institutions

often seem remote and lethargic to the ordinary police officer. The methods of the private investigator—going into foreign jurisdictions without any legal authority, but often with the cooperation of the foreign authorities to investigate suspects and criminal acts—are often an essential element of the investigation of complex cases. In the past this was actually done by private investigators, such as the well-known Pinkerton agents in the nineteenth and early twentieth centuries. In contemporary circumstances, the actions of DEA officials in conducting surveillance and in paying informers come into this category. These activities run the risk of crossing the boundary into illegality and creating tensions among states. A graphic illustration of this was the torture and murder of undercover DEA agent Camera in Mexico in 1985. The case became notorious in 1990 when the U.S. government arranged for the kidnapping on Mexican territory of one of those suspected of involvement in the murder. The U.S. Supreme Court ruled narrowly that this did not violate the United States–Mexican Extradition Treaty. Mexican opinion was outraged by the cavalier infringement of Mexican territorial and sovereign rights, while the DEA accused the Mexican authorities of repeatedly protecting traffickers.

In general, the obstacles to international cooperation are legal, organizational, and operational. The classic, long-standing legal difficulty is the delay, expense, and technicalities involved in extraditing persons and evidence from one jurisdiction to another. Extradition of persons often fails, even between neighboring countries such as Britain and Ireland, which have the same legal tradition, because the form of the request does not satisfy the authorities of the country to whom the request is made or for reasons of policy. Countries routinely have legislation (for example, eight out of the twelve members of the European Community at the time of this writing) that forbids the extradition of their own nationals to other jurisdictions to stand trial. Extradition is often refused on the basis of doubts about the possibility of a fair trial, fears of an inappropriate punishment, or for reasons of foreign policy. There are other formidable legal obstacles. Joint operations performed by police forces of different countries are often made very difficult by different police powers, different police–judiciary relations, and different criminal procedures. What are called joint operations are often national enquiries with the advice and support of police officers from another jurisdiction. No country yet allows police officers from another country to exercise police powers on their territory.

Difficulties also occur because police forces are organized in very different ways in different countries. The militarized police forces of the southern part of Europe—the Gendarmerie Nationale, the Guardia Civil, the Carabinieri—have no counterparts in the Anglo-American tradition. The independent local police forces in the United Kingdom have no parallels in most European countries. These factors make it difficult for police officials to understand the professional ethos of foreign forces and their modus operandi when they come into contact. When direct relations are established in frontier regions, for example, it is frequently difficult to find equivalent officials in the respective police forces who can liaise with one another. The interface between police and political authorities also creates difficulties both within and among jurisdictions. When police officers suspect that their opposing counterparts are controlled too tightly by politicians or too inclined to take instruction from them, cooperation is likely to be withheld.

Operational difficulties in cooperation are usually highly specific. They can include the lack of efficient communication because of a lack of equipment or of a mutually comprehensible language, less commitment in pursuing an enquiry on the one side rather than the other; and the absence of a common policy in investigating particular forms of crime. For example, in France the police have a policy of never allowing a ransom to be paid for a kidnapped victim, whatever the circumstances. It is claimed that this policy has had an important deterrent effect, a view supported by the sharp decline in this type of offense. The Netherlands police, on the other hand, often allow a ransom to be paid so that a surveillance operation can be mounted to increase the chances of apprehending the criminal. When the Netherlands police asked the French authorities to mount a surveillance operation on the payment of a ransom in a Strasbourg hotel, this request was refused. Analogous refusals have been made in the area of controlled delivery of goods, because in many European jurisdictions in the past, a police officer could refrain from taking action if he or she knew that a crime was being committed.

None of these legal, organizational, and operational difficulties is insuperable. They are well known and taken into account throughout the developed world through improved training, more international contacts, and the greatly increased problem posed by international crime. Ignorance of the problem is no longer a barrier to improved cooperation. But the sine qua non of improvement is political stability based on cooperative political relations among states. If improvements are to gain legitimacy and win acceptance, they must be transparent, and those who operate them must be accountable in a way that guarantees the respect of individual rights.

Malcolm Anderson

Bibliography

Anderson, Malcolm. *Policing the World: Interpol and the Politics of International Police Co-Operation.* Oxford: Clarendon Press, 1989.

Bayley, David H. *Patterns of Policing: A Comparative International Analysis.* New Brunswick, NJ: Rutgers University Press, 1985.

Den Boer, M. "European Policing after 1922." *Journal of Common Market Studies* 31 (1993): 3–28.

Fignaut, C., ed. *The Internationalization of Police Cooperation in Western Europe.* The Netherlands: Gouda Quint and Kluwer, 1993.

———, and R.H. Hermans, eds. *Police Cooperation in Europe.* The Netherlands: Lochem, 1987.

Fooner, Michael. *Interpol: Issues in World Crime and International Criminal Justice.* New York: Plenum Press, 1989.

International Criminal Police Review. Official Publication of the International Criminal Police Organization and Interpol, 1946–.

Interpol: Global Help in the Fight Against Drugs, Terrorists, Counterfeiters. Washington, DC: U.S. Department of Justice, National Institute of Justice, 1985.

Meldal-Johnsen, Trevor, and Vaughn Young. *The Interpol Connection: An Enquiry into the International Criminal Police Organization.* New York: Dial Press, 1979.

Nadelmann, Ethan A. *Cops across Borders: The Internationalization of U.S. Criminal Law Enforcement.* University Park: Pennsylvania State University Press, 1993.

*United States Participation in Interpol, the
International Criminal Police Organization*. Washington, DC: Department of
the Treasury, General Accounting Office,
1976.

Interrogation

An interview is a nonaccusatory conversation in
which, through question and answer, the police
interviewer tries to develop investigative and
behavioral information that will test the veracity of statements made by a suspect, victim, or
witness. Interrogation, in contrast, is an accu-
satory procedure designed to elicit from the
subject an acknowledgment that he or she did
not tell the truth during an initial statement,
whether that person be a suspect who originally
denied involvement in the issue under investigation, or a victim who fabricated the nature of
the alleged offense.

Preliminaries
Privacy is the principal psychological factor
contributing to the successful outcome of an
interview or interrogation. Typically, interrogator and suspect sit in similar chairs, directly
facing each other approximately five feet apart,
without any physical barrier (such as a desk)
between them. Furthermore, the interrogator
tries to minimize distractions that may disrupt
privacy, such as phones ringing or interruptions
by other people entering the room.

In a custodial setting, the interrogator must
advise the suspect of his or her rights and obtain the proper waiver before asking any questions. If it is not a custodial setting no warnings
are required. The 1966 U.S. Supreme Court
decision in *Miranda v. Arizona* (384 U.S. 436)
established the rule that before a person in police custody (or otherwise deprived of freedom
"in any significant way") could be interrogated,
he or she must be given the following warnings:

1. That he has the right to remain silent and
   that he need not answer any questions;
2. That if he does answer questions his answers can be used as evidence against
   him;
3. That he has a right to consult with a
   lawyer before or during the questioning
   of him by police;
4. That if he cannot afford to hire a lawyer
   one will be provided for him without
   cost.

All of the warnings must be given in such a
way that the suspect clearly understands what
he or she is being told, and the interrogation
may be started only if he or she has indicated
willingness to answer questions. The interrogator is not allowed to talk the suspect out of
his or her refusal to talk. If at any time the
suspect says that he or she wants a lawyer the
interrogation must cease; the interrogator cannot talk the suspect out of his or her desire for
a lawyer.

In the 1979 case of *North Carolina v. Butler* (441 U.S. 369) the U.S. Supreme Court ruled
that the waiver needed before initiating any
questions does not have to be a written one; an
oral waiver is sufficient.

In the 1976 case of *Beckwith v. United
States* (452 U.S. 341, 347) the U.S. Supreme
Court held that focus of suspicion does not require the issuance of the warnings, only custody.

Interrogation of a suspect occurs only
after a nonaccusatory interview and when
the investigator is reasonably certain of the
suspect's involvement in the issue under investigation.

The Positive Confrontation
Most interrogators enter the interview/interro-
gation room with a file summarizing results of
the investigation. After an exchange of greet-
ings, the interrogator confronts the suspect with
a statement of guilt. This type of accusation is
made only when the suspect's guilt seems very
clear. Otherwise, the statement should be less
direct. Following this confrontation, the interrogator pauses to evaluate the suspect's reaction
to the statement. Then the interrogator responds by repeating the initial statement of involvement, places the investigation file aside,
sits down directly opposite the suspect, and
makes the transition to a sympathetic and understanding person.

Theme Development
The interrogator then presents "moral justification" for the suspect's criminal behavior. One
way of doing this is to place moral blame for an
illegal activity on another person or an outside
set of circumstances. This appeals to a basic
aspect of human nature. Many people tend to
minimize responsibility for their actions by
placing blame on someone or something else.
The interrogator suggests in a theft case, for
example, that the suspect was not paid enough

by an employer or that someone left money where it was an open temptation. Often the suspect will say that other employees also stole, thereby making him or her just one of several thieves. Other moral justifications for criminal behavior include unusual family expenses, desperate circumstances, a friend came up with the idea, retribution for an argument, or alcohol/drug dependency.

The interrogator presents this moral justification in a sympathetic and understanding way; an interest in working with the suspect to resolve the problem breaks the ice. The justification is voiced in a monologue, not giving the suspect an opportunity to speak until he or she is at the point of admitting guilt.

Handling Denials

The more often the suspect denies guilt, the more difficult it becomes for him or her to admit guilt later. Therefore, the interrogator interjects a blocking statement whenever the suspect enters an "I didn't do it" plea. By keeping fast and hard to theme development, the interrogator weakens the guilty suspect's denials. Many guilty people will change from a defensive position to an offensive one—offering objections. The innocent suspect, however, will generally not ask to make a statement. Instead, he or she will, without any display of etiquette, promptly and unequivocally maintain innocence. An innocent suspect never moves past this denial stage. He or she remains steadfast in the assertion of innocence.

Overcoming Objections

Most suspects' objection statements can be categorized into two general groups: 1. trait objections ("I loved her," or "I wasn't brought up that way," or "A person who would do something like that is really sick"); and 2. factual objections ("I don't even own a gun," or "I didn't even know him," or "I don't need the money"). Statements from either group are feeble explanations even when they may be partly true. In any event, the interrogator should not argue with the suspect over the statement or show surprise or irritation. Such a reaction discourages the suspect, who perceives that he or she has made the wrong statement, or at least an ineffective one. If the interrogator overcomes a suspect's objections, the suspect often withdraws into a shell and focuses on impending punishment.

Keeping a Suspect's Attention

Following the objection stage, the guilty suspect often becomes pensive, apathetic, and quiet. It is most important during this stage that the interrogator procures the suspect's attention so that he or she listens to the theme (psychological justification for the suspect's behavior) and does not concentrate on punishment (which would only serve to reinforce resolve to deny the crime). To do this, the interrogator draws nearer to the suspect. This closer proximity often regains the suspect's attention, and he or she will watch and listen to the interrogator more intently. Verbally, the interrogator begins to channel the theme down to the probable alternative components.

Handling Suspect's Passive Mood

At this stage, the suspect may cry, which often expresses remorse. Many other suspects do not cry but express their emotional state by assuming a defeatist posture—slumped head and shoulders, relaxed legs, and a vacant stare. In order to facilitate the impending admission of guilt, the interrogator intensifies the theme presentation and concentrates on the psychological justification for the unlawful act. Gestures of sympathy, such as a hand on the suspect's shoulder, aid truth-telling.

Presenting an Alternative Question

The alternative question is one in which the interrogator presents to the suspect two incriminatory choices concerning some aspect of the crime. Elements of the alternative are developed as logical extensions of the theme. If the theme focuses on contrasting behavior that is impulsive and spur-of-the-moment with planned and premeditated acts, the alternative question is: "Did you plan this thing out or did it just happen on the spur of the moment?" Either choice is an admission of guilt. The alternative question should be based on an assumption of guilt; it should not be a direct questions such as "Did you do this or didn't you?" A misphrased question invites denial. When the suspect accepts one alternative, he or she has made a first admission of guilt. The interrogator's task is then to develop this admission into an acceptable confession.

Having the Suspect Orally Relate Details of the Offense

The alternative question answered, the interrogator responds with a statement of reinforcement. This essentially is a statement that acknowledges the suspect's admission of guilt. The interrogator's objective is to obtain a brief oral review of the basic sequence of events, while obtaining sufficient detail to corroborate the suspect's guilt. Questions asked at this time should be brief, concise, and clear, calling only for limited verbal responses from the suspect. It is premature to ask such an all-encompassing question as "Well, just tell me everything that happened." Furthermore, questions should be open-ended and devoid of emotionally charged terminology. Once the interrogator has obtained a brief verbal statement about the crime sequence, he or she should ask detailed questions so as to obtain information that can be corroborated by subsequent investigation. After this full verbal statement has been completed, it may be necessary to return to the suspect's choice of alternatives, or to some other statement that the suspect has made, to establish his or her actual purpose and intent at the time of the crime.

Converting an Oral Confession into a Written One

After advising the suspect, the interrogator leaves the room, purportedly to check on something. The interrogator returns with a witness who may be introduced as someone who has been involved in the investigation. The interrogator then repeats the essential details of the suspect's confession, after which the witness asks a few confirming questions. Now is the time to convert an oral confession into a written one. Basically, four formats can be used:

1. A statement written by the suspect;
2. A statement written by the interrogator and read and signed by the suspect;
3. A statement taken down by a secretary or stenographer that is then transcribed into a typed document for the suspect to read and sign; or
4. A tape-recorded or video-recorded statement.

Fundamental guidelines should be followed. In a custodial setting, even though the *Miranda* warnings have been given and the appropriate waiver obtained, it is advisable to repeat the warnings at the beginning of the confession, referring to the fact that the suspect had received them earlier.

The interrogator should keep in mind that the statement of guilt must be readable and understandable by someone who is not familiar with what the suspect has done. Leading questions should be avoided, the confessor's own language should be used, and full corroboration should be established. Certainly any errors, changes, or crossed-out words should be initialed with an "OK" written in the margin by the suspect. The statement should reflect the fact that the suspect was treated properly, that no threats or promises were made, and that the statement was freely given by the suspect. When the suspect has completed reading the written statement he or she is instructed to "write your name here" (while pointing to the place for the signature). The interrogator avoids asking the suspect to "sign here" because the word "sign" connotes too much legalism. The suspect signs each page of the statement in the presence of the interrogator and a witness, who can then sign each page as well.

Obtaining the written confession at the end of interrogation is, of course, not the capstone. Every effort should be made to subject the statement to verification and to obtain the supporting evidence necessary for trial.

Joseph P. Buckley, III

Bibliography

Aubry, Arthur S., and Rudolph R. Caputo. *Criminal Interrogation.* Springfield, IL: Charles C. Thomas, 1980.

Baker, Liva. *Miranda: Crime, Law, and Politics.* New York: Atheneum, 1983.

Kamisar, Yale. *Police Interrogation and Confessions: Essays in Law and Policy.* Ann Arbor: University of Michigan Press, 1980.

Reid, John E., Fred E. Inbau, and Joseph P. Buckley. *Criminal Interrogation and Confessions.* 3d ed. Baltimore, MD: Williams and Wilkins, 1986.

Royal, Robert F., and Steven R. Schutt. *The Gentle Art of Interviewing and Interrogation: A Professional Manual and Guide.* Englewood Cliffs, NJ: Prentice-Hall, 1976.

Van Meter, C.H. *Principles of Police Interrogation.* Springfield, IL: Charles C. Thomas, 1973.

J

Jail

Jail is the point of entry into the criminal justice system, the place where arrested persons are booked and held pending court appearance if they cannot arrange bail. Jail is also the city or county detention facility for persons serving misdemeanor sentences, which in most states cannot exceed one year. Prison, on the other hand, is a state or federal institution that holds persons serving felony sentences generally running to more than one year.

The public impression is that jails hold a collection of dangerous criminals, predators who seriously threaten the lives and property of ordinary citizens. In fact, most persons incarcerated belong to a different social category. Some students of the jail politely refer to them as the poor. "American jails operate primarily as catchall asylums for poor people," says Ronald Goldfarb in *Jail: The Ultimate Ghetto of the Criminal Justice System* (1975). "With few exceptions, the prisoners are poor, undereducated, unemployed, and they belong to minority groups," adds Edith Flynn in *Prisoners in America* (1977). Other more imaginative labels for the jailed are "social refuse," "social junk," and "street people." Labels such as "riff-raff," "social trash," and "dregs" continue to suggest lack of social worth and moral depravity. Within the jail itself labeling is cruder and more derogatory.

Beyond poverty and its causes—undereducation, unemployment, and minority status—those jailed share two essential characteristics: detachment and disrepute. They are detached because they are not well integrated into conventional society, are not members of conventional social organizations, have few ties to conventional social networks, and subscribe to unconventional values and beliefs. They are disreputable because they are perceived as irksome, offensive, threatening, capable of easy arousal, even protorevolutionary. These two features—detachment and disrepute—lead the police to watch and arrest the "rabble" frequently, regardless of whether or not they are engaged in crime, or at least in serious crime. (Most of these people commit petty crimes, such as drinking on the street, and are usually vulnerable to arrest.)

The basic purpose of the jail differs radically from the purpose ascribed to it by government officials and academicians. It is this: The jail was invented and continues to be operated in order to manage society's rabble. Society's impulse to manage the rabble has many sources, but the subjectively perceived "offensiveness" of the rabble is at least as important as any real threat it poses to society.

Who Goes to Jail?

Most persons who are arrested, booked, and held in jail are not charged with serious crimes: They are charged with petty ones or with behavior that is no crime at all. In a study of San Francisco city and county jails a sample of one hundred male felony arrests, selected over a one-year period from the intake population, showed that in making arrests "offensiveness" of acts was a more important factor than crime severity. For example, there were more arrestees in jail for disturbing the peace and purse-snatching than for rape and assault (Irwin, 1985). Offensiveness is a definition that conventional witnesses or their agents (the police) impose upon events. An act performed by a disreputable person—one who is deemed worthless or of low character—is not viewed in the same way as an identical act performed by an ordinary citizen. Hollywood celebrities snorting cocaine in an expensive Malibu Beach home are viewed quite differently from lower-class Chicanos shooting heroin in a skidrow "shooting gallery."

Most prisoners are petty hustlers, derelicts, junkies, outlaws, corner boys, lowriders, and prostitutes. Membership in these visible categories makes them peculiarly liable to arrest and incarceration. The function of the jail, then, is more to manage these disreputables than to combat crime.

What Happens to People in Jail
When the police bring arrested persons to the jail, their obvious intention is that the "offenders" be held there, tried for their crimes, and, if found guilty, punished. This is the official purpose for jailing people. But, the jail—like most public institutions—has other, unstated purposes as well: These often produce undesirable, unintended consequences.

Reputable people commit crimes and are occasionally arrested, but it has never been social policy to keep them in jail while they await trial. When the jail first came into use in England in medieval times, bail to assure a court appearance was used more often than jail. Today, in addition to setting bail, most jurisdictions systematically release many persons on their own recognizance. The decision is directly related to reputability. Recently, many cities have introduced "citation" programs in which police officers may treat some misdemeanors as if they were traffic violations; they may simply issue a citation that requires the offender to pay a fine or appear in court. The decision to cite is usually discretionary and is related to repute. Consequently, when reputable people are arrested, they are almost always cited, bailed out, or released on their own recognizance. The only significant exception is when they are arrested for drunk driving, for which most state laws require a short period of detention for sobering up. Many persons who build and manage jails assume that the jail is almost exclusively for rabble.

Because many rabble are not trusted to appear at their court hearings or even to stay in jail, security has been the fundamental concern in the design of jails. This concern almost invariably results in the erection of massive buildings with complicated locking systems and elaborate surveillance. These not only increase security but also restrict prisoners' movements and form almost impassable barriers between them and outsiders. Second, because rabble are not expected to behave themselves in jail, they must be controlled; it is believed that some prisoners may harm others and destroy property. This concern for control, however, stretches far beyond protecting life and property. It extends to enforcing behavioral conformity for managerial convenience, and even beyond that. Hans Mattick in his article "The Contemporary Jails of the United States: An Unknown and Neglected Area of Justice" (1974) notes that

> Some jail administrators go overboard when it comes to the smaller details of jail security. Instead of relying on good peripheral security and the rational internal deployment of staff, they deplete the time and energies of their limited staffs by harassing the inmates in the details of daily living by frequent head counts, strip searches, cell "shakedowns," and the censorship of prisoner mail. In general, this is a wasteful use of scarce personnel. There is also a general tendency to treat all prisoners, except "trustees," as maximum security cases, while "trustees" are given too much freedom and responsibility because they are the de facto operators of the jail.

Concern for control is also expressed in extensive measures to prevent "immoral" behavior by prisoners, such as drinking, gambling, taking drugs, and engaging in sex. When officials plan jails they go to great lengths to keep prisoners out of sight. The jail, however, because of its relationship to the court, must be in or near the center of the city. Prisoners have therefore been hidden deep within a massive building. Recently, architects have hidden even the jail itself by placing it out of public view at the top of a building, for example, and disguising its special features (such as barred windows).

The purpose of punishment manifests itself both in the structure of the jail, which has less space and fewer physical resources and material amenities than other "total institutions," and in the jailers' general management style, which is one of "malign neglect." Official policies, informal custodial practices, and much of the interaction between jailers and jailed disguise only thinly an intentional meanness. This is so because most jail policymakers, jail managers, and the general public believe that prisoners are disreputables who deserve to be treated with malign neglect.

Unintended Consequences

One consequence of these structural features and processes is that a jail prisoner generally experiences more punishment than a convict in a state prison. This punishment is intentional. Several unintended and socially undesirable processes also occur. Jail tends to maintain people in rabble status or convert them to it. To avoid rabble status, a person must sustain a conscious commitment to a conventional set of social arrangements. However, when persons are jailed, their ties and arrangements with people outside very often disintegrate. In addition, they are profoundly disoriented and subjected to degrading experiences that corrode their general commitment to society. Jail prepares them for rabble life by supplying them with the identity and culture required to get by as a disreputable.

Disintegration, disorientation, and degradation are malignant processes. Jailed prisoners often lose their property: Their cars are impounded, they lose their tools, their clothes, and their place of residence, if they had one. Their communication with friends, employers, creditors, and organizations is almost entirely cut off. Their social relations deteriorate. Finally, they cannot take care of ordinary business that is necessary to maintain a viable, conventional life. Disorientation makes many jailed prisoners dispirited and less able to cope with the complexities of modern society. Subjection to the abrupt and harsh experiences of arrest, booking, and placement in the "tank" often produce feelings of malaise, anxiety, disillusionment, despondency, and profound confusion. This disorientation impairs jail prisoners' ability to get themselves and the pieces of their lives back together after release.

Degradation of jail prisoners usually occurs every step of the way from arrest through detention to court appearance. They are degraded by the hostility and contempt directed at them by police officers, deputies, and other criminal-justice functionaries. This degradation can lead to the rejection (or further rejection) of conventional values and loss (or further loss) of commitment to society. Preparation, the last of the malignant processes, happens when jailed persons already living on the margins of society are introduced to the rabble life and are prepared for rabble existence. They lose conventional sensibilities and acquire rabble mentality. Moreover, they learn rabble definitions and skills, and make friends with members of rabble networks.

With their commitment to dominant cultural values damaged or destroyed and their ties to conventional society shaken loose, many failed persons drop out; they migrate to deviant worlds and rabble status. Consequently, the jail, which is intended to control the rabble, actually increases its numbers.

John K. Irwin

Bibliography

Feeley, Malcolm. *The Process is the Punishment.* New York: Russell Sage, 1979.

Flynn, Edith. "Jails and Criminal Justice." In *Prisoners in America.* Ed. Lloyd Ohlin. Englewood Cliffs, NJ: Prentice-Hall, 1977.

Goldfarb, Ronald. *Jails: The Ultimate Ghetto of the Criminal Justice System.* New York: Doubleday, 1975.

Irwin, John. *The Jail: Managing the Underclass in American Society.* Berkeley: University of California Press, 1985.

Mattick, Hans. "The Contemporary Jails of the United States: An Unknown and Neglected Area of Justice." In *Handbook of Criminology.* Ed. Daniel Glaser. Chicago: Rand McNally, 1974.

Moynahan, J.M., and Earle K. Stewart. *The American Jail: Its Development & Growth.* Chicago: Nelson-Hall, 1980.

Mullen, Joan, et al. *American Prisons and Jails.* 5 vols. Washington, DC: U.S. Department of Justice, NIJ, 1980.

Rothman, David. *The Discovery of the Asylum.* Boston: Little, Brown, 1971.

Thompson, Joel A., and G. Larry Mays, eds. *American Jails: Public Policy Issues.* Chicago: Nelson-Hall, 1990.

Jail Assaults

Violence in prisons has been extensively studied, but assaults in pretrial detention or police lockups have not. Most studies of inmate assaults have been done in prisons for male inmates. Assault rates can be an important concern in the management of pretrial and long-term facilities, small jails, and police lockups (cf. Sechrest, 1991). Since research on assaults in jails and lockups is quite limited, studies of prison assaults in relation to crowding or population density are most often utilized instead.

Population Density

Increased institutional violence in jails or prisons may be related to the effects of increased social density or increased spatial density. Social density refers to placing increased numbers of inmates in existing space; spatial density refers to reduced space for the same number of inmates (cf. Nacci, Teitlebaum, and Prather, 1977:26). Increased density in prisons has been linked both to increased assaults (Gaes, 1985; Megargee, 1977; Nacci, Teitlebaum, and Prather, 1977:29) and to fewer assaults (Innes, 1986; Jan, 1980). Innes (1986:5–6) defined density in state prisons for men as the "percentage of inmates in regular housing in each prison in less than 60 square feet for more than 10 hours per day." His comparisons by security grades (minimum, medium, maximum) for four density levels showed that the highest rates of inmate-on-inmate assaults occurred at lowest density across all security grades and that assault rates were highest in maximum security prisons at all densities (Innes, 1986:6).

Megargee (1977:294) examined incident rates in a federal medium-minimum security institution for men aged eighteen to twenty-five and found that the less space available for inmates the higher the incident rates. Megargee (1977:293) noted that his results may be confounded by the fact that prison inmates are out of their cells much of the day. Sechrest (1989) found a significant relationship between jail density and the rate of inmate-on-inmate assaults for male but not female inmates; age and race were not found to be significantly related to jail assaults.

Gaes (1985:136) found fewer effects of crowding in prisons, stating that research on prison crowding has not convincingly demonstrated the adverse effects of crowding, although he agreed that dormitories produced more clinic visits, higher blood pressure, and slightly higher assault rates (Gaes, 1985:136; cf. Paulus, Cox, and McCain, 1977, 1984). Gaes (1985:95) concluded that prisons housing significantly more inmates than a design capacity based on sixty square feet per inmate were likely to yield high assault rates, a finding directly contradicted by Innes (1986). Gaes (1985:134) concluded that crowding, not age or transiency, was the best predictor of assaults.

Location

Kratcoski (1988) found that 71 percent of all assaults occurred in a few locations in the federal facility and 68 percent of them occurred in the cell block area of the state facility (Kratcoski, 1988:28). Most assaults occurred on the day shifts, higher rates of assault were sustained by trainee officers and male officers, and the age of the officer assaulted was not a factor (Kratcoski, 1988:29–30). However, regarding age of the assailant, 75 percent of those in federal prison and 56 percent of those in state prison were twenty-five years of age or under. Thus assaults on staff were concentrated among inmates in that age category.

Sechrest (1991) found that inmate assault rates in a pretrial facility can be better explained in terms of their location in the facility, which suggested that particular types of inmates were most involved in assaults. Inmates are classified based on behavior characteristics. Therefore, assaults on other inmates tended to occur on the floors of the jail that held the most troublesome inmates—not necessarily the youngest or those of any particular racial group—or in the most crowded areas.

Sechrest (1991) found that the highest staff assault rate was in the misdemeanant quarters. This area held citizens arrested for such offenses as drunk driving, misdemeanor battery on a spouse, and child support, as well as the mentally ill and public inebriates. These individuals presented more problems for staff. While only 5.5 percent of all assaults in the facility occurred in this area, *almost half were against staff* (47.4 percent, with seven of these requiring medical attention). However, the intake processing areas had the lowest inmate and staff assault rates, possibly due to the greater officer movement, availability of law-enforcement personnel, higher levels of supervision during intake processing, and the temporary nature of this detention.

Age

Nacci, Teitelbaum, and Prather (1977:29–30) did not find a direct relationship between age and assaults, although they reported that "the relationship between density and misconduct was strongest in institutions with young adults." Eckland-Olson, Barrick, and Cohen (1983) found age to be more critical than crowding in producing prison assaults and disciplinary actions, with the relationship between density and misconduct highest in prisons holding first-term youths and young adults.

Kratcoski (1988) examined questions regarding inmate-on-staff assaults using incident report data from a state and a federal prison. Concern was with the location of assaults and the age of assaulting inmates, among other things. He found that inmates aged twenty-five or younger were more likely to be involved in assaults on correctional officers, with most minor assaults occurring when the officer was alone, but major assaults occurred when other officers were present. Gaes (1985:103) found only limited support for crowding-age interaction on inmate assault levels.

Race/Ethnicity

The race of inmates may be a determinant of assaultive behavior toward other inmates or staff. The influence of race is not widely studied, although Gaes and McGuire (1985) appear to support the possibility that a more homogeneous population, racially and ethnically, will lead to more assaults against staff and fewer against inmates. They speculate that "as a racial mixture tends toward equality, there is less intimidation of other inmates resulting in violence; however, the level of violence is redirected toward staff as a catharsis or displacement effect" (Gaes and McGuire, 1985:61). This thesis was supported in part by Sechrest (1991).

Racially heterogeneous inmate populations were not found to be more assaultive to staff or fellow inmates (Sechrest, 1991). At a population "mix" of no more than 60 percent black or white inmates (inclusive of Hispanics), inmate-on-inmate assaults did not decline precipitously (they rose slightly), nor did inmate assaults on staff rise. Moreover, at 60 percent or greater of black predominance the mean number of inmate assaults decreased slightly and staff assaults declined to below the overall population mean assault rate. Also, when blacks were in the minority (under 40 percent) assaults against other inmates were below the population mean and staff assaults were above the mean. Although Gaes and McGuire's "racial homogeneity" observation was not supported for jail inmates overall, it received some support where the population was predominately white and Hispanic. That is, where white and Hispanic inmates predominate in a jail setting there may be a tendency for them to redirect their hostility toward staff rather than other inmates.

Gender

Most studies of assaults by inmates have been done in men's prisons. A Georgia study found that the rate of disciplinary infractions in a women's facility was associated with several variables, including number of arrests, age, density of home county, history of violence, and average population (Ruback and Carr, 1984:60). Gaes (1985:103) cited laboratory studies showing that under certain conditions women reacted positively to crowding and males negatively.

Sechrest (1989) found that in a women's facility density alone predicted assaults. However, neither the number of assaults nor assault rates could be predicted when controlling for the percentage of white inmates on a unit, mean age of assaulters, and the size of the total population of the unit. However, a curvilinear pattern for women's assaults was found. Assault rates could be either low or high at low densities but assaults clearly increased at very high densities. Megargee (1977:294) found a similar curvilinear pattern for all incidents on density and disciplinary violations in a men's facility. That is, during months when density was relatively low the violation rate could be high or low, but when density was high misconduct rates were high. Sechrest (1989) did not find that age was a factor in inmate-inmate assaults at a facility for women. Factors other than age appeared to be operating in conjunction with increased density to produce assaults in men's and women's jails, as suggested by Gaes and McGuire (1985:58–59).

Type of Supervision

Since the late 1960s managers of jail and prison living units have been experimenting with different types of supervision practices in order to control violence and disruptive behavior on inmate living units. These new practices emphasize staff training in new inmate management practices intended to reduce tension and better control increasing prison populations. These newer types of supervision are called "podular/remote" and "podular/direct" supervision. The term "podular" refers to the architectural design that has developed with these innovative practices (Nelson, 1988:8). While much has been written on the successes of these innovative management concepts in jails or local detention facilities, little has been done to compare assault rates in inmate living units that use different supervision practices. The greatest interest is for "podular/direct" supervision, also called "third generation," "new generation" management, or simply "direct" supervision.

The direct supervision design has been found by its practitioners to be more effective in supervising inmates. That is, they find less violence on the units, essentially fewer inmate-on-inmate or inmate-on-officer assaults. To date, however, the documentation of this reduction is largely anecdotal or incomplete. Research using appropriate comparisons has not been done. For example, one report provides reduced assault and suicide rates for "new generation" jails in comparison with "traditional jails," but does not use rates based on the inmate populations involved (Nelson, 1988:13). Another article notes that a third generation jail has had no homicides, sexual assaults, or suicides, but no time frame or rates are provided (Black and Nesterode, 1989:109).

A facility using direct supervision for nineteen months was cited as having less graffiti and defaced walls, substantial reductions in "inmate-upon-inmate" violence and minor fights, and marked improvements in staff safety (Wallenstein, 1987:36). One facility (Pima County Sheriff's Department, 1989) reported a drop in incidents of violence (assault, arson, self-mutilation, suicide and attempts, escapes and attempts, disturbances, and instigating a fight) of 1.4 to .53 per 100 inmates from 1985 to 1988 based upon the use of direct supervision in contrast to traditional supervision. This occurred on thirty-six-bed living units (eighteen cells double-bunked) as the average population increased from 1,271 to 2,503 inmates. An overall 59 percent decrease in incidents of violence is claimed for the "last six months" of 1988; assaults in the old linear jail were thirty-two per month, and direct supervision had thirteen to twenty-two per month, depending on the unit (Pima County Sheriff's Department, 1989).

Dale K. Sechrest

Bibliography

Black, J.W., and Nesterode, W. "Accreditation: Setting a Standard for Excellence." *Corrections Today* (February 1989): 8–109.

Eckland-Olson, S., D.M. Barrick, and L.E. Cohen. "Prison Crowding and Disciplinary Problems: An Analysis of the Texas Prison System." *Journal of Applied Behavioral Science* 19(2)(1983): 163–76.

Gaes, G.G. "The Effects of Overcrowding in Prison." Eds. Michael Tonry and Norval Morris. *Crime and Justice: An Annual Review of Research* (1985).

———. and W. J. McGuire. "Prison Violence: Crowding versus Other Determinants of Prison Assault Rates." *Journal of Research in Crime and Delinquency* 22(1)(1985): 41–65.

Innes, C.A. "Profile of State Prison Inmates, 1986." *Bureau of Justice Statistics Special Report No. NCJ-109926.* Washington, DC: U.S. Department of Justice, 1986.

Jan, L. "Overcrowding and Inmate Behavior." *Criminal Justice and Behavior* 7(3)(1980): 293–301.

Kratcoski, P.C. "The Implications of Research Explaining Prison Violence and Disruption." *Federal Probation* 52(1)(1988): 27–32.

Megargee, E.I. "The Association of Population Density, Reduced Space and Uncomfortable Temperatures with Misconduct in a Prison Community." *American Journal of Community Psychology* 5(1)(1977): 289–98.

Nacci, P.L., H.E. Teitelbaum, and J. Prather. "Population Density and Inmate Misconduct Rates." *Federal Probation* 41(1977): 26–31.

Nelson, W.R. "The Origins of the Podular Direct Concept." *American Jails* (Spring 1988): 8–14.

Paulus, P.B., V. C. Cox, and G. McCain. "Effects of Crowding in Prisons." Washington, DC: U.S. Department of Health, Education and Welfare, National Institute of Education, 1977.

———. "Prison Crowding Research." *American Psychologist* 39(10)(October 1984): 1148–60.

Pima County Sheriff's Department Corrections Bureau. Facility description provided at May 1989 American Jail Association Conference, Hollywood, Florida, c. 1989.

Ruback, R.B. and T.S. Carr. "Crowding in a Woman's Prison: Attitudinal and Behavioral Effects." *Journal of Applied Social Psychology* 14(1)(1984): 57–68.

Sechrest, D.K. "Population Density and Assaults in Jails for Men and Women." *American Journal of Criminal Justice* 14(1)(1989): 87–103.

———. "The Effects of Density on Jails Assaults." *Journal of Criminal Justice* 19(1991): 211–23.

———. and W.C. Collins. *Jail Management and Liability Issues.* Miami: Coral Gables, 1989.

Wallenstein, A.M. "New Generation/Direct Supervision Correctional Operations in Bucks County, Pennsylvania." *American Jails* (Spring 1987): 34–36.

Juvenile Diversion

Although the figure varies widely from one department to another, it is generally concluded that police departments officially release about 50 percent of juveniles who could be detained for a law violation (the term "arrest" for juveniles is avoided in many states). Another large but undocumented number of detainable juveniles are contacted and released informally—on the street, on school grounds, in stores, and so on. In this sense, police normally *divert* the majority of juvenile suspects who could be detained. This "diversion" shows that in most states a great deal of discretion is given to police officers handling juveniles.

With impetus provided by the President's Crime Commission in 1967, by the growing acceptance of labeling theory (the theory that society's reaction to a criminal act is more important in determining the perpetrator's future than the act itself), and by a growing concern that the judicial processing of juvenile offenders has not reduced propensities for further offending, diversion has been offered as a more humane approach. The term "diversion" has taken on two rather distinct colorations.

Diversion as Treatment

The first is very similar to the notion of community treatment (Kobrin and Klein, 1983). Juveniles are referred by the police (or probation or the court) to agencies that attempt to correct those factors thought to cause delinquency. These agencies, more often private than public, generally stress psychological counseling. Other treatment procedures—recreation, job training, educational tutoring—also generally assume that the juvenile needs remedial help. Less common are services that locate the problems elsewhere—in the structure of the school, absence of job opportunities, or in various forms of racial or ethnic discrimination.

This form of diversion faces several serious problems. One of these is that the views of the diverters—the police, usually—yield a rather narrow range of "acceptable" community agencies to which referrals are readily made (Klein, 1976). This limits the amount of diversion that can take place.

A second problem is that this form of diversion-to-treatment is seen as particularly appropriate principally for minor or first-time offenders. These are, of course, the very kinds who constitute the usual 50 percent or more who would not be detained in any case (Klein and Teilmann, 1980). This redundancy makes a formal treatment process out of an informal release process—few additional offenders are actually turned away from the juvenile system.

A third problem is that treatment of these "diverted" youngsters has not yet proved that it reduces their recidivism or improves their lives (Klein, 1979). There are even some indications that providing such treatment to those having questionable needs for treatment can be harmful (Kobrin and Klein, 1983).

These three problems stem in part from weak theoretical foundations for diversion-as-treatment and in part from failures to implement diversion programs in accordance with good intervention models. Thus the problems are not endemic to the concept, but are understandable and predictable correlates.

"True Diversion"

This term was coined to describe a more rigid form of diversion: rejection by the system of a client who would clearly otherwise be inserted into it (Cressey and McDermott, 1973). This diversion is more difficult to implement because it requires the will and the mechanisms to release more serious or repeat offenders (Dunford, Osgood, and Weichselbaum, 1982). Police often feel uncomfortable with such a policy, seeing it as a failure to deter future delinquency or even as an implied reward for delinquent behavior.

There are still two forms of true diversion. In the first, offenders are arrested and the determination made that they should be petitioned to the court. Instead, they are referred for treatment to public or private agencies. In the second, arrest and petition determination are followed by outright release with no referral for treatment. Quite obviously, this latter version is less favored by most police officers since it seems to be letting offenders off the hook altogether, without any accountability for their delinquent behavior. There are conflicting experimental reports about the efficacy of these two forms of true diversion. One (Klein, 1986) reports lower recidivism resulting from outright release, while the other (Dunford, Osgood, and Weichselbaum, 1982) finds no differences associated with release versus treatment.

Normalization

A final, even more radical form of diversion that is most in line with the tenets of labeling theory is called "normalization." The attempt here is to treat a delinquent incident as *normal*, the sort of behavior that is so common or harmless that it needs no formal response. Almost by definition, normalization can only take place in the community setting, since police custody or citation is a formal response.

In states that allow considerable discretion to police officers, normalization is fairly common: Many minor incidents are seen but not acted upon. Normalization as a form of diversion is therefore deliberate nonresponse to incidents. Diversion can only be separated from regular discretionary activity by applying lesser responses to acts formerly eliciting active processing. One can "divert" from street contacts, physical arrests, detentions, and petition filings by taking a lesser action for each level of response. Whether or not any such form of diversion is accompanied by a treatment option is a connected but logically separate issue.

Trends in Diversion

Prior to the urgings of the President's Crime Commission in 1967, most police diversion was of the "normal" sort—regular releases on the street or at the station. During the 1970s, federal and state funds enabled agencies to couple diversion with treatment (and thereby confused the two practices). Most referrals were to outside agencies but some were to treatment specialists employed by or located in police stations. The amount of such referral activity varied widely but was generally far less common and less intensive than had been anticipated (Carter and Klein, 1976; Klein and Teilmann, 1980).

In the late 1970s and early 1980s, other philosophical and organizational developments in the police world changed the potential for diversion activities. National attitudes and the justice system's response to delinquency became more conservative. A stronger distinction was made between "real" delinquents and "status offenders," such as runaways, truants, and incorrigible minors. The former were less likely to be judged eligible for nonjustice treatment, while the latter were increasingly seen as not the police's business.

A decrease in specialized juvenile units and juvenile officers accompanied new legislation to deinstitutionalize (Kobrin and Klein, 1983) or even decriminalize status offenders (Schneider and Schram, 1983). Programs continued to treat minor offenders but failed also to rehabilitate their clients. This failure lowered concern for divertible juveniles.

In the early 1980s both the mass media and public officials heeded the drama of missing, abused, homeless, and abducted children. New hot lines, centralized data banks, and identification programs emerged more in proportion to the media hype than to prevalence of the problem; juvenile officers and units increasingly concentrated their efforts on child victims. For many police, this trend was seen as fortuitous; they could turn their attention from minor offenders to innocent victims, from diversion to criminal investigation. Federal and state funds poured into child-victim programs reducing the money available for other activities, including diversion.

Police diversion practices may have peaked and perhaps will decline until the national mood again shifts in the liberal direction and criminologists produce more convincing data about the effectiveness of diversion, with or without referral to treatment programs.

Malcolm W. Klein

Bibliography

Carter, Robert M., and Malcolm W. Klein. *Back on the Street: The Diversion of Juvenile Offenders.* Englewood Cliffs, NJ: Prentice-Hall, 1976.

Cressey, Donald R., and Robert A. McDermott. *Diversion from the Juvenile Justice System.* Ann Arbor: National Assessment of Juvenile Correction, University of Michigan, 1973.

Dunford, W. Franklyn, D. Wayne Osgood, and Hart Weichselbaum. *National Evaluation of Diversion Projects: Executive Summary.* Washington, DC: U.S. Department of Justice, National Institute of Juvenile Justice and Delinquency Prevention, 1982.

Klein, Malcolm W. "Issues and Realities in

Police Diversion Programs." *Crime and Delinquency* 22 (1976): 421–27.

———. "Deinstitutionalization and Diversion of Juvenile Offenders: A Litany of Impediments." *Crime and Justice: An Annual Review of Research*. Vol. 1. Eds. Norval Morris and Michael Tonry. Chicago: University of Chicago Press, 1979. 145–201.

———. "Labeling Theory and Delinquency Policy: An Experimental Test." *Criminal Justice and Behavior* 13 (1986): 47–79.

———, and Teilmann, Kathie S. "Pivotal Ingredients of Police Juvenile Diversion Programs." *Juveniles in Justice: A Book of Readings*. Ed. H. Ted Rubin. Santa Monica, CA: Goodyear. 1980. 168–81.

Kobrin, Solomon S., and Malcolm W. Klein. *Community Treatment of Juvenile Offenders: The DSO Experiments*. Beverly Hills, CA: Sage, 1983.

President's Commission on Law Enforcement and Administration of Justice. *Task Force Report: Juvenile Delinquency and Youth Crime*. Washington, DC: Government Printing Office, 1967.

Schneider, Anne L., and Donna D. Schram. *An Assessment of Washington's Juvenile Justice Reform*. Vol. 10. Eugene, OR: Institute of Policy Analysis, 1983.

J

L

Law-Enforcement Accreditation

The Commission on Accreditation for Law Enforcement Agencies, Inc., works to promote and maintain excellence, efficiency, and professionalism in law-enforcement agencies through administering an accreditation program. The commission was formed in 1979, utilizing the expertise of four major law-enforcement associations: the International Association of Chiefs of Police (IACP), National Organization of Black Law Enforcement Executives (NOBLE), National Sheriffs' Association (NSA), and Police Executive Research Forum (PERF). The commission began its work by developing a set of law-enforcement standards to achieve several purposes. First, to increase agency capabilities to prevent and control crime; second, to enhance agency delivery of law-enforcement services; third, to improve cooperation and coordination with other law-enforcement agencies and other components of the criminal-justice system; and fourth, to increase citizen and staff confidence in the goals, objectives, policies, and practice of the agency. In addition to developing standards the commission established and administers an accreditation process by which law-enforcement agencies can demonstrate "voluntarily" that they meet professional criteria.

Broadly representative, the twenty-one-member commission is composed of eleven law-enforcement professionals and ten representatives from the public and private sectors. The latter includes leaders in government, education, the judiciary, labor, and business. The four law-enforcment associations previously mentioned appoint commission members for three-year terms. The commission is autonomous and not obligated to any governmental unit. It was founded by, exists for the benefit of, and derives its authority from the law-enforcement community. Voluntary participation in the accreditation program constitutes the continuing source of the commission's authority.

Standards

The standards address six major law-enforcement concerns: (1) role, responsibilities, and relationships with other agencies; (2) organization, management, and administration; (3) personnel administration; (4) law-enforcement operations and operational support; (5) prisoner and court-related services; and (6) auxiliary and technical services. Designed to reflect the best professional practices in each of the six areas, the standards deal with the "what to," leaving the decisions of "how to" up to the agency. The standards have undergone extensive drafting and review before approval. The commission-approved standards were then submitted to law-enforcement agencies and individuals for examination and comment. Standards were also subjected to a structured field review by more than 300 agencies of various types and sizes. The end result of the process was the commission's promulgation of more than 900 standards, which continue to be revised and grow in number.

Total compliance with the large number of standards presents a near impossible goal for most law-enforcement agencies. Therefore agencies that seek accreditation need only comply with the standards specifically applicable to them. Applicability is based on an agency's size and the function it performs. For example, small agencies cannot reasonably be expected to employ the range of specialists/experts/technicians that large agencies can. The standards that are applicable to an agency fall into two categories: mandatory and optional. To achieve initial accreditation agencies need to comply with all mandatory standards and 80 percent of the optional standards, although they are encouraged to exceed the mark. Each agency selects the 80 percent optional with which it will comply. The standards are designed so that compliance is attainable and not an unreasonable burden on any well-managed law-enforcement agency. Below is an illustration of the opening standards in Chapter 84.

Chapter 84: PROPERTY MANAGEMENT

Law enforcement agencies generally have in their keeping three types of property: (1) that which is owned or used by the agency; (2) that which is in the custody of the agency; and (3) that which is acquired by the agency as found, recovered, or evidentiary property.

A well-structured system for managing property owned or used by the agency involves two phases: (1) the initial identifying, labeling, and recording of existing capital assets and (2) the maintenance of the system as assets are added, transferred, replaced, or destroyed. The system should identify each item of agency property, its cost and date of acquisition, its location, its condition, usage data, relevant maintenance and repair data, and the person responsible for the item.

The property management system should also provide for the management and control of found, recovered, and evidentiary property and property in the custody of the agency. This is critically important in investigative areas and in the proper administration of agency resources.

It is readily apparent that a law enforcement agency's property management system must develop and maintain strict measures with respect to the handling, security, and disposition of property.

84.1 Acquired and In-custody Property

84.1.1 A written directive regulates control of property held by the agency.

Commentary: Written directives outlining the functioning of the property management system are necessary to ensure continuity and consistency of operation. The establishment and maintenance of correct evidence-handling procedures are most important to the successful prosecution of a case in court. Law enforcement agencies should establish procedures for the prompt photographing and return of property to victims, with the prosecutor's approval.

(M M M M M M)

84.1.2 A written directive designates one person as responsible for each property management activity.

Commentary: Only when property accountability is vested in one person for each property management activity can centralized control of property be realized for agency property, property in custody, and for found, recovered, or evidentiary property.

(M M M M M M)

["M" stands for mandatory; "O" for optional. These two standards are mandatory for all six categories of law enforcement agencies—hence the six Ms.]

The Process

Once an agency submits a formal application for accreditation, the commission determines whether the agency meets eligibility criteria and, if so, requests that the agency complete an agency profile questionnaire. The questionnaire is designed to elicit information about the agency's size, responsibilities, function performed, organization, management, etc. This information permits the commission to reconfirm the agency's eligibility and to determine which standards are applicable to the agency. With instructional guidance supplied by the commission, the agency conducts its own assessment to determine the extent to which it meets applicable standards and assembles the necessary proofs of compliance. The time period for completion of self-assessment varies depending on the agency's resources, the chief executive officer, the accreditation manager, and other factors. Then, experience shows that agencies with a full-time accreditation manager take from one year to eighteen months to complete self-assessment.

Upon reviewing the agency's self-assessment report and finding it acceptable, the commission sends a team of assessors to the agency to verify its compliance with standards. Assessors examine the proofs of compliance that the agency assembled during the self-assessment phase and, in keeping with the commission's desire to maintain an open accreditation process, provide agency employees and the general public with an opportunity to comment on the agency's compliance through a public forum, phone and personal interviews, and letters. After the commission's staff reviews the assessment team's report, it is forwarded to the commission, which either awards or defers accreditation. If the latter happens, the agency is given an outline of the steps required to gain full compliance with the standards. At any point in the accreditation process decisions by the commission, its staff, and its assessors may be appealed by the agency pursuant to procedures established for this purpose. Experienced law-enforcement practitioners and persons with demonstrated knowledge of the field are recruited, selected, and trained by the commission to conduct the on-site assessments. Assessors are not assigned to an assessment within their own state. An agency is notified in advance of the names and backgrounds of potential assessors. The commission accepts comments from the agency about conflicts of interest and other circumstances indicating that an assessor should not be assigned.

Benefits of Accreditation

The commission cites the following as direct benefits of the entire eighteen-month-to-two-year accreditation process:

- Recognition of professional excellence
- Continued professional growth and improvement
- Community understanding and advocacy
- Employee pride and confidence—esprit
- Government officials' trust and support
- Liability insurance costs contained or decreased
- Liability litigation deterred
- State-of-the-art impartial guidelines for evaluation and change

- Proactive management systems, documented policies and procedures
- Coordination with neighboring agencies and other components of the criminal justice system
- Access to the latest law enforcement practices

The application fee is $250 and is not refundable unless the agency is ruled ineligible. The commission has established two payment plans. Option A fees do not include on-site costs, which are negotiated on an agency-by-agency basis and are payable to the commission prior to the assessment. Examples of Option A fees: a law-enforcement agency with one to nine employees would pay $4,675; an agency with 3,000+ employees would pay $18,700. Option B covers all commission services including on-site assessment. Examples of Option B fees: a law-enforcement agency with one to nine employees would pay $5,845; an agency with 3,000+ employees would pay $23,375. (Note: these figures were in effect as of January 1993.)

Reaccreditation

An accredited law-enforcement agency must seek reaccreditation every five years. The commission recommends beginning the process before the thirty-seventh month. Reaccreditation is easier than accreditation because the agency submits detailed annual reports each year that already comply with commission standards. Again, agencies undergo an on-site evaluation in which assessors examine proofs of compliance with the standards, observe agency operations, conduct a public hearing, and produce a report for review and vote by commission members before the end of month sixty following accreditation. Reaccreditation is easier but not by any means a walk-through.

Accreditation Statuses

The five statuses are:

- Accredited. The agency is in full compliance with all applicable mandatory standards and with the required percentage of applicable other-than-mandatory standards.
- Accredited-with-a-time-limit. The agency has not achieved the required compliance with applicable standards. This may result from circumstances beyond the agency's immediate control. The com-

mission continues to recognize the agency's accredited status, but only for a specified period not to exceed nine months, during which the agency must remedy deficiencies.

- Accredited-with-condition(s). The commission designates the agency as accredited but requires that the agency take specified actions.
- Accreditation lapsed. The agency has not achieved required compliance with applicable standards and is no longer accredited.
- Accreditation withdrawn. Apart from the above four commission-initiated designations, an agency may decide to discontinue its participation in the accreditation program.

As of January 1993, more than 912 law-enforcement agencies in the United States, Canada, and the Caribbean and Pacific Islands are in some stage of the accreditation program; and 244 are currently accredited.

Law Enforcement Assistance Administration

The 1968 Omnibus Crime Control and Safe Streets Act (Public Law 90-351) was meant to be the battle plan for a "national war on crime." Among its other provisions, the Act created the Law Enforcement Assistance Administration (LEAA) to support state and local governments' crime-control measures. From an initial appropriation of $60 million, the agency grew until, by the time of its demise in 1982, it had spent over "$7 billion for research, development and evaluation of various programs in criminal justice, hardware, and police education through the Law Enforcement Education Program" (Reid 1987:130). Although the LEAA was not the first federal funding program directed at the criminal-justice system, it was the largest in terms of both money and personnel, and perhaps one of the most criticized.

Two events in 1965 significantly contributed to the creation of LEAA: establishment of the Office of Law Enforcement Assistance (OLEA), directed by the U.S. attorney general; and the appointment of the President's Commission on Law Enforcement and Administration of Justice. The OLEA, although shortlived, provided the federal government with experience in administering grant programs to local criminal-justice agencies. Perhaps more important, however, it allowed the federal government to ease into a new role of intervention and assistance in an area that traditionally had been considered the responsibility of state and local governments. One major obstacle for federal interdiction in this area was the fear that there would be a loss of local control over criminal-justice agencies.

In 1967 the President's Commission released its voluminous report, which detailed much of what members thought was wrong with the criminal-justice system. The commission found that there was no systemwide criminal-justice planning, that personnel and training were inadequate, and that law enforcement was poor. The commission recommended that the federal government provide substantial financial assistance to state and local agencies, thereby facilitating rather than controlling their activities.

As initially conceived by President Lyndon Johnson, the LEAA would have underwritten the cost of preparing and implementing comprehensive plans for tackling local crime. The program would have been administered by the Office of Law Enforcement Assistance under the direction of the attorney general, who would have had wide discretion in funding decisions.

As finally passed, Title I of the Omnibus Crime Control and Safe Streets Act significantly altered the president's proposed program. Each state would create a state planning agency (SPA) to develop comprehensive criminal-justice plans. Up to 90 percent of the cost of operating the SPAs would be paid by the LEAA. Action grants were provided to cover operational costs of projects developed pursuant to the comprehensive state plans. Provisions were also made for establishment of regional planning units (RPUs), which would cover a number of local jurisdictions within each state. Each RPU would prepare regional plans and review grant applications before their submission to the SPA for funding. Thus, while the federal government would provide the funding, responsibility for development and implementation of crime-control strategies remained primarily at the state and local level through the operation of the SPAs and RPUs.

The act required the LEAA to develop a discretionary grant program and to establish a National Institute of Law Enforcement and Criminal Justice. The LEAA would retain 15 percent of all action grant monies and develop its own program to fund exemplary projects which fell outside the scope of the states' comprehensive plans. Prior to 1978 the discretionary grant program was administered by regional offices of LEAA. After the regional offices were abolished, the program was operated directly from Washington, D.C.

The National Institute of Law Enforcement and Criminal Justice was created to encourage research and provide funding for the training and college education of criminal-justice personnel. Criminal-justice employees and preservice students were encouraged to obtain college degrees by the awarding of grants and loans through the Law Enforcement Education Program (LEEP).

Throughout its history LEAA underwent numerous changes. In the beginning it was governed by an administrator and two associates appointed by the president subject to approval by the Senate. Under a 1973 amendment to the Safe Streets Act, authority was given to a single administrator.

LEAA's initial efforts were understandably slanted toward law enforcement. Social unrest had helped create the agency, and better funded police were to be the agents of change. A 1971 amendment, though, mandated that a quarter of all action grant monies were to be spent on corrections programs. Additional funds reimbursed up to 75 percent of the cost of renovation and construction of prisons. Amendments in 1974 and 1976 earmarked funds for juvenile-justice programs and the courts.

In 1982 federal funding for LEAA was withdrawn and this vital organization ceased to exist. Programs that can trace their origin directly to the LEAA, however, still exist within the Justice Department, most notably the National Institute of Justice, the National Institute of Corrections, the Bureau of Justice Statistics, and the National Institute for Juvenile Justice and Delinquency Prevention.

Joseph B. Vaughn

Bibliography
Feeley, Malcolm M., and Austin D. Sarat. *The Policy Dilemma: Federal Crime Policy and the Law Enforcement Assistance Administration, 1968–1978*. Minneapolis: University of Minnesota Press, 1980.
Reid, Sue T. *Criminal Justice Procedures and Issues*. New York: West, 1987.
Safe Streets Reconsidered: The Block Grant Experience, 1968–1975. Washington, DC: Advisory Commission on Intergovernmental Relations, 1977.
Twentieth Century Fund. *Law Enforcement: The Federal Role*. New York: McGraw-Hill, 1976.
White, Susan O., and Samuel Krislov, eds. *Understanding Crime: An Evaluation of the National Institute of Law Enforcement and Criminal Justice*. Washington, DC: National Academy of Sciences, 1977.

Los Angeles Police Department

California was admitted to the Union in 1850, the same year that Los Angeles was incorporated as a city. Within that year the city, which boasted a population of 1,610, elected A.P. Hodges as mayor, Samuel Whiting as city marshal, and George T. Burrill as the first elected sheriff. The duties assumed by the sheriff and marshal included the collection of local taxes. The sheriff's obligations required him to traverse a vast area on horseback, fighting bands of Indians and marauding desperadoes. Lacking paid assistants, the marshal was permitted to deputize citizens whenever necessary to maintain order. In lurid contrast to the peace and tranquility of the pueblo days (under Mexican rule), the city of 1852 became the scene of turbulence and bloodshed, a condition that lasted many years. Lawlessness swiftly developed into a major social problem as the thirst for quick wealth in the goldfields brought many a rogue to California. In 1853 City Marshal Jack Whaling was assassinated in broad daylight by a desperado named Senati. The need for an effective law-enforcement agency became increasingly urgent. In June 1853 a police force of one hundred volunteers was authorized by the common council. They were the first designated police officers and wore white ribbon badges bearing the words "City Police—Authorized by the Council of Los Angeles" in both English and Spanish. Known as the Los Angeles Rangers, they served for approximately four years and disbanded.

Another group of Los Angeles lawmen made their debut in March 1855. They were the Los Angeles City Guards, organized to represent city authorities when called upon to maintain the peace. The guards, who wore smartlooking blue uniforms, may be regarded as Los

Angeles' first uniformed policemen. They patrolled the numerous saloons and gambling halls scattered throughout the city. But it was not until 1869 that the police force was changed from a voluntary organization to a paid city department. In the following year, a city ordinance established the first Board of Police Commissioners out of the common council's committee on police. The city marshal had jurisdiction over the department, subject to the approval of the mayor and common council. The population of the city at this time neared five thousand. In 1871 Los Angeles remained wide open in the fullest sense of the word. Fortunes were being made in real estate, mining, transportation, and agriculture. Hordes of rough-and-ready individuals looking for a chance to make easy cash continued to pour in. Prostitution and gambling flourished without a single controlling law or ordinance. In 1876 City Marshal Juan Carrillo became chief of police, as well as dog catcher and city tax collector. The latter duty was decidedly profitable. It netted him 2.5 percent of all tax money collected, a responsibility that obviously tended to distract him from establishing an effective police agency.

During this time Chinese were brought to California in shiploads, so that by 1880 their number had reached 228,899. They were virtually slaves made to work the gold fields, the railroads, and whatever other enterprises were afoot. Exploiting the Chinese came easily and many arguments erupted over ownership of the few native women allowed in their camps. City Marshal William C. Warren died in a shootout involving a Chinese prostitute; in another dispute concerning an intercompany marriage, known as the "Chinese Massacre," nineteen Chinese were lynched. In the end no one had to pay for this abhorrent crime, which disgraced the city, its law-enforcement officers, the courts, and those in political power. It was an episode worth remembering as a low point in California history.

In 1875 the first mounted police force was organized. Foot patrolmen received ninety dollars per month and the mounted officer an additional five dollars. It may be well to note that the city marshal received only ten dollars more. Jacob F. Gerkins was appointed the first chief of police and coinciding with this historic change members of the force began to wear a regulation uniform. It consisted of a felt hat of the old frontier type and an ordinary, hip-length, blue serge coat. An eight-pointed silver star, considered quite elegant at the time, was purchased by the patrolmen at a cost of six dollars. Chief Gerkins wore the first "gold badge"—a shield displaying an eagle and the word "Chief." Included among the duties of Chief Gerkins and his men was the enforcement of laws prohibiting the grazing or herding of cattle in the streets, the sale of opium except for scientific or medical purposes, and the speed of steam trains at more than six miles an hour within city limits. Officers were also instructed to pick up loose paper blown about the streets, lest it cause horses to run away. It is interesting to note that in 1885 the department's equipment had a total value of $354; this included a horse and saddle, six dark lanterns, thirteen police stars, twenty rogue pictures, seven sets of nippers (handcuffs), old belts and clubs, and the newly invented telephone.

The Era of Chief John M. Glass

In 1889 Chief John M. Glass, a truly notable individual, took over the department. Chief Glass can be credited with the first organizational development of the department. He also developed the first time book and the first systematic supervision of personnel by dividing the city into four police districts. In turn, these four districts were split and numbered from one to eight. By this method, the sergeants, or "roundsmen" as they were called, were able to maintain a record of their patrolmen's beats. In those days sergeants depended upon the flashing of a red light atop a telephone box to alert them to an emergency. The police force had only one division—patrolmen. However, between the late months of 1888 and the end of 1889, Charles O. Moffet acted as a one man detective bureau. Shortly thereafter, Chief Glass organized the first detective bureau, which consisted of Moffet and three officers. The number was increased to six the following year. Other innovations included the appointment of the first police matron, the introduction of the first patrol wagon, the first substation, the first alarm system, and the adoption of the first entry-level standards for recruits. Glass was the first chief in California to adopt the use of the Bertillon system of identification. The Records and Identification Division came into being in 1890 when officers were required to write and submit reports of investigations to the chief. These reports were hung on a hook outside the office of Chief Glass. Under his direction, what had essentially been a group of watchmen became a formal group of professional lawmen striving to make Los Angeles a safe place to live. After eleven years as chief, Glass retired on the last day of the nineteenth century.

A New Century

In 1903 the city sprawled across vast distances and the areas assigned to each officer were tremendous by necessity. The sworn force numbered seventy-nine, including the chief, two captains, six sergeants, and two matrons. Officers walked a beat and rode a streetcar when responding to a distant call; bicycles were used on the larger beats. Civil service first spread its protecting hand over the department in 1903. Records show that of the 139 employees, 112 were certified as permanent with the remainder on probation. Mental aptitude for patrolmen was considered half as important as physical requirements. The mental aptitude rating assigned six points for duties, one for spelling, one for penmanship, one for arithmetic, and one for information about the city.

The position of chief was a transitory one at this time. Former Chief Walter H. Auble, back on patrol, was killed in the line of duty while attempting to arrest two burglary suspects. Then followed a succession of five chiefs in as many years. Political control of hiring was at fault; the men selected were inexperienced and nonprofessional. Without needed reform policies the department stood still. Finally, Charles E. Sebastian was appointed to the office and brought stability. In his first year, 1911, the fingerprint file was inaugurated; two years later it contained 290,000 records of individuals either under the Bertillon system or with photographs and fingerprints. Chief Sebastian established such a solid reputation for his crusade against vice that he became the first police officer to be elected mayor.

World War I depleted the force somewhat as policemen were granted leaves without pay to "join the colors." By war's end only one officer was killed while serving abroad. At home, ironically, the number of officers killed in the line of duty—seventeen—was exceptionally high for the six-month period between October 1918 and March 1919. The department's thin ranks and an accelerated level of criminal activity took a toll.

Beginnings of a police school arose in 1916 under the directorship of Captain R. Lee Heath, an attorney. Chief John L. Butler was respon-

sible for the instigation of the formal training program. The program had an average monthly enrollment of 573, with classes scheduled to "interfere as little as possible with the officers' off-duty time." The school offered classes in discipline, patrol duty, fires, first aid, care of lost children, law, traffic enforcement, morals, and physical conditioning. In addition, educators of national importance instructed officers on specially selected topics including criminal psychology.

The Dark Days

The 1920s and 1930s were turbulent, controversial years for the Los Angeles Police Department. Corruption existed in the city and in the department, but its degree and scope will probably never be completely known. For some, the Roaring Twenties provided the opportunity to acquire quick wealth. But on a policeman's salary, especially when outside jobs were rigidly prohibited, this was nearly impossible. Inevitably some went astray. For example, a group of detectives were cited for operating funeral parlors and paying commissions to officers who directed bodies to their places of business. Other officers were involved with extortion against bootleggers and some took bribes. During one fifteen-month period, more than 100 of the 1,200 sworn personnel were discharged for cause. As can be imagined, the incentive to easy gain disrupted the department, affecting its leadership. From 1920 to 1923 five police chiefs came and went. Chief James W. Everington, who served only three months, stated on his way out, "I haven't run the department since I was appointed. An honest man can't do that." He referred to the dictatorial manner of the police commission, which had compelled him to leave. When he had demanded all brothels and gambling houses closed, he had asked too much, since they provided a good source of extra income for some police.

After years of leadership turnover and a loosely knit organization, reform was badly needed. On August 1, 1923, with the appointment of August Vollmer as chief, police professionalism began in earnest. The forty-seven-year-old reformer had led a comfortable life as police chief of Berkeley and lecturer on criminology prior to his arrival in Los Angeles. His desire to test his theories of police administration in a large department attracted him to the job. His reorganization of the department included two key ingredients: efficient administration and scientific investigation. He required that professional officers be completely free of political influence, and he wanted to obtain the most intelligent, dedicated individuals available. He also sought to inform the citizenry that higher taxes were the only way to pay for improved police service. As he put it, "How can you expect to get intelligent men for $120 a month when they can make $165 driving a milk wagon?" A new concept of his that brought attention was the "Crime Crushers" division. This three-hundred-man mobile force was armed with the knowledge of when and where crimes were most frequently committed. Their job was to saturate those areas and make instant arrests. The Crime Crushers also went after organized crime syndicates and shot it out with mobsters, giving credence to Vollmer's warning, "Many will die." Actual reorganization of the department took this configuration: Eleven divisions were created, each uniting similar functions under a single head to provide more efficient leadership and clarify lines of authority; the eleven executives reported to the chief but handled day-to-day administration themselves. After one year of service, August Vollmer, true to his word, resigned as chief and returned to Berkeley. In that short time he had made lasting improvements in the department and had shown Los Angeles, if not all of America, that police could be reliable and honest.

But a few years later Mayor George E. Cryer stunned Chief James E. Davis by slashing the department's budget by 27.5 percent. This caused the elimination of the police school and eventually destroyed most of the innovations Vollmer had worked so hard to institute. No matter, Davis would not be daunted. Many "firsts" can be traced back to him, a number of which made the street policeman's job easier. He initiated the use of "hot sheets" bearing license numbers of stolen or wanted cars. These were carried on the handlebars by every motorcycle officer and inside every patrol car. A 900 percent increase in the arrest of car thieves resulted. He introduced the dragnet system for hunting wanted criminals, whereby the city was staked off into sections in which officers stopped and examined all motorists and detained suspicious characters. He developed a passion for crime statistics and for charts showing trends, tendencies, and yearly comparisons of number, types, and distribution of crimes. Comparing these with those of other cities, he was elated to find

the crime rate decreasing to the lowest it had ever been. For all the good Chief Davis brought about he could not erase police corruption. With ten police trials in session and constant media coverage of his few bad men, public support to dispose of him grew stronger. On October 31, 1929, the police commission charged Davis with incompetence and neglect of duty. Faced with the negative publicity of a public trial, and to protect his pension, he accepted a demotion to deputy chief in charge of traffic.

Police corruption continued, as did the battles between the incumbent chief and the police commission for some time to come. One bright spot in the 1930s was the 1932 Olympic Games held in Los Angeles. The police moved in and provided safety; only two robberies, eight burglaries, thirty-nine thefts, and thirty traffic accidents were reported during the entire games. The next year, however, saw the arrival of Joe Shaw, the iron-fisted boss of the police and fire departments. His brother, Mayor Frank Shaw, allowed him a free hand in running the departments. Joe soon learned that selling promotional examinations was lucrative, along with other shameless practices. The Shaws ruled city government until in 1938 Frank became the first mayor in the nation ever recalled, and Joe was convicted of sixty-six offenses in connection with the sale of jobs and promotions.

Age of Reform

In 1939 the department was completely overhauled and reorganized under the command of a reform-minded new chief, Arthur Hohmann, who was a former military lieutenant and a graduate of Chief Vollmer's original police academy. Specifically, overall functions were divided into three entities: field operations, functional operations (personnel, property, jail, etc.), and investigational operations, each with a deputy chief in command. Each divisional captain was made accountable for all patrol duties, traffic control, vice enforcement, and preliminary crime investigations. Hohmann centralized a number of other operations, disbanded the vice squad, and abolished several hundred acting ranks, which in effect had denied advancement to qualified officers displaced by the "scabs." His downfall came after two years of successful administration, when he opposed the use of police to break strikes. He handled the North American Aviation labor strike and riot by ordering his officers to stand their ground despite management's insistence that police should disperse the strikers. A riot broke out, the Fifteenth U.S. Infantry stepped in, and Hohmann landed in court to contest his demotion back to lieutenant. He won and was reinstated by the California Superior Court to deputy chief with restitution of all lost salary. His victory did not sit well with the political machine, which banished him to an obscure office with no subordinates, no desk, and no work to do.

World War II ushered in a set of new problems: drafted officers, fewer qualified recruits, a city swollen by newcomers to start up war production, and mass hysteria after the attack on Pearl Harbor. On February 23, 1942, a Japanese submarine surfaced off the coast of Santa Barbara and shelled an oil installation. This prompted residents all along the California coast to arm themselves in preparation for the "inevitable" attack. Rabid emotionalism spread into ethnic corners of Los Angeles and soon racial incidents marred the city. The most famous one was the "Zoot Suit" riots in which Mexican Americans robbed some sailors, and a subsequent rash of assaults instigated by both sides bloodied the streets. Later, the Brenda Allen case focused public attention on the police again. More corruption—this time a vice sergeant was selling protection to Madam Allen, the owner of a brothel, and in the ensuing investigation other police crimes were discovered. For the remainder of the 1940s a holding pattern prevailed, with the police doing their job as best they could under difficult circumstances. The decade ended on a good note as William A. Worton, a hard-bitten administrator and retired Marine Corps general, took over as interim chief. He served for one year during which he established a planning office to chart the city's crime and growth trends and introduced a military-style intelligence squad to scout the underworld and keep abreast of mobsters' plans. But more important, he hand-selected William H. Parker to assist him in rebuilding the department.

The Era of Chief William H. Parker
When Parker was sworn in on August 9, 1950, there were 4,895 employees under his direction; 4,189 sworn and 706 civilians. He had a budget of $200 million. The yearly salary for an officer was $3,480; Parker's, $12,480. The city was divided into twelve divisions, and its population of almost 2 million ranked fourth in the nation. Total crimes in 1950 were about 51,000. There were almost 1 million vehicles in the city, the greatest number of registered vehicles of any city in the nation. There were also more than 34,000 traffic accidents. During the year Parker took office, the department logged approximately 500,000 calls for service.

His first official act was to release a list of promotions and transfers, making it a point to promote those highest on the civil service list without favor. Next he cut his staff officers from fourteen to eight, thereby gaining better control over them and ensuring that critical information was more forthcoming. He established the Bureau of Administration, which brought together five existing divisions and created a new one, the Planning and Research Division consisting of statistical, legal services, analysis, forms design, manuals and orders, and field services units. Also in his first year Parker almost lost his life. He was to speak before Senator Estes Kefauver's committee concerning organized gambling in the Los Angeles area when an informant tipped off the intelligence unit that Chief Parker was to be killed. The murder attempt was foiled and later another plot to bomb Parker's home was averted.

The chief's thrift was his hallmark at budget sessions. He was a constant watchdog on wasteful spending. The city's money was expended as frugally as his own. Another achievement for which he was commended was the creation of a rehabilitation center for the treatment of alcoholics. In the fight against drug trafficking, he scored a success to the extent that Chief H.J. Anslinger of the Federal Bureau of Narcotics said, "Los Angeles has the only adequate narcotics squad." Further innovations garnered more success for Parker, and after thirty-nine previous chiefs who had averaged less than two years in office, he was to stay in power for sixteen years. His death in 1966 ended an era, possibly the most productive and renowned in the history of American municipal law enforcement.

The Era of Chief Edward M. Davis
Chief Davis was one of the department's more flamboyant and outspoken chiefs, frequently being quoted in the news media for various "outrageous" statements. A strong, no-nonsense leader, he once confided that to be a good chief in Los Angeles, "You had to be a tough son of a bitch." He implemented the Basic Car Plan concept, bringing the police officer and the citizen closer together. An officer was no longer

subject to a rapid succession of reassignments. Instead, he was given an area of responsibility, a piece of real estate, and told: "This is your district and your people. Get to know them, the geography, the problems and help to solve them. The lives and the property of the people who live here are in your hands. Take good care of them." A series of technological advances greatly aided Davis and his officers, such as computerization of criminal "want and warrant" information with access to statewide files on stolen vehicles. Management development was begun under Davis, which provided talented officers with the opportunity to acquire a management degree at nearby Pepperdine University. Other educational programs designed for potential lieutenants and captains evolved at the California Institute of Technology and at California State University, Northridge. Team policing gained a foothold during this time, as did the SWAT team. The Venice Beach riots, a severe earthquake, a Symbionese Liberation Army confrontation, and the Alphabet Bomber all sorely tested both new team concepts. Upon retiring from police service in 1978, Chief Davis entered politics as a state senator.

The Present Day LAPD
Daryl F. Gates became the city's forty-ninth chief of police on March 28, 1978, after participating in a unique and highly competitive examination process, which for the first time had been opened up to executive-level police personnel nationwide. As it turned out he inherited adversity—reduced resources and demands for increased police services have slowed his plans for the department. He has faced a court-ordered hiring injunction and a debilitated pension system. Massive tax cuts have severely limited money needed for improvements and morale has been low. Still, Chief Gates has tried to do more with less in a city that bursts at its seams. An indication of his vision was made evident in August 1982 when the department established the Human Resources Development Committee. Its purpose was to support alignment of all department employees on the LAPD; to encourage a people-oriented managerial environment and an expanded sense of personal responsibility for the well-being of the department and the community; and to increase participation of all employees in management of the department, with particular emphasis on open communication, trust, and full self-expression.

The highly publicized Rodney King incident in which LAPD officers beat King for resisting arrest reflected badly on Chief Gates and almost obliterated any accomplishments he claimed. From the day of the incident in March of 1991 until his retirement in the summer of 1992, Chief Gates endured constant questioning about his handling of the officers involved. Once the worst race riot in U.S. history occurred in reaction to the not-guilty verdict that cleared the officers of wrongdoing, Chief Gates took more pounding from just about everyone. The main charge was that he had not acted quickly enough to put officers in place to prevent the L.A. riots; secondary charges had to do with his creating a climate in which such beatings could flourish; and to the satisfaction of few outside the LAPD, he steadfastly denied any breach of training and operational procedure on the part of his officers. A 1991 investigation of the LAPD led by Warren M. Christopher had recommended that Gates retire. With Chief Gates still in office and defiantly opposed to leaving except on his own terms, Philadelphia Police Commissioner Willie L. Williams accepted the job to head the LAPD.

Abridged from the Official History Provided by the Los Angeles Police Department

M

Manpower Allocation

In its broadest definition manpower allocation includes determining adequate staffing levels, deploying officers to patrols, and then scheduling officers for duty. Attention to staffing only began to take on significant importance in the 1960s. This coincided with the public's increasing demand for greater accountability in the use of public funds to provide better police service. Historically, deployment of officers has been a major concern of police managers because patrol is a visible product of police work. Innovative managers such as O.W. Wilson provided administrators with tools to guide deployment decisions. The same was not true for staffing. First, managers had to convince the public that the police were understaffed. When funds became available officers were added. Police staffing got a substantial boost during the Law Enforcement Assistance Administration years. Second, simple methods to help managers justify their staffing needs were not available. Even when managers had the methods they did not always use them. Public demand for police presence affected manpower allocation and increased budgets. Since patrol took a sizeable bite out of the budget, justifying increased funding meant justifying the patrol function.

Staffing

As motorized patrols replaced foot patrols staffing became a serious issue. Either by managerial decision or by contract, the larger cities began to employ two-officer units for patrol. In the 1970s several studies examined the effectiveness of the tandem units. While some conflicting results appeared, most of the more careful research, e.g., Boydstrun et al. (1977), found no differences in safety and efficiency between two-officer and one-officer units. More important, one-officer units were found to be more productive. Although such findings may not have made radical changes in police staffing methods, they lent guidance to management decisions regarding patrol staffing. In rural areas two-officer units are an unaffordable luxury. A rural officer's main duties are to enforce traffic laws, respond to traffic accidents, and assist motorists. Handling citizen complaints is not a priority due to the fact that in rural areas calls for service are few. Whereas urban staffing is driven by workload and response, rural staffing is driven by coverage and availability.

Deployment

An early rationale for deploying officers to beats was based on calls for service. Officers were assigned to beats according to the degree of activity in the area. Around 1941 O. W. Wilson introduced the concept of "hazard scores." The scores gave greater weight to calls that incurred more work or hazard for the responding officers. For example, a robbery would have a higher hazard score than a citizen complaint. Officers were deployed to beats not only by the number of calls received, but also by an estimation of police resources required. In theory this placed officers where they were needed the most. Yet, often the hazard scores were arbitrary. The need for officers did not always equate with the weights given. Police specialization, greater officer mobility, and automated statistics soon replaced older, less defensible methods of manpower allocation.

Time spent on calls became the most commonly used replacement for hazard scores. Generally, the amount of time spent per call was easy for managers to measure and figure into the equation. Time as a measurement also reflected the amount of resources required and used. However, like most workload-based measures the time method looked back historically and in certain ways was inefficient. As demand for patrol became more complex and as managers had to make do with less funding, manpower allocation underwent change to incorporate another measure—performance.

Mathematical Models

When police radio became the standard for deployment, it provided more accurate data regarding patrol and response. Then, with the advent of computers, police managers could engage in more sophisticated mathematical modeling. IBM's Law Enforcement Manpower Resource Allocation System (LEMRAS) was one such early advancement. The Saint Louis Police Department employed LEMRAS in the 1960s to modernize its manpower allocation (Crowther 1964). Later, Larson showed how queuing theory, a branch of mathematics, could assist patrol deployment. Larson in his text *Police Patrol Analysis* (1972) formalized the "hypercube model." Hypercube deployed patrols to minimize travel time or workload based on call-for-service data and detailed street maps. It allocated a fixed number of patrol units to beats in order to minimize delays in reponse time. Chelst (1975) applied hypercube to the New Haven Police Department, to little avail since the results were discarded because of changes in patrolling philosophy.

In a federally funded study that focused on New York City, Chaiken and Dormont (1977) developed another model that simulated response in terms of units busy and patrolling frequency. Their Patrol Car Allocation Model (PCAM) included a measure that showed the likelihood of a call not being answered immediately. In addition to simulating response the model also examined various schedules for tours of duty and the effect those schedules had on response and delayed calls. Later, Green and Kolesar (1989) revised PCAM because it underestimated delays. Similar automated methods have been used to deploy fire engines and other emergency services.

Hypercube and PCAM have remained the primary sources for mathematical deployment of patrols in urban areas. Urban police generally respond to almost every call. Preventive patrol is deemed necessary, though this was questioned in the Kansas City experiment (Kelling, et al. 1974). Until recently, rural policing has not embraced automated deployment. Rural law enforcement differs from urban in that greater distances must be covered and patrol is directed toward traffic control and officer visibility. Rural deployment concentrates on miles of road traversed, rather than on rapid response to calls for service. Usually only one patrol officer is available regardless of the expected level of activity. Urban cross-beat dispatching to handle calls cannot be achieved in rural areas. Lee et al. (1979) studied optimizing road patrol in Nebraska based on traffic densities. Working under the assumption that traffic density correlated highly with the number of accidents, the researchers attempted to equate patrol deployment with accident reduction. However, they failed to consider the need for police presence and regular patrol coverage beyond accident reduction.

The hypercube model and PCAM not only allowed managers to examine urban deployment schemes, but could also show the differences adding or subtracting officers would make. Managers could justify additional officers, for example, as a means to reduce response time. Such an assessment had to be done separately because the mathematical models were not designed to suggest staffing levels. Raub and Sweat (1981) first described a method for the Illinois State Police to meet the specific needs of rural policing. Their model initially was designed to deploy officers to patrol and could also translate rural policing needs into staffing numbers. Raub (1988b) refined the model and made it available to other departments through a microcomputer program. Parallel to Raub's efforts, the Northwestern University Traffic Institute taught a similar model. The two models merged to become the Police Allocation Model in 1990. A subsequent grant produced an extension of the model to assist the sheriffs' department in addition to statewide law enforcement agencies.

Models such as hypercube and PCAM do a good job of designing patrol territories in urban areas. In rural areas results are different. Boundaries such as rivers, railroads, and large tracts of developed or undeveloped land present obstacles. For rural police managers sophisticated methodology often requires more work than doing it by hand or with the assistance of a simplified computer program. For either type of policing, management sets the objectives for

M

the agency. Then management designs the patrols and deployment to meet those objectives. The models and mechanical aids only provide management with a "snapshot" of what could happen under certain circumstances. A different set of circumstances produces a different snapshot. Thus, manpower allocation depends on the planning capabilities of the manager and his or her recognition of how the agency should operate.

Richard A. Raub

Bibliography

Bammi, Deepak. "Allocation of Police Patrol Beats to Patrol Units to Minimize Response Time to Calls for Service." *International Journal of Computers and Operations Research* 2 (1975): 1–12.

Birge, J.R., and S.M. Pollock. "Using Parallel Iteration for Approximate Analysis of a Multiple Service Queuing System." *Operations Research* 37 (1989): 769–99.

Boydstrun, J.E. *Hypercube Queuing Model: Executive Summary.* Washington, DC: U.S. Department of Housing and Urban Development, 1975.

———, et al. *Patrol Staffing in San Diego: One- and Two-Officer Units.* Washington, DC: Police Foundation, 1977.

Chaiken, J., and P. Dormont. "A Patrol Car Allocation Model: Background, Capabilities, and Algorithms." *Management Science* 24 (1988): 1280–300.

———. "Patrol Car Allocation Model." Washington DC: Department of Housing and Urban Development, 1977.

Chelst, K. *Implementing the Hypercube Queuing Model in the New Haven Department of Police Services: A Case Study in Technology Transfer.* Washington, DC: U.S. Department of Housing and Urban Development, 1975.

Clawson, C., and S. Chang. "Relationship of Response Delays and Arrest Rates." *Journal of Police Science and Administration* 5 (March 1977): 53–68.

Crowther, R.F. *The Use of a Computer System for Police Manpower Allocation in St. Louis, Missouri.* Bloomington: Indiana University, 1964.

Green, L., and P. Kolesar. "Testing the Validity of a Queuing Model for Police." *Management Science* 35 (February 1989): 127–48.

Kaplan, F.H. "Evaluating the Effectiveness of One-Officer vs. Two-Officer Patrol Units." *Journal of Criminal Justice* 17 (1979): 325–55.

Kelling, G., et al. *The Kansas City Preventive Patrol Experiment: A Technical Report.* Washington, DC: The Police Foundation, 1974.

Kolesar, P. "Ten Years of Research on the Logistics of Urban Emergency Services." *Operations Research* (1981): 557–60.

———, et al. *Guidelines for Scheduling Police Patrol Cars.* New York: The Rand Institute, 1976.

Larson, R.C. *Police Patrol Analysis.* Cambridge, MA: MIT Press, 1972.

———. *A Hypercube Queuing Model for Facility Location and Redistricting in Urban Emergency Services.* Washington, DC: U.S. Department of Housing and Urban Development, 1975a.

———. "What Happened to Patrol Operations in Kansas City? A Review of the Kansas City Preventive Patrol Experiment." *Journal of Criminal Justice* 3 (1975b): 267–97.

———, and M.F. Cahn. *Synthesizing and Extending the Results of Police Patrol Studies.* Washington, DC: U.S. Department of Justice, 1985.

Lee, S.M., et al. "Optimizing State Patrol Manpower Allocation." *Journal of the Operations Research Society* 30 (1979): 885–96.

McLaren, R.C. "Allocation and Distribution of Police Patrol Manpower." *Law Enforcement Science and Technology.* Washington, DC: Thompson Book Company, 1968.

Police Allocation Manual: Determination and Allocation of Personnel for Police Traffic Services for State-Wide Agencies. Evanston, IL: Northwestern University Traffic Institute, 1990.

Raub, R.A. "Projecting Police Traffic Enforcement Workload: An Empirical Analysis." *Transportation Quarterly* 42 (April 1988a): 279–87.

———. "Staffing a State Police Agency for Service and Patrol." *Journal of Police Science and Administration* 16 (December 1988b): 255–63.

———, and G.L. Sweat. *A Method for Allocating State Police Officers in Illinois.* Springfield, IL: Illinois State Police, 1981.

Schumate, R.P., and R.F. Crowther. "Quantitative Methods for Optimizing the Allocation of Police Resources." *Journal of Criminology, Criminal Law, and Police Science* 57 (June 1967): 197–206.

Wilson, O.W. "Distribution of the Police Patrol Force." Chicago: Public Administrative Service, Publication 74, 1941.

———. *Police Planning*. Springfield, IL: Charles C. Thomas, 1958.

Media Relations

Law-enforcement officials probably place second only to politicians in having a difficult time coping with the news media. Police/media communications result in frequent misunderstandings, often because neither party fully appreciates the job the other has to do. This lack of comprehension breeds fear and mistrust. Generally speaking, law-enforcement officials tend to look upon news reporters as snoopers poking their noses into things that are none of their concern. A ready quip is that some reporters "never let the facts get in the way of a good story." Moreover, many law-enforcement officials believe that reporters are extremely liberal and permissive and actually fight or frustrate police investigations. Traditionally the media have zealously sought to expose alleged internal police corruption, which almost always garners headlines and television attention. This glaring exposure has often resulted in law-enforcement agencies becoming wary of media personnel since such news coverage reflects adversely on the agencies.

Part of the problem is that reporters often believe that the police routinely withhold information from them, or worse yet regularly release inaccurate information. Sometimes this causes a reporter to "dig" for the "real" story when, in fact, there is none. This tends to polarize the police and the media. Also, police executives wary of being misquoted tend to respond in a reticent manner and are thus perceived as uncooperative. Since successful working relationships cannot be founded on mutual mistrust, many police/media interactions deteriorate into an exchange of noncommittal responses, which further exacerbates the misunderstanding. When this happens the reporter after a story might just go ahead and fill in the blanks. This reinforces law enforcement's perception that regardless of what one tells a reporter, the story will reflect that reporter's personal beliefs. So the cycle of mistrust continues.

Freedom-of-information acts have been codified in many states and localities. These statutes were originally enacted to counteract government abuses of power. But, as with many well-intentioned legal changes, this one soon backfired. Volumes of once-classified information useful to foreign governments and organized crime became readily available to anyone who requested it, including the media. The rift between the police and the media grew that much wider due to the declassification. Now a reporter can confront a law-enforcement official with documented evidence of an investigation planned or in progress and request confirmation. The law-enforcement official must then deny any knowledge of the investigation, thereby driving an additional wedge between these two groups. When confidentiality is at stake rules are often skirted.

Federal Guidelines

The National Advisory Commission on Criminal Justice Standards and Goals of 1973 clarified the police/media issue in Standard 1.7:

> Every police executive immediately should acknowledge in written policy statements the important role of the new media and the need for the police agency to be open in its relations with the media. The agency should promote an aggressive policy of presenting public information rather than merely responding to occasional inquiries.

1. The news media relations policy should be included in the agency training curricula, and copies of it provided to all agency personnel, media representatives, and the public. The policy should acknowledge:
   a. The right of the press to obtain information for dissemination to the public;
   b. The agency's responsibility to respond to inquiries from the media, subject to legal restraints and the necessity to preserve evidence, to prevent interference with police investigations and other operations, and to protect the constitutional rights of persons accused of crimes;

M

c. The agency's responsibility to seek the cooperation of the media to delay publication—rather than imposing censorship or unilateral news moratoriums—when immediate reporting of certain information may be detrimental to the community, to victims of crime, or to an investigation; and

d. The mutual benefits to the police agency and the media when relations between the two are characterized by candor, cooperation, and mutual respect.

2. The news media relations program should provide regular liaison between the agency and the media through an officer or unit, depending upon the size of the agency and the nature and frequency of local news media demands.

3. Every police chief executive should establish a means of local, regional, or state accreditation of legitimate news media agencies to assist media representatives in receiving police cooperation.

4. Every police chief executive, in cooperation with the media, should prepare a written policy establish the relationship between his agency and the news media during unusual occurrences.

Standard 1.7 went on to define what a written media policy would include, the relations officer, how to obtain accreditation of media representatives, and how to handle media relations during unusual occurrences. Since 1973 law-enforcement officials, drawing on practical experience, have amended this set of guidelines only slightly.

Model Police Guidelines
Gerald W. Garner in his book *The Police Meet the Public* sets forth the press-related policies and procedures of the nationally recognized Lakewood, Colorado, Department of Public Safety. The following are established guidelines for the release of information to the press "before" an arrest:

Release
1. A description of the exact offense, including a brief summary of events
2. Location and time of offense
3. Injuries sustained or damages resulting from the action

4. Identity of the victim, except for a sex crime victim
5. Whether or not there are suspects
6. Information about unidentified suspects, such as physical description, vehicle description
7. Identification of fugitive suspects for whom a warrant has been issued
8. Criminal background of a fugitive when the public should be alerted to danger
9. Method of complaint (officer observation, citizen, warrant, indictment)
10. Length of investigation and name of officer in charge of investigation (undercover operations may require withholding the officer's identity)

Nonrelease
1. Identity of suspects who are interviewed but not charged
2. Identity of witnesses where such information could subject them to danger or extreme embarrassment
3. Identity of sex crime victims (general information is sufficient: race, sex, age)
4. Exact address of a sex offense, where such information could lead to the identity of the victim
5. Exact identifying information about the weapon or other physical evidence
6. Any information that could be known only to the guilty party, i.e., "investigative keys"
7. Information about valuable items not stolen
8. Conjecture about suspects or fugitives
9. The amount taken in a robbery or burglary
10. Identity of victims in death investigations until notification of relatives has been made
11. Misleading or false information ("planted stories")

The following are established guidelines for the release of information to the press "after" an arrest:

Release
1. Time and place of arrest
2. Defendant's name, age, residence, usual occupation, marital status, and similar background
3. The exact charge

4. Facts and circumstances relating to the arrest, such as resistance, pursuit, possession or use of a weapon, description of contraband discovered
5. Identity of the agency or unit responsible for the arrest, including the name of the arresting officer (undercover operations may require withholding the officer's identity)
6. Duration of the investigation
7. Pretrial release or detention arrangements (including amount of bond, location of detention)
8. Scheduled dates for various stages in the judicial process

Nonrelease
1. Name of the defendant's employer
2. Comments about the character or reputation of the defendant
3. Names of juvenile defendants except where charges involve only traffic code violations or violations of game and fish statues
4. Prior criminal record of defendant (Records Section may release such information on request of news media in accordance with state and federal statutes)
5. Information about the existence or content of a confession, admission, or statement by the accused
6. The refusal of the accused to make a statement
7. The refusal of the accused to submit to tests or examinations
8. Results of any examinations or tests
9. Description or results of laboratory examinations of physical evidence
10. Reenactment of the crime
11. Revelation that the defendant directed investigators to the location of a weapon, contraband, or other evidence
12. Any remarks about the assumed guilt or innocence of the defendant
13. Comments about the credibility of testimony
14. Whether the information for the arrest was derived from an informant

Other strictures apply, such as not providing photographs of subjects in custody to the news media "without first consulting the prosecuting attorney having jurisdiction over the matter." The Lakewood guidelines are exemplary and foster the best possible relationship between the police and the media.

Joseph E. Scuro, Jr.

Bibliography
Barber, Carter. "A Magna Carta for Media-Police Relations." *Police Chief* 37 (9) (1970): 28–31.
Fishman, M. "Police News: Constructing an Image of Crime." *Urban Life* 9 (January 1981): 371–94.
Garner, Gerald W. *The Police Meet the Press.* Springfield, IL: Charles C. Thomas, 1984.
Geberth, Vernon J. "The News Media in Homicide Investigations." *Law and Order* 29 (7) (1981): 46–53.
Wilson, J.V., and P.Q. Fuqua. *The Police and the Media.* Boston: Little, Brown, 1975.

Military Model

The term *military model* as it is applied to law enforcement refers to the adoption of ideas and practices that originated in the armed forces and the adaptation of these to a law-enforcement program.

The interaction and exchange between the military and law-enforcement functions of society has been an ongoing one from the Anglo-Saxon period to the present. The origins of this relationship predate the existence of the army and the police as separate, formal units of society.

Historical Antecedents

In England, following the end of Roman rule (about A.D. 450), the island's Roman-Celtic culture was invaded by a host of migrants from northern Europe. Territorial wars ensued over the next several hundred years, but these were accompanied by a striving for social order within the various cultures. The island became dominated by an Anglo-Saxon culture in its heartland with a Celtic fringe surviving in Wales and Scotland. During the period of Anglo-Saxon dominance, roughly A.D. 700–1000, the individual male citizen had civic responsibilities imposed upon him by his leaders. As a member of the *fyrd* (a kind of militia) the citizen was obliged to bear arms in defense of the kingdom. As a resident of a *tithing* (a group of ten families) he was also responsible for obeying the law *and* pursuing lawbreakers. Thus in the Anglo-Saxon period, military defense and law enforcement were simply civic responsibilities of the male members of the society. The title of sheriff first appeared in the reign of Canute (1016–1035), but his duties in those days seemed primarily administrative and judicial.

Among many changes caused by the Norman Conquest was the beginning of specialization in military and law-enforcement functions. The knight, originally a professional soldier, became part of a social elite in the counties from whose ranks the leadership of government developed. The constable and marshal (both Norman in origin) began as a kind of captain and lieutenant, respectively, who were responsible for defense of a medieval castle. The constable was designated by Edward I in 1285 as the one responsible for a semi-annual inspection of each household to see that heads of families in his area were maintaining the supply of arms prescribed by law. Thereafter the military duties of the constable gave way to an increasing number of peacekeeping duties in his district. Constables were elected by freeholders in the parish or village for a one-year term of unpaid service.

The Normans retained the position of sheriff—and its Anglo-Saxon title—first as a prestigious administrator of royal interests in the county (or counties) as well as presider over the county court. The development of the manorial and royal court systems eroded the judicial component of the sheriff's duties, just as the abuse of power and authority by individuals in that office in the reigns of Henry II and Edward I brought a diminution of their administrative status. At the Council of Clarendon (1164), Henry II bestowed extensive law-enforcement powers and responsibilities upon the sheriff, which thrust him into the midst of the crime problem then plaguing England. Under these provisions each sheriff was responsible for seeing to the construction of a jail in his county. The medieval sheriff was also expected to make a biannual tour of his county. The purpose of this tour (the Sheriff's Tourn) was to administer the Oath of Frankpledge to all male citizens of the county. The oath committed the citizen to obey the law and to assist in the apprehension of lawbreakers. Thus, despite the creation of specific offices in which some law-enforcement duties were vested, the medieval English kings continued to rely upon the individual male citizen for maintenance of social order.

The military duties of the citizen were carried out as a member of the local militia, but a decree in 1327 forbade the use of county militia for campaigns outside the county. Reliance upon mercenaries for military manpower had been building for some time, and the actual involvement of the ordinary citizen in the many English conflicts of the Middle Ages became increasingly rare. Nevertheless, illegal personal armies composed largely of professionals were maintained by many nobles throughout the Middle Ages until the reign of Henry VII (1485–1509). The existence of these armies is considered a major factor in the crime problem of the Middle Ages and during the Wars of Succession in the fifteenth century.

Emergence of an Organized Force
In modern England Cromwell is said to have initiated the use of uniforms for soldiers in his army during the English Revolution. This important component of the military model remained as a hallmark of the English soldier thereafter.

Following the restoration of the monarchy in 1660, crime in the English countryside dictated continued reliance upon the law-abiding tendency of the average citizen under the eye of the village or parish constable. He, in turn, was responsible to the gentry of the county who administered the county's affairs. In London it was a different story. The urban setting, bustling with commerce and industry, was densely crowded, and the rising crime rate of the eighteenth and nineteenth centuries was no match for a law-enforcement system geared to a medieval, rural society. While the rural constable appears to have been a reputable member of his community who conscientiously pursued his duties (Kent, 1980), in London, particularly in the eighteenth century, the upstanding citizen's responsibility to police his parish for one year as a constable too often became an irritant to be casually passed off to some lesser person. A call for professional, paid, supervised personnel to carry out the law-enforcement task was issued in the 1700s by William Pitt, the prime minister, as well as by Henry Fielding and Patrick Colquhoun, magistrates in Westminster and London, and no doubt by many others, but to no avail.

In the desire for more order in government, reputable officers of the military were increasingly placed in responsible civilian government positions as forerunners of the civil service in the eighteenth and nineteenth centuries. As Parliament designed new legal machinery to bring order to urban and industrial society, more and more often an army or naval officer was selected to assemble and oversee that machinery, especially in law enforcement and prisons. Some government leaders advocated a paid, full-time police force. However, opponents in Parliament to the creation of a paid constabulary pointed repeatedly to the police of Paris, already in existence, as a repugnant example of a militarized civilian police force. When the London Metropolitan Police were authorized in 1829, two commissioners—one military, one civilian—were named to oversee the force despite a very skeptical and at times hostile public. A uniform was deemed essential to identify the patrolling constable, and the color chosen was blue because the army used red. A blue uniform topped with a stovepipe hat—mixing civilian and military dress—was meant to help placate opposition to a military organization. The City of London—one mile square—was exempted from the Metropolitan Police jurisdiction at the insistence of the city's powerful delegation in Parliament. They retained a city marshal as head of an unpaid constabulary until 1839. It was the City of London model that was used by many cities in the United States prior to the creation of paid, full-time police departments.

The "Model" in America

When the British established colonies in the New World, they imposed the peacekeeping tradition from England, i.e., an unpaid constable elected from the citizenry and a militia for civil defense that also obligated the male citizenry to participate. American policing moved city by city from a voluntary service into a paid service beginning with larger, mostly eastern cities during the period of 1830–1860. The eastern urban areas rapidly increased in population in that period, and the rurally spawned model for maintaining social order proved inadequate, as it did in London. The power of ward and precinct officials in American city governments prevented the establishment of a strong police administrator, and the authority to appoint and supervise police was often relegated to the ward and precinct level in the nineteenth-century American city. Concern over rising crime and the lack of control of "the dangerous classes" caused the creation of investigating boards of citizens. New York's Lexow Commission was the first, but eight or more other major cities followed within a ten-year period at the turn of the twentieth century. Fogelson identifies the period of 1900–1930 as the time in which the "military analogy" developed hand in hand with the effort to reform law enforcement. The analogy likened crime to an enemy and the police to the nation's defense. Although the uniform had been grudgingly adopted by the police in the nineteenth century, little else of the military model was common before World War I. Titles used by the American police forces in cities—patrolman, roundsman, etc.—were distinctly unmilitary. The urban policeman's crime-control function had been diluted in the 1800s by extensive social-service duties, which ranged from feeding and housing transients to apprehending stray animals. The "war on crime" followed America's victorious emergence as a world power from World War I. From that time to the present the military uniform has been joined in law enforcement by other military traditions such as close-order drill, replacement of nineteenth-century police titles with army ranks and insignia (corporal, sergeant, lieutenant), shoulder patches, the use of a military salute as the proper courtesy to a superior officer, and even the traditional military funeral for those felled in the line of duty.

During the 1960s, a few departments experimented with the use of a nonmilitary uniform (slacks and blazer of prescribed color and cut), but few cities joined the experiment.

Although there has been no significant recruitment of military leadership to fill police manpower needs, American policing seems to view prior honorable experience in the military as an asset for those recruited at the patrol level.

At present, the relationship of law enforcement with the military seems to have reached a plateau, with no evident trend toward significant further identification with the military establishment.

Donald J. Weisenhorn

Bibliography

Fogelson, Robert M. *Big City Police.* Cambridge, MA: Harvard University Press, 1977.

Joliffe, J.E.A. *The Constitutional History of Medieval England from the English Settlement to 1485.* New York: Norton Library, 1969.

Keir, Sir David Lindsey. *The Constitutional History of Modern Britain Since 1485.* New York: Norton Library, 1969.

Kent, Joan. "The English Village Constable,

1580–1642: The Nature and Dilemmas of the Office." *Journal of British Studies* 20 (1980): 26–49.

Military Police

The term "military police" fails to convey the complexity and diversity of the policing tasks performed by the approximately 94,000 men and women assigned to military police and investigative units. Policing in the military has all the variety found in civilian policing, plus some unique aspects. For example, in all four branches of the military, law-enforcement units are in one organization and major investigative units are in another. Military police and investigators must be familiar with federal, state, county, and municipal laws. They must also know the laws promulgated in the Uniform Code of Military Justice and the laws of those foreign nations in which they may be assigned. In addition to traditional police functions the military police also perform tasks that are unique to the military, such as maintaining security of nuclear weapons and defending bases during times of war. Military law-enforcement personnel must also be cognizant of U.S. Code 18, Section 1385, which precludes their use as a posse comitatus to execute the law against civilians. This section does not apply to civilians who have contracts with the military services, nor does it prohibit actions against civilians committing offenses that have a direct bearing on military operations or personnel.

History

The roots of the American military police can be found in Europe, where in the eighteenth century two elite French military units, the Gardes Suisses and the Gardes Françaises, were used to police the streets of Paris. In America, the first "police" in New Amsterdam (New York City) were members of military units that provided patrols and watches on a random basis from the city's founding through 1761. However, the modern-day military police trace their origins to 1776, when General George Washington established the first provost marshal (military police officer) of the U.S. Army. This was followed in 1778 by the formation of the first military police unit, the Marechaussee Corps, whose police functions included apprehending deserters, drunks, and stragglers; patrolling the camp; and maintaining control of prisoners. The history of the military police was very erratic from the disbanding of the Marechaussee Corps in 1783 until the beginning of World War II. Military police units were formed during the Civil War and again in World War I; however, these units were disbanded upon the cessation of hostilities. During those times, military policing duties were performed as additional duties and investigative requirements were filled by civilian agencies such as the Pinkerton Detective Agency. The outbreak of World War II resulted in the permanent establishment of the U.S. Army Military Police Corps (MPC) on September 26, 1941. This was followed by the establishment of the Army Criminal Investigation Division (CID) in 1944, the Air Force Security Police in 1947, and the Air Force Office of Special Investigations (AFOSI) in 1948. The Naval Investigative Service (NIS), which was established in 1966, can trace its origins to 1882 when the Office of Naval Intelligence (ONI) was created. The Marine Corps' Military Police (MP) in its modern form was created in 1970, and the navy's police personnel, the Master-at-Arms (MA), was established in 1973.

Mission

The missions of the military police and investigative organizations are manifold. Each entity must fulfill traditional police or investigative functions as well as those functions that are peculiar to their parent service. Most of the organizations have "wartime" missions for which they must train, in addition to the training required to maintain their traditional police skills in a professional manner. The basic law-enforcement functions of the military police organizations, regardless of their branch of service, include such tasks as traffic management and control, crime prevention activities, and order maintenance on their respective military installations or aboard ship. They also must train for combat defense, riots, and antiterrorist activities. The security of United States nuclear and conventional weapons is a major responsibility of the military police organizations. Military police from the army and the air force are also responsible for the corrections and rehabilitation programs in their respective services. Police personnel from the army, air force, and marine corps serve on the correctional staff at the U.S. Military Disciplinary Barracks, Fort Leavenworth, Kansas, the Department of Defense's maximum-security confinement facility.

All the investigative organizations have criminal and fraud missions; the navy and air force also have counterintelligence missions. The traditional criminal and fraud investigative responsibilities include such offenses as murder, rape, computer crimes, and contractor fraud. In addition, the three military investigative organizations conduct protective-service operations for military and civilian dignitaries. They also have antiterrorist missions and, when requested, they support the U.S. Secret Service in the protection of the president and other high-ranking government officials.

Jurisdictional Authority
The authority of military police organizations, with a few exceptions due to mission or organizational differences, is generally the same. For example Title 10 USC Section 807 authorizes military police to apprehend individuals that are subject to the Uniform Code of Military Justice; Title 10 USC Section 809 authorizes military commanders to order the arrest of military and civilian individuals residing, working, or visiting at their installations, based on probable cause. Torres (1985) provides a more complete listing of the U.S. codes that pertain to the individual organizations. Personnel assigned to these organizations are authorized to carry weapons and to administer oaths.

The investigative branches have more varied jurisdictions, as they provide investigative support to all elements of their respective services at the request of responsible commanders. Among the major crimes they investigate are all major offenses contained in the Uniform Code of Military Justice; fraudulent acts on the part of military members and civilian contractors; and narcotics offenses. The Air Force Office of Special Investigations and the Naval Investigative Service also have counterintelligence missions including the protection of military resources and personnel from the threats of sabotage, espionage, subversion, or terrorism.

Organization
Military police and investigative organizations are as varied as the missions they must perform. For example, there are more than 26,000 officers, warrant officers, and enlisted personnel assigned to the Army's Military Police Corps. These individuals are stationed around the world, and they normally work a three-shift rotation. The commanding officer of each military police unit is responsible to a post com-

mander. The Military Police Corps' field units receive staff guidance from the Office of Army Law Enforcement, which comes under the deputy chief of staff for personnel. In addition to performing traditional police functions, Military Police Corps personnel also establish and maintain liaison with their civilian counterparts.

The Air Force Security Police's force of nearly 50,000 members is comprised of active duty and reserve officers and enlisted personnel, National Guardsmen, and a number of Department of Defense and contract civilian employees. These personnel are assigned to one of two functional specialties: security or law enforcement. A major responsibility of personnel assigned to the security specialty is the protection of the air force's nuclear and conventional weapons systems. Personnel assigned to the law-enforcement specialty perform traditional police functions, in addition to establishing and maintaining liaison with local, state, and federal civilian law enforcement agencies. Like their army counterparts they normally work a three-shift rotation. The Air Force Office of Security Police is a separate operating agency under the air force inspector general. The Air Force Office of Security Police, with headquarters at Kirtland Air Force Base, New Mexico, provides staff and administrative guidance to security police personnel in the field; however, security police commanders in the field come under the direct supervision of the senior air force commander at their assigned location.

Approximately 2,400 marine corps officer and enlisted personnel are assigned to the military police. Their duties and shift rotations are similar to those of the air force and army law-enforcement units. The head of the Law Enforcement and Physical Security Section, at U.S. Marine Corps headquarters, is on the staff of the marine corps commandant. The Law Enforcement and Physical Security Section provides staff guidance to military police field units, such as proposing policy and procedural changes. Military police commanders in the field come under the direct authority and supervision of the senior commander of the local marine corps installation.

The navy has approximately 2,500 personnel performing law-enforcement functions. They receive administrative and staff guidance from the Law Enforcement and Security and Investigative Command (NSIC) in Washington, D.C. The commander of NSIC reports to the chief of naval operations. Naval law-enforcement personnel in the field come under the supervision of their installation's senior navy commander. The navy also employs the services of Department of Defense civilian police personnel at selected installations.

The Army Criminal Investigation Command (USACICD) has 2,132 assigned personnel of whom 1,118 are special agents. The other personnel provide support and administrative services. This command has only a criminal investigation mission. The commander of the Criminal Investigation Command reports directly to the army chief of staff. Unlike the military police, the investigative organization has direct command over its subordinate units in the field. The Criminal Investigation Command headquarters is located in Washington, D.C., and provides command supervision and staff guidance to more than 135 geographically separated units located at army posts around the world. Thus the local field units provide investigative support and service to the local post commander, but do not come under that commander's direct supervision. The USACICD also commands three crime laboratories that are located in the United States, Germany, and Japan. These laboratories support all other military law-enforcement organizations and some federal investigative agencies. The laboratories provide scientific investigative services in five broad areas: fingerprinting, firearms, photography, chemistry, and questioned documents.

The Air Force Office of Special Investigations (AFOSI) has approximately 2,900 assigned personnel of whom about 2,100 are special agents and the remainder are administrative and support personnel. AFOSI special agents are located at every major air force installation and in selected cities around the world. AFOSI is a separate operating agency and the commander reports to the air force inspector general. AFOSI units provide criminal investigative services and counterintelligence support to local air force commanders; however, the AFOSI commander whose headquarters are located at Bolling Air Force Base, Washington, D.C., retains both supervisory and staff control over AFOSI field units.

The Naval Investigative Service (NIS) has approximately 1,000 special agents assigned worldwide to marine corps and navy land installations as well as selected navy ships. Unlike their army and air force counterparts, NIS special agents are predominantly civilians. The NIS is an operating element of the Naval Security and Investigative Command (NSIC). The civilian director of NIS reports to the commander of the Naval Security and Investigative Command, who reports to the commander of Naval Operations. NIS special agents provide criminal investigative services and counterintelligence support to navy and marine corps commanders; however, staff functions and supervision over the NIS field units are retained by the director of the Naval Investigative Service.

Personnel Qualifications
Minimum qualifications for enlisted members of the individual military police organizations are similar. Individuals must be at least eighteen years old and in general must not have a criminal record, must not have used drugs, must pass a physical exam, must pass a background investigation, and must qualify with firearms. The requirements for officer personnel in military police forces are essentially the same as those for enlisted members, with the primary difference being that military officers generally have a college degree.

Personnel qualifications for the military investigative organizations are as diverse as the missions of the organizations themselves. In general, special agent applicants must pass written and oral examinations, be of high moral character, be emotionally stable, and qualify for appropriate security clearances. NIS applicants must have a college degree, be between the ages of twenty-one and thirty-five, be a United States citizen (may be naturalized), and must pass a federal civil service exam. CID applicants must be twenty-one years old and have the same basic qualifications as members of the Army's Military Police Corps. Enlisted personnel must have a minimum of two years of college and must have served for at least six months in the Military Police Corps. All personnel, whether officer, warrant officer, or enlisted, must be U.S. citizens who evidence high moral character and emotional stability. The AFOSI has similar physical, moral, and psychological requirements; however, active duty applicants can come from any air force career specialty, not just the Security Police. The AFOSI has both active duty and reserve enlisted and officer special agents and approximately 200 civilian special agents. AFOSI special agents must be U.S. citizens, and the twenty-one-to-thirty-five-year-old age restriction for the civilian agents is generally applicable to the military agents. Civilian agents normally have a college degree; however, this may be waived in lieu of experience or special needs of the air force. AFOSI civilian agents must also pass the federal civil service exam.

Training

All personnel assigned to the Army's Military Police Corps must attend a twelve-week military police training course at the Military Police School, Fort McClellan, Alabama. Air Force Security Police and Marine Corps Military Police personnel receive their training at the Air Force Security Police Academy, Lackland Air Force Base, Texas. Upon completing the seven-week basic course, air force personnel receive an additional six weeks of training in either security or law enforcement. After completing the basic course, Marine Corps Military Police personnel attend the law-enforcement course. The Navy conducts a ten-week master-at-arms course for its law-enforcement personnel at the Army Military Police School. The Air Force Security Police Training Academy is located at Lackland Air Force Base in San Antonio, Texas. The academy provides initial police training for air force and navy personnel. Personnel attending the basic military police courses receive training in such areas as military law, traffic enforcement, firearms qualification, riot control, and report writing. Advanced courses include military police investigation, correctional facility administration, and working with police canine units. Military police personnel also attend many civilian police schools such as the FBI National Academy and the Northwestern Traffic Institute.

All special agents assigned to the AFOSI must complete the eleven-week basic investigator's course at the AFOSI Academy, Bolling Air Force Base, Washington, D.C. Upon completion of the basic coursework each agent must complete one year's probation before becoming fully accredited as a special agent. Qualified special agents who have completed their probationary period may apply for duty as a polygraph examiner, which requires fourteen weeks of Department of Defense polygraph course work, plus a specified period of certification training in the field. Other qualified agents may apply for training in several special areas such as linguistics, forensic science, or computer science.

CID special-agent applicants must complete an eleven-week criminal investigator's course at Fort McClellan, Alabama. They too must serve one year's probation. Upon successful completion of the probationary period, the qualified CID special agent may attend a number of Department of Defense and federal law-enforcement courses. One elite specialty of the U.S. Army is the criminal laboratory technician, which requires two years of training in one of the five scientific categories provided by the laboratories.

NIS agent applicants must complete a seven-week criminal-investigator course given at the Federal Law Enforcement Training Center (FLETC), Glynco, Georgia. NIS agents subsequently attend a two-week in-house course where they receive instructions on navy policies and procedures and complete firearms qualification. Upon completion of a probationary period, qualified NIS agents may attend a number of specialty courses in subjects such as polygraphy, antiterrorism, and hostage negotiation.

During their basic investigator courses, all special agents assigned to military investigative organizations receive several hundred hours of instruction on such diverse topics as military law, administration, investigative techniques, photography, firearms, crime-scene searches, interviewing techniques, and report writing. Military investigators, like their police counterparts, also attend courses sponsored by the civilian schools and law-enforcement agencies.

Harry L. Marsh

Bibliography

Barnett, R.W. "The U.S. Navy's Role in Countering Maritime Terrorism." *Terrorism* 6(3) (1983): 469–80.

Braithwaite, L., and S.R. Sonnad. "Cynicism Amongst Military Police Personnel in Western Europe." *Justice Quarterly* 1(3) (1984): 413–36.

Military Police Journal. Fort McClellan, AL: U.S. Army Military Police School, 1973–ongoing.

Moore, R.H., Jr. "Posse Comitatus Revisited: The Use of the Military in Civil Law Enforcement." *Journal of Criminal Justice* 15(5) (1987): 375–86.

Smith, B.L., and R.M. Ward. "Maladaptive Behaviors Among Military Police Personnel and Implications for Administrative Policy." *Journal of Criminal Justice*

14(4) (1986): 307–17.

Torres, Donald A. *Handbook of Federal Police and Investigative Agencies.* Westport, CT: Greenwood Press, 1985.

Money Laundering

Money generated by narcotics trafficking and other profit-motivated crime in the United States is estimated at $300 billion annually. Although analysts have difficulty accurately counting well-hidden crime proceeds, the amounts are staggering. Moreover, the effects of "dirty money" on legitimate commerce are grave. Convenience, relative anonymity, and universal acceptability make hard cash the preferred medium of exchange in illegal transactions. Drug traffickers and other racketeers who accumulate large cash inventories face serious risks of confiscation and punishment if considerable, unexplained cash hoards are discovered. For these criminals to fully benefit from their illicit activities, they must first convert those cash proceeds to an alternative medium—one that is both easier than cash to use in everyday commerce and that avoids pointing, even indirectly, to the illegal activity that produced it.

Money laundering is a term that describes the process of converting illegally earned assets originating as cash to one or more alternative forms to conceal such incriminating factors as illegal origin and true ownership. Recently, through heavy colloquial use, the term's meaning has broadened to refer not only to individual acts of laundering but also to many complex steps of illegal asset conversion, beyond the basic exchange of cash, for less conspicuous and more socially acceptable methods of payment. Despite saturation by the media on the topic of money laundering, our knowledge remains limited and stems mainly from federal enforcement efforts. While state and local agencies in Florida, Arizona, and several other states have been increasingly active in combating money laundering offenses, leadership is still exercised by the federal government. The main reason is that tracking the international movement of drug money back to a Colombian cartel or to another foreign source is a federal task and a priority.

The Money-Laundering Process

The number of steps involved in a money-laundering scheme is directly related to the distance that criminals desire to put between their illegally earned cash and the laundered asset into which that cash is converted. The most basic factor in a laundering scheme is the conversion of cash to another asset—usually an alternative payment medium—so that criminals can more easily conceal its origin and spend it more freely, when desired. Banks and a number of other financial institutions routinely issue negotiable instruments such as cashier's checks and money orders in exchange for cash. From the perspective of drug traffickers and other organized criminals and the money launderers who serve them, preferred negotiable instruments meet two basic criteria: (1) they are bearer instruments, or are made out to fictitious payees, entitling the holder to use them in commerce without inviting questions of true ownership; and (2) they are liquid assets, enabling owners to use them immediately, if desired, avoiding unacceptable personal inconvenience. Although transactions with financial institutions are the most common basic step in money laundering, the services of other commercial institutions are also required if illegally earned wealth is to be further converted to make it more difficult to trace.

The next step involves using the laundered funds to acquire one or more types of assets. Asset acquisition provides criminals with a source of income that appears to have been generated independent of any criminal activity. The use of legitimate businesses and business transactions to launder funds is one of the oldest methods of choice for several reasons. Legitimate business offers criminals a source of employment in the community and helps to cultivate an image of respectability. It creates reportable income for tax purposes, although criminals drastically underreport their true income. Particularly popular for laundering are businesses that deal in substantial numbers of cash sales, making accurate audits of business volume very difficult. High cash turnover businesses include bars, restaurants, entertainment establishments, and vending machines. Legitimate business produces a base of legal operation and a secure planning site for a variety of criminal activities, such as fencing stolen goods. Real estate purchases are also attractive money laundering vehicles for at least two reasons. First, as an investment real estate has traditionally held and usually increases its value (less so recently). Real estate represents a fixed asset that offers an array of tax benefits, ranging from property depreciation over the life of the asset to tax deductions for reported interest payments (which in fact may be fictitious because of the fraudulent basis of the real estate loan). In addition, as a steady producer of income, real estate rentals may be altered on the books.

A subsequent step is liquidating laundered assets by reconverting them to their original cash form. This step completes most standard money laundering processes by reconstituting the asset into a liquid form for use in criminal or legitimate activities or for the consumption of goods or services that leave little if any traceable documentation. Criminals are increasingly using banks to wire transfer their funds out of the locality, often to another country where the funds are converted to cash at their final destination.

Laundering Specialists
Features of convenience, speed, and privacy associated with modern-day financial transactions place "self-laundering" within easy reach of most criminals. However, because many criminals fear detection from exposing themselves in their money-laundering transactions, they have begun to employ a variety of laundering specialists. These specialists sell their services to criminals, often in the form of multi-service packages, or they may simply assist in one or two independent steps of a more complex laundering process.

There are three basic types of specialists. "Couriers" arrange for the transport of currency to a laundering site where it is converted to another method of payment, such as money orders. Couriers working for foreign traffickers may smuggle the currency out of the United States to a safe foreign jurisdiction, where the laundering transactions are completed on foreign soil. The value of couriers lies in their apparent legitimacy and lack of any obvious connection to the true owner of the currency. They may not even know the owner of the money they are transporting. "Currency exchange specialists" operate formal or informal businesses that can either be ostensibly legal or dedicated solely to service an illegal clientele. The most formalized exchanges, *casas de cambio*, exchange dollars for pesos. Usually, the *casas* are legitimate foreign currency exchange houses that are used by criminals seeking quasi-banking services. "White-collar professionals," such as attorneys and accountants, provide investment counseling, create nominee trust accounts, handle international funds transfers, and exploit tax avoidance schemes in foreign jurisdictions. Their main service is the manipulation of financial, commercial, and legal procedures to conceal the origin or true ownership of the assets under their control.

Specialists who launder funds for large criminal organizations often create informal organizations to provide their services. Unlike the Mafia, which is held together by rigid hierarchical rules, these are loose coalitions united by consensus and related to a common objective—the pursuit of steady, lucrative income. Only rarely do the laundering organizations operate as subordinate units of the criminal organization they serve. Rather, they function as loose clusters of free agents who may sell their services on a one-time or longer-term basis to such organizations. These specialists may work for more than one criminal organization, as well as for high-level individual criminals who manage independent organizations, such as drug importers and first-tier wholesalers who amass substantial assets.

Tracking Operations
Organized criminals at almost all levels of operation desire ready access to, and use of, their illicit proceeds (cash). Primarily at the wholesale level, local racketeers and drug dealers, who keep their funds close to their bases of operation, also launder a portion of their funds. This fact may be easily obscured by the focus of media and federal-enforcement attention given to the international dimensions of laundering operations. Due to variations in the spending practices of criminals, as well as incomplete and otherwise poor intelligence on sophisticated criminal operations, it can be difficult to estimate the size and scope of a particular illegal operation. Although it may be difficult to obtain information on the number of transactions in which a subject is involved during any given time period, intelligence on laundering activities provides one of the best indicators of the true range of criminal activities. Treasury Department officials obtained Al Capone's conviction for tax evasion when they could not successfully prosecute him for racketeering, murder, and sundry other crimes. A focus on money laundering enables state and local law enforcement to follow a similar approach to supplement an investigation for substantive organized crime or narcotics violations with tax fraud and business fraud aspects.

Sustained enforcement campaigns against money laundering may encourage white-collar professionals to withdraw their illegal services or demand more exorbitant fees. This situation could encourage the increase of greedy newcomers whose inexperience may expose criminal profits to more frequent confiscation through, for example, asset forfeiture actions. An increasing number of states now have laws that allow for the confiscation of property obtained, either directly or indirectly, with funds derived from criminal activities. Enforcement personnel who have seized property used purely as conveyances may now have the option, under broadened state laws, of also seizing more expensive assets, such as luxury homes, high-priced automobiles, bank and securities accounts, and real property. Asset forfeiture represents one of the most potent weapons available to law enforcement against economically motivated crime. In addition to generating funds for law enforcement, forfeiture allows government agencies to strip criminals of the profits of their crimes and seize assets such as equipment and supplies that are used to facilitate the manufacturing, distribution, and sale of illegal commodities. At its best, this approach can subject criminals to a 100 percent tax on their earnings—a clear disincentive for them and others to remain in that business.

Initiatives for Detection
The paper trails surrounding the different steps in the money-laundering process are prime candidates for intelligence collection efforts. A comprehensive money-laundering intelligence effort should include these steps.

- Encourage financial institutions to report large cash transactions.
- Identify money-laundering specialists whose presence might indicate a developed local market for services.
- Continue to follow financial and commercial transactions arranged by individuals known or suspected of specializing in money-laundering services.
- Investigate assets acquired with large amounts of cash or other arrangements that depart from routine practices for conducting similar kinds of transactions.

To comply with federal laws, currency transactions made through financial institutions must be recorded on Federal Currency Trans-

action Report (CTR) forms. To minimize the risk of detection associated with compliance, criminals who launder their own money and professional launderers who do it for them often falsify information on CTRs or try to avoid completing them altogether. Some of the more common evasive techniques include:

- Concealing or misrepresenting the ownership of the funds being exchanged or providing false identification data.
- Entering into corrupt relationships with employees of financial institutions to avoid completing CTRs or to ensure that completed forms will not be forwarded to the Treasury Department.
- Changing couriers frequently to conceal the large number of transactions being conducted for the benefit of one person.
- Breaking large volumes of currency into lots smaller than the $10,000 sum that triggers the CTR requirement, and arranging for currency transactions under the $10,000 amount. (These are called "structured transactions" or "smurfing," and are now illegal under federal law.)

To get a strategic picture of large cash transactions that may mask laundering activities, a number of state enforcement agencies have entered into agreements with the Treasury Department to obtain computer tapes of CTR data involving such transactions for their states. The tapes are analyzed for patterns and trends that identify both financial institutions with high volumes of cash transactions and individuals making the transactions. In addition, several states have passed laws patterned after federal legislation that provide financial institutions that report suspicious transactions with immunity from lawsuits. Preliminary reports suggest that the quantity of suspicious transaction reports is fairly low (in comparison to the volume of CTRs), but the quality is high in terms of pointing to probable laundering activity. The suspicious transaction reports help agencies to find the "needle in the haystack."

Investigative Techniques
Investigation of money laundering usually applies white-collar crime investigative techniques. It is essential that agencies track financial and ownership patterns for subsequent auditing and accounting. This helps investigators document discrepancies between the

amounts of income and other assets accumulated by suspects, compared with the reported amounts that can be verified through records of legitimate employment. Such evidence builds upon a variation of an IRS investigative technique known as the "net worth" method and is used increasingly in federal and state money laundering prosecutions. Sting operations are also employed to good advantage. Undercover personnel pose either as criminals in search of laundering services or, more frequently, as launderers willing to provide their services to drug traffickers to help the latter transport their currency and deposit it in banks or other institutions.

Court-authorized electronic surveillance is a potentially effective technique for laundering investigations. However, this technique is extremely labor-intensive and time-consuming, and many agencies have little experience using it against white-collar criminals. In cases where statutory, staff, and other restrictions make direct money-laundering investigations difficult, violations can be investigated indirectly as part of the investigation of the substantive crime. There are two advantages to incorporating laundering investigations into other criminal investigations. First, a financial investigative approach is added to investigations of drug trafficking and organized crime. This "second front" presents an additional opportunity to generate evidence for both the targeted activity and related offenses. Another advantage is that the financial investigation facilitates asset-forfeiture actions that may follow on the heels of criminal charges.

Legal Framework

Depending on a state's legal framework, traditional statutory violations that are involved in money laundering may include conspiracy, aiding and abetting, fraud, and tax violations. A number of innovative state statutes have been patterned after the 1986 federal laundering statute and a variety of other antiracketeering laws. California, Arizona, New York, Florida, and fourteen other states have enacted laws that specifically penalize the conversion of criminally derived property into other forms of assets. The Arizona statute is one of the most comprehensive. Since money laundering is a predicate offense under Arizona's Racketeering Act, substantial criminal and civil remedies are available. These remedies include a personal civil judgment equal to the amount of the ille-

gal gain, forfeiture of the proceeds of money laundering and of the underlying criminal acts, and forfeiture of the defendant's interest in any enterprise used for money laundering. The Arizona statute also enhances the degree of the money-laundering offense if a person "knowingly initiates, organizes, plans, finances, directs, manages, supervises, or is in the business of money laundering." This provision is aimed at specialists such as attorneys, financial advisers, real-estate brokers, bankers, and operators of *casas de cambio*. In addition, several states have passed laws that are either patterned after the Bank Secrecy Act of 1970 and require the reporting of large cash transactions, or that otherwise proscribe activities that facilitate laundering. Such activities are the unregulated operation of a business that performs financial services—check cashing and currency exchange—and failure to disclose owners and interested parties in the formation of corporations. At least sixteen states have enacted laws that address the specific offense of money laundering.

Once drug traffickers shift operations away from locations that have grown hazardous from enforcement pressure, their money-laundering operations will follow suit. As laundering operations are transacted within more states and extend into still more local communities, a nationwide problem, whose magnitude has strained federal resources, will fall more squarely on the shoulders of state and local law-enforcement agencies.

Clifford Karchmer
Douglas Ruch

Bibliography

Block, Alan A. *Masters of Paradise: Organized Crime and the Internal Revenue Service in the Bahamas.* New Brunswick, NJ: Transaction Publishers, 1991.

Ehrenfeld, Rachel. *Evil Money: Encounters along the Money Trail.* New York: Harper Business Books, 1992.

Hughes, S.J. "Policing Money Laundering through Funds Transfers: A Critique of Regulation under the Bank Secrecy Act." *Indiana Law Journal* 67 (Winter 1992): 283–330.

Karchmer, Clifford. *Illegal Money Laundering: A Strategy and Resource Guide for Law Enforcement Agencies.* Washington, DC: U.S. Department of Justice, Bureau of Justice Assistance, 1988.

————, and Douglas Ruch. "State and Local Money Laundering Control Strategies." *NIJ Report*. Washington, DC: U.S. Department of Justice, National Institute of Justice, 1992.

Morgan, P.T. "Money Laundering: The Internal Revenue Service, and Enforcement Priorities." *Florida Law Review* 43 (December 1991): 939–90.

Naylor, R.T. *Hot Money and the Politics of Debt*. New York: Linden Press, Simon and Schuster, 1987.

Powis, Robert E. *The Money Launderers: Lessons from the Drug Wars, How Billions of Illegal Dollars are Washed through Banks & Businesses*. Chicago: Probus, 1992.

Multi-Ethnic Communities: Barriers to Policing

Jacob (1984) concludes from a study of crime rates in several American cities that criminal-justice policy-makers suffer from a lack of knowledge on which to base policy decisions. He points out that police administrators cannot tell with any accuracy the nature or amount of crime in their jurisdictions or to what extent it is changing over time. In recent years the racial and ethnic composition of many urban areas has changed dramatically, and the police are not familiar with the cultural diversity of new immigrant groups (Moore and Trojanowicz, 1988). The police have purposively maintained a low visibility in these communities since their lack of awareness or understanding of local problems makes benign neglect a more viable law-enforcement policy. Thus, to residents of these neglected communities, the police are perceived as insensitive to their needs (Bahn, 1974; Kelling, 1987). Since unresponsive policies may heighten community tensions and conflict, Wasserman (1982) argues that law-enforcement policy "must be constantly revised to reflect changing social conditions within the community."

Police departments are public agencies that exist to carry out public policy. Unlike other public agencies, however, police departments have traditionally operated largely independent of effective public and legislative oversight. Police officials acting alone determine the distribution of manpower resources within their communities. By deciding how and where personnel will be utilized, these officials in fact establish community priorities in law enforcement. Consequently, the police have frequently been criticized for their lack of commitment to developing and maintaining community-based programs with a meaningful component for community input and control.

Minority communities have contended that police fail to consider local conduct norms and community-specific problems involving order maintenance and informal social control (Bahn, 1974). The role of police as enforcers of local community standards is thus undermined. Police-initiated programs that focus on community involvement—such as Neighborhood Watch—are viewed with suspicion and resisted. In general, minority residents are reluctant to cooperate with police efforts to institute such community-oriented programs since these programs appear based not on local concerns but on law-enforcement's concern with crime (Kelling, 1987; Skogan, 1989). These police–community relation problems have led to an increased emphasis on citizen participation in law-enforcement policy-making.

The Asian-American Community

Many Asian immigrants have no knowledge of American criminal law or their legal rights and obligations and little understanding of the operation of the American system of criminal justice. Some do not even know how to call the police. Another major problem is communication. Immigrants are often reluctant to call the police because of the language barrier; furthermore, for those who do call the police for assistance, communicating their needs over the phone is a major obstacle to receiving an appropriate response. On those rare occasions when Asian victims do report crimes, they do not understand why action is not taken immediately. Very often Asians will demand that those who have harmed them be arrested and incarcerated quickly. They do not understand the legal process that a suspect has to go through in order to be found guilty and sentenced. Since the process seems inconsistent with their expectations, Asian victims are left feeling dissatisfied with the police.

Finally, there are distinct cultural barriers. Many immigrants distrust and avoid the police because of their negative conceptions of and experiences with police in their native countries, i.e., law enforcement in many Asian countries is largely seen as part of a corrupt political system. Also, there are perceived risks of retaliation if offenses are reported and if victims identify and testify against offenders. In so doing, victims face the threat of retaliation not only against themselves but against members of their families as well. And this threat may come from both the accused offender and/or his or her relatives. These barriers reinforce a sense of powerlessness within the community. Individuals are in effect inhibited from speaking up, demanding their rights, and believing they have a role in determining the quality of police service available.

Law-Enforcement Initiatives

The first order of police work, legally sanctioned since the origins of policing in England, has been the preservation of peace. But the police cannot preserve the peace without public input in defining the police role in order maintenance, crime control, and community service activities. Failure to consider community sentiments and concerns in law-enforcement policy is likely to produce irrational responses to rational problems. Thus promoting community participation in the policy-making process initially rests with the viability of police–community-relations programs (Wasserman and Moore, 1988).

A police agency's community-relations program is more than a public-relations program to "sell the police image" to the community. It is a long-range, full-scale effort to acquaint the police and the community with each other's problems and to stimulate action aimed at solving those problems. Community relations should not be the exclusive business of specialized units but rather the business of the entire department from the chief to the patrol officer. Community relations are not a matter of special programs but should encompass all aspects of police work—from the selection, training, assignments, promotion of personnel field procedures, staff policy-making and planning—to the handling of citizens' complaints.

Specialized Training

The traditional approach to addressing problems in police–community relations has been through specialized training of officers. The goal is to promote an appreciation of cultural diversity and to foster an understanding of different community values and lifestyles. Alpert and Dunham (1989) report that matching police activities to community expectations improves citizen satisfaction with the police.

Training in human relations, conflict resolution, and minority cultures and languages should be offered to prepare officers to deal with a pluralistic constituency. Neglect of this area feeds a general attitude of isolation and prejudice among the police. An ability to communicate with persons whose backgrounds and languages differ from those of the officer not only increases the rapport between the police and community residents who can provide assistance and information, but also decreases the chance that conflict will develop due to misinterpretation. It has been pointed out that the insensitivity or ignorance of police officers to cross-cultural meanings of verbal and nonverbal communications is responsible for a great deal of police–citizen conflict (McEvoy, 1976). If police are to be successful in dealing with communities embracing different cultures and lifestyles, they must work at understanding and then avoiding behavior, including language, offensive to residents of those communities.

Community Outreach

Law-enforcement officials need to reach out to the community through such means as bilingual resource materials and education sessions on criminal-justice operations—including crime reporting, accessing victim-witness assistance programs, obtaining an attorney, and appearing/testifying in court. Visibility in the community is critical in order to develop trust and understanding on the part of the residents and to confront many of their negative perceptions of the police. Functions should include developing positive crime-prevention programs in conjunction with civic groups or schools; arranging tours of criminal-justice facilities; offering a "speakers bureau" for requests for public presentations on law-enforcement issues; and coordinating a liaison-referral network for community groups and other human service organizations. Periodic seminars on community-relations policies and programs should also be arranged utilizing resources from the community. Such forums should maximize the opportunity for frank exchange between concerned citizens and the police. These efforts may in turn serve to inhibit officers from dismissing departmental policies as "just talk," since officers are sensitized to the problems these policies are intended to address in the communities that they serve.

In recent years there has been a significant trend at the federal, state, and local levels to

M

provide greater citizen input in the development of policy by public agencies through administrative rule-making procedures. Davis (1975) suggests that by requiring municipalities to adopt the provisions of the Federal Administrative Procedure Act, in regard to rule making by their police departments, communities would have the opportunity to review and comment on rules and rule changes. The procedure for determining policy and codifying that policy in rules and regulations would thus become a visible process potentially involving the entire community, not merely designated ad hoc community leaders. The benefit of providing the police with clear guidelines that reflect genuine public policy is obvious.

Citizen Complaint Processing

Perhaps the most valuable asset that a police agency can possess is credibility with the community it serves (Kelling et al., 1988). Effective policing depends to a large degree on the cooperation and support of residents, and these can be obtained only where the community perceives the police force as working on its behalf, not as an "enemy" to be feared and avoided. The public credibility of any police agency depends largely on the integrity of the internal disciplinary process, i.e., the degree of public confidence in the ability of the police to police themselves (Kerstetter, 1985). Even a police agency exemplary in most areas of practice can experience incidents of abuse of authority or be perceived as abusing its authority. Therefore it is essential that every agency take the steps necessary to enforce its regulations and to maintain its credibility.

An underlying validity of any successful internal disciplinary process depends upon the existence of clearly defined policies, rules, regulations, and guidelines, so that every officer knows what conduct is expected and what will not be condoned (Police Executive Research Forum [PERF], 1981). Although it is not always possible to provide for every conceivable situation with which an officer may be confronted, precise policies with careful training and supervision can effectively reduce incidents of bad decisions being made in the stress of emergency situations.

Not only must policies be clearly articulated, but their breach must be readily ascertained and appropriately disciplined. Since most police work is not directly supervised, the best information a police agency has regarding its officers' conduct is obtained through a citizen complaint system. For the system to operate effectively, the community must perceive that it is fair, thorough, timely, and worthy of public trust. A prerequisite to a successful citizen complaint process is that citizens be informed about the complaint system and be encouraged to use it. A public education effort is recommended for explaining the complaint process and utilizing the media, various civic organizations, libraries, schools, and community service centers for public announcements, lectures, posters, and brochures. Police substations, storefronts, and community relations offices should have complaint forms and explanatory literature available (in all languages used to a significant extent in the community) and should be able to assist citizens in making complaints. Every effort should be made to reduce any intimidating features that might discourage complainants from reporting incidents, and possible language and literacy barriers should be taken into consideration at each step. Complete records of complaint reception, investigation, and adjudication should be maintained; moreover, statistical summaries should be published regularly and made available to the public.

Community-Based Initiatives

Empowerment in the Asian-American community refers to a process of enabling the community to increase its collective influence and participation in the political system. Its principles further American democratic ideals of exercising one's rights to speak and assemble freely. The strength of community organizing derives from the participation of people who lack individual power and come together out of shared interests and concerns. Empowerment in the Asian community can be viewed as a step-by-step process involving: (1) identification of Asian-immigrant issues; (2) broad-based participation despite political, social, and economic differences; and (3) effective indigenous leadership. These requisite conditions may be achieved through education and networking.

An important objective of education is to enable members of the Asian community to draw on tools and resources in managing local crime problems through institution building, such as neighborhood associations, gang-prevention programs, and storefront outreach-referral services for citizens who are fearful or victims of crime. Networking helps to ensure a broad representation of the views of various neighborhood constituencies, a coordination of community initiatives, and an institutional means of monitoring governmental policy response. Finally, the establishment of Asian-American organizations, with pan-Asian consciousness, serves as an important focus in developing intercommunity cohesion.

Neighborhood Coalitions
Often neighborhoods that have differed along social, economic, or ethnic lines have come together around a single issue because it has broad implications for the community as a whole. Anti-Asian violence has been one such issue. All Asians are subject to attack, regardless of culture, language, or nationality. Asians who have involved themselves in the various struggles against anti-Asian violence have recognized the racist roots of violence. Struggling against racist forces requires resistance to common perceptions and attitudes about Asians in favor of those based on the community's own perceptions. Identifying oneself as an Asian-American affirms a relationship to the social, cultural, and historical experience of Asians in America. It places individual experience in the context of the collective. At the same time, it underscores the common treatment of all racial minorities in America and leads to identification with other people of color as well.

Citizen Advisory Councils
Citizen input into the police policy-making process has most frequently been encouraged through ongoing neighborhood advisory committees (Fink and Sealy, 1974). While "blue-ribbon" citizens' panels consisting of community leaders appointed during periods of crisis are often not in touch with real concerns of neighborhoods, a continuing advisory committee which is made up of a cross section of neighborhood residents can provide assistance to the police department both in developing appropriate police policy and in helping to resolve conflicts between citizens and police. These advisory councils are seen as essential in providing the police force with information about community sentiments, ensuring that the police are responsive to the needs of the neighborhoods, and improving communication between citizens and the police. Such committees are intended to be neither passive recipients of imposed police practices, nor passive groups on which police policy established elsewhere is merely explained and justified. Rather, such groups are intended

to be active participants in the identification of priorities, formulation of policies, and evaluation of the adequacy of police services being administered in their particular communities.

Eric D. Poole
Mark R. Pogrebin

Bibliography
Alpert, G.P., and R.G. Dunham, eds. *Critical Issues in Policing: Contemporary Readings*. Prospect Heights, IL: Waveland, 1989.
Bahn, C. "The Reassurance Factor in Police Patrol." *Criminology* 12 (1974): 338–45.
Bittner, E. *The Functions of Police in Modern Society*. Washington, DC: National Institute of Mental Health, 1970.
Davis, K.C. *Police Discretion*. St. Paul, MN: West, 1975.
Fink, J., and L.G. Sealy. *The Community and the Police: Conflict or Cooperation?* New York: John Wiley and Sons, 1974.
Jacob, H. *The Frustration of Policy: Responses to Crime by American Cities*. Boston: Little, Brown, 1984.
Kelling, G.L. "Acquiring a Taste for Order." *Crime and Delinquency* 33 (1987): 90–102.
———, and J.K. Stewart. "Neighborhoods and Police: The Maintenance of Civil Authority." *Perspectives on Policing* 10. Washington, DC: National Institute of Justice and Harvard University, 1989.
———, et al. "Police Accountability and Community Policing." *Perspectives on Policing* 7. Washington, DC: National Institute of Justice and Harvard University, 1988.
Kerstetter, W.A. "Who Disciplines the Police? Who Should?" In *Police Leadership in America: Crisis and Opportunity*. Ed. W.A. Geller. Chicago: American Bar Foundation, 1985.
McEvoy, D.W. *The Police and Their Many Publics*. Metuchen, NJ: Scarecrow Press, 1976.
Moore, M.H., and R.C. Trojanowicz. "Corporate Strategies for Policing." *Perspectives on Policing* 6. Washington, DC: National Institute of Justice and Harvard University, 1988.
Police Executive Research Forum. *Police Agency Handling of Officer Misconduct: A Model Policy Statement*. Washington, DC: PERF, 1981.

Skogan, W.G. "Communities, Crime, and Neighborhood Organization." *Crime and Delinquency* 35 (1989): 437–57.

Taub, R.P., et al. *Paths of Neighborhood Change: Race and Crime in Urban America.* Chicago: University of Chicago Press, 1984.

Wasserman, R. "The Government Setting." In *Local Government Police Management.* Ed. B.L. Garmire. Washington, DC: International City Management Association, 1982.

———, and M.H. Moore. "Values in Policing." *Perspectives in Policing* 8. Washington, DC: National Institute of Justice and Harvard University, 1988.

Multi-Ethnic Communities: Interactive Model

A major issue facing modern policing is how to operate effectively in light of the ever-increasing ethnic diversity of our population. History has demonstrated that most police issues, ranging from personnel to excessive use of force, are linked closely to the challenges that result from the increasing ethnic diversity found in our cities and suburbs. The difficult challenge of policing in rapidly changing multi-ethnic communities has resulted in riots triggered by conflict between police officers and members of ethnic communities, including those in Los Angeles and Miami (Alpert and Dunham, 1992; Porter and Dunn, 1984).

Leaders of metropolitan areas with less ethnic diversity than Los Angeles and Miami may think that these types of problems do not concern them. However, these ethnically diverse cosmopolitan areas are prototypes of the American urban scene. In most communities, ethnicity seems to complicate police procedures and encounters between the police and the public. Progressive police administrators have been searching for solutions to the problems inherent in this type of potentially explosive interaction. Improved policies, training, enhanced supervision, and the decentralization of administrative duties are just some of the solutions that have been attempted. However, it must be realized that information about potential clients, i.e., members of the various ethnic groups and their views toward police and policing, is necessary to guide these solutions. Questions such as the following need to be answered by the police to help design their new approach to policing: How do members of each ethnic community conceptualize the police? What are their cultural expectations? Which policing procedures will receive community support and the cooperation of the law-abiding residents and which will be rejected with noncooperation and perhaps violence?

At the same time, the police come to view the ethnic community and its members as antagonistic to the police and their role in the community. Police feel like they have no citizen support in the area and begin to focus more and more on the lack of respect for the police, refusals to cooperate with the police, and antagonistic bystanders taunting police officers while an investigation or arrest is in process. This type of reciprocal mistrust can develop into a cycle that escalates into the extreme conflict manifest in the Rodney King case.

Formal and Informal Social Control

To couch the multi-ethnic policing problem in sociological terms, it is one of disjuncture between formal and informal social control structures. Further, when all is said and done, it is the informal social control structure that revolves around intimate or primary relationships that has the greatest impact on social control. In fact, for the formal control structure (i.e. the police and courts) to have any degree of effectiveness, it must be supported and given credibility by the informal structure.

When the intimate relationships of the primary groups are weakened, social control is gradually dissolved. The resulting indirect or secondary relationships have a much different effect on social control. As Park (1925:26) noted almost seventy years ago:

> It is characteristic of city life [in the absence of neighborhood cohesion] that all sorts of people meet and mingle together who never fully comprehend one another. The anarchist and the club man, the priest and the Levite, the actor and the missionary who touch elbows on the street still live in totally different worlds. So complete is the segregation of vocational classes that it is possible within the limits of the city to live in an isolation almost as complete as that of some remote rural community.

Park observed differences between social control based on mores and neighborhood cohesion, and social control based on indirect and secondary relationships and positive law. The latter is much weaker and less capable of establishing order.

More recently, Greenberg and Rohe (1986:79) have reviewed the empirical research on the relationship between informal control and crime. They concluded that emotional attachment to the neighborhood, perceived responsibility for the control over the neighborhood, and the expectation that oneself or one's neighbors would intervene in a criminal event are associated with low crime rates. This evidence suggests a relationship between the informal control of a cohesive neighborhood and crime.

Informal social control in the residential context refers to the development, observance, and enforcement of local norms for appropriate public behavior (Greenberg and Rohe, 1986:80). It is the process by which individual behavior is influenced by a group and usually functions to maintain a minimum level of predictability in the behavior of group members and to promote the well-being of the group as a whole.

Formal social control is based on written rules or laws and prescribed punishments for violating these rules and laws. The police and the courts are the institutions most directly charged with maintaining order under formal social controls. The means of formal social control are not very effective without the direct support of the informal means of control. The combination and the interaction of the two is central to establishing effective social control.

The stigma of a police car in one's driveway, being handcuffed and placed in a police car in front of family members and long-time friends and neighbors, and the sting of gossip is feared much more in cohesive neighborhoods than the actual punishments of the formal system. Of course, maximum effectiveness of the control system requires that the norms and values of the informal system be consistent with those of the formal system. Wilson and Kelling (1982:34) advocate this level of integration:

> The essence of the police role in maintaining order is to reinforce the informal control mechanisms of the community itself. The police cannot, without committing extraordinary resources, provide a substitute for that informal control. On

the other hand, to reinforce those natural forces the police must accommodate them.

If the local values and customs of a neighborhood dictate that the police are outsiders and arrest is the imposition of unfair and biased rules on fellow residents, then the stigma of arrest is absent and the informal control system works against the formal system.

Informal social control is not present in every neighborhood, rather it is a variable that differs both in form and degree among neighborhoods. Many lack any degree of fundamental integration and thereby the means for an effective informal social control system. More specifically, the results of research on neighborhoods indicate that shared norms are less likely to develop in low-income neighborhoods that are heterogeneous with regard to ethnic composition, family type, or lifestyle, than they are in low-income, culturally homogeneous neighborhoods or in middle-class neighborhoods (Greenberg and Rohe, 1986; Merry, 1981). Residents of low-income heterogeneous neighborhoods tend to be more suspicious of each other, to perceive less commonality with other residents, and tend to feel less control over their neighborhood than do the residents of more homogeneous areas. For example, many inner-city black neighborhoods lack a dominant cultural group. Even though the residents are all black, housing discrimination and other factors result in neighborhoods that vary considerably in the social values, lifestyle, and family type characteristic of its residents (Erbe, 1975). As a result of this diversity, residents have little consensus on conceptions of appropriate public behavior, and informal social control within the neighborhood tends to be weak. In extreme cases, the conceptions of appropriate public behavior are in conflict among neighborhood residents.

The situation in predominately white, middle-class neighborhoods is much different. These neighborhoods tend to be more homogeneous due to self-selection resulting from the greater freedom of choice in locating a residence. Residents tend to self-select their location based upon similarities of other residents to their family type, lifestyle. and values. This process tends to group residents according to their basic underlying assumptions of appropriate public behavior and values. Therefore, informal social control tends to be much more developed in these types of neighborhoods, when compared to low-income neighborhoods.

An Interactive Model

The neighborhood unit still is a social unit as well as an ecological category, even though neighborhoods have undergone considerable change in the past fifty years. These changes have resulted in considerable variation among neighborhoods in their degree of cohesiveness and the strength of their informal social control systems. It is still true that neighborhood context can provide an important source of integration into the larger society for its residents. In fact, cohesive neighborhoods provide alternative means for residents to respond to and adapt to the larger, more complex society. In addition, cohesive neighborhoods incorporate an important system of informal social control that can be crucial to establishing order and controlling crime, if it is integrated into the formal social control system involving the police and the courts. The key is the interaction between the formal social control system of the larger community, and the informal control systems operating in the various neighborhoods.

One of the early functions of developing urban police forces was to establish social regulation to supplement law-enforcement duties. This need developed when police effectiveness declined, as urbanization increased and as communities became more cosmopolitan (Black, 1980; Kelling, 1985). In the most disorderly parts of American cities, the traditional police officer became an "institution" who responded to a "moral mandate" for informal social control in situations where individuals violated community or neighborhood norms and impinged on the personal and property rights of others. "Street justice" was another name for this function (Sykes, 1986) "Street justice," then, is a response to a community or neighborhood mandate that something be done about situations where formal institutions cannot or will not act for a variety of reasons. When this function became linked to ethnic and racial prejudice in the 1950s and 1960s, however, it ushered in decades of reform.

Skogan (1990) has analyzed indicators of neighborhood decline that lead to disorder. These include public drinking, corner gangs, street harassment, drugs, noisy neighbors, commercial sex, vandalism, dilapidation/abandonment, and rubbish. Other research has also revealed that neighborhoods are declining but the community-policing philosophy is still appropriate for many areas. Further, it is possible to create community spirit in those areas that never had any or that have lost it (Alpert and Dunham, 1988).

The traditional model of policing, whether it is labeled "street justice" or "order maintenance," represents a model of policing that integrates the informal control system of the local community with the formal control system of the police. The more recent model of policing, whether it is called "law enforcement" or "professional," attempts policing with minimal integration between the formal control system of the police and the informal control system of the local neighborhood.

The interactive model calls for policing strategies that integrate formal procedures and practices with the informal social control system operating within the various neighborhoods. To reach maximum effectiveness, police discretion and strategies must be organized within the established norms of public behavior in the neighborhood. Policies must be developed with an understanding that the neighborhood has established alternative ways which residents adapt to and cope within the larger social system, including the police, and the laws they enforce.

Community-Oriented Policing

There has been a resurgence of interest in this policing strategy and a recent increase in the number of programs that have been initiated in agencies around the country. This interest may be more a function of the failure of the "law-enforcement" or the "professional" model discussed earlier than an increase in support for this type of policing. Regardless of the reasons, significant attention and resources are being allocated to community-oriented policing. The purpose of the model is to place a greater emphasis on nonadversarial problem-solving in lieu of traditional strategies that conflict with normative structures in the neighborhood. Nonadversarial policing is achieved through the development of specific tasks and policing strategies, which are based upon a combination of law-enforcement requirements, community needs, and techniques of problem-solving. The question still remains: How can the police gain a greater understanding of the unique characteristics of specific communities so that a bond will form?

Neighborhood Intervention and Community Evaluation

During the past fifteen to twenty years, many large, urban police departments have adopted some sort of team policing in response to the demand for decentralization of their police operations. In theory, team policing is an excellent way to increase the efficiency and effectiveness of policing, both proactive and reactive. Neighborhood Intervention and Community Evaluation has several organizational elements that should be added to the traditional components existing in many team policing units. Most departments stress the need for police officers to return to the old meaning of "beat officer." That is, to learn about the residents and business people in their neighborhoods and to see them and be seen in situations that are not always defined as negative or at best neutral. To reduce isolation officers must first be assigned to community beats for an extended period, supervised by command staff. This move toward stability will increase the identification of an officer with the residents, geography, politics, and other issues of a given neighborhood. Second, there must be the traditional police–community relations meetings or citizens' advisory groups. Even when these two elements are operating, successful community policing requires proper training, feedback mechanisms, and an institutionalized reward system.

Neighborhood Training

Neighborhood training can effectively inform the officer as to what he or she can expect from the residents, physical surroundings, or other influences. This in-service training introduces officers to community characteristics while working the streets under supervision (in a way similar to a field-training officer). Clear differences divide officers and citizens concerning style of policing. To match style of policing with community needs, knowledge of community values and beliefs as well as the attitudes and priorities of police officers must be part of the training mix.

The needs of the community can be determined by periodic social surveys that, if linked to census data and local planning information, can inform officials of the changing nature of a given neighborhood. While it is relatively easy to identify what constitutes negative behavior, it is difficult to ascertain exemplary behavior. A Blue-Ribbon Committee studying the Miami Police Department came to a similar conclusion. In its final report (Overtown Blue Ribbon Committee, 1983:199), it noted:

> It is our conclusion that a minor organizational change can have a major impact on community relations and on the interrelationships between citizens and police. We believe that confidence in the police will be enhanced if the police measure and make more visible the activities they perform. Moreover, police work is usually rewarded by the gratitude an officer receives from those who he or she helps. Status in the department, promotions, raises, commendations, etc., rest largely on his or her crime-fighting activities, the number of arrests, crimes he or she solves, etc. As a result, the patrol officer may regard service calls as a necessary evil.

Both the crime fighting and the service function of the police need to be evaluated on the institutional and individual levels. First, an ongoing study of victimization can provide police with data on how well their agency provides services. Usually, this information is gleaned from official crime statistics (UCR), but victimization data can be misleading. Second, a random survey of consumers of police services can provide administrators and planners with feedback on their services and the officers who provide them.

Rewarding the Police Officer

Most police departments provide incentives for their officers. These include traditional promotions, merit increases, and "officer-of-the-month" recognition. Traditionally, these rewards have been based on aggressive actions that have led to an arrest(s), the capture of a dangerous felon, or some other heroic activity. These criteria for rewarding police officers are important and serve to encourage similar actions from others. Yet other types of police behavior deserve recognition, such as exemplary service to the community and the diffusion and reduction of violence. The actions of an officer who avoids a shooting or talks a suspect into custody may not be known to his or her superiors, and when they are, the officer may be labeled a "chicken" or one who cannot provide needed backup to fellow officers. This type of nonaggressive behavior—consistent with neighborhood norms—deserves attention and reinforcement.

Toward an Interactive Model
The model will work most effectively in homogeneous neighborhoods and in areas where police administrators have strong control of their officers. It is important that police officers work for the community, not merely to impress their supervisors. Some cities will find it quite reasonable to split police jurisdictions to use the proposed model, as many geographic locations attract or limit certain groups of people. Other cities may find their demographic mix too complex to divide for this type of policing. Regardless of the administrative level of commitment, patrol officers are in the best position to understand the varied and changing needs of the community.

Roger Dunham
Geoffrey P. Alpert

Bibliography
Alpert, Geoffrey, and Roger Dunham. *Policing Multi-Ethnic Neighborhoods.* Westport, CT: Greenwood Press, 1988.
———. *Policing Urban America.* Prospect Heights, IL: Waveland Press, 1992.
Black, Donald. *The Manners and Customs of the Police.* New York: Academic Press, 1980.
Dukes, Richard, and Geoffrey Alpert. "Criminal Victimization from a Police Perspective." *Journal of Police Science and Administration* 8 (1980): 21–30.
Erbe, Brigette. "Race and Socioeconomic Segregation." *American Sociological Review* 40 (1975): 801–12.
Furstenberg, Frank, and Charles Wellford. "Calling the Police: The Evaluation of Police Service." *Law and Society Review* 7 (1973): 393–406.
Greenberg, Stephanie, and William Rohe. "Informal Social Control and Crime Prevention in Modern Neighborhoods." In *Urban Neighborhoods: Research and Policy.* Ed. R. Taylor. New York: Praeger, 1986.
Greene, Jack. "Foot Patrol and Community Policing: Past Practices and Future Prospects." *American Journal of Police* 6 (1987): 1–18.
Kelling, George. "Order Maintenance, the Quality of Urban Life, and Police: A Different Line of Argument." In *Police Leadership in America: Crisis and Opportunity.* Ed. William Geller. New York: Praeger, 1985.
Mastrofski, Stephan. "Police Knowledge on the Patrol Beat: A Performance Measure." In *Police at Work: Issues and Analysis.* Ed. R. Bennett. Beverly Hills: Sage Publications, 1983.
Merry, Sally E. *Urban Danger: Life in a Neighborhood of Strangers.* Philadelphia: Temple University Press, 1981.
Moore, Mark. "Problem-Solving and Community Policing." In *Modern Policing.* Ed. Michael Tonry and Norval Morris. Chicago: University of Chicago Press, 1992.
———, and George Kelling. "To Serve and Protect: Learning from Police History." *The Public Interest* 70 (1983): 49–65.
Overtown Blue Ribbon Committee. Final Report. Miami: City of Miami, 1983.
Park, Robert, et al. *The City.* Chicago: University of Chicago Press, 1925.
Porter, Bruce, and Marvin Dunn. *The Miami Riot of 1980.* Lexington, MA: Lexington Books, 1984.
Skogan, Wesley. *Disorder and Decline: Crime and the Spiral of Decay in American Neighborhoods.* New York: Free Press, 1990.
Steinman, Michael. "Officer Orientations Toward the Community." *Urban Affairs Quarterly* 21 (1986): 598–606.
Sykes, Gary. "Street Justice: A Moral Defense of Order Maintenance Policing." *Justice Quarterly* 3 (1986): 497–512.
Walker, Samuel. "Broken Windows and Fractured History: The Use and Misuse of History in Recent Police Patrol Analysis." *Justice Quarterly* 1 (1984): 75–90.
Wilson, James Q., and George Kelling. "The Police and Neighborhood Safety." *Atlantic Monthly* (March 1982): 29–38.

Multijurisdictional Drug Law Enforcement

Federal, state, and local law enforcement agencies increasingly recognize the value of coordinating efforts for reducing drug abuse. Interagency cooperation for drug law enforcement has existed for more than twenty years, but recently the nature and goals of these cooperative efforts have changed dramatically in some jurisdictions. Three types of enforcement strategies prevail. First, case-oriented is essentially reactive and seeks sufficient evidence to arrest, prosecute, and convict known drug distributors. Methods for building cases include use of informants, undercover and surveillance, and "buy and bust" operations. Virtually all police departments with narcotics or dangerous drug units carry out this type of enforcement. Second, network-oriented is a proactive effort in which distribution is traced from street-level drug sellers through mid-level and high-level distributors, and at times to top-level kingpin distributors. This type of enforcement also requires the use of undercover and surveillance methods but often also involves complex financial investigations to build prosecutable interlocking cases. Third, comprehensive problem-reduction strategies are proactive initiatives taken to reduce injury to the community resulting from both the supply and demand for drugs. They typically involve not only law-enforcement agencies but also community members and relevant community agencies such as those providing education, health, and mental health services for high-risk populations. Law-enforcement agencies that participate in comprehensive problem-reduction strategies ordinarily also participate simultaneously in case-oriented and network-oriented strategies.

Maricopa County, Arizona
This county, whose major city is Phoenix, started its drug demand reduction program in March 1989. Its components are:

- Periodically (usually two or more times each month) a location in the county where drugs are known to be used openly is targeted for a "user accountability" strike. During the selected time period, ranging from several hours to a few days, a task force of law-enforcement officers from nearby communities arrests persons at the targeted location for drug possession. Additionally the task force begins proceedings for seizing the persons' vehicles and other property related to their drug possession.
- Each of the county's law-enforcement agencies has instituted a policy of en-

couraging arrests to be made under any circumstances when a person is found to possess illegal drugs (e.g., during the course of routine traffic stops). These offenses are all felonies in Arizona.
- Persons arrested on drug charges are formally booked (not given a summons or otherwise diverted from the arrest process), so they necessarily spend some time locked up in the county's jail intake facility.
- The county prosecutor's office screens arrest reports for drug offenses to determine whether the arrestee meets criteria specified for participation in drug treatment as an alternative to prosecution. Typical arrestees who meet the criteria are first-time felony drug offenders over the age of eighteen without a prior history of other felonies or recent misdemeanors involving drugs. Prosecution is temporarily suspended for qualifying arrestees, who are later sent a letter from the county attorney explaining the conditions that they must meet in order to avoid subsequent filing of criminal charges.
- The alternative offered to the arrestee typically entails filing a written "statement of facts" admitting to the offense charge, participating in a period of drug-abuse treatment and mandatory drug testing, paying a treatment program fee, paying additional fees and assessments, and paying the sheriff for the costs of having been housed in the county jail's intake facility.
- Eligible arrestees who opt for the treatment alternative undergo up to two years of group therapy, seminars, and routinely repeated urinalysis. At the end of the assigned period, arrestees who complete the treatment program and remain drug-free have their charges dropped.
- Arrestees who are eligible for the treatment alternative or who fail to complete it successfully are handled by the county attorney's normal procedures for prosecuting drug arrests. Arrestees who do not respond to the letter offering them the treatment alternative have an arrest warrant or summons issued against them.
- An imaginative media campaign continually reminds the county's populace about

the program through television, billboards, and print media. The message: If you're caught with drugs, you're going to jail. "You then face felony charges, a prison sentence, and stiff financial penalties. Or pay to enter a year-long rehab program." The media are well informed about task force operations in progress, and their coverage helps demonstrate that the "Do Drugs. Do Time" campaign is more than rhetoric.

The Maricopa program is based on the assumption that a large proportion of drugs purchased in the county are consumed by casual or infrequent drug users. By reducing the number of casual drug users, law-enforcement agencies hope to disrupt the drug markets in their communities. Surveys have shown very high public awareness of the demand-reduction strategy and its slogan. A potentially conflicting goal of the county attorney's office is to avoid processing increasing numbers of persons arrested for drug possession or use. The key ingredient in this aspect of the program was prefiling diversion—eligible arrestees' cases are not filed in court at all if arrestees accept the conditions of the diversion program. Whether the reduction in prosecutor's workload can continue over the long term is not yet clear. Arrestees on minor drug possession charges who fail to respond to the letter offering the diversion option must be rearrested and prosecuted, and they represent a potential future burden on the criminal-justice system.

The treatment component of the program is operated under a county contract by TASC, an incorporated, private, nonprofit, outpatient facility. TASC stands for "Treatment Assessment Screening Center," but the organization is otherwise similar to the Treatment Alternatives to Street Crime units found in many other jurisdictions. The main problem faced by TASC management in providing drug treatment is covering the expenses of indigent clients. A Drug Enforcement Administration (DEA) agent in Phoenix coordinates education by supplying schools and other community agencies with DEA materials.

Juvenile arrests are uncommon under the demand-reduction program because the task force targets are places frequented by adults. Still, juvenile arrestees are unlikely to go undetected; Maricopa has one of the few programs in the country for universal urinalysis of juveniles who enter detention. The drug test results of arrested juveniles are made available to assigned probation officers, who may make the information available to others, such as parents, teachers, or attorneys, at their discretion. Prior to establishing the urinalysis program, probation staff reported they had trouble distinguishing drug abusers from nonusers.

Federally Organized Efforts
Drug task forces are the principal vehicles of federally organized cooperation and are mainly of two types: DEA state and local task forces created by DEA; and Organized Crime Drug Enforcement Task Forces (OCDETFs) centered in selected U.S. attorney's offices in major cities throughout the country. The precursors of DEA state and local task forces were actually launched in 1970 prior to DEA's inception. In that year a pilot federal task force was set up in New York City by DEA's predecessor, the Bureau of Narcotics and Dangerous Drugs (BNDD). The impetus for BNDD was to respond to drug traffic that spilled beyond municipal, county, and state boundaries in metropolitan New York. The early state and local task forces were based on the concept of "creative federalism." In order to foster mutual respect among levels of government, with each treated as an equal, creative federalism relied heavily on the notion of coordination, which was never formally defined and led to frustration. Nowadays, formal cooperation in DEA state and local task forces has matured into a routine bureaucratic arrangement documented by compacts, memoranda of understanding, and sometimes contracts binding federal and nonfederal jurisdictions.

Beginning in 1985, the DEA task forces received a line-item federal appropriation to support overtime and investigative expenses. From that year, when the appropriation stood at $13.5 million for twenty-six DEA task forces, the separate funding grew to $32 million for forty-four task forces in fiscal year 1989. In 1986 Congress passed the Anti-Drug Abuse Act, which in part mandated that the DEA integrate the task forces into its overall national drug-enforcement program. Together with the increased appropriation, that legislation institutionalized the DEA-SL task forces and in one section provided state and local task force participants with federal investigative and arrest powers. By receiving federal investigative authority, the nonfederal investigators have arrest powers throughout the country.

Granting task force investigators federal enforcement powers was a significant development. Since the early 1970s, DEA task force participants had been deputized as U.S. marshals, a controversial status that conveyed sweeping investigative and arrest powers far beyond the enforcement of drug-related federal statutes. After 1986 designation as a state or local DEA task-force investigator carried federal enforcement authority that was limited to drug-related violations of federal Title 21 of the U.S. Code. Thus, DEA-SL task force personnel had the same powers as DEA agents, no more or less.

Organized Crime Drug Enforcement Task Forces (OCDETFs), begun in 1984 as a presidential initiative, are charged with targeting major national and international trafficking organizations, the highest levels of importing and wholesale distribution. OCDETFs are administrative clusters of federal investigative and prosecutive agencies. The U.S. attorney's office that has an OCDETF designates coordinators who oversee investigations. The coordinators work with both the participating federal law-enforcement agencies and the leading assistant U.S. attorney to see that cases are developed in a prosecutable manner. In contrast with DEA-SL task forces, it is the exception rather than the rule for OCDETFs to involve nonfederal investigators. Generally this is because the high level of trafficker upon which OCDETFs focus usually are one or two trafficking levels above those targeted by state or local investigators. However, it is important to understand the instances of state and local involvement in OCDETFs, since they represent the only other major example of formalized federal task force cooperation with nonfederal agencies in drug enforcement.

An example of an OCDETF case involved the FBI and a Baltimore city detective. An FBI task force was formed to target long entrenched managers of heroin distribution organizations who used young gang members to kill off competitors. Instead of trying to solve the drug homicide cases alone or to apprehend the leaders through conventional narcotics investigation, the Baltimore FBI office enlisted the assistance of a local detective. The detective had specialized expertise that was valuable to the FBI, having served tours in the Baltimore Police Department's homicide and narcotics squads. The detective used his extensive local informant contacts, and after a protracted undercover and grand jury investigation the FBI developed evidence that resulted in the arrest of several suspected assassins on federal firearms charges (which carry a fifteen-year mandatory minimum sentence). Faced with the certainty of long-term punishment, some assassins became government witnesses and worked with the FBI to implicate the drug kingpins. The first defendant who pleaded guilty, the ringleader, received a seventy-year prison sentence. At the close of this investigation, the Baltimore detective returned to his department.

Benefits of Cooperation

Several basic factors are associated with positive task force experiences and help account for the continued operation of DEA state/local task forces, OCDETFs, and informal, ad hoc modes of cooperation:

- Pooling federal and local agency resources ensures broad geographic coverage for investigations, helps build a critical mass of resources (starting with intelligence information), and provides each participating agency with an investigative capability that can enter its jurisdiction when need be, bringing the full force of a mobile strike team.
- Participating local investigators become exposed to cases usually more complex and demanding than those they had been working. This provides investigators with valuable on-the-job training and the opportunity to develop or refine such specialized skills as report writing, testifying before grand juries, use of court authorized electronic surveillance, working closely with an experienced prosecutor from the inception of a case, and seeking hidden assets through financial investigations.
- Participating agencies also stand to benefit from a portion of the assets seized from criminals. In many cases the agency's cost for the loss of an investigator to a task force is made up out of forfeiture proceeds, although the agency

may have to wait for adjudication of the forfeitures so that the assets can be liquidated.

Organizational conflicts and questions over leadership still occasionally surround efforts to establish task force cooperation. Many of the problems that are labeled "political" in nature may actually stem from local reaction to the federal agency's selection of a task force commander with limited experience in dealing with nonfederal investigators. Hence, plans to prevent or reduce task force problems need to incorporate a process of careful leadership selection.

Jan Chaiken
Marcia Chaiken
Clifford Karchmer

Bibliography
Chaiken, Jan, and Marcia Chaiken. "Drug Use and Predatory Crime." *Drugs and Crime*. Eds. James Q. Wilson, and Michael Tonry. Chicago: University of Chicago Press, 1990.
———, et al. *Multijurisdictional Drug Law Enforcement Strategies: Reducing Supply and Demand*. Eds. James Q. Wilson, and Michael Tonry. Washington, DC: National Institute of Justice, 1990.
Connors, Edward F., III, and Hugh Nugent. *Street-Level Narcotics Enforcement*. Washington, DC: Bureau of Justice Assistance, 1990.
Coyle, Kenneth R., and Chip Coldren. *Case Studies in Multijurisdictional Task Force Implementation and Operation*. Washington, DC: Criminal Justice Statistics Association, 1990.
Eck, John E., et al. *Taking a Problem-Oriented Approach to Drug Enforcement*. Washington, DC: Police Executive Research Forum, 1989.
Ferris, Janet E. *Starting Forfeiture Programs: A Prosecutor's Guide*. Washington, DC: Police Executive Research Forum, 1989.
Gallagher, G. Patrick. *The Management and Disposition of Seized Assets*. Washington, DC: Police Executive Research Forum, 1988.
Holmes, Cameron H. *Developing Plans to Attack Drug Traffickers' Assets*. Washington, DC: Police Executive Research Forum, 1989.
Wexler, Harry K., et al. *A Criminal Justice Strategy for Treating Drug Offenders in Custody*. Washington, DC: National Institute of Justice, 1988.

National Crime Victimization Survey

The National Crime Victimization Survey (NCVS) reports unoffical crime statistics collected from victims of crime by the Bureau of the Census for the Bureau of Justice Statistics (BJS). Unofficial statistics differ from official data in that they are produced independently of the records of a government crime-control agency. (For an example of official crime statistics see Uniform Crime Reporting System.)

While official statistics (those maintained by police agencies, courts, or correctional institutions) document the amount of crime reported to the police or the manner in which an apprehended offender is processed, unofficial statistics attempt to show the amount of crime that occurs in the United States even though the incidents cited were not reported to or recorded by a crime control agency. Unofficial statistics like those contained in the NCVS indicate that a considerable number of crimes—often referred to as the "dark figure of crime"—are not reported to the police.

Historical Development

The measurement of criminal victimization other than through official crime statistics is a relatively new endeavor in the United States. In 1965 President Lyndon B. Johnson created the Commission of Law Enforcement and the Administration of Justice, which was, among other duties, to determine the amount of crime that occurred in the United States. In their examination of crime the Commission wanted to gather victim-based statistics to supplement the information available from the *Uniform Crime Reports (UCR)* published by the FBI. They sponsored three victimization studies: the Bureau of Social Science Research Study, commonly referred to as Field Survey I (Biderman et al., 1967); the National Opinion Research Center Study, commonly referred to as Field Survey II (Ennis, 1967); and the University of Michigan Survey Research Center Study, commonly referred to as Field Survey III (Reiss, 1967).

The results of these three studies indicated that a significant portion of the crimes that occur (as high as 51 percent) are not reported to the police. However, the most frequently occurring crimes reported in the victimization studies closely paralleled the crimes previously shown to occur most often by the UCR.

In 1969 the BJS began exploring the feasibility of an ongoing national victimization survey with the Bureau of the Census. A pilot project was conducted during which surveys were conducted in five major cities, in addition to a national survey. Based upon those pilot surveys, the NCVS was instituted in 1972.

Method of Data Collection

The NCVS program currently conducts a national survey of households and individuals to measure the amount of crime that occurs in the United States (see Tables 1 and 2). Every six months approximately 60,000 household interviews and 135,000 personal interviews are conducted. The same sample (households and/or individuals) is interviewed twice a year for a three-year period about their victimization experiences over the preceding six months. In past years surveys of businesses were also conducted to determine the extent of their victimization. The commercial survey was suspended in 1977 (U.S. Department of Justice, 1985).

Initially the NCVS program sends an introductory letter explaining the purpose of the study and advising the individual that an interviewer will be contacting them. The initial interview with the household is a personal interview conducted by Census Bureau personnel. Follow-up interviews may later be conducted by telephone. All people interviewed for the study are advised that their answers are confidential by law and may be reviewed only by a sworn employee of the U.S. Bureau of the Census.

Household Surveys

Information is obtained on each household member who is twelve years of age or older. Anyone within the household who is fourteen years or older can be interviewed to obtain this information. For purposes of this survey, members of a household are categorized in one of three different ways: household respondents, self-respondents, and proxy respondents. Household respondents answer questions that pertain to everyone in the household, such as whether the home is owned or rented, total income, or whether anyone in the household had been the victim of a crime in the last six months. Self-respondents, who are at least fourteen years old, answer questions that relate directly to themselves and any crimes that they may have been the victim of in the last six months. Proxy respondents provide information for household members aged twelve or thirteen, or for members of the household not available for interviews at the time of the survey.

Data are collected on six of the eight crimes that make up the Part I offenses reported in the Uniform Crime Reporting System by police agencies. Because the survey is based on interviews of the victim, data on homicide are obviously not collected. The crime of arson is excluded from the NCVS because it is often difficult to determine whether a household member was in fact the person responsible for committing the offense. For each household, information is recorded on the number of burglaries, larcenies (thefts), or vehicle thefts that occurred during the previous six months. Within each household, information is recorded on each individual who was the victim of a rape, robbery, assault, or personal larceny.

A separate report form is filled out for each victim and each crime reported to the interviewer. Information on attempted crimes is also recorded. For example, if an armed robbery occurred in the home during which three persons were robbed, three separate reports would be completed, one on each victim. This differs significantly from the police statistics collected by the UCR, which would reflect only one incident.

Additionally, information is collected on whether the victim attempted to protect self or property during the commission of the crime.

Business Surveys

Prior to being suspended in 1977, business surveys were conducted as part of the national survey. Interviewers from the Census Bureau contacted the owner or manager of the commercial establishment. If the interviewer was unable for some reason to obtain information from either the owner or manager, he attempted to obtain it from another employee, such as an assistant manager. Excluded from the survey were government office buildings, farms, and household "cottage" industries. Information was collected on attempted or actual burglaries and robberies.

Criticisms of the NCVS

Victimization studies like the National Crime Victimization Survey are subject to a number of criticisms and concerns. In times of fiscal constraint the NCVS will be vulnerable to concerns about cost effectiveness.

There are a number of methodological problems inherent in research of this type, many of which were identified in the early field surveys conducted for the Commission on Law Enforcement and the Administration of Justice. Family members are not necessarily a reliable source of information on other family members. Individuals have a tendency to remember events as having occurred at times other than when they actually occurred. The further removed an incident is from the time a survey is conducted, the less accurate the memory of an individual will be. Like the UCR, the NCVS shows only the number of crimes that have occurred or been reported, not how many crimes can be attributed to the same offender.

The present NCVS requires respondents, after the initial contact, to be interviewed once every six months for three years, resulting in their having to complete seven interviews. There is a danger that the respondents will grow tired of the process and underreport crimes merely to reduce the amount of time required to complete the interview. As with any type of survey research that utilizes personal interviews, the NCVS is subject to bias introduced by the person who conducts the interview.

Implications for the Police

NCVS results have a number of implications for the police, primarily in those areas that explore the reasons crimes either are or are not reported to them. The specific reasons for not reporting a crime vary with the type of offense and whether or not the crime was completed. For crimes of theft or household crimes, the more frequent reason for not reporting was that the victim did not think the crime was serious enough to call the police. For personal crimes of violence, however, most frequently the victims considered the crime a private/personal matter or took care of it themselves. In some instances the victims felt that nothing could be done, or that the police would not do anything

TABLE 1

1973–90 Trends   Personal and Household Crimes: Victimization Levels and Rates

Year		All Crimes	Victimizations			Population	
			Crimes of Violence	Personal Theft	Household Crimes	Number of Persons	Number of Households
1973	Number	35,681,030	5,350,550	14,970,570	15,339,910	164,362,900	70,442,400
	Rate		32.6	91.1	217.8		
1974	Number	38,441,090	5,509,950	15,889,010	17,012,130	167,058,400	72,162,900
	Rate		33.0	95.1	235.7		
1975	Number	39,266,130	5,572,670	16,293,720	17,399,740	169,671,500	73,559,600
	Rate		32.8	96.0	236.5		
1976	Number	39,317,620	5,599,330	16,519,380	17,198,910	171,900,500	74,956,100
	Rate		32.6	96.1	229.5		
1977	Number	40,314,380	5,901,510	16,932,910	17,479,960	174,092,700	76,412,300
	Rate		33.9	97.3	228.8		
1978	Number	40,412,370	5,941,080	17,050,240	17,421,050	176,214,600	77,980,400
	Rate		33.7	96.8	223.4		
1979	Number	41,249,320	6,158,790	16,382,170	18,708,360	178,284,500	79,498,600
	Rate		34.5	91.9	235.3		
1980	Number	40,251,630	6,130,060	15,300,240	18,821,330	184,324,000	82,753,100
	Rate		33.3	83.0	227.4		
1981	Number	41,454,180	6,582,310	15,862,850	19,009,020	186,336,000	84,094,600
	Rate		35.3	85.1	226.0		
1982	Number	39,756,400	6,459,020	15,553,030	17,744,350	188,496,600	85,210,700
	Rate		34.3	82.5	208.2		
1983	Number	37,001,200	5,903,440	14,657,300	16,440,460	190,504,010	86,635,240
	Rate		31.0	76.9	189.8		
1984	Number	34,543,500	6,021,130	13,789,000	15,733,370	191,962,210	88,039,320
	Rate		31.4	71.8	178.7		
1985	Number	34,863,960	5,822,650	13,473,810	15,567,500	194,096,690	89,262,830
	Rate		30.0	69.4	174.4		
1986	Number	34,118,310	5,515,450	13,235,190	15,367,670	196,160,150	90,394,710
	Rate		28.1	67.5	170.0		
1987	Number	35,336,440	5,796,070	13,574,720	15,965,650	197,726,980	91,823,260
	Rate		29.3	68.7	173.9		
1988	Number	35,795,840	5,909,570	14,056,390	15,829,880	199,412,460	93,362,150
	Rate		29.6	70.5	169.6		
1989	Number	35,818,410	5,861,050	13,829,450	16,127,910	201,375,630	94,899,080
	Rate		29.8	70.2	169.9		
1990	Number	34,403,600	6,008,790	12,975,320	15,419,490	203,273,870	95,762,680
	Rate		31.7	68.3	161.0		

Note: Rates for crimes of violence and personal theft are the number of victimizations per 1,000 persons aged 12 or older; rates for household crimes are per 1,000 households. Detail may not add to total because of rounding.

about the crime because they would not feel it was important or that they were inefficient or insensitive. Infrequently mentioned as the most important reason for not reporting a crime were unwillingness to take the time or fear of reprisal by the offender.

When victims were asked why they did report a crime to the police a significant number responded that they did so for economic reasons, either to collect the insurance money or to recover stolen property. A large number of individuals answered that the most important reason for reporting a crime to the police was a sense of personal obligation; that it was their duty to report crimes, or that by reporting they could prevent it from happening again to them or to another person. When there is no loss or damage, crimes are more likely to be reported out of a sense of personal obligation. As financial loss increases, however, economic

TABLE 2

1973–1990 Trends   Number and Percent of Victimizations Reported to the Police

Year		All Crimes	Crimes of Violence	Personal Thefts	Household Crimes
1973	Number	11,543,630	2,434,930	3,312,400	5,796,300
	Percent	32.4	45.5	22.1	37.8
1974	Number	12,853,890	2,581,570	3,902,430	6,369,890
	Percent	33.5	46.9	24.6	37.4
1975	Number	13,700,830	2,629,100	4,279,810	6,791,920
	Percent	34.9	47.2	26.3	39.0
1976	Number	13,703,120	2,732,610	4,389,070	6,581,440
	Percent	34.9	48.8	26.6	38.3
1977	Number	13,508,590	2,722,090	4,203,570	6,582,930
	Percent	33.5	46.1	24.8	37.7
1978	Number	13,171,610	2,626,510	4,198,800	6,346,300
	Percent	32.6	44.2	24.6	36.4
1979	Number	13,510,250	2,774,660	3,932,550	6,803,040
	Percent	32.8	45.1	24.0	36.4
1980	Number	14,411,330	2,889,820	4,109,450	7,412,060
	Percent	35.8	47.1	26.9	39.4
1981	Number	14,711,170	3,065,590	4,241,510	7,404,070
	Percent	35.5	46.6	26.7	39.0
1982	Number	14,175,230	3,113,150	4,180,080	6,882,000
	Percent	35.7	48.2	26.9	38.8
1983	Number	12,804,180	2,784,420	3,881,990	6,137,770
	Percent	34.6	47.2	26.5	37.3
1984	Number	12,515,250	2,835,620	3,623,090	6,056,540
	Percent	35.2	47.1	26.3	38.5
1985	Number	12,490,520	2,789,950	3,688,870	6,011,700
	Percent	35.8	47.9	27.4	38.6
1986	Number	12,678,300	2,734,360	3,707,990	6,235,950
	Percent	37.2	49.6	28.0	40.6
1987	Number	12,926,960	2,758,730	3,742,080	6,426,150
	Percent	36.6	47.6	27.6	40.2
1988	Number	13,032,470	2,829,900	3,859,600	6,342,970
	Percent	36.4	47.9	27.5	40.1
1989	Number	13,174,870	2,630,700	3,972,400	6,571,770
	Percent	36.8	44.9	28.7	40.7
1990	Number	12,961,910	2,886,960	3,705,990	6,368,940
	Percent	37.7	48.0	28.6	41.3

Note: The numbers for crimes of violence and personal theft are for persons aged 12 or older. Detail may not add to total because of rounding.

factors become the most important reason for an individual to report a crime (Harlow, 1985).

The NCVS provides information that cannot be obtained from the UCR about the nature and extent of criminal victimization in the United States. Of primary benefit to law-enforcement agencies is the information regarding the reporting habits of victims and the relationship between the victims and offenders.

Joseph B. Vaughn

Bibliography

Biderman, Albert D., L.A. Johnson, J. McIntyre, and A.W. Weir. *Report on a Pilot Study in the District of Columbia on Victimization and Attitudes Toward Law Enforcement.* Field Surveys I, President's Commission on Law Enforcement and the Administration of Justice. Washington, DC: Government Printing Office, 1967.

Biderman, Albert D., L.A. Johnson, J. McIntyre, A.W. Weir, and Albert J. Reiss. "On Exploring the Dark Figure of Crime." *Annals of the American Academy of Political and Social Science* 374 (1967): 16–33.

Doleshal, Eugene. "Hidden Crime." *Crime and Delinquency Literature* 2 (1970): 546–73.

Ennis, P. H. *Criminal Victimization in the United States: A Report of a National Survey.* Field Surveys II, President's Commission on Law Enforcement and the Administration of Justice. Washington, DC: Government Printing Office, 1967.

Garofalo, James. *An Introduction to the National Crime Survey.* National Criminal Justice Information and Statistics Service, LEAA. Washington, DC: Government Printing Office, 1977.

Harlow, Caroline W. *Reporting Crime to the Police.* Bureau of Justice Statistics Special Report. Washington, DC: Government Printing Office, 1985.

Levine, James P. "The Potential for Crime Overreporting in Criminal Victimization Surveys." *Criminology* 16 (May 1978): 25–38.

Reiss, Albert J. *Studies in Crime and Law Enforcement in Major Metropolitan Areas.* Volume I, Field Surveys III, President's Commission on Law Enforcement and Administration of Justice. Washington, DC: Government Printing Office, 1967.

U.S. Department of Commerce. Bureau of the Census. *National Crime Survey—National Sample Survey Documentation.* Washington, DC: Government Printing Office, 1976.

U.S. Department of Justice. *Sourcebook of Criminal Justice Statistics, 1984.* Washington, DC: Government Printing Office, 1985.

Zedlewski, Edwin W. "Deterrence Findings and Data Sources: A Comparison of the Uniform Crime Reports and the National Crime Surveys." *Journal of Research on Crime and Delinquency* 20 (July 1983): 262–76.

New York City Police Department

The New York City Police Department is perhaps unique in American history, having existed in one form or another for more than three hundred years. The history of the New York police involves many successes and scandals, innovations as well as investigations. Both the good and bad aspects of policing are evident in the department's three-century lifespan. It is important to remember that if the society the police are charged with guarding is itself corrupt and scandalous, the police themselves may reflect that morality or lack thereof.

Dutch and British Influences

The Dutch were the first colonists in present-day New York and they developed the first New York police. The colony, called New Amsterdam, on the south end of Manhattan Island, was administered by Peter Minuit, the director general of New Netherlands, a territory extending from Albany, New York, to Gloucester, New Jersey. In 1624 Minuit created the post of "schout fiscal" (sheriff attorney) to enforce the rules and laws of the Dutch West India Company in the New Amsterdam colony. This officer served a dual function as both policeman and prosecutor enforcing both civil and military laws and ordinances established by the Dutch monarchy. In 1632 Minuit was succeeded by Wouter van Tiller, who expanded the police penal functions in the colony. Tiller's administration saw the introduction of a gibbet, or whipping post, built near the docks, from which lawbreakers were suspended as a public deterrent to other potential criminals. A "burgher guard," an early form of municipal police, was established in 1643. New Amsterdam became a city in 1653 (population 800), and the burgher guard was advanced to a *rattel wacht*, or rattle watch, a night-patrolling force equipped with rattles to summon aid. By 1658 the rattle watch became profession-alized, as eight men were paid to perform this duty. This group of paid watchmen became, in effect, the first police department. The captain of this pioneer force was named Ludowick Post.

In 1664 the British took over New Amsterdam and renamed the port town New York. With a population of only 1,500, the town was initially governed under combined Dutch and English laws. The first high constable of New York was Obe Hendrick. The first uniformed police officer, a "bellman," appeared in New York as a substitute for the night-time rattle watch in 1693. Four years later the streets of New York were lighted at night for the first time. A constable's watch was created by Mayor Isaac De Reimer in 1700. This police force consisted of one constable and twelve watchmen who were ordered to protect the population of lower Manhattan, which then numbered 5,000. The first watch house, forerunner of the police station, was constructed at Wall and Broad streets in 1731.

From Watchmen to NYPD
With the winning of American independence in the Revolutionary War, the British withdrew from New York in 1783 and the city established its first American police force. New York City was the first capital of the United States, and the city fathers created a police force—primarily still a night-watch force—composed of one captain and twenty-eight men—for a population that had reached 25,000 by 1786. The captain received eight English shillings a night and a watchman three shillings (New York City still used the English currency). Within a few years a fee system was established that raised the watchmen's incentive and income. Constables received one shilling, sixpence for each warrant served, with an additional sixpence for each mile traveled. An officer received one shilling for collecting a twenty-shilling fine and received an additional shilling for either taking a suspect into custody or transporting him to the jail.

The growing population of immigrants created unique social problems, and the New York police tried to keep up with the burgeoning crime and vice rates. In 1789, the last year New York served as the nation's capital, the population numbered 33,000. These people were protected and served by a police force of fifty-two men, who were paid four shillings a night. By 1801 two more captains were added; the force also had two deputies and seventy-two watchmen, all supported by an annual budget of $21,162. Watchmen now delivered a summons for 19 cents, took a man into custody for twelve-and-a-half cents, and collected twelve-and-a-half cents on every $2.50 fine. Because of the low wages most of the watchmen's positions were filled by teamsters, stevedores, and mechanics who worked for the police force at night, many of whom slept on the job. During 1802 records show 120 instances of watchmen caught sleeping on the job were fined; the following year 140 similar cases were noted. In an attempt to overcome the poor performance of some of these night officers, bonuses were offered for "good arrests." On July 8, 1805, $23 was awarded to a group of marshals and watchmen who captured "the Portuguese Francisco," an alleged murderer. An officer named Richard Nixon received $5, and all the other officers received a $2 bonus, while Francisco went to the gibbet. The responsibility of the night watch was extended to cover the protection of Potter's Field, because student doctors were stealing corpses from graves for their anatomy studies.

The watchmen normally wore their own clothes, frequently the work clothes of their day jobs. This made it difficult for the public to recognize the watchmen in their official capacities, so identifying headgear and uniforms were proposed. A styled hat was suggested in 1820 but the watchmen uniformly rejected it. As a compromise, for a time a painted plate was fixed on the watchmen's caps. Finally late in 1827, the watchmen adopted the traditional leather headgear of the firemen, winning them the nickname Leatherheads. As these hats were varnished twice a year, they soon became as hard as iron helmets. Additionally, the Leatherheads were issued thirty-three-inch wooden clubs to help them maintain order. It is perhaps important to note that the duties of this generation of New York policemen mainly consisted in keeping the thieves, rioters, and purveyors of vice out of the more respectable parts of the city, a policy that remained basic to police thinking throughout the nineteenth century and well into the twentieth.

At the turn of the nineteenth century, daytime law enforcement owed its survival mainly to one man, High Constable Jacob Hays, referred to as "a police force all himself." Patrolling on his own some eighteen hours a day, Hays developed a unique method of breaking up street arguments before they could evolve into riots. When a belligerent crowd gathered around a fight, Hays would circle the perimeter knocking off hats with his wooden club. As the men stooped to pick up their hats, Hays would shove them with his foot or hand, a tactic that piled up bodies in a form of barricade that contained the original fighters until Hays could either arrest them or summon additional officers.

In 1836 the first attempt was made to establish a detective squad. These officers were called Roundsmen. The following year regular police day patrols were established. The actual birth of the New York City Police, with such a name, was very near. In 1844 the Municipal Police Act abolished the night-watch system and empowered the mayor to select 200 men to police the city twenty-four hours a day. George Matsell, a police magistrate since 1840, was named superintendent. Matsell's salary was set at $1,250 a year; patrolmen were to receive $500 annually. The act also designated that officers wear an official uniform—a single-breasted blue frock coat, buttoned to the neck with the initials M.P. on the collar.

Due to blocked appropriations by city aldermen, the New York City Police Department was not actually established until 1845. By this time, 800 men were authorized to wear the blue uniform and the eight-pointed copper-star badge on their left breast. These policemen were first known as the Star Police, but were soon greeted with nicknames such as Harper's Police, owing to their creation by Mayor Harper, or the lasting epithet "coppers," or "cops." There is some difference of opinion over whether the nickname coppers resulted from the badge itself or from a theatrical term of the day for captures or arrests—the suspect being "copped." The 1845 law creating the police force also resulted in the creation of station houses, which served a dual purpose. Originally designed as a place where citizens could go to find a policeman, they also served as a lodging place for indigents.

In their first six years of operation, the New York police force, totaling 1,000 officers at its height, made 144,364 arrests. Of these, 13,896 were for assault and battery; 20,2532 for disorderly conduct; 36,675 for intoxication; 29,290 for intoxication and disorderly conduct; and 14,454 for picking pockets. Among the more exotic arrest charges were 187 for bastardy and 171 for something called "constructive larceny." Additionally, there were 1,484 arrests for insanity; 64 for murder; 68 for rape; 138 for insulting females in the street; and 11,347 for vagrancy. Conspicuous by their absence are any sizable numbers of arrests for crimes against property.

Requirements for joining the police force in 1853 were simple. A prospective officer had to be a citizen, be able to read and write, and know the "first four rules of arithmetic." A doctor's certificate was needed to attest to one's physical fitness and twenty-five character references from citizens were required. Now the police patrolled in their own clothes, as uniformed officers were frequently targeted by mobs. But uniforms again became mandatory in 1854 and were seen as a means of instilling pride and discipline in the police ranks. A rise in arrests during the first six months of 1854—25,000, up 2,800 over the previous six-month period—was attributed to the officers' pride in their uniforms.

Besetting Problems

The Tammany Hall era in New York resulted in a bitter division over who had ultimate power over the police. Mayor Fernando Wood, known to many as "the model mayor," who was in fact a corrupt, power-hungry official, used the municipal police to achieve his own ends. However, his administration was also marked by scandals, as he openly sold jobs in city departments. Such behavior forced the state legislature to establish the Metropolitan Police Force, which was not responsible to Mayor Wood. The jurisdiction of this force corresponded roughly to the precinct boundaries of Greater New York. A dispute between the state legislature and Mayor Wood over the appointment of a city street commissioner resulted in near anarchy in New York, as metro police were sent to city hall to arrest Mayor Wood for inciting a riot. The metros were attacked by the Woods faithful, including members of the municipal police. Eventually, the National Guard was called in to restore order.

One of the greatest challenges to the New York police came during the 1860s, as men were called for the army draft during the Civil War. In July 1861 a riot broke out when attempts were made to draft able-bodied men. Draft offices were burned and life and property throughout the city was threatened. In several skirmishes with rioters policemen were beaten savagely. When government arsenals came under attack by rioters, the Union Army was called in to assist the police in putting down the riot. Armed soldiers followed by club-wielding police broke the back of the riot. Casualties were heavy across the board; fifty soldiers and three policemen killed; three hundred soldiers wounded; two thousand rioters killed, another eight thousand injured or maimed.

The 1870s were marred by two persistent problems in New York City. The first was the deep-seated ethnic hostilities of the various immigrant and citizen populations. The second was the involvement of many in the police department in the systematic looting of the city and its residents. Ethnic, nationalist, and religious hatreds boiled over in 1871 between Protestant Northern Irelanders and Catholic Irish. A traditional Orangeman parade, celebrating the Protestant victory over the Catholic Irish, resulted in a riot leaving eleven civilians and two policemen dead, and sixty-seven civilians wounded. The police were again criticized for being unable to handle a civic disorder. The police role in the looting of the city was directly tied to the similar tactics of the Tammany Hall political bosses in office. Police officers were increasingly appointed as political favors, and lenient laws permitted the police extremely broad search-and-seizure powers. The superintendent or a captain within a precinct could, in writing, empower any patrolman or detective to search the books or shop of a pawnbroker, vendor, junk dealer, auctioneer, or secondhand dealer if the officer sought property that he suspected had been illegally obtained. On a complaint of two or more homeowners, the superintendent could permit police to conduct a raid on gambling dens or whorehouses. Much of the illegal gains of such establishments found their way into the hands of the confiscating officers. Conversely, however, in 1872 a "flag of honor" was presented to the police in recognition of their bravery, attesting to the growing reputation of the New York City police. In 1875 the police received their lasting nickname, The Finest, by Mayor William Havermeyer.

Police indiscretions resulted in attention from reformers like the Rev. Charles Parkhurst and the Society for the Prevention of Crime. His investigations into the vice operations in the city led indirectly to the first investigation of the New York City police, conducted by the Lexow Committee, chaired by Republican Senator Clarence Lexow, which began hearings in March 1894. Testimony was introduced that showed the police encouraged conspiracy and collusion with saloon operators and whorehouse madams, resulting in the payment of protection money for continued operation. Police involvement in the "shakedown" of merchants and both overt and covert participation in many gambling and confidence enterprises were also exposed before the committee. However, the committee's revelations of police brutality aroused the greatest indignation among the public. A previously unknown group of policemen, known as "the clubber's brigade," was exposed. However, the committee's and journalists' exposure of the clubbers was only intended to stop such attacks on so-called respectable citizens, including peaceful strikers. All agreed that young toughs and petty criminals should still be subjected to the club.

The committee's reforms resulted in the appointment of Teddy Roosevelt as police commissioner in 1895. Although he was actually one of four commissioners, almost everyone agreed that "T.R." ran the show. A school of pistol practice was established, and all uniformed officers were required to carry a .32 caliber Colt revolver, the first standardization of police sidearms. The same year the Bicycle Squad (the "bike cops") was created, the most famous member of which was "Mile-a-Minute" Murphy. In 1896 the Bertillon system of identification was adopted. With the ratification of the Greater New York Charter in 1897, the merger of the park police and regular police took place. Perhaps the most important innovation by T.R. was the imposition of strict discipline from above. His honest, firm hand forced every man in the department to accept responsibility for his own actions.

Corruption, Reform, and Modernization
The twentieth century dawned on New York City with a population of 4 million people and 6,400 police officers, serviced by an annual budget of $11.5 million. The police board was replaced by a single police commissioner in 1901. Police Chief William Devery brought back much of the institutionalized graft that had been stopped during the Roosevelt administration. A major police scandal of the early 1900s was the Becker–Rosenthal case. Police Lieutenant Charles Becker, a member of Special Squad No. 1, was named a partner to a notorious gambling hall owner, Herman Rosenthal. After Rosenthal complained to the press that

Becker was getting almost $10,000 a week in protection money, Rosenthal was gunned down by four hoods. When the district attorney offered the gunmen immunity for their testimony, they fingered Becker as the man who masterminded the shooting. Becker and four of his colleagues were convicted and sentenced to death in the electric chair. Becker was executed in 1915, still protesting his innocence.

While there was a short-lived police-reform movement in New York following the Becker–Rosenthal case, the passing of the Eighteenth Amendment—ushering in Prohibition—plunged the city back into wholesale corruption. Bootlegger Arnold Rothstein, famous for fixing the 1919 World Series, made pervasive, if not permanent, partnerships among organized criminals, the police, and unscrupulous politicians. More positively, however, the early decades of the twentieth century witnessed the introduction of modern technology in police work in New York. In 1919 an automobile patrol was initiated. Specialized services were created with the Aviation Bureau in 1929, the Crime Prevention Bureau in 1930, the Narcotics Squad in 1933, and the Police Laboratory in 1934. Radios were first installed in patrol cars in 1932.

The seesaw battle between the reformers and corrupters in New York politics continued to influence the role of the police. The election of reform-minded Mayor Fiorello LaGuardia resulted in an investigation into New York corruption by Governor Franklin D. Roosevelt in 1929. Focusing mainly on magistrates, the investigation revealed that connections among criminals, judges, and the police were too evident. Police Commissioner Lewis Valentine, a tough, loyal, and honest policeman, noted that for many years police officers had believed that racketeers and other criminals with political pull had to be treated with kid gloves. Valentine ordered the gloves be taken off, but said this was not a call for "general police brutality." Unfortunately, neither LaGuardia or Valentine could insure that after they left office the old ways of graft and corruption in the police department would not creep back in.

There were New York policemen who put their duty above any financial or political consideration. In 1928 seven men were nominated for posthumous honors for valor. Two died attempting to rescue fire victims; five fell in their efforts to stop holdups. Another thirteen officers survived gun battles with criminals. Such

real-life tough cops were led by the likes of John Cordes, two-time winner of the department's medal of honor; Barney Ruditsky; and John Broderick. Broderick joined the police force in 1923 and retired twenty-four years later.

Civil Disorder
The 1930s and 1940s saw another burden added to the police function of maintaining order in New York. Civil disorder among workers and labor-union members, or among the black communities, threatened the policemen's idea of themselves as the first and last bastion of social order. Communist-inspired dissent among 1930s labor unions resulted in frequent clashes between workers and the police. Far more troublesome to the police were frequent racial outbursts among the black communities. A 1935 riot in Harlem resulted in deaths and injuries. In 1943 Harlem erupted again, and 5,000 policemen were needed to restore order. Five people were killed, and 500 blacks were arrested for looting.

Additional civil disorders swept through New York City in 1964, 1967, and 1968. The first involved the fatal shooting of a black teenager by a seventeen-year police veteran. The officer said the youth attacked him with a knife and he was forced to defend himself. The resultant rioting spread out of Harlem and into Bedford-Stuyvesant in Brooklyn, resulting in one death and thirty injuries. The 1967 troubles were touched off when an officer tried to arrest two knifefighters in a Puerto Rican neighborhood. The officer, slashed by one of the participants, shot and killed his assailant. The 1968 disorders followed the assassination of Martin Luther King, Jr. There were no fatalities but 400 arrests were made.

The Knapp Commission and Innovation
In 1973 the Knapp Commission was convened to once again discuss the pervasive graft and corruption in the New York City Police Department. The commission classified abusers on the force as belonging to two categories: "meat eaters" and "grass eaters." Meat eaters aggressively misused police power for personal gain by soliciting bribes or by cooperating with criminals. Grass eaters accepted payoffs when their everyday duties put them in a tempting position to take bribes without soliciting them. The Knapp Commission concluded that the vast majority of police officers "on the take" were grass eaters, although the few meat eaters who

were periodically caught captured all the headlines.

The New York City Police Department pioneered the techniques of hostage siege and negotiation. In 1972 they formed a special unit, named the Hostage-Negotiating Team, under the command of Frank Bolz. The team consisted of seventy officers, including women, who were all members of the Detective Bureau, selected after psychiatric tests for steadiness. Then-commissioner Patrick Murphy, head of the police department, supplied the rationale for creating such a unit, dispelling the image of "trigger-happy" officers always ready to attack. "There can be no more use of firepower, considering the carrying strength of the average bullet. It can travel further than the limits of where the problem exists and is a serious danger in the crowded urban conditions under which we live." Between 1974 and 1977 Bolz personally handled eighty hostage-taking situations, all of which were resolved without any deaths.

The creation of such specialized units as the Hostage-Negotiating Team, and the progress made in hiring and promotions of minorities (women were first promoted in 1965 and Benjamin Ward was named the department's first black police commissioner in 1984) indicate that despite periodic, historical problems related to graft and corruption, the New York City Police Department retains its position on the cutting edge of American law enforcement.

Present Day

The year 1990 marked a new beginning for the NYPD. On January 22 Dr. Lee P. Brown was appointed commissioner. Dr. Brown came to New York from Houston, having served as chief of the Houston Police Department for eight years. Well-known for his unswerving belief in community policing, Commissioner Brown's first administrative move was to change the NYPD from the traditional model of policing to a community-based model. He and Mayor David N. Dinkins instituted a program called "Safe Streets, Safe City" to form the cornerstone of a crime control plan. With guaranteed funding, one precinct switched immediately to community policing, to be followed by all precincts in due time. Commissioner Brown made other notable changes to realize his vision of more cops in the community. He insisted that his management team act like a corporate board and operate as one unit rather than as separate entities. One premise of community policing is that everyone works together, because competing or fractious groups are unproductive. In a surprise move, Brown selected a civilian to restructure police training for the conversion to a community-based system.

The 1990 Staffing Study of the NYPD measured calls for service, crime, and arrest activity and compared them to the experience of fifteen and twenty years ago. The study found that radio runs per precinct had increased by 132 percent between 1974 and 1989. For every police officer, the number of crimes he or she had to deal with had increased by 60 percent over the last twenty years. During the same period, the uniformed strength of the department fell by 19 percent. Under Commissioner Brown the department plans to gain 23 percent in uniformed officers. However, through civilianization, redeployment, and the consolidation and elimination of specialized units, patrol strength will increase by 50 percent.

Statistically, New York City ranked fifteenth among major U.S. cities for total crime in 1990. Arrests for murder and nonnegligent manslaughter, grand larceny, and grand larceny involving a motor vehicle remained high. All other types of arrests, including narcotics, showed a reduction from the previous year. Calls to 911 totaled 8,63,627; radio runs generated by the calls amounted to 4,128,323 for a daily average of 23,736. Under Commissioner Brown's redirected police force, regular officers accounted for 69.9 percent of staffing, detectives, 13.2 percent, and administrative officers, the remainder. Female officers comprised 11.9 percent of the force. The ethnic breakdown was 75.2 percent white, 12.6 percent Hispanic, 11.3 percent black, .8 percent Asian, and .1 percent Native American.

Due to the illness of his wife, Lee Brown cut short his five-year appointment as police commissioner. It is now up to his successor, Raymond Kelly, either to fully implement community policing or to go in a different direction.

Paul Louis

Bibliography

Astor, Gerald. *The New York Cops: An Informal History.* New York: Charles Scribner's Sons, 1971.

Costello, A.E. *Our Police Protectors.* New York: C.F. Roper, 1885.

Crump, Irving, and John Newton. *Our Po-*

lice. New York: Dodd, Mead, 1935.

Klein, Herb. *The New York Police: Damned If They Do, Damned If They Don't.* New York: Crown, 1968.

Niederhoffer, Arthur. *Behind the Shield.* New York: Doubleday, 1967.

Radano, Gene. *Walking the Beat.* New York: World, 1968.

Arthur Niederhoffer

Arthur Niederhoffer (1917–1981), a street cop turned sociologist, was revered as a charismatic role model by thousands of police officers and other students that he taught, advised, and inspired. His multifaceted career in law enforcement as police officer, attorney, professor, author, and researcher broadened and sharpened his in-depth perspectives on the police.

Born in New York City, Niederhoffer, interestingly, as a child loved walking past the neighborhood police station. Educated in the city's public schools, Niederhoffer was encouraged in academics and athletics by his parents. His father, Martin, a court interpreter, graduated from City College in New York City. A brilliant student, Niederhoffer entered Brooklyn College at the age of fifteen and competed on the football and handball teams. After his graduation in 1937, he went on to Brooklyn Law School where he earned his LL.B. cum laude (later converted to J.D. cum laude). In 1940, the same year that he was admitted to the New York State Bar as an attorney, he joined the New York City Police Department. As a result of the depressed economy there were fewer opportunities for lawyers; and he thought that as a policeman he would be able to put his legal background to use.

"I learned about police work by pounding a beat," Niederhoffer often candidly admitted. He rose through the ranks—appointed sergeant in 1951, promoted to lieutenant in 1956. He achieved four departmental recognition awards for meritorious performance. In two separate incidents he rescued suicidal women—each 250 pounds—from drowning in the East River. After both acts of heroism he had to be hospitalized briefly due to the effects of submersion. In addition he won a tuition grant for outstanding educational attainment in police-related studies.

During the final period of his twenty-one-year police career, Niederhoffer instructed, supervised, and trained recruits at the New York City Police Academy. As curriculum-develop-ment officer in charge, he raised the educational level and requirements of the training program. He also lectured to community groups and did psychological testing, personnel evaluation, and research into the quality and performance of police at the academy.

In 1960 he served as executive aide to the police liaison officer of the American Institute for Research (AIR), a nationally known research group cosponsored by the Russell Sage and Rockefeller foundations. AIR conducted a long-range research program in the New York City Police Department aimed at improving selection and training procedures.

While still on the force, Niederhoffer returned to Brooklyn College and in 1956 earned a master's degree in sociology and was conferred summa cum laude, an honor rarely bestowed by the department. His first book, *The Gang: A Study of Adolescent Behavior* (Philosophical Library, 1958), written with the sociologist Herbert A. Bloch, is based on Niederhoffer's masters thesis. From their extensive study of adolescent behavior in a variety of cultures, the researchers theorized that when a society does not make adequate provisions for the passage of adolescents into adult status, youths create equivalent groups to fill the void. Sometimes these groups become subverted into delinquent gangs. Bloch and Niederhoffer's theory is recognized in the field as an important explanation for juvenile delinquency.

Inspired by his successful return to academia, Niederhoffer continued his studies at New York University's Graduate School of Arts and Science. He was granted his Ph.D. in 1963, two years after his retirement from the police department.

"The job controls a police officer's life when he is on the force, and it haunts him when he leaves. Once a cop, always a cop," he asserted. Underscoring this credo, he drew upon his police career as a frame of reference for his doctoral dissertation, "The Mobile Force: A Study of Police Cynicism." He devised a questionnaire consisting of twenty open-ended statements about significant areas of police work to test eleven hypotheses concerning cynicism in an urban police department and administered it to a sample of 220 police officers.

From the analysis of his data, Niederhoffer concluded that cynicism becomes part of the occupational ideology learned by socialization into the police force. It is in the police academy that recruits initially acquire the stereotyped patterns of cynical attitudes, which are reinforced in the course of their police careers. He pointed out, however, that a police officer's attitude toward his role can change over time and can vary with his experience and background. For example:

> The brand new recruit will be less cynical than the more seasoned recruit. The recruit will be less cynical than the more experienced police officer. Superior officers will be less cynical than patrolmen. Patrolmen with a college education will be more cynical than their counterparts without education.

From this research study, Niederhoffer devised a Cynicism Scale, a linear causal model, which has been widely replicated to gauge cynicism in other urban police department as well as in other occupations and professions.

Niederhoffer had always wanted to teach upon his retirement from the department. "I always had the vision of the scholar. To me the greatest honor is to be a man of learning and have people come to you and learn from you," he said. Consequently, the former police officer launched his professorial career with teaching stints at Queens, Brooklyn, and Baruch colleges of the City University of New York (CUNY); Hofstra University; Long Island University; and New York University. To his subject matter—courses in police administration, delinquency, police science, human relations, criminal justice, and sociology/anthropology—he contributed original thinking, historical and sociological perspectives, and an insider's down-to-earth overview, undergirded by his more than twenty-one years of police experience, with the added perk: a storehouse of colorful police anecdotes to enhance his teaching. He understood the problems of law enforcement, its stresses and pressures. He had not been just a participant/observer riding along for several months in a radio patrol car. In 1967 he moved permanently to John Jay College of Criminal Justice (CUNY) as a professor of sociology, where he taught for fourteen productive years—stimulating, enriching, and inspiring his students and colleagues. Significantly, he was much appreciated as a conciliator able to link police science and more traditional academic branches of the college.

On the fifteenth anniversary of the founding of John Jay College, Niederhoffer was awarded the college's presidential medal; not only was he the first and only member of the faculty to receive this honor, but he was also unanimously chosen. President Gerald W. Lynch, when presenting the award, described Niederhoffer as an "individual who exemplifies the genius of our faculty, who personifies the best tradition of the great scholar, teacher, and counselor to student and colleagues alike. He is a wonderful human being and one of the loveliest people I know." The citation reads:

> For your extraordinary and continuing career as a scholar, teacher, researcher, and author, for your outstanding contributions to the intellectual development of the field of criminal justice; for your seminal scholarship and numerous publications in sociology and criminology, and for your example to us all in the great tradition of the scholar professor.

With his students and colleagues he discussed topical and perplexing police questions such as: How does an idealistic rookie become cynical? Why are police vulnerable to corruption? Does police authoritarianism come into the force along with the recruits? Exploring these issues and probing some of the internal problems of police work motivated Niederhoffer to write his next book, *Behind the Shield: The Police in Urban Society* (Doubleday, 1967). Grounded in his police experience and insights and supplemented by intensive interviews with police officers in other cities, the retired police officer/professor lifted the "blue curtain" of secrecy that had screened police work until then. Although it is an insider's view of an urban police department, it is not a critique or an exposé. Rather, it is a thoughtful, meticulously researched and documented study of the sociology of the police, written by a practicing sociologist, but without the sociological jargon.

In *Behind the Shield* Niederhoffer delineates a psychological and sociological profile of the urban police officer and the social forces that mold his personality. He examines a variety of police activities and describes in a series of vignettes the making of and molding of police officers—the rookie, the detective, the college man, the supervisor, and the old-timer. Niederhoffer analyzes and evaluates why they choose a police career, how they are trained, and what pressures they encounter. And he concludes that "it is the police system, not the personality of the candidate, that is the more powerful determinant of behavior and ideology." For example, on authoritarianism he comments:

> . . . Police authoritarianism does not come into the force along with the recruits, but rather is inculcated through strenuous socialization and experience in the police social system.

> . . . The police occupational system is geared to manufacture the "take-charge guy," and it succeeds in doing so with outstanding efficiency.

> . . . The hostility and fear that press almost palpably against a policeman in lower-class areas aggravates his impulse to get tough.

> . . . Since the policeman feels justified and righteous in using power and toughness to perform his duties, he feels like a martyr when he is charged with brutality and abuse of power.

Behind the Shield had been published shortly after racial riots—which many were convinced were triggered by police action—in Rochester, New York; Philadelphia; New York's Harlem; the Watts section of Los Angeles; and Newark, New Jersey. Consequently, the spotlight of the nation focused on the police. As a former police lieutenant, Niederhoffer had been able to put into words, with empathy and respect for the police image, what police officers actually live through. And as a professor of sociology he had the clout and credibility to clarify controversial police issues, tempered by his sociological insights. His national reputation escalated to the point where he was recognized as one of the foremost experts on police problems. A dynamic down-to-earth, and provocative speaker, he was invited to lecture, participate in conferences on the police, and evaluate law-enforcement programs all over the United States and in Canada.

Moreover, he was never afraid to step over the official "blue" line to express his convictions that targeted controversial police issues. Consider for instance, his comments on crime:

> . . . crime is a community problem, not a police problem. A larger police force is not the answer.

On the legal system:

> . . . police are solidly aligned against the U.S. Supreme Court, which they suspect is slowly but surely dismantling the hallowed foundation of law enforcement. I do not feel that Supreme Court decisions shackle police. Police will develop new techniques of investigation that will make them more effective.

On professionalism in police work:

> . . . the great stumbling block is in police work's traditionally low status in our culture. The public holds fast to the derogatory stereotypes of the grafting cop, the sadistic cop, the dumb cop, the chiseling cop, and the thick-brogued cop. There can be no profession where the public refuses to grant high status and prestige.

> . . . the rookie police officer is faced with the dilemma of choosing between the professional ideals acquired during his academy training and the pragmatic approach of the precinct—the requirements of the job.

On college education:

> . . . We can't assume that education makes "A" a better police officer than "B," but education can improve a person. College can increase knowledge and give one a more open mind—perhaps more tolerant and sophisticated in what to look for—with more insights and alternatives for action.

> . . . I feel that there is a danger in having an elite police force. I believe that the police force should be more representative of the population at large and permit a great number of persons without college degrees to enter. Although I would encourage every department to encourage as much as possible the study and improvement of the force by education at every rank.

And finally, with prophetic vision on the future of policing in America:

... There are three things that are very important: first, unionization. There is a split in the ranks over professionalism and unionism. (My prediction is that unionism will win because it appeals more and gives more protection to the officer at the lower echelon.) Next is the introduction of women into police work. And the third is the spread of college training for police.

... police will be at the storm center of each episode of crisis or catastrophe that is bound to occur in the ghetto, on the campus, at demonstrations, or wherever social protest is most threatening. ... Society is asking the police not only to protect it, but also to preserve it. The people of America turn to them as saviors and demand an end to lawlessness and violence.

Additionally, Niederhoffer applied his perceptions concerning law enforcement in a concrete way to the escalating problems of crime and violence in inner cities. He participated in several hands-on projects with the same objective—to build a bridge between the police and the community. Under the aegis of New York city's then-mayor John V. Lindsay, Niederhoffer in 1968 helped to organize and supervise a community police corps to combat crime in Harlem. This innovative plan established a youth patrol using local residents to assist the police by performing certain street-patrol functions to prevent crime. In the same year he was recruited, along with Alexander B. Smith, by the U.S. Department of Health, Education, and Welfare to submit a report entitled "The Development and Impact of the Police–Community Relations Project of the Office of Juvenile Delinquency." To assess the project, Smith and Niederhoffer visited eight police–community relations programs, conducted extensive interviews, and observed the plan in action.

In his most ambitious research to date, Niederhoffer functioned as director of research in a two-year-long major study during 1970–1971, sponsored by the U.S. Department of Justice's Law Enforcement Assistance Administration (LEAA), National Institute of Law Enforcement and Criminal Justice Technical Assistance in Criminal Justice, Washington, D.C. Niederhoffer critiqued, evaluated, and commented on more than three hundred proposals on police, courts, criminal justice, crime prevention, and other subjects, already submitted to the institute for funding by LEAA and on ongoing and/or completed activities of institute grantees and contractors.

This in-depth project for LEAA underscored for him how strands of police action are inextricably intertwined with law enforcement and the fate of society. In his view:

Responding to this mandate in his own way, the retired police lieutenant published three more books and numerous articles in professional journals related to police and law enforcement (see bibliography that follows). Long Island University honored Niederhoffer with its Distinguished Service Award in recognition of his achievements in criminal justice.

In *The Ambivalent Force: Perspectives on the Police* (Ginn and Company, 1970), a book of readings edited by Niederhoffer and Abraham S. Blumberg, the coeditors examine the harsh ambiguities and ambivalences of the police role. As a result of the tensions and conflicts of the occupation, police officers need more than technical and legalistic training. To broaden police perspectives, Niederhoffer and Blumberg present police in their anthology in a social, historical, and comparative setting, assembling articles by experts in their fields—the academic behavioral scientist, the journalist, the lawyer, the psychologist, the police officer, and the historian.

Building on their mounting interest on police–community relations, Niederhoffer and Smith wrote *New Directions in Police–Community Relations* (Rinehart Press, 1974). Previously the researchers had jointly paid on-site visits to police–community relations projects for their evaluation report to the Office of Juvenile Delinquency, U.S. Department of Health, Education, and Welfare. And, as research director for the LEAA study, Niederhoffer had reviewed numerous police–community programs. Smith, too, had been involved with community-relations units of the police department when he headed a study of law-enforcement efforts to prevent and control the illegal distribution and sale of pornography. *New Directions in Police–Community Relations* offers a practical guide to police–community relations, utilizing case studies, questionnaires, and interviews. To observe programs in action, the coauthors visited sites in New Orleans; Wilmington, Delaware; Houston, Texas; Enfield, Connecticut; Philadelphia; and New York City.

Niederhoffer subsequently explored the personal side of life on the force by contemplating such varied questions as: How does police work affect family relationships? Does the occupation precipitate suicide, marital instability, or divorce? Niederhoffer and his wife, Elaine, investigated these complex and pressing problems in *The Police Family: From Station House to Ranch House* (Lexington Books, 1978). In their well-documented book, the coauthors employed questionnaires, interviews, surveys, and rap sessions with officers in major police departments, their spouses, and their children, and with police chaplains, revealing a behind-the-scenes view of the pressures on the families of police officers. Moreover, because the Niederhoffers lived for more than twenty years within the "blue circle," they were able to enliven their empirical study with personal anecdotes.

Admittedly, the couple wrote, "the shadow of the job darkens family relationships"; the omnipresent sense of danger arouses fear for the safety of loved ones; the oppressive revolving duty chart disrupts family routines; the high visibility of the police family's activities promotes surveillance by the community and media. But the Niederhoffers found that, by and large, police families made peace with the occupation; they cope with the distressing problems endemic to police work. The job "may be a jealous mistress," but "if the marriage is O.K., the job is O.K." Of course, marital dissatisfaction and unhappiness can affect working satisfaction, and occupational demands can cause marital dissatisfaction. "The rate of divorce for the occupation as a whole rises no higher than the average level of divorce in the United States. Divorce police-style equates with divorce American-style." And similarly, ". . . the rate of police suicide is about the same as that for the national adult male population."

Niederhoffer read what was to be his last paper, "Myths and Realities in Criminal Justice," at a meeting of the American Society of Criminology (ASC) in November 1980, feeling as vigorous as ever. He was elected a fellow of the ASC by his colleagues. Shortly after his return he was hospitalized, losing his heroic eight-year battle with lymphoma, and died on January 14, 1981. (In his typical courageous and dedicated way, he managed to grade papers and write to his students during the January intersession.)

At his memorial service, President Gerald W. Lynch said:

> . . . Arthur is the prototype of what John Jay College is; the practitioner who stood on the front line of police work; the thinker and explainer to us all of the reasons for social deviance and the proper responsibilities and limits of social control; the man of strong compassion for his fellow human beings who strove to help us understand police work and its stress, as well as the criminals the police must deal with.

In loving tribute, his colleagues, friends, and relatives established the Arthur Niederhoffer Memorial Fellowship, awarded annually to students in the doctoral program in criminal justice at John Jay College who "best epitomize in academic achievement and in the promise of future fulfillment the professional accomplishments of Arthur Niederhoffer."

Elaine Niederhoffer

Bibliography

Books

Niederhoffer, Arthur. *Behind the Shield: The Police in Urban Society*. Garden City, NY: Doubleday, 1967.

———, and Herbert A. Bloch. *The Gang: A Study of Adolescent Behavior*. New York: Philosophical Library, 1958.

———, and Abraham S. Blumberg, eds. *The Ambivalent Force: Perspectives on the Police*. Waltham, MA: Ginn and Company, 1970; Corte Madera, CA: Rinehart Press, 1973; New York: Dryden Press, 1976.

———, and Elaine Niederhoffer. *The Police Family: From Station House to Ranch House*. Lexington, MA: Lexington Books, 1978.

———, and Alexander B. Smith. *New Directions in Police-Community Relations*. Corte Madera, CA: Rinehart Press, 1974.

Monographs

Niederhoffer, Arthur. *Criminal Justice Higher Education*. New York: Advanced Institutional Development Program (AIDP),

John Jay College of Criminal Justice, 1976.

———, and Alexander B. Smith. *Police–Community Relations: A Study in Depth*. Washington, DC: Office of Juvenile Delinquency, Department of Health, Education, and Welfare, 1971.

Articles
Niederhoffer, Arthur. "Police." *Encyclopedia Americana*. Danbury, CT: Grolier, 1971.
———. "Prisons." *Encyclopedia Americana Annual*. Danbury, CT: Grolier, 1972.
———. "Modern Prisons." *Encyclopedia Americana*. Danbury, CT: Grolier, 1974.
———. "Police." *World Book Encyclopedia*. Chicago: World Book, 1977.

Nonlethal Weapons: Empirical Evidence

Compared to the number of arrests made by police officers, violent altercations are relatively few in number. Los Angeles Police Department (LAPD) records for the first half of 1989 indicate that incidents requiring a level of force intended to cause the suspect to fall to the ground occurred just once in every 128 arrests. Incidents involving the use of firearms are not included in these figures. Many police use-of-force situations are sudden close-contact situations requiring immediate, instinctive response. Other situations begin as "standoff" situations (with time for planning and maneuvering), but change to immediate-response situations if the suspect increases resistance, if officers approach the suspect without formulating a plan, or if officers do not take aggressive actions to control the suspect before the standoff situation deteriorates.

In 1982, in response to public pressure, the LAPD virtually eliminated use of the upper-body control holds ("chokeholds"), which had been used with great regularity for decades. (They are still used elsewhere by many law-enforcement and corrections agencies.) Loss of the upper-body control holds created a significant gap in the escalation/de-escalation of force scale for situations requiring immediate response in close-contact situations.

The term "nonlethal weapons" is used generically to identify innovative alternatives to traditional nonfirearm weapons and tactics (such as batons, flashlights, martial-arts techniques, and miscellaneous bodily force) that police have used for more than 150 years of organized municipal law enforcement in the United States. (Others may prefer the terms "less lethal weapons," "reduced lethality weapons," or "suspect control devices" to describe these alternatives.) Nonlethal weapons have also been defined in terms of the tactics and situations for which they are appropriate:

> Devices which may be used to aggressively take control of a deteriorating tactical situation prior to that point in time when control holds, batons, or deadly force may become necessary; and when it is unsafe for an officer to move to within contact range of the suspect; and when attempts by officers to control the suspect by conventional means will likely result in serious injury to officers, suspects, or both. (Meyer et al., 1981)

Research and Testing

In 1979 and 1980 the LAPD researched more than a dozen innovative devices to attempt to control violent people (especially those under the influence of PCP) in a way that would reduce injuries to suspects and officers. The following devices were subjected to intense evaluation, including field testing by the LAPD and the Los Angeles County Sheriff's Department: Taser (a stun gun that delivers a 50,000-volt shock), chemical irritant spray, capture nets, leg grabbers, and the Immobilizer (a combination of poles and chains). It was found that the Taser and chemical irritant spray were weapons of temporary incapacitation, while the others would contain the suspect's movements but would not render the suspect helpless (frequently meaning that there would still be a violent confrontation when the still-unhandcuffed suspect was "unwrapped" from the device). Further, although an officer would ideally have a backup officer present during any violent confrontation, the Taser and chemical irritant spray had the advantage of being hand-held, one-officer operations that allowed the officer to stay six to fifteen feet away from the suspect. The other devices required setup and application by trained teams to operate. In 1981 the LAPD adopted Taser and chemical irritant sprays of the CS and CN types. Currently the LAPD is testing two types of cayenne pepper, or OC, spray in an effort to find a spray device with greater officer acceptance than the older CS and CN spray types.

Tactical Scenarios

During the 1970s many officers around the country received major incapacitating injuries while attempting to take into custody persons under the influence of PCP, an animal tranquilizer known for giving human users "super-human" strength. It was not unusual for the most aggressive efforts of five or six officers to be inadequate to control a single PCP suspect without serious injury to several of the involved parties. A decade ago some researchers saw nonlethal weapons scenarios as limited to violent mental cases or persons under the influence of alcohol or narcotics who were unresponsive to verbal commands, but who were not at the moment attacking someone or otherwise presenting a threat that required an immediate application of force to control the situation. One group of criminologists pointed out that practitioners must distinguish between scenarios in which nonlethal weapons are appropriate and those in which they are not:

> In most instances assaults and attacks on law enforcement agents are spontaneous events that are precipitated by some stressful or emotional confrontation. Frequently, however, there has been ample time for a dialogue between the officer(s) and the assailant. (Meyer et al., 1981)

However, nonlethal weapons can also be successful as shooting avoidance tools in some situations, early in the confrontation before an unarmed but resisting suspect has the opportunity to become armed and attack the officer. Also, a suspect who is armed with less than a firearm (for example, a knife, bottle, or club) could be "zapped" with a nonlethal weapon before the suspect could attack.

It was in this context that the LAPD believed that "any weapon was worth looking into if it could stop incidents from escalating to a point where deadly force may have to be used." Time (sudden attack versus a standoff situation) and distance between the officer and the suspect are the crucial factors in determining whether nonlethal weapons are appropriate for the situation. During the past twelve years, the Taser and chemical irritant spray have been used in thousands of standoff situations. Such situations frequently deteriorate into immediate-response, deadly force situations if the suspect attacks with a knife or a club (or other dangerous implement amounting to less than a firearm), and if the suspect is not quickly controlled.

Experience throughout the 1980s has also shown that officers are sometimes successful using nonlethal weapons in sudden-attack scenarios. There have been instances where standoff situations involving the use of knives and other weapons that appeared about to be used against officers, as well as a number of suicide threats, were brought to swift conclusion through aggressive use of the Taser. Burglary and car theft suspects have been flushed from positions of cover and concealment by use of chemical irritant spray.

The vast majority of nonlethal weapon incidents involve unarmed suspects who exhibit resistive, violent, or bizarre behavior, thus presenting a significant safety threat to themselves, others, and the officers whose job it is to intervene.

Critique of the Literature

It has been widely speculated that Taser and close-contact devices such as Ultron II and Nova (which use Taser circuitry) can induce a heart attack, cause severe burns, or cause electrocution. This speculation is likely based upon the human fear of electricity and our lack of knowledge about different types of electrical currents and their effects upon the body. The literature cites cases where a suspect died sometime after the Taser was used. However, medical authorities generally do not believe that Taser was the cause of death in these cases, and they argue over whether it was a contributing factor.

In 1980 the supervising physician of the Medical Services Division, Los Angeles City Personnel Department, wrote that the Taser was "reasonable and feasible and presents no undue risk to the recipient." In 1985, after the LAPD had used the Taser hundreds of times, a medical journal article concluded that "major injuries, either primary to the [electrical] current or secondary to [falling down], have not been reported" (Koscove, 1985). The need for effective nonlethal weapons is also demonstrated by expensive litigation, which results from injuries produced by conventional tactics. Americans for Effective Law Enforcement, a Chicago-based legal and law enforcement educational association, has documented a number of out-of-court settlements and jury awards in amounts ranging from tens of thousands of dollars to millions of dollars to compensate people for injuries they received from conventional tactics such as batons and flashlights.

In a landmark nonlethal weapons case in 1988 (*Michenfelder v. Sumner*, 860 F.2d 328), a federal appellate court found that

> . . . authorities believe the Taser is the preferred method for controlling prisoners because it is the "least confrontational" when compared to the use of physical restraint, billy clubs, mace, or [beanbag] guns. . . . When contrasted to alternative methods for physically controlling inmates, some of which can have serious after effects, the Taser compared favorably.

The Meyer Study

LAPD records show that 1,160 of the reports for the first half of 1989 documented incidents in which officers attempted to control the suspect by causing the suspect to fall to the ground. These incidents were below the level of deadly force (which, by LAPD policy, includes firearms and upper-body control holds or "chokeholds"), but above the level of generally minor, supposedly noninjurious applications of physical force (compliance holds, for example) in which nonlethal weapons might not be expected to be a reasonable option.

A stratified sampling procedure yielded 395 reports in which any of six conventional force types (baton, kick, punch, flashlight, swarm technique, or miscellaneous bodily force) was documented as the effective force that controlled the situation; eighty-eight reports where Taser was the effective force; and nineteen reports where chemical irritant spray was the effective force. Thus a total of 502 reports were subjected to analysis. Sixty-six of these documented more than one force type that fit the research scenario (i.e., listed at least one force type that was ineffective in addition to the force type that succeeded), and care was taken to avoid double counting.

Variables were coded from each of the 502 reports in the sample and the data were entered into Stata, a statistical computer program, and subjected to analysis. Selected pairs of variables were cross-tabulated and subjected to "chi-square" testing to determine if statistically significant relationships existed. The purpose of such testing was to rule out as much as possible the hypothesis that the relationships that appeared to exist between tested variables were due to chance, i.e., that there was no actual relationship. All of the relationships were of such significance that there was not one chance in two thousand that the relationships were due to chance.

Meyer created the injury classification scheme depicted in Table 1.

Findings

Table 2 reports injuries to suspects from the Effective Force Types (i.e., the force type that brought the incident to a conclusion).

Table 3 reports the number of injuries to officers that resulted from each Effective Force Type.

Table 4 shows the varying success rates (i.e., the percentage of incidents for which a given weapon or tactic was the Effective Force Type) achieved by different force types, along with corresponding injury rates to officers and suspects.

The data clearly demonstrate that the Taser electronic weapon and chemical irritant spray caused fewer and less severe injuries than conventional force types. The data did not suggest any other rival hypotheses that might account for the results.

There is a clear implication from these findings that police officers should use nonlethal weapons as the first resort during violent confrontations, which require using sufficient force to cause the suspect to fall to the ground. This implication is reinforced by the findings of a survey of 395 randomly selected field officers

TABLE 1

Injury Reporting Designators Used in This Study

Injury Designator	Definition
None	No injury
Taser/Gas	Effects from Taser or chemical irritant spray only
Minor	Complained of pain, minor scratches, skin redness
Moderate	Small lacerations, welts, contusions, bruises
Major[a]	Breaks, concussions, large lacerations or contusions, sprains, strains

[a] To qualify for the "major" injury category, officers had to have been placed off-duty or on "light" (nonfield) duty; suspects were usually hospitalized.

TABLE 2

Injuries to Suspects by Effective Force Type[a]

Effective Force Type	None	Taser/Gas	Minor	Moderate	Major	Total
Baton	24	0	24	66	7	121
Kick	20	0	9	12	0	41
Punch	6	0	5	15	1	27
Misc. Force	51	0	20	58	6	135
Flashlight	4	0	0	14	6	24
Swarm	33	0	3	10	1	47
ChemSpray	0	18	1	0	0	19
Taser	0	88	0	0	0	88
Total	138	106	62	175	21	502

[a] Taser/Gas means effects of Taser or chemical irritant spray only; minor, moderate, and major injuries are defined in Table 1.

TABLE 3

Injuries to Officers by Effective Force Type[a]

Effective Force Type	None	Taser/Gas	Minor	Moderate	Major	Total
Baton	99	0	4	10	8	121
Kick	36	0	0	3	2	41
Punch	19	0	0	5	3	27
Misc. Force	109	0	5	13	8	135
Flashlight	20	0	3	1	0	24
Swarm	39	0	1	6	1	47
ChemSpray	14	5	0	0	0	19
Taser	88	0	0	0	0	88
Total	424	5	13	38	22	502

[a] Taser/Gas means effects of Taser or chemical irritant spray only; minor, moderate, and major injuries are defined in Table 1.

TABLE 4

Success Rates of Force Types, with Corresponding Injury Rates

Force Type	Study Cases[a]	Success Cases	Success Rate	Major/Moderate Injuries[b] Officers	Suspects
Baton	143	121	85%	16%	61%
Kick	47	41	87%	11%	26%
Punch	36	27	75%	36%	64%
Misc. Force	143	135	94%	15%	46%
Flashlight	25	24	96%	4%	80%
Swarm	51	47	92%	16%	24%
ChemSpray	21	19	90%	0%	0%
Taser	102	88	86%	0%	0%
Total	568	502	88%	13%	39%

[a] Includes Effective and Ineffective Force Types.

[b] Percentage of major and of moderate injuries, regardless of whether force was effective.

from fifteen subelements of the LAPD in October 1990 (Meyer, 1990).

The officers were asked to respond anonymously on a Likert scale to a series of written statement-questions regarding use-of-force issues. Prominent among the findings were that 77 percent of the officers believed that more aggressive use of nonlethal weapons would result in fewer and less severe officer injuries during confrontations; 68 percent encouraged the development of a *Star Trek*–style "ray gun"; and 66 percent expressed confidence in the Taser. It is noteworthy that only 14 percent expressed confidence in chemical irritant spray. The injury effects of the Taser and chemical irritant spray should be considered to be at or below the "minor" level. Arguably, critics could elevate the temporary pain and discomfort to the "moderate" level on the injury scale, but doing so and then reexamining the statistical results (i.e., considering only the major-injury columns of Tables 2 and 3) would still lead one to the conclusion that the nonlethal weapons produced fewer and less severe injuries than the conventional force types.

In police confrontations that cannot be controlled by verbalization, nonlethal weapons should be used early and aggressively to bring the situation to a conclusion as quickly as possible before it deteriorates into a confrontation requiring a greater level of force. This concept is the key to significantly reducing injuries to officers and suspects. Moral and legal constraints require officers to use the minimum amount of reasonable and necessary force to control a confrontation. It hardly needs to be noted that whatever force types are effective and result in the least severe injuries to officers and suspects are more reasonable than those that result in greater injuries.

Greg Meyer

Bibliography

Casey, Joe D. "Research and Development Needed for Less-Than-Lethal Weapons." *Police Chief* 55 (February 1988): 7.

Geis, Gilbert, and Arnold Binder. "Non-Lethal Weapons: The Potential and the Pitfalls." *Journal of Contemporary Criminal Justice* 6 (1990): 1-7.

Geller, William A., and Michael S. Scott. *Deadly Force: What We Know*. Washington, DC: Police Executive Research Forum, 1992.

Kornblum, Ronald N., and Sara K. Reddy.

"Effects of the Taser in Fatalities Involving Police Confrontation." *Journal of Forensic Sciences* 36 (1991): 434–48.

Koscove, Eric M. "The Taser Weapon: A New Emergency Medicine Problem." *Annals of Emergency Medicine* 14 (December 1985): 112.

Meyer, C. Kenneth, et al. "A Comparative Assessment of Assault Incidents: Robbery Related, Ambush, and General Police Assaults." *Journal of Police Science and Administration* 9 (1981): 1–18.

Meyer, Greg. "Your Nonlethal Weapons Alternatives." *Journal of California Law Enforcement* 15 (1981): 125–36.

———. "A Survey of 395 Los Angeles Police Officers on the Subject of Nondeadly Use of Force." Los Angeles: California State University, 1990.

———. *Nonlethal Weapons vs. Conventional Police Tactics: The Los Angeles Police Department Experience*. Los Angeles: California State University, 1991.

Peak, Ken. "The Quest for Alternatives to Lethal Force: A Heuristic View." *Journal of Contemporary Criminal Justice* 6 (1990): 8–22.

Reddin, Thomas J. "Non-Lethal Weapons—Curse or Cure?" *The Police Chief* 34 (December 1967): 60–63.

Scharf, Peter, and Arnold Binder. *The Badge and the Bullet*. New York: Praeger, 1983.

Sweetman, Sherri. *Report on the Attorney General's Conference on Less than Lethal Weapons*. Washington, DC: U.S. Department of Justice, National Institute of Justice, 1987.

Nonlethal Weapons: History

Since the dawn of time people have sought to control the behavior of their fellows. Our recorded history is full of accounts of the need to protect ourselves from a hostile environment. All of these functions—social control, punishment, and protection—have involved tools and weapons of both a lethal and nonlethal nature. Both lethal and nonlethal devices evolved from simple beginnings. Fire, stone, hemp, and water have been used to punish and control people. Most societies have for more than a century and a half allowed their police to enforce and legitimize their mores and laws through physical means (Peak, 1990:8).

This entry traces the evolution of nonlethal weapons used by international police forces to protect themselves and the public at large. Although the term "nonlethal weapons" is used throughout, note that this term may be somewhat inappropriate; *any* tool or weapon can be lethal if used in an improper or unintended manner. For those reasons, the National Institute of Justice uses the term "less-than-lethal" to designate a weapon where there is only a temporary effect and minimal medical implications to normally healthy persons (Sweetman, 1987:4–5).

Nonlethal Weapons Unveiled, 1829

When London's new bobbies began patrolling the streets in September 1829, they were armed with a baton ("truncheon") that still today is a standard-issue weapon; it was made of hardwood, rubber, or plastic, two to four centimeters in diameter, and thirty to sixty-five centimeters in length. Swords, although not a standard issue to the bobbies in the nineteenth century, were kept in most police armories for possible use during riots or large demonstrations (Peak, 1990:10).

Social turmoil in America between 1840 and 1870 brought increased use of force by the police—themselves frequent victims of assault. The New York City police and other departments were armed with thirty-three-inch clubs, which officers were not reluctant to use. Charges of police brutality were common in the mid-1800s, when officers allegedly clubbed "respectable" citizens with frequency (Peak, 1990:10).

Police and Nonlethal Force, 1860 to 1959

International policing from 1860 to 1959 witnessed only one major addition to the small array of nonlethal police tools: chemical weapons. "CN" gas was synthesized by a German chemist in 1869 and was the first "tear gas," producing a burning sensation in the throat, eyes, and nose. CN became available for use in aerosol cans in 1965, with "Chemical Mace," the most well-known variety. By 1912 there was increased use of chemical weapons for riot situations and subduing criminals (Peak, 1990:11).

"CS" gas was first synthesized in 1928 as a white powder that stored well. It was adopted by many police forces as it had a greater affect than CN, causing a very strong burning sensation in the eyes that often caused them to close involuntarily. Severe pain in the nose, throat,

and chest, and vomiting and nausea are also associated with its use (Crockett, 1968:9).

After the turn of the century, the baton remained a staple tool among American police. As late as 1900, when the Chicago Police Department numbered 3,225 officers, the only tools given to the new patrolman were "a brief speech from a high-ranking officer, a hickory stick, whistle, and a key to the call box" (Haller, 1976:303). Charges of police brutality continued, even from within. In 1903 a former New York police commissioner stated:

> "For three years, there has been through the courts a dreary procession of citizens with broken heads and bruised bodies against few of whom violence was needed to effect an arrest. Many of them had done nothing to deserve an arrest and if the victim complains, his charge is generally dismissed. The police are practically above the law" (Lundman, 1980:274–75).

A Technological Explosion: The 1960s

The 1960s witnessed major technological advances in nonlethal weaponry but profiteering was a major inducement for developers. As technologist/inventor William Shaw observed, "Inventors were concerned with producing devices and products that would sell. Neither the inventor nor the potential manufacturer worried about the negative effects of the new products" (Shaw, 1973:84).

This was the age of rioting, both on domestic and foreign soil, and it seemed that everyone—from presidential commissions to civilians on the street—was debating how much and what kind of force should be exerted by the police toward bringing rioters under control. Aerosol chemical agents, developed to provide alternatives to police batons and firearms, became the most widely used nonlethal weapons to emerge for police use. Mace seemed like "manna from heaven" (Coon, 1968:46). Mace-squirting nightsticks were issued in the District of Columbia, and thousands of law-enforcement agencies later adopted Mace in some form.

A chemical wand was also developed, touted as "burning for five full minutes . . . about as long as seven burning type grenades . . . giving off a steady stream of CS" (Peak, 1990:13). "CR" gas appeared in 1962; six times more potent than CS and twenty times more potent than CN, it caused extreme eye pressure and occasional hysteria. CS gas cartridges, fired by shotguns at a range of 125 meters, were used in the United States and Great Britain as early as 1968. Soon, however, there was international concern about the use of these gas-emitting weapons. For example, Los Angeles Chief of Police Thomas Reddin argued that the weapons carried the inherent risk of inciting further violence. He also contended that further research was needed into these police weapons.

In 1967 alternatives to lethal lead bullets were first attempted in Hong Kong. Wooden rounds, fired from a signal pistol with a range of twenty to thirty meters, were designed to be ricocheted off of the ground, striking the victim in the legs. The wooden rounds proved to be fatal, however, and direct fire broke legs at forty-six meters (they were also deemed unacceptable by the Northern Ireland police). Rubber bullets were developed and issued to British troops and police officers in 1967, only a few months after the wooden rounds appeared. Intended to deliver a force equivalent to a hard punch at twenty-five meters, the rubber bullets caused severe bruising and shock. Also intended to be ricocheted off of the ground, the rubber bullet was designed so that riot police could outrange stone throwers (Manwaring-White, 1983:140).

British riot police also employed watercannons, designed to fire large jets of water at demonstrators on the streets of Derry in 1968 and later in Northern Ireland. Resembling armored fire engines, watercannons were also used in Germany, France, Belgium, and the United States. Nontoxic blue dye was added to the water for marking the offenders; for a time the firing of a CR solution was contemplated. The overall efficacy of watercannons was questionable, however, as it was often observed that demonstrators simply avoided the jets of water by hiding behind makeshift shields (Manwaring-White, 1983:141–42).

In 1968 another unique riot-oriented weapon was unveiled in America: the "Sound Curdler," consisting of amplified speakers that produced loud, shrieking noises at irregular intervals. Attached to vehicles or helicopters, the device was first used at campus disturbances. Thirteen of these devices were purchased by the British for possible use in Northern Ireland, at a cost of 2,000 pounds each.

Beanbag Guns, Strobe Lights, and "New-Age" Batons: The 1970s

Another unique nonlethal weapon was literally unfurled in 1970, following the killing of four protesters by armed national guardsmen at Kent State University: a gun that shot beanbags rather than bullets. The apparatus resembled a large billy club with spiral grooves in the barrel; it fired a pellet-loaded bag that unfurled into a spinning pancake, capable of knocking down a 200-pound person at a range of 300 feet. Although its manufacturer warned that it had potentially lethal capabilities, it quickly became popular in several countries, with South Africa, Saudi Arabia, and Malaysia purchasing hundreds of thousands of them (Peak, 1990:15–16).

Several other inventions were added to the nonlethal arsenal of the police in the 1970s. The "Photic Driver," first used by police in South Africa, produced a strobe effect, its light causing giddiness, fainting, and nausea. A British firm developed a strobe gun, which operated at five "flickers" per second. Some of these devices also had a high-pitched screamer device attached. Another apparatus known as the "Squawk Box" had two high-energy ultrasound generators operating at slightly different frequencies, which produced sounds that also caused nausea and giddiness (Peak, 1990:16).

Another invention of the early 1970s included injector dart guns, adapted from veterinarians' tranquilizer guns that, when fired, injected the drug they carried. Other developments included an electrified water jet and a baton that carried a 6,000-volt shock; shotgun shells filled with plastic pellets; plastic bubbles that immobilized rioters; a chemical that created slippery street surfaces for combatting rioters; and an instant "cocoon," which was an adhesive substance that, when sprayed over crowds, made people stick together (Manwaring-White, 1983:145–46).

A substantive change occurred with the police baton in 1972. While the "typical" baton had been about one inch in diameter and ten to thirty inches in length, this new baton had a handle about six inches from its grip end, which allowed (according to its manufacturers) its versatility to be virtually unlimited (Folley, 1972:46–47). This "side-handle" baton did indeed become popular and remains popular among police officers today.

Two new types of projectiles very different in nature were developed in 1974: the plastic bullet, and the Taser. Because rubber bullets often led to the disability of targeted individuals, further research in England resulted in a seemingly "softer" plastic bullet. Made from hard, white PVC, four inches in length, one-and-a-quarter inches in diameter, and weighing about five ounces, the bullet resembled a blunt candle and could be fired from a variety of riot weapons. Their speed of 160 miles per hour and range of thirty to seventy meters made them attractive to riot police. However, the plastic bullet proved fatal as well. Between January and August 1981, seven persons in Northern Ireland died after being struck with these bullets; all were struck in the head. About 25,000 plastic bullets were fired by the British army and the Northern Ireland police during that period, causing many serious head and kidney injuries (Manwaring-White, 1983:142–43).

The Taser, patented by a Los Angeles firm, resembled a flashlight and shot two tiny darts into its victim. Attached to the darts were fine wires through which a transformer delivered a 50,000-volt electrical shock, which would knock down a person at a distance of fifteen feet. Police officers in every state except Alaska had used the device by 1985, but its use has not been widespread because of limitations of range and on persons under the influence of drugs. Heavy clothing can also render it ineffective. The primary manufacturer of Taser filed for bankruptcy in 1985, underscoring the problem of funding the research and development of high-tech, nonlethal weaponry (Sweetman, 1987:4–5).

The stun gun, also introduced in the mid-1970s, initially competed with the Taser as the nonlethal weapon of choice for police personnel. Slightly larger than an electric razor, it delivered a 50,000-volt shock when its two electrodes were pressed directly against the body. Like the Taser, its amperage was so small that it did not provide a lethal electrical jolt. Its target, rendered rubbery-legged and falling to the ground, was unable to control physical movement for several minutes. Several abuses of the stun gun were documented in 1985. Five New York City police officers were indicted for using the stun gun to torture four men arrested on minor charges; a San Antonio sheriff's lieutenant was sentenced to two years' probation for repeatedly shocking a handcuffed suspect. The criminal element also had access to the device; in Dallas two supermarket robbers used one to disable a clerk (Serrill, 1985:59).

The Continuing Quest: The 1980s

There was little abatement in the number of newly developed nonlethal police weapons during the 1980s. Flashlights were marketed that had stun capacity or contained chemical agents. However, studies showed that when these flashlights were used as a baton, with 425 pounds of force and very likely to fracture the skull, the potential for injury and liability was quite high (Cox, Fauch, and Nixon, 1985:245).

Some "tools" which seem very unusual today were created for police use in the early 1980s. The "entanglement net" and the "action chain control device" each required four officers to operate, in what seems today much like a "Keystone Cops" scenario. (Officer No. 1, armed with a long baton, distracted the suspect while Officer No. 2 sprayed him with a fire extinguisher; thus diverted, the suspect was then encased with a net thrown over him by Officers No. 3 and No. 4. Any weapons possessed by the suspect were then knocked away by Officer No. 1, using the long baton.) (Peak, 1990:18).

Also marketed were an expandable baton (from six to sixteen inches "with a flick of the wrist") and a six-inch steel whip which, when opened to its thirteen-inch length, projected three steel coils and was transformed into something resembling the Medieval "cat-o-nine-tails." In 1987 the zenith of baton technology was reached, perhaps, with the invention of a model shaped like a Colorado mountain highway. The "twelve-grip action" baton was short-handled and was advertised as having "incorporated many of the leverage techniques used in the martial arts." Advertised as "question-mark shaped," this baton actually had four bends and curves at its business end (Peak, 1990:18).

Summary

This entry traced international attempts over the course of a century and a half to arm the police with effective alternatives to lethal force; most of those attempts either failed utterly or were fraught with serious problems. Many manufacturers, motivated by potential profits, often engaged in little product research.

The quest remains for effective alternatives to lethal force. It is a paradox in this "high-technology" age that we have not been able to develop reliable substitutes for lethal police weapons. The above chronology shows that past attempts to do so were inefficacious and, at times, even humorous.

Society—especially the scientific community—and the police must endeavor to continue working together to succeed in discovering non-lethal means of legitimate physical control. There is much to be gained and, if the quest fails, much to be lost.

Kenneth J. Peak

Bibliography

Coon, T.F. "A Maze of Confusion Over Amazing Mace." *Police* (November–December 1968): 45–47.

Cox, T., J.S. Fauch, and W.M. Nixon. "Police Use of Metal Flashlights as Weapons: An Analysis of Relevant Problems." *Journal of Police Science and Administration* 13, 3 (1985): 244–50.

Crockett, T.S. "Riot Control Agents." *Police Chief* (November 1968): 8–18.

Folley, V.L. "The Prosecutor: The New Concept Police Baton." *Law and Order* (September 1972): 46–50.

Haller, M.H. "Historical Roots of Police Behavior: Chicago, 1890–1925." *Law and Society Review* 10 (2) (1976): 303–23.

Lundman, R.J. *Police Behavior: A Sociological Perspective.* Oxford: Oxford Press, 1980.

Manwaring-White, S. *The Policing Revolution: Police Technology, Democracy, and Liberty in Britain.* Brighton, Sussex: The Harvester Press, 1983.

Peak, K. "The Quest for Alternatives to Lethal Force: A Hueristic View." *Journal of Contemporary Criminal Justice* 6 (1) (1990): 8–22.

Reddin, T.J. "Police Weapons for the Space Age." *Police Chief* 33 (11) (1967): 10–17.

Serrill, M.S. "ZAP! Stun Guns: Hot But Getting Heat." *Time* (May 1985): 59.

Shaw, W. "Should We Develop a Non-lethal Sidearm for Police Use?" *Law and Order* (June 1973): 84–89.

Sweetman, S. *Report on the Attorney General's Conference on Less Than Lethal Weapons.* Washington, DC: Department of Justice, National Institute of Justice, 1987.

Northwestern University Traffic Institute

The Traffic Institute (TI) was established at Northwestern University in 1936 for the purpose of expanding the scope of university-level education and training in traffic safety. Since that time TI has broadened its original objective to include training in accident investigation, transportation engineering, criminal investigation, and police operations and management, and to address urgent issues in criminal justice and law enforcement. Representatives from federal, state, and local police agencies, as well as members of foreign agencies, attend the institute's many and varied programs. TI also serves the law-enforcement community through research, publications, and on-site assistance.

History

The advent and proliferation of automobiles made crossing streets a terrifying proposition. Even where "slow" signs existed they were useless since there was no general understanding of what "slow" meant on a speedometer. By the 1930s death and injury from traffic accidents throughout the country had become a major problem for unprepared law-enforcement agencies. A young Evanston patrolman named Frank Kreml grew concerned and with the help of Illinois state leaders imposed a method on the madness. Kreml devised a balanced law-enforcement program of accident investigation involving records, analyses, and selective enforcement that proved sound in Evanston. Cities like Syracuse and Louisville requested that Kreml install similar programs in their police departments. With Kreml's assistance, ten cities adopted a variation of the plan between 1930 and 1936. Accidents decreased in these cities, demonstrating to skeptics that the plan was not just a local phenomenon in "that suburb north of Chicago." With Frank Kreml as director, a two-week Traffic Officer's Training School (TOTS) began in 1932 and made an impact.

TOTS ran annually until 1936, when the Automotive Safety Foundation (ASF) came into being. ASF leaders met with the president of Northwestern University to strike a deal. ASF would donate $5,000 if the university would match the amount, institutionalize TOTS, and give housing to the newly founded Traffic Safety Division, a field service approved by the board of directors of the International Association of Chiefs of Police (IACP). With a handshake the agreement was made and the Northwestern University Traffic Institute, along with the Traffic Safety Division of the IACP, became a reality. As a team the IACP and TI began to assist state law-enforcement organizations, such as the California Highway Patrol (administrative reorganization); the Wisconsin Highway Patrol (total reorganization from 73 to 350 men); and the Illinois State Police (completely deactivated and reactivated). In municipal areas, Detroit for example, over a nineteen-month period the team produced a 61 percent reduction in traffic fatalities. Los Angeles, Atlanta, Chicago, Cleveland, and other cities likewise benefited.

In the years just prior to World War II, TI's agenda expanded beyond traffic. Having perfected the nine-month Police Administration Training Program and a growing short-course program, both at the institute and in the field, TI staff expressed the need for texts and other training materials. Writers started to work to fill the need. Two of the best-known texts to have come out of the early years were *Evidence Handbook* and the first of its kind, *The Traffic Accident Investigation Manual*. In the years just prior to World War II TI's agenda expanded beyond traffic. The U.S. Army asked the institute to observe and analyze its movements during maneuvers. In a bold report the institute pointed out the gross inefficiencies in safety, in the movement of vehicles and people, in supervision, and in dealing with environmental problems. Moreover, the report called for a total reorganization of the Corps of Military Police, including the establishment of a school for military police. The school, envisioned by TI, carries on to this day.

By 1945, TI staff outgrew their original building at 1827 Orrington and moved to 405 Church Street, a location earmarked for the institute by Northwestern University President Franklyn Bliss Synder. As further expansion and activity followed the war, the institute gained national prominence. J. Stannard Baker, who was to become the foremost authority on traffic accident investigation, joined the institute staff in 1946. Baker was appointed director of research and development, thus greatly strengthening TI's teaching, research, field service, and publications programs. That same year the American Bar Association requested a partnership with TI to establish the Traffic Court Judges and Prosecutors Program of one-week conferences given across the country. A third major development in the late 1940s was the creation of a program for Chief Drivers' License Examiners, funded by a grant from Farmers Insurance Group of Los Angeles.

To combat motor vehicle accidents on an industry-wide front, the Insurance Institute for Highway Safety commenced operations as part of TI in January 1959. Then, given generous federal funding during the 1960s, TI experienced even more rapid growth. In 1966 the National Highway Traffic Safety Administration (NHTSA) became an agency within the U.S. Department of Transportation. NHTSA fostered state and local highway safety programs and authorized the setting of vehicle standards to unite federal and private efforts, increasing traffic safety nationally. The major legislation brought more prominence to TI. The 1970s also produced dynamic change. The International Branch was established as a section of the Training Division in 1975. Its first mission was to design and implement a twenty-two-month training program for Saudi Arabian police officers. With increasing enrollments came added monies. Construction began on a new building at 555 Clark Street.

In 1978 Noel C. Bufe became the ninth director of the Traffic Institute. He was chosen because of his work on the federal level as deputy director of NHTSA and his extensive experience in state and local government, highway safety, and criminal-justice program management.

Liberal federal funding ceased beginning in the late 1970s. The cutbacks caused the institute to diversify in order to open new avenues for financial backing. More attention was given to areas for research; a ten-week School of Police Staff and Command was added; consulting services were increased nationally and internationally; and training materials and correspondence courses were developed to stimulate income. In 1981 the newly created Accident Investigation Division revised its classic *Traffic Accident Investigation Manual* and adopted an "accident reconstruction" approach. J. Stannard Baker and Lynn B. Fricke updated the internationally acclaimed *Manual* in 1986. The National Committee on Uniform Traffic Laws and Ordinances transferred to the institute in 1982. The committee maintains the Uniform Vehicle Code and the Model Traffic Ordinance for all the states, a task it had accomplished for more than fifty years prior to joining TI. In 1988 the Circuit Court of Cook County chose TI to develop and manage a pilot program for a court-sponsored Traffic Safety School for drivers convicted of moving traffic violations. The program will assist in bringing under control the traffic court's 850,000 annual caseload of moving traffic violations. Facing the future, TI still has public safety problems to solve. Among the most troublesome are high-risk driving, driving under the influence of alcohol or other drugs, endless highway congestion, adverse vehicle and pedestrian mix, gross variations in law enforcement and adjudication, state-to-state law disparities, mechanical defects in vehicles, electronic means of hindering enforcement, and declining funds for highway construction and maintenance.

The Twelve Divisions
Each of the Traffic Institute's twelve divisions is a vital component in its efforts to educate personnel involved with traffic safety, law enforcement, criminal justice, and highway transportation. The divisions are:

- Police Administration Training Program (PATP). Through the exploration of public safety and law-enforcement issues that confront police managers, students develop the analytical and leadership skills necessary to perform as administrative staff officers. Nine months' duration.
- School of Police Staff and Command (SPSC). The program prepares first- and second-level police management for senior-level positions in their agencies. Ten weeks long.
- Police Training Division. Not strictly for management training like the PATP and SPSC, the division offers seminars and workshops for officials in law enforcement, civil service, the judiciary and administration, and for private sector individuals. The curriculum addresses current issues in the field and is redeveloped annually to reflect advancements in research and technology.
- Field Services Division. Its two primary functions are to administer and present Traffic Institute on-site training programs throughout the United States and its territories, and to research and evaluate municipal, county, and state law enforcement agency management including field operation systems and procedures. Annually TI trains over 6,000 police officers and conducts over 150 on-site programs.
- Transportation Engineering Division. Engineers with extensive backgrounds in the planning, design, and operation of transportation systems disseminate information about, and facilitate the

application of, recent developments in the field.
- Accident Investigation Division. This division's seven-course series is the most comprehensive training program of its kind, beginning with the basics and culminating in traffic accident reconstruction.
- Motor Vehicle Administration Division, which provides training and continuing education for drivers license administrators and U.S. Armed Forces police personnel.
- Research and Development Division. This division supports TI through program and publication development, classroom instruction in specialty areas, and research in applied transportation engineering and law enforcement.
- Legal Division, which creates and reviews course outlines, texts, and other publications; provides legal instruction on- and off-campus; and in a consultant role prepares field surveys for law enforcement agencies involved in criminal or civil lawsuits. It specializes in administrative law, traffic law, evidence law, equal opportunity requirements, and civil liability.
- Traffic Safety School (TSS) offers classroom courses designed to create a positive attitude toward safe driving and to improve driving skills. TSS includes a major research and evaluation component to measure driving records before and after course attendance and to identify which instructional methodology and content are most effective in changing driver behavior.
- Public Information and Publications Division. This division is responsible for all promotional activities including media relations, advertising, training/reference manuals, textbooks and audio-visual materials, course brochures, and the Alumni Association newsletter. It also produces independent-study courses.
- Research Center for Aviation Safety and Security. The newest division serves as a clearinghouse to advance knowledge of aviation safety and security nationally and internationally. This departure from a concentration on highway safety demonstrates respect for TI's ability to solve mass-transportation problems.

The Traffic Institute's faculty and staff have advanced degrees in such disparate areas as law, engineering, educational administration, and the social sciences. Faculty and staff have written numerous books and articles and serve at high levels in government agencies and professional associations. Along with the FBI Academy and the Southern Police Institute, the Traffic Institute forms the trinity of the "big three" law-enforcement training centers.

N

Occupational Culture

The concept of culture has a long and distinguished history, and like most sociological concepts is subject to wide variations in definition and application. Like role, group, rule, and collective behavior, it has been both widely and inconsistently used. It retains its hold on the imagination for its common sense relevance, not for its sociological precision or elegance of reference. A cautious and working definition of police occupational culture is advanced here in order to explicate the term and examine its utility in explaining police behavior.

Comparative Studies

An *occupational culture* is a reduced, selective, and task-based version of culture that is shaped by and shapes the socially relevant worlds of the occupation. Embedded in traditions and a history, occupational cultures contain accepted practices, rules, and principles of conduct that are situationally applied, and generalized rationales and beliefs. Such cultures highlight selectively the contours of an environment, granting meaning to some facts and not others, and linking modes of seeing, doing, and believing. To some extent, occupational culture contains what is taken for granted by members, invisible yet powerful constraints, and thus it connects cognition and action, environment and organization, in an entangling and interwoven tapestry. They act as socially validated sources one for the other.

The principal works on the police vary in method, in conceptual focus, in depth of analysis, and in the degree to which they are comparative. A brief review of these studies will establish the outlines of the relevance of the concept of occupational culture. In a comparative study of Scottish and American police roles Banton (1964) focuses on two functions of policing, peacekeeping and law enforcement, in societies with relatively high or low social integration (characterized by density of social interaction). The higher the level of social integration, the more the culture arises in lower density settings as a substitute for the social integration of the officer in high density (rural) settings. Westley, in the first American research of note (a dissertation completed in 1951 and published in 1970) relies on policing culture as a primary explanatory concept. Because the public is seen as hostile and distrusted, even potentially violent, the occupational culture emphasizes the themes of self-protection in the forms of secrecy, violence, and maintenance of respect for officers (Westley, 1970: chap. 4). Westley states these as variable features; they arise more in large American urban departments than elsewhere (cf. Westley, 1970:xxi, with Holdaway, 1983).

Cain (1973) compared a rural with an urban English force using interviews and observations. Her focus was on how role definers (e.g., the public, one's colleagues) constrain actions of officers, given varying degrees of dependency. She found higher dependency on other officers in the urban force where the public were seen as unsupportive. There, the radio and the police vehicle became primary tools. Echoing Banton she found the rural force less dependent on other officers (and more on the public) and less concerned with action, risk, excitement, and crime-fighting. Cain saw these *role configurations* as the basis for a network of meanings that differentially bound the two forces.

Rubinstein (1972) and Skolnick (1966) echo Westley's themes of violence, secrecy, distrust, collegial orientation, and dependency among American urban police. Rubinstein's very insightful ethnography details the resultant tactics—the lies, the violence, the deception and self-deception; the quasi-paranoid world of a segment of urban policing. Skolnick's sociolegal treatise poses a contradiction between features of the occupational culture and the resultant "working personality" on one hand, and the "democratic rule of law" on the other. In Skolnick's eyes urban policing and many of the procedural guarantees provided in American law are often in conflict. The conflict is resolved in favor of the guidelines of the culture. Pressures to act to maintain respect for the law and the officer, reinforced by culturally validated beliefs in the dangerousness and violence of the public, mean that police tend to act to control crime and to produce "justice without trial." Skolnick's ideas, as Holdaway (1980, 1983) has shown, have been rather too widely accepted as characteristic of American policing and even generalized without data to characterize British forces.

Wilson (1968) viewed police work as an administrative problem. How does one command and control police when there is no adequate theory of the causation of events and no technology for coping with the vagarious nature of human existence? Wilson argues that organizational structures are responses to the degree of uncertainty in the environment. He emphasizes the uncertainty that pervades the work from both administrative and line-worker's perspectives.

Bittner (1967, 1970, 1974), takes the phenomenological *field* of the officer as central and sees policing as the competent application of violence to coerce order in a situation (1974). Thus competence, creating public compliance, and force are intertwined themes in Bittner's work. Bittner elegantly depicts this defining facet of police work but makes little reference to administration or occupational culture.

Manning's view (1977, 1979) of police occupational culture is premised on the existential proposition that life is uncertain. Uncertainty blurs the tendency of social actors to distinguish public from private actions and the front from the back stage of any setting. The inherent uncertainty of police work and the need to control information to maintain public fronts increases the likelihood of police teamwork that in turn generates collective ties and mutual dependence. The themes of secrecy and violence, the face-to-face character of police work, and the here-and-now nature of social reality are amplified by this structuring of experience. Rituals, ceremonies, and myths fix and order the nature of policing uncertainty and in turn structure the perception of the world as risky and uncertain (e.g., in *Narcs' Game* [1980] Manning illustrates the enacted nature of the environment by an occupational culture, a set of shared understandings about skills, roles, people, and organizations). These ideas are often in conflict with the organization's strategies and tactics of public dramaturgical management, which, at least in America, are keyed by the idea of "police professionalism."

Simon Holdaway's important summary and critique of the idea of occupational culture (1980) clarifies the essential British policing experience, as well as explores themes of risk, violence, hedonism, and crime-control found in both American and British research. He makes central *typification* of time, space, and work (strategies and tactics). For him, as with Manning, the degree of focus on risk and disorder (or chaos) is unique to the policing culture. Uncertainty is transformed by the police into a kind of impending moral chaos. In that sense, Holdaway, Bittner, and Manning accept the centrality for police of controlling and ordering public scenes (cf. Reiner, 1985, on "ordering").

Structurally grounded explanations for police culture are contained in the historical works of Brogden (1982) and the work of Jefferson and Grimshaw (1984). In their view, the primary forces shaping policing are the dual structures of "class" and "the law." The occupational culture, police administration, and police behavior are seen as direct consequences of the constraints of law. The law guides managers and police administration including the decisions of chief constables, middle managers, and police in the streets. This rather unicausal view has found little support among police researchers and working police officers, nor is it reflected in collected data. The determinant character of the law is not evidenced in studies of arrest behavior, corruption, or administrative behavior. Nevertheless, further investigation is needed on the patterning effect of law upon behavior and in shaping the occupational culture.

These works, primarily ethnographic, based upon diverse data, and spanning more than twenty-five years of police research in Anglo and American societies echo many themes. All grant the occupational culture a significant place in determining officer behavior. In some works, it stands in a dialectical relationship to the law, the organization, or other aspects of the social structure (race, class, sex, age). It mediates the environment on the one hand and actions on the other. It is a kind of *symbolic mediator*. It is widely used as an explanatory concept. This is true whether the consequences of the culture are seen as negative, as for example when it is seen to support lying, corruption, or violence; or positive, for example, in providing support, colleagueship, insulation against stress, and standards of competent practice.

Social Structure

Three features of social structure are poorly integrated in studies of police occupational culture. The first is the Anglo-American preoccupation with equality combined with the consistent themes and realities in those societies of class dominance, racism, and sexism. The combination is explosive, since both are enstructured into policing: practices of exploitation of the (relatively) powerless and the use of the law to maintain that balance; and a public espousal of equality of opportunity, procedural, and substantive justice. The second is the structure of democratic Anglo-American societies, which restricts police access to private places. While law guarantees a variety of procedural protections to citizens, these societies seek to define policing as a function of criminal law (and link this with morality and the state). Third, the structure of modern Anglo-American policing has evolved to produce characteristic organizational features and careers (Manning, 1983). These features include broad recruitment and a pyramid-shaped organizational structure, flat organizational hierarchy, little interorganizational mobility, limited vertical and extensive horizontal mobility, characteristic formal and informal specialization, and bases of job-attachment/commitment (Van Maanen and Schein, 1979). Furthermore, features of the occupation *qua* occupation must also be considered in describing the occupational culture. The salience of these features varies as well as does the overall importance attributed to the occupational culture.

Constructs of Occupational Culture

Occupational culture arises from a set of *tasks* that are repeated and routinized in various degrees, and a *technology* that is various and indirect in its effects (it is mediated by the organizational structure), producing a set of *attitudes* and an explanatory structure of *belief* (ideology). The tasks of policing are *uncertain*; they are various, unusual, and unpredictable in appearance, duration, content, and consequence. They are fraught with *disorderly potential*. The police officer is *dependent* on other officers for assistance, advice, training, working knowledge, protection in the case of threats from internal or external sources, and insulation against the public and periodic danger. The occupation emphasizes *autonomy*, both with respect to individual decision-making or what lawyers term "discretion"; the public it serves and controls (officers will routinely experience adversarial relations with the public); and the rigid authority symbolized by the paramilitary structure of the organization. Finally, the occupational culture makes salient displaying, creating, and maintaining *authority*. The sources of the authority theme are multiple insofar as they draw on the state's authority, the public morality of the dominant classes, and the law.

Conclusion

Police occupational culture in Anglo-American societies is a product of social structure and the evolution of the police organization. The organization of policing subscribes to a set of characteristics that might best be considered a *symbolic form* that is both paramilitary and dominated by a dispersed group of autonomous officers making independent decisions. The characteristic themes of the police occupational culture—dependence, uncertainty, autonomy, and authority—are found in their two social worlds, that of the officers and that of administration. A social world includes more than the occupational culture; it encompasses themes from the larger culture about the meaning of work generally and types of job attachment and commitment. It includes meta-themes that mark and dramatize one or more features of the shared occupational culture.

Peter K. Manning

Bibliography

Banton, M. *The Policeman in the Community*. New York: Basic Books, 1964.

Bittner, E. "The Police on Skid Row." *American Sociological Review* 32 (October 1967): 699–715.

———. *The Functions of Police in Urban Society*. Bethesda: National Institute of

Mental Health, 1970.

———. ". . . A Theory of Police." In *The Potential for Reform of Criminal Justice*. Ed. H. Jacob. Beverly Hills: Sage, 1974.

Brogden, M. *The Police: Autonomy and Consent*. New York: Academic, 1982.

Cain, M. *Society and the Policeman's Role*. London: Routledge and Kegan Paul, 1973.

Holdaway, S. "The Occupational Culture of Urban Policing: An Ethnographic Study." Ph.D. diss., University of Sheffield, 1980.

———. *Inside the British Police*. Oxford: Basil Blackwell, 1983.

Jefferson, T., and R. Grimshaw. *Controlling the Constable: Police Accountability in England and Wales*. London: Cobden Trust, 1984.

Jermeir, J., and L. Berkes. "Leader Behavior in a Police Command Bureaucracy: A Closer Look at the Quasi-Military Model." *Administrative Science Quarterly* 24 (March 1979): 1–23.

Manning, P.K. "Police Lying." *Urban Life and Culture* 3 (1974): 283–306.

———. *Police Work*. Cambridge, MA: MIT Press, 1977.

———. "The Social Control of Police Work." In *British Police*. Ed. S. Holdaway. London: Edward Arnold, 1979.

———. *Narcs' Game*. Cambridge, MA: MIT Press, 1980.

———. "Organisational Work: Enstructuration of the Environment." *British Journal of Sociology* 33 (March 1982): 118–34.

———. "Police Careers." In *The Encyclopedia of Crime and Justice*. Eds. S. Kadish et al. New York: Macmillan, 1983.

———. "British Police: Continuities and Changes." *Journal of the Howard League* 25 (November 1986): 261–78.

Muir, W.K., Jr. *Police: Street Corner Politicians*. Chicago: University of Chicago Press, 1977.

Preiss, J.J., and H. Ehrlich. *An Examination of Role Theory*. Lincoln: University of Nebraska Press, 1966.

Punch, M. *Conduct Unbecoming*. London: Tavistock, 1986.

Reiner, R. *The Politics of the Police*. New York: St. Martin's, 1985.

Reiss, A.J., Jr. "Strategies of Control Over Organisational Life." In *Control in the Police*. Ed. M. Punch. Cambridge, MA: MIT Press, 1983.

Rubinstein, J. *City Police*. New York: Farrar, Straus and Giroux, 1972.

Skolnick, J. *Justice Without Trial*. New York: John Wiley and Sons, 1966.

Tifft, L. "The 'Cop Personality' Reconsidered." *Journal of Police Science and Administration* 2(3) (1979): 266–78.

Van Maanen, J. "Working the Street." In *Prospects for Reform in Criminal Justice*. Ed. H. Jacob. Beverly Hills: Sage, 1974.

———. "Notes on the Production of Ethnographic Data in an American Police Agency." In *Law and Social Enquiry*. Ed. R. Luckham. Uppsala, Sweden: Scandinavian Institute of African Studies, 1981.

———. "The Boss: First Line Supervision in an American Police Agency." In *Control in the Police Organisation*. Ed. M. Punch. Cambridge, MA: MIT Press, 1984.

———, and E.H. Schein. "Toward a Theory of Organization Socialization." In *Research in Organizational Behavior*. Ed. B. Staw. New York: JAI Press, 1979. 209–69.

Weick, K. *The Social Psychology of Organizing*. 2d ed. Reading, MA: Addision Wesley, 1979.

Westley, W. *Violence and the Police*. Cambridge, MA: MIT Press, 1970.

Wilson, James Q. *Varieties of Police Behavior: The Management of Law and Order in Eight Communities*. Cambridge, MA: Harvard University Press, 1968.

Offender Profiling

Offender profiling, or psychological criminal profiling as it is often called, is a method of identifying the perpetrator of a crime based on an analysis of the nature of the offense and the manner in which it was committed. Specifically it is the process of determining various aspects of a criminal's personality makeup from his or her choice of actions before, during, and after the criminal act. This information, combined with all other pertinent details and physical evidence, is then compared with the characteristics of known personality types and mental abnormalities to develop a practical working description of the offender.

The origins of psychological profiling are a matter of some conjecture. It is possible to find references to a type of criminal psychology in the literature as early as 1803; however, virtually all of these works were legalistic discussions of the insanity plea and did not concern themselves with the individual. Perhaps the first student of criminology to relate the nature of the crime to the personality of the individual was Jacob F. Fries, an obscure author who wrote a handbook on criminal anthropology in 1820. While this seemed to signal a new emphasis on the individual, most of his insights were lost as criminal psychology attempted to relate criminal behavior to heredity, mental retardation, epilepsy, and physical appearance throughout the latter half of the nineteenth century.

Another reference to the relationship between the crime and the personality of the criminal appeared in the teachings of Dr. Hans Gross, an Austrian magistrate and professor of criminal law in the 1870s. Unfortunately his book *Criminal Psychology*, published in 1897, contained only scant reference to the subject.

Interestingly enough, the writings of Arthur Conan Doyle may have been one of the more important springboards in bringing psychological profiling into existence. It is well known that the Sherlock Holmes series served as the seminal base for many of the modern scientific methods used in criminal investigations. His use of tobacco, dust, plaster casting, and even document examinations to identify perpetrators prompted Dr. Edmund Locard, a leading criminologist of the time, to comment, "Sherlock Holmes was the first to realize the importance of dust. I merely copied his method." A careful reading of the mysteries suggests that Sherlock Holmes also used a form of psychological profiling. For example, in "A Scandal in Bohemia," he comments:

> "When a woman thinks that her house is on fire her instinct is at once to rush to the thing which she values most. It is a perfectly overpowering impulse, and I have more than once taken advantage of it. A married woman grabs her baby— an unmarried one reaches for her jewel box."

In most cases Sherlock Holmes tracked the master criminal. He describes him clearly in story after story as an intelligent man without a conscience who operates according to his own set of rules and enjoys his role as villain. These characteristics today describe the psychopathic personality.

Whatever the origins of the technique are, the first practitioner in modern times was Dr. James Brussel, a New York psychiatrist. Dr. Brussel was in many ways the true pioneer of the field. A former assistant commissioner of the New York State Department of Mental Hygiene, he assisted the New York City police and other law-enforcement agencies on numerous occasions between 1957 and 1972. Some of the more famous cases in which he developed profiles included the "Mad Bomber of New York" and the "Boston Strangler."

In 1971, the author, already involved in criminal profiling to a limited extent, met with Dr. Brussel and with his assistance was eventually able to combine the advantages of the psychiatric approach with insights derived from traditional crime-scene investigations and criminal statistics.

The resulting procedure proved to be quite effective for certain types of crimes. Moreover, in the last decade the technique has been further refined by FBI agents in the Behavioral Sciences Unit of the FBI Academy at Quantico, Virginia, and is now an even more valuable investigative tool.

This was made evident in an evaluation of the value of profiling conducted by the author in 1981. At that time the results of profiling in 193 cases were reviewed. Eighty-eight, or 45 percent, of the cases were found to have been resolved. Investigators stated that in 77 percent of these cases psychological profiling had been of significant assistance in the investigation and in 17 percent it had actually identified the suspect.

Depending on the amount of information that can be derived from the crime scene, a psychological profile can often provide an investigator with the probable sex and age of the perpetrator as well as his or her ethnic background, relative social status, marital situation, level of education, occupational category, possible criminal background, and potential for continued criminal activities. Even an individual's tastes in clothing and vehicles can occasionally be deduced. Under certain circumstances the profile can also provide information concerning the probable characteristics of any future attacks, and the most productive investigative strategies for locating, apprehending, and interviewing the offender.

A major advantage of this procedure is that it can—and should—be utilized only after all other investigative methods have been tried. Utilized in this manner, psychological profiling not only provides additional leads and direction but forces the investigator to reexamine all existing data on the case. Experience has shown that the comprehensive review necessary for preparing the profile will in itself sometimes result in the discovery of previously overlooked clues and investigative leads.

Unfortunately, this advantage can be completely nullified by a poor or incomplete crime-scene investigation. The lack of complete crime-scene descriptions, sketches, and photographs as well as accurate autopsy results and thorough background investigations of the victim(s) will severely limit the ability of the profiler to construct a usable description of the perpetrator. This requirement for a truly complete and productive crime-scene investigation is vital to the procedure.

The usual crime-scene investigation concentrates on the collection and preservation of physical evidence. Offender profiling simply carries the process one step further. Using the same evidence found at the scene plus additional data about the particular type of crime and the victim, the profiler attempts to collect information relating to personality and motives. Both techniques have the same goal and both are dependent upon the ability and thoroughness of the crime-scene investigator. Therefore, while it is theoretically possible to prepare an accurate profile of the perpetrator in any type of crime, it is not feasible. Psychological profiling should be utilized only in those types of crimes where the crime-scene investigation is as complete and thorough as possible.

As a practical matter, this procedure can be expected to provide usable data in only a few highly specific types of crimes. Even then it is totally dependent upon the psychological value of the evidence collected. Most of the offenses, to be appropriate for profiling, must feature some form of overt sexual activity or a loss of contact with reality. Generally speaking, the types of crimes in which profiling has been most successful include:

Homicides that involve sexual activity, or appear to be sex-related
Forcible rapes
Sexual molestations
Indecent exposures

Some forms of arson
Homicides involving the parents, children, or a majority of the members of a family
Deaths by hanging

Perhaps the most limiting factor associated with psychological profiling is the amount of training and preparation necessary to develop the skills to accurately profile a crime. The profiler must possess an excellent knowledge of abnormal psychology, human nature, crime-scene investigative procedures, and forensic medicine. Further, he or she must review countless cases before an awareness of the underlying relationships between the perpetrator's psychological status and the details of the criminal act begin to emerge. An additional problem is the emotional turmoil that results from continual exposure to the violent types of crimes being examined. This is an extremely corrosive reaction and unless properly controlled can cause severe mental anguish for the profiler.

Howard D. Teten

Bibliography

American Psychiatric Association. *Diagnostic and Statistical Manual of Mental Disorders (DSM-II)*. Washington, DC: APA, 1968.

———. *Diagnostic and Statistical Manual of Mental Disorders (DSM-III)*. Washington, D.C.: APA, 1970.

Camps, Francis E., ed. *Gradwohl's Legal Medicine*. 3d ed. Bristol, England: John Wright and Sons, 1973.

Cleckley, Hervey. *The Mask of Sanity*. St. Louis, MO: C.V. Mosby, 1964.

Hazelwood, Robert R. "The Behavior-Oriented Interview of Rape Victims: The Key to Profiling." *FBI Law Enforcement Bulletin* 52(9) (1983): 8–15.

Pinizzotto, Anthony J. "Forensic Psychology: Criminal Personality Profiling." *Journal of Police Science and Administration* 12(1) (1984): 32–40.

Reese, James T. "Obsessive-Compulsive Behavior." *FBI Law Enforcement Bulletin* 48(8) (1979): 6–12.

Ressler, Robert K., John E. Douglas, Nicholas Groth, and Ann Burgess. "Offender Profiles: A Multidisciplinary Approach." *FBI Law Enforcement Bulletin* 49(9) (1980): 16–20.

O

Operational Costs

Effective law-enforcement management is vastly different in today's difficult economic times. Gone are the days when the traditional response of meeting crime control problems and community service needs was to hire more officers and purchase more equipment. Now there is a critical need for managers to promote efficiency and effectiveness. As this almost impossible responsibility of providing more service with less funding falls on the chief of police or sheriff, the easy way out is to tighten administrative screws and allow the burden to fall on the employees. However, this shortsightedness may well lead to resentment, labor/management conflicts, or serious morale and job satisfaction problems.

Administrators must be sensitive to the feelings and sentiments of the work force in order to implement the types of changes necessary to streamline law-enforcement services. To achieve cooperation managers should ask employees for cost-cutting ideas and maintain high visibility to facilitate formal and informal discussions. Furthermore, management should seek advice from other law-enforcement agencies concerning their successes and failures in cost-cutting.

NEI Survey

The FBI National Executive Institute (NEI) recently queried more than 100 law-enforcement executives in the United States and Canada on how to increase productivity while curtailing costs. Due to decreasing tax revenues, rising costs, and a down-turned economy, the executives were eager to share their experiences. Upon reviewing the survey results, the NEI found the areas that provided the greatest opportunity for cost reduction involve overtime, vehicles, volunteers, civilian participation, automation, reducing false alarms, increased use of federal forfeiture funds, service fees, and subcontracting for services.

The following list illustrates specific measures suggested for cost reduction.

Automation
- Decentralize entry of police incident reports to reduce lag time and the number of mail runs to headquarters.
- Install phone mail on department telephone systems to automatically direct outside callers to the proper extension.
- Implement automation of tasks where feasible.

Administration
- Eliminate unnecessary business and training expenses.
- Delay promotions for forty-five days.
- Streamline administrative positions.
- Consolidate various job responsibilities.
- Increase use of civilian volunteers, auxiliary police officers, and cadets.
- Reduce overtime.
- Use flexed work schedules for some units, where possible.

Maintenance
- Use jail maintenance personnel and/or inmate labor to maintain grounds and buildings, to build K-9 pens for dogs, or to build a tactical recovery vehicle from an old patrol car and old bullet-proof vests.
- Delay or cut back renovation projects not necessary to the department's mission.
- Repair radios in-house.
- Subcontract for services.

Training
- Use video technology for roll-call training.

Automobiles
- Implement an accident reduction program consisting of pursuit policy training and high performance driving techniques and sanction against negligent drivers.
- Remove roof-mounted emergency lights from a significant number of marked vehicles.
- Switch from premium to regular-grade gasoline.
- Install sophisticated radio equipment in operational vehicles only.
- Reduce the number of take-home cars.
- Defer replacing vehicles for one more fiscal year.
- Change marked vehicles from traditional two colors to less expensive and more visible single white color.
- Downsize investigative and administrative (unmarked and nonpursuit) vehicles to smaller, less expensive models.

Other
- Institute service fees for special events and extraordinary nonemergency services.

- Minimize police response to false alarms.
- Implement bicycle patrol in congested areas.
- Prohibit use of alcohol in park and beach areas to reduce calls for service.
- Use federal forfeiture funds to purchase computers, office equipment, and protection and enforcement-related equipment.

Case Studies

1. Colorado State Patrol Photo Lab Cash Funding

Situation: The Colorado State Patrol has historically charged citizens and attorneys for copies of photographs of accidents and other incidents in which the private sector has a vested interest. All fees collected from the sale of photographs were deposited in the patrol's budget to be distributed as needed. Although fees collected exceeded the annual operating budget allocation, new expenditures were limited to essential needs only.

Solution: Proposals were submitted to the Office of State Planning and Budgeting to allow the photo lab to become fully cash funded. The process was complex, requiring justification and a guarantee that the arrangement would work. Few state agencies have cash-funded operations, but such arrangements are advantageous to both the agency and the state. The proposals were granted. So far revenue generated has resulted in covering operation expenses, the upgrade of photographic equipment, and expansion into areas such as video. Moreover, the budget previously shared by the photo lab and the Education and Safety Unit now has one less user, leaving more money for improving safety and education programs.

2. Knoxville Police Department Work Scheduling

Situation: In 1982 Knoxville hosted the World's Fair, creating a demand for greater police service. To meet the demand the Knoxville Police Department changed its shift rotations. Since that time the department has continued to maximize use of patrol personnel while reducing overtime and call-in costs.

Solution: The Uniform Division works a six-day-on, four-day-off schedule with five detachments. The morning and night shift are nine hours and ten minutes and the evening shift is ten hours and ten minutes. The advantages of such an arrangement are two overlapping periods—one in the afternoon between 1400 and 1540, and one in the evening between 2145 and 0010. The afternoon overlap helps with court duty and allows two detachments to be on the street at once. The night overlap takes care of peak time hot calls for service. The overlap also adds flexibility to bring a shift in early or later by several hours to handle special events (football games, parades, etc.) without having to pay overtime. A power shift works from 1600 to 0200 (four on, three off) to supplement the patrol detachments during the busiest hours of the evening.

3. Utah Law Enforcement Intelligence Network

Situation: No centralized coordination of narcotics and criminal intelligence existed in the State of Utah. The Utah Department of Public Safety, the Utah Division of Investigation, and the Utah Department of Corrections joined for such a purpose to form the Utah Law Enforcement Intelligence Network. Federal funding assisted the formation of the network but did not pay all costs. Essential to the network, data-entry personnel to feed network computers with information were one of those extra costs.

Solution: To remedy the shortfall of funds, the Utah Division of Investigation contacted the Utah National Guard and proposed a pilot program. The program called for the National Guard to provide select individuals to perform data entry. After background checks and clearance the individuals were placed on active duty under the direct supervision of a criminal information technician and the section sergeant. Since August of 1990 the computer database of approximately 2,500 names and intelligence data has grown to near 10,000—due to National Guard assistance.

4. Nassau County Police Department Automatic Alarm Permit System

Situation: Within Nassau County jurisdiction there are more than 120,000 individual alarm subscribers. In excess of 100,000 alarm transmissions are received annually from either central stations or through automated dialing mechanisms. Each incident results in the dispatch of two police officers to investigate. Records show fewer than 1 percent of the alarms to be actual emergencies, with the major cause of the problem attributable to human error and to a much lesser degree the forces of nature, power disruptions, and mechanical failures. Some 40,000 premises a year are judged to be "alarm abusers," each having transmitted at least three false alarms within a ninety-day period.

Solution: As proposed, all alarm users register with the police department and after paying the prescribed fee be issued a permit that is subject to suspension and/or revocation contingent on the number of false alarms. Following the revocation, the alarm owner is required to reapply for a permit, which will only be issued upon the satisfaction of all outstanding penalties, submission of proof that the alarm system has been inspected and found to be in proper order, and the payment of an additionally prescribed alarm permit fee. Those not complying will no longer receive police response when their alarm is activated. A revenue enhancer, the new system should produce for Nassau County $1 million in its first year and nearly $400,000 in subsequent years.

5. Cooperative Agreement for Shared Law Enforcement Services

Situation: The Hennepin County Sheriff's Department and the Minneapolis Police Department each needed special expertise and better equipment to strengthen their operations. Hennepin County wanted to add a bomb squad and Minneapolis—which had a decent water rescue unit—sought superior equipment.

Solution: Hennepin County and Minneapolis entered into a formal agreement to provide services to each other. The Minneapolis Police Bomb Squad, because of a higher frequency of response, offered exactly what the Sheriff's Department needed. The Sheriff's Department, because of a statutory responsibility for water rescue, had developed a state-of-the-art underwater recovery unit. Capital expenditure estimates were as high as $75,000 for basic bomb squad equipment plus maintenance costs of $5,000 per year. Equipment and maintenance costs for an improved underwater recovery unit approached $10,000. Factoring in training and overtime expenses inflated the figures more. Both total amounts were saved.

Law-enforcement leaders who tackle the problem of managing with less will be truly successful only when they recognize that the issue, much like violent crime, illegal drugs, and community unrest, requires long-term commitment and planned action.

For specific examples on how various law-enforcement agencies have cut costs, contact the Chief of the Education and Communication Arts Unit at the FBI Academy in Quantico, Virginia. This entry is an abridgment of a report on cost reduction, which is an ongoing interest of the FBI Academy.

Richard M. Ayers

Organizational Structure: Theory into Practice

Organizational structure is basic to the success of any police department. Its utility, however, must be viewed from a number of different and increasingly complex perspectives. In its theoretical sense, organizational structure can be defined as a blueprint of departmental relationships based on a network of control mechanisms conducive to the overall direction of the organization. The design of such a blueprint in police administration has its conceptual roots in the influential classical school of organizational theory.

The classical school of organizational theory has been resolutely dependent upon the formal and impersonal approach to work and its corollary of strict compliance with departmental policies. Its emphasis on rules and procedures is exemplified in the writings of Max Weber, the "father of modern bureaucracy." While the classical school and its principles dominated the early views of police organizations, many police agencies have since introduced less stringent means of organizational control with variable degrees of success. Among those are the participative-management model, the behavioral approach through its focus on systems analysis, and other morale-boosting alternatives like team policing.

The Classical School of Police Organizational Structure

American police institutions have traditionally drawn on the classical view of organizational structure and its principles of work coordination as advanced in the Weberian school of classical organizational theory (Wilson and McLaren, 1972). In the absence of alternative methods for self-discipline and appropriate accountability, police agencies—although influenced by the church and military models of organizational structure—have opted to follow the classical model. With its emphasis on rationality, impersonality, and coercive control, it provided the central method for controlling police activities and effectively achieving departmental goals. Working from this Weberian perspective of organizational structure and from a Taylorist approach to systematizing work flow, formal authority becomes the dominant feature by which labor is divided, tasks are assigned, coordination is maintained, and responsibilities are exacted among the agency population. Such a network of authority is most commonly depicted in complex organizational charts, sets of rules and regulations, strict supervisory measures, and a formal communication procedure by which all personnel are instructed on how to handle their duties. The pyramid shape of police organizations that essentially transpires reflects these formal lines of authority and responsibility from the chief of police to commanders, and from first-line supervisors to front-line operatives.

Early police organizations continued to adopt the strict principles associated with the classical/scientific view of organizational theory (Bittner, 1970) later labeled as "Theory X" (McGregor, 1960). Abidance with Theory X has been seen as the most efficient method by which to coordinate complex and rather dangerous police activities. These principles include (1) a hierarchy of authority, (2) division of labor, (3) unity of command, (4) specialization, (5) span of control, (6) delegation of authority, and (7) formal communication (Souryal, 1977). These principles collectively gave rise to a formal paramilitary environment considered most conducive to discipline, standardization of work steps, and control of police operations, all in the name of order, legality, and effectiveness.

In order to better understand the dynamics of traditional police organizational structure, it is necessary to clearly define the principles that inform such a model and to articulate the contribution made by each.

Authority, the backbone principle, is preeminent and omnipresent. No police department, regardless of nature, location, or size, could function without it. In its theoretical sense, it is the cultural as well as the administrative right of a superior to command a subordinate to carry out a task and the latter's obligation to comply with such a command without unnecessary questions (Barnard, 1938; Souryal, 1977). For example, the chief of police exercises the authority to direct all activities of the department through policy-making, job assignment, rotation of personnel, supervisory measures, as well as the ultimate weapon, disciplining insubordinate or negligent behavior on the part of subordinates. The superior's role at all levels of the department is thus characterized by the right to direct subordinates, and the sub-

ordinates' role is characterized chiefly by a duty to comply.

While authority is, by nature, a formal relationship between two or more levels within the organization, it should not be confused with influence, which also permeates police departments on an informal basis at all times. The principle of influence implies the right of the superior officer to persuade, win over, or to suggest a response by a subordinate. But since influence is informal in nature, it does not establish a duty to comply, because the subordinate maintains the right of choice and may opt not to oblige if not convinced. Nevertheless, the use of influence in police organizational structure through the medians of advice and counseling has been common and is highly recommended at all levels of the organization. Influence serves the organizational needs for collaboration, common understanding, and motivation, without which the police department would be performing in a rigid manner with its members uninformed, unmotivated, and unproductive.

Division of labor is the basic method of allocating work into meaningful functions like patrol, traffic, criminal investigation, and jail staffing. Conversely, it is also the practice of grouping compatible police tasks in one division and under one supervisor. Therefore, criminal investigation, evidence collection, intelligence-gathering, and undercover activities would form an independent division. Traffic regulation, accident investigation, and parking enforcement would form another. Methods normally include division by place, process, major purpose, clients, and under exceptional conditions, by special duties performed. Although division of labor in police organizations obviously varies from one department to another on the basis of size, goals, tradition, budget, and special mandate, proper division of labor normally reflects the department's concern for specialization, for accountability, and for maximum productivity.

Unity of command is the principle by which each person in the organization must have one designated superior from whom orders are regularly received and to whom reports are made (Souryal, 1977). The principle establishes a clear and direct chain of command within the agency through which authority and communication flow from superiors at the top of the organization to all operatives at the lower levels. The absence of a well-defined chain of command may create confusion as to who is in charge, who should issue orders, and who the reporting authority is.

Span of control is a principle that determines the maximum number of officers a supervisor can manage effectively. In order to ensure control and adequate accountability within the department, every officer must be supervised at all times. But in order to minimize the cost of supervision within the department, the number of officers assigned to each supervisor must be maximized. This should be done without undermining the quality of supervision, which, in turn, depends on the nature of the job and the ability of the supervisor. Thus a patrol sergeant might supervise ten to fifteen patrol officers in a large city, but the head of a SWAT team is limited to four or five team members.

Specialization in police organizational structure is an overriding principle that promotes optimal functioning of the department. The principle is based on the rationale that some police officers would be more productive in manual tasks, others in technical tasks, and still others in mental tasks. Police personnel are therefore divided into line officers, staff officers, and auxiliary officers. Line officers include all functionaries from the chief of police to patrol officers who (1) carry out the major purpose of the department, (2) deliver the services, (3) face the clientele, and (4) make their own decisions as they go (Souryal, 1977). These include, for example, patrol officers and supervisors, traffic officers and detectives, and their respective commanders. Staff officers usually handle intellectual functions like planning and research, legal advising, public relations, etc. These officers, however, are not independent in their decisions since they must check their final plans with the head of the department for approval and authorization. Auxiliary officers are assigned to routine functions of a housekeeping nature. Their primary function is to relieve the line officers of time-consuming tasks such as dispatching, motor pool, property room, and data processing. While the segregation of line, staff, and auxiliary in police organizational structure is necessary to enhance the overall productivity of the department, it can mistakenly be perceived as reflecting on the status and prestige of the officers involved. This can be corrected through the formal, as well as informal, socialization of the officers and the creation of a shared awareness of their collective contributions.

Delegation of authority is the principle of conferring certain power on commanding officers and supervisors throughout the department. The rationale behind this practice lies in two concepts. The first is the "exception principle," which indicates that the chief executive officer of any agency does not have the time to attend to every decision personally. The second is the need to grant certain powers to the lower level commanders and supervisors, without which their authority may be rendered ineffective. Therefore, and depending on the size, nature, and tradition of the department, sergeants may be delegated to authorize certain schedule changes or reprimand certain behaviors, lieutenants may be authorized to coordinate certain projects, captains to authorize certain transfers, and deputy chiefs to approve certain purchases, and the like. Although the principle of delegation of authority in police organization, as in military organizations, prohibits the superior's delegation of responsibility, most chief executives in police departments today are not held administratively responsible if their delegation of authority was appropriately made to the appropriate personnel under appropriate checks.

Formal communication—the necessary relaying of information from one level to the next and integrating all departmental activities in a well-informed entity—is the critical thread that binds the organization together. Proper communication enhances the coordination of departmental functions by stimulating the motivation of department members. In traditional police organizations, communication is strictly formal and limited to downward and upward channels. The former is in the order of commands or instructions, and the latter is in the form of reports or petitions. In progressive police departments, on the other hand, multiple-directional communication is allowed. This includes horizontal, diagonal, and circular communication, in addition to the traditional vertical direction. Furthermore, progressive police departments appreciate and encourage informal communication. This method, labeled "managerial communication," is perceived to be far more conducive to shared understanding since it allows for face-to-face impressions, instant feedback, deliberation, and freedom to express oneself in a democratic environment. Most progressive police departments today apply the managerial-communication method by instituting regular sergeant meetings, staff meetings, and irregular meetings for task-force members and project coordinators.

As noted at the outset, the seven principles just discussed inform the basic and traditional structure of police organization. Activation of these principles creates coordination from the narrowest point of the organization at the top to the broader, lower levels at the bottom. Simultaneously, the pyramid shape of the organization evolves. Its horizontal differentiation is caused by the principles of the division of labor and specialization, and its vertical differentiation by the principles of delegation of authority and span of control. Because of the pyramid mode's relative simplicity and lack of ambiguity, most police departments have found it plausible to adopt and easy to follow. Consequently, this view of organizational structure has had the strongest impact on the development of police departments and law-enforcement agencies throughout the country since their inception in the mid-nineteenth century.

However, critics of the classical theory of police organization abound (Angell, 1971; Kimble, 1969; Myron, 1980). It has been pointed out that the traditional model is too authoritarian, inefficient, impersonal, stagnant, stifling to creativity, and possibly costly and ineffective. As a case in point, critics disputed the standard argument contending that the war on crime requires a paramilitary-type organization since that position cannot be supported either by facts or by historical evidence of its success in fighting crime.

But the debate on the value of the model began much earlier when Chester Barnard (1938) pointed out in his definitive work, *The Functions of the Executive*, that in addition to formal structures there exist informal arrangements that are imperative to the progress of organizations and to the development and growth of their members. Organizational structure, according to Barnard, is "a system of consciously coordinated activities of forces of two or more persons," and not merely a strict formal structure based upon clear-cut lines of responsibility and authority. From this humanistic view of organization comes a recognition of the roles of the individual and the environment, both of which must affect organizational structure directly and indirectly.

The Human Relations Approach to Police Structure

The human relations approach views the organization as a social group with its chief executive officer as a team builder who creates a co-operative effort among subordinates through a democratic management process. Influenced by the teachings of Abraham Maslow, Douglas McGregor, Chris Argris, Elton Mayo, and others, progressive police administrators were encouraged to modify organizational structure in favor of a participative management model. Also, in response to the publication of the powerful report by the President's Commission on Law Enforcement and Administration of Justice (1967), serious attempts to incorporate a participative systems approach in police organizations were accelerated. Two basic innovations were attempted: a move toward the democratization and liberalization of police structure; and the development and application of team policing by a large number of police departments. The first innovation was to be achieved primarily by developing clear policy statements and enunciating guidelines for increased police discretion, by refining police human resources and creating administrative boards in large departments, by improving police education and training, and by enhancing meaningful communication within, and without, the police department. Success in that endeavor, however, was contingent upon the managerial skills of the department's chief administrators, who were expected to create a working environment of openness and sincerity. Such an environment was to enhance motivation and provide informal guidance so that all police personnel could realize their potential in contributing to the organization.

The second innovation attempted was team policing, which works on the premise that the police administrator (sergeant, lieutenant, or the equivalent) is a *primus inter pares* (first among equals) rather than the traditional autocratic administrator. This practice called for several organizational changes. These include (1) reducing the size of work groups and decentralizing their operations, (2) maximizing communication among team members and between them and their leaders, (3) allowing team members and their leaders to adjust their tactical objectives and operational priorities, (4) maximizing interaction between the team and the community, and (5) assigning teams to their respective districts for a longer period of time.

In theory, the human relations model attempts to alleviate the major problems of the traditional approach to police organization. It advocates decentralization, distribution of authority, motivating career paths, workers' participation, and informal communication, in addition to other humanistic programs. Patrol positions under this model, for example, came to be seen as positions to be used as boundary roles from which the organization could receive information and through which it could respond effectively to changes in the environment.

While the organizational philosophy expressed in the human relations approach is admirable and probably the first recognition of behavioral forces in police structures, it fell short of realistically addressing the need for organizational responsiveness. The results of team policing programs, for example, were surprisingly disappointing. White (1977) reports that team policing could not be shown to increase officers' job satisfaction or increase the public's satisfaction with police performance. Other critics revealed inherent problems associated with decentralization of the police function—mainly, its inefficiency. Reppetto (1980) noted that "decentralization often is directly opposed to specialization." He argued that in "a police department with many decentralized subdivisions . . . it is uneconomical for each subdivision to have its own specializations." Other problems were noted regarding the performance of middle management personnel. Consequently, and with few exceptions, most police departments that had resorted to team policing returned to the traditional model of police structure.

The Systems School and Police Structure

From the systems perspective of organization that emerged in the late 1960s came the view of organizations and organic wholes. Faced with the need for more police productivity, the organization could no longer be viewed as merely the sum of its parts but rather a product of the unique aspects of each part, their arrangement, and the effects of the environment in which they operate. According to this perspective, positions are considered interrelated to such an extent that a change in one position would necessarily affect the operation of the other positions. Furthermore, the cohesion of the organization and its productive potential came to be seen as substantially dependent on the external environment. Consequently, organizational structure had to adapt to the demands and supports in its environment as well as to the responses generated from within. This view has been especially reinforced by the recommendations of the National Advisory Commission's *Report on Criminal Justice Standards and Goals* (1973). Furthermore, encouraged by the success of systems analysis and computer technology in private businesses, progressive police agencies began to carefully incorporate elements of the new systems approach in their organizational structure (Coffey, 1974).

It must be noted, however, that the systems approach to police administration did not change the basic organizational structure of police departments in any tangible manner. Conventional control mechanisms—authority from above and compliance at the lower levels—as well as the practices of supervision, specialization, and discipline, remained unchanged. The most important changes produced by the systems model were, in fact, of a behavioral nature rather than mechanical. Gains from these changes, moreover, were limited mostly to larger and more progressive departments that had the fortitude to adopt them and the means and skills to make them work. Nevertheless, the managerial impact of the systems approach on police organizations in America (federal, state, or local) has been substantial and durable. For example, the perception of authority merely as a demonstration of autocratic power came to be seen as obsolete, and the routinization of tasks and overattachment to procedures were regarded as a waste of valuable resources. The use of the military model in police organization also came to be seen as an example of overorganization, and streamlining work flow became logical and desirable. Reorganization of police functions along the lines of input and output with an eye to cost effectiveness became a challenge to progressive agencies. Progressive departments focused on planning and research functions, task-force projects, problem-solving and the improvement of productivity, adaptation to the environment, and interdependence among other criminal-justice agencies.

One theoretical model of the systems-analysis approach to police administration was amply presented by Alan Coffey (1974) in his work *Administration of Criminal Justice: A Management Systems Approach*. His model stresses that police organizational structures should be flexible and dynamic to accommodate, integrate, and achieve four major managerial objectives: (1) synchronization of "what" functions are needed, to be accomplished in a "how" manner, by "whom," in order to accomplish "which results"; (2) interfacing among the roles and functions of police personnel to optimize the department's overall productivity; (3) development of the managerial skills of all police personnel to enhance service delivery; and (4) maintaining a "cost-effectiveness" monitoring instrument to measure the quantitative and qualitative output of the agency on the basis of structural-functional schema.

Some of the more effective tools introduced by the systems approach to police organizations include Management by Objectives (MBO), Program Evaluation and Review Techniques (PERT), Programming, Planning and Budgeting Systems (PPBS), Zero-Based Budgeting (ZBB), and Organizational Development (OD). These tools have been instrumental in maintaining a higher level of fiscal accountability, organizational responsiveness, and productivity.

While the systems approach to police organization does not explicitly call for a standard set of structural changes, police agencies that adopt such an approach find such changes unavoidable. The nature of the changes and their extent must be determined by police leaders based upon the individual adequacies and inadequacies of each department at the time of change. Consequently, a uniform shape and style of systems-oriented departments does not exist, but characteristically all progressive departments share the common features of scientific management, flexibility, responsiveness, productivity, and civility.

Sam S. Souryal

Bibliography

Angell, J.E. "Toward an Alternative to the Classical Police Organizational Arrangements: A Democratic Model." *Criminology* 9 (1971): 185–206.

Barnard, C. *The Functions of the Executive.* Cambridge, MA: Oxford University Press, 1938.

Bittner, E. *The Functions of the Police in Modern Society.* Washington, DC: Government Printing Office, 1970.

Coffey, A. *Administration of Criminal Justice: A Management Systems Approach.* Englewood Cliffs, NJ: Prentice-Hall, 1974.

Kimble, J. "Daydream, Dogma, and Dinosaurs." *Police Chief* 36 (1969): 12–15.

McGregor, D. *The Human Side of Enterprise.* New York: McGraw-Hill, 1960.

Myron, R. "A Crisis in Police Management." *Journal of Criminal Law, Criminology,*
and Police Science 50 (1980): 600–05.

Reppetto, T.A. "Police Organization and Management." In *Progress in Policing: Essays on Change.* Ed. R.A. Staufenberger. Cambridge, MA: Ballinger, 1980. 65–85.

Souryal, S.S. *Police Administration and Management.* St. Paul, MN: West, 1977.

Staufenberger, R.A. *Progress in Policing: Essays on Change.* Cambridge, MA: Ballinger, 1980.

White, T. *Evaluation of LEAA's Full Service Neighborhood Team Policing Demonstration.* Washington, DC: Urban Institute, 1977.

Wilson, O.W., and R.D. McLaren. *Police Administration.* 3d ed. New York: McGraw-Hill, 1972.

Organizational Structure: Three Models with International Comparisons

Police agencies in industrialized countries throughout the world tend to follow one of three basic organization models: centralized, coordinated, and fragmented. The model associated with a country is influenced by a variety of factors. The more significant of these are usually derived from answers to the following questions: What was and is the nature of a country's past and present political ideology? How did the historical evolution of police in a country take place? How do citizens of a country perceive issues of governmental authority in general and the role of police in particular? What are some of the key social characteristics that are inherent in a particular country and that might influence attitudes about a particular model of policing?

The Centralized Model

The centralized model of police organization and administration is found in both democratic and nondemocratic countries. France, Japan, and the former Soviet Union illustrate variations of this model. From a Western perspective this model has its origins in the ancient Roman style of police administration. It necessitates the central government creating a police force and then imposing it on the community. Since the eighteenth century, this model has been the creation of national governments for the general welfare of citizens, and it has been national governments that centrally administer, supervise, and coordinate their police. In such a model the police are viewed as representatives of the state and perceive themselves as such.

For centuries the police of France have been associated with the central government. Today, the two principal police agencies of France are the National Police and the Police Gendarmerie. Both are organized and administered by the national government.

The National Police is the largest of the two and is responsible for policing any town with a population exceeding 10,000. The National Police falls under the administrative arm of the Ministry of the Interior and of Decentralization. This ministry is considered an important one within the Council of Ministers. The minister who is responsible for this ministry is a civilian who has had an extensive career as a civil servant. Another senior administrator of the National Police is the director general, who is responsible for central administration. The director general is also a career civil servant who has spent some time in the civilian branch of French law enforcement.

The National Police is divided into several operational directorates. These directorates illustrate the nature of the French approach to law enforcement. Among the more obvious is the Urban Police, which is the uniform branch responsible for patrolling urban areas of the country. The Counter-Espionage Directorate is devoted to state security and counterespionage activities. The Air and Border Police handle security at airports and along France's extensive borders. The Office of the Inspector General is responsible for the oversight of police units throughout the country with the goals of investigating internal or external complaints and of improving the efficiency of police.

The Criminal Investigation Directorate includes the judicial police, who are responsible for investigations into serious crime. In terms of accountability the judicial police are unique, because the French legal system requires that police investigators work closely with prosecutors and magistrates who are either conducting or overseeing criminal investigations into serious cases. The General Intelligence Directorate is often referred to as the political police, for they are responsible for collecting information for the national government. Finally, the Republican Security Company (CRS) is a highly disciplined militaristic unit. The CRS is called upon to handle public disorders, natural disasters, and rescue missions. They are employed as traffic specialists who are responsible for patrolling the highways on the outskirts of large cities. The CRS also has a special duty to assist in the reduction of juvenile delinquency. As such, they patrol campsites and beaches during the summer and establish clubs to provide constructive leisure time activities for young people.

The work of the National Police is coordinated at the local level by commissioners of the republic. For administrative purposes France is divided into ninety-five departments, which are similar to counties. The chief executive officer within each department is called a commissioner of the republic. The commissioner is accountable to the central government for the general administration of his department. This includes law enforcement.

The National Gendarmerie is the other principal police force of France. It is accountable to the Ministry of Defense because it is a military police force. The Gendarmerie is responsible for policing towns and rural areas where the population is under 10,000. The minister of defense is assisted in the administration of this force by the director of the gendarmerie and by the inspector general of the gendarmerie. The director is trained in law and is concerned with central administration, while the inspector general is an army general concerned with improving the effectiveness of the force.

The gendarmerie is divided into three kinds of operational units. The Department Gendarmerie is primarily responsible for providing police services to small towns. The Mobile Gendarmerie is composed of regional units that offer the same kinds of services to rural areas that the Republic Security Company provides to the communities that it serves. Finally, the Republican Guard has three regiments that are located in Paris to serve both as honor guards and as security for government officials.

The Coordinated Model
The second organizational model is a coordinated system. It is characterized by a shared or cooperative effort between the central government and various local communities to provide police services. This model has long been associated with England and Wales, which at present have forty-three police forces. The principal elements in this coordinated system of organization include the home secretary, the police authority for each force, and the chief police executive of each force.

The home secretary is a senior member of the British prime minister's cabinet. He is a civilian politician who sits atop the police organizational hierarchy. The responsibilities charged to the home secretary epitomize the centralized administrative characteristics of policing in the country. To illustrate, the home secretary has the authority to remove any senior official from his position within any of the forty-three police forces; he can appoint people to investigate any issue dealing with any of the police forces; he makes regulations concerning the organization and administration of all police forces; and he provides 51 percent of the budget for each of the forces.

While the role of the home secretary illustrated how the police of England and Wales possess some of the attributes of a centralized model, two other elements indicate that the English police organization is also decentralized from an administrative perspective. For example, each of the forty-one provincial police forces has a police authority, which is usually a committee composed of local politicians and magistrates. The exceptions to this rule are the City of London Police, in which the City Council of London serves as the police authority, and the London Metropolitan Police, where the home secretary serves alone in this capacity. The duties of a police authority explain how a police organization is also influenced by local factors. For example, the police authority appoints all senior-level administrators to their force; they determine the overall manpower needs of their force; they also provide the necessary equipment and buildings for their force; and they provide forty-nine percent of the funds for the budget of their force.

The other element in this coordinated model of police administration is the chief executive of the force, who is usually referred to as the chief constable. Statute law clearly spells out the fact that each police force is under the direction and supervision of its chief constable. Thus the chief constable, who is appointed by the police authority but who is also held accountable to the home secretary, administers and manages the daily operations of his force.

The Fragmented Model

The third model of police organization is the fragmented system, and it is found in only a few countries. The United States appears to have developed this model more extensively than other countries that are associated with it. The emergence of this fragmented system is attributed directly to the federated nature of the political system of the country. A basic feature of this federated system is that a citizen of the United States is also a citizen of the specific state in which he or she resides. The United States presently consists of fifty states.

The fragmented system is also influenced, at least in the United States, by local communities asserting their legal right to home rule. Home rule is a long-standing political belief that maintains local governments should have the authority and responsibility to provide certain governmental and social services to the community that they serve. In this context local government refers to county and municipal, or city, government. The kinds of services local governments would expect to provide include building roads, providing fresh water and sewage treatment facilities, establishing elementary and secondary educational systems, and offering police services. In such a model the police are viewed as representatives of both the organization and the specific community that they serve.

The manner in which police have evolved is tied very closely to the political ideology of the United States. One of the principal features of that ideology is reflected in how people view governmental authority. It is important to remember that the primary reason for the American Revolution (1775–1783) was to overthrow the centralized authority of the British Crown that the colonists found too arbitrary. After gaining independence from Great Britain, the founding fathers had to grapple with the question of what form of government should be established. Despite the fact that there was a need to establish a national government to represent the collective interests of the states, the political leaders adopted two very important political tenets.

The first of these was that governmental power and authority at the national level would be separated. The Constitution would spell out the authority of the executive, legislative, and judicial branches of government, so that power would be divided among the three. This idea came from the French Enlightenment philosopher, the Baron de Montesquieu (1689–1755). The other basic political tenet stressed the importance of local self-government. This view essentially stated that each citizen should have the opportunity to become actively involved in the conduct of government, and that the bulk of governmental authority should be found at the local level. Local meant the municipal and county levels of government. The leader of this position was Thomas Jefferson (1743–1826), who would eventually become the third president of the United States. The source of Jefferson's inspiration for this position came from the political writings of the British philosopher John Locke (1632–1704), one of the early political writers associated with the era of the Enlightenment.

The manner in which policing has emerged in the United States is intricately tied to these two political tenets. For the most part it is a fragmented system. What this means is that there are more separately and publicly funded police agencies in the United States than in any other country in the world today. The total number is approximately 40,000. A little over half of these agencies possess only quasi-police functions, such as alcohol beverage control boards and state game and fish departments. The other agencies, almost 20,000 total, are viewed primarily as police agencies that have the responsibility of enforcing the law and maintaining order in their respective jurisdictions and also in providing social services to the citizens of their jurisdiction.

When one considers the total number of agencies, it might appear rather difficult to understand the manner in which police are organized and administered in the United States. In fact, it is fairly simple because each of the 20,000 police agencies falls under one of four categories: federal, state, county, or municipal.

Federal Law Enforcement
As was indicated earlier, the Founding Fathers feared the creation of a strong centralized government. This was illustrated by the fact that when they wrote the Constitution they provided very narrow police powers to the national government in the hope of reserving most of these powers to the individual states. The founders originally vested the national government with only four police powers: to collect taxes, to regulate commerce, to establish post offices and postal roads, and to punish counterfeiters. Since the establishment of these powers, but especially during the twentieth century, Congress and the federal courts have had to interpret what these terms mean, in particular as new legislation was passed to deal with taxation and the regulation of commerce. The result has been an expansion of the national government's policing authority.

Another unique American feature relates to how federal police agencies are organized and administered at the national level. Those countries that have a national police agency usually place that agency administratively under the jurisdiction of one member of the cabinet government, such as a minister of interior, a minister of justice, or a minister of public security. The reason for this approach is that it is designed to ensure greater efficiency and effectiveness. That approach has not been followed in the United States. Although Americans are interested in efficient and effective police agencies, there is a much more important consideration that has its roots in the political ideology of the country. Because Congress feared that the executive branch of government might become too powerful, in other words replacing an arbitrary English king with an arbitrary American president, Congress purposely attempted to fragment the national police authority by distributing that power among several government departments.

Admittedly, all these government departments are within the executive branch and subject to the presidential chain of command. Nevertheless, the belief was, and remains true to this day, that if you distribute this power among several departments and then specifically limit each department's enforcement authority to only a select group of federal criminal offenses, you will prevent the executive branch from becoming too powerful with its police powers. The underlying rationale for this was based on what appears to be a universal trait of human nature. That is, when two or more agencies are responsible for basically the same thing, in this case law enforcement, they tend to become competitive. One way for an agency to maintain a competitive edge is not to cooperate with its competition, and this is graphically illustrated by an unwillingness at times to share information with one another. This kind of attitude breeds a degree of inefficiency, but Americans are willing to accept that in light of the higher or more important political objective of not allowing police forces that are at the disposal of the chief executive from becoming too powerful.

Problems related to a lack of cooperation have been long-standing among all law-enforcement agencies throughout the United States. One possible exception to this rule has emerged recently, however, that involves the greater cooperation among agencies in attempting to curtail illegal drug trafficking. Even in this instance though, there are still cases in which a lack of cooperation has lead to inefficiency in dealing with this very serious problem.

What follows are some illustrations of the role of federal law-enforcement agencies in this fragmented approach to policing. There are presently sixty-one federal agencies that are considered to have federal law-enforcement responsibilities. Of these, thirty-seven have fairly specific police authority, while the others have only quasi–law-enforcement duties. Only a few that are considered among the most significant of these law-enforcement agencies are briefly mentioned here.

Federal Bureau of Investigation
The chief administrative officer of the Department of Justice is the attorney general of the United States. This person is appointed by the president of the United States and is a member of the president's cabinet. Within the Justice Department there are several important federal law-enforcement agencies. Undoubtedly, the most famous is the Federal Bureau of Investigation (FBI). The FBI or Bureau, as it is often referred to, is the largest of all the federal law-enforcement agencies and has the most extensive responsibility for the prevention and detection of federal criminal offenses. For example, it has jurisdiction over more than 200 kinds of federal crimes. Among the more important are kidnapping; robbery, burglary, or embezzlement of funds from either a federal bank or a bank that is insured by the federal government; theft, embezzlement, or robbery of federal property; piracy and other crimes aboard an aircraft; violations of civil rights; and interstate gambling and organized crime.

The chief administrative officer of the FBI is the director. The Bureau is organized into several divisions, and some of the more prominent of these are identified here. For example, the Identification Division is a national repository and clearinghouse for fingerprints. Local law-enforcement agencies have access to this information. The Training Division trains all new recruits to the Bureau, and it also offers specialized courses for state and local law-enforcement officers. The Laboratory Division provides a wide range of scientific expertise to assist in the investigation and prosecution of crimes, and local law-enforcement agencies can avail themselves of this facility. The Technical Services Division is responsible for computerized data systems. Among the more significant features in this division is the National Crime Information Center (NCIC), which contains information about stolen property, persons wanted for major crimes, and missing persons. Once again, local law-enforcement agencies can utilize this service. The Criminal Investigative Division conducts investigations of most crimes that fall under the jurisdiction of the FBI. Finally, the Office of Congressional and Public Affairs collects and publishes crime data that are published in the *Uniform Crime Reports*. In addition to these divisions there are over fifty field offices that are scattered throughout the United States.

Drug Enforcement Administration
The Drug Enforcement Administration (DEA) was created in 1973 to consolidate efforts toward the control of the illegal distribution of drugs. Until that time, the enforcement of drug laws had been a shared responsibility of several federal agencies. Organizationally, the DEA is found within the Department of Justice, and since 1982 it has been placed under the administrative command of the FBI. The DEA's basic responsibility is to control the distribution and use of dangerous drugs. It is primarily concerned with the major national and international cartels that manufacture and distribute illicit drugs. It also assists local law-enforcement agencies throughout the country in combating illicit drug sales.

Immigration and Naturalization Service
Also within the Department of Justice is the Immigration and Naturalization Service (INS). It is responsible for enforcing the immigration and naturalization laws that relate to the admission, exclusion, deportation, and naturalization of aliens. Within the INS is a law-enforcement unit called the Border Patrol, which is designed to prevent the illegal entry of aliens and the smuggling of illegal goods into the United States. The Border Patrol is principally concerned with guarding the Canadian and Mexican borders for possible illegal entries. The most serious problem is found at the Mexican border, where people from South America, Central America, and Mexico attempt to enter the United States illegally.

Not all federal police agencies are administered from one government department, although all those referred to thus far have been organized within the Department of Justice.

Another government department that also has law-enforcement units within its organization is the Department of the Treasury. The chief administrative officer of this department is the treasury secretary. Like the attorney general, this person is appointed by the president of the United States and holds a cabinet-level position within the government.

Secret Service

The Secret Service is one of the police agencies found in the Treasury Department. The original purpose of the Secret Service was to control the making and distribution of counterfeit money and it retains that responsibility. For most Americans the Secret Service is best known as the agency that protects the president and his family from assassination attempts. Since the death of President John F. Kennedy, the responsibilities of the Secret Service have been expanded to include protecting all former presidents, their wives, and any of their children under the age of sixteen.

Internal Revenue Service

The Internal Revenue Service (IRS) is another unit within the Department of the Treasury that has law-enforcement authority. The most visible responsibility of the IRS is to see to it that all citizens pay their federal taxes and do not attempt to evade this responsibility.

There are far too many federal law-enforcement agencies to mention all of them. the ones identified here offer some sense of the responsibilities associated with federal law enforcement and how some are organized.

State Law Enforcement

The United States consists of fifty states. The government for each state essentially mirrors that which is found at the federal level. Each state has its own executive branch of government, with the chief executive officer being titled the governor; each has a legislative branch that enacts state laws, among other things; and each has a state court system that enforces and interprets the state constitution and any other law that has been passed in the state legislature.

With the exception of the state of Hawaii, all the states have some type of state law enforcement agency or agencies. State law-enforcement agencies are a twentieth-century invention. Although the reasons for creating such agencies have varied with each specific state, there were some common concerns that initi-

ated the early movement to establish state law enforcement. First, there was a need to establish an agency that had authority to enforce state laws throughout the state, as county and local police departments were limited to enforcing the law within their particular geographical jurisdiction. Second, with the invention of the automobile, there was a need to provide traffic enforcement on state roads that connected various cities and towns. Third, during the first few decades of this century, there was a good deal of labor unrest. The classic example of this was found in mining towns. In these small communities local law-enforcement officers were often related to the miners who were participating in the labor unrest. The officers were obviously unwilling or reluctant to enforce the law against their own relatives. As a result, there was a need to dispatch a police force to these towns that could maintain law and order during labor disputes.

Several states created a state police agency that would not only be responsible for enforcing all state laws throughout the state but would also specialize in the enforcement of state traffic laws. Those states that adopted this approach obviously gave rather broad responsibilities and authority to their state police agency. Other states were reluctant to follow this example. One of the principal concerns, already alluded to, was familiar to the history of American politics. People were concerned about establishing a police force that was too powerful and would ultimately be controlled by the chief executive officer of the state. The fear was that a governor might use the state police force to enhance his own political power. As a result, some states created an agency called a highway patrol. Its responsibility was essentially limited to enforcing traffic laws on state highways.

As this century progressed, states that had established only a highway patrol gradually saw the need to have an agency that could investigate certain crimes throughout the state. Instead of enhancing the authority of the highway patrol to handle such matters, these states created another enforcement agency that is usually called a state bureau of investigation.

Therefore, some states have a state police force that has very broad enforcement responsibilities, while other states have created two state law-enforcement agencies: a highway patrol to handle traffic enforcement and a bureau of investigation to address other law-enforcement needs throughout the state. Although these are the principal law-enforcement agencies with statewide jurisdiction, each state also has several boards or commissions that have quasi–law-enforcement authority within the state. Examples include state alcoholic beverage boards or commissions and state game and fish departments.

County Law Enforcement
One of the principal tenets of American politics, alluded to earlier, is the notion that local governments assert their right to home rule. This means that local governments exercise the authority and responsibility to provide certain governmental and social services to the community that they serve. The next two examples of this fragmented police system illustrate the significance of home rule quite well, for one of the earliest forms of asserting the right of home rule was in the establishment of law-enforcement services. Local police agencies are responsible for enforcing most of the criminal laws of a state, and they are frequently called on to resolve most of the daily incidents or problems related to order maintenance throughout the country.

County law enforcement is one kind of local law-enforcement. By adhering to the notion of home rule and for purposes of local administration, each state is divided into several counties. The responsibility for providing law-enforcement services to most counties rests with the sheriff's department, and there are over 3,000 of these throughout the United States. The office of the sheriff dates back to the eighth century in England and was brought over to America with the colonists.

Today the sheriff has three primary responsibilities. The first is essentially to provide law-enforcement services for the rural areas of the county. The second is to maintain a county jail, which is used to house people who have been charged with a crime but who have not as yet appeared in court. The jail is also used to house prisoners who have been convicted of a crime and whom the court has sentenced to less than a one-year term of incarceration. (In the United States, the facilities that are used to house prisoners who have been convicted of a crime and sentenced to more than one year of incarceration are called prisons. Whereas jails are generally administered by counties, prisons are administered by either a state or the federal government.) The third responsibility of the sheriff is to serve as an officer of the court. This means that the sheriff's department provides the court with bailiffs who maintain order in the courtroom. The sheriff's department also transports prisoners to the court and from the jail, transports people who have been sentenced to a term of incarceration at a facility other than the sheriff's jail, and serves legal documents to people that the court has so ordered.

In most counties the sheriff is elected by the people of the county. Although some sheriffs have had a prior background in law enforcement, many have not. As such, they are elected politicians first and law enforcement agents second. Because of this fact, sheriff's departments are often the least professional of all the law-enforcement agencies in the United States, but there are exceptions to this rule. Another factor that hinders the effectiveness of the sheriff in the area of law enforcement is that he is also responsible for the county jail. In other words, while deputy sheriffs should be trained as both police officers and correctional officers, they frequently are not. This has led on occasion to some degree of inefficiency and a lack of professionalism within the sheriff's department.

To avoid the problem of giving too many responsibilities to the sheriff, some counties, at present almost one hundred, have taken the responsibility of law enforcement away from the sheriff. In those instances the sheriff remains responsible for the jail and for serving as an officer of the court. The county has then established another agency which is usually called the county police. It is that agency that has the responsibility of enforcing the laws and maintaining order throughout the county.

Municipal Law Enforcement
The other kind of local law enforcement is municipal or city police, and there are approximately 16,000 of these. The reason for their creation goes back to the issue of home rule. As villages and towns developed, the citizens determined that they wanted to establish their own law-enforcement agency and not be dependent on the sheriff of the county. Usually the citizens were prompted to create their own police department in the hope that it would assure greater efficiency and effectiveness in law-enforcement service. Today, all cities, many towns, and some villages have their own police department. In the larger cities of the

United States the police department may employ several thousand officers, while a village may have only one or two officers. In any event their responsibility is to enforce the laws of the state in their particular geographical jurisdiction.

In most municipal police departments the chief administrator of the department is referred to as the chief of police. He is appointed to this position by either the mayor, with the approval of the city council, or by a board of city commissioners. Unlike the county sheriffs, chiefs of police usually have had extensive careers in law enforcement.

Municipal police departments that have at least seventy-five to one hundred officers are organized in a similar fashion. This would include a patrol unit, which would consist of approximately 50 percent of the police officers and would patrol the city twenty-four hours a day. A separate traffic unit that specializes in traffic enforcement and investigations is usually found in only the larger cities. A criminal investigation unit is responsible for investigating all serious crimes after they have occurred. A vice, organized crime, and intelligence unit enforces the vice laws in the community, deals with any ongoing problem of organized crime cartels in the community, and gathers intelligence on crime trends in the community. A juvenile unit specializes in dealing with juvenile offenders and in developing programs to discourage juveniles from a career of delinquent behavior. Finally, a community relations and crime prevention unit attempts to improve relations between the community and the police department. One way in which this is done is to establish programs that explain how citizens can assist the police in preventing crime from occurring in the community.

With each type of police agency in the United States—be it federal, state, county, or municipal, it is the responsibility of the geographical jurisdiction in which the particular agency functions to provide funding for the agency. Each agency is also responsible for the recruitment, selection, and training of the officers employed. Moreover, they are responsible for establishing all rules and procedures for the particular agency. Although this is only a brief overview, it illustrates why this approach to law enforcement is categorized as a fragmented model.

Richard J. Terrill

Bibliography

Alderson, J.C., and W.A. Tupman, eds. *Policing Europe After 1992*. Exeter, England: University of Exeter, 1990.

Cario, R. "French Police: General Organization and Tasks. *Revue Internationale de Criminologie et de Police Technique* 44 (1991): 418–32.

Fijnaut, C. "The Police and the Public in Western Europe: A Precarious Comparison." *Police Journal* 63 (1990): 337–45.

Kurian, George T. *World Encyclopedia of Police Forces and Penal Systems*. New York: Facts on File, 1988.

Loveday, B. "The New Police Authorities in the Metropolitan Counties. The Cost and Consequences of Abolition of the Metropolitan County Authorities." *Policing and Society* 1 (1991): 193–212.

Mawby, R.I. *Comparative Policing Issues: The British and American Experience in International Perspective*. London: Unwin Hyman, 1990.

"Police Agencies in Europe." *Les Cahiers de la Sécurité Interieure* 7 (1991–1992): 13–175.

Stead, Philip J. *The Police of France*. New York: Macmillan, 1983.

Terrill, Richard J. "Organizational Change for England's Police: An American Perspective." *Policing and Society* 2 (1992): 173–91.

———. *World Criminal Justice Systems: A Survey*. 2d ed. Cincinnati: Anderson, 1992.

Torres, Donald A. *Handbook of Federal Police and Investigative Agencies*. Westport, CT: Greenwood Press, 1985.

———. *Handbook of State Police, Highway Patrols, and Investigative Agencies*. Westport, CT: Greenwood Press, 1987.

Organized Crime

The examination of organized crime by law enforcement is made more difficult by the lack of any agreed upon, legally accepted definition of the phenomenon. In 1976 the Federal Strike Forces defined organized crime in the broad manner typical to law enforcement: "The term 'organized crime' for the purpose of these guidelines includes all illegal activities engaged in by members of criminal syndicates within the United States."

This not very useful definition simply stresses the syndicated nature of organized criminal groups. In 1983 Judge William H. Webster, director of the Federal Bureau of Investigation, provided a more detailed definition:

An organized crime investigation is targeted against any member or members of an organized crime group involved in the violation of Federal Statute(s) specifically aimed at racketeering activities. For the purpose of managing investigations, an organized crime group is defined as any group having some manner of formalized structure whose primary objective is to obtain money through illegal activities and maintains its position through the use of violence or the threat of violence, corrupt public officials, graft or extortion, and has an adverse effect on the people in its locale or region, or the country as a whole. The thrust of the organized program is targeted against individuals comprising major crime groups across the country.

This definition contains many important elements of organized crime for law-enforcement practitioners to study. (A) Organized crime is a group activity or process. (B) It possesses some form of regularized interaction, roles, and structure. (C) It has continuity over time. (D) It has goals and objectives, strategies and tactics, to attain these ends and to minimize risks, such as (E) using violence and the threat of violence, (F) using corruption, graft, and (G) extortion.

One may also note that Judge Webster's definition also directly stresses his agency's mission with reference to (1) the Federal Racketeering statutes, (2) the prosecutorial emphasis, and (3) the targeting of individuals.

The definition only indirectly hints at several additional elements of importance: (1) Organized criminals tend to be lifetime careerists; (2) illegal activities are directed toward wealth and power, not just to the direct proceeds of the illegal act; (3) organized crime possesses capital for complex, long-term, planned enterprises and operations; (4) its operations tend to be interjurisdictional—interstate and often international in scope; (5) key members are protected, insulated, and buffered by forms of organizational structuring and by the use of "fronts" and nonmember associates;

and (6) long-term goals stress the maximization of profit and power through the cartelization, or monopolization, of criminal enterprises and markets, as well as control over legitimate (noncriminal) businesses and sectors of the economy.

Judge Webster's definition is also important for what it does not say. It does not say that organized crime is limited to any specific ethnic or racial group. It does not say organized crime is only the Mafia or La Cosa Nostra, or only twenty-four Italian-American crime families.

Organized Crime: A Brief History
Organized crime is as American as apple pie. Lincoln Steffens noted in *Shame of the Cities* that "the spirit of graft and lawlessness is the American spirit." He was probably correct. Certainly we can find counterfeiting, smuggling, prostitution, extortionate usury, labor racketeering, protection through graft, corruption, and influence peddling prior to the American Revolution and long before the massive waves of European immigration of the last quarter of the nineteenth century.

Most histories of organized crime, however, overlook this. For much of this early organized crime was protected or controlled by indigenous elites, often politically influential individuals, who controlled the local press and were able to stay out of jail. Violence was used selectively, and often so delegated as to be ignored, or placed on minor figures or sensationalized "outlaws," without recognition of any ties to the larger political system. Close examination of the lives of men like John Hancock and his father, the Yazoo land fraud, the Crédit Mobiler scandal, or the era of the robber barons illustrates this point.

Conventional histories of organized crime usually begin with either the Italian immigration or the "Black Hand," and the discovery of Sicilian secret society "Mafia" members in New Orleans in the 1890s. A few emphasize the development of the ethnic street gangs in the large urban ghettos throughout the nineteenth century. The latter stress on street gangs is the better one. It is the more historically accurate, emphasizing the Irish, German, and Jewish street gangs of the 1840s and 1850s. And it is more useful, for it points out a key social phenomenon, the street gang, which has often been an important incubator of criminal organizations and organized criminals.

A more unified theoretical approach is to view the emergence of organized crime after the mid-nineteenth century in the United States in terms of stages, and thus avoid the common overidentification with a particular ethnic, religious, or racial group. This approach also eliminates the ethnic or alien conspiracy thesis that some analysts feel dominates police thinking on this subject.

The first stage in the development of organized crime can be called the *Predatory Stage*. Its hallmark is the street gang that has become strong enough to prey upon the local neighborhood or community. The extortionate street gang uses violence and the threat of violence to obtain regularized income. Also typical is the use-oriented consumption of proceeds, or stealing for personal need, from episodic crimes typical of street gangs. This is a first step in the embryonic development of the organized criminal group.

Regularized income provides discretionary capital for the group's expansion into planned endeavors, such as running illegal card games. It also provides the opportunity for role specialization within the gang as well as opportunities for interaction with the professional "service crime" underworld.

In the street gang, leadership is based on a combination of street skills, physical prowess, and toughness. In the predatory stage some additional interpersonal and business skills are also required of the leader. Now, not only must the group selectively use violence and threats, it must possess negotiating and diplomatic skills.

The predatory street gang is useful to the existing criminal infrastructure in the neighborhood or community, especially the professional criminals, gamblers, brothel-keepers, bootleggers, and others, because gang members can serve as bouncers, collectors, lookouts, private security, and eliminators of rivals and competitors. In this latter role they are also useful to legitimate businessmen. Also, having the extortionate or predatory street gang so employed and co-opted avoids having them used against one.

In the late nineteenth century both businessmen and trade unionists found the predatory street gangs a useful source of head breakers for their individual causes. This established a pattern that continued well into the twentieth century and formed ties that helped lead to organized crime penetrations of legitimate businesses and trade unions. This is important because it underscores the essential "patron–client

relationships" that are fundamental to the structuring of organized criminal groups.

Ties to the "service" underworld increased the learning and sophistication among predatory street gang leaders. But it was the existence of political machines in many nineteenth-century cities that provided the most important contacts. For with them came protection and employment for predatory street gangs that could turn out the vote and intimidate the opposition.

But it is also important to note that the predatory street gang was subservient to the politician and the political machine. The gang could work for the politician and receive some benefits from the relationship, but at this stage the politician was in control. He was the patron. Through the political machine's control of the police, the street gang remained a client to his rule.

The second stage in the development of organized crime is the *Parasitical Stage*. In order for this to occur there must be some "window of opportunity" through which the predatory street gang can travel to emerge as a parasitical organized criminal group. Changes in power, rule shifts, regulation alterations, economic crises, war, and even natural catastrophes can create such windows, but other situational variables have to be present so they can be exploited.

In the United States, such a condition was created with the regulation and prohibition of alcohol, which went into effect in January 1920. Without this window it is likely that traditional organized crime as we know it would never have emerged from the predatory street gang and hoodlum stage.

Prohibition provided the incentive for collaboration and organization beyond the neighborhood and city, as well as its vast profits, which facilitated the transformation of the predatory street gangs into criminal organizations and syndicates. Most important, it provided the means to reverse the patron–client relationship to the political system. Now the organized criminal possessed the resources, money, and organization to corrupt and control politicians and influence elections and the political machines in many cities across the United States. Where they did not, the syndicated, organized crime group at least had the resources and power to buy some time and immunity from prosecution while they sought to control the illicit service economies of gambling, loan-sharking, prostitution, labor racketeering, and drug trafficking.

It is during the parasitical stage that organized crime groups seek to expand further into the legitimate sectors of society. Prohibition had provided both the necessity and opportunity for gangs to form loose confederations, syndicates, and alliances to pool capital and resources, regionalizing and nationalizing markets and activities. The end of Prohibition meant the legalization of many previously illicit holdings of organized crime members and their associates, but it did nothing to break up the networks and patterns of association that had developed in that period.

Changes in technology and society also assisted the expansion of organized crime. Telephonic wire services made possible the nationalization of gambling and the creation of "layoff" services (a hedging bet made by one bookie with another to protect the first, who has taken more bets on one contestant than he wants to carry on himself) to reduce bookmaking risk, just as television helped create a wider market for professional sports and a vast new industry and pool of clients for sports bookmakers.

In the fully matured parasitical stage one begins to see an increased blending of previous illegal activities with legitimate enterprises. This further legitimates the place of the organized criminal group within the political system. At this point many forms of gambling (horse racing, lotteries, etc.) are legalized and former bookmakers become businessmen. Over time, this legal gambling goes public and becomes a publicly traded stock issue, and organized crime blends further into the upperworld. Law enforcement then faces even greater problems in combating organized crime. At this point law-enforcement resources frequently shift to focus on those criminal organizations that have not attained such a degree of social, economic, and political integration with the larger society.

The third stage is the *Symbiotic Stage*. Here, organized crime increasingly moves from opposition to interaction with the state. In the United States there are only fragmentary signs of this occurring, and thus it is less important to us here. In Japan and Italy there are more obvious indications of this. In Japan, for example, organized crime groups, collectively known as Yakuza, turned out 18,000 gangsters at the behest of the government to protect the travel route of President Eisenhower in 1960. More recently, Japanese organized crime figures assisted in channeling the Lockheed scandal payoffs to Japanese government officials.

In Italy the Sicilian Mafia has strong ties to the dominant Christian Democratic party, particularly the Andreotti wing in Sicily. This creates an interactive relationship and mutual profit-making as policies and programs are developed that promote Mafia domination of certain aspects of the marketplace, and permit them to enforce it with extralegal violence.

Organized Crime: A Law-Enforcement Perspective

A growing variety of organized crime groups confronts law enforcement today. They range from the traditional, well-known La Cosa Nostra (LCN) Italian-American families to the less well known Israeli "Mafia," Russian "Mafia," and Nigerian "Mafia." In addition, from the Far East there come the Japanese Yakuza, the Chinese Triad groups, and the Vietnamese gangs, which are frequently overseas Chinese-Triad connected. Within the Western Hemisphere today, and arising from the window of opportunity of drug trafficking, there are Cuban, Colombian, Mexican, Canadian, and other ethnic organized crime groups, as well as black, white, and outlaw motorcycle gang organizations.

Given this assortment of groups, it is often wiser for law enforcement to look for patterns of attributes and identifiers of organized crime, rather than to focus on a particular group unless it is reacting to a specified target or prosecutorial objective.

There is a variety of perspectives from which law enforcement can focus on organized crime. One, it can target individuals, such as John Gotti or Nicky Scarfo. Two, it can target an entire criminal group or organization, such as the Hererra family, or Ghost Shadows outlaw motorcycle gang. Three, it can target an activity such as heroin dealing. Four, it can target keystone activities such as fencing, which affects residential burglary, or "chop shops," which affect car theft, motor vehicle department corruption, and insurance fraud. Five, it can target keystone, organized crime predictor activities, such as intimidation-arson, extortion, extortionate assault and "bustouts" (the point in a swindle or confidence game where the victim surrenders money or other valuables), and loan-sharking, all of which often point to organized crime penetrations into the community.

Or it can target patterns of violence, such as murders of known drug dealers, independent bookmakers, pornography store operators, union officials, or local criminal financiers, any and all of which may indicate changes in patterns of organized crime. Six, it can target entire criminal markets, such as the exploitation of the private carting (refuse) industry in a given community or region, by combining several of the available approaches.

Whatever approaches law enforcement chooses it should keep in mind the following patterns and attributes common to organized criminal groups. There is ongoing interaction by members of the group over time. These interactions develop into patterns, roles, divisions of labor, status relationships, and the like. The group members tend to identify with each other as a subculture and to develop a long-term careerist attitude toward a criminal lifestyle. Violence, the threat of violence, or a reputation for violence serves as a halo surrounding the activities of the group.

In addition groups that have reached the parasitical stage will possess capital for entering new criminal markets. They have resources for investment and the know-how to undercut competition, penetrate legitimate business, and they will use fronts, buffers, and nonmember associates to expand their influence and power. They will also engage in long-term planning for complex crime scenarios and develop political connections and influence. A major question at present is, Will the new nontraditional organized criminal groups establishing themselves in the United States be able to establish the political ties and corruption networks to insulate themselves from prosecution? If and where they do, they obviously will be much harder for law enforcement to deal with successfully.

Law-Enforcement Tools for Combating Organized Crime

Police agencies with proactive intelligence units using the above patterns and indicators should be able to track and develop intervention strategies for limiting the scope of organized crime in their community. Having the best intelligence unit possible, run by first-class, long-term professionals and used and listened to by the departmental administration is, of course, the basic tool for fighting organized crime. Next comes a series of laws that are vital to enhancing the enforcement goals of the police. A look at federal law enforcement illustrates this.

The Federal Bureau of Investigation under Director Webster has made great strides in fighting traditional (LCN) organized crime. It has succeeded for the following reasons: (1) a commitment to long-term (multiyear), deep, undercover investigations; (2) active use of electronic surveillance legislation; (3) use of the Racketeer Influenced Corrupt Organization (RICO) statute; (4) use of witness immunity statutes and the Witness Protection Program; and (5) use, and threat of use, of criminal forfeiture laws. These are essential tools for combating organized crime that must be available to every state and local law-enforcement agency. One cannot expect to adequately combat organized crime without them, and they must be aggressively lobbied for in all jurisdictions where they are not currently available. In addition, at the state level, a statewide grand jury system is critical to combating corruption and organized crime. And again, it must be strongly lobbied for by police professionals everywhere.

Law enforcement can combat organized crime only with the tools it is given and within jurisdictional constraints. Organized crime, on the other hand, typically operates across jurisdictions, states, and even national boundaries. This means organized crime investigations require interagency cooperation. They often require strike forces or joint task forces, and always active liaison. It means that to deal with organized crime, the law-enforcement professional must be professional in every sense of the word. Organized crime will never be eliminated but it can be limited. It can be prevented from reaching the advanced parasitic or symbiotic stage, wherein the mission of law enforcement may be perverted.

Peter A. Lupsha

Bibliography

Abadinsky, Howard. *Organized Crime*. Boston: Allyn & Bacon, 1981.

Albini, Joseph. *The American Mafia*. New York: Appleton-Century Crofts, 1971.

Browning, F., and J. Gerassi. *The American Way of Crime*. New York: G. P. Putnam's Sons, 1980.

Dintino, J., and F. Martens. *Police Intelligence Systems in Crime Control*. Springfield, IL: Charles C. Thomas, 1983.

Kelly, Robert, ed. *Organized Crime: A Global Perspective*. Totowa, NJ: Rowman & Littlefield, 1986.

Kwitny, Jonathan. *Vicious Circles: The Mafia*

in the Marketplace. New York: W. W. Norton, 1979.

Pace, D., and J.C. Styles. *Organized Crime: Concepts and Control.* Englewood, NJ: Prentice-Hall, 1975.

Peterson, Virgil. *The Mob: 200 Years of Organized Crime in New York City.* Ottawa, IL: Green Hill, 1983.

Salerno, Ralph. *The Crime Confederation.* New York: Popular Library, 1969.

U.S. President's Commission on Organized Crime. *The Impact: Organized Crime Today.* Washington, DC: Government Printing Office, 1986.

O

P

William Henry Parker

William Henry Parker (1902–1966), former chief of the Los Angeles Police Department, was born in Lead, South Dakota. His grandfather, a frontier law-enforcement officer, influenced the boy in his choice of professions, and not his father, who was superintendent of the Homestake Mine, the largest gold mine in America. It is unknown why in his mid-twenties Parker left the Black Hills of South Dakota to travel as far away as Los Angeles. But he did, joining the police force there in 1927 and receiving his LL.B. degree in 1930 from the Los Angeles College of Law. Again, for an unknown reason, he decided not to practice law but to stay with the police department, where he advanced rapidly. Eager to learn, he increased his knowledge of police work by attending a variety of specialized police training courses given across the country. He served in all ranks of the department, absorbed the idiosyncrasies of each, and thereby made himself indispensable. So when he became chief of police he could legitimately say that he had seen it all—a claim not every police administrator could make.

World War II presented him with an unusual opportunity. Upon enlistment he studied overseas administration and Italian at Harvard University in preparation for service with the military government branch of the U.S. Armed Forces. Once in Europe life quickened: he took part in the Normandy Invasion (wounded, awarded the Purple Heart); he participated in the liberation of Paris (awarded the Croix de Guerre with Silver Star by the Free French Government); he went to Sardinia (awarded the Star of Solidarity by the Italians for restor-

ing civil government); and he stayed over in occupied Germany where he created democratic police systems for Munich and Frankfurt. Parker was discharged in November 1945, an army captain.

Back from the war Parker returned to the Los Angeles Police Department and in 1950 was appointed chief. As chief, he delivered many speeches to foster cordial relations between police and the public. *Parker on Police* (1957) collects his philosophy/working principles. A few excerpts will highlight his beliefs about law enforcement:

> As policemen we are guided by an artificial definition of right and wrong—the law. We do not pretend that it is all-wise, all-inclusive, or all-just. . . . Law exists, not because we do agree on what is right and wrong, but because we do not agree.

About police discretion:

> In a perfect system of civil administration, the function of the police is to interfere with the liberty of the individual only when it degenerates into license, and any material variation from this standard is to be deprecated as being arbitrary and tyrannical.

About police image:

> Public attitudes toward the police directly affect crime rates. Disrespect for law enforcers breeds disrespect for law. A child who is raised to laugh at "cops" is not likely to grow up with any great respect for the laws which the police enforce.

About the police–citizen bond:

> Law enforcement is so dependent upon
> the cooperation of the individual citizen
> that credit for police progress must go
> primarily to the citizen. . . . Largely by
> his political ethics, the citizen determines
> the ethics of the police.

About stringent ethics:

> If it is a valid premise that Religion and
> Morality are indispensable to human
> welfare, it must be concluded that Reli-
> gion and Morality are indispensable to
> each other. Therefore, the leadership we
> require in this compelling return to fun-
> damental virtues must lie among those
> men who have been privileged to under-
> stand the true relationship between God
> and man.

Chief Parker's accomplishments were many. He
created and developed the Internal Affairs Division (for handling complaints leveled at police), was coauthor of the Board of Rights procedure (guaranteed separation of police
discipline from municipal politics), created the
Bureau of Administration (known nationally
for the competency of its Intelligence and Planning and Research divisions), assisted in designing a new Police Administration Building (a
marvel of functional purpose), and promoted
professionalism throughout the Los Angeles
Police Department. The Kefauver Crime Investigation (1952) commended Parker for his
crime-fighting ability, as did other police observers who considered Los Angeles the "white
spot" in American's crime pattern.

Controversy marred the last stage of his
career. Branded a racist for his supposed inequitable treatment of minorities, blacks in particular, civil rights groups demanded his resignation. The Watts Riot (1965) was his undoing.
In a Los Angeles ghetto, with an estimated
population of 90,000 blacks, state highway
patrolmen chased a drunk driver onto the un-
friendly turf. Cries of police brutality sparked
a melee with these results: 36 people dead, 900
reported injured, more than 4,000 arrested, and
$200 million worth of property damage. Parker
responded at a news conference, "One person
threw a rock and then, like monkeys in a zoo,
others started throwing rocks." That unfortunate blunder in speech etched his epitaph;

within a few months of the riot he was on leave
from the department for "health reasons."
Previously, he had also made news by calling
Chief Justice Earl Warren's "legal idealism" a
social danger. Parker's conservative bent just
could not tolerate the liberalization of American life, which to him meant a slackening of
morals and, eventually, increased crime.

Art imitated life when the television program *Dragnet* aired (first radiocast, 1949; first
telecast, 1952). Jack Webb as Sergeant Joe Friday always unnerved a negligent officer by telling him bluntly, "The chief wants to see you."
Fans in the Los Angeles area knew, of course,
that the chief was the stern William H. Parker;
fans on the outside may not have known his
name but easily understood the evocation of a
hard-nosed, no-nonsense boss. Incidentally,
Parker's office supplied the technical advice for
Dragnet, the most popular police program ever,
renowned for its realism.

Parker did not waste time on mental diver-
sions. He labored at administering a large police department, writing speeches, and bettering
community relations. He was married to Helen
Schwartz. They had no children. On the evening
of July 16, 1966, at a testimonial dinner in Los
Angeles, he walked to the dais to receive a
plaque citing him as one of the nation's foremost police chiefs. Returning to his table, esteemed man of the hour, he collapsed. Heart
surgery for removal of an aneurism of the aorta,
months before, had not prevented his sudden
death.

Bibliography

"After the Blood Bath." *Newsweek* 66(9)
(August 30, 1965): 13–19.
New York Times 8 (August 14, 1965): 7; 68
(July 17, 1966): 2.
Wilson. O.W., ed. *Parker on Police.* Spring-
field, IL: Charles C. Thomas, 1957.

Patrol

Ever since Boston, Massachusetts, authorized
the first permanent Night Watch in 1801, when,
where, and how to patrol have preoccupied
police management. No different now, the same
questions have to be answered on a daily basis.
Over the past century and a quarter machines
invented for the public have assisted patrol. The
first breakthrough came with the call box, or
street phone, about 1867. Placed in strategic locations, call boxes allowed citizens to report

crime, potential crime, and emergencies; patrol officers also used call boxes to communicate with one another. More technically advanced telephones appeared in Washington, D.C., in 1878. The Detroit Police Department initiated bicycle patrol in 1897 and was likewise the first to supply an officer with a Model-T Ford soon afterward. Moving ahead into the twentieth century, radio, walkie-talkies, and computerized dispatching aided patrol immeasurably. Besides machines, horses and dogs have been staples of patrol. In fact, even with major advances in technology, horses, dogs, and shoe leather are still important manifestations of keeping watch.

Techniques
On foot is the most expensive method of patrol because it is labor intensive. Moreover, officers walking beats cannot cover as much ground as their cohorts using transportation. Foot patrol's main advantage is that it helps to bond neighborhoods and foster improved community relations. If the expense involved is measured in relation to crime prevention and heightened community trust of law enforcement, then foot patrol usually comes out ahead of other types of patrol and is money well spent. It is not uncommon for police who have become machine dependent to have to relearn the rudiments of foot patrol. Donald T. Shanahan (1975), who wrote the basic text on patrol administration, gives these police academy instructions:

> Know the people on your beat; their occupations, and their habits; know personally night watchmen, janitors, and all other persons who may be working at unusual hours of the day and night; acquaint yourself with operators of taverns, pool rooms, and clubs and all laws relating to the proper conduct of such establishments on your beat; know where your call boxes are located and your firealarm boxes. Additionally, officers should know the same information about the adjoining beats. Be so intimately involved with the residents of your beat that knowledge of when they are away on vacation and advice about the safeguards they should take to insure the protection of their property can be given freely, and accepted sincerely. Officers should know not only those proven law-abiding residents but also those of questionable character.

The instructions demand a lot from an officer. He or she must be eagle-eyed, possess a facile memory, be everyone's friend, sort out those who may be suspect, and accomplish all this in a tireless manner while on foot. Shanahan's last requirement is that the officer project himself or herself as an "exemplary member of the community" both on and off duty.

Estimates of workload continue to suggest that officers spend between 70 and 80 percent of their time on noncriminal activities. That being so, the figures confirm foot patrol as good management because officers are on the street, in the schools, and at public gatherings "in person." They are not "detached" in cars and bored waiting for something to happen. Seemingly old-fashioned, progressive police departments boast of their "new" foot patrols. City government in metropolitan areas practically mandates their use. To increase tax bases, cities are reclaiming their downtown areas by making them more attractive to business and residents. Highly visible foot patrol is one of the best ways to demonstrate the city's commitment to safer streets.

An axiom of foot patrol is: Its one regularity is its irregularity. Officers avoid established routine so criminals cannot get a fix on them. British Prime Minister Sir Robert Peel (1788–1850), who established the first police force in London, said of foot patrol, "They may not be everywhere, but they may be expected anywhere." Peel's pithy remark is still the goal today and puts added pressure on police to be visible, invisible, and like a genie—revisible, all at the same time. To hone their craft, foot patrol officers imagine vicarious or hypothetical situations. They envision how things could happen on their beat, noting physical objects (e.g., entrances, exits, blind alleyways), social patterns (e.g., hours of the day, hangouts, frequent faces), and crime patterns (e.g., holdups, burglaries, auto theft). Once a hypothetical situation becomes real, the officer relies on what is called "proper" observation. Clearness and quickness of mind determine success. Shortly after a crime has occurred the officer begins to assimilate information. Everything related to the crime gets noted, at first mentally, then in a written report. Sights, sounds, weather, eyewitness accounts (including the emotional state of witnesses, age, language used, etc.), distinguishing features of the suspect, and generally everything to make the case. If the officer sees the offender briefly without making an arrest, a quick eye for physical characteristics is requisite. Foot-patrol officers learn that the nose and ears offer the most reliable mnemonic device for remembering a face.

While on foot the officer can patrol either conspicuously or inconspicuously. Conspicuous patrol tells the public and the criminal who the officer is and where he or she moves. An officer who looks physically out-of-shape or otherwise not up to the job will be taken advantage of. Whereas a physically fit, active, and alert officer will command respect. To make the most of the 70–80 percent time spent on noncriminal activities, conspicuous patrol is community-oriented policing with the addition of even more shoulder-rubbing and hand-shaking. One disadvantage of high visibility is that the public calls on the officer for everything from a missing pet to stopping domestic violence. Inconspicuous patrol is employed when a masterful or hard-to-catch criminal works an area. At such times the officer must rely on shadow tactics to throw off the criminal. The proverbial saying "If you want the best coffee in town, look for cops in the shop" is antithetical to crime prevention. A combination of conspicuous and inconspicuous patrol is best, though change from one to the other presents problems. The trick in realizing Peel's remark is for the officer to appear idiosyncratic in habits and means of covering the beat. It is management's job to analyze crime data to demarcate beats that can be effectively patrolled by foot. Community stability also affects the size of a beat. In volatile parts of the community the mere presence of an officer can spark an attack or a riot.

Motorized Patrol
Rapid response with much less fatigue makes motor patrol more attractive than foot patrol. In a car an officer arrives on the scene fresh and unwinded to close in quickly on the criminal. A regular tour of duty in a car is not seen as an endurance test requiring the officer to have legs of steel. Cars assist idiosyncratic patrol strategy with use of double-back, concentric, stationary, and zigzag driving patterns that can be executed slowly for observation or rapidly for crime investigation. Cutting off escape routes—called quadrant response—can be accomplished only with cars. Civil disorders necessitate motorized patrol for a show of force; the lone foot patrol officer would be ill-advised to step into the middle of an unruly crowd. The loud sirens and flashing lights of police cars attune the public

to police action. Pavlovian in effect, the assault on the senses halts bystanders and freezes or disorients criminals. More so than on foot, motorized patrol officers must know the lay of the land and traffic patterns. A car speeding around corners can become an instrument of death.

Police still debate whether the one-officer car is better than the two-officer car, or vice versa. Putting two officers—two salaries—in one car is costly and dilutes patrol coverage. One-officer cars patrol more area because more cars are in use and response to calls for service are doubled with twice as many cars on the street. The single officer feels like an indispensable part of the team, since he or she must be ready to give assistance at any time. The officer remains more alert and is not distracted by conversation. The officer does not have to prove his or her worth (show off) to a second officer and can be evaluated more easily on individual performance. Accepting the authority to act alone, assuming responsibility for one's actions, and knowing he or she will be held accountable for individual actions are strong motivational factors. Objections to the one-officer car are threefold. First, there is safety in numbers; two officers per car are more formidable and can cover each other in dangerous situations. While this seems apparent, FBI reports on the number of law-enforcement officers killed and assaulted have not always supported the notion. In the 1970s one-officer cars appeared to be safer. Recent data suggest that two-officer cars are now less apt to incur injury or death. The reason that single officers may be more protected is that they do not take chances. Officers on their own call for assistance and weigh decisions carefully. Their hesitancy to act in a rash manner raises the second objection—that single officers do not patrol aggressively. Again, when looked at closely the notion evaporates; the experience of police departments has been that officers who work alone develop more cunning and insight than when given a partner. Self-reliance forces them to be better patrol officers. The third objection is that it is nearly impossible for a single officer, who must pay attention to driving, to observe the passing scene. A second officer is in a much better position to keep a watchful eye. This objection also fizzles; experience shows that officers operating alone concentrate more and develop observational powers beyond normal—reliance on a partner causes them to relax too much. Success with the one-officer car hinges on expert dispatching of information from department headquarters, rather than on having to weigh a second opinion voiced by a partner.

With so much in favor of the one-officer car, what is there to debate? Officer safety is the overwhelming factor on the side of the two-officer car. Even though FBI data have varied on this point, certain situations call for double strength and the use of different tactics that only one officer cannot supply, e.g., youth gang activity. As mentioned, police departments conduct manpower-workload studies in conjunction with crime analysis and geographic mapping to determine patrol needs. Patrol assignments change often; foot patrol, one-officer cars, two-officer cars, and foot-and-auto combinations are employed as needed.

Canine and Horse
Well-trained police dogs are indispensable for patrol. Dogs are used primarily for crime prevention, crowd control, building searches, and security. As all film buffs know dogs have a highly developed sense of smell and can trail escaped convicts, detect crimes, and locate drugs, explosives, and missing persons. Dog training involves obedience and scenting classes, along with crime scene investigation. Selection of a handler is as important as dog selection. Both handler and dog undergo psychological testing. The handler must like and be willing to work with dogs and test positive for an even temperament undeterred by any annoyance the dog might present. The dog must not be gun shy and test positive for aggressive instincts controlled by self-protection. Dogs usually go on patrol eight hours a day with an additional hour devoted to feeding, grooming, and exercise. Keeping and training dogs is expensive, but because their sense of smell and hearing are much more acute than humans, cost is relative to performance.

If dogs are thought high maintenance, horses are surely a luxury. Horse patrol is limited to crowd control and for trotting through downtown areas. People respect tall, powerful horses the way they respect fierce-looking dogs. An officer mounted on horseback has an unobstructed view of things, and in parks can gallop across the green whereas a car might have to take a circuitous route. Perhaps the main attraction of horses is for police parades. Nothing beats a team of stalwart officers in riding boots atop well-groomed animals for building public confidence. Although it appears that economic restrictions will phase out horses, they will be missed by everyone at parade time.

Helicopter
Police use helicopters to augment ground forces in the following situations: to bring about arrest, for car and pedestrian checks, for roof inspection/building checks, for area illumination, to recover stolen cars, for prowler and robbery calls, for car chases, for detection of fires, and for aerial surveillance and traffic control. Air-ground coordination spells the difference between success and failure. In addition to a command unit providing coordination based on technical data and known patrol patterns, a procedure as simple as painting car numbers visible to the pilot ensures proper response. Patrol patterns can be either "mesh"—the helicopter flies north-south, then east-west; or "concentric"—the pilot flies to the crime scene then makes 360-degree turns enlarging the perimeter for a systematic search. If two or more helicopters are sent to the scene, coordination of their flight patterns is even more critical. As with the one-officer/two-officer car debate, certain dangerous situations require two pilots and dual controls in the helicopter. Civil disorders, flood, and rescue operations place a lone pilot in jeopardy without in-flight assistance. Except in emergencies the command unit and pilots know exactly where to land because all landing sites are preselected. Police pursuit in cars concerns police management, the public, and local government. The liability issue restrains some police departments from engaging in high-speed ground pursuit. Helicopters make pursuit less perilous and more effective. Fleeing felons cannot shake a helicopter, and pilots from their vantage point can radio ahead for interception.

Bicycle, Scooter, Motorcycle
Still in use as a viable means of patrol the bicycle grants these advantages: It is less physically taxing and more expedient than foot patrol; it can maneuver where a car cannot (alleyways, beaches, around obstacles); and officers stay fit from the exercise. Beat size can be increased and still allow for concentrated patrol while providing diversion from boredom experienced by foot patrol officers. Scooters also achieve greater mobility but, being motorized, do not provide exercise. Unlike bicycles, scooters are enclosed to protect the officer during bad

weather. Not enclosed, motorcycles give the patrol officer mobility with the speed of a car and are in this respect more dangerous.

Marine

The U.S. Coast Guard enforces federal laws in territorial waters. Coastal marine patrol, especially for port cities, is responsible for enforcing state laws and county ordinances, promoting water safety, conducting vessel safety inspections, performing routine patrol, removing navigational hazards, towing disabled craft if possible, and assisting federal and other law-enforcement agencies. Inland water patrol, e.g., along the Ohio and Mississippi rivers, is seen less frequently than marine patrol. Once a quiet job, marine patrol now entails extensive drug-enforcement stops.

Experiments

Beginning in the 1970s police scholars and progressive police administrators took it upon themselves to examine the conventional wisdom of patrol. Before this period of scrutiny police felt they patrolled effectively. However, it was more from a gut feeling of self-satisfaction than from hard evidence. The first attempt to dissect patrol became the most famous—the Kansas City Preventive Patrol Experiment (1971). For the experiment patrol levels were increased in some areas of Kansas City, reduced in others, and remained the same in a third part for the control group. The results surprised practically everyone. On the whole citizens were unaware of the level of patrol around them. Even though the number of police differed considerably from one area to another, few people took notice. Reported crime and victimizations did not differ significantly in the three areas. Nor did citizen satisfaction with police service or citizen fear of crime. For the moment it appeared that patrol practices had little impact on crime prevention and community relations. The Kansas City Preventive Patrol Experiment did not go unchallenged. Some police leaders vehemently questioned the methodology and results. Others accepted the fact that something was amiss with patrol and initiated their own experiments.

Chief William Kolander in San Diego followed up Kansas City with a study of one-officer versus two-officer cars. At the time many police managers took for granted that two-officer cars were superior. Kolander's results demonstrated the reverse: One-officer cars were as safe and productive as two-officer cars. Over the next fifteen years more experiments probed conventional wisdom. Chief Hubert Williams in Newark, New Jersey, and Chief Max Durkin in Flint, Michigan, tested hypotheses about foot patrol. Chief Anthony Bouza in Minneapolis focused on alternative means for handling domestic violence. And Chief Lee Brown in Houston put to trial fear reduction in high-crime neighborhoods. Detective productivity and rapid response to calls for service were other police functions subjected to experimentation. During this time of sifting out verifiable from presumed truth, disillusionment set in. As with Kansas City many of the studies showed that preventive patrol made little difference, that officers appeared to be largely unproductive, and that rapid response to calls for service failed to net more arrests or make the public feel more secure.

On the brighter side, over fifteen years of experimentation yielded some usable results. While the major conclusions were disappointing much had been learned along the way. Police scholar George Kelling enumerated the positive aspects—what works—absorbed from this period of inquiry.

- One-officer cars can patrol safely and be just as productive as two-officer cars.
- In nonemergency situations citizens who call police for service are as satisfied with alternative responses to calls for service (e.g., telephone counseling, delayed response) as they are with rapid response if the reasons for providing alternatives are carefully explained to them.
- Foot patrol reduces citizen fear of crime, increases citizen satisfaction with police, and improves police morale.
- Arresting assailants in domestic disputes reduces the likelihood that they will assault their spouses in the future.
- If police officers carefully gather information after the commission of a crime, communicate it to detectives, and detectives use it, the productivity of detectives can be improved.
- Police methods that increase the quantity and improve the quality of police–citizen interaction reduce citizen fear of crime.
- Police, working with citizens, can help citizens define the nature of community problems and devise methods for solving those problems.

Studies of police patrol are more intricate now than when the Kansas City experiment took place. For example, in 1992 political scientist G.A. Gianakis examined performance appraisal methods, the types of instruments used to make the appraisals, and the kinds of performance categories included in the instruments. Gianakis measured personality traits, physical appearance, workload, police skills, overall knowledge required for patrol, and outcomes to form his selected criteria. He then used the criteria and shift-rotation data to determine performance in accredited versus nonaccredited law-enforcement agencies. After manipulation of mountainous data, Gianakis concluded that agency accreditation had beneficial effects but performance appraisal in law enforcement continued to be "as confused as performance appraisal in general." Since any experimentation is never the final word new studies need to be undertaken. As society changes, so too does patrol rationale.

Bibliography

Boydstun, J.E., et al. *Patrol Staffing in San Diego*. Washington, DC: Police Foundation, 1977.

Decker, S.H., and A.E. Wagner. "The Impact of Police Patrol Staffing on Police-Citizen Injuries and Dispositions." *Journal of Criminal Justice* 10 (1982): 375–82.

Gianakis, G.A. "Appraising the Performance of Police Patrol Officers: The Florida Experience." *Journal of Criminal Justice* 20 (1992): 413–28.

Kaplan, E.H. "Evaluating the Effectiveness of One-Officer versus Two-Officer Patrol Units." *Journal of Criminal Justice* 7 (1979): 325–55.

Pate, Anthony M., et al. *Three Approaches to Criminal Apprehension in Kansas City: An Evaluation Report*. Washington, DC: Police Foundation, 1976.

Police Foundation. *The Newark Foot Patrol Experiment*. Washington, DC: Police Foundation, 1981.

Rich, T.F. *Revealed Preferences of the Criminal Justice System During A Period of Workload Scheduling. Report No. II: National Survey of Police Departments*. Washington, DC: National Institute of Justice, 1984.

Shanahan, Donald T. *Patrol Administration: Management by Objectives*. Boston: Holbrook Press, 1975.

Sherman, Lawrence W. "Policing Communities: What Works?" In *Crime and Justice: An Annual Review of Research*. Vol. 8. Eds. Michael Tonry and Norval Morris. Chicago: University of Chicago Press, 1986.

Wilson, L.A., et al. "Situational Effects in Police Officer Assaults: The Case of Patrol Unit Size." *Police Journal* 63 (1990): 260–71.

Performance Measurement

Performance measurement is the use of social science methods to learn how well an agency is doing its job. Since police departments do many different jobs, it is difficult to measure their performance. Moreover, given the current state of knowledge about policing, performance measurement is able to provide only partial knowledge about the operations of a police department and their effects on the community. It also should be noted that performance measurement, no matter how exact, cannot replace discussion, negotiation, and judgment in reaching policy decisions about policing.

Early Years

August Vollmer is widely credited with fostering the first police performance measurement program in the United States. He became chief of the Berkeley Police Department in 1905, and during the next quarter of a century developed the department's data collection and evaluation methods far beyond those of any other local, state, or federal agency. The major milestone for systematic data collection, however, was the introduction of the *Uniform Crime Reports* (UCR) in 1930—Vollmer played a prominent role in the inception of this measure. Some American police chiefs had expressed a desire for the compilation of crime statistics since 1871, but the political and administrative obstacles had been too great until numerous commissions in the 1920s heightened public awareness of crime. In 1928, the International Association of Chiefs of Police (IACP), with support from the Rockefeller Foundation, devised a standardized crime-reporting system for police departments throughout the country. The IACP wanted the Federal Bureau of Investigation, with its new reputation for effectiveness and integrity, to have responsibility for managing data collection. The IACP issued its recommendations in 1929, and Congress and President Herbert Hoover assigned this responsibility to the FBI the following year. The FBI's role in producing crime statistics was twofold: It established crime classifications and coding rules, and it served as a clearinghouse to tally and publish the statistics.

Early criticisms of the UCR went unheeded. A technical report for the Wickersham Commission in 1931 pointed out that decentralized data collection would result in inaccurate data and suggested the responsibility be transferred to the Bureau of the Census. The Wickersham Commission report included two other caveats: (1) that crimes reported to police did not accurately indicate the true occurrence of crime; and (2) that the causes of crime were difficult to determine and the fluctuation of the crime rate could not be attributed solely to police activities. Twenty years later Thorsten Sellin, the eminent criminologist, pointedly criticized the UCR for failing to be more specific about the potential criminal population, rather than using the general population to estimate crime rates. In 1957 Sellin's widely publicized statement in *Life* magazine that American crime statistics were worse than any other country's led FBI Director J. Edgar Hoover to institute some changes to provide more precise methods of estimating the population base for between-census years. Some adjustments to the crime classification definitions were also made. To this day, however, valid criticisms of the UCR remain:

1. *The crime categories lack conceptual focus.* Local jurisdictions vary in the way they treat some crime categories. More important, legal crime categories tell the analyst very little about why a crime was committed or how it might have been prevented.
2. UCR *reports require the cooperation of the local police departments and citizens who report crimes to the police.* Crimes that citizens do not report or police do not record are omitted. The data are thus more accurate in depicting police activities than patterns of crime.
3. *The UCR is open to abuse by agencies that want to appear to be doing better than they are.* Agencies charged with reducing crime should not be given the responsibility for collecting data used to assess their own crime control performance. A separate statistical agency that obtained data independent of police

agencies would be less tempted to bias the data and would present information more widely usable for the public.

Despite criticism of the UCR, the measures have gained widespread use. In 1968, though, the Omnibus Crime Control and Safe Streets Act called for the establishment of the National Criminal Justice Information and Statistics Service (NCJISS). Its purpose was to collect information on criminal-justice agencies and to sponsor a nationwide survey on criminal victimization. The NCJISS sponsored several surveys before instituting the annual National Crime Victimization Survey in 1972. Conducted by the Bureau of Census, the National Crime Victimization Survey includes interviews with national samples of approximately 60,000 households and 39,000 business conducted at six-month intervals.

The most important finding of early victimization surveys was the confirmation of the suspicion that UCR statistics greatly underestimated the occurrence of crime. The extent of the discrepancy varied according to type of crime and by city. Despite the considerable attention given to these findings by the research community, most police departments continued to rely heavily upon UCR statistics to evaluate their programs. This is due in part to administrative inertia and also to the high cost of conducting periodic victimization surveys.

Attempts to Specify Standards and Goals
The period from 1965 to 1973 saw no fewer than six national commissions on crime, violence, and criminal justice, plus innumerable state and local commissions on these topics. A major problem with the commissions' reports as a basis for performance measurement was the lack of research on policing. Despite the lack of research to support their recommendations, they set detailed standards, goals, and objectives and offered an array of programs and approaches to achieve them. The National Advisory Commission report, for example, stated that a realistic goal for its recommended program was to cut high-fear crimes by 50 percent within a decade. They expected too much based on too little evidence. A second major problem was that the commissions tried to bring order to priorities for an occupation that, despite previous impressive efforts to achieve nationwide professional standards, remains a local, particularistic enterprise. Although the commissions

attempted to establish clear priorities, their recommendations invariably included something for everybody.

Two National Projects
In 1970 President Richard Nixon appointed members to serve on the National Commission on Productivity. The commission established a special advisory group for police comprising twenty law-enforcement professionals and researchers. The advisory group focused on three patrol objectives: deterrence of crime, apprehension of criminal offenders, and satisfaction of public demand for noncrime services. But the result of their work fell far short of their aspirations and was quite narrow. They relied primarily on easily quantifiable measures of police activities. The suggested measures reflected more the quantity of police activities than the quality of service.

The second project was conducted by the American Justice Institute (AJI) and funded by the Law Enforcement Assistance Administration. AJI produced an interim report in 1976 and a final report in 1978. Unlike the Productivity Commission's product, AJI's 1978 report made a concerted effort to provide a detailed structure for performance measurement in police departments. This program, called the Police Program Performance Measurement System (PPPm), identified forty-six police agency objectives that were grouped into five categories: crime prevention, crime control, conflict resolution, services, and administration. To measure the accomplishment of each objective, PPPm provided definitions of measures, instructions on data collection and statistical computations, and standards for judging success. Recognizing that a police department might not find all objectives desirable nor all measures feasible, the authors devised a "cafeteria of measurement tools" to permit agencies flexibility in choosing some objectives and measures while rejecting others. Included in the package were cost estimates for implementing each measurement technique. Despite the greater sophistication of PPPm, it still had its drawbacks, such as misleading claims of comprehensiveness and lack of attention to measures of police service equity.

Current Practices
Many police departments have not modified their performance measurement systems despite the efforts of commissions and researchers. In fact, many administrators are still diligently trying to institute changes from previous reform eras. A dominant feature of most current police agency performance measurement is the overriding concern that it be guided by a coherent framework of police goals and objectives. Another characteristic of many current programs is the reliance on one statistic—or a few—to indicate performance, rather than making an attempt to develop a greater number of indicators that shed light on many aspects of the agency's operations.

Most of the current problems with police agency performance measurement come from inappropriate views of what actual police work is like. One relevant simile suggests that measuring performance is like scoring a game. We should score competing police agencies, divisions, or strategies to determine which is the best and how much better it is. Presumably the best will be rewarded, providing incentives for the others to improve. Another frequently used simile is that a performance program is like a thermometer, or even a thermostat, not only accurately and independently reflecting changing conditions, but even indicating the sorts of responses to make. In this view, the program is set into operation after careful design and testing, and continues to produce information to policy-makers, requiring only routine maintenance and minor repairs. Neither simile is appropriate. Treating performance measurement like a game limits the uses to which measures can be put, because the emphasis is placed on getting higher scores rather than on understanding how those scores are generated and whether, in fact, they are worth achieving. The "packaging" of program evaluation and performance measurement programs tends to foster the second simile. Such packages are likely to necessitate substantial and continued redesign. Practices originally regarded as essential to police performance may later be shown as irrelevant. Both similes assume a greater knowledge of policing than is currently available.

A Learning Process
As a learning process, performance measurement can serve three functions: problem identification, program development, and theory building. Each local police agency in the United States has a number of constituents whose views on what police should do are relevant to the identification of problems requiring police attention. Learning what constituencies value

about policing is only part of the process of identifying problems. Police must also be aware of changes in and outside their community that may affect their work. It is difficult for police planners and executives to monitor circumstances or events that do not fall into the agency's current problem definitions. The initial stimulus for identifying new problems for police thus often comes from elsewhere. Newspaper articles, interest group lobbying, demonstrations, riots, and other dramatic occurrences are the usual "triggers" for the process that illuminates a new police problem. Often it is a change in values, not circumstances, that is behind the identification of a long-standing situation.

If learning what police problems are is one important aspect of performance measurement, learning how to deal with them is another. It is not enough to implement a new high-visibility, antiburglary program and then compile crime statistics. The steps in its implementation must be studied and assessed lest success or failure be incorrectly attributed. Many factors besides patrol visibility contribute to fluctuations in crime rates and must not be overlooked. In the end, performance measurement should tell police constituents not only whether the problem is getting better or worse, but also to what degree the changes are due to police efforts.

Theory building can evolve out of the everyday work of police. One would think that police—immersed in their organization and employment—would have a comprehensive knowledge of the processes through which their work affects the public, but systematic, theory-based knowledge of policing is only beginning to emerge. Performance measurement contributes to the development of theories and is likewise dependent upon those theories, forming a symbiotic relationship. Interpretation of data about performance depends on our understanding of causal associations; therefore a key element for improving measurement is the continual exchange of ideas and information between those who measure police performance and those who study policing and its social effects.

Types of Information Collected and Recorded
Most information collected by police is gathered for purposes of case management and personnel supervision. Many records are generated by operational units of the agency as the personnel in those units note information required for conducting service activities or initiating legal proceedings. Other data are collected from individual employees in order to review their activities:

1. *Calls for service.* A citizen requests police assistance.
2. *Offense and investigation reports.* A patrol officer records data gathered from the complainant(s), witness(es), and initial inspection of the scene.
3. *Arrest reports.* When a suspect is taken into custody and charged by the police, a record is made.
4. *Personnel activity reports.* The format and types of information collected daily on patrol activity vary by police agency. Usually there are spaces for officers to identify themselves and their assignments and to record the date, condition of vehicle and equipment, and mileage figures, among other notations.
5. *Field interrogation.* These forms are filled out for each field stop made by officers when no arrest or other formal action is taken. Field stops include the halting of suspicious vehicles or persons on the street.
6. *Vehicle and traffic reports.* Stolen and recovered vehicles, traffic accidents, and traffic citations comprise this category.
7. *Other police reports.* Recovered and impounded property, personnel actions, vehicle acquisition/use/maintenance, registration of private weapons, and issuance of various licenses are examples of miscellaneous report writing.

Despite this wealth of information, police performance measurement is not easy. Many police agencies in the United States have developed computer systems that allow the rapid search of files for information related to outstanding arrests, stolen or missing vehicles, missing persons, and other records. But computers have been used less for retrieving summary statistics from police records. This is because records are commonly filed as descriptive or narrative information, rather than as precoded information that can be readily counted or sorted. Moreover, police data typically do not include information about citizens' reactions to police service or other consequence of police activities. And, of course, data alone tell us nothing. Only as we use theories to interpret data can we measure performance.

Current police records provide a place to begin in designing performance measurement programs, but they must be examined critically. Simply because a department has been collecting data and has particular kinds of information available is not sufficient reason to conclude that those data measure important aspects of agency performance, or that the data accurately reflect conditions they are supposed to represent.

Gordon P. Whitaker
Stephen Mastrofski
Elinor Ostrom
Roger B. Parks
Stephen L. Percy

Bibliography

Jacob, Herbert, and Michael J. Rich. "The Effects of the Police on Crime: A Second Look." *Law and Society Review* 15 (1980): 109–22.

Silberman, Charles E. *Criminal Violence, Criminal Justice*. New York: Random House, 1980.

Skogan, Wesley G., and M.S. Maxfield. *Coping with Crime: Victimization, Fear, and Reactions to Crime*. Beverly Hills, CA: Sage, 1981.

Warr, Mark. "The Accuracy of Public Beliefs about Crime: Further Evidence." *Criminology* 20 (1982): 195–204.

Whitaker, Gordon P., et al. *Basic Issues in Police Performance*. Washington, DC: National Institute of Justice, 1982.

————, ed. *Understanding Police Agency Performance*. Washington, DC: National Institute of Justice, 1984.

Personnel Selection

Personnel costs typically account for more than eighty of every hundred taxpayer dollars expended in a police department budget. Thus effective personnel management in the police service is a crucial area of responsibility for managers both inside and outside the department.

Peter F. Drucker, management consultant and professor, has pointed out that managers are fond of saying, "Our greatest asset is people." He went on to add, however, that most managers know perfectly well that of all the resources, people are the least utilized and that little of the human potential of any organization is tapped and put to work. Indeed, he proposes that managers—private and public alike—in reality view their personnel in terms of problems, procedures, and costs, and he adds that contemporary personnel management has been heavily imbued with such thinking. As a result, personnel management policies and practices typically have been designed to categorize and control employees. While the traditional approach has its place, personnel management should begin to lead and to train in light of the new challenges confronting public organizations. Clearly such a recommendation, if implemented, would measurably stand to benefit the police service and would be significantly helpful during a period of unprecedented inquiry and concern over increasing the cost effectiveness of the police service versus an emphasis on the privatization of our government-produced police services.

Research shows that you can increase productivity by millions of dollars through the use of valid tests to select workers. Some readers may be skeptical of this statement. They know that many people who score poorly on a job-related test will do great work, and other people with high test scores perform poorly. However, on the average, an increase in one score point on a valid test increases the probability of good work performance by a measurable amount.

Issues and Standards

Issues usually emanate from standards, and goodness knows police personnel management has more than its fair share of both. The more contemporary and challenging issues and standards are as follows.

Merit Versus Representation. First there is the issue of merit versus representation. Simply stated, in personnel parlance merit denotes the principle that only "the best shall serve." This tenet was advanced by the National Civil Service League in 1881 and was promulgated by Congress in the benchmark Pendleton Act of 1883. Shortly before 1900 most local governments had followed suit by establishing similar charters or statutes. In 1970 Congress established as national policy six merit principles under the Intergovernmental Personnel Act, which served to promote a professional system of personnel administration.

The 1960s (particularly with the enactment of the Civil Rights Act of 1964) gave impetus to increasing the representation of minorities in private and public organizations. The term *affirmative action* is omnipresent in the minds of personnel managers. Today, to "the best shall serve" the words "on a representative basis" have been added. The theory and ethics involved are sound and are commendable, but the application of the principle has been filled with ambiguity and argument.

The Civil Rights Act of 1991 expanded the importance of the earlier acts by including discrimination in: (1) conditions of employment; (2) formation of the employment contract; and (3) compensatory and punitive damages for intentional discrimination. The Equal Employment Opportunity Commission (EEOC) issued a decision that compensatory damages for intentional discrimination can be awarded in an administrative proceeding. All of this means accidentally or intentionally discriminating against someone can be very costly to the offending agency.

Within the above acts and associated court case law is the growing litigation over sexual harassment in the work place. Similar to the above comment, it has cost the jobs of some police managers and officers. And it has cost some cities and counties a lot of money in the payment of damages to the victims. The main reason for mentioning this in this section is that the personnel unit and training unit in a police agency must coordinate their efforts to avoid such cases by appropriate training programs.

Sworn Careers versus Civilian Careers. Basically there are three reasons that police agencies employ civilian workers: (1) they're cheaper; (2) they have a unique job skill; and/or (3) they're performing tasks that the sworn complement dislike.

Many police agencies now count their number as 20 percent and growing. A few agencies have promoted civilians into supervisory and management positions. A few are accepted to full empowerment as a member of the police management team. Unfortunately, many civilians receive little or no recognition for the work they perform, have no career path, and are disparaged by their sworn counterparts. This must change.

Equal working conditions, opportunities for professional growth and personal achievement must be available to each and every civilian employee. They must be encouraged to comment on decisions that affect them. Artificial status barriers must be removed. "Glass ceilings" must be eliminated and "comparable worth" among jobs must prevail. With one in five, in some cases one in three, nonsworn people working within a police department today, this situation must be assessed and corrected as needed.

Civil Service Commissions versus Personnel Departments. In 1970 the National Civil Service League produced the sixth edition of its *Model Public Personnel Administration Law.* The proposed model law set the stage for a second dispute—that of civil service commissions versus personnel departments. Those defending the retention of civil service commissions underscore their past successes and the threat of political patronage. In turn, those advocating strong personnel agencies emphasize the increasing legal and administrative requirements for bureaucratic change. It appears that the trend is in favor of the model law mentioned above, and thus the responsibilities (if not the number) of commissions have been on the decline. Both have presented differing hurdles and frustrations to police agencies seeking fast, efficient, and effective selection and promotion of personnel.

Home Rule versus the Law. A third controversy roughly encompasses the claims of local autonomy (home rule) versus those of legal and/or statutory decisions. On the one hand we see the closely guarded sovereignty of state and local government; on the other we observe legalistic reforms emanating from the courts and political bodies—reforms that explicitly question the authority and independence of home rule. With respect to public personnel, for example, there has been a tendency to require different agency action programs to implement each of the multitude of special-interest employment provisions adopted in recent years. The question thus basically revolves around a matrix of administrative objectives (effectiveness) and legal requirements (social equity).

Labor's Rights versus Management's Prerogatives. The significance of a fourth debate—labor rights versus management prerogatives—has increased as the focus has shifted from the fundamental question of whether public employees should unionize to the current quandary over determining what is bargainable. We frequently see employee demands invading the domain of management prerogatives. At times the very essence of the merit principle has come under attack.

There are few more provocative subjects in police personnel administration today than the relationship between collective bargaining and merit. The probability of conflict between these two systems has hung like a dark cloud over the new collective-bargaining systems in public jurisdictions. Both systems have irreproachable objectives—in the case of collective bargaining, the participation by police employees in setting the terms and conditions of their work; and with regard to merit principles, the staffing of police agencies with the most able persons from all parts of our society.

In addition, public labor unions are frequently at odds with affirmative action laws. A tug-of-war is developing between the new laws forbidding discrimination in employment and such long-accepted labor union practices as seniority and fair representation. Seniority provisions, long considered a mainstay of the union contract, can be construed as inhibiting women and minorities from advancing up the ladder. Affirmative action plans to eliminate employment discrimination conflict in some cases with the rights and interests of employers and unions as stated in contract negotiations and in labor agreements.

Central Personnel Agency versus Departmental Unit. The last of the five issues focuses on the respective roles and responsibilities of the central (city-wide, countywide) personnel agency and the departmental personnel unit or specialist. Both should address the four subject areas just described. The larger the police agency the more likelihood of a departmental personnel unit. Whether there is a unit or a person assigned part-time to the personnel function, the following responsibilities should be considered as falling within the purview of the police agency:

1. Develop policies and instructions in all areas of police human resources administration, subject to the approval of the chief.
2. Serve as advisor to the chief and other line officials on personnel matters.
3. Develop an integrated management information system that includes all necessary personnel data, such as reporting of individual activity or performance.

4. Develop programs for the effective recruitment of qualified police and civilian applicants, including women and minorities.
5. Develop and administer systems of selection for appointment to the police service, including a program of background investigation and possibly psychiatric appraisals.
6. Develop criteria for promotion and a system of determining the relative qualifications of eligible officers in accordance with these criteria.
7. Administer a training program for all ranks (sworn and civilian), including entry training of recruits, in-service training of experienced officers, and training for advancement.
8. Develop a system of performance evaluation, including, where legal, an evaluation of promotion potential.
9. Develop and administer a system of position classification and assignment analysis to assure equal pay for equal work, as well as to form the basis for staff assignment and evaluation.
10. Develop a plan of adequate compensation, fairly distributed among ranks and assignments, including provision for differentials based on special hazards, shifts, or outstanding performance.
11. Represent the agency in negotiations or other meetings with representatives of organized employees, and develop a grievance procedure to minimize conflict within the agency.
12. Administer a program of exit interviews of resigning personnel, using information thus gathered to adjust unsatisfactory working conditions.
13. Develop a high level of morale and strong motivation among police personnel in order to obtain their greatest commitment to the goals of the agency.
14. Provide advice to line police managers at all levels concerning human resources problems, with special attention to leadership and disciplinary problems; and administer a program review of disciplinary actions and appeals.
15. Conduct a personnel research program.
16. Represent the police agency to the central personnel agency or civil service commission.

Old Standards versus New Standards: Americans with Disabilities Act (ADA) and the Age Discrimination in Employment Act of 1967 (ADEA). On July 26, 1994, all organizations were legally obligated to comply with ADA parameters. The purpose of the ADA is *not* to require police employers to recruit and hire a less-qualified candidate who is disabled over a more qualified candidate who is not. The operative word is "qualified." "Qualified individuals" means those people who can perform the essential requirements of the job with or without *reasonable accommodation.* Note that the "requirements" must not be arbitrarily constructed to exclude otherwise qualified individuals. The law basically says "an individual must satisfy the position's requirements in the areas of educational background, employment experience, and skills and/or requisite licenses." The person also must be able to perform the essential functions of the position with or without reasonable accommodation. Personnel managers should focus on what the job's requirements are *rather than on how the requirements are achieved.*

The two key issues with ADA are: (1) reasonable accommodation; and (2) what does "disability" mean. Reasonable accommodation is defined as modifying or adjusting the *job application process* and *work environment* to enable a qualified disabled person to perform the essential tasks of the job. If, however, the department can clearly demonstrate that the accommodation would present an "undue hardship" for the organization, then there is reasonable grounds for denying employment of that individual.

Congress opted for a very broad definition of disability to both physical and mental impairment that substantially limits one or more of the major life activities. Impairment ranges from AIDS to orthopedic to many more ailments but excludes sexual orientation and disorders due to drug abuse. Case law will soon expand and further refine what is and is not a disability.

Police personnel selection policies and procedures must be examined in light of ADA. Job requirements must be documented and factually demonstrated when necessary. Reasonable accommodations must be subjected to careful inquiry. Undue hardships in terms of accommodation must be identified and substantiated. Plainly put, *police organizations will be testing and hiring more and more people who would have been rejected in the past.*

In regard to ADEA, the personnel unit must experience both selection and retention policies and procedures. Mandatory retirement ages (e.g., 55) are being subjected to court scrutiny. It appears that the courts are rejecting mandatory retirement ages in favor of fairer (although more cumbersome) physical fitness standards and tests.

Some Workplace Diversity versus a Lot of Workplace Diversity. If you think your department consists of worker diversity now, just wait a few years and look back. Three influencing forces will cause even greater complexity in work force composition. First, our courts and our laws compel police departments to be "equal opportunity employers." In certain cases, we see police organizations being ordered to hire more of a particular type of person. Initially, the types were according to race or gender. A new type was identified a few years ago—disabled. There are likely to be more types added in the coming years.

Second, many new Americans have arrived and are continuing to make their home in the United States. Many of them originate from such Pacific Rim nations as the Philippine Islands, Cambodia, Laos, Vietnam, Taiwan, Hong Kong, and Korea. South of us, we see the Mexicans and Central Americans moving north. In the past few years, Eastern Europeans have also started to immigrate. The majority of them will enter the job market in the mid-1990s, and some will opt for police careers.

Third, it appears that our society is discounting unity or sameness in favor of diverseness or uniqueness. For example, the label of "American" is frequently being hyphenated to emphasize one's uniqueness (Irish-American, Italian-American, African-American, Mexican-American, Korean-American). Rather than clinging to the delusion of a "melting pot," we should recognize that many people are endeavoring to maintain their uniqueness—to make certain they get their fair share of the pie. And a major ingredient in this "pie" is one's opportunity to work.

It seems to me that the police manager will become responsible for leading police personnel who, while different in many ways, must learn to respect one another, work in harmony, and accept our interdependence and similarities as humankind. This will tax the best of leaders but it has been done before and must be accomplished now.

Manpower Planning: The Cornerstone of Successful Recruitment and Selection

Manpower planning includes the development, maintenance, and utilization of the skills of actual and potential members of the police agency. Moreover, it addresses the bottom-line question of *how many* and *who*, in terms of actual and potential employees, ought to be selected, trained, and utilized.

In the vast majority of police agencies the manpower planning process is divided between training of actual employees and personnel management of potential employees. While it is not essential that the process be performed by a single unit, the overall manpower policy should control and coordinate the individual activities.

Both training and personnel management require policy direction on at least three important issues. The first of these is the upgrading of the work force (e.g., upgrading the amount of in-service level of skill training, the minimum entry-level educational requirement, and the job-related, physical-strength standards). The second is the development and maintenance of a viable manpower resource pool (e.g., qualified and certified police-service candidates immediately ready to enter and effectively serve the agency on a full-time basis). The third is the implementation of equal employment opportunity programs (e.g., job-related testing; and elimination of cultural biases in recruitment, selection, assignment, and promotion). With all of this in mind, police service manpower planners have a major responsibility to have the *right number* of qualified people available to be hired and deployed at the *right time*.

Equal Employment Opportunity: Affirmative Action. The current state-of-the-art in affirmative action has resulted, ironically, in a "damned if you do, damned if you don't" situation. Most police agencies have developed active support for equal employment opportunity—as have police unions. In many cases this active support has been genuine and persistent. Unfortunately, in a few instances this has taken the form of cosmetic slogans, with very little substantive progress. So much of personnel management today (and this will apply well into the future) is affected by explicit affirmative action requirements that this subject is best discussed before other, more traditional components. Indeed, nondiscriminatory hiring, assignment, discipline, and promotion procedures are judged by many police chiefs and personnel managers as the most perplexing and frustrating of administrative decisions.

Title VII of the Civil Rights Act of 1964, as amended by the Equal Employment Opportunity Act of 1972, has become the modern civil rights muscle. Both its congressional history and its ramifications should be understood by police administrators when they formulate affirmative action policies, goals, and programs. Significantly, Title VII prohibits any discrimination on the basis of race, color, religion, sex, or national origin in all employment practices (including hiring, promotion, firing, compensation, and various other terms and conditions of employment) for employers having fifteen or more employees. In 1964 the U.S. Equal Employment Opportunity Commission (EEOC) was established to investigate violations of the Civil Rights Act of 1964. These guidelines became applicable to the public sector in 1972. The Civil Rights Act of 1991 adds further muscle to antidiscrimination efforts.

At the heart of the continuing controversy lies *test validation*. Test validation means that documented proof must exist showing that the test does in fact examine for job-related skills, knowledge, abilities, and for job behavior (SKA/JB). Selection criteria, methods, and instruments are being challenged in the courts—in other words, the validity of the tests used in selecting, assigning, and promoting employees is under close scrutiny. Validity may be expressed thus: Does the test in reality measure what it was intended to measure? One does not measure weight with a yardstick. Associated with the concept of validity are the equally important subjects of *job task analysis* and *cultural impartiality*.

Recruitment: Attracting Qualified Resources

The fundamental goal of recruitment is to attract qualified people to serve as sworn and civilian police employees. The term *qualified* denotes persons who possess, or can acquire through entry-level training, the requisite SKA/JBs to effectively perform the assigned tasks/duties. When there are difficulties with the image of the police agency, low salaries, and fringe benefits, and/or a shortage of people with existing or innate qualifications, constraining residency requirements, and complicated administrative procedures, quite obviously there will be burdensome hurdles confronting any recruitment effort.

Fortunately, the police service is looked upon as the source of a highly important helping activity—the protection of life and property. Thus any potential limitations on a successful recruitment program may be offset by the following incentives: a purposeful job, a stimulating set of responsibilities, a collegial working environment, reasonable pay and benefits, opportunities for career advancement, and job security. The 1990s may see *fewer* qualified people applying for police agency positions than there are job openings. The key, therefore, will be to attempt to attract the *most qualified* for purposes of the next phase—selection: hence the continuing paramount significance of recruitment. The quality and the effectiveness of the police service, then, starts with recruitment.

Sources of the Resources. Those responsible for recruiting may find potential applicants through a variety of sources, including current police employees and other city/county employees, walk-ins and write-ins, educational institutions, employment services, and consultants and professional job recruiters. Attractive, imaginative, and current literature and application forms should be available at all times.

Interaction with the Resources. Among the ways of making contact with potential police personnel are the following: posted and mailed job vacancy announcements; advertising (newspapers, radio, and television); recruitment task force teams; visits, displays, and open houses; work-study programs and internships; cooperative recruiting efforts; and professional associations. These techniques are equally applicable to recruiting for entry-level and supervisory and management police personnel. In addition to making any printed information attractive, it is important that such information clearly expresses minimum job requirements, the duties/tasks of a police officer, the working environment, the pay and benefits, and other relevant employment conditions and expectations.

Management Responsibility. The recruitment and selection of personnel for the police service is a basic responsibility of management. This responsibility can no more be farmed out to other government agencies than can management's responsibility to organize, plan, or budget. To do so is to abdicate a management func-

tion that is crucial to the proper operation of any organization.

The primary concern of police agencies should be the quality rather than the residence of police personnel. Artificial preemployment residency requirements limit the number of applicants from among whom qualified candidates may be selected.

One of the most effective recruiting techniques is to involve *all* police agency personnel in recruitment activities by providing incentives for their participation. The benefits of such a program are twofold: more personnel become involved in recruiting than could be assigned specifically to such duties by the agency; and because of their professional interest, police personnel generally recruit better qualified candidates.

Selection and Assignment

Police personnel selection denotes the preferential choosing of human talent for the police service in accordance with the tasks/duties of the job. As has been mentioned earlier, the selection process actually begins with recruitment. The succeeding stages are examination, certification, and assignment (placement). The traditional point of emphasis, as it will be here, is examination. The primary intent of an examination or test is to identify those applicants who possess or are likely to possess the highest degree of SKA/JBs needed to fulfill the job requirements. (It should be remembered that tests throughout the recruitment sequence—both before and after the training or academy program—must be validated and must be planned in relation to the training skills taught.)

The purpose of the test is the key to deciding what type, format, and content to administer. A brief discussion of traditional merit-system tests appears immediately below. Following this, a newer method of examining is explored—the use of assessment centers.

Traditional Testing. The four major categories of testing in terms of police agency personnel decisions are the following: (1) entry level (for new employees); (2) lateral entry (for experienced police personnel acquired from other police agencies—for the same position and for promotion); (3) promotional (open or closed to external competition); and (4) specialized assignments (e.g., crime prevention and narcotics). Table 1 shows the typical examination techniques as they relate to these four categories.

It is significant to note the last two techniques cited in Table 1: training and probation. The frequency of application is poor except under entry-level decisions. Ironically, these techniques have consistently demonstrated their highest reliability in predicting a new employee's job effectiveness (the main reason being that there is a much longer exposure to an individual's SKA/JBs in a learning and job-related environment—or training—and in actual on-the-job performance). Fortunately, some police agencies have recognized the immense utility of training and probation as mechanisms for selection. Applied in tandem they significantly increase a department's accuracy about a person's talent to successfully perform the duties/tasks of a police officer.

Assessment Center. Briefly, an assessment is a carefully planned process composed of situation-based tests that are clearly job related and are administered in a single and expanded time frame. Many of the traditional techniques of testing are also present in an AC. The answer to the query "Why ACs?" seems self-evident. First and foremost, the traditional civil service paper/pencil and oral board interviews and other appraisal processes are just not cutting it. Concisely put, they inculcate too many inadequacies. In fact, some have accused the present system of inadvertently fostering the Peter Principle (promoting—or in some cases retaining—people to their highest level of incompetency). Second, the majority of those who have experienced the traditional means of having one's skills tested are vociferously asking for a more accurate method of doing so. Third, to these two concerns I would add those of the police manager, which can be posed as follows: "I am in need of a decidedly better process—legally, ethically, and politically—for making personnel decisions. Decisions that, in turn, explicitly impact such organization-wide concerns as affirmative action, productivity, and social equity."

An AC can be used for a variety of purposes and structured in an infinite number of ways. Typically, however, assessment spans one to two days. The latter is preferable in that the candidates spend more time with the assessors. The ratio of assessor to candidate is important: The more assessors to the assessees, the better. One assessor per two candidates is ideal, although in some cases a higher ratio—if carefully planned and if the assessors are experienced—can be effective. Basically there are five major

TABLE 1

Types of Selection Techniques as Applied to Testing Categories

	Category of Testing			
Selection Technique	Entry Level	Lateral Entry	Promotional	Specialized Assignments
Application verification	F	F	F	R
Paper and pencil test	F	F	F	O
Physical agility	F	O	R	R
Panel interview (oral board)	F	F	F	O
Medical	F	F	O	R
Psychiatric	F	O	O	R
Background inquiry	F	F	F	R
Performance ratings	N/A	F	F	F
Appraisal of promotability, assignment	N/A	N/A	F	F
Rating of résumé	N/A	F	F	O
Professional search agency	R	R	O	R
Exempt appointment	R	R	O	F
Training	F	O	O	O
Probationary period	O	O	O	O
Assessment centers	R	R	O	R

Key: F = frequently   O = occasionally   R = rarely   N/A = not applicable considerations to be dealt with in establishing an AC: (1) job requirements—skills, knowledge, and abilities; (2) methodology—exercises and instruments; (3) training of assessors; (4) time frame; and (5) ratio of assessors to candidates. Decisions on these elements directly and primarily influence the costs and benefits of an AC.

To the Year 2000
On its path to the year 2000, police personnel management is likely to experience a confluence of challenges that will tax its stamina and acumen:

- The professionalization of the *police* personnel manager. (Incidentally, this person is apt to be a civilian with a rank equivalent to a police manager.)
- A constantly changing workplace (e.g., decentralization, computers) and work force (e.g., older workers, racial minorities, females, paraprofessionals, and the handicapped).
- Personnel management will increasingly encompass and emphasize *human resource management.*
- New and improved alternative testing methods and technological support for these methods (e.g., computers, audiovisual aids, and assessment centers).
- A requirement for greater innovation and success in attracting and employing people. (As of 1983 we entered the "baby bust" era; therefore, until 2000 there are fewer people available for the growing number of jobs.) Fortunately, the majority of our police managers are adept problem-solvers and competitive by nature.

Paul M. Whisenand

Bibliography

Bopp, William J., and Paul Whisenand. *Police Personnel Administration*. 2d ed. Boston: Allyn & Bacon, 1980.
Dunnette, Marvin D., et al. *Police Selection and Career Assessment*. Washington, DC: U.S. Department of Justice, LEAA, 1976.
Felkenes, George T., and Peter C. Unsinger. *Diversity, Affirmative Action, and Law Enforcement*. Springfield, IL: Charles C. Thomas, 1992.
Kelly, Michael J. *Police Chief Selection: A Handbook for Local Government*. Washington, DC: Police Foundation, 1975.
More, Harry W., and W. Fred Wegener. *Behavioral Police Management*. New York: Macmillan, 1992.
O'Leary, Lawrence R. *The Selection and Promotion of the Successful Police Officer*. Springfield, IL: Charles C. Thomas, 1979.
Special Data Issue: Police Personnel Recruitment and Special Training Programs. Washington, DC: International City Management Association, 1991.
Spielberger, Charles D., ed. *Police Selection and Evaluation: Issues and Techniques*. New York: Hemisphere, 1979.
Talley, Joseph E. *Performance Prediction of Public Safety and Law Enforcement Personnel: A Study in Race and Gender Differences and MMPI Subscales*. Springfield, IL: Charles C. Thomas, 1990.

Physical Fitness Standards

There was a time when police officers were chosen because of appearance. One of Sir Robert Peel's requirements was that the "policeman must maintain a good appearance, which commands respect of citizens." Scholars may surmise that he intended for them to be physically fit, i.e., "good in appearance," but was that in fact what he meant? A cursory review of basic fundamental requirements of police officers shows that "physical requirements" more often refers to height, weight, eyesight, etc. Occasionally it was stated that strength and agility must be demonstrated by running, jumping, and weight lifting tests.

Throughout law-enforcement history, especially in the United States, little emphasis has been placed on the police being physically fit. Up until the latter part of the twentieth century police for the most part have remained "fat, dumb, and happy."

In recent years there has been an increased interest in the physical fitness of police officers but little research has been done. A major research effort in physical fitness was accomplished by Price et al. (1976), which resulted in the document "Physical Fitness Programs for Law Enforcement Officers: A Manual for Police Administrators." This research was one of the first studies that presented a systematic plan for the development and evaluation of programs and methods that could be used to ensure

P

a high level of physical fitness among police personnel.

A more recent study by Tracy and Burns (1992) is called "Health and Fitness Changes: A Two-and-a-Half Year Study" and was conducted for the Idaho Department of Law Enforcement. This study resulted in the department's health and wellness program policies and procedures.

It is a well-documented fact that police officers live in an extremely stressful environment from a psychological point of view, yet little is done to mandate physical fitness standards for police officers. There are no standards among agencies and no emphasis on physical fitness other than a physical exam and a physical fitness/agility exam as part of the testing procedure. Even the Commission on Accreditation for Law Enforcement Agencies (1984:32) does not address the issue of physical fitness beyond requiring agencies to have a "physical fitness exam using valid useful and non-discriminatory procedures." With this in mind, let us review the current state of physical fitness and present data for trainers and administrators regarding mandatory fitness programs.

The Current State of Fitness
A review of the literature indicates that although there is some discussion related to physical fitness, much of the material is descriptive in nature and the topic lacks a primary focus. The available literature does, however, present some interesting research results.

Tracy and Burns (1992:4) state that a 1981 study of the Idaho Department of Law Enforcement medical examinations confirmed the need for fitness programming by revealing significant health risks among commissioned employees: 51 percent were overweight, 35 percent had elevated blood lipids, 32 percent were smokers, 20 percent had a family history of heart disease, 16 percent were hypertensive, and 2 percent were diabetic. The goal of the Idaho Department of Law Enforcement's Health and Wellness Program is simply to enhance the health status and quality of department employees and their families. The department has twenty-two fitness coordinators located at duty stations around the state. They educate peers, administer physical fitness assessments, provide individualized fitness and nutrition counseling, monitor progress, report results, and encourage employees and dependents to make healthy lifestyle choices.

Quire and Blount (1990) present research results that clearly indicate that police officers can reduce their cholesterol level and risk of heart attack. They state that heart disease has been identified as the leading cause of death or retirement among police officers. Their study examined officers from the St. Petersburg, Florida, Police Department, who received medical examinations every two years. These examinations were part of a physical fitness program developed by the Department's Research and Development Section. The results showed that when the average total cholesterol levels were compared to general population standards, all of the age groups were found to have a low coronary risk. The age group that differed the most favorably were those persons forty to forty-nine years of age. Quire and Blount attribute the results to the efforts made by the department to make its officers aware of the steps they can take to reduce the risk of heart disease through a program that is entirely personal and virtually impossible to ignore, and that provides the means to control and reduce their risk.

Farenholtz and Rhodes (1990) completed a comprehensive task analysis of the physical work associated with the performance of Canadian police officers in their duties. The purpose of the study was to develop a physical test to measure the minimal physical abilities required for police tasks. The data collected led to the development of the Police Officers' Physical Abilities Test (POPAT), which involves a 440–yard run and includes tests of jumping, lifting, carrying, mobility and agility, stair-climbing, obstacle avoidance, and cardiovascular fitness.

In 1989 the Governors Panel to Review Police Training Programs in Massachusetts offered recommendations to tighten medical and physical screening requirements and to improve physical fitness and reduce health risk during training.

McDermott (1986) found the existence of a wide variety of programs designed to address the mental and physical stress of the police environment. He suggested that the national interest in fitness is directly related to evidence that police officer's health is deteriorating. McDermott's analysis led to the development of future scenarios, the most optimistic of which suggests mandated physical fitness standards as a condition of employment. He also theorizes specific steps police departments could use in implementing a fitness program.

In 1986 the Federal Bureau of Investigation's Training Division Research and Development Unit mailed a training needs survey packet to 2,497 police agencies across the United States. The survey had been requested by the United States Department of Justice in order to prioritize the allocation of federal funds in the area of training. The survey results indicated that handling personal stress and maintaining an appropriate level of physical fitness ranked one and two, respectively, in programs most requested by police officers. In the Price et al. (1976) study regarding police department–sponsored physical fitness programs, over 1,900 officers participated in the survey. Ninety percent of the officers responding were in favor of a department-sponsored physical fitness program. These surveys reflect that the vast majority of officers want physical fitness programs and have for some time.

T.R. Collingwood, in a lecture at the Cooper Institute for Research, stated that police officers in the United States are about ten years behind the active population in the area of physical fitness. Collingwood (1988) also stated that physical fitness programs were now being viewed as a necessity within the law-enforcement community and that mandatory physical fitness standards were becoming institutionalized. Bracy (1988:2) found in a recent study that "due to largely poor diet and lack of exercise, a significant sample of American police possessed a body composition, blood chemistry, and general level of physical fitness greatly inferior to that of a similar sized sample of convicts." To emphasize this point, Healey (1981) asks the questions, "What healthy 40-year-old police officer would bet he could win a foot race with a healthy 20-year-old suspect when the police officer has an additional 18 pounds of clothing and equipment to contend with?" (p. 67).

Healey also presents a convincing argument that management has a fitness responsibility. He suggests that physical fitness is a "tool" and is an extension of the most important unit of the police department, the individual. Healey exhorts that "without police fitness standards, a police department has too many 'loose wires' to account for. It is unfair to place the burden of quality effectiveness on each individual without presenting a plan that will achieve these goals" (67). In conclusion, Healey remarks that it is ironic that "elected officials can crack jokes concerning an officer's death due to a lack of fitness" (68), but not take any

steps to mandate fitness for the police. In other words, nobody seems to take responsibility for physical fitness: not management, applicants, or incumbents.

Nay (1989) cites several court cases that even challenge physical fitness standards for recruits. To further illustrate this attitude of nonresponsibility, the courts have carefully noted that in some instances, incumbents do not have to be examined annually for physical fitness.

It is difficult to understand why officers are lagging behind in fitness when they and management have at their beck and call numerous publications about fitness and nutrition. There are fitness centers in low density population areas and there are numerous television programs on fitness, yet officers are not motivated by police managers and local politicians to become physically fit, even though they know the risks.

However, several articles have appeared that indicate there might be a change. Grimes and Shaw (1991) state that in order to assess a police officer's muscular and aerobic fitness levels and to influence the health risk factors that impact on their cardiovascular health, the University of Delaware and the New Castle County Police Department have adopted the diagnostic and preventive approach developed by Cardio-Kinetics, Inc.

This method of evaluation employs sophisticated testing equipment and includes follow-up testing every six to twelve months. The benefits to the department include reduced absenteeism, improved morale, and decreased disabilities and health-care expenditures (45).

Arliss (1991) outlines a cardiovascular risk assessment initiated by the New York Police Department. The risk assessment is available to all officers and all precincts and is performed by a team of civilian registered nurses. Funding for the cardiovascular risk assessment program comes from police unions through the Police Relief Fund. Cost savings realized with the program include a reduction in days lost due to illness and a decrease in injuries and their attendant costs (22).

Firearms and Fitness
Many police officers consider themselves invincible because they are the police (police mentality). They believe that their training with firearms will answer a majority of situations. In a study by Ness (1989) of the Illinois Minimum Standards Basic Law Enforcement Curriculum, it was found that officers rated their training in

physical activity as inadequate, while their training in firearms was rated as adequate and in some academies it was rated more than adequate. A study by Talley (1984) revealed similar results of the Michigan basic training curriculum. It can be readily concluded that police academies, and consequently the police, tend to rely more on firearms training than physical fitness training.

Relying on firearms as a means to protect officers and to apprehend offenders will many times fall short. In 1985, the Supreme Court in *Tennessee v. Garner* restricted the use of deadly force in apprehending a fleeing, nondangerous felon. Now officers must be in adequate condition to enable them to pursue and subdue without "firearm dependence."

To illustrate the fact that officers are physically unfit and reliant on firearms, some officers are having their own weapons taken from them in the line of duty and then are being shot with that weapon. According to the *International Chiefs of Police Newsletter* (1988), from January to November 1988 a total of twelve officers were slain with their own weapon. According to the FBI *Uniform Crime Reports*, a total of sixty-nine officers were killed in the line of duty in 1991.

The question then arises, do officers have the strength, flexibility, endurance, and the necessary weapons retention training to prevent their weapons from being taken? If officers cannot protect themselves, they cannot protect the public they serve.

In instances where officers have used firearms inappropriately, a common thread seems to emerge. Specifically, officers believe they are not physically able to do anything else but shoot, which creates panic and bad judgment. Fitness could possibly give these officers the confidence, ability, and endurance to try other alternatives, which could include defense tactics and/or impact weapons. Firearms expertise alone is not enough. Special Agent Bob Rogers of the physical training unit at the FBI Academy remarked at one of his lectures that "some officers have their fitness program on their hip."

Detriments and Benefits to Fitness
The Surgeon General of the United States stated in a press release in early 1988 that smoking remains the single most important preventable cause of death in the United States. It is a well-documented fact that smoking causes approximately 390,000 deaths annually, that smoking is a major cause of strokes, and that among women, lung cancer exceeds breast cancer. Although the authors do not know of any study relating to police officers and smoking, how many officers are seen smoking and drinking a cup of coffee? Lifestyle and poor food choices are other areas of concern for police officers and the general public. Police officers literally kill themselves with their lifestyle.

Another detriment to not being fit is vulnerable appearance. The vulnerable appearance that some officers have may actually encourage others to "try" them. Strong-arm robbers, who were interviewed after their apprehension, suggested that they chose their victim because they would not offer resistance. This "vulnerability" is determined by the victims' overall appearance, stance, alertness, and demeanor. Which raises the question: Do some officers look so vulnerable that they actually invite an attack or challenge? Fitness could possibly remove the perception that potential offenders have of some police officers.

The adverse effects of the lack of fitness are overwhelming, the positive benefits are often overlooked. According to an article in the *New England Journal of Medicine*, a person can expect to live an additional one or two hours for every hour spent on physical fitness. Physical fitness is also known to reduce stress, and an officer tends to be more confident in confrontations. Being physically fit also promotes self-esteem, improves the quality of life, improves firearms accuracy, and allows officers to be more effective with impact weapons and defense tactics.

Not only does the individual benefit from fitness but the agency also benefits. Physically fit officers use less sick time, they increase public respect for the agency, and they show improved attitudes toward others. Physically fit officers also tend to be involved in fewer lawsuits in the area of excessive force and show increased productivity. There is a tendency in agencies promoting physical fitness for an increased rapport between the administration and other personnel because of the perceived caring attitude demonstrated by the agency. Finally, the agency benefits from physically fit officers in that fitness tends to prevent premature retirement and on-the-job injuries.

Mandatory Programs versus Voluntary Programs
There are numerous areas to consider when implementing mandatory physical fitness pro-

grams. Law-enforcement administrators must be aware of the legal aspects, the cost factors, safety of officers, morale, and collective bargaining agreements. All of these areas will have an impact on the program. Perhaps it will be more workable and desirable to have only voluntary fitness programs. However, conversations with various police agencies and reviews of the literature indicate that voluntary physical fitness programs do not have a consistent majority of officers participating. There may be an initial rush into a program but the interest is not maintained. About 10 to 15 percent may become involved for a time. Officers who really need a program will not participate voluntarily.

The lack of volunteer participation may sound contradictory from the survey results just mentioned; however, there is a vast difference between knowing that a program should be implemented and actually maintaining involvement in the program, particularly when there is no support from the top. In addition, not knowing how to begin a program, the lack of attainable goals, and the intimidation factor also cause officers to stay uninvolved in physical fitness programs.

Legal Considerations
To accomplish police tasks, officers at any given time may have to run, jump, wrestle, shoot, push, swim, and punch. In essence police officers are athletes. We expect the high school, college, and professional athlete to be fit; however, there is no demand or expectation that police officers be fit, even though they may have to engage in all of those physical activities without warning.

Courts are beginning to recognize that police officers are "athletes" and must perform certain physical tasks to be effective. In *United States v. City of Wichita Falls.* (1988), the court held that the City of Wichita Falls could conduct physical assessment tests for persons seeking employment with the police department, and in addition, the training academy could require physical agility testing after the recruits had entered the academy. The United States, through the Department of Justice, alleged that Wichita Falls had been engaged in the practice of sex discrimination, which was in violation of Title VII of the Civil Rights Act of 1964.

The physical assessment test at Wichita Falls is a test of general physical condition in which the applicant is tested in five areas of fitness:

1. Cardiovascular function
2. Body composition
3. Flexibility
4. Dynamic strength
5. Absolute strength.

The physical agility test is a test of specific strengths and motor abilities, which is related to the police function.

The court found that the tasks performed during physical agility testing are the tasks that a police officer should perform. Furthermore, the court found that tests are "operational necessities for a Wichita Falls police officer." The court concluded that the tests conducted by Wichita Falls were valid tests and stated that officers are confronted daily in situations where "they move rapidly, use physical force and stress their cardiovascular system."

Thomas, Means, and Brandon (1989) state that the legal risk is great where agencies determine who the unfit officers are through mandatory health or fitness assessment testing and do not have a remedial program, which improves the officer's fitness level and/or removes the officer from street duty. The documentation as to the test results and assignment would be available to plaintiffs in litigation matters.

In a 1988 case, *Parker v. District of Columbia*, an officer shot an offender whom the officer could not subdue. The offender was not armed. The court found in favor of the plaintiff after considering two issues: failure to train in arrest procedures and deficient physical fitness programs. The court concluded that the officer's condition posed a foreseeable risk of harm to others due to his inadequate physical condition. Records indicated that the officer had had no training in these areas for years.

Physical Fitness Test vs. Physical Ability (or Job Task Performance Test)
A battery of tests for physical fitness would involve the items listed below:

a.	Strength	Bench Press
b.	Flexibility	Sit and Reach
c.	Muscular Endurance	Sit-ups
d.	Cardiovascular Endurance	1.5 Mile Run
e.	Body Fat Percentage	Skinfold Test

Normative tables that are adjusted for age, sex, and weight are compared for results to establish a level for scoring. Each separate test result is averaged for a total fitness score. There may be less of a risk for lawsuits than the job task test, due to the comparison to others of their own weight, sex, and age (Thomas, Means, and Brandon, 1989:2).

The job task performance (or ability) test is based on specific physical tasks that a police officer must be able to learn during his or her tour of duty. Examples include pushing a vehicle, climbing over a wall, and carrying a 150-pound person twenty yards. All officers must perform these tasks regardless of age, sex, or weight, as these tasks are necessary to their job. To clarify, a physical ability test involves the performance of a job task, whereas a physical fitness test measures one's health status.

Mandatory Testing and Enforcement of Standards

According to Schofield (1989), to be enforceable, mandatory standards must be reasonable and rational. The Supreme Court states that the Constitution allows enforcement on the standards that have a rational basis, that consist of documented logic on health needs, and are "fairly implemented."

Under Title VII, the legality of a specific standard depends upon the impact. Job-related proof is required where mandatory standards have a disparate impact on women. Standards with no disparate impact under Title VII are constitutional if related standards are used rationally.

Schofield further states that the courts' using the "rational basis" analysis initially assumes the validity of the standards utilized, such as a nonsmoking rule, as it has a rational relationship to a governmental interest of employee's health and safety. Another example is visual acuity testing.

Steps to a Program

Legal counsel at the FBI Academy in Quantico, Virginia, suggests the following recommendations for a fitness program:

1. Start a mandatory wellness program as a first step, which would include information on a healthier lifestyle, such as nutrition, stopping smoking, and the benefits of exercise. In addition a physical exam could be included.
2. Be aware of and avoid any negative impact that might occur, particularly on a protected group until the program is deemed job related.
3. Before any mandatory standard is implemented, consult with fitness experts and legal counsel to ensure its legality.

Chronology of Litigation Involving Physical Fitness Testing

The following is a short chronology of litigation involving the Illinois Local Governmental Law Enforcement Officers Training Board and the challenge they faced involving the power test.

September 3, 1987, the Training Board established implementation date for Power Test as January 1, 1988.

December 3, 1987, Chicago officials appeared before the Training Board to delay the implementation of the Power Test. The Chicago Police Department was concerned that a pending case, *Dyer-Neely v. Chicago,* which involved the city's selection standards, would conflict with the state-mandated Power Test requirement.

June 2, 1988, the Training Board agreed to halt the Power Test of recruits as an academy entrance requirement pending outcome of the *Dyer-Neely* class suit.

August 26, 1988, the federal court in *United States v. Wichita Falls,* Texas, issued its order ruling the Cooper Aerobic Test created no adverse impact and met appropriate testing standards. The Training Board decided to reinstate the Power Test.

The City of Chicago backed the Training Board in its decision to resume the test, and the Power Test was not challenged by the *Dyer-Neely* class action suit in federal court.

July 26, 1990, the Americans with Disabilities Act (ADA) was signed into law, effective July 26, 1992.

Years of study and review by the Training Board, and in accordance with the consultants' opinion (Cooper Aerobic Institute), indicate that the Power Test is job related.

In light of the Civil Rights Act of 1991, the deputy chief of Litigation at the U.S. Department of Justice advises that the act may not apply to the Power Test because of "inherent differences" in the physical ability of genders. The purpose of the law is understood to address different treatment when inherently similar abilities are being measured.

Legal counsel for the Training Board advises that the Civil Rights Act of 1991 should not affect the administration of the Power Test as the Training Board is not the employer and the test uses the same measurement level of fitness for all applicants—40 percent. To require a numerical standard for both sexes not based on the same level of fitness would discriminate between the sexes.

In 1992, legal counsel for the Training Board states that in his opinion there does not appear to be a reason to discontinue the Power Test at this time.

Some Current Programs in Effect

Federal Bureau of Investigation
The FBI requires physical fitness testing for special agent applicants, trainees, and those agents on the job. A pre-employment physical fitness test is administered in four areas: body fat measurement, one minute of sit-ups, the maximum number of push-ups, and a 1.5 mile walk-run. Applicants must be in excellent physical condition with no defects that could hamper firearms use, defensive tactics or raids, and dangerous assignments. Vision and hearing requirements are strict. The new special agent is taught how to proceed with conditioning to meet the fitness tests and rating scales used to determine whether the person stays in the training program. During training the trainee is administered a fitness test that includes pull-ups, push-ups, sit-ups, a 120-yard shuttle run, and a two-mile run.

Special agents on the job receive fitness-for-duty physical examinations once every three years until the age of thirty-three. Then they are examined annually. There are fitness advisers in each of the field offices and at headquarters in Washington.

Idaho Department of Law Enforcement
The Idaho Department of Law Enforcement Health and Wellness Program was implemented in April 1991 to improve the employees' health, decrease disabilities, and enhance job performance. The program is available to and for the benefit of all full-time and part-time employees, their spouses, and in some instances other dependents. Periodic medical examinations, physical fitness assessments, individualized exercise and nutrition prescriptions, and fitness standards are mandatory for commissioned personnel. Noncommissioned personnel, employees' spouses, and excepted commissioned personnel may participate on a voluntary basis.

For commissioned personnel there are mandatory medical screenings (every three years for those under the age of thirty-five; every two years for those thirty-five to forty-nine; and every year for those over fifty). The department fitness assessment test battery measures five components. They are:

1. Skinfold measurement to measure body composition
2. Push-ups (sixty seconds) to measure upper body muscular strength and endurance
3. Sit-ups (sixty seconds) to measure abdominal muscular strength and endurance
4. Sit and reach test to measure flexibility at hip joint
5. 1.5 mile run/walk, one mile walk, or stationary bike test to estimate cardiorespiratory endurance.

Officers are required to attain and maintain themselves at or above the fiftieth percentile level for each fitness test. There are also incentives with the program such as using duty time for physical conditioning training.

Knoxville, Tennessee, Police Department
The Knoxville, Tennessee, Police Department developed a physical conditioning manual that contains the department's general order establishing guidelines for officers' physical qualifications and standards and includes a job-related physical fitness program for officers.

The general order explains procedures for the physical qualifications tests for applicants, recruits, and officers. It also describes the physical fitness incentive program and physical examinations. Exercises for the job-related physical fitness program are designed to improve officers' physical ability to perform physically demanding job tasks and enhance general fitness.

Ohio State Patrol
The Ohio State Patrol has implemented a health and fitness program for all of their officers. Participation in mandatory physical fitness and a progressive discipline policy is currently in effect. Their policy is also part of their labor contract.

The Ohio program is geared toward a "high quality of life during the trooper's active career period and into retirement." Incumbent troopers who fail minimum fitness standards will be subject to discipline in March of 1991. New recruits are subject to the entire program after graduation from the academy. In June of 1989 the program was implemented for all nonbargaining unit supervisors.

St. Louis Police Department

In October of 1986, the St. Louis, Missouri, Police Department began mandatory physical fitness testing and a voluntary wellness program for police officers. The fitness program requires that officers be tested annually for certain physical abilities to determine a fitness level. Any officer who fails to meet minimum standards is placed on limited duty for a period of ninety days. If no improvement is shown after ninety days, the officer is removed from active duty as the officer is considered a risk. The officer has a choice of using vacation time, personal time, or sick time; if none of these is available the officer must request a furlough without pay.

California Highway Patrol

The California Highway Patrol has been physically testing officers since 1979. Currently mandatory tests are administered annually. There are minimum job standards for officers hired after January 1, 1984. Officers appointed prior to this date may lose benefits if the exam is failed, as the tests are considered job related. All entry level tests and mandatory tests for uniformed personnel are based on job-related physical activities that officers are routinely involved in.

In January of 1984, the Highway Patrol was involved in court action brought by the California Association of Highway Patrolmen. The association was granted a preliminary injunction that prohibited any demotion or dismissal of officers. Prior to the trial the association and the Highway Patrol reached an agreement, as follows:

1. Mandatory physical performance testing for all traffic officers.
2. Officers who fail and were appointed prior to January 1, 1984, shall be denied special assignments, promotion, and voluntary overtime opportunities if they fail the tests.
3. Officers who fail and are appointed after January 1, 1984, shall be denied special duty assignments, promotion, overtime programs, merit raises, transfers, second-

ary employment, and are subject to other action, including dismissal.

The physical performance program consists of the work task, the test for the task, and the standard required for that test.

The State of Illinois

Like many states, the state of Illinois has instituted a back-door approach to physical fitness for entry-level police officers. While most law-enforcement training academies have physical fitness testing, the vast majority of police agencies do not require officers to keep physically fit after returning from recruit training. The Illinois Local Governmental Law Enforcement Officers Training Board (1987) instituted fitness testing for recruits at the various training facilities. These physical fitness standards consist of five areas:

- Aerobic Capacity or Cardiovascular Endurance
- Strength
- Flexibility
- Abdominal Muscular Endurance
- Body Weight and Body Composition.

All of the above tests are conducted according to age and sex.

Great Bend, Kansas, Police Department

The Great Bend, Kansas, Police Department began a five-year implementation program in 1984. The physical agility test is administered to all commissioned police officers twice per calendar year. The stated purpose of the test is to promote fitness among officers through exercise, to promote good health, decrease the use of sick leave and job related accidents, improve alertness, and to maintain a comfortable appearance.

The physical agility events include the following:

1. Push-ups
2. Sit-ups
3. Vertical Jump
4. Agility Run
5. 1.5-Mile Run.

Officers are divided into categories based on age and must score a specified number of minimum points to pass. Failure to meet the standards results in disciplinary action. For the first failure officers receive a written warning; for the third failure officers receive a five-day suspension.

Hazelwood, Missouri, Police Department

The Hazelwood Police Department has a physical fitness program that involves health screening, individualized health programs, and physical fitness testing. This city of 16,000 crafted a mandatory fitness program designed to meet legal challenges if personnel must be disciplined when failing to meet standards. Each officer participates in a two-part health screening that consists of obtaining medical information from the officer through questionnaires and interviews. Medical tests include measures of heart rate and blood pressure as well as an exercise stress test. Based on screening, officers undertake individualized physical fitness rehabilitation. To ensure that officers maintain a fitness standard, an annual physical fitness test includes a timed 1.5-mile run or 3-mile walk, a bench press, sit-ups, and a sit and reach test. After initial screening officers have three years to pass the test before being disciplined.

Collective Bargaining Agreements

Should a law-enforcement agency's physical fitness program be a part of the collective bargaining agreement? Ayers and Coble (1987) state that a police administrator's primary obligation is the protection of life and property. To fulfill this obligation the administrator must have the rights and freedom to accomplish this.

Some of the basic rights that could be affected by a fitness program as part of a collective bargaining agreement are:

1. Planning, directing, and controlling department operations
2. Disciplining and firing officers
3. Determining performance standards
4. Training officers and determining criteria. (6)

Ayers and Coble further write that "managers who cannot discipline and even fire employees who refuse to conform to departmental directives cannot maintain the public's trust"(7).

Even if an adequate fitness program is agreed upon by all parties to the bargaining agreement, is this a further erosion of management's rights? Could any change or improvement in the program be implemented by management in the future without labor disputes and/or court action?

Americans with Disabilities Act (ADA) Civil Rights of 1991 Considerations

The 1991 Civil Rights Act (Amendment to Title VII) prohibits adjusting scores (norming) for hiring or promotion. Specifically, the physical performance tests such as "timed runs" that allow more time for females due to physiological differences violates the Amendment to Title VII. The act requires agencies to use a single physical performance standard for men and women. The results of this would have a disparate impact on women. If this occurs, the agency must prove that the standard used is necessary to perform the duties of the job. A recent report by Susan Johnson of the Cooper Institute (1992) acknowledges that the Americans with Disabilities Act (ADA) has caused some concern with police agencies that have implemented physical fitness standards and testing.

According to Johnson too many times agencies (primarily the legal department) shy away from litigation in the area of fitness as they may not understand the need for fitness, what fitness is, and how to implement it. A legal misinterpretation then results. The ADA does not in certain respects require anything that has not already been required through the Civil Rights Act of 1964 or the Rehabilitation Act of 1973. Agencies can set standards even if adverse impact does occur. If it does then it can be upheld as long as it is job related. However, one change that agencies should be aware of is in the requiring of medical exams (unless informed consent is given) prior to an offer of employment and inquiries as to the disability status of potential employees. These are prohibited by ADA.

Even though the ADA has a higher burden of proof in documentation and rationale as essential job requirements, this does not require major changes in existing tests or programs. Rationales such as trying to justify fitness as an essential job factor relating to medical status, wellness, or disability protectors are faulty according to Johnson (1992). A valid rationale that justifies fitness as being job related is that it pertains to the physiological readiness in performing critical essential functions. According to Johnson fitness is aerobic capacity, strength, flexibility, and body composition. These areas are predictive factors in officers' being able to perform the essential job tasks and are job related.

Physiological readiness can justify fitness with the ADA. Courts in recent years have been accepting general standards in organizations, which relieves every agency of validating fitness programs individually. The Cooper Institute has validated fitness with the physiological readiness rationale for numerous police agencies.

In summary, Johnson (1992) and the Cooper Institute advise that the ADA does not require anything new than what has been required by previous legislation, only the burden of defending the programs may be higher. Additional planning will be required as to when to implement testing and health inquiries.

Conclusion

The well-being, safety, and productivity of police officers can be greatly enhanced through a total program of fitness that includes strength, flexibility, endurance, proper nutrition, and education on maintaining a healthy lifestyle.

To ensure that a total fitness program is successful, the head of the agency must be very supportive and participate in the program. In addition, the program should be reasonable, fairly implemented, and legally defensible, by utilizing persons of expertise in program development.

We live in, and the police work in, a violent society. The training in impact weapons, firearms, defense tactics, and weapon retention, along with a strong physical foundation, will enable police officers to do what they are sworn to do.

James J. Ness

Bibliography

Arliss, R.M. "Healthy Hearts for New York City Cops." *Police Chief* 58(7) (1991): 16–22.

Ayers, R.M., and P.R. Coble. *Safeguarding Management's Rights*. Gaithersburg, MD: International Association of Chiefs of Police, 1987.

Bracy, D. "The Decline of the Vaccination Model: Criminal Justice Education for a Changing World." *C.J. The Americas* 1(2) (1988): 1.

California Highway Patrol Physical Performance Program Manual. HPM 70.9 (September 1984).

Collingwood, T.R. "Implementing Programs and Standards for Law Enforcement Physical Fitness." *Police Chief* 55(4) (1988): 20–24.

Commission on Accreditation for Law Enforcement Agencies. *Standards for Law Enforcement Agencies*. Fairfax, VA: Commission on Accreditation for Law Enforcement Agencies, 1984.

Farenholtz, D.W., and E.C. Rhodes. "Recommended Canadian Standards for Police Physical Abilities." *Canadian Police College Journal* 14(1) (1990): 37–49.

Getz, R. "You Can't Afford Not to Have a Fitness Program." *Law and Order* 38(6) (1990): 44–50.

Grimes, J., and R.R. Shaw. "Fitness and Health Evaluations for Law Enforcement Officials." *National FOP Journal* 20(4) (1991): 41–45.

Healey, B. "The Aerobic Cop." *Police Chief* 48(II) (1981): 67–70.

International Association of Chiefs of Police. Newsletter. Gaithersburg, MD (December 1988).

Johnson, S. *Perspectives on the ADA*. Report to the Illinois Local Governmental Law Enforcement Officers Training Board. Gaithersburg, MD, February 14, 1992.

McDermott, B. *What Will Be the Future of Police Fitness Programs By the Year 2000?* Sacramento: California Commission on Peace Officer Standards and Training, 1986.

Nay, W.E. "A Review of the Full Range of Abilities and Characteristics in Police Selections Tests." Paper presented at the annual meeting of the Academy of Criminal Justice Sciences, Washington, DC, March 1989.

Ness, J.J. "Graduate Police Officer Perceptions of the Illinois Minimum Standards Basic Law Enforcement Training Curriculum." Paper presented at the annual meeting of the Academy of Criminal Justice Sciences, Washington, DC, March 1989.

Ohio State Patrol. *Health and Physical Fitness Manual*. Columbus: Ohio State Patrol, 1988.

Price, C.S., M.L. Pollock, L.R. Gettman, and D.A. Kent. "Physical Fitness Program for Law Enforcement Officers: A Manual for Police Administrators." (Grant No 76–NI–99–0011.) Washington, DC: Law Enforcement Assistance Administration, 1976.

Quire, D.S., and W.R. Blount. "Coronary Risk Profile Study of Male Police Officers: Focus on Cholesterol." *Journal of*

Police Science and Administration 17(2) (1990): 89–94.

St. Louis Police Department. *Physical Fitness Manual.* St. Louis, MO: St. Louis Police Department, 1986.

Schofield, D.L. "Establishing Health and Fitness Standards." *FBI Law Enforcement Bulletin* (June 1989): 26.

Slahor, S. "Focus on Fitness: The FBI Way." *Law and Order* 38(5) (199): 52–55.

Talley, R.A. "A Task Inventory Follow-up Examination of the Oakland Basic Police Academy: A Survey Study." Ph.D. diss. Michigan State University, East Lansing, 1984.

Thomas, R.T., Jr., R.B. Means, and M.R. Brandon. "Designing Public Safety Physical Fitness Programs: Legal and Protocol Perspectives, Part II." *Police Law Journal* (March 1989): 2.

Tracy, T.J., and D.A. Burns. "Health and Fitness Changes: A Two-and-a-Half Year Study." Boise: Idaho Department of Law Enforcement, 1992.

U.S. Department of Justice. Federal Bureau of Investigation. Training Division. *State and Local Law Enforcement Training Needs in the United States.* Vol. 1. Washington, DC: U.S. Department of Justice, 1986.

Allan Pinkerton

In February 1855 Allan Pinkerton established the Northwest Police Agency in Chicago, Illinois. It was to be a regional police system for the fledgling railroad industry, extending over an area consisting of Illinois, Indiana, Michigan, Ohio, and Wisconsin. Shortly it would grow to cover the entire nation and eventually became the present-day Pinkerton, Inc., the world's largest private security and detective firm. Since federal detection was scant and city police were inefficient or corrupt, Pinkerton became the nation's preeminent detective force in the nineteenth century. In many respects Allan Pinkerton was to his century what J. Edgar Hoover was to the twentieth.

Pinkerton was born in Glasgow, Scotland, on August 25, 1819. Although his father had been a police officer, Allan apprenticed as a cooper. Young Pinkerton soon became involved with the Chartists, a workers' movement in Great Britain that was increasingly interpreted by officials as radical. Local political and police pressure compelled Allan Pinkerton and his new bride to flee Scotland in 1842. After a short stay in Canada and in Chicago, he settled in a small Scottish settlement called Dundee, forty miles northeast of Chicago. He opened a cooperage and employed eight apprentices.

Throughout the 1840s numerous counterfeiters passed spurious money and made business haphazard in much of the rural Midwest. Out on an expedition in 1847 hunting wood to be used as barrel staves, Pinkerton stumbled upon a camp of counterfeiters. He returned with the local sheriff to make the arrest and was heralded as a hero. Itinerant rogues nevertheless continued to travel the area selling bundles of fake money to those rustics wanting to turn a fast profit. Constables seemed powerless and a delegation of Dundee merchants pressured Pinkerton into watching for counterfeiters as a part-time deputy sheriff. A number of arrests followed and Pinkerton began to be weaned away from barrel making.

By 1850 Pinkerton had given up his Dundee business and moved to Chicago. He was an avid abolitionist, but most Dundee residents were conservative on slavery. In his only bid for elective office in Dundee, Pinkerton had come in last in a field of nine candidates. He was convinced that his poor showing was due to his abolitionism. Chicago had a sizable abolitionist population, and he felt his views would be more acceptable there. More important, requests for his services had increased. For example, the national government became interested in the counterfeiting problem in the Midwest. Because the Treasury Department would not have Secret Service agents to combat counterfeiting until after the Civil War, the Secretary of Treasury had Pinkerton investigate the problem in Illinois in 1851 and 1853. In 1852 Cook County sheriff William Church asked Pinkerton to rescue two kidnapped Michigan girls who had been taken westward. By 1854 he was an official deputy to the Cook County sheriff in Chicago. At the same time, the U.S. postmaster appointed him to be a special agent in the Chicago postal system. He was to investigate mail theft. In several spectacular cases he discovered postal employees stealing mail, and local newspapers proclaimed that "as a detective police officer Mr. Pinkerton has no superiors and we doubt that he has any equals in the country." By mid-decade, as an official in the Cook County sheriff's office, which did much unofficial detecting, Pinkerton hovered between public and private policing. Then in February 1855 Pinkerton opened his agency. He made a commitment to private policing, but in a country with little official law enforcement his duties took him across geographic and jurisdictional boundaries.

There was an explosion of railroad building in the 1850s. Illinois had ninety-eight miles of railroad track in 1851. Five years later that figure jumped to 2,086 miles. The figure would more than double by decade's end. The railroads faced the dual problems of rapid growth and America's "home rule" conception of law enforcement. Much vandalism and crime occurred on railroad property in the rural areas. Buildings and bridges were burned and trains were derailed. In addition there were problems with railroad employees far from direct supervisory control. Railroad conductors, in their capacity of selling tickets on board the train, could take money and admit passengers but not issue tickets. With no record of a transaction conductors could pocket the fare. Opportunities were great. For example, in 1857 Illinois Central conductors sold $147,856 worth of tickets—officially, at least. Railroad management wanted to control their workers who were far away from headquarters. Pinkerton was to provide that control. A spying system—Pinkerton called it a "testing program"—was devised to watch conductors. Either Pinkerton himself or one of his employees (there were three at first, but the number grew rapidly in the next five years) boarded the trains, posed as a passenger, and watched the conductors. Immediately Oscar Caldwell was spotted taking money. An arrest, trial, and conviction followed. Caldwell's trial aroused considerable interest in Chicago and divided employee and employer. Most railroad workers in 1855 took sides against their bosses and this newly invented spy system. Shortly, Allan Pinkerton devised a symbol for the agency, the all-seeing eye. The eye began to convey double meanings. For railroad workers it meant distrust and deception; for the owner it meant accountability and control. In the next five years Pinkerton's testing program uncovered numerous cases of conductor dishonesty. In the same period railroad workers began to form unions. It seemed that war between the workers and the capitalists might erupt but then another war got in the way.

Tensions between the northern and southern states over slavery continued to increase in the late 1850s and peaked with the election of Abraham Lincoln. The threat of secession was ominous and so was the possibility of presidential assassination. One such attempt had occurred earlier, during Andrew Jackson's presidency. Rumor reached Pinkerton that Lincoln would be murdered as he traveled from Illinois to Washington, D.C. Pinkerton intercepted the president-elect in Philadelphia with the news that a murder conspiracy was afoot in Baltimore. Only with great effort did Pinkerton persuade Lincoln to be disguised and secretly escorted through Maryland. It was never proven that a real plot existed, however, and Pinkerton was accused of manufacturing one for his own benefit.

War broke out shortly after Lincoln's arrival in the nation's capital, and Pinkerton returned to Chicago. One of Pinkerton's close friends, George McClellan, became a general in the Midwest and used the detective to gather enemy intelligence. When McClellan was given command of all the Union forces, Pinkerton headed the spy service. A cause célèbre occurred when one of his agents, Timothy Webster, was discovered and executed by the Confederate government. The agency continued to spy on conductors and uncover government corruption in the awarding of wartime contracts. When McClellan was dismissed in 1863 Pinkerton returned to his private practice.

After the war Pinkerton's agency expanded. Offices opened in New York City (1865) and Philadelphia (1866). Testing the honesty of railroad employees continued but emphasis shifted to the pursuit of train robbers. Kinship gangs such as the Renos, the Youngers, and the Daltons plagued the railroads. Frank and Jesse James emerged as folk heros, especially after Pinkerton agents botched an ambush and injured the bandits' mother. Pinkerton continued to chase the railroad robbers, but as happened with the testing programs, the desperadoes made many think that detectives were merely representatives of the moneyed classes who were against the common people.

Although much of the animosity between Pinkerton agents and organized labor would occur after Allan Pinkerton's death in 1884, there were harbingers. A secret Irish fraternity named the Molly Maguires terrorized the Pennsylvania coal mines between 1867 and 1877. A Pinkerton agent infiltrated and exposed the organization, and several miners were tried, convicted, and executed. Coal workers claimed that Pinkerton's men were agents provocateurs while mine owners felt terrorism had been dealt a decisive blow. In the twenty years following the Civil War the Pinkerton agency grew and was more visible. Agents served as private police who traveled across many boundaries doing very public acts. For many people, especially as Pinkerton and other private detective firms became more established, the entire profession hovered on the border of respectability.

As businesses grew so did the number of Pinkerton operatives. By 1870 there were twenty detectives and sixty watchmen. In spite of economic recession and depression the number would almost double in the next decade. The number of other detective agencies increased rapidly as well. Besides combating criminality and radicalism, Pinkerton set out to forge a profession. First, in a series of in-house publications, he defined business philosophy and employee conduct. This was done to control his own operatives and provide guidelines of behavior for other detective agencies. Like any respectable business, the Pinkerton agency worked for fees instead of rewards. Pinkerton would not accept disreputable work like so many divorce detectives did. Employees had to subscribe to a puritanical lifestyle. In short, his business—and by implication all proper private detectives—was to be a carbon copy of other respectable businesses. Contradicting prevailing attitudes that it takes a thief to catch a thief, Pinkerton told his operatives that "the profession of the detective is a high and honorable calling."

Second, Pinkerton tapped into a growing popular literature coming out of Edgar Allan Poe's earlier detective puzzles and the sensationalist, cheap "yellow book" publications. Both genres distorted real detectives and detection. To exploit this popularity and correct misperceptions, Pinkerton published sixteen detective books between 1874 and 1884. Actually, the literary output was a corporate endeavor: several different authors, under his editorial supervision, put Pinkerton's memoirs to paper. Two types of publication resulted. The detective stories were matter-of-fact retellings of past cases. They were marked by a lack of excitement and sensation. The second type were not stories; they were descriptions of various crimes and criminal menaces in America. This allowed Pinkerton to pose as an expert on crime in America. Such knowledge was based on his

"rogues' gallery" and network of agents throughout the country.

When Allan Pinkerton died in 1884, the management of the agency passed to his two sons, William and Robert. Much stormy history remained to be written in the late nineteenth century. But at his funeral Pinkerton was eulogized as a reformer because "the profession in this country of which, in its true dignity, he was the honored founder, is no mean profession. It is a social protector." Of course, not everyone shared that view.

Frank Morn

Bibliography
Horan, James. *The Pinkertons: The Detective Dynasty That Made History*. New York: Crown, 1968.
Morn, Frank. *"The Eye That Never Sleeps," A History of the Pinkerton National Detective Agency*. Bloomington: Indiana University Press, 1982.
Rowan, Richard. *The Pinkertons: A Detective Dynasty*. Boston: Little, Brown, 1931.

Police Academy

In discussions of police training and academies, the problem of generalizing is no less complicated than when covering other aspects of policing in the United States. However, most police scientists agree that police training as such had changed little from the constabulary and night-watch system of 1636 through the mid-1900s. The night-watch person, the sheriff, or the constable may have been given a brief set of directions and sent out on his own. The police officer, even through the 1940s and 1950s, may have, in addition, had the opportunity to accompany a more experienced officer for a week or more before patrolling alone. Some agencies offered no buffer; others, such as those in New York City and Chicago, offered at least several weeks of full-time training. Nevertheless, it was not until 1959 that New York and California became the first of many states to require a minimum basic-training period for all police agencies within their jurisdiction.

Task Force on Police—1967

The Task Force on Police, sponsored by the 1967 President's Commission on Law Enforcement and the Administration of Justice, directed its attention to the parallel low expectations of a recruit's minimal formal educational requirements and the quality of basic training. It was disappointed to find that in the previous ten to forty years of supposed increasing modernization and upgrading of local police agencies, improvements had little to do with recruitment practices and training. The task force reported that 70 percent of police agencies required only a high-school diploma, and 25 percent of the agencies required merely an elementary education at a time of increasing educational requirements in many other occupations.

In its survey, the task force found that of the 269 responding police agencies, 97 percent had recruit-training programs lasting from one week to twelve weeks. Those agencies reporting the longer training periods were municipalities with populations of 250,000 or more; the average training period of municipalities with populations below 250,000 was only three weeks. In the early 1970s twelve weeks of training was considered quite progressive; by 1986 six months of basic training was considered advanced.

The task force on Police seemed concerned about instilling in police recruits an appreciation for enforcing the law and maintaining peace within a democratic, pluralistic society. It believed police officers in the United States should be committed without resentment to upholding the due process of law that protects the rights of the accused, and it recommended that they must be sensitized to the differing norms and values of ethnic groups and minorities. The task force concluded that most training programs were disjointed, run by unmotivated part-timers who had little time to prepare their presentations, and inadequate for preparing a recruit to police within a democratic political context.

Recommendations. The task force made recommendations about training that would guide the police officer's tremendous discretionary power in everyday policing, the type of instruction that many programs seemed to neglect in favor of detailed study of substantive law and police science. It encouraged training programs that would teach respect for the rights of civilians and would teach options available to officers other than the criminal-justice processes for resolving problems. Finally, it recommended a college degree as a minimum requirement for all police applicants. Its recommendations seemed prophetic, particularly in view of what the Walker Report submitted by Daniel Walker,

director of the Chicago Study Team, to the National Commission on the Causes and Prevention of Violence, appraised as a "police riot" in summer 1968 over a generally peaceful demonstration against the war in Vietnam during the Democratic National Convention in Chicago.

Police Task Force—1973
Six years later the Task Force on Police of the 1973 National Advisory Commission on Criminal Justice Standards and Goals made its own suggestions for improving police training. Less specifically oriented toward a philosophical or moral position vis-à-vis democracy or pluralism as was the 1967 task force, this group seemed more interested in upgrading police training for pragmatic reasons. It affirmed the view of police administrators, who asserted that the quality of education provided their recruits was reflected in more efficient performance and fewer unnecessary complaints or litigation by citizens. It seemed more practical to avoid citizen hostility and promote more community respect both by raising educational requirements and by emphasizing psychological and sociological principles of human behavior.

Recommendations. The task force made several suggestions concerning police training: that all agencies gradually increase minimum educational requirements until, by 1982, all applicants would have to possess a four-year degree. Also, that agencies require a minimum of forty in-service training hours per year for each police officer and require a period of formal training before promoted officers assumed their new responsibilities. Further, the task force recommended a required ten-week basic training curriculum for all recruits (specific elements will be outlined under "Curriculum"). Finally, it would require each state to establish police academies or criminal-justice training centers so that by 1978 every police officer in every state would have access to either an academy or training center.

Police Academies and Training Centers
A police academy is basically a school established to accommodate classroom teaching of recruits as well as physical and self-defense training, and parade or field maneuvers. Some academies include firing ranges, combat courses, and high-speed driving areas. State police academies have dormitories for their re-

cruits and follow the military model for training. Criminal-justice training centers are academies that also include in-service training for all elements of the criminal-justice system, e.g., judges, prosecuting attorneys, and defense attorneys. The police academy in Dayton, Ohio, serves such a dual purpose.

Academies are usually established in city, county, or regional areas whose tax resources permit the construction and fairly constant use of the academy, although nonagency personnel may also use the facilities. For example, a county-level academy may permit independent village or town police to accompany its own recruits, or an academy may serve as a training center for a particular region of a state. An academy not only trains its recruits before they are assigned to active duty, it also provides in-service training for veteran officers.

Characteristics of Police Recruits
Only one study (Harris, 1973), conducted in 1969, has detailed the characteristics of police recruits. Focusing on one of the most advanced police agencies in the country, the study found that recruits, on average, were twenty-five years old, that 75 percent were married, and 47 percent of those who had no previous police experience cited job security as a reason for applying. Excluding their military service, the recruits averaged 3.2 jobs per person: 88 percent increased their monthly salaries by an average of 35 percent, and the remaining 12 percent—mostly recruits who had been correctional or police officers in other departments and who were joining for expected advancement opportunities—had an average salary decrease of 10 percent.

Training Themes
The Harris study identified three themes that cut across all categories of recruit training. One of the themes, defensiveness, was expressed by both instructors and recruits. Instructors stressed the importance of careful note-taking and the need to follow department rules and procedures at all times. Recruits heard stories of officers who had been guided by decent motives winding up dead, paralyzed, or faced with legal or departmental charges. They were warned not to act in a forthright manner with reporters, minorities, women, lawyers, politicians, the general citizenry, and even, at times, the departmental hierarchy—many of these would, it was predicted, turn on the police,

watch complacently when others turned on the police, or sacrifice the line officer to relieve community tension.

The second theme was professionalization. The academy staff tried to instill a sense of special pride within the recruit class. They talked about the need for ethical police behavior, sensitivity to the public, impartial enforcement of the law, and displays of confidence, leadership, and self-control. Indeed, the recruits came to believe that, of all major professions, the police should be at the apex.

Depersonalization was the third theme. Depersonalization referred to the subjective experience of being stereotyped and stereotyping in return, instead of interacting as one individual to another. Recruits were cautioned against the tendency to distrust the motives of others while romanticizing one's own motives, which leads to emotional detachment and defensiveness in order to avoid being exploited. Interestingly, the study revealed that several presentations by the Community Relations Squad designed to increase the recruit's cognitive flexibility and to alter his or her prejudices backfired, producing the opposite effects in the classes.

Curriculum
The curriculum of the academy examined in the 1969 study covered twelve weeks of full-time training, one week of which was a precinct assignment under direct supervision of a veteran police officer. The curriculum was broken down into several categories. The relative weight is computed for comparative purposes.

- Department structure and sub-structures (9 percent), inspection and drill (6 percent), regulations and forms (6 percent):   21%
- Law and the courts (excluding traffic):   23%
- Police proficiency: self-defense and riot control (8 percent); first aid (5 percent); driving skills, traffic law, reports, and procedures (12 percent):   25%
- Patrol procedures, including forty field hours: 26%
- Community relations, police ethics, and professionalism: 5%

The Police Task Force of the 1983 National Advisory Commission had maintained that the minimum length of recruit training should be 400 hours (ten weeks) with a suggested curriculum along the following lines:

- Introduction to the criminal-justice system — 8%
- Administration — 9%
- Law — 10%
- Police proficiency — 18%
- Human values and problems — 22%
- Patrol and investigation procedures — 33%

It is not known how much the police proficiency category may overlap with patrol procedures, departmental structures, or administration, which makes definitive comparisons difficult between the two curricula. But the contrast between the 5 percent allocated to "community relations, police ethics, and professionalism" in the actual 1969 curriculum relations and the 22 percent allocation for "human values and problems" recommended by the task force in 1973 is quite telling. Indeed, community relations, personal values, and discretionary power are the areas that generate much internal and external conflict within North American policing.

In some academies, such as New York City's, social science and community relations lessons comprise from 25 to 33 percent of recruit training. Unfortunately, such courses are often taught by officers who are building seniority in order to teach either law or police science. It is not unusual for social science or community relations lessons to be experienced as boring or superfluous by many recruits; in one academy that will remain anonymous, it was estimated that from 50 to 70 percent of the recruits never broke the strap surrounding the reading material. Obviously, increasing the length of recruit training does not automatically lead to better teaching of interpersonal skills, principles of human behavior, or reasonable guidelines for policing within a pluralistic society.

Police Training versus Police Mandates
An FBI survey found that, regardless of size, type, or geographic location of the police agency, the majority of training needs reported by police officials themselves concerned basic law-enforcement skills. The top fourteen of the twenty-five priorities cited included only two items that could be interpreted as interest in

community relations and interpersonal skills: "handling personal stress" and "promoting a positive image." The rest included such areas as physical fitness, conducting of interviews, weaponry, report writing, intelligence gathering, court testimony, high-speed driving, and drug searches. Since advancement and days off for good felony arrests are linked to the law-enforcement mandate of police work instead of to the peace-maintenance mandate, it is not surprising to find police officers having more incentive to increase their law-enforcement competencies instead of those related to peace maintenance.

Critics within and outside police agencies are aware that both the culture and social structure of the United States buttress, indeed, require the bias toward law enforcement. However, the critics realize that competent police work also requires communication skills and interpersonal sensitivity, as police interact with people whose problems have deep emotional significance attached to them. An estimated 50 to 80 percent of police calls (depending on which study is used) involve maintaining the peace and providing personal services, e.g., interviewing in cases of domestic violence, rowdiness by juveniles, public nuisances and squabbles, unruly crowds, and providing lifesaving services. For this reason, the more astute police scientists and administrators advocate a training structure that reflects the skills necessarily proportionate to the actual role most officers play. Some suggest an organizational and training distinction similar to the difference between New Scotland Yard and the municipal police of Great Britain.

The Police Response
Training programs, at least in the more advanced agencies, are trying to bring the law-enforcement and peace-maintenance functions into better balance. In 1969 one of the most enlightened departments in the country devoted 5 percent of its training to community relations and the like; by 1981 the New York State Municipal Police Training Council (MPTC) (now the Bureau of Police Training) required that about 10 percent of its curriculum be devoted to community and social relations. Although the MPTC's program was considered the standard for the 1980s, the community and social relations portions were still less than half of the National Advisory Commission's standard. New York City's academy, which usually

spends approximately 19 percent of its recruit training on what it categorizes as social science, seems to come closest to what the commission had in mind.

Innovations and the Future

Within budgetary considerations, police administrators for the most part continue to provide what they think will best make the recruit more competent once he or she is in the field. Generally, training programs have been lengthened, and forty hours of required annual in-service training is fairly common. Training styles have shifted from the more militaristic stress-training to the more collegiate non-stress teaching techniques. Most departments realize the benefit of having full-time, committed, and well-prepared training staff, and focus more attention on interpersonal skills, crisis intervention, stress management, and self-defense.

In the 1970s, the Dayton, Ohio, academy under Police Chief Robert Igleberger, which required all recruits to be assigned to a social service agency, such as a hospital or state mental facility, as part of their basic training. Unfortunately, after his tenure the requirement was eliminated when the training program was reduced from six months to seventeen weeks. The police department in Greensboro, North Carolina, under Police Chief William Swing instituted a multiphased, staff development training program that provided training for each job placement according to the staffing needs of the department.

The Nassau County, New York, Police Department under Police Commissioner Samuel Rozzi began two reforms in the early and mid-1980s. Since the county police department provided most ambulance services in the county, each recruit became a certified emergency medical technician before leaving the academy. Also, the academy assigned each recruit to a state-certified field trainer during his or her field assignment prior to graduation. The New York Police Department initiated stress management for its recruits, a phase of training that major police agencies such as Los Angeles's have included in their programs. The Denver Police Department was one of the first in the country to establish a program aimed at intervening in spousal abuse calls. Finally, the curriculum of the Suffolk County, New York, Police Department includes conflict and stress management such as crisis intervention in general and domestic violence in particular, as inherent aspects of recruit training.

The debates and criticisms about recruit training that plagued police administrators during the 1960s and 1970s still existed in the 1980s. Currently the movement is toward even more expanded curriculums promoting a greater understanding of human behavior, and with that an enlarged expectation of recruits. Computer simulations of crowd behavior, leadership decisions, hostage negotiations, and more are currently in use. For example, Firearms Training Systems of Norcross, Georgia, has developed a computer-simulated training aid that tests the wisdom and accuracy of employing disabling or deadly force. Common law-enforcement situations play across a 10-foot screen for police trainees to react to instantly. A life-size gunman runs out of a store firing in the direction of the police officer. Is he the robber or the store owner? An innocent-looking woman is stopped for speeding and when the officer approaches she reaches inside her purse. Is she after identification or a small pistol? The police trainee either doesn't fire or fires blanks along with a laser beam at the screen, depending on the next few seconds of action and his or her visual acuity and judgment. The laser beam bullets leave their mark as the simulator freezes the action to show if the officer reacted correctly, and in the case of being fired on, if the officer survived the ordeal.

Greater understanding of human behavior is achieved through training programs such as those that emphasize diversity awareness and race relations. The resurgence of community-oriented policing mandates the enlarged focus. Also clearly a priority, since youth gangs and juvenile crime in general have shown a marked increase, police academies expend more effort in preparing officers to handle wayward and dangerous youth. Greater educational expectations challenge police academies to teach more than ever before, and police recruits to learn more than ever before. Such a detail as having Chevrolet send a videotape explaining the antilock braking system on its automobiles can and does save lives.

In 1989 the Law Enforcement Information Network (LETN), founded by a former Dallas chief of police, went on the air. LETN began broadcasting five days a week, twenty-four hours a day, offering a wide variety of training programs. The network was founded in response to the issue of police civil liability, that is, finding a police department negligent in training its officers and the subsequent high-dollar settlements. Many small police departments, especially rural agencies, do not have well-staffed and well-equipped police academies for training purposes, nor do they have the funds to send out trainees. A network like LETN is beneficial to them and may become a standard training device in the future for every size police department and law-enforcement agency.

Richard N. Harris

Bibliography

Berkley, George. *The Democratic Policeman.* Boston: Beacon Press, 1969.

Bittner, Egon. *The Functions of the Police in Modern Society.* Cambridge, MA: Oelgeshlager, Gunn, and Hain, 1979.

Earle, Howard H. *Police Recruit Training.* Springfield, IL: Charles C. Thomas, 1973.

Elliott, J.F. *The New Police,* Springfield, IL: Charles C. Thomas, 1973.

Favreau, Donald F., and Joseph E. Gillespie. *Modern Police Administration.* Englewood Cliffs, NJ: Prentice-Hall, 1978.

Franks, Helen. "Softly, Softly." (Police Training in Race Relations). *New Statesman and Society* 3 (February 23, 1990): 20–21.

Harris, Richard N. *The Police Academy: An Inside View.* New York: John Wiley and Sons, 1973.

Hilton, Phil. "A Match for the Crowd." (Computer Simulation of the Behavior of Crowds). *Personnel Management* 24 (June 1992): 57–58.

McNamara, John H. "Uncertainties of Police Work: Recruits' Backgrounds and Training." In *The Police.* Ed. David J. Bordua. New York: John Wiley and Sons, 1967. 163–252.

National Advisory Commission on Criminal Justice Standards and Goals. *Task Force Report: The Police.* Washington, DC: Government Printing Office, 1967.

Thibault, Edward A., et al. *Proactive Police Management.* Englewood Cliffs, NJ: Prentice-Hall, 1985.

Willmer, M.A.P., and Kevin Gaston. "Developing Police Leadership." (Computer Simulation Training Aid). *Leadership and Organization Development Journal* 11 (July 1990): 10–17.

Police Brutality

On March 3, 1991, all of America and much of the world was exposed to the videotape of a black man in Los Angeles being viciously beaten by several white police officers. Since that time the name "Rodney King" has become synonymous with police brutality in the minds of most Americans. Subsequent to the removal of the state trial to Simi Valley, a virtually all white suburb, a jury of ten whites and two minority women acquitted four of the officers on virtually all of the charges connected to the beating. The jury verdict sparked the most deadly riot in our history, leaving fifty-four dead and over a billion dollars in property damage.

While the rubble in Los Angeles was still cooling, on November 6, 1992, a thirty-five-year-old black motorist, Malice Green, was beaten to death by two white police officers in Detroit using lead-weighted flashlights. Both officers were convicted of the offense, one receiving 12 to 25 years in prison, the other 8 to 18.

These two highly publicized incidents only serve to illustrate that the problem of police misconduct and police brutality as a specific form of racial misconduct continues to be a serious problem facing the criminal-justice process nearly thirty years after the wave of urban disturbances that shook the nation in the 1960s. These riots, in Los Angeles, Newark, Cleveland, and Detroit, were all sparked by routine police contacts with black citizens. The Kerner Commission, which investigated these riots, and later the President's Commission on Law Enforcement and the Administration of Justice established by President Lyndon Johnson, emphasized the strained relationship that existed between the police and the minority community and recommended urgent remedial action. The issue of police brutality became a focus of attention for police professionals and academic researchers for the ensuing decade. A number of studies emerged documenting the existence of police brutality (e.g., Kirkham, 1976; Reiss, 1976; Rubenstein, 1973; Westley, 1953). Numerous recommendations were made including the need to increase minority representation on police forces and to improve police training especially in the areas of cultural understanding and the use of force. Obviously, as the King and Green cases illustrate, the problem of police brutality continues to exist. Further, we must assume that these cases represent only the "tip of the iceberg" having been fortuitously documented and well publicized. Since police forces maintain the records on citizen complaints and conduct their own internal investigations, statistics which might document the extent of police brutality are virtually unattainable by either researchers or the general public. If nothing else, these cases and the violent response provoked by the verdict in the King case illustrate that police brutality as a critical issue in law enforcement has yet to be adequately addressed. The reasons for this failure lie in sociopolitical changes in American society since the initial flurry of attention, differential perceptions of the police role by citizens, and in the nature of law enforcement itself.

Since the 1960s and early 1970s, when concerns about police violence were first raised, a number of changes have occurred in American society to push the issue of police misconduct far from the spotlight of scholarly and political concerns.

The election of Ronald Reagan in 1980 ushered in an era of political conservatism, which affected not only the economic and political institutions but the justice institution as well. The resulting conservative atmosphere that resulted not only removed police behavior from public scrutiny but also expanded police powers and elevated their daily operations beyond legitimate critique. At the same time, increasing drug abuse especially the use of "crack" cocaine and escalating rates of interpersonal violence served to reinforce the image of the police as a besieged minority defending the majority against spreading social disorganization. A secondary, but nevertheless highly significant impact of these problems (including the arrival on the scene of the AIDS epidemic) was to shift already shrinking research funds away from the social issues facing the poor and minority citizens—including that of police misconduct—to these issues.

In short, the impetus created by events in the 1960s and 1970s that led to critical analysis of police behavior in an attempt to understand the nature of policing, and that might have led to changes in police behavior, was stymied by events in the 1980s. Since a very broad segment of American society has always viewed the police as the "thin blue line" standing between them and those segments of society they view as being responsible for crime and disor-der, and who have been willing to accept police conduct uncritically, these trends served only to reinforce their position and to increase the numbers in their ranks. These individuals generally give unqualified support to police actions and discourage any criticism of police behavior by labeling it "antipolice" and supportive of disorder and anarchy.

Working Definition

Much of the difficulty in establishing a serious dialogue on police violence lies in the problems surrounding the definition of the proper role of the police in a democratic society. The traditional approach has been to define policing from a functional perspective. From this point of view, the role of the police is often seen as consisting of three basic functions: law enforcement, order maintenance, and service. Historically both the police institution and the public have emphasized the law-enforcement function. Despite the fact that enforcing the criminal code, investigating crime, and apprehending criminals occupy far less police time and resources than do responding to domestic disputes, quelling public disturbances, and curbing a wide variety of disorderly conduct, the image of the police as "crime-fighters" is perpetuated by the police themselves and reinforced by the mass media through television, movies, and news reporting. Clichés such as the "war on crime" and the "war on drugs" are used to describe their work. These cliches and the corresponding images created only serve to provide a narrow and superficial basis for a critical examination of their conduct. One rarely questions how wars are to be won and then only after the fact.

The definition of the police role supplied by Egon Bittner (1980:39) provides an alternative to the traditional approach. He argues that "it makes much more sense to say that the police are nothing more than a mechanism for the distribution of situationally justified force in society. He points out that this definition of the police role cuts across all traditionally identified police functions. It reinforces the reality that the police may use force to overcome resistance to their commands in any situation. Carl Klockars (1993:1) further supports Bittner's argument:

> It is their [police] general right to use coercive force which defines police and distinguishes them from all other citi-

zens. It is the special competence of police and what police and no one else make available to us in modern society.

To define the police mandate in this manner focuses attention on the issue of police violence and especially the excessive application of it in the form of police brutality. If, as Bittner and Klockars suggest, the authorized use of force is the core of the police mandate, then a critical examination of how police actually utilize force, against whom, and under what circumstances becomes legitimate in the process of evaluating police performance (Bittner 1980:39–46). Unfortunately, as Thomas Barker (1978) observes, the definition of police brutality as the application of unnecessary and unjustified use of force is not very helpful since these terms are, in themselves, ambiguous. As Manning (1993:1) points out:

> The law provides little guidance as to where, when, and in what quantity it [force] should be applied. In the nation state context, policing serves the state, but the state's interests are rarely directly served. The police, as the behavior of Chief Daryl Gates and the LAPD illustrates, also serve frequently their own political and moral interests in a rather complex fashion.

However, as he goes on to say, "the police mandate is constrained by two matters: the right to apply violence and the grounding norm of state authority" (1993:1). Since the street milieu of the patrol officer presents numerous situations for the use of force, each situation must be evaluated within its own context. Critical to the evaluation of police use of force within a given context are two factors: the legal right to use force in that situation and the extent to which that force serves the state's interest. If the legal right to use force in that situation is absent or if the force exceeded the amount necessary to effectuate an arrest and, at some point, began to serve the personal interests of the officer or officers involved, then that force is unnecessary and unjustified and can be characterized as police brutality. For example, following *Tennessee v. Garner,* police may no longer use deadly force simply because an alleged offender is attempting to evade capture. Any situation in which an officer uses deadly force

against an alleged offender in the absence of threat to life is not supported by law and is unjustified. In the Rodney King incident, the police had an initial right to take Mr. King into custody; however, from the videotape it appears that at some point, the violence used served the personal needs and interests of the officers involved.

The Reiss Study and Racism

Probably the most widely known empirical study of police violence is the work of Albert Reiss (1971) who studied police behavior in Washington, D.C., Boston, and Chicago with the aid of observers riding in police cars. His findings indicated an abuse rate of 41.9 per 1,000 white citizens and 22.6 per 1,000 black citizens. He concludes:

> If one accepts these rates as reasonably reliable estimates of undue force against suspects, then there should be little doubt that in major metropolitan areas the sort of behavior commonly called "police brutality" is far from rare. (1971:339)

In evaluating Reiss's data, one should bear in mind that the incidents recorded involving excessive or undue force occurred in front of observers, therefore, it is likely that the Reiss study underestimates rather than overestimates the occurrence of excessive force. Unfortunately, his data are more than twenty years old and have not been replicated. Lundman (1980:160) concludes:

> It is true that most defiant citizens are not assaulted by police. To this we can now add: It is also true that in absolute terms it appears that many cities contain relatively large numbers of citizens who have experienced needless police force.

Who are the most likely targets of police brutality? As Swain (1974:120) points out:

> Thus violence or rough behavior is used by the police against certain people and in certain communities. The police do not deny that they use violence against certain citizens; rather they defend it on the grounds of its effectiveness in dealing with what they define as violations and problems.

From the literature, a fairly consistent pattern emerges as to who these "certain people" are. Those who openly defy police authority, fail to demonstrate proper respect, resist arrest, or who fall into certain classes—drunks, street addicts, homeless people, or sexual deviants— are the most likely recipients of police abuse. As Lundman (1980:162) indicates:

> Because authority is so central to the police role, citizens who question or resist authority represent a very serious challenge to patrol officers. As a consequence, intense verbal coercion is used to establish police authority, and if that is not effective, physical force is used to elicit citizen acceptance of authority.

Historically, the black community has been the most critical of the police abuse of force. The National Advisory Commission on Civil Disorders (1968:302–09), which reported the findings of an investigation into the wave of urban disturbances that occurred across the United States in 1967, concluded that tensions between the black communities and their police departments created by unresolved grievances over police practices were a significant factor in escalating these disorders. While racist behavior of individual police officers cannot be discounted as a factor, other factors affecting the black community and its citizens are probably more significant. The disproportionate distribution of black citizens in the poverty class brings them more in contact with police, relative to middle-class citizens living in middle-class communities. Pervasive feelings of oppression experienced by black citizens and directed at the police increase the likelihood that these encounters will become hostile.

Van Maanen and the Police Subculture
Prior research into police use of excessive force has approached the problem from a number of different perspectives. Four main factors have emerged as explanations for police violence: psychological, sociological, occupational, and class-conflict. The psychological approach has focused on the question of a "police personality." As Kania and Mackey (1977:28) state:

> The psychological approach to police personality has focused on those individuals with personalities which are thought to be attracted to police

work . . . Thus it is theorized that police work, by attracting and retaining persons with these personalities, develops a concentration of individuals who are prone to use violence.

While some research has supported the conclusion that recruits to the occupation do possess values that are somewhat different from the general population, the research results are neither consistent nor are they strong enough to provide an explanation that would account for the persistence of police violence over time and its distribution across departments. As Kania and Mackey (1977:32) go on to point out:

> Psychological theory suggests that a generally uniform personality type is attracted to and retained by police departments. If this is true, then the psychological theory has no predictive value by itself. A uniformity in police personality should logically produce a uniform set of rates for police violence in the 50 states, if personality type were the only significant factor in police violence. Since the rates are far from uniform, one must conclude that other factors of greater significance are involved.

Despite its weakness, the psychological explanation is the one most widely accepted by the police themselves and by a large percentage of the general public. The idea that police violence is perpetrated by the few relatively violent persons who become police officers is appealing since an individualistic account of the behavior allows police organizations to perpetuate the myth that the conduct is relatively rare and, at the same time, to avoid organizational scrutiny. In fact, police screening procedures are developed with an eye toward eliminating the maladjusted or flawed personalities from the ranks of police applicants. Psychological and psychiatric screening permits police departments to argue that they are taking measures to prevent police brutality and since, admittedly, these measures are not perfect, when incidents do occur, they can argue that occasionally the "bad apple" slips through. Certainly, although some instances of police brutality can be attributed to the pathological tendencies of some officers (just as some crime can be attributed to mentally ill persons), a psychological explanation does not provide an adequate theoretical explanation of police brutality.

A much sounder approach requires an institutional perspective with a focus on the role played by the police subculture. This approach brings us to the sociological and occupational variables of police work.

Before developing the sociological and occupational perspectives, we might first examine the class conflict theory. This explanation, derived from a Marxist point of view, sees the police as the tool of the powerful used to suppress the powerless and maintain the existing social order. This point of view really provides no new insights into police brutality since it merely describes the role of the police since the inception of the first modern police forces in Great Britain. That police derive their authority to use force from the existing sociopolitical structure and use it to support the legal norms primarily created by the rich and powerful tells us very little as to why they often employ that authority in a brutal and violent fashion. To observe that their authority and the majority of police violence is directed against poor people rather than against the upper and middle classes with whom they identify does not necessarily imply a class bias. As Klockars (1993:3) points out:

> What is often spoken of as the ideological bias of police, their unwillingness to focus on crimes of the rich and their disproportionate attention to the behavior of the poor is largely without a political dimension. Such behavior on the part of the police does not stem from ideology but from the special competence of police.

In short, the poor are disproportionately involved in traditional or "street crime," which is the specific target of patrol officers. Again, the continuous interaction between the police and the poor merely provides ample opportunity for the exercise of authority and force against lower-class persons. Their day-to-day activities provide the necessary but not the sufficient conditions which create the opportunity for the abuse of authority and the emergence of police brutality disproportionately directed at some citizens.

However, we ought not to dismiss class conflict theory as being irrelevant to the issue of police brutality. While it may not furnish a satisfactory explanation of the motivation of police officers to engage in excessive violence against poor and minority citizens, it does help us to understand society's failure to adequately respond to the problem. The failure of the jury to convict any of the police officers involved in the Rodney King case in the state trial can be understood from a social conflict perspective. From their point of view, King merely represented the type of individual that the police are supposed to control and, if in doing so, they reacted in an overzealous fashion, it was obvious from the attempt on his part to evade capture and from portions of the videotape that he challenged their authority. In short, King could be viewed as a "deserving victim" and therefore beyond the protection of the law. Given the fact that the response of the King jury was really not unique since police officers are rarely convicted of criminal charges stemming from acts of excessive force—at least at the local level—the message that is conveyed to the law-enforcement community is that they may act with virtual immunity. The rationalization that is provided to individual police officers to neutralize any guilt which they might feel in committing acts of police brutality is that they are simply "doing the job which the public expects." The police and the public tend to share a distorted "definition of the situation." This distorted view is further strengthened by the emphasis that both the police and the mass media place on the dangers of the occupation.

The interrelationship between the organizational and occupational perspectives provides the best approach to an understanding of police brutality. Two key elements of the police organization are danger and authority. Because of the danger inherent in the occupation, police officers are taught to be suspicious; because authority is viewed by police as the key to their occupational success and self-esteem, they learn to be aggressive and authoritarian. The occupation produces a subculture whose most salient norms are secrecy and solidarity. Overall it creates a feeling of "us versus them" in which "them" represents a dangerous and threatening category of persons. The subculture also provides a "worldview" which categorizes these persons and furnishes rationalizations for their devaluation.

As Van Maanen (1978:224) observes, police categorize their world into "suspicious persons," "know-nothings," and "assholes," the latter being the most likely targets of police brutality. He further notes:

> It is the asshole category which is most combined with moral meaning for the patrolman—establishing for him a stained and flawed identity to attribute to the citizen upon which he can justify his sometimes malevolent acts.

The function of the police in society to enforce laws and maintain order through the legally mandated use of force combined with their special competence to deal with traditional or "street crime" places them in the position of exercising their authority principally against poor and minority citizens. When they receive any challenge to their authority or disrespect for their commands, excessive force can be the result. Since the middle and upper classes generally support their actions on behalf of maintaining social order, police may act with relative immunity. In addition, the secrecy and solidarity characteristic of the police subculture serve to conceal most instances of police brutality. Since most police encounters, even those in which their authority is challenged, do not provoke excessive violence, we must examine other elements of the police subculture. Here, the suspicious nature of the police personality and the tendency to perceive some persons as unworthy of legal safeguards become significant factors. When individuals thus labeled challenge police authority, excessive force is frequently the result. The administration of "street justice" in the form of beatings administered to sex offenders, unruly drunks, and street junkies is a consequence of police perceptions of unworthiness.

The values and norms of the police subculture are learned in the process of socialization into the occupation. Learning the content of the police subculture begins in the training academy through the informal interaction between the recruit and veteran officers. This process continues during the rookies' field training and is completed "on the streets" with the assignment of the new officer to a veteran officer. In short, the values and norms of the police subculture identify the targets and the situations where excessive force may be appropriate. The centrality of the use of force in the occupation combined with the constant awareness of the need to maintain control and impose his/her authority creates the potential for police brutality. As Westley (1953:41) notes:

> The policeman uses violence illegally because such usage is seen as just, acceptable, and, at times, expected by his colleague group because it constitutes an effective means for solving problems in obtaining status and self-esteem which policemen as policemen have in common.

Administration's Responsibility

Police administrators and political leaders must begin to view the problem of police brutality as an institutional one rather than an individual one rooted in the attitudes and behavior of a "few bad apples," Clearly the problem of excessive and unwarranted police violence is a form of organizational deviance described by Lundman (1980:140–42). The role police administrators play in supporting organizational deviance is clear. In the case of police brutality, it is probably more informal through the lack of adequate and responsive action to citizen complaints rather than formal through manifestly encouraging illegal practices. To recognize the significant role that socialization into the police subculture plays is to understand the need for developing means of retarding the internalization of the negative elements by new officers as they are assimilated into the police agency. In short, the primary responsibility for curbing police brutality rests with police administrators. Since the bulk of police violence is directed at essentially powerless people, the police hierarchy must take action to protect all of its constituents against police misconduct, not just those who are viewed as worthy. To accomplish this, police administrators must take all citizen complaints seriously, must initiate thorough and honest investigations, and must level meaningful sanctions against offending officers. The community, through the local prosecutor and the courts, must also send a message to the police that contravenes the message that they have been historically receiving— that police brutality against certain citizens is acceptable—by vigorously prosecuting and convicting officers involved in the use of excessive force. The long-range benefit of these proposals will be the creation of an atmosphere that will weaken the support for police brutality within both the community and the police subculture itself.

Donald B. Walker

Bibliography

Barker, Thomas. "An Empirical Study of Police Deviance Other Than Corruption." *Journal of Police Science and Administration* 6(3)(1978): 264–72.

Bittner, Egon. *The Functions of Police in Modern Society.* Cambridge, MA: Oelgeschlager, Gunn and Hain, 1980.

Kania, Richard, R.E., and Wade C. Mackey. "Police Violence as a Function of Community Characteristics." *Criminology* 15(1)(1977): 27–48.

Kirkham, George. *Signal Zero.* New York: Ballantine, 1976.

Klockars, Carl B. "The Legacy of Conservative Ideology and Police." *Police Forum* 3(1)(1993): 1–6.

Lundman, Richard J. *Police and Policing: An Introduction.* New York: Holt, Rinehart and Winston, 1980.

Manning, Peter K. "Violence and Symbolic Violence." *Police Forum* 3(1)(1993): 1–6.

National Advisory Commission on Civil Disorders. *Report of the National Advisory Commission on Civil Disorders.* New York: Bantam Books, 1968.

Reiss, Albert J. *The Police and the Public.* New Haven, CT: Yale University Press, 1971.

———. "Police Brutality—Answers to Key Questions." In *Ambivalent Force: Perspectives on the Police.* 2d ed. Eds. Arthur Niederhoffer and Abraham Blumberg. Hinsdale, IL: Dryden Press, 1976. 333–42.

Rubenstein Jonathan. *City Police.* New York: Ballantine, 1973.

Swain, L. Alex. "The Politics of Identification." *Crime and Delinquency* 20(2)(1974): 119–28.

Tennessee v. Garner (1985) 471 U.S. 1, 105 S.Ct. 1694, 85 L. Ed. 2nd.

Van Maanen, John. "The Asshole." In *Policing: A View From the Street.* Eds. Peter K. Manning and John Van Maanen. Santa Monica, CA: Goodyear, 1978. 221–38.

Westley, William A. "Violence and the Police." *American Journal of Sociology* 59(1953): 34–41.

Police Budgeting

In the most general sense, police budgeting is merely an agency-specific form of public administration budgeting, and its development corresponds to budgetary development throughout the public sector. The only way in which police budgeting might be distinguished from other public budgeting is in the programmatic materials required to support budget requests within the most recent forms of budgeting—Planning Program Budgeting Systems (PPBS) and Zero-Based Budgeting (ZBB).

The historical derivation of modern budgeting has been a cumulative working out process resulting from the sequential emergence or "discovery" of fiscal management problems and solutions to those problems. As each problem has become clearly identified and resolved by means of new approaches to the management of public funds, the older techniques, by and large, have been absorbed and continued within the new techniques and formats. The following description of events and concepts rests upon this view of a derived, evolutionary, and cumulative public-budgeting system.

Major Periods of Budgetary Development

Allen Schick has identified three periods of budgetary reform, each named after the major *purpose* of the reform or the *problem* that led to the reform (Schick, 1982).

The Pre-Reform Spoils Era

Although the local, state, and national governments of the United States have collected taxes and expended revenues since revolutionary times, budgeting as we conceive of the term today was not practiced until early in the twentieth century. Prior to that the collection and spending of public funds were pretty much ad hoc practices, with little attention given to accounting for funds, at either the points of collection or expenditure. The lack of controls permitted carelessness and more than a little dishonesty in the handling of public funds at all levels of government. Fiscal abuses (as well as nepotism) during the Grant administration gave rise to major reform efforts during the Reconstruction era, but it was not until 1906 that budget reform became a serious force in public administration.

Reform for Control

New York City was the first American city to establish a consolidated line-item budget, following the creation of the New York Bureau of Municipal Research in 1906. President Taft appointed a Commission on Economy and Efficiency in 1909, whose work prompted Congress to pass the Budget and Accounting Act in 1921. The first consolidated federal budget was realized soon afterward. These earliest line-item budgets were designed almost solely to establish *control* over public funds—to require *accountability* of public funds from collection through expenditure. Although controls were focused primarily upon integrity problems, there were also increased efforts to ensure that funds were spent for the purposes intended by the appropriating officials. The expenditure categories of *personnel, equipment, supplies, contractual services*, and *capital expenditures* were devised at this time for control purposes.

This initial period of budgetary reform extended from approximately 1910 to the mid-1930s. The *line-item budget* was originated during this period, and the skills of *accountants* were predominantly required to support the new system.

Reform for Management

For about three decades, beginning in 1930, public administration burgeoned with the invention, development, and refinement of management techniques. The emphasis was upon efficiency, and the primary budgetary format that emerged, at the behest of the Hoover Commission in 1949, was the *performance budget*. The control emphasis of the previous era was continued and absorbed into a new mode of budgeting, which required the administrator to submit budget documentation showing efficient programmatic elements, in addition to the line-item controls of the previous era.

Reform for Planning

Systems theory contributed to the development of administrative concepts in both business and the public sector after World War II. By 1954 the Rand Corporation had presented *program budgeting* to the U.S. Department of Defense, and DOD Comptroller Charles Hitch had instituted the *Planning, Programming, Budgeting System* (PPBS) by 1961. Although this new system included the former requirements of *control* and *management*, it emphasized the clear statement of agency objectives and expectations of results, all quantifiable as inputs and outputs. It also required cost-benefit analyses of alternative approaches to the accomplishment of agency goals.

President Lyndon Johnson generalized PPBS to most departments of the federal government and the new system soon spread to some progressive state and local governments.

Zero-Based Budgeting (ZBB) was originated at Texas Instruments by Peter Phyrr and introduced into the Georgia state government and then the federal government by Jimmy Carter. It is a derivative of PPBS, but an elaborate one, emphasizing the setting of objectives, detailed planning, and essentially placing all program elements of an agency in competition with each other for funding on the basis of their comparative contributions to the agency's goals.

PPBS and ZBB are said to raise the visibility of an agency's operations, and the level of the political debate over the allocation of fiscal resources.

State-of-the-Art Budgeting and Current Police Practices

In most respects police agencies are required to use whatever budgeting format has been adopted by the city, county, or state government of which they are a part. Following the initiative of the federal government in the early 1960s, some of the more progressive states, counties, and cities, large and small, adopted varied forms of PPBS, often applying a localized name to the new approach. As this increasingly occurred, the police administrators in those jurisdictions were required to make strategic decisions about the goals of their departments, to quantify those goals in multiyear formats, and to relate proposed expenditures to expected levels of goal-achievement (e.g., a patrol plan would specify a percentile reduction in business burglaries for the next budget cycle, if funded at a requested level; a new investigative unit, a specific clearance rate for a given offense; a traffic enforcement unit, a reduction in fatal collisions). This new practice was found to be difficult, time-consuming, and expensive in terms of analysis and data requirements.

As those local police agencies gained experience with programmatic budgeting, they built the requisite databases and adapted to the system's greater requirements of data and administrative work. Soon, however, ZBB overtook PPBS and was considered by many to be more useful than PPBS, while costing no more to administer.

Many state and local governments have adopted only a few elements of PPBS or ZBB, avoiding their more ponderous analytic requirements, and thus have produced hybrids of line-item and programmatic budgeting techniques under a variety of localized titles. Some sophisticated police chiefs and sheriffs have adopted the analytic techniques associated with PPBS and ZZB even though their parent governments have been unable to adopt the advanced budgeting systems jurisdiction-wide. In these cases, it should be pointed out, the benefits to the agency consist largely of internal improvements in administrative quality, rather than improved budgeting practices of the jurisdiction.

Despite almost three decades of adaptation to the PBBS and ZBB systems by many sophisticated local governments, both large and small, indications are that most of the approximately 17,000 local police and sheriff's departments continue to utilize *line-item* budgeting systems, consistent with the practices of their parent governments.

In summary, police budgeting in the United States is a rich mix of all the conceptual approaches, methods, and techniques devised since the founding of the nation, with the greater number of local governments continuing to stress *control* of public funds over the more recent concerns with *management*, and *planning*. It is expected that the more recent concepts of budgeting will continue their diffusion into the many thousands of local law-enforcement agencies of the United States.

Victor G. Strecher

Bibliography
Kelly, Joseph A., and Joseph T. Kelley. *Costing Police Services*. Washington, DC: National Institute of Justice, 1984.
Lyden, Fremont J., and Ernest G. Miller, eds. *Public Budgeting*. 4th ed. Englewood Cliffs, NJ: Prentice-Hall, 1982.
Miron, Jerome H. *Managing the Pressures of Inflation in Criminal Justice: A Manual of Selected Readings*. National Criminal Justice Executive Training Program. Washington, DC: National Institute of Law Enforcement and Criminal Justice, 1979.
Sabo, Lawrence D., and Peter C. Unsinger. "Zero-Based Budgeting: Its Application in a Patrol Division of a Small Department." *Police Chief* 44(5) (May 1977): 60–62.
Schick, Allen. "The Road to PPB: The Stages of Budget Reform." In *Public Budgeting*. Eds. Fremont J. Lyden and Ernest G. Miller. Englewood Cliffs, NJ: Prentice-Hall, 1982. 46–68.

Police Chief

Executive Responsibilities

Few public agencies have as many challenging and important jobs as the police. They range from the obvious (managing traffic) to the dangerous (protecting us from danger) to the humane (helping those unable to care for themselves) to the constitutional (protecting our rights) to the omniscient (identifying potential problems, preventing crime, and making us feel secure). Given these jobs, the chief's is, by definition, at least as challenging and important. A call for applications to a vacant chief's position makes the job sound like one for a superhuman:

> Ten to 20 years of law enforcement experience; proven ability, and preferably a master's degree in personnel management and administration; a personal capacity to deal frequently and effectively with the public; demonstration of an ability to work "under heavy fire"— political or social, internal or external; a broad background in the technical and legal aspects of the criminal justice system; willingness to work the long hours of a top business executive for a fraction of the salary of those executives; openness to much-needed change and innovation in law enforcement; and an ability to earn the respect and confidence of the rank-and-file policemen and the taxpaying public (Kelly, 1975:11–12).

While this job description is demanding, it nonetheless covers the major elements of the police chief's job. A "good" chief knows what people expect of the police and can get rank-and-file officers to follow his or her leadership. A chief is expected to be responsive to the public, as represented by elected and appointed officials, and to be nonpolitical.

This expectation originated in the nineteenth century and grew into conventional wisdom during the twentieth. Driven by the Progressive or reform movement, it transformed the chief into a nonpolitical law-enforcement specialist instead of the crony of local politicians. August Vollmer played a major role in this change in the first third of this century. He thought the police had to be divorced from politics and have professional status to be effective and have a good image. To help accomplish this, he argued that chiefs had to be secure from removal for political reasons: because they did

Police Corruption

Police corruption takes place when an officer receives or is promised significant advantage or reward (1) for doing something that he or she is under duty to do anyway, (2) for doing something that he or she is under duty not to do, (3) for exercising a legitimate discretion for improper reasons, or (4) for employing illegal means to achieve approved goals (Punch, 1985:14). Use of this definition provides clarification of a number of issues that have surrounded discussions of police corruption. For example, the reward may be personal (money, gifts, access to power) or organizational (promotion, peer support, approval of superiors). The reward may also be other than material; it may consist, for example, of professional preferment resulting from advancing the agency's goals through illicit means. At the same time it distinguishes corruption from other forms of police misconduct. These include brutality that is not in furtherance of the organization's goals; "cooping" (sleeping on the job); performing private errands during one's shift; and "landing a cushy detail"—getting a comfortable assignment—or pilfering; absenteeism; and cutting administrative corners. Corruptions, as opposed to other forms of misconduct, always involves a benefit for the police officer in exchange for an abuse of the officer's power.

Typologies

This definition recognizes that there are many analytical types of police corruption. In 1974 Barker and Roebuck offered a typology of police corruption that identified eight categories of corrupt acts. In slightly modified form, these are:

1. Corruption of authority—accepting or demanding free meals, liquor, services, or discounts.
2. Kickbacks—accepting or demanding money, goods, and services from towing companies, ambulances, garages, lawyers, doctors, bondsmen, undertakers, taxicabs, service stations, moving companies, etc.
3. Opportunistic theft—thefts from suspects, victims, crime scenes, or unprotected locations.
4. Shakedowns—taking money from criminals or traffic violators in return for overlooking the offense.

5. Protection of illegal activities—taking money or other reward from vice operators or from legitimate companies operating illegally in return for protecting them from law-enforcement activity.
6. The fix—taking money or other rewards for quashing prosecutions that have already been initiated or for disposing of traffic tickets that have already been issued.
7. Direct criminal activities—committing crimes such as burglary or robbery that may make use of information known to the police but do not otherwise involve the abuse of police power.
8. Internal payoffs—sale of work assignments, off-days, holidays, vacation periods, evidence, and promotion.

The definition of corruption offered earlier dictates the addition of another category to those listed above, in order to account for corrupt activity designed to enhance the effectiveness of law enforcement and the advancement of the corrupt officer's career (Punch, 1985:11):

9. Combative corruption—planting or adding to evidence, falsifying testimony, intimidating witnesses, or paying informants with illegally obtained drugs in order to make arrests, obtain convictions, or get longer sentences for criminals.

Another typology utilizes the pervasiveness of corruption, the degree of organization, and the sources of bribes (Sherman, 1974:7). A department in which most officers do not condone corruption may nevertheless occasionally produce the "rotten apple," the uniformed officer who accepts an occasional bribe while on such assignments as traffic patrol. "Rotten pockets" are small groups of officers, typically assigned to enforce vice laws, who cooperate in low-level corruption.

The second type, "pervasive unorganized corruption," occurs when a large percentage of the department is corrupt, but officers act independently and there is little if any collusion among them. Finally, "pervasive organized corruption" includes situations in which corruption is not only widespread but in which both police officers and corruptors are organized. This type of corruption may extend into the department's highest ranks and permits the influence of organized crime in law enforcement.

International Perspectives

Until the mid-1970s, studies of police corruption tended to focus on the United States. America's high and highly visible rate of police corruption seemed consistent with the corruption in governmental and business circles that had been described at least since the turn of the century (Steffens, 1957). Although extensive corruption of the police had been noted in India (Bayley, 1969), Saigon (McCoy, 1972), Singapore (Jeffries, 1952), Hong Kong (Davies and Goodstadt, 1975), and rural Italy (Banfield, 1958), the assumption had always been that northern Europe, with its well-developed tradition of government service, its lack of political machines, and a rigid class structure that made tipping the police acceptable but prevented tipping from becoming extortion, was virtually free of police corruption (Fosdick, 1915). Since that time, major scandals in the police of London (Cox, Shirley, and Short, 1977) and Amsterdam (Punch, 1985) have led many observers to conclude that no police force can be guaranteed to be free of corruption—or at least of the potential of corruption.

History

Nevertheless, America's experience with police corruption and the response to it has been unique, and the American history of corruption has influenced the character of American law enforcement in a number of ways.

Historically, urban American police officers bought their jobs, their assignments, and their promotions; they expected to recoup the costs and make a tidy profit from graft. The vice laws—those regulating alcohol, gambling, and prostitution—were the most common source of such graft, which was supplemented by violators of regulations pertaining to traffic, health, building codes, and Sabbath closings. Less common but not unknown were shakedowns, extortion, sale of information and protection to criminals, armed robbery, auto theft, and looting. A series of postwar scandals did not eliminate corruption, and in 1979 a federal prosecutor indicted the entire Philadelphia police force for its methods and its unwillingness to cooperate in the investigation of corruption. The same decade found a long-standing relationship among police, municipal government, and organized crime in Chicago (Beigel and Beigel, 1977). But the most famous scandal and the one with the farthest-reaching impact was the Knapp Commission investigation of the New York City Police Department. By televising its hearings, the commission focused national and international attention on the widespread and highly organized corruption it uncovered, corruption that reached into the upper ranks and was commonly accepted by police officers as "clean money," that led to a comfortable standard of living and an undemanding work situation. It also revealed how the traditional distinction between "clean" and "dirty" money had become blurred in practice with the introduction of the buying, selling, and stealing of narcotics. Finally, the Knapp Commission introduced the memorable terms "grass-eater" and "meat-eater" to describe officers who, respectively, simply accepted whatever corrupt money came their way as opposed to those who actively sought out corruption opportunities.

Theories of Corruption

One frequent analysis of corrupt practices involves the contradictions and difficulties that characterize the relationship between the police and the population, particularly in a democratic society. Police officers are directed to enforce the law, to maintain order, and to do both of these without infringing upon the rights of the individual. The inconsistencies and conflicts among these goals, often resulting in a failure to fulfill any of them, produce what Bruce Smith has described as the "police problem" (1960: 2–3). Goldstein (1977:163) has suggested that the demands made upon the police are so diffuse and contradictory that their job is actually unworkable and that this leads to an atmosphere of "duplicity and hypocrisy" that, in turn, leads to a police subculture that is characterized by strong internal solidarity, the sense of an adversarial relationship with the rest of society, its own value system, and a process for socializing recruits. This subculture is supported by a hierarchy that emphasizes efficiency rather than legality and whose leadership, drawn largely from the ranks, shares their values and perceptions.

It is against this background that most attempts to establish empirical associations between police corruption and particular social, political, economic, historical, and cultural factors take place. Such factors include the influence of organized crime, the need to enforce unpopular laws, recruitment of inferior personnel, police abuse of their discretionary powers, poor training of recruits, poor leadership, inadequate administrative control, low pay, the low status of police officers, political corruption, corruption in other areas of the criminal-justice system, low moral standards in other parts of society, and the conflict police experience in their roles while exercising their day-to-day functions (Simpson, 1977:87).

The most commonly used theoretical frameworks for explaining police corruption are the sociological, the sociopsychological, and the organizational (Simpson, 1977:112). Sociological theories often emphasize the "code," the unwritten rules that prescribe what is permitted and what is required and that are enforced by the police peer group. The code, which enjoins solidarity and secrecy in the face of a public believed to be either indifferent or actively hostile to the police, allows and may even demand that the police participate in the corrupt activities that the low moral climate of society makes possible. Some of these theories suggest that corruption supports values that are basically the same as those of the larger society and allows the police to accumulate wealth while they are regulating and controlling the activities—gambling, commercial sex, narcotics—that an ambivalent society has made illegal but does not really want eliminated. It allows them to accommodate the conflicting desires of a pluralistic society (Bracey, 1976) and—by manipulating evidence and testimony—lets them make arrests that can be successfully prosecuted in a legal system that makes it difficult to make such arrests (Manning, 1974).

A variant of this approach emphasizes the police subculture, an occupational culture characterized by the frustrations of police work. Wilson (1963:138) stresses the functional aspect of this subculture in providing the police with "a basis for self-respect independent to some degree from civilian attitudes." Socio-psychological theories focus on the interaction between the individual and the environment. They do not seek to explain why corruption occurs initially, but rather why some officers become corrupt while others do not. One such explanation is based on the concept of the "moral career" (Stoddard, 1968:204), a process by which the officer begins with relatively minor offenses and progresses gradually to more serious acts. This view of corruption explains why some police administrators are concerned about acts as trivial as accepting a free cup of coffee from a restaurant; they are afraid that such an act is the first step in a process in which the officer increasingly accepts the values of the "code."

Competing with the code are the standards set by society to regulate the conduct of the police as well as the individual's own system of morality "gained from prior socialization in family, religious, educational, and peer group interaction." Because each officer combines and applies these sets of standards differently, structural factors alone will not determine whether or how deeply he or she participates in corrupt activities.

The organizational analysis of police corruption suggests that the bureaucratic and paramilitary structure of police departments provide a setting that produces corruption or, at the very least, is tolerant of it. For example, by institutionalizing managerial secrecy and discouraging officers from bringing complaints against their colleagues, the police hierarchy encourages the use of the "rotten apple" defense against charges of corruption brought by the press, citizens, or other outside agencies (Misner, 1975). The inflexibility of the traditional police bureaucracy leads to a system of organizational control based on authoritarianism and threat, while its reward system encourages loyalty to the organization and individuals within it rather than to the principles of morality and professionalism.

Corruption Prevention
American police have experimented with a number of measures designed to prevent, detect, and punish corruption. Several of these have been identified as being particularly successful (McCormack and Ward, 1979).

1. *Positive Leadership.* The effective chiefs show by example and support, as well as by their statements, that their anti-corruption policies are important to them. In departments with a reputation for misconduct, new chiefs have found that it is important to take steps early in their administration and that waiting too long may make it impossible to overcome the hostility that forceful anti-corruption methods will produce in those who subscribe to the "code."

2. *Political Influence.* Politics intrudes upon police administration primarily when politicians ask that certain laws not be enforced, that violations of law be ignored, or that they be allowed to influence the assignment and promotion of police personnel. Since most American

police chiefs report to an elected official, it has proven impossible and perhaps undesirable to eliminate politics entirely. Nevertheless, chiefs successful in fighting corruption have observed that when external political influences dictate their decisions, they lose the confidence of their officers and the public, and they have made it clear that responsibility for managing their departments rests with them.

3. *Authority and Responsibility.* The Knapp Commission recommended that primary responsibility for all but the most serious corruption investigations be vested in the commands concerned, rather than in headquarters. Thus, all members of the department, including first-line supervisors, have the duty to take action against corruption, and failure to do so results in disciplinary action against all officers in the chain of command.

4. *Policies and Procedures.* Effective anti-corruption policies are clear, unambiguous, and systematically disseminated to all members of the department. Careful planning results in a set of procedures that makes it clear which areas of action are handled by supervisors or command officers and which are handled by the internal-affairs unit.

5. *Internal-Affairs Units.* Most departments with more than a hundred sworn personnel include an internal affairs or inspection unit in their organizational structure. The unit provides an ongoing effort to detect actual or potential problems of police misconduct and investigates the more serious cases. The unit generally reports to the chief or deputy chief; its size is dictated by such factors as the size of the department, the number of complaints received, the number of cases handled, the actual responsibilities of the unit, and the nature of the department's misconduct problems.

6. *Field Associates Programs.* In these programs, selected recruits and veteran police officers are given special responsibility for covertly obtaining and reporting information on corruption or other misconduct. Although the program itself is well publicized internally, the identity of the field associates is kept secret. Such programs are particularly useful in departments where reporting fellow offic-

ers has been rare and is considered an offense against the "code," although the personnel of such departments can be expected to be most hostile toward them.

7. *Turning.* "Turning" occurs when an officer who is discovered to be corrupt is promised immunity or some other inducement in exchange for collecting evidence against other corrupt officers; this may involve wearing a recording device. This has often proven to be an effective way of uncovering and prosecuting systemic corruption, although the ethics of encouraging an officer to continue in corrupt activities has been debated.

8. *Integrity Testing.* This consists of exercises such as leaving wallets full of cash in places where police officers will find them and waiting to see if the officers return the "found" property; department personnel may or may not be informed that such a program is being carried out. Although departments with corruption problems may find integrity testing worthwhile both as an investigating device and as a deterrent, it is open to both ethical and legal charges of entrapment.

Dorothy H. Bracey

Bibliography

Banfield, Edward C. *The Moral Basis of a Backward Society.* New York: Free Press, 1958.

Barker, Thomas, and Julien B. Roebuck. *An Empirical Typology of Police Corruption: A Study in Organizational Deviance.* Springfield, IL: Charles C. Thomas, 1974.

Bayley, David H. *The Police and Political Development in India.* Princeton, NJ: Princeton University Press, 1969.

Beigel, H., and A. Beigel. *Beneath the Badge: A Story of Police Corruption.* New York: Harper & Row, 1977.

Bracey, Dorothy H. *A Functional Approach to Police Corruption.* New York: John Jay Press, 1976.

Cox. B., J. Shirley, and M. Short. *The Fall of Scotland Yard.* Harmondsworth, England: Penguin, 1977.

Davies, Derek, and Leo Goodstadt. "Crawling out of the Woodwork." *Far Eastern Economic Review* 87 (March 7, 1975): 10–12.

Fosdick, Raymond B. *European Police Systems*. Montclair, NJ: Patterson-Smith. 1969 (Reprint of 1915 ed.).

Goldstein, Herman. *Policing a Free Society*. Cambridge, MA: Ballinger, 1977.

Jeffries, Sir Charles. *The Colonial Police*. London: Max Parrish, 1952.

McCormack, Robert, and Richard H. Ward. *An Anti-Corruption Manual for Administrators in Law Enforcement*. New York: John Jay Press, 1979.

McCoy, Alfred, et al. *The Politics of Heroin in Southeast Asia*. New York: Harper & Row, 1972.

Manning, Peter K. "Police Lying." *Urban Life and Culture* 3 (1974): 283–306.

Misner, Gordon E. "The Organization and Social Setting of Police Corruption." *Police Journal* 48 (1975): 45–51.

Punch, Maurice. *Conduct Unbecoming*. New York: Tavistock Publications, 1985.

Sherman, Lawrence W. *Scandal and Reform: Controlling Police Corruption*. Los Angeles and Berkeley: University of California Press, 1978.

———, ed. "Toward a Sociological Theory of Police Corruption." *Police Corruption: A Sociological Perspective*. Garden City, NY: Anchor, 1974.

Simpson, Antony E. *The Literature of Police Corruption*. New York: John Jay Press, 1977.

Smith, Bruce. *Police Systems in the United States*. 2d ed. New York: Harper & Row, 1960.

Steffens, J. Lincoln. *The Shame of the Cities*. New York: Hill and Wang, [1903] 1957.

Stoddard, E.P. "The Informal Code of Police Deviancy: A Group Approach to Bluecoat Crime." *Journal of Criminal Law, Criminology and Police Science* 59(2) (1968): 201–13.

Wilson, James Q. "The Police and Their Problems: A Theory." *Public Policy* 12 (1963): 189–216.

Police Ethics

The word *ethics* has a number of meanings, each of which is sufficiently distinct from the others to require specification. In its most general sense *ethics* is the sum total of human duty, the moral obligation of human beings to act in ways that are good and just and proper. When, for example, we speak of a person who tries to lead an "ethical life" it is this sense of ethics that we employ. A second and narrower sense of *ethics* confines its meaning to the systematic study or logic of human duty. When *ethics* is used in this sense, it is often understood to be a branch of philosophy and its practice the province of philosophers. However, there is a sense in which all people are philosophers and employ this kind of ethics when they try to think through moral problems that confront them in their daily lives. Finally, *ethics* sometimes refers to both the systematic study of human duty and to the human duties themselves in certain limited areas of human conduct or enterprise. The reason that both of the above meanings of *ethics* combine in this third meaning is that the people who do the work in these limited areas are usually the same ones who develop the area's formal ethics. It is this meaning of ethics that is implied when, for example, we speak of "legal ethics," "medical ethics," or "police ethics."

Why "Police Ethics?"

Some areas of human conduct or enterprise develop their own distinct ethics while others do not. There is no special ethics of grandparents, cooks, bus drivers, or college presidents even though all of them do important work and have the capacity to behave in morally exemplary or morally reprehensible ways in the course of doing it. In order for a special ethics of a limited area to arise and develop, certain conditions have to be satisfied.

First and probably most important, the area must have some special features to it that make it difficult to bring under the domain of general, conventional ethics. The ethics of that area must in some way be different from those of conventional morality. In the case of police ethics, police possess at least two capacities the use of which raises special ethical problems. Police are entitled to use coercive force and to lie to and deceive people in the course of their work. Moreover, as sociologist Egon Bittner reminds us, while "few of us are constantly mindful of the saying, 'He that is without sin among you, let him cast the first stone . . . ,' only the police are explicitly required to forget it" (Bittner 1970:8–9).

Second, the special ethics of the area must be of such a character and have such consequences that they become an issue of concern not just to those who practice them but to others outside the limited area. Principles of medical, legal, journalistic, and police ethics arise not only because practitioners in those areas employ extraordinary means and inherit distinctive ethical obligations, but also because each of those areas has been subject to all sorts of moral controversy. In fact, it is probably safe to say that the existence of a special ethics for a given area of activity is a certain sign that practitioners of that activity have engaged in practices that have seriously offended the moral sensibilities of sizable numbers of people.

Third and finally, a special ethics develops in areas where certain types of misconduct cannot be or are thought better not controlled by other means. In general, this means areas of activity that cannot be effectively controlled by law, regulatory systems, supervisory review, market pressures, or public opinion. In specific, this typically means areas of professional activity that are highly discretionary and in which consumers of that activity must place a relatively large degree of trust in the conduct of those who practice that activity.

In certain areas such as law and medicine, canons of formal ethics have been developed to such a point that they assume the force of law. That is, practitioners can be formally charged with violations of ethical rules, have the charges against them adjudicated, and, if found guilty, be punished for their misconduct. In most police agencies ethical violations of this formal kind are tried and punished under charges of "conduct unbecoming a police officer." Such provisions in departmental regulation are extremely general and have been applied to behavior as diverse as off-duty drinking and gambling, political campaigning, marital infidelity and fornication, fixing traffic tickets, theft of department property, and fraternization with felons or other persons of bad character. A substantial body of case law has developed bearing upon police-agency capacities to enforce such standards of officer conduct.

In addition to this formal, administrative variety, police ethics include a number of other types of moral discourse. While all of them are ultimately concerned with what is right and wrong for police to do, each is distinguished from the others both in its content and in the rhetorical terms with which it speaks to moral questions. At least three relatively distinct types of police ethical discourse exist and merit separate consideration. We shall refer to them as: (1) The Public Ethics of Moral Uplift, (2) The Theoretical Ethics of the Exercise of

Coercion, and (3) The Working Ethics of Police Practitioners.

The Public Ethics of Moral Uplift

Although it rarely receives attention from philosophers, and when it does it is often disparaged for its emotional tones, an important variety of police ethics is conducted in invigorating metaphors and impassioned rhetoric whose purpose is to instil pride and virtue into police officers and garner support for police from the public. Sociologically and psychologically, this rhetoric is necessary for police as a way of reconciling their obligations to use coercive force and deception with general cultural norms that find violence and deception to be morally unsatisfactory means of resolving difficulties. In American police history the most distinctive moral rhetoric of this type has sought to understand police in terms of a military analogy and their work as fighting a "war on crime."

The Military Analogy. One occasion upon which American society is prepared to accept the use of force and deception by its agents is the condition of war. Under conditions of war, when an enemy threatens the very existence of society, when a society is in danger of losing everything, moral reservations about using virtually any means, no matter how morally distasteful, to defeat that enemy tend to dissolve. It is for this reason, as well as others, that American police have long promoted a public understanding of their role as fighting a "war on crime."

Equating the police role with that of the military also has the advantage of celebrating and advancing a variety of military virtues of police officers. Like good soldiers, police officers possess the virtues of courage, bravery, honor, and self-discipline. Therefore under dangerous conditions they would earn the respect and gratitude of a public whose life and property they keep safe from predators. Far from being morally suspect because they traffic in force and fraud, the military analogy envisions a police of morally exemplary officers who earn honor, respect, and gratitude from a public whose lives and property they protect from malevolent forces.

While the military analogy and the metaphor of the "war on crime" charge the work of policing with military virtues and enhance public support for police, the long-term consequences of wrapping policing in military rhetoric have created more problems than the metaphor solved. The fundamental problem is with the whole idea of a war on crime. It is a war that police not only cannot win but cannot, in any real sense, fight. They cannot win it because it is simply not within their power to change those things like unemployment, the age distribution of the population, moral education, freedom, civil liberties, ambition—and the social and economic opportunities to realize it—that influence the type and amount of crime in any society. Moreover, any kind of real "war on crime" is something no democratic society would be prepared to let its police fight. It would simply be unwilling to tolerate the kinds of abuses to the civil liberties of innocent citizens that fighting any kind of real war would inevitably involve.

A further difficulty of working under the crime-fighting rhetoric of the military analogy derives from the fact that the vast majority of what police officers do day in and day out is not, by any stretch of the imagination, crime-fighting. If one excludes traffic enforcement, the tour of duty of the typical patrol officer in the high-crime areas of our nation's largest cities might not involve the arrest of a single person (Reiss, 1971). In a study of 156 full-time patrol officers in a very high crime area of New York City during 1980, Walsh (1986) found that 68 percent of the patrol officers made three or less felony arrests per year and that 40 percent made no felony arrests whatsoever during the entire year.

For patrol officers, most of what they are actually called upon to do is mundane community service. If they understand "real police work" to be fighting crime, they may come to see much of what they do as "bullshit" or mere "PR" (public relations). It is not uncommon for patrol officers to come to see the chief administrators of their department as hypocritical promoters of a crime-fighting image far removed from what patrol officers know to be the reality of police work. So while it is the case that the military analogy and war-on-crime rhetoric seek to promote the virtues of courage, bravery, discipline, and honor—uplifting virtues which should promote pride among police officers and respect from citizens—both often end up engendering feelings of cynicism, frustration, resentment, and despair because they misrepresent the nature of police work.

The Theoretical Ethics of the Exercise of Coercion

A second and very different variety of police ethics seeks to understand and explain the unique ethical implications that flow from the police obligation to use coercive force to achieve just ends. The pioneering work in this area is found in a book entitled *Police: Streetcorner Politicians* by William K. Muir, Jr. (1977).

The Extortionate Transaction. Muir's analysis of police ethics is derived from a simplified model of coercive relationships that Muir calls the "extortionate transaction." This model holds that all coercive relationships are composed of five elements: a victim, a victimizer, a threat, a hostage, and a ransom. The elements are necessary whether the coercive relationship is morally desirable, as in the case of a government "victimizer" who threatens a citizen "hostage" with loss of freedom or property unless the citizen "victim" delivers the "ransom" of law-abiding behavior; or morally undesirable, as in the case of the kidnapper who threatens to kill an innocent hostage unless a cash ransom is paid.

The power of Muir's model to promote understanding of police ethics is based on the fact that it is the simplest possible model of coercive relationships. This means that if any one of the five terms in the model is eliminated, the coercive relationship disappears. Simply put, one cannot have a coercive relationship if there is no victim, no victimizer, no hostage, no ransom, or no threat.

For police, whose responsibility it is to coerce others and keep from being coerced themselves, Muir's model offers a number of disturbing conclusions. It advises police to have nothing that can be taken from them, either because they possess nothing, fortify it heavily against threats, or do not value anything enough to make it worth threatening. Similarly, the model of the extortionate transaction advises police to be irrational in their willingness to carry through on threats and to develop a reputation for nastiness that will not only make their threats more credible but deter others from threatening them.

These strategies for success in coercion create a moral environment for police that is distinctly different from the moral environment of civilized society. While the rest of society can value possessions, accumulate them, enjoy them openly, and develop and celebrate the virtues of rationality, restraint, generosity, and compassion, these civilized virtues and values compromise the police obligation to exercise their coercive responsibilities. In coercive relationships the virtues of civilized society become liabilities that the officer's moral obligation to coerce effectively advises him or her to abandon.

At the core of the ethical life of the officer is a profound moral dilemma. On the one hand, the officer's obligations to the values of civilized society oblige him or her to coerce people effectively. On the other hand, the officer's obligation to coerce people effectively requires that he or she suspend the very values that civilized society treasures. For Muir, the moral career of the police officer is a process of attempting to understand and reconcile the conflicting demands of the morality of coercion and the morality of civilized society.

The Working Ethics of Police Practitioners

Although in recent years some police academies have begun to teach police ethics in a systematic fashion and to give to police officers the analytical tools that will help them sort through the paradoxical moral demands of their occupation, most of the ethical discussions of police officers do not take place in formal ethical terms. The most common vehicle for ethical dialogue among working police officers is the "war story," the parable police use to teach one another the moral and practical complexities of the police world.

It will be helpful to consider two examples of police war stories, each of which contains an example of a means of morally reconciling a police officer's right to lie with civilized morality's obligation to be truthful.

The Police Placebo. The Smith brothers are two men in their middle fifties who have spent at least the past decade of their lives on skid row. They are familiar figures to police, who refer to them as "10–81s," the police code for the mentally ill.

Among the Smith brothers' problems, as they see them, is that from time to time they are pursued by invisible agents from outer space. These agents have powers that are literally unbelievable. Among them is the ability to insert fine wires in a person's head, through which they can control him.

The Smith brothers have managed to avoid the victimization largely through the efforts of a sympathetic police sergeant. The sergeant had

the good sense to report the invasion to Washington, which immediately responded to his report by dispatching a squad of equally invisible investigators who were especially trained—and armed—to deal with such intruders. Needless to say, this operation is highly confidential and outside of the Smith brothers, the sergeant, and a handful of persons with the highest of security clearances, no one knows about it. (Klockars, 1984:534).

For police the moral lesson of the Smith brothers' tale is the virtue of the placebic lie. Such lies have a self-evident morality to them: Police officers find it ethically defensible to lie when the lie is told to benefit the person lied to and no more effective means of dealing with the problem is available. This is, of course, the same moral justification physicians draw on when they choose to treat certain patient complaints with medical placebos.

Less elaborate but more common examples of police placebos include all sorts of promises to keep a close watch on an area or dwelling after a person has been victimized or has become fearful of being victimized by media reports of crime; assurances that burglaries with all the earmarks of a professional job were probably the work of "just kids"; advising a seriously injured child or spouse of an accident victim that the deceased is all right or receiving expert medical attention; telling the family of a fatally injured accident victim that their loved one died instantly and painlessly when the officer knows the death was neither quick nor painless; and attribution of a decision not to arrest to some generous or kindly motive rather than admitting the futility of doing so in the face of inadequate evidence.

Blue Lies. The demonstrator was a middle-class white woman in her late forties. She had entered the abortion clinic anteroom and had begun pleading with the women present not to go through with the acts of murder they were contemplating. The receptionist barred the door to the procedure room and called the cops.

When they arrived the women seated herself on the floor and refused to move. The press, including a photographer, was present. The woman stated that she had thought a lot about what she was doing and that she would not leave under her own power. If the police wanted her out of the clinic, they were going to have to carry her out.

The shorter of the two policemen in the anteroom, which by now had been cleared of both press and patients, kneeled down slowly next to her and explained: "Look ma'am. I understand what you are trying to do here and even though it's against the law I can respect it. But the problem is that this is my first day back to work after being off for a hernia operation. I've got twenty-two stitches and I'm afraid that if I have to carry you out of here they might just open up."

"You're not lying to me, are you?" asked the woman.

"No, I'm not," said the policeman. "I'll show you my stitches if you want," he offered, reaching for his belt.

"That's O.K. I believe you. I don't want you to hurt yourself because of me. I'll go with you." (Klockars, 1984: 536)

"Blue Lies," such as the one above, are different from police placebos in that they are not told to help or comfort the person lied to but, rather, to exert control. Police understand the legitimacy of such lies to derive in a general way from their right to use coercive force. In the working ethics of police practitioners, police are justified in lying to achieve any ends they are justified in using coercive force to achieve. In fact, as the war story above seeks to illustrate, lying is preferable, on both moral and practical grounds, to physical coercion.

Neither "blue lies" nor "police placebos" exhaust the types or varieties of lies that the working culture of police practitioners find to be ethically legitimate. They are offered here only as examples of the *form* in which the ethics of working police officers are typically developed, the "war story," and the unique ethical problems police officers must address. Policing is the only domestic occupation that is given the legitimate right to use force and fraud to achieve just ends. And, by and large, it is left to police themselves to work through the ethical contours of that obligation in their own vocabularies.

Carl B. Klockars

Bibliography

Bittner, E. *The Functions of Police in Modern Society.* Cambridge, MA: Olegeschlager, Gunn & Hain, 1970.

Muir, W.K., Jr. *Police: Streetcorner Politicians.* Chicago: University of Chicago Press, 1977.

Klockars, C.B. "Blue Lies and Police Placebos." *American Behavioral Scientist* 27 (March–April 1984): 529–44.

Reiss, A.J. *The Police and the Public.* New Haven, CT: Yale University Press, 1971.

Walsh, W.F. "Patrol Officer Arrest Rates: A Study of the Social Organization of Police Work." *Justice Quarterly* 3 (September 1986): 271–90.

Police History
Early American Policing (1600–1860)

Police departments as we know them—organized, salaried bureaucracies, most of whose members wear uniforms—began in the United States in the generation before 1860. From the outset, the police department has been a multipurpose agency of municipal government, not just a component of the criminal justice system. New York police officers in the 1850s spent more time on stray horses and lost children than they did on burglaries, just as their counterparts a century later labored to keep traffic moving and initiated the paperwork on fender benders. Understanding the origins of American police therefore requires attention to the general context of urban government, as well as official responses to crime and disorder.

The earliest inhabitants of colonial cities in the seventeenth century still had at least one foot in the Middle Ages. Their worldview was dominated by scarcity. Government's most important task was to regulate economic life so that strangers did not usurp work rightfully belonging to residents, or wandering poor gain the right to local relief, or greedy men take undue advantage of consumers. Public officials did not think of government as a provider of services financed through the collection of taxes. Government did encourage private interests to undertake necessary projects, like streets and wharves, for which the public purse was inadequate. In New York City one mechanism to achieve such goals was to transfer public land to private ownership in return for specific commitments to the construction of public facilities.

In the late eighteenth and early nineteenth centuries, a new worldview came to prevail, at least among the elite, one characterized by the prospect of growth and perhaps even of abundance rather than scarcity. Adam Smith's *Wealth of Nations*, published in 1776, gave a convincing theoretical statement of how the pursuit of individual interests could lead to general economic growth if the market were free of government-granted monopolies or private combinations in restraint of trade. In this intellectual climate, government would be more a promoter of growth than a regulator of scarcity by helping provide what modern economists know as social overhead capital and what the nineteenth century called improvements. Thus government now paid for new wharves and streets, built canals, and promoted the development of railways. Tax-supported schools, at least in theory, produced a disciplined and literate labor force; gas lamps made night a little less gloomy and fearful; and publicly equipped, although not yet paid, fire companies provided some protection against this major urban hazard. By 1860 twelve of the sixteen largest cities had public water systems to aid in firefighting and to give residents something to drink other than alcohol or possibly fouled well water.

Urban Growth and the Need for Police

Between 1820 and 1860 American cities attracted unprecedented numbers of migrants, whether from rural America, Ireland, or Germany. Growth was the reality as well as a theoretical possibility. Whereas only one of twenty Americans lived in an urban settlement in 1790, the ratio was one in five in 1860. New York and Brooklyn together accounted for more than a million people, Philadelphia more than one-half million, while Chicago, incorporated only in 1833, had more than one hundred thousand residents in 1860. By the early 1870s the city of Chicago was spending in a day what had sufficed for an entire year in the late 1840s.

When municipal governments examined growth and its consequences, they were both exhilarated and fearful. Historian Edward Pessen has demonstrated that the business elite exercised disproportionate influence on urban government throughout the so-called age of the common man. When city councils became less patrician and more plebeian in the late 1840s and 1850s, they also lost many of their former functions. Independent boards and commissions replaced council committees as the overseers of public services while the mayor, almost invariably a leading business or professional man, became a more powerful figure. Council, usually elected by wards, more often reacted to external initiatives than proposed measures of its own, at least for anything that went beyond the neighborhood level. Most members of the elite liked growth; their businesses and real-estate holdings appreciated in value with more

people and higher levels of economic activity. They did not like some of the negative consequences, such as larger numbers of strangers, immigrants of alien tongue, customs, and religion who did not always recognize the cultural superiority and natural goodness of old-stock American Protestants. Some members of the elite were also troubled by the visible increase in the number of poor and dependent people who neither benefited from the city's growth nor seemed able to cope with its complexity.

Establishing a police department was one response to these concerns. When New York created its modern department in 1845, the city made the police responsible for a wide range of services, from inspecting hacks and stages to lighting the gas lamps in the evening. Over time many of these functions were transferred to other agencies, but the point remains that the police were never thought of exclusively as a crime-fighting and order-maintaining group.

The police did have important responsibilities in keeping the peace and dealing with criminals. In the colonial period order maintenance and crime-fighting were more individual and communal responsibilities than the purview of a bureaucratic agency. The colonists brought with them such traditional English institutions as elected constables and the night watch. In theory constables had extensive legal responsibilities and powers, although rarely did their prestige and authority match their legal position. The watch, often made up of reluctant citizens, kept a lookout for fire as well as crime and disorder. In the case of crime the aggrieved party bore the burden of initiating the processes of apprehension and prosecution. By the early nineteenth century, New York had more than one hundred persons with police powers, either as elected constables or appointed mayor's marshals. These officers spent much of their time in the service of civil processes, although they were available for hire by victims of theft. They made a specialty of returning stolen property in exchange for a portion of the recovery. Early nineteenth-century police officers were thus fee-for-service professionals rather than salaried bureaucrats.

Riots, often with specific political targets and goals, were recognized features of pre-industrial urban life. Rioters rarely took life although they often destroyed considerable property. The most famous riots were those associated with the American Revolution, such as the protests over the Stamp Act of 1765, the

Boston Massacre of 1770, and the Boston Tea Party of 1773. The decades before the revolutionary agitation also experienced periodic urban disorders. The most savage reprisals were directed at slaves thought to be plotting against whites, such as in New York City in 1712 and 1741. In most instances rioters seemed content to disperse once they made their point, whether it was antipopery or a protest against body snatching by doctors and medical students. But by the 1820s, middle- and upper-class urbanites no longer seemed willing to accept levels of unseemly behavior in public places previously thought unavoidable.

From the early eighteenth century onward, urbanites like Benjamin Franklin organized voluntary societies to achieve desirable social goals. The pace of this activity accelerated in the generation after 1815, especially under the auspices of religious groups who wished to spread the good news of salvation through the publication and distribution of bibles and tracts, to reach children in Sunday schools, to uplift the poor, and to reform juvenile delinquents and fallen women. Whenever families failed in their tasks of nurturing and disciplining their members, other institutions had to step in to remedy the deficiencies. A case in point is New York's House of Refuge, founded by the privately established Society for the Reformation of Juvenile Delinquents in 1825, which received state support for this purpose.

The English Example

In these activities American institution builders looked to England for both general inspiration and specific models to emulate. The American elite considered the Atlantic to be a highway as well as a barrier (indeed in the early nineteenth century it was cheaper to cross the Atlantic than to move any distance at all on land), so that books, ideas, and people moved freely between London, Boston, New York, and Philadelphia.

One of these ideas was that government in some instances would have to assume direct responsibility for social well-being. In 1829 Sir Robert Peel put through Parliament a bill for the creation of the London Metropolitan Police, a salaried bureaucracy responsible for the maintenance of order and the prevention and detection of crime. The London Metropolitan Police served as a direct model for police departments subsequently established in American cities.

Peel's bill was preceded by a half-century of debate and discussion, parliamentary inquiries, and the creation of numerous voluntary societies to reform public morals. During these decades London also relied on fee-for-service police officers while the watch was organized and paid for on a parish-by-parish basis with consequent wide variations in numbers and effectiveness. Civil authorities were virtually helpless to deal with such outbreaks as the Gordon Riots of 1780, while senior army officers objected to being called upon to suppress riots because of the possible impact upon morale and discipline. As evangelical religious ideas became more popular in England, there was greater concern for the state of public morality. Prostitution and drunkenness came to be thought of as social problems to a greater extent than they had been in earlier decades. This is not to say that rates of disorder, crime, or behavior contrary to evangelical notions of propriety were necessarily rising, but that influential figures were less tolerant, accepting, or stoic about such matters. The French Revolution and its aftermath seems to have convinced the upper classes that they needed to exercise firmer control over the lower. To some extent the more orderly people became, the higher the level of expectations among the propertied and respectable.

The London Metropolitan Police Bill thus represented the convergence of three streams of social concern. The first was for a public agency other than the army that could be mobilized to deal with civil disorder. Policemen would be uniformed, subject to quasi-military discipline, and sufficiently removed from civilians to act as a riot-repressing force; but there would not be the potential morale problems associated with the use of the army or the possible class bias of the militia. If the militia were recruited from the same groups as rioters, it might join in. If, like England's mounted yeomanry, the militia came from landowners, urban workers and farm laborers would hardly accept it as legitimate. The police would be recruited from the people, but not locally, so that their loyalties would be more to their organization and their superiors than to the people they policed.

The second stream of concern was crime. Pre-Peel police officers, such as the famous Bow Street Runners, might deal efficiently with property crimes after victims hired them. Unfortunately, they also found consorting and conspiring with criminals to be in their interests. The line between cops and robbers was a fuzzy one at best and easily crossed. Moreover, even the best officers acted only after the crime had occurred and when there was sufficient monetary incentive. Peel's police were to be preventive, a word used frequently and loosely. Ideally the very presence of such a force would lead criminals to accept honest toil as a way of life and would keep young people from ever straying from that path.

Finally, the police could deal with the "police" of the city in its generic sense. When early nineteenth-century figures referred to the "police" of the city, they had a broad conception in mind, akin to the later judicial notion of police power, the ability to legislate for the public welfare. Policing involved keeping city streets clean as well as the good order and discipline of its residents. The presence of a police officer might deter residents from airmailing their garbage into the streets, as well as keep streetwalkers from plying their trade. We can subsume these activities under the heading of "preventing unseemly behavior in public places." In the absence of salaried bureaucrats entrusted with keeping the peace and imposing a moral code, what could sober people do about drunks except step over them or avoid where they congregated? The establishment of the police meant an active group patrolling the streets on the lookout for breaches of the moral code as well as common-law crimes, thus extending the authority of the state into the daily lives of the people.

The London police were not universally accepted in their first years. The slang term *crushers* gives some sense of lower-class response. The leaders of the force worked hard to get citizens to acknowledge the moral authority of the police. The first commissioners, recruited from outside London where possible, dismissed many of their early appointees for drunkenness and tried to maintain tight administrative control. The lines of authority ran to a cabinet minister, the home secretary, not to locally elected officials.

The Rise of American Urban Police Departments

The existence of the London police stimulated American urban leaders to think about establishing similar institutions, especially since their own cities were experiencing rapid growth and social change. New York City's population had grown almost four times between 1790 and 1820; between 1820 and 1860 the growth was more than sevenfold. Before the mid-1820s, city officials considered their problems of crime and

disorder to be manageable, but by the mid-1830s they worried about endemic street violence. Indeed, 1834 was long remembered in the city's history as the year of riots. When the great fire struck a year later, authorities could neither fight the fire effectively nor control looting without calling out the militia. Sensational murder cases went undetected and largely uninvestigated unless someone put up substantial reward money. Periodic economic panics and crises meant thousands of unemployed men and women on the margins of subsistence would fall below it without some form of assistance. Boston and Philadelphia also experienced conflict among religious, ethnic, and class rivals, while cities with substantial slave populations were concerned above all else with controlling their blacks.

After a decade of debate and the forging of a consensus that New York City needed a police force, the state legislature adopted legislation in 1844 creating the police department and setting forth its powers and structure in detail. The law required municipal approval before it became effective. This approval was granted in 1845. Increasingly, both legal theorists and municipal officials took the position that any extension of municipal powers required direct action by the state legislature. For the remainder of the nineteenth century, state legislatures sometimes exercised their prerogative to intervene in urban police departments in a heavy-handed fashion.

The New York Police Department, established in 1845, was a salaried bureaucracy, but it differed in significant ways from the London police, even though its first set of rules and regulations was largely copied from London's. The New York police were not uniformed, although members did carry a star-shaped badge for identification. Originally the term of office was one year, raised to two in 1846 and four in 1849. The alderman of the particular ward had the most to say about who should serve as police officers. If an alderman was voted out of office, most of the police officers he appointed lost their jobs. The force was decentralized in that each ward constituted a patrol district with little central supervision.

A new state law in 1853 made major changes in the organization and administration of the police. It established a board of police commissioners, consisting of the mayor, the city judge, and the recorder (a judicial official), thus reducing the aldermen's role in appointments and administration. Police officers now could be removed only for cause, thus making police work a career. The practice of naming people to senior positions without prior police experience died out, and the standard became entry at the bottom and promotion from within. The new commissioners put the police into uniform, an innovation resisted without success by some men who cherished their anonymity.

Although the New York police now looked like their London counterparts, there were still substantial differences between the two departments. London's administrators stressed careful control of the use of police powers and tried to keep the police from having to perform unpopular tasks like closing drinking places on Sunday. In New York ultimate authority over the police lay in the hands of locally elected officials who, along with New York's judges, were more prone to let the police take a tougher approach than their counterparts in London. Historian Wilbur Miller, Jr., has documented how the New York police were more inclined to use force and make arrests on suspicion than London's. Despite police rhetoric about judicial intervention or not being backed up, they were rarely disciplined for such actions or discouraged from using such tactics. London's police were generally more circumspect in their dealing with citizens because their superiors wanted them to be embodiments of the moral authority of the state, with the uniform accepted as its legitimate symbol.

An obvious and very important difference was the unarmed police of London compared with the armed police of New York. Throughout the nineteenth century and for most of the twentieth, English police officers were not armed; in recent years a rising volume of violent crime has led to serious questioning of this policy. In New York the police were not armed early in their history. Officers began to carry weapons without legal authorization to do so because they perceived their working environment as dangerously unpredictable. Samuel Colt's technological innovations made handguns cheaper and more readily available in the 1850s. New York newspapers complained in the mid-1850s that the streets of New York were more dangerous than the plains of Kansas, while historians Roger Lane and David Johnson have noted the prevalence of violent crime in Philadelphia during these years.

The arming of American police, begun by officers without legal authorization, soon became enshrined in custom. Unlike their British counterparts, American public authorities took the position that the tough, armed cop was the best response to the pervasive problems of crime and disorder within their cities.

Police departments joined other public institutions such as school systems as instruments of order, stability, and uplift to cope with an explosively growing and often disorderly urban environment. Within the ranks, station house socialization passed the norms of the veterans along to the rookies, norms that had less to do with law enforcement than with maintenance of group solidarity and respect. "Don't talk about police business to outsiders" and "Don't take any guff from civilians" were more important than the statute books or the rules and regulations of the department set forth in such minute details.

At top levels, such as among board members and commissioners, political winds could blow harshly. In 1857 the New York state legislature abolished the municipal police and substituted a new department, the Metropolitan Police, with responsibilities for an enlarged district. New York City still had to pay for the officers assigned within its boundaries. This arrangement lasted for thirteen years. In other states as well, legislatures stepped in and replaced individuals holding senior administrative positions. These interventions were usually related to some hope of partisan advantage or distaste for the way city police were or were not enforcing liquor and vice laws.

One branch not always provided for in the first stages of a bureaucratic policy were the detectives. If a preventive police were fully effective, there would be no need for detectives. Establishing a detective squad was an admission that the police had not lived up to expectations. And there was the old fear that detectives and criminals were much too close. Roger Lane has shown how slow Philadelphia was in assigning police officers to work as homicide specialists.

Marxist scholars treat American police within a conceptual framework of class analysis. Historians such as Sidney Harring and Sean Wilentz look at the police as an instrument created by the owners of the means of production to control workers' behavior. The most obvious instances of such control came in strikes, where the police aided owners who wished to keep operating despite turnouts of their workforce. In such situations, say these scholars, the naked realities could not be disguised under such formulae as enforcing the law or protecting life and property. One does not have to be a Marxist to acknowledge that in large cities at least local police departments were seldom neutral in labor disputes.

Just as London provided the model for New York, Boston, and Philadelphia, these eastern cities served as models for other American communities. Historian Eric Monkkonen sees the establishment of bureaucratic police departments as an innovation beginning in the older and larger cities and then diffusing surprisingly quickly out and down the urban hierarchy. According to Monkkonen, fifteen cities had adopted uniforms—his key indicator of a bureaucratic police—by 1860 while another twenty-four joined them in the following decade. Evidently, the salaried, bureaucratic police was an idea whose time had come between 1840 and 1870. Later decades were to see the maturation and expansion of the patterns established during these formative years.

James F. Richardson

Bibliography

Jonson, David R. *Policing the Urban Underworld: The Impact of Crime on the Development of the American Police, 1800–1887*. Philadelphia: Temple University Press, 1979.

———. *American Law Enforcement: A History*. St. Louis, MO: Forum Press, 1981.

Lane, Roger. *Policing the City: Boston, 1822–1885*. Cambridge, MA: Harvard University Press, 1967.

———. *Violent Death in the City: Suicide, Accident, and Murder in Nineteenth Century Philadelphia*. Cambridge, MA: Harvard University Press, 1979.

Miller, Wilbur R. *Cops and Robbers: Police Authority in New York and London, 1830–1870*. Chicago: University of Chicago Press, 1977.

Richardson, James. *The New York Police: Colonial Times to 1901*. New York: Oxford University Press, 1970.

———. *Urban Police in the United States*. Port Washington, NY: Kennikat, 1974.

Walker, Samuel. *A Critical History of Police Reform: The Emergence of Professionalism*. Lexington, MA: Lexington, 1977.

———. *Popular Justice: A History of American Criminal Justice*. New York: Oxford University Press, 1980.

The Police in Urban America, 1860–1920

During the period following the Civil War, American policing developed the form and character that was to carry it into the 1980s. Uniformed police departments in the fifty-seven largest cities had been established between 1850 and 1880 (Monkkonen, 1982:54–57). Most cities had their own municipal police departments by the end of the nineteenth century. The social, political, and economic forces of the period between 1860 and 1920 defined the nature and scope of the police institution. By the 1920s an outline of the parameters of police authority, a blueprint of the administrative structure of the police organization, and a rough approximation of the police function had emerged. Although these characteristics developed more as a result of historical trial and error than careful planning, they collectively represented a foundation of policing that is recognizable to most people today. It is not an overstatement to say that in order to understand the strengths and weaknesses of American policing in the 1980s, one must be knowledgeable about the complex history of the police institution.

The purpose of this section is to present a historical analysis and overview of the significant themes surrounding the history of the police between 1860 and 1920. Details of that history will not be presented here, since they are available in the sources cited. Although much work remains to be done, available historical research provides a rich source of information about specific departments (Conley, 1977; Monkkonen, 1982).

Urban Conditions

Cities created police departments during a period of American history characterized by massive social change brought about by industrialization, immigration, and urbanization. Between 1860 and 1910, the modern American city emerged as the total population of the United States tripled to 92 milion. The number of people living in cities grew from a low of 5 percent in the early nineteenth century to over 45 percent by 1910. The largest cities—Boston, New York, and Philadelphia—had less than 100,000 people in the early nineteenth century and more than 1 million by 1890 (Johnson 1979:4; Lane 1975:161). This growth did not occur just on the eastern seaboard. Midwestern cities such as St. Louis, Cleveland, and Detroit ranked fourth, sixth, and ninth, respectively, by 1910. Chicago, which was eighth in 1860 with a population of 100,000 moved to second place by 1910 with a population of over 2 million.

Population shifts and immigration rates increased during prosperity and decreased during economic recessions. The resultant strains produced by these economic and population shifts created new challenges for the cities that had been organized and operated on a model more appropriate to the preurban period of the eighteenth century. One of the new challenges was the need to address the problem of maintaining order in the cities. Cities like New York, Boston, and Philadelphia created their uniformed police organizations during a period of great social and political turmoil. Some cities experienced riots, others saw rising property crimes, still others had social problems with immigrants and a mobile population. Each of these problems varied in intensity and importance from city to city. But all cities experienced the effects of industrialization and urbanization in some form. Population growth mushroomed and the demands on urban government for services increased dramatically.

There was a need for an effective order-maintenance institution. The constable and watch systems of the eighteenth century did not contribute to a sense of security for the community and were not designed to address a preventive role. The constable was attached to the courts and did not serve as an official of city government. The constable-watch system did not act to prevent crime but operated on a reactive basis. For a fee, constables would investigate a crime after the fact and report to the victim who was paying the reward. This form of entrepreneurial policing, although beneficial to some, simply could not address the changing levels of disorder and crime (Lane, 1975:8–10, Richardson, 1978:17–19).

Theories on the Creation of Police
Historical research on the police has increased in quantity and quality in the past decade. Prior to the 1970s, histories of the police fell into the category of anecdotal or organizational descriptions with little analytical content or generalization (Conley, 1977). Recent research has attempted to place police development in a larger context of the times, but more work on synthesizing and generalization is needed (Monkkonen, 1982:575).

There are currently three standard conceptual frameworks for examining the history of the police (Monkkonen, 1981b:49–61). One

explanation for the rise of the urban police is that crime rose to such unprecedented levels that the constable-watch system collapsed and was incapable of adjusting to the pressures of industrialization and urbanization (Johnson, 1979). There is no historical evidence that crime was rising, and if the evidence existed, it would have been verified by arrest data, which in turn would argue for the effectiveness of the traditional constable-watch system.

A second explanation argues that the riots of the early nineteenth century created such fears among the populace that alternative means of riot suppression were sought. Not willing to establish a standing army because of its potential threat to liberty, Americans created a paramilitary organization. This new police force contributed a visibility and continuity lacking in the traditional constable-watch system, presented an organized show of force when required during civil disorders, but also allowed for civil control over the organization. The difficulty with this appealing interpretation is that only a few cities had riots before they established the new police, and even in these cities there was no connection between the riots and the creation of the police. The causal connection between riots and the establishment of the American police has yet to be proven.

Another explanation is that the elites feared the rising number of and threat from the poor immigrants (Lane, 1975:23–25; Richardson, 1970:23–50). Whether it was a fear of the destruction of their societal values, a fear for their property, or a fear of the loss of control of the urban social order, the argument is that the elites established the police to control the "dangerous classes." This interpretation claims that the police served a social-control function, while others claim a class-control function (Harring, 1983). The social-control interpretation lacks evidence that connects this goal to the intent of the nineteenth-century proponents of the police.

The newest explanation for the creation of a uniformed police argues that the police represented just one of many urban government agencies created to provide services to meet the changing demands on city governments—just one example of the growth of "urban service bureaucracies" (Monkkonen, 1981b:55), such as those concerned with health, fire, and sewage. As city governments began to absorb a variety of these services once provided by entrepreneurs, they established bureaucracies to deliver them. Once larger cities adopted these models other cities followed. Smaller cities learned of the innovation and established uniformed police organizations as part of the national movement of expanding city government. Urban uniformed police emerged as part of the movement that increased governmental responsibility for a variety of direct services to the public.

Although public concern with order, riots, and crime—as well as a growing fear of the "dangerous classes"—played a role in shaping the new police, these issues did not dominate the debate around the establishment of the police. These specifically threatening social problems contributed to the debate and subsequent development of the police, but they served as precipitating events in most cases and not as preconditions to the establishment of the police. Finally, there is no historical evidence to support the theory that any one or any combination of these social problems caused cities to create a uniformed police. In fact, most cities did not experience these social problems, yet they also created uniformed police organizations during the late nineteenth century. We have been too quick to seek out some catastrophic event as a causal factor for the origin of a uniformed police when the historical evidence suggests that its development was an innovation that followed a process of expanding urban government.

Decentralization and Authority

The police in America are unique in the Western democracies in that they are organized at the level of local government with no formal connection to a central government. The nature of federalism in the United States and the inherent deep distrust of a central government dictated that governments be as close to the people as possible. For this reason police departments across the country are organized along the jurisdictional lines of the municipal government, not those of the county, the region, or the state. The decentralized nature of the American police, to a degree unheard of in Western Europe, dates back to the late nineteenth century (Fogelson, 1977:14–15).

Another characteristic of the American police was deep partisan ties. Unlike their counterparts in England, the American police fulfilled the society's expectation that the police be organically involved in the local community. This expectation was a local extension of the American commitment to democratic government. In order to control the potentially awesome power of the police, Americans placed administrative responsibility in locally elected officials, aldermen, rather than in mayors or police chiefs. As a result, police officers not only actively participated in local politics, they also gave their allegiance to locally elected officials. Local ward bosses appointed police officers, controlled promotions, and held police accountable. There was no bureaucratic buffer between the public and the police and, as a result, the police reflected and acted out community tensions.

They also reflected the political conflicts of the day. Political power and the control of the cities shifted back and forth between the coalition of white Anglo-Saxon Protestants and rural legislators, and the urban political machines dominated by ethnic immigrants. The political struggle between these power groups directly shaped the police in modern America. Unlike their counterparts in England, who attempted to remain neutral, the American police sided with the majority during political conflicts. First, American police lacked any identification with a national symbol of law and thus had no formally defined authority upon which to base a position of neutrality. Political disorders were local in nature, and the threat was to local institutions and values. Second, conflicts in urban America were ethnic-based, not class-based, so the visibility and identity of the majority was clear. Workers joined the upper class in their fear of and willingness to control the foreign elements with their strange cultures and different religions. As a result of these conditions, the police represented the majority and upheld the existing political institution of representative democracy. They felt little pressure to remain neutral to transcend social conflicts. This historical context had long-term implications because these conditions shaped the definition of authority of the police that is still applicable today.

The distinguishing characteristic of American policing is that police authority is personal and guided by popular control rather than the formal standards of the rule of law. Police authority emanates from the political majority of the citizens, not from abstract notions of law. Authority rested on a local and partisan base within limited legal and symbolic standards, and was legitimized by informal public expectations (Haller 1976:303–24). Because the police rested their authority on the basic principles of democratic government, closeness to the citizens, and informal power rather than bureaucratic rules and legal standards, they did not represent an impartial legal system and they had wide discretionary powers (Johnson, 1979:184–85; Richardson, 1978:285). This combination of the need to rely on personal authority and their wide discretionary powers led the police to develop an "arrogant insistence on a respectful acknowledgment of their authority" (Johnson, 1979:136). Failure to give prompt attention to police commands could result in an arrest or physical harm to a citizen. Police had only vague notions of how to do their job and thus "personalized decision became the fundamental tool of policing" (Johnson, 1979:141–85). Yet the police also relied on cooperation from the public partly because of their close social and political ties to the people on their beats and partly because of their need to maintain a level of order defined by the local neighborhood. As a result of these structural influences on the definition of police authority and the use of discretion, the application of police power resulted in a growing "dependence on the police to regulate the tensions of urban society" (Johnson, 1979:143).

The combination of decentralization, local political ties, and a reliance on popular authority shaped how the police performed, or didn't perform, their functions. Brutality was widespread and was either generally accepted or ignored by the larger community. Although corruption contradicted official morality, it existed on such a large scale that it was not difficult for a reformer to raise a hue and cry. Inside police departments, promotions were bought and sold, retirements with full pensions could be had for a fee, and even assignments that had the potential for graft carried a price in the corrupt market. Outside the departments, employers and factory owners bought the services of the public police to break labor picket lines by dispersing or arresting picketers. In some situations the police actually worked for the employer or company owner as antilabor enforcers. The police also used their official role in counting ballots, selecting polling sites, and verifying voter registration lists to guarantee that their alderman won the election. There is no question that the historical record is peppered with examples of brutality and corruption and that many people suffered at the hands of the police. What we don't know is how functional this corruption may have been. One author suggests that it was a functional and also a logical extension of the informal political process of the time. Corruption provided a way of benefiting politicians for public service to their constituency, of providing a degree of flexibility in order to allow a wide variety of cultures and lifestyles to coexist in the urban environment, and it helped to modify official behavior (Richardson, 1978:186–287).

In spite of the contemporary charges and countercharges of corruption in the urban policing of the last half of the nineteenth century, which have to be viewed in the context of the intense political atmosphere of the era, there is evidence that support for the police institution did exist. The record, of course, is not clear. Competent and compassionate policing, heroic acts, and trustworthy officers who had good relationships with the citizens are not the stuff that ends up in official records, newspaper editorials, or reports of investigating committees. Yet from about 1860 until 1900, police departments had hundreds more applicants than positions available and the earlier high turnover of officers subsided and stabilized by the last decade of the century. Although politicians viewed urban police departments as agencies for the distribution of patronage, the competency and intelligence level of officers appeared to be average. The taxpayers approved attractive retirement pensions and paid salaries that competed well with contemporary wage rates. For example, the average police officer earned an annual salary of about $1,200 in the 1870s, which was $400–$600 more than that earned by skilled tradesmen and workers in manufacturing. These wages and the attractiveness of the job deteriorated around the turn of the century. Much of that change was probably due to the constantly changing economic conditions and the difficulty of performing the police function.

Role

If the police role originally was to prevent crime, there is little evidence that it became their primary function between 1860 and 1900. Indeed, created in the midst of social upheaval from rising immigrant populations and from the effects of the industrial revolution, the police absorbed tasks related more to social services than crime control. "Demands of the populace and by representatives of local government" shaped the duties of the police (Lane, 1975:119). The police responded to the demands of the urban poor in a variety of ways.

They provided free overnight lodging to the homeless immigrants, managed soup kitchens, responded to inquiries from mothers about their lost children, participated in controlling local elections, controlled the distribution of vice through their arrest patterns, and otherwise absorbed a variety of functions that tended to serve the lower classes. By performing these tasks the police of the late nineteenth century contributed to urban order by mediating class conflicts and managing tensions in the urban community. Crime control was neither a primary function of the police nor was it a primary contributing factor to urban order.

This is not to say that nineteenth-century American police did not address criminal behavior in urban America. The data on the exact level of criminal activity for this period are either not available or very unreliable, but it acknowledged that crime peaked in the 1860s and 1870s (Lane, 1975:144). As is true today, crime patterns varied spatially and changed over time. Most of the criminal activity occurred in the heart of the city, which created some problems for the police. If they concentrated their forces in that area, citizens in outlying areas complained of not being sufficiently protected. On the other hand, commercial leaders obviously demanded more police in the center of the city. The police constantly had to balance their response to these contrasting political pressures.

Criminal activity was lively and the police did respond. In the early nineteenth century the primary crimes were burglary and arson. The later period saw increased activity in pickpocketing, theft, burglary, and vice. Criminals plied their trade, but there was no attempt to eradicate crime. The police regulated crime, which seemed to satisfy the community and to serve police objectives. The police worked closely with the criminal element to keep crime at an acceptable and nonthreatening level to avoid a public outcry or pressure from community elites. Vice was not suppressed; it was licensed by the police. Some of these conditions included payoffs to officers, keeping undesirable establishments out of middle- and upper-class neighborhoods, and maintaining an orderly place of business. The criminal was not totally secure, however, for there was a political need to make arrests, not all cops were crooked, and periodic enforcement crackdowns did occur. The overall evidence, however, does not portray the urban police as a crime-fighting or primarily law-enforcement institution.

From 1900 to 1920 and beyond, reformers attempted to change the police from a catch-all service agency of urban government to a specialized crime-control bureaucracy. This transformation occurred in reaction to larger changes in urban America. The constituency of the police—the sick, poor, migrants, unemployed, mentally ill—began to have their own agencies of assistance because of the development of specialized organizations in the broad social services area. The change resulted, in part, from a national reform movement led by the Progressives, who argued for clean government, professional government employees, and rationalized and specialized governmental structure. The result was a reversal of the precinct-based, decentralized structure of the police organization, an upgrading of personnel through civil service requirements, and a change in function from maintaining urban order to crime control (Fogelson, 1977:92–116).

By the early twentieth century this impetus for police reform came from within its ranks. The coalition of civic, religious, and commercial groups that led the reforms of the late nineteenth century gave way to leaders from the police field after the turn of the century. This period of reform has been labeled the second wave of reform (Fogelson, 1977:166–82) or the second transformation of the police (Monkkonen, 1981b:148–50). These leaders concluded that the police function was spread too thin and that the organization was a catch-all agency that absorbed too many social service responsibilities. They argued that these responsibilities detracted from what they saw as the primary goal of the police, crime control. Relying on a model of professionalism, police leaders pushed for more centralization in the administration of the departments by lengthening the chief's tenure, developed a model that organized the departments along functional rather than geographic lines in order to close precincts and lessen the political influence of ward aldermen, and hoped to insulate the administration from politics by demanding more autonomy in controlling the police. These reformers hoped to remove police decision-making from the ordinary citizen and place it in a rule-bound bureaucracy. They also proposed higher entry requirements, increased salaries, and expanded promotional opportunities. These changes established a new image of the police based on a vocational, not a political, model and demanded a commitment from the officers in the organization.

The result of these reforms carried the police into the 1980s. They narrowed their functional responsibility to crime control and they changed their image from a social service agency to that of a crime-fighting organization. The cost of that success was high, however, and for the past two decades those reforms have been questioned. The police succeeded in not only insulating themselves from the public, but they have also become isolated. The image of a crime control agency has had to be manipulated because of the impossibility of achieving that self-imposed mandate. The professional model they advocated has developed only at the top of police organizations; rank-and-file unions have filled the gap at the lower levels. The challenge of the next generation of police leaders will be to address the legacy of the reforms implemented between 1860 and 1920.

Conclusion
The formation of the urban police in American in the nineteenth century and the reforms attempted through 1920 represented a societal acknowledgment that the police function is vital to the well-being of the cities. This vitality emanated from the role played by the police in contributing to an orderly environment within which cities expanded, populations grew, and political processes developed. That role, although cloudy, is still vital today. The lessons and legacy of the period from 1860 to 1920 are crucial to an understanding of the current pressures on the police. The reliance on personal authority rather than formal standards of the legal culture, combined with the American citizen's unwillingness to accept governmental power without question, places the police in the position of having to justify their actions in each police–citizen encounter. This climate contributes to an increase in community tensions and confrontations. The historical record shows that over time the police have learned to use their wise discretionary powers to ameliorate that tension.

The close linkage between the police and local politics, a linkage that relies on a process of informal political influence, allows the various publics to influence police policy and actions, but it also places the police in the position of choosing between groups. History informs us that the American urban police emerged as representatives of the political majority and have always sided with that majority. Again, the historical record suggests strongly that the police used their wide discretion and their capacity to provide immediate service to minority groups to forestall and ameliorate the potentially harsh effect of unchecked majority political rule.

The failure of the professionalism movement to become institutionalized and to permeate the organization, let alone the whole field, created a natural tension between administrators and the rank-and-file. In addition, the historical record makes it clear that at best the professionalism movement masked many of the inherent characteristics of urban policing such as its parochialism, its basis in local politics, and its inability to prevent crime. Current reformers who ignore that historical record are doomed to limited success or, quite possibly, failure.

John A. Conley

Bibliography
Carte, Gene, and Elaine H. Carte. *Police Reform in the United States: The Era of August Vollmer.* Berkeley: University of California Press, 1975.
Conley, John A. "Criminal Justice History as a Field of Research: A Review of the Literature, 1960–1975." *Journal of Criminal Justice* 5(1) (1977): 13–28.
Fogelson, Robert M. *Big-City Police.* Cambridge, MA: Harvard University Press, 1977.
Haller, Mark. "Historical Roots of Police Behavior: Chicago, 1890–1925." *Law and Society Review* 10 (Winter 1976): 303–24.
Harring, Sidney L. *Policing a Class Society: The Experience of American Cities, 1865–1915.* New Brunswick, NJ: Rutgers University Press, 1983.
Johnson, David R. *Policing the Urban Underworld: The Impact of Crime on the Development of the American Police, 1800–1887.* Philadelphia: Temple University Press, 1979.
———. "The Origins and Structure of Intercity Criminal Activity 1840–1920: An Interpretation." *Journal of Social History* 15(4) (1982): 593–605.
Lane, Roger. *Policing the City: Boston, 1822–1885.* New York: Atheneum Press, 1975.
Monkkonen, Eric H. "A Disorderly People: Urban Order in the Nineteenth and

Twentieth Centuries." *Journal of American History* 68(3) (1981a): 539–59.

———. *Police in Urban America, 1860–1920*. Cambridge, MA: Harvard University Press, 1981b.

———. "From Cop History to Social History: The Significance of the Police in American History." *Journal of Social History* 15(4) (1982): 575–91.

Richardson, James F. *The New York Police: Colonial Times to 1901*. New York: Oxford University Press, 1970.

Schneider, John C. *Detroit and the Problem of Order, 1830–1880: A Geography of Crime, Riots, and Policing*. Lincoln: University of Nebraska Press, 1980.

Walker, Samuel. *A Critical History of Policy Reform*. Lexington, MA: Lexington, 1977.

Police 1920 to the Present

Historians tend to assign labels to specific time periods. Admittedly, there is a danger in this, because arbitrary dates or events that mark the contours of an era can sometimes omit the contributions of important historical antecedents. Despite this concern, the identification of specific periods continues because it makes the study of the past more manageable and generally more intelligible.

Jacques Barzun, the historian, has suggested that what distinguishes one period from another is often the principal issue raised and its ultimate resolution. Which idea emerges as the central issue? What are people's perceptions of the idea? How does the idea move from thought to action? These are the historians' critical concerns as they seek to identify and understand the principal issue of an era. It is important to keep in mind, however, that it is the issue raised and not the individual resolutions offered that form the boundaries of an age. In this light, a case can be made for characterizing the history of American police from the 1920s to the present as the era of professionalism.

Students of political science and public administration can easily appreciate this characterization. Since Woodrow Wilson's famous article, "The Study of Administration" (1887), a significant body of work has emerged that seeks to explain why and how government agencies have focused so much attention on improving administrative efficiency throughout the public sector. Indeed, most scholars have suggested that the aim of public administration in the twentieth century has been to achieve a level of professional stature through a greater degree of autonomy, centralized authority, and objective rationality. For our purposes, the history of American law enforcement can serve as an excellent illustration of that movement.

In addition to the conceptual basis used for analysis, another preliminary concern involves the matter of definition. What do we mean by the terms *police* and *professionalism*? Police forces are governmental organizations that are accountable to the executive branch (mayor, governor, or president). They are afforded the principal discretionary authority to utilize legal force or the threat of force to maintain the public order and to enforce the law. Most of their time, however, is spent providing a myriad of social service activities that have been deferred to them.

While professionalism in law enforcement could be defined in several ways, a generic approach appears most appropriate. Professionalism is usually characterized by a reliance upon a core of scientific-based knowledge. It naturally follows that there is a degree of training that often occurs at a university and that is designed to assure a level of technological sophistication and social awareness. That training contributes to a distancing between the professional and layperson, however, giving the professional a greater level of knowledge on a given subject. In turn, professionals create organizations and associations that limit employment opportunities to fellow professionals. In addition, laypersons are afforded less opportunity for input in the formation of policies for the bureaucracy.

During the past seventy-five years, American law enforcement has been grappling with the dilemma of how to gain recognition as a profession. Although a portion of this campaign has been directed at the general public, much energy has been focused on the membership within the law-enforcement community. The reason for this is fairly straightforward. Since the nineteenth century, when law enforcement became a full-time job, it has been viewed as a blue-collar occupation. The recruitment process bolstered this view further, as it placed more emphasis on physiological traits such as agility and endurance than on more intellectual qualities, such as social consciousness and psychological understanding. Although noteworthy events surrounding the police of this century have not always been directed solely at achieving the goal of professionalism, a case can be made for several of them either supporting this idea or creatively enhancing the effort.

As is the case with any movement that extends over several decades, there are phases of the movement that are clearly more dominant than others. To date, the emphasis on professionalism in law enforcement has been most prevalent during the periods of the 1920s and 1930s and the 1960s and 1970s. What follows is an examination of the move toward professionalism during those periods.

1920s and 1930s

It is both interesting and important to note that these two periods were preceded by confrontations. The confrontations were often quite violent, which is consistent with the historical record, as it is replete with examples of change initiated by conflict. Before the onset of the 1920s, the law-enforcement community was rocked by at least two types of confrontation: (1) The efforts of some rank-and-file officers to assert themselves through union activity was soundly defeated with the Boston Police Strike of 1919; and (2) that same year also marked the culmination of approximately two decades of sporadic race riots in several cities in which the police were often active or passive participants.

These confrontations may have played some role in encouraging professionalism in law enforcement, but the movement received its principal impetus from other factors. For example, following the conclusion of World War I, the country embarked upon an effort to transform itself from a rural, agrarian society into an urban, industrialized nation. The scope and level of governmental involvement in that process was significant. As government defined its ever-expanding role, the administrative problems of most public-sector organizations became evident.

One item on this new agenda for the country that influenced law enforcement was the tremendous need for paved highways. The decade of the 1920s witnessed a significant increase in such roads. Paved highways enhanced the sale of automobiles (another new feature of the American landscape), which in turn created several new law-enforcement problems. The police agencies at that time, generally county and municipal law enforcement, were incapable of handling these traffic problems totally. This helped promote the argument for the establishment of statewide law-enforcement departments. A few states had already created state police forces, but these were usually not established for traffic-related purposes. Traffic enforcement simply provided another reason for those states that had not already developed a state police agency or a highway patrol to do so.

For the federal government, the problem of roads and automobiles was viewed in a slightly different light. In 1919 Congress enacted the National Motor Vehicle Theft Act. This expanded the policing powers of the Bureau of Investigation (the name was changed to the Federal Bureau of Investigation in 1935). This legislation is indicative of how Congress used the commerce and tax clauses of Article I of the United States Constitution either to expand the policing powers of existing federal agencies, like the FBI, or to create new agencies, such as the Border Patrol or the Bureau of Alcohol, Tobacco, and Firearms. Part of the reason for the willingness of Congress to create new federal law-enforcement agencies was the concern, at the time, over centralizing too much power in just a few agencies. Another justification, however, was the recognition that an autonomous agency with a narrow enforcement focus was more apt to cultivate an efficient professional approach with regard to its particular mandate.

The manner and extent to which some police began to utilize science and technology was another indication of their desire to achieve professional standing. Two of the basic technological developments of the time, the automobile and the telephone, were to have a significant impact on how police would assist citizens. By 1930 the use of the two-way radio had been perfected and would also influence the manner in which police performed their duties. In that same year, the *Uniform Crime Reports* (UCR) were introduced as the first national crime-reporting system.

Interest in utilizing scientific techniques to detect crime was, for the most part, haphazard during the first two decades of this century. Information was available, though, for several Europeans had been conducting important experiments and making significant discoveries regarding photography, the preservation of footprints, handwriting analysis, criminalistics, and modern fingerprinting. As the nation developed a serious concern over crime in the 1930s, the FBI started to appreciate the value of scientific policing. Before these efforts evolved, however, August Vollmer had already been arguing for the use of scientific techniques by the police. Vollmer, who many consider the father of modern professional policing in this country, contended that the scientific method was superior and more in harmony with the law than some of the more popular interrogation techniques of the day. He advocated using "lie detectors," fingerprinting, and the scientific evaluation of physical evidence, and, as a consultant to several law-enforcement agencies, he encouraged the establishment of crime labs. Vollmer was convinced that, with proper training, the police would be able to maximize the effectiveness of these new techniques. He was therefore a strong supporter of police officers pursuing what is now termed a traditional liberal arts education. He believed that scientific knowledge, the training in that knowledge at a university, and the belief in a level of technological sophistication were each imperative if law enforcement was to assume the stature of a profession. One must keep in mind that although these intentions and efforts were sincere, the results were modest and would remain so for several decades.

Science and technology brought a new and welcome dimension to policing, but the extent to which politics hindered professionalism continued to be a problem. Throughout most of the nineteenth century, reformers had attempted to deal with the more blatant examples of police department manipulation as a result of the spoils system. By the early twentieth century several critics had focused their attention on politics within the administration of law enforcement. What they were principally concerned about was the failure of police departments to employ modern methods of organization and management. It is fitting that Raymond Fosdick represents that perspective here, for he published his now famous *American Police Systems* in 1920. Fosdick illustrated how the American political system complicated and at times hindered efforts to improve the efficiency of law enforcement. He pointed out how police departments had failed to adopt modern ideas about administration that were exemplified in the principles of scientific management. In addition, he was particularly concerned about the lack of attention and direction paid to the establishment of professionalism among the executive leaders within police departments.

Last, during the late 1920s and early 1930s, a national concern with crime emerged that was reflected in a proliferation of commissions to study crime and the institutions of criminal justice. While most commissions were created at the local level, President Herbert Hoover did establish the National Commission on Law Observance and Enforcement (1929–1931). This commission identified several obvious problems within the justice system and offered recommendations to rectify them. The national concern with crime also prompted a new image for law enforcement. Prior to that time, the aims of police were essentially a combination of law enforcement, order maintenance, and social service support. This general view, however, was to be replaced with an image of police as professional crime-fighters. The rationale for this new image was that the police would be portrayed as efficiently tackling the crime problem. While the development of this image was initiated by J. Edgar Hoover at the FBI, the idea of police as professionally trained crime-fighters would also become evident at the local level.

The expansion of autonomous, centralized agencies, the use of science and technology, and the emphasis on organization and management principles were among the means undertaken to achieve a level of professionalism during this first phase. Each of these factors stressed the importance of efficiency. And what amounted to almost a blind faith in efficiency would dominate this move toward professionalism and would persist throughout the 1940s and 1950s.

1960s and 1970s

The second phase was similar to the first in that it was initially marked by violent confrontations. Images of the police dominated the headlines in the 1960s as they attempted to cope with the civil rights movement, protests against the war in Vietnam, and urban riots. Unlike the first period, when the confrontations were largely ignored, the violence of the 1960s proved quite instrumental in shaping the agenda for professionalism in law enforcement. In fact, with one possible exception, it dominated the effort.

That one exception was the important role the Supreme Court played in supervising the manner in which state courts applied constitutional due process protections to criminal cases. For the first time in its history, the Court focused a good deal of its attention on criminal justice in general and law enforcement in particular. The Court was especially interested in reviewing Fourth, Fifth, and Sixth Amendment issues. Among the cases entertained by the Court having a significant impact on police were: *Mapp v. Ohio* (1961), search and seizure; *Escobedo v. Illinois* (1964) and *Miranda v. Arizona* (1966), self-incrimination; *Katz v. United States* (1967), electronic surveillance; *United States v. Wade* (1967), lineups; and *Terry v. Ohio* (1968), stop-and-frisk. With each of these cases, the Supreme Court was putting the law-enforcement community on notice: The legal mandate to enforce the law and maintain order was to be exercised within the due process constraints of the Constitution.

The unrest of the 1960s led to the establishment of several national commissions that were mandated to investigate the causes of violence and/or to recommend reforms. These included the President's Commission on Law Enforcement and the Administration of Justice, the National Advisory Commission on Civil Disorders, and the National Advisory Commission on Criminal Justice Standards and Goals. Each report focused a considerable amount of attention on the police, which renewed interest in professionalism within law enforcement. In some respects the second phase of the movement was similar to the first. It emphasized the importance of autonomy, science and technology, and the principles of organization and management. Where the second phase differed from the first, however, was in the importance placed on the democratization of the movement and in balancing the concern for efficiency with one for effectiveness.

In this context, democratization means that all levels within the police were to benefit from the move toward professionalism. (Prior to this time, only upper management were viewed as professionals.) There were at least three instances in which the movement was democratized. First, the opportunities for the line officer to pursue a college education were expanded considerably, and a significant number took advantage of this opportunity. This feature is basic to any attempt at professionalism.

Second, the line officer became the focus of some of the most significant research ever conducted on police officers. For example, we learned a good deal about the extensive discretionary authority of the line officer, about the police subculture and how that limits the impact of the organization's policies on the patrol officer's behavior, and the effect that police relations have on the various sentiments of the community. While all of this research was significant, the most important discovery (or rather rediscovery) was that the police did not have just a single professional duty, such as that of crime-fighters. That image had been suspect for some time, but it took the reports of the national commissions and the research efforts of several scholars to illustrate the various functions of the police. These include the duties of law enforcement, order maintenance, and social service. Of these three duties, it is interesting to note that the last offers law enforcement the greatest hope for acceptance as a profession. What makes this observation interesting is that since the 1930s a significant segment within the law-enforcement community has attempted to disassociate itself from that aspect of the work.

The third aspect of democratization was reflected in a renewed interest in unionization. As is the case with any attempt to organize labor, economic factors played an important role. For police, however, there were also complex social and political factors that related to the various commission reports. The police felt that they were being singled out as the principal cause for the disorder and unrest. Even though that was not the case, the police felt politically and socially ostracized. To overcome this sense of isolation, some officers joined unions in an attempt to protect their interests. As the rank-and-file of the unions increased, they became a formidable power that any move toward professionalism had to reckon with.

Finally, during the first phase, efficiency was singled out for particular edification. In fact, it epitomized the move toward professionalism. While efficiency remains an important characteristic during this second phase, research has suggested that its significance should be put into perspective. That research includes the now-familiar reports on preventive patrol, response time, and detective studies, which added to our understanding of the limited capacity of the police to prevent and reduce crime. These findings helped focus attention on the effectiveness of law enforcement. Peter Drucker, the management expert, notes that efficiency is concerned with doing things right, whereas effectiveness is concerned with doing the right things. Doing the right thing is based on sound judgment and creative insights. The future standing of law enforcement as a profession may rest on how seriously it strives to become more effective.

Richard J. Terrill

Bibliography

Bittner, Egon. *The Functions of the Police in Modern Society: A Review of Background Factors, Current Practices, and Possible Role Models.* Cambridge, MA: Oelgeschlager, Gunn & Hain, 1980.

Carte, Gene, and Elaine H. Carte. *Police Reform in the United States: The Era of August Vollmer, 1905–1932.* Berkeley: University of California Press, 1975.

Fogelson, Robert M. *Big-City Police.* Cambridge, MA: Harvard University Press, 1977.

Neiderhoffer, Arthur. *Behind the Shield: The Police in Urban Society.* Garden City, NY: Doubleday, 1967.

Reppetto, Thomas A. *The Blue Parade.* New York: Free Press, 1978.

Ries, Albert J. *The Police and the Public.* New Haven, CT: Yale University Press, 1971.

Skolnick, Jerome H. *Justice Without Trial: Law Enforcement in Democratic Society.* New York: John Wiley and Sons, 1975.

Smith, Bruce. *Police Systems in the United States.* 2d ed. New York: Harper & Row, 1960.

Walker, Samuel. *Popular Justice: A History of American Criminal Justice.* New York: Oxford University Press, 1980.

Police Legal Liabilities: Overview

Police legal liabilities emanate from a variety of sources ranging from state to federal laws and carrying civil, criminal, and administrative sanctions. For the purpose of an overview, legal liabilities may be classified as in the accompanying table.

These liabilities apply to all public officers, not just to law-enforcement personnel. Probation and parole officers, jailers, prison officials, and other personnel in the criminal-justice system are liable under the provisions of the accompanying table. An officer may be liable under any or all of the categories, based on what may essentially be a single act, if the act is serious and all elements that trigger liability are present. The double jeopardy prohibition of the Fifth Amendment does not apply because double jeopardy arises only in criminal prosecutions for the same offense by the same jurisdiction.

Although various legal remedies are available to the public, as the categories in the table indicate, plaintiffs are inclined to use two remedies against police officers. This discussion will therefore focus on those two liability sources to the exclusion of others. These sources are: (1) civil liability under state tort law; and (2) civil liability under federal law (42 U.S. Code, Section 1983—also known as Civil Rights Cases).

Civil Liability under State Tort Law

Tort is defined as a civil wrong in which the action of one person causes injury to the person or property of another, in violation of a legal duty imposed by law. Three general categories of state tort based on a police officer's conduct are: (1) intentional tort, (2) negligence tort, and (3) strict liability tort. Of these, only intentional and negligence torts are used in police cases. Strict liability torts are applicable in activities that are abnormally dangerous, such that they cannot be carried out safely even with reasonable care. Police work does not fall under strict liability tort, hence that category will not be discussed.

Intentional Tort

This occurs when an officer intends to bring some physical harm or mental effect upon another person. Intent is mental and difficult to establish; however, courts and juries are generally allowed to infer the existence of intent from the facts of the case. In police work, the kinds of intentional tort often brought against police officers are:

False Arrest and False Imprisonment. In a tort case for false arrest, the plaintiff alleges that the officer made an illegal arrest, usually an arrest without probable cause. False arrest also arises if the officer fails to arrest the "right" person named in the warrant. An officer who makes a warrantless arrest bears the burden of proving that the arrest was in fact based on probable cause and that an arrest warrant was not necessary because the arrest came under one of the exceptions to the warrant rule. If the arrest is made with a warrant, the presumption is that probable cause exists, except if the officer obtained the warrant with malice, knowing that there was no probable cause (*Malley v. Briggs,* 106 S.Ct. 1092 [1986]). Civil liability for false arrest in arrests with warrant is unlikely unless the officer serves a warrant that he or she knows to be illegal or unconstitutional.

False arrest is a separate tort from false imprisonment, but in police tort cases the two

	I. Under State Law	II. Under Federal Law
A. Civil Liabilities	1. State tort law	1. Title 42 of U.S. Code, Section 1983—Civil Action for Deprivation of Civil Rights.
	2. State civil rights law	2. Title 42 of U.S. Code, Section 1985—Conspiracy to Interfere with Civil Rights.
		3. Title 42 of U.S. Code, Section 1981—Equal Rights under the Law.
B. Criminal Liabilities	1. State penal code provisions specifically aimed at public officers for such crimes as (a) official oppression, (b) official misconduct, and (c) violation of the civil rights of prisoners.	1. Title 18 of U.S. Code, Section 242—Criminal Liability for Deprivation of Civil Rights.
	2. Regular penal code provisions punishing criminal acts as assault, battery, false arrest, serious bodily injury, homicide, etc.	2. Title 18 of U.S. Code, Section 241—Criminal Liability for Conspiracy to Deprive a Person of Rights.
		3. Title 18 of U.S. Code, Section 245—Violation of Federally Protected Activities.
C. Administrative Liabilities	1. Agency rules or guidelines on the state or local level—vary from one agency to another.	1. Federal agency rules or guidelines—vary from one agency to another.

are virtually identical in that arrest necessarily means confinement, which is in itself an element of imprisonment. In both cases, the individual is restrained or deprived of freedom without legal justification. They do differ, however, in that while false arrest leads to false imprisonment, false imprisonment is not necessarily the result of a false arrest.

The best defense in false arrest and false imprisonment cases is that the arrest or detention was justified and valid. An officer who makes an arrest with probable cause is not liable for false arrest simply because the suspect is later proven innocent, nor does liability exist if the arrest is made by virtue of a law that is later declared unconstitutional. In the words of the United States Supreme Court: "We agree that a police officer is not charged with predicting the future course of constitutional law" (*Pierson v. Ray*, 386 U.S. 555 [1967]). In these cases, however, the officer must believe in good faith that the law was constitutional. Also, the fact that the arrested person is not prosecuted or that he or she is prosecuted for a different crime does not make the arrest illegal. What is important is that there be a valid justification for arrest and detention at the time those took place.

Assault and Battery. Although sometimes used as one term, assault and battery represent two separate acts. Assault is usually defined as the intentional causing of an apprehension of harmful or offensive conduct; it is the attempt or threat, accompanied by the ability to inflict bodily harm on another person. An assault is committed if the officer causes another person to think that he or she will be subjected to harmful or offensive contact. In contrast, battery is the intentional infliction of a harmful or offensive body contact. Given this broad definition, the potential for battery exists every time an officer applies force on a suspect or arrestee. The main difference between assault and battery is that assault is generally menacing conduct that results in a person's fear of imminently receiving a battery, while battery involves unlawful, unwarranted, or hostile touching—however slight. In some jurisdictions, assault is attempted battery.

The police are often charged with "brutality" or using "excessive force." In police work, the improper use of force usually constitutes battery. The general rule is that nondeadly force may be used by the police in various situations as long as such force is reasonable. Reasonable force, in turn, is that force that a prudent and cautious person would use if exposed to similar circumstances and is limited to the amount of force that is necessary to achieve valid and proper results. Any force beyond that necessary to achieve valid and proper results is punitive, meaning it punishes rather than controls.

The defense in assault and battery cases is that the use or threat of the use of force by the police was reasonable under the circumstances; however, what may be reasonable force to one judge or jury may not be reasonable to another. The use of reasonable force includes self-defense or defense of others by the police. The defense is available not only when an officer is actually attacked, but also when the officer reasonably thinks he or she is in imminent danger of an attack.

Wrongful Death. This tort, usually established by law, arises whenever death occurs as a result of an officer's action or inaction. It is brought by the surviving family, relatives, or legal guardian of the estate of the deceased for pain, suffering, and actual expenses (such as expenses for the funeral), and for the loss of life to the family or relatives. In some states, the death of a person resulting from the police's use of deadly force comes under the tort of misuse of weapons. An officer has a duty to use not merely ordinary care but a high degree of care in handling a weapon, otherwise he or she becomes liable for wrongful death.

The use of deadly force is governed by departmental policy or, in the absence thereof, by state law that must be strictly followed. The safest rule for any agency to prescribe is that deadly force should be used only in cases of self-defense or when the life of another person is in danger and the use of deadly force is immediately necessary to protect that life. Agency rules or state law, however, may give the officer more leeway in the use of deadly force. These rules are to be followed unless declared unconstitutional.

The use of deadly force to apprehend fleeing felons has been severely limited by the U.S. Supreme Court in *Tennessee v. Garner* (471 U.S. 1 [1985]). In that case the Court said that deadly force is justified only when the officer has probable cause to believe that the suspect poses a threat of serious physical harm, either to the officer or to others. Thus, if the suspect threatens the officer with a weapon or there is probable cause to believe that the suspect has committed a crime involving the infliction or threatened infliction of serious physical harm, the officer may use deadly force if necessary to prevent escape, and if, when feasible, some warning has been given. Therefore, "fleeing felon" statutes in many states are valid only if their application comports with the requirements of *Tennessee v. Garner.* The use of deadly force to prevent the escape of a misdemeanant should not be resorted to except in cases of self-defense or in defense of the life of another person.

Intentional Infliction of Emotional Distress. This takes place when an officer inflicts severe emotional distress on a person through extreme and outrageous conduct that is intentional or reckless. Physical harm need not follow. What is extreme and outrageous is difficult to determine; moreover, the effect of an act may vary according to the plaintiff's disposition or state of mind. Most state appellate courts that have addressed the issue have held, however, that more than rudeness or isolated incidents is required. There is need for the plaintiff to allege and prove some kind of pattern or practice over a period of time rather than just isolated incidents. The case law on this tort is still developing, but it has already found acceptance in almost every state.

Negligence Tort

For tort purposes, negligence may be defined as the breach of a common law or statutory duty to act reasonably toward those who may foreseeably be harmed by one's conduct. This general definition may be modified or superseded by specific state law that provides for a different type of conduct, usually more restrictive than this definition, in particular acts.

Some of the negligence torts to which police officers may be exposed are:

Negligent Operation of Motor Vehicle. Police department manuals usually provide guidelines on the proper use of motor vehicles. These guidelines, if valid, constitute the standard by which the actions of police officers are likely to be judged. In some states departmental policies are admitted in court merely as evidence, while in other states the departmental policy is controlling.

Negligent Failure to Protect. Police officers in general are not liable for injury to someone whom the police failed to protect, neither is any duty owed by the police to specific individuals to prevent crime. The police, however, have a general duty to protect the public as a whole and to prevent crime. What this means is that the police generally cannot be held liable if a member of society becomes a victim of crime. The exceptions, based on developing case law, are:

(a) If a "special relationship" has been created. Example: The police told a mother that there was nothing they could do when she asked them to protect her daughter from her father. A court order for protection had been issued by a family court, hence a "special relationship" had been created because of such judicial order (*Sorichetti v. City of New York*, 482 N.E. 2d 70 [1985]). Some states, however, are doing away with the requirement of "special relationship" and are following a trend toward liability based mainly on the general duty of police to protect the public at large. Should this trend continue, possible liability based on negligent failure to protect will be an even bigger concern for officers in the future than it is now.

(b) Where the police affirmatively undertake to protect an individual but negligently fail to perform. Example: The police assure a victim, who calls on a 911 emergency line, that assistance will be forthcoming; the victim relies on the promised assistance but the assistance never comes and damage is suffered.

Whether or not the police are liable for injuries to third parties caused by drunken drivers who are allowed by the police to drive has caused a split in court decisions; some courts impose liability while others do not. This area of law is fast developing and changes may be forthcoming in the immediate future.

Civil Liability under Federal Law (Civil Rights or Section 1983 Cases)

The Law

Liability under federal law is based primarily on Title 42 of the U.S. Code, Section 1983, entitled *Civil Action for Deprivation of Rights*. This law provides as follows:

> Every person who, under color of any statute, ordinance, regulation, custom, or usage, of any State or Territory, subjects, or causes to be subjected, any citizen of the United States or other persons within the jurisdiction thereof to the deprivation of any rights, privileges, or immunities secured by the Constitution and laws, shall be liable to the party injured in an action at law, suit in equity, or other proper proceeding for redress.

This law, usually referred to as the Civil Rights Law or Section 1983, is the most frequently used remedy in the arsenal of legal liability statutes available to plaintiffs. The law, originally passed by Congress in 1871, was then known as the Ku Klux Klan law because it sought to control the activities of state officials who were also members of that organization. For a long time, however, the law was given a limited interpretation by the courts and was seldom used. In 1961, the Court adopted a much broader interpretation, thus opening wide the door for liability action in federal courts. Among the reasons for the popularity of this statute are that Section 1983 cases are usually filed in federal court where discovery procedures are more liberal and attorney's fees are recoverable by the "prevailing" plaintiff in accordance with the Attorney's Fees Act of 1976.

Basic Elements of a Section 1983 Lawsuit

The two basic elements of a Section 1983 lawsuit are: (1) the defendant must be acting under color of law; and (2) there must be a violation of a constitutional or of a federally protected right.

The Defendant Must Be Acting under Color of Law. This means that the misuse of power possessed by virtue of the law and made possible only because the wrongdoer is clothed with the authority of the state cannot be tolerated. The difficulty is that while it is usually easy to identify acts that are wholly within the term "color of law" (as when an officer makes a search or an arrest while on duty), there are some acts that are not as easy to categorize. Examples: P, a police officer, works during off-hours as a private security agent in a shopping center. While in that capacity, P shoots and kills a fleeing shoplifter. Was P acting under color of law? Or suppose an officer arrests a felon during off-hours and when not in uniform. Is the officer acting under color of law? The answer usually depends upon job expectation. Many police departments (by state law, judicial decision, or agency regulation) expect officers to respond as officers twenty-four hours a day. In these jurisdictions any arrest made on- or off-duty comes under the requirement of color of law. In the case of police officers who "moonlight," courts have held that their being in police uniform while acting as private security agents, their use of a gun issued by the department, and the knowledge by department authorities that the officer has a second job, all indicate that the officer is acting under color of law. On the other hand, acts by an officer that are of a purely private nature are outside the color of state law even if done while on duty.

The courts have interpreted the term *color of law* broadly to include local laws, ordinances, or agency regulations; moreover, the phrase does not mean that the act was authorized by law. It suffices that the act appeared to be lawful even if it was not in fact authorized; hence, an officer acts under color of law even if he or she exceeds lawful authority. Moreover, it includes clearly illegal acts committed by the officer by reason of position or opportunity.

There Must Be a Violation of a Constitutional or of a Federally Protected Right. Under this requirement, the right violated must be given by the U.S. Constitution or by federal law. Rights given only by state law are not protected under Section 1983. Example: The right to a lawyer during police lineup prior to being charged with an offense is not given by the Constitution or by federal law; therefore, if an officer forces a suspect to appear in a lineup without a lawyer, the officer is not liable under Section 1983. If such right is given by state law, its violation may be actionable under state law or agency regulation, not under Section 1983.

Defenses in Civil Liability Cases

Various legal defenses are available in state tort and Section 1983 cases. Three of the most often used defenses are (1) probable cause, (2) official immunity, and (3) good faith.

The Probable Cause Defense

This is a limited defense in that it applies only in cases of false arrest, false imprisonment, and illegal searches and seizures, either under state tort law or Section 1983. For the purpose of a legal defense in Section 1983 cases, probable cause simply means "a reasonable good faith belief in the legality of the action taken" (*Rodriguez v. Jones,* 473 F.2d 599 [5th Cir. 1973]). That expectation is lower than the Fourth Amendment definition of probable cause, which is that probable cause exists "when the facts and circumstances within the officers' knowledge and of which they have reasonably trustworthy information are sufficient in themselves to warrant a man of reasonable caution in the belief that an offense has been or is being committed" (*Brienigar v. United States,* 338 U.S. 160 [1949]).

The Official Immunity Defense

Official immunity is composed of three categories: absolute, quasi-judicial, and qualified.

Absolute Immunity. This means that a civil liability suit, if brought, is dismissed by the court without going into the merits of the plaintiff's claim. Absolute immunity does not apply to police officers. It applies only to judges, prosecutors, and legislators. There is one instance, however, when police officers enjoy absolute immunity from civil liability. In *Briscoe v. LaHue* (460 U.S. 325 [1983]), the Supreme Court held that police officers could not be sued under Section 1983 for giving perjured testimony against a defendant in a state criminal trial. The Court said that under common law, trial participants—including judges, prosecutors, and witnesses— were given absolute immunity for actions connected with the trial process. Therefore, police officers also enjoy absolute immunity when testifying, even if such testimony is perjured. The officer may be criminally prosecuted for perjury, but that seldom happens.

Quasi-Judicial Immunity. This means that certain officers are immune if performing judicial-type functions, but not when performing other functions connected with their office. An example is a probation officer when preparing a presentence investigation report upon order of the judge. Quasi-judicial immunity does not

that the city itself could not invoke the good faith defense.

In a 1985 decision, the Supreme Court ruled that a money judgment against a public officer "in his official capacity" imposes liability upon the employing agency, regardless of whether or not the agency was named as a defendant in the suit (*Brandon v. Holt,* 105 S.Ct. 873 [1985]). In *Brandon,* the plaintiff alleged that although the director of the police department had no actual notice of the police officer's violent behavior, administrative policies were such that he should have known. The Court added that although the director could be shielded by qualified immunity, the city could be held liable.

In a 1986 case the Court decided that municipalities could be held liable in a civil rights case for violating constitutional rights on the basis of a single decision (as opposed to a "pattern of decisions") made by an authorized municipal policy-maker (*Pembaur v. City of Cincinnati,* 475 U.S. 469 [1986]). In this case the county prosecutor in effect made official policy and thereby exposed his municipal employer to liability, by instructing law-enforcement officers to make a forcible entry, without search warrant, of an office in order to serve capiases (a form of warrant issued by the judge) on persons thought to be there. The case was brought by a Cincinnati, Ohio, physician, based on an incident where law-enforcement officers, under advice from the county prosecutor, broke down the door in his office with an ax. The officers were trying to arrest two of the doctor's employees who failed to appear before a grand jury. The Court decided that this violated the Fourth Amendment rights of the office owners and concluded that the City of Cincinnati could be held liable.

Can the Police Sue Back?

Can the police strike back by suing those who sue them? The answer is yes, and some departments are in fact striking back. The number of civil cases actually brought by the police against the public, however, has remained comparatively small. The reality is that although police officers may file tort lawsuits against arrestees or suspects, there are difficulties in doing that. One is that in a tort case the officer will have to hire his or her own lawyer. This necessitates financial expense that the officer cannot recover from the defendant. Should the officer file a tort case for damages, the chances of meaningful success may not be good because most of those who run afoul of the law and have encounters with the police are too poor to pay damages. Moreover, officers oftentimes refrain from filing civil cases for damages because it is less expensive and more convenient to get back at the suspect in a criminal case. Almost every state has provisions penalizing such offenses as deadly assault of a peace officer, false report to a police officer, resisting arrest or search, hindering apprehension or prosecution, and aggravated assault. These can be added to the regular criminal offense against the arrested person, thereby increasing the penalty or facilitating prosecution. Finally, many officers feel that the harsh treatment they sometimes get from the public is part of police work and is therefore to be accepted without retaliation. Whatever the attitude, the police do have legal remedies available should they wish to exercise them.

Conclusion

Liability lawsuits have become an occupational hazard in policing. The days are gone when the courts refused to entertain cases filed by the public against police officers and agencies. The traditional "hands-off" policy by the courts is out; conversely, "hands-on" is in and will be with us in the foreseeable future.

The effects of liability litigations on policing are significant and controversial. Advocates maintain that liability lawsuits afford the public a needed avenue for redress against police excesses and that this, in turn, has led to accelerated police professionalization. Opponents argue, however, that liability lawsuits hamper police work and curtail police effectiveness and efficiency. Whatever the real or imagined effects, liability lawsuits are here to stay. It is a reality that has become part of the price we pay for policing a free society.

Rolando V. del Carmen

Bibliography

Butler, E. "Liability of Municipalities for Police Brutality." *Tennessee Bar Journal* 19 (May 1983): 21–29.

del Carmen, Rolando V. *Criminal Procedure for Law Enforcement Personnel.* Monterey, CA: Brooks/Cole, 1987.

Elliott, C.J. "Police Misconduct: Municipal Liability Under Section 1983." *Kentucky Law Journal* 74(3) (1985/1986): 651–66.

Higginbotham, J. "Defending Law Enforcement Officers Against Personal Liability in Constitutional Tort Litigation. Parts I and II." *FBI Law Enforcement Bulletin* 54(4) (1985): 24–31; 54 (5) (1985): 25–31.

Littlejohn, E.J. "Civil Liability and the Police Officer: The Need for New Deterrents to Police Misconduct." *University of Detroit Journal of Urban Law* 58 (Spring 1982): 365–431.

McCoy, C. "Lawsuits Against Police—What Impact Do They Really Have?" *Criminal Law Bulletin* 20(1) (1984): 49–56.

"Municipal Liability for Requiring Unfit Police Officers to Carry Guns." *Fordham Urban Law Journal* 11 (1982/1983): 1001–38.

Rittenmeyer, S.D. "Vicarious Liability in Suits Pursuant to 42 USC 1983: Legal Myth and Reality." *Journal of Police Science and Administration* 12(3) (1984): 260–66.

Silver, I. *Police Civil Liability*. New York: Matthew Bender, 1986.

"When Police Lie: Federal Civil Rights Liability for Wrongful Arrest." *Ohio Northern University Law Review* 10 (Summer 1983): 493–518.

Police Legal Liabilities: Use of Force

Police work inevitably involves the use of two types of force: nondeadly force and deadly force. Nondeadly force is defined as force that when used, is not likely to result in or produce serious bodily injury or death. By contrast, deadly force is force that, when used, would lead a reasonable police officer to conclude that it poses a high risk of death or serious injury to a human target.

Use of force by the police is actionable under state tort law, federal law (42 USC Section 1983), or both. Most plaintiffs allege violations of both laws in the same complaint, particularly in the use-of-deadly-force cases. In most states, a complaint containing both types of law may be heard either in a state or federal court. Liability under the state tort law is governed by state statutes (examples are wrongful death statutes found in all states) and court decisions; liability under Section 1983 comes under federal law and federal court decisions.

Since a federal civil suit under Section 1983 succeeds only if there is a violation of a constitutional right or of a right given by federal law, the plaintiff would likely allege that the use of excessive or deadly force violates such constitutional rights as the prohibition against illegal seizure (Fourth Amendment), the right to due process (Fifth and Fourteenth Amendments), and constitutes cruel and unusual punishment (Eighth Amendment). Failure to recover under state law does not mean that the federal case also fails; conversely, success in one does not mean success in the other. Although alleged in the same complaint, the two causes of action can have different results because they are based on different laws, the plaintiff in a state or federal court.

Nondeadly Force
General Rule and Definition in State Tort Cases. The general rule in state tort cases is that nondeadly force may be used as long as it constitutes reasonable force. Reasonable force, in turn, is defined as force that a prudent and cautious person would use if exposed to similar circumstances and is limited to the amount of force that is necessary to achieve legitimate results. Anything beyond what is necessary to achieve legitimate results is unreasonable.

For purposes of field operations, it is best to think of nondeadly force as either reasonable or punitive, rather than as reasonable or unreasonable. In any areas of police work, the use of reasonable force is legal, whereas the use of punitive force is always illegal and exposes the officer and the department to civil liability. The problem, however, is that the term "reasonable force" is subjective, and thus what is reasonable force depends on the circumstances in each case and the conclusion drawn by a judge or jury from a specific set of facts. The officer must take careful note of the circumstances that led to the use of a certain level of force in hopes that the judge or jury will find such use of force reasonable.

Different circumstances justify the use of varying degrees of force. For example, an arrest made by three or more officers of a single suspect in a crowded street at noontime calls for a different amount of force than an arrest of a dangerous suspect in the suspect's apartment late in the evening. Similarly, the arrest of a dangerous parolee who has just committed another murder requires an escalated level of force that is unnecessary in the arrest of a "hot-check" writer. Both situations are governed by the same "reasonable force" rule, but the circumstances differ.

Assault and Battery Cases

Most lawsuits against the police alleging use of excessive nondeadly force take the form of assault and battery allegations. These are tort cases brought under state law in which the plaintiff seeks damages from the police officers and other defendants for violations of rights. In assault and battery cases, both of which have their origin in common law instead of statutory law, the basic standard for reasonableness during arrest is the Restatement (Second) of Torts, Section 134, which provides: "If the actor is privileged to take custody of another, he is privileged, if necessary, (a) to use, for the purpose of maintaining his custody, such force. . . . as he would be privileged to use to effect the other's arrest."[1] As is usually the case in the state tort claims, this standard is vague and conducive to subjective interpretation, which often accounts for cases that are difficult to reconcile.

Assault. Although sometimes used as one term, assault and battery refer to two separate acts. Assault is usually defined as the intentional causing of an apprehension of harmful or offensive conduct; it is an attempt or threat accompanied by the ability to inflict bodily harm on another person. An assault is committed if the officer causes another person to think that he or she will be subjected to harmful or offensive contact. For example, for no justifiable reason, Officer X draws her gun and points it at another person. This constitutes assault because the act is intentional and causes an apprehension of harmful or offensive conduct. In many jurisdictions, words alone do not constitute assault. There must be an act to accompany the threatening words.

Battery. Battery is the intentional infliction of harmful or offensive body contact. Given this broad definition, the potential for battery exists every time an officer uses force on anybody. The main difference between assault and battery is that assault is generally menacing conduct that results in a person's fear of imminently receiving battery, whereas battery involves unlawful, unwarranted, or hostile touching, however slight. In some jurisdictions, assault constitutes attempted battery.

The police may use reasonable force when making an arrest, but unreasonable force constitutes battery. If the arrest by the police is improper or invalid, the handling and handcuffing of the arrestee constitutes a technical battery.[2] In one case the court found that the police had used excessive force on a family when responding to a call to settle a neighborhood dispute, and they were made to pay $10,000. The court said that excessive force was used on the father, who was not of great physical strength and who was already being subdued by his brother when the police kicked him in the groin and struck him on the head with a nightstick. It was alleged that the officers kicked the mother on the back and buttocks after she was handcuffed and lying face down in the mud. The son was also injured during the arrest process.[3] In another case, the evidence clearly showed that the plaintiff had been repeatedly and severely hit, at times with a nightstick, and had been slammed against the trunk of the car. The amount of force used was considered excessive, hence damages were awarded.[4]

In assault and battery cases against the police, most courts have held that the burden of providing that excessive force was used lies with the plaintiff. Once that is established during the trial, however, the burden shifts to the defendant officer to prove that such use of force was justified—if that be the defense. This means that the officer must prove that under the circumstances the amount of force used was reasonable. In contrast, a California appeals court has taken a different course. In one case involving battery, the court required the police to bear the burden of proving that the force used was reasonable.[5] The court added that "the officer is not entitled to a presumption a battery is justified simply because of his or her official position." The California decision, however, is the exception rather than the rule.

Deadly Force

The rules on the use of deadly force are often precise, strict, and limiting. Deadly force is defined as force that, when used, would lead a reasonable police officer objectively to conclude that it poses a high risk of death or serious injury to its human target. Firearms are obviously instruments of deadly force, as are long knives, daggers, and lead pipes. A nightstick may be considered an instrument of deadly force, depending upon how it is used. An arm or fist may be a deadly weapon, depending upon its likelihood to produce death or serious injury. For example, the fist of a professional heavyweight boxer is a deadly weapon, whereas the fist of a ten-year-old boy would be considered nondeadly.

Police officers are different from other public officials in that in some instances they are allowed to use deadly force. The authority to use such force is necessary in police work, but it also carries serious responsibilities and the potential for high-profile liability lawsuits. A potential lawsuit exists every time a police officer uses any type of deadly force. Liability may arise under intentional tort (specifically the use of excessive force and wrongful death), or negligence tort (when negligence in the handling of firearms results in injury to a suspect or a third party). Liability may also arise under federal law because a plaintiff might allege that the use of deadly force by the police under the circumstances constituted a violation of constitutional rights. Police officers are advised to observe utmost care when using deadly force and must abide strictly by prescribed departmental rules.

Although variations exist from state to state and according to departmental regulations, the general rules on the use of deadly force are summarized as follows:

Misdemeanor Cases

The safest practice for police officers is not to use deadly force in misdemeanor cases. The only exception is if deadly force is necessary for self-defense or defense of the life of a third person. The use of deadly force in misdemeanor cases always raises questions of disproportionality because the designation of the offense as a misdemeanor means that society does not consider that offense serious in that state. If the offense is not considered serious, using deadly force to prevent possible escape is a disproportionate sanction.

In Felony Cases

General Rule. The safest rule is to use deadly force only when the life of the officer or another person is in danger and the use of such force is immediately necessary to preserve that life. In all other cases—such as resistance to arrest or escape from custody—the use of deadly force poses liability risks for the police officer. If authorized by state law or departmental policy, the use of deadly force in instances other than self-defense or defense of third persons is valid as long as it is not so disproportionate to the severity of the offense committed as to constitute cruel and unusual punishment. For example, a state law or departmental policy that allows the use of deadly force to prevent the escape of a dangerous murder suspect will likely be constitutional because of the seriousness of the crime of murder. On the other hand, if the crime was shoplifting, serious constitutional questions would arise from the use of deadly force because of its disproportionality to the nature of the offense. One writer summarizes the current case law on the use of deadly force to prevent the commission of a felony as follows: "There is no dispute that such force may be used to prevent the commission of a felony which threatens the life or safety of a human being, including the burglary of a dwelling house. . . . As to felonies which involve no such danger, the tendency in the modern cases is to say that the use of deadly force is unreasonable in proportion to the offense."[6]

Tennessee v. Garner: The Leading Case on the Use of Deadly Force to Prevent Escape of Fleeing Felons. Until 1985 there were no guidelines whatsoever from the United States Supreme Court on the use of deadly force by police officers. The limits for such use were set instead by state law or departmental rules. That changed in 1985 when the Court decided *Tennessee v. Garner,*[7] a case that sets guidelines for the use of deadly force to prevent escape of fleeing felons.

In *Garner,* two Memphis police officers one evening answered a "prowler inside call." Upon arriving at the scene, they saw a woman standing on her porch and gesturing toward the adjacent house. The woman said she had heard glass shattering and was certain that someone was breaking in. One police officer radioed the dispatcher to say that they were on the scene, while the other officer went behind the neighboring house. The officer heard a door slam and saw someone run across the backyard. The fifteen-year-old suspect, Edward Garner, stopped at a six-foot-high, chain-link fence at the edge of the yard. With the aid of a flashlight, the officer saw Garner's face and hands. He saw no sign of a weapon and admitted later that he was reasonably sure Garner was unarmed. While Garner was crouched at the base of the fence, the officer called out, "Police, halt!" and took a few steps toward him. Garner then began to climb over the fence. The officer shot him. Garner died; ten dollars and a purse taken from the house were found on his body.

In using deadly force to prevent the escape, the officer was acting upon the authority of a Tennessee statute and pursuant to police department policy. The Tennessee statute provided that "if after notice of the intention to arrest the defendant, he either flees or forcibly resists, the officer may use all the necessary means to effect the arrest." The police department policy was slightly more restrictive but still allowed the use of deadly force in cases of burglary even if there was no danger to the officer. The Court concluded that the facts did not justify the use of deadly force under the circumstances and therefore remanded the case for further proceedings on the issue of liability. *Garner* set the following guidelines on the use of deadly force to prevent escape: Where the officer has probable cause to believe that the suspect poses a threat of serious physical harm, either to the officer or to others, it is not constitutionally unreasonable to prevent escape by using deadly force.

Worded affirmatively, it is constitutionally reasonable for an officer to use deadly force to prevent escape when the officer has probable cause to believe that the suspect poses a threat of serious physical harm, either to the officer or to others. The Court opined that "if the suspect threatens the officer with a weapon or there is probable cause to believe that he has committed a crime involving the infliction or threatened infliction of serious physical harm, deadly force may be used if necessary to prevent escape, and if, where feasible, some warning has been given."

According to one writer, three elements may be deducted from the above quotation that should offer some guidance in assessing situations to determine whether the officer's belief that a suspect is dangerous is in fact justified:[8]

1. The suspect threatens the officer with a weapon;
2. The officer has probable cause to believe that the suspect has committed a crime involving the infliction or threatened infliction of serious physical harm;
3. The officer has given some warning, if feasible.

The writer goes on to say that either (1) or (2) above would satisfy the requirement of dangerousness but (3) applies to both (1) and (2), meaning that some warning must be given, if feasible, in either instance.

The Court in *Garner* also concluded that the use of deadly force to prevent the escape of an apparently unarmed suspected felon is constitutionally unreasonable. The Court emphasized that "where the subject poses no immediate threat to the officer and no threat to others, the harm resulting from failing to apprehend him does not justify the use of deadly force," adding that "a police officer may not seize an unarmed nondangerous suspect by shooting him dead."

The *Garner* decision rendered unconstitutional the then existing "fleeing felon" statutes in nearly half the states insofar as those statutes allowed the police to use deadly force to prevent the escape of a fleeing felon regardless of circumstances. Fleeing felon statutes are constitutional only if they are consistent with the requirements set by the Court in *Garner*. The Court based its decision on the Fourth Amendment, saying that "there can be no question that apprehension by the use of deadly force is a seizure subject to the reasonable requirement of the Fourth Amendment." It follows that if an arrest of a suspect with the use of nondeadly force is governed by the Fourth Amendment, the use of deadly force to make an arrest should also be so governed.

What Rules Govern the Use of Deadly Force? Numerous cases of legal liability resulting in multimillion-dollar damage awards arise from the use of nondeadly or deadly force. Officers must therefore exercise utmost caution and know the limits within which they work. The use of force, nondeadly or deadly, is governed by the following sources (in descending order of importance):

1. Departmental or agency rules or guidelines, which can be more limiting but not more permissive than state law or court decisions;
2. State law, usually the Penal Code or the Code of Criminal Procedure;
3. Judicial decisions by federal and state courts; and
4. The United States Constitution, particularly the Fourth Amendment prohibition against unreasonable searches and seizures and the due process clause.

Officers must be familiar with all of the above, particularly with departmental rules on the use of force. Those rules are often more limiting than state law and are binding on the officer regardless of what state law or court decisions provide. For example, state law may allow the use of deadly force to protect property, but if departmental policy allows the use of deadly force

P

only for self-defense, an officer who shoots a potential burglar runs the risk of liability.

Wrongful Death Lawsuits. This tort, usually established by law, arises whenever death occurs as a result of an officer's action or inaction, be it felony or misdemeanor cases. It is brought by the surviving family, relatives, or legal guardian of the estate of the deceased for pain, suffering, and actual expenses (such as expenses for the funeral and hospitalization) and for the loss of life to the family or relatives. Examples include shooting and killing a fleeing suspect, firing shots at a suspect in a shopping center that result in death of an innocent bystander, or using a chokehold that results in the death of the arrestee. In some states, a death resulting from a police officer's use of deadly force comes under the tort of misuse of weapons. An officer has a duty to use not merely ordinary care but a high degree of care in handling weapons, otherwise he or she becomes liable for wrongful death.

Test to Determine Civil Liability Under Federal Law in Excessive Use-of-Force Cases: Graham v. Connor
An important question for police officers is this: What test will the courts use to determine whether the use of force amounts to a violation of a constitutional right so that the officer can then be held civilly liable under federal law? In a case decided in 1989, the Supreme Court said that allegations that law-enforcement officers used excessive force in arrests, investigative stops, or other forms of seizure must be analyzed and judged under the Fourth Amendment "objective reasonableness" standard rather than under the "substantive due process" clause of the Fourteenth Amendment.[9]

The facts of *Graham v. Connor* are as follows: Graham, a diabetic, asked a friend to drive him to a convenience store to buy orange juice to counteract the onset of an insulin reaction. Upon arrival at the store, Graham saw a lot of people ahead of him, so he asked his friend to drive him to another friend's house. Connor, a police officer, saw Graham enter and leave the store hastily. Suspicious, Connor stopped the car and ordered Graham and his friend to wait while he ascertained what happened in the store. Backup police arrived, handcuffed Graham, and ignored explanations about his diabetic condition. A scuffle ensued and Graham sustained multiple injuries. Gra-ham was released when the officer learned that nothing happened in the store. He later sued, alleging excessive use of force by the police. On appeal, the Court held that police officers may be held liable under the Constitution for using excessive force, but such liability must be judged under the Fourth Amendment's "objective reasonableness" standard, rather than under the Fourteenth Amendment's "substantive due process" standard used in previous lower court cases.

The result of that decision is that *Graham* now sets the legal standard by which allegations of excessive use of force by police officers are determined for civil liability purposes, that standard being "objective reasonableness" under the Fourth Amendment. This is significant because in a case decided earlier,[10] the Second Circuit Court of Appeals had enumerated four factors that courts were to use in determining constitutional violations in use-of-force cases, which are:

1. the need for the application of force;
2. the relationship between the need and the amount of force that was used;
3. the extent of the injury inflicted; and
4. whether force was applied in a good faith effort to maintain or restore discipline or maliciously and sadistically for the very purpose of causing harm.

These factors required consideration by the court whether the officer acted in "good faith" or "maliciously and sadistically for the very purpose of causing harm," obviously a difficult and subjective task for the fact-finder. Nonetheless, the majority of lower federal courts applied this test to all excessive force claims against law enforcement and prison officials filed under Section 1983. That was changed by *Graham*.

Aside from abandoning the motive test, *Graham* is also significant because it explicitly states that the reasonableness of a particular use of force by the police, deadly or nondeadly, "must be judged from the perspective of a reasonable officer on the scene, rather than with the 20/20 vision of hindsight." This is important because it sets the standard the trier of fact must use when determining reasonableness, that standard being the perspective of a reasonable officer on the scene. This is considered more equitable by the police, whose main complaint in use-of-force cases was that they were second-guessed by judges or juries, sitting in the comfort of an air-conditioned room, with a lot of time to spare, and "using the 20/20 vision of hindsight." Officers understandably reject conclusions about reasonableness of the use of force drawn by individuals who have never been on the streets and who do not know the pressure involved in making split-second decisions with an officer's life at stake. They would rather be judged by their own peers, who presumably know whereof they speak because they have been through a similar experience. In reality, however, this "reasonable officer on the scene" test boils down to having a parade of "experts" on the witness stand, who have had police experience, being presented with both sides, but drawing opposite conclusions from the same set of facts. Nonetheless, the *Graham* standard conveys to defendant officers a sense of realism and fairness.

The Court in *Graham* did not specify factors that might lead to a finding of objective reasonableness by a judge or jury. All it said was that this should be judged from the perspective of a reasonable officer on the scene. Although a new standard has thus been set, the standard nonetheless leaves room for subjectivity because even reasonable officers can differ as to what action ought to have been taken under the circumstances. The Court stated, however, that "the calculus of reasonableness must embody allowances for the fact that police officers are often forced to make split-second judgments—in circumstances that are tense, uncertain, and rapidly evolving—about the amount of force that is necessary in a particular situation." Although that does not set a definitive guideline, it narrows discretion by the fact-finder and is less likely to result in blatantly arbitrary decisions.

The *Graham* test applied only to Section 1983 cases, a required element of which is a violation of a constitutional right. It does not apply to cases brought under state tort law, such cases being governed by standards set under state law. Some lower courts have applied the *Graham* test retroactively; others have not. Moreover, *Graham* applies only to "warrant, investigative steps and other forms of seizure" situations. Thus, if the use of force takes place in other situations the *Graham* test does not apply. For example, in cases of crowd dispersal or the use of force in jails, the old substantive due process test still applies.

Summary and Conclusion

Use of force is an inevitable part of policing that carries immense potential for liability. Civil liability looms every time any type of force is used, whether that force be nondeadly or deadly. It is imperative that officers know the limits of the use of force. In cases of nondeadly force, that limit is reasonableness; in deadly force cases, that limit is usually set by departmental policy and, in the absence of that, by state law and the United States Constitution.

The Court has not specified precise limits on the use of force, but two cases have laid out important principles. *Tennessee v. Garner* allows the use of deadly force to prevent escape only where the officer has probable cause to believe that the suspect poses a threat of serious physical harm either to the officer or to others. The second case, *Graham v. Connor*, holds that the use of force in arrests, investigative stops, or other forms of seizure must be analyzed and judged under the "objective reasonableness" standard of the Fourth Amendment rather than under the "substantive due process" clause of the Fourteenth Amendment. Gone under the new test is the relevance of police motive for the use of force. *Graham*, moreover, states that the reasonableness of a particular use of force by the police must be judged from the perspective of a "reasonable officer on the scene," rather than with the "20/20 vision of hindsight." Although discretion has been curtailed by *Graham*, subjectivity has not been completely eliminated.

Use of force is an emotional issue usually pitting police departments against the community and is a flashpoint for potentially explosive police–community relations. To minimize lawsuits, police officers must know the proper limits of the use of force, the department must lay out clear guidelines for such use, and police supervisors must appreciate the importance of proper training in this sensitive and crucial area of police work. Failure to know the proper limits of the use of force leads to civil liability that can impose heavy burdens on the officer, the supervisor, and the agency.

Rolando V. del Carmen

Notes

1. As quoted in I. Silver, *Police Civil Liability: Law and Practice*, 1991 Supp., at 6–5.
2. *Budgar v. State*, 414 N.Y.S. 2d. 463 (1979).
3. *Lewis v. Downs*, 774 F.2d 711 (6th Cir. 1985).

4. *Bustamente v. City of Tucson,* 701 P.2d 861 (Ariz. App. 1985).
5. *Valdez v. Abney,* 227 Cal. Rptr. 707 (1986).
6. Supra note 1, at 5–9.
7. 471 U.S. 1 (1985).
8. J.C. Hall. "Police Use of Deadly Force to Arrest: A Constitutional Standard." (Part II). *FBI Law Enforcement Bulletin* (July 1988):23.
9. *Graham v. Connor,* 109 S.Ct. 1865 (1989).
10. *Johnson v. Glick,* 481 F.2d 1028 (2nd Cir. 1973).

Bibliography

Aaby, D.A. "Scope of the Public Duty/Special Duty Doctrine in Illinois: Municipal Liability for Failure to Provide Police Protection. *Northern Illinois University Law Review* 10 (1990): 269–301.

Aaron, T. "Federal Due Process Limitations on the Termination of State and Municipal Law Enforcement Officials." *American Journal of Police* 11 (1992): 53–63.

Berringer, H.G. *Civil Liability and the Police.* Evanston, IL: Northwestern University Traffic Institute, 1987.

"Constitutional Law: The Viability of Section 1983 Actions in Response to Police Misconduct." *Annual Survey of American Law* 1990 (April 1992): 747–79.

del Carmen, Rolando V. *Civil Liberties in American Policing: A Text for Law Enforcement Personnel.* Englewood Cliffs, NJ: Prentice-Hall, 1991.

Kappeler, Victor. "Police Liability." *Police Liability Review* 4 (Fall 1992): complete issue.

Meadows, R.J. "Likelihood of Liability." *Security Management* 35 (July 1991): 60–66.

More, Harry W., and P.C. Unsinger. *Managerial Control of the Police: Internal Affairs and Audits.* Springfield, IL: Charles C. Thomas, 1992.

Roberts, B.E. "Legal Issues in Use-of-Force Claims." *Police Chief* 59 (February 1992): 16, 20, 22–24, 28–29.

Police Misconduct: The Rodney King Incident

On March 3, 1991, several officers of the Los Angeles California Police Department (LAPD) were videotaped beating motorist Rodney G. King following a police pursuit. The graphic images of this display of police force incited reactions from the public and the police community. Although any brutality of this nature is repugnant, the incident raised larger questions and concerns about the pervasiveness and tolerance of such police conduct, as well as the impact on the fragile image of the police in America. Immediately accusations of ineptness, neglect, and unprofessionalism were lodged against Los Angeles area law-enforcement agencies. These once renowned icons of professionalism and innovation were scrutinized and chastised as unfit for permitting such police misconduct to become customary.

In response to the Rodney King incident, Mayor Tom Bradley of Los Angeles assembled a commission to conduct an internal investigation into the infrastructure and ethos of the LAPD. Warren Christopher chaired the Independent Commission on the Los Angeles Police Department, thus the "Christopher Commission" evolved as the name of the report. At the same time, the Los Angeles County Sheriff's Department (LASD) was experiencing similar difficulties with chronic incidents of excessive force followed by citizen complaints. Sheriff Sherman Block of Los Angeles County responded to the events surrounding his own deputies, the King incident, and the formation of the Christopher Commission by creating an internal commission to examine the operations of the LASD. Block named Judge James G. Kolts to act as chair and special counsel on this internal commission. Together, these commission reports painted a grim picture of pervasive tolerance by both the LAPD and the LASD of chronic misconduct by a core group of officers.

The Rodney King Incident

On the morning of March 3, 1991, at approximately 12:40 A.M. a California Highway Patrol (CHP) unit attempted to stop Rodney King's vehicle, which was observed traveling at speeds in excess of one hundred miles per hour. Rodney King failed to stop and fled from the CHP unit, which resulted in a prolonged vehicle pursuit. Several other police vehicles joined in the chase including officers of the Los Angeles Police Department. After a short while King was stopped and ordered to exit his vehicle. The officers reported that King resisted their efforts to arrest him. They stated that the resistance was of such magnitude that they chose to use a

Taser electric stun-gun to subdue King. Near this point in the incident, a nearby witness, George Holliday, began to videotape the arrest unbeknownst to the police officers. With King still on the ground, LAPD officers Laurence Powell, Theodore Briseno, and Timothy Wind began to strike King repeatedly with batons and kicked him under the direction of LAPD Sergeant Stacey Koon. Once the arrest was consummated, King was treated at an area hospital and charged with evading arrest. Medical records showed that King received twenty stitches, including five on the inside of his mouth, and suffered a broken cheekbone and right ankle. Body fluid tests revealed that King had a blood/alcohol level sufficient to constitute legal intoxication, along with trace amounts of marijuana. Important to the subsequent officers' trial, there was no indication of PCP or any other illegal drug in King's blood and urine samples. After being held for four days King was released and the charges were dismissed for lack of evidence. Shortly after the incident, area television media distributed George Holliday's videotape resulting in widespread exposure. Within a matter of days most of America had seen the videotape, which was played repeatedly on news broadcasts.

General Findings of the Christopher and Kolts Commissions

Soon after the King incident, the Christopher Commission began an internal investigation of the Los Angeles Police Department; in July 1991 it published its findings and recommendations. One year later in July 1992, the Kolts Commission released its findings. Although the two commissions were not collaborative, the Kolts Commission indicated that its investigation of the Los Angeles County Sheriff's Department was influenced by the Christopher Commission. Furthermore, although the two commissions investigated different agencies—LAPD and LASD—the departments shared many elements in common. Such factors as indigenous residential populations, similar agency practices, adjacent and overlapping police jurisdictions, operational collaboration between agencies, and police subcultural customs were the most obvious.

Initial impressions of the Rodney King incident suggested that police use of excessive force might be an aberration or isolated event. Members of the Christopher and Kolts commissions, Mayor Bradley, and law-enforcement

advocacy groups nationwide hoped the King incident was indeed an anomaly of police behavior. However, many Los Angeles City and County residents held different views about the incident and described the agencies as callous, unresponsive, and often abusive (Christopher Commission, 1991; Kolts Commission, 1992; Ricker, 1991).

As indicated by Table 1, the problem of excessive force in the LAPD was not customary for all officers, but rather for a core group of chronic violators. In a random survey of 960 LAPD officers administered by the Christopher Commission, respondents indicated mixed values about use of excessive force.

What is most striking are those officers who candidly supported use of excessive force or "street justice" added to those officers who expressed no opinion. Together their responses supporting excessive force either directly or tacitly equaled almost 16% of LAPD. Also fully 70% of the officers surveyed indicated directly or tacitly that no excessive force problem existed in LAPD. Yet citizen complaint data showed 24.7% of the 8,274 complaints filed between 1986 and 1990 were for excessive force, with another 14.5% of the complaints for improper tactics. (Christopher Commission, 1991 [includes LAPD Complaint Database, 1986–1990]). All told, improper methods of arrest, improper search and seizure, and misuse of force accounted for 39% of the total citizen complaints filed between 1986 and 1990. The data suggested that contrary to the perception of many of the officers surveyed, an excessive

TABLE 1

Officer Responses to Commission Survey*

	Agree	Disagree	No Opinion
Use of excessive force is a serious problem in LAPD	30%	53%	17%
An officer is justified in administering physical punishment to a serious crime suspect or one with an attitude problem	4.9%	84%	11%

* This table presents only two of the questions asked in the survey. Source: Christopher Commission, 1991.

force problem did exist within LAPD. Overall data indicated that only 1% of all LAPD arrests resulted in a use of force report being filed. The commission expressed concern about the lack of reports being filed in compliance with policy. Again, data indicated that 6,000 officers were involved in one or more use-of-force incidents between 1987 and 1991, which belied the lack of reports filed.

Table 2 shows the frequency of complaints against a core group of officers from 1986 to 1990. Upon compiling the data from citizen complaints, use of force reports filed by officers, and use of excessive force allegations, the commission established a very troubling pattern of misconduct that had developed within the LAPD. The data indicated that the most excessive individuals could be narrowed to a "group of forty-four." For example, one officer had thirteen allegations of excessive force and improper tactics, five other complaint allegations, twenty-eight use of force reports, and one shooting ascribed to him alone.

Departmental Liability for Officer Misconduct

Officers and agencies are subject to various types of liability claims involving police use of excessive force. These include both individual and departmental liability, as well as state tort, federal civil rights, and other actions arising from vicarious liability. Recent attention has been focused on the extent of redress against police departments through interpretation of 42 U.S.C. Section 1983. Circumstances surrounding the King incident have raised many questions involving the extent of liability exposure of LAPD as a departmental entity under Section 1983.

In the post–Civil War era Congress passed three separate federal statutes prohibiting deprivation of constitutional protections and federally protected rights by agents of government acting under "color of law"—18 U.S.C. Section 241, 18 U.S.C. Section 242, and 42 U.S.C. Sec-

tion 1983. As a result of overt acts of discrimination and deprivation of civil rights by southern states following the Civil War, Congress passed the Ku Klux Klan Act of 1871, which was later codified into 42 U.S.C. Section 1983. Relying on those protections espoused in the Fourteenth Amendment, Section 1983 afforded claimants redress from constitutional deprivation by state agents of government. Further, the language of the Section 1983 statute directed attention to not only the states and constitutional protection but also to the designation of certain "persons" as being prohibited from depriving others of civil rights. As can be seen by the verbiage of the statute, the interpretation of "person" is central to the legislative intent underlying Section 1983.

In the Dictionary Act of 1871 "person" extended to cover "bodies politic and corporate . . . unless the context shows that such words were intended to be used in a more limited sense." Because of the proximity of the writing of the Dictionary Act to the Fourteenth Amendment and Section 1983, the courts have used this definition of "person" for interpreting the extent of liability for police agencies and municipalities.

Development of the Monell Doctrine

Early courts excluded municipalities and/or their extended agents, e.g., police departments, from liability exposure under Section 1983 as evidenced by the ruling in *Monroe v. Pape* (1961). The *Monroe* holding was subsequently replaced by dicta in *Monell v. Department of Social Services of the City of New York* (1978). *Monell* established that municipalities were liable under Section 1983 for constitutional rights deprivations that arose from official policy, regulation, ordinance, or custom of the governmental entity. Thus the municipality and/or agency could be held liable if the officers' actions were linked to official policy or custom.

Elements of Customary Behavior

As indicated in *Monell*, custom can be established through several methods: either those that emanate from official policy or those that emanate from custom. Official policy has been defined by some courts as that which is a result of promulgated rules, ordinances, or policies by a lawmaking body or that which evolves from customary behavior or "widespread practice" (e.g., *Bennett v. City of Slidell*, 1984).

TABLE 2

	Number of Allegations			
	1–2	4 or more	6 or more	8 or more
Number of Officers	1,400	183	44	17

Source: Christopher Commission, 1991.

Official policy that evolves from customary acts is more problematic to interpret inasmuch as it emanates from certain patterns of practice rather than from written rules. These "unwritten rules" can become official policy by virtue of becoming accepted practice among officers. Official policy by custom is extremely difficult to define and thus the courts have provided little clarity. Aside from a promulgated unconstitutional policy as established by the court in *Oklahoma v. Tuttle* (1985), a single act cannot establish customary behavior. Custom evolves from a discernible pattern of conduct (*Fiacco v. City of Rensselaer*, 1986; *Patzner v. Burkett*, 1985; *Languirand v. Hayden*, 1983; *Springfield, Mass. v. Kibbe*, 1987). The pattern is not merely one which evolves from one individual but rather from several officers. Rudosky (1982) suggests that patterns of police misconduct arise through chronic practices by officers that are tolerated by the department.

In order for this conduct to develop, the behavior is not only tacitly approved by the department through inaction but further becomes a matter of common knowledge among officers such that the conduct propagates itself (*Webster v. City of Houston*, 1984). The pattern of behavior continues to evolve and grow through repeated use, as well as through supervisory inaction. The courts have not specifically clarified the extent to which supervisors or other officers must be cognizant of standard practices in order for them to become considered custom. Widespread participation and awareness indicate both direct and indirect culpability respectively.

Deliberate Indifference Standard
In *City of Canton, Ohio v. Harris* (1989) the court established a bright-line standard which held that liability exists when circumstances indicate the police department showed "deliberate indifference" to officer training resulting in constitutional deprivation. Further, if a causal linkage can be shown between departmental indifference and police misconduct then there exists the implication that the department made a "conscious choice" that is tantamount to the establishment of a de facto policy. Therefore the court held that the police department has an obligation to take the necessary measures to insure proper training and supervision of its officers. Department responsibility also extends to maintaining awareness of customary officer practices. Failure to be proactive in responding to violations of policy or misconduct can be construed as deliberate indifference.

Liability for failure to properly train personnel has been established in several cases (*Wierstak v. Heffernan*, 1986; *Davis v. Mason County*, 1991; *City of Canton, Ohio v. Harris*, 1989). Justice O'Connor noted in *Harris* that responsibility may be imposed on policy-makers and administrators when they "are aware of, and acquiesced in, a pattern of constitutional violations involving the exercise of police discretion." Therefore, common knowledge of unfit behavior can promote the development of customary conduct and supervisory disregard of that knowledge can create deliberate indifference.

Failure to Discipline
Customary behavior can also evolve through tacit approval from supervisors by failing to properly investigate and discipline officer misconduct. Departmental tolerance can exacerbate police misconduct in several ways. First, the courts have held that hesitancy to investigate citizen complaints and claims against officers implies tolerance of the officers' behavior (*Fiacco v. City of Rensselaer*, 1986; *Wierstak v. Heffernan*, 1986). Agencies that demonstrate a complaisant or nonresponsive attitude toward police misconduct tacitly approve the behavior by not investigating claims against officers.

Second, once agencies have investigated and sustained claims against officers they must initiate disciplinary or remedial action against those officers. Failure to take disciplinary or corrective action can infer approval of the questioned behavior and perpetuate the conduct through omission. According to the LAPD database, the department only sustained 2% of complaints against officers in five years and as indicated in Figure 1 only 9% of those sustained force complaints resulted in officer removal.

Figure 2 indicates the apportionment of unsustained citizen complaints for use of excessive force.

Findings of the Christopher Commission suggested that investigation of these complaints may have been less than aggressive and thus may explain the high rate of exoneration of accused officers. The LAPD data suggested significant laxity in pursuing officer misconduct through internal investigation. Rudosky (1982) maintains that such departmental lack of responsiveness causes the spread of police misconduct because of a lack of deterrence.

FIGURE 1

Penalties for Sustained Force: Complaints, 1986–1990

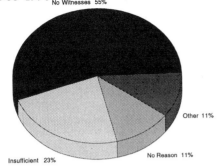

No Witnesses 55%

Insufficient 23%

Other 11%

No Reason 11%

Source: LAPD Database.

FIGURE 2

Reasons for Unsustained Force: Complaints, 1988–1990

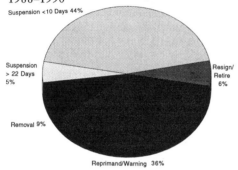

Suspension <10 Days 44%

Suspension > 22 Days 5%

Resign/ Retire 6%

Removal 9%

Reprimand/Warning 36%

Source: LAPD Database.

Third, consistent with deterrence theory, the efficacy of departmental sanctions against officer misconduct is based not only on the celerity of sanctions but also on the certainty and severity of discipline against officers. The absence of adequate sanction controls, which are administered with a degree of severity, can perpetuate officer misconduct. If officers who are willfully engaged in excessive force or misconduct are aware that the departmental response will be timid or nonexistent, then there exists no deterrent effect on their behavior.

Commission Findings as Indicators of Departmental Custom

Inasmuch as internal practices of the police department can be indicators of departmental ideology, the Christopher Commission findings identify several philosophies and operating practices that are considered indicative of the LAPD ethos. As mentioned previously, the commission observed that the same group of officers were subject to use of excessive force and complaints. Those officers were known to department supervisors both by reputation and work style. The commission indicated it was common practice in LAPD to transmit electronic MDT (mobile data terminal) messages between patrol units in a conspicuous manner. Other officers and supervisors should have been readily aware of the practice. Some officers exchanged vulgar, racially insensitive, and gender-biased communications. The commission cited examples of vulgar communications such as "sounds like monkey slapping time" and "I would love to drive down Slauson with a flame thrower . . . we would have a barbeque." Among the LAPD officers surveyed, 25% agreed that significant racial prejudice existed between officers and minority citizens, and 28% agreed that "an officer's prejudice towards the suspect's race may lead to the use of excessive force." Further evidence of the acceptability of such conduct was that the officers with the most egregious records continued to receive satisfactory evaluations by supervisors.

FTOs (field training officers) perpetuated these attitudes and practices during indoctrination of probationary officers. FTOs are charged with the responsibility of instructing new officers in proper procedures and practices. The commission findings suggest that several of the FTOs had themselves been involved in repeated excessive use of force incidences and likely imparted those same attitudes to the probationary officers.

General Recommendations of the Christopher Commission

First, the commission found there existed a lack of adequate emphasis on a community-based policing ideology in the LAPD. Rather emphasis was on a strict crime control ideology, which tended to divide and alienate the community and the police officers. The commission recommended there be an ideological transition in the LAPD to a more community-based approach to policing with emphasis placed on creating a better working relationship between police and community.

Second, more emphasis needed to be placed on the recruiting and selection process of officers. Prospective recruits should be subjected to an intensive background investigation to discover any history of deviance or violent behavior. The commission indicated that the LAPD relied too heavily on psychological examination to detect past violent or deviant behavior among recruits. Increased efforts should be placed on extensive background investigation rather than on merely testing to detect deviance or tendencies.

Third, academy training plays a crucial role in indoctrinating recruits into a proper perspective about policing and appropriate behavior. Because of the formative state of early trainees, it is critical to impart the proper attitude and role expectations from the beginning. In addition to the appropriate indoctrination, the commission recommended that additional emphasis be placed on verbal skills training rather than the traditional emphasis on physical skills. Additional training should be provided on cultural, ethnic, and gender awareness/sensitivity.

Fourth, FTOs must be expected to stand as an appropriate role model for probationary officers. FTOs should be of stellar character and advocates for department policy. They should also demonstrate attitudes and work styles that are conducive to promoting sensitivity toward the community and its diversity, rather than to stressing a crime control perspective.

Fifth, citizen complaints—especially excessive use of force complaints—should be entered into the personnel files of officers and should be a consideration in assignments, promotions, and other personnel matters. The Commission noted that no unsustained citizen complaints were entered in the personnel files of officers. Although unsustained complaints should not impair an officer's ability to be reassigned or promoted, past work history, including complaints, should be evaluated in any pending change in officer status.

Last, it is incumbent on any department to aggressively investigate citizen complaints of excessive force. Internal affairs should discover all relevant facts concerning the complaints and insure that an adequate and in-depth investigation has been conducted. If the allegation is sustained, it is incumbent on the leadership of the department to discipline the officer(s) involved. Discipline should be carried out with celerity, certainty, and severity in order to preclude other officers from engaging in similar misconduct.

The Trials and Their Aftermath

Following the King incident of March 3, 1991, LAPD officers Powell, Briseno, Wind, and Sergeant Koon were charged in California State Court with criminal assault and assault under color of authority based on excessive force. Because of concern over the ubiquitous media coverage of the event, attorneys for the officers sought a change of venue outside of Los Angeles. Their request was granted by a California appeals court and the trial was moved to Simi Valley, California, a nearby suburb in Ventura County. Critics claimed the change of venue to this predominantly white middle-class area would obscure the racial and inner-city context of the King incident.

Los Angeles Superior Court Judge Stanley Weisberg presided over the trial that began in March 1992. After almost a month of testimony, the presentation of six prosecution witnesses (Rodney King was not called to testify)—and forty-nine defense witnesses, the jury comprised of ten whites, one Asian, and one Hispanic began their deliberation. On April 29, 1992, the jury acquitted the officers on ten of eleven charges against them. Immediately after the news of the verdict became known, Los Angeles erupted into one of the worst incidences of civil unrest in U.S. history. The riots lasted for more than forty-eight hours and resulted in more than 3,700 fires, fifty-three deaths, and millions of dollars in property damage.

Following the state trial, the U.S. Justice Department conducted its own investigation and indicted the four officers for depriving Rodney King of his civil rights under 18 U.S.C. Section 242, as well as aiding and abetting one another. A more ethnically diverse jury, including several black members, was impaneled in federal court in Los Angeles to hear the second trial. The prosecution relied heavily on a computer enhanced version of the George Holliday videotape, as well as the testimony of Rodney King, who this time took the stand. After deliberation, the federal jury on April 16, 1993, rendered a mixed verdict concerning the multiple charges against the officers. Their verdict found Sergeant Koon guilty of both charges, Officer Powell guilty of deprivation of civil rights only, and Officers Briseno and Wind innocent of charges. The federal trial verdict met with a calm, mostly celebratory reaction across the country.

William P. Bloss

Bibliography

Alpert, Geoffrey. "*City of Canton v. Harris* and the Deliberate Indifference Standard." *Criminal Law Bulletin* 25 (1989): 466–72.

———, et al. "Law Enforcement: Implications of the Rodney King Beating." *Criminal Law Bulletin* 28 (1992): 469–78.

Bennett v. City of Slidell (1984). 735 F2d 861 (5th Cir.).

Bloss, William. "The Net Widens on Personal Liability for State Officers. *Police Liability Review* 4 (1992): 1–3.

City of Canton, Ohio, v. Harris (1989). 109 S.Ct. 1197.

Christopher Commission. *Report of the Independent Commission on the Los Angeles Police Department*. Los Angeles: The Commission, 1991.

Davis v. Mason County (1991). 927 F2d. 1473 (9th Cir.).

del Carmen, Rolando V. *Civil Liberties in American Policing: A Text for Law Enforcement Personnel*. Englewood Cliffs, NJ: Prenice-Hall, 1991.

———. *Criminal Procedure Law and Practice*. 2d ed. New York: Brooks-Cole, 1991.

———, and Jeffrey Walker. *Briefs of 100 Leading Cases in Law Enforcement*. Cincinnati, OH: Anderson, 1991.

Fiacco v. City of Rensselaer (1986). 782 F2d. 319 (2nd Cir.).

Garner v. Tennessee (1985). 471 U.S. 1.

Graham v. Connor (1989). 109 S.Ct. 1865.

Hughes, James. "The Will Decision-Freedom for States to Discriminate." *Mississippi College Law Review* 11 (1990): 157–72.

Joyner, Irving. "Litigating Police Misconduct in North Carolina." *North Carolina Central Law Journal* 19 (1991): 113–45.

Kappeler, Victor. *Critical Issues in Police Civil Liability*. Prospect Heights, IL: Waveland Press, 1993.

Klotter, John, and Jacqueline Kanovitz. *Constitutional Law*. 4th ed. Cincinnati: Anderson, 1981.

Kolts Commission. *Internal Report on the Los Angeles County Sheriff's Department*. Los Angeles: The Commission, 1992.

Languirand v. Hayden (1983). 717 F2d 220 (5th Cir.).

Larez v. City of Los Angeles (1991). 928 F2d 112 (9th Cir.).

Los Angeles v. Heller (1986). 475 U.S. 796.

Los Angeles v. Lyons (1983). 461 U.S. 95.

Monell v. Department of Social Services of the City of New York (1978). 436 U.S. 658.

Monroe v. Pape (1961). 365 U.S. 167.

Oklahoma v. Tuttle (1985). 471 U.S. 808.

Patterson, Amy. "Comments Made by LAPD Chief Become Focus of Appeal." *Police Liability Review* 3 (1992): 6–7.

Patzner v. Burkett (1985). 779 F2d 1363 (8th Cir.).

Ricker, Darlene. "Behind the Silence." *ABA Journal* (July 1991): 44–49.

Roberg, Roy, and John Kuykendall. *Police and Society*. Belmont, CA: Wadsworth, 1993.

Rudosky, Leonard. *The Politics of Law*. New York: Pantheon Books, 1982.

Shoop, Julie. "Police Misconduct Cases: A Growing Industry." *Trial* (August 1991): 11–12.

Springfield, Mass. v. Kibbe (1987). 480 U.S. 257.

Webster v. City of Houston (1984). 735 F2d 838.

Wierstak v. Heffernan (1986). 789 F2d. 968 (1st Cir.).

Police Mortality

A once-popular misconception was that premature police deaths were attributable to homicide, occurring as a result of the dangers of police work. In reality, a large percentage of police officers die prematurely from stress-related disease and other causes. Evidence from research indicates an increased risk of disease and mortality among those in the police profession and suggests that police officers, on the average, die at a much younger age than others in the general population. Guralnick (1963), for example, found that the overall mean age of death for police officers in the United States is fifty-nine. The average death age for the general population is seventy-three for males and seventy-seven for females.

Evidence of Police Mortality

Background Research. Few major studies have been done on police mortality. In a mortality study of 149 occupations, Guralnick (1963) found police officers to have a significantly high incidence of heart disease, diabetes, and suicide. The data were taken from 1950 census information and death certificates. Milham (1983), in a Washington state study, suggested that police have an increased risk of cancer of the colon and liver, diabetes, and heart disease. Mortality ratios for heart disease were highest among younger police officers (thirty to forty-four years of age). A study that suggested contradictory results was the normative aging study (Sparrow, Thomas, and Weiss, 1983). This study found that police officers in the sample had heartdisease rates similar to those of persons in other occupations. It was noted, however, that police subjects for this study were a group of very healthy veterans who volunteered, and no information was given concerning variables that would confound the results.

The most recent study on police mortality was that of Vena et al. (1985). This study involved 2,376 police officers who worked in a city police force between 1950 and 1979. Findings revealed significantly high rates among police officers for cancer, heart disease, and suicide. These findings are discussed below in detail.

Cancer. Police mortality from cancer at specific body sites was significantly higher than expected when compared with the general work population. In particular, cancers of the digestive organs, especially the esophagus and colon, were the highest.

The length of police service appeared to have an effect on cancer mortality rates. Overall elevated mortality rates from cancer were influenced heavily by the increased risk among officers with ten to nineteen years of service and those with forty years of service. In the ten-to-nineteen-year-employed group, there was a threefold risk for digestive cancer and a fourfold risk for cancer of the lymphatic and blood-production tissues. In the over-forty-year-employed group of officers, there was a fourfold risk for bladder cancer, a twofold risk for cancer of the digestive organs, and a threefold risk for cancer of the lymphatic and blood-production tissues. A statistically significant fourfold risk of brain cancer was found in the twenty-to-twenty-nine-year-employed group of officers.

Heart Disease. Past research on police mortality indicates that heart disease seems to be prevalent among the police population. Early studies show police officers ranked at or near the top of occupations for mortality from heart disease. More recent studies show similar results, demonstrating that heart disease among police appears to generally increase with increasing years of service.

For the most part, young police officers have lower heart disease mortality due to the stringent physical requirements for recruit officers. However, by the time officers have forty years in service, the risk increases significantly. Suggestions from research indicate that stress, poor diet, lack of exercise, and carbon-monoxide exposure may be contributing factors to this increased risk.

Suicide. The majority of police mortality studies completed thus far have indicated an increased risk of suicide among police officers. Guralnick's data from 1950 show a significantly high rate of suicide for police when compared with 148 other occupations. More recently, Vena et al. (1986) found data evidencing the suicide rate among police to be three times that of other municipal workers. This is an unusual finding, since suicide rates in the working population are generally lower than the general population.

Police suicide rates vary throughout the United States, but one thing remains constant: The police rate is always higher than that of other working populations. A dismaying fact is that even these high rates for suicide may actually be underestimated. The official causes of police deaths, as listed on death certificates, depend largely upon the investigation by local police agencies. The fact that the victim is a police officer and the stigma associated with suicide may influence the kind of data eventually recorded. Recent studies have shown that coroners' reports involving police deaths of a suspicious nature are often presented vaguely.

Reasons discussed in the literature for high rates of police suicide are frustration with the police and criminal-justice system, reactive depression, demands of the police marriage, and loss of personal control. The majority of police suicides involve the use of the officer's own service firearm. Police suicide appears to be an occupation-specific problem and needs to be examined by further research.

Antecedents of Police Mortality

There exists a good probability that high mortality rates for cancer, heart disease, and suicide are related to police occupational factors and accompanying lifestyle habituation. Risk factors evident thus far in the literature include a high-stress work environment, irregular sleeping and eating habits, poor health practices, and lack of sufficient exercise.

Stress. Police work has been implicated as one of the most stressful occupations in the world, and stress has been linked to many of the diseases that police officers die from—e.g., heart disease, diabetes, high-blood pressure, and ulcers. Hans Selye (1978) described "diseases of adaptation," where stress disrupts the regulatory functions of the body and eventually leads to a breakdown of affected organs. A related condition brought on by stress is suppression of the immune system. This may lead to a lowered immunity to disease-producing viruses and cancer-causing agents. The connection between cancer and stress is not yet clear, but future research may confirm this relationship. Related environmental factors thought to be related to job stress are smoking, caffeine use, and alcohol consumption. These factors appear to exacerbate the deleterious health effects that stress has on police officers.

Diet. Cancers of the colon and digestive organs have been found to be related to diet. The ingestion of high-fat foods and lack of vegetables, for example, has been associated with increased colon cancer risk. Other foods that increase risk are fried foods, high meat and animal fat consumption, and bacon. These types of foods are commonly eaten by police officers on duty. Often police rotate shifts and do not have access to proper foods. Many times, officers fit in their meals whenever possible during tours of duty.

Exercise. The majority of police officers in the United States do little or no meaningful exercise. Surveys of police show that approximately 86 percent report lack of exercise and that 25 percent are overweight. These may be important antecedents of disease progression among police. Lack of exercise has been pointed out as a risk factor in heart disease, diabetes, and colon cancer.

Shift Work. Working different shifts on a rapid rotation basis may have adverse effects on the health of police officers. Shift work is thought to cause an imbalance in many of the body's normal regulatory functions, such as temperature, electrolyte balance, and heart rate. Officers generally experience poor sleeping and eating schedules, a common feeling of dullness, and family problems as a result of shift work. Medical evidence exists that cardiovascular disease is associated with shift work.

Alcohol Use. Cancers of the esophagus and cirrhosis of the liver have been associated with alcohol use. Police officers have an increased mortality risk for both of these diseases. Police officers appear to depend heavily upon alcohol as a coping technique to deal with job stress. Besides causing physiological anomalies, alcohol abuse among police may lead to family and job difficulties.

Personality Factors. The type-A behavior pattern, characterized by high striving, achievement, time urgency, competition, anger, and hostility, has been associated with an increased risk of heart disease. Police officers tend to be type-A individuals.

Prevention
Whether or not the aforementioned factors are causally related to police mortality awaits future research. At present these factors have been proposed as playing a part in the increased risk of disease.

In today's work environment, there is a renewed emphasis on prevention of disease at the workplace. Prevention may be best accomplished in police work through education and organizational policy. Police agencies have been encouraged to initiate exercise and fitness standards; to promote dietary education; to make available medical screening for heart disease, high-blood pressure, and certain types of cancers; and to create awareness of the police mortality problem. Improved health among police officers should become an important goal for both the individual officer and the police organization.

John M. Violanti

Bibliography

Dash, J., and M. Reiser. "Suicide among Police in Urban Law Enforcement Agencies." *Journal of Police Science and Administration* 6 (1964): 18–21.

Grencik, L. "The Physical Fitness of Deputies Assigned to the Patrol Function and Its Relationship to Formulation of Entrance Standards." Washington, DC: U.S. Department of Justice. LEAA, 1973.

Guralnick, L. "Mortality by Occupation and

Cause of Death among Men 20–64 Years of Age: United States, 1950." *Vital Statistics—Special Reports* 53. Bethesda, MD: USDHEW, 1963.

Hurrell, J.J., and W.H. Kroes, eds. "Job Stress and the Police Officer." *DHEW Publication (NIOSH) 76–187*. Washington, DC: Government Printing Office, 1977.

Kroes, W.H. *Society's Victim: The Police Officer*. Springfield, IL.: Charles C. Thomas, 1976.

Milham, S., Jr. "Occupational Mortality in Washington State, 1950–79." *DHHS (NIOSH). Publication 83116*. Washington, DC: Government Printing Office, 1983.

Richard, W.C., and R.D. Fell. "Health Factors in Police Job Stress." In *Job Stress and the Police Officer DHEW (NIOSH), Publication 67–118*. Eds. W.H. Kroes and J.J. Hurrell, Washington, DC: Government Printing Office, 1977.

Selye, Hans. "The Stress of Police Work." *Police Stress* 1 (1978): 7–9.

Sparrow, D., H.E. Thomas, and S.T. Weiss. "Coronary Disease in Police Officers Participating in the Normative Aging Study." *American Journal of Epidemiology* 118 (1983): 508–13.

Vena, J.E., J.M. Violanti, J. Marshall, and R. Fiedler. "Mortality of a Municipal Worker Cohort: Police Officers." *American Journal of Industrial Medicine* 10 (1986): 383–97.

Vena, J.E., S. Graham, M. Zielezny, K. Swanson, R. Barnes, and J. Nolan. "Lifetime Occupational Exercise and Colon Cancer." *American Journal of Epidemiology* 122 (1985): 357–65.

Violanti, J.M., J.E. Vena, and J. Marshall. "Disease Risk and Mortality among Police Officers: New Evidence and Contributing Factors." *Journal of Police Science and Administration* 14 (1986): 17–23.

Police Officers: Gender Comparisons

Police officers are part of a highly organized and traditional structure that makes heavy demands on its members. Their emotional and psychological energies are drained from dealing with irate citizens, human tragedies, unpredictable crises, boredom, threats to their own health and life, and rotating shifts that create an unhealthy life rhythm. For most police these stressors are secondary to those experienced in the court system and within their own department. Organizational stressors vary, but most commonly they involve departmental politics, administrative policies that are incongruent with street realities, limited promotion opportunities, poor pay, excessive paperwork, inadequate equipment and training, lack of administrative support, and the frustration of seeing repeated offenders back on the street.

Additional stressors emerged with the influx of women into the male-dominated patrol force. Responding to the pressures of the civil rights and feminist movements of the 1960s and 1970s, a series of congressional mandates paved the way for equal job opportunities and career advancement for women. Thus legally, police departments were pressured to include women in all facets of policing. Psychologically, however, most police were unprepared for this change. The transformation from male- to mixed-gender patrol compelled both genders to adapt to a new order of psychosocial reality.

Sex-Role Spillover

This new reality is best understood in the context of sex-role and work-role expectations. Gender identity is the most basic cognitive category in our society. It is the person's gender that makes a difference in virtually every aspect of human interaction, both males and females learn to relate as men and women first and as workers second. Until recently, however, the majority of women did not engage in paid employment; thus, men more frequently experienced women in the nonwork context of lovers, mothers, and spouses (Guteck and Morasch, 1982).

Although today the majority of women are employed, most are in traditional female occupations such as nursing, social work, clerical, and other service jobs. These "pink" occupations are consistent with society's prescribed role for females: submissive, supportive, and nonaggressive. But what about women in the masculine world of policing? It is estimated that about 6 percent of United States sworn police officers are women, and several urban departments report having more than 10 percent. However, these women are overrepresented in clerical, secretarial, and administrative jobs, and in those assignments that give them authority over other women or children (Bell, 1982;

Glaser and Saxe, 1982; Greene, 1987).[1] Few are in patrol where officers make authoritative decisions, battle crime, and compete with rough street offenders. In essence, the work roles assigned to females merely broaden the scope of their traditional roles while preserving male authority and dominance.

In contrast, the world of street policing has a set of work-role expectations that is associated with the traditional male cultural traits of competitiveness, strength, aggressiveness, and a military regimentation. Unlike most women, most men's experience with contact sports or the military prepares them for the regimentation and physical endurance of police training. Although 50 to 90 percent of police calls are of a social service nature, police are popularly viewed as constantly responding to life-threatening situations and physical challenges. This image is exemplified by one officer who said, "I am not here to be a social worker with a nightstick. I am here to stop the bad-guys." The mass media keep this impression alive through romanticizing the gun-toting, quick-draw, "make my day" law-enforcement heroes of Hollywood screen and television dramas. These traits have traditionally been considered desirable or essential for effective policing. In fact, historically, the person most likely to advance up the ranks has been the "felony cop." Thus, many officers are reluctant to relinquish the "crime-stopper" role.

Since the stereotypical female traits are diametrically opposed to these characteristics, many male officers have greeted women newcomers less than enthusiastically (Kroes, 1982; Wexler and Logan, 1983). And here lies the basis of a cultural contradiction: the spillover of female gender-role expectations into a masculine workplace. For women patrol officers this spillover is evident in four areas: coworkers' attitudes, citizens' attitudes, gender-work role dilemmas, and stress management.

Coworkers' Attitudes

Policemen's negative attitudes toward women police officers are well documented (Balkin, 1988; Johnson, 1990). The most common reason given for antiwomen attitudes is that women are not physically strong or aggressive enough for patrol duty (Vega and Silverman, 1982). Despite the numerous studies of the 1970s showing women officers performing their work effectively, resistance to women persist (Bloch and Anderson, 1974; Sichel et al.,

1978). In a 1985 study of 525 male and 155 female urban and suburban police officers, nearly half the males felt that as a result of women not carrying a fair workload their work had become more dangerous (Johnson, Nieva, Wilson, 1985).[2] Compounding their frustration with women was their belief that the administration goes easy on women who do not perform their duty. Not surprisingly, acceptance of women as an immediate boss found resistance from a large number of these officers.

The women officers, on the other hand, sensed their socially disadvantaged status and resented it. They felt overprotected, closely watched, intimidated by other officers, and believed that, compared with males, their mistakes were more apt to be penalized. The constant testing of their loyalty and the pressure to prove themselves with male qualities of fighting and cussing were major contributors to their burnout level. Another study of twenty-five women police officers showed that 80 percent felt that being a woman in a predominantly male department was stressful. After six years on patrol these women did not feel accepted but rather ignored, sexually harassed, and gossiped about (Wexler and Logan, 1983).

Citizens' Attitudes

On the street, women are both advantaged and disadvantaged by their gender. Generally, when a male perpetrator is arrested by a male officer, the male ego is challenged—battle lines are immediately drawn. In contrast, many suspects find little challenge in fighting a woman. Some offenders comply because they assume that woman officers are more likely to use a gun to compensate for their weaker body strength, or they believe that women with guns are unpredictable. As Sherman (1975) has noted, women tend to have a "gentling" effect on potentially explosive situations (Johnson, 1990).

While males may not be challenged by fighting a woman, challenging her authority is seen as more legitimate than challenging a male officer's authority (Sterling and Owen, 1982). When one female officer arrived on the scene of a traffic accident in her district, the citizen refused to cooperate until she called her male supervisor. In general, citizens who see police primarily as crime-fighters are most likely to resist the idea that policewomen are competent (Homant, 1983). These varying public reactions indicate that women officers are seen as women first and law enforcers last.

Gender–Work Role Dilemmas

One of the stressful conditions women patrol officers face is the task of deciphering the mixed and incompatible messages as to whether to act like a woman and deprofessionalize their role or to act like an officer and defeminize their role. It is a long understood fact that lack of clarity about one's role in an organization (role ambiguity) creates stress-related maladies— low morale, withdrawal, overaggression, and coronary heart disease (Beehr, Walsh, and Taber, 1976; French 1975; Kahn et al. 1964). More recent reports find that one's role identity and role performance are important factors affecting psychological well-being (Thoits, 1992). This lack of job role clarity is perceived by both males and females as a problem for female officers. Interviews with women police officers are replete with stories about the stress women experience trying to deal with gender work-role conflicts (Johnson, 1990; Martin, 1979).

Many policewomen feel that the constant pressure to prove themselves is frustrated by the realization that their best efforts and contributions go unnoticed by their fellow male colleagues (Balkin, 1988; Johnson, 1990). Entering at the onset of women's influx into patrol work, one woman began hanging out at the bars with her male squad colleagues. The more she matched their walk, cussing, and lifestyle, the more they resented her presence. She eventually entered professional counseling to regain her self-identity. This example may be extreme, but in the few studies available on women officers, the majority of women report discomfort in being pressured to curse more than they would like or act tougher than they feel. Ironically, the more they behave like women, the more they are perceived as incompetent; yet the more they behave like men, the more they threaten the male officers' sense of masculinity. Striking a delicate balance between masculinity and femininity is a challenge.

Stress Response

What does all this mean in terms of the mental and emotional strains experienced by male and female officers? Given the added stress women encounter, one should expect them to show higher levels of burnout than the males. This is not clearly the case. Both males and females show moderately high levels of burnout. However, burnout is expressed differently by gender. Women officers are more likely to report feelings of being drained and used up by their job (internal burnout); men are more likely to externalize their burnout by treating citizens like impersonal objects and becoming callous or violent toward family members or citizens.

There is reason to assume that the lower external burnout of females is due to the lower exposure to the harshness of street life and, from the males' view, the administration's leniency toward women. After all, compared with men, women officers experience significantly fewer personal assaults and shootings and are less likely to be investigated for a criminal or departmental offense. An important question is why do women have lower exposure in the first place?

Given that females are relatively new to patrol duty and are generally younger than their fellow male officers, their lower rate of external burnout may result from less exposure to the stressors of working with citizens. If this is the case, women and men with an equal amount of time on the force should have similar burnout rates. However, regardless of time on the force the stress of women is internalized and that of men externalized.

It is possible that their status as women and sex-role socialization protects them regardless of time on the force. If, as Sherman (1975) notes, women tend to have a "gentling" effect on potentially explosive situations, then regardless of tenure, this effect will persist. Stereotypical thinking facilitates this effect. For example, male offenders, who find no challenge in fighting a female or who acquiesce because they believe that women with guns are hysterical, are in essence reducing the incidence of women officers' exposure to violence. Further, those women who use their mental strength and psychological techniques to verbally talk offenders into submission are also reducing their exposure. As one woman officer stated,

> Some of the roughest guys see me as a mother rather than a police officer. I then talk to them as a son. I use it to my advantage. I'm able to use psychology to make them comply.

Fellow officers who allow sex-role expectations to spill over into their work experience also contribute to protecting women from the full harshness of street realities. It is not uncommon for women police officers to report that male officers often do not know whether to treat them as a lady or a police officer. One reported that:

> I was just about to enter a dark alley to investigate a robbery in progress, when my male backup motioned for me to fall back. He said I might get hurt. I did not know whether to be flattered at his chivalry or angry at his lack of confidence in me!

These examples suggest that the reason why women's external burnout remains relatively lower than men's throughout their career is because their policing style or their status as women reduces the number of physical confrontations or harsh encounters relative to those experienced by their male colleagues. They appear to be shielded by their socialization and the social attributes assigned to women in our society (Johnson, 1990).

Still another factor is the lifestyle of women officers relative to those of their male coworkers. Women officers are less likely to have all their eggs in one basket. More women than men are involved in activities outside of policing (often their families), perceive that their law-enforcement skills can be applied to other jobs, feel untrapped by the job, and are able to shut off the job when off duty. Unlike the men, they do not eat, sleep, and breathe their job. In sum, they are more likely to compartmentalize their lives (Johnson, unpublished data). When they leave their jobs, they become emerged in another world of nonpolice friendship and family ties—a world that provides a vacation from the intense world of policing. While they still experience internal burnout symptoms, their stress level seldom reaches the level of callous behavior typified by those manifesting external burnout (e.g., treating people as impersonal objects).

Finally, with regard to role ambiguity, most women officers do manage to resolve the inherent conflict between femininity and masculinity. Because gender is the most basic cognitive category, policewomen seldom relinquish femininity; they merely add masculine traits to their repertoire. Some women strike a balance with what they wear. Those who find their uniform too compromising of their femininity will wear fancy lacy undergarments or color their nails. Many women merely compartmentalize their lives. Off duty they wear perfume, a dress, and high-heels; femininity is accented. On the job they suppress all elements of femininity and adopt purely masculine forms of behavior.

Still other women suppress their femininity depending upon their activities on the job. As one women states:

> I am a woman and I want to be treated like a woman. However, this does not mean that when my partner is in trouble I think first about my fingernails. No, I will do anything physical or otherwise to back him up. After a physical fight and things are under control I want to be treated as a woman.

In interviews conducted by the author, several males stated that they are most comfortable with this type of woman, that is, one who does not deny her femininity but who at the same time is willing to put her life on the line if needed.

Social Support

Social support has long been known to be a buffer against a variety of stressful life events (Caplan et al., 1980; Gottlieb, 1981). Studies vary on whether coworkers, supervisor, or spouse are the most useful in reducing job strain and physiological stress (Burke and Bradshaw, 1981; House, 1981; Pinneau, 1976). However, with only a few exceptions all agree that social support is beneficial (Gertsel, 1988; Shinn, Lehman, and Wong, 1984; Wilcox, 1981).

Within the police culture, support for women officers generally differs from that for men. On the average, female officers compared with males receive less support from their supervisors, squad members, and spouses. It is spousal support, however, that shows significant gender differences. When a male officer goes home, his family is willing to listen to him and lets him know that he is doing meaningful and important work. He can count on help in rearranging his schedule to meet personal problems or to get him out of tight spots. Consistent with gender-role expectations, far fewer females can count on this type of family support. A classic example comes from a female officer married to another police officer:

> We can work the same beat, experience similar traffic violations, and the same number of irate citizens, but when we get home he expects me to listen to him. He says my day could never be as unpleasant as his; and even if it was, it is my job to listen.

Some women say that when they joined the force, their spouses told them they were on their own. They did not want to have any "shop-talk" at home, and above all they did not want to socialize with any of their police coworkers.

For many women this lack of support began during the academy training period. Recruit training intrudes on family time; it is often fifteen hours a day. Typically, married male recruits come home to prepared meals, clean children, and private time to study. In contrast, many women continue to assume major responsibility for maintaining their house and children (Glaser and Saxe, 1982). Too often the husband will not take up the slack. Numerous studies show that the husband's contribution to household work does not significantly increase if his spouse is employed (Strong and DeVault, 1992). Wives are left to search for help from relatives or outsiders or find it necessary to lower their domestic standards. In short, most women officers neither get nor expect spousal support, and they learn to function without it. This is evident by the fact that lack of spousal support only makes a difference in the job burnout level of male officers, who expect and count on it (Johnson, Nieva, and Wilson 1985).

Although employed mothers work out child-care arrangements, they are not always satisfactory, and parent-child time is limited. Giving 100 percent at work and 100 percent at home generally results in dissatisfaction with their parenting role. Rotating shifts mean that child-care providers are needed for odd hours. Both those with and without children know that this can be difficult. Thus it is not surprising that most women would consider quitting the force if they had a child or another child. Few males see an additional family member as problematic. Moreover, relative to females, fewer of them are dissatisfied with their parenting role (Johnson, unpublished data).

The combination of minimum support, work stress, and changes in gender-role behavior creates havoc on a significant number of policewomen's marriages. Some husbands become threatened by their wives' growing assertiveness. A turning point for many was the day their wife came home in full uniform; particularly intimidating was the gun and nightstick. Unexpectedly, they were shaken by the realism of her authority. Others became jealous of her new male colleagues, whom they envisioned as having a more glamorous job than they themselves. Not every relationship can

survive these tensions. In a sample of 137 women (most under age thirty), 13 percent were currently divorced; compared with 4 percent of the 451 males (most over age thirty). They were also twice as likely as the males to be separated. Thus, by age thirty, one-fifth of women officers were either separated or divorced, and a number of others were in their second marriage. A fifth of these women believed that police work was definitely a factor in the break-up of their marriage; another fifth were unsure (Johnson, Nieva, and Wilson, 1985). Regardless of reasons given for relationship break-ups, their marital instability is definitely above the national average. In sum, women patrol officers encounter sex-role spillover in all aspects of their lives.

Conclusion

In spite of their growing presence, the number of women in United States patrol cars is low and the average tenure is brief. Those who apply too often drop out because of misconceptions about the training program, unrealistic assessments of the time commitment, and personal or interpersonal problems unique to female recruits (Glaser and Saxe, 1982). Once employed they are subject to the same stressors as males. However, while most cops manifest strong symptoms of burnout by the seventh year, this is especially the case for females. No doubt this reflects both low social support and the added stress from the antifemale environment that inspires disbelief in their ability to physically and emotionally function in the streets. In a profession where peer support is a strong factor in boosting one's confidence and self-esteem, it takes an emotionally and psychologically strong person to withstand the pressure. Similar to men, not all women are fitted for the police profession. Unfortunately, society's depiction of women as the "weaker sex" leads many to assume that all women are unfit for patrol duty (Washington, 1975).

Objections to women based on their strength are unwarranted. Such oppositions have been unjustified since the 1960s and 1970s, when height and strength requirements were abolished. Further, only a handful of departments require their officers to stay in condition. Even in light of this knowledge, many males still use women's physical "inferiority" as an excuse for barring them from patrol work. On the other hand, the same opposition is not directed at the many male officers who enter the profession in great shape and then rapidly become overweight and out of shape. Certainly if acceptance is given to these officers, the objection based on female physical weakness seems unreasonable (Bouza, 1990). This is not to undermine the importance of proper physical fitness but to emphasize its importance for both genders.

Women cannot escape the physical aspects of the job. Pound for pound the average woman cannot compete as effectively as men. Regardless, studies show that given a progressive program women can be made to be as physically fit as their male peers (Charles, 1982). It is also important to keep in mind that when it comes to dexterity, flexibility, and endurance, women officers do equally well or even better than men if they use leverage. A greater appreciation for the presence of women will no doubt develop as male patrol officers become more accepting of the minimum need for "brutal force" or muscular strength and weight (Bouza, 1990; Washington, 1975).

In addition to being effective patrol officers, women provide a unique way of policing. In the midst of cries against police brutality, all police training programs would do well to cultivate in their male officers a male version of the "gentling" techniques of women. On the other hand, women must adapt some aspects of male behavior for effective policing. Most women are products of early and often subtle socialization, which cultivates the appearance of weakness. For example, projecting authority is more difficult for women than men. Given the sex-role typing that is prevalent in our society, the legitimacy of women's authority in the workplace is bound to be challenged. Thus for those who need it, training academies must retrain them in a mode of communication that projects confidence and authority in their demeanor and voice (Glaser and Saxe, 1982). In the process, however, it is important that women not feel that their basic sense of self is being subverted.

Women recruits need to be aware of the potential for inner conflicts between their femininity and their career choice. Progressive police departments are providing individual counseling and peer group sessions to allow discussion of this unique issue, as well as others (Glaser and Saxe, 1982; Washington, 1975). In addition, given the struggles women have in balancing work and family, workshops particularly tailored to male spouses would go a long way in sensitizing them to potential role

changes and the need for adaptation. Innovative training programs for women can reduce the attrition rate of women and ease their burnout. The Los Angeles Police Department instituted such a program and reduced female recruits' attrition rate from 50 to 7 percent (Glaser and Saxe, 1982).

Most women pursue an occupation not to compete like a man, but to lend their skills in getting a job done (Washington, 1975). In order to fully appreciate the capabilities as well as the unique contributions of women, it is essential to drop the notion that a difference is tantamount to weakness. There is strength in diversity. It is the differences between males and females that provide the greatest promise for more effective law enforcement.

Leanor Boulin Johnson

Notes

1. For a historical discussion of women in law enforcement, see "A Century of Women in Policing." B.R. Price and S. Gavin. In *Criminal Justice System and Women*. Eds. B.R. Price and N.J. Skoloff. New York: Clark Boardman, 1982.

2. Citations for all single-authored or co-authored L.B. Johnson studies—as well as Johnson's unpublished data—refer to a major project funded by the National Institute of Mental Health. In 1983 over 728 male and female police officers employed in two major eastern cities were administered a 333–item questionnaire (topics included work experiences/satisfaction, work-family issues, social support, coping strategies, physical and mental health). In addition, 479 male and female police spouses completed a 254-item survey. The questionnaires reflected input from many sources, including an advisory panel, police ride-along experiences, workshops for police officers and their spouses, formal and informal interactions with ethnic minority and gender-based police organizations, over sixty intensive interviews with police officers and spouses, and pretesting in one rural and two urban departments. During a data feedback workshop in 1987, administrators and officers from the participating departments commented on the results, further refining the analyses.

Bibliography

Balkin, J. "Why Policemen Don't Like Police-women." *Journal of Police Science and Administration* 16 (1988): 29–36.

Beehr, T.A., J.T. Walsh, and T.D. Taber. "Relationship of Stress to Individually and Organizationally Valued States: Higher Order Needs Strength as a Moderator." *Journal of Applied Psychology*, 61 (1976): 41–47.

Bell, D.J. "Policewomen—Myths and Reality." *Journal of Police Science and Administration* 10 (1) (March 1982): 112–20.

Bloch, P.B., and D. Anderson. *Policewomen on Patrol: Final Report.* Washington, DC: Police Foundation, 1974.

Bouza, A.V. *The Police Mystique: An Insider's Look at Cops, Crime, and the Criminal Justice System.* New York: Plenum Press, 1990.

Burke, R.J., and P. Bradshaw. "Occupational and Life Stress and the Family." *Small Group Behavior* 12 (1981): 329–75.

Caplan, R.D., S. Cobb, J.R.P. French, Jr., R.V. Harrison, and S.R. Penneau, Jr. *Job Demands and Worker Health: Main Effects and Occupational Differences.* Ann Arbor: Institute for Social Research, 1980.

Charles, M.T. "Women in Policing: The Physical Aspect." *Journal of Police Science and Administration* 10 (2) (July 1982): 194–205.

French, J.R.P., Jr. "A Comparative Look at Stress and Strain in Policemen." In *Job Stress and the Police Officer.* Eds. W.H. Kroes and J.J. Hurrell. Washington, DC: U.S. Department of Health, Education and Welfare. 1975. 60–71.

Gertsel, N. "Divorce and Kin Support: The Importance of Gender." *Journal of Marriage and the Family* 50 (1) (1988): 209–19.

Glaser, D.F., and S. Saxe. "Psychological Preparation of Female Police Recruits." *FBI Law Enforcement Bulletin* (January 1982): 5–7.

Greene, R.L. "Psychological Support for Women Entering Law Enforcement, Police Managerial Use of Psychology and Psychologists." In *Police Managerial Use of Psychology and Psychologists.* Eds. H.W. More and P.C. Unsinger. Springfield, IL: Charles C. Thomas, 1987. 171–87.

Gottlieb, B.H. *Social Network and Social Support.* Beverly Hills, CA: Sage, 1981.

Guteck, B.A., and B. Morasch. "Sex-Ratios, Sex-Role Spillover, and Sexual Harassment of Women at Work." *Journal of Social Issues* 38 (4) (1982): 55–74.

Homant, R.J. "Impact of Policewomen on Community Attitudes toward Police." *Journal of Police Science and Administration* 11 (1) (March 1983): 16–22.

House, J.S. *Work Stress and Social Support.* Reading, MA: Addison-Wesley, 1981.

Johnson, L.B. "Job Strain and Police Officers: Gender Comparisons." *Journal of Police Studies* 14 (1990): 12–16.

———. *On the Front Lines: Police Stress and Family Well Being. Congressional Technical Testimony Before the Select Committee on Children, Youth, and Families.* (May 20, 1991): 36–48 ff.

———, V.F. Nieva, and M. Wilson. *Police Work-Home Stress Study: Interim Report.* Maryland: Westat, Winter 1985.

Kahn, R.L., D.M. Wolf, R.P. Quinn, J.D. Snaek, and R.A. Rosenthal. *Organizational Stress: Studies in Role Conflict and Ambiguity.* New York: John Wiley and Sons, 1964.

Kroes, W.H. "Job Stress in Policewomen: An Empirical Study." *Police Stress* 5 (3) (1982): 10–11.

Lefkowitz, J. "Psychological Attributes of Policewomen: A Review of Research and Opinion." *Journal of Social Issues* 31 (1975): 3–26.

Martin, S.E. "Police**women** and **Police**women: Occupational Role Dilemmas and Choices of Female Officers." *Journal of Police Science and Administration* 7 (3) (September 1979): 314–23.

———. *Breaking and Entering: Policewomen on Patrol.* Berkeley: University of California Press, 1980.

Maslach, C., and S.E. Jackson. "Burn-out Cops and Their Families." *Psychology Today* (May 1979): 54–62.

Pinneau, S.R., Jr. "Effects of Social Support on Occupational Stresses and Strains." Paper presented at the 84th Annual American Psychological Association Meetings, September 1976.

Sherman, L.J. "Evaluation of Policewomen on Patrol in a Suburban Police Department." *Journal of Police Science and Administration* 3 (1975): 434–38.

Shinn, M., S. Lehman, and N.W. Wong. *Social Interaction and Social Support* 40 (4) (1984): 55–76.

Sichel, J., L.N. Friedman, J.C. Quint, and M.E. Smith. *Women on Patrol: A Pilot Study of Performance in New York City.* Washington, DC: Government Printing Office, 1978.

Sterling, B.S., and J.W. Owen. "Perceptions of Demanding Versus Reasoning Male and Female Police Officers." *Personality and Social Psychology Bulletin* 8 (2) (June 1982): 336–40.

Strong, B., and C. DeVault. *The Marriage and Family Experience.* 5th ed. New York: West, 1992.

Thoits, P.A. "Identity Structures and Psychological Well-Being: Gender and Marital Status Comparisons." *Social Psychology Quarterly* 55 (3) (1992): 236–56.

Vega, M., and R.A. Silverman. "Female Police Officers as Viewed by Their Male Counterparts." *Police Studies* 5 (1) (Spring, 1982): 31–39.

Washington, B. "Stress Reduction Techniques for the Female Officer." In *Job Stress and the Police Officer.* Eds. W. Kroes and J.J. Hurrell. Washington, DC: U.S. Department of Health, Education, and Welfare, 1975. 35–49.

Wexler, J.G., and D.D. Logan. "Sources of Stress among Women Police Officers." *Journal of Police Science and Administration* 11 (1) (1983): 46–53.

Wilcox, B.L. "Social Support in Adjusting to Marital Disruption: A Network Analysis. In *Social Networks and Social Support.* Ed. B.H. Gottlieb. Beverly Hills, CA: Sage, 1981.

Police Organizations

The International Association of Chiefs of Police (IACP) was founded in 1893. Headquartered in Alexandria, Virginia, the organization today has 13,000 members. Police executives—commissioners, superintendents, chiefs, and directors of national, state, provincial, and municipal departments; assistant and deputy chiefs; and division or district heads—comprise this exclusive group. The mission of the IACP is to provide consultation and research services in all phases of police activity. Additionally, the IACP raises funds for the betterment of law-enforcement management and operates a speakers' bureau. Each year it presents the Parade Policeman of the Year Award, a high honor. The IACP maintains a 1,000–volume library on criminology and law enforcement and publishes *Police Chief* (1934–), the annual *Police Buyers' Guide,* and the *Police Yearbook.*

The Police Executive Research Forum (PERF) had its beginnings in 1975. It is based in Washington, D.C., with a membership of 320. This group includes 150 executive heads of large public police agencies, 130 executives other than department heads and executives of criminal-justice agencies, and 40 former members who no longer qualify for general membership. PERF's function is to stimulate public understanding and discussion of important criminal-justice issues. To achieve this it fosters cooperation throughout the criminal-justice system and encourages development of new knowledge. Once research has been completed, PERF disseminates its findings to all concerned. *Asset Forfeiture Bulletin, Problem Solving Quarterly,* and *How to Rate Your Local Police* are regular publications. Other special studies and monographs appear frequently.

The Police Foundation (PF), also located in Washington, D.C., initiated its activities in 1970. PF sponsors projects that examine traditional police crime-control practices, test new ways of delivering police services, and improve the quality of police personnel and officials. PF conducts forums for the debate and dissemination of ideas and offers a wide range of technical assistance, training, and consulting services.

The American Federation of Police (AFP), now in Miami, Florida, commenced operation in 1961. Its 104,000 members of governmental and private law-enforcement officers make it one of the largest organizations of its kind in the country. The AFP bestows service and bravery awards in twenty-four categories. Its main publication is the *Police Times Magazine* (1964–).

The National Association of Police Organizations (NAPO), after its founding in 1979, has grown to a sizable membership of over 200,000. From its Detroit, Michigan, base NAPO promotes the needs of its members on a national level, and because of its size and united front exerts considerable influence when endorsing candidates for national office.

The National Black Police Association (NBPA) was formed in 1972 to improve relationships between police departments and the black community, to recruit minority police officers on a national scale, and to eliminate police corruption, brutality, and racial discrimination. Located in Washington, D.C., the NBPA has 35,000 members. The National Organization of Black Law Enforcement Executives (NOBLE) has similar aims but does not restrict its endeavors just to bettering the life of the minority police officer. Having begun in 1976 and with a present membership of 1,300, NOBLE also researches crime prevention, offers on-site technical assistance and training to citizen-based, crime-prevention programs, and conducts management surveys, among other activities. NOBLE publishes several bulletins of which *NOBLE Actions* is the best known.

The National Sheriffs' Association (NSA) is in Alexandria, Virginia, and has a membership of 25,000. Founded in 1940, NSA sponsors the National Neighborhood Watch Program, certifies jail technicians, and operates the National Sheriff's Institute. The NSA also sponsors insurance programs, bestows awards, and runs a children's service. It publishes *Sheriff* (1948–), the *Annual Directory of Sheriffs*, newsletters, training manuals, monographs, and guidelines. The NSA is particularly interested in aiding victims of crime through an assistance program.

A number of other police organizations exist to express a diversity of law-enforcement concerns. With their growing memberships they underscore the fraternal nature of the police community. Following are some of them:

American Police Academy (1977)
American Society of Law Enforcement
  Trainers (1987)
Association of Professional Police Investigators (1987)
Blacks in Law Enforcement (1986)
Commission on Accreditation for Law
  Enforcement Agencies (1979)
Firearms Instructors (1981)
International Law Enforcement Stress
  Association (1978)
National Constables Association (1976)
Police Marksman Association (1976).

Police Pursuit

Actuarial statisticians and safety engineers have estimated the extent and costs of accidents, injuries, and deaths for many activities and occupations for more than a century. While their facts and figures may deter some organizations and individuals from participating in risky tasks

and activities, others continue to take risks, play the odds, and enjoy the challenge.

A classic example of a cost-benefit analysis in the construction industry is the planning, insuring, and building of the Bay Bridge from San Francisco to Oakland, California. The dangers of building an unprecedented suspension bridge, including job tasks and other types of risk, interrelationships among risk factors, and opportunities to reduce risk and error were analyzed and computed. The nature and extent of accidents, injuries, and deaths were estimated and costs associated with those values were added to the construction costs. Obviously, the policy-makers determined that the benefits of building the bridge were worth the expected and foreseeable human and financial losses.

The concept of calculated risk refers to the ratio of costs and benefits. The critical issue is to identify and measure accurately the costs and benefits. When the potential or anticipated benefits outweigh the risks, then a planned course of action will be acceptable. Risk analysis includes risk assessment and risk management; risk is best understood as "the likelihood of injury, harm, damage or loss multiplied by its potential magnitude" (Grose, 1987:25).

To understand risk analysis, the organizational contexts in which things exist must be understood. In the construction industry, the bottom line is (hopefully) the quality of the product and the financial profit. Other organizational contexts are more complicated. For example, police work includes many high-risk activities, which move beyond financial considerations and include the balance of law enforcement and public safety (Alpert and Fridell, 1992). Police administrators and policy-makers must accept, attempt to reduce, or avoid physical risk and transfer financial risk. Too often these two types of risk are managed as separate entities, with the former controlled by administrators and the latter in the domain of an insurance carrier.

This actuarial approach to risk management and the probabilistic risk-assessment approach can be applied to the analysis of risk in police activities. The actuarial approach as noted above requires that the expected value of the event and the undesirable consequences be measured and evaluated. In the case of police-pursuit driving, the number of events and undesirable consequences can be derived from research. The critical assumption is that the causal agents of the undesirable consequences or negative effects remain stable over time. Probabalistic risk assessments attempt to predict the likelihood and foreseeability of safety failures of complex systems. The success of these methods depends on the information used for estimating the elements of the events. Unfortunately, the lack of large-scale, complex, and comparative data sets on police-pursuit events reduces the ability to forecast disaggregated outcomes.

Pursuit Driving

Because of the complex nature of pursuit, the various actors, unpredictable actions, and a lack of data, the risk-assessment techniques perform better for the construction industry than they do for analyses of pursuit driving. One of the major impediments to accurate risk assessment is the unpredictable innocent bystander. When only the police officer and the suspect are considered, the actuarial and probabalistic assessments are powerful. However, these are only two of the three points on an interactive triangle, which has at its remaining corner the environment, including conditions, innocent drivers, passengers, and pedestrians. A definition of pursuit and a discussion of the power and influence of each point of the interactive triangle follows.

A pursuit is an event in which the suspect is attempting to elude capture and avoid arrest. Unless the suspect has a death wish he or she will run until safety is reached. In either scenario the suspect will eventually surrender, return to a safe speed, or become involved in an accident. It is the police officer and the supervisor who must decide very quickly whether to continue or terminate the pursuit.

The suspect, who has refused to heed the commands of the officer, has the primary responsibility to stop the chase by pulling over. The suspect is also directing the pursuit by selecting the course, speed, and recklessness of the driving. However, the suspect is influenced psychologically by the police officer.

It is only the police driver who is subject to direct control during the course of police pursuit. The goal of the officer is to apprehend the suspect and make the arrest. Accordingly, it is the officer who must become aware of personal capabilities and take into account environmental conditions, which may affect accomplishing the police mission, to protect lives. Decisions must be based on information beyond personal safety and include the risk to the motoring pub-

lic. The police officer must factor into the decision-making process the risk created by the suspect's driving; the potential of innocent bystanders, passengers, and others becoming involved; and how his driving influences the suspect's driving. In other words, the officer must understand that when a suspect refuses to stop for the emergency lights and siren, a routine encounter turns quickly into a high-risk and dangerous event. The officer must understand how a "show of authority" involving emergency equipment will affect the suspect's driving. If the suspect becomes reckless or refuses to stop, it is the officer and his or her supervisor who must determine the value of continuing the pursuit and the risk of the pursuit to the officer, innocent bystanders, passengers, and pedestrians. The officer and the supervisor must also understand the influence of the chase on the participants. The need to "win" and make that arrest is often influenced by the adrenaline rush felt by the officer. A pursuit is an exciting event and involves one person running to escape and another chasing to catch. If it continues, it resembles a drag race until one party terminates or there is a crash.

One reason for this competition is the fact that police officers order thousands of motorists to pull over without complication. Most law-abiding citizens accept the warning or ticket or do not fight with the officer when an arrest is made. Certainly, the officer becomes used to the compliance and when a suspect does not submit to the wishes and orders of the officer, it is perceived as "contempt of cop."

The final corner of the interactive triangle, the environment including the innocent bystander, is uncontrollable. Yet, elements of this factor are predictable. Road conditions, the likelihood of traffic and other matters can be assessed to determine risk. However, an innocent bystander or passenger may not have knowledge of what is taking place and may just be at the wrong place at the wrong time.

It is obvious that an officer is better able to control personal actions, reactions, and communication than to change the weather, road conditions, population density, or the capabilities of the police cruiser. Unfortunately, most law-enforcement driving programs view their mission as one of skill development and emphasize exercises designed to hone the trainee's mechanical skill to control the multiton guided weapon known as the police cruiser. The unfortunate reality is that much less effort is devoted to training *when* to use those acquired skills than *how* to use them. Comparatively, a pursuit is at least as dangerous to the public as the use of a firearm (Alpert and Fridell, 1992). The potential for physical and human injury becomes frightening where the kinetic energy of a 3,500-pound projectile is unleashed. Similarly, the danger of pursuit is multiplied with each vehicle encountered and frequent assessment of the risk of continuation is paramount (Alpert and Dunham, 1990; Alpert and Fridell, 1992).

Three factors are traditionally identified as comprising the police-driving triangle, and it is clear that only one can be subject to control in the heat of the pursuit. Therefore, the police driver is the focus of effective pursuit policy and risk management. What we know about these factors specifically and pursuit in general has been learned from evaluation.

Evaluation of Pursuit
A police pursuit is an attempt by a police officer to apprehend a suspect by ordering the suspect to halt by use of emergency equipment (lights and sirens). A pursuit is begun only after an officer initiates a traffic, felony, or investigatory stop of a vehicle and the suspect refuses to obey the order to stop. Although there are other derivations of the definition, the basic elements of a pursuit, including a suspect fleeing to escape and a police officer chasing to apprehend, are the critical ones.

The evaluation of pursuit driving has only a brief history. Precious little research was conducted on pursuit until the 1980s when pursuit driving was seriously questioned by victims, concerned citizens, and progressive police administrators (Alpert and Fridell, 1992). In the 1980s, police pursuit was identified as "The Most Deadly Weapon" (Alpert and Anderson, 1986). Most recently, individual agencies are conducting their own data-collection efforts and evaluating their findings. In 1993 it is appalling that only one state, Minnesota, is required to collect and analyze state-wide data on pursuit. The specific numbers and conclusions from these studies have been reviewed elsewhere (Alpert and Dunham, 1990; Alpert and Fridell, 1992). However, it must be emphasized that the originating crime in most pursuits is a traffic offense. Also it is important to understand that pursuits in urban areas pose far greater risks than those conducted in rural areas and freeways. Therefore, aggregate statistics mask the very real danger of urban pursuits and those conducted on streets likely to encounter traffic. The research conducted on pursuit all points to the same issue: the balance between the enforcement of laws and the safety of the public. In other words, it is an accepted fact that pursuit driving is a dangerous police tactic and presents risk to the public. Driving on public streets at excessive speeds or in an erratic manner is dangerous to all involved—officer and suspect—and to those who are in the path—passengers and innocent bystanders. The main question is, Is it worth enforcing the law for which the suspect is wanted compared to the risk created by that process? Stated in a different way, pursuit driving must be evaluated by balancing the need to immediately apprehend the suspect with the likelihood of accident or injury (risk). To understand pursuit is to understand both concepts.

It is clear that both the goals of law enforcement and public safety are significant. Unfortunately, to achieve one goal the other may have to be sacrificed. On the one hand, if the enforcement of a particular law were treated to the exclusion of public safety, then any cost of pursuit driving would be justified. On the other hand, if public safety were considered paramount and laws were to be enforced only when there was no risk to the public, no pursuit would be justified. Obviously neither of these two extremes is acceptable. Proper police conduct must balance the two goals after considering the mission of police: to protect life. Although no one has seriously advocated taking firearms away from the police, the trend has been to restrict their use to defense or preservation of life situations. Similarly, it would not be in society's best interest to take the ability to pursue criminals from the police, but as in the use of firearms, there is a trend to restrict its use (Alpert and Fridell, 1992). There exists a need to balance these two critical social demands: the need to immediately apprehend a suspect and the risk to the public created by a pursuit.

The Need for Immediate Apprehension
The argument is clear: Police have the duty to enforce the law and one aspect of that duty is to arrest known violators. A police officer has the authority if not the duty to issue citations for traffic violations. Upon observation or reasonable suspicion of such a violation, the officer may initiate a traffic stop (*Delaware v. Prouse*, 1979). Similarly, if an individual suspected of a criminal act is observed in a vehicle, then the

officer may initiate a "felony" stop. The initiation of these traffic and felony stops is a routine task expected, if not demanded, of police officers. As noted, most citizens acknowledge the request by an officer to stop and pull off the road when the officer turns on emergency lights and siren. In the infrequent situation when the suspected law violator decides not to stop and increases speed or takes evasive actions, in other words, initiates a chase, the officer must do everything possible to stop the violator from creating havoc on the roadway, without driving recklessly her- or himself. The only other option would be to terminate the attempt to make a traffic or felony stop and hope the law violator will not commit some heinous act.

There is legal support for the continued pursuit of law violators as long as the police officer does not drive recklessly. The theme among these cases is that the police should not be responsible for the outcome of the reckless behavior of the pursued and that the police should not be the insurer of this highly irresponsible person. In one of the earliest and most cited cases, the Kentucky Court of Appeals (then Kentucky's highest court) heard *Chambers v. Ideal Pure Milk Co.* (1952: 590–91), a case where a traffic violator was pursued, drove recklessly, and was involved in an accident with an innocent third party. The court ruled that even if a police officer *causes* a violator to increase his level of recklessness, the officer should not be responsible. Charged as they (the police) were with the obligation to enforce the law, the traffic laws included, they would have been derelict in their duty had they not pursued him. The police were performing their duty when Shearer, in gross violation of his duty to obey the speed laws, crashed into the milk wagon. To argue that the officers' pursuit caused Shearer to speed may be factually true, but it does not follow that the officers are legally liable for the results of Shearer's negligent speed. Police cannot be made insurers of the conduct of the culprits they chase.

In another interesting case, *West Virginia v. Fidelity Gas and Casualty Co. of New York* (1967: 90–91) the court said in essence we are not prepared to hold an officer liable for damages inflicted by the driver of a stolen vehicle.

Both the *Chambers* and *West Virginia* cases were used as precedents in one of the most cited decisions from a state court, *Thornton v. Shore* (1983). This case, from the Kansas Supreme Court, has become essential for munici-

pal defense attorneys as it uses as its rule only the actual driving of the officer as a measuring rod, and it relies upon deterrence theory, which suggests that all violators will flee if they are not chased. In this case the trial court issued a summary judgment for a Kansas University Police Department officer who was sued pursuant to a chase that resulted in the death of two law-abiding motorists. The plaintiffs in this lawsuit argued that the police officer should have terminated the pursuit based on the extreme reckless behavior of the individual being pursued and should have recognized the foreseeability of an accident and likelihood of injury. The defendant police officer argued that he was immune from liability pursuant to the state law permitting him to disregard certain traffic laws, but not to disregard the duty to drive with due regard for the safety of all persons. The trial court ruled that the officer's driving was reasonable and granted summary judgment. On appeal, the Kansas Supreme Court affirmed the summary judgment for the officer.

In the dissenting opinion of *Thornton* is a more modern and likely scenario for the 1990s. Justice Herd's dissent in *Thornton* (1983:668) exemplifies a more contemporary view:

> . . . Even with the [emergency] warnings, however, the driver must operate the [police] vehicle with due regard for the safety of all persons. The majority holds whenever a high speed chase results in a collision between the person pursued and a third party, the pursuing officer has, as a matter of law, met the "due regard" standard . . . by merely turning on his warning signals . . . There are numerous scenarios where an accident is caused by one not a party to a collision. It is a question of causation.

While there are numerous other cases from a variety of jurisdictions that could be cited, they would add precious little and would basically repeat the arguments made above (Alpert, 1991; Alpert and Fridell, 1992; Urbonya, 1991). These arguments for the need to continue a pursuit and immediately apprehend the law violator focus on:

1. the officers' obligation and duty to apprehend suspects;
2. the dereliction of duty if the police do not pursue;

3. that the police should not be responsible for the outcome of the reckless behavior of the pursued; and

4. that police should not be the insurer of this highly irresponsible person.

The decisions state directly or infer that information known about pursuit indicates that the law violator who is aware that an officer will terminate the pursuit simply will increase his or her speed or recklessness to avoid capture. Interestingly, these cases acknowledge that the police officer may cause a violator to increase the level of recklessness and the general risk to the officer, law violator, and motoring public, but for the sake of law enforcement some danger or risk is necessary. One example of this philosophy has been stressed by the California Highway Patrol (1983). The general opinion of the California Highway Patrol (CHP) based upon its data is that pursuits are worth the inherent risks. The CHP report concluded:

> Attempted apprehension of motorists in violation of what appear to be minor traffic infractions is necessary for the preservation of order on the highways of California. If approximately 700 people will attempt to flee from the officers who participated in this six-month study, knowing full well that the officers would give chase, one can imagine what would happen if the police suddenly banned pursuits. Undoubtedly, innocent people may be injured or killed because an officer chooses to pursue a suspect, but this risk is necessary to avoid the even greater loss that would occur if law enforcement agencies were not allowed to aggressively pursue violators (1983: 21).

In fact, a recommendation made in the California Highway Patrol report (1983:17) reads: "[A] very effective technique in apprehending pursued violators may be simply to follow the violator until he voluntarily stops or crashes."

The Need for Public Safety

The argument is clear: Life is more important than property and public safety is more important than the immediate apprehension of a law violator. Certainly the public is better served by minimizing risks and maximizing police tactics that permit the safe apprehension of law violators or permit them to escape. Perhaps these issues have best been summarized in a Florida Supreme Court case, Brown v. City of Pinellas Park (1992:12–14):

> Solely because a man ran a red light, suddenly the innocent citizens of Pinellas County were subjected to a threatening stream of publically-owned vehicles hurtling pell-mell, at breakneck speed, down a busy roadway in one of Florida's most densely populated urban areas. . . . In the balance, the desire to bring Deady [suspect] to justice for running a red light is far less important than the lives of the Brown sisters. . . . Experience and foresight support the conclusion that Deady engaged in such reckless conduct primarily because he was being chased by police, and that this misconduct would have ceased had the police discontinued the pursuit.

In other words, when the risks of pursuit driving become so great that an accident or injury becomes likely, then it is more important to reduce the risks and terminate the pursuit than to apprehend the violator. Of course, if the violator is a known serial murderer, the risks can be increased in a pursuit beyond that of a traffic offender, but the murderer is likely to take more risks to escape than the minor offender and his will to escape must be considered.

Another recent example comes from the Texas Supreme Court decision in *Travis v. City of Mesquite* (1992). The case involved a familiar fact pattern. The police engaged in a chase and the pursued vehicle collided with a third party. The issues included whether the police should be responsible for their decision to engage in a pursuit, regardless of the risks involved, and whether, as a matter of law, the police officers' decisions both to initiate and continue chase were the proximate cause of the collision. The court reported that "the decision to initiate or continue pursuit may be negligent when the heightened risk of injury to third parties is unreasonable in relation to the interest in apprehending suspects" (1992:8). The court noted that "police officers must balance the risk to the public with their duty to enforce the law to choose an appropriate course of conduct. Public safety should not be thrown to the winds in the heat of the chase" (1992: 6–7).

In a recent federal case, *Groves v. United States of America* (1991:8 fn. 2), Judge Sporkin wrote:

> The principle of proportionality cannot be ignored in this case. A police officer cannot be allowed to risk the lives of innocent people traveling the public roads simply to pursue a car that runs a red light. There is no doubt that a number of traffic regulations should be waived when an emergency vehicle needs to make its way through the streets to protect lives. But the police must remember that the traffic regulations themselves exist to protect lives, and they cannot be hastily ignored when the police witness a minor infraction.

The critical issue is one of foreseeability. Common sense supported by empirical research indicates that traffic congestion, weather, road conditions, speed, recklessness, likelihood of apprehension, and other conditions and circumstances help determine the risk of pursuit driving. Even when an officer is exempt from the laws regulating traffic flow (stop signs and traffic lights), and is authorized to drive faster than the speed limit, by state statute he or she must drive with *due regard* for the safety of all persons using the roads. This regulation arguably places a special responsibility on the driver of an emergency vehicle who chooses to exercise this privilege. The driver of the emergency vehicle may be held to a higher standard than a citizen, as he is a professional, assumed to have the proper training and experience to warrant the special exemption. The "due regard" criterion is not always limited to situations where police are directly involved in accidents and may extend to the totality of the situation and the driving of the offender as well as the officer. In other words, physical force used by the officer who crashes into another vehicle is likely to violate the "due regard" criterion. In addition, psychological force, or pressure placed on a suspect to flee, may be considered as a violation of "due regard" for the safety of the motoring public. It is an officer's driving and its impact that will be judged by the reasonable person who is faced with the question: Should this pursuit have taken place the way it did, with the risks it created, and for the potential results it could have yielded?

Balancing Law Enforcement with Public Safety

The purpose of pursuit is to apprehend a suspect within the mission of police, to protect lives. Tactics and activities undertaken must consider apprehension secondary to public safety. One way to help officers understand this balance is to have them apply the same standards used in weighing the alternatives to firing a weapon in a situation where innocent bystanders may be endangered. Whenever an officer fires a weapon, he or she must be concerned that the bullet may accidentally hit an unintended target. By comparison, in pursuit the officer has not only his or her own vehicle to worry about but also must consider the pursued vehicle creating dangerous situations and other vehicles creating danger by attempting to get out of the way.

Pursuit driving has been available to the police in the fight against crime. Unfortunately, the inherent nature of pursuit creates a significant danger to the officers, law violators, and general public. Whether or not this danger and the resulting injuries and deaths is worth the benefits is the question police administrators and policy-makers have been examining for years. As in other applications of force, the courts have been establishing standards of proximate cause and reasonableness as the acceptable parameters for pursuit driving.

Police officials must determine whether they want to restrict pursuit by the type of offense known to the officer or some other criterion. Some jurisdictions have rules and regulations that do not permit pursuit of a suspect who has only committed a traffic offense. Other jurisdictions limit pursuit to violent felons. Still other agencies do not permit pursuits for any offense without a supervisor's permission. However, most departments permit pursuit for most offenses but require the officer (and supervisor) to balance the need to immediately apprehend the suspect with the risk created by the pursuit. Pursuit policies are categorized into the following scheme (see Alpert and Fridell, 1992:118–19):

1. *Judgmental*: allowing officers to make all major decisions relating to initiation, tactics and termination;
2. *Restrictive*: placing certain restrictions on officers' judgments and decisions; and
3. *Discouragement*: severely cautioning or discouraging any pursuit, except in the most extreme situations.

Police departments operating under regulations that emphasize judgmental decision making provide only guidelines for their officers. Usually these warnings require officers to weigh various factors before initiating a pursuit, to consider their safety and the safety of others during a pursuit, and to terminate a chase when it becomes too risky.

Departments that operate under restrictive regulations or specific rules limit an individual officer's discretion. For example, these orders can restrict officers from initiating pursuits when the law violators are juveniles, traffic offenders, or property offenders. Similarly, in-pursuit driving behavior may be regulated. Specific speed, distance, or time limitations may be ordered. Additionally, a rule may restrict some types of driving, such as going the wrong way on a one-way street, driving over curbs, or trespassing on private property.

Discouragement policies only allow pursuit driving under specific conditions. Examples include chasing a known murder suspect or a suspect who has been observed committing a violent crime by the officer. These policies are very specific and leave little room for discretion.

In other words, there exists a policy continuum, ranging from detailed and controlled to general and vague. The latter emphasizes officer discretion and the former has reduced the discretionary decisions made on the street and provides the officers with more structure. Discretion, whether controlled by the command staff through policies and procedures or left up to the line officer, must be reasonably exercised within the rule of law and expectations of the community.

Pursuit Policy: General Principles and Specific Rules

The purpose of a policy is to reduce officer discretion and can include specific requirements and prohibitions as well as general guidelines. The restriction of specific actions such as limiting the maximum speed and the duration of a pursuit can be controlled independently by specific rules, which will be discussed below under "Termination of the Pursuit." Similarly, these actions can be considered within the context of other variables, depending upon the type of policy that is desired and the type of training provided. The variables to be considered include:

1. Officer's background and preparation
   a. tactical preparation (training, experience, and familiarity with area including escape routes);
   b. type of vehicle (condition, equipment, etc.).
2. Nature and characteristics of incident, area, and conditions
   a. traffic conditions (density, speed, etc.);
   b. pedestrian traffic;
   c. road conditions (width, lanes, fitness, surface);
   d. geographic area (hills, sidewalks, curb breaks, etc.);
   e. weather and visibility;
   f. location of pursuit (residential, commercial, freeway, school zones, etc.);
   g. time of day; and
   h. speed of each vehicle.
3. Information pertaining to offender
   a. the offense committed by the offender;
   b. likelihood of successful apprehension (identification of offender, type of vehicle, probability of apprehending offender at a later time, and extent to which offender will go to avoid capture);
   c. age or maturity of offender; and
   d. effect of officer's driving on offender's driving (i.e., is the officer's action the moving force of the offender's recklessness?).

The policy can help create tactical knowledge and advanced preparation, which involves knowing as much as possible about a situation before taking or continuing action to resolve it. The pursuing officer may be familiar with the area and may even be familiar with the likelihood of pedestrian or vehicular traffic, but does not make the decision regarding the exact route to be taken or the spontaneous driving maneuvers taken by the law violator. A strong policy and training, however, can control the overall risk, the most critical factor of a police pursuit.

All pursuits involve risk. Fortunately, there are specific ways to decrease and control the omnipresent risk. Improving knowledge and preparation can achieve this goal. The following elements are necessary parts of a plan:

1. A clear and understandable policy delineating departmental requirements within the context of state laws and the police mission;

2. Specific *training* to the policy, using examples of risk assessment;
3. A detached supervisor, trained in risk assessment, who takes *control* over the pursuit, who assumes its *supervision* and who will terminate it when it becomes too risky; and
4. *Accountability*, by requiring officers to complete pursuit critiques and have the forms reviewed individually to determine if the pursuit driving was within policy, and collectively to provide information to trainers and policy-makers. Additionally officers must receive feedback on the appropriateness of their pursuit driving.

The organizational and incident specific elements are incomplete without the consideration of the actions of at least the three actors in a pursuit scenario. This complexity creates uncertain events and unpredictable contingencies. If police officers are regulated by a strong policy, follow that policy, and are controlled by their supervisors, they will rarely become involved in accidents. If problems occur, their behavior can be observed, reported, and modified. The driving behavior of the law violator appears to be the most significant factor involved in the outcome of the pursuit. Once a person decides not to stop for a police vehicle that is displaying its emergency lights and siren, it is difficult to predict how that person will drive, the degree of recklessness he or she will display, and whether or not concern will be shown for personal welfare. *There are no rules for the law violator.* However, if the law violator has recklessly evaded the police in congested traffic for even a short period of time, it is safe to predict that he or she will continue to do so. The few offenders who voluntarily terminate their pursuit do so after a relatively small amount of risk has been taken and most often within a minute or so (Alpert and Dunham, 1990). It is the driving actions of the pursued law violator that the police cannot control and, consequently, it is the law violator who ends up in accidents more often than anyone else. It is a natural urge for an officer to respond in a reflexive manner to this driving, but a reflexive action must be replaced by knowledge and preparation through training to reduce risk and officer's blame.

Examples of principles and rules include the number of vehicles authorized to become involved in a pursuit—and their role in the pursuit. These vehicles must operate in an emergency mode, with lights and siren. A limited number of back-up vehicles can position themselves at strategic locations and can parallel the route. This number and their specific function must be determined by policy and the vehicles must be assigned, controlled, and justified by a supervisor. It is important that officers recognize the impact of their decisions during a pursuit and that they are not engaged merely in a contest to win. Officers must continually re-evaluate the situation to determine the need to immediately apprehend a suspect balanced against the danger created by the pursuit. For example, if there is no realistic way to apprehend or capture the suspect, there must exist some reason or justification to take risks. Also, as officers may be caught up in the moment, it is important that the supervisor take control of the pursuit. But the supervisor must rely upon the information provided by the lead officer in order to make proper decisions. This requires that sufficient information be provided by the pursuing officer. Communication at a minimum includes:

1. The crime for which the suspect is wanted;
2. What is known about the suspect and his or her actions;
3. Location and direction;
4. Environment in which the pursuit is taking place, including vehicular or pedestrian traffic—likelihood of traffic increasing;
5. Speed of both vehicles;
6. Driving behavior of the pursued; and
7. Any description of vehicle and passengers.

It is essential to stress that officers cannot assume that an individual observed for a traffic violation must be involved in something more serious because he or she is fleeing. Officers must rely on what they know not what they think or sense. Increasing risks during a pursuit can only be justified by what is known (Alpert and Smith, 1991).

The purpose of pursuit is to apprehend a suspect. Within the mission of police, to protect lives, this purpose must be kept in mind at all times and all tactics or activities undertaken must be with safety and apprehension in mind. It is necessary for officers and supervisors to ask themselves: If this pursuit results in an injury or a death, or even property damage, would a reasonable person understand why the pursuit occurred, why it was continued, or why it was necessary? This question will ultimately be asked and it is appropriate to have it in the guidelines. A policy should include the warning that the officers' behavior will likely be reviewed and analyzed by a "common man" mentality. Will the officer be able to convince a group of nonpolice that his or her behavior and the risks taken were reasonable under the conditions?

Termination of the Pursuit

The need to immediately apprehend a suspect must be balanced against the danger created by the pursuit. When the dangers or risks of a pursuit, or the foreseeability or likelihood of a collision outweigh the need to immediately apprehend the suspect, the lead officer or the officer's supervisor must terminate it. This is usually dictated by the nature of the offense for which the law violator is wanted and the recklessness of his or her driving. Other considerations, however, are also important:

1. An analysis of whether speed dangerously exceeds the normal flow of traffic;
2. The type of vehicle being pursued (i.e., motorcycle or muscle car);
3. The likelihood and extent of pedestrians or vehicular traffic;
4. The danger of erratic maneuvering by the violator, such as driving the wrong way on a one-way street, driving without lights, over curbs, or through private property;
5. The distance between the officer and the offender;
6. The danger of exceptional speed;
7. The identification of the suspect as a juvenile;
8. Whether a clear and unreasonable hazard exists to the officer, law violator, or members of the public; and
9. The totality of the hazards created during a pursuit.

There are many other questions that must be addressed by policy. These include the use of offensive tactics, passing and the spacing of vehicles, the use of roadblocks, and ramming, among others. The specific responsibilities of the supervisor and the possibilities of an interjurisdictional pursuit must be considered and addressed in a policy (Alpert and Dunham, 1990).

Defensible Training: Translating Policy into Practice

Pursuit training must provide more than mere lip service to the principles embodied in the policy. Similarly, departmental disciplinary actions must reflect any differences in the actions taken in pursuit with the policy even if no accident or injury results. Any officer who violates policy must be disciplined and must receive further training and education. Results of current police litigation stress that courts look not only to the existence of training but to its sufficiency. The holdings in cases such as *City of Canton v. Harris* (1989), *Davis v. Mason County* (1991), *Frye v. Town of Akron* (1991), and *Rivas v. Freeman* (1991) demonstrate that management of police pursuit risks requires an in-depth analysis of the elements of the pursuit. That is, tactics authorized by the agency for its officers must be a critical and integral part of the training process as well as policy. For example, to authorize by policy the use of roadblocks or "ramming" techniques without corresponding training is a grievous invitation to a "deliberate indifference" claim if injury to a suspect or officer should occur.

At the heart of defensible pursuit training is instruction in risk identification and assessment. The training must not be delivered from a purely theoretical standpoint but must integrate practical illustrations of risks which are unacceptable under agency policy. It must also be understood by the risk manager that the restrictiveness of the policy will help determine the degree of risks which will be taken. Officers must, by second nature, come to recognize which offender and environmental factors should trigger a decision to terminate a chase. Split-second decisions made by police officers must be reduced.

The training must integrate all departmental responsibilities, even those that may be mandated under directives or policies other than the pursuit policy. Obvious examples are departmental communications directives and deadly force policies (Alpert and Fridell, 1992).

Finally, training must address the need to modify unacceptable pursuit behavior and to create awareness of the needs and expectations of the public. It is an axiomatic truth that policing is a balance of law enforcement and public safety. Unnecessary risk to the public violates the nature of the police mission. Training can help control the adrenaline-created disregard for public safety that, in some instances, accompanies the pursuit and the overreaction that is exhibited in its culmination when a suspect is taken into custody (Alpert and Smith, 1991).

A Concluding Observation
Pursuit driving is one tactic that police have relied upon for the apprehension of suspects. Until the 1980s very little was known about the risks and benefits of pursuit. The trend, balancing the enforcement of laws with the safety of the public, has resulted in a number of restrictions being placed on pursuit. In fact, the more that is learned about pursuit the more control is placed on it. The analogy of a pursuit to the use of a firearm has demonstrated the potential deadly consequences. In 1990, the International Association of Chiefs of Police published a model policy and a policy, concepts, and issues paper evaluating pursuit driving. While they have maintained a middle-of-the-road posture, they have summarized the need for reform:

> The policy issue confronting law enforcement and municipal administrators is a familiar one of balancing conflicting interests: One side there is the need to apprehend known offenders. On the other side, there is the safety of law enforcement officers, of fleeing drivers and their passengers, and of innocent bystanders. . . . The model policy is relatively restrictive, particularly in prohibiting pursuit where the offense in question would not warrant an arrest. Most traffic violations therefore, would not meet these pursuit requirements. It is recognized that many law enforcement officers and administrators may find this prohibition difficult to accept and implement, particularly where a more permissive policy has been traditionally accepted.

> But in this critical area of pursuit driving, law enforcement administrators must be prepared to make difficult decisions based on the cost and benefits of these types of pursuit to the public they serve.

Geoffrey P. Alpert

Note
Portions of this chapter have appeared in W. Smith and G. Alpert, "A Critical and Constructive Look at the Defensability of Police Pursuit Training." 172–93. In J. Bizzack, *Is-*

sues in Policing. Lexington, KY: Autumn House Publishing, 1992.

Cases
Brown v. City of Pinellas Park, Supreme Court of Florida, No. 75,721, 75,722 & 75,726 (decided July 23, 1992).
Chambers v. Ideal Pure Milk Co. 245 S.W. 2d 589 (1952), 590–91.
City of Canton v. Harris 109 S. Ct. 1197 (1989).
Delaware v. Prouse, 440 U.S. 648 (1979).
Groves v. United States of America, Civil Action No. 90–2695 (decided in 1991).
Travis v. City of Mesquite, Supreme Court of Texas, No. C-8576 (decided May 20, 1992).
Thornton v. Shore 666 P.2d 655 (1983).
West Virginia v. Fidelity Gas and Casualty Co. of New York, 263 F. Supp. 88 (1967), 90–91.

Bibliography
Abbott, Les. "Pursuit Driving." *FBI Law Enforcement Bulletin* (November 1988): 7–11.
Alpert, Geoffrey P. "Analyzing Police Pursuit." *Criminal Law Bulletin* 27 (1991): 358–67.
———. "Police Pursuit: Linking Data to Decisions." *Criminal Law Bulletin* 24 (1988): 453–642.
———. "Questioning Police Pursuit in Urban Areas." *Journal of Police Science and Administration* 15 (1987): 298–306.
Alpert, Geoffrey P., and Patrick Anderson. "The Most Deadly Force: Police Pursuits." *Justice Quarterly* 3 (1986): 1–14.
Alpert, Geoffrey P., and Roger G. Dunham. *Police Pursuit Driving: Controlling Responses to Emergency Situations.* Westport, CT: Greenwood Press, 1990.
———, and Roger Dunham. "Policing Hot Pursuits: The Discovery of Aleatory Elements." *Journal of Criminal Law and Criminology* 80 (1989): 521–39.
———, and Roger Dunham. "Research on Police Pursuits: Applications for Law Enforcement." *American Journal of Police* 7 (1988): 123–31.
Alpert, Geoffrey P., and Lorie Fridell. *Police Vehicles and Firearms: Instruments of Deadly Force.* Prospect Heights, IL: Waveland Press, 1992.
Alpert, Geoffrey P., and William Smith. "Be-

yond City Limits and into the Wood(s):
A Brief Look at the Policy Implications
of *City of Canton v. Harris* and *Wood v.
Ostrander.*" *American Journal of Police*
10 (1991): 19–40.

Auten, James. "An Analysis of Police Pursuit
Policy." *Law and Order* 38 (1990): 53–
54.

California Highway Patrol. *Pursuit Study.*
Sacramento: California Highway Patrol,
1983.

Charles, Michael, David Falcone, and Ed-
ward Wells. *Police Pursuit in Pursuit of
Policy: The Pursuit Issue, Legal and Lit-
erature Review, and an Empirical Study.*
Washington, DC: AAA Foundation for
Traffic Safety, 1992.

Farber, William. "Negligent Vehicular Police
Chase." 41 *Am. Jur. Proof of Facts* 2
(1985). 79–132.

Fennessy, Edmund, Thomas Hamilton, Kent
Joscelyn, and John Merritt. *A Study of
the Problem of Hot Pursuit by the Police.* Washington, DC: U.S. Department
of Transportation, 1970.

Glines, Carroll. *Jimmy Doolittle: Master of
the Calculated Risk.* New York: Van
Nostrand Reinhold, 1980.

Grose, Vernon. *Managing Risk: Systematic
Loss Prevention for Executives.*
Englewood Cliffs, NJ: Prentice-Hall,
1987.

"High-Speed Pursuits: Police Officers and
Municipal Liability for Accidents Involv-
ing the Pursued and an Innocent Third
Party" [unsigned comment] *Seton Hall
Law Review* 16 (1986): 101–26.

Koonz, Joseph, and Patrick Regan. "Hot Pursuit: Proving Police Negligence." *Trial* 21
(1985): 63, 65–69.

Nowicki, Ed. 1989. "The Heat of the
Chase." *Police Magazine* (March 1989):
24–26, 45–46.

Patinkin, H.P., and H. Bingham. "Police Motor Vehicle Pursuits: The Chicago Experience." *Police Chief* 53 (1986): 61–62.

Schofield, Daniel L. "Legal Issues of Pursuit
Driving." *FBI Law Enforcement Bulletin*
57 (1988): 23–30.

Silver, Isadore. *Police Civil Liability.* New
York: Matthew Bender, 1986.

Solicitor General. A Special Report from the
Solicitor General's Special Committee on
Police Pursuits. Ontario, Canada: Solici-
tor General's Office, 1985.

Territo, Leonard. "Citizen Safety: Key Elements in Police Pursuit Policy." *Trial*
(August 1982): 31–34.

Urbonya, Kathryn. "Establishing a Deprivation of a Constitutional Right to Personal Safety under Section 1983: The
Use of Unjustified Force by State Officials in Violation of the Fourth, Eighth
and Fourteenth Amendments." *Albany
Law Review* 51 (1987): 171–235.

———. "Problematic Standards of Reasonableness: Qualified Immunity in Section
1983 Actions for a Police Officer's Use
of Excessive Force." *Temple Law Review*
62 (1989): 61–116.

———. "The Constitutionality of High-Speed
Pursuits Under the Fourth and Fourteenth Amendments." *St. Louis Law Review* 35 (1991): 205–88.

Zevitz, Richard. "Police Civil Liability and
the Law of High Speed Pursuit." *Mar-
quette Law Review* 70 (1987): 237–84.

Police Reform

The term *police reform* refers to action taken to
change police behavior considered inappropriate or unlawful. This includes matters related to
abuse of police status, such as brutality, questionable use of deadly force, searches without
warrants, or illegal detention or questioning of
suspects; improper conduct while on duty, such
as drinking, use of police vehicles or equipment
for activities not related to police work, or in-
attention to police matters; or personal conduct
by officers, including gambling, involvement in
disposal of stolen property, or conduct regarded
as immoral in a particular community. When
police misconduct is discovered in a certain
department and a response is called for by specific events, internal disciplining of officers or
administrators is the common course of action.
If the problem is defined as serious or far-reaching enough to require extensive investigation
and sweeping changes, modification of police
behavior may include changes in a department's
organizational structure of systems of control,
or even a redefinition or refocusing of the police role in that community.

Police reform movements have generally
arisen during periods in American history when
it was felt that political control, graft, brutality,
or incompetence permeated police departments.
Generally, reform movements have been initiated in large cities, where corruption or dys-

function were most obvious or most serious. Mass media exposure of improper police activities has frequently led to citizen initiated demands for changes in the administration or operation of certain departments. In some cases, civilian review boards were established as a result of criticism that police departments were not effectively disciplining officers or changing internal procedures. The power of such boards was advisory only, and the final decisions on reform activity remained in the hands of the police chiefs or commissioners.

Early Professional Development
The career activity of August Vollmer illustrates the direction of reform in the early twentieth century. Between 1905 and 1932 Vollmer played a major role in changing the nature of policing from an occupation entered through political patronage and characterized by corrupt and brutal dealing with the public to one moving toward acceptance as a profession. Beginning with his election as town marshal of Berkeley, California, in 1905, Vollmer sought to reduce vice and corruption. His efforts included increasing the size of the force, introducing night patrols in addition to day patrols, and moving aggressively against gambling and drug-dealing establishments. He sought to speed reaction and availability time by having officers ride bicycles while patrolling their beats, and when automobile use became widespread he instituted the first totally mobile police patrol unit in the country. During the nearly thirty years he served as police chief of Berkeley and Los Angeles and as a special consultant to other departments, he introduced many innovations, including upgraded filing and classification systems, use of radios in police cars, gathering intelligence information through use of ex-offenders, using scientific information to establish innovative crime detection and solution techniques such as the "lie detector" test, and recruitment of college graduates as officers. However, his most far-reaching contribution resulted from his effort to establish professional standards for police and to lead the public to view policing as an occupation worthy of professional stature. He created a police training school in 1908 that acquainted officers with a wide range of subject matter related to police work and also pioneered efforts to create police education programs in colleges and universities. Vollmer believed that police training should include knowledge of the natural and social sciences as well as technical expertise in fingerprinting, first aid, report writing, and firearm use, and he lobbied for cooperation between the police and social service agencies.

In the early 1900s, when Vollmer initiated efforts toward reform in California, the problems identified as existing in many departments across the nation centered around the control of local police by politicians. Since political patronage, graft, and bribery were regarded as the result of the close ties between police and politicians, reformers sought to establish independent police organizations that were directed by nonpartisan police commissions and administrative boards.

Federal Bureau of Investigation
The creation of the Federal Bureau of Investigation in 1908 and the appointment of J. Edgar Hoover as its director in 1924 helped advance the concept of police work as a profession. Under Hoover's leadership, the Bureau recruited well-educated personnel who were able to utilize the latest technological advancements. Their image was enhanced by their use of street clothes as worn by professionals, rather than the typical police uniform. In the 1930s the image of police officers as crime-fighters and protectors of the public interest was furthered by the FBI's well-publicized efforts to bring notorious outlaws to justice and to enforce federal laws.

By the end of World War II, a high-school diploma was considered the appropriate educational attainment for police officers, but the climate of political and social unrest in the 1960s again set in motion calls for police reform and for increased professionalization of police forces. The civil rights disturbances, in particular, demonstrated that many police departments were inadequately prepared to handle their responsibilities. Overreaction and use of excessive force often resulted in physical injuries to citizens and officers. Frequently, control functions were assigned to poorly trained officers who were not knowledgeable of the values, cultures, and lifestyles of the groups they were required to control. The President's Commission on Law Enforcement and the Administration of Justice noted that such police actions as the use of racial slurs, profane and abusive language, interrogation or arrests as harassment, and lack of sensitivity to citizens' demands or needs were key factors in provoking violent reactions toward police (President's Commission on Law

Enforcement and the Administration of Justice, 1967:178–79). The Law Enforcement Assistance Administration (LEAA) and the National Institute of Justice (NIJ) were created in response to the commission's findings, and enormous financial resources were placed at their disposal. Program development, research, and training in all areas of policing were promoted and given support. These LEAA- and NIJ-sponsored programs served as the foundation for many new community-responsive police reforms that evolved.

Police Reform Equated with Professionalism

Police reforms ultimately became equated with efforts to establish professionalism within the organizational structure, administrative policies, and police functions. As the innovations gained acceptance, strides in the professionalization of law enforcement included a code of ethics; a clearly defined body of knowledge; uniform minimum standards of excellence for recruitment, education, and performance; and an emphasis on the development of specialists in law-enforcement technology.

The centralized administrative core of the police organization facilitated the growth of specialized task units within the bureaucratic structure. The paramilitary hierarchical structure encouraged adherence to professional standards by granting promotions to officers with exemplary crime-fighting records. The prevalence of reforms aimed at professionalism can also be seen in the adoption of standardized entrance exams and the recruitment of college graduates by police academies, the requirement of civil service examinations by some police organizations, and the growth of police unionization.

Disillusionment with the Professional Model

Gordon Misner, a prominent criminologist, warned the National Commission on the Causes and Prevention of Violence (1969) that the distancing of politics and policing that had occurred might be detrimental to effective reform because political leadership had not been given a voice in the long-range planning and policy development of departments. It was noted that police effectiveness is a legitimate concern of political leaders. Other objections to increased professionalization of police work in the early 1970s centered on the fact that requiring higher education for entry into the occupation might automatically exclude members of lower-class, ethnic, and racial groups, who could have performed effectively as officers, and that college education was not necessary for the tedious, boring, repetitive activities that make up a large portion of police work. It was also noted that increased professionalization had not put an end to corruption and incompetence in police departments in large cities, and that the huge amounts of funds spent in developing crime labs, innovative equipment, and organizational innovations had not put an end to crime in the streets.

In spite of the efforts at police reform over the years, police corruption and brutality continued. Citizens' reliance on community policing, self-defense courses, and private security was evidence that there was a lack of confidence in police effectiveness and responsiveness.

Skolnick and Bayley (1986:212) noted that professionalism among police has taken a new direction in recent years. They characterized the "old" professionals as persons well trained in penal law, firearm use, and search and interrogation procedures, who view their work from a legalistic, law-enforcement perspective and do not consider the needs of the public as a primary concern of policing. In contrast, they described the "new" professionals as committed to a more service-oriented style, grounded in the notion that police serve the community and are accountable to it. Police departments that follow the "new" professional orientation would be likely to develop their organizations and procedures to take into account the changing natures and needs of the communities they serve.

The New Community-Service Orientation

Current innovations in policing may best be understood by an examination of the trend toward a community-service orientation that is emerging as the new objective in law enforcement. The traditional goal of policing in the United States has been that of fighting crime, with an emphasis on professional and legalistic behavior by officers. Movement away from this combative orientation in favor of crime-prevention and order-maintenance objectives can be found in many current policies. In pursuing this goal of community-oriented law enforcement, contemporary police reform is characterized by a movement toward a greater reciprocity between the police and the community, with the police taking on a more active role of service. The "crime-fighters" are now being replaced with more generally intentioned public servants. This new community orientation for law enforcement is exemplified through changes found in the structure of police administration, organizational policies, enhanced community involvement, and procedures for patrol.

The Structure of Police Administration

Efforts are underway to accomplish a radical reorganization of the structure of police administration that will be more conducive to achieving the prevailing goal of community service. The traditional organizational structure of the police has emphasized a powerful administrative core with authority over the entire paramilitary hierarchy. There is a trend away from this insulation of the police organization toward a decentralized structure directed at improved community service. The emphasis being placed on team-policing strategies[1] and the establishment of storefront police substations are indicative of community-oriented policing and dissemination of decision-making authority beyond the administrative core.

Many police organizations are adopting participant-management philosophies in which patrol officers and other lower-level personnel are encouraged to participate in policy decisions. Job enrichment techniques aimed at increasing levels of productivity and motivation are also prominent among current police administration strategies.

Organizational Policies

The new humanistic orientation is clearly evident in changes found in organizational policies. The preservation of public order through preventive policing strategies is a recurring theme within contemporary law-enforcement administration. The battle with crime historically waged by police in the United States is now placed within the overall perspective of order maintenance. The policing techniques that are perceived as best capable of executing policy directives are those that provide far-reaching assistance to the most citizens and reduce barriers created by the old policing philosophies, which have fostered community resentment.

In accord with the effort to minimize conflict, many police departments have attempted to reduce citizen fear of police by adopting deadly-force policies such as placing limitations on riflery, bans on carrying heavy weaponry, and restrictions on the discharge of all firearms.

Measurement of police efficiency by the absence of crime and public perceptions of safety, rather than by high rates of arrest, also reflects the new administrative policies aimed at preserving social order. Modifications in investigation procedures aimed at a more personal approach during the interrogation of witnesses and victims, and a willingness to divert cases from the system and refer them to social service agencies, further illustrate the community service policy in effect.

Community Involvement

Police reform is very evident in the new emphasis placed on community involvement. The police are often responsible for intensive efforts being made at community mobilization for self-defense and crime prevention. Many police organizations have established special patrol units directed to enhance community awareness of crime by conducting crime-prevention programs, establishing neighborhood crime-watch networks, and sponsoring social or charity events that promote interaction between the police and the community. Community mobilization is also apparent in the visible increase of civilian personnel functioning within police organizations. This effort aimed at greater citizen involvement has been called "civilianization" (Skolnick and Bayley, 1986) and ranges from use of citizens as research and planning personnel to deployment of civilian patrol units that respond to requests for police in noncrime situations.

Patrol Procedures

Current innovations in police patrolling procedures reflect the movement away from crime-fighting and toward a sensitivity to the local community. The prevalence of the reactive-patrolling approach to crime control and reports that rapid response time is of little consequence have created concern about the effectiveness of random patrolling procedures and have subsequently led the way for directed patrolling practices with a narrower focus. The objectives in these structured patrol procedures typically include the concentration on high crime areas or specific offense types. In an additional effort to remove the old barriers between the community and police, police organizations have incorporated not only a more extensive use of foot patrol, but also other alternatives to squad cars, such as patrolling on horseback, motor scooters, and even on ten-speed bicycles.

Police training now emphasizes respect for neighborhoods served and the importance of having police actions reflect this value of community. In accord with the human services emphasis, officers are trained in the more effective handling of child abuse, domestic violence, missing children cases, and empathetic treatment of victims during crime investigations. This new service-oriented professionalism expands the job definition from law enforcement and order maintenance to include all community problems and encourages police officers to assist in neighborhood improvements. This extension of patrol training to the climate and needs of the community is intended to better equip the officers for the social work duties that have always consumed much of their time.

Prospects for the Future in Police Reform
Police reform is a dynamic process affected by the social or political climate reflecting community needs and by the presence of resources required to facilitate change. The success of reform efforts depends not only on the effective mobilization of available resources, but also on public support of the innovations. In view of the current situation in policing, it is likely that the prospects for police reform in the near future will concentrate on two areas: (1) encouraging a greater commitment from individual police officers to serve, learn from, and be accountable to the community, and (2) more involvement of the community in the police mission.

No single program can ever satisfy all areas in which there is a perceived need for police reform. Effective change is more likely to result from independent efforts to assist police officers in accepting the worthiness of community service–oriented police work. A growing recognition that officers with demographic characteristics similar to those of the citizens they work with can improve community relations and reduce racial or gender tensions has paved the way for equal-employment opportunities and the recruitment of more minority officers. Training programs will likely expand the attention they give to strategies for dealing with human problems. Job enrichment efforts and the provision of inner-organization mechanisms to assist officers in coping with job-related stress are apt to become a priority among police administrations. Monetary and promotional incentives for higher education will continue because the motivational level of college graduates is considered to be higher. However, adjustment in the nature of police work must also be made. In an effort to make their tasks more interesting, patrol officers will probably be given increased investigative responsibilities and empowered to establish a working network of community contacts. Reorientation of the police role is more likely to occur after the image of the crime-fighter has been replaced, not with that of the diminutive public servant, but rather with one of a skilled administrator specializing in community health.

As public acknowledgement of community service as the preferred objective of the police grows, greater citizen involvement is also likely to occur. Whether this public support takes the form of civilians working within the police organization, or the growth of resources provided by the responsive social climate, enhanced reciprocity between the police and the community will no doubt have positive consequences.

Peter C. Kratcoski
Kimberley L. Kempf

Note
1. This technique involves the identification of a group of specially trained patrol officers with a specific area of the community, and a directive to perform any patrol activities needed to maintain a safe and orderly environment. Various terms have been used to describe this innovation in patrol procedure, including: "team policing," "community service policing," "the neighborhood police team," the "beat commander project," and "community-based policing."

Bibliography
Bloch, P.B., and D. Specht. *Neighborhood Team Policing*. Washington, DC: Government Printing Office, 1973.
Cho, Y. *Public Policy and Urban Crime*. Cambridge, MA: Ballinger, 1974.
Gay, W.G., H.T. Day, and J.P. Woodard. *Neighborhood Team Policing*. Washington, DC: LEAA, 1977.
President's Commission on Law Enforcement and Administration of Justice. *Task Force Report: Police*. Washington, DC: Government Printing Office, 1967.
Schwartz, A.L., and S.N. Clarren. *The Cincinnati Team Policing Experiment: A Summary Report*. Washington, DC: Police Foundation, 1977.
Sherman, L.W., C.H. Milton, and T.V. Kelly.

Team Policing: Seven Case Studies.
Washington, DC: Police Foundation,
1973.

Skolnick, Jerome H., and David H. Bayley.
The New Blue Line. New York: Free
Press, 1986.

Walker, Samuel. *A Critical History of Police
Reform.* Washington, DC: Heath, 1977.

Wasson, D.K. *Community Based Preventive
Policing: A Review.* Toronto: John D.
Crawford, 1975.

Police–Social Work Team

The Concept

The addition of social work service in police
departments is part of a larger development of
special units that began about 1950 and included community relations, computer-based
probability forecasting, crime solvability factors, and a host of other areas.

When Are Social Work Services Needed?

Examples of predicaments in which police and/
or citizens may request social work intervention
are: mental health problems, neighbor disputes,
domestic disturbances, parent-child problems,
runaways, alcoholism, suicide, aggravated
battery, emergency transportation services,
death notification, abuse and neglect, shoplifting, well-being check, criminal damage to property, and temporary and minimal financial assistance for transients in need of emergency
lodging.

Social work services are provided to citizens by experienced social workers with master's degrees. Services include assessment, crisis
intervention, counseling (individual, family, and
marital), and referral to other community services. The majority of interviews may be held
in the police department or in the citizen's
home, depending on the citizen's situation and
attitude about receiving services in a police setting. Senior citizens are almost always seen in
their homes. The advantage of holding interviews in the police department is that the setting
can offer controls in a situation where it is indicated, i.e., people may benefit from structure
to help them control harmful behavior, while
home visits provide the opportunity for social
assessment of the home and community resources.

The police-referred client can obtain important benefits by having immediate services
available from a social worker. "Families who

might not seek out an agency are seen in their
homes at a time when denial is impossible"
(Burnett et al., 1976). At the point of police
contact, people may be more emotionally accessible than usual since they are in trouble and
may welcome assistance. When a helping relationship is established at a time of crisis, the
citizen and his or her family may have a stronger desire to continue this relationship than if
the referral process has necessitated a break in
continuity of service (Michaels and Treger,
1973). In the initial contact, social workers
must move quickly to relate to areas of anxiety
so that people will feel social service has been
useful. Although clients should have the option
to go elsewhere, rather than use social services
in a police department, experience indicates that
citizens who refuse service associated with the
police department are unlikely to use service
elsewhere. The reluctant families have probably
resisted referrals by police and schools before.
It has been observed that parents are more often at the core of such resistance than are young
offenders (Michaels and Treger, 1973). Police
and social workers need to recognize that the
officers' authority can serve as a legitimate catalyst in encouraging people to initiate contact
with a social worker. When internal motivation
is not present, external authority can be useful
in getting people started when treatment appears necessary to ensure public safety and to
protect individuals from their own destructive
behavior.

Police, social workers, and the community
all gain by cooperative relations. The police will
have an alternative resource for dealing with
social and mental health problems; social workers expand their services to new populations;
and community safety is extended as a result
of improved functioning of vital groups of its
citizens.

The History

The literature in police and social work cooperation reveals a practice and knowledge gap.
Many social workers believe that differences in
orientation preclude constructive cooperation.
It has been suggested by Parkinson (1980) that
sex-role barriers may lie at the root of problems
in interagency cooperation since most social
workers are female while most police officers
are male. Others believe that police work and
social work are like oil and water and do not
mix. For example, police focus on law enforcement and public safety, while social workers

focus on problem resolution—even though community service is a shared goal.

Police work and social work also have different time frames. Police work frequently deals with the immediate and life-threatening situation, while social workers tend to work more in longer range, ongoing relationships and predicaments. The lack of contact and in some instances negative experiences, biases, and hostility between social workers and police reinforce the distance between the two groups. Police officers perceive that social workers are never available when they are needed and that they never communicate information about people referred for services (Bard 1970; Treger et al., 1975). Social service and mental health agencies are frequently unresponsive to police requests for services and consultation to police-referred clients who require crisis and early intervention services, while police officers are not always aware that family problems are not easily and quickly solved, that improvements are not immediately visible, and that some families do not respond to referral and so cannot be helped. In mental health cases and in family and neighbor disputes, timely social work consultation and intervention can often be useful to the police and the community.

Police have a long history of providing services related to health, education, and welfare. Over the years many of these functions have been taken over by social agencies (Schrag, 1971). Still, 50 to 90 percent of police calls are of a social service nature. Many people think of the police first when they are in trouble that requires help outside the family, especially at times when social agencies are closed—evenings, weekends, and holidays. As a result police often find themselves dealing with situations that require social work training. Many officers enjoy these roles and derive satisfaction in the feeling that comes from helping people just as social workers do. Social workers need to be sensitive to these feelings on the part of police, to prevent role conflict and to utilize police expertise in areas that will strengthen social work services.

The experience in working with the police has changed social work practice to become more proactive by intervening early rather than waiting for the client to come to them. Police benefit by having an alternative resource and disposition. As a result, police officers share in the process of providing needed services to people and learn of the more positive aspects of people's functioning. Experience indicates that interpersonal contact between police and social workers can help dispel some myths about each. The citizen is offered social work services and an alternative to the justice system when it is appropriate and public safety is not compromised.

Problems and Issues in Cooperation
The experience in several different communities with populations from 30,000 to 100,000 illustrates the kinds of problems and issues that emerge as a result of cooperation.

Police are concerned with dependability, response time, confidentiality, and whether social workers will supplant police services and replace police officers. A request for personal counseling by police personnel can also be an issue. Police want cooperating professionals to understand and be sensitive to their subculture, the nature of their work, the kinds of problems they are dealing with, and their needs for specialized services. They seek to preserve their areas of decision-making and authority under the law. Providing quality public service is a high priority for the police agency and an area of common ground for initiating police and social work cooperation. Emphasis on commonalities between police work and social work will reduce conflict and tend to facilitate cooperative efforts. Since suspicion and unfamiliarity exists between the two groups, personal contact should be a first step in initiating cooperation. Apart from labels and titles people have much in common. When social workers are physically in the police department, they and their services are more likely to be accepted as part of the team; when they are outside the department they are more likely to be looked upon as outsiders. Police have a special need to have their own social workers, individuals they know and can depend on. Dependability is an important factor in police work. It is also possible for social workers to establish positive relationships with the police when social services are outside the department. However, this requires more planning for interpersonal contact and consultation with the police.

Relations between police and social workers will be strengthened if social workers have a positive attitude toward police services, are available to receive referrals, give feedback on clients' participation and response to services, and offer consultation and training. Police and social workers need to develop realistic expectations of each other by learning what each can do and appreciating the need for each other's services. Social workers can best be oriented to police work, the organization of the police department, and the community by the police they intend to work with. In this way the police will be aware that the social worker knows their organization and orientation. Social workers can best maintain their own integrity and avoid unnecessary conflict by being clear and definite about their own role. For example, social workers decide how they want referrals made, who they will offer services to, and what services will be offered. Yet there needs to be some flexibility and accommodation by both professions. Social workers should be careful not to involve themselves in police roles even though they may be invited by the police as a way of testing out the relationship. Police will learn best about social work by observation and experience. Too much talk about the social work role can impede development of positive relations. The police will be convinced of the value of social work services when they see the results of treatment—i.e., behavior and attitude change—and experience the benefits of consultation as a useful input into police decision-making.

Another key issue in police–social work relations is communication. Can police and social workers exchange information while maintaining professional standards? Experience in police-social work cooperation (Treger et al., 1975) reveals that exchange of information helped to close a long-standing gap and that misuse of information feared by both police and social workers never materialized.

Both social work and law enforcement have codes of ethics that relate to the protection of information. It is a matter of mutual concern. In a model project (Treger, 1976) the social assessment and service plan was shared with the clients' signed consent as is common practice among social agencies. At the outset clients were informed that whatever was specifically discussed with the social worker was confidential unless behaviors violated a law or were injurious to them or others—in which case the client was encouraged to inform the police. In this project social work practice was guided by the view that "to conceal law-violative behavior may be destructive in its outcomes: It places the social worker in the position of an accomplice; it does not protect the community; and it defeats the goal of developing more socially responsible behavior in the client. Further, a person may benefit from coming to grips with the consequences of their behavior." The laws between states and countries regarding police and social work information exchange may vary; thus communication patterns may be developed within these constraints. For example, in West Germany the law provides for information exchange in one direction only—from police to social workers. State social work registration acts also provide guidelines in this vital area.

Many social workers believe that guidelines in regard to confidentiality should be developed. Undeniably there is some loss of confidentiality normally associated with a client seen in a police agency. Police administrators believe that for the police–social worker relationship to be successful there must be a willingness on the parts of the police officer and social worker to openly discuss the various facets of the case for the benefit of the client and the community.

One of the early issues in a police–social work team program (Treger, 1981) was: Can police and social workers establish a program of mutual interdependence without co-optation? Sometimes police are concerned that social workers will supplant police services and ultimately replace police officers. This may be especially true with juvenile officers. There is some basis in reality for this concern since juvenile officers also interview youths and parents and are knowledgeable about community resources. Police officers sometimes think they are giving up their cases by referring them to social workers. Experience indicates that issues of co-optation and negativity by both police and social workers are best addressed by positive experiences in cooperation. Emphasizing differences can be counterproductive in initial stages of cooperative relations. Involvement in professional reference groups provide support for the professional role, while attendance at programs of each other's professional organizations can further interprofessional cooperation.

In some police departments, social workers are participating in training police in stress management and are assisting police families in group discussion meetings on how to cope with living amid the stresses of the police officer's job. Police officers also provide support for social workers. In one police department several officers confronted a social worker (who was experiencing burnout) with the seriousness of her constant fatigue. As a result she recognized the need to take corrective steps.

Another issue is: Can social workers counsel police officers and still maintain a working relationship? The social worker's role in working with the police sometimes extends to providing informal personal services to police personnel and their families. Police administrators frequently support personal and job-related counseling for their officers, thus strengthening the social worker's value to the department. The provision of services to cooperating personnel may be an important factor in the success of interprofessional efforts. Often police officers develop more trust in a police social worker than a treatment-oriented person outside the department. Since a long-term coworker and counselor relationship could precipitate problems in the working area, an outside referral should be encouraged when ongoing services are indicated and desired. When a departmental need for personal social services is great enough, a social worker can be engaged from another police department (Treger, 1981).

One criticism of police–social work cooperation is that it may bring more people into the justice system. In one study (Thomson and Treger, 1973) it was determined that over a three-year period one community (Wheaton, Illinois) with a police–social service program experienced a sharp decrease in juvenile court referrals, while sixteen other towns in the same county (for which completed data were available) experienced a sharp increase. Wheaton's referrals declined 41 percent and the other towns' referrals increased 32 percent. A significant portion (35 percent) of the decline in juvenile court referrals by the Wheaton Police Department was directly attributable to the program.

A preliminary study of parents' attitudes (in two upper-class communities) about their receiving social services for themselves and their children in a police department concluded that "most families have a positive attitude toward receiving social work services in a police department, that coercion in the referral process is not perceived by parents whose children become involved with the police (except in 5.8 percent), and that the environment of a police department does not impede parents' willingness to accept social work services, but may actually enhance the social worker's acceptability as a helping agent" (Curtis and Lutkus, 1976). Further evaluation of this question and the effects of social services on the police-referred client is needed. The resolution of these issues and others resulting from differing orientations, values, and professional needs will either inhibit or encourage cooperative efforts.

Arrangements for Cooperation
Police and social work cooperative programs will tend to develop in communities where there is an identified need and citizen expectation that the political structure support such efforts. A number of arrangements inside and outside police departments are possible (Levens, 1978; Treger et al., 1975) and depend upon what community decision-makers believe will work best in a particular community. Arrangements for new services should be planned to fit in with existing police services and community resources so there is little disruption and duplication (Treger, 1980). A good fit will increase the prospects for program acceptance and support by the police and the community. Although the program has been operational in mostly medium sized-communities, it can be designed for larger populations.

Since the inception of the social worker in the police department program, a proliferation of arrangements for services has emerged. Some programs have remained traditional with the social worker physically located in the police department. Over time the social service unit has become an integral part of police services to the community. Occasionally the social worker also offers services to people in other departments of municipal government. As police officers and social workers cooperate they get to know one another, to trust and become friends as well as coworkers. Both have become aware that most of their work involves dealing with people in crisis. Advocates for the social worker in the police department arrangement believe that distance between the police officer and social worker lessens communication and referrals and breeds unfamiliarity and distrust. The social worker in the department shortens response time and increases availability, two important concepts in police work.

Another arrangement for police–social work cooperation is the social worker in the community social agency. Frequently, chronically mentally ill individuals create management problems for the community that result in a request for police assistance. The police look toward the community mental health agency as a resource to deal with the mentally ill. Police do not view ongoing services to the mentally ill as part of the police role. Most officers prefer to have mental health professionals diagnose and decide on the appropriate agency for referral. Frequently, chronically mentally ill individuals do not advise the police of their involvement with community agencies. As a result the police do not contact the agency for assistance and both are left without appropriate services.

A key issue for community social agency–police cooperation is the discomfort each has in working with the other. Many social workers in community agencies are uncomfortable with mandated treatment. They believe that if people are coerced to accept services, their right to self-determination is seriously constrained. Police officers see social workers as "bleeding hearts" who are out to get everyone "off the hook," put criminals back on the street, and undo the work of the police.

Social workers in a community social agency are more likely to be viewed by the police as outsiders with whom it is more difficult to establish trust and confidence. When cooperation with social workers is sanctioned by the police chief and community officials, the development of trust and confidence is facilitated. The incentive to cut down on the usage of police time in areas where other services may be more appropriate could result in police and social workers spending their time in new roles and relationships.

The most recent arrangement for police–social work cooperation to emerge is in the private, for-profit corporation, e.g., the crisis consultant in private practice. This model grew out of an in-house service in two suburban communities that had financial problems maintaining their police–social work programs.

The differences in the private for-profit models and other models are:

1. Cost is based on village population—contract costs change in the direction of population change.
2. The corporation absorbs all overhead costs, e.g., office space, telephone, secretarial services, pagers, liability insurance, etc.
3. Police must accompany social workers on all crisis calls.
4. All juveniles are seen at the police department. The corporation handles all status adjustment assessments.
5. Some contracts provide for services to police officers and their families or any village employees at no additional charge.

6. The corporation will provide police training or community education upon request. Each community can select from the services available.

In this service arrangement the social worker is accountable only to the contract and not to the police chain of command. The contract specifies twenty-four-hour availability, a response time of no more than ten minutes by phone, and no more than one hour in person. All clients are referred for ongoing services to public and private practitioners based on their ability to pay.

Two troublesome areas are:

1. Social workers must be comfortable about being in business. They are in a competitive market with public and private agencies and need to place an appropriate dollar value on services.
2. Police struggle with control. They believe the social workers' loyalty is spread thin. This can be overcome by demonstrated availability and service provision (Treger et al., 1985). Although operators of the for-profit model claim this model costs less than other arrangements, they are reluctant to disclose the details of their operation, citing competition. This constraint could make comparisons difficult.

The development of arrangements for social work cooperation with the police is a dynamic process that will change over time as a result of experience and evaluation, as well as be characterized by the unique qualities and resources of a particular community.

Social workers and the police share a common goal of community service and protection of citizens. Both groups have different but complementary roles. Ongoing experience and evaluation of the issues in cooperation may help to strengthen both police work and social work, as they together provide a more useful community service than either could provide alone.

Harvey Treger

Bibliography

Bard, M. *Training Police as Specialists in Family Crises Intervention.* Washington, DC: Government Printing Office, 1970.

Burnett, B., J. Carr, J. Senapi, and R. Taylor. "Police and Social Workers in a Community Outreach Program." *Social Casework* 57(1) (1976): 41–49.

Curtis, P., and A.M. Lutkus. "Attitudes toward Police Social Work." San Francisco, CA. Paper presented at the twenty-eighth annual meeting of the American Association of Psychiatric Services for Children, November 1976.

Levens, B.R. "Domestic Crises Intervention—A Literature Review of Domestic Dispute Intervention Training Programs." *Canadian Police College Journal* 2(3) (1978): 299–328.

Michaels, R.A., and H. Treger. "Social Work in Police Departments." *Social Work* 18(5) (1973): 67–75.

Parkinson, G. "Cooperation between Police and Social Workers: Hidden Issues." *Social Work* 25(1) (1980): 12–17.

Schrag, C. *Crime and Justice: American Style.* Washington, DC: Government Printing Office, 1971.

Thomson, D., and H. Treger. "Police Social Work Cooperation and the Overburden of the Juvenile Court." *Police Law Quarterly* 3(1) (1973): 28–39.

Treger, H. "Wheaton-Niles and Maywood Police–Social Service Projects: Comparative Impressions." *Federal Probation* 40(3) (1976): 33–39.

———. "Guideposts for Community Work in Police–Social Work Diversion." *Federal Probation* 45(3) (1980): 3–8.

———. "Police–Social Work Cooperation: Problems and Issues." *Social Casework* 62(7) (1981): 426–33.

Treger, H. and Associates. *The Police–Social Work Team.* Springfield, IL: Charles C. Thomas, 1975.

Treger, H., J. Cousins. S. Silvin, K. Risdon, and C. Emrickson. Panel Discussion on Public Safety and the Individual: Social Work Practice and the Police. National Association of Social Work Professional Symposium, November 8, 1985, Chicago, IL.

Police Solidarity

The sociological concept of solidarity refers to the unique sense of identity, belonging, and cohesion that one develops as part of a group of colleagues who share in common social roles, interests, problems, concerns, and even lifestyles. Since solidarity refers to loyalty to one's colleagues instead of loyalty to an organization, community, or set of principles, it involves emotional ties and commitments rather than formal or contractual relationships. A sense of solidarity or unity as it is alternatively called is the pivotal feature that pervades the police subculture and sustains its integrity. It derives from both common experiences police officers encounter in their working environment and from the socialization or social learning process inherent to the police subculture, which involves the transmission of social norms, values, and beliefs. It is *both* a consequence of other basic features of police subculture, such as a sense of social isolation, *and* a cause of other basic features, such as secrecy.

Solidarity as Loyalty to Colleagues Rather Than Loyalty to the Police Organization

As officers move into higher ranks, solidarity tends to decline. Conversely, members of the police administration are frequently seen by line officers in much the same way they perceive members of the community and other outsiders—as threatening the police subculture. Michael Brown (1981:82) and Peter Manning (1978:85–86) remark on how police loyalty and social bonds provide police safety from the arbitrary authority and power of aggressive administrators and supervisors. The very fact that officers feel detached from their departmental administrators and supervisors, and consequently develop in-group bonds as a collective protective response, may indicate that police solidarity is inversely related to organizational loyalty and respect for administrative authority. In his study of civilianization of the communications division of police departments, Shernock (1988b) found that interpretations of membership in the police department differed for sworn and civilian communications personnel. Sworn personnel tended to interpret their membership in terms of their group identification with fellow officers, whereas civilian personnel tended to interpret their membership in terms of their identification with the organization itself.

In her study of police in New York City precincts, Elizabeth Reuss-Ianni (1983) concluded that there are two distinct cultures in policing: a street cop culture and a management cop culture, which have conflicting perspectives on policy, procedure, and practice in policing. The particularistic values of the street cop culture—the "we-they" worldview, secrecy, and solidarity—are juxtaposed against the new bureaucratic values of police reform that the management cop culture has adopted, where the rule book presumably takes precedence. In contrast to street cops, management cops take community relations, public opinion, and politics seriously and are concerned with public accountability, productivity, and cost effectiveness. Consequently they are seen by street cops as not having loyalty to people but instead to social and political networks.

Shearing (1981) and Ericson (1981) argue, on the other hand, that what first might appear to be a conflict between subcultural and formal organizational norms can actually involve a complementarity between these ostensibly different norms. These authors interpret subcultural norms as providing direction and guidance for the real work of policing, while formal departmental rules provide the framework used in legitimating this work. In turn, top administrators support and reward those who are successful in managing both the "back-stage" work carried out according to subcultural norms and the "front-stage" appearances of abiding by departmental rules. Leonard (1980:67) adds that although police officers frequently complain about their agencies to their peers, any external complaint against or adverse publicity about their department often results in an increased sense of solidarity among all members of the department.

In his empirical study on police solidarity, Shernock (1988a) found the organizational loyalty of his respondents was not related to solidarity measured by either an index of "toleration toward the misconduct of and unequivocal trust toward fellow officers" or by the comparative value placed on loyalty to fellow officers. On the other hand, he found two separate measures of subordination to authority inversely related to solidarity. Obedience to superiors was negatively correlated with both measures of solidarity, and opposition to greater supervision was positively correlated with both measures of solidarity.

Although there has been some disagreement regarding solidarity between line officers and police administrators, there is virtually no such disagreement regarding solidarity between sworn officers and civilians within the police department. In his study of civilianization, Shernock (1988b) concluded that patrol officers were disingenuous when they remarked that "civilians can't be trusted to the same degree as sworn officers because they lack street and police background." The underlying problem of

trust would not seem to reflect civilians' response to the pressures of their work, given their significantly lower levels of reported stress in their work compared to that of sworn communications personnel. The problem of trust also would seem to be based only minimally on civilians' perspectives toward work values and police functions, inasmuch as sworn officers performing the same work as these civilians do not differ significantly from them on these values and functions. Instead, given the significant differences in expressions of solidarity and loyalty between civilians and sworn officers in both similar and complementary positions to these civilians, the underlying problem of trust appears to be the threat of civilization to "the indescribable bond between police officers."

Solidarity as Loyalty to Colleagues Rather Than Loyalty to the Community
Police solidarity has been most commonly seen as the consequence of a need for insulation from perceived dangers and rejection of the community. Even though actual violence occurs in probably fewer than 2–3 percent of police–civilian encounters, the highly unpredictable but potentially dangerous scene is always a part of police patrol. In order to deal with this constant threat of being in a potentially dangerous situation involving persons who cannot be identified in advance, patrol officers come to view everyone with suspicion. This omnipresent suspicion, in turn, serves to isolate police from the rest of society. This sense of isolation is reinforced by citizens' failure to help the police in fights. The police officer's lack of confidence in receiving help from the public in dangerous situations leads officers to believe that the only people who can be counted on in tight or problematic situations are other police officers and to equate the very essence of survival with the existence of an unquestioned support and loyalty among fellow officers. Since the successful officer needs the full support of his or her partners in order to act in dangerous situations, to violate the sanctity of solidarity by reporting a fellow officer leads one to be viewed as an unsafe officer.

Probably the factor in the external working environment most frequently cited as contributing to both police solidarity and a negative community orientation is the police perception of public hostility toward law enforcement and police officers. During the 1960s, Skolnick (1966:225) reported that the

Westville police he studied felt the most serious problem they had was not race relations but some form of public relations, lack of respect for police, lack of cooperation in enforcement of the law, and lack of understanding of the requirements of police work. In his interviews of police officers, Westley (1970:107) found that 73 percent of the officers interviewed believed that the public liked and supported the police. Similarly, Skolnick found that 70 percent of the 282 officers in the Westville police believed that the public rated the prestige of police work as either poor or only fair, while only 2 percent felt that the public rated it as excellent.

If this perception of hostility by the public toward the police is realistic, public hostility becomes an environmental precondition for police isolation and solidarity. On the other hand, if the perception is mistaken, it may indicate that the dynamic characteristic of the occupational subculture itself, which includes a sense of minority group status and solidarity, leads to the projection of hostility and, in turn, contributes to a negative community orientation.

Van Maanen (1978:119) states that "in general there is little to link patrolmen to the private citizen in terms of establishing a socially satisfying relationship," and that "patrolmen recognize accurately that few civilians are likely to return favors." The long and often irregular working hours, particularly as a result of shift schedules, do not allow police to develop off-duty friendships with nonpolice and thereby contribute to police isolation. Ferdinand (1980) found that until the age of forty much of a police officer's social life is spent within the confines of the police subculture. Police suspicion itself is reinforced by officers' work experiences where they are so frequently in an adversarial relationship with the public and where they are confronted daily by people who are weak or corrupt, as well as dangerous. Lundman (1980:85) notes further how the public stereotypes and depersonalizes the police, conferring on them a master status that leads them to feel a loss of identity and a sense of being stripped of their individuality.

In contrast, Walker (1992:226–27) states that police officers do not have an accurate perception of citizen attitudes and that survey data indicate citizens are supportive of police. He cites the 1975 National Crime Survey, which found that 84 percent of whites and 74 percent of blacks rated the police as good or average. Although Lundman (1980:83–84) recognizes some factual basis to the police perception of public hostility, he also finds that the police academy and the field training experience communicate a defensiveness theme to recruits, emphasizing distrust of persons and organizations outside the police department. The defensiveness theme is communicated by seasoned officers in their war stories and in their interpretations of both the community relations unit as merely functioning to deflect public criticism and of the internal inspection squad as merely functioning to protect the department from attempts to create a civilian review board. Thus recruits are presumably cautioned that "the only people to be trusted are other police officers."

As an outsider group, the patrol officer's occupational identity and subculture crystallize, wherein isolationism, secrecy, strong in-group loyalties, sacred symbols, common language, and a profound estrangement from the larger society intensify. Like other minorities, police officers not only tend to distrust members outside their in-group, but, moreover, tend to fraternize, both on and off the job, with members of their own minority group in order to avoid unpleasant interactions with civilians who view them only in terms of their police identity. Thus, isolated by the hostility and stereotyping they perceive, the police compensate by developing an intense solidarity for self-protection and moral support (Westley, 1970:111). The consequent unity enables them to tolerate isolation from, hostility of, and disapproval of citizens. Police loyalty then can be seen as assuaging real and imagined wrongs inflicted by a hostile public. As the police bonds to the public become weaker and their in-group activities and cohesiveness become greater, the police become more suspicious of and more polarized from the public, wherein the police-public relationship often turns from supportive to adversarial.

In his study on the relationship between police solidarity and community orientation, Shernock (1988a) found that solidarity as measured by an index of "toleration toward the misconduct of and unequivocal trust toward fellow officers was weakly related to less support for the service function and to the comparative value placed on respect for citizens, but not related to the comparative importance of the community relations function. On the other hand, when solidarity was measured as the comparative ranking of the value "loyalty to other police officers," it was found strongly related to a lower comparative value placed on respect for citizens and moderately related to less importance placed on the community relations function, but not related to less support for the service function when controlling for age and police experience and not related to defensiveness toward the media. Shernock also found that antagonism toward externally imposed control over police discretion was found to be highly correlated with the first measure of solidarity and weakly to moderately correlated with the second measure of solidarity. There appears to be a definite tendency for solidarity among police to increase as their level of antagonism toward externally imposed control over police discretion increases.

Solidarity as Loyalty to Colleagues Rather Than Loyalty to Ethical Principles

As a shield against the attacks of the outside world and against public criticism, the police place a high value on secrecy within their subculture. This code of secrecy among police officers, which is not confined to American policing alone, appears to be the strongest code adhered to within the police agency and, according to Goldstein (1977:165), stronger than similar tacit norms in the highly regarded professions of media and law. The perceived hostility toward the police fosters an "us versus them" attitude and a feeling that officers must stick together even to the point of lying about the misconduct of other officers. Secrecy is thus seen by Westley (1970:111) as solidarity insofar as it represents a common front against the outside world. Blumberg (1976:15) concurs, stating that "secrecy provides the glue that binds police solidarity." It maintains group identity and supports solidarity since it gives something in common to those who belong to the police subculture and differentiates those who do not. The sense of unity and loyalty that results from the demand for conformity to the values of the police subculture can someday be invoked by any officer to cover a serious mistake or to help him or her out in serious trouble.

Yet, as Westley (1970:112) significantly observes, secrecy does not apply to achievement but to mistakes, to plans, to illegal actions, to character defamation. Because the police subculture requires that its members be loyal and trustworthy, officers feel obligated to cover up a fellow officer's brutal acts, petty thefts, extor-

tionate behavior, abuses of police power, and other illegalities. "Blowing the whistle," "finking," and "squealing" are breaches of the code of silence and secrecy that represent the most heinous offense in the police world. It is an unwritten law in police departments that police officers must never testify against their fellow officers. Every officer tacitly agrees to uphold the secrecy code in order to claim solidarity rights to the unit or agency to which he or she belongs.

It is still uncertain, however, whether those conforming to the "code of silence" disapprove of the misconduct of fellow officers, and whether tolerance of that misconduct indicates how individual officers themselves can be expected to behave. The answer from a number of students of police misbehavior is that there is a connection between an officer's own values and behavior and his or her tolerance of the misconduct of fellow officers. Noting the effects of police subcultural expectations on recruits, Savitz (1970), in a longitudinal study at three different time periods, found that recruits not only became more permissive toward corrupt police conduct but approximated the values of experienced officers over time. More specifically, Barker (1978) has observed that those police officers who believe that certain forms of misconduct will not be reported are probably more likely to engage in such misconduct. Stoddard (1968) has gone even further, noting that "whether one can inform on his fellow officers is directly connected with the degree of his illegal involvement prior to the situation involving the unlawful act." Likewise, Muir (1977:67, 72) believes that once a police officer has violated a standard or rule, he or she is bound to remain silent regarding others' violations, even if they are more serious. It would thus appear, according to these critics, that tolerance toward the misconduct of other officers is more likely to be based either on a more complete socialization to the subcultural value systems or on complicity that develops as a result of one's own misconduct than on mere conformity to the "code of silence."

Conclusion

Some degree of solidarity may be very positive. Loyalty to fellow officers may bolster officers' self-esteem and confidence and may call forth a courageous reaction to threats to the interests of a member of a group to which one belongs. Nevertheless, attention has been focused on the police subcultural attribute of solidarity because of its perceived negative consequences for organizational control and change, public accountability, and ethical conduct. The particularistic value placed on loyalty to colleagues often comes into conflict with the bureaucratic values of police reform, and police solidarity itself often undermines supervisory control by police administrators. The isolation associated with police solidarity may undermine loyalty to the community insofar as it influences officers to develop attitudes that are essentially different from those of the wider society within which the police function and are charged to protect, and may create and sustain negative perceptions toward and hostile encounters with members of the public. Excessive loyalty to colleagues also has been seen as inconsistent with loyalty to the high ideals of the ethical canons of the profession, and, consequently, as militating against the obligation impelled by a regulatory code of ethics to identify and mete out professional sanctions against those fellow practitioners who have failed to perform their duties properly.

While police officers might continue to express solidarity with fellow officers by maintaining the "code of silence," there are some indications that there are changes in patterns of fraternization among police that have bolstered solidarity in the past. Blumberg states that regardless of what a number of dated studies may show, his experience in contact with a variety of police departments would lead him to believe that the new generation of police recruits has developed a more expanded friendship network than their predecessors and that the social isolation of police is somewhat exaggerated. There are also some indications, despite the need for more research, that the recruitment of women and African Americans has modified police solidarity. Martin found that the entrance of women into policing has diminished the traditional solidarity of the group because expressions of friendship that are acceptable between two males are problematic between officers of different sexes, and also because women officers do not share the same off-duty interests as male officers. While it might be assumed that increased educational qualifications and professionalization of the police might lead to conflicts between old-line officers, and thus at least temporarily weaken solidarity among police officers, the effects of these changes, as well as others, must be determined by future empirical research studies.

Stan Shernock

Bibliography

Alpert, Geoffrey, and Roger Dunham. *Policing Urban America.* 2d. ed. Prospect Heights, IL, 1992.

Barker, Thomas. "Peer Group Support for Police Occupational Deviance." *Criminology* 15 (1977).

———. "An Empirical Study on Police Deviance Other Than Corruption." *Journal of Police Science and Administration* 6 (1978): 264–72.

Bedrosian, Albert. "An Occupational Hazard—The Subculture of Police." *Journal of California Law Enforcement* 15 (1981): 95–101.

Blumberg, Abraham. "The Police and the Social System: Reflections and Prospects." In *The Ambivalent Force: Perspectives on the Police.* Eds. Abraham Blumberg and Arthur Niederhoffer. New York: Dryden Press, 1976.

Brown, Michael. *Working the Street: Police Discretion and the Dilemmas of Reform.* New York: Russell Sage, 1981.

Conser, James A. "A Literary Review of the Police Subculture: Its Characteristics, Impact, and Policy Implications. *Police Studies* 2 (1978): 46–54.

Ericson, Richard. "Rules for Police Deviance." In *Organizational Police Deviance: Its Structure and Control.* Ed. Clifford Shearing. Toronto: Butterworth, 1981.

Ferdinand, T.H. "Police Attitudes and Police Organization: Some Interdepartmental and Cross-Cultural Comparison." *Police Studies* 3 (1980): 46–60.

Gaines, Larry K., Victor E. Kappeler, and Joseph B. Vaughn. *Policing in America.* Cincinnatti: Anderson, 1994.

Goldstein, Herman. *Policing in Free Society.* Cambridge, MA: Ballinger, 1977.

Leonard, V.A. *Fundamentals of Law Enforcement: Problems and Issues.* St. Paul, MN: West, 1980.

Lester, David, and William Tom Brink. "Police Solidarity and Tolerance for Police Misbehavior." *Psychological Reports* 57 (1985): 326.

Lundman, Richard. *Police and Policing: An Introduction.* New York: Holt, Rinehart and Winston, 1980.

Manning, Peter. "Rules, Colleagues, and Situationally Justified Actions." In *Policing: A View From the Street.* Eds. Peter

Manning and John Van Maanen. New York: Random House, 1978.

Martin, Susan. *Breaking and Entering: Police Women on Patrol*. Berkeley: University of California Press, 1980.

Muir, William. *Police: Streetcorner Politicians*. Chicago: University of Chicago Press, 1977.

Reuss-Ianni, Elizabeth. *Two Cultures of Policing: Street Cops and Management Cops*. New Brunswick, NJ: Transaction Books, 1983.

Savitz, Leonard. "The Dimensions of Police Loyalty." *American Behavioral Scientist* (May–June, July–August 1970): 693–704.

Shearing, Clifford. "Deviance and Conformity in the Reproduction of Order." In *Organizational Police Deviance: Its Structure and Control*. Ed. Clifford Shearing. Toronto: Butterworth, 1981.

Shernock, Stan. "An Empirical Examination of the Relationship Between Police Solidarity and Community Orientation." *Journal of Police Science and Administration* 16 (1988a): 182–94.

———. "The Differential Significance of Sworn Status and Organizational Position in the Civilianization of the Police Communications Division." *Journal of Police Science and Administration* 16 (1988b): 288–302.

Skolnick, Jerome. *Justice Without Trial*. New York: John Wiley and Sons, 1966.

Stoddard, Ellwyn. "'The Informal Code' of Police Deviancy: A Group Approach to Blue Collar Crime." *Journal of Criminal Law, Criminology, and Police Science* 59 (1968): 201–13.

Van Maanen, John. "Kinsmen in Repose: Occupational Perspectives of Patrolmen." In *Policing: A View From the Street*. Eds. Peter Manning and John Van Maanen. New York: Random House, 1978.

Walker, Samuel. *The Police in America: An Introduction*. 2d ed. New York: McGraw-Hill, 1992.

Watkins, C. Ken. *Social Control*. London: Longman, 1975.

Westley, William. "Secrecy and the Police." *Social Forces* 34 (1956): 254–57.

———. *Violence and the Police*. Cambridge, MA: MIT Press, 1970.

Police Suicide

Policing has frequently been cited as a uniquely stressful occupation (Kroes, 1976; Somodevilla, 1978). Studies indicating that police officers have especially high rates of disorders, both physical and psychological, have been used to support this contention (Kroes, 1976; Singleton and Teahan, 1978). These disorders include digestive, respiratory, and cardiovascular problems as well as divorce and suicide.

Suicide, the most dramatic manifestation of the toll extracted by these disorders, is also one of the most difficult to study for a number of reasons. In our culture, where suicide is stigmatized and results in loss of life insurance for the survivors, there is a tendency for medical personnel to list a suspicious death as an accident if at all possible. The suicidal person may seek to spare his or her family and make the death seem accidental, for example, by driving a car into a tree or turning over a boat in deep water. Most experts estimate conservatively that the number of actual suicides is at least twice as high as the number reported. A study in Michigan estimated that two-thirds of police suicides had been reported as accidental or natural deaths, but one in Chicago claimed that "most cases of suicide were clearly apparent" (Wagner and Brzeczek, 1983).

Any consideration of suicide must also take into account unsuccessful attempts. These figures are even more difficult to obtain, but Gottesfeld (1979) estimates that about ten times as many people attempt suicide as succeed. There are no studies of attempted suicide among police.

Some people actively try to kill themselves, while others may try passive, indirect means. They take unnecessary risks, allow themselves to die by failing to attend to health problems, or abuse drugs and alcohol. Such behaviors, which Farberow (1980) has called indirect self-destruction, is seldom included in suicide statistics, and there is no hard evidence to indicate how common it is. Allen (1986:414), however, believes that

> for police officers, the likelihood of developing indirect self-destructive behavior is great. Risk-taking in its positive qualities has played a prominent role in the development of their identity as police officers especially in the form of mastering fear-provoking situations, and in facilitating ambitious achievement. In

short, risk-taking for the individual police officer has established the predominant motives of excitement and mastery.

Several studies seem to show that, compared with workers in other occupations, police officers are particularly prone to suicide. Indeed, some data show that officers are more likely to die by their own hands than to be killed by others (Kroes, 1976).

However, these studies are often so seriously flawed as to bring their conclusions into doubt. For example, although women are more likely than men to attempt suicide, men are more likely to succeed. The findings of a study that compares a primarily male occupation, such as policing, with a primarily female one, such as teaching, will be more likely to reflect sex differences than occupational ones. Other factors related to suicide rates, such as social class, may further complicate the ability to make meaningful comparisons. Police have more control of reporting than other occupations, and Lester (1987) has attributed the lack of recent research into police suicide to the desire of police forces to protect their images.

Because of their ready access to guns, police may be more likely to succeed at suicide than other groups. Wagner and Brzeczek (1983) and Aussant (1984) found that the majority of police officers who committed suicide used a firearm. Indeed, the common police slang for suicide is "to eat your gun."

Incidence of Police Suicide in Relation to Other Occupations

With these cautions in mind, we may examine the information that does exist. Using data gathered during periods ranging from the 1930s through the 1960s, several authors have found high rates of police suicide. These include Heiman (1975), who studied officers in Chicago, San Francisco, and New York; Niederhoffer (1967), who studied New York officers; Nelson and Smith (1970) for Wyoming; Richard and Fell (1975) for Tennessee; and Guralnick (1963) and Labovitz and Hagedorn (1971), who used United States census data.

These studies vary, however, in the ranking of the police suicide rate among the occupations studied. Guralnick found police to have the highest rates. Kroes reported that police committed suicide less frequently than laborers and lumbermen, but somewhat more frequently than physicians; Labovitz and Hagedorn said

that only self-employed manufacturing managers surpassed police. Richard and Fell found police third behind laborers and pressmen.

Rates also seem to vary tremendously from department to department. Despite Joseph Wambaugh's frequent inclusion of police suicides in his novels about the Los Angeles Police Department, Dash and Reiser (1978) argued that the LAPD had low suicide rates. Denver and London also are reported to have few police suicides (Terry 1981), and Heiman (1975) concludes that, in general, police suicides are less common in the Midwest and South than in the East and West.

Analysis of Suicides in Two Police Departments

Much of the work cited above studied incidence of suicide, with little attention paid to individual cases. Some relatively recent studies have concentrated on the specifics of confirmed cases. In Chicago Wagner and Brzeczek (1983) analyzed the twenty cases of suicide by police officers in the years 1977 to 1979; Aussant (1984) looked at twenty-seven cases in Quebec between 1973 and 1983.

These studies had several similar findings. Both found that firearms were used about 80 percent of the time. More than half the subjects had a history of medical and/or psychiatric problems, and many (44 percent in Chicago, 30 percent in Quebec) had a severe drinking problem.

The majority in both studies had had problems at work. In Chicago seven of the subjects had had serious disciplinary problems, and "in almost every case, there was a notable drop in the victim's performance ratings within a period of six months to two years before the suicide." Fourteen of the officers had been injured on duty at least once. In Quebec, work-related problems were the most common precursors to suicide. Most commonly listed were professional failure, problems in adapting to a transfer, feelings of uselessness and dissatisfaction with use, and not fitting into the police organization.

Prevention

Although all these studies give some idea of the conditions surrounding police suicide, they can only give circumstantial evidence about cause, and therefore about possible strategies for prevention. New evidence (Slater and Dupue, 1981) supports one of the earliest conjectures on the cause of suicide that it is related to a lack of group cohesiveness, which Durkheim called "anomie." Thus the greatest deterrent to suicide is a sense of personal involvement and identity with others. This work is particularly important, because many studies have revealed feelings of isolation in officers (Lewis, 1973; Niederhoffer, 1967).

Prevention is very difficult to measure. However, in hopes of decreasing stress-related disorders in their members, an increasing number of police departments are providing psychological services (see Reese and Goldstein, 1986). These services include monitoring officers' performance for warning signs of suicide and providing stress-management training and crisis-intervention counseling, including counseling after potentially traumatic incidents.

Although many claims have been made for the benefits of these programs (see Reese and Goldstein, 1986), there is little solid, unbiased evidence to substantiate these claims. Even the best may have serious flaws. Unfortunately, most of these programs focus on the individual officer; few address the organizational factors that have been considered the greatest stressors in policing (Ellison and Genz, 1983). There are also serious practical and ethical considerations when the person who is doing counseling also has the power to deprive the officer of his or her job. Officers often are loath to discuss problems with a person whom they see, quite rightly, as a representative of the department.

Summary
Many questions remain about the nature and causes of police suicide and the best strategies for prevention. However, there is a general agreement that it is a serious enough problem to warrant continued study and an increase in efforts at prevention. These efforts must be multifaceted. Of course they must include procedures for selecting the most appropriate individuals for the job and helping those later found to be in trouble. They must also work to provide optimal organizational conditions that help to ameliorate the impact of the extrinsic stressors of the occupations.

Katherine W. Ellison

Bibliography
Allen, S. "Suicide and Indirect Self-Destructive Behavior among Police." In *Psychological Services for Law Enforcement*. Eds. J. Reese and H. Goldstein. Washington, DC: Government Printing Office, 1986.

Aussant, G. "Police Suicide." *RCMP Gazette* 46 (1984): 14–21.

Danto, B. "Police Suicide." *Police Stress* 1 (1984): 32–36, 38, 40.

Dash, J., and M. Reiser. "Suicide among Police in Urban Law Enforcement Agencies." *Journal of Police Science and Administration* 6 (1978): 18–21.

Ellison, K., and J. Genz. *Stress and the Police Officer*. Springfield, IL: Charles C. Thomas, 1983.

Farberow, N. *The Many Faces of Suicide*. New York: McGraw-Hill, 1980.

Gottesfeld, H. *Abnormal Psychology: A Community Mental Health Perspective*. Chicago: Science Research Associates, 1979.

Guralnick, L. "Mortality by Occupation and Cause of Death among Men 20–64 Years of Age." *Vital Statistics: Special Report* 53 (1963).

Heiman, M. "The Police Suicide." *Journal of Police Science and Administration* 3 (1975): 267–73.

____. "Suicide Among Police." *American Journal of Psychiatry* 134 (1977): 1286–90.

Kroes, W. *Society's Victim—The Policeman*. Springfield, IL: Charles C. Thomas, 1976.

Labovitz, S., and S. Hagedorn. "An Analysis of Suicide Rates among Occupational Categories." *Sociological Inquiry* 41 (1971): 57–71.

Lester, David. *Suicide as a Learned Behavior*. Springfield, IL: Charles C. Thomas, 1987.

Lewis, R. "Toward an Understanding of Police Anomie." *Journal of Police Science and Administration* 1 (1973): 484–90.

Nelson, Z., and W. Smith. "The Law Enforcement Profession: An Incidence of High Suicide." *Omega* 1 (1970): 293–99.

Niederhoffer, A. *Behind the Shield*. Garden City, NY: Doubleday, 1967.

Reese, J., and H. Goldstein. *Psychological Services for Law Enforcement*. Washington, DC: Government Printing Office, 1986.

Richard, W., and R. Fell. "Health Factors in Police Job Stress." In *Job Stress and the Police Officer*. Eds. W. Kroes and J.

Hurrell. Washington, DC: Government Printing Office, 1975.

Singleton, G., and J. Teahan. "Effects of Job-Related Stress on the Physical and Psychological Adjustment of Police Officers." *Journal of Police Science and Administration* 6 (1978): 355–61.

Slater, J., and R. Dupue."The Contribution of Environmental Events and Social Support to Serious Suicide Attempts in Primary Depressive Disorder." *Journal of Abnormal Psychology* 90 (1981): 275–85.

Somodevilla, S. "The Psychologist's Role in the Police Department." *Police Chief* 45 (1978): 21–23.

Terry, W. "Police Stress: The Empirical Evidence." *Journal of Police Science and Administration* 9 (1981): 61–75.

Wagner, M., and R. Brzeczek. "Alcoholism and Suicide: A Fatal Connection." *FBI Law Enforcement Bulletin* 52 (1983): 7–15.

Policewomen

Within the last two decades, American society has experienced a social revolution of yet unmeasured sociocultural, political, and economic magnitude. The activism and egalitarianism engendered by the civil rights movement, the Berkeley free speech movement, the Vietnam War protests, and women's liberation have caused a questioning of the basic underpinnings of some of our fundamental belief structures, as well as the very legitimacy of some of our political and social institutions. One consequence of this revolutionary period was the redefining of a "woman's place" and the corresponding proper scope of her employment activities in certain nontraditional occupations. Women's entry into the sordid world of "street policing" as patrol officers has remained one of the more controversial deviations from traditional gender-prescribed occupational roles.

Women are a reality in today's workplace in both traditional and nontraditional occupational categories. Their presence in the marketplace can be attributed to a multiplicity of factors: (1) a new image–woman as a person; (2) frustration with the role of wife-companion; (3) new or expanded employment opportunities for women; (4) improved contraceptive methods; (5) economic downturns; and (6) the national commitment to eliminating prejudice and discrimination (Chafe, 1972; Friedan, 1963, 1981; Giele, 1978; Rothman, 1978). However, despite the fact that nearly 50 percent of the female population is currently in the workforce, women continue to be victimized by social and institutionalized discrimination and prejudice (Chafe, 1972; Friedan, 1981; Rothman, 1978). As a whole, women continue to earn significantly less than their male counterparts. Researchers in the early 1970s found that women workers earned only 57 percent of what their male counterparts did (Sawhill, 1973; Suter and Miller, 1973). After two decades that condition is finally improving. Women remain generally clustered in low-status, service-type occupations, where there is little opportunity for self-growth or professional advancement. Admittedly, though, women are becoming increasingly represented in the legal and medical professions, the boardrooms of private enterprise, and public-sector administration. What remains to be seen is whether this increased presence is truly attributable to social change or solely reflective of bureaucratic tokenism.

History

The past and present experience of women entering law enforcement is quite illustrative of the organizational dilemmas and social difficulties confronting women entering nontraditional occupational roles, as well as the legal remedies that have been utilized to facilitate their movement toward parity in the workplace. The appearance of women within the sphere of criminal justice was triggered by a series of social forces in the late 1800s and early 1900s. The surge toward industrialization, the expansion of the western frontier, the development of the steam engine, the extension of political democracy, and the development of new economic institutions all encouraged intellectual debate about traditional values and lifestyles (North, 1974; Rothman, 1971). This was an era of religious revivalism, utopian experiments, and an increased social consciousness and conscience. People banded together to encourage temperance; institute public education; develop humane management systems for the deviant, delinquent, and insane; and abolish slavery (Chafe, 1977; Ditizion, 1969; Giele, 1978; Platt, 1969; Rothman, 1971).

The experience of the female abolitionists as well as the host of social problems caused by rapid industrialization—the breakdown of the family, endemic poverty, child labor, and an increase in youth- and female-related crime—provided the catalyst for the appearance of a fledgling women's movement (Price and Gavin, 1982). The primary goal of the suffragettes, as they came to be called, was the attainment of the franchise and the elimination of some of the social ills besetting women and children. Enter the "child-saving movement," the precursor to our current juvenile justice system, which "was a reputable task for any woman who wanted to extend her housekeeping functions into the community without denying antifeminist stereotypes about women's nature and place" (Platt,1969:76). Women's entry into law enforcement in a custodial or social worker mode during this era constituted an official recognition of the problems associated with the supervision of women in custody (Bell, 1982; Higgins, 1961; Price and Gavin, 1982). Women were able to make these early inroads into policing due to the reformist zeal of the period, an acceptance of a limited and special role for women in law enforcement, and the efforts of a few dedicated progressive reformers (Horne, 1980).

In 1905 the Lewis and Clark Exposition in Portland, Oregon, saw the first documented appointment of a woman with police powers. Lola Baldwin was hired to deal with the problems of juveniles and young women. She was so successful in her efforts that a permanent Department of Public Safety for the Protection of Young Girls and Women was created (Price and Gavin, 1982). The first actual recognition of a regularly rated policewoman came in 1910 with the hiring of Alice Stebbin Wells by the Los Angeles Police Department. She had as her chief duties the supervision and enforcement of laws concerning women and juveniles at dance halls, skating rinks, movie theaters, and other places of public recreation (Bell, 1982; Horne, 1980). Alice Wells was also the driving force behind the first national policewomen's organization. In May 1915 the International Association of Policewomen was founded and Wells was installed as its first president (Price and Gavin, 1982).

During the next two decades, women expanded their presence within law enforcement, but they remained primarily in custodial, clerical, or counselor-type positions that were consistent with the prevailing perceptions of women's roles beyond the hearth. Unfortunately, with the advent of the Great Depression and the New Deal's focus on finding employ-

ment for men, women were once again relegated back to the home and childrearing.

The United States entry into World War II marked a major turning point for women, not only in law enforcement but in all areas of economic endeavor. With the men on the front lines and war supplies in acute demand, officials and organizations had little choice but to employ women in all sorts of positions that had never before been deemed appropriate for women. Despite their able performance in all aspects of employment during the war years, it was abundantly clear following the war that the American people were not ready to dispense with the sexual division of labor nor to accept the demise of traditional values (Chafe, 1972, 1977; Rothman, 1978). A woman was not to be thought of as an equal in the workplace, and many of the policewomen of this era preferred that they be considered unique and different—as social service workers rather than "cops" (Horne, 1980). Most of these women had bachelor's degrees or more and had a background in either social work, teaching, or nursing. The prevailing male attitude was that so long as the policewomen kept out of their way and stayed in the women's bureau under the supervision of a woman, they could be retained as a link between the police and social service agencies (Milton, 1975). "Real" police work, with its focus on punitive rather than preventative methodologies, would remain the province of male officers.

The early 1960s marked a period of profound social experimentation for the United States—the Kennedy administration's vision of Camelot set the stage for a nationwide quest for equality and brotherhood. In keeping with these philosophies, the civil rights movement and the women's movement fueled the demands of women in the law-enforcement community for equal opportunity and career advancement. Meanwhile, other developments within the greater social infrastructure were assailing the traditional methodologies and values of American peacekeeping.

During the early 1960s and early 1970s, the United States Supreme Court, under the direction of Chief Justice Earl Warren, initiated the "due process revolution," which compelled law enforcement to reexamine its traditional philosophy and modes of operation (Cox, 1968; O'Brien, 1974). Concurrent with these changes in criminal defendants' rights was a growing interest in police professionalism. Reformers like August Vollmer, O.W. Wilson, and Bruce Smith pioneered the concept of the professional law-enforcement agency with an emphasis on individual integrity, higher education, improved training, operational efficiency, and clean-cut lines of organization (Goldstein, 1977; Horne, 1980; Roberg, 1976). Lastly, there was finally a recognition of the "service" aspect of the law-enforcement function—that despite the prevailing mythologies and media depictions, only some 15 percent of an officer's time was actually spent "crime-fighting" (Goldstein, 1977). Thus the old "tough cop" mentality of punitive authoritarianism began a gradual transition to a more service-directed and humanistic orientation. It would have seemed, then, that with the increased movement of law-enforcement agencies toward professionalism, legalism, and a service model of policing, women police officers would have been a welcome presence. This was not the case, and it took a battery of legal mandates to secure women's rights to equal opportunity within American law-enforcement agencies.

In 1961 a New York policewoman sued for the right to compete in a promotional examination process. She was successful and four years later became the Big Apple's first female sergeant (Bell, 1982). The impetus for removing the artificial employment barriers for women came primarily from the federal government. In 1972, through the Equal Employment Opportunity Act, Congress amended Title VII of the 1964 Civil Rights Act to prohibit discrimination by public as well as private employers. The creation of the Equal Employment Opportunity Commission (EEOC) in 1968 as the executor of Title VII provisions provided the needed push to move women cops into more meaningful roles and out onto the street. Executive Orders 11246 and 11375 prohibited discrimination by federal agencies, contractors, and subcontractors on the basis of race, religion, color, national origin, and sex. Executive Order 11478 further prohibited discrimination in federal government employment on the basis of race, color, religion, sex, or national origin (Bell, 1982). The Equal Protection Clause of the Fourteenth Amendment has also provided authoritative rulings whereby for an employer to require a candidate to meet height or other requirements, the employer must show that the policy is necessary for the safety and efficiency of business operations so as to mitigate its discriminatory effect. In a similar vein several federal Supreme

Court decisions paved significant pathways for women desiring a career in law enforcement: (1) in November 1971, in *Reed v. Reed* (404 U.S. 71), the Court held that the Fourteenth Amendment prohibited discrimination on the basis of sex; and (2) the *Griggs v. Duke Power Company* (401 U.S. 424 [1971]) decision stated that any test for hiring "must measure the person for the job, and not the person in the abstract [and that] any educational requirement or test score must be shown to be significantly related to successful job performance" (Stuart, 1975:61). The Crime Control Act of 1973 brought with it the persuasive power of the federal purse. Any law-enforcement agency with fifty or more employees that received $25,000 or more in federal monies was required to implement women's equal opportunity programs or policies. Other judicial rulings have specifically addressed such issues as selective procedures and hiring (*Weeks v. Southern Bell Telephone and Telegraph*, 408 F. 2d 228 [1969], *Bowe v. Colgate-Palmolive*, 416 F. 2d 711 [1969]), and promotion (*Shriptzer v. Lang*, 234 NYS. 2d 285 [1962]). The collective impact of these legislative and judicial rulings has been the reduction of administrative and social barriers for women in professional career tracks (Bell, 1982).

Unwelcome Anomalies
Despite the foregoing legal remedies, Catherine Milton's historic 1972 study for the Police Foundation reported that women officers were being utilized almost exclusively in clerical or juvenile functions, were required to have additional education or meet other special entrance requirements, were regulated by hiring quotas, and were allowed to compete for promotions or openings only in the women's bureau. In 1974 women officers made up approximately 2 percent (2,859) of the nation's 166,000 sworn strength (Eisenberg, Kent, and Wall, 1973). Researchers found that a significant number of these individuals were assigned primarily to clerical or secretarial functions, even though women had been "on the street" since September 1968 in Indianapolis (Horne 1980). Today, women officers are found in all aspects of law enforcement and in all sizes and types of agencies at the federal, state, county, and municipal levels. Figures for 1983 suggest that women police officers constitute some 6 percent of the total sworn officer population at all levels of enforcement (Stinchcomb, 1984). If one holds this figure as a constant and interfaces it against

the U.S. Department of Justice's 1985 figure of 389,808 sworn peace officers, it appears that there are some 23,000 female officers nationwide. Generally, it is the larger urban police departments that have significantly higher representations of female officers within their ranks. For example, as of September 1986, 11 percent of the San Diego Police Department's total sworn officers were women. Yet despite women's increased nationwide patrol presence and satisfactory performance in the field, women officers remain unwelcome anomalies to a large percentage of their male peers (Martin, 1980; Niederhoffer, 1978).

In assessing the continued existence of this generalized feeling of resentment, skepticism, and/or hostility toward women officers by their male peers, several factors need to be identified and discussed. First of all, one must recognize the prevailing mythology that contemporary police work is largely dominated by tasks requiring physical strength and courage. Although easily refuted through empirical documentation, this belief remains entrenched in the historical beginnings of police work where the ability to "mix it up" was deemed to be of primary importance. Then one must look to the opportunity and organizational structure of most police organizations. The paramilitary hierarchical structure limits the vertical mobility available to individuals. This is further complicated by a lack of meaningful criteria by which to evaluate employees for management positions. Historically, it has been the "felony cop" who has rapidly advanced through the ranks, and many times the same skills that served these individuals so well on the streets contribute to their ineffectiveness and demise in a managerial role. The interrelationships of the foregoing factors contribute to and support the notion that police work is a man's work (Price and Gavin, 1982). Therefore, women who have entered the field of law enforcement have been handicapped by a set of historically conceived social stereotypes of women and the corresponding social mythologies about what has constituted a "woman's place." Women were seen as too emotional, too irrational, too illogical, and too lacking in objectivity to handle the day-to-day sordidness of street policing (Bell, 1982). Furthermore, women were perceived as less powerful, less well-trained in the use of force, and less willing to use it—in general, as being too soft. And last, women peace officers violated the cultural stereotypes that women

didn't carry guns, women didn't fight, women didn't arrest men, and women didn't earn substantial incomes (Charles, 1982; Dreifus, 1980).

Stereotypic thinking is beset by many hidden dangers, the first being that it does not result from a fresh appraisal of each phenomenon or situation, but rather from a routinized habit of judgment and expectation. Stereotypes are a type of attitude, one that can result in gross oversimplification of experience and can fortify the cognitive component of prejudice (Allport, 1935; Doob, 1935). Unfortunately, stereotypes have often been reinforced by seemingly self-fulfilling behavior on the part of the stereotyped population. This has significant implications for women police officers, particularly those in the predominantly smaller (fewer than fifty sworn officers) law-enforcement agencies. Current research has suggested that the number of women present in an organization is more critical than their socialization or gender per se (Kanter, 1976). Tokens, because of their scarcity, stand out and are thus likely to be evaluated more extremely and more likely to be cast in stereotypic roles. This does not happen to minority individuals in fully integrated groups and suggests that it is uniqueness rather than minority group status that affects the token (Wexler and Quinn, 1985). As has already been suggested, sexist stereotypes influence people's expectations so that they remember behaviors that agree with the stereotype. These sexual expectations of behavior become self-fulfilling prophecies (Brown, 1965). Individuals who feel or know they are deemed marginal employees are anxious and likely to react in an inappropriate or undesirable fashion. Thus the circle has been completed—there existed the sexist assumption that elicited the stereotypic behavior that in turn confirmed the original assumption.

In spite of a new array of liberal values, most men and women still tend to think of people who are intellectual, independent, and ambitious as masculine and people who are supportive, emotional, and interdependent as feminine (Broverman et al., 1970). These traditional definitions of feminine behavior encourage the development of interpersonal skills/social skills as a primary area of feminine "expertise." Bardwick (1971) concluded that "women are able to successfully compete in the masculine occupational world to the extent that they can bring 'masculine' personality qualities to the role. . . by temperament and socialization, relatively few women have these personality characteristics."

All too often the achievement-oriented woman has found herself typecast as pushy, aggressive, and unfeminine. Research conducted by Stein and Bailey (1975) contradicted this by finding that identification with a "masculine" role (competency, independence, intelligence) did not correlate with low femininity. A 1983 study of women police officers in a major southern California department similarly found that although women officers identified with the personality-trait cluster typically associated with males, they still viewed themselves as being highly feminine (Lord, 1986). A similar 1982 study of female police recruits reported that they appeared to add masculine traits (assertiveness, forcefulness, and risk-taking) into their personal style without compromising their femininity (Lester et al., 1982). This brings us back to the dilemma confronting both male and female officers in contemporary law-enforcement organizations.

Male Response

The traditional police attitude about the inherently masculine nature of law enforcement makes the prospect of a female partner or coworker particularly offensive to some male officers. The presence of women on uniformed patrol is viewed by these individuals as not only an unpleasant reality, but also as patently unwise. Both the male and female officer become caught up in a quixotic double-bind with the men demanding a tough, assertive, physical partner who will cover them at all costs. Stereotypically though, women are not supposed to fight, act aggressive, or protect a man. However, for the female officer to be accepted as effective and competent, she must behave less as a woman and more as a man, which can in turn threaten the male officer's sense of masculinity. Should the female officer behave as a "woman," she is perceived as inadequate and a safety hazard. This catch-22 situation that confronts women officers has some potentially very dangerous implications for both the health of the police organization and that of the individual officer.

Peace officer occupational-related stress has been recognized as a significant problem by law-enforcement administrators and researchers alike. Studies have indicated that police officers, as an occupational category, are highly at risk as a population because (1) they are more likely to develop or die from circulatory and digestive disorders than most occupational groups; and (2) they are 6.5 times more likely to commit suicide than their civilian counterparts (Richard and Fell, 1975). Additional research in the area has acknowledged that women and other minority officers are especially vulnerable to the psychological and physiological consequences of sustained exposure to job-related stress (Eisenberg, 1975; Martin, 1980; Wexler and Logan, 1983). The generally low acceptance factor for women in most aspects of the police function is further exacerbated by women's usual lack of access to the peer-group support structure of fellow male officers. Over the years, much has been written about the police personality and the tendency for officers to turn inward and form their own subculture with the ensuing "we-they" attitude framework (Skolnick, 1969, 1975; Van Maanen, 1978). Women officers' access to this peer-group support structure is critical in that it helps to mitigate the strain and consequences of occupational-related stress. The existence of the police subculture often functions as a stress-reduction mechanism since it provides individual officers a forum within which they can safely ventilate. Wexler and Logan's (1983) study of the occupational-related stress experiences of women officers in a major California metropolitan department suggested that women's greatest obstacle was in demonstrating that they could be effective officers without compromising their femininity. They concluded by saying:

> . . . the most significant stressors seem to be ones in which others were denying them as officers, as women, or both. It is psychologically a very threatening and uncomfortable situation when one's self-perception is substantially different from the perception of others. This is particularly the case when such fundamental identities are at stake as one's gender and profession.

So while they remain highly visible, much gossiped about, and feared as competitors, women officers will have to continue to perform their peacekeeping tasks with a minimum of social and organizational support. The confounding factor in this whole contradictory state of affairs, myths and stereotypes aside, is that the empirical evidence overwhelmingly supports the presence of women officers in uniformed patrol.

Empirical Evidence
In 1967 the President's Commission on Law Enforcement and the Administration of Justice unequivocally stated: "Policewomen can be an individual asset to modern law enforcement, and their present role should be broadened." However, despite all the positive rhetoric about their utility and job performance, women officers remain overrepresented in the supportive and clerical functions within the law-enforcement milieu; almost any discussion involving the effectiveness, competency, or appropriateness of women peace officers seems to revolve around the central issue of strength or brute force. Michael Charles (1982:203), in his rigorous evaluation of women's physical capabilities, argued that this focus on stature and brawn is self-defeating and

> while fitness is important to the health and safety of police officers, it is even more important that they have the ability to plan their actions and utilize their skills with maximum efficiency. . . . Developing alternative procedures . . . will allow officers to maximize their effectiveness and therefore accomplish tasks otherwise beyond their capacity.

What we do know about the physical capabilities of women affirms the argument that pound for pound, women are weaker than men and that when it comes to a display of brute strength, they cannot compete as effectively as their male counterparts. However, when it comes to muscular dexterity, flexibility, and endurance, women can do equally well, particularly if leverage is involved (Washington, 1975). An experimental program conducted at the New Jersey State Police Academy in 1980 showed that with the proper training, a progressive development orientation, and a supportive environment, women cadets could: (1) be made as physically fit as their male peers; (2) handle stress as effectively; and (3) be as willing as the male cadets to utilize force (Patterson, 1980; Townsey, 1982). Charles (1982) concluded his study on the physical aspects of women in the patrol function by saying that while not generally as physically strong as their male peers, women officers can attain a level of fitness that is well within the demands of contemporary street policing.

During the 1970s several major scientific studies were conducted to assess women officers' field performance using such indices as supervisory evaluations, patrol observation of policing style, citizens' opinions, arrest rates, sick time, complaints, and commendations. The studies were conducted for Washington, D.C.; New York City; Denver, Colorado; Newton, Massachusetts; Philadelphia, Pennsylvania; California State Highway Patrol; Pennsylvania State Police; and St. Louis County, Missouri. The overall conclusions of these eight profiles was that women were able to perform the police function as ably as men. There were identifiable differences in (1) the numbers of arrests made; (2) the style of policing and intervention; (3) shooting ability; (4) use of sick time; (5) sustained disciplinary actions; and (6) strength and agility (Townsey, 1982). Unfortunately, these same study results often contradicted one another, lacked rigorous scientific control, and contained a distinguishable element of sexual bias. For example, the findings from the two-year preliminary study of the Philadelphia experience were reported under the following headline in the June 20, 1978, edition of the *San Diego Union*: WOMEN COPS LESS EFFICIENT IN KEY DUTIES, STUDY CLAIMS:

1. Women were not as efficient in the following categories:
   (A) required more assistance to make arrests
   (B) were assaulted more often
   (C) had more vehicle collisions
   (D) sustained more injuries
2. Women were as efficient in the following types of calls:
   (A) handling an assist to another officer
   (B) handling a mentally deranged person
   (C) making an arrest
   (D) responding to an in-progress felony
   (E) handling a highway disturbance
   (F) transporting a prisoner
3. Women were more efficient in the following situations:
   (A) responding to a "man with a gun" call
   (B) handling a domestic disturbance
   (C) making a traffic stop

Other studies indicated that women used more restraint in using their firearms and managing family disturbances; did as well as men in driving, writing reports, and handling medical emergencies; were perceived as being more sensitive to citizens' needs; and were seen by the community as equally competent to men, although a male officer was still preferred in a violent fistfight confrontation (Glassman 1980; Kerber, Andes, and Mittler 1977). The 1973 Police Foundation Report found that the arrests made by female officers were equally likely to result in convictions, that they made fewer arrests, and that male and female officers were equally represented in the areas of police equipment collisions, injuries, and resignations. These researchers concluded that gender was not a bona fide occupational qualification for field assignment (Block, Anderson, and Gervais 1973). In a recent study of the attrition rates for male and female officers, it was found that female officers' turnover rate only slightly exceeded that of male officers (1.2 percent). This finding helps to discredit the commonly held perspective that women are less committed to their careers and less involved in their work than their male counterparts (Fry, 1983). This same body of research found that women deputies were less likely to retire, less likely to become disabled, and less likely to be fired or forced to resign in lieu of termination. Given the foregoing information, it seems reasonable to conclude that the policing styles and strategies of male and female officers are more alike than they are different. To persist in the current state of affairs is a no-win situation because consistently evaluating women "by the male standard distracts society's attention from the competence of male officers and reduces society's ability to identify and analyze problems or implement and formulate solutions" (Bell, 1982:120).

Succeeding in a Difficult Career Path

Despite the sometimes formidable resistance to their presence within law-enforcement organizations, women officers have remained upbeat not only about their current capabilities, but their futures as well. Some of this can be attributed to the type of women who choose law enforcement as a career path. As has been discussed earlier in this article, policewomen tend to incorporate more male personality traits into their repertoire of social behaviors. Other studies have suggested that women officers were more daring, changeable, outspoken, and restless, and that they reported more "masculine interests" and were more open to new experiences (Kennedy and Homant, 1981). O'Block and Abele (1980) and Price (1974) found that

female police executives, as a group, exhibited more strength in leadership-associated personality traits than did male police executives. Specifically, the women exhibited significantly more strength in the following areas: emotional independence, verbal aggressiveness, concern with appearance (self-confidence and self-image), and the seeking of social roles. The males scored significantly higher in only one trait, persistence.

Both men and women identify effective leadership with the masculine character/personality traits (Wexler and Quinn, 1985). This contributes to the difficulties women are confronted with when they assume leadership or supervisory roles within the police organization. This, coupled with the traditional perceptions of "police work as men's work," makes the notion of a female sergeant particularly offensive to some male officers. Therefore, it becomes incumbent on the police organization to reinforce the perception that a female officer's promotion to sergeant or above was based on her achievements (merit), not her sex (affirmative action).

> Such support will increase the women's security in their positions and their exhibition of leadership behaviors. It will also enhance the men's perceptions of the women sergeants; an individual cannot be an effective manager unless he or she is perceived as having power in the organization. (Wexler and Quinn, 1985:105)

Most of all, though, the police agency must demonstrate a philosophical commitment to the thorough integration of women within the formal and informal organizational structure. For to the extent that women are denied access to the informal channels of information gathering and conflict resolution, the more they are compelled to respond formally with its associated implications of lesser control/power (Wexler and Quinn, 1985).

The presence of women in what has long been an exclusively male occupation poses a multitude of individual and organizational conflicts. A generally accepted principle in organizational theory is that the workplace functions as a complex occupational and organizational entity that shapes workers' perceptions of self and others. The relationship between gender and organizational status suggests that those work roles assigned to women are seen as appropriate extensions of women's more diffuse social role of nurturance. These arrangements can act to reflect, magnify, or distort gender differences, which then confirm existing stereotypes and existing organizational norms. This has culminated in law-enforcement administrators' limited and often inaccurate appraisal of women officers' true potential and capabilities in the field. By way of illustration, in December 1986 the author responded to a survey from a major midwestern department that was evaluating "the various types of duty assignments appropriate for female officers."

Conclusion

The nature and scope of police work will continue to be a reality with which women must necessarily cope. Women officers must become comfortable not only with the physical aspects of the job, but also with the requisite "command presence" that directs rather than asks and that encourages aggressive assertiveness rather than passivity. Some women will not be able to meet this challenge. Police work is a very demanding profession, and not everyone is physically or psychologically equipped to handle its rigors and abuse, male or female. As Anthony Bouza (1978) noted, the fact that certain male officers have been found unsuitable for police work has not provided a compelling reason for discontinuing the use of men in police work. The same should hold true for women peace officers. However, the reality remains that law enforcement is still a traditionally male-dominated occupation in which men, through their psychological characteristics, socialization processes, and social acceptance, remain at a distinct advantage. The author remains optimistic that future sociocultural and organizational changes will promote the development of an androgynous police force where an individual officer's success is predicated on ability, rather than sexual physiology. Until such time, "female officers will be pressured to think like men, work like dogs, and act like ladies" (Martin, 1980:219).

Lesli Kay Lord

Bibliography

Allport, G.W. Handbook of *Social Psychology*. Ed. C. Murchison. Worcester, MA: Clark University Press, 1935.

Bardwick, J. *Psychology of Women*. New York: Harper & Row, 1971.

Bell, D.J. "Policewomen: Myths and Reality." *Journal of Police Science and Administration* 10(1) (1982): 112–20.

Block, P., D. Anderson, and P. Gervais. *Policewomen on Patrol*. Washington, DC: Police Foundation, 1973.

Bouza, A.V. *Police Administration*. New York: Pergamon Press, 1978.

Broverman, I.K., et al. "Sex Role Stereotypes and Clinical Judgments on Mental Health." *Journal of Consulting and Clinical Psychology* 34(1) (1970): 1–7.

Brown, R.W. *Social Psychology*. New York: Free Press, 1965.

Chafe, W.H. *The American Woman*. New York: Oxford University Press, 1972.

———. *Women and Equality*. New York: Oxford University Press, 1977.

Charles, Michael T. "Women in Policing: The Physical Aspect." *Journal of Police Science and Administration* 10(2) (June 1982): 194–205.

Cox, A. *The Warren Court*. Cambridge, MA: Harvard University Press, 1968.

Danto, B. "Police Stress." *Police Product News* 3(10 (1979): 56–60.

Ditizion, S. *Marriage, Morals and Sex in America*. New York: W.W. Norton, 1969.

Doob, L.W. *Propaganda, Its Psychology and Technique*. New York: Henry Holt, 1935.

Dreifus, C. "People Are Always Asking What I'm Trying to Prove." *Police Magazine* 3(2) (1980): 19–25.

Eisenberg, T., D.A. Kent, and C.R. Wall. *Police Personnel Practices in State and Local Governments*. Washington, DC: Police Foundation, 1973.

———. "Job Stress and the Police Officer: Identifying Stress Reduction Techniques." Paper presented to National Institute of Occupational Health and Safety Symposium, May 1975: Cincinnati, OH.

Friedan, B. *The Feminine Mystique*. New York: W.W. Norton, 1963.

———. *The Second Stage*. New York: Summit Books, 1981.

Fry, L. "A Preliminary Examination of the Factors Related to Turnover of Women in Law Enforcement." *Journal of Police Science and Administration* 11(2) (1983): 149–55.

Giele, J.Z. *Women and the Future*. New York: Free Press, 1978.

Glassman, C. "How Our Lady Cops are Doing." In *Parade Magazine, San Diego Union* (July 27, 1980): 4.

Goldstein, H. *Policing a Free Society*. Cambridge, MA: Ballinger, 1977.

Higgins, L. *Policewoman's Manual*. Springfield, IL: Charles C. Thomas, 1961.

Horne, P. *Women in Law Enforcement*. Springfield, IL: Charles C. Thomas, 1980.

Kanter, R.M. "Why Bosses Turn Bitchy." *Psychology Today* 9 (1976): 56–57, 59, 88–89, 91.

Kennedy, D.B., and R.J. Homant. "Nontraditional Role Assumption and the Personality of the Policewoman." *Journal of Police Science and Administration* 9(3) (1981): 346–55.

Kerber, K., S.M. Andes, and M.B. Mittler. "Citizen Attitudes Regarding Competence of Female Police Officers." *Journal of Police Science and Administration* 5(1) (1977): 337–40.

Kroes, W., B. Margolis, and J. Hurrell. "Job Stress in Policemen." *Journal of Police Science and Administration* 2(4) (1974): 301–07.

Lester, D., et al. "The Personality and Attitudes of Female Police Officers: Needs, Androgyny and Attitudes toward Rape." *Journal of Police Science and Administration* 10(3) (1982): 357–60.

Lord, L.K. "A Comparison of Male and Female Peace Officers' Stereotypic Perceptions of Women and Women Peace Officers." *Journal of Police Science and Administration* 14(2) (1986): 83–97.

Martin, S.E. *Breaking and Entering*. Berkeley: University of California Press, 1980.

Milton, C. *Women in Policing*. Washington, DC: Police Foundation, 1972.

———. "Women in Policing." In *Police and Law Enforcement, 1973–1974*. New York: AMS Press, 1975.

Niederhoffer, A., and E. Niederhoffer. *The Police Family*. Lexington, MA: Lexington, 1978.

North, D.C. *Growth and Welfare on the American Past*. Englewood Cliffs, NJ: Prentice-Hall, 1974.

O'Block, R.L., and V.L. Abele. "Emerging Role of the Female Detective." *Police Chief* 47(5) (1980): 54–56.

O'Brien, C.A. "Dilemmas of Criminal Justice in a Democratic Society." In *Judicial Crimes: The Supreme Court in a Changing America*. Ed. Richard Funston. New York: John Wiley and Sons, 1974.

Patterson, M.J. "Training Tailored for Women." *Police Magazine* 3(5) (1980): 22–26.

Platt, A. *The Child Savers*. Chicago: University of Chicago Press, 1969.

Price, B.R. "A Study of Leadership Strength of Female Police Executives." *Journal of Police Science and Administration* 2(2) (1974): 219–26.

———, and S. Gavin. "A Century of Women in Policing." In *The Criminal Justice System and Women*. Eds. B.R. Price and N.J. Skoloff. New York: Clark Boardman, 1982.

Reiser, M. "Some Organizational Stresses on Policemen." *Journal of Police Science and Administration* 2(2) (1974): 156–59.

Richard, W.C., and R.D. Fell. "Health Factors in Police Job Stress." Paper presented to National Institute of Occupational Health and Safety Symposium, May 1975, Cincinnati, OH.

Roberg, R. *The Changing Police Role*. San Jose, CA: Justice Systems Development, 1976.

Rothman, D.G. *The Discovery of the Asylum*. Boston: Little, Brown, 1971.

Rothman, S.M. *Women's Proper Place*. New York: Basic Books, 1978.

Sawhill, I.V. "The Economics of Discrimination against Women: Some New Findings." *Journal of Human Resources* 8(3) (1973): 383–95.

Skolnick, J.H. *Politics of Protest*. New York: Simon and Schuster, 1969.

———. "Why Police Behave the Way They Do." In *Police in America*. Eds. J.H. Skolnick and T.C. Gray. Boston: Educational Associates, 1975.

Stein, A.H., and M.M. Bailey. "The Socialization of Achievement Motives in Females." In *Women and Achievement*. Eds. M.S. Mednick, S.S. Tangri, and L.W. Hoffman. New York: John Wiley and Sons, 1975.

Stinchcomb, J.D. *Opportunities in Law Enforcement and Criminal Justice*. Lincolnwood, IL: VGM Career Horizons, 1984.

Stuart, C.G. "Changing Status of Women in Police Professions." *Police Chief* 42(4) (1975): 61.

P

Suter, L.E., and H. Miller. "Income Differences between Men and Career Women." *American Journal of Sociology* 78(4) (1973): 962–74.

Townsey, R.D. "Female Patrol Officers: A Review of the Physical Capability Issue." In *The Criminal Justice System and Women*. Eds. B.R. Price and N.J. Skoloff. New York: Clark Boardman, 1982.

Van Maanen, J. "The Asshole." In *Policing: A View from the Street*. Eds. P.K. Manning and J. Van Maanen. Santa Monica, CA: Goodyear, 1978.

Washington, B. "Stress Reduction Techniques for the Female Officer." Paper presented to National Institute of Occupational Health and Safety Symposium, May 1975, Cincinnati, OH.

Wexler, J.G., and D.D. Logan. "Sources of Stress among Women Peace Officers." *Journal of Police Science and Administration* 11(1) (1983): 46–53.

Wexler, J.G., and V. Quinn. "Considerations in the Training and Development of Women Sergeants." *Journal of Police Science and Administration* 13(2) (1985): 98–105.

Police Workload

In the face of the commonsensical notion that excessive workload on police patrol officers causes them to experience stress, recent research (Stotland and Pendleton, 1989) has indicated that the effect that workload has on police patrol officers is not straightforward and simple. Instead, the heaviness of the workload determines which of a number of possible causes of stress will actually affect these officers. When the workload is heavy, one set of causes is effective; when the workload is light, another set of causes is effective. Workload in this context refers to the amount of felony crime generally occurring in a given officer's precinct, divided by the number of officers assigned to that precinct.

When the police workload is light, the major source of stress is rejection or derogation by sergeants. This derogation can be shown in poor evaluations, criticism, unwillingness to support an officer in "official trouble," etc. This leads to a drop, or at best prevents a rise, in the low workload officers' self-esteem. Consequently, the officers have poor interpersonal relations with their peers and the public. This globally experienced syndrome leads to increased sick days, high anxiety both on and off the job, problems with alcohol, a variety of physical ailments, and psychological difficulties. The key to low workload police officers' well-being thus is positive relationships with others, especially their sergeants. Furthermore, these officers are more accepting of departmental rules and more interested in promotions than are high workload officers. In short, these officers are oriented to their departments, as well as to their sergeants.

On the other hand, high workload police officers do not suffer stress as a consequence of derogation by their sergeants or poor interpersonal relationships with their peers or the public. Their stress stems from a high number of difficult events in their work, such as a shooting, a racial incident, being sued or investigated, or from a high number of changes in their general life situation which demand readjustment. A high number of such difficult police events or life changes leads to more sick days, anxiety, physical complaints, drinking problems, automobile accidents, and citizen complaints. These high workload officers' vulnerability to stress from difficult police events is consistent with their relatively greater focus on traditional police work than on their departments. They are less interested in promotions and have greater disdain for departmental rules and policies.

The differences between the high and low workload police officers apparently lies in the greater opportunity that the former have to evaluate their abilities as traditional crime-fighting police officers. They do not need to turn to their sergeants, peers, or departments as sources of evaluation, as do the low workload officers. The high workload officers have the day-to-day activities of policing as the more or less objective measures of professional competence. Without as much opportunity to gauge their abilities by such activities, the low workload officers turn to the implicit and explicit evaluations made by others in their squads and in the department.

Another apparent reason for the differences between the high and low workload officers is that the latter work closer to the ceilings of their capacities and therefore have less reserve energy to cope with additional demands placed on them. The low workload officers do not appear to be working continuously close to the top of their capacities and therefore have more reserves.

the police as crime-fighters instead of community servants. It was during this era that J. Edgar Hoover assumed control of the Federal Bureau of Investigation and Harry J. Anslinger served as commissioner of the Bureau of Narcotics. History suggests that as "moral entrepreneurs" these and other individuals influenced the perception of the police role as being primarily one of law enforcement.

An analysis of the police reform movement shows that police professionalism, in the truest sense of the term, has been—and will probably continue to be—unattainable. It is worth noting that the movement—in its attempt to create independence from partisan politics—served to isolate the police from the community. Other factors have contributed to police independence, such as the passage of the Political Activities Act of 1939, more commonly known as the Hatch Act. This act prohibited civil service employees from active participation in elections and protected them from reprisal for failing to support a candidate.

The isolation of the police was seriously challenged during the 1960s and 1970s. As a result of racial and student confrontations with the police, these and other groups demanded access to the decision-making process in order to make the police more accountable for their actions. The prevailing assumptions that the police existed primarily to enforce the law made it difficult, if not impossible, for these groups to have any input into police policy formulation.

Yet some change did occur in that the perception of the police as crime-fighters was modified to include community-service and order-maintenance functions. Such change was supported by academic research showing, for example, that the police actually spend approximately 20 percent of their time enforcing the law and that high police visibility does not significantly affect the rates of certain crimes.

Thus some inroads have been made by citizens in their effort to influence police policies. As citizens have become increasingly aware that the police mandate extends beyond the crime prevention/crime repression aspect, accountability has, to an extent, been forced upward in the police hierarchy. This has been accomplished as a result of citizen interest, court decisions (e.g., *Miranda*, *Mapp*, *Wade*), and the imposition of liability via Title 42 Section 1983 of the U.S. Code.

Conclusions

The struggle for control of the police is far from being decided in one direction or the other. The police still demand independence from outside influences in carrying out their mandate. Special-interest groups, from downtown business associations to national civil rights groups, still seek to gain control of or influence over police policies.

Unquestionably, one outcome of this ongoing evolution has been the recruitment, training, and retention of better qualified police officers. The original goal of police accountability has not, however, been achieved.

Herman Goldstein has commented that part of the problem lies with misguided efforts on the part of the community. He argues that the attempt to make the police responsive to the demands of the community is simply an exercise in majority control. If a police agency is to be viable in a democratic society, then it must be responsive to legitimate demands from minority segments of the population as well. Thus the police should not always be responsive to community or special-interest demands but must always be accountable to the community for their actions.

Michael B. Blankenship

Bibliography

Bittner, E. *The Functions of the Police in Modern Society*. Cambridge, MA: Oelgeschlager, Gunn, & Hain, 1980.

del Carmen, R.V. *Criminal Procedure for Law Enforcement Personnel*. Monterey, CA: Brooks/Cole, 1987.

Goldstein, H. *Policing a Free Society*. Cambridge, MA: Ballinger, 1977.

Johnson, D.R. *American Law Enforcement: A History*. Arlington Heights, IL: Forum, 1981.

Klockers, C.B. *The Idea of Police*. Beverly Hills, CA: Sage, 1985.

Manning, P.K. "The Police: Mandate, Strategies, and Appearances." In *Policing: A View from the Street*. Eds. P.K. Manning and J.V. Maanen. New York: Random House, 1978. Pp. 1–31.

Monkkonen, E.H. *Police in Urban America, 1860–1920*. Cambridge, England: Cambridge University Press, 1981.

Reiss, A.J. *The Police and the Public*. New Haven, CT: Yale University Press, 1971.

Wilson, J.W. *Varieties of Police Behavior*. New York: Atheneum, 1968/1971.

Polygraph

The polygraph has been used by the police in the investigation of serious crimes since at least the early 1900s. Historical development in the field can be traced along two lines, one involving changes in instrumentation and the other changes in testing techniques.

Polygraph Instrumentation

Historically, the most dramatic attempts at "lie detection" relied upon ordeals such as placing hot irons on the tongue of suspects—who would presumably be protected by their innocence or burned by their guilt. It was not until 1895, when Cesare Lombroso, an Italian criminologist, and a student of his named Mosso, used the hydrosphygmograph and the "scientific cradle," which revealed that objective measurement of physiological changes were associated with the detection of deception. Following Lombroso and Mosso, H. Munsterberg and others noted the effect of lying on breathing, cardiovascular activity, involuntary movements, and the galvanic skin response (GSR)—changes in electrical resistance in the skin. In 1917 W. Marston reported success at detecting deception with discontinuous measurements of blood pressure. In 1921 J. Larson, under the guidance of August Vollmer, a pioneer in applying science to police work, devised an instrument for making continuous recordings of both blood pressure and breathing. In 1930 L. Keeler, generally credited with developing the prototype of the present-day polygraph, refined Larson's apparatus by adding a device for measuring GSR.

Although modern polygraphs represent considerable technical improvements over earlier devices, it is true, nevertheless, that the physiological measures incorporated by Keeler are essentially those used today. The modern polygraph is a briefcase-sized device that, in most field settings, records changes in skin resistance (GSR) by means of two electrodes attached to the fingertips. A standard medical blood pressure cuff, which is partially inflated during testing, is used to record changes in relative blood pressure and pulse rate. Finally, changes in breathing activity are recorded by hollow, corrugated rubber tubes, one placed around the abdomen and one around the upper thorax, which expand and contract with chest cavity movement during inspiration and expiration. Activity in each of these physiological measurements is monitored by either electronic or mechanical means and is permanently recorded on a paper chart by a pen-and-ink system.

Testing Techniques

Although commonly referred to as a "lie detector," neither the polygraph nor any other device available today is capable of detecting when a lie is told. Moreover, there is no known physiological response that is unique to lying. Lie detection, therefore, is in fact an inferential process in which "lying" is inferred from comparisons of physiological responses to questions that are asked during polygraph testing. It is for this reason that polygraph techniques—that is, the way in which testing is administered and polygraphic data are interpreted—have shown more dramatic changes than the polygraph instrument itself.

There are two major testing techniques in use today, the relevant/irrelevant (R/I) and the control question technique (CQT). A third format, the so-called peak-of-tension (POT) test, is infrequently encountered in the field.

The R/I technique was widely used by early practitioners and, although in less favor today, it is still the procedure of choice among some schools of examiners. This technique consists of a pretest interview and a polygraphic testing. During the interview the examiner discusses with the subject background information relative to the investigation at hand and attempts to become familiar with the subject's language and personal history in order to ensure that the test questions, which may or may not be reviewed before testing, are properly worded.

In its simplest form polygraph testing in the R/I technique consists of the asking of a series of relevant questions interspersed among irrelevant questions. Relevant questions are those pertinent to the crime at hand (e.g., "Did you shoot John Doe?"); irrelevant questions are not crime related (e.g., "Are you over eighteen years of age?"). The series of test questions may be repeated two or more times during the testing.

An assumption implicit in the R/I technique is that truthful persons will not react differentially to a great degree to relevant and irrelevant questions, while people lying will. This assumption has been seriously challenged and is the reason that the preferred technique of most examiners today is the CQT.

The CQT was first developed in 1950 by John E. Reid. Today there are numerous variations of the CQT, all similar in principle.

The CQT, like R/I testing, consists of a pretest interview and polygraph testing. During the pretest interview the examiner discusses with the subject the purpose of the examination and the nature of the polygraph instrument. Also, the exact test questions are prepared and reviewed with the subject. The question list consists of irrelevant, relevant, and control questions, although other types of questions (e.g., "guilt complex") may also be asked. The relevant and irrelevant questions are similar to those asked during R/I testing. Control questions deal with matters similar to, but of presumed lesser significance than, the offense under investigation. The examiner seeks to frame these questions so that the subject will, in all probability, lie in answer to them or will be concerned about the accuracy of the answer. Examples of control questions in a theft case would be: "Did you ever steal anything?" and "Before you were eighteen years old, did you steal anything?"

In the CQT, the question list, typically not more than ten or eleven questions, is read to the subject while the polygraph instrument monitors the subject's physiological activity. There are two or more repetitions of the question list during an examination. Simply stated, in the CQT more consistent and greater physiological responses to relevant questions than to control questions indicate lying on the relevant issues: conversely, consistently greater physiological responses to control than to relevant questions indicate truthfulness in the matter under investigation.

The third type of testing format, infrequently encountered in field settings, is the POT test. Although there is general agreement that the POT format is of great value, its use is limited to situations in which specific details of a criminal offense are not made available to the suspect. A POT test consists of the asking of a stem question and multiple options. The stem might be: "Do you know if John Doe was killed with a _____?" The options might be the names of various weapons, e.g., gun, knife, club, etc., including the actual one used. The guilty person, recognizing the correct option, would be expected to show a greater physiological response to that one than to the others whereas an innocent person would not. Typically, a series of three or more such multiple choice tests would be carried out, usually after initial testing by either the R/I or CQT procedures, provided that sufficient detailed information about the offense is known.

Uses of Polygraph Testing

In police work there are two major uses of polygraph testing. The first of these is referred to as specific issue testing. Here polygraph testing is used to investigate whether a particular person is responsible for or involved in the commission of a particular offense. Because polygraph testing has been shown to be extremely valuable in this regard, almost every large- and medium-sized police agency employs one or more full-time polygraph examiners. In addition to helping the police to identify criminal offenders, it is also well established that polygraph testing often exonerates persons against whom the circumstantial evidence appears quite incriminating. Thus, it is claimed that there are great savings of investigative time and effort due to the use of polygraph examinations.

The second use of polygraph testing is in preemployment screening of applicants for police work. The use of the polygraph for this purpose is very controversial and is, in fact, illegal in some jurisdictions. When used, however, preemployment polygraph testing helps to substantiate information collected during traditional background investigations and to uncover information not otherwise available. A number of studies support the effectiveness of the polygraph for these purposes.

Accuracy of Polygraph Testing

Field practitioners maintain that their accuracy is between 90 percent and 95 percent; errors tend to be of the false negative type rather than false positive. (A false positive error is made when a truthful person is found to be "deceptive" during polygraph testing. A false negative error occurs when a person who lied is reported to be "truthful.") A great deal of controversy surrounds these claims because the scientific research is unclear.

Much of the relatively small body of research that addresses the accuracy of polygraph testing has been carried out in controlled laboratory studies. Even though these studies show that polygraph procedures may yield an accuracy of about 90 percent, the ability to generalize on the basis of these studies to field settings is problematic. On the other hand, good field-based research is quite limited and very controversial.

Because there are differing views in the scientific community about the nature and value of the research evidence, it is unlikely that the controversy over accuracy will be settled soon. In addition to this general concern, there is evidence suggesting that polygraph testing may be more accurate in certain kinds of field situations (criminal investigations) than in others and may vary somewhat with the technique used to carry out the testing. In spite of these problems, many observers believe that the accuracy of polygraph testing compares favorably with that of other commonly used investigative methods.

Training and Regulation of Examiners

There are more than thirty private and governmental schools in the United States and other countries, including Canada, Japan, Israel, and Korea, that serve as training facilities for polygraph examiners. Admission requirements and the nature and quality of the training vary considerably since there is not mandatory, uniform regulation of the field. The American Polygraph Association (APA), the major professional organization in the United States, accredits training facilities but only those choosing membership in the APA.

APA-accredited schools must be at least seven weeks in length and devote a specified minimum number of hours of instruction in topics such as psychology, physiology, legal issues, ethics, and polygraph techniques. In addition, a supervised internship is required after the completion of academic instruction. In the most rigorous schools, applicants must hold a bachelor's degree in an appropriate area, undergo a personal interview, and pass written psychological tests and a polygraph screening examination.

About forty states now regulate the activity of polygraph examiners. In some of these, mandatory licensure requirements are set out by statute. In others, the kinds of situations in which polygraph testing may be used are proscribed; preemployment testing, for example, may be prohibited in private sector employment but not in public employment. The lack of uniform regulation, particularly with respect to licensure requirements, is seen by many as a serious problem in the field.

Legal Status of Polygraph Examinations

The commonly held belief that polygraph examination results are not admitted into courtroom proceedings is not true. The initial judicial decision of *Frye v. U.S.* (293 F. 1013 [1923]) did exclude polygraph evidence. That decision, however, is not followed in a number of jurisdictions. Some permit polygraph evidence even over the objection of counsel. In many others polygraph results are admitted by stipulation. At the federal level there is no single standard governing admissibility; some courts have permitted polygraph evidence while others have denied it.

Court rulings on the admissibility of polygraph results generally have little effect on other uses in the administration of justice. It is very common, for instance, for prosecutors to use polygraph results to decide whether and which charges to file. It is also common for some judges to use polygraph results in sentencing decisions. In addition, defense attorneys rely on polygraph testing to plan their defense and to negotiate pleas. Thus, the polygraph plays an important role in the justice system quite apart from its use by the police.

Frank Horvath

Bibliography

Ansley, N., and J. Pumphrey. *Justice and the Polygraph: A Collection of Cases.* Severna Park, MD: American Polygraph Association, 1985.

Barland, G., and D. Raskin. *Validity and Reliability of Polygraph Examinations of Criminal Suspects.* (Contract No. 75–N1–99–0001) Washington, DC: National Institute of Justice, Department of Justice, 1976.

Horvath, F. "The Police Candidate Polygraph Examination: Considerations for the Police Administrator." *Police* 16 (1972): 33–39.

———. "Polygraphy: Some Comments on the State of the Art." *Polygraph* 9 (1980): 34–41.

———. "Detecting Deception in Eyewitness Cases: Problems and Prospects in the Use of the Polygraph." In *Eyewitness Testimony: Psychological Perspectives.* Eds. G. Wells and B. Loftus. New York: Cambridge University Press, 1984. 214–55.

———. "Job Screening." *Society* 22 (1985): 43–46.

Larson, J. *Lying and Its Detection.* Chicago: University of Chicago Press, 1932.

Lykken, D. *A Tremor in the Blood.* New York: McGraw-Hill, 1981.

Trovillo, P. "A History of Lie Detection." *Journal of Criminal Law, Criminology,* and *Police Science* 29 (1939): 848–81.

Widacki, J., and F. Horvath. "An Experimental Investigation of the Relative Validity and Utility of the Polygraph Technique and Three Other Common Methods of Criminal Identification." *Journal of Forensic Sciences* 23 (1978): 596–601.

Posse Comitatus

According to *Black's Law Dictionary* (1979), the "posse comitatus" (power of the county), a venerable English and American institution, consists of the entire population of a county over fifteen years of age, which the sheriff may deputize to assist in keeping the peace or capturing felons. "Posse Comitatus" also has been adopted as the name of a group of American tax protestors.

The current Federal Posse Comitatus Act (18 U.S.C. section 1385 [1988]), prohibits anyone from "willfully us[ing] any part of the Army or the Air Force as a posse comitatus or otherwise to execute the laws" absent express constitutional or statutory authorization.

The antecedents of the act go back to the London riots of 1780, when Lord Chief Justice Mansfield fashioned a new doctrine to meet the contingency. Working without the aid of precedent because the mob had burned his law library along with his house, Lord Mansfield authorized deputizing soldiers as members of a posse comitatus to assist constables in enforcing the Riot Act. This "new doctrine" of posse comitatus theory rapidly took root in American soil. The Judiciary Act of 1789 empowered U.S. marshals to "command all necessary assistance" to help them enforce the laws and subsequent Congresses during the early presidential administrations further responded by passing laws authorizing the use of troops to suppress rebellions and enforce the laws (Engdahl, 1971:31–49). Some later representative mid-nineteenth-century uses of posse comitatus theory include suppression of South Carolina's nullification ordinances by President Jackson; enforcement of the Fugitive Slave Act during the 1850s; President Lincoln's April 15, 1861, call for 75,000 volunteers to meet the threat of southern secession; and, after the Civil War, the maintenance of order during Reconstruction by Presidents Johnson and Grant (Furman, 1960:87–95).

During the 1850s Republicans advocated a national statute to prohibit the use of the army to return fugitive slaves to their masters. Two of the more egregious examples of this were the Anthony Burns affair in Boston and the suppression of free soilers in Kansas Territory (Nevins, 1947:150–54, 412–50). By the 1870s the Democrats came to champion a federal posse comitatus act in order to end Reconstruction.

By 1874 the Democrats achieved their first postbellum majority in the House and by 1878 were strong enough to pass the first Posse Comitatus Act, which became law on June 18, 1878, over President Hayes's signature. As originally enacted, the statute made it a misdemeanor punishable by a fine of up to $10,000 or imprisonment of up to two years or both to use the army to enforce the civil laws. Under current rules the potential term of imprisonment makes it a felony.

Notwithstanding the arguments put forward by Lorence (1940) and other commentators, the act has been so generally accepted and observed that its constitutionality has never been seriously challenged. Apparently no one has ever been convicted of violating it. In fact the act was so rarely employed during the first ninety years of its existence that, except for a handful of early cases, it was all but forgotten when it was discovered by defense lawyers as a potential shield (a new exclusionary rule) to avoid prosecution for violation of other federal laws ("The Posse Comitatus Act," 1976:716–30).

The act has been amended three times; the unruly Alaska Territory was exempted from it in 1900. Although the act applied to the air force as a spin off from the army, the air force was formally included in it in 1956 as the act was moved from Title 10 to Title 18. The Alaska exception was removed in 1959 on that state's admission to the Union. It is arguable whether any constitutional exemptions to the act exist (House of Representatives, 1981:6, n. 3). Corwin (1974:149) argues that Article II, Section 3, authorizes by implication the president to do what is necessary and not forbidden by statute to protect those great interests confided in the national government by the Constitution and thereby ensure that the laws are faithfully executed. Among numerous recognized statutory exceptions are: (1) actions in furtherance of a military or foreign affairs purpose; (2) Department of Defense inspector general audits and investigations; (3) actions to protect federal personnel, property, or functions; (4) actions taken pursuant to specific statutory authority to act in the event of insurgency, domestic violence, rebellion, or a conspiracy that cripples the government; and (5) actions taken under other express statutory authority. A complete list of current exceptions is contained in Department of Defense Directive 5525.5.

As stated above the act emerged from relative obscurity in the early 1970s, not as a criminal statute to punish the guilty but as a defendant's shield to avoid prosecution. While federal judges have reflected the general temper of the times, for the most part they have not responded favorably to defense arguments to create a new basis to invoke the exclusionary rule.

Doss (1989) divides the Posse Comitatus Act cases chronologically among three categories: early (pre-1971), middle (1971–1981), and recent (post-1981). While the early cases largely treated jurisdictional issues, the two later periods are dominated by a mixture of the "Wounded Knee" cases and "drug" cases, with the former figuring most significantly during the middle period and the latter throughout both periods.

The Wounded Knee cases created three separate tests to determine whether the military has executed the laws: the "pervasive use" test (*United States v. Jaramillo*, 380 F.Supp. 1375, D.Neb [1974] *appeal dismissed*, 510 F.2d 808, 8th Cir. [1975]); the "direct active use" test (*United States v. Red Feather*, 392 F.Supp. 916, D.S.D. [1975]; and the "regulatory, proscriptive or compulsory use" test (*United States v. McArthur*, 419 F.Supp. 186, D.N.D., *aff'd sub nom. United States v. Casper*, 541 F.2d 1275, 8th Cir., *cert. denied*, 430 U.S. 970 [1975]). The "drug" cases involve some form of military/civilian interface (generally including either military law-enforcement agencies, military personnel in the capacity of informants, both, or some other form of military support) in the enforcement of either military or civilian criminal laws, the majority of which have involved drugs or some other form of contraband.

For the most part the courts have found the claimed violation of the Posse Comitatus Act did not occur using some combination of the judicially formulated Wounded Knee tests and the "military purpose doctrine," which permits incidental or indirect aid to civilian law enforcement when the primary aim of the questioned act is to achieve a legitimate military purpose

(Meeks, 1975:124–26; "The Posse Comitatus Act," 1985:123–24).

Further examination of the cases indicates the Posse Comitatus Act does not apply to the coast guard, civilian investigators employed by defense, or military investigators responding to on-base criminal violations committed by civilians (Doss, 1989:72). The courts generally applied the act to the naval services between 1974 (*United States v. Walden*, 490 F.2d 372, 4th Cir., *cert. denied*, 416 U.S. 983, *reh. denied*, 417 U.S. 977 [1974]) and 1986, only because the secretary of the navy ordered its observance as a precautionary measure. Since 1986 the courts have held the act expressly excludes the navy (*United States v. Roberts*, 779 F.2d 565, 9th Cir., *cert. denied*, 107 S.Ct 142 [1986]).

In the few cases such as *Walden* in which the act was found to have been violated, the courts have generally refused to apply a per se exclusionary evidence rule. Through 1992 the main impact of the act has been to produce a "chilling effect" on military managers to exercise extreme caution in cooperating with or providing assets to civilian law-enforcement agencies. And while it has not resulted in any significant acquittals of criminal defendants, it may have prevented some cases from ever going to court, particularly during the 1970s.

During the 1960s and 1970s there was strong pressure to strengthen the act to make it more restrictive. Major amendments would have given the act extraterritorial application and extended it to include all the armed forces.

By 1981 the mood had changed. Motivated by increased concern over the drug threat and a more conservative criminal-justice philosophy, the courts added a new statutory exception to Title 10 authorizing "military cooperation with civilian law enforcement officials." This new Chapter 18 permitted civilian use of information collected during military operations, military equipment and facilities, military training and advice, and other military assistance just as long as military personnel did not become directly involved in actual civilian law-enforcement activity, the assistance rendered was subject to reimbursement, and did not directly affect military preparedness (18 U.S.C. sections 371–78 [1982]).

Empowered by Chapter 18, the federal government created the South Florida Task Force (SFTF) to coordinate federal, state, and local law enforcement, including military support thereto, in that geographic region. The

SFTF concept was expanded into the whole National Narcotics Border Interdiction System (NNBIS), which for a time provided regional coordination for various aspects of military assistance for drug interdiction.

Chapter 18 was amended several times in 1986 to authorize coast guard law-enforcement activities from naval vessels; in 1987 to require the Defense Department to submit an annual plan for civilian drug law-enforcement assistance; and in 1988 to change the emphasis from authorizing cooperation to requiring "military support for civilian law enforcement agencies," as the chapter was retitled (18 U.S.C. sections 371–80 [1988]). In addition to significantly revising Chapter 18, Public Law 100–456 (1988) strengthened the drug interdiction program by enhancing the role of the national guard and requiring the secretary to integrate defense assets into an effective communications support network.

Thus far, the venerable Posse Comitatus Act has withstood the test of time and achieved its intended purpose: to keep civil authorities from arbitrarily using the military to enforce civil laws. Other statutes permit the military to cooperate with and support civilian law-enforcement agencies so long as the military directly performs civilian law-enforcement functions.

Marion T. Doss, Jr.

Bibliography

Corwin, E. *The Constitution and What It Means Today*. Princeton, NJ: Princeton University Press, 1974.

Doss, M. "The Federal Posse Comitatus Act: Guardian of America's Civil Criminal Justice System." *American Journal of Police* 8(2) (1989): 63–91.

Engdahl, D. "Soldiers, Riots, and Revolution: The Law and History of Military Troops in Civil Disorders." *Iowa Law Review* 57 (October 1971): 1–73.

Furman, H. "Restrictions Upon Use of the Army Imposed by the Posse Comitatus Act." *Military Law Review* 7 (1960): 85–129.

House Judiciary Committee. *Posse Comitatus Act: Hearing on H.R. 3519 Before the Subcommittee on Crime, 97th Cong., 1st Sess.* Washington, DC: Government Printing Office, 1982.

House of Representatives. *Department of Defense Authorization Act of 1982: H.Report 97–71, Part 2, 97th Cong., 1st Sess.* Washington, DC: Government Printing Office, 1981.

Lorence, W. "The Constitutionality of the Posse Comitatus Act." *University of Kansas City Law Review* 8 (1940): 164–91.

Meeks, C. "Illegal Law Enforcement: Aiding Civil Authorities in Violation of the Posse Comitatus Act." *Military Law Review* 70 (1975): 83–136.

Nevins, A. *Ordeal of The Union Vol. II: A House Dividing, 1852–1857*. New York: Charles Scribners' Sons, 1947.

"The Posse Comitatus Act: Reconstruction Politics Reconsidered" [note]. *American Criminal Law Review* 13 (1976): 1467–93.

"The Posse Comitatus Act as an Exclusionary Rule: Is the Criminal to Go Free Because the Soldier Has Blundered?" [note]. *North Dakota Law Review* 61 (1985): 107–38.

Post-Shooting Trauma

The human and emotional consequences of posttraumatic stress have received increasing attention in the media. Initially highlighted as the post-traumatic stress syndrome of military personnel in Vietnam, the issue of post-traumatic stress has since been significantly explored (Seligman and Maier, 1967; Strayer and Ellenhorn, 1975; Wilson, 1980).

For some police officers, one of the most difficult situations they may have to face is one requiring them to shoot a suspect to protect other people's lives or their own. Several early studies have delineated various demographic and personal effects of shootings on police officers (Fyfe, 1978; Milton et al., 1977). Various emotional responses to traumatic events have also been discussed in some detail (Stratton, 1984).

Eric Nielson (1980) reported the relative frequency of perceptual distortions, including a sensation of slow motion, tunnel vision, and auditory blocking. The most prevalent experience was the slowing of time. Emotional symptoms included thought intrusions, depression, anxiety, sleep disturbances, fatigue, and the inability to focus thoughts.

Shooting and killing or wounding another human being can be a traumatic event for some police officers, especially if they have entered the profession in order to help people. However, there are procedures and professionals available that can enable these officers to regain good feelings about themselves and their work and continue productively in their careers.

Over the years there has been an increased awareness of the unique stressors and particular problems confronting law-enforcement officers and their agencies. This awareness has evolved through the consultation of psychologists and other behavioral science specialists with law-enforcement personnel.

Until Dr. Martin Reiser's pioneering work with the Los Angeles Police Department, which began in 1968, law-enforcement agencies provided very little actual assistance for their employees. As of 1974 there were still only a few agencies that had implemented a formal psychological counseling service for employees.

In recent years, these services for police departments and their employees have mushroomed. At a national symposium on police psychology sponsored by the Federal Bureau of Investigation in September 1984, there were 166 psychologists who were working directly with law enforcement. And there is now a police-psychology section in the American Psychological Association.

A psychologist who has seen numerous officers involved in shootings has a good idea of the various reactions such officers can have. He or she can help them by sharing this knowledge and by suggesting coping skills they can use to adjust to the possible trauma.

Currently in the United States, estimates show that police officers kill about three hundred suspects and injure another three hundred every year.

Dealing with the Crisis

The evidence is clear that people experiencing crisis or trauma do better with guidance. Thus formalized procedures should be developed for officers involved in shootings, as well as for officers experiencing other traumas. Departments should recognize that abnormal reactions to abnormal circumstances are normal; it is acceptable for officers to have emotional reactions; and officers should be encouraged to seek assistance from psychologists or trained peers.

Officer Reactions

Awareness of shooting-related police traumas began to emerge at the same time that post-traumatic stress disorder (PTSD) was being recognized and accepted as a phenomenon in Vietnam veterans. Initially officer reactions were discussed in anecdotal ways by a few psychologists and described by Strayer and Ellenhorn (1975) and Stratton (1984).

Just as not every Vietnam veteran experiences PTSD, not all officers involved in shootings experience traumatic reactions. Our own research and clinical experience indicate that approximately one-third have minimal or no problems, one-third have a moderate range of problems, and one-third have serious problems. However, almost all officers return to work and perform effectively again. The intensity of the difficulties is generally related to personality, current life situations, personal history, available support systems, and particular aspects of the incident (closeness to the subject, goriness of the incident, etc.).

The first major study was done by Nielson (1980). Initially, all sheriffs and police departments in cities of 20,000 or more were sampled in the states of Colorado, Mississippi, North Dakota, Washington, and Maryland. Nielson found that 54 percent of the sheriff's departments and 88 percent of the police departments had a written policy regarding the use of deadly force.

Nielson also studied the demographics of sixty-three officers involved in shootings and their reactions. Similar studies were made by Soskis, Soskis, and Campbell (1983) of fourteen special agents in the Federal Bureau of Investigation and by Stratton, Parker, and Snibbe (1984) involving sixty Los Angeles County deputy sheriffs. Although the studies did not cover all areas in the same manner, Table 1 demonstrates the commonality of reactions of officers involved in shootings.

Officers report that during a shooting every sense is heightened and they experience everything in slow motion, like viewing a movie frame by frame. They have reported seeing the bullet leaving the gun or entering the victim's body; seeing the contortions on the victim's face; watching the body break and bend and palpitate before the final collapse. They hear screams and blood-curdling yells, and they record all these events in their mind like videotapes ready to play back at any time.

Emotional releases sometimes occur immediately. However, they often occur after the fact and away from the police environment because when they are on duty officers believe they must be in control. Behavioral scientists generally believe that emotional release is better than keeping feelings bottled up and can help prevent stress-related diseases. Yet law enforcement is an occupation that demands that people be objective and unemotionally involved.

Recurring thoughts or flashbacks occur without exception, and anniversary dates of the incident (or holidays close to it) are often reminders of the event. When officers drive by a location where a shooting occurred, they tend to be reminded of the incident and may even have the same bodily and emotional responses they did at the time of the shooting. Whenever anyone experiences a significant emotional event—whether it be something tragic, like a shooting, or something joyful, like the birth of a child—they do not forget the details or the emotional experiences. Officers have refused to work anniversary dates of traumatic incidents because of the feelings they generate.

A common type of flashback occurs in dreams or nightmares. Dreams can be seen as a way for feelings and thoughts to surface that we can't acknowledge in our waking state but that need to be addressed. Issues we cannot handle consciously such as fear, weakness, anger, or depression can often be dealt with in our sleep. Officers have been awakened by their spouses because they are thrashing around, sitting straight up in bed, or yelling profanities and shaking. Others have broken out in sweats ("like having buckets of cold water thrown on me") and have awakened to find their beds soaked.

Forty-seven percent of the sixty officers we surveyed experienced new fears related mostly to legal entanglements or job security, with 14 percent concerned about the department's reactions to them. As our society relies more and more on the courts to settle disputes, the possibility of civil suits or the district attorney filing criminal charges against officers increases.

Being involved in situations where people are alive one minute and dead the next confronts officers directly with the finiteness of life. When their lives are threatened or they've been nearly killed or seriously injured, they may question the way they are leading their lives. Dealing with death has caused significant changes in officers' behavior and ideas regarding life and death.

The sheer shock of killing another person, even when seemingly justified, has often led to intense consideration of anyone's right to take another human life. Sometimes an officer wants to know more about the dead suspect's family or other aspects of the person's life, and sometimes the officer feels an increasing sense of guilt depending on what these private investigations turn up.

If an officer has been in a tense situation where he or she was expected to shoot someone and was unable to, returning to work is difficult, if not impossible.

With all the attention given to them by fellow cops, many officers begin to feel that they are being looked at as heroes. Often their feelings are the exact opposite. They wish they could totally forget the incident. However, as their actions are reviewed by the media, the district attorney, the training staff, and others, the process seems to drag on forever with the officers often feeling guilty.

The life of the officer's family is also disrupted. The lengthier the process, the more pressure is added to the family unit and to the relationships within it.

Often the strongest guilt reactions occur when an officer's partner has been shot, especially if he has been killed. The surviving officer often feels responsible, believing that if he had taken a different action, been more careful, or said something different the entire misfortune could have been avoided. Officers risk their lives to protect and cover for one another, and when one dies the partner presumes the surviving officer did his best for his partner, and yet he refuses to relinquish responsibility.

Generally, officers whose partners are killed feel more guilt than those who experience other types of police tragedies. Even worse can be the accidental shooting of one's partner, a fellow officer, or an innocent victim. Constant reconstruction of the incident—looking at ways it could have been handled differently—only adds to the guilt and frustration.

When a partner has been killed, the surviving officer may try to help with some of the partner's responsibilities. He or she might try to help out the widow and children and take care of other things that were important to his or her partner.

Summary
The data cited herein suggest some significant demographic and psychological reactions of officers involved in shootings. Seventy-three percent of the shootings involved other police officers and 91 percent of the incidents occurred on duty. A variety of psychological reactions

TABLE 1

Reactions of Officers Involved in Shootings

	12/80 Nielson	7/24 Soskis et al.	Stratton et al.
Population	63 Police officers involved in shootings	14 Special agents involved in 17 shootings	60 Deputy sheriffs involved in shootings 6 months to 3 yrs. prior
Age	Majority 29 or younger	24–25	
Experience	4 years or less patrol	9 months to 15 years	0–5 years 14% / 6–10 years 41% / 11–15 years 37% / 16+ 8%
Time	79% between 8 p.m. –5 A.M.	1:30 A.M. to 11:05 P.M.	
Shots fired by officers	3.7	17 (1) Shot each incident	
Shots fired by suspects	1.5	14 (1) Shot by each suspect	
Results		8 Killed 4 Wounded	45% Killed 55% Wounded 9% Off Duty
Prior Shootings			0 1 2 3 4+ / 32% 39% 17% 8% 6.6%
Last shootings occurred			1 yr 2 yr 3 yr 4 yr / 35% 31% 29% 5%
Other officers			1 2 3 4+ / 53% 6% 18% 23%

During incident

	12/80 Nielson	7/24 Soskis et al.	Stratton et al.
Emotional and psychological reaction	64% Slow motion / 27% Auditory blocking / 43% Tunnel vision	59% Slow motion / 65% Auditory blocking / 53% Tunnel vision	79% Slow motion / 26% Speed up
Emotional and physical reactions		65% Disbelief it was happening / 59% Automatic response (result of training) / 59% Rush of strength or adrenaline / 29% Fear	
General psychological reactions/attitudes	51% More cautious / 28% Increased apathy, negative response to job / 24% Embittered / 14% Increased interest in family	Most remember as if yesterday / 65% More cautious / 47% Regret or sympathy for subject / 50% Re-evaluated important life, values, goals / 41% Helped growth and maturity / 29% Made me better person, optimistic about coping with future stress, could trust others and count on them in a crisis	45% Changes in way see self, life, or job / 37% Greater caution / 22% Importance of training/preparedness / 19% New problems in street / 60% Felt threatened and endangered, distrust DA / 46% Became overbearing developed new attitudes / 48% Suspicious, vigilante, / 24% On guard toward gun / 18% Career believed affected, guilty feelings even if more confident

(continued)

Reactions of Officers Involved in Shootings *(continued)*

	12/80 Nielson	7/24 Soskis et al.	Stratton et al.
	Some "met the test," have more confidence, are less pressed to prove self, few harmful involvments with subject's family		
Physical	92% Nausea/upset stomach	29% Fatigue	Sleep problems
	35% Stress symptoms	18% Stress symptoms	Nightmares
	25% Headaches	5% Headaches	Loss of appetite
	14% Fatigue	0% Nausea/vomiting	Increased drinking
Emotion/psychological reactions following shooting	59% Thought intrusions	47% Sleep problems	57% No problems
	52% Depression	41% Anxiety/tension	63% — Yes
	33% Anxiety, agitation	35% Sadness crying	28% Anger
	27% Sleep disturbances	depression	23% Mixed
	25% Fatigue, inability to focus	24% Disturbing thoughts	18% Elation
	22% Thoughts		18% Confusion
			18% Anxiety
			13% Depression
			25% Fear, worry, anxiety
			7% Fear of lawsuit
			100% Flashbacks, recurring thoughts:
			30% Affected greatly
			33% Affected moderately
			35% Affected little or not at all
Family aspects		59% Wife worried/upset	76% Reaction from spouse or relatives: Yes
		33% Subsequent marriage problems	48% Supportive
		6% Divorced since incident	21% Tension, fear, worry
			10% Glad officer not hurt
			8% Avoidance, disinterest
Peer reactions	41% Support	77% Support	
	41% Curiosity	18% Curiosity	
	19% Aggravation	13% Aggravation	
	7.9% None reported	6% None reported	
Support/talked to most	57% Peers	100% Fellow agents	98% Other deputies
		53% Wife/girlfriend	80% Station supervisors
		12% Clergy	75% Station brass
		6% Other family	70% Department brass
		6% Supervisor	
Sources of aggravation	42% Press coverage unfair	Prolonged nature of investigation and fragmentary information (Paramount)	47% New fears or doubts
	42% Threats against self/family	55% Supervisor's concern for self or position	30% Legal entanglement
	19% Fellow officers	41% News media	30% Job related
		29% Other bureau officials	17% Dept's reactions
		12% Suspects' family and friends	
		6% Supervisor	
		6% Suspects' attorneys	
		6% Other agents	

was described, such as time distortion, sleep difficulties, and fear of legal consequences, as well as various emotional reactions, such as anger, elation, or crying. Approximately 30 percent of the respondents felt that the shooting incident affected them greatly, about 33 percent only moderately, and about 35 percent not at all. The emotional responses to shootings appear to be as varied as the individual people involved.

John G. Stratton

Bibliography

Brooks, P.R. *Officer Down, Code Three.* Schiller Park, IL: Motorola Teleprograms, 1975.

Fyfe, J. *Shots Fired: An Examination of New York City Police Firearms Discharges.* Ann Arbor, MI: University Microfilms International, 1978.

Milton, C., J.W. Halleck, J. Lardner, and G.L. Albrecht. *Police Use of Deadly Force.* Washington, DC: Police Foundation, 1977.

Nielson, E. *Salt Lake City Police Department: Deadly Force Policy—Shooting and Post-Shooting Reactions.* Salt Lake City, UT: Salt Lake City Police Department, December, 1980.

Seligman, M.E.P., and S.F. Maier. "Failure to Escape Traumatic Shock." *Journal of Experimental Psychology* 74 (1967): 1–9.

Soskis, D.A., C.W. Soskis, and J.H. Campbell. "An Analysis of the Effects of Post-Shooting Trauma on Special Agents of the Federal Bureau of Investigation." Unpublished manuscript, 1983.

Stratton, J.G. *Police Passages.* Manhattan Beach, CA: Glennon, 1984.

Stratton, J.G., J.R. Snibbe, and K. Bayless. "Police in a Violent Society." *FBI Law Enforcement Bulletin* 54(1) (1985): 1–7.

Stratton, J.G., D.A. Parker, and J.R. Snibbe. "Post-Traumatic Stress; Study of Police Officers Involved in Shootings." *Psychological Reports* 55 (1984): 127–31.

Strayer, R., and L. Ellenhorn. "Vietnam Veterans: A Study Exploring Adjustment Patterns and Attitudes." In *Soldiers in and after Vietnam.* Eds. D.M. Mantell and M. Pilisuk. *Journal of Social Issues* 31(4) (1975): 81–93.

Wilson, J.P. "Conflict, Stress and Growth: The Effects of the Vietnam War on Psychosocial Development among Vietnam Veterans." In *Strangers at Home: Vietnam Veterans Since the War.* Eds. C.R. Figley and S. Leventman. New York: Praeger, 1980.

Private Security

Security provides those means, active or passive, that serve to protect and preserve an environment and that allow for the conduct of activities without disruption. Careful analysis of this basic definition can broaden one's understanding of private security. The "means" depend first of all on the goals of the organization and the clientele served. If the organization is service-oriented, security must necessarily be unobtrusive and suggestive, since the clientele must be free to partake of services, such as those at a resort hotel or amusement park. At the other extreme, if the organization is an industrial plant producing materials under a classified government contract, security will be quite intrusive and highly visible, given the extremely limited nature of the organization's clientele—namely, the Department of Defense. In either case, the means employed should reflect legal, moral, and ethical restrictions. Private security practitioners, it should be noted, are not bound by the same legal restrictions that affect the operations of their counterparts in public law enforcement. For example, private security officers do not have to invoke the *Miranda* warning when questioning a suspect. Other due process procedures can be similarly affected.

Our definition next mentions "active and passive" means. Active means include such things as security education, employee searches, and surveillance operations. Passive measures include fences, lights, alarms, and other devices. Some elements such as identification control involve interaction between passive (identification cards, keys, lock) and active (security police scrutinizing identification cards) measures. The words *protect* and *preserve* are sometimes referred to as the "hallmarks of security," as well they might be. For in protecting the environment (whatever that environment might be) security administrators preserve it so that the "bottom line" can be realized: The organization can survive and prosper as a profit-making enterprise. Next we further delineate the word "environment" itself.

The security environment can range from tight to relaxed. To some extent this environment is influenced by the structure involved (single or multiple facility, for example), the service or product being produced or offered, and management policies. The phrase "conduct of activities without disruption" signals the essential equation that security directors must constantly balance: productivity and security. "Perfect" security might dictate a complete body and vehicle search of every employee entering and leaving the facility every day, but such a practice might adversely affect productivity. Thus the security professional must, with crucial input from management, maintain what can be a constantly shifting balance between security and productivity.

Historical Antecedents
Probably the earliest manifestation of "modern security," the "watch and ward" system in England and later in the United States, involved private citizens sharing, on a rotating basis, responsibility for night security of the town. Increasing urbanization and the resultant crime necessitated the establishment of the first full-time police departments in the 1840s, whose officers were paid to discharge the "safety" duties formerly performed by private citizens. Early on came the realization that public law-enforcement officers could not possibly meet all the safety requirements in the community. This prompted Allan Pinkerton in 1855 to establish the first private security company in this country, involved initially in hunting outlaws, providing railroad security, and handling other security functions. Now Pinkerton's ranks as the largest private security enterprise in the world. Capitalizing on the same requirement for a private security effort, Edwin Holmes founded the country's first burglar alarm company in 1858, a harbinger of today's multimillion-dollar protective alarm industry. Washington P. Brink was not far behind when he inaugurated a truck delivery service in 1859 that later evolved into the present Brink's Armored Car Company. Perhaps World War I and World War II—creating extensive needs for defense plant guards and security—exerted the most significant impact on the dramatic growth of the private security industry. Out of World War II, in fact, emerged two Department of Defense programs: the DOD Industrial Security Program, which affects defense contractors with classified contracts; and the DOD Industrial Defense Program, which transmits security recommendations based on on-site inspections of facilities on the DOD Key Facilities List. Both programs have contributed on an ongoing basis to an expansion of the need for private security resources. Many observers contend that the so-called crime waves that have erupted since World War II have exerted an even more pronounced influence on the growth of the private security industry by prompting business and industry into the realization that the police cannot deal with a rising crime rate and protect private concerns as well. This more than any other phenomena, such observers argue, has resulted in transforming private security from a merely peripheral industry to a dominant one of today.

Components of the Private Security Industry
The Private Security Task Force Report of the National Advisory Committee on Criminal Justice Standards and Goals (1976) offered the following description of the elements of the private security industry.

Guard and Patrol Services and Personnel. Guard and patrol services include the provision of personnel who perform the following functions, either contractually or internally, at such places and facilities as industrial plants, financial institutions, educational institutions, office buildings, retail establishments, commercial complexes (including hotels and motels), health-care facilities, recreation facilities, libraries and museums, residence and housing developments, charitable institutions, transportation vehicles and facilities (public and common carriers), and warehouses and goods distribution depots:

- Prevention and/or detection of intrusion, unauthorized entry or activity, vandalism, or trespass on private property;
- Prevention and/or detection of theft, loss, embezzlement, misappropriation or concealment of merchandise, money, bonds, stocks, notes, or other valuable documents or papers;
- Control, regulation, or direction of the flow of movements of the public, whether by vehicle or otherwise, to assure the protection of property;
- Protection of individuals from bodily harm; and
- Enforcement of rules, regulations, and policies related to crime reduction.

These functions may be provided at one location or several. Guard functions are generally provided at one central location for one client or employer. Patrol functions, however, are performed at several locations, often for several clients.

Investigative Services and Personnel. The major services provided by the investigative component of private security may be provided contractually or internally at places and facilities, such as industrial plants, financial institutions, educational institutions, retail establishments, commercial complexes, hotels and motels, and health-care facilities. The services are provided for a variety of clients, including insurance companies, law firms, retailers, and individuals. Investigative personnel are primarily concerned with obtaining information with reference to any of the following matters:

- Crime or wrongs committed or threatened;
- The identity, habits, conduct, movements, whereabouts, affiliations, associations, transactions, reputation, or character of any person, group of persons, association, organization, society, other group of persons or partnership or corporation;
- Preemployment background checks of personnel applicants;
- The conduct, honesty, efficiency, loyalty, or activities of employees, agents, contractors, and subcontractors;
- Incidents and illicit or illegal activities by persons against the employer or employer's property;
- Retail shoplifting;
- Internal theft by employees or other employee crime;
- The truth or falsity of any statement or representation;
- The whereabouts of missing persons;
- The location or recovery of lost or stolen property;
- The causes and origin of, or responsibility for, fires, libels or slanders, losses, accidents, damage, or injuries to real or personal property;
- The credibility of information, witnesses, or other persons; and
- The securing of evidence to be used before investigating committees, boards of award or arbitration, or in the trial

of civil or criminal cases and the preparation thereof.

Detective or investigative activity is distinguished from the guard or watchman function in that the investigator obtains information; the guard or watchman usually acts on information (or events).

Alarm Services and Personnel. Alarm services include selling, installing, servicing, and emergency response to alarm signal devices. Alarm devices are employed in one of four basic modes: local alarm, proprietary alarm, central station alarm, or police connected alarm. Alarm signal devices include a variety of equipment, ranging from simple magnetic switches to complex ultrasonic Doppler and sound systems. Various electronic, electromechanical, and photoelectrical devices and microwave Dopplers are also utilized.

Alarm personnel include three categories of employees: alarm sales personnel, alarm systems installers and/or servicers, and alarm respondents. Those persons in alarm sales engage in customer/client contact, presale security surveys, and postsale customer relations. Alarm installers and servicers are trained technicians who install and wire alarm systems, perform scheduled maintenance, and provide emergency servicing as well as regular repair of alarm systems. (Alarm installers and servicers may be the same depending on the employers.) Alarm respondents respond to an alarm condition at the protected site of a client. The alarm respondent inspects the protected site to determine the nature of the alarm, protects or secures the client's facility for the client until alarm system integrity can be restored, and assists law-enforcement agencies according to local arrangements.

Armored Car and Armed Courier Services and Personnel. Armored car services include the provision of protection, safekeeping, and secured transportation of currency, coins, bullion, securities, bonds, jewelry, or other items of value. This secured transportation, from one place or point to another place or point, is accomplished by specially constructed, bullet-resistant armored vehicles and vaults under armed guard. Armed courier services also include the armed protection and transportation, from one place or point to another place or point, of currency, coins, bullion, securities, bonds, jewelry, or other articles of unusual value. Armed courier services are distinguished from armored car services in that the transportation is provided by means other than specially constructed bullet-resistant armored vehicles. There are also courier service companies that employ nonarmed persons to transport documents, business papers, checks, and other time sensitive items of limited intrinsic value that require expeditious delivery. Those services concerned merely with expeditious, unarmed delivery are not intended to be covered by this report's standards and goals.

The major distinction between the services provided by armored cars and armed couriers and those furnished by guards and watchmen is liability. Armored car guards and armed couriers are engaged exclusively in the safe transportation and custody of valuables, and the firms providing these services are liable for the face, declared, or contractual value of the client's property. These service companies are bailees of the valuable property, and the guards and couriers are protecting the property of their employer. This liability extends from the time the valuables are received until the time a receipt is executed by the consignee at delivery. Except for war risks, the armored car company is absolutely liable for the valuable property during such protective custody. Conversely, guards, watchmen, and their employers do not assume comparable liability for the property being protected.

Private Security Interface with the Criminal-Justice System

An examination of recent history reveals that before 1967 we did not "officially" have a criminal-justice system (CJS). What did we have? Many contend that we were shackled with separate, semiautonomous feifdoms, each largely hidden from public scrutiny, each going its own way. Anything systematic about their functioning, critics said, was more accidental than planned.

But the turbulent 1960s changed all that, shaking "establishment" institutions to their very foundation. Spiraling crime waves, civil rights demonstrations, the Vietnam War, the counterculture, all added impetus to publication of *The Challenge of Crime in a Free Society* (1967), a report by the President's Commission on Law Enforcement and the Administration of Justice. Foremost among the Commission's findings was the assertion that "the system of criminal justice . . . is not a monolithic, or even a consistent, system!" These findings, combined with the subsequent resulting establishment of the Law Enforcement Assistance Administration, precipitated a searching, critical examination of the CJS that continues unabated to this day.

The police-courts-corrections triumvirate cited by the Commission in 1967 began almost immediately to expand. First to be added was an office with virtually unlimited discretionary powers—the office of the public prosecutors. Subsequent "counsel for indigents" court decisions added the office of public defender. The system now had five elements.

Efforts to relieve overcrowded prisons, coupled with the acknowledgement that America's fortress prisons can do little to correct their "clients," focused increasing attention on two alternatives: probation and parole. Now considered separate (from corrections) and distinct CJS elements, they expand the system to seven.

Increasing pressure not only to find alternatives to incarceration as a punishment but also to devise better means of insuring a defendant's court appearance has led to a continuing development of pretrial intervention strategies. Indeed, the establishment of the National Association of Pretrial Services Agencies, dedicated to expanding the use of such strategies, argues convincingly for the inclusion of pretrial intervention as a separate CJS element.

The move toward decriminalization of public drunkenness and marijuana possession, together with diversionary efforts directed toward such offenders, makes inclusion of substance-abuse agencies in the CJS not only logical, but essential. In fact, *The Connection*, a periodical published by the National Institute on Drug Abuse, is dedicated to linking criminal-justice and substance-abuse agencies in a true CJS partnership.

Recognition that the police spend approximately 80 percent of their time handling noncriminal matters has pointed increasingly to the conclusion that the police function primarily as "social service brokers." Expanding this idea to encompass the entire CJS, Abadinsky (1979) notes that "it is only a broader theoretical and methodological approach that will enable the social services to be more responsive to the nuances and variations that are encountered in criminal justice settings."

The most significant addition to the CJS for our purposes is that of the private security industry.

Commenting in the preface of the report of the Task Force on Private Security of the National Advisory Committee on Criminal Justice Standards and Goals (1976), task force chairman Arthur J. Bilek asserted that "the private security industry, with over one million workers, sophisticated alarm systems and perimeter safeguards, armored trucks, sophisticated minicomputers, and thousands of highly skilled crime prevention experts, offers a potential for coping with crime that cannot be equaled by any other remedy or approach." That the National Advisory Committee commissioned the *Private Security Task Force Report* as an integral part of its overall publication of criminal-justice standards and goals solidly confirms Mr. Bilek's statement.

The International Association of Chiefs of Police (IACP) added its prestigious endorsement through two editorials in its publication *Police Chief* by its then-president, Howard Shook. Editorially reminding IACP members that modern public policing traces its beginnings to the private security industry, Shook (1978) asserted that "millions of tax dollars are saved annually through the partnership of security and public safety." In an earlier editorial Shook (1977) stated that "public police should do everything possible to encourage and support the concept of professional private security." The IACP president, elected for a one-year term, published twelve editorials during his tenure. The fact that two of the twelve were devoted to private security attests to the clinical importance with which the industry is viewed by the police profession.

The Public-Private Police Relationship
The public-private relationship deserves special attention because private security's link to the criminal-justice system is through public security; that is, through the public police. This relationship has at times proven to be tenuous at best, for to deny that problems exist between the two is to evade reality. Many potential problems exist that, if left to fester, would prevent true cooperation and integration of the private security practitioner with his or her colleague, the public police officer, and through the police officer with the entire criminal-justice system. Unfortunately, this relationship has sometimes been characterized by a lack of mutual respect, emanating primarily from the public police side.

The police have traditionally viewed themselves as a well-trained and motivated group of professionals. Indeed, all the states require completion of formal instruction and certification, some quite extensive, before a candidate for the police service can become a sworn officer. Since most states do not demand similar qualifications for private security police, the public police have naturally looked upon their "cousins" with disdain, disdain only thinly disguised in many cases. This and other factors have prevented meaningful, effective cooperation and coordination between the two groups in some jurisdictions. Part of this problem stems from a serious misunderstanding each has of the other's mission and functions. Again, the police are principally to blame in that most departments do not include instruction or orientation in recruit training concerning the role of the private security industry. In many cases, this derives from a case of marked shortsightedness on the part of the police concerning how much private security can reduce the public security workload. Perhaps nothing disturbs public police agencies more than the problem caused by false alarms due to malfunctioning alarm systems. Devices installed and serviced by the private security industry have a nasty habit of sounding when any number of events occur, most of which are unrelated to a burglary, robbery, or any other criminal activity. Because these malfunctions cause an often significant drain on police resources, the false alarm problem constitutes perhaps the greatest wedge between closer public- and private-police cooperation.

There are, however, many areas where public-private police cooperation has proven most productive. Principal among these is the sharing both of investigative and intelligence expertise. Certainly many investigations initiated by practitioners within the private security industry are subsequently worked jointly with public security agencies and are finally taken forward (in the sense of referral to the appropriate prosecutor's office) by the public security agency. The benefits to be gained in such joint enterprises are obvious. Given the increasingly ominous rise in crime rates since World War II, police intelligence has loomed ever more critical as a tool. With their unique yet complementary perspectives, these two security forces can forge a significant intelligence linkage.

This cooperative intelligence effort can prove most productive, perhaps, in the area of white-collar and corporate crime. FBI Director William Webster reoriented his agency's investigative resources toward this pervasive activity, calling for heightened cooperation between public law-enforcement agencies and the private security industry in uncovering, investigating, and ultimately prosecuting this corrosive variety of criminal activity. Reasoning that the private security industry serving business and industry is "on the front lines" where white-collar and corporate crime is actually occurring, Webster voiced an eloquent, convincing appeal for private security to come to the aid of its public counterpart in this vital area. In so seizing the initiative, Webster was merely reflecting the position of IACP President Shook, who had recently declared that the "public police should do everything possible to encourage and support the concept of professional security."

Public police leaders who clearly perceive the importance of community involvement in crime control efforts have been quick to recognize the role of the private security industry in involving the private sector in crime prevention—the ultimate aim of any police–community relations effort. Private security has a captive audience. It works with and has access to the nation's workforce. This workforce, a captive audience in the sense that it must be physically present at the workplace usually for an eight-hour day, represents a fertile breeding ground for a community-based, crime prevention effort. In many areas private security professionals, usually in cooperation with local police–community relations units, are "mining" this potentially productive employee population in an effort to get across the community crime prevention message. Properly coordinated and orchestrated, this effort can be expanded to include homes and neighborhoods to actively foster a truly effective police (public and private) community crime prevention effort. Shook again put it most succinctly when he observed that

> the business of the private security sector is not only to sell safety and security but to educate people in the many ways they can protect themselves. This important service makes private security a natural ally of the police and formidable foe of the criminal. Together we can fashion a program which will foster public understanding and enlist public assistance in combating crime. Both police and private

security stand to gain, but more importantly, the public stands to gain the most: a safe and tranquil community in which to live and work.

Perhaps the most promising and fastest growing (in terms of publicity and interest) area of potential public-private police cooperation lies in the area loosely dubbed "hostage-terrorist operations." Although not nearly as prevalent in this country as it has been overseas, hostage-taking and terrorist-oriented activities show tremendous potential for escalation here as well. Because top executives of large U.S. corporations view this spreading cancer as a highly personal threat, not only to themselves but to their families as well, they have made it a priority for their private security services. Since public police forces, particularly those serving large urban areas, have had antiterrorism plans in place for many years, the private sector has naturally gravitated to the public police for help and support. Out of this marriage of convenience, even necessity, have evolved many joint training efforts that have proven most productive not only in enhancing joint protective strategies, but also in improving overall relations.

The private security industry stands firmly anchored within the "criminal-justice family." Increasingly active efforts by professional organizations in the private and public sectors, including the International Association of Chiefs of Police and the American Society for Industrial Security, can only serve to solidify this relationship.

The Security System

Too often in the past "security" was seen from a "single entity" viewpoint, that is, in terms of guards or burglar alarms or some other security element. But to be recognized as a viable part of any corporation or business, security must be seen from a systems-approach perspective, as a component that can be translated into return on investment (ROI). Today's modern corporate security/loss prevention director, is, first of all, a competent, well-rounded business executive and, second, a "security expert."

The first task of the security director is to conduct a searching risk analysis to pinpoint those areas/functions/hazards that might adversely impact ROI and then to design a dynamic security system approach to protect against potential adverse impacts. In doing so, the director integrates the major elements of security (barriers, lighting, alarms, key-lock systems, identification/movement control systems, and the security force) into a smoothly functioning security system designed to enhance the organization's ROI.

Today, the security/loss-prevention arena includes responsibility for safety, fire control, document security, personnel security (clearances), executive protection, "fitness for duty" assessments, health services, substance-abuse programs, government regulation implementation, disaster/emergency operations, process monitoring, protection against industrial espionage and "insider trading" abuses, and trademark protection—to name only the *major* responsibilities. Security executives of multinational organizations, moreover, are being called upon to perform comprehensive, highly sophisticated, strategic global risk analysis upon which corporate management can base business decisions such as where (in what country in the Middle East, for example) to locate an expansion facility. Seen from this perspective, "security" belongs in the corporate boardroom as an integral and crucial part of American business.

Donald C. Becker

Bibliography

Abadinsky, Howard. *Social Service in Criminal Justice.* Englewood Cliffs, NJ: Prentice-Hall, 1979.

Cole, Richard B. *The Application of Security Systems and Hardware.* Springfield, IL: Charles C. Thomas, 1970.

Green, Gion, and Raymond C. Farber. *Introduction to Security.* Los Angeles: Security World, 1975.

Healy, Richard J. *Designing for Security.* New York: John Wiley and Sons, 1968.

Hemphill, Charles F., Jr. *Security for Business and Industry.* Homewood, IL: Dow Jones–Irwin, 1971.

National Advisory Committee on Criminal Justice Standards and Goals. *Private Security Task Force Report.* Washington, DC: Government Printing Office, 1976.

President's Commission on Law Enforcement and the Administration of Justice. *The Challenge of Crime in a Free Society.* Washington, DC: Government Printing Office, 1967.

Shook, Howard. "Untapped Resources of the Private Security Sector." *Police Chief* (December 1977): 9.

———. "Police and Private Security." *Police Chief* (June 1978): 8.

Probation and Parole

Probation and parole are two different methods of dealing with convicted criminal offenders. Confusion over the nature of probation or parole, however, often results in the two terms being incorrectly used interchangeably. Briefly, the distinction involves time and jurisdiction. With regard to time, probation is granted to a criminal offender without the requirement of a period of incarceration in a correctional facility—probation is "before" prison; parole is a form of release granted to an inmate who has served a portion of his or her sentence in a correctional facility—parole is "after" prison. Jurisdiction-ally, probation is a judicial function of the courts; parole is an administrative function of an executive agency. For a more complete understanding of the nature and differences of probation and parole and the relative functions of each within the criminal-justice system, it is necessary to examine the history, concepts, and processes of each system in some detail.

The History of Probation

Probation, the practice of maintaining convicted criminal offenders in the community under supervision of court authority, traces its history back to the English common law traditions. Judges in the Middle Ages who might wish to spare convicted offenders from the then commonly used forms of punishment—torture, mutilation, and death—had the power of clemency and the judicial reprieve. While clemency might remove the threat of punishment entirely, judicial reprieve merely allowed the offender's punishment to be suspended while new evidence could be gathered or a full pardon sought. The practice of recognizance allowed convicted offenders to avoid punishment or imprisonment by entering into a debt obligation with the state, the debt being collected only if the offender engaged in future criminal conduct. Sureties were required for some offenders—sureties being people who made themselves responsible for the behavior of the offender after release from the court.

Early American courts continued the practices of their English forefathers in giving some criminal offenders what amounted to a second chance prior to imprisonment or other forms of punishment. John Augustus, a Boston businessman, is generally given credit for creating the modern concept of probation in 1841. Augustus offered to supervise offenders released into his custody by a Boston judge, and over an eighteen-year period he supervised about two thousand probationers, assisting them in finding jobs and living accommodations.

The success of Augustus' experiment resulted in the Massachusetts state legislature creating a paid probation officer position for Boston in 1878. By 1880 probation spread to other Massachusetts jurisdictions and was extended to felony court offenders in 1898. Other states followed this example, and by 1925 the federal government had adopted a probation system for federal district courts.

The Concept of Probation

The concept of probation varies in relation to how and when the term is used, and by whom. Probation can refer to a *sentence*—a convicted criminal offender is placed and maintained in the community, as opposed to prison, under the supervision of an authorized agent of the court. Probation can refer to a *status or process*—the probationer is subject to specific rules and conditions that he or she must follow to avoid prison and remain in the community. Probation can also refer to an *organization*—a probation department manages, supervises, and attempts to rehabilitate offenders, and also carries out court-ordered investigations into the backgrounds of persons considered as candidates for probation. Whatever the conceptual description, probation is normally indicative of a nonpunitive philosophy of sentencing for selected convicted criminal offenders that stresses keeping the subject in the community and possibly offering treatment without an institutional setting or added forms of punishment associated with correctional facilities.

The philosophy behind the concept of probation is that the average criminal offender is not a particularly dangerous person or a menace to society. Probation advocates emphasize that the incarceration of criminal offenders creates negative influences for an individual that may make it more difficult, if not impossible, to readjust to society upon release. Probation, therefore, is seen by its advocates as providing a needed "second chance" for convicted offenders to prove themselves worthy of remaining in society through their association with their family, the community, and a supervising probation officer.

In actual practice, probation is normally seen in a dual perspective. While the obvious practice remains closely aligned to the philosophy of a second chance, whereby a convicted offender's prison sentence is suspended for a probated sentence in return for a promise of good behavior in the community, a less obvious but just as effective use of probation is its strategy to control prison overcrowding. Less dangerous offenders are more likely to receive probation in some cases so limited prison space may be maintained or reserved for violent or dangerous offenders. Whatever the practice, probation carries with it the possibility of a prison sentence if the terms of the court-ordered supervision are violated. If these rules are broken, especially if the probated offender commits another crime, probation may be revoked and the original prison sentence may be enforced. Each probationary sentence is established for a fixed time period, depending on the seriousness of the crime and the statutory law of the jurisdiction. Probation is considered completed when the offender fulfills the court-ordered conditions for that fixed time period. Upon completion of the probationary sentence, the offender is allowed to live in the community without court supervision.

Conditions of Probation

A probation sentence is normally viewed as an act of clemency on the part of the court and is indicative, in this sense, of a rehabilitative sensibility in the criminal-justice system. As previously mentioned, the continuing problem of prison overcrowding is also a factor in the granting of probation in some jurisdictions, though this may not be evidence of a rejection of a rehabilitation ethic. Therefore, there are two sides of a probationary contract between the court and the convicted offender. One involves the treatment and rehabilitation of the offender through regularly scheduled meetings with trained probation officers or other designated personnel; the other side of the contract reflects the supervision and enforcement aspects of probation. Standard probation rules may include all or some of the following in some form or another:

1. Commit no offense against the laws of this state or any other state or of the United States.

2. Avoid vicious or injurious habits.
3. Avoid persons or places of disreputable or harmful character.
4. Report to your probation officer as directed.
5. Permit the probation officer to visit you at home or elsewhere.
6. Work faithfully at suitable employment as much as possible.
7. Remain within a specified area or jurisdiction.
8. Pay assessed fines, court costs, restitution, or other payments that the court shall determine (including lawyer's fees, probation fees).
9. Support your dependents.
10. Participate in any specified community-based program (work, drugs, etc.).

In addition, a judge may decide to impose special conditions that apply only to a specific convicted criminal, such as ordering a drug or alcohol abuser to give up the use of these substances, or possibly take regular tests to determine if the offender is "chemical free." Likewise, probationers may have their interpersonal relationships limited, if, for instance, they have been involved in continued disputes or violence with certain family members or friends. Also, probationers may be required to periodically report on their personal practices—for example, tax evaders may be required to submit their tax returns and other valid papers.

The History of Parole

Parole, the planned community release and supervision of incarcerated offenders prior to the actual conclusion of their court-imposed prison sentences, also has its roots in the English legal tradition. In 1617 the privy counsel of the British Parliament standardized the previously purely subjective practice of some English judges to spare the lives of condemned felons by exiling them to the newly created overseas colonies. The privy counsel order established procedures for the transportation and overseas supervision of these exiled felons. Early forms of parole involved the sale of prisoners to colonial businessmen as indentured servants. By the mid-1800s, English public support for this form of penal slavery had fallen off and reform efforts were considered. One such reformer, Alexander Maconochie, was appointed director of an infamous Australian penal colony on Norfolk Island. He established a system of classification for prisoners that emphasized rehabilitation and provided for "tickets of leave" to the mainland for deserving inmates. This informal system of parole was later improved upon by a disciple of Maconochie's, Sir Walter Crofton, director of the Irish Convict Prisons. Crofton's parole tickets of leave program utilized private volunteers or policemen who could monitor the activities of released Irish convicts in the community, an early form of parole officer.

In the United States, the first real parole system was begun in Philadelphia in 1822. By 1851 the Philadelphia system included two appointed parole officers; Massachusetts had initiated a similar program in 1845 that had one officer charged with assisting released inmates to obtain work, clothing, and transportation. The driving force behind American parole efforts, however, was Zebulon Brockway, a prison reformer who became warden of New York's Elmira Reformatory in 1876. Brockway utilized a well-developed screening process that selected rehabilitated offenders for early release to volunteers known as guardians. The parole officers met with the released inmates at least once a month and submitted written reports on the parolee's progress. The process spread quickly thereafter; Ohio created the first parole agency in 1884, and by 1901 twenty states had some type of parole system.

The Concept of Parole

Parole is normally considered to be a method of completing a prison sentence—though in the community instead of a correctional facility—and is not the same as a pardon, which terminates the remainder of a prison sentence. The paroled offender can legally be recalled to prison to serve the rest of the sentence if the parole officer finds that the parolee's adjustment to community life is inadequate, or, more likely, if the paroled offender commits another crime.

The decision process involved in parole is determined by a legal statutory requirement and normally involves completion of a minimum sentence or percentage of the total imposed sentence. Parole is normally granted by a parole board, which is an executive committee of men and women who determine whether a specific offender has reached a level of rehabilitation sufficient for return to the community. The board also dictates specific parole conditions, or rules, which the parolee must obey to avoid a return to prison. Federal prison systems have a federal parole board that serves the same functions.

When a parolee is released into the community, his or her activities are supervised by a parole officer. The officer's duties include helping the parolee maintain a place in the community, assisting him or her in finding employment, and monitoring the parolee's behavior.

Parole is generally seen as an act of grace on the part of the criminal-justice system. As such, it represents an actual manifestation of the stated rehabilitative philosophy of returning the incarcerated offender to the community. There are, however, two conflicting points of view concerning the true nature of parole. On one hand, the paroled offender is said to have received a break from society and is allowed to return to the community to serve the remainder of a court-imposed sentence. On the other hand, the perspective exists that maintains that parole is a privilege, not a right, and that the parolee is in reality an unreformed, dangerous criminal who must be carefully watched and supervised in the community. This latter perspective is particularly prominent in states or jurisdictions in which prison overcrowding has resulted in frequent or mass paroles of inmates in an attempt to make room for incoming prisoners. This conflict between the "treatment" perspective and the "enforcement" perspective has not been solved either in the criminal-justice system or by the public. This conflict has resulted, instead, in a trend toward determinate, flat, or mandatory sentences, and a movement to abolish parole practices entirely.

Conditions of Parole
Before release into the community, a parolee is given a standard set of rules and conditions that must be obeyed. As with probation, these rules and conditions must be strictly followed, as violations may result in a return to prison. Parole rules may curtail or prohibit certain types of behaviors while demanding others; such rules may be moralistic or strict in nature to prohibit or at least severely inhibit a return to former criminal tendencies. But parole rules are frequently designed to be punitive without rehabilitative aspects. The variety of philosophies behind the creation of parole rules directly reflects the ideology of the jurisdiction of separate parole boards. Some states may expressly prohibit specific types of behavior, while another state may require the parolee to seek permission for it—an example would be a parolee's desire

to marry. Allowing for these stated differences, parole rules generally follow the patterns, if not the spirit, of the following:

1. A condition of every parole is that the parolee not commit another offense or act of delinquency during the parole term.

In addition, the parolee must:

2. Work or pursue a course of study or vocational training.
3. Undergo medical or psychiatric treatment, if necessary, or treatment for drug or alcohol addiction.
4. Attend or reside in a facility established for the instruction or residence of persons on probation or parole.
5. Support your dependents.
6. Do not possess firearms or other dangerous weapons.
7. Report as ordered to your parole officer.
8. Permit the parole officer to visit you at home or elsewhere.
9. If a minor, the parolee will, in addition to the above, reside at home with parents or foster parents; attend school; attend required nonresidential programs for youth; contribute to his or her own support at home or in a foster home.
10. The conditions of parole will be communicated to the parolee prior to release, in writing, and he or she shall sign a copy of the same before being released. A signed copy will be kept by the parolee and a copy will be forwarded to the parole officer. After a designated hearing, the parole board may meet again to review and modify the conditions of parole.

Parole supervision often begins in the correctional facility where specified agents assist the inmate in creating a parole plan. The adequacy of the plan is an important element in the parole board's decision to grant community release.

Effectiveness of Probation and Parole
A careful review of probation's effectiveness was prepared for the federal government by Carlson and Parks in 1979. Among the findings of the researchers was the conclusion that probation seems to be effective primarily for first offenders. The study noted that regardless of effectiveness overall, probation was more cost

effective than incarceration, especially when considering the maintenance of the offender's community ties. Employment was deemed a major factor in the success or failure of a probationer's completion of his sentence. The effectiveness of probation officers was reported to be directly tied to a probationer's success or failure—misdemeanor offenders might be served as well on unsupervised probation; caseload reduction is not the answer to effective probation, rather there is a need to match offender types and treatment needs with different types of officers; probation officers are not necessarily lenient, as judges' sentencing decisions frequently correspond closely with probation officers' presentence report recommendations. Finally, the study concluded that probation may not have a better rate of success than incarceration, but it certainly did no worse and was at least as effective. Also, there were indications that probationers would, overall, succeed or fail on their own, regardless of the amount of attention received from the probation officer.

There is stronger disagreement over the effectiveness of parole—a Newsweek magazine poll in 1982 showed that it is popularly believed that recidivism rates are very high, approaching 70 percent. Research designed to study the effectiveness of parole has produced a wide variety of results. The National Council on Crime and Delinquency collected data (Gottfredson et al., 1973) from every state adult parole authority. Its findings showed that parole was more effective than believed, based on the type of offense, ranging from a high of 90 percent successful to a low of 65 percent successful. In a 1977 study by the same agency (National Council on Crime and Delinquency, 1982), researchers found that after three years, 12.8 percent of parolees had returned to prison as technical violators, and 12.3 percent were recommended for return to prison for committing new offenses, a total of 25 percent failure. In both samples, the relationship between the commitment offense and parole success was remarkably similar. Offenders who committed the most serious offenses were most likely to be successful on parole, while those with prior conviction records were more likely to violate parole conditions than first-time offenders.

However, not all research has been so supportive of parole. A 1980 study by Sacks and Logan compared groups of parolees with inmates who were discharged outright from prison to determine whether parole made a difference

in lowering recidivism rates. After two years the recidivism rate was 70 percent, and after three years it was 77 percent. Of those discharged outright from prison, the two-year recidivism rate was 82 percent, and climbed to 85 percent after three years. Parolees who recidivated did manage to stay in the community longer than those discharged without parole supervision (8.3 months). Therefore, it is obvious that a sharp disagreement exists over the future of parole, with studies variously reporting upwards of 70 percent success rates for parolees or 70 percent recidivism, or failure rates.

Paul Louis

Bibliography

Carlson, Eric, and Evelyn Parks. *Critical Issues in Adult Probation: Issues in Probation Management*. Washington, DC: Government Printing Office, 1979.

Carter, Robert M., et al. *Probation, Parole, and Community Corrections*. 3d ed. New York: John Wiley and Sons, 1984.

Gottfredson, Donald, et al. *Four Thousand Lifetimes: A Study of Time Served and Parole Outcome*. Hackensack, NJ: National Council on Crime and Delinquency, 1973.

Hussey, Frederick, and David E. Duffee. *Probation, Parole, and Community Field Services: Policy, Structure, and Process*. New York: Harper & Row, 1980.

National Council on Crime and Delinquency. *Characteristics of the Parole Population*. Hackensack, NJ: NCCD, 1982.

Nelson, E. Kim, et al. *Promising Strategies in Probation and Parole*. Washington, DC: National Institute of Law Enforcement and Criminal Justice, LEAA, 1978.

Newsweek. "American Justice" (November 1982): 47.

Sacks, Howard and Charles Logan. *Parole: Crime Prevention or Crime Postponement?* Storrs: University of Connecticut Law School Press, 1980.

Professionalism

Professionalism is that state of mind, that standard of behavior, that image of competency and sensitivity, and that constellation of attitudes that one equates with the finest persons who follow a calling; who practice the art and science of a vocation; and who perform the functions of a job.

Professionalism in police work reflects these attitudes and manner of performance in carrying out the awesome responsibility of protecting the lives and liberty of the public being served. It creates in the public mind the image of the agency. It implies that an officer has reached a level of expertise through education, training, and experience that separates him or her from others who are less qualified or less dedicated to public service. It also implies that a professional will strive to achieve the highest standards of behavior and performance. This effort distinguishes the professional from the nonprofessional, whose attitude is one of getting by with less than optimum standards of ethics, behavior, and competence.

The Uniqueness of Policing

While every profession has suffered from the inappropriate behavior of one or more of its members, most outside observers do not measure the total worthiness of a legal, medical, educational, or theological organization by the singular incidents of one of its members. Any unprofessional act by a peace officer, however, brings the spotlight of notoriety to focus on the entire service. Where the traditional professions have, over the years, achieved prestige in the community at large, policing has not enjoyed this level of esteem. The traditional professions have schools of higher education dedicated to the teaching of acceptable practices and behavior. Such schools have only recently begun to emerge for the police function.

In addition to advanced training methods within each of these professions, there are governmental bodies that judge the degree to which a supplicant meets clearly defined criteria for acceptance in the profession. Also, each of the traditional professional organizations has internal control devices to regulate the practice of its members. Until recent times, these control mechanisms remained the exclusive province of the respective professional bodies, with little influence exerted by the public at large. Now, however, the public has become more active in the regulatory process and is beginning to exert some pressure on the governing bodies of law, medicine, education, and theology.

This public input has always been present in police service. Since its earliest time in America, and certainly during most of the twentieth century, police service has operated under close political and societal scrutiny, quite often in the glare of media exposure. All too often this exposure failed to address the major issue: the quality or lack thereof of personnel charged with police responsibilities. For too long police were controlled from without with little regard for professional standards.

The Decision Process

The nature of the police function has an even greater impact on professionalism. An officer's decision, made in seconds, may have an influence on policing throughout the nation (e.g., the *Mapp* and *Miranda* controversies), and it must withstand scrutiny by many experts over extended periods of time. The patrolman cannot afford an error in judgment because all of his or her actions are subject to review by the media, the community, and diverse elements of the criminal-justice system. For example, a patrolman has between two and ten seconds to decide whether to stop, arrest, subdue, or shoot an offender to protect others, with only knowledge and experience to aid decision-making. Next, the patrolman's superior must pass judgment on whatever action was taken, either upholding or countermanding it. Then the police commander assesses the situation and acts accordingly, possibly even recommending prosecution. Thus from two to ten days after the first two-to-ten-second decision the patrolman learns the consequences of having acted.

Not only is the patrolman expected to react within time constraints, he or she is also expected to be able to shift psychological gears at a moment's notice; one moment operating in a proactive, supportive role, the next involved in a life-threatening reactive response mode. Therefore he or she must:

1. be familiar with criminal law,
2. be able to provide early medical assistance,
3. be knowledgeable in scientific investigative techniques,
4. be prepared to use force and/or firearms to overcome resistance and protect life,
5. be able to present the facts in court,
6. know and practice police courtesy to benefit all classes of persons.

If policing is to become professional, then the charge is to develop qualified personnel to assume the above awesome responsibilities.

History of Professionalism

Peel's Reforms. Proper selection and preparation of patrol officers was a keystone of the

Peelian reform movement. Sir Robert Peel's success in 1829 in moving the Metropolitan Police Act through the British Parliament was a culmination of effort begun long before 1816, when the Parliament released a study on crime conditions in England. The Industrial Revolution, with its massive social upheavals, had created conditions demanding attention from the government. By 1842 the Metropolitan Police Force of London had become the model for modern police agencies.

Early American Departments. By the middle of the nineteenth century, full-time paid police forces were a reality in several larger cities of America. Boston and New York adopted the Peelian model, but many of Peel's principles were not integrated into the daily operation of the agencies. Londoners soon referred to their officers as "Bobbies" (after Sir "Robert" Peel) with esteem and affection. This was not the case in the early American departments. The patrolman became subservient to the detective, as the "gold" badge of the detective was far more prestigious than the "tin" badge of the police officer.

Twentieth-Century Agencies. When August Vollmer was elected marshal of the town of Berkeley, California, on April 18, 1905, a new and powerful voice was added to the professionalization movement in American policing. He was not alone in his efforts, although he is frequently credited with being the father of modern American policing. His success appears to have been based upon several of Peel's principles, and apparently Vollmer adopted several of the Londoner's reform actions, most notably the manner in which a patrol officer was selected, trained, and assigned. Vollmer went on to become a leading authority in the police reform movement, and his department stood out as a role model garnering national and international acclaim.

Vollmer's Impact. In 1908 Vollmer began what can best be described as a move toward providing a strong educational base for developing patrol officers. This early training effort led to the Berkeley Police School in 1913 and the initiation of college classes in police administration at the University of California in 1916. This educational base was anchored in more effective screening of people entering the service in his department. As early as 1906 Vollmer had

instituted intelligence and psychological testing for new recruits. By 1919 he gave complete responsibility to his patrolmen for investigation and presentation in court of all offenses occurring on their beats. The patrolman was given support by various specialists inside and outside the department, but the basic responsibility for successfully concluding a case rested with him.

College Cops. In that same period, Vollmer turned to the University of California as a recruiting pool to obtain the quality of manpower his new system of policing demanded. He was successful in convincing a number of students to enter his department as full-time patrol officers. They were subjected to rigorous intelligence, psychological, medical, and personality screening tests prior to being accepted in the force. A number of these men, who served as patrolmen in the Berkeley Police Department (1919–1925) later went on to other agencies and institutions of higher learning as disciples of the Vollmerian system.

The Training Move. While Vollmer expanded the educational base for developing police practitioners on the West Coast, several departments in the Midwest and East used a different method. The Detroit Police Department initiated a training academy in 1911, and New York City began its training academy in 1914.

The Wickersham Commission. During the Depression, a public outcry over crime led to President Herbert Hoover's decision to appoint a federal commission to study the problem of crime in America. A number of recommendations were made, but the most telling statement related to the need for improved methods of selecting, training, and educating police officers.

The Challenge of Crime. Crime was a major issue in the presidential election campaign of 1964. In 1965 President Lyndon B. Johnson appointed the Commission on Law Enforcement and the Administration of Justice. With several task forces studying diverse aspects of crime, the commission was able to compile a comprehensive report entitled *The Challenge of Crime in a Free Society* (1967). The task force report on the police made a number of recommendations but two deserve special mention. The first dealt with the need for more federal support and involvement in addressing the problem of crime at the local level. This led to formation of the Office of Law Enforcement Assistance (OLEA), which later came to be identified as the Law Enforcement Assistance Administration (LEAA). The second recommendation related to the need for upgrading the police service through higher education. The Law Enforcement Education Program (LEEP) was created to implement this idea.

The Return to Policing. Regardless of titles and descriptive terms, a large proportion of the students in the programs who benefited from LEEP entered into public service as law-enforcement officials. An even larger percentage of LEEP participants became actively engaged in police work. With the move toward better educated police came the problem of accommodating different attitudes and philosophies about crime control as debated between the "academics" and the "practitioners." Both camps did, however, support the movement toward greater professionalization of the police service.

Professional Organizations
One mark of professionalism in a given group is the existence of an organization or association that represents its membership in a professional mode, such as the American Medical Association or the American Bar Association. No such singular group provides this service for police officers. The organization that comes closest to achieving this goal is the International Association of Chiefs of Police (IACP). It was started in 1893 and has grown from a loosely knit fraternity of police leaders into a more broadly based practitioner oriented voice on the international scene.

Two major academic organizations concerned with criminal justice are also involved in the professionalization process. The American Society of Criminology (ASC) was founded in 1941 under the direct influence of August Vollmer and several of his disciples. On May 13, 1963, a group of academics formed the International Association of Police Professors, which in 1970 became the Academy of Criminal Justice Sciences (ACJS).

Standards for Professionalism
First and foremost there must be a concern for ethical and moral requirements in accepting an individual into the police service. Second, some organization must take the lead in specifying the standards of performance that will identify an officer as a recognized member of the profession. Third, the educational base by which concepts, knowledge, techniques, and tools used in police work are learned must be strengthened to ensure that persons entering the service demonstrate a capacity to perform the awesome task of policing. Fourth, a certification or licensing procedure must be initiated to confirm that each applicant has achieved the required level of competence. Methods must also be devised whereby a hearing and discrediting process can be instituted should an officer fail to live up to his or her moral and performance obligations. Finally, the various levels of government must work with concerned interest groups to verify that such standards are both equitable and adhered to. The nature of the police function, with its myriad responsibilities and pitfalls, has made attainment of any kind of high status elusive. But now that political control of police has become less of a problem, Vollmerian principles have become engrained, educational reform has reshaped the police, and professionalism is an achievable goal.

Edward A. Farris

Bibliography
Chapman, Samuel G. *Police Patrol Readings.* Springfield, IL: Charles C. Thomas, 1964.

Eastman, George D., and Esther M. Eastman. *Municipal Police Administration.* 6th ed. Washington, DC: International City Management Association, 1969.

Farris, Edward A. *A New Vista for Sheriffs— New Mexico.* 3d ed. Las Cruces, NM: New Mexico State University Cooperative Extension Service, 1985.

Leonard, V.A. *Police Organization and Management.* 2d ed. Brooklyn, NY: Foundation Press, 1964.

Perkins, Rollin M. *Elements of Police Science.* Brooklyn, NY: Foundation Press, 1941.

Vollmer, August. *The Police and Modern Society.* Berkeley: University of California, 1936.

Vollmer, August, and Frank Boolsen. *Police Organization and Administration.* Sacramento, CA: California State Department of Education, 1950.

Property Crime Program (Stings)

Stings involve federal, state, or local law-enforcement officials, often in joint actions, posing as fences and conducting stolen property and contraband transactions with thieves, fences, and other criminals associated with the organized handling and disposal of property. The Law Enforcement Assistance Administration (LEAA), through its Criminal Conspiracies Division, initiated the Anti-Fencing Program in late 1974 to address the problem of escalating property crime (e.g., burglary, larceny, theft, and auto theft) in the United States. Property crime makes up over 90 percent of all crimes committed each year. In 1979, more than 10 million property crimes were reported, resulting in the loss of over $11 billion worth of stolen property. Some experts have placed the loss figure closer to $20 billion annually. The Property Crime Program was developed on the premise that theft is "only the beginning of a very intricate system in which stolen property is acquired, converted, redistributed, and reintegrated into the legitimate property stream." This system is known as the stolen property distribution system (SPDS). The Property Crime Program is designed to penetrate the SPDS through two mutually supportive and interrelated thrusts: enforcement and intelligence. The enforcement component involves the incrimination of thieves, generating fear and apprehension in the criminal community. Experience has demonstrated that these thieves are career criminals and are highly skilled, predatory, and professional. The intelligence component takes advantage of the unique position of a fence dealing with thieves to gain information to be used in the identification and incrimination of active fences and other key actors in the system.

The Property Crime Program stands in stark contrast to the traditional view of property crime enforcement. Unlike the static approach employed by most law-enforcement agencies, "It does not pin all its chances for successful performance on the ability to identify the thief at the original crime scene. Rather, by understanding and following the course of the crime, it provides additional opportunities for success" (Walsh, 1978). During the past seven years, more than forty jurisdictions have conducted property crime projects. The combined results are impressive:

1. the arrest of 9,970 property criminals;
2. the development of solid evidence against these individuals, with a 90 percent conviction rate;

3. the savings of an estimated $109 million in court costs, due to the fact that the vast majority of these convictions were obtained through guilty pleas;
4. the recovery of $300 million in stolen property, almost all of which has been returned to the rightful owners; and
5. the acquisition of valuable insights into the property crime problem.

Perhaps the paramount benefit of the special undercover operations has been the insights that have been obtained about property crime. Several of the most important lessons are outlined below:

1. The sophistication of thieves and fences in the theft, storage, transportation, and sale of stolen property is generally greater than previously expected.
2. Interagency cooperation is absolutely essential to effectively attack the property crime problem.
3. There are strong connections between property crime and other serious criminal activity (i.e., murder, rape, narcotics trafficking, racketeering).
4. Individuals involved in other forms of criminal activity cannot long resist the temptation to commit property crimes. Persons undetected by law-enforcement agencies while committing one or a variety of crimes can often be identified through an antifencing program.

Examples of how these "stings" work will clarify the overall design of the Property Crime Program.

Washington, D.C.
Washington, D.C.'s Metropolitan Police Department, in conjunction with the Federal Bureau of Investigation, conducted four widely publicized antifencing operations over a period of two years, from October 1975 to September 1977. The first operation is perhaps the best known, largely because it was the first to use the name "Sting" after the popular book and movie. The target of the operation was the escalating theft activity in the downtown business district. A high volume of office equipment was being stolen from office buildings despite an increase in law-enforcement personnel assigned to the area. Known as PFF, Inc. (Police FBI Fencing Incognito), undercover operatives from

both the police department and the FBI posed as fences of Italian descent with connections to an organized crime syndicate in New York. PFF, Inc., utilized a number of proven techniques and safety measures to achieve success. It required customers to call ahead, admitted only limited numbers to the locked dealing room, used a visible armed security man, offered customers a drink to get their fingerprints on a glass, feigned an interest in astrology to determine birth dates of customers, and held a party at the end to gather them together for a mass arrest. After nearly a year in operation, the first sting party in the nation was held on February 26, 1976. The sting task force collared 108 thieves and within a few days the total rose to 180. These included a number of individuals who had volunteered to act as "hit men" for "the mob." Most were street-level thieves, many of whom had expensive drug habits. Over 60 percent qualified as career criminals. Only a handful of those charged chose to go to trial, and of those only one was found not guilty.

A second sting terminated four months later. This operation, known as GYA for Got You Again, utilized a trucking firm as a front and netted 150 more thieves, including nine that had been arrested in the first sting. A third, Hi-Roller, culminated in twenty arrests and the clearance of ninety-three crimes. The final and most ambitious sting was called Triconn. The objective of the new storefront warehouse was to gain intelligence on and apprehend other fences working in the area. Sixteen scouts infiltrated the stolen property distribution system. They employed mobile units including an ice cream truck and a souped-up van to make transactions in the street. Undercover officers sold ice cream to children while purchasing checks and stolen credit cards from prostitutes and street people. Special audiovisual equipment in the truck recorded the exchanges. Other illicit goods were bartered in the van and likewise taped. Altogether, 125 people were arrested and $1.2 million in stolen property recovered.

Los Angeles, California

One of the most successful antifencing operations was conducted by the Los Angeles County Sheriff's Department and the Federal Bureau of Investigation from July 1976 to May 1978. The twenty-two-month project, code named Operation TARPIT, was responsible for the recovery of $42 million worth of stolen property and the arrest of 256 individuals. The undercover operatives utilized a team concept, working in small groups out of storefronts, apartments, warehouses, and mobile units. Instead of targeting a specific crime, the teams targeted crime in a specific area. The teams bought everything from automobiles to home entertainment equipment and during their fencing activities made some unusual discoveries. They exposed a scam in which painted lead was sold as platinum; they secured pirated films such as *Star Wars*; they recovered valuable Mexican artifacts and German stocks and bonds; they took in a national treasure of Thailand; they arrested the perpetrator of a highly publicized murder in the Los Angeles area; and they revealed a sophisticated bank fraud network. A side operation established a phony consulting firm known as Pinnacle Professional Consultants. An FBI agent and an informant staffed the consulting firm. The informant directed individuals involved in illegal activities such as land scams to the office for consultation. Once an individual had said too much in an incriminating way, an investigation commenced. One lead resulted in the arrest of several suspects who had fraudulently transferred the titles of twenty pieces of property and thirty-five vacant lots in a three-county area. In addition, a cohesive surveillance operation was initiated to monitor sophisticated hotel burglary and jewel thieves. Using this method, a ring of burglars trading from Texas to Las Vegas was broken, and over $120,000 worth of stolen jewelry recovered.

Honolulu, Hawaii

Project Hukilau consisted of three major operations and a number of ancillary investigations that grew out of the sting experience. The three major operations were undertaken by the Honolulu Police Department and the Honolulu field office of the FBI. Hukilau I started with two storefronts. The first storefront opened in July 1977 and was in a warehouse complex located in a heavy industrial area. The front, Ad-Venture, Inc., was run by two undercover officers posing simply as fast-talking West Cast "haoles" with a great deal of money. The front itself had a traditional counter with two-way mirrors, two manual video cameras, three fixed video cameras, and two hidden microphones (one placed in a nonfunctioning adding machine). Certain savvy thieves recognized Ad-Venture, Inc., as a police setup and avoided it. So to gain credibility authorities arranged a mock raid that even the raiding police were unaware of while making arrests. The scam worked and the undercover officers opened up a new site in January 1978. This time it was a pornographic photo studio with separate offices. The traditional storefront arrangement was scrapped in lieu of a more open officer lounge, and studio layout. Pinhole lenses replaced two-way mirrors to aid the deception. While the sound and picture on the videotape suffered somewhat, the thieves and fences were noticeably more relaxed. Hukilau I produced indictments against 113 defendants and resulted in clearing 651 offenses. Over 90 percent of the 97 subjects ultimately arrested were convicted.

After Hukilau I, the criminal community was understandably unsettled and extremely cautious. In Hukilau II, an attempt was made to establish a more native flavor for the next sting. A bicycle shop, Bob's Pedals, was established in a predominantly apartment and condominium neighborhood. The shop was small, allowing for only one camera, though three undercover officers and a confidential informant staffed the operation. The thieves fell for "Bob's" with an arrest figure of 51 and an indictment count of 229. Operation Aloha followed to catch the more discerning and intelligent subjects. Because the operation was designed to trap those at the highest level of the stolen property distribution system, the outcome was less dramatic. The travel agency front did draw in upper-echelon thieves but on the whole secured more names than indictments. Another sting, Hana Hou, commenced in a four-apartment unit located on the Leeward Coast of Oahu. The local crime problem had intensified to such an extent that during the operation the undercover premises were robbed twice. The officers employed there endured the interruptions well and arrested sixty-nine subjects, forty-nine of whom were identified as major offenders (the individuals who unwittingly burglarized the apartment were also apprehended). Over $300,000 worth of stolen property was recovered.

A final note, and one of enormous interest: the LEAA Property Crime Program in six years spent only $30 million (roughly the cost of one-and-a-half fighter aircraft) to reduce the number of thieves in American cities.

Catherine A. Cotter
James W. Burrows

Bibliography

Bowers, R.A., and J.W. McCullough. *Assessing the "Sting"—An Evaluation of the LEAA Property Crime Program*. Washington, DC: Department of Justice, NIJ, 1983.

Chaiken, J.M., and M.R. Chaiken, *Varieties of Criminal Behavior*. Santa Monica, CA: Rand Corporation, 1981.

Conconi, Charles, and Toni House. *The Washington Sting*. New York: Coward, McCann, and Geoghegan, 1979.

Cotter, Catherine A., and James W. Burrows. *Property Crime Program. A Special Report: Overview of the Sting Program and Project Summaries*. Washington, DC: Department of Justice, LEAA, 1981.

Law Enforcement Assistance Agency. *Strategies for Combatting the Criminal Receiver of Stolen Goods: Anti-Fencing Manual*. Washington, DC: Government Printing Office, 1976.

———. *Taking the Offensive*. Washington, DC: Government Printing Office, 1978.

Schaeffer, R., and A.E. Lewis. *Surprise—Surprise—How the Lawmen Conned the Thieves*. New York: Viking Press, 1979.

Walsh, M.E. *Reassessing Your Agency's Property Crimes Enforcement Mission*. Washington, DC: Government Printing Office, 1978.

Weiner, Kenneth, et al. "Stinging the Detroit Criminal: A Total System Perspective." *Journal of Criminal Justice* 12 (1984): 289–302.

Prostitution

Prostitution is the performance of sexual acts with another person in exchange for money or other compensation. The acts may be heterosexual or homosexual and may be performed by a male or a female. Prostitution has traditionally involved a female prostitute and a male client, referred to as a "trick," or "john." Today, however, male prostitutes are as available as female prostitutes in many metropolitan areas. Prostitutes are commonly referred to as whores, hustlers, hookers, or harlots.

Prostitution has flourished in many cultures. Relationships with prostitutes (*hetaeraes*) in Babylonia were used in religious rites to bring a man closer to his god. The early Greeks had their hetaeraes, or "good friends," high-class prostitutes who were required to wear distinctive clothing and dye their hair blond or red.

The economic benefits of the "world's oldest profession" have enabled it to prevail in spite of religious and societal pressures. Historically, prostitutes have received varying degrees of respect and protection from society, at times enjoying high social status, at other times reviled, as they were during the venereal disease epidemic of Western Europe during the sixteenth century. During this epidemic and afterward, prostitutes were driven from brothels and subjected to strict medical inspections.

Prostitution in the United States has followed basically the same acceptance-rejection patterns as it has in other parts of the world. While the West was being won, prostitution followed the migration. First, there were the "hog ranches" to service the westward movement. Then there were the "floating hog ranches," or riverboat brothels that moved westward with the flow of immigrants. These flat boats were turned into "bagnios," with prostitutes entertaining customers in narrow cubicles built within the cargo boxes. When there were no rooms the "mattress girls" of New Orleans and other cities carried their own mattresses around on their heads or their backs.

In the early nineteenth century, "grabber" gangs in New York City procured girls for madams such as "Red Light Lizzie" and Jane "the Grabber" Haskins. In Chicago in the 1800s Lizzie Allen was proclaimed the most successful madam of the nineteenth century. After the Chicago fire of 1871 hers is said to have been the first business restored to full operation. In the 1800s Sam Purdy's gang of white slavers roamed the great rivers of mid-America stealing young girls for the "white slave" trade in the West. Today, forms of prostitution range from the "mustang ranches of Nevada" to the high society call girl operations of the "Mayflower Madam" of New York.

A study of street prostitution in San Francisco during the early 1980s by the National Institute of Mental Health showed that 60 percent of the prostitutes were under sixteen years of age. Many were as young as ten or twelve. They hustled primarily for economic reasons. Sixty-nine percent were white, the remainder varied racially.

The major police interest in the enforcement of prostitution laws has been to protect the prostitute from allied crimes and to protect the public from venereal diseases through less frequent contacts. With the advent of Herpes Genitalia II and AIDS (Acquired Immune Deficiency Syndrome) both incurable, contagious and sexually transmitted diseases, more stringent laws may be forthcoming.

Common Types of Prostitutes

A prostitute at some time in her or his career may work within each of many classifications of prostitution. Some of the more common classes of prostitution are:

The Streetwalker. Streetwalking is the most common class of prostitution. It is the most visible form of operation and the type of prostitution causing the most concern to the police. In poor neighborhoods the streets are full of persons who are in the business full-time or use streetwalking as a means to supplement other income. In the age of the automobile, the streetwalker is an instant business success.

The Call Girl/Boy. The telephone offers the prostitute a degree of sophistication in contacting clients. It also offers large organized operations clandestine protection from discovery. The telephone serves to maintain a wide circle of contacts for the prostitute. If discreetly used the telephone offers a certain degree of security from enforcement.

The working prostitute maintains a "black book" of customers. When the prostitute wishes to work, she uses the phone to contact listed prospects. From a black book the prostitute can quickly establish or reestablish a business. Thus, the black book has a high monetary value and frequently is sold to other prostitutes.

The Electronic Call Girl/Boy. A popular new device for the prostitute is the installation of an electronic answering device. The communication between prostitute and clientele is then screened through the medium of a recording device. The same basic service may be carried on through an answering service where calls are screened and caller identities are verified before callbacks.

The Lonely Hearts Hustler. Enterprising prostitutes have always found clever ways in which to obtain new clients. The pages of pulp magazines are full of cases where boy meets girl through the lonely hearts club. The numerous contacts made by a prostitute in this manner are seldom reported, and they very seldom come to the attention of the police.

The Computer-Selected Date. Computerized dating firms are in the business of introducing couples. Illicit operators can take advantage of the situation and contact cash customers through this medium. Prostitutes pay the nominal fee, submit a questionnaire, and let the computer select the customers. This automatic matchmaker not only selects congenial prospects, but categorizes as to financial endorsement.

The Public Relations Gimmick. The line between legitimate and illegitimate enterprises is frequently so fine it is not a matter of law but one of morality. The public relations "action" is so covert and the mating of the male and female so shrewd the customer frequently believes the romance is for love. The sponsoring company paying the public relations firm must have a satisfied client, so the amount of money spent is not a factor.

The Photo Studio. Photo studios operate in areas that are liberal in certain types of conduct. The operator puts up colorful signs advertising nude models to photograph. He then waits for lonely males to beat a path to the door. In many instances the models may be legitimate and the photographer may actually take pictures. In many cases the model uses the posing session to make contact with a photographer who never bothers to put film in the rented camera.

The Secretarial Service. Most secretarial services are legal, well-supervised, and render a vital service. Occasionally, however, illicit operators will have business connections and begin contracting secretarial services to unethical clients.

The Housewife. It is not unusual among the ranks of prostitutes to find housewives who supplement the family income. This is fairly common among impoverished minorities who must either assist or entirely support a family. When this amateur activity threatens the professionals, the professionals immediately inform the police, who quickly jail the trespassers.

The Massage Parlor. The most obvious inroads of organized crime into prostitution during the past two decades have been through the massage parlor. Wherever a corrupt government agency can be found, there will shortly follow a colony of fixed massage parlors or the more "mobile variety," each catering to prostitute–client relationships.

This list by no means includes all of the innovative ways in which prostitutes and clients are brought together.

Prostitution will always be a difficult crime to control. In the Kinsey report, *Sexual Behavior in the Human Male* (1948), about 69 percent of all males reporting indicated they had some experiences with prostitutes.

Laws Controlling Prostitution

All states have laws governing the activities of the prostitute. Most states look upon prostitution as a minor *mala prohibita* crime and attach a minor fine to the violation. Some states also require a medical examination prior to appearing before a judge on a case. Minimal penalties attached to prostitution make it almost decriminalized. Prostitution thus supports the medical profession with required medical examinations and the legal profession, which must process the cases.

Because of public apathy and the decriminalized nature of the crime, most police believe prostitution should be legalized. Legalization would put the activity under government control through licensing and medical examination, and the activity would be restricted to certain business-zoned areas of a city. College-level students surveyed in 1987 almost unanimously agreed that prostitution should be legalized. This sanction will probably vary for different demographic groups and within different regions of the country.

Allied illegal activities associated with prostitution include pandering, which is the securing of clients for a prostitute, and pimping, which is living off the earnings of a prostitute. Both are felonies in most states. There are rarely prosecutions on these crimes because the prostitute refuses to testify against her "man."

The Federal Mann Act of 1910, "The White Slave Traffic Act," prohibited the interstate transportation of women for immoral purposes and curbed the flow of large groups of prostitutes operating on an interstate circuit. The Omnibus Crime Bill of 1965 (as amended in 1986) defines organized crime as a continuing conspiracy, and organized groups headed by pimps and panderers can now be prosecuted under that act.

Most communities in the United States are committed to the suppression rather than the regulation of prostitution. Community attitudes tend to govern the amount of enforcement that prostitution will receive. Thus there has been a willingness on the part of many law-enforcement agencies to actively enforce prostitution laws.

The United National General Assembly in 1949 adopted a convention for the suppression of prostitution worldwide. Thus, a wide variety of control systems operates to prohibit or limit the activities of the prostitute. Worldwide and in the United States there is little consistency in the control of prostitution.

Denny F. Pace

Bibliography

Bullough, Vern L. *Prostitution: A Guide to Sources, 1960–1990.* New York: Garland, 1992.

Bullough, Vern L., and Bonnie Bullough. *Women and Prostitution: A Social History.* Prometheus Books, 1987.

Decker, John F. *Prostitution: Regulation and Control.* Littleton, CO: Rothman, 1979.

Pace, Denny F., and Jimmie C. Styles. *Organized Crime: Concepts and Controls.* 2d ed. Englewood Cliffs, NJ: Prentice-Hall, 1983.

Reynolds, Helen. *The Economics of Prostitution.* Springfield, IL: Charles C. Thomas, 1985.

Sion, Abraham. *Prostitution & the Law.* Winchester, MA: Faber & Faber, 1978.

Weatherford, Jack M. *Porn Row: An Inside Look at the Sex-for-Sale District of a Major American City.* New York: Arbor House, 1986.

Weisberg, D. Kelly. *Children of the Night: A Study of Adolescent Prostitution.* Lexington, Mass.: Lexington, 1984.

Psychological Attributes

The question of whether there is a distinctive police personality is one that has occupied students of policing for some time. The answers to this question are fraught with methodological and interpretative problems, not the least of which is the often hidden assumption that police work represents a deviant career or is populated by individuals who are somewhat unbalanced or otherwise prone to misbehavior, if not outright violence. On the whole, however, this view of police work is but a reflection of cultural and social stereotypes of policing, for there is considerable evidence supporting the view that police officers are much like other occupational groups.

Kates's study (1950:2) of police officers found them to have "as many signs of maladjustment as may be found in other groups." Matarazzo et al. (1964) found that their police applicants scored at the healthy end of three personality scales compared with normal and patient groups. Using the MMPI (Minnesota Multiphasic Personality Inventory), Hooke and Krauss (1971) found that the police officers they studied, compared with the general population, were a "normal lot." Symonds (1970:16) was "impressed with the degree of maturity, good judgment, and mental health" of the ordinary police officer. Lefkowitz (1971:9) observed that police officers are "not particularly cynical regarding police work, not dogmatic in their thinking" (cf Lefkowitz, 1973; 1974). Baehr et al. (1968), and Matarazzo et al. (1964) found that officers' IQ scores were consistently within the average range. Reiser (1972:21), found police officers to be "above the norm in intelligence, have better than average emotional stability, like working with people in a service function, and have a strong desire to contribute to the betterment of community life." Similar findings were reported by Baehr et al. (1968)

There is, of course, some evidence contrary to these findings. Preiss and Ehrlich (1966) found about 35 percent of a group of police recruits to be "probably maladjusted" or "doubtful" on the measures of emotional adjustment used. Chwast (1965) found police officers to be suffering from feelings of powerlessness and self-hate. Becker (1963), Pfiffner (1967), Riess (1967), Westley (1951), and Wilson (1963) found officers not only suffering from low self-esteem, but also being preoccupied with the importance of having respect for the law. Reporting on his psychiatric counseling of police officers, Shev (1977) observed that a third of the officers treated by him were so unstable they should not be police officers.

Police Personality

In order to avoid a controversial area of police study, certainly one caught in a quagmire of definitional and methodological problems, there is perhaps a tendency to either avoid this topic altogether or to diffuse it in one fashion or another. Murphy (1965) and Radano (1968), for instance, view police officers as being like everyone else. In a similar fashion, Reiser

(1972:21) argues that "there are as many personality types and individual differences among a large population of policemen as among engineers, teachers, lawyers, or psychologists." This statement differs little from an earlier and simpler statement he made in this same book, namely: ". . . there is no such thing as a police personality" (81). Nevertheless, the existence of a police personality has been the subject of considerable research and comment.

Rokeach, Miller, and Snyder (1971) provide perhaps the best evidence supporting the existence of a police personality. They note that "police [are] generally homogeneous in their attitudes and beliefs . . . [and] that policemen have attitudes and personality characteristics that are distinctly different from other occupational groups" (156). Compared with matched civilian controls, they note, officers with little education "place a relatively lower value on freedom, equality, independence, and a world of beauty and . . . place a relatively higher value on obedience, self-control, a comfortable life, and pleasure" (164). That there are many significant differences on personality-trait scores between a group of police recruits at the beginning of training and both general populations and college students has been verified by other researchers.

The most far-reaching conclusion of Rokeach et al. (1971) is the notion that "personality factors and social backgrounds are more important than occupational socialization in understanding police value systems" (155). Bayley and Mendelsohn's findings (1969) that experienced police officers scored lower on anomie, authoritarianism, prejudice, and social distance than control groups supports the findings of Rokeach and his associates that police socialization may not be as important as many commentators have thought. Not everyone agrees with these findings and their interpretation.

After reviewing the existing literature and after pointing out many of its methodological flaws, Balch (1972:110) notes that "the evidence—by its very inconsistency, if nothing else, does not indicate the existence of a police personality, authoritarian or otherwise." Many commentators who disagree with the notion that there is a police personality agree that police officers share a common set of ideas about themselves, the world within which they live, and their work. These attitudes, however, are largely the result of their socioeconomic backgrounds and work experience. But Niederhoffer (1967:159–60) argues: "It is the police system, not the personality of the candidate, that is the more powerful determination of behavior and ideology."

Authoritarianism. Of all the psychological traits attributed to officers, perhaps none has received more attention than the authoritarian personality. As defined by Adorno and his associates (1950), an authoritarian person is an individual who adheres to conventional middle-class values, who is submissive and uncritical toward the idealized moral authority of the in-group, who wants to find and punish persons violating conventional values, who is opposed to the subjective, imaginative, and tender-minded, who believes in the mystical determinants of a person's fate, who thinks in rigid categories, who identifies with power figures, who gives exaggerated assertion to notions of strength and toughness, who is generally cynical and hostile, who believes that wild and dangerous things go on in the world, and who is overly concerned with the sexual goings-on of others. Given police work's support of a legally conventional view of the world, its search for wrongdoers (i.e., law violators), and its seemingly continual preparation and training for the use of force, it is easy to understand how police officers and police work come to be viewed as authoritarian.

The primary questions raised by the issue of authoritarian personalities are: (1) Do police officers possess such a personality? (2) Are authoritarian personalities more attracted to policing than to other occupational pursuits? and (3) Does police work itself teach or heighten individual authoritarian tendencies?

Matarazzo et al. (1964), Niederhoffer (1967), and McNamara (1967) found police scores on authoritarian, dogmatic, and other related scales similar to and sometimes lower than those obtained by other groups, especially groups with comparable educational levels. Niederhoffer and McNamara found police-recruit authoritarian scores similar to those of the working class studied by Adorno et al. (1950).

Other studies have shown police officers to be impulsive risktakers, prone to act out their impulses in physical aggression. Mills (1969) found police officers projecting aggressiveness onto others as a means of justifying their own assertive actions. Matarazzo et al. (1964), Trojanowicz (1971), and Walther et al. (1973)

argued that their police officers were markedly self-assertive and concerned with maintaining a virile self-image. Trojanowicz and Walther et al. noted, however, that officers they studied generally did not respond with above-average forcefulness to the aggression of others. These same officers were seen to be lacking in self-confidence, preferring to be supervised, and preferring to supervise others, in a highly directive manner. Rokeach et al. (1971) reported similar findings vis-à-vis a lack of independence and desire for structured work environment. Marshall and Mansson (1966) reported that their sample of police officers was more rigid, punitive, and more easily influenced by a status figure than their comparison groups.

Inasmuch as the authoritarian scores of police officers are similar to those of the working class from which many of them are recruited, and inasmuch as the authoritarian scores of the working class are higher than middle- and upper-class scores, it appears that police departments recruit members from a relatively authoritarian class of people, rather than serving as a general magnet attracting a broad range of individual authoritarian personalities per se. As such, and as Wilson (1968:33–34) noted, the police " . . . bring to the job some of the focal concerns of working-class men—a preoccupation with maintaining self-respect, proving one's masculinity, 'not taking any crap,' and 'not being taken in.'" Although the evidence is somewhat inconsistent, it appears that police experience intensifies the authoritarianism inherent in the backgrounds of police recruits.

Cynicism. Cynicism, as defined by Niederhoffer (1967:96) is "a loss of faith in people, of enthusiasm for the higher ideals of police work, and of pride and integrity." Niederhoffer found that cynicism was related to length of police service, as did Regoli and Poole (1978a). It was lowest at the recruit stage, reached its peak during the seven to ten year service period, and declined until retirement. Niederhoffer (76) also reported that the most cynical officers were often the most successful; they made the most arrests.

Regoli's (1976) examination of Niederhoffer's cynicism scale found it invalid and unreliable. Rather than being a single variable, he found it to consist of the following five variables: (1) cynicism toward relations with the public, (2) cynicism toward organizational functions, (3) cynicism about police dedication to duty, (4) cynicism about police social solidarity, and (5) cynicism about training and education. Regoli and Poole (1978b) also suggest that cynicism differs among different organizational types of law enforcement. They found that city officers were more cynical toward relations with the public; whereas county officers were more cynical about police dedication to duty.

As with authoritarianism, questions may be raised as to whether cynical individuals become police officers, whether cynicism is a characteristic of certain socioeconomic classes, or whether it is the result of job demands. Regoli and Poole's (1978b) finding that cynicism does not increase significantly with length of service favors the first two views. The weight of commentary, however, favors the latter view.

Suspiciousness. Cynicism and suspiciousness represent complementary, albeit distinct, ideas. As with cynicism the existence of suspiciousness is widely believed. The question of interest here is whether this suspicion is an individual personality trait or one that is job specific. Although some studies hint that new recruits are the source of this suspiciousness, most analysis and commentary focus upon the job-specific demands underlying it. Lipset (1969:78) notes that a police officer's job requires him or her to be suspicious of human behavior, to be able to sense plots and conspiracies based upon the smallest of indicators. That suspiciousness even extends to suspicion of other officers. In a similar vein, the longer police officers had served on the force, the readier they were to perceive danger in twenty different situations.

Suspiciousness and cynicism are thought to lead to perceptions of low occupational prestige, a sense of being shunned by acquaintances and neighbors, and a sense of isolation. While these perceptions may be viewed as the consequences of ambiguous and often conflicting role expectations, as may cynicism and suspiciousness, they form the basis of a binding police subculture thought by many to strongly affect police attitudes. Further research may strengthen research findings supporting the idea of a police personality; nevertheless, the weight given to this subculture as a formative milieu of ideas and actions cannot be ignored.

Low Occupational Prestige. Being suspicious and cynical of the very persons officers are pledged to serve may underlie perceptions of citizens failing to hold their occupation in high regard. Watson and Sterling (1969:9) found that only 40 percent of their sample felt that the police image in their community was favorable. Although McNamara (1967) reported that 75 percent of his experienced police officers felt police work should be ranked alongside medicine and the legal profession, he found, as did Reiss (1967), that they also felt their occupational prestige was on the decline.

Despite the prevalence of these sentiments, Bayley and Mendelsohn (1969) found that the Denver police officers felt they received higher than average respect from the public. Preiss and Ehrlich (1966) reported similar findings. Moreover, there is considerable evidence that the public views the performance of police duties rather favorably.

Pariah Feeling. In addition to feeling that the public has little appreciation of their occupation and services, some officers feel that they are social undesirables. The pariah feeling is the feeling of being "scorned by citizens who are more respectable but no more honest." They are, in other words, isolated from their friends, as well as from the public.

Contrary to this trend of thought, Bayley and Mendelsohn (1969) reported that only 12 percent of their Denver police officers had difficulty making friends with nonpolice families and less than 25 percent complained of difficulties in their social relationships because of their job. As many as 68 percent said they associated primarily with nonpolice friends.

Isolation. The pariah feeling coupled with serving ambiguous and unappreciated organizational goals leads to isolation and the formation of a subculture. Police thus afflicted become defensive in the face of citizen uneasiness and seek out the company of one another where they are able to reinforce one anothers' thoughts and values, thus enhancing and perhaps even exaggerating them.

The clannishness attributed to police work may also be found in other occupations. However in comparison, policing tends to be more isolated. Under many circumstances police officers need to be isolated in order to perform their duties effectively and in order to reduce the cognitive strain of their work. Where such isolation develops, and it must perforce develop to

some extent everywhere, it affects such personal attributes as authoritarianism, cynicism, and suspiciousness regardless of whether they belong to a person's individual makeup or to the structure of the socioeconomic groups from which they come.

Conservatism. Police have been described as conservative and moralistic, typically approaching problems with black and white solutions. According to Lipset (1969:76) William Parker said that the majority of the nation's police officers were "conservative, ultraconservative, and very right wing." Skolnick (1975:61) concluded that Goldwater conservatism represented California police. Wilson (1968) observed that Chicago police officers were unreceptive to social change. Bayley and Mendelsohn (1969) reported that Denver police were more conservative and more Republican than the community as a whole. Niederhoffer (1967:117) indicated a reasonably large number of New York City police officers belonged to the John Birch Society. Watson and Sterling (1969:9) noted that 65 percent of officers queried said that punishment is an effective measure in crime control, while 82 percent indicated that punishment for crime should be severer. Respondents to their nationwide survey tended to side with a sample of civilian conservatives more often than with a sample of civilian liberals.

As with the other psychological attributes, it is uncertain whether conservatism is a manifestation of personality, social background, or police socialization. Inasmuch as conservatism may be attached to authoritarianism, its origins might lie with personality factors. Inasmuch as there is some evidence that political conservatism is unaffected by a police officer's age (Bayley and Mendelsohn, 1969), its derivation might lie within the social backgrounds of police recruits. Then again, its origins may lie within the very demands of police work itself or a combination of the above. As Lipset (1969:76) has argued, police officers are conservative because police officers are recruited largely from undereducated and typically conservative working-class populations, and because their job stresses toughness, authority, and a skeptical view of human nature.

Conclusion

Although much of the evidence bearing upon psychological attributes is conceptually problematic, methodologically flawed, and sometimes inconsistent, a few researchers, especially Rokeach and his associates (1971), appear to have demonstrated that individuals possessing certain types of personality attributes are attracted to police work. Nevertheless, neither they nor any other student of this topic has been able to disentangle the effects of a person's socioeconomic background from the demands that police work and its subculture place upon individual officers. Future research within this area may shed further light upon these mutually interdependent relationships.

W. Clinton Terry, III

Bibliography

Adorno, T.W., et al. *The Authoritarian Personality.* New York: Harper and Brothers, 1950.

Baehr, Melany, et al. *Psychological Assessment of Patrolmen's Qualifications in Relation to Field Performance.* U.S. Department of Justice, LEAA. Washington, DC: Government Printing Office, 1968.

Balch, Robert W. "The Police Personality: Fact or Fiction?" *Journal of Criminology Criminal Law and Police Science* 63(1) (March 1972): 106–19.

Bayley, David H., and Harold Mendelsohn. *Minorities and the Police: Confrontation in America.* New York: Free Press, 1969.

Becker, Howard S. *The Outsiders: Studies in the Sociology of Deviance.* New York: Free Press, 1963.

Chwast, Jacob. "Value Conflicts in Law Enforcement." *Crime and Delinquency* 11 (April 1965): 151–61.

Dodd, David J. "Police Mentality and Behavior." *Issues in Criminology* 3(1) (Summer 1967): 47–67.

Hooke, James F., and Herbert H. Krauss. "Personality Characteristics of Successful Police Sergeant Candidates." *Journal of Criminal Law, Criminology, and Police Science* 62 (March 1971): 104–06.

Kates, Solis L. "Rorschach Responses, Strong Blank Scales, and Job Satisfaction among Policemen." *Journal of Applied Psychology* 34 (August 1950): 249–54.

Lefkowitz, Joel. *Job Attitudes of Police.* National Institute of Law Enforcement and Criminal Justice. U.S. Department of Justice. Washington, DC: Government Printing Office, 1971.

———. "Attitudes of Police Toward Their Job." In *The Urban Policeman in Transition.* Eds. J.R. Snibbe and H.M. Snibbe. Springfield, IL: Charles C. Thomas, 1973. 203–32.

———. "Job Attitudes of Police: Overall Description and Demographic Correlates." *Journal of Vocational Behavior* 5 (October 1974): 221–30.

———. "Psychological Attributes of Policemen: A Review of Research and Opinion." *Journal of Social Issues* 31(1) (Winter 1975): 3–26.

Lipset, Seymour M. "Why Cops Hate Liberals—and Vice Versa." *Atlantic Monthly* 223(3) (March, 1969): 76–83.

McNamara, John H. "Uncertainties in Police Work: The Relevance of Police Recruits' Background and Training." In *The Police: Six Sociological Essays.* Ed. David Bordua. New York: John Wiley and Sons, 1967.

Marshall, James, and Helge Mansson. "Punitiveness, Recall, and the Police." *Journal of Research Crime and Delinquency* 3(2) (July 1966): 129–39.

Matarazzo, Joseph D., Bernadens V. Allen, George Saslow, and Arthur N. Wien. "Characteristics of Successful Policemen and Firemen Applicants." *Journal of Applied Psychology* 48 (April 1964): 123–33.

Mills, Robert B. "Use of Diagnostic Small Groups in Police Recruit Selection and Training." *Journal of Criminal Law, Criminology, and Police Science* 60(2) (1969): 238–41.

Murphy, Michael J. "Improving the Law Enforcement Image." *Journal of Criminal Law, Criminology, and Police Science* 56(1) (1965): 105–08.

Niederhoffer, Arthur. *Behind the Shield: The Police in Urban Society.* Garden City, NY: Doubleday, 1967.

Pfiffner, John McDonald. *The Functions of the Police in a Democratic Society.* Los Angeles: Civic Center Campus, Center for Training and Career Development, University of Southern California, 1967.

Preiss, Jack J., and Howard J. Ehrlich. *An Examination of Role Theory: The Case of the State Police.* Lincoln: University of Nebraska Press, 1966.

Radano, G. *Walking the Beat.* New York: World, 1968.

Regoli, Robert M. "An Empirical Assessment

of Niederhoffer's Police Cynicism Scale."
Journal of Criminal Justice 4(3) (1976):
231–41.

Regoli, Robert M., and Eric D. Poole. "Specifying Police Cynicism." *Journal of Police
Science and Administration* 6(1) (1978a):
98–104.

———. "Explaining Cynicism among City
and County Police." *Criminal Justice
Review* 3(1) (1978b): 93–99.

———. "Measurement of Police Cynicism: A
Factor Scaling Approach." *Journal of
Criminal Justice* 7(1) (1979): 37–51.

Reiser, Martin. *The Police Department Psychologist.* Springfield, IL: Charles C.
Thomas, 1972.

Reiss, Albert J. "Career Orientations, Job
Satisfactions, and the Assessment of Law
Enforcement Problems by Police Officers." *Studies of Crime and Law Enforcement in Major Metropolitan Areas.* Vol.
1. Washington, DC: Government Printing Office, 1967.

Rokeach, Milton, Martin G. Miller, and John
A. Snyder. "The Value Gap Between Police and Policed." *Journal of Social Issues* 27(1) (1971): 155–71.

Shev, Edward E. *Good Cops, Bad Cops.* San
Francisco: San Francisco Book Company, 1977.

Skolnick, Jerome H. *Justice Without Trial:
Law Enforcement in a Democratic Society.* New York: John Wiley and Sons,
1975.

Symonds, Martin. "Emotional Hazards of
Police Work." *American Journal of Psy-
choanalysis* 30(1970): 155–60.

Trojanowicz, Robert C. "The Policeman's
Occupational Personality." *Journal of
Criminal Law, Criminology, and Police
Science* 62(4) (December 1971): 551–59.

Walther, Regis H., et al. "The Contrasting
Occupational Cultures of Policemen and
Social Workers." In *The Urban Police-
man in Transition.* Eds. J.R. Snibbe and
H.M. Snibbe. Springfield, IL: Charles C.
Thomas, 1973. 260–80.

Watson, Nelson A., and James W. Sterling.
Police and Their Opinions. Washington,
DC: International Association of Chiefs
of Police, 1969.

Westley, William A. "The Police: A Sociological Study of Law, Custom, and Morality." Ph.D. diss. Chicago: Department of
Sociology, University of Chicago, 1951.

———. *Violence and the Police: A Study of
Law, Custom, and Morality.* Cambridge,
MA: MIT Press, 1970.

Wilson, James Q. "The Police and Their
Problems: A Theory." *Public Policy* 12
(1963): 189–216.

———. *Varieties of Police Behavior: The
Management of Law and Order in Eight
Communities.* Cambridge, MA: Harvard
University Press, 1968.

Psychological Fitness for Duty

Fitness for duty evaluations refers to the formal
psychological assessment of law-enforcement
personnel to address in specific terms their ability to reliably and safely perform law-enforcement functions. This type of evaluation is well
established in occupational medicine, e.g., return to work exams and "for cause" evaluations. Law-enforcement agencies increasingly
use fitness exams in order to assure that personnel in sensitive positions have the mental and
emotional ability to handle all aspects of their
jobs, in addition to keeping their own behavior
controlled and lawful. In a 1988 survey 193
municipal police departments and 39 state police agencies responded to a questionnaire concerning psychological services. The fitness for
duty question was: Does your department/
agency offer "special examination for suspended and problem police officers?" In answer, 38.91 percent said yes, they currently used
such a service and 67.11 percent perceived the
need for a special examination service (Delprino
and Bahn, 1988). An earlier survey conducted
by Parisher et al. (1979) found that only 20
percent of the department/agencies contacted
used any type of psychological services, whether
for evaluating fitness for duty or not.

The International Association of Chiefs of
Police (IACP), Psychological Services Section,
published fitness for duty guidelines in 1991.
Since the IACP is a leader in the profession the
guidelines will be listed in full:

1. Only qualified psychologists and/or psychiatrists should be responsible for psychological fitness for duty evaluations.
2. If professional licenses are required by
   the state, they should also be required
   for the mental health professional conducting any fitness for duty evaluations.
3. Mental health professionals who conduct
   fitness for duty evaluations should be

experienced in the field of police and/or public safety psychology and familiar with the research on testing and evaluation in this field.

4. Evaluators who have a dual relationship (e.g., as the officer's past therapist or counselor) should refrain from conducting fitness for duty evaluations in these cases, whenever feasible.

5. The client in fitness for duty evaluations is the referring agency, not the officer/employee.

6. An informed consent and release form advising of the limits of confidentiality should be obtained from the officer/employee prior to any assessment for fitness to duty.

7. A description of the reason(s) for referral for a fitness for duty evaluation, including the questions to be addressed, should be obtained prior to any assessment.

8. Fitness for duty assessments should include: (a) at least one in-person interview with the officer/employee; (b) a battery of psychological tests; and (c) review of any other information deemed appropriate.

9. Whenever possible, fitness for duty evaluators should go beyond standard clinical testing and interviewing techniques to include a review of relevant background information such as personnel records and investigator's reports.

10. If information deemed necessary for review by the evaluator cannot be obtained, any recommendations should include the comment that the evaluation is based on available data and might be affected by specific additional information that was requested but not obtained by the evaluator.

11. A written report documenting the findings of the evaluation along with specific recommendations regarding the officer/employee's ability to meet responsibilities of continued employment and/or retraining/rehabilitation suggestions should be provided to the agency.

12. The written report should provide reason(s) for any determination about an officer/employee's fitness for duty. Administrative decisions based on the report are the responsibility of the referring agency.

13. The agency is responsible for safeguarding the confidentiality of the evaluation.

14. A policy for providing the fitness for duty evaluation results to the officer/employee should be developed with the agency prior to any evaluations. Whenever possible, the evaluator or another qualified mental health professional should be available to interpret results if they are shared with the officer/employee.

A review of these guidelines shows that past evaluation practices may have been negligent or inept, and needed stronger restatement.

Legal Developments
Court decisions have made it clear that law-enforcement agencies can be held liable for the behavior of their officers, even in off-duty situations (e.g., *Bonsignore v. City of New York* [1980]). In legalese the term is "vicarious liability." Another legal development is the recent passage of the Americans with Disabilities Act (ADA). The Act establishes the principle that employers must make "reasonable accommodation" for employees with mental and physical impairments. These two developments when taken together form an adversarial relationship. On the one hand, law-enforcement agencies must protect the public from officers who behave irresponsibly, inappropriately, or use poor judgment due to mental impairment; on the other hand, agencies are required to accommodate impaired personnel within reason. The IACP Psychological Services Section studied the implications of ADA with great interest. The IACP concluded, "It appears that there is nothing in this law that would impede the continued utilization of job-related psychological screening." The IACP interpreted the ADA to mean that for police officers psychological screening could be conducted before employment, and that administering psychological tests during screening would not violate the ADA. Questions asked relating to prior mental illness or psychiatric history would also be permissible and in line with inquiring about past alcohol and drug use/abuse.

The Evaluation
Law-enforcement agencies determine fitness for duty using a variety of practices and policies. Clearly some agencies do not employ professional help but rely on discipline to address fitness for duty problems, or simply cover them

up. If psychological examinations are administered, variation occurs according to whether a psychologist is on staff or an external consultant, the size of the agency, the availability of light duty stations (for rehabilitation), municipal policies, the presence or absence of an Internal Affairs Unit, and the like. No matter what the practices and policies are, they should be formalized and uniformly applied.

A psychological fitness for duty evaluation typically involves acute or chronic deviant behavior on the part of an employee (often an officer but also emergency dispatchers and other civilian personnel). Examples of such behavior are manifest in frequent citizen complaints for excessive use of force, evidence of alcohol problems, obvious emotional turmoil and bizarre behavior, complaints of domestic violence by the spouse, or a history of exhibiting poor judgment. Once superiors note the behavior a risk management issue arises. The risk may be to the person, to the public, to colleagues, to property, or to the reputation of the agency. Psychological problems may or may not be associated with violations of the law or infractions of policy and can be dealt with independently of the fitness for duty evaluation. If the agency is to fire the employee anyway, the evaluation is unnecessary. The fitness-for-duty examination is a disability evaluation. A key difference between a disability evaluation and other kinds of psychological exams is that the issue is very narrowly defined: Can this person do the job or perform the range of jobs safely?

To begin with, the evaluator makes a preliminary assessment of the individual based on personnel records and interviews with other employees. A complete evaluation is costly to the agency and could be discontinued if deemed unnecessary. Perhaps more important, a complete evaluation often represents an ordeal for those involved and should be conducted only when warranted. As mentioned earlier, agencies should have policies and procedures in place regarding the evaluations as they frequently become embroiled in legal controversy. Once the agency decides to proceed, it is proper to order the employee to undergo the evaluation. Per IACP guidelines, a qualified evaluator ordinarily means a licensed doctoral level practitioner with experience in law-enforcement fitness-for-duty examinations. After the preliminary assessment, the evaluator meets with the employee to explain the procedure. This requires delicate handling. The employee is told that in

order to continue the evaluation he or she must waive the privilege of confidentiality by signing a form. Most agencies having procedures require the employee to cooperate with the examination and, by extension, require waiving confidentiality. Once the waiver is signed psychological testing commences using whatever instruments are appropriate to the referral issue. The battery of appropriate tests can include paper and pencil personality tests (e.g., Minnesota Multiphasic Personality Inventory) and projective tests, such as the Rorschach. Next, the evaluator conducts the clinical interview in which the employee talks about the incident(s) that precipitated the need for an evaluation. Then the employee's history in and out of the agency is weighed to project a clear picture of character and motivation. Any current history including medications taken, alcohol or drug involvement, and medical status is also considered. Therefore, a minimally acceptable procedure for conducting the evaluation comprises a review of relevant documents and/or collateral contact with relevant parties, the administration of a battery of psychological tests, a clinical interview with the employee, and ascertaining all employee histories.

Once completed, the evaluator issues a report to the agency that addresses the employee's ability to perform on the job, covering such functions as:

- making critical decisions;
- exercising good judgment in a pressured and unpressured situation;
- dealing appropriately with the chain of command, with peers, and with citizens;
- having adequate sensory and motor skills to drive an emergency vehicle in a safe manner, engage in physical confrontations, and handle weapons;
- avoiding the use of force in personal matters;
- obeying the law; and
- abstaining from excessive use of intoxicants.

In addition to indicating which functions are compromised, the report should unambiguously state whether or not the officer is fit for duty and give reasons for that determination. Any psychological diagnosis must use nomenclature taken from the American Psychiatric Association Diagnostic and Statistical Manual. The evaluator recommends appropriate treatment and/or reassignment to light duty. For example, an employee with a drinking problem might be considered unfit for duty until he or she completes treatment and submits to taking Antabuse (a drug that, when combined with alcohol, produces nausea). Finally, with the implementation of the Americans with Disabilities Act in mind, the evaluator should indicate ways in which the agency can reasonably accommodate the individual, if possible.

Anthony V. Stone

Bibliography

Burke, Ronald J. "Type A Behavior, Occupational and Life Demands, Satisfaction, and Well-Being." *Psychological Reports* 63 (1988): 451–58.

Delprino, Robert P., and Charles Bahn. "National Survey of the Extent and Nature of Psychological Services in Police Departments." *Professional Psychology: Research and Practice* 19 (1988): 421–25.

Flanagan, Catherine L. "The ADA and Police Psychology." *Police Chief* 58 (1991): 15–16.

Grossman, Linda S., et al. "Sensitivity of MMPI Validity Scales to Motivational Factors in Psychological Evaluations of Police Officers." *Journal of Personality Assessment* 55 (1990): 549–61.

Janik, James. "Considerations of Returning a Law Enforcement Officer to Duty After Inpatient Treatment for Substance Abuse." *Forensic Reports* 4 (1991): 367–78.

Ostrove, Eric. "Police/Law Enforcement and Psychology. Special Issue: Psychology in Law Enforcement." *Behavioral Sciences and the Law* 4 (1986): 353–70.

Parisher, D., et al. "Psychologists and Psychological Services in Urban Police Departments." *Professional Psychology: Research and Practice* 10 (1979): 6–7.

Stone, Anthony V. "Psychological Fitness-for-Duty Evaluation." *Police Chief* 57 (1990): 39–42, 53.

Zelig, Mark. "Ethical Dilemmas in Police Psychology." *Professional Psychology: Research and Practice* 19 (1988): 336–38.

Psychological Services Units

Psychological services units (PSUs) are a recent development in policing. Police agencies have now recognized the wide spectrum and potential worth of the services and activities that such units can provide. While psychological services for offenders have long been the norm in criminal justice, similar services for police officers were unknown until the late 1960s. Most of the largest departments now have such units. A national association of police psychologists was formed in 1984.

Throughout the early 1970s, the police literature frequently contained references to the need for psychological services for police officers, such as the following:

> There is nothing to fear in discovering that a law enforcement officer has emotions, feelings, prejudices, and the like. The only thing to fear is not recognizing that he is not a superhuman being. He must understand himself in order to survive. In understanding himself he will be able to cope with the task at hand and provide to the community the kind of law enforcement we all talk about but find hard to implement. (Kreins, 1974)

Other writers noted the many stress factors in police work (Blanch, 1977; Cruse and Rubin, 1972; Hillgren and Bond, 1975; Kroes, 1976; Kroes and Hurrell, 1975; Reiser, 1972, 1973, 1975; Straton, 1984) recognized the value of psychological services in interpersonal communications, mental health, referral services, and chemical dependency. Moreover, spouses also needed psychological services:

> To improve morale and efficiency—and indeed for humanitarian reasons—police departments must develop programs and policies cognizant of their employees' spouses. In the future, fringe benefits may even include support for psychological services, such as marriage counseling. (Rafky, 1974)

The necessity for psychological services in the areas of police officer selection and training has also been pointed out:

> The selection of police officers is perhaps the most critical part of the prowess of law enforcement. Poor selection procedures may have implications for many years into the future. Selection is much too important a decision to be made haphazardly. (McCreedy, 1974)

Psychology must be an integral part of every police training course, not only for dealing with others in crisis situations, but also for helping officers deal with their own personal problems. (Blanch, 1977)

Police Psychological Services Units have been the increasingly popular answer to these vari-ous problems. Numerous effects upon police operations have resulted. Very quickly, PSUs have found themselves with responsibilities expanded beyond officer counseling. In Houston, for instance, 302 successive hostage negotiation incidents were handled without injury with the help of the PSU—contrasted to previous frequent violence. In Tucson, the psychologist can order the transfer of officers with no

---

TABLE 1

Police Psychological Services

Personnel Selection
Recruit Interviews
Psychological Testing
Selection Criteria Development
Specialized Function (SWAT, Hostage Team) Selection

Employee and Family Counseling
Personal Problems
Family Problems
Marital Adjustment
Job Stress
Mental Health
Referral Services

Other Counseling Services
Voluntary Group Counseling
Family Counseling
Stress Programs
Weight Reduction
Alcoholism
Chemical Dependency

Preservice Training
Crisis Intervention
Family Dynamics
Basic Psychology
Adjustment to Police Career
Design Training Models

In-Service Training
Family Dynamics
Mental Health
Stress Programs
Specialized Functions
Training Designs
Roll-Call Training
Develop Training Models

Investigative Consultation
Case Consultation
Offender Profile Analysis
Pattern/Modus Operandi Analysis
Hostage/Terrorist Situations

Management Consultation
Policy Development/Input
Problem Officers
Promotion Screening
Lobbying/Legislative Witness

Research
Surveys
Mental Health Studies
Designing Training Programs
Videotape Roll-Call Vignettes

Public/Community Relations
Public Appearances (TV, radio)
Interviews
Conferences
Public Education (rape, terrorist, hostage)

Crisis Intervention
Hostage Negotiations
Suicide Prevention
Mentally Disordered
Other Crises

Administrative Functions
Policy Development
Personnel Supervision
Internal Programs
Peer Counseling Directives
Chaplain Programs
Coordination with Other Police Agencies
Coordination with Other Governmental Agencies
Coordination with Private Agencies
Supervise Interns

questions asked. In most jurisdictions with PSUs, all officers who use deadly force must now see the psychologist for assessment and/or counseling.

As depicted in Table 1, PSUs provide a broad spectrum of services. Some of the existing units provide most or all of these diverse activities, while others are more restricted in scope of service.

Several other points should be noted:

- The demand for police psychologists is extensive and extends across a number of functional areas. Without exception, the work time of each PSU psychologist is oversubscribed.
- Not all police PSUs have the resources to perform all of the various potential functions.
- Many larger departments with PSUs are routinely approached by neighboring jurisdictions for assistance in dealing with critical behavioral problems.
- The police psychologist cannot be categorized in a simple typology; he/she is a counselor, a trainer, an investigator, a consultant, a public-relations person, and an administrator.

Police Psychological Services Units are recent innovations, and, as with many innovative programs, wide variance has developed in functions and management. It is important to note that units established for *one* purpose; e.g., counseling police and their families, have very quickly become involved in virtually all aspects of police operations.

Larry T. Hoover

Bibliography

Blanch, M.H. "Psychology for Law Enforcement—Service and Survival." *Police Chief* 44(8) (1977): 66–68.

Cruse, Daniel, and Jesse Rubin. *Determinants of Police Behavior*. Washington, DC: National Institute of Law Enforcement and Criminal Justice, LEAA, U.S. Department of Justice, 1972.

Hillgren, J.S., and R.B. Bond. "Stress in Law Enforcement: Psycho-physiological Correlates and Legal Implications." *Journal of Forensic Psychology* (1975): 25–32.

Kreins, Edward S. "The Behavioral Scientist in Law Enforcement." *Police Chief* 41(2) (1974): 46–48.

Kroes, William H. *Society's Victim the Policeman: An Analysis of Job Stress in Policing*. Springfield, IL: Charles C. Thomas, 1976.

———, and J.J. Hurrell, eds. *Job Stress and the Police Officer: Identifying Stress Reduction Techniques*. Washington, DC: U.S. Department of Health, Education and Welfare, National Institute for Occupational Safety and Health, 1975.

McCreedy, Kenneth R. "Selection Practices and the Police Role." *Police Chief* 41(7) (1974):41–43.

Mann, Philip A. "Establishing a Mental Health Consultation Program with a Police Department." *Community Mental Health Journal* 7 (1971): 118–26.

Monahan, John, ed. *Community Mental Health and the Criminal Justice System*. New York: Pergamon Press, 1976.

Rafky, David. "My Husband the Cop." *Police Chief* 41(8) (1974): 62–65.

Reiser, Martin. *The Police Department Psychologist*. Springfield, IL: Charles C. Thomas, 1972.

———. *Practical Psychology for Police Officers*. Springfield, IL: Charles C. Thomas, 1973.

———. "A Psychologist's View of the Badge." In *Criminal Justice as a System: Readings*. Eds. Alan R. Coffey and Vernon E. Renner. Englewood Cliffs, NJ: Prentice-Hall, 1975.

Straton, J. *Police Passages*. Manhattan Beach, CA: Glennon, 1984.

P

Public Opinion

Law enforcement receives wide coverage in polling data. Both academic criminologists and journalists are today interested in public opinion toward the police as evidenced by the amount of survey data and empirical research on the topic. Polls and surveys regarding the police "assess the mood of the public toward [law enforcement] agencies and provide data upon which to formulate policy recommendations and decisions" (White and Menke, 1978:204). The types of polls administered to the public vary from large-scale polls such as the Roper and Gallup polls to moderate-sized polls found in magazines and newspapers. Opinions and attitudes of residents in a particular region are also obtained through television polls, university polls, or surveys conducted by small independent agencies. Through these polls and surveys, respondents relate their attitudes and opinions about criminal justice in general as well as specific attitudes toward the police. The longest running poll on public opinion toward the police is the National Opinion Research Center's General Social Survey, which has collected annual longitudinal data since 1973 (Flanagan and Maguire, 1992; Flanagan and Vaughn, 1994).

While a few annual and biannual polls and surveys on the police exist, most are administered only sporadically, typically after a volatile issue heightens public focus and sparks heated debate. Public opinion on the police is most frequently gauged after a highly publicized and shocking event galvanizes the nation's attention. Thus the police receive more scrutiny through public opinion polls when they are involved in highly publicized and shocking events such as the Jeffrey Dahmer murders in Milwaukee, the Rodney King beating in Los Angeles, and the deaths of cult members at the Branch Davidian compound near Waco, Texas.

This entry discusses attitudes toward the police. After identifying various factors that influence public opinion of the police, including race, age, gender, ties to society, and previous experiences with law enforcement, the discussion focuses on the media's impact on public opinion toward the police and the consequences of public opinion polls on police procedures. The entry closes with an examination of how the police attempt to improve their public image, and how public opinion has changed the operational realities of contemporary police work with specific examples of how police executives can foster positive public opinion in crisis situations.

Factors Influencing Public Opinion of the Police
Although positive public opinion is important for all components of the criminal-justice system, it is especially crucial for law-enforcement agencies because citizens initiate police activity and provide information useful in making arrests (Zamble and Annesley, 1987). For example, a study by Black (1970) revealed that in three U.S. cities 76 percent of police activity was initiated by citizen phone calls. Further, citizens who believe that the police can "do something" are more likely to report victimizations than

those who lack confidence in the police (Block, 1974). Confidence in law enforcement leads to public support of the police and promotes citizen cooperation in crime prevention, order maintenance, and criminal investigation.

Most research on public attitudes toward the police reveals "high levels of satisfaction with the police and their performance" (White and Menke, 1978:206; Zamble and Annesley, 1987). However, Decker (1981) reports that individuals with more negative experiences and antagonistic police contacts tend to be less satisfied with police performance. He thus argues that the nature of police–citizen contact is an important factor determining attitudes toward the police (ATP). ATP are more negative among individuals in which the police initiate contact, highlighting the tension and negativism surrounding police initiated encounters (Jacob, 1971).

In addition to experiential factors that affect ATP, demographic, residential, and life-stage characteristics are also important in shaping public perceptions of law-enforcement officers. Attitudes toward police are least favorable among African Americans and youths (Decker, 1981). Campbell and Schuman (1972) found that in comparison with whites, African Americans are twice as likely to classify themselves as very dissatisfied with police services. Further, Hirschi (1969) theorized that youth are more prone to participate in delinquency because of weak social bonds to conventional society. Decker (1981) claims that under Hirschi's bonding theory, delinquency leads to negative encounters with the police, and in turn these youths are more likely to hold negative ATP. There is also evidence to suggest that persons living in cities perceive the police more negatively than persons living in rural areas. Zamble and Annesley (1987), for example, report that those who reside in urban areas hold significantly less favorable attitudes toward the police than residents of small cities. There are several explanations for urban-rural differences. First, people residing in smaller cities tend to be more conservative (Stephan and McMullin, 1982), and more favorable attitudes toward the police are held by conservatives (Larsen, 1968). Second, because crime is less prevalent in smaller areas there is greater satisfaction with police services (Zamble and Annesley, 1987). Third, increased confidence in the police by small-area residents may result from familiarity with police; a familiarity unattainable in large urban cities (Zamble and Annesley, 1987).

Further, researchers report the existence of a positive relationship between social class and evaluations of the police (Walker et al., 1972). More specifically they found that individuals with incomes less than $3,000 are more dissatisfied with police encounters and give lower evaluations of police performance. Also, a review of the literature indicates that although males have higher crime rates and more contact with the police (Decker, 1985), the variation in ATP between males and females was only minutely related to sex (Campbell and Schuman, 1972; Winfree and Griffiths, 1977).

The attitudes the elderly hold toward the police have recently received much attention. Because citizens over the age of sixty-five now make up a large proportion of the U.S. population, police agencies have a heightened awareness and concern for the needs of the elderly. Zevitz and Rettammel (1990) report that elderly victims of serious crime have disproportionate personal contact with the perpetrator compared to other age groups. Accordingly, the Canada Solicitor General (1985) says that the elderly fear victimization more than any other age group in society. Furthermore, Arcuri (1981) found that older persons, regardless of race or social class, with direct police contact possess less favorable ATP. Also, Morello (1982) noted that attitudes toward the police by the elderly are more likely to become less favorable as the frequency of police contact increases. Thus the research indicates that individuals from the following groups possess the least favorable ATP: the young, the old, the poor, African Americans, individuals who possess weak social bonds, individuals with previous contact with the police, and individuals with formal police–citizen interaction.

The Media's Influence on Public Opinion of the Police

Public opinion about the criminal-justice system and its components is largely a byproduct of public beliefs about crime. An analysis of the literature reveals that "there is a marked discrepancy between public beliefs about crime and objective conditions" (Warr, 1980:457), leading many to claim that this discrepancy is traceable directly to the media (Surette, 1992). For example, data show that violent crime is a rare event. Yet the public believes that there is an epidemic of violent crime (Warr, 1980). Research indicates that media coverage of violent crime, particularly television coverage, gives the public an unrealistic and inflated perception of the prevalence and incidence of predatory crime. The media's importance should not be underestimated, however; Graber (1979) reports that the primary source of information about crime for 95 percent of the general population is the mass media. Consequently there is an exaggerated fear of crime by the public due to media reports that lack historical perspective and are dramatized (Warr, 1980).

Sabato's (1991) "feeding frenzy" concept helps explain how sensational media coverage drives public opinion of the police. The police are susceptible to "feeding frenzies," in which multiple news organizations focus on a specific theme, resulting in intense media scrutiny. For example, after the motorist Rodney King was stopped by the Los Angeles Police Department and pulled from his car and beaten, the media were saturated nationwide with the videotaped beating and a glaring focus upon the topic of police brutality. Immediately after the incident, a *Los Angeles Times* poll reported that 66 percent of the city's residents believed that brutality by the LAPD was common, and 50 percent of the respondents claimed that the King beating caused them to lose confidence in the police (Flanagan and Vaughn, 1994). Thus the King incident illustrates the potentially powerful effect of the media upon public opinion about the police.

Consequences of Public Opinion on Policing

Plainly, there are inaccurate beliefs about the police in society, and the consequences of such public beliefs are far reaching because they affect the quality of people's lives. If individuals believe that the police cannot offer protection, they are more likely not to report criminal incidents to the police (Skogan and Klecka, 1977). Moreover, the private security industry thrives with security systems in businesses, homes, and cars because people live in fear of victimization. Weapons, especially handguns, are purchased in order to allay feelings of apprehension and vulnerability. Constant fear of violent victimization may lead to self-imposed isolation and migration to the suburbs from inner-city neighborhoods. Because confidence and trust in law enforcement is eroded, citizens believe they must provide for their own protection and preservation.

How the Police Attempt to Improve Their Public Image

Although public opinion toward the police is generally positive, the police foster their public image by tailoring police services to specific citizen needs. Law-enforcement agents are entrusted with extraordinary responsibility and authority, exposing them to situations and pressures civilians do not encounter. Reactive and routine patrol further separate law enforcement agents from private citizens. As a result, a police subculture forms with its own "language," norms, mores, and customs. This includes wearing a uniform. Even though the uniform is a symbol of the occupational authority of the police, Bell (1982) claims it affects both citizen attitudes toward the police as well as officer self-esteem. Research indicates that the military-style police uniform gives many officers a sense of increased power over civilians (Howton, 1969), and that citizens respond more favorably to officers in civilian-style uniforms (Bell, 1982). Bell concludes that civilian ATP are most positive toward nonauthoritarian police officers. Likewise, Smith and Hawkins (1973:147) report that citizen impressions of police beat behavior affects ATP; hence, the "police must take greater care in their on-duty behavior."

Civilian Review Boards

Further, civilian review boards originated and were established in several U.S. cities in the 1960s to process citizen complaints of police misconduct. Review boards were designed to ease the tension between the police and their constituents. However, the police objected to civilian review boards because they believed that civilians could "neither comprehend nor appreciate" the nature of law enforcement (Skolnick and Fyfe, 1993:221) . Moreover, civilians were divided over the issue. Members of the white working class and suburbanites opposed civilian review boards, while minorities and residents of the inner cities favored them (Skolnick and Fyfe, 1993). The opposition prevailed; consequently review boards were defunct for a number of years. Recently, in the 1980s and 1990s, civilian review boards have become more acceptable to the police and demanded by citizens in many jurisdictions historically opposed to the concept. This is a reflection of greater representation by minorities and women in local government (Skolnick and Fyfe, 1993). Due to their resurrection, civilian review boards have been the subject of empirical research. Decker, Smith, and Uhlman (1979:97) collected data concerning operation of these boards in thirteen large American cities and found they had only a "negligible effect" on citizens' ATP. Walker and Bumphus (1992) cite research, however, that identified increased positive ATP in jurisdictions that implement civilian review compared to those that do not. Because there has been a limited amount of research in this area, further study is required to form sound conclusions.

Community Policing

Another tactic to increase public support of the police is the concept of community-oriented policing. Trojanowicz and Bucqueroux (1990) contend this style of policing fosters quality police–community relationships through increased communication between citizens and law enforcement officers. They note that the police have traditionally been a reactive organization, responding only to calls for service. The goal of community-oriented policing is to be proactive so that the police form partnerships with citizens to prevent crime. Community-oriented policing encourages the police and citizens to adopt problem-solving techniques, which focus on the development of intimate relationships between citizens and the police to allow optimal communication to solve the immediate needs of the community (Trojanowicz and Bucqueroux, 1990). Questions remain, however, as to whether community-oriented policing programs increase positive ATP. Studies conducted in cities implementing community-oriented policing report inconsistent findings. For instance, Kelly (1975) and Eisenberg, Fosen, and Glickman (1973) found no change in ATP. Conversely, Houston's neighborhood-oriented policing project and Newark's Foot Patrol Experiment reported an increase in positive ATP (Trojanowicz and Bucqueroux, 1990). Therefore more research must be conducted on existing community-policing programs with greater focus on the more successful programs to identify the characteristics that enable them to thrive.

Elderly Programs

Senior citizen anticrime programs are also designed to increase positive ATP. The personnel of these units receive specialized training in interviewing the elderly and are more knowledgeable than most officers about available community resources for older persons in need. Zevitz and Rettammel (1990) report that this specialized service promotes the elderly's perception that police are sensitive and responsive to their crime-related needs and problems.

Education and Diversity
Finally, law-enforcement agents today are more educated and better trained than at any time in the history of policing (Carter, Sapp, and Stephens, 1989) For instance, a college education is a prerequisite for application to some police departments around the country. Moreover, the recruitment and hiring of more women, minority, and ethnic officers makes police agencies more like the public they serve. Research shows that increased educational requirements and multiculturalism in policing is advantageous (Carter, Sapp, and Stephens, 1989). Moreover, many believe that the addition of more minorities and women have made law-enforcement agencies more effective and responsive to community problems (President's Commission, 1967). Further, Andrews (1985) reports citizens believe that today's law-enforcement officers are less confrontational and more "open-minded and sensitive" than yesteryear's, bolstering the positive public image of and support for the police.

How Public Opinion Affects Police Work: Two Contemporary Examples
Although direct causal relationships are difficult, if not impossible to demonstrate, there is evidence to suggest public opinion affects change in police behavior. Public opinion is most crucial after a cataclysmic event focuses scrutiny on the police. The most immediate and obvious change departments pursue is job suspension, demotion, or termination. Firing a few officers may serve to immediately quell public dismay with police service, but it may not address systemic, enduring, and structural departmental deficiencies. As a general rule, if community relations are good before a crisis erupts, departments that act quickly to remedy crises of public opinion can diminish negative ATP.

Two contemporary examples serve as guides for how a police chief can promote positive ATP during crisis situations. The Rodney King beating in Los Angeles and the Malice Green murder in Detroit became symbols of urban violence and police brutality reflected in public opinion polls. On March 3, 1991, the motorist Rodney King was stopped by the LAPD after a car chase of speeds over 100 mph.

The beating King suffered as he was taken into custody was captured on videotape. Within days, the videotaped beating was broadcast over the world, sparking heated debate on police brutality.

From the outset, Chief Daryl Gates and the LAPD were under siege. Chief Gates initially said that he was shocked, but "would withhold judgment on the behavior of the officers until the incident could be investigated" (Independent Commission, 1991:12). Although Chief Gates called for an investigation, his inflammatory statements and apparent insincerity sparked public animosity, resulting in very negative ATP. Chief Gates's long-standing antagonistic relationship with the minority community in Los Angeles made public relations difficult. There were complaints of excessive force in the LAPD during the thirteen-year tenure of Chief Gates. For many, the videotape provided the evidence to show that Chief Gates tolerated, even rewarded, police brutality. Public opinion polls after the incident showed that throughout the nation many believed that the police were brutal (Gallup, 1991). A *Time/CNN* poll reported that 48 percent of blacks believed they were at risk of being treated unfairly by the police; however, 72 percent of whites did not believe they were at risk (Shulman, 1992). In Los Angeles public opinion toward the police would not turn positive until the city charter was amended, a new chief was hired, and the department's use of force policy was rewritten. Daryl Gates's response to the Rodney King incident is the worst type of crisis management in which an antagonistic chief fueled negative public opinion, perhaps contributing to the worst rioting in the nation's history, as well as driving officer morale to an all-time low.

Contrast what happened in Los Angeles to the Malice Green incident in Detroit. On November 5, 1992, Green, a thirty-five-year-old black man, was sitting in a parked car in front of a known crack house when approached by two undercover officers. A struggle ensued with four officers because Green resisted arrest. After Green was hit in the head and killed with a heavy police flashlight, all four officers were charged with felonies, including second-degree murder, felonious assault, involuntary manslaughter, and a misdemeanor charge of willful neglect of duty (Levin, 1992).

Perhaps most important, Chief Stanley Knox's reaction to the Green murder was much different than the reaction of Chief Gates to the King beating. Chief Knox's reaction was swift, decisive, and unwavering as he acted immediately to fire the officers and take responsibility for their actions. At a news conference shortly after the incident, Chief Knox expressed grief and outrage, saying that the incident brought tears to his eyes. This decisive and swift action immediately stemmed the flow of negative public opinion (Salholz and Washington, 1992), which deflated public outcries of police insensitivity and abuse. To be sure, the Green incident had the potential to evolve into a public-relations nightmare, but similarities between the Green and King situations stopped with the beating because city officials in Detroit earnestly reached out to the minority community. This was possible because Chief Knox had a good history of relations with the minority community, the very persons who traditionally hold the most negative ATP. As a result the public in Detroit believed that the Green incident was an isolated incident, whereas public opinion in Los Angeles indicated that police brutality was rampant.

Conclusion

This entry discusses influences upon public opinion of the police such as demographics, contact with police, and the media. Moreover, the consequences of public opinion on police work are shown as are attempts by the police to improve their image. Finally and most important, it is shown that public opinion of the police is directly related to the efficiency of law enforcement. Without the public's confidence in the police, citizens may not report crimes or give information to the police. Thus the police would be ineffective in finding and apprehending criminals.

In assessing public opinion data on the police, attention must first be paid to the methodology used in opinion polls and surveys. Even though public opinion is important to policy and decision-makers, not all public opinion surveys are scientifically suitable to base policy decisions. White and Menke's (1982) review, for example, found that surveys aimed at evaluating the mood of the public toward the police were atheoretical. They pointed out that the methodological problems in many public opinion surveys make meaningful data interpretation difficult. For example, methodological problems such as localized and noncomparable samples, indeterminate response categories, and vague questions have plagued some public opinion data. For the suggestions and proposals of policy- and decision-makers to be of value, it is imperative that the research they rely upon be guided by sound methodology and theory (White and Menke, 1982).

Christine Rose Ramirez
Michael S. Vaughn

Bibliography

Andrews, P. "Mellow Attitude Helps Police Gain Structure." *Seattle Times,* August 18, 1985.

Arcuri, A.F. "The Police and the Elderly." In *The Elderly Victim of Crime.* Ed. D. Lester. Springfield, IL: Charles C. Thomas, 1981. 106–28.

Bell, D.J. "Police Uniforms, Attitudes, and Citizens." *Journal of Criminal Justice* 10 (1982): 45–55.

Black, D. "The Production of Crime Rates." *Journal of Police Science and Administration* 9(1) (1970): 80–87.

Block, R. "Why Notify the Police: The Victim's Decision to Notify the Police of an Assault." *Criminology* 11 (1974): 555–69.

Campbell, A., and H. Schuman. "A Comparison of Black and White Attitudes and Experiences in the City." In *The End of Innocence: A Suburban Reader.* Ed. C.M. Haar. Glenview, IL: Scott Foresman, 1972. 97–110.

Canada Solicitor General. *Criminal Victimization of Elderly Canadians.* Ottawa: Department of Supply and Services, 1985.

Carter, D.L., A.D. Sapp, and D.W. Stephens. *The State of Police Education: Policy Direction for the 21st Century.* Washington, DC: Police Executive Research Forum, 1989.

Decker, S.H. "Citizen Attitudes toward the Police: A Review of Past Findings and Suggestions for Future Policy." *Journal of Police Science and Administration* 9(1) (1981), 80–87.

———. "The Police and the Public: Perceptions and Policy Recommendations." In *Police and Law Enforcement, 1975–1981.* Eds. R.J. Homant and D.B. Kennedy. New York: AMS Press, 1985, 89–105.

Decker, S.H., R.L. Smith, and T.M. Uhlman. "Does Anything Work? An Evaluation of Urban Police Innovations." In *Evaluat-*

ing *Alternative Law Enforcement Policies*. Ed. R. Baker. Lexington, MA: Lexington, 1979. 43–54.

Eisenberg, T., R. Fosen, and A.S. Glickman. *Police Community Action: A Program for Change in Police–Community Behavior Patterns*. New York: Praeger, 1973.

Flanagan, T.J., and K. Maguire, eds. *Sourcebook of Criminal Justice Statistics—1991*. United States Department of Justice, Bureau of Justice Statistics, Washington, DC: Government Printing Office, 1992.

Flanagan, T.J., and M.S. Vaughn. "Public Opinion about Police Abuse of Force." In *Public Use of Excessive Force and its Control: Key Issues Facing the Nation*. Eds. W.A. Geller and H. Toch. Washington, DC: PERF/NIJ, 1994.

Gallup, G. *The Gallup Poll*. Princeton, NJ: Gallup Poll, March 20, 1991.

Graber, D. "Evaluating Crime-Fighting Policies. In *Evaluating Alternative Law Enforcement Policies*. Eds. R. Baker and F. Meyer. Lexington, MA.: Lexington, 1979. 179–200.

Hirschi, T. *Causes of Delinquency*. Berkeley: University of California Press, 1969.

Howton, W.F. *Functionaries*. Chicago: Quadrangle, 1969.

Independent Commission on the Los Angeles Police Department. *Report*. Los Angeles: Independent Commission on the Los Angeles Police Department, 1991.

Jacob, H. "Black and White Perceptions of Justice in the City." *Law and Society Review* 5 (1971): 69–89.

Kelly, R.M. "Generalizations from an OEO Experiment in Washington, DC. *Journal of Social Issues* 31 (1975): 57–86.

Larsen, K.S. "Authoritarianism and Attitudes toward Police." *Psychological Reports* 3(2) (1968): 349–50.

Levin, D.P. "Four Detroit Officers Charged in Death: Two Facing Counts of Murder in Police Beating of Motorist." *New York Times* (November 17, 1992): 1–A, 10–B.

Morello, F. *Juvenile Crimes against the Elderly*. Springfield, IL: Charles C. Thomas, 1982.

President's Commission on Law Enforcement and Administration of Justice. *Task Force Report: The Police*. Washington, DC: Government Printing Office, 1967.

Sabato, L.J. *Feeding Frenzy: How Attack Journalism Has Transformed American Politics*. New York: Free Press, 1991.

Salholz, E., and F. Washington. "Detroit's Brutal Lesson: Why Its Police Beating Case Isn't Like L.A.'s." *Newsweek* 120(30) (1992): 45.

Shulman, T.C. *Time*/CNN Poll. "The Fire This Time." *Time* 139(19) (1992): 18–25.

Skogan, W.G., and W.R. Klecka.*The Fear of Crime*. Washington, DC: American Political Science Association, 1977.

Skolnick, J.H., and J.J. Fyfe. *Above the Law*. New York: Free Press, 1993.

Smith, P.E., and R.O. Hawkins. "Victimization, Types of Citizen–Police Contacts, and Attitudes toward the Police." *Law and Society Review* 8(1) (1973): 135–52.

Stephan, G.E. and D.R. McMullin. "Tolerance of Sexual Nonconformity: City Size as a Situational and Early Learning Determinant." *American Sociological Review* 45(3) (1982): 411–15.

Surette, R. *Media and Criminal Justice: Images and Realities*. Pacific Grove, CA: Brooks/Cole, 1992.

Trojanowicz, R., and B. Bucqueroux. *Community Policing: A Contemporary Perspective*. Cincinnati, OH: Anderson, 1990.

Walker, D., R.J. Richardson, T. Denyer, O. Williams, and S. McGaughey. "Contact and Support: An Empirical Assessment of Public Attitudes toward the Police and the Courts." *North Carolina Law Review* 51 (1972): 43–79.

Walker, S., and V.W. Bumphus. "The Effectiveness of Civilian Review: Observations on Recent Trends and New Issues Regarding the Civilian Review of the Police." *American Journal of Police* 11(4) (1992): 1–26.

Warr, M. "The Accuracy of Public Beliefs about Crime." *Social Forces* 59(2) (1980): 456–70.

White, M.F., and B.A. Menke. "A Critical Analysis of Surveys on Public Opinions toward Police Agencies." *Journal of Police Science and Administration* 6(2) (1978): 204–18.

———. "On Assessing the Mood of the Public toward the Police: Some Conceptual Issues." *Journal of Criminal Justice* 10(3) (1982): 211–30.

Winfree, T.L., and C.T. Griffiths. "Adolescent Attitudes toward the Police." In *Juvenile*

Delinquency: Little Brother Grows Up. Ed. T. Ferdinand. Beverly Hills: Sage, 1977. 79–99.

Zamble, E., and P. Annesley. "Some Determinants of Public Attitudes toward the Police." *Journal of Police Science and Administration* 15(4) (1987): 285–90.

Zevitz, R.G., and R.J. Rettammel. "Elderly Attitudes about Police Service. *American Journal of Police* 9(2) (1990): 25–39.

R

Repeat Offender Programs

Repeat Offender Programs (ROP) and/or Targeted Offender Programs (TOP) represent recent special collaborative police and prosecutorial initiatives designed to selectively incapacitate career criminals using pre-arrest targeting, warrant services, and/or post-arrest case enhancement strategies.

Background

Recent empirical studies have established what police officers and administrators have long suspected: A relatively small number of offenders commit a disproportionate share of all crime in the United States. Specifically, the most active 10 percent of offenders are responsible for over 50 percent of all reported crimes committed (Blumstein et al., 1986; Wolfgang, Figlio, and Sellin, 1972). Yet this subpopulation of high-rate offenders, often labeled "career criminals" (Petersilia, Greenwood, and Lavin, 1978; Chaiken and Chaiken, 1982) represent only about 15 percent of those sentenced to prison each year (Gay and Bowers, 1985). Even so, in what Pontell (1984) describes as "a limited capacity to punish," demand for prison space is outpacing prison capacity.

Furthermore, crime occurs in major cities with such frequency and volume that it has become impossible for local law-enforcement agencies to respond to *each* crime occurrence. This is particularly true under the traditional *case*-oriented strategy wherein the amount of time an investigator allocates to a case is affected by the perceived seriousness of the *offense*, the probability of an arrest, and the likelihood of positive prosecutorial review. Throughout this process, it is the *case* and its quality that receives the attention of the inves-

tigator, not characteristics of the *suspect*, whose identity and criminal history are usually unknown.

Together, these facts suggest that if law-enforcement agencies are to be successful in policing career criminals, they should concentrate their scarce, limited resources on selectively targeting the most active and dangerous repeat offenders and collaborate with prosecutors in selectively incapacitating them.

As a result, many police departments have begun seeking proactive alternatives to the traditional reliance on random patrol visibility and case-oriented investigative methods.

Enforcement Initiatives

Since the mid-1970s, police administrators and scholars have been advocating that informationally directed methods of policing (i.e., addressing specific problems and/or offenders) would enhance police performance and citizens' expectations, and reduce overall crime (Cordner and Hale, 1992). Some examples of innovative initiatives include community policing, crackdowns, hot spots, directed patrol, split-force patrol, profiling, perpetrator and location-oriented patrol, sting operations, team policing, and the Felony Augmentation Program.

Developing coterminously with directed intervention strategies and in response to the problem posed by career criminals, the Department of Justice in the mid-1970s, through the Law Enforcement Assistance Administration (LEAA), supported various local Comprehensive Career Criminal Programs (CCCP). The CCCP was initially designed to enhance, coordinate, and integrate police and prosecutorial efforts in apprehending and convicting the habitual, serious repeat offender. The CCCP was a dual-focused, ambitious program composed of the Integrated Criminal Apprehension Program (ICAP) for police agencies and the Career Criminal Program (CCP) for prosecutors (Chelimsky and Dahmann, 1981).

ICAP sought to increase the efficiency and effectiveness of all police services by directing patrol deployment and related field activities based on systematic data collection, crime analysis, and structured planning. The use of crime analysis and sound management principals in structuring police field activities and criminal investigations were the pivotal aspects of ICAP. Unfortunately, however, there is only limited evidence that proactive strategies or tactical decisions resulted from crime analysis efforts or that this information was used to support specific *suspect-oriented* apprehension strategies (Gay, Beall, and Bowers, 1984). Although patrol and investigative personnel demonstrated varying degrees of awareness concerning identified career criminals, other routine duties stifled any concerted career criminal activities on their part.

Similarly, prosecutorial CCPs were career criminal programs *in name only*, lacking specific procedures and monitoring systems for career criminal identification and prosecution (Springer, Phillips, and Cannady, 1985; Chelimsky and Dahmann, 1981) Thus, despite the stated objectives and employed mechanisms, an intensive evaluation of four of these CCPs by LEAA found that they did *not* increase convictions or incarceration rates. Moreover, evaluators of the CCP found that the police–prosecutor liaison was limited primarily to post-arrest activities (Chelimsky and Dahmann, 1981).

Police Repeat Offender Programs
Almost immediately after the disappointing evaluations of ICAP and CCPs (regarding the identification and incarceration of career criminals), police agencies started experimenting with a variety of repeat offender programs, or ROPs in the late 1970s and early 1980s. Although these ROPs used some of the same techniques to identify and incarcerate career criminals, they were smaller and more specialized, as opposed to the broad systemic efforts advocated under the CCCP.

A nationwide random survey conducted in 1984 by Gay and Bowers (1985:8) found thirty-three law-enforcement agencies running ROPs, all of which fell into one or more of three program types: (a) pre-arrest targeting—utilizing

intensive surveillance and informants; (b) warrant services—to locate and arrest those wanted on felony warrants; and (c) post-arrest case enhancement strategies—to increase the likelihood of conviction and lengthier sentences.

In their evaluative conclusion, Gay and Bowers favorably described post-arrest enhancement programs (particularly those operating in Baltimore County and New York City) and, with some provisos, pre-arrest programs operating in San Diego, St. Louis, Washington, D.C., and West Covina.

Gay and Bowers' survey indicated significant variability in the orientation, administration, and intensity of the ROPs, each type having its own advantages and disadvantages. Still, two elements were common to all program types: (a) a specific set of *offenders* was selected for special targeting, and (b) the police went beyond normal routine procedures to ensure that those targeted would be apprehended and incarcerated for their crimes.

The best-known repeat offender program, and until 1990 the only ROP extensively researched, was established by the Metropolitan Police Department in the District of Columbia in 1982. The objective of the Washington ROP unit was to increase the apprehension rate of targeted offenders based on informants, previous crime patterns, and other types of police intelligence. When initial attempts at direct surveillance proved too frustrating and too time-consuming, the Washington ROP unit shifted most of its attention to serving outstanding felony warrants.

An evaluation by Martin and Sherman (1986) found that the Washington ROP increased the likelihood of arrest, prosecution on a felony, felony conviction, and length of term for those sentenced to prison. Overall, for ROP-initiated targets, 47 percent of the targets in the experimental group were arrested, while only 6 percent of those assigned to the control group were arrested. These results, however, may be biased because of the target selection practices of the Washington ROP and the criteria used for prioritizing potential candidates for apprehension. According to Martin and Sherman (1986:9):

> Although officers were expected to select criminally active targets, ROP *did not establish formal indicators* of activity or any system for prioritizing among potential candidates. Selection was based on

informal understandings about what makes a "good" target.

This lack of control by management in allowing ROP squads to largely develop their own criteria resulted in three types of ROP squads: "hunters" (focusing on warrant service), "trappers" (specializing in surveillance, decoys, and other covert proactive operations), and "fishers" (who brought back whatever they could find). The activities of these squads contributed to a more serious problem emphasized by the evaluators:

> By casting the net widely, the ROP increased the danger of informally labeling as "repeat offender" many individuals who, in fact, are not highly active and undermine efforts to get the U.S. Attorney to give its arrestees special consideration by presenting many cases that appear to be trivial. (Martin and Sherman, 1986:10)

Still, the Washington ROP was considerably more successful than prior pre-arrest programs and demonstrated that pre-arrest targeting could be used to identify and apprehend career criminals effectively. This paved the way for subsequent repeat offender programs that have employed more formalized candidate selection criteria. By collaborating with prosecutors in formalizing candidate selection criteria, agencies have more narrowly defined *who* qualifies for pre-arrest targeting and post-arrest case enhancement prosecution. This in turn has allowed for a more efficient use of limited resources and the avoidance of draconian activities that may violate the civil liberties of those designated for special attention.

Current Research on ROPs
A recent study of a ROP was conducted by the Rand Corporation to empirically evaluate the impact of a *post-arrest* case enhancement strategy being utilized by the Phoenix Police Department (Abrahamse et al., 1991). The randomized field experiment lasted one year (1987 through 1988) ending with 480 assignments (257 to the experimental group and 223 to the control group).

Analysis of case disposition patterns showed no significant increase in conviction rates for the experimental (ROP) cases, but revealed significant increases in the likelihood of commitment to prison and in the length of sentences imposed (Abrahamse et al., 1991:155)

Lessons learned from these early ROP efforts suggested that these programs would be more efficient and effective in dealing with the career criminal if three overriding problems were addressed: (a) the information problem, (b) the mobility problem, and (c) the chain problem (Spelman, 1990).

The information problem pertains to "turf" management and poor inter- and intradepartmental communications and coordination, especially with the prosecutorial component of the justice system. Moreover, because frequent, experienced offenders are also likely to be the most mobile, no single police agency (or no single prosecution or probation agency or no single ROP unit) will have full information about an individual offender's activities. Therefore, criminal-justice agencies must work together to identify, arrest, convict, and incapacitate the serious repeat offender.

Finally, in order for the criminal-justice system to function at peak efficiency and effectiveness it must be remembered that police, courts, and corrections are all links in a chain, and that each component directly and indirectly impacts upon the other components of the system. If the chain is broken at any point, by any agency, career criminal apprehension and incapacitation will be hindered.

In an attempt to overcome some of the weaknesses and criticisms of earlier repeat offender programs, the Police Executive Research Forum (PERF), in conjunction with the Bureau of Justice Assistance (BJA), designed a "model" repeat offender program that was responsive to these specific problems, yet general enough to allow adaptability at the local level by police, prosecutors, and correction officials (Spelman, 1990). PERF researchers then selected three jurisdictions (Kansas City, Missouri; Rochester, New York; and Eugene, Oregon) to implement and test the model.

After reviewing a number of existing ROPs, the PERF researchers concluded that a more systemic, comprehensive approach in targeting career criminals (as opposed to the fragmented, specialized unit approach) would be more effective (Spelman, 1990:65). The resulting conceptual design focused on the internal integration, horizontal integration, and vertical integration activities among and within criminal-justice agencies. Spelman (1990:66) explains:

Internal Integration. Prior repeat offender programs were confined to special units, but information, expertise, and other resources were broadly distributed throughout the criminal justice agencies involved. Special units would be more effective if agency members outside the unit were involved in program development and operations.

Horizontal Integration. Most prior efforts were confined to a single police department or prosecutor's office, but repeat offenders often committed crimes in several jurisdictions. Thus, ROPs would be more effective if all municipal and county law enforcement agencies within the metropolitan area participated.

Vertical Integration. The prosecutor's participation in target selection decisions and in tactical operations would help to ensure that most, if not all, repeat offenders received special attention. Formal involvement of probation and/or parole officers could similarly ensure that repeaters were supervised more closely while they were on the street.

Although an in-depth empirical or evaluative assessment is not yet available on the implementation of this model, the proposed system-wide model has initially demonstrated in all three case studies that a successful ROP can be mounted with a modicum of specialization and centralization. According to Spelman (1990: 70), collaboration within each agency and between agencies was the key in each of these three cities. Although these ROPs relied on different administrative structures and tactics, "an integrated, system-wide approach was common to them all."

The most recent attempt to empirically analyze repeat offender programs, utilizing pre-arrest targeting and post-arrest case enhancement strategies, was conducted by Gay in 1993. Gay's research involved a statewide analysis of ROPs of several major police departments in the State of Texas including a process and impact assessment of the Houston Police Department's Targeted Offender Program.

In summary, repeat offender programs are recent innovations specifically designed at targeting, apprehending, and selectively incapacitating the career criminal. As with other types of innovative police strategies, ROPs have meet with varying degrees of success. However, given the problem posed by career criminals, it is expected that ROPs and TOPs will continue to proliferate among law enforcement agencies throughout the 1990s.

Bruce W. Gay

Bibliography

Abrahamse, A., P. Ebener, P. Greenwood, N. Fitzgerald, and T. Kosin. "An Experimental Evaluation of the Phoenix Repeat Offender Program." *Justice Quarterly* 8 (1991):141–68.

Blumstein, A., J. Cohen, J. Roth, and C. Visher, eds. *Criminal Careers and Career Criminals*. Vol. 1. Washington, DC: National Academy Press, 1986.

Chaiken, J., and M. Chaiken. *Varieties of Criminal Behavior*. Santa Monica, CA: Rand Corporation, 1982.

Chelimsky, E., and J. Dahmann. *Career Criminal Program National Evaluation: Final Report*. U.S. Department of Justice, National Institute of Justice. Washington, DC: Government Printing Office, 1981.

Cordner, G., and D. Hale, eds. *What Works in Policing: Operations and Administration Examined*. Cincinnati, OH: Anderson, 1992.

Gay, Bruce W. "Policing Hard Core Offenders: An Analysis of Targeted Offender Programs in Texas That Use Pre-Arrest Targeting and Post-Arrest Case Enhancement Strategies to Selectively Incapacitate Career Criminals." Unpublished Ph.D. diss. Huntsville, TX: Sam Houston State University, 1993.

Gay, W., T. Beall, and R. Bowers. *A Four-Site Assessment of the Integrated Criminal Apprehension Program*. Washington, DC: University City Science Center, 1984.

Gay, William, and Robert Bowers. *Targeting Law Enforcement Resources: The Career Criminal Focus*. Washington, DC: U.S. Department of Justice, National Institute of Justice, 1985.

Martin, Susan, and Lawrence Sherman. *Catching Career Criminals: The Washington, D.C. Repeat Offender Project*. Report No. 3. Washington, DC: Police Foundation, 1986.

Petersilia, J., P. Greenwood, and M. Lavin. *Criminal Careers of Habitual Felons.* Santa Monica, CA: Rand Corporation, 1978.

Pontell, Henry. *A Capacity to Punish: The Ecology of Crime and Punishment.* Bloomington, IN: Indiana University Press, 1984.

Spelman, William. *Repeat Offenders.* Washington, DC: Police Executive Research Forum, 1990.

Springer, J., J. Phillips, and L. Cannady. *The Effectiveness of Selective Prosecution by Career Criminal Programs.* Washington, DC: EMT Group, 1985.

Wolfgang, M., R. Figlio, and T. Sellin. *Delinquency in a Birth Cohort.* Chicago, IL: University of Chicago Press, 1972.

RICO

Title IX of the Organized Crime Control Act of 1970 speaks to Racketeer Influenced and Corrupt Organizations. Better known as RICO, the statute's original intent was "to seek the eradication of organized crime in the United States by strengthening the legal tools in the evidence gathering process, by establishing new penal prohibitions, and by providing enhanced sanctions and new remedies to deal with the unlawful activites of those engaged in organized crime." At the time of enactment organized crime meant Mafia-type extended families that engaged in multifarious criminal activities. RICO targets were well-defined and had been since the days of Al Capone in the 1920s and 1930s. What RICO was supposed to do—"seek the eradication of organized crime in the United States"—has instead over the past two decades become in one judge's words, "the monster that ate jurisprudence."

Controversy

That is not to say that RICO has been a total failure. Many racketeers, including kingpins, have been prosecuted and imprisoned using RICO. What has happened to dampen enthusiasm is that since 1980, and especially after 1985, prosecutors have applied RICO to every type of white-collar crime imaginable. While this may seem a good thing, it deviates far from the original intent to prosecute Mafia-type extended crime families. What the anti-RICO legal establishment calls garden variety violations continue to clog the courts. An example of such a violation would be a business competitor who claimed that a rival engaged in "racketeering" by trying to buy-up all raw materials for a product. An actual, more substantial case occurred when Eastern Airlines brought a racketeering suit against its unions for conspiring to impede management, asking for $1.5 billion in damages. The American Bar Association follows RICO suits and has determined that between 1970 and 1985 approximately 270 cases per year were filed; after 1985 that number jumped to more than 1,000 filed per year. Obviously, the recent rash of cases has not focused on organized crime only. In 1985 the U.S. Supreme Court ruled to let RICO's broad application stand, and if the law needed reform Congress should amend it. With sanction from the high court to proceed, prosecutors reveled in civil RICO and the treble damages they could claim.

Again, why should a statute that aids law enforcement call for immediate reform? Supreme Court Justice Antonin Scalia has threatened to find RICO unconstitutionally vague when the appropriate test case comes along; and with boundless energy prestigious law journals dedicate hundreds of pages to dissecting RICO. The list of racketeering activites prosecutable under RICO is lengthy and has been added to since 1970. It includes the following:

- Any act or threat involving murder, kipnapping, gambling, arson, robbery, bribery, extortion, or dealing in narcotics or other dangerous drugs that is chargeable under state law.
- Any act that is indictable under federal law Title 18, United States Code, relating to bribery; sports bribery; counterfeiting; theft from interstate shipment; embezzlement from pension and welfare funds; extortionate credit transactions; the transmission of gambling information; mail fraud; wire fraud; obstruction of justice; obstruction of criminal investigations; obstruction of state or local law enforcement; interference with commerce, robbery or extortion; racketeering; interstate transportation of wagering paraphernalia; unlawful welfare fund payments; prohibition of illegal gambling businesses; interstate transportation of stolen property; and white slave traffic.
- Any act that is indictable under federal law Title 29, United States Code, relating to restrictions on payments and loans to

labor organizations, and embezzlement from union funds.

- Any offense involving bankruptcy fraud; fraud in the sale of securities; or the felonious manufacture, importation, receiving, concealment, buying, selling, or otherwise dealing in narcotics or other dangerous drugs.

Additions to RICO as of 1993:

- Dealing in obscene matter;
- Financial institution fraud;
- Tampering with a witness, victim, or an informant;
- Retaliating against a witness, victim, or an informant;
- Laundering of monetary instruments;
- Engaging in monetary transactions in property derived from specified unlawful activity;
- Use of interstate commerce facilities in the commission of murder-for-hire;
- Trafficking in certain motor vehicles or motor vehicle parts;
- Trafficking in contraband cigarettes; and
- Any act indictable under the Currency and Foreign Transactions Reporting Act.

Such a comprehensive list for making indictments should nullify organized crime. Hand-in-hand with RICO, the Comprehensive Crime Control Act of 1984 enhanced the government's ability to seize assets gained through racketeering activities. Practically everything a defendant owns may be forfeited if the court decides the gains were ill-gotten. Most controversial, assets needed by a defendant to pay an attorney can be frozen before the trial starts, as can all personal assets in an effort to cripple racketeering activities that might be ongoing. RICO reformers argue that freezing all assets violates the defendant's Sixth Amendment right to counsel. More punitive, under RICO an individual "injured in his business or property" may bring a civil action to recover damages from the racketeer. If convicted in a criminal action, the defendant faces fines, imprisonment, and/or mandatory asset forfeiture. If convicted in a civil action, the defendant may have to comply with orders of divestiture, face restrictions on future activities, or reorganize/dissolve the enterprise, in addition to paying treble damages to the private individual. The treble damages amount to compensation for court costs, attorney fees, and

"general equitable relief." RICO reformers argue these are draconian penalties that strip the defendant of any means to survive.

Other criticisms of RICO are more legalistic and can only be glimpsed at here. Justice Scalia's insistence on the vagueness of RICO has to do with the pattern requirement. At least two predicate acts of racketeering must occur to constitute a pattern, which should show "continuity plus relationship." Without continuity plus relationship—in direct reference to organized crime—no concrete pattern is established. Another vagueness of RICO is that a person must acquire interest in, or administer, an enterprise to be in violation. The word "enterprise" should have kept the courts on track but to the contrary has confused matters. "Enterprise," originally signified a well-established crime syndicate. If the presence of an enterprise is not proven, then RICO must be abandoned. Depending on the case, different courts have found individuals, private businesses, sole proprietor-ships, foreign and domestic corporations, labor organizations, government agencies, and other associations to be enterprises. Thereby some courts have turned vagueness to their advantage and opened their doors to garden variety violations not intended to be RICO.

The savings and loan scandals of the 1980s increased use of RICO. People hurt by the S&L mess have been able to recoup some of their money through civil RICO, even though organized crime was not to blame. The magnitude of the financial crime and its devastating effect on trustful citizens has caused legislators to wait and see if and how long civil RICO redresses what the federal government cannot in paybacks. Other uses of civil RICO are not so commendable. An attorney can "terrorize" a defendant by simply mentioning RICO. Few legitimate business owners want to bear the stigma of having been accused of racketeering; so they settle quickly out of court even if the case has no merit.

Law Enforcement and RICO
RICO has garnered mixed reviews from law enforcement. In 1980 over one hundred La Cosa Nostra members, associates, union officials, and co-conspirators received prison sentences for racketeering in connection with the International Longshoremen's Association. The FBI conducted a follow-up study some time later and discovered to its dismay that the

dockside racket continued to flourish. New racketeers stepped in immediately, and even worse those removed from the scene were small fry who by their absence strengthened the criminal organization. Moreover, the organization went to school and learned from court proceedings how to avoid future indictments. After completing their sentences, the small fry who maintained the code of silence returned to racketeering as heroes. Results like these frustrate law enforcement. In its opinion RICO greatly assists bringing "individuals" to justice but fails to eradicate organized crime.

RICO investigation begins with a review of intelligence. The crime organization's structure, membership, and activities must be clear in mind before going further. FBI Special Agent Donald V. North (1988) outlines other procedural steps:

> The next step is to conduct a background investigation through agency file reviews, agency and public record checks, and available informants of the group on the individual members and their criminal activities. During this stage, the investigator attempts to identify individual and group assets, as well as proprietary interests. All structured criminal groups must have some type of chain of command whereby directives flow down and financial gain is shared upwards. The next investigative phase involves the use of toll records, pen registers, physical surveillance, and analyses of prior arrests and associates to identify meeting places, methods of communication between group members and entities utilized to facilitate their criminal activities. At this stage the investigator evaluates and defines the criminal group, the enterprise(s) that may be the investigative focus, and the potential predicate criminal acts.

During investigation the concept of enterprise is multifaceted. It may consist of the structured group using a respectable front, i.e., licit; or acting as criminals, i.e., illicit. The enterprise may also be the crime victim, the vehicle used to commit the crime, or the benefit derived from the criminal act. Investigators must separate and catalogue the evidence for each type of enterprise. Prosecution and forfeiture actions depend on careful preparatory work. Ideally,

every member of the enterprise will be identified and brought to justice, so as not to repeat the longshoremen's embarrassment. To achieve this, investigators decide whether to pursue an overt or a covert plan. For an overt plan, interviews are sought to produce witnesses, records are subpoenaed, expert witnesses arranged for, and a grand jury brought to fore. When dealing with sophisticated organized crime groups, covert techniques are the better choice, e.g., telephone and microphone electronic surveillance, closed-circuit television, consensual recordings made by victims, and the use of undercover agents. For covert techniques to stand up in court, investigators must record and separate each direct and circumstantial piece of evidence. Not only that but they must also record and separate each piece by enterprise, assets involved, illegal profit generated, RICO predicates, and support for civil relief. Because RICO aims to eradicate organized crime by removing its economic base and incentive, an accurate accounting of assets is foremost in the investigation. If not frozen upon indictment, any unknown assets will be liquidated and transferred to keep the enterprise going. Unlike RICO reformers who would not freeze all assets, law enforcement and many judges would exact the full measure of the law.

For assistance in a case, federal authorities reward local law enforcement by sharing or remitting seized assets. With so much money at stake the temptation is for local law enforcement to shift more officers to drug and white-collar crime investigation. The lure of seized assets might also tempt police to reap the riches any way they can. The *Houston Chronicle* ran a probing article on asset forfeiture May 17, 1992, entitled "Legal Larceny?" The newspaper report took over sixteen months to write while the reporter waited for the U.S. Marshals Service to release data under the Freedom of Information Act. Finally released, the data listed cars, cash, and other property seized in the Southern District of Texas from Houston to Laredo to Brownsville for the years 1986–1989. After data analysis the *Houston Chronicle* published these findings:

- Seizures rose dramatically in the four-year period to more than $38 million a year for the Houston region, which federal officials attribute not to an increase in drug cases or other crimes but to a widening use of the forfeiture laws.

- Some properties were seized from citizens who were never charged with the crimes.
- The sharpest increases were in seizures of vehicles—quick-money items that are easiest for the government to keep because many owners cannot afford to fight for return of inexpensive cars.
- The more property the government seized, the bigger the share it had to give back. In 1986, for example, the government kept 80 percent of all vehicles seized. By 1989, it had to give back more than half.
- Federal agencies kept increasingly expensive items for themselves, even while the values of items sold by the government fell.
- While mortgage companies and other lien holders receive special handling from the government, [mostly innocent] individuals must endure a lengthy and invasive process that opens them up to scrutiny by the IRS and other federal agencies before winning release of their goods.

In a continuance of the report on May 19, a photo showed Houston Police Chief Sam Nuchia accepting a U.S. government check for $1.9 million. The hefty reward was for services rendered in the war on drugs. The *Houston Chronicle* reported fairly by also including a story of "The General," a drug kingpin in the Rio Grande Valley. Once caught, Librado Perez forfeited $4.9 million in assets and is a sterling example of why the forfeiture laws were passed in the first place.

On June 29, 1993, the U.S. Supreme Court ruled unanimously that the Constitution limits the amount of money and property government may seize from suspected narcotics dealers. The Eighth Amendment prohibits the imposition of "excessive fines" and also the infliction of "cruel and unusual punishment." Now the lower courts must decide the exact limits of asset forfeiture case by case. Slated for reform, RICO will undoubtedly see changes in its language to avoid vagueness and forfeiture laws will become less draconian. As a law-enforcement tool RICO has done an admirable job of granting the wherewithal to convict organized crime members; but as a mainstay of prosecutors to exact treble damages in civil cases it has been abused. In a little over two decades the

simple acronym has created quite a stir. Perhaps in the future RICO will engender disgust only among crime bosses and not throughout the legal profession.

Bibliography

Baker, J.S. "Nationalizing Criminal Law—Does Organized Crime Make It Necessary or Proper?" *Rutgers Law Journal* 16 (Spring/Summer 1985): 495–588.

Fassett, D.W. "Mother of Mercy, Is This the End of RICO?" *Criminal Justice* 6 (Spring 1991): 12–17.

Lichtenberger, John, ed. *Readings in White-Collar Crime.* Westport, CT: Meckler, 1991.

Magarity, G.T. "RICO Investigations—A Case Study." *American Criminal Law Review* 17 (Winter 1980): 367–78.

McMillion, Rhonda. "ABA Seeks End of Civil RICO Abuses." *ABA Journal* (October 1991): 112.

North, Donald V. "RICO: A Theory of Investigation." *Police Chief* 55 (January 1988): 44–47.

"Symposium. Reforming RICO: If, Why, and How?" *Vanderbilt Law Review* 43 (April 1990): 621–1101.

"Symposium. The 20th Anniversary of the Racketeer Influenced and Corrupt Organizations Act (1970–1990)." *St. John's Law Review* 64 (Fall 1990): entire issue.

Van Houten, Paul, Robert T. Murphy, and Rena Johnson. "RICO." *American Criminal Law Review* 28 (1991): 637–77.

Role of the Police

The enforcement of the law is one of the most influential mechanisms for social control. In fact, there exists no governmental function that controls or directs the activities of the public as much as law enforcement. Law enforcement is a government service with which the public has frequent contact. Such contact and control is constant, and, if it is not experienced directly through personal contact, it is at least felt indirectly through the visible or implied presence of police personnel.

To most people the phrase *law enforcement* relates directly to the responsibility of uniformed police officers or to police activities in the community. This relationship is correct since the police are most surely involved in the enforcement of the law and, by definition, police officers are persons employed by municipal, county, or state government and charged with the responsibility of enforcing the law and maintaining order. Typically, they are referred to as city police, county sheriffs and deputies, and state police or highway patrol officers.

Not valid, however, is the tendency to think of crime control and the maintenance of order as the exclusive responsibility of the police. This misconception is easily understood, however, when we consider the visible activities of the police. The police have the responsibility for dealing with crime and traffic on a twenty-four hour basis, are usually conspicuously visible to the public, and are the agents that immediately respond when violations of the law occur. The police, however, are just one segment of the mechanism our society uses to maintain the standards of conduct necessary to protect individuals in the community. This system has four generalized and separately organized units: police, prosecution, courts, and corrections. Generally speaking, the police are charted with the detection, identification, and apprehension of law violators. The prosecutor's office will determine whether to charge or not charge the offender; if a charge is filed, what to charge; if appropriate, to plea bargain; and if a charge is filed, to prosecute. Courts hear cases, weigh evidence, interpret law, and determine guilt or innocence. When guilt is the finding, the sentence may be suspended or, if a sentence is imposed, it may be probation, a fine, incarceration, or some combination of these. Corrections is charged with detention and rehabilitation of the offender. This is obviously an oversimplification of the process, but it does place in perspective the special generalized role of the police in conjunction with the other segments of the system.

Types of Police
City police derive their authority from the state constitution, and their administrative operations are defined by each municipal government. Municipal police are granted full police powers.

In addition to municipal police there are county sheriffs' departments, which in large parts of the United States constitute full-fledged police organizations. In some states, however, they are restricted to the administration of the county correctional facility, the serving of court orders and documents, and provision of security for courts.

State police units exist in all but a few of the states. They may be called state police, public safety departments, or highway patrols. In some states they practice full police activities, but typically they limit their function to highway traffic control, enforcement, and accident investigation.

Although the Constitution did not specifically establish federal police agencies, Congress created them for the enforcement of specific legislative acts. For example, the Constitution stipulates that Congress has power to coin money and punish counterfeiters (Article I, Section 8). Concurrently, Congress has the authority to establish the Secret Service to detect and arrest counterfeiters. Other examples of federal police agencies include the Federal Bureau of Investigation, Internal Revenue Service, and the Drug Enforcement Administration.

The Police Responsibility
The municipal, county, and state police of the United States are charged with responsibilities that rank second to none in importance in our democratic society. The police service is that branch of government that is assigned the awesome task of securing compliance to the multitude of laws and regulations deemed beneficial to society. Since law is society's means of achieving conformance to desired norms, the police are society's agents for the maintenance of harmony within the community.

Within this broad context the police are charged with: (1) safeguarding of lives and property, (2) preservation of the peace, (3) prevention of crime, (4) suppression of crime through detection and arrest of violators of the law, (5) enforcement of the law, (6) prevention of delinquency, (7) safeguarding the constitutional rights of individuals, (8) control of vehicular traffic, (9) suppression of vice, and (10) provision of public services.

The police have not always had these broad responsibilities. For years the police, and even the public, generally believed the police were fulfilling their responsibility by investigating crime and attempting to apprehend criminals. There was no thought given to the concept of prevention, and most certainly citizens did not expect the police to intervene in domestic disputes or problems related to their youngsters. Police officers saw themselves as "crime-fighters" and in fact many officers still hold to such provincial thinking. Role conflict is unavoidable as the police oscillate between competing traditions such as control of the public versus social service to the public. So strong is the influence of the past that typical police officers show deep resentment when an outsider attempts to confront them with evidence of the change.

Although the police function is old, it has begun, of necessity, to change in order to meet changing needs. The process of law enforcement has gone through a gradual development along with the country's urbanization, which has enlarged the police role significantly.

Even though the police of this country are changing, there are certain societal expectations beyond their capability. For example, even under the most favorable conditions the police cannot eliminate crime. The police do not create the social conditions conducive to crime nor can they resolve them. The police do not enact the legislation that they must enforce. They do not adjudicate the offenders they arrest, and they are only one of the agencies of criminal justice.

Most certainly the police role still involves their being "crime-fighters," but in a much broader context. In addition to the suppression of crime and enforcement of the law the police are becoming increasingly involved with crime prevention and public service. Theirs is an expanding role and now includes such activities as family crisis intervention, juvenile diversion, social agency referral services, youth programs, rape victim assistance, and other public service functions. Since *Miranda v. Arizona*, requiring police officers to inform suspects of their constitutional rights before questioning, the police have come to recognize their role in safeguarding the constitutional rights of individuals.

It is even being suggested by some criminologists and a few police administrators that police organizations should become known as "departments of police services" rather than police departments or, worse yet, police forces. They suggest that law enforcement is a "police service" rather than a "police force." By definition, the word *force* denotes coercion, power, compulsion, brawn, might, and generally refers to troops of an army. Service on the other hand denotes help, duty, and aid, which is a more appropriate description of the police function. In support of this view, some police organizations have recognized law enforcement as a community responsibility, with the police assuming a leadership profile rather than an autocratic role.

Police Power/Authority

The concept of "police service" must not, however, infer erosion of the authority of the police officer in terms of the legal definition of his or her responsibility for enforcement. Unfortunately people have demonstrated their inability to live in harmony with their neighbors, thus the need for exercising police authority and the legal power of arrest. In conjunction with the "power to arrest" the police do have the authority to use force in securing compliance with the law and this authority is in fact basic to their role in maintaining public order. This awesome but essential authority carries with it the responsibility of using only that force absolutely necessary in any given situation in order to achieve a legal objective. The possible consequences of the use of force demand that it be exercised with the greatest degree of discretion. The police officer should always try for voluntary surrender in any arrest situation, but need not retreat or desist from his/her efforts by reason of the resistance or threatened resistance of the person being arrested.

To really understand the role of the police in achieving their objectives it is necessary to review operational "line" functions. Line functions are police activities directly related to the achievement of objectives. They are, typically, patrol and criminal investigation.

Patrol. Patrol refers to moving on foot or by vehicle around and within an assigned area for the purpose of providing police services. Police officers are usually in uniform, and when a vehicle is used, it is usually conspicuously marked. The purpose of patrol is to distribute police officers in a manner that will eliminate or reduce the opportunity for citizen misconduct, increase the probability of apprehension if a criminal commits a crime, and provide a quick response when a citizen requests police assistance. The patrol unit is the backbone of police operations and operates twenty-four hours each day.

The patrol function is so basic to fulfilling the police responsibility that its goals are essentially synonymous with the total police objective. As such, the patrol officer is the most important position of the police organization. The patrol officer is responsible for all activities within his/her geographical assignment and will respond to all situations related to police service. He/she will institute constant surveillance techniques, arrest violators when he/she observes the commission of a crime, respond to radio dispatched calls as requested by citizens, control vehicular and pedestrian traffic, direct traffic, enforce traffic regulations, investigate traffic accidents, conduct preliminary investigations following the commission of a crime, investigate public accidents involving personal injury, mediate family disputes, search for lost children, refer people to social agencies able to offer specialized assistance outside the realm of police services, give directions to motorists, and provide a wide variety of other public services.

Criminal Investigation. The investigation of crime becomes necessary when patrol has failed as a deterrent or has been unable to apprehend the criminal immediately after the commission of a crime. The initial purpose of investigation is to identify, locate, and arrest the perpetrator of the crime. The secondary but equally important purpose is to prepare the case for court and assist in the prosecution of the offender.

The police officer who investigates such crimes is usually referred to as a detective. Generally the detective goes to work after the fact and must rely on such things as physical evidence, witnesses, and information obtained from various sources. As a general rule, the detective works in civilian clothing so that he/she is inconspicuous when moving about the community in pursuance of the investigative task.

Unlike patrol officers, detectives are not usually involved in crime prevention but with the repression of crime through the subsequent arrest of offenders. Briefly stated, the detective becomes involved in such activities as searching the crime scenes, securing physical evidence, interviewing witnesses, interrogating suspects, obtaining warrants of arrest, taking suspects into custody, preparing written reports for prosecution, and testifying in court.

Crime Prevention

As stated previously, in recent years the police have become more involved with crime prevention. Crime prevention is primarily an additional responsibility of uniformed patrol officers and personnel assigned to a specialized crime-prevention organizational unit.

The primary means by which patrol prevents crime is through being conspicuous and available. The obvious presence of the police discourages the criminal from committing a crime for fear of being caught. This indicates the importance of the conspicuously marked vehicle. Not only does this show their presence, but it also gives the impression of police saturation. Patrol officers also prevent crime by becoming familiar with juveniles within their patrol area or beat. A healthy relationship built on mutual respect between the patrol officers and juveniles will do more toward the prevention of delinquency than any other police activity. The patrol officer is the person the juveniles see and identify as the authority symbol. Respect for the officer promotes respect for the law, and such respect will discourage unlawful conduct.

A very important, but often overlooked, role of patrol in crime prevention is the securing of information that can be passed to other units of the police department. With such information the specialized units can work on a potential problem prior to its actually becoming a problem. The patrol officer is on the street and is in the best possible position to obtain information on such things as the formation of a juvenile gang, the underlying frustrations of the community, the use of narcotics, etc.

A specialized unit for crime prevention may become involved with such things as coordination of neighborhood watch programs, diversion programs for juveniles, public education, improving community relations, involvement with community organizations, youth programs, and working with other public agencies.

Support Services

Other police officers work within organizational units that exist to assist the line activities of the police organization. These men and women may be assigned to the crime laboratory, communications center, records, equipment maintenance, research and planning, inspections, jail, identification center, property management, personnel recruitment and selection, and training.

Police Role in the Protection of Individual Freedom

In effect, people of the community realize their civil rights through the interpretive actions of the police. In other words, police procedures and policies are in a sense telling the public what they can or cannot do. There are, of course, many controls from the federal level relative to civil rights, but implementation is the major responsibility of the local police departments, and they must be totally cognizant of the ramifications and importance of these rights.

In addition to interpretive actions defining civil rights, the police have the role of instructing citizens with regard to their duties, obligations, rights, and privileges in terms of the law. They should, for example, publish pamphlets that describe the citizens' rights under the Constitution of the United States, the state, and the municipality within which they live. The police might also stress the public's responsibility in relation to those protective privileges that they have under the law.

Vern L. Folley

Rural Law Enforcement

The study of police and policing in the United States concentrates primarily on urban areas. This is justified by the generally higher levels of crime and concentration of police activity in metropolitan areas. However, there is increasing evidence that rural crime and law enforcement are worthy subjects of attention. This is due to the large number of citizens served by rural law-enforcement personnel and the particular difficulties faced by those personnel. Rural law enforcement occurs in those areas of the country that lie outside Standard Metropolitan Statistical Areas (SMSA) and have been demographically designated as rural in nature. Most of these areas are far from cities, not linked economically or socially to the everyday life of the city. In addition, these areas tend to be dominated by agricultural or recreational economics. They are served by small, sometimes part-time, police departments.

There are many dilemmas that rural law enforcement faces that are not part of the urban scene. The first is the problem of open space. Police in rural areas are responsible for patrolling large expanses of area and road. The difficulty is compounded by the fact that the number of police per thousand citizens in rural areas is lower than in urban areas. Thus rural police are expected to cover more territory (both in square miles and road miles) than their urban counterparts as well as to serve more citizens. These two facts create difficulties in the provision of service in that service areas are sometimes quite substantial and considerable driving time between calls may slow response time significantly. Because there tends to be less crime in rural areas, rural police officers generally possess less of the constant wariness that characterizes their urban counterparts. This leads to considerable potential difficulties for a number of reasons. The first is that backups are seldom nearby when trouble develops. Second, encounters in rural areas are less visible, thus jeopardizing the officer's safety in a way not typical of urban encounters. Third, officers in rural areas are more likely to ride alone than those in cities. Finally, handguns are owned at disproportionately higher rates in rural areas. Thus officers in the "hinterlands" are more likely to approach a dangerous situation, less likely to expect trouble, less likely to be able to count on support in the immediate future, and more likely to encounter armed citizens.

In addition, rural police and rural criminal-justice agencies in general have even lower levels of funding than those in cities. This is evidenced by the lower number of officers per thousand citizens. The level of technology seldom approaches that of urban areas. Police training and education also tend to be somewhat less comprehensive, creating situations where officers are less prepared to deal with the multitude of situations that they must face. Rural police are also less likely to have specialists on the force because of the smaller number of cases seen in each particular category. The highly specialized nature of crime in the modern world thus poses significant problems for rural policing. Compounding these difficulties is the fact that many rural communities are served by a larger, geographically distinct police force, either the state police or a county police force. Many rural towns employ part-time officers or constables to provide the bulk of their policing needs.

The primary form of police service provided in rural areas is through the office of the sheriff. This is usually a county-level organization. The sheriff is most often an elected official, which has benefits and drawbacks for the citizens of the county. On the one hand, the sheriff is usually not a professional law-enforcement officer, and therefore lacks much of the training and values usually associated (positively) with the profession. On the other hand, the will of the electorate often influences the sheriff to act in ways consistent with the needs and demands of the citizenry, but often absent in the professional model. Certainly a larger degree of community control can be exerted over the police in these circumstances.

Rural police tend to resemble the citizenry that they serve more than their urban counterparts. Indeed, several commentators have noted the extent to which police in rural areas are integrated into the communities they serve. This is largely because rural police are drawn from the more consistent fabric of rural society, which does not hold for their urban counterparts. And the nature of rural law enforcement does not isolate the rural police officer from the community in the same way that it tends to in urban areas. The homogeneity of rural communities does a lot to explain this integration.

The Image of the Sheriff

The small town police officer or sheriff is regularly portrayed by the entertainment media in one of three quite different but equally inaccurate fashions. The first is the heart of gold, low-profile officer who solves everyone's problems with a bit of folksy wisdom and a few laughs. Andy Griffith's television sheriff helped launch this characterization, and its apparent popularity is attested to by the widespread syndication of the show. A second common portrayal of the rural law-enforcement officer finds him rushing from crime to crime, confronting murder, mayhem, and robbery. The *Walking Tall* films exemplify this approach. The final image frequently offered to the public is of the always inept, usually corrupt, and inevitably corpulent small town cop who must be rescued or punished by a "supercop" from the big city as in the film *In the Heat of the Night*. The impact of these popular views of rural law enforcement is difficult to measure. In fact, one might reasonably ask whether popular perceptions make any difference. Unfortunately, they are important because there is some evidence to suggest that they influence decisions made about the law-enforcement needs of rural communities.

The National Sheriffs Institute in 1976 compiled a profile of 167 first-term county sheriffs, the majority of them from rural areas. The profile disclosed a mean age of just over forty-one years and 12.3 years of experience in law enforcement. Forty-nine percent were high-school graduates, and 68 percent of those had attended at least some college; 18 percent had earned an associate of arts or bachelor's degree. So it seems safe to say that law-enforcement officers in the rural community reflect the characteristics of the majority populace. Salaries and highly localized recruiting practices restrict the applicant pool for most positions in the immediate area. Lateral movement between agencies, when it occurs, tends to be within the same state and is generally caused by salary considerations.

The Reality of Rural Law Enforcement

Obviously rural law-enforcement agencies are small. They usually lack the scale to provide significant differentiation of tasks among personnel. Specialists (e.g., homicide investigators, traffic accident investigators, crime prevention officers, youth officers) are seldom economically feasible. Knowledgeable staff and auxiliary service experts (e.g., statistical analysts, crime scene technicians) are also unavailable. Equipment and facilities are frequently inadequate or nonexistent. Major crimes are particularly demanding and complex service problems require borrowing the expertise of a larger neighboring department or a state agency. The alternative is to muddle through, perhaps with disastrous results.

Many agencies are too small to provide round-the-clock service seven days a week. They commonly rely on reserve or auxiliary officers (many of whom are untrained) or on a call-back system, which requires that a regular officer be available to respond from home to any calls for assistance. The volume and seriousness of rural crime in a given area may not merit more personnel or more sophisticated equipment if measured by standards of cost efficiency. The fact that police spend most of their time providing services other than crime-fighting is especially true in rural settings. Given this, efficiency may not be the most appropriate criterion by which to measure agency scale. Effectiveness would seem to be a more appropriate criterion. In one respect, money spent on law enforcement is spent on its potential. It is invested to ensure that when police service is needed it will be forthcoming, with that measure of sensitivity, boldness, or courage appropriate to the situation. Rural citizens have a right to expect the same level of preparedness as urban dwellers. The frequency with which it is actually required should be one—but not the sole—criterion for measuring its value. This is an important consideration, one that might help discourage response to the problem of inadequate scale by blindly consolidating local agencies or supplanting with state-provided services. There are values to smallness that should be preserved.

One of the major advantages of smallness is the familiarity that officers have with the citizens they serve and with the people who staff other local criminal-justice agencies. The American justice system, as frustrating as it can often be, was designed to diffuse power among multiple agencies and actors. When their number is relatively few, necessary coordination may be effected without surrendering the advantages of this power diffusion. It is also easier to measure productivity in a small system or agency. In this era of diminishing resources and expanding competition for the tax dollar, it is critical to provide government services in a timely and accurate fashion. Individual and unit productivity are more visible in small-scale operations, as is progress toward goals. Smaller agencies tend to generate higher levels of interaction with the community. When every officer is expected to be able to handle every call from every neighborhood, a sensitivity to the true character of those neighborhoods results. The democratization effect this has should not be minimized. It is ironic that the concept of "team policing," which is being attempted by numerous urban police agencies, has as a core principle the need to get officers back in touch with the people they serve.

The Changing Scene
Crime—in fact, all manner of social problems—is on the rise in rural America. Increased leisure time, higher levels of education, enhanced expectations of affluence and position, mobility, and the economy are putting a strain on traditional forces of social control in small towns and in the country as well. This vulnerability is in its early stages as compared with urban centers. It is and can be only partly influenced by law-enforcement practices. It seems important, then, to avoid putting the lion's share of responsibility for dealing with increased levels of deviance and crime on the local police. Rather, enhanced police performance must be viewed in the context of the community's efforts to deal with more fundamental causes. Unlike their urban counterparts, who can only repress crime by patrol or control it by investigations and arrests, rural law-enforcement practitioners still have an opportunity for prevention through the timely and sensitive provision of the full range of community-oriented services they are capable of delivering.

The obvious problems of rural and small-town law enforcement, such as low population density, frequently huge geographic jurisdictions, low tax bases, and lack of economy of scale, must be addressed by any proposed improvement strategy. To do so in a meaningful fashion, however, requires more information on rural crime and law-enforcement problems than is currently available. Agency planners must demand with all the force they can muster that proper attention be focused on rural problems including consideration of funding and resource-sharing mechanisms that will enhance local capabilities without subverting local control.

Scott H. Decker
Steven M. Ward

Bibliography

Bartol, Curt R. "Psychological Characteristics of Small-Town Police Officers." *Journal of Police Science and Administration* 10(1) (March 1982): 58–63.

Bristow, Allen P. *Rural Law Enforcement.* Boston: Allyn and Bacon, 1982.

Cain, Maureen. "On the Beat: Interactions and Relations in Rural and Urban Police Forces." In *Images of Deviance.* Ed. S. Cohen. Baltimore, MD: Penguin, 1971.

Cronk, Shandler D. et al. *Criminal Justice in Rural America.* Washington, DC: U.S. Department of Justice, National Institute of Justice, 1982.

Decker, Scott H. "The Working Personality of Rural Policemen." *LAE Journal of the American Criminal Justice Association* 41(3) (1978): 19–28.

____. "The Rural County Sheriff: An Issue in Social Control." *Criminal Justice Review* 4(2) (1979): 97–111.

Esselstyn, T.C. "The Social Role of a Rural County Sheriff." *Journal of Criminal Law, Criminology, and Police Science* 44(2) (1953): 177–84.

Kowalewski, David et al. "Police Environments and Operational Codes: A Case Study of Rural Setting." *Journal of Police Science and Administration* 12(4) (December 1984): 363–72.

S

St. Louis Police Department

The Constabulary

The origin of the St. Louis Police Department is traceable to the turn of the nineteenth century, when the city began its first police patrol. The Constabulary, as this founding force was called—its name attributable to French influence—was officially established in 1808 through the efforts of the board of trustees of the "Town of St. Louis." The creation of this force came five years after the U.S. purchase of Louisiana and fifteen years prior to the granting of the city's first "town" charter in 1832. This modest beginning of a police force (although they would not be termed "police" until 1818) antedated similar actions by older, more established eastern cities by twenty years. While a forerunner in police service, the Constabulary had, by today's standards, a meager beginning.

Four armed officers, one of whom received the distinction of captain's rank, comprised the small initial force. These original St. Louis officers, who received no compensation for their services, were required to furnish their own weapons. Police ranks at this time were filled by conscription; white males between the ages of eighteen and sixty were liable to serve four months a years without exception. Refusal to satisfy the often capricious call to service was punishable by the imposition of a one dollar fine.

This ever-changing group of police-citizens was charged with providing safety and security for the approximately one thousand inhabitants of the growing frontier town. Additionally, these first officers were charged with enforcement of local ordinances prohibiting trespass and establishing curfew, ordinances enacted primarily to control the behavior of slaves, who comprised approximately 25 percent of the city's population. Accordingly, the founding force had simple duties and operated under simple circumstances, remaining relatively unchanged and without documented incident until 1818, when the need to expand the police became paramount.

The Force of 1818

St. Louis experienced great expansion during the decade of 1810 to 1820, expansion both in the form of population and the size of the city itself. With increased population came the proliferation of residential areas outside the existing bounds of the city. The population, approximately 1,400 in 1810, grew to 4,598 during the 1920s. An influx of immigrants with differing religious and social backgrounds prompted the city's growth and increased its cosmopolitan character. With these changes, the need for additional police services became apparent. The Constabulary of 1808, no longer sufficient, was thus expanded in 1818 by the addition of two men and the support of a night watch. While the practice of conscription was still the predominant mode of police staffing, a paid captain and officer positions were created by the city board. These new positions were filled by the city board selecting individuals from a roster of available citizenry. The first paid police position was held by Captain Mackery Wherry, who was compensated $100 a year for his services.

On February 23, 1826, the force underwent additional expansion. Under the direction of the mayor and board of aldermen, a captain and twenty-six police lieutenants were selected to perform the police function. The selection process remained the same—selection by list.

City ordinance exempted clergy, indigents, and minorities from service. Under these same ordinances the first guardroom was established providing the officers with furniture and a source of heat; this guardroom was one of the first St. Louis police facilities.

St. Louis saw additional growth of its police in 1839; the City Guard was founded with sixteen men. The guard, functioning to support the night watch, consisted of two officers, a one-armed man named Gabes Warner and a constable. Warner held the position of night chief. Night police were under the direction of the city marshall, who also held the position of captain of the guards. The captain was provided with a salary of $50 per month; officers were paid about $500 a year. The force, then termed "police," expanded at a rapid rate. By 1841 the police force consisted of forty-one men: one captain, three lieutenants, twenty-eight privates, and eleven guards.

Reorganization aimed at consolidating police services began in 1846. Under this plan the city marshal, the city guard, and the police were consolidated into one department; however, a distinction still remained between day police and night police. The night police consisted of six lieutenants and forty-eight officers, collectively called the Guards. The day police consisted of one lieutenant and seven officers. The department would not adopt eight-hour shifts until 1854 and would abolish that practice two years later under Chief Rawls—the first chief. Little change in the operation or size of the department ensued until the social turbulence of the Civil War in 1861.

Metropolitan Police System
The Metropolitan Police System was established on March 27, 1861. The Missouri General Assembly created the police system through legislation, removing control of the police from the mayor and establishing a board of police commissioners who were appointed directly by the governor. In the wake of the Civil War, this legislation was seen as a method to achieve stability and depoliticize the St. Louis police. Neither goal was to come to immediate fruition.

The first board of police commissioners was known as the Brownlee Board (1861) and it named James McDonough the first chief of the Metropolitan Police. However, ensuing political turmoil led to the division and replacement of both the board and chief during the same year of their appointment.

The succeeding How Board was appointed by Governor Gamble on September 10 of 1861 and served until February 3, 1865. This board appointed the city's second chief, J.E.D. Couzins, who resigned shortly after being charged by the mayor with receiving and failing to account for reward monies. Couzins later failed to appear before a committee charged with the investigation of police corruption.

Between 1861 and 1870 St. Louis saw at least six police chiefs come and go; James McDonough, the first chief, was reappointed in 1870 and served four years. At least three totally different police boards were utilized during this ten-year period and numerous resignations and appointments occurred.

Stability and depoliticizing did not come to either the board or the police ranks; for on March 26, 1868, the Missouri General Assembly appointed a committee to investigate charges of fraud and corruption on the part of the board of police commissioners, police chiefs, and individual police commanders.

Charges brought against the board of police commissioners and police officers by Mayor James Thomas ranged from fraud and the misappropriation of property to failure to serve warrants, drunkenness, and the visitation of houses of ill repute. One notable incident involved Captain William Lee. On October 10, 1866, Lee, while in uniform and in a drunken state, was said to have mounted a horse at the St. Louis fairgrounds and rode into a public saloon, endangering the patrons and disturbing the peace. Ironically, Lee was appointed chief of the Metropolitan Police two years after the incident. Other less flamboyant charges were brought against the department, including the improper search of a female prisoner, allowing a prisoner to escape, interfering with elections, and the failure to enforce a ban on Sunday liquor sales.

The investigative committee's report, while valuable as a historical document, failed to refute many of the charges levied by the mayor and attempted to present the police and board in the most favorable light. The committee concluded that the department was "now" keeping accurate records of transactions, and while some of the incidents charged had in fact occurred, the department's character was above reproach—"having made but few mistakes." It was recommended that the mayor's executive powers and his involvement with the police be curtailed.

During this turbulent period from 1861 to 1870, even the department's personnel strength did not remain stable. Departmental strength fluctuated from 320 men at the beginning of 1862 to 25 at year's end; military guards were enlisted to assist the St. Louis police.

Innovations
The period from 1861 to the later half of the 1900s was also marked by many improvements and innovations in policing. Great strides were made by the St. Louis Police Department in the development of police technology, education, and human-resource development programs.

In March 1867 legislation was enacted providing for mounted police whose primary mission was to deal with and apprehend horse thieves. Four districts were established, and an equal number of mounted officers were assigned to patrol each of these areas—always riding in pairs. Later in November 1892, land and stables were set aside for the training of the department's mounted police. Although the use of mounted police was abolished in 1948, its value was rediscovered and the program was reintroduced in 1971.

The first police telephone was installed in 1881 and utilized on an experimental basis; the first police alarm was installed the following year. In 1897 the Bertillon system was adopted, to be replaced with the Henry fingerprint system in 1927. St. Louis's first police patrol car was procured in 1903 and the maiden use of motorcycles occurred four years later. A research bureau was established and subsequently became St. Louis's first police laboratory, where police experimentation with color photography began. The department began a radio station in 1930 and opened the first department-owned television station in 1970.

Vast improvements in human-resource development programs took place. A school of police instruction began in 1889, but it was not until 1969 that the Greater St. Louis Police Academy was established. Scholarships and educational pay incentive plans were developed and a forty-hour workweek was adopted. A police library was opened, one that has become the nation's largest department-owned library housing over thirty thousand volumes. The first police-initiated detoxification center went into operation in 1966, and the department instituted a police-employees' assistance program in 1983, designed to assist police officers in coping with stress.

Present day
In the fall of 1991 Col. Robert E. Scheetz retired from his position as chief of police after a long and distinguished career. Colonel Clarence Harmon became the new chief and the first African American to head the St. Louis Police Department. Also in 1991, the St. Louis City and County Police Departments signed a Mutual Police Services agreement that formalized joint "most wanted" fugitive identification, cooperative auto theft investigations, shared radio communications, joint purchases of equipment, and other reciprocal endeavors. Community involvement programs continue to produce results. Combat Auto Theft (CAT) allows citizens to register their automobiles with the police department. Each citizen agrees not to drive his or her car between the hours of 1 A.M. and 5 A.M. and receives a decal. If police spot a car on the street with the CAT decal during those hours, the driver is automatically pulled over. The Street Corner Apprehension Team (SCAT) is used in drug-infested neighborhoods to demonstrate highly visible police action. SCAT officers make arrests to draw maximum attention, and equally attention-getting, conviction rates are around 97 percent. Another program, We Are Responsible (WAR), employed a different kind of eye-striking tactic. A Corvette sports car seized under the Asset Forfeiture Program was painted with the police department logos and the message "Drug Users Are Losers" and driven around St. Louis. But of these and other programs, the Gun Buy Back program got national media coverage. The most visible sign of police–community cooperation yet seen perhaps anywhere in the United States, Gun Buy Back paid a bounty to citizens who voluntarily turned in guns. In just thirty days in 1991 citizens surrendered more than 7,500 firearms, with handguns comprising approximately 67 percent of the total.

Victor E. Kappeler

Bibliography
Bellairs, K.G. "From Wherry to Gerk, 1808–1931." *St. Louis Police Journal* 29 (August 1931): 4–9.
Missouri Joint Committee of the General Assembly, 1868. *Report of the Joint Committee of the General Assembly Appointed to Investigate the Police Department of the City of St. Louis.* New York: Arno Press, 1971.
St. Louis Board of Police Commissioners.

History of the Metropolitan Police De-
partment of St. Louis, 1818–1910. St.
Louis, MO: privately published, 1910.
St. Louis Police Department Past and
Present. St. Louis, MO: St. Louis Police
Library, 1984.
Troen, S. K., and G. E. Holt, eds. St. Louis.
New York: New Viewpoints, 1977.

Search and Seizure

All search and seizure law springs forth from
the Fourth Amendment to the U.S. Constitution, which provides that:

> The right of the people to be secure in
> their persons, houses, papers and effects,
> against unreasonable searches and sei-
> zures, shall not be violated, and no war-
> rants shall issue, but upon probable
> cause, supported by oath or affirmation
> and particularly describing the persons
> or things to be seized.

This provision has led to the vast body of law
designating what is constitutionally permissible
behavior by law-enforcement officials in the
search and seizure area.

The Fourth Amendment itself applies to
activity by federal officials, but the U.S. Supreme Court has held that it also protects
against unreasonable searches and seizures by
state officials to the same extent that it protects
against such activity by federal officials (*Ker v.
California*, 374 U.S. 23 [1963]). Most states
have separate constitutional measures that mirror the Fourth Amendment but are only applicable to state officials. These state measures
may be more restrictive of police practices than
the Fourth Amendment. Simply put, a state law
cannot constitutionally offer less in the way of
Fourth Amendment protection to its citizens
than the Fourth Amendment itself.

Standing

When a court determines that a search or seizure was unreasonable, the usual remedy is the
exclusion of the evidence seized pursuant to the
illegal search or seizure, as well as the exclusion
of any evidence that is the fruit of the illegal
search or seizure. The party seeking the remedy
of exclusion must qualify as having an appropriate standing to assert the claim for relief. To
qualify as the proper party, the claimant "must
have been a victim of the search or seizure"

(*Jones v. United States*, 362 U.S. 257 [1960]).
Often this requires that the court find that the
individual asserting the claim had an expectation of privacy in the thing seized or the area
searched. If the evidence being offered by the
prosecution against the defendant was acquired
by the police through a search or seizure of
someone other than the defendant, normally the
defendant will not have standing to assert the
Fourth Amendment claim and the evidence will
be admitted against him or her.

Searches—The Reasonable Expectation of Privacy

The Fourth Amendment protects only against
unreasonable searches and seizures. Historically, the Supreme Court has held that a search
was unreasonable, and thus illegal, if it consisted of a warrantless physical intrusion into an
area specifically enumerated (or a logical extension thereof) in the Fourth Amendment itself.
The protected areas were "persons, houses,
papers, and effects." Logical extensions of
"houses" were, for example, apartments or
hotel rooms.

In 1967 the Supreme Court shifted the focus of Fourth Amendment protections when it
decided *Katz v. United States* (389 U.S. 347
[1967])

> [T]he Fourth Amendment protects
> people, not places. What a person know-
> ingly exposes to the public, even in his
> own home or office, is not a subject of
> Fourth Amendment protection. . . . But
> what she seeks to preserve as private
> even in an area accessible to the public,
> may be constitutionally protected.

The *Katz* opinion also described the analysis
currently used by the Supreme Court in determining when a search has, in fact, been a reasonable one:

> [T]here is a twofold requirement, first,
> that a person have exhibited an actual
> (subjective) expectation of privacy and,
> second, that the expectation be one that
> society is prepared to recognize as rea-
> sonable.

Katz, then, stands for the proposition that in
order for a search to have occurred, the person
searched must have a reasonable expectation of
privacy in the place searched. If no such expec-

tation of privacy exists, the Fourth Amendment protections do not come into play.

Search or No Search

Often officers inadvertently happen to see a person walking along with a gun extending from his pocket, or encounter the smell of marijuana being smoked nearby. Discovery of evidence in this manner does not normally involve Fourth Amendment protections, because these situations are not considered searches or seizures for Fourth Amendment purposes. Often officers will utilize the "plain view" doctrine (discussed *supra*) to avoid Fourth Amendment problems and the operation of the exclusionary rule, excluding evidence from the fact finder.

Similarly, the use of routine *or common* enhancement devices does not constitute a search. Use of binoculars or a flashlight, for example, does not invalidate surveillances that, without use of such devices, would be more difficult for officers to conduct. In *Dow Chemical Co. v. United States* (106 S. Ct. 1819 [1986]), the Court held that the use of a telescopic camera lens by officers in taking aerial photographs of an industrial complex does not constitute a search. Enlargement of standard photographs of an industrial complex does not constitute a search. Enlargement of standard photographs by blowup procedures is also not characterized as a search for purposes of the Fourth Amendment. The Supreme Court did distinguish, however, between the use of highly sophisticated surveillance equipment not generally available to the public (which would constitute a search) and the more conventional devices used in *Dow*.

The Court has also held that when officers flew over a defendant's land and happened to see marijuana plants growing thereon, such conduct did not constitute a search (*California v. Ciraolo*, 106 S.Ct. 1809 [1986]).

Use of specially trained police dogs to sniff luggage to detect narcotics or other contraband has been held not to constitute a search: this use of dogs is considered routine or common. However, a different result would be reached if the dogs were used to sniff people for the same purposes without a search warrant. In this instance the use of dogs is not common and therefore would constitute a search (*United States v. Place*, 462 U.S. 696 [1983]).

Officers' observation of "physical characteristics . . . constantly exposed to the public" do not constitute a search for Fourth Amendment purposes (*Cupp v. Murphy*, 412 U.S. 291 [1973]). Citizens cannot raise Fourth Amendment claims when police take exemplars of their voices, as there is no reasonable expectation of privacy in a voice that is constantly used in public (*United States v. Dionisio*, 410 U.S. 1 [1973]). The same is true of handwriting exemplars and fingerprints (*United States v. Mara*, 410 U.S. 19 [1973], *Cupp v. Murphy*, supra).

Officers may constitutionally extract blood samples and/or breath samples in certain situations without violating Fourth Amendment rights. Although it is preferred that the officer obtain a search warrant to extract these items, often time is of the essence, as the evidence may disappear quickly. In *Schmerber v. California* (384 U.S. 757 [1966]), the Supreme Court set forth guidelines. First, there must be a "clear indication" that the sample will show evidence of the crime. In *Schmerber*, the defendant was arrested for drunk driving. Second, the test must be "reasonable," meaning that it causes "virtually no risk, trauma, or pain." Third, the test must be "performed in a reasonable manner . . . taken by a physician (or medical personnel) in a hospital environment according to accepted medical practices." It is important to note that, although the Supreme Court characterized the taking of blood in *Schmerber* as a search and seizure under the Fourth Amendment, the warrantless search and seizure was reasonable in that it was made "incident to the arrest" of the defendant at a time when "exigent circumstances" existed regarding the quick disappearance of the evidence through passage in the bloodstream. Warrantless searches "incident to arrests" and searches made under "exigent circumstances" will be discussed, infra.

Some bodily intrusions by officers are considered so violative of a person's constitutional rights that they are unreasonable notwithstanding the presence of a search warrant. Among these constitutionally impermissible instructions are those that have been characterized by the Court as "bound to offend even hardened sensibilities" and "shock[ing] to the conscience." The Supreme Court determined in *Rochin v. California* (342 U.S. 165 [1952]) that when officers, without a warrant but with probable cause, broke into the defendant's home and forcefully attempted to extract certain pills he had taken, then took him to a hospital where doctors forced the substance out with a stomach pump, the officers violated defendant's right to due process.

Police use of an electronic tracing device or "beeper" is not a search if it merely enables police to monitor the movement of contraband in a vehicle. This is merely an "enhancement" of what the police could accomplish by mere visual surveillance (*United States v. Knotts,* 460 U.S. 276 [1983]). However, if the contraband is brought into a residence (expectation of privacy) and the police use the beeper to monitor the movement of the contraband from room to room, such conduct constitutes a search "when it reveals information that could not have been obtained through visual surveillance." A search warrant must be obtained in order for this police activity to be classified as legally permissible.

When police activity does constitute a search, the search will be valid if it is reasonable. A reasonable search is one based on probable cause.

Probable Cause

There are two types of probable cause. The first is probable cause to issue an arrest warrant; the second is probable cause to issue a search warrant. Normally, determinations that probable cause exist must be made by a neutral, detached, and impartial magistrate. However, the approach will differ when an officer, because of time constraints, must make an on-the-spot analysis to determine whether to search or arrest a suspect.

Probable cause to arrest requires that an officer or affiant have facts within his or her own personal knowledge that are sufficient to convince a reasonably cautious person that an offense has been, is being, or is about to be committed by the accused. This determination is the same whether the officer is on the scent analyzing the situation or relaying a factual scenario to a magistrate.

Probable cause to search, however, requires a slightly different assessment of the facts. Here, there must be a substantial probability that certain items are fruits, instrumentalities, or evidence of crime and that these items are presently to be found in the place to be searched.

Basically, there is not a problem if the facts comprising probable cause are within the personal knowledge of the officer requesting the search warrant. Many times, however, the bulk of information police officers acquire comes from anonymous "tips" or police informants.

Police informants and "tipsters" are not always consistently reliable. Prior to 1983, the courts used a two-pronged test to determine whether there was probable cause to search or to arrest when the source of information was an informant. This test is known as the *Aguilar-Spinelli* test (*Aguilar v. Texas,* 378 U.S. 108 [1964], *Spinelli v. United States,* 393 U.S. 410 [1969]).

The first prong of the test requires analysis of the "basis of the knowledge" of the informant. The relevant inquiry here requires the officer to explain how the informant acquired knowledge. "[T]he informant must declare either (1) that he has himself seen or perceived the fact or facts asserted; or (2) that the information is hearsay, but there is good reason for believing it—perhaps one of the usual grounds for crediting heresay information."

The second prong of the test requires study of the "veracity" of the informant. In other words, is the informant reliable? Usually an informant's veracity will be established if information he or she previously provided has led to arrest or perhaps convictions.

In 1983 *Illinois v. Gates* (462 U.S. 213 [1983]) changed the test. The proper analysis is now focused on the "totality of the circumstances." The more mechanical operation of *Aguilar-Spinelli,* while still an operative test in evaluating informant information, has given way to the less stringent dictates of *Gates.* Much less is required under the totality of circumstances approach; courts are freer to consider and use informant information.

Search Warrants

A search warrant must be grounded on probable cause. Generally, the police cannot search without a search warrant but, of course, as noted earlier, there are exceptions to this rule. In order for a search warrant to be valid, it must comply with the requirements set forth in the Fourth Amendment. It must particularly describe the place to be searched as well as particularly describe the things to be seized. The purpose of these particularity requirements is to preserve "the right of the people to be secure in their persons, houses, papers, and effects . . ." by preventing overbroad warrants and general searches.

The particularity of the description of the place to be searched is usually "enough if the description is such that the officer with a search warrant can, with reasonable effort, ascertain and identify the place intended" (*Steele v. United States*, 267 U.S. 498 [1925]). If a warrant is sufficiently particular on its face but results in confusion when it is carried out, it is permissible to allow an officer to use common sense to resolve the confusion. However, if the warrant is overly broad on its face, it will be void despite the fact that the officers confine their search to the express area where probable cause to search existed.

"[T]he warrant must be sufficiently definite so that the officer executing it can identify the property sought with reasonable certainty" (*Marron v. United States*, 275 U.S. 192 [1927]). If the items sought are contraband, the warrant need not describe them in the same amount of detail as is necessary for an item that is not contraband. For instance, a warrant may properly describe the items being sought as narcotics and narcotic paraphernalia, whereas a general description of stolen property may well prove insufficient.

A search warrant that authorizes a search for narcotics would permit the police to search most anywhere in the place described since narcotics can be easily hidden. If, instead, the warrant authorizes the police to search for a large stolen vase, they would not be authorized to search through desk drawers or medicine chests, since the items could not reasonably be found in those places and, hence, no probable cause would exist to search there.

Search warrants must be issued by an impartial magistrate. This magistrate must make two separate findings, both of which must be supported by the evidence. First, he or she must consider from the facts presented that there is a sufficient connection between the item sought and the illegal activity. Second, the magistrate must conclude that there is substantial probability that the items sought can be found in the place to be searched. A warrant that complies with these two requirements is a valid warrant based on probable cause.

If an officer conducts a search believing in good faith that the search warrant was valid (i.e., that there was probable cause to issue the warrant), evidence obtained through such a search generally will be admissible against the accused even though the warrant is later found to be defective (*United States v. Leon*, 468 U.S. 897 [1984], *Mass v. Sheppard*, 468 U.S. 981 [1984]).

A search warrant must be executed on a timely basis. This means that probable cause to

search must exist at the time of execution, as well as at the time of issuance. Usually execution must take place within ten days of issuance, but the important factor is that probable cause still exist at the time of execution, even within the 10 days. Furthermore, most states provide that a warrant be executed during the daytime although nighttime service of the warrant can be arranged under certain circumstances. The policy behind this rule is that there is more risk of mistake or harm occurring at night.

Finally, in order to execute any warrant, be it arrest or search, the police must comply with the "knock and notice" rule. First, the officer must knock and identify him- or herself. Second, the officer must state his or her purpose, that is, execution of the warrant. Third, the officer must wait for a reasonable period of time before entering uninvited. Exceptions allowing police to enter premises without complying with the "knock and notice" rule exist when the police reasonably believe that the people within the premises can frustrate the purpose of the search or arrest if they have advance notice, such as by destroying evidence. In addition, if an officer courts danger by complying with "knock and notice" requirements, he or she can enter without giving notice.

Sometimes it is unnecessary for police to obtain a search warrant because a person consents to the search. When a person does consent, it may later become difficult to determine if the consent was voluntary. If consent was not voluntary, any evidence or fruits obtained pursuant to the search will be inadmissible at trial. In *Schneckcloth v. Bustmonte* (412 U.S. 218 [1973]), the Court held that "the question whether consent to search was in fact 'voluntary' or was the product of duress or coercion, express or implied, is a question of fact to be determined from the totality of the circumstances."

Usually, consent to a search will be found voluntary if an officer *reasonably believes* that a person has consented to the search. However, courts do look at specific factors to determine such voluntariness. First, courts will consider the *age* of the person consenting. A very young or very old person might be more likely to consent simply because he or she is intimidated by the officer's request to search. Second, courts will look at the personality of the consenting party. Education, intelligence, and timidity are all relevant considerations. Third, a court would be concerned about whether the consenting party has the knowledge of the right to refuse the search, although in *Schneckcloth* the Court held that "the prosecution is not required to demonstrate such knowledge as a prerequisite to establishing a voluntary consent." Fourth, different rules apply if the consenting party was in police custody at the time consent was given. The basic presumption is that consent given in an area such as a public street may be determined to be voluntary whereas consent given "in the confines of the police station" would be involuntary (*United States v. Watson,* 423 U.S. 411 [1976]).

When a party gives consent for an officer to search for a particular item, the officer can look only in the area where the item can be found. Once again, the officer cannot reasonably search a desk drawer for a stolen refrigerator. Likewise when a person gives consent to search a particular place or area, the officer is limited to that place or area.

Another type of consent issue arises when a third party consents to the search of a common area. In *United States v. Matlock* (415 U.S. 164 [1974]), the Supreme Court held:

> The authority which justifies the third party consent rests . . . on mutual use of the property by persons generally having joint access or control for most purposes, so that it is reasonable to recognize that any of the co-inhabitants has the right to permit the inspection in his own right and that the others have assumed the risk that one of their number might permit the common area to be searched.

A person who shares a common area with another may consent to the search of that area but may not consent to the search of an area within the "exclusive control" of the other person. For example, if two people share an apartment and have separate bedrooms one tenant generally cannot consent to a search of the cotenant's private bedroom.

Exceptions to the Warrant Requirement
Several exceptions to the rule that searches and seizures be supported by a warrant based on probable cause have been discussed, supra. "Searches made under exigent circumstances," "incident to arrest," and "in plain view" have been briefly mentioned, as has the concept of police intrusions that have been the product of consent given by the target.

These "exceptions" will now be more carefully surveyed.

The "plain view" exception arises when an officer, subsequent to a justified prior intrusion and situated in a place in which he or she has a legal right to be, comes upon evidence that with probable cause is incriminatory. The officer may, under these circumstances, conduct a search without a warrant. The "plain view" exception also empowers an officer to seize the evidence come upon inadvertently.

A second exception is known as the "open fields" exception to the warrant requirement. In *Oliver v. United States* (466 U.S. 170 [1984]), the Supreme Court held that "[o]pen fields do not provide the setting for those intimate activities that the [Fourth] Amendment is intended to shelter from government interference. . . . There is no societal interest in protecting the privacy of those activities . . . that occur in open fields." Since there is no reasonable expectation of privacy in "open fields," that which an officer observes in such a place is seizable without a warrant since no search has occurred.

A third exception involves "exigent circumstances." If an officer is in "hot pursuit" of a suspect for whom the officer has probable cause to arrest, and the suspect runs from a public area into a private building to avoid arrest, the officer may follow the suspect and search for him or her without a warrant. The delay caused by requiring the officer to obtain a warrant under these circumstances may well allow the suspect to escape or destroy evidence.

Similarly, if during an arrest that takes place inside a house, the officers have a reasonable suspicion that others are in the house and associated with the criminal enterprise, they may make a protective sweep to locate the others. During the sweep, contraband observed in "plain view" may be seized (*Maryland v. Buie,* 494 U.S. 325 [1990]).

It is also an exigent circumstance if an officer is lawfully positioned outside an apartment and hears sounds that indicate that a life-threatening situation has developed therein. The officer may enter without a warrant, the exigent circumstance being the protection of life. Once inside, contraband that the officer observes in "plain view" may be seized lawfully. Once the "exigent circumstances" terminate, of course, the officer may no longer lawfully search or seize.

A fourth exception to the warrant requirement for a search or seizure involves motor vehicles. Although the law of search and seizure in this area was quite complex, recent Supreme Court cases have substantially simplified the "car search" exception.

Realizing that motor vehicles are, by their nature, easily movable and that, by venturing out on a public street in a vehicle, a person naturally holds a reduced expectation of privacy in his or her vehicle and its contents, the Supreme Court long ago held that if an officer has probable cause to believe that contraband or evidence of crime is in the vehicle, the officer may conduct an immediate warrantless search of the vehicle, including glove boxes and the trunk, where there is probable cause to believe such items might be stored (*Carroll v. United States,* 267 U.S. 132 [1925] and *Chambers v. Maroney,* 399 U.S. 42 [1970]). For example, if an officer believes a vehicle contains illegal aliens who have been smuggled across the border and are thus evidence of a crime, the officer may stop the vehicle and immediately search all areas of the car that may reasonably be used to secrete the evidence. A warrantless search for illegal aliens in the glove box of the car, however, would be considered unreasonable, and thus violative of the Fourth Amendment (*United States v. Ross,* 456 U.S. 798 [1982] and *California v. Acevedo,* 111 S.Ct. 1982 [1991]).

In addition to the *Ross*-type vehicle warrantless search, officers may legitimately search the entire passenger compartment of a vehicle, as well as containers therein, if they are in the process of conducting a lawful custodial arrest of a person in the vehicle. This official conduct is considered a "search incident to arrest," to be discussed, infra, and does not apply to non-custodial arrests, such as the cite and release arrest (*New York v. Belton,* 453 U.S. 454 [1981]).

Finally, in some situations, a vehicle may be legally "impounded" by officers and the vehicle's contents inventoried without a warrant. If a vehicle is determined to be abandoned or for some other legitimate reason, such as public safety, is properly placed in police custody, an officer may, without a warrant, conduct an inventory as long as it is carried out in accordance with standard acceptable police procedures and is not used as a pretext for avoiding obtaining a search warrant (*South Dakota v. Opperman,* 428 U.S. 364 [1976]). Such warrantless inventory "searches" are considered reasonable because they allow the police to protect the citizen's property from theft, and, in addition, deter citizens from alleging that the officers converted the property to their own use. Inventories have also been supported as reasonable for public safety reasons if, for instance, a vehicle might contain a weapon that could fall into the wrong hands if not inventoried (*Cady v. Dombrowski,* 413 U.S. [1973]).

A fifth and major exception to the warrant requirement for a search is the "search incident to arrest." Before we analyze this exception, a brief explanation of the law of arrest and/or detention is appropriate.

An arrest or detention is a seizure for Fourth Amendment purposes and thus must be supported by a warrant. If an arrest or detention is *not* supported by a warrant, the arresting or detaining officer must, at the time of the warrantless arrest or detention, have either probable cause to arrest or reasonable suspicion to detain the suspect in order for the officer's conduct to be considered reasonable under the Fourth Amendment. Since the law of arrest is quite different from that of detention, a comparison of the two areas of the law follows.

As stated, an officer may arrest a person if he or she has probable cause to believe that person has committed a crime. Probable cause requires a showing that the officer has facts within his or her own personal knowledge that are sufficient to convince a reasonably cautious person that an offense has been, is being, or is about to be committed by the suspect.

An officer who has probable cause to arrest a suspect, with or without a warrant, also has the right to conduct a full search of the suspect and to open any containers (e.g., a wallet) found thereon (*United States v. Robinson,* 414 U.S. 218 [1973]). Such an arrest "is a reasonable intrusion under the Fourth Amendment, that intrusion being lawful, a search incident to the arrest requires no additional justification."

In *Chimel v. California* (395 U.S. 752 [1969]), the Supreme Court held that the purpose of such a search is "to remove any weapons that the [suspect] might seek to use in order to resist arrest or effect his escape" and "to search for and seize any evidence on the [suspect's] person in order to prevent his concealment or destruction."

Chimel held that if a suspect is placed under custodial arrest, not only can the police conduct a full contemporaneous search of his or her person, they can also search the area within the suspect's immediate control. Thus the area within the suspect's arm's length or "lunging" radius may be searched as well as any containers in that area. The concern is that the arrestee might gain control of weapons or destroy evidence if these items remain accessible at the time of arrest. The language of *Chimel* however contains limitations:

> There is not comparable justification, however, for routinely searching any room other than that in which an arrest occurs—or, for that matter, for searching through all the desk drawers or other closed or concealed areas in that room itself. Such searches, in the absence of well-recognized exceptions may be made only under the authority of a search warrant.

With respect to the less intrusive seizure known as a "detention" or "stop and frisk," officers need not possess probable cause. *Terry v. Ohio* (392 U.S. 1 [1968]) detailed the situation in which a stop and frisk is permissible and the quantum of proof, reasonable suspicion, needed to justify such a seizure:

> [W]here a police officer observes unusual conduct which leads him reasonably to conclude in light of his experience that criminal activity may be afoot and that the persons with whom he is dealing may be armed and dangerous, where in the course of investigating this behavior he identifies himself as a policeman and makes reasonable inquiries, and nothing in the initial stages of the encounter serves to dispel his reasonable fear for his own or others' safety, he is entitled for the protection of himself and others in the area to conduct a carefully limited search of the outer clothing of such persons in an attempt to discover weapons which might be used to assault him.

> Such a search is a reasonable search under the Fourth Amendment and any weapons seized may properly be introduced in evidence against the person from where they were taken.

The standard of proof necessary to justify such a stop and frisk has come to be known as "reasonable suspicion"; that is, the officer must have a "particularized and objective basis for suspecting the particular person stopped of criminal activity" (*United States v. Cortez*, 449

U.S. 411 [1981]). In *Adams v. Williams* (407 U.S. 143 [1972]), the Supreme Court extended the *Terry* rule to a situation where a reliable informant gives police information of suspected criminal activity nearby (see also *Alabama v. White,* 110 S.Ct. 2412 [1990]).

Traditionally, the *Terry* "stop and frisk" has been used to prevent a crime from occurring. However, *United States v. Hensley* (469 U.S. 221 [1985]) would authorize police, during an investigation of a crime, to stop and frisk "a person suspected of involvement" in that crime. This type of detention is permissible only when police are investigating "felonies or crimes involving a threat to public safety."

If a *Terry* stop becomes overly intrusive or extends beyond the time period within which probable cause for arrest should reasonably have developed, the detention will become an illegal arrest and any evidence obtained thereby will be excluded at trial. "[T]he investigative methods should be the *least* intrusive means reasonably available" (*Florida v. Royer,* 460 U.S. 491 [1983]), and *United States v. Sharpe,* 470 U.S. 675 [1985]). The purpose for the frisk is *solely* to discover weapons or hidden instruments that might be used to assault the police officer. If, during the frisk, the officer feels what appears to be a weapon, he or she may seize it. The finding of a weapon, then, usually constitutes probable cause to arrest the suspect, which, in turn, authorizes the officer to conduct a more extensive search incident to arrest. But if the officer feels an object that could not possibly be a weapon, but that may, for example, be narcotics, the officer has no right to seize the object without a warrant.

Finally, courts distinguish between a *Terry* stop and the situation where a police officer approaches a person or stops a person and asks a question or two. The latter is considered a mere unprotected encounter and is not considered a seizure under the Fourth Amendment.

In conclusion, a search incident to arrest can be quite extensive in that the officer may properly seize evidence, including weapons, narcotics, etc., not only from the person of the arrestee but also from within the area in the arrestee's immediate control. If a *Terry* detention is involved, the officer is restricted to a frisk of the outer clothing of the suspect for weapons. The law of search and seizure is a complex subject that changes on an almost daily basis.

Harry M. Caldwell
Paul G. Flynn

Bibliography

Hall, John W. *Search and Seizure*. Annual Supplements. Rochester, NY: Lawyers Co-Op, 1982.

Hirschel, Joseph D. *Fourth Amendment Rights*. Lexington, MA: Lexington, 1979.

"'Knock, Knock: Who's There?' Does Police Entry of Premises by Ruse Violate the Individual's Fourth Amendment Rights in Light of *Katz v. United States?*" *Criminal Justice Journal* 12 (Spring 1990): 167–84.

Misner, Robert L. "Justifying Searches on the Basis of Equality of Treatment." *Journal of Criminal Law and Criminology* 82 (Fall 1991): 547–78.

Ringel, William E. *Searches and Seizures, Arrests and Confessions*. 2 vols. New York: Clark Boardman, 1980.

Slobogin, Christopher, and Joseph E. Schumacher. "Rating the Intrusiveness of Law Enforcement Searches and Seizures." *Law and Human Behavior* 17 (August 1991): 881–943.

Williams, Gregory H. "The Supreme Court and Broken Promises: The Gradual But Continual Erosion of *Terry v. Ohio*." *Howard Law Journal* 34 (1991): 567–88.

Wilson, Bradford P. *Enforcing the Fourth Amendment: A Jurisprudential History*. New York: Garland, 1986.

Serial Murder

Working Definition

Only a few attempts have been made to define serial murder. Frequent references to serial murder are made using the term *mass* to depict a number of victims. This misuse of the term *mass* has resulted in general confusion as to what is meant by serial murder. The following working definition by Egger (1984) provides the most extensive definition available:

> Serial murder occurs when one or more individuals (males in most known cases) commit a second murder and/or subsequent murder; is relationshipless (victim and attacker are strangers); is at a different time and has no apparent connection to the initial (and subsequent) murder; and is usually committed in a different geographical location. Further, the mo-tive is not for material gain and is believed to be for the murderer's desire to have power over his victims. The series of murders which result may not appear to share common elements. Victims are perceived to be prestigeless and in most instances, are unable to defend themselves, and are powerless given their situation in time, place, or status, within their immediate surrounding (such as vagrants, prostitutes, migrant workers, homosexuals, missing children, and single and often elderly women).

Some better known examples of serial murderers are Ted Bundy, John Wayne Gacy, Henry Lee Lucas, and Ken Bianchi and Angelo Buono, the Hillside Stranglers.

Extent and Prevalence

There have been numerous estimates regarding the incidence of serial murder and the number of serial murderers at large. However, these estimates are based upon extrapolations from total reported homicides in a given year or from identified serial murderers. Most of the serial murders are believed to be encompassed within the total number of reported stranger-to-stranger homicides for which the relationship of victim to offender is unknown or that of a stranger, as presented in the *Uniform Crime Reports*. Estimates of the number of serial murder victims are based only upon the confessions of serial murderers or when a pattern of serial murders is identified.

Whether the phenomenon is on the increase in this country has not been empirically determined. Many references are made by the mass media to such an increase but research is limited by the fact that the serial murder, per se, is not reported in official crime or mortality statistics. Media reports are currently the only source from which to determine increase as well as the actual incidence of the phenomenon. Such information lacks reliability and validity. Historical research by Eric Hickey and others reveals numerous reports of serial murder and refutes the notion that serial murder is a contemporary phenomenon. Cross-national comparisons, although limited, indicate that serial murder is not strictly an American phenomenon either.

People Who Kill Serially

Research on serial murder, although limited,

shows it to be a stranger-to-stranger crime. Practically all of the psychological research attempting to explain the causes of the serial murderer's acts is conducted from a case-study-specific approach. There has been little or no effort to combine this research into an aggregate description so that etiological theories can be derived, or to facilitate general observations on the serial murderer. Terms most frequently used to describe the serial murderer are *psychopath* or *sociopath*; however, the meaning of these terms is subject to a great deal of disagreement among psychologists and psychiatrists and the terms are no longer used in the *Diagnostic and Statistical Manual for Mental Disorders*. General etiological theories of inadequate socialization are the most frequently cited explanations of the serial murderer's behavior (i.e., child abuse and neglect, broken home, alcoholism, etc.).

Developing Taxonomies
Legal classifications of homicide are not useful in describing or categorizing serial murder or the serial murderer. The range of geographical and chronological patterns identified provide only a few typologies or categories that are limited in nature and scope. Many serial murderers are very mobile and roam across state lines while others act within a relatively small geographic area. Motive typologies such as "lust," "sex," or "sadistic" are not unique to serial murder. The "organized nonsocial" and the "disorganized social" dichotomy developed by Robert R. Hazelwood and John E. Douglas is currently being used by the FBI in their psychological profiling program.

The Victims
There is an even greater paucity of research on the serial murder victim. In almost all cases the victims have been strangers to the serial murderer. Victim selection would appear to be random in nature. Limited research indicates victim selection may be based upon the murderer's perception of the victim as vulnerable or as a symbolic representation.

Current Investigative Strategies
There are currently six general responses by law enforcement to the serial murderer: conferences, information clearinghouses, task forces, investigative consultant teams, psychological profiling, and the centralized investigative networks. Conferences, information clearinghouses, and task forces require coordination and cooperation among law enforcement officers on an intraagency or interagency basis within a relatively limited geographical area. Conferences have, at times, been provided on a national as well as a regional basis. The investigative consultant team is a somewhat unique response found only in response to the Atlanta Child Murders. Psychological profiling is a recent development to assist criminal investigators. The most active research and development of this investigative tool has been conducted by the FBI's Behavioral Science Unit. A centralized investigative network is the most recent response to serial murder. On a national level, the Violent Criminal Apprehension Program (VICAP), a component of the FBI's National Center for the Analysis of Violent Crime, is collecting information on unsolved homicides, missing persons under suspicious circumstances, and unidentified dead bodies in order to search for patterns and alert the appropriate police agencies regarding these patterns. On a state level, New York State is currently developing the Homicide Assessment and Lead Tracking System, which will be compatible with VICAP and operate in a similar fashion on a state level. In each instance, state-of-the-art computer software is being developed for use by crime analysts.

The Problem of Serial Murder: Linkage Blindness
With the exception of psychological profiling, a specific investigative tool, the above law-enforcement responses to serial murder have all been attempts to increase common linkages or networks among law-enforcement agencies or officers regarding unsolved homicides or in instances where a serial murderer has been apprehended. For the latter, the focus is not on pattern similarity but on the identification, documentation, and verification of the serial murderer's trail of victims across numerous jurisdictions. By definition, all the responses involve stranger-to-stranger homicides, which greatly increases the investigator's need for information not readily available. Thus, the lack of any prior relationship between the serial murderer and his victim and the high rate at which multiple jurisdictions are involved in a serial murder mean that the central problem of serial murder investigation in this country is the lack of information.

Information is necessary to establish that a single homicide event is part of a series of events. Second, information is necessary to establish modus operandi patterns. Information is also necessary to evaluate the physical evidence from identified series. To obtain access to this kind of information, an investigator or agency must expand and develop new sources of information beyond jurisdictional boundaries. The obvious sources of this information are law-enforcement counterparts in other jurisdictions that encompass the series of common homicide events.

The lack of law-enforcement efforts to expand sources of information to other jurisdictions has been characteristic of most of the incidents of serial murder in this country. The nation's law-enforcement community very infrequently makes the necessary effort to seek sources of information outside their respective jurisdictional boundaries because of blindness, forced or intentional, to the information linkages necessary to respond effectively to the serial murderer. This does not mean that law-enforcement agencies intentionally keep valuable information on unsolved homicides from other agencies. However, this "linkage blindness" means that the police in this country do not seek such information beyond the structural purview of their work environments.

Simply stated, there is a lack of sharing or coordination of investigative information relating to unsolved murders and a lack of networking among law-enforcement agencies in the United States. The greatest cause of this linkage blindness is the fact that American policing is very decentralized and fragmented. Other critics would attribute such blindness to a jealousy and competitiveness among law-enforcement officers and agencies. The point is that no structure or formal network currently exists to allow officers in different agencies and in different states to share information on criminal investigations.

The Future: Expanded Research and Correcting Police "Vision"

There has been precious little money, talent, or time devoted to research of the serial murder phenomenon. Research and systematic study of this phenomenon in addition to increased communication, coordination, and cooperation to reduce linkage blindness and increase police "vision" must occur in order to better understand serial murder and develop more effective tactics and strategies for reducing its prevalence and increasing the identification and apprehension of serial murderers.

Steven A. Egger

Bibliography

Abrahamsen, D. *The Murdering Mind.* New York: Harper & Row, 1973.

Egger, Steven A. "A Working Definition of Serial Murder and the Reduction of Linkage Blindness." *Journal of Police Science and Administration* 12(3) (1984): 348–57.

———. "Serial Murder and the Law Enforcement Response." Ph.D. diss. Huntsville, TX: College of Criminal Justice, Sam Houston State University, 1985.

———. "Law Enforcement's Response to Serial Murder: A Communication Problem." *New York Law Enforcement Journal* 1(2) (June 1986):27–33.

———. "A Challenge to Academia: Preliminary Research Agenda for Serial Murder." *Journal of Ideology* 10(1) (1986).

Fox, J.A., and Levin, J. *Mass Murder: America's Growing Menace.* New York: Plenum, 1985.

Guttmacher, M. *The Mind of the Murderer.* New York: Grove Press, 1960.

Lunde, D.T. *Murder and Madness.* Stanford, CA: Stanford Alumni Press, 1976.

Office of Juvenile Justice and Delinquency Prevention. *National Missing/Abducted Children and Serial Murder Tracking and Prevention Program.* Washington, DC: U.S. Department of Justice, 1983.

Sheriff

The *Corpus Juris Secundum* states: "The sheriff ordinarily is an elective public officer and chief executive officer in his county, is an officer of the court and subject to its orders and directions, and is made responsible by common and statutory law as conservator of peace within his jurisdiction." Presently, thirty-five state constitutions mandate the office. Deputy sheriffs, constables, and even coroners often perform duties assigned to the sheriff. The deputy sheriff can act as the sheriff's alter ego, though cannot do so in name, person, or right. The sheriff appoints two types of deputies: a general deputy or undersheriff and a special deputy. The deputies carry out what the sheriff assigns them and are hired and fired by the sheriff. Constables resemble sheriffs in their duties though their powers are less and their jurisdictions smaller (see "Constable").

History

The office of sheriff derives from Anglo-Saxon England around the ninth century. Reeves who were caretakers for the king over his dominion gave rise to the office. The king's reeves, then as sheriffs, exercised judicial, financial, and administrative power that over time became imperious. Some sheriffs abused the community at large with impunity, such was their disregard for any authority other than themselves. Thus the legal principle of the sheriff as servant of the crown, and not as independent ruler, had to be reestablished. Familiar to all, the tales of Robin Hood who continually clashed with the Sheriff of Nottingham were not pure fiction. Whether Robin Hood actually existed or not, his ruthless adversary did to embody despotic governance. The medieval sheriffs fought so fiercely to dominate that it took several centuries for the monarchy to regain its authority. Once the monarchy consolidated its power the office of sheriff resumed its supportive responsibilities: conserving the peace, suppressing disorder by forming "posse comitatus," receiving writs, summoning juries, and executing judgments. In the sixteenth century the office of lord lieutenant replaced the office of sheriff, which was not done away with completely. In England today the sheriff presides over elections and courts as a chiefly ceremonial officer.

American government adopted the sheriff model early on. In 1705, Pennsylvania, and shortly thereafter other states, made the office of sheriff elective. Where larger units of local government prevailed, not centered in towns but in rural areas, the sheriff soon became the leader of the county. Later sweeping across the country to the west the office supplanted the *alguacil* of Spanish and Mexican rule. United States sheriffs were given much the same responsibilities as the medieval English sheriffs: to maintain the peace, to serve as the executive officer of the county and district courts, to serve writs and processes of the court, and to supervise the jail and its prisoners. In small counties the office also acted as tax assessor and collector—the part of the job the sheriff of Nottingham relished. The first sheriffs whether elected or appointed were bound to serve. Statutes providing for a penalty in the event of nonservice are a matter of legal history. A candidate was eligible for the office by being a qualified voter, a resident of the county, and a property owner. A candidate was ineligible if he had misused public money, was an attorney at law, had been convicted of crime, or already served in a federal office. By statute the sheriff periodically had to prove that his dealings with public money were above board. Evidently, medieval England had taught American government a cautionary lesson. Moreover, to strengthen government's hold over the office the sheriff-elect in most jurisdictions had to put up a bond. The collateral security required was to ensure "the faithful performance of the duties of the office" and "to protect and give indemnity to all persons who may be damnified by neglect or failure in the performance of such duties." The amount of the bond was fixed by statute. The office of sheriff has remained practically unchanged in the intervening years.

Current Controversy

There are increasing fears that the office of sheriff is under attack. As states consolidate their law enforcement units into departments of public safety the sheriff loses ground. The national publication *Sheriff*, in the March–April 1993 issue, devoted its entire contents to the debate, or in its view—the coming debacle. The National Sheriffs' Association (NSA) President, Frank Policaro, Jr., speaks to the point:

> You would think that with skyrocketing crime statistics, sheriffs' offices and their personnel would be welcome in the law enforcement arena to augment other police agencies. After all, there is enough crime to go around for everyone. However, the Fraternal Order of Police has a different opinion. They are threatened by the sheriffs, afraid that we are going to erode their power.

NSA Executive Director Bud Meeks is likewise on the defensive:

> The office of sheriff in some states is being called an antiquated position and some say it should be eliminated. Over the past few years, we have heard arguments that the sheriff is too powerful; the position is too subject to political pressures; or the office of sheriff should not be an elected position, but appointed. We regard the individuals who

make such comments as enemies to the office of sheriff.

Proof of tangible discontent has surfaced in the State of Hawaii, where the legislature abolished the office of sheriff, to be replaced by the Department of Public Safety; and in Pennsylvania, where the Fraternal Order of Police fails to recognize the office and fights against its continuance in the state supreme court.

When actions taken are not so spiteful and drastic as in Hawaii and Pennsylvania, part of the controversy stems from nomenclature. Sheriffs insist on retaining their independence through the governmental entity of the "office." A sheriff's "department" is unacceptable. An office confers a public charge, a public trust, and the most important grant, "an authority to exercise some portion of the sovereign power, either in making, executing, or administering laws" (*Black's Law Dictionary*). A department is merely an offshoot of an executive branch that is delegated to, subordinate, and essentially powerless given that a state or county administrator makes the decisions.

In Massachusetts not only is the office of sheriff at risk of being abolished but also county government in toto. Plans have been advanced to transfer county functions and employees to state jurisdiction. What that could mean for Massachusetts sheriffs—from painful to severe—is threefold: (1) a change from elective to appointive status to increase accountability; (2) a reduction of duties to process serving and prisoner transportation; and (3) a straight out abolition of the office and integration into the state's prison system. Since Massachusetts sheriffs are constitutional officers it would take a constitutional convention and a voter-approved amendment to realize option three. The Massachusetts debate is not unique. Other states are examining the same three options. Option one is repugnant to sheriffs because appointment spawns favoritism and allows policy-makers to choose someone outside the county who is a stranger. Option two is no less obvious in its attempt to diminish the sheriff's power and influence. As serious as recent attacks have been on the office of sheriff, it seems unlikely at this time that American sheriffs will go the way of their English antecedents. High crime rates in America, not confined to metropolitan areas but extending far and wide into rural communities, should safeguard the office indefinitely.

Bibliography

Brown, D.L. *Model Plan for Police Agencies Facing Major Community Development by the Year 2000*. Sacramento: California Commission on Peace Officer Standards and Training, 1991.

Lee, Captain W.L. Melville. *A History of Police in England*. Montclair, NJ: Patterson Smith, [1901], 1971.

Los Angeles County Sheriff's Department Year in Review. Los Angeles: Los Angeles County Sheriff's Department, 1992. (Note: This annual publication is book-length; the 1991 *Review* contains 326 pages, making it much more informative than standard police department annual reports.)

Reaves, Brian A. *Sheriffs' Departments 1990: A Lemas Report*. Washington, DC: U.S. Department of Justice, Bureau of Justice Statistics, 1992.

"Sheriffs' Offices Under Attack." *Sheriff* 45 (March–April 1993): 1–32.

Strandberg, K.W. "Sheriffs on Management." *Law Enforcement Technology* 18 (1991): entire issue.

Bruce Smith

Bruce Smith (1892–1955), police consultant and criminologist, was born in Brooklyn, New York, the son of a banker and real estate operator. He was regarded as something of a rebel, even from his first collegiate experience at Wesleyan University. While there he delighted in rolling cannonballs down the main street and in firing a shotgun from his dormitory window. He was expelled in his senior year for publicly ridiculing the college chaplain because he had conducted a prayer that went on for more than seven minutes—Smith had clocked him with a stopwatch. Moving on to Columbia University, presumably a more serious student, he earned his B.S. degree in 1914. One of his professors, Charles A. Beard, also director of the New York Bureau of Municipal Research, acted as his mentor and convinced him to remain at Columbia for graduate study. In 1916 Smith was granted both the LL.B. degree and the M.S. in political science. After graduation he worked with Beard at the Bureau of Municipal Research, later renamed the Institute of Public Administration. That same year he was assigned to study the police department in Harrisburg, Pennsylvania. Unfamiliar with police operations, he wondered why he had been chosen. About the Harrisburg experience he reflected, "That's how I got into police work. I was dragged in squealing and protesting. I knew nothing about cops. Boy, how I hated to leave those actuarial tables."

Soon World War I intervened and as a second lieutenant Smith served in the United States Air Force from 1917 to 1919. The war over, he returned to the Institute of Public Administration and quickly rose to the position of manager, which he held from 1921 to 1928. During those hectic years he acquired invaluable knowledge collaborating with the Missouri Association for Criminal Justice, the National Crime Commission, and the Illinois Association for Criminal Justice. From 1941 to 1946 and from 1950 to 1952 he was acting director of the institute; in 1954 he became director until his death, thus fulfilling the promise Charles Beard had seen in him.

Throughout the second half of his life, Smith was associated with so many commissions on the administration of justice and on law revision that it would take a catalog to enumerate them, and a book to cite his many contributions. But the keystone of his career was his monumental work in surveying police departments in about fifty leading American cities and in eighteen states, in creating the *Uniform Crime Reports* (1930)—devised after an exhaustive study of Western European practices and adopted by the Federal bureau of Investigation—and in writing several police treatises, most notably *Police Systems in the United States*.

Smith, who never wore a police uniform, nonetheless earned the respect of the cop on the beat. In such statements as this about protracted entrance exams, he championed the recruit: "I don't care if a rookie thinks the duke of Wellington is a man, a horse, or a smoking tobacco. . . . What counts is a man's character." His sympathy for the job of policing ran deep: "Rarely does a major piece of police work receive the accolade of general approval. . . . The environment in which police must do their work is therefore certain to be unfavorable." And he saw clearly the obstacles to improvement, "No police force . . . is ever quite free of the taint of corruption; none succeeds in wholly repressing or preventing criminal acts, or in effecting arrests and convictions in any large portion of the total offenses reported; many are deeply involved in political manipulations of

various kinds." So he fought for better methods of selection and training of personnel, a different system of promotion, increased discipline, and severance from political control and the Civil Service Commission, to name a few of his reforms. Furthermore, he encouraged police departments to give civilians the desk jobs, thereby returning police to the streets. Interestingly, as a consultant to the U.S. Army Air Force during World War II, he advocated the same tactic; because of him 350 colonels were reassigned from offices to field duty.

But Smith did not always meet with success. Even though he was mostly welcomed by police departments, revered by the officers, and acknowledged as an authority, he became a Sisyphus-like figure. In 1923 he made sweeping recommendations for reform of the New Orleans Police Department; in 1946 upon his return he found almost the same disgraceful situation in the department as had appeared earlier—a disheartening déjà vu. In another instance, fourteen years after analyzing the St. Louis Police Department, when asked for further guidance, he suggested reform measures nearly identical to the ones he had offered before since little had changed. Often, in the case of Smith, it seemed that his sound advice went too much against the grain for the entrenched police departments to carry out.

Smith contributed regularly to professional journals, both American and British. He wrote the standard articles on police for the *Encyclopedia Britannica*, *Encyclopedia Americana*, *Collier's Encyclopedia*, and the *Encyclopedia of Social Sciences*. In tribute, O.W. Wilson wrote: "Smith combined the best qualities of policeman, executive, statesman, and scholar." He was married in 1915 to Mary Rowell; they had two children. Late in life Smith purchased a yacht—the *Lucifer*—and indulged his passion for sailing. While aboard the *Lucifer* he was stricken by a lung ailment, later dying in Southampton Hospital in New York of a heart attack. At the time of his death he was writing a book about British police, whose organization he wanted to elucidate for American police. He died a young sixty-three.

Bibliography

Current Biography, 1953. New York: H.W. Wilson, 1954. 577–79.

Smith, Bruce. *Police Systems in the United States*. 2d. ed. New York: Harper and Brothers, 1949.

Watts, Eugene J. "Bruce Smith." *Dictionary of American Biography* 14(5) (1977): 638–39. New York: Charles Scribner's Sons.

Wilson, O.W. "Bruce Smith." *Journal of Criminal Law, Criminology and Police Science* 47(2) (July–August 1956): 235–37.

Social Support

The "stress cycle," at least as a general concept, is familiar to the average layperson. Certain life events or experiences disrupt life patterns, cause an imbalance in an individual's ability to cope, and ultimately affect the individual's physical and psychological well-being. For law-enforcement officers those consequences are believed to include high rates of heart disease and stomach disorders, rates of divorce twice as high as those in most other occupations, and suicide rates that are two to six times the national average (Axelber and Valle, 1979; Blackmore, 1978).

Fortunately, research indicates the untoward effects of stress are not inevitable. People who are subjected to the same stressors experience different outcomes—some people appear to suffer few if any effects, while others suffer debilitating effects. In other words, there is reason to believe that other factors intervene and moderate the ultimate effects of stress. Not surprisingly, there has been considerable interest and activity among researchers who study stress, particularly among high-stress occupations such as law enforcement, in identifying and understanding factors that can moderate the effects of stress. In this section we will discuss one of the most widely studied possible moderators—social support.

Conceptualizing the Stress Cycle: Definitions, Models, and Processes

In order to understand how social support might moderate the effects of stress, one needs to go beyond the general outline of stress offered above. It is important to understand the processes that occur between being presented with a stressor and experiencing strain, the negative physical and/or psychological effects. McGrath (1970) and Cohen and Wills (1985) have presented models that provide such a framework.

McGrath (1970) developed a stress cycle model within which the relationship of stress,

strain, and social support can be examined (Figure 1). The model begins with a situation or set of circumstances (A). If the situation is perceived by the individual as possibly leading to some undesirable conclusion, it becomes a "stressful situation" (B). The individual then chooses some response (C). The response is executed with the intention of changing his or her relation to the "stressful" situation (D).

FIGURE 1

McGrath's Paradigm for Analysis of the Stress Cycle

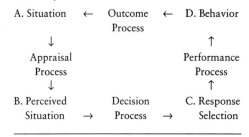

These four stages are connected by four linking processes: appraisal, decision, performance, and outcome. These processes are dynamic, allowing for the possibility of other factors like social support to affect the final consequences of the individual's behavior.

Within the model, stress is defined as the state of imbalance between perceived threat and coping capacity of the individual. Stressors are defined as the stimuli that have been perceived as stressful. The responses to the variety of specific behavioral adjustments or changes in the individual's physical or psychological well-being related to stress is defined under the concept, strain.

For example, law-enforcement officers are expected to fulfill a number of roles: law enforcer, service provider, peace-keeper, etc. In some situations, these roles may be in conflict (stressor). An officer responding to a domestic violence complaint might arrest the assaultive spouse. The victim (and usually the children) may become upset and perhaps threatening when the assailant is arrested. The officer may perceive the conflict inherent in this situation as stressful. The cumulative effect of having to handle these kinds of situations may result in physical distress (e.g., ulcers), lowered job satisfaction, and eventually burnout (strain).

Social Support and the Stress Cycle

Operational definitions of social support vary in the degree of specificity. Cobb (1976) defines social support as information from others, which leads the person to believe that he/she is cared for, loved, and esteemed and is a member of a network of mutual obligations. House (1981) adds that social support must involve supportive relationships characterized by the willingness to give emotional, informational, instrumental, or appraisal aid in times of need. Cohen and Wills (1985), in a review of the social support literature, conclude that specific types of social support are needed by specific types of stressful situations (e.g. fellow law-enforcement officers' emotional support in helping another officer deal with a child abuse case or the use of deadly force). Measures that assess only general availability of social support resources may not provide evidence that social support has an effect on well-being.

Cohen and Wills's model (Figure 2) explicitly proposes social support to be a viable factor in aiding stress resistance and decreasing strain. First, the perception that support sources can provide necessary resources may redefine the potential for harm posed by the situation and/or reinforce the individual's perceived ability to cope with the situation. This provision may prevent a particular situation from being appraised as stressful. The officers who responded to the domestic complaint described earlier may receive informational support from other officers that decreases the responding officers' discomfort when interacting with domestic violence victims, or provides insights into how to handle the situation more effectively. This support may prevent future domestic complaints from being appraised as stressful. Second, as outlined by Cohen and Wills's model, adequate support might actually intervene between the appraisal of the situation as stressful and the onset of the pathological outcome by providing a solution to the problem, by reducing the perceived importance of the problem, or by facilitating healthful behaviors.

Main Effect or Buffering Effect?

The exact process through which social support affects well-being and/or psychological outcomes remains a subject of considerable debate, but two mechanisms have been hypothesized and have been widely examined. One mechanism, a main effect, proposes that social support has a generalized beneficial effect regardless

FIGURE 2

Social Support's Role in Coping with Stressful Situations

support may prevent stress appraisal	support may result in reappraisal, inhibition, maladjustive responses, or facilitation of adjustive responses
↓	↓
situation or demand → event appraised	physiological → illness or response or illness stressful behavioral behavior adaptation

of whether a person is under stress. In other words, social support enhances well-being in general. The alternative mechanism, buffering, proposes that social support doesn't provide a generalized beneficial effect but rather only serves as a "buffer" under high stress situations.

Acquisition of Social Support in Law Enforcement

Although most officers perceive the need for work social support, they do not always believe it is available. In Graff's study (1986) 43 percent of the officers who responded indicated that they did not have a support person at work. A number of individual and organizational factors may affect the amount of social support one perceives to be available and/or actually receives.

Individual Characteristics

For instance, there's reason to believe that one's personality may have an influence. Individuals with high negative affectivity (NA) scores are individuals who are more likely to experience significant levels of distress and dissatisfaction at all times even in the absence of any specific stressful event. They tend to see the negative side of others and the world and are less satisfied with themselves and their lives. Both Sarason et al. (1985) and Hobfoll and Stokes (1988) noted individuals high in NA tend to be unattractive to others and may be unsuccessful at creating or sustaining stable relationships necessary to foster social support.

There's also speculation, some of it within law-enforcement research, that demographic characteristics like gender and race may affect the availability of social support. Charles

(1981) concluded that new officers were evaluated by their male and female peers not only on performance but also on their ability to "fit into" the social setting. The nonacceptance of females into the social culture of the work group creates obstacles that might further hinder their performance and further substantiate their peers' negative perceptions of their performance. These differences between male and female acceptance into law enforcement suggest that gender may be a factor in the ability to develop work-related support in law enforcement. Bennett (1984) found a negative association between minority status and general behaviors that new officers value to attain personal or social goals. Bennett concluded that this negative association indicated that the minority members did not accept the expected modes of conduct by the new officer in a predominantly white working environment. Similar to Charles's conclusion that female officers were evaluated on their ability to "fit into" the social setting was Bennett's speculation that the negative association with the identified behavior might affect the acquisition of social support by minorities.

Organizational Characteristics
There's also reason to believe that amount and sources of social support available to an officer may change during different stages of their training and career.

During the first six to eight months of their probationary period, recruits appear to continue to report social support from family members and nonlaw-enforcement friends, as well as increasing levels of social support from other law-enforcement officers (Fuehrer, 1982). The perceived social support from law-enforcement supervisors actually may decrease during the formal training period and then increase when the recruit begins field training (Lord, 1992). There is reason to believe similar changes occur during later stages of an officer's career. Although only exploratory, this research also provides evidence that law-enforcement training sites differed substantially in the amount of social support perceived to be available by new officers. There are a number of reasons for possible differences among departments, including instructor–student ratios, instructors' efforts to facilitate group cohesiveness but also to encourage competition among the recruits, and the degree to which the new officers were accepted by veteran officers.

Stress, Social Support, and the Law-Enforcement Officer: A Research Perspective
Does social support moderate the effects of stress? If so, does social support provide a generalized beneficial effect (main effect) or does it act as a buffer against the effect of stress? Unfortunately, the literature on social support and stress is quite complex and at times contradictory, and there is not an easy, unequivocal answer to these questions.

With respect to the main effect versus buffering effect debate, there is support for both positions. The limited law-enforcement research supports only main effect (Fuehrer, 1982; and Lord, 1992). On the other hand, Cohen and Wills (1985) concluded that studies on occupational stress provide evidence for both the main effect and buffering effect of social support. Some attribute these discrepancies to lingering disagreements on how to best define and measure stress, social support, and strain and to the actual complexity of their relationships.

More seriously, a growing number of researchers question the validity of findings showing a stress–social support relationship. They base their reservations on a variety of concerns including the use of unvalidated subjective measures; the confounding of stress and social support measures (e.g., some events like the death of a loved one or divorce are simultaneously considered a stressor and a social support loss); the failure to control for third variables like personality traits (e.g. negative affectivity), which might explain observed effects; and the use of inferentially weak cross-sectional designs.

In spite of some supportive findings, the research literature leaves us with more questions than answers. Thus there is clearly a need for additional research on the role social support plays in moderating the stress–social support relationship.

Conclusion
In spite of these methodologically based reservations and concerns, social support is considered by many as the most promising moderator of the effects of stress. In fact some law-enforcement systems have begun to take action to enhance the availability of social support.

In Lipson's report to the California Commission on Peace Officer Standards and Training (1987), an eight-person panel recommended support groups to help retain patrol officers. According to the report, by the tenth year of employment a large number of police officers make the decision that patrol work is not appropriate for them and they decide to leave police work. This is precipitated by the officers' own feelings of dissatisfaction, failure at home, and a search for other opportunities. To retain the motivated officer, Lipson's report recommends the development of social support groups that would be available to the officer throughout his or her career.

While this seems like a promising development, law-enforcement administrators should not lose sight of the fact that a number of factors affect the availability of social support during an officer's career and that social support is usually provided in personal and private ways. Establishing formal social support groups is likely to be an important but inadequate step. Attention also needs to be paid to the possibility that various organizational factors (e.g., policies and practices) might promote or hinder the creation of natural support systems and that some recruits, most notably women and minorities, may not be spontaneously accepted into these systems.

Vivian B. Lord
Denis O. Gray

Bibliography

Axelber, M., and J. Valle. "South Florida's Approach to Police Stress Management." *Police Stress* 1 (1979): 13–14

Bennett, R.R. "Becoming Blue: A Longitudinal Study of Police Recruit Occupational Socialization." *Journal of Police Science and Administration* 12(1) (1984): 47–58.

Blackmore, J. "Are Police Allowed to Have Problems of Their Own?" *Police Magazine* 1 (1978): 47–55.

Burke, R.J. "Burnout in Police Work." *Group and Organizational Studies* 12(2) (1987): 174–88.

Charles, M.T. "The Performance and Socialization of Female Recruits in the Michigan State Police Training Academy." *Journal of Police Science and Administration* 9(2) (1981): 209–23.

Cobb, S. "Social Support as a Moderator of Life Stress." *Psychosomatic Medicine* 38 (1976): 300–14.

Cohen, S., and T.A. Wills. "Stress, Social Support, and the Buffering Hypothesis." *Psychological Bulletin* 98(2) (1985): 310–57.

Fell, R., W. Richard, and W. Wallace. "Psychological Job Stress and the Police Officer." *Journal of Police Science Administration* 8 (1980): 139–43.

Fuehrer, A.E. "Occupational Stress, Social Support and Job Satisfaction among Police Recruits." *Dissertation Information Service* (University Microfilms International no. 8304233), 1982.

Graff, F.A. "The Relationship between Social Support and Occupational Stress among Police Officers." *Journal of Police Science and Administration* 14(3) (1986): 178–86.

Hobfoll, S.E., and J.P. Stokes. "The Process and Mechanics of Social Support." In *Handbook of Personal Relationships*. Ed. S.W. Duck. New York: John Wiley and Sons, 1988. 497–517.

House, J.S. *Work Stress and Social Support.* Reading, MA: Addison-Wesley, 1981.

Kroes, W.H., J.J. Hurrell, Jr., and B.L. Margolis "Job Stress in Police Administrators." *Journal of Police Science and Administration* 2(4) (1974): 381–87.

Lipson, G. "What Will Be the Future Impact of Patrol Officer Retention Programs by the Year 2000?" Unpublished study for the California Commission on Peace Officer Standards and Training, 1987.

Lord, V. "Changes in the Social Support Sources of New Law Enforcement Officers." *Dissertation Information Service* (University Microfilms International no. 9220199), 1992.

McGrath, J. *Social and Psychological Factors in Stress.* New York: Holt, Rinehart, and Winston, 1970.

Maslach, C. and Jackson, S.E. "Measurement of Experienced Burnout." *Journal of Occupational Behavior* 2 (1981): 99–113.

Sarason, B.R., I.G. Sarason, T.A. Hacker, and R.B. Basham. "Concomitants of Social Support: Social Skills, Physical Attractiveness, and Gender." *Journal of Personality and Social Psychology* 49(2) (1985): 469–80.

Stevenson, T. "Stress among Police Officers: Burnout and its Correlates." *Dissertation Abstracts International* 49 (1988): 11–B.

Van Maanen, J. "Police Socialization: A Longitudinal Examination of Job Attitudes in an Urban Police Department." *Administrative Science Quarterly* 20 (1975): 202–28.

Van Maanen, J.V. and E.H. Schein. "Toward

a Theory of Organizational Socialization." *Research in Organizational Behavior* 1 (1979): 209–64.

Southern Police Institute

The original idea for the establishment of the Southern Police Institute did not germinate in the mind of a police administrator, a practicing lawyer, or a learned jurist. A Swedish economist developed the concept that such an institute would be both practical and beneficial. Gunnar Myrdal, in his 1944 book, *An American Dilemma,* planted a seed when he wrote:

> It is my conviction that one of the most potent strategic measures to improve the Southern interracial situation would be the opening of a pioneering modern police college in the South, which would give a thorough social and pedagogical training as well as a technical police training.

Dr. Joseph D. Lohman (formerly Chairman, Illinois Division of Corrections; Sheriff, Cook County, Illinois; and Dean, School of Criminology, University of California) first suggested organizing the Southern Police Institute (SPI) to David A. McCandless in 1949. Mr. McCandless, at the time Director of Public Safety with the City of Louisville, Kentucky, carried through on the idea. He held a series of discussions with university and city officials in Louisville until his proposals began to take root. A short time later a committee was appointed to develop plans for the institute. The committee recommended the annual presentation of three twelve-week courses for twenty-five student officers. The courses were designed primarily for an audience of commanding, supervising, and administrative police officers from southern and bordering states. Named dean, McCandless and a former police sergeant, Rolland L. Soule, opened the first SPI class in 1951.

Formative Years
The original training program consisted of twenty-one topics for a total of 420 hours of instruction. Fieldwork and simulated incidents supplemented the classroom lectures. One full-time instructor and approximately forty-five visiting lecturers made up the teaching staff during the first year and a half of the institute's

operation. A second full-time instructor doubled faculty strength for fall 1952. During 1955 the program underwent review. Four two-week seminars were added and the winter term for the administrative officers' course was discontinued. Acknowledging the influence of Gunnar Myrdal, the institute pioneered in presenting conferences that examined police responsibility for maintaining racial harmony, among other related interests. Within the first ten years of offering the short-term courses, officers attended from 167 municipalities, 38 states, and 22 foreign countries.

At the suggestion of the Southern Police Institute faculty, a group of police administrators met with University of Louisville administrators and faculty during 1961 to review the SPI program of instruction. As a result of their assessment, a significant change in curriculum appeared in 1962. Emphasis in the curriculum shifted to more instruction in police administration, personnel management, and business procedures, without reducing the time allotted for instruction in the social and behavioral sciences or in criminal or constitutional law. The number of hours of classroom instruction was reduced from 420 to 300, but more individual study and library work were required. The modified (hours) and expanded (learning load) twelve-week course earned the approval of the university's Curriculum Committee of the College of Arts and Sciences. Thereafter student police received twelve semester hours of university credit through SPI. Thus the Southern Police Institute became the first school in the United States to offer college credit for in-service police education.

As the number of faculty continued to increase, guest lecturers became fewer, though they still contributed significantly to the program. Class size grew to sixty officers during 1967, and a series of workshops added a new dimension. The School of Police Administration, a degree-granting unit of the University of Louisville, was established in 1969, and with that move SPI became a division of the newly formed school and an integral part of the university. The National Crime Prevention Institute was added in 1971.

Another major review of SPI's program occurred in 1972. The evaluators determined that graduate-level courses should be made available to student officers holding a baccalaureate degree. Since 1973 graduate courses have been offered to SPI students who qualify for graduate study under university requirements. In 1978 the faculty, recognizing that the designation "School of Police Administration" was not descriptive enough, recommended a name change. The new name, the School of Justice Administration, was approved by the Board of Trustees the next year. The most recent organizational change has been to place the school in the College of Arts and Sciences (1992).

SPI Today

The Southern Police Institute has graduated more than 10,000 police officers from the United States and foreign countries. Demand for the on-campus Administrative Officers Course continues to run high. Charges for the course, the cornerstone of SPI, were $2,790 per individual in 1993, excluding meals. Tuition is $1,225; books and supplies, $400; housing, $1,100; and parking/student fees, $65. The overall goal of instruction has always been to strengthen the individual both mentally and ethically in administrative leadership. Additional seminars on and off campus are well attended and are tailored to meet the needs of an agency or region. SPI conducts career development programs in locations such as Greensboro, North Carolina; Ft. Lauderdale, Florida; Las Vegas, Nevada; Boulder, Colorado; Bismarck, North Dakota; and Grand Island, Nebraska. Seminar topics range from "Solving Unresolved Homicides" to "Planning the Effective Use of Financial Resources" to "Investigation of Sex Crimes." The Southern Police Institute has survived when police education and training were not popular, when money for training was sparse, when federal grants were available/unavailable, and during periods of national economic recession. As one of the "big three" law-enforcement training centers in the United States, SPI flourishes because of its original commitment to create better understanding between police and the public.

Special Function Police

Special function police forces are agencies that have full police powers but are responsible for law enforcement and security to specific institutions rather than general state and local governments. Special function police forces include railway, transit, harbor, and university police as well as housing, school district, and hospital district police.

History

The earliest special function police forces in the United States were the railway police forces established in the late nineteenth century. As the West was settled, railroad companies often found themselves operating in frontier areas where local authorities were few, poorly organized, and unable to maintain law and order. Train robberies, assaults on passengers, and nonpaying stowaways interfered with the provision of effective railroad service. As a result, every state legislature except Minnesota passed legislation authorizing railroad companies to raise, equip, and operate their own police forces and gave the officers of these forces full police powers under state law. Today, forty-two railroad companies, which together own 82 percent of the nation's rail mileage, continue to maintain their own police forces under this legislation. These departments total 2,820 sworn officers and 129 nonsworn personnel.

Transit police forces developed more recently. In 1901 Pennsylvania authorized the establishment of "street railway police" to deal with the growing problem of crime, especially pickpocketing, on its urban trolley lines. New Jersey next established such a force in 1904. Currently transit police operate in fifteen jurisdictions including San Francisco, Boston, Chicago, Dallas, Houston, New Jersey, and the Washington D.C., area. The largest such department is the New York City Transit Police Department, which employs more than 4,000 sworn officers. Transit police are responsible for security and law enforcement on the subways, buses, and facilities operated by the transit authority that they serve.

Similarly, port authority and harbor police forces provide protection to the facilities and waterfronts of major seaports. The most important of these is the Port Authority of New York and New Jersey police force. This force was founded in 1928 with forty men and at that time provided police service and protection to several important bridges in the New York–New Jersey metropolitan area; thus, the officers were originally titled "Bridgemen" while the sergeants were called "Bridgemasters." Today, the Port Authority police force has approximately 1,200 sworn officers, who by interstate compact have full police powers in both New York and New Jersey. Their jurisdiction includes not only the bridges and tunnels of the Port Authority but the cargo terminals, railheads, and airports within the Port District, a zone of operations approximately twenty-five miles in radius centered on the Statue of Liberty. The facilities entrusted to their protection include the World Trade Center.

Many smaller harbor police forces exist in U.S. seaports, sometimes as a component of the metropolitan police force rather than as independent organizations. For example, the New Orleans Police Department operates a Harbor Police division with about seventy sworn officers having full state police authority.

A related but distinct type of special purpose police agency is the marine patrol forces maintained by states with large coastlines, such as the Connecticut Marine Patrol, the Florida Marine Patrol, and the Maryland Natural Resources Police. The earliest such force was probably the Maryland State Oyster Police, founded in 1868 to prevent illegal oyster fishing in the Chesapeake Bay area. Today, such agencies are frequently responsible for enforcing environmental protection laws as well as for providing police protection and rescue services to coastal and recreational shipping. For example, the Florida Marine Patrol serves as the law-enforcement division of the Florida Department of Natural Resources. Besides being vested with full state police powers, it is provided with U.S. Department of Commerce credentials for the purpose of enforcing federal laws designed to protect marine wildlife.

The widest recent expansion of special function police forces has taken place in the formation of college and university police forces. While such forces date from at least 1894, when the Yale Campus Police Force was formed by hiring two New Haven police officers, most educational institutions relied on private security guards lacking police authority until the early 1970s. The increase of crime on campus, particularly theft and rape, led to the formation of a variety of university police forces empowered under either local ordinance or state statute. With the passage of the Crime Awareness and Campus Security Act in 1990, universities were required to report crime statistics to the FBI. The resulting publicity and increased exposure to civil liability for inadequate protection are expected to motivate more universities to form their own police forces under state statute.

Duties

Special purpose police forces have general law-enforcement responsibilities to protect the institutions they serve. However, unlike municipal police agencies, they face tasks directly related to the function of the institutions they serve and must plan their operations accordingly.

For example, railroad police emphasize the prevention of trespassing and vandalism. While these are comparatively trivial offenses to most municipal police, railroad facilities pose an increased risk of injury to the trespasser and railroad operations can be easily disrupted by simple acts of vandalism. A special problem faced by both railroad and port police is the prevention and investigation of cargo theft. Both types of police therefore operate more sophisticated surveillance and alarm systems than most municipal police functions require. Careful record-keeping of cargo seals is necessary as a basis for investigating thefts that have already been carried out. Procedures for dealing with large-scale accidents must also be well established. For example, the Port Authority of New York–New Jersey maintains a special unit cross-trained as firefighters and emergency rescue teams to respond to airplane crashes at Port Authority airports. Additionally, since both port and railway police serve interstate transportation networks, both must be particularly concerned with attempted shipment of illegal drugs through their facilities. For example, a multiagency operation on Amtrak's eastern passenger lines in 1983 was coordinated by the Amtrak police using drug courier profiles and resulted in 107 arrests over a four-month period.

Transit police face the problems of vandalism and trespassing as well, but must also prioritize the prevention and investigation of robberies of passengers. In some jurisdictions, such as Detroit, plainclothes as well as uniformed officers have been detailed to personally ride the buses servicing high-risk areas.

Marine patrol police have such varied duties that a high degree of specialized training is necessary for each officer. Seamanship, first aid, and rescue skills are as necessary as basic law-enforcement procedures to their tasks. Most commonly, such forces employ the twenty-five-foot Boston Whaler type of patrol boat with two-man crews. Thus each patrol officer must be highly competent in all aspects of the marine patrol mission.

University police, operating as they do in places of higher education, generally adopt a service-oriented rather than confrontational style of policing. Moreover, university police devote great resources to theft prevention and campus escort programs. Narcotics use and unruly crowd situations are among the problems university police must confront without alienating the faculty or student bodies with overly authoritarian methods.

Thus, for all types of special function police the smooth and safe functioning of the parent institution is the central concern that shapes the law-enforcement response. Special function police must seek to prevent rather than respond to disruptive activies. This requires methodical proactive planning.

Coordination

Frequently special function police forces share police responsibility with other law-enforcement agencies serving the general area in which the special function institutions are located. A transit line may pass through several counties and cities, while railroad operations are interstate in nature. Universities are often located in areas also served by a municipal police or sheriff's department. In such cases coordination between the various law-enforcement agencies is essential, including a clear understanding of which agency is responsible for responding to different types and locations of incidents. In some cases, special function police are given multijurisdictional authority by state legislation. For example, the Houston Metro Transit Police are empowered to act in each jurisdiction through which the metro operates by Texas statute. The Washington, D.C., Metro Area Transit Authority Police Force, which operates in Virginia and Maryland as well, has concluded memoranda of understanding with local law-enforcement agencies such as the Arlington County, Virginia, Police and Sheriffs' department defining in detail the scope of the transit police operations in those jurisdictions. As noted above, Maryland Natural Resources Police have some federal authority, while the New York–New Jersey Port Authority Police have full police powers in both states.

In some cases, special function police face coordination problems with each other. For example, a cargo theft from one railroad company's freight car may take place on rail lines owned by a different railroad company. Thus railroad police inspect cargo seals at each station within their jurisdiction whether or not the train is owned by their employer. Any discrepancies are reported back to the railroad control center.

A problem related to coordination is certification. In many states all police officers must attain certain state-mandated standards of training. Special function police force officers are no exception. These officers will be trained to the same standard of general law-enforcement competence as municipal officers, despite the often limited nature of their duties, which strongly emphasizes the security function. However, in states lacking certification requirements, special function police, particularly if organized under local ordinance, may lack training commensurate with their authority.

Eric W. Moore

Bibliography

Ball, E.R. "Railroad Police." *Law and Order* 38(4) (1990): 62–66.

Clede, B. "Marine Police Are Down Home." *Law and Order* 34(11) (1986): 37–40.

Dewhurst, H.S. *The Railroad Police.* Springfield, IL: Charles C. Thomas, 1955.

Hinkle, O.D., and T.S. Jones. "Security Guards or Real Cops? How Some Major Universities are Facing the '90's." *Law and Order* 39(9) 1991: 141–48.

Powell, J. W. *Campus Security and Law Enforcement.* Woburn, MA: Butterworth, 1981.

Rafter, R.W. "Maryland's Natural Resources Police." *Police Chief* 51(12) (1984): 42–44.

Special Weapons and Tactics (SWAT)

In 1964, the Philadelphia Police Department, in response to an alarming increase in bank robberies, established a one-hundred-man Special Weapons and Tactics Squad. The purpose of this unit was to react quickly and decisively to bank robberies while they were in progress, by utilizing a large number of specially trained officers who had at their disposal a great amount of firepower. The tactic worked.

Shortly after the successes of the Philadelphia SWAT team were publicized, other departments formed similar special units, most notably the Los Angeles Police Department (SWAT). Many different names were given to these teams: SRT (Special Reaction Team), Los Angeles Sheriff's Department; MUST (Metro Unique Situation Team), Nashville Police Department; HRT (Hostage Rescue Team), to name a few.

The formation of SWAT teams by major police departments marked a departure from traditional police service and the advent of a new method of crisis management by modern police executives. Many rank-and-file police officers were slow to see these teams as the most ideal element of a department to correctly handle certain high-risk situations. But police executives were quick to recognize that the use of highly motivated, specially armed, specially trained, and exceptionally well-led reams of officers, when faced with heavily armed criminals or media happenings such as hostage incidents, usually reduced civil liability and complemented public relations when the incident was resolved successfully in favor of the police with little or no loss of life. By the end of the 1970s all major departments across the United States had formed SWAT teams, and the rank-and-file police officers of America had accepted them as an integral part of police service.

Staffing
SWAT teams are staffed by regular police officers selected for the teams after meeting certain stringent criteria. SWAT team members are required to have a normal psychological profile with emphasis on the ability to work well as a member of a team. Without question each member must be physically fit and not have any limiting physical characteristics, such as hearing loss or extreme myopia. Team members must be able to react well under stress and conditions of extreme fatigue. They must be capable of following orders without question and at the same time demonstrating the ability to lead others when called upon.

Equipment
Because SWAT teams are required to tackle situations that demand unorthodox entry into structures under extremely adverse conditions, they must be adept in the use of special equipment such as ropes and rappelling paraphernalia, which they can use to enter a structure from a rooftop or from a hovering helicopter. They must be able to use explosives to blast doors, walls. or roofs in order to make a quick and safe entry.

The SWAT team uniform must provide all-weather protection. It must be able to be worn at night without making the officer an easily identifiable target. It must be loose-fitting in order to allow the officer freedom of movement. Many teams have opted for a ski-mask type wool cap, which can be rolled up during hot days and let down at night for concealment.

Team members usually wear military-type boots. In recent years the outfitting of SWAT teams has become a fast-rising business in America, with companies developing an exotic assortment of uniforms, SWAT weaponry, and even SWAT vehicles.

The weapons of a SWAT team are dictated by tactical necessity. In assaults on defended properties, teams use automatic rifles, usually stockless and short-barreled, with a high rate of fire. A shotgun is usually brought along on every operation to provide long-range delivery for tear gas or smoke. Teams will employ sharpshooters against snipers and to cover the movement of other team members. Sharpshooters use high-powered, long-range rifles, usually fitted with high-resolution scopes that can be used day or night. As a rule, teams will issue automatic pistols to each member as personal, close-in weapons, because of their rapid fire and quick and easy reload capabilities.

Other equipment possessed by teams include gas masks for each member, starlight scopes for night vision, flashlights attached to weaponry for nighttime target acquisition, bulletproof vests, SWAT vests that fit around the body and are capable of carrying everything from extra ammunition to water canteens, leg holsters for pistols to allow for quick draw, and high-band, voice-activated, silent listening radios for instant interteam communication that may be employed even while a team member is under fire. Last, teams have special SWAT vehicles, usually vans, that are brought to the scenes of incidents and provide command post and logistic center functions.

Training
Because SWAT teams are required to perform the most hazardous of tasks, such as freeing hostages, it is of paramount importance that they be well trained. Each team should have a clearly defined yearly training program dictated by their potential missions. Types of training required for teams include the use of explosives for controlled entry into structures; live-fire target recognition and acquisition; day and night movement procedures in all types of terrain and in all types of weather; entry procedures for all types of structures; envelopment techniques; room- and building-clearing techniques; rappelling from buildings, cliffs, and helicopters; use of flash-bang and smoke grenades to cover movement and facilitate entries; physical conditioning; hand-to-hand combat;

radio and nonverbal communication procedures in daylight and darkness; quick-kill techniques; antisniper and sniper techniques; small-unit organizational concepts; antiambush procedures; chemical agent use and recognition; cover, camouflage, and concealment use; movement under cover of fire; and small unit leadership.

Team Characteristics

SWAT teams are characterized by several features that other police units do not possess. Regardless of their size (most teams average twelve members), teams are usually organized into two distinct groups: the assault group, whose function it is to enter and clear structures; and the cover group, whose function it is to cover the assault group and protect team perimeters. SWAT teams have clearly defined chains of command that flow from the team leader directly to the head of their department, thus eliminating intermediate commanding officers whose interference during critical calls could be disastrous. SWAT teams are on twenty-four-hour call and have a clearly defined call-up procedure that automatically goes into effect whenever a department dispatcher receives a potential SWAT call.

Uses

SWAT teams are used exclusively in any of five incidents: (1) they are used in hostage-related incidents. While negotiation is the ideal method of resolving hostage situations, negotiations will sometimes break down and the crisis will have to be resolved tactically. (2) Sniper situations pose a great threat to innocent civilians and must be resolved quickly and decisively. (3) Barricaded suspects often have to be overcome or arrested in order for public tranquility to return to a neighborhood or commercial area. (4) Sometimes other police units will call upon SWAT teams to aid in the arrest of subjects who are heavily armed. Usually a team will have the upper hand in firepower. (5) Teams are usually called upon to provide antisniper protection for dignitaries.

Evolution

Since the advent of transnational terrorism with the massacre of Israeli athletes at the 1972 Olympic games in Munich, major countries have developed special units designed for counterterrorist duties. Great Britain utilizes the SAS (Strategic Air Service), West Germany its

GSG-9 (Border Police Unit 9), France the Groupe D'Intervention Gendarmerie Nationale (National Police Intervention Group), and the United States formed its Delta Force. All of these units are in the most fundamental sense large SWAT teams. They are direct descendants of the Philadelphia Police Department's one-hundred-man unit. They receive similar training, wear the same uniforms, use the same weapons, equipment, and organization, and have similar missions. The only real difference is that they operate on a much larger scale with a wider jurisdiction.

Future Use of SWAT Teams

Most jurisdictions throughout America have formed SWAT teams to handle hazardous situations. Teams with as few as five members function extremely well with adequate training. With any rise in domestic terrorism, specially trained units such as Special Weapons and Tactics teams will be needed to maintain order.

Phillip A. Davidson

Bibliography

Beckwith, Charles A., and David Knox. *Delta Force*. New York: Harcourt Brace Jovanovich, 1983.

Cappel, Robert P. *S.W.A.T. Team Manual*. Boulder, CO: Paladin Press, 1979.

Davidson, Phillip L. *S.W.A.T.* Springfield, IL: Charles C. Thomas, 1979.

Jacobs, Jeffrie. *S.W.A.T. Manual*. Boulder, CO: Paladin Press, 1983.

Kolman, John A. *A Guide to the Development of Special Weapons and Tactics Teams*. Springfield, IL: Charles C. Thomas, 1982.

Miller, Abraham H. *Terrorism and Hostage Negotiation*. Boulder, CO: Westview Press, 1980.

State Law-Enforcement Agencies

A variety of state agencies provides law-enforcement services. Many of these agencies have wide law-enforcement or peacekeeping powers; others are restricted to the enforcement of specific statutes or investigation of certain offenses. In the United States there are sixty-six state agencies classified as separate state police, highway patrol, or state investigative agencies, or listed as such under a larger department or umbrella agency, such as a department of public safety or division of criminal justice. There are also a great number of other specialized investigative agencies, both uniformed and nonuniformed, operating at the state level, such as an office of fire marshal, state revenue or excise tax office, department of wildlife or natural resources, division of consumer affairs, or even investigators assigned to the attorney general's office. Many states have employees who are assigned investigative duties or functions for regulatory agencies, but do not perform true law-enforcement or criminal investigative functions. In other states many of these "investigative" matters may fall under the jurisdiction of a state law-enforcement or state criminal investigative agency.

Historical Perspective

It is clear from a historical perspective that county and local police agencies were given the mandate for ensuring public safety duties and enforcing statutes. This system was transferred from England and adapted to the American colonies. The Texas Rangers were apparently the first state-level law-enforcement group established in North America, although the agency was developed in 1835 as a semimilitary state police/militia force rather than a police/criminal investigatory unit. In 1865, both Connecticut and Massachusetts appointed state constables, but neither was a large, wide-ranging state police law-enforcement agency. The United States basically lacked efficient state police or investigative agencies to enforce state laws, and it was not until 1905 that the first modern, uniformed state police force was established in Pennsylvania.

The establishment of state police, highway patrols, and state investigative agencies was predicated on many factors, including economic, political, geographic, and legal. These agencies were created in most situations because the state governors did not have anyone to enforce state law in municipal or county areas; they were often seen as a security force of the governor's office. Except in certain situations, such as corruption, strikes, disaster, or riots, these state enforcement agencies were not empowered to replace municipal or county enforcement officers. In 1935, the New York State Legislature imposed a state police on the City of New York but eventually returned general police functions to the city administration. In some states, such as Rhode Island and Connecticut, there is an extensive rural state trooper program in lieu of a police force.

The development of state police, highway patrol, and state investigative agencies has been inconsistent for many reasons. They are often controlled directly by the governor or placed under umbrella agencies, yet most receive funds through the state legislature, which also provides their enforcement powers or investigative authority. Thus in some states a variety of agencies is centralized into one department or agency, while others have these state criminal investigative or police functions spread among many agencies, sometimes independent of one another. For example, in Oklahoma there is a State Highway Patrol, State Bureau of Investigation, and State Bureau of Narcotics and Dangerous Drugs control, each of which is a separate agency; the State Bureau of Investigation reports to a commission and the other two agencies report to the governor.

Personnel Employment

State law-enforcement personnel include armed uniformed officers and criminal investigators, or a combination of both, that (1) effect arrests or provide investigative assistance to all law-enforcement officers in the state on request and have primary jurisdiction in certain types of offenses; (2) operate communications and computer services on the intrastate and interstate levels with other law-enforcement agencies (federal, state, county, or municipal); (3) provide training or instruction at a state-level academy, which may or may not be controlled by the state police, highway patrol, or state investigative agency; (4) provide a forensic laboratory to conduct analysis of evidence through scientific means (in some states the laboratory may be a state-level independent agency); and (5) maintain a central records repository for fingerprints, background data, and records of criminal and noncriminal information available to state criminal-justice agencies.

Specifically, a separate state police or division of state police is defined as having statewide police or arrest powers for both traffic and criminal offenses. Most state police agencies have both uniformed and plainclothes personnel, although there are some exceptions. State police also provide auxiliary services in the areas of forensics, communications, records, and training, and may provide specialized services such as fixed-wing aircraft or watercraft patrol, depending on geographic location. In some state enforcement systems, the fire marshal may be an independent investigative unit or segment while in others the office may be part of the state police, highway patrol, or state investigative agency.

A state highway patrol is defined as an agency with statewide authority to enforce traffic regulations and arrest nontraffic violators who fall under their jurisdiction, and with powers to assist any law-enforcement officer upon request, including federal, and other state, county, and municipal officers. Most highway patrol agencies do not utilize plainclothes investigators or have limited investigator personnel and do not investigate criminal cases throughout the state. One exception, although there are others, is the Washington Highway Patrol, which operates as a state police agency except that it is called a highway patrol; it has wide-ranging criminal and traffic-enforcement authority and utilizes plainclothes criminal investigators.

A state investigative agency is defined as one that has statewide arrest authority and primary jurisdiction in specific criminal investigations; provides criminal investigative assistance to all law-enforcement agencies upon request; has no uniformed personnel (or limited uniformed personnel); and provides a variety of auxiliary services to criminal-justice agencies as indicated previously under state enforcement agencies in general. By definition, it excludes state agencies with a narrow purpose, such as those who have personnel with limited arrest powers, or who function as a very specific uniformed force within the state, such as alcoholic beverage control board agents or fish and game inspectors.

Most states confer the powers of sheriffs, chiefs of police, or constables on members of highway patrol, state police, or state investigative agencies, although others place limitations on these powers. In Missouri the State Highway Patrol, which performs as a state police agency, does not have the power of serving civil process; the authority has historically been conferred on the county sheriff.

Organization
Specifically, there are twenty-six highway patrols and twenty-three state police agencies; Hawaii is the only state that does not possess a state police, highway patrol, or state investigative agency. There are also thirty-five state investigative agencies or established investigative segments that are not under a state police or highway patrol, or are a separate division

within a larger department. The state police agencies in Michigan, New Mexico, New York, Oregon, Pennsylvania, Rhode Island, and Virginia operate as independent organizations responsible to the governor; the remaining sixteen state police agencies operate under a larger umbrella agency that is responsible to the governor. Only six state highway patrol agencies operate under a department of safety, department of transportation, or other traffic-oriented department.

Some highway patrols operate under a larger department that has both a public safety and traffic function, such as the North Carolina Highway Patrol (under the Department of Crime Control and Public Safety) or the Nevada Highway Patrol (under the Nevada Department of Motor Vehicles and Public Safety). Even though the North Carolina Highway Patrol operates under a larger umbrella agency, the North Carolina State Bureau of Investigation exists as a separate agency responsible to the governor. In Nevada the highway patrol and a division of investigation are both under the Department of Motor Vehicles and Public Safety, which is responsible to the governor.

Highway patrol personnel generally possess statewide powers of arrest in relation to state traffic offenses or criminal acts committed on state highways or property, as well as authority to assist other officers on request. However, the Mississippi Highway Patrol and the Missouri State Highway Patrol (each under the Department of Public Safety), the Nebraska State Patrol, the Ohio State Highway Patrol, and the Washington State Patrol perform duties associated with a state police force rather than a general highway patrol. These five highway patrol agencies utilize both uniformed and plainclothes personnel to effect arrests for a variety of nontraffic-related offenses and perform other duties associated with a defined state police force. Ohio is the only state of the five that also has a Bureau of Criminal Identification and Investigation, which is under the office of attorney general.

The states that have a highway patrol or state police agency separate from a state bureau of investigation are California, Florida, Georgia, Kansas, North Carolina, North Dakota, Tennessee, Wisconsin, and Wyoming. The states that utilize a state police or highway patrol and a separate division of investigation (or similar designation), both under a larger umbrella department, are Alabama, Arizona, Colorado,

Idaho, Illinois, Iowa, Minnesota, Mississippi, Montana, Nevada, Texas, and Utah. Idaho is unique in that the Idaho Department of Law Enforcement has both an Idaho State Police, without any plainclothes investigators or detectives, and a separate nonuniformed police services division that investigates state criminal offenses and assists county or municipal police departments on request. The South Carolina State Law Enforcement Division (SLED) is the only state law-enforcement agency in the United States that does not have any field or regional offices and operates only from a headquarters location. The SLED transports personnel, which may include handlers and their canines, from the headquarters office to the appropriate location, and they return there upon completion of the assignment.

The states having a state police that performs both traffic-related functions and criminal investigative duties under a larger umbrella organization are Alaska, Arkansas, Connecticut, Delaware, Indiana, Kentucky, Louisiana, Maine, Maryland, Massachusetts, New Hampshire, New Jersey, Vermont, and West Virginia. The states having a highway patrol under a larger umbrella organization are Alabama, Arizona, California, Colorado, Florida, Georgia, Iowa, Minnesota, Mississippi, Missouri, Montana, Nevada, North Carolina, Ohio, Oklahoma, South Carolina, South Dakota, Tennessee, Texas, Utah, Wisconsin, and Wyoming. The states with highway patrols not under a larger department and responsible directly to the governor are Kansas, Nebraska, North Dakota, and Washington.

The state law-enforcement agencies responsible to the state attorney general, rather than to a larger department or directly to the governor, are the California Division of Law Enforcement, Kansas Bureau of Investigation, Montana Department of Justice, New Jersey Department of Law and Public Safety (includes the state police), North Carolina State Bureau of Investigation, North Dakota Bureau of Criminal Investigation, Ohio Bureau of Criminal Identification and Investigation, Wisconsin Department of Justice, and the Wyoming Criminal Investigation Division.

The state with the largest highway patrol is California; the smallest is Wyoming (each highway patrol operates as a traffic-oriented force, and there is a separate state investigative agency responsible to the attorney general). The largest state police agency is in Pennsylvania;

the smallest is in Idaho. In Pennsylvania the criminal investigators are part of the state police; in Idaho the Police Services Division is separate from the state police but under the same umbrella agency. The largest state bureau of investigation is the Florida Department of Law Enforcement; the smallest are the South Dakota Division of Criminal Investigation and the North Dakota Bureau of Criminal Investigation.

Record Maintenance and Other Services
In most states the state police, the highway patrol, or state investigative agency is responsible for collecting and reporting crime statistics for the state and transmitting that data to the FBI, which publishes the Uniform Crime Reports. In only a few states are the statewide criminal statistics gathered directly from local agencies rather than from the state-level law-enforcement or criminal investigative agency. Most, but not all, state-level enforcement agencies issue an annual or fiscal crime index report. Every state has a computer-assisted information network for processing criminal records, fingerprints, driver's licenses, registrations, or other information, although they may not always be located in one agency. Every state law-enforcement or criminal-justice agency also has access to the National Crime Information Center (NCIC) operated by the FBI, as well as a state-level computer information system. The NCIC, established in 1967, provides information through NCIC terminals of criminal histories on convicted felons and fugitives, arrest warrant data for persons sought on extraditable offenses, "lookouts" for wanted individuals on extradictable violations, identifying numbers for stolen properties—such as vehicles, boats, aircraft, weapons, and securities—and missing persons.

Every state, whether it be through a state police, highway patrol, or state investigative agency, provides forensic services to its personnel and to other state law-enforcement or criminal-justice agencies. In some states, such as Illinois, six satellite Department of State Police forensic laboratories perform more routine or frequently requested analysis of evidence; the main laboratory in Springfield conducts more complex, arduous forensic evaluations. Generally, state forensic laboratories receive evidence for testing only from authorized law-enforcement personnel or specified criminal-justice agencies such as probation or parole. One exception is the forensic laboratory in the Wyoming Criminal Investigation Division under the attorney general, which performs forensic analysis for defense attorneys as well. More agencies are adopting the single-fingerprint system for identification rather than the ten-fingerprint system in wide use in 1987. Most state-level forensic examiners and identification specialists are civilians, a practice that will continue in the future.

Operational Differences
The state police or highway patrol uniforms differ tremendously from state to state, including the color of the pants, jacket, or shirt; type of hat (standard short-brim, medium-brim Stetson, or peaked campaign); use of short-waisted or thigh-length dress tunic, use of across-the-shirt leather shoulder strap; and the wearing of boots rather than shoes. Only a minority of departments do not wear issued badges on uniforms since the agency patch and collar/hat insignia on the uniform constitutes identification. This is the case with the Missouri State Highway Patrol, New Jersey State Police, New York State Police, and Pennsylvania State Police. In most states other police and all private police personnel by statute must wear a uniform different in color or style from that worn by state law-enforcement officers.

State law-enforcement agencies also use a wide variety of differently colored vehicles, which do not always correspond to the uniform colors. The gamut of colors utilized varies from the traditional black and white used by the New Mexico State Police to the nearly all red vehicles used by the Minnesota Highway Patrol. There is no standard type or make of vehicle used consistently by all state law-enforcement agencies and most are equipped with the standard red lights, with only a minority of agencies using red and blue or only blue emergency lights. Usually state enforcement vehicles are assigned to the trooper or investigator on a twenty-four-hour basis; there are some exceptions.

As of 1987, nearly all state police, highway patrol, or state investigative agencies required only a high-school degree or its equivalent as a minimum for employment. Only the Wisconsin Division of Criminal Investigation and the Connecticut State Police had no minimum educational requirements for employment. Only five agencies (all state investigative agencies) required a four-year college degree; five agencies required two years of college or sixty college credits as a prerequisite for employment; one

department provided an eight-month training period after which the officer was awarded an associate's degree; three departments required thirty semester hours (one department waived this provision on certain conditions); sixteen departments required 120 credits but waived the requirement with appropriate enforcement or criminal investigative experience; and forty-three agencies required only a high school degree or its equivalency.

All state law-enforcement agencies had a certification program for officers and many arranged for college credit for academy training. Only in a few states did officers receive reimbursement for college tuition or higher pay after attaining an associate or bachelor's degree. Only the West Virginia State Police had their training certified by a college so that all state police academy graduates received an associate's degree, a very innovative program.

Donald A. Torres

Bibliography
Floherty, John J. *Troopers All—Stories of State Police*. Philadelphia: Lippincott, 1954.

Fosdick, Raymond B. *American Police Systems*. New York: Century Press, 1920.

Johnson, David R. *American Law Enforcement—A History*. St. Louis: Forum Press, 1981.

Monroe, David G. *State and Provincial Police*. Chicago: International Association of Chiefs of Police and Northwestern Traffic Institute, 1941.

Smith, Bruce. *The State Police: Organization and Administration*. New York: Macmillan, 1925.

Torres, Donald A. *Handbook of State Police, Highway Patrols, and State Investigative Agencies*. Westport, CT: Greenwood Press, 1987.

Vollmer, August, and Alfred E. Parker. *Crime and the State Police*. Berkeley: University of California Press, 1935.

Strategic Planning

There is a growing and rather extensive literature on strategic planning. For example, the Learning Resource Center at the FBI Academy has compiled a ten-page bibliography on strategic planning. This bibliography lists items available at the FBI Academy Library. Melcher and Kerzner (1988:20), while tracing the evolution of strategic planning theory, write that the first interest in the subject can be traced to the Harvard Business School in 1933, when top management's "point of view" was added to the business policy course. This perspective emphasized incorporating a firm's external environment with its internal operations.

George Steiner's classic work, *Strategic Planning: What Every Manager Must Know,* was published in 1979 and is generally considered to be the bible of strategic planning. Steiner asserts that strategic planning is inextricably interwoven into the entire fabric of management. Steiner lists fourteen basic and well-known management processes (e.g., setting objectives and goals, developing a company philosophy by establishing beliefs, values, etc.) that make up the components of a general management system, and links them to a comprehensive strategic planning process (7–8).

There are many different models or approaches to strategic planning. Melcher and Kerzner's book *Strategic Planning: Development and Implementation* provides an excellent description and review of various models. In essence, strategic planning is a highly rational approach to the management process. It seeks to answer the following questions: Why does the organization exist? What is the organization doing today? What should the organization be doing in the future? What short-term objectives and longer-term goals must be accomplished to bridge the gap from the present to the future?

There is some debate among strategic planners as to whether this analysis can be meaningful without identifying the organizational culture, its values and norms, and the values of critical decision-makers. Thus a number of models of the strategic planning process include a values identification, audit, and analysis step. Many other models do not include this step. The writer's experience has been that many law-enforcement officials are turned off by what they see as "mushy, touchy-feely, organizational psychology concepts" intruding into the planning process.

The writer believes that an understanding of the organizational culture is extremely important to the success of any attempt to change an organization. Strategic planning is such an effort—changing the organization from its present to its future. Nevertheless, many organizations and their members are not ready for this kind of self-examination. Strategic planning can assist law-enforcement agencies in perform-

ing their mission without including the values analysis step.

Evolution of Management Thought
Up until the 1950s organizations were governed by one set of rules. There were a variety of highly respected theories about organizations, including Henry Fayol's classical organization theory/administrative science, Max Weber's bureaucratic theory, and Frederick Taylor's scientific management, but all prescribed the same set of rules. First, simplify work as much as possible. Second, organize to accomplish routine activities. Third, set standards of control to monitor performance. Finally, take no notice of any changes in the world at large that might affect the organization. There was very little expectation of change and no effort made to anticipate it.

However, these theories with their "principles" of administration did result in dramatic gains in productivity. In fact, these ideas led to substantially enhanced profits and corresponding salary increases for workers. Why? Because they placed a premium on a rational approach to organizing work, and they stressed the importance of qualified and competent managers—a definite departure from earlier approaches that encouraged nepotism and amateurism.

Unfortunately for these ideas the world changed. In the latter half of the twentieth century, change itself became the critical variable. Once we could safely wager that tomorrow would be like today in all important respects; today it is a fool's bet.

Beginning around 1950 we saw the development of administrative philosophies that recognized this new pervasiveness of change. Change was viewed as a certainty, not as an anomaly. It was not to be treated normatively (i.e., as either good or bad) but was seen as inevitable. Thus organizations had to be structured to accommodate and anticipate change. Also the focus was shifted from the routine duties that employees perform each day to the results that were expected to flow from all this effort. The new buzz phrase was "manage for results." The new paradigm called for flexible or ad hoc organizational structures that organized for desired results, developed goals to direct or focus effort, and anticipated changes.

Many readers are familiar with some of these new paradigm theories: management by objectives (MBO); planning, programming budget system (PPBS); zero-based budgeting (ZBB); contingency approaches; and situational theories. For a variety of reasons these administrative efforts met with varying levels of success—mostly disappointing—when implemented by organizations. For example, the federal government tried and abandoned PPBS, then MBO, and finally ZBB. Even so, management philosophies that emphasize end results have remained popular.

As a next step managers not only wanted to know the future direction of their organizations, they also wanted to identify their strengths and weaknesses. This approach is called long-range planning. In the United States, long-range planning became a popular management philosophy in the early to middle 1970s.

Long-range planning, however, also has its shortcomings, primarily because it ignores external factors that affect an organization's performance. Some people felt that long-range planning focused too exclusively on internal factors and created an introspective mind-set. Strategic planning, by contrast, is conceived as a management-for-results philosophy that uses both an internal assessment and an environmental assessment.

A major difficulty in understanding these different managerial philosophies is that writers use different names for these ideas and they also develop unique definitions for them. Nevertheless, almost all are in agreement that strategic planning is a results-oriented philosophy that employs both an internal organizational assessment and an external environmental analysis.

Models of Strategic Planning
As detailed earlier there are a number of different approaches to strategic planning, requiring varying levels of resource commitments; and each organization needs to adapt or modify these different ideas to fit its unique situation. There is no universal "best way."

In this section two models will be described. The first of these, applied strategic planning, is defined as "the process by which the guiding members of an organization envision its future and develop the procedures and operations necessary to achieve that future" (Pfeiffer et al., 1986:1). The definition is a mouthful, but a picture of the process provided in Figure 1 is clear. A few of the steps deserve comment. Note that on the right side of Figure

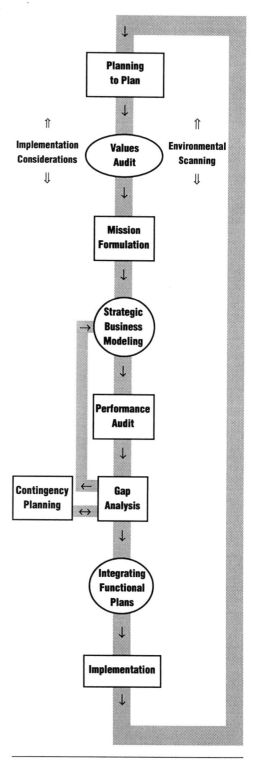

FIGURE 1

The Applied Strategic Planning Model

research literature, however, has not demonstrated that policing is any more or less stressful than other occupations either inside or outside the criminal-justice system. Prison guards are also subjected to a variety of occupational stressors: role conflict between custody and rehabilitation, shift work, limited career advancement, and a potentially explosive inmate subculture.

A number of studies have concluded that correctional work may even be more stressful than policing. Cheek and Miller (1983) report that heart disease, alcoholism, and emotional disorders accounted for 60 percent of the disability time for New York state correctional officers, which is 300 percent higher than comparable time for other state employees. The divorce rate for New Jersey officers has been observed to be twice as high as the state average, and prison guards have been found to have more instances of sickness, ulcers, hypertension, and heart disease than a comparable sample of police officers (Cheek, 1983; Cheek and Miller, 1982, 1983).

There is also evidence that occupations outside the criminal-justice system experience considerable stress. Emergency room surgeons temper hospital regulations with personal judgments of what is in the best interest of the patient. In addition they make decisions with life and death outcomes and labor long hours at inconvenient times and locations. A growing number of ministers are suffering from stress and burnout. The "walk on water" syndrome refers to an expectation that ministers can accomplish almost anything: teaching, delivering inspirational sermons, counseling, fund-raising, and competently administering their churches. One organization estimates that at least 17 percent of all ministers suffer from long-term stress or burnout. In one year alone, stress-related illnesses among ministers constituted the second leading category of medical claims for people working in this profession (Whittemore, 1991).

A recent national survey conducted by Northwestern National Life Insurance Company, as reported in the *Albany Herald*, underscores the pervasiveness of stress in a wide variety of occupational settings. Seven of ten employees sampled perceived job stress to be a major health-related problem; one-third were seriously considering a job change; 14 percent had adapted to stress by changing jobs during the reporting period; and, last, over one-third of the employees expected to experience job burnout in the near future.

How stressful is policing? How does the occupation of police officer measure up to other occupations on the amount of stress experienced? In attempting to answer this question, the author conducted a preliminary study that compared police officers to prison guards on the same measurement of stress. No significant differences were found between the two groups on the amount of stress they experienced, but differences were observed on the specific stressors affecting both groups. Police officers rated racial conflict, political pressure, court appearances, and lack of promotional opportunities to be more stressful than did guards. Shift work, role conflict, and the risk of physical attack were perceived to be just as stressful to the sampled guards as they were to the police. In a more extensive follow-up study, the author compared police officers to prison guards, probation officers, firefighters, and emergency medical technicians on multiple measures of stress and burnout. Police officers, prison guards, and probation officers were comparable on the magnitude of stress they experienced (see Table 1). All three groups, scored higher on the multiple measures of stress and burnout than emergency medical technicians and firefighters. The data suggested that policing is indeed stressful but perhaps no more stressful than other people-processing occupations in the criminal-justice system. However, these conclusions are tentative, as comparative studies are the Achilles heel of the police stress literature.

Police managers have implemented various practices in responding to the problem of stress. At least forty-two states administer psychological tests to police applicants in an effort to weed out applicants who are prone to overreact to stressful law-enforcement situations (Inwald and Shusman, 1984). Test results may be supplemented with clinical interviews, preemployment histories, or information relating to previous criminal histories. Psychological testing, however, poses a number of legal and ethical issues. Test results are imperfect predictors of subsequent recruit performance, and otherwise competent candidates may be wrongfully denied employment. Psychological measures of personality characteristics may be unnecessary intrusions into the privacy of job applicants, especially given the weight attached by police managers to the test results. In addition, lower test scores by minorities and unequal job classification between black and white officers may be the basis of charges of racial discrimination (Inwald, 1984, 1985). The upshot is that psychological testing may reduce police misconduct, prevent negative publicity stemming from illegal use of force, and save valuable department time and resources in conducting training programs.

At least seventy-five police departments nationwide have their own stress unit programs, which sponsor workshops by department psychologists, outside consultants, or local college professors (*USA Today*, 1986). Officers are acquainted with the symptoms of stress, its causes and effective methods of adaptation, for example, relaxation, meditation, and exercise. Peer group counseling, another in-house program, employs veteran police officers who are recovering alcoholics, divorced, or in other ways have experienced the negative effects of stress. The rationale for using police counselors is that "fellow officers are more likely to accept them" (Leonard and Tully, 1984). In 1986, New York City's department responded to seven police suicides by training one hundred officers as peer counselors. Telephone hot lines in four precincts enabled officers under stress to reach the counselors on a twenty-four-hour basis (*New York Times*, 1986).

Intensive physical exercise reduces stress and increases an officer's ability to adapt to organizational stressors. The Dallas Police Department implemented a physical exercise program and studied the overall effects on officer job performance. Officers who participated in a consistent and rigorous physical exercise regimen demonstrated a 42 percent decrease in sick days, while officers who had little or no exer-

cise experienced a 5 percent increase. After completion of the exercise program, citizen complaints declined and supervisory commendations increased. Overall, job performance improved by 15 percent (Swanson and Territo, 1984). In recognizing the beneficial effects of physical exercise on officer performance, some police departments have implemented some rather creative and innovative practices. The Lexington, Kentucky, Police Department purchased a gymnasium for its officers. The Bowling Green, Kentucky, Police Department pays officers' membership fees to a local health club (Gaines et al., 1991).

There is no question that police officers experience unique stressors that ultimately result in burnout, rapid turnover, and physical symptoms. As severe as the problem may appear, however, people in other occupations, especially those dealing with life-threatening situations and decisions, also experience high levels of stress. Although the sources of stress for these occupations may be different, the consequences are likely to be the same. Although police stress is an important problem in its own right, there is an urgent need for research demonstrating that policing as a profession is intrinsically more stressful than other occupations.

Richard H. Anson
Nancy C. Anson

Bibliography

Albany Herald. "Stress Wears Down Workers." (May 12, 1991): 5b.

Anson, Richard, and Mary E. Bloom. "Police Stress in an Occupational Context." *Police Science and Administration* (December 1988): 229–35.

TABLE 1

Occupational Differences for Stress and Burnout

	Police	Guards	Probation Officers	Fire-fighters	EMTs
Episodic stress	645	653	322	604	430
Chronic stress	42	43	40	35	38
Tedium	74	74	76	60	67
Physical exhaustion	25	26	27	21	24
Mental exhaustion	23	23	23	19	21
Emotional exhaustion	21	22	22	9	19
Depersonalization	14	13	12	6	11

Source: Richard H. Anson and Mary Ellen Bloom. "Police Stress in an Occupational Context." *Journal of Police Science and Administration* (December 1988): 232.

Axelberd, M., and J. Valle. "Stress Control Program for Police Officers of the City of Miami Police Department." Concept paper 1. City of Miami Florida Police Department, November 1978.

Bartol, Curt. *Psychology and American Law*. Belmont, CA: Wadsworth, 1983.

Blackmore, J. "Are Police Allowed to Have Problems of Their Own?" *Police Magazine* (July 1978): 47–55.

Cheek, Frances E. "Correctional Officer Stress." *Corrections Today* (February 1983): 14–24.

Cheek, Frances E., and M. Miller. "Reducing Staff/Inmate Stress." *Corrections Today* (October 1982): 72–78.

———. "The Experience of Stress for Correctional Officers: A Double-Bind Theory of Correctional Stress." *Journal of Criminal Justice* 11(2) (1983): 105–20.

Dash, J., and M. Reiser "Suicide among Police in Urban Law Enforcement Agencies." *Journal of Police Science and Administration* 6 (1978): 19–20.

Eisenberg, Terry "Labor-Management Relations and Psychological Stress—View From the Bottom." *Police Chief* (April 1975): 59–60.

Gaines, Larry K., Mittie D. Southerland, and John E. Angell. *Police Administration*. New York: McGraw Hill, 1991.

Goodin, C.V. "Job Stress and the Police Officer: Identifying Stress Reduction-Techniques. Eds. Wilt-Kroes and J.J. Hurrell. Proceeding of symposium, Cincinnati, Ohio, May 8–9. Washington, DC: Government Printing Office, 1975.

Gudjonsson, Gisli, and K.R.C. Adlam. "Occupational Stressors among British Police." *Police Journal* (January 1985): 77.

Heiman, M.F. "Police Suicides Revisited." *Suicide* 5 (1975): 15–20.

Inwald, Robin. "Pre-Employment Psychological Testing for Law Enforcement: Ethical and Procedural Issues. What Administrators Should Do." *Training Aids Digest* (June 1984): 1–3.

———. "Administrative, Legal and Ethical Practices in the Psychological Testing of Law Enforcement Officers." *Journal of Criminal Justice* 3 (1985): 368–70.

Inwald, Robin and Elizabeth Shusman. "The IPA and MMPI as Predictors of Academy Performance for Police Recruits." *Journal of Police Science and Administration* 12 (1984): 1.

Kreitner, Robert, Margaret Sova, Stephen Wood, Glenn Friedman, and William Reid. "A Search for the U-Shaped Relationship Between Occupational Stressors and the Risk of Coronary Disease." *Journal of Police Science and Administration* (June 1985): 123.

Labovitz, S. and R. Hagedorn "An Analysis of Suicide Rates among Occupational Categories." *Sociological Inquiry* 41 (1971): 67–72.

Leonard, John and G. Patrick Tully. "Occupational Stress and Compensation in Law Enforcement." *Law Enforcement Bulletin* (July 1984): 25.

Maynard, Peter, and Nancy Maynard. "Stress in Police Families: Some Policy Implications." *Journal of Police Science and Administration* 10 (1982): 309.

New York Times (September 15, 1986): 14.

Pendergrass, Virginia, and Nancy Ostrove. "A Survey of Stress in Women in Policing." *Journal of Police Science and Administration* 12 (1984): 307.

Rafky, David (1974) "My Husband the Cop." *Police Chief* (August 1974): 65.

Robin, Gerald, and Richard Anson. *Introduction to the Criminal Justice System*. New York: Harper and Row, 1991. 113–16

Selye, Hans. *The Stress of Life*. New York: McGraw-Hill, 1976.

Shook, H.C. "Pitfalls in Policing." *Police Chief* 5 (1978): 8–10.

Somodevilla, S.H. "The Psychologist's Role in the Police Department." *Police Chief* (April 1978): 21.

Stenmark, David, Linda DePiano, John Wackwitz, C.D. Cannon, and Steven Walfish. "Wives of Police Officers: Issues Related to Family—Job Satisfaction and Job Longevity." *Journal of Police Science and Administration* 10 (1982): 230.

Stratton, John. "Police Stress: An Overview." *Police Chief* (April 1978): 59–60.

Swanson, Charles R., and Leonard Territo. *Police Administration: Structures, Processes and Behavior*. New York: MacMillan, 1984.

USA Today (September 15, 1986): 3.

Violanti, John. "Stress Patterns in Police Work: A Longitudinal Study." *Journal of Police Science and Administration* 11 (1983): 213.

Violanti, John, James Marshall, and Barbara Howe. "Police Occupational Demands,

Psychological Distress and the Coping Function of Alcohol." *Journal of Occupational Medicine* 25 (1983): 455–58.

———. "Stress Coping and Alcohol Use: The Police Connection." *Journal of Police Science and Administration* 2 (1985): 108.

Webb, S.D., and D.L. Smith. "Police Stress: A Conceptual Overview." *Criminal Justice Review* 8 (1980): 251–57.

Wexler, Judie G., and Deana Logan. "Sources of Stress among Women Police Officers." *Journal of Police Science and Administration* 11 (1981): 46-53.

Whittemore, Hank. "Ministers under Stress." *Parade Magazine* (April 14, 1991): 4–6.

Stress: Coping Mechanisms

Over the past several years, society in general and a number of professional fields in particular have shown an increasing concern over the concept and manifestations of stress (Sewell, 1983). Some consider stress to be the events external to the organism that make demands on it, while others suggest that it is the organism's response to challenging events (Selye, 1978). Finally, others view both the external and internal events as the stress and emphasize the interaction between the environment and the response (Lazarus and Launier, 1978). Taken as a whole this research has shown a relationship between stress and physical illness, as well as stress and physical trauma. This is particularly true of people in what are considered to be the "front line" occupations: air-traffic controllers, hospital emergency room staffs, social workers, and police officers. Of particular interest is the special concern that law-enforcement officers have received in regard to their stressors.

Police work is highly stressful since it is one of the few occupations where an employee is asked to continually face physical dangers and to put his or her life on the line at any time. The police officer is exposed to violence, cruelty, and aggression, and is often required to make extremely critical decisions in high-pressured situations (Goolkasian et al., 1985; Territo and Vetter, 1983). Officers are often called upon to maintain social order while working long hours, experiencing conflicts in their job demands, and having to face hostile feelings of an unusually nonsupportive community (Fell, Richard, and Wallace, 1980).

Stressors have been identified by Kroes (1976), Roberts (1975), Terry (1981), and several others who have conducted extensive studies into law-enforcement occupational stressors. They have grouped the stressors into four broad categories: (1) organizational practices and characteristics, (2) criminal-justice system practices and characteristics, (3) public practices and characteristics, and (4) police work itself (Territo and Vetter, 1983). All of these pressures combine to create unusual occupational stressors in addition to whatever individual stress the officer may be experiencing. When individual stress reaches certain levels it may lead to illness by (1) disrupting tissue functions through neurohormonal mechanisms, (2) causing the choice of coping activities that are inappropriate and/or damaging to one's health, or (3) causing the person to minimize the significance of his or her disease symptoms (Farmer and Monahan, 1980).

The emphasis of police officer stress, to date, has focused on one dimension of the stress process: stressors. The coping element of the process has been largely overlooked. Coping behaviors are an important aspect of the stress process. Coping refers to both overt and covert behaviors that reduce or eliminate psychological distress and stressful conditions (Fleishman, 1984). Coping represents the things that people do to deal with life strains they encounter. Pearlin and Schooler (1978) have classified coping behaviors into three categories: (1) responses that change the situation, (2) responses that alter the meaning or appraisal of the stress, and (3) responses intended to control distressful feelings. Other researchers have offered similar typologies consisting of active-behavioral (problem-focused), avoidance (emotion-focused), and active-cognitive coping (Billings and Moos, 1981; Moos and Schaeffer, 1986). The active-cognitive coping category includes trying to interpret the meaning of the event, logical analysis, and mental preparation. Problem-focused coping involves the practical aspects of seeking information and support, taking action, and identifying alternative rewards. These are adaptive strategies. Emotion-focused coping is affective regulation, emotional discharge, and resigned acceptance of the stress, and it is oftentimes maladaptive.

The way an individual copes depends on his or her understanding of the stressful situation, making sense of it, and developing appropriate responses to it (Lazarus 1967). Research by Violanti and Marshall (1983) has indicated that police officers utilize coping mechanisms that increase the stress rather than alleviate it (Violanti and Marshall, 1983; Violanti, Marshal, and Howe, 1985). This research showed that police officers used maladaptive coping mechanisms such as alcohol, drugs, deviance, and cynicism. The use of these emotion-focused solutions has a tendency to change the law-enforcement officer into a law violator, thus increasing not only their personal stress but also that of the department and fellow officers.

Additional research has shown that law-enforcement officers have no preference for adaptive coping mechanisms over maladaptive coping mechanisms, and in many instances could not identify coping mechanisms that were maladaptive (Fain and McCormick, 1988). Adaptive coping is characterized as problem-solving approaches to deal directly with the stressful situation by seeking and implementing solutions. Maladaptive coping, on the other hand, does not deal directly with the problem and therefore is not likely to relieve the individual's anxiety. Indeed, maladaptive coping is more likely to exacerbate stress and have a negative effect on job satisfaction (Parasuraman and Cleek, 1984). Research by Kirmeryer and Diamond (1985) indicates that the personality type of the police officer strongly dictates their selection of a coping mechanism. Police officers who have a type A personality are more likely to make emotive-focused coping decisions, while type B personality types are more likely to react slowly to the stress and maintain

their emotional distance. All of this research indicates that police personnel are experiencing high levels of stress without a clear understanding of how to alleviate that stress in acceptable ways.

It has been suggested that one of the functions of coping behaviors is to decrease the impact of the demands of stress (Marshall, 1979; Pearlin and Schooler, 1978). Therefore, the use of an appropriate coping strategy might function as a buffer against stress, both present and future, and limit the negative impact of the stress. A model offered by Zeitlin (1984) depicts coping as a process in which personal resources are used to manage stress. This model approaches coping from a cognitive and behavioral standpoint and emphasizes the importance of both external and internal resources for coping with stress (Figure 1). Adaptive coping mechanisms are derived from these two main resources.

Coping is proposed in this model to be an interrelated four-step process. The first step is the cognitive appraisal of the stress-causing event and its meaning. The significance of the stress is widely influenced by the beliefs, morals, values, and expectations of the person. As police officers are generally more conservative than the general population, their values may sway them away from seeking help or convince them that there is nothing wrong. The second step consists of decision-making, which is dependent upon the external and internal resources of the person experiencing the stress. These resources include personal beliefs and

FIGURE 1

Coping with Stress Model

EXTERNAL RESOURCES
Support Systems
Material Resources
↓

PERCEPTION OF STRESS → DECISION MAKING
Analysis of • Determine Plan
Resources • of Action
→ COPING EFFORT

↑
INTERNAL RESOURCES
Beliefs and Values
Physical and Psychological Status
Coping Behavior Patterns

value systems, coping behavioral patterns, physical and psychological status (internal resources), and social support systems and material resources (external resources) (Ellis and Greiger, 1977; Lazarus, 1966; McCubbin and Patterson, 1981; Zeitlin, Williamson, and Rosenblatt, 1987). It is in this area that law-enforcement agencies should place the greatest emphasis in providing assistance. The lack of positive external and internal resources, or the reluctance to depend on those available, is a primary stumbling block in the path for police officers coping with stress.

The third step in the coping process involves action on the decision reached, either by making a reappraisal of the stressful event or by implementing some type of coping effort. Because this is greatly influenced by the resources available to police officers, any changes implemented in stage two will affect this subsequent stage. Finally, the fourth step is an evaluation of the outcome of the coping effort and its effectiveness in relieving the stressful event. The coping process is offered in four steps, however, each step in the process is dependent upon the preceding step. Hence, any change or intervention that can be initiated at any point in the coping process will alter the outcome of the coping effort and ultimately the coping behavior (Zeitlin, Williamson, and Rosenblatt, 1987). Law-enforcement officers appear to have a deficiency of external or internal resources or at least have difficulty accessing these resources. Research has shown that when using these resources, police officers will choose coping behaviors that do not appropriately relieve the situation and oftentimes enhance the stress (Fain and McCormick, 1988; Violanti and Marshall 1983). Fortunately, as Zeitlin and her colleagues (1987) have pointed out, the internal and external resources can be changed and this will impact upon the police officers' coping efforts.

The internal resources, beliefs and values, physical and psychological status, and coping behavior patterns can be altered by the use of staff counselors, psychologists, and psychiatrists. Police officers originally rejected the notion of talking to outsiders about their personal and occupational problems but have become more open in this type of response. Anderson and Bauer (1987) offer advice for professionals in the mental health field who treat police officers, as well as in those areas in which law-enforcement officers may need assistance. One of the counseling programs that they offer and recommend for law-enforcement officers is a stress management session. In addition to counseling by professionals, the use of police peer counseling has become increasingly popular. Klein (1989) describes the training program that eligible police officers go through, under the guidance of a clinical psychologist, to be trained as a peer counselor. These peer counselors are trained to help officers with developing constructive ways of dealing with stress, and with recognizing what they can change and what they cannot. Peer counselors also make recommendations for further counseling or other types of mental health assistance.

Programs that affect the internal resources must deal directly with the police officer. That is not to minimize the importance of the family or friends but to emphasize the importance of the police officer. In addition to the assistance offered by these professionals, the internal resources of the police officer can be enhanced by training programs to improve their use of adaptive coping skills rather than maladaptive skills. Ellison and Genz (1983) offer techniques for individual stress management that include goal setting, time management, financial planning, and physical fitness. Norvell and Belles (1987) have designed a forty-hour training program for supervisory personnel. The purpose of this training program is to reduce the stress of the participating officers, and at the same time provide them with information that will allow them to observe stressful behavior in fellow officers.

An example of a training program that has proven successful with other professionals in high-stress occupations is the Stress Management Workshop. This four-hour workshop focuses on the individual and attempts to increase the participants' awareness of stresses both at work and at home. The majority of the training involves helping the professional learn techniques for healthy coping. The areas emphasized are personal management skills, relationship skills, outlook skills, and stamina skills.

Personal management skills include time and energy management. The participants are taught the importance of setting personal goals and working toward them, the importance of time management and prioritization skills, even in the face of not being able to plan their work day, and the importance of pacing themselves even when the schedule they have is set by someone else. Relationship skills involve ways to create a supportive environment for others, learning contact skills to help form friendships, listening skills to attend to others, as well as assertiveness skills to address self needs. Outlook skills are taught to enable the participant to view life from different perspectives, to learn what situations must be surrendered to, and what situations must be taken on faith. However, it also includes learning how to use positive self-reaffirming statements, imagination, and humor effectively. Finally, stamina skills involve learning how exercise, relaxation, and nutrition will fortify the participant to resist stress and relieve tension when they arise.

Of equal importance are the external resources that a police officer can depend upon. Social supports play a "buffering" role in the potential impact of stressor events, contribute to overall improved physical health by placing the individuals in a better position to cope with the stress, and, finally, provide a preventive role in reducing the number of stressful events that one experiences (Steinglass, Weisstub, and De-Nour, 1988). Many times police officers hold their families and spouses at bay, not allowing them to experience the hardships that accompany being a police officer (Besner and Robinson, 1982; James and Nelson, 1975; Stratton, 1984). This can be alleviated in part by providing the same training to family and spouses that is provided to police officers for stress management. In addition, social support systems should receive additional training in the recognition of the danger signs of burnout from occupational stress (Stratton, 1984).

The recognition of stress in police work has increased the need for effective coping on the part of police officers. Coping is a product of both personal and situational influences, and a better understanding of police officer coping will enhance their ability to face stressful situations. Further, the learning and use of adaptive coping responses may diminish the amount of stress that the officer faces in the future. Presently there are several training programs in place for police officers and other professionals in stress prone areas, but little research is available on the effectiveness of these programs.

Following an existing model of stress and coping responses, emphasis in any police training program should focus on improving the internal processes of officers and prepare their external support systems for the potential problems they will face. These programs should focus on personal and situational management techniques that will adapt to the confined environment situations facing police officers. In addition, the training and/or counseling should emphasize coping situations that will deal with solving the stress problem or deal directly with the stressor, rather than allowing a response that masks the situation. Only when these types of programs are widely accepted in law enforcement, and by the officers employed, will there be any possibility of reducing stress through appropriate and acceptable coping mechanisms.

Dawn B. Young

Bibliography

Anderson, W., and B. Bauer. "Law Enforcement Officers: The Consequences of Exposure to Violence." *Journal of Counseling and Development* 3 (1987): 65, 381–84.

Besner, H.F., and S.J. Robinson. *Understanding and Solving Your Police Marriage Problems.* Springfield, IL: Charles C. Thomas, 1982. 40–54.

Billings, A.C., and R.H. Moos. "The Role of Coping Responses and Social Resources in Attenuating the Stress of Life Events." *Journal of Behavioral Medicine* 4 (1981): 139–57.

Ellis A., and R. Greiger, eds. *Handbook of Rational-Emotive Therapy.* New York: Springer, 1977.

Ellison, K.W., and J.L. Genz. *Stress and the Police Officer.* Springfield, IL: Charles C. Thomas, 1983. 106–34.

Fain, D.B., and G.M. McCormick. "Use of Coping Mechanisms as a Means of Stress Reduction in North Louisiana." *Journal of Police Science and Administration* 16 (1988): 121–28.

Farmer, R.E., and L.H. Monahan. "The Prevention Model for Stress Reduction: A Concept Paper." *Journal of Police Science and Administration* 8 (1980): 55–60.

Fell, R.D., W.C. Richard, and W.L. Wallace. "Psychological Job Stress and the Police Officer." *Journal of Police Science and Administration* 8 (1980): 139–44.

Fleishman, J.A. "Personality Characteristics and Coping Patterns." *Journal of Health and Social Behavior* 25 (1984): 229–44.

Goolkasian, Gail A., et al. 1985. *Coping with Police Stress.* Washington, DC: National Institute of Justice, U.S. Department of Justice, J-LEAA-013-78.

James, P., and M. Nelson. *Police Wife: How to Live with the Law and Like It.* Springfield, IL: Charles C. Thomas, 1975. 13–26.

Kirmeryer, S.L., and A. Diamond. *Journal of Occupational Behavior* 6 (1985): 183–95.

Klein, R. "Police Peer Counseling." *FBI Law Enforcement Bulletin* 10 (1989): 1–5.

Kroes, W.H. *Society's Victim—The Policeman: An Analysis of Job Stress in Policing.* Springfield, IL: Charles C. Thomas, 1976.

Lazarus, R.S. *Psychological Stress and the Coping Process.* New York: McGraw-Hill, 1966.

———. "Cognitive and Personality Factors Underlying Threat and Coping." In *Psychological Stress.* Eds. Appley and Trumball. New York: Appleton-Century Crofts, 1967. 151–81.

Lazarus, R.S., and R. Launier. "Stress-Related Transactions between Persons and Environment." In *Perspectives in Interactional Psychology.* Eds. L.A. Pervin and M. Lewis. New York: Plenum, 1978. 287–327.

McCubbin, H., and J. Patterson. *Systematic Assessment of Family Stress, Resources and Coping.* St. Paul: University of Minnesota, 1981.

Marshall, J.R. "Stress, Strain and Coping." *Journal of Health and Social Behavior* 20 (1979): 200–01.

Moos, R.H., and J.A. Schaeffer. "Overview and Perspective." In *Coping with Life Crises.* Ed. R.H. Moos. New York: Plenum, 1986.

Norvell, N., and D. Belles. "A Stress Management Curriculum for Law Enforcement Personnel Supervisors." *Police Chief* 8 (1987): 57–59.

Parasuraman, S., and M.A. Cleek. "Coping Behaviors and Managers' Affective Reactions to Role Stressors." *Journal of Vocational Behavior* 24 (1984): 179–93.

Pearlin, L.I., and C. Schooler. "The Structure of Coping." *Journal of Health and Social Behavior* 19 (1978): 2–21.

Roberts, M.D. "Job Stress in Law Enforcement: A Treatment and Prevention Program." In *Job Stress and the Police Officer: Identifying Stress Reduction Techniques.* Eds. H. Kroes and J. Hurrell. Washington DC: U.S. Department of Health, Education and Welfare, 1975.

Selye, H. "The Stress of Police Work." *Police Stress* 1 (1978): 7–9.

Sewell, J.D. "The Development of a Critical Life Events Scale for Law Enforcement." *Journal of Police Science and Administration* 11 (1983): 109–16.

Steinglass, P., E. Weisstub, and A.K. De-Nour. "Perceived Personal Networks as Mediators of Stress Reactions." *American Journal of Psychiatry* 145 (1988): 1259–64.

Stratton, J.G. *Police Passages.* Manhattan Beach, CA: Glennon Publishing, 1984. 101–48, 287–318.

Territo, L., and H.J. Vetter. "Stress and Police Personnel." *Journal of Police Science and Administration* 11 (1983): 195–207.

Terry, III, C.W. "Police Stress: The Empirical Evidence. *Journal of Police Science and Administration* 9 (1981): 61–75.

Violanti, J.M., and J.R. Marshall. "The Police Stress Process." *Journal of Police Science and Administration* 11 (1983): 389–94.

Violanti, J.M., J.R. Marshall, and B. Howe. *Journal of Police Science and Administration* 13(2) (1985): 106–10.

Zeitlin, S. *The Coping Inventory.* Bensenville, IL: Scholastic Testing Service, 1984.

Zeitlin, S., G.G. Williamson, and W.P. Rosenblatt. *Journal of Counseling and Development* 65 (1987): 446.

Strikes and Job Actions

Strikes and job actions are intentional alterations, disruptions, or suspensions of the work roles of a significant number of employees for the purpose of forcing employers to satisfy worker demands. Among public safety employees these actions have included a number of *covert* job actions and *overt* strike tactics. The former category includes principally the "ticket blizzard," in which the issuing of traffic citations reaches epidemic proportions, and the "blue flu," or sick-ins, during which extraordinary numbers of officers report themselves ill and unable to work, as well as other speed-up and slow-down tactics. The latter category is reserved for the strike, in which significant numbers of officers overtly refuse to work in order to achieve their collective goals. Such activities have been widely and popularly perceived as disruptive of and an interference with, if not a grave threat to, commonwealth interests. The following paragraphs focus principally on the *overt* strike, and only incidentally address covert forms of job action.

Arguments: Pro and Con

At the outset it is well to recognize that "unionization" and "strikes" are not coextensive phenomena. Nonetheless, in the public perspective on these matters, fear of strikes by police often appears to dominate the collective consciousness. Anticipation of the strike, then, necessarily influences attitudes toward unions. For that reason, arguments regarding the propriety of police unionization and the right of officers to strike are intimately related. Publicly accepted understandings of the purpose and role of unions, on the one hand, and the importance assigned to the role of police (as well as firefighters and some other public employees), on the other, have often led "unions" and "police" to be seen as incompatible. As a result, the unionization of and strikes by public-sector employees, e.g., sanitation workers, schoolteachers, firefighters, and police, have traditionally been regarded as outrageous and inappropriate. The core of the opposition to police involvement in such activities was succinctly expressed by then-governor (of Massachusetts) Calvin Coolidge when he fired striking Boston police officers in 1919. He stated: "There is no right to strike against the public safety by anybody, anywhere, anytime." For several decades following the Boston police strike, public and official opposition to police unionization and, of course, to their striking, was overwhelming. Only since the 1960s and 1970s has this attitude tended to soften and become less rigid. The opposition has several facets.

An early argument against strikes by public-sector employees invoked the element of legal sovereignty. Based on the political philosophy of Thomas Hobbes, the sovereignty argument contends that government has the sole power and authority to determine public policy. Granting the right to negotiate the terms of that policy to any lesser interest group—as would be the case if an organization (union) representing public-sector workers were afforded the right to strike—negates the authority and power of the state. Accordingly, that condition would threaten the "whole people" and the commonwealth, and risk a decline in the democratic political process since, at least in theory, that process precludes sharing public authority with private groups. In short, the sovereignty argument rests on the notion of political elitism as well as on an implied intolerance of dissent and democratic principles.

Over time there have been several challenges to the sovereignty argument. First, since legislatures have allowed private individuals to sue governmental bodies for negligence, governmental sovereignty has already been breached. Second, if in a democracy the sovereignty of government reflects the will of the ruled, it is plausible for that will to support the right of private groups to strike against, bargain with, or otherwise negotiate public policy with government. Further, it is argued that the state's legal sovereignty or supremacy should not be confused with political sovereignty, i.e., the processes by which public policy is created and conducted. Given the distinction between legal and political sovereignty, then, in principle, collective bargaining with its employees neither diminishes government's ultimate legal authority nor conflicts with the ideals of a democratic society.

When applied specifically to public-safety workers such as police, the foregoing arguments have been refined and supplemented. Of particular importance is the issue of strikes among employees who provide allegedly essential services, i.e., those regarded as indispensable for maintaining the health, safety, and well-being of the populace. There are several facets to this issue: First is the concern over the fear generated in the population by the suspension of such services; second, there is concern that the supposedly essential nature of their duties affords these workers undue influence in the collective-bargaining process; finally, the concern is that taken together these and other matters put government at a disadvantage in negotiations. However logical, evidence (see below) suggests the basis on which much of this concern rests, i.e., the dire consequences of suspending essential services, including injury, loss of life, destruction of property, loss of property, loss of profits and revenue, and a decline in public order, are more anticipated than real.

Additionally, arguments developed in opposition to specific reforms sought by line officers have frequently been converted into arguments opposing unionization of police officers. For example, efforts to establish a dues-checkoff system, of great help in maintaining organizational stability and rank-and-file solidarity, were attacked on the grounds that government agencies cannot be used to collect private debts; line officers' quests for the establishment of formal grievance procedures were opposed by many police administrators as a threat to the civil-service system and to the customary lines of authority in police departments; and efforts to secure collective-bargaining agreements have been beaten back as unconstitutional delegations of authority. Further, granting police the right to unionize and engage in collective bargaining has been staunchly opposed by those who regard police in the military/soldier model. Given that perception, police are not entitled to the same rights granted other public-sector employees. Finally, the alternative model of police, that of professional, has also been used to argue against police unionization, on the grounds that such an arrangement is inimical to professionalization.

History

Rhetoric concerning the issue of police unionization and related matters exaggerates the number and frequency of job actions engaged in by police officers. By the early 1900s police were unionized in no fewer than thirty-seven American cities. However, in the years following the Boston police strike of 1919, the legitimacy and hence the organizational basis necessary for initiating successful job actions by police were largely extinguished in the United States. Thus, despite efforts to restore police unions prior to mid-century, it was not until the 1950s and 1960s that police fraternal and benevolent associations and other labor organizations experienced significant official (though begrudging) approval in the form of dues-checkoff systems, formal grievance procedures, and collective-bargaining rights. To be sure, such recognition and concessions were not won without the threat and/or use of job actions such as sick-ins, slowdowns, and ticket blizzards in places such as Atlanta, Boston, Detroit, New York, and Pittsburgh. However, it was not until the decade of the 1970s that police strikes occurred in any regular way. Let's examine the record of job actions, both overt and covert.

One of the earliest and most indelible American experiences with a police strike was the 1919 walkout of Boston police due to dissatisfaction with wages and general working conditions (police in Cincinnati, Ohio, had struck in September 1918). For three days thereafter, Boston was the scene of an inordinate degree of robbery, vandalism, petty theft, looting, and general mob behavior. In all, eight persons were killed. Order was not restored before

the mayor's request for the mobilization of the state guard was met by then-Governor Calvin Coolidge. Beyond the riotous actions of citizens, this strike ushered in several decades of strongly negative sentiment regarding unionization of public employees in general and police officers in particular. In some jurisdictions, even police-benevolent and fraternal societies were outlawed.

Such antiunion sentiment did not survive, however, and during the post–World War II period, the unionization of police officers was again being pursued with growing vigor. By the late 1960s and the 1970s the "ghost" of 1919 had been dispelled. To no small degree, the aggressiveness of the increasing number of police unions at this time was matched and likely encouraged by similar activity among sanitation workers, schoolteachers, firefighters, prison/jail personnel, public hospital nurses, and other public employees, Indeed, the militance of public workers during the 1970s was in keeping with the generally militant, anti-establishment attitude that prevailed during that and the preceding decade. Thus, relative to other categories of public employees, police job actions at that time were hardly unique.

The precise number of covert police job actions occurring during the 1960s and 1970s is not known. Many of these were either threatened actions or were so brief or subtle in character as to escape widespread attention and recording. More accurate is the record of overt actions—police strikes—during recent years. According to the Bureau of Labor Statistics, between 1970 and 1980 no fewer than 215 police strikes occurred in U.S. cities, and job action was threatened in several others. Examination of this matter in terms of refined statistical data is in order.

Data compiled by the Bureau of Labor Statistics of the U.S. Department of Labor shed considerable light on work stoppages among government employees ("stoppages" being defined as all interruptions of employee activity lasting a full day or shift or longer and involving six workers or more). Examination of these data for the eleven-year period of 1970 through 1980 (see Table 1) indicates that police strikes constitute a very small proportion of all work stoppages among local government employees. For example, during these eleven years of heightened job actions, police strikes annually averaged only 4.9 percent of all local government strikes. During this same period the annual average number of police officers on strike comprised a mere 2.9 percent of all local government workers on strike, and contributed a mere 1.2 percent to the employee days lost due to such strikes. Let's refine these remarks slightly.

As these data indicate, in only two years, 1971 and 1979, did the number of striking police officers comprise more than 2 percent of all local government workers engaged in work stoppages, and in four of these years they represented fewer than 1 percent of all striking local government workers. (The highly exceptional figures for 1971 reflect the single strike of New York City police officers. That strike, January 14, 1971, involved approximately 2,100 officers, or about 89.7 percent of all police officers on strike during that year.) Further, during nine of these eleven years striking police officers constituted substantially fewer than 2 percent of all striking local government workers.

Equally important are comparative data on the duration of police strikes and those of other local government employees, as measured by the number of employee days idle due to strikes. Thus in only two of the eleven years (1971 and 1979) did the number of employee days idle due to police strikes exceed 2 percent of total days idle due to all local government work stoppages. Of the total number of employee days lost due to local government strikes during this period, police strikes contributed a mere 1.2 percent. Stated differently, the average number of employee days lost per annum due to police strikes is about .51 percent of the mean number of employee days lost due to all local government work stoppages. Taken together, except for the few inflated instances resulting from atypical conditions, these data justify the conclusion that, statistically, and relative to other local government agencies, job actions among police are piddling. Nonetheless, for many observers the importance of police strikes is not a matter of relativism but one of consequences. We now turn to that matter.

Consequences

The consequences of strikes by police may be assessed in any of several ways. One is to examine their effects on working conditions for officers, including changes in wages or benefits, and other work-related issues. A second area of assessment is the influence of these actions on law and public policy pertaining to such job action among public-sector employees. Finally, one may assess their consequences vis-à-vis alteration in crime patterns and, relatedly, the

---

TABLE 1

Work Stoppages by Police and Local Government Workers, 1970–1980

(Workers Involved and Employee Days Idle in Thousands)

Year	Stoppages			Workers Involved			Employee Days Idle		
	Police		Local	Police		Local	Police		Local
	No.	%	No.	No.	%	No.	No.	%	No.
1970	28	7.25	386	1.6	.35	168.9	6.8	.51	1,330.5
1971	17	5.59	304	23.4	17.06	137.1	110.6	13.63	811.6
1972	15	4.47	335	.6	.52	114.7	1.6	.16	983.5
1973	5	1.40	357	.6	.32	183.7	1.7	.07	2,166.3
1974	12	3.44	348	1.5	1.10	135.4	4.5	.34	1,316.3
1975	11	2.46	446	2.1	.83	252.0	5.9	.31	1,903.9
1976	15	4.26	352	1.9	1.20	146.8	3.2	.21	1,542.6
1977	19	5.17	367	2.2	1.61	136.2	7.8	.49	1,583.3
1978	21	4.82	435	3.1	1.81	171.0	5.9	.39	1,498.8
1979	35	6.52	536	9.5	4.62	205.5	55.9	2.26	2,467.1
1980	37	7.5	493	3.7	1.74	212.7	11.5	.51	2,240.9

Source: U.S. Department of Labor, Bureau of Labor Statistics. *Analysis of Work Stoppages*, 1970, Bulletin 1727; *Analysis of Work Stoppages*, 1971, Bulletin 1777; and *Work Stoppages in Government*, 1973, Report 437; 1974, Report 453; 1975, Report 483; 1976, Report 532; 1978, Report 582; 1979, Report 629; 1980, Report 2110.

meaning of police strikes for the security of persons and property in our society. In brief, do police strikes jeopardize commonwealth interests? Given the public apprehension over that matter, and the popular idea that police are indispensable for the prevention and control of crime, assessment of the consequences of police strikes will be limited to the third area of concern.

There are two schools of thought concerning the effects of police strikes on criminal activity. First is the view that during the police's absence, the criminal and lawless elements are free to indulge their perversities and pose a threat to social orderliness, and that police stand as a "thin blue line" between civility and savagery. The disorderly conditions during and allegedly because of the Boston and Montreal (1969) police strikes are often cited to support this perspective. The second and competing perspective suggests that, in fact, police have less influence on fluctuations in the rates of crime than any of several other factors, and that police have little or no way of preventing or controlling criminal behavior. In an effort to test the validity of these conflicting perspectives, particularly as they pertain to four major types of crime (burglary, larceny, auto theft, and robbery), the author gathered and analyzed relevant FBI data for eleven U.S. cities experiencing police strikes during the decade of the 1970s. Special attention was given to comparing the official rates of these four major types of crime during three two-month intervals, regarded as the prestrike, strike, and poststrike periods. Logically, the perspective suggesting the absence of police (as during a strike), resulting in a breakdown in public order, leads to the prediction that crime rates would rise from the prestrike to the strike period, and decline upon the termination of the strike when ordinary police patrols, etc., are resumed. On the other hand, the competing perspective suggests that offense rates would fluctuate rather independently of police strikes. That is, rates during strike periods may rise, fall, or remain constant relative to pre- and poststrike periods.

The experience of the eleven cities studied provides only minimal support for the "police presence" argument. That is, of the forty-four instances (eleven cities times four offenses) that might have yielded evidence supporting that perspective, only seventeen instances (38.6 percent) did so. And of the seventeen, only eleven (25 percent of the original forty-four tests) were

sufficiently strong to be regarded as other than chance variations. More refined consideration of these results for cities having longer and shorter police strikes, for cities of varying size, and in terms of the specific offense categories revealed no patterned data supportive of the "police presence" perspective.

The data generated in this investigation challenge the view that police strikes jeopardize the well-being of persons and property; they lend validity to the belief that police strikes have little or no impact on rates of reported crime. One possible explanation for the lack of civil disorder or a rise in crime rates during strike periods is that municipalities often use contingency policing plans and employ surrogate forces to fill the gap created by striking personnel. Use of these forces, it is argued, creates the impression that policing goes on as usual and rule violators are thus kept in line. Consistent with that theme, it has been argued that it was the absence of these plans and forces that led to the violence and property destruction in the Boston and Montreal strikes. However, careful examination of the experience of cities using and not using these plans and forces reveals little evidence in support of this explanation. In terms of strike-related changes in crime rates, cities lacking such plans fared no worse than those employing them.

An added concern over the consequences of police strikes rests on their supposed impact on municipal revenues and the "ripple effect" of this on various other government programs and operations. For example, what is lost when police officers refuse to write traffic citations, when nonstriking personnel must be recruited and paid (often at overtime wage levels), etc.? Examination of this matter suggests the economic effects of work stoppages are less than anticipated, with one study reporting a loss of about .20 percent of a city's annual revenue due to a ticket strike lasting one month. This has led observers to conclude that, unlike civilian strikes, among police these are political rather than economic phenomena.

In summary, careful investigation rather than speculation suggests that the presumed socially destructive consequences of police strikes are seldom realized. Just as the police presence is not a deterrent to crime, neither is its absence an inducement. This interpretation accords with other research concluding that (1) with the exception of saturation methods, variation in the intensity of police patrols has little effect on rule-violating behavior, and that (2) in most instances of police strikes there is little or no increase in the incidence of disorderly behavior. Finally, these data on the consequences of police strikes suggest that at least some of the arguments against police unionization and the use of the strike as a means of bargaining are without foundation in fact. Not only do such arguments rest on a questionable understanding of the basis of unlawful conduct, they also rest on an apparent overstatement of the role of police and an understatement of the importance of informal means of social control. Particularly the "essential services" argument seems to rest on questionable grounds. On these grounds, then, it appears safe to conclude that police strikes are unlikely to have the dire consequences anticipated by Calvin Coolidge.

Conclusions

It is apparent that these few paragraphs stand as the briefest survey of a complex, highly emotional issue. We may nonetheless conclude that, characteristically, the politicization of police, including the resort to unionization and strikes, rests on the same general issues leading other workers to take similar action—wages, benefits, and general work conditions. Despite this common element, a resort to unionization and striking by police (and a few other categories of public workers) has been defined and evaluated in qualitatively different terms and almost exclusively on the basis of short-run, parochial interests. On that basis, job actions among police have been the topic of far more discussion and resistance, and the basis of more public anguish than their scope and consequences would necessitate.

To a marked degree, the perceived differences between police and other segments of the work force, and the resulting public anguish over police strikes, rests on a widespread, taken for granted (but unfounded) belief in the indispensability of police, that in their absence society would soon revert to a condition of savagery. On such grounds, public policy has been created and administered, though perhaps unintentionally, so as to penalize both the police as well as the general population in this democratic society. Police have been penalized by being subject to policies denying them the opportunities for self-determination enjoyed by other working groups. There is a dual paradox involved in this matter. On the one hand, to the degree that police helped generate and perpetu-ate the myth of their indispensability, they contributed to their own "victimization" by creating an atmosphere inimical to union activity. On the other hand, by its failure to more carefully evaluate the myth of indispensability as a factor in formulating public policy, the public has contributed to its own anguish.

By far the greater price has been paid by the general citizenry, which, historically, has been influenced by and experienced the effects of an ill-advised policy in this area. Ours is regarded as a democratic society. Logically, that should lead to organizational management policies and operational styles of policing that would promote their democratization, including, among other things, greater opportunity for self-governance, greater police–citizen interaction, and the encouragement of police identification with pro-democratic (rather than right-wing) forces in society. Unions promote such democratization. Yet what we have experienced historically and what continues to the present is an organizational style and policies that promote a military/professional model of policing quite at odds with the ideal of a democratic society. The prevailing model of police is one that promotes elitism and authoritarianism, fosters the use of deadly force (e.g., SWAT teams that cannot be distinguished from the armed forces), that segregates or isolates citizens from their police, and promotes an atmosphere of mutual suspicion and distrust. This is a model of policing more consistent with totalitarianism than democracy. We might conclude, then, with the thought that to the degree that it promotes democratization, the effort to promote police unionization in our society, including the right to strike, may prove to be one of the healthiest contributions to the future of the American system of policing.

Erdwin H. Pfuhl, Jr.

Bibliography

Bopp, William J., and Michael Wiatrowski. "Police Strike in New Orleans: A City Abandoned by Its Police." *Police Journal* 55 (April 1982): 125–35.

Burpo, John H. *Police Unions in the Civil Service Setting.* Washington, DC: U.S. Department of Justice, Law Enforcement Assistance Administration, October 1979.

Gammage, Allen Z., and Stanley L. Sachs. *Police Unions.* Springfield, IL: Charles C. Thomas, 1972.

Gentel, William D., and Martha Handman. *Police Strikes: Causes and Prevention.* Gaithersburg, MD: International Association of Chiefs of Police, 1979.

Grimes, John A. *Work Stoppages: A Tale of Three Cities.* Washington, DC: Labor Management Relations Service, 1970.

Juris, Hervey A., and Peter Feuille. *Police Unionism, Power and Impact in Public Sector Bargaining.* Lexington, MA: Lexington, 1973.

Larson, Richard E. *Police Accountability, Performance Measures and Unionism.* Lexington, MA: Lexington, 1978.

Pfuhl, Erdwin H., Jr. "Police Strikes and Conventional Crime: A Look at the Data." *Criminology* 21 (November 1983): 489–503.

Swank, Calvin J., and James A. Coner. *The Police Personnel System.* New York: John Wiley and Sons, 1983.

Wellington, Harry H., and Ralph K. Winter, Jr. *The Unions and the Cities.* Washington, DC: Brookings Institution, 1972.

Supreme Court Decisions

While often characterized as enforcers of the law, the police in America must also be upholders of the law. In carrying forth their law-enforcement functions the police are mandated to operate under a series of legal guidelines that have been created by statute or by case decisions of courts, or that flow from the U.S. Constitution as well as individual state constitutions. These legal rules establish the procedures under which the police are to operate and often provide sanctions for breaches of these rules. The exclusion from court use of evidence obtained in an unconstitutional manner is perhaps the best known of the sanctions against improper police conduct.

Until the middle of the twentieth century, the law regarding police procedures was fairly staid; most states followed the English common law rules concerning arrest, search and seizure, use of force, confessions, and the like and little thought was given to development of a unique set of American legal aspects of policing. State legislative enactments in the field of criminal law related largely to what constituted illegal conduct, not how that conduct was to be investigated or how offenders were to be dealt with by the police. Similarly, state appellate courts reviewed relatively few criminal convictions, and those that did receive review often turned upon an interpretation of state statute or a determination of the authority of a "constable" at common law. Civil suits against police officers for improper conduct were rate, though not unheard of. Most important, the federal court system, including the U.S. Supreme Court, rarely became involved in review of state criminal convictions; the notion of federally protected rights being applied to defendants in state criminal proceedings was simply not considered. The few state criminal cases that were reviewed by the Supreme Court considered primarily whether the state had exercised jurisdiction properly. The constitutional doctrine of "due process" as a direct element of the penal relationship between the state and its citizens was not even successfully advanced before the Supreme Court until 1927.

The "hands-off" approach of federal courts was to change drastically following World War II. The federal courts' enforcement, led by the Supreme Court, of various due process rights in state criminal cases changed the nature of American policing. Process became as important as product; adherence to proper police procedure became as important as the factual guilt of the suspect. This entry will highlight the prime court decisions that have most affected the way in which police officers perform their law-enforcing role. The case decisions examined will cover the topics of arrest and detention of suspects, search and seizure, confessions, and use of force.

Arrest and Detention of Suspects

Perhaps the best known police activity is the arrest of criminal suspects. Law-enforcement officers apprehend offenders primarily in order to take them to court to answer to a criminal charge. Today, the circumstances under which an arrest may lawfully be made are normally dictated by state statute. For many years all jurisdictions have required the minimal constitutional standard of "probable cause" in order to make a valid warrantless arrest or a sworn statement of probable cause in order for a magistrate to issue an arrest warrant. Consequently, the validity of arrests has received scant court attention other than in circumstances where the suspect's right to a fair trial is affected (such as the finding of evidence incident to the arrest).

However, the Supreme Court has indicated that the law of arrest does have constitutional dimensions beyond merely the requirement of probable cause. In *United States v. Watson* (423 U.S. 411 [1976]), postal inspectors developed Watson as a suspect in a stolen credit-card ring. Arrangements were made for an undercover inspector to meet with Watson in a restaurant. Following the purchase of additional stolen credit cards from Watson, the officer made a warrantless arrest of the suspect. Following conviction, the matter reached the Supreme Court on the issue of whether the postal inspector should have obtained an arrest warrant prior to arresting Watson. It was conceded that the government had sufficient probable cause for a warrant and that the officers had plenty of time to obtain a warrant prior to the restaurant meeting. The Court ruled, however, that while the preferred practice would be to obtain an arrest warrant if possible prior to making an arrest and judgments about probable cause would be more readily acceptable when backed by a warrant, the Constitution does not require issuance of an arrest warrant prior to arresting a suspect in a public place even if officers had the time and opportunity to obtain a warrant.

What of an arrest not made in a public place? Is a pre-issued warrant required? The answers to these questions were delivered in *Payton v. New York* (445 U.S. 573 [1980]). After several days of investigation, detectives had developed probable cause to believe that Payton had murdered a gas station attendant. Without an arrest warrant, officers entered Payton's apartment intending to arrest him. Payton was not at home, but the officers seized a cartridge case that was in open view in the apartment. The cartridge case was subsequently introduced as evidence against Payton at his murder trial. On appeal to the Supreme Court Payton contested the lawfulness of the police officers' entry into his apartment. The Court examined the trend of decisions in state courts on this issue and ruled that absent exigent circumstances or consent, police officers may not enter a private home to make a warrantless arrest. Issuance of an arrest warrant is a prerequisite to a valid entry in nonemergency circumstances. Failure to comply with this constitutional requirement will result in any evidence seized incident to the arrest being inadmissible in court. In a later decision, *Welsh v. Wisconsin* (466 U.S. 740 [1984]), the Court ruled that in determining whether an emergency exists in order to excuse the warrant requirement, the severity of the offense is the prime consideration. Normally, a warrantless entry of a home

to arrest an individual for a minor offense will never be admissible.

Additionally, barring an emergency, even the possession of an arrest warrant will not legally justify entry into the home of a person other than the party named in the warrant. If a suspect is in the home of another, not only must an arrest warrant be obtained by the police but so must a search warrant, ruled the Supreme Court in *Steagald v. United States* (451 U.S. 204 [1981]).

On occasion, the police find it necessary to detain individuals without making a full custody arrest of them. This procedure has its origins in "suspicious persons" laws that for many years authorized the police to make an inquiry of suspicious persons who were found in suspicious places. The criticism of these laws lay in the notion that "suspicion" is a lower standard than the Fourth Amendment seizure requirement of "probable cause." Additionally, the police were the sole determiners of what constituted "suspicious" behavior because the judgment of a magistrate never came into play during these on-the-street encounters.

Recognizing the need to balance reasonable police procedures against the constitutional right of citizens to be free from unreasonable seizures, the Supreme Court granted a limited right to police to conduct temporary detentions in a case styled *Terry v. Ohio* (392 U.S. 1 [1968]). In *Terry* a city detective observed two men acting in an unusual manner on a downtown street. Basing his decision on his training and experience, the officer concluded that the two men were quite likely "casing" a retail store prior to robbing it. The two men were subsequently joined by a third person. The detective approached the individuals, identified himself as a policeman, and asked for identification. Upon receiving a mumbled response to his inquiry, the detective "frisked" the individuals and discovered two of them to be carrying pistols. The individuals were charged and convicted of carrying concealed weapons. They appealed, contesting the authority of the detective to stop and frisk them. The Supreme Court ruled the temporary detention practices valid even on grounds less than probable cause. The Court ruled that when an officer has reasonable suspicion to believe criminal activity is afoot and offers identification, he or she may lawfully stop an individual for questioning. If the results of the inquiry do not dispel fears that the person is armed, the officer may conduct a frisk for weapons in the name of self-protection. The Court noted that the "stop and frisk" procedure is necessary in order to resolve ambiguous situations and separate innocent behavior from possible criminal activity. The process is a "minor inconvenience" to the citizen.

The authority to detain on less than probable cause does not, however, permit a "shakedown" of everyone at a scene (*Brown v. Texas,* 443 U.S. 47 [1979]), or a roundup and stationhouse detention for fingerprinting of several individuals who meet a general description of an offender (*Davis v. Mississippi,* 394 U.S. 721 [1969]).

Search and Seizure

A prime investigatory activity of law enforcement is the gathering of evidence to aid in case solution and prosecution. Such seizures of physical evidence may occur as an adjunct to an arrest for some viewed offense or may be the result of direct questing for previously identified items such as a murder weapon. Concurrently, due to the potentially violent circumstances in which the police become involved, safety of the officer from those he or she seeks to arrest or detain is of major concern to the police and the courts. It is in this area of search and seizure of items for prosecutorial purposes and officer safety that the day-to-day work of police officers has been most affected by Supreme Court opinions over the last forty years.

Police officers desire to search for physical objects in one of several circumstances. First, officers desire to search arrested persons in order to protect themselves from potential harm or escape of the arrestee. Such searches may reveal weapons but may also produce evidence for court purposes. The arrest of a dangerous fugitive would be followed by a search of his or her person by the arresting officer. Second, officers desire to quest for physical evidence when the circumstances, oftentime of arrest, indicate a likelihood of the presence of evidence that will aid in courtroom prosecution. For example, the arrest of a robber in an automobile might lead an officer to conclude that the evidence of the robbery was in the vehicle. Third, as a result of prior investigative effort, premises may need to be searched to yield physical evidence believed to be located there. In each of the previous circumstances the courts have attempted to balance the citizen's Fourth Amendment right against unreasonable search and seizure against the government's authority to maintain law and order and need to successfully prosecute criminal offenders.

Search Incident to Arrest. The authority of a law-enforcement officer to conduct a search of the surrounding area incident to the arrest of a criminal suspect has long been recognized. For a substantial portion of this country's history the view was held that a valid arrest was a substitute for the general constitutional requirement of a warrant as a predicate to searching. Thus, for many years an officer who arrested a suspect would use the circumstances as an opportunity to search not only the individual but the surrounding environs for evidence relevant to the criminal offense. Such a rule often dictated the time when it was most advantageous for an officer to arrest an offender. If the officer waited until the offender entered his home before arresting him, the officer was legally authorized to search the entire house as it was the "area within the control of the suspect."

The rules concerning search incident to arrest changed, or at least were redefined, by the Supreme Court in 1969. A case styled *Chimel v. California* (395 U.S. 752 [1969]) presented the opportunity to clarify the rule. Police armed with an arrest warrant, but no search warrant, entered Chimel's home and subsequently arrested him for burglary of a coin shop. The officers searched the entire house adjunct to the arrest and found coins from the burglary. The evidence was introduced at Chimel's trial. Following his conviction, the Supreme Court reviewed the case on the issue of the lawfulness of the search and seizure. The Court rejected the notion that an arrest is a constitutionally permissible substitute for a search warrant. Rather, the authority to search incident to arrest is protective in nature. A peace officer may conduct a search of the person and the area within his or her immediate control contemporaneous with an arrest for the purpose of removing weapons, preventing possible escape, and locating evidence that might otherwise be destroyed. The scope of the search is limited to the body of the arrestee and the armspan area. Since the search is protective in nature, absent a search warrant there is no constitutional justification for extending the search further.

Chimel did little to clarify the authority of police officers to conduct protective searches of persons stopped for traffic violations. Courts across the country disagreed as to whether such a detention for the purpose of issuing a traffic citation was an "arrest" under the search-incident-to-arrest-doctrine, and if the detention did constitute an "arrest," the permissible scope of any search. The high court clarified the issue in *United States v. Robinson* (414 U.S. 218 [1973]), wherein an officer made an arrest of a driver who had no operator's license. A subsequent search of his person revealed an illicit drug in his pocket. The Supreme Court ruled that the search-incident-to-arrest doctrine applied to any "full custody" arrest, regardless of the severity of the offense. Thus, an arrest of a traffic offender who will be taken to jail justifies a search, but mere detention for issuance of a ticket, without more, does not warrant a search. Additionally, in *New York v. Belton* (453 U.S. 454 [1981]), the Court ruled that following a lawful arrest of the driver, the interior of an automobile may be searched incident thereto.

Warrantless Searches for Evidence. "We do not retreat from our holdings that the police must, whenever practicable, obtain advanced judicial approval of searches and seizures through the warrant procedure," the Supreme Court has stated. The use of a magistrate as an intervening arbiter between the police and the citizen is a matter of continuing emphasis by modern courts. However, courts recognize circumstances do exist where requiring the obtaining of judicial approval prior to questioning for evidence would be impractical if not impossible. While these circumstances are viewed by the courts as exceptions to the general requirement of a search warrant, to a uniformed police officer the "exceptional circumstances" are more common than situations where a warrant is appropriate.

Searching of motor vehicles for evidence is likely the most frequent application of an exception to the warrant requirement. Since 1925 the Supreme Court has authorized warrantless searches of motor vehicles for evidence of a crime. Because one has a lesser expectation of privacy and because a motor vehicle could flee the jurisdiction while officers sought a search warrant, police officers are permitted to conduct warrantless vehicle searches when probable cause exists to believe the automobile contains evidence. In *United States v. Ross* (456 U.S. 798 [1982]), police had probable cause to believe Ross was selling drugs out of his automobile. Ross was arrested and the vehicle trunk was opened. A bag containing heroin was dis-

covered. The vehicle was towed to the police headquarters and another warrantless search produced other evidence. On appeal the Supreme Court ruled that when officers have probable cause they may search a vehicle, including its trunk, glove box, and any packages therein that could reasonably contain the evidence for which they have grounds to search. The scope of the search is dictated by the type of evidence sought. A stolen television set might reasonably be found in the trunk, but not in the glove box.

Search under a Warrant. Courts have jealously protected individual privacy rights when a search of a person's residence is involved. Barring an emergency such as a crime in progress or the immediate destruction of evidence, the courts require a search warrant to enter a residence without the resident's consent. The Supreme Court reiterated this cardinal principle in *Mincey v. Arizona* (437 U.S. 385 [1978]), where an undercover police officer was found murdered in the suspect's apartment. Following the suspect's arrest, homicide investigators without benefit of a search warrant spent several days processing the apartment for evidence. Following his conviction for murder, Mincey contested the validity of the warrantless search. The Supreme Court ruled the warrantless search for evidence unconstitutional. While the officers had plenty of probable cause, no emergency existed that would excuse obtaining a warrant from a magistrate prior to searching—the suspect was in custody and the scene secured. Likewise, the gravity of the offense, in this case murder, does not create an exception to the application of constitutional rights. A suspect's Fourth Amendment rights are the same in murders of police officers as in petty theft cases.

The mandate of acquiring a warrant prior to searching for evidence in non-emergency circumstances has required police officers to justify their behavior to an impartial magistrate before intruding into a citizen's privacy. This legal rule has forced officers to preplan many of their investigative actions and to maintain close liaison with the judiciary.

Confessions

The Fifth Amendment to the Constitution provides that no person may be compelled to be a witness against her- or himself. Historically, this right prohibited the government from calling a criminal defendant as a witness at his or her own trial. The protection had no relationship to pretrial statements and confessions made to the police by criminal suspects. Rather, court admissibility of such statement turned upon whether the confession had been voluntarily made. At a minimum, physical abuse and torture were not permissible under American law (*Brown v. Mississippi,* 297 U.S. 278 [1936]).

In the 1960s the Supreme Court evidenced concern that the voluntariness standard of confession admissibility did not provide sufficient citizen protection in cases of psychological coercion on the part of the police. Following a finding that the Fifth Amendment also encompassed a pretrial right to absolute silence (*Malloy v. Hogan,* 378 U.S. 1 [1964]), the Court through review of several state confession cases sought to develop a bright-line rule to provide police officers guidance when interrogating criminal suspects. The rule came in one of the most controversial court decisions in American legal history: *Miranda v. Arizona* (384 U.S. 436 [1966]). The decision substantially altered American police practices in the interviewing of criminal suspects by effectively eliminating the tactic of "squeezing a confession out of a suspect." Many police officers charged that the decision would "handcuff" officers in the investigation of crime. Civil libertarians hailed the ruling as a long overdue effort to protect citizens from coercive police behavior.

Ernesto Miranda was arrested and taken to police headquarters to be questioned on kidnapping and rape charges. He was a poor man who lacked even a high school education. Following a two hour interrogation session that did not involve brutality or other physically coercive behavior, Miranda confessed. Conviction at trial followed. On appeal to the Supreme Court, his case was considered with three other cases involving police interrogation tactics. The justices reviewed police interrogation tactics through the examination of published training materials. The majority of the Court concluded that any questioning of a person who is under arrest is inherently coercive and jeopardizes the free exercise of the constitutional right to silence. A divided Court ruled that the prosecution may not use statements that are the product of custodial interrogation of a suspect unless it proves that the suspect's Fifth Amendment privilege was protected and a knowing waiver of the privilege was made. Protection of the privilege against self-incrimination was to be accomplished by first orally advising the in-cus-

tody suspect that he had the right to remain silent, anything said may be used against him in court, he had the right to talk to a lawyer prior to questioning, and if he could not afford a lawyer, one would be provided. If a suspect did confess, the burden fell upon the state to prove the warning had been given and a knowing waiver of rights had occurred.

The ruling in Miranda has resulted in virtually all police officers advising everyone who is arrested, not just those to be interrogated, of the so-called Miranda warning. Dispute still rages among scholars over whether the ruling has, in fact, reduced the number of confessions given to the police. At a minimum, the legacy of *Miranda* is that in the prosecution of criminal offenders guilt often must be proven with evidence independent of the defendant's own words. Consequently, police officers have had to become better trained in alternative investigative tactics.

Subsequent court rulings have clarified the scope of coverage of the *Miranda* holding. Many scholars believe that Supreme Court rulings in the mid-1980s have actually eroded a citizen's Fifth Amendment rights as established under the Miranda decision.

Use of Force
In providing police officers with the authority and duty to enforce the criminal law, the government has granted them the privilege to use reasonable force against persons and property to carry out that responsibility. The privilege may also involve the authorization to use force capable of causing death. Normally, state law defines the circumstances under which police officer use of force in the areas of arrest, search, and seizure is justified. If the conduct is justified, the officer is not subject to criminal prosecution for his or her behavior or liable for civil damages. If in enforcing the law the officer engages in unjustified use of force, he or she may be subject to criminal charges and money damages. For example, the beating of a criminal suspect who is offering no resistance may subject an officer to criminal prosecution for assault and battery. Conversely, a peace officer's use of the same amount of brute force against a subject resisting a lawful arrest will likely be excused under the criminal law.

Over the years courts largely deferred to the legislature to define the level of force that police officers were permitted to use in enforcing the law. Little judicial attention was given to the scope of statutes authorizing the use of force. In the last decade many police departments, fearing civil suits in the area of excessive force, established use-of-force policies more restrictive than permitted by use of statute. However, a few even continued to follow use-of-force rules that had their origins in common law. It was the latter circumstance that prompted the Supreme Court's first examination of the constitutionally permissible scope of police authority to use deadly force.

In *Tennessee v. Garner* (471 U.S. 1 [1985]), police officers responded to a "prowler inside" call. Upon arriving at the scene, officers saw a young man flee the house toward a fence. When the young man failed to stop on one of the officer's commands, the officer fired a shot at him. The shot struck and killed the individual. He was determined to be fifteen years old and unarmed. A purse and ten dollars from the house were found in his possession. Under Tennessee state law, the officer was legally justified in using deadly force to stop the "fleeing felon." The decedent's parents sued the officer and the police department contending the state law was unconstitutional. When the matter reached the Supreme Court, a majority ruled that such blanket authorization for police officers to use deadly force against any felony offender was unreasonable and thereby unconstitutional. The Court noted that it is not better that all persons die than that they escape. Deadly force may constitutionally be used only if the officer has probable cause to believe the suspect poses a serious threat of harm to the officer or another person.

The *Garner* decision altered the law on the use of deadly force by police officers in nearly two dozen states.

Supreme Court Decisions, 1989–1992
Fourth Amendment

In *Maryland v. Buie* (110 S.Ct. 1093 [1990]), the Court ruled that police may conduct a protective sweep of closets and adjoining spaces of a home after an arrest in the home without any reason or suspicion to believe others are present who pose a threat. Also, according to the decision, police may conduct a protective sweep of other rooms or spaces in the home if they have reasonable suspicion someone is present who poses a threat.

In *Horton v. California* (110 S.Ct. 2301 [1990]), the Court ruled that the Fourth Amendment does not prohibit the warrantless seizure of evidence in plain view, even though the discovery of the evidence is not inadvertent.

In *Michigan Department of State Police v. Sitz* (110 S.Ct. 2481 [1990]), the Court ruled that the Fourth Amendment does not forbid the initial stop and brief detention of all motorists passing through a highway checkpoint established to detect and deter drunk driving.

In *Illinois v. Rodriguez* (110 S.Ct. 2793 [1990]), the Court ruled that a warrantless entry into a residence based upon the consent of a third party is legal if police, at the time of entry, reasonably believe that the third party possesses common authority over the premises, even if the third party in fact does not.

In *United States v. Verdugo-Urquidez* (110 S.Ct. 1056 [1990]) the Court ruled that the Fourth Amendment does not apply to the search and seizure by U.S. agents of property owned by a nonresident alien that is located in a foreign country.

In *Alabama v. White* (110 S.Ct. 2412 [1990]) the Court ruled that an anonymous tip, which is corroborated by independent police work, can in some cases exhibit sufficient indicia of reliability to provide reasonable suspicion for an investigatory stop.

In *Florida v. Wells* (100 S.Ct. 1632 [1990]), the Court held that the opening of a closed container by a Florida Highway Patrol trooper for inventory purposes was illegal, because the Florida Highway Patrol had no policy concerning the opening of closed containers encountered during an inventory search.

In *Florida v. Bostick* (111 S.Ct. 2382 [1991]), the Court ruled that law-enforcement officers who approach a seated bus passenger and request consent to search the passenger's luggage do not necessarily seize the passenger under the Fourth Amendment. The test applied in such situations is whether a reasonable passenger would feel free to decline the request or otherwise terminate the encounter.

In *California v. Hodari D.* (111 S.Ct. 1547 [1991]), the Court ruled that a Fourth Amendment seizure does not occur when law-enforcement officers are chasing a fleeing suspect, unless the officers apply physical force or the suspect submits to an officer's show of authority.

In *County of Riverside v. McLaughlin* (111 S.Ct. 1661 [1991]), the Court ruled that a person arrested without a warrant must generally be provided with a judicial determination of probable cause within forty-eight hours after arrest, including intervening weekends or holidays.

In *California v. Acevedo* (111 S.Ct. 1982 [1991]), the Court overruled its prior decision in *Arkansas v. Sanders* (442 U.S. 753 [1979]) and upheld, under the automobile exception to the warrant requirement, the warrantless search of a container placed into a vehicle, even though the probable cause to search was focused exclusively on that container.

In *Florida v. Jimeno* (111 S.Ct. 1801 [1991]), the Court held that a person's general consent to search the interior of a car includes, unless otherwise specified by the consenter, all containers in the car that might reasonably hold the object of the search.

Fifth Amendment

In *Illinois v. Perkins* (110 S.Ct. 2394 [1990]), the Court ruled that an undercover law-enforcement officer posing as a fellow inmate need not give Miranda warnings to an incarcerated suspect before asking questions that may elicit an incriminating response.

In *New York v. Harris* (110 S.Ct. 1640 [1990]), the Court ruled that an illegal warrantless arrest of a suspect in his home does not require the suppression of an incriminating statement given by the suspect outside his home.

In *James v. Illinois* (110 S.Ct. 648 (1990]), the Court held that the impeachment exception to the exclusionary rule, which allows the prosecution to introduce illegally obtained evidence to impeach the defendant's testimony, should not be extended to allow impeachment of all defense witnesses.

In *Pennsylvania v. Muniz* (110 S.Ct. 2638 (1990]), the Court ruled that videotaped evidence of an arrestee's slurred speech in response to routine booking questions and of his performance of sobriety tests is nontestimonial and not within the scope of the Fifth Amendment privilege against compelled self-incrimination.

In *Minnick v. Mississippi* (111 S.Ct. 486 (1990]), the Court ruled that once a custodial suspect requests counsel in response to Miranda warnings, law-enforcement officers may not attempt to reinterrogate the suspect unless the suspect's counsel is present or the suspect initiates the contact with law enforcement.

In *McNeil v. Wisconsin* (111 S.Ct. 2204 (1991]), the Court held that an in-custody suspect who requests counsel at a judicial proceeding, such as an arraignment or initial appearance, is only invoking the Sixth Amendment right to counsel as to the charged offense and is not invoking the Miranda Fifth Amendment–based right to have counsel present during custodial interrogations. Thus, officers are not prohibited from later approaching the in-custody suspect for interrogation about uncharged crimes.

In *Arizona v. Fulminate* (111 S.Ct. 1246 [1991]), a divided Court decided that a confession between prison inmates was involuntary and inadmissible in this case. However, the Court also noted that in certain cases, the admission into evidence of an involuntary confession may be harmless error if the involuntary confession's admission is harmless beyond a reasonable doubt.

In *White v. Illinois* (112 S.Ct. 736 [1992]), the Court upheld the admissibility of out-of-court statements made by a child sexual assault victim to her babysitter, her mother, the police, and medical personnel who treated her. The Court decided that a witness need not be unavailable before her out-of-court statements can be admitted as exceptions to hearsay evidentiary rules.

In *United States v. Felix* (112 S.Ct. 1377 [1992]), the Court dealt with the effect of the Double Jeopardy Clause of the Fifth Amendment on two overlapping drug prosecutions. This case arose out of a federal drug investigation of a methamphetamine manufacturing facility operated by the defendant in Oklahoma, which law-enforcement officers raided and shut down. The defendant evaded arrest and moved his operation to Missouri.

Sixth Amendment

In *Michigan v. Harvey* (110 S.Ct 1176 [1990]), the Court held that the prosecution may use a defendant's statement to impeach the defendant's testimony at trial, even when the statement is taken in violation of the defendant's Sixth Amendment right to counsel.

In *Maryland v. Craig* (110 S.Ct. 3157 (1990]), the Court ruled that the Sixth Amendment does not invariably require face-to-face confrontation between a defendant and a child abuse victim-witness at trial, if the child abuse victim-witness will suffer emotional trauma by testifying in the presence of the defendant.

In *Idaho v. Wright* (110 S.Ct. 3139 [1990]), the Court held that an out-of-court statement by an alleged victim of child sexual abuse did not possess sufficient guarantees of trustworthiness to be admitted at trial, but ruled that an out-of-court statement may be admitted if it is determined that the child making the statement was particularly likely to be telling the truth when the statement was made.

In *Doggett v. United States* (112 S.Ct. 2686 [1992]), the Court determined that a delay of eight and one-half years between a defendant's indictment and trial violated his Sixth Amendment right to a speedy trial. In this case the defendant was indicted in 1980 on drug charges but left the country for Panama four days before police officers arrived at his home to arrest him.

First Amendment

In *Osborne v. Ohio* (110 S.Ct. 1691 [1990]), the Court held that an Ohio statute prohibiting the possession and viewing of child pornography does not violate the First Amendment.

In *Jacobson v. United States* (112 S.Ct. 1535 [1992]), the Court overturned the federal child pornography conviction of a Nebraska farmer because he was entrapped by a U.S. Postal Service child pornography sting operation. The case began in 1984, when the defendant legally ordered and received two magazines containing photographs of nude preteen and teenage boys from a California adult bookstore. Subsequently, Congress changed the law and made it illegal to receive sexually explicit depictions of children through the mail.

In *R.A.V. v. City of St. Paul, Minnesota* (112 S.Ct. 2538 [1992]), the Court struck down a city ordinance designed to prevent the bias-motivated display of symbols or objects, such as Nazi swastikas or burning crosses. The case concerned the prosecution of a teenager who assembled a crudely made cross and burned it on the front lawn of an African-American family.

Extradition

In *United States v. Alvarez-Machain* (112 S.Ct. 2188 [1992]), the Court found that the United States–Mexico Extradition Treaty said nothing about the obligation of the two countries to refrain from forcible abductions, and, thus, did not govern the jurisdiction of a U.S. court to try the defendant. In 1990 Alvarez-Machain was forcibly kidnapped at the behest of the DEA from Mexico, flown to El Paso, Texas, and arrested by DEA officials. The Mexican government officially protested the abduction.

Conclusion

The last thirty years have seen the legal authority of police officers significantly influenced by judicial decisions. Foremost have been the opinions of a Supreme Court that adopted an aggressive, proactive stance in the articulation of citizen rights and corresponding restrictions on the authority of the government and its agents, the police. Return by the courts to a hands-off policy concerning police procedures is unlikely to occur; police officers will continue to see the process of enforcing the law directed by state statute, but most important, refined by the courts.

Jerry L. Dowling
William U. McCormack

Bibliography

Baker, Liva. *Miranda: Crime, Law and Politics.* New York: Atheneum, 1983.

Galloway, John, ed. *The Supreme Court and the Rights of the Accused.* New York: Facts on File, 1973.

Graham, Fred P. *The Self-Inflicted Wound.* New York: Macmillan, 1970.

Leonard, V.A. *The Police, the Judiciary and the Criminal.* Springfield, IL: Charles C. Thomas, 1975.

McCormack, William U. "Selected Supreme Court Cases: 1989–1990 Term." *FBI Law Enforcement Bulletin* 59 (November 1990): 26–32.

———. "Selected Supreme Court Cases: 1990–1991 Term." *FBI Law Enforcement Bulletin* 60 (November 1991): 26–32.

———. "Supreme Court Cases: 1991–1992 Term." *FBI Law Enforcement Bulletin* 61 (November 1992): 25–31.

Nagel, Stuart S., ed. *The Rights of the Accused.* Beverly Hills, CA: Sage, 1972.

Television Police

In daily life most people living in the United States are far more likely to encounter the television police than actual police officers. It is reported that 97 percent of 95 million American households are equipped with at least one television set and that 50 million of this total receive cable programs (Bagdikian, 1991:22). With average daily household viewing time at just under seven hours, television has become a very influential purveyor of cultural values, norms, and status-roles (Maguire 1988:168). Because so many television programs are framed around a crime/police focus, one of the most popular status-roles on television is that of the police officer. For most people, then, general attitudes about the police are probably shaped in part by what is seen on television.

Police and Police-Related Programs

For decades policing has been a main theme of many prime-time television programs. Programs with a direct or indirect focus on policing typically fall into one of five general categories. A first category of programs are those which offer a serious and dramatic presentation of character(s) vocationally identified as police officers (see Table 1 for a list of examples).

Because these programs offer the most explicit and detailed representation of police work, they are most crucial to an understanding of the topic at hand, that is, television police. A second category of programs are those highlighted by a serious and dramatic presentation of character(s) vocationally identified as private detectives. Some of the most successful examples of this type have been *Peter Gunn, Mannix, Barnaby Jones, The Rockford Files, Magnum, P.I., and Murder, She Wrote.*

A third genre of police programs are those that consist of a humorous presentation of character(s) vocationally identified as police officers. The most prominent historical examples of this type are *Car 54, Where Are You?, The Andy Griffith Show, and Barney Miller.* A fourth kind of police program revolves around a spy or secret agent. These shows highlight a sort of international policing and may be presented humorously (e.g., *Get Smart*), seriously (e.g., *The Six Million Dollar Man* or *Mission: Impossible*), or with a combination of humor and seriousness (e.g., *The Man From U.N.C.L.E.*). Finally, a fifth category of police program is characterized by the lawman set in the time period of the Old West. Examples of this type are *The Lone Ranger, The Life and Legend of Wyatt Earp*, and *Gunsmoke.*

The foregoing paragraph indicates both the varied nature of police and police-related programs as well as the fact that policing has become a staple topical theme of much prime-time television programming. Despite the diversity and popularity of police programs, however, television is seldom faithful to real life. Research over the course of several decades, dating back to the mid-1950s, has consistently shown that police and policing are presented in stereotypical ways (Dominick 1973; Smythe 1954). The stereotypes are either excessively positive or excessively negative. As a starting point let us consider the positive stereotypes that are most likely to be found in the first category of program mentioned above—that is, police shows where the principal character or characters of the program is/are police officers and the plot of the show is serious in nature. Table 1 is an extensive, but by no means exhaustive, listing of such programs. Program titles are presented in a rough chronological order beginning with shows of the 1950s.

When characterized in positive terms, the police tend to be portrayed as unusually bright, talented, courageous, and virtuous. Historically, in most of these category one police programs the chief protagonist is a white male police officer whose image is generally advanced as a super crime-fighter. The police officer is intelligent, well-read, and keenly observant. He is a crime-solver who invariably prevails in a battle of wits with a highly clever, if sinister, villain. It is also the case that the police protagonist possesses impressive physical talents including hand-to-hand combat skill, the ability to use weapons with speed and effectiveness (particularly a gun), and the capacity and daring to handle a car moving at high speed (Kaminsky and Mahan, 1985:64). Furthermore, the police hero is depicted as having uncommon courage, as a person willing to risk life and limb time after time. Finally, the police officer is shown as a person above reproach, as someone who could never be bought off by the forces of darkness, although many attempts to do just that are showcased.

From the viewpoint of the audience it is all very well that the television police hero has so many positive features; they are all needed because the criminal offender is typically a very formidable foe. Most of the time the villain is one or more of the following: a member of organized crime, a genius mastermind, and/or an individual obsessed by greed, revenge, or general madness. Organized crime figures are difficult to defeat because they are members of a team and have economic and political power behind them. A genius mastermind is difficult

to defeat for the reason that this type of criminal is highly intelligent and the criminal act undertaken is the product of careful and imaginative preparation. In addition, the offender who is driven by greed, revenge, or mental/emotional pathology is extremely dangerous, a person willing to chance everything to bring off the crime and avoid apprehension. To capture this type of offender the police officer must show tremendous courage, even a courage that borders on becoming foolhardy at times.

With these personality characteristics of the police officer and criminal offender in mind, it remains only to describe the typical nature and setting of the criminal act. It is a point of consensus among all scientific studies of television crime/police programs that the most frequent type of criminal offense depicted is an act of interpersonal violence, with murders and attempted murders being the most common. Moreover, these violent offenses are most often set in urban areas. Large American cities are often described by television characters as urban jungles where danger is lurking at every turn. The television police are characterized as last-order champions of law and order; without the police the violence of the urban jungle would overtake the innocent members of society.

The aforementioned have been the predominant ingredients of police program plots played out by notable leading characters such as Joe Friday of *Dragnet*, Steve McGarrett of *Hawaii Five-O*, Lieutenant Columbo of *Columbo*, and dozens more television police stars. Indeed, the television police are so good at crime investigation and offender apprehension that television criminals rarely elude capture. In Maguire's (1988:178–79) study of

---

TABLE 1

Forty-One Past or Current Television Police Programs

1. *Dragnet*	12. *The Rookies*	22. *Police Story*	33. *Crime Story*
2. *Highway Patrol*	13. *Kojak*	23. *Police Woman*	34. *Downtown*
3. *The Naked City*	14. *The Streets of*	24. *Joe Forrester*	35. *Heart of the City*
4. *M-Squad*	*San Francisco*	25. *The Blue Knight*	36. *In the Heat of*
5. *The Untouchables*	15. *Toma*	26. *Serpico*	*the Night*
6. *The FBI*	16. *S.W.A.T.*	27. *T.J. Hooker*	37. *Cops*
7. *Ironside*	17. *Starsky and Hutch*	28. *CHIPS*	38. *Top Cops*
8. *Hawaii Five-O*	18. *Baretta*	29. *Hunter*	39. *The Hat Squad*
9. *Mod Squad*	19. *McCloud*	30. *Miami Vice*	40. *American Detective*
10. *Felony Squad*	20. *Columbo*	31. *Hill St. Blues*	41. *NYPD Blue*
11. *Adam-12*	21. *McMillan and Wife*	32. *Cagney & Lacey*	

forty-six hours of prime-time television crime and police programs, it was found that only two out of ninety-nine television offenders "got away" with their crimes.

As indicated earlier, it is not always the case that the television police are featured in positive terms. Indeed, occasionally police officers are shown engaged in illegal behavior of their own, including the commission of ordinary crimes or the taking of bribes. Moreover, the police are sometimes depicted as agents of search and seizure violations and/or excessive use of force (Arons and Katsh 1977:13; Simon and Fejes 1980:68). Seldom would the police program hero be involved in such misdeeds, however. It is far more likely to be some other member of the police force, now and then it might even be the partner of the police hero. When the main police protagonist commits a wrongdoing it is usually a procedural law violation and the act is often explained as the product of being frustrated by legal bureaucracy (Ericson, 1991:224–25).

It is furthermore the case that in programs where a private detective is the star of the show it is not uncommon for police officer characters to come across in negative terms. For example, in pursuing a case a private detective may have to overcome a bumbling, cowardly, corrupt, and/or overly rigid police officer who is conducting an official investigation of the same case. In such instances where the police officer actually becomes an impediment to solving the case, the detective is portrayed as an even more impressive figure. After all, it is not just the criminal who has to be overtaken, but the police officer too must be surmounted. Predictably, by the end of these program episodes it is the detective who is most likely to solve the case and/or shoot the criminal (Maguire, 1988:178–79).

When it comes to the television police there is little middle ground or room for realistic characterization; police officers tend to be either heroic or extremely flawed. Television, not unlike film, appears to thrive on exciting stories that present a stark contrast between good and evil. Unfortunately, when such an overly simplistic theme is used to frame a television police program, certain negative consequences emerge.

Authenticity and Consequences of TV's Display of Policing

Prime-time television police and police-related programs project numerous distortions about policing in the United States. The most egregious distortions include the following: Most television crime is violent interpersonal crime; the police officer nearly always solves the case and apprehends the offender; police officers spend almost all of their time on law-enforcement activities; the police officer is routinely involved in fisticuffs and gunplay; and the stock setting for televised crime and police work is the big city. All of these characteristic features are just plain wrong or at the very least misleading (see Dominick, 1973:247–49; Maguire, 1988:181–85; Walker, 1983:53–55). First, most actual crime does not involve interpersonal violence; only a tiny percentage of crime is of this type. Second, real police officers are not nearly as proficient as the television police are at solving cases and apprehending offenders. In fact, the actual police solve only about 20 percent of the most common real crimes, for example, robbery and burglary. Third, virtually all studies of police job-time show that the real police spend a minority of time in direct law enforcement. Most police time is spent on mundane tasks such as patrolling, writing reports, and directing traffic. Fourth, real police officers rarely exchange gunfire with suspects; it happens, but not nearly as often as television suggests. Finally, television's concentration on big city crime and policing ignores the entire world of rural and suburban crime and policing. In general, for reasons of their own, most notably ratings, television producers take excessive liberties in police and police-related programs.

What are the negative consequences of television's misrepresentation of police officers and police work? There is, first of all, the simple fact that television presents a distorted image of actual policing. To project to millions of viewers an inaccurate image of any social phenomenon is a problem in and of itself. It becomes an especially serious problem not just because the phenomenon is police work but because the programs are often promoted as authentic depictions of real-life policing (Oates, 1985). A second negative consequence of television's characterization of policing is that the viewing audience, that is the general public, may come to expect too much from actual police. This could be a direct result of the portrayal of the television police as supercops who solve cases in brilliant fashion and invariably apprehend criminals. A third negative consequence, just the opposite of the second possibility mentioned, is that viewers may expect the worst out of the real police. This could happen when the police are depicted stereotypically at the negative extreme, as crooks, bullies, and/or imbeciles. In either case, the extreme positive or extreme negative, the viewing public may form an unflattering estimation of real police officers and thereby make actual police work more difficult than it already is. It is possible that there may be some positive consequences of television's portrayal of the police and policing, but if there are, it is likely that they would be outweighed by the negative consequences just discussed.

Recent Developments

In the early 1990s television producers advanced a new genre: reality-based programming. Nowhere is this type of program more conspicuous than in police shows such as *Cops, Top Cops,* and *American Detective.* Whereas traditional police programs provide a dramatic reproduction of something supposedly resembling everyday life, these new shows promise viewers an actual look at breaking events in the real world, as television crews accompany the police while they work. Not only is this a new hook with which to lure viewers, but producers are pleased that the cost of these reality-based programs are much less than the average sitcom or drama (O'Connor, 1992:C:11). It may be illustrative to examine what one reviewer had to say about the reality-based program, *COPS:*

> Raw, abrasive, edgy, this series forcibly drags you into the street to look over the shoulders of police officers confronting the barbarians poised at our gates. From policing Mardi Gras ("a controlled riot") to a coke bust in a Miami-area mansion, this pioneering reality is, appropriately, excruciatingly real in form and content (Sauter, 1992:19).

Because the television camera follows the police in their natural work settings, there is no disputing the fact that the reality-based police programs do capture real situations. Nevertheless, there is still an element of orchestration to these programs. When a drug bust is featured, for example, there is no coverage of the days, weeks, or months of preparation that precede the bust. The camera does not show police officers simply sitting, observing, and recording the behavioral patterns of the suspects. All of the dull, time-consuming (and necessary) aspects of police work are left unseen. Only the most exciting interruptions to the ordinary flow of police work are highlighted on television and even these segments are, to some extent, choreographed and edited. The so-called reality-based police programs, then, do not present a generally representative image of actual policing.

Summary

For decades crime/police shows have been an integral part of prime-time network programming. Apparently seeking more to entertain audiences than inform them, television producers have typically stereotyped police officers and police work. Police officers tend to be presented in extremely positive or extremely negative ways. Moreover, television policing is almost always defined in terms of crime-fighting that in reality is just one of many functional duties of actual police officers. Unfortunately, this emphasis on the most dramatic and spectacular features of police work promotes a display of policing that is at odds with real police work. As discussed earlier, it is likely that this misrepresentation results in several negative consequences for the police and the general public. Although researchers as well as experienced police officers and police trainees are critical of such shows (Simon and Fejes, 1980), this type of programming is not likely to be discontinued any time soon.

Brendan Maguire

Bibliography

Arons, Stephen, and Ethan Katsh. "How TV Cops Flout the Law." *Saturday Review* (March 19, 1977): 11–18.

Bagdikian, Ben. "Television Journalism in the '90s: Stay Tuned. Or Will You?" *Television Quarterly* 26 (1991): 21–28.

Dominick, Joseph. "Crime and Law Enforcement on Prime-Time Television." *Public Opinion Quarterly* 37 (1973): 241–50.

Ericson, Richard. "Mass Media, Crime, Law, and Justice." *British Journal of Criminology* 31 (1991): 219–49.

Kaminsky, Stuart, and Jeffrey Mahan. *American Television Genres.* Chicago: Nelson-Hall, 1985.

Maguire, Brendan. "Image vs. Reality: An Analysis of Prime-Time Television Crime and Police Programs." *Crime and Justice* 11 (1988): 165–88.

Oates, Joyce. "For Its Audacity, Its Defiantly Bad Taste and Its Superb Character Studies." *TV Guide* (June 1, 1985): 4–7.

O'Connor, John. "A TV 'Reality' of Dramatizations and Platitudes." *The New York Times* (April 20, 1992): C: 11.

Sauter, Van Gordon. "Rating the Reality Shows." *TV Guide* (May 2, 1992): 18-21.

Simon, Rita, and Fred Fejes. "*Real Police on Television Supercops.*" *Society* 17 (1980): 68–70.

Smythe, Dallas. "Reality as Presented by TV." *Public Opinion Quarterly* 18 (1954): 143–56.

Walker, Samuel. *The Police in America*. New York: McGraw-Hill, 1983.

Terrorism

Terrorism in the United States can generally be divided into two broad categories: (1) those acts sponsored by or connected to terrorist groups having mainly foreign interests, and (2) those acts sponsored by or connected to domestically oriented groups. In the latter category one would include racist organizations that resort to violence. For effective law enforcement, however, this dichotomy is somewhat artificial and meaningless. A bomb placed by a terrorist group centered ten thousand miles from our shores, but pursuing an international political issue in this country, is as deadly as a bomb placed by a local racist organization, and sometimes the motivations overlap.

Thus far domestic terrorism has been relatively nonexistent. The Federal Bureau of Investigation, in conjunction with state and local police agencies, has prevented its spread, and numerous members of terrorist groups have been arrested, tried, and convicted. Prudence does dictate, though, that we should take no great comfort from the fact that, up to now, our cities have escaped most of the extreme examples of international terrorist violence.

Rely on the Basics

As a police concern, terrorism is neither a mystery nor a particularly esoteric discipline nor an invincible onslaught. American police currently have the wherewithal to cope with terrorism. Since terrorists replicate and intensify normal criminal actions, successful anticriminal tactics can be easily adapted to subdue them. A run-through of basic police functions will clarify this assertion. Police officers are selected for duty because they possess these attributes: self-control, self-motivation, ability to work alone, emotional stability, intelligence, physical fitness, mental alertness, bravery, patience, and open-mindedness. Therefore, selection of such individuals insures a personal readiness to perform well under extreme conditions. Police of this caliber who often confront dangerous felony situations will have no trouble when up against a terrorist attack.

The primary training offered police at present is sound. But it does need certain additions in emphasis and expenditures of time. Recruit training curricula should include stress marksmanship for one. Under circumstances of great stress, police must be able to inflict fast, disabling wounds (this does not mean using faster and/or heavier ammunition). In the midst of grenade explosions and submachine-gun fire, and to avoid hitting innocent bystanders, a police marksman should remain calm and disable the terrorists only. Observational skill is also important. Terrorists, like other criminals, most often plan ahead. They survey the area of their intended actions. They take pictures, make both mental and written notes, and return to do so again and again. In many cases, they at least slightly disrupt the normal pattern of existence in their target area. The question is, can police be trained to detect such slight changes in an area's pattern? The obvious answer is, not always. But the more familiar an officer is with an area, the more likely observational training will enable him or her to detect unusual or suspicious changes. In addition to learning how to observe acutely, knowing the enemy is a must. This is gained through study of the particular terrorist psychology, philosophy, and machinations. Of chief importance in the battle against terrorism, intelligence gathering faces some difficulty. Penetration of a criminal activity with political or ethnic overtones is conditional because the U.S. Constitution purposely protects political actions. Police have to prove that political actions are also criminal before intelligence activities can be initiated.

When one speaks of police counterterrorist/antiterrorist actions, unfortunately there appears to be a gross overemphasis on the part of the media on highly militarized weapons and equipment. The hooded, booted, fatigue-uniformed, automatic-weapons-carrying SWAT team supported by one or more helicopters and military armored cars seems to be a common media-induced picture. Indeed, this picture may be relevant when all other police measures have failed and a group of terrorists have barricaded themselves in an airplane or a building. But for the most part, the application of sound, professional, day-to-day police work will suffice before such a situation reaches the extreme.

A Concentrated Effort

Terrorists hope to influence the minds and resolve of not only their targeted victims but also of the world at large. They desire to convey these ideas: (1) the terrorist is all powerful, (2) the terrorist's opponents are weak, brutal, corrupt, and inept, (3) the tide of history is with the terrorists, not with their opponents, and (4) meeting the demands of the terrorist is the only solution to the terrorist problem. This is psychological warfare, and as Hitler demonstrated in the 1930s, a war is first won in the minds of the opponents. Police behavior must be such that the terrorist effort to discredit them and the government they represent will, in turn, be discredited. Police efficiency has to be superior to that of the terrorists. If a police department is capable of preventing street crimes, it will also be capable of preventing terrorist acts on the streets. Conversely, if a police department is deficient in patrol effectiveness, the same department will be deficient in combating terrorism through the use of patrol.

Investigation of terrorists is no different from that of regular investigations; police employ informants, crime-stopper tips, interviews, surveillances, record checks, scientific evidence, information gathered by patrol personnel, and other means to learn all they can. Terrorist groups will, however, normally be highly insulated against penetration by outside informants and the accidental view of ordinary citizens. This only indicates that the police investigator will have to work harder, smarter, and more imaginatively. Interagency liaison is of invaluable assistance here. Local police will not have a wide-ranging picture of terrorist capabilities without access to information held by federal and state law-enforcement agencies having broader jurisdiction. Cooperation is thus essential; where interagency work has been close and forthcoming the terrorists have lost.

There is enough of a bloody track record available to enable police to analyze the potential for terrorist attacks and the form such attacks will take in their respective jurisdictions. After intelligence has provided information on which terrorist groups might be active, consideration then must be given to the point of attack, if actualized. Past targets have included police stations, airports, airliners, public buildings, public personalities, churches, synagogues and mosques, multinational businesses, political party headquarters, ethnic group organizations, "soft" military installations, banks, and armored cars. Knowing what targets are favored, what modi operandi are standard, and what level of terrorist activity is present, police can narrow their focus and modify their tactics to deal with the threat. Of course, no counterterrorist action will be guaranteed free of casualties, but preventive action will achieve five objectives:

1. Make it harder for terrorists to act in the first place;
2. Stop some terrorist actions cold and cut others short;
3. Reduce friendly casualties while inflicting costs on the terrorists;
4. Curtail somewhat the mission of the terrorist group; and
5. Arouse resistance in vocal members of the public and in some public officials.

Emergency Planning and Practice

Police cannot be expected to act expeditiously upon notification of a building or aircraft takeover unless they are prepared beforehand. Prior planning should include organizing the reaction team, equipping the team, and organizing the command and control structure to run it. Also, equipping the command post—communication links being the most important factor—is necessary. Next, establish ground rules for interaction with the press, insure that police shifts can be restructured, and that a contingency plan is manifest and known to key personnel.

Terrorists are not supermen; they are not usually well trained; they are not always soldiers, heroes, or warriors—except to themselves; they are fanatics and zealots. Because they are willing to risk, and even to sacrifice, their lives for their beliefs, they are doubly dangerous. Nonetheless, thinking police can outwit them.

David G. Epstein

Bibliography

Burton, Anthony M. *Urban Terrorism: Theory, Practice & Response.* New York: Free Press, 1975.

Hacker, Frederick J. *Crusaders, Criminals, Crazies: Terror and Terrorism in Our Time.* New York: Norton, 1976.

Hoffmann, Bruce, et al. *Terrorism in the United States and the Potential Threat to Nuclear Facilities*. Santa Monica, CA: Rand Corporation, 1986.

Kobetz, Richard W., and H.H. Cooper. *Target Terrorism: Providing Protective Services*. Gaithersburg, MD: International Association of Chiefs of Police, 1978.

Motley, James B. *United States Strategy to Counter Domestic Political Terrorism*. Washington, DC: Government Printing Office, 1983.

Terrorism: Definitional Problems

Von Clausewitz (1976) stated that terrorism is the continuation of politics by other means. The political content of the act of terroristic violence distinguishes it from such ordinary violent criminal activities as murder, kidnapping, hijacking, robbery, arson, and extortion, all of which are committed with far greater frequency by "nonterrorists" for motives of simple revenge, profit, or passion.

The political nature of the motivation, purpose, and origin of terrorist groups is the most important characteristic shared by such disparate groups as the PIRA, Sendero Luminoso, RAF, PFLP, Red Brigades, Sikh extremists, WUO, JDL, and a variety of neo-fascist groups.

There are, of course, other characteristics that distinguish terrorism from other forms of violent crime. Wilkinson (1976) identifies the following:

1. The systematic use of murder, injury, or threats to achieve *political* ends, e.g., government repression, revolutionary activity, or recognition.
2. The focus, direction, and purpose of terrorism is to create *fear, insecurity and panic.*
3. Terrorism is inherently indiscriminate and random. Terrorism is deliberate attacks on civilian (noncombatants) targets. This strategy spreads fear, for none in particular is the target; therefore, no one is safe and the individual is unable to avoid being a victim. The strategy of terrorism is directed toward "soft" targets.
4. Terrorism involves barbaric methods of destruction, e.g., car bombs, nail bombs, and double bombs are preferred. Terrorism recognizes no rules or conventions of warfare.
5. Terrorism is more expressive than violence; thus terrorists need an audience and the media. Without the media, terrorism is an exercise in futility. The Palestine question, the Irish troubles, or the dreams of South Moluccans are given substance by the media. The combination of outrageous demands and outrageous behavior commands our attention.
6. Terrorist acts are well planned rather than spontaneous acts of criminal violence.

The political dimension of terrorism confounds our attempts to study it in a scholarly fashion. The word "terrorism" itself is hopelessly loaded and is normally applied only to activities of which we disapprove. Even those who practice terrorism and who openly seek credit for bombings, skyjackings, assassinations, and other violent criminal acts prefer to be known by other, less pejorative titles, such as freedom fighters, guerrillas, commandos, revolutionaries, insurgents, or armies of national liberation. The word terrorism can produce extreme emotions, partly as a reaction to the indiscriminate nature of the violence and fear associated with it and partly because of its philosophical substance. The search for a definition which is both concise enough to provide an intelligent analytical premise yet general enough to obtain agreement by all parties in the debate is laden with complexity. As a result of this problem, many observers and analysts get around the definitional problem by referring to one of several preemptive phrases, such as "one person's terrorist is another person's freedom fighter," "terrorism to some is heroism to others," "today's terrorist is tomorrow's freedom fighter," and so on. These phrases, aphoristic though they may seem, outline the problem facing scholars who have attempted to define the limits of terrorism either for the purpose of developing some type of international agreement or to conduct scholarly research. Terrorism wears many hats and only recently has it become a central concern of democratic governments. In one respect, terrorism is the use of unlawful means to achieve legitimate ends (Poland, 1988; Wardlaw, 1982).

The problem of definition is further exacerbated by observers who frequently engage in the familiar rhetorical tactic of answering a question or a charge by leveling a countercharge. The key to this tactic is the speed and facility that the "but what about" phrase can be

TABLE 1

Chronological Summary of Confirmed Incidents

Date	Location	Type	Group Attributed To
1987			
4/16	Davis, CA	Arson	Animal Liberation Front
5/25	Mayaguez, PR	Pipe Bombing	Guerrilla Forces of Liberation
5/25	Caguas, PR	Pipe Bombing	Guerrilla Forces of Liberation
5/25	Ponce, PR	Pipe Bombing	Guerrilla Forces of Liberation
5/25	Aibonito, PR	Pipe Bombing	Guerrilla Forces of Liberation
5/25	Mayaguez, PR	Attempted Pipe Bombing	Guerrilla Forces of Liberation
5/25	Carolina, PR	Attempted Pipe Bombing	Guerrilla Forces of Liberation
5/25	Cidra, PR	Attempted Pipe Bombing	Guerrilla Forces of Liberation
10/?	Flagstaff, AZ	Malicious Destruction of Property	Evan Mecham Eco-Terrorist International Conspiracy (EMETIC)
1988			
1/12	Rio Piedras, PR	Fire Bombing (2 incidents)	Pedro Albizu Campos Revolutionary Forces
5/26	Coral Gables, FL	Bombing	Organization Alliance of Cuban Intransigence (OACI)
7/22	Caguas, PR	Pipe Bombing	Ejercito Popular Boricua-Macheteros
9/19	Los Angeles, CA	Bombing	Up the IRS, Inc.
9/25	Grand Canyon, AZ	Sabotage	Evan Mecham Eco-Terrorist International Conspiracy (EMETIC)
10/25 or 10/26	Flagstaff, AZ	Malicious Destruction of Property	Evan Mecham Eco-Terrorist International Conspiracy (EMETIC)
11/01	Rio Piedras, PR	Pipe Bombing	Pedro Albizu Campos Revolutionary Forces
11/04	Rio Piedras, PR	Attempted Pipe Bombing	Pedro Albizu Campos Revolutionary Forces
1989			
4/03	Tucson, AZ	Arson	Animal Liberation Front
6/19	Bayamon, PR	Pipe Bombing (2 incidents)	Ejercito Popular Boricua-Macheteros
7/03 or 7/04	Lubbock, TX	Malicious Destruction of Property	Animal Liberation Front
1990			
1/12	Santurce, PR	Pipe Bombing	Pedro Albizu Campos Revolutionary Forces
1/12	Carolina, PR	Pipe Bombing	Pedro Albizu Campos Revolutionary Forces
2/22	Los Angeles, CA	Bombing	Up the IRS, Inc.
4/22	Santa Cruz County, CA	Malicious Destruction of Property	Earth Night Action Group
5/27	Mayaguez, PR	Arson	Unknown Puerto Rican Group
9/17	Arecibo, PR	Bombing	Pedro Albizu Campos Revolutionary Forces
9/17	Vega Baja, PR	Bombing	Pedro Albizu Campos Revolutionary Forces
1991			
2/03	Mayaguez, PR	Arson	Popular Liberation Army
2/18	Sabana Grande, PR	Arson	Popular Liberation Army
3/17	Carolina, PR	Arson	Unknown Puerto Rico Group
4/01	Fresno, CA	Bombing	Up the IRS, Inc.
7/06	Punta Borinquen, PR	Bombing	Popular Liberation Army

(in Arizona and California) and two took place in the southern region (one each in Florida and Texas). Bombing attacks (including explosions, attempted bombings, pipe, tear gas, and fire bombings) dominated the type of attack during this period (twenty-three of thirty-four). Also included were four acts of malicious destruction of property, one act of sabotage, and six arsons. Surprisingly, no deaths or injuries resulted from the incidents.

In addition, the FBI recorded thirty-one suspected acts of terrorism. Similar to confirmed incidents, the use of an explosive device, both detonated and undetonated, was the most popular weapon. Targeted areas included California, Florida, Illinois, Montana, New York, and Puerto Rico. Three injuries resulted from these suspected terrorist acts. In a third category, twenty-four potential acts of terrorism were prevented.

The FBI recognizes two types of terrorism in the United States. Domestic terrorism involves groups or individuals whose terrorist activities are directed at elements of our government or population without foreign direction. International terrorism is terrorist activity committed by groups or individuals who are foreign-based and/or directed by countries or groups outside the United States or whose activities transcend national boundaries.

Financing of Terrorist Groups
Domestic terrorist groups, indigenous to the United States, have engaged in a variety of activities to support themselves. This has included bank robberies, armored car robberies, member contributions, extortion, counterfeiting, money laundering, credit card fraud, and fund-raisers. For example, on September 7, 1988, five members of a splinter group of Aryan Nations were prosecuted on counterfeiting charges. During the past several years, dozens of members of "The Order" (Silent Brotherhood) were convicted on counterfeiting and armed robbery charges, their largest undertaking being the 1984 multimillion-dollar Brink's armored car robbery in Ukiah, California. In a similar manner, leftist revolutionary groups such as the United Freedom Front, which was Marxist-Leninist in its ideals, financed their bombing campaigns in the early 1980s through bank and armored truck robberies which they termed "expropriations." Domestic terrorist groups have also turned to foreign sponsors of terrorism to fund their operations. In 1986 members

of the El Rukn Street Gang were arrested in conjunction with an FBI undercover operation in which El Rukn members purchased an inert, light antitank weapon (LAW). The LAW rocket was allegedly to be used in the commission of a terrorist act in the United States in return for funding of the El Rukn Street Gang by the government of Libya. A deceptive means of obtaining money for terrorist activities is through fund-raisers. These affairs sponsored by organizations affiliated with terrorist groups include rallies, conventions, dinner parties, and mass mailings. Prime contributors to these affairs are members of emigre communities and emigre student organizations, who are advised that the funds are being obtained for such causes as war orphans and widows of the "struggle movement." Any effective law-enforcement campaign against terrorism requires an understanding and targeting of the financial resources of terrorist groups. Simply stated, a common recurring ingredient for all terrorist groups is the need to obtain funding for weapons, training, and supplies for its members.

By far the most imposing terrorist threat is the possibility of nuclear terrorism. Recent events in global affairs, such as the disintegration of the Soviet Union/Eastern bloc and the discovery of Iraq's substantial nuclear program, have heightened awareness of the threat overseas. The tremendous volume of nuclear weapons scheduled to be removed for eventual dismantlement has generated fears that these weapons while in transit might be vulnerable to terrorists. At home U.S. nuclear facilities are no less attractive targets for making an indelible political statement. The FBI has a Nuclear Crisis Response Plan to be implemented immediately upon receipt of information relating to a nuclear terrorism incident. The plan marshals specialized resources and personnel from the Department of Energy, the Department of Defense, and other federal agencies who possess technical expertise to assist the FBI. All FBI field offices with DOE and/or Nuclear Regulatory Commission facilities within their territory maintain site-specific nuclear contingency plans, which are updated regularly. These, of course, are reactive measures. Each U.S. nuclear facility maintains its own security force in a proactive mode.

World Trade Center Incident
The foregoing chronology of terrorism in the United States comes from the most recent FBI

report, ending in 1991. Since then the unthinkable has happened—the perpetration of a major act of international terrorism in the most populous American city. On February 26, 1993, a bomb detonated inside the World Trade Center in New York City killed five people and injured over 1,000. The cost of structural damage that disabled the building and business time lost in an active commercial center could not be estimated accurately. When the FBI began its investigation an early break in the case appeared unlikely. But break it did in less than a week. Forensic evidence found in the extensive rubble of steel and concrete and a daisy-chain paper trail led the FBI to Mohammed Salameh. In what the media termed an amateur act, Salameh had used his own name to rent a van to carry the bomb into the World Trade Center. At the Ryder Truck Rental Agency he had left a phone number where he could be reached, and he had returned to Ryder no fewer than three times to collect a refund on his deposit. The bomb itself was a crude device made with agricultural fertilizer. Although the bomb lacked sophistication it did its job well enough and a better bomb might have toppled the building. The FBI learned that Salameh was Jordanian by birth with ties to Iraq. In rapid succession, other coconspirators emerged revealing a network of terrorists active on the East Coast. By following wire transfers of money to Germany, the FBI produced solid evidence linking Salameh to terrorist funding. The amount of money involved was just under $10,000 per transfer to avoid federal reporting requirements. Those aspects of the case cropped up early and easily. What then remained was for the FBI to pursue the case most likely into the Middle East, where success is much harder to come by, and prosecution in this country for the crime. After the World Trade Center bombing the United States joined Great Britain, Germany, Italy, Greece, and other nations around the world as having been violated by a major international terrorist attack.

Bibliography

Adams, James. *The Financing of Terror: How the Groups That are Terrorizing the World Get the Money to Do It.* New York: Simon and Schuster, 1986.

Hoffmann, Bruce. *Terrorism in the United States and the Potential Threat to Nuclear Facilities.* Santa Monica, CA: Rand Corporation, 1986.

Motley, James B. *U.S. Strategy to Counter Domestic Political Terrorism.* Washington, DC: National Defense University Press, 1983.

Poland, James M. *Understanding Terrorism: Groups, Strategies, and Responses.* Englewood Cliffs, NJ: Prentice-Hall, 1988.

Rubin, Barry, ed. *The Politics of Counterterrorism: The Ordeal of Democratic States.* Washington, DC: Johns Hopkins University Foreign Policy Institute, 1990.

Technology Against Terrorism: The Federal Effort. Washington, DC: U.S. Congress, Office of Technology Assessment, 1991.

Terrorist Research and Analytical Center. *Terrorism in the United States 1991.* Washington, DC: U.S. Department of Justice, Federal Bureau of Investigation, 1992.

Texas Rangers (1823–)

In its duties this unique law-enforcement body operates somewhere between the military and local authorities. Historically, Texas Rangers have "ranged" over the state of Texas assisting city and county officials with peacekeeping, investigations, and general cleanup of outlaws. As stated in Art. 4413 (11) of the Texas *Revised Civil Statutes*:

> They shall have authority to make arrests, and to execute process in criminal cases; and in civil cases when specially directed by the judge of a court of record; and in all cases shall be governed by the laws regulating and defining the powers and duties of sheriffs when in the discharge of similar duties; except that they shall have the power and shall be authorized to make arrests and to execute all process in criminal cases in any county in the state.

Since there are 254 counties in Texas stretching across 266,807 square miles, canvasing the state takes some doing.

Early History

In 1823 Stephen F. Austin, civil and military leader of the Anglo-American colonists in Texas, employed ten men to serve as peace officers, naming them Rangers. Three years later Austin added to their number in a written agreement with six militia districts to keep "twenty to thirty Rangers in service all the time." The force gained legal status in 1835 with the outbreak of the Texas Revolution. War with Mexico drained manpower from the western frontier, leaving settlers vulnerable to Indian attack, so a larger corps of Rangers was assembled to patrol the borderland. Then from 1836 to 1845, the period of the Republic, Texas, having won independence from Mexico, was fearful that the Mexicans no less than the Plains Indians would seek to recapture their land. How to handle the threat of encroachment was the burning question. Eminent Texas historian Walter Prescott Webb tells what was decided by the leaders of the fledgling Republic:

> Experience proved that the most effective force was a squad of well-mounted men who would ride the great distances along the two frontiers and repel or destroy raiding parties. Legally these forces were given all sorts of titles, such as mounted gunmen, spies, mounted riflemen, etc., but it became the custom to refer to them in common parlance as Texas Rangers. (Webb, 1952:756)

During this time men such as Ben McCulloch, Samuel H. Walker, W.A.A. (Big Foot) Wallace, and John Coffee Hays earned reputations as gutsy Rangers able to surmount whatever odds were against them. For instance, McCulloch and a group of Rangers rode alongside a volunteer army in pursuit of Comanches who had stolen from and murdered settlers in the Guadalupe Valley. They all met on August 12, 1840, in what was to be called the Plum Creek Fight. There the Rangers fought boldly, and the surviving Comanches retreated farther west out of Texas. Hays, equally a hero, also beat back Indians by using the newly developed Colt revolver.

Two Wars
In 1845 Texas entered the Union and on the heels of that event a second war with Mexico commenced. John Coffee Hays, made a colonel, was ordered to raise a regiment of five hundred Texas Rangers to assist in the war effort. For the first time in their history the Rangers fought as a unit in the United States Army. It was to be something of a drawback, though, because they were not military per se but free spirits; they lacked spit-and-polish discipline and tended to

despise the Mexicans to a degree beyond that generated by mere warfare. Another development concomitant with entry into the Union was that Texans expected federal troops to take over defense of the borderlands. This relief never materialized; the federal troops remained stationary, not riding roughshod across the dusty miles meting out justice as did the Rangers. As a result, in the minds of many Texans, their Rangers were irreplaceable.

During the Civil War the Rangers lost some of their luster, since they stayed at home to continue guarding the Indian frontier while other Texans trudged east to the real battle. After the Civil War, Reconstruction governor E.J. Davis oversaw legislation to create the first state police for Texas, which would overshadow the Rangers. Davis' intention was to make sure that Reconstruction policies would be adhered to, but what Texas got was three years of police corruption, culminating in Chief James Davidson's absconding to Belgium with $37,434.67 of the state's money. On April 22, 1873, the act authorizing the state police was repealed and the force abolished.

Rise to Greatness
Between 1874 and 1890 the Texas Rangers knew glory enough to fill a hundred legends. Lawlessness in the state had grown to alarming proportions before Governor Richard Coke charged the state legislature with enactment of a legal remedy. Out of its deliberation came the creation of two fighting forces. Major John B. Jones commanded the larger of the two, the Frontier Battalion, composed of six companies, each under the command of a captain. The battalion roamed the border to repulse any Indian uprising, although Major Jones and his Rangers spent more time correcting civil matters: riots, feuds, murders, and train robberies. Captain L.H. McNelly led the second contingent, called the Special Force, comprised of about thirty men. Its duty was to suppress cow theft and brigandage. One of McNelly's most famous actions was the Las Cuevas affair. In it sixteen bandits paid with their lives for driving stolen cattle into Mexico. The Texas Rangers were not to be trifled with, and almost any crime committed near the border was dealt with harshly—that was the widespread warning of Las Cuevas.

Men from these forces achieved even greater notoriety by hunting down and capturing such outlaw killers as John Wesley Hardin and Sam Bass when it appeared that no one else could stand up to them. The anecdote of the day was that in a small Texas town an angry mob was about to destroy the place when, livid with fear, the mayor sent for the Texas Rangers. At noon a train arrived and off stepped a lone man armed with a Winchester rifle, his steely eyes fixed on the mob. The mayor asked, "Who are you?" "I'm a Texas Ranger," he replied. Hoots and laughter shook the town. "What, only one Ranger? When we've got a mob! Where are your men?" The Ranger answered in a calm, clear voice, "You've got only one mob, haven't you? Now what's the ruckus?"

A Well-Established Institution
Into the twentieth century the Texas Rangers still maintained border patrol even though Indian raids had stopped and cattle rustling was on the decline. In 1911 Pancho Villa's bandits were smuggling guns from Texas into Mexico and had to be stopped. A few years later in 1918 with Prohibition the contraband reversed direction; this time illegal liquor flooded into Texas from Mexico. Both unlawful activities kept the Rangers more than busy. Then, perhaps the single greatest search for a band of criminals on the loose occurred in 1934. Destiny ordained that the Barrow gang, led by Clyde Barrow and Bonnie Parker, was to meet head-on with Frank Hamer, the quintessential Texas Ranger. When Hamer got the assignment to go after them, the gang had already killed twelve people in cold blood. Hamer, a superlative looking man, reported to have killed sixty-five outlaws in thirty years of law work, caught up with Bonnie and Clyde in Louisiana. He had stalked them for 102 days. From ambush he and other lawmen blasted the couple in their Ford, riddling metal and flesh with bullets, thus ending their spectacular crime spree. For bringing Bonnie and Clyde to justice the State of Texas paid Hamer at the rate of $180 a month for the time he was on their trail.

But such heroics were not enough to sustain the life of the Texas Rangers, or so it seemed. In 1932, two years before Hamer's historic confrontation, during the gubernatorial race, the Rangers supported Ross Sterling in opposition to Miriam "Ma" Ferguson. When "Ma" won the election she fired all forty-four Rangers in service and replaced them with her appointees. Her vendetta tarnished the good name of the force, built up over 110 years, as Texans witnessed one of her "Rangers" convicted of murder, several others declared guilty

of using confiscated equipment to rig their own gambling hall, and a captain arrested for theft and embezzlement. Understandably, after such misuse of authority, high-level talk centered around abolishing one of the best-known law enforcement bodies in the world. Only the election of a new governor, James V. Allred, saved the day. Governor Allred appointed Albert Sidney Johnson chairman of the new Public Safety Commission to resuscitate the Texas Rangers. Before Johnson was through he had erected new quarters at Camp Mabry, placing the State Highway Patrol and the Rangers under one roof, had beefed up personnel, and had purchased every description of crime-solving equipment.

Today, the Texas Rangers operate as a part of the Texas Department of Public Safety and are still considered second to none in their role as free-agent lawmen. They carry on the tradition of their past brethren James B. Gillett, Ira Aten, Buck Barry, Captain John R. Hughes, Captain Bill McDonald, James Pike, and others who traversed Texas to make it a safe place to live. All of the Rangers mentioned in this brief history can be read about in colorful biographies that challenge any Western novel for genuine gallantry.

Bibliography
Douglas, Claude Leroy. *The Gentlemen in the White Hats: Dramatic Episodes in the History of the Texas Rangers.* Dallas, TX: South West Press, 1934.
Mason, Herbert Molloy, Jr. *The Texas Rangers.* New York: Meredith Press, 1967.
Webb, Walter Prescott. *The Texas Rangers: A Century of Frontier Defense.* Austin, TX: University of Texas Press, 1935.
———, ed. *The Handbook of Texas.* 2 vols. Austin, TX: Texas State Historical Association, 1952.
———. *The Story of the Texas Rangers.* Austin, TX: Encino Press, 1957.

Traffic Radar
Since its introduction to traffic law enforcement in 1948, radar (*ra*dio *d*etection *a*nd *r*anging) has been an integral component of vehicular speed measurement. Each year hundreds of thousands of dollars are collected in courts throughout the nation from motorists whose vehicular speed was monitored with the aid of this electronic instrument.

Today, with the evolution of radar into a technologically sophisticated device, its overall efficiency and effectiveness have been greatly enhanced. In spite of vast improvements, radar is currently being scrutinized, questioned, and challenged, not only for its reliability but also for the quality of operator training.

The use of radar first came into prominence during World War II when it was developed by the British to measure the distance, speed, and direction of enemy aircraft and naval vessels. Early military radar was a pulse type that transmitted its signal at intermittent intervals. An object's distance was measured by the length of time it took the signal to leave, travel to the object, and return to the radar signal receiver. Direction, on the other hand, was determined by comparing the angle of the signal transmittal with its angle on return.

The police radar units of today differ from the earlier pulse-type radar in that they use a constant wave signal to measure speed or relative motion. For example, a signal is sent out from the transmitter, strikes an object in motion, and part of the signal reflects back to a receiver in the radar unit. The shift or change in signal frequency is then measured and converted by the unit into a speed reading.

Police radar operates using the "Doppler effect," named after the Austrian physicist Christian Johann Doppler, who is credited with its discovery in 1842. This scientific principle states that the frequency of sound waves will vary as the distance between a transmitter and receiver is either increased or decreased. In addition to sound waves, this effect also applies to light waves, radio waves, or any others.

Traffic radar units used in speed monitoring activities today transmit radio waves at a rate of ten billion or more per second on two primary radar frequencies, X- and K-band. An X-band radar unit transmits its signal at a frequency of 10.525 GHz (gigahertz) or 10,525,000,000 waves per second. The K-band radar unit transmits its signal at a frequency of 24.150 GHz or 24,150,000,000 waves per second. Both signals travel at the speed of light or 186,000 miles per second.

A beam that strikes a stationary object will be reflected to the receiver at the same frequency at which it was originally transmitted, and no speed measurement will be shown. However, an object moving toward the radar's transmitter will compress the signal, causing a higher returned frequency. An object moving away will cause a lengthened signal, thereby returning the signal at a lower frequency. In the latter two instances, there is a definite change between the transmitted and received signal, representing relative motion that will result in the radar unit displaying a vehicular speed measurement.

How much of a change is needed to register a speed reading? For every one mile per hour with an X-band radar unit there must be a shift in frequency of 31.4 waves per second; whereas a shift in frequency of 72.0 waves per second is necessary with a K-band radar unit. It is important to remember that police traffic radar will register a speed measurement only when there has been a change in the frequency between the transmitted and reflected signal caused by the relative motion of an object capable of reflecting the radar signal.

At the present time, what is the state of the art for radar and radar operator training? To give us some sense of perspective, we need to examine the course of events that has transpired at the federal level.

In August 1977 the National Highway Traffic Safety Administration (NHTSA) entered into an interagency agreement with the National Bureau of Standards (NBS) in hopes that such a collaboration would produce performance standards for police speed-measuring devices.

During the next three years, the National Bureau of Standards tested both radar and nonradar speed-measuring devices and in November 1980 presented a draft copy of performance standards for radar devices to the National Highway Traffic Safety Administration. The goal of this joint effort was to publish a "Qualified Products List" of those devices that met or exceeded these standards.

On January 8, 1981, the NHTSA published a Notice of Proposed Rulemaking in the *Federal Register* requesting comments on performance requirements and methods for evaluating speed-measuring devices. Benefits from this proposal would be measured in terms of definitive specifications for use by state administrators and purchasing agents. It was also hoped that compliance with such standards would result in better quality radar devices, and additional courts would accept radar-based evidence because of better equipment.

However, with the national election came a change in federal administration philosophy and, as one NHTSA representative termed it, "upon further consideration" a Notice of Termination of Rulemaking was issued in the November 19, 1981, *Federal Register*. There would be no "Qualified Products List"; instead the states were given the benefit of the National Bureau of Standards test results in order to adopt their own specifications for radar devices. It was quite clear that the issuance of any kind of performance standards on radar units could become a "hot potato" that might prompt challenges of prestandard devices.

In October 1982 the International Association of Chiefs of Police (IACP) entered into an agreement with the national Highway Traffic Safety Administration and the Law Enforcement Standards Laboratory of the National Bureau of Standards for the purpose of conducting a radar research and testing program. This project was undertaken to determine the compliance of currently marketed radar devices with the previously established "Model Performance Specifications for Police Traffic Radar Devices," set forth by the National Bureau of Standards. The end result was a "Consumer Products List" to assist law-enforcement agencies throughout the country in making future radar purchases.

The IACP solicited and received more than fifty requests for testing program documents from independent organizations. After careful review, they selected Dayton T. Brown, Inc., Bohemia, New York, and the Department of Electrical Engineering and Systems Science, Michigan State University.

During the preliminary testing phase, each laboratory was given one radar device to test under the watchful eye of technically qualified persons from the National Highway Traffic Safety Administration, the National Bureau of Standards, and the International Association of Chiefs of Police. This was done to ensure that the laboratory personnel were competent, the testing equipment was appropriate, and the tests conducted were done in the proper manner.

In June and July of 1983, the test laboratories were given the remainder of the radar units and testing was completed on a total of twenty-four devices in October. At the completion of this initial phase, it was reported that none of the radar units totally complied with the model performance specifications.

For example, some units were not accompanied by an operator's manual, tuning-fork certificates, or even the correct tuning fork; some failed to meet certain labeling requirements; others were deficient in signal-processing channel sensitivity, frequency stability under conditions of high humidity or extreme temperature, and display readability, i.e., numerical height and luminescence.

As a result of these and other shortcomings, the IACP then made a recommendation to the NHTSA and NBS to allow the radar manufacturers to make the necessary modifications to bring each unit into full compliance.

This recommendation was accepted, but not without certain conditions for each manufacturer to meet. It was set forth that (1) required modifications were to be performed on the same unit tested during the initial phase, (2) modifications must be made in the presence of laboratory testing personnel, (3) the NBS technical staff was to be provided with information on any circuit modification in order to determine if additional testing would be required, and (4) the manufacturer would be required to pay for any additional testing upon completion of the modifications. All participating radar manufacturers agreed to comply with these conditions and resubmitted their units for the final phase of testing, which was completed in January 1984.

The final analysis showed all radar devices tested to be in full compliance with the model performance specifications. A listing of each device was published in April 1984 by the International Association of Chiefs of Police in the form of a "Consumer Products List." Along with this, the IACP also published a detailed explanation of the entire testing program in a set of summary documents entitled *Testing of Police Traffic Radar Devices—Volumes I and II.*

In 1986, the IACP and NHTSA testing program was reinstated and three new radar models were added to the "Consumer Products List," bringing the total of approved units to twenty-seven.

The National Highway Traffic Safety Administration has also been active in the preparation of a comprehensive radar operators' training program for use by law-enforcement agencies and training institutions. Their recommended forty-hour program, which was distributed in September 1982, consists of twenty-four hours of classroom instruction and sixteen hours of supervised practical application. This program has become the training standard for radar operators nationwide.

There is no doubt that the cooperative efforts of the National Highway Traffic Safety Administration, the National Bureau of Standards, and the International Association of Chiefs of Police in testing police traffic radar have indeed provided much worthwhile and needed information for the benefit of all law-enforcement agencies. Without equivocation, government-sponsored radar-testing programs, improvements in equipment, and the establishment of a standardized training program have all had a positive impact on both a unit's reliability and an operator's credibility.

Traffic radar has come a long way since its introduction and early use in speed-monitoring activities. The radar units of today are more technologically sophisticated and the operators much better trained; however, in spite of these advancements, radar is often unduly criticized. Regardless of this criticism, the fact still remains that in the United States, traffic radar and its application play an integral part in providing a safe, efficient, and economical system of transportation for the entire motoring public.

Robert E. Nichols, Jr.

Bibliography

Basic Training Program in Radar Speed Measurement. Washington, DC: U.S. Department of Transportation, National Highway Traffic Safety Administration, September 1982.
Field Strength Measurements of Speed Measuring Radar Units. Washington, DC: U.S. Department of Transportation, National Highway Traffic Safety Administration, June 1981.
Model Performance Specifications for Police Traffic Radar Devices. Washington, DC: U.S. Department of Transportation, National Highway Traffic Safety Administration, March 1982.
Nichols, Robert E., Jr. *Police Radar: A Guide to Basic Understanding.* Springfield, IL: Charles C. Thomas, 1982.
———. "Police Radar: The State of the Art." *Wisconsin Law Enforcement Journal* (Summer 1983).
———. "A 1984 Update on Police Traffic Radar." *Wisconsin Law Enforcement Journal* (Winter 1984).
Police Traffic Radar. Washington, DC: U.S. Department of Transportation, National Highway Traffic Safety Administration, February 1980.
Testing of Police Traffic Radar Devices, Volume I—Test Program Summary. Gaithersburg, MD: International Association of Chiefs of Police, April 1984.
Testing of Police Traffic Radar Devices, Volume II—Test Data. Gaithersburg, MD: International Association of Chiefs of Police, May 1984.

Traffic Services

Traffic services encompasses one of the broadest and most important areas of law enforcement. Often referred to as PTS (Police Traffic Services), the field covers everything the police do that relates to highway and traffic safety.

The importance of PTS can be seen by the magnitude of the losses suffered through traffic crashes. More than three times as many people are killed every year in crashes as are killed through criminal activity. Many times more people are injured in crashes than in criminal assaults. The value of property damaged in crashes is far higher than the value of property stolen or damaged by criminal acts. The primary purpose of PTS is to stem these losses.

PTS has a relatively short history. While traffic control dates back to horse and buggy days, PTS as a concept dates from the 1920s. It was then that the public first began to notice the toll exacted by traffic crashes and began to demand some action. The first conference on PTS was sponsored by the National Safety Council and was designed to devise methods for reducing accidents in cities. It was also during this era that the first state highway patrol type agencies were formed.

Over the years there has been a lot of involvement in highway safety by government at all levels. Concern with the loss of life and property from traffic accidents has prompted implementation of a variety of programs and efforts, the expenditure of large sums of public money, and the generation of new laws.

Occasionally, as during the oil embargos of the 1970s, some reduction in traffic accidents was visible, but there was little or no agreement on the specific causes of the reduction. One need only turn to the literature to realize that even among experts there is no overriding consensus.

One of the problems facing PTS is the lack of a universal definition. Arbitrarily, the following definition from the IACP will be used:

All activity performed by the police to assist in the safe, rapid, and efficient movement of persons and goods on this nation's streets and highways.

It is equally difficult to find agreement on the elements or activities that are logically placed within the realm of PTS. The following elements or subfunctions have been selected as constituting police traffic services :

Traffic Law Enforcement
Accident Investigation and Management
Traffic Direction and Control
Traffic Engineering
Traffic Ancillary Services
Police Traffic Services Administration

These are also the six subgroups within PTS that are used by the Commission on Accreditation for Law Enforcement Agencies (CALEA) in standards that they have developed. The following sections elaborate on these six elements.

Traffic Law Enforcement

Enforcement of traffic laws is a primary responsibility in the effective delivery of police traffic services. It involves identifying and apprehending traffic offenders, taking enforcement action against them, and participating in the adjudication of charges brought. Enforcement is a unique police contribution. It is the keystone of the entire structure of PTS.

The basic purpose of Traffic Law Enforcement (TLE) is to reduce accidents and control congestion. However, police action must be directed to the entire spectrum of infractions so that a climate of general compliance with traffic laws can be achieved.

The test of effectiveness of any enforcement effort is in the reduction of infractions. It must not be assumed that the failure to reduce accidents is necessarily a failure of the police effort. There are many variables that contribute to accidents, and while the police effort may not show reductions in incidents, it may keep the problem from getting worse.

Because of the limited resources available for enforcement, the selection of activities must necessarily be limited to those with the greatest potential for success. Analysis of traffic data will generally indicate the type, time, and locations of violations most frequently associated with vehicular and pedestrian accidents.

The driving public, in general, has a poor perception of the risk of having an accident. Many drivers feel that they will not incur damage, injury, loss of life, or economic loss as a result of their driving style. TLE is one way of increasing the perception of risk.

A traffic citation is of little use unless it results in a conviction. The judicial process sometimes dilutes the effect of the citation by plea bargaining, minimum sentences, or findings of "not guilty" because of a legal technicality. Enforcement agencies should provide rigorous training for officers to minimize the number of convictions lost as a result of some mistaken action or inaction on the part of the arresting officer.

When motorists are stopped for an infraction, an opportunity is present to educate them so that they will be less likely to violate again. Such things as information on violations as factors in accidents and general safe-driving practices are often as effective as the issuing of a citation in curbing unsafe driving activity.

Treating violators fairly enhances the image of law enforcement. If they are informed both of their rights and responsibilities they will be less likely to resent the process of being cited.

Enforcement must be uniform in its application. *Nothing is more damaging* to the police image than the suspicion that certain elements of the population are "picked on" or victimized by enforcement action. The seriousness of the offense, the degree of violation, the conditions and circumstances surrounding the offense, and the available evidence should be the controlling factors to support the action.

Traffic enforcement should not be the exclusive province of officers assigned to traffic safety duty. All officers should be involved in some traffic enforcement, particularly when a violation occurs in their presence.

While officer discretion should not be unduly constrained, because of the wide variety of circumstances under which traffic violations occur, specific guidelines should be provided for enforcement actions to ensure the uniformity and appropriateness of their application. It is extremely important to observe the constitutional rights and privileges of all citizens. No compromise with consistent and uniform enforcement should be influenced by the age, sex, race, or other characteristics of the offender.

An officer who issues a traffic citation accepts the obligation to pursue that action through the courts by preparing evidence, obtaining witnesses, testifying, and performing the necessary functions to ensure a conviction.

Agencies coordinate with local courts to ensure that officers need appear only when a case is actually going to be heard; appearance in court by officers is mandated under those circumstances; and complete case files are provided to the prosecutor well ahead of trial dates.

Agencies have a specific policy on pursuit. They use fixed-point selective enforcement to save energy and to increase police visibility. They also have specific enforcement plans in place such as truck and weight enforcement, hazardous materials transportation, DWI enforcement, and bicycle/pedestrian programs.

Accident Investigation and Management
Police respond to a traffic accident in two different ways. As scene managers they are concerned with the preservation of human life, the speedy clearing of unsafe conditions, and the reduction of confusion. Every law-enforcement officer is responsible for such measures. Accident investigation, however, can prove to be a complex and demanding responsibility to be carried out only by someone with specialized training.

Accident investigations are conducted to collect data to determine contributing factors in the incident, to establish prevention programs, and to take appropriate legal actions. Data needs vary widely from a multifatality accident to one in which the only damage is a scratch that can be repaired at little cost. Regardless of severity, the value of the data for uses other than legal action should be explored to the fullest extent.

Data must be gathered with maximum accuracy and uniformity of definitions, categories, and formats. The information will be used to discover patterns that assist in reducing future accidents. It will also provide the basis for enforcement actions where violations have occurred, and will be useful to a variety of potential users, including state and local highway departments, parties involved in the accident, and the agency itself. The need for such various uses must be anticipated. This sets a requirement that data must be reliable and uniform. Local definitions and nonstandard forms can make the task of analysis difficult if not impossible.

While an enforcement action is usually appropriate at an accident scene, it is most important that there be sufficient evidence available to support the action. Police must make a

maximum investigative effort whenever an accident involves substantial damage or injuries, and in particular when criminal or civil legal actions are anticipated.

The completeness and accuracy of reports are mandatory if analysts are to determine accident patterns, contributing factors, and accident investigation principles and procedures. Individual reports must be considered in aggregate so that those responsible for safety actions can benefit from the information.

There are a number of follow-up activities to complete the handling of an investigated accident. Every effort must be made to identify and apprehend drivers who leave the scene of accidents without fulfilling their legal responsibilities. Such drivers are a serious threat to the goals of traffic safety.

Persons involved in accidents must be provided information concerning their rights and responsibilities. This includes the completion of forms, the exchange of identifying information, and other matters specified by law. They also have the right to obtain information and avoid self-incrimination.

After taking an enforcement action at an accident scene, an officer has the obligation to pursue court action by assisting in prosecution, subpoenaing witnesses, preparing evidence, and performing other necessary functions.

Minor accidents, as defined by law or policy, usually do not need investigation. It is only necessary to ensure that the involved parties have exchanged required information, and that required forms are completed.

Accident scene management is a critical action because the most severe results of an accident situation can occur after the initial collision has taken place. This can include the injured not being properly or promptly cared for, other vehicles becoming involved in the accident, fires starting, hazardous materials leaking, or other matters that increase the probability of injury or property loss and increase congestion.

A major concern of police at an accident scene is the immediate care of the injured. The ability of officers to handle such cases varies widely. In rural areas, where emergency medical service personnel may not be readily available, officer competency must be high. In urban situations Emergency Medical Service personnel may be at the accident scene before the police.

Another important action is the clearing of the accident scene and its restoration to normal conditions. The longer a road is closed or traffic is restricted, the greater the possibility of additional accidents and delay to other motorists. However, the need to collect data must not be discouraged by a zeal to get traffic moving again.

Traffic Direction and Control

Traffic conditions may necessitate the physical presence of a control officer. The need may arise on a regular basis in circumstances such as at busy downtown intersections, school crossings, factory gates, and during rush hours. Control may also be needed for such events as athletic contests or parades.

Traffic Direction and Control (TD&C) is sometimes needed unexpectedly under hazardous conditions such as at accident scenes, in adverse weather conditions, and during other natural or civil disturbances. In all such circumstances, safety is a primary goal. While many TD&C assignments are scheduled daily, unexpected events require command officers to divert the necessary manpower quickly.

While the maintenance of safe conditions is of primary importance in PTS, it is also important to maintain the flow of traffic. Emergency regulations, such as street closings and parking bans, are a necessary part of TD&C in hazardous and/or special circumstances. When possible, they should be anticipated and plans made accordingly.

Traffic Engineering

Although traffic engineering is not a primary function of Police Traffic Services, it is nonetheless an influencing element. While police do not have a professional engineering background, they do have one area of expertise that not all traffic engineers possess: a thorough knowledge of the roadway conditions and hazards in their jurisdiction.

In most jurisdictions professional engineering help is available. However, if other agencies are not willing or able to address roadway environment problems, the law-enforcement agency must get involved because of its concern for highway safety and efficiency. The degree to which a department is involved, either as a primary or supplemental agent, can vary considerably, but it is important that police traffic agencies be involved.

A primary function is to assist in identifying engineering-related hazards and reporting them to the appropriate authorities. In most cases the hazards referred to are those not requiring immediate emergency actions. When the hazard is critical, it may require protective measures to be established until public works personnel can assume responsibility for the condition.

When a condition has been identified that requires traffic engineering remedial action, the law-enforcement agency should be involved in the planning as well as the implementation of the remedy. The potential impact upon the agency must be planned for, and the ability of the agency to accomplish what is necessary for the success of the planned action must be assessed.

In some jurisdictions, total transportation system planning, programming, and regulating are sometimes carried out without law-enforcement agency involvement. There are a variety of reasons or excuses for such exclusion, most of which are without merit. The law-enforcement agency should make known its availability and willingness to assist where necessary or appropriate for two reasons:

1. Its unique contribution (knowledge of roadway conditions and hazards) to the total system makes its perspective valuable.
2. Decisions that affect the transportation system have a significant impact on the smooth functioning of PTS operations.

A police agency should develop such data as will be needed for traffic engineering decisions. In some cases the law-enforcement agency must perform simple traffic engineering actions such as taking traffic counts and doing other survey work.

Traffic Ancillary Services

Over time, police have provided various services to the public apart from law-enforcement functions. These services have become both popular and necessary and have been made a permanent part of the agency's responsibilities.

Traffic safety education is one area where police can make a valuable contribution. The extent to which a department can be involved depends on local needs and the participation of other agencies in the education process.

Officers, for example, can work with children of all grade levels, beginning with bicycle and pedestrian safety and emphasizing auto and motorcycle safety in the later grades. Specific topics such as drinking and driving, safety-belt usage, and a driver's rights and responsibilities can be explained. Police can also be active in community safety education through media articles, speakers' bureaus, and related programs.

One of the factors leading to unsafe driving and accidents is a poor perception of risk. Drivers generally consider their driving habits to be safer than they really are. Traffic safety education is one means of increasing the perception of risk. In such training the basic factors causing poor perception must be emphasized. Instilling good traffic safety habits and attitudes in individuals before they are drivers is one of the most important safety roles that a law-enforcement agency can assume.

Agencies should announce specific enforcement programs that they will be implementing. A majority of drivers should take such programs into consideration when they get behind the wheel. Many organizations become interested in traffic safety issues and programs. Law-enforcement agencies should be represented to such organizations as a resource, recommending ideas and programs rather than commenting on the recommendations of others.

Police assistance is most welcomed by the motorist in situations where breakdowns, lack of information, or other problems occur that can interfere with a safe and efficient trip. Such help may include providing trip directions, obtaining gasoline or necessary supplies, or summoning specialized assistance for a variety of mechanical or medical problems. The level of assistance provided will vary by area served. In urban areas appropriate private individuals or organizations are available to help. In rural areas where such services are scarce the agency will play a more active role. Agencies should have a policy that states the services available and the level at which they will be provided.

Police Traffic Services Management
Management and *administration* are terms that are often used interchangeably unless an author wants to apply a unique definition to one or the other. For the purposes of this section, assume that they embrace the same activities: operations, research and planning, personnel administration, evaluation, and information management. Three of these activities are vital to PTS: the management of resources, development of personnel, and the flow and use of information.

If traffic operations are to be at all successful, they must utilize the limited resources made available to obtain maximum operational effectiveness. One of the first steps in this process is to identify traffic problems that are conducive to corrective action. Determining key problem characteristics allows the traffic supervisors to deploy resources in a manner that impacts on operational objectives. The end result of the analysis is to maximize the presence of personnel and equipment at locations and times conducive to enhancing traffic safety and flow.

As with other facets of police work, specialized units may be required for some tasks. In PTS these can include accident investigations, hit-and-run follow-up, drinking and driving enforcement, traffic records analysis, and selective enforcement. Officers may be assigned to these units either full- or part-time, but specific, rigorous training is necessary for such personnel to accomplish their tasks in an effective manner.

When resources for any purpose are limited, it is necessary to conduct evaluations of current programs to determine whether they are meeting their objectives. The department cannot afford to continue programs that fail in their purposes regardless of the worthy intentions involved.

The management procedures and guidelines that direct specific programs should not be considered fixed for all time. They should be subjected to scrutiny at regular intervals. The rationale for such action is continual adaptation to changing conditions. As evaluation results flow in and conditions change, there must be modifications to keep programs and procedures at maximum effectiveness.

A few cautions about evaluation are in order. It is performed at set times, uses objective criteria and measures, is open to outside inspection, and considers overall agency objectives. PTS programs can be too easily planned and implemented without the evaluation to determine if agency resources are being used wisely.

One of the most important management functions is the maintenance of personnel competence. Formal academy training, field training, periodic in-service training, and attendance at such institutions as the Northwestern University Traffic Institute are the customary methods used.

While PTS specialists are necessary, this does not reduce the obligation of all agency personnel to perform PTS functions associated with their positions in an efficient and effective manner. Training in some aspects of PTS is necessary for a wide range of agency employees.

Patrol officers usually have operational PTS responsibilities for which they should be trained and evaluated. Patrol supervisors and command-level personnel must plan, evaluate, and coordinate operations. Performance training standards should guide their effort.

No PTS system can operate effectively without data for the purpose of identifying problems and to support actions taken. A key principle in information system design is that data collected must be organized in such a way that they are readily available to potential users in a format useful to them. The agency's PTS records are a primary component of such a system. This includes accident reports, citations, and miscellaneous traffic-related incident reports. The data required to conduct evaluations of programs and operations are another important element.

One problem with information systems is that they generate many reports that nobody reads or uses. Regular review of user needs and uses is important so that system managers may produce the most useful management information.

There are several characteristics of a data system that are critical. If the data system is not readily accessible, the potential user may decide to do without it. If response (turnaround) time is excessive, this may discourage its use. If the system fails to produce requested data within a reasonable time, this too may discourage its use. It is important, then, that user needs be reflected in the system design and reports.

Difficulties in the Delivery of PTS

There has been and continues to be a pervasive notion that Police Traffic Services is a low-priority function and that PTS is not and should not be a principal law-enforcement goal. The critical role of PTS must be continually emphasized by law-enforcement and other public officials. Support from public and private highway safety interest groups can also have a positive impact on budget allocations for traffic control, and on agency commitment and organization.

Lack of commitment to the traffic problem is the first obstacle that must be overcome. Because citizens fear the criminal and crime, they support a strong effort against crime. They have no sense of fear about traffic crashes. Yet, as mentioned earlier, more lives are lost and people destroyed by injuries in traffic than in crime. There is no glamour to traffic—only hard work. Because the motor vehicle is so much a part of every individual's daily life, there is a reluctance to pass tough traffic laws to deal with those involved in traffic crashes, first, because most people have a poor perception of risk; and second, because most people resent strict control on their ability to drive as they see fit.

Support for Traffic Services. Budget and commitment are almost universally cited as the chief problem facing the police traffic manager. Commitment and budget are almost synonymous terms. The commitment to Police Traffic Services by the legislating authorities is reflected by the budget they appropriate for those services. Unfortunately, as the budget tightens nationally, Police Traffic Services are placed in competition with all other government agencies for available tax dollars.

The highest priority should be given to the PTS budget. Attention should be addressed to (a) convincing citizens, public officials, and law-enforcement officials that greater commitment to traffic safety must be reflected in public budgets; and (b) determining how more effective and efficient uses of budget resources can be made for traffic safety.

Conclusion

Police Traffic Services is one of the broadest areas of law enforcement. Nationally, more officer time is spent on PTS (including routine traffic patrol) than any other activity. It is one of the key areas in which police practice both parts of the motto "To serve and protect."

The field of PTS faces difficulties in that it is not a "glamorous" part of law enforcement and often lacks a strong public mandate. People demand their "right to drive" and often resent police interference over what they consider trivial infractions. The PTS budget is also often the first to be cut. People fear crime more than crashes, even though they are more likely to be involved in the latter. Therefore, they will support cuts in PTS before other programs.

Fortunately, increased public awareness in such areas as drunk-driving enforcement has focused new attention on PTS and increased the mandate for more visible enforcement and action. Since it is unlikely that traffic deaths and other traffic-related problems will substantially decrease in the near future, the demand for improved PTS is all the greater.

Noel C. Bufe

Bibliography

Baker, J. Stannard, and Lynn B. Fricke. *Traffic Accident Investigation Manual*. Evanston, IL: Northwestern University Traffic Institute, 1986.

Booth, Weldon L. *Police Management of Traffic Accident Prevention Programs*. Springfield, IL: Charles C. Thomas, 1980.

Borkenstein, Robert F., and Kent B. Joscelyn. *Recommendations for the Development of the Police Traffic Function*. Hartford, CT: Travelers Research Center, 1968. Prepared by Indiana University Department of Police Administration under Travelers Research Center/National Highway Safety Bureau contract FH-11-6604.

Buren, R.M., R.E. Lucke, and R.C. Pfefer. *Development of Performance Measures for Police Traffic Services*. Washington, DC: U.S. Department of Transportation, April 1984.

Hand, Bruce A., Archible W. Sherman, Jr., and Michael E. Cavanagh. *Traffic Investigation and Control*. 2d ed. Columbus, OH: Merrill, 1980.

International Association of Chiefs of Police. *Model Police Traffic Services*. Gaithersburg, MD: IACP, 1975–1977. Vol. 1. *Policies*. Vol. 2. *Procedures*. Vol. 3. *Rules*. Manual updated, 1985.

———. *Police Traffic Responsibilities*. IACP, Highway Safety Program Management Series, Vol. 2, 1976. Gaithersburg, MD.

Leonard, V.A. *Police Traffic Control*. Springfield, IL: Charles C. Thomas, 1971. (Written for the chief of a small department with staff under 75).

Northwestern University Traffic Institute. *Traffic Patrol*. 3d ed. Traffic Patrol and Direction Series, P.N. 400. Evanston, IL: Northwestern University, 1981.

Weston, Paul B. *The Police Traffic Control Function*. 4th ed. Springfield, IL: Charles C. Thomas, 1978.

Transit Police, New York City

History

The New York City Transit Police Department is the second largest police force in New York State, and one of the largest law-enforcement agencies in the country. It is comparable in size to municipal police departments in Houston, Detroit, and Washington, D.C. The department traces its origin to 1936 when Mayor Fiorello LaGuardia signed a resolution creating the post of "special patrolman" on the subway system. By 1940 the city had taken over all the private subway lines and more special patrolmen were hired. The first promotional exam for these officers was given in 1942, the same year that summons books were first issued. The special patrolmen were granted peace officer status in 1947, giving them the same powers as members of the New York City Police Department. After much public discussion, the department was made a separate entity in 1955, and Thomas O'Rourke became the first chief of the department. By 1975 the force had grown to 3,600 officers, but the onset of the city's fiscal crisis in that year caused a reduction in hiring that thinned their numbers to about 2,600 officers by 1980. The first police "sweep" of the subways was conducted on June 4, 1982; the technique employs a large number of officers to search an area for criminals. On January 13, 1986, more than 500 recruits were sworn in, bringing the department's strength to an all-time high of more than 4,000 officers. The 250 female officers now on the force also represent an all-time high.

Duty

The department is responsible for policing a subway system that carries about 3.5 million riders daily on more than 6,000 subway cars over 700 miles of track serving 460 stations. To accomplish this mission, the department has formed a network of police districts similar to police precincts, as well as system-wide patrol forces and specialized units. The twelve districts are divided into three board zones, and each zone has a commanding officer who reports to the chief of patrol. The four districts in Manhattan comprise Zone 1, the four district in Brooklyn make up Zone 2, and the two districts in the Bronx and the two in Queens fill out Zone 3. Each district is then divided into patrol posts. The subway system is patrolled twenty-four hours a day, seven days a week, primarily by uniformed officers, but also by plainclothes officers. All deployment is based on crime patterns and other needs, which are reviewed daily.

Each officer carries a walkie-talkie radio to communicate with the Transit Police Operations Unit. Subway motormen and bus drivers also rely on radios to contact the Transit Police through their own command centers. Special antennas and base stations make radio communication possible. The Tactical Patrol Force ensures that a uniformed officer is on every subway train between 8 P.M. and 4 A.M. Another unit, City-Wide Patrol Services, responds to problems that cross district lines. At one time it concentrated on stations and trains where schoolchildren caused problems. As that was corrected the unit turned its attention to preventing graffiti. The Detective Division investigates every major crime that is not accompanied by an arrest. Detectives also conduct follow-up investigations when there is an arrest, so that the strongest possible case can be presented in court. A specialized unit within the Detective Division works to educate the riding public on how to avoid becoming the victim of crime.

A task force of plainclothes officers concentrates on one high-priority problem—the crime of passenger robbery. The Canine Unit now numbers forty-three teams. An Emergency Medical Rescue Unit, formed in 1977, provides aid to sick and injured passengers and to fellow officers in need of care. All of these line units are backed up by support services, and the Inspectional Services Division bears the responsibility for investigating civilian complaints against officers and for conducting spot checks of officers in the field.

Bill Murphy

Transnational Crimes

Unlike criminal investigations coordinated within the jurisdiction of a particular country, the international law-enforcement community faces two formidable obstacles when developing prosecutable cases against criminal enterprises with tentacles that extend throughout the world. First, evidence admissible in one country may be suppressed in another with more restrictive procedural standards. Second, the doctrine of sovereignty, or self-government within national boundaries, limits the ability of law-enforcement officers in one country to investigate and prosecute criminal activities that extend into another. Because of the enormous damage caused by international crime cartels, legal systems throughout the world are changing to facilitate the international efforts of police agencies.

Applying the Bill of Rights to Foreign Investigations

The Fourth Amendment of the U.S. Constitution requires law-enforcement officers in the United States to conduct searches and seizures in a "reasonable" manner. The U.S. Supreme Court has held that as a general rule, a reasonable search is one conducted with a search warrant requiring a judicially approved showing of probable cause and limitations on the scope of the search. In addition, the Court recognizes a number of exceptions to the warrant requirement as reasonable, namely, emergency searches, searches based on consent, the motor vehicle exception, and search incident to arrest. As a deterrent to unreasonable searches by police officers, the Court adopted the exclusionary rule, which requires the suppression of evidence derived from investigations that violate the Constitution. Because police in foreign countries are generally unaware of the procedural standards of the American judicial system, the danger exists that under certain circumstances, evidence collected by foreign police will be suppressed in this country.

In many instances the exclusionary rule does not apply to searches and seizures conducted in foreign countries. Since the Bill of Rights applies only to the actions of the U.S. government and its employees, evidence independently acquired by foreign police for their own purposes is admissible in U.S. courts, despite the fact that such evidence, if seized in the same manner by American police, would be excluded as violative of the Fourth Amendment. This rule applies even when the evidence is seized from American citizens. An exception to the rule, though infrequently applied, occurs when the behavior of the investigating officers is so inhumane or outrageous that a court, exercising its supervisory responsibilities, suppresses evidence obtained pursuant to the offending action. Another exception occurs when there is substantial participation in the search by U.S. law-enforcement agents, thereby converting the investigation into a joint venture implicating the Fourth Amendment and the exclusionary rule. Recently the Supreme Court limited this exception by determining that the Fourth Amendment does not apply to the search and seizure by U.S. authorities of property owned by a nonresident alien and located in a foreign country.

In *United States v. Verdugo-Urquidez* (110 S. Ct. 1056), Verdugo-Urquidez, a Mexican national suspected of the torture-murder of an undercover DEA agent, became a fugitive after being charged by the DEA with numerous drug violations in the United States. Based on the outstanding American warrant, Verdugo-Urquidez was arrested in Mexico by the Mexican Federal Judicial Police (MFJP) and remanded to U.S. marshals at the California border. The next day the director of the MFJP, at the request of DEA agents, authorized a warrantless search of Verdugo's two residences in Mexico. During the searches, conducted by both MFJP officers and DEA agents, one of the DEA agents found and seized documents allegedly reflecting the volume of marijuana smuggled into the United States by Verdugo's organization. Because the searches, which were unrelated to any contemplated Mexican prosecution, were initiated and participated in by DEA agents (who also took custody of the evidence), the lower courts found that the participation of the DEA agents was substantial enough to make the joint venture searches subject to the strictures of the Fourth Amendment. Holding that a warrant was required to ensure reasonableness in the search of the Mexican premises of Verdugo-Urdquidez, the lower courts suppressed the evidence. The Supreme Court reversed, stating the protections of the Fourth Amendment were not intended by the framers of the Constitution to apply to U.S. government action against foreign nationals on foreign soil. Conversely, U.S. agents who participate to a substantial degree in a search or seizure of a U.S. citizen with foreign police in a foreign country must comply with the U.S. Constitution or risk exclusion of any evidence obtained thereby in American courts.

Fifth Amendment protection against self-incrimination is another issue. This protection requires that all confessions must be voluntary and that custodial interrogations must be preceded by constitutional warnings in accordance with *Miranda v. Arizona*. Foreign officials certainly cannot be required to adopt the criminal procedure of the United States during the questioning of suspects. In the absence of succinct judicial guidance concerning the extraterritorial application of the Bill of Rights during interrogations, it would seem prudent to consider the protection against self-incrimination as a necessary constitutional principle whenever prosecution in the United States is sought.

U.S. Statutes That Provide Extraterritorial Jurisdiction

The traditional limitations on a sovereign state to assign criminal liability to acts outside its territorial jurisdiction has undergone dramatic changes in the United States. The following statutes are among those that appear most useful to the international law-enforcement community:

- Subchapter II, entitled "Import and Export," of the Controlled Substances Act (Title 21, U.S. Code) regulates the methods by which controlled substances enter and leave the United States. Of particular interest is section 959, which is intended to permit extraterritorial application of laws proscribing the distribution or manufacture of controlled substances outside the United States intended for importation to the United States Section 959(b) addresses any person aboard an American aircraft anywhere in the world who possesses a controlled substance with intent to distribute.

- Title 18 of the U.S. Code provides American courts with jurisdiction to try cases involving several types of violent acts occurring outside the United States. This provision covers crimes falling with-in the special maritime and territorial jurisdiction of the United States, including any place "outside the jurisdiction of any nation with respect to an offense by or against a national of the United States" (section 7[7]); crimes aboard aircraft (section 32); murder or attempted murder of certain federal employees (section 1114); kidnapping of certain federal employees or "internationally protected" persons (section 1201); hostage taking outside the United States when either the hostage or the hostage taker is a U.S. national (section 1203); terrorist acts against U.S. nationals (section 2331).

- Federal conspiracy statutes may often allow prosecution of foreign nationals who have engaged in a conspiracy outside the United States.

One of the best methods of combating large-scale international crime is through the seizure and forfeiture of assets associated with illegal activity. Although the U.S. government cannot lawfully seize assets located within the territorial borders of other countries, foreign criminals often attempt to hide illegally gained profits from the authorities of their countries by transferring funds to the United States. To attack this problem, Congress enacted 18 U.S.C. section 981(a)(1)(B), which permits the forfeiture of assets located inside the United States that are derived from drug trafficking abroad. In an effort to encourage international cooperation, Congress enacted several more federal statutes that permit the sharing of the proceeds of U.S. forfeiture actions with countries that facilitate the seizure of those assets under U.S. law.

International Cooperation

The doctrine of sovereignty generally prevents police officers of one country from conducting investigations in another. In fact, unauthorized overseas investigations can result in denial of access to the evidence, diplomatic protest, or even arrest of the visiting agent. Fortunately, a number of formal and informal methods have been developed for criminal investigators to obtain assistance from their colleagues in other countries. Many federal agencies have representatives—FBI legal attachés (Legats) and DEA country attachés, for example—stationed in American embassies abroad for the purpose of maintaining liaison with foreign police. While such personnel have no investigative jurisdiction in their host countries, they can aid inquiry. Examples of frequently requested assistance coordinated through Legats are name checks and fingerprint searches in the files of the FBI's Identification Division, interviews with witnesses, and identifying the location of suspects or assets. These informal requests have the advantage of being more expeditious and flexible, though with limitations. Information that cannot be furnished to foreign police without a court order includes federal grand jury proceedings and interceptions of wire, oral, and electronic communications under the provisions of the Electronic Communications Privacy Act. Examples of formal requests for assistance are the transmittal of certain types of business documents, such as bank or telephone records; executing a search or arrest warrant; freezing assets; and compelling testimony.

Another means of formal request is to write a letter rogatory to the judiciary of another country asking for information about official acts. Such requests not only involve the cooperation of judges or magistrates but also require approval by the Office of International Affairs at the U.S. Department of Justice and the Department of State, as well as their foreign counterparts. Because a letter rogatory involves diplomatic channels, the procedure often results in a slower response than desired by police agencies conducting criminal investigations. However, mutual legal assistance treaties (MLATs) permit prosecutors to expedite international cooperation by eliminating many of the time-consuming diplomatic requirements of letters rogatory. The United Nations Convention Against the Illicit Traffic in Narcotic Drugs and Psychotropic Substances or the "Vienna Convention" is another important step toward reconciling legal systems throughout the world. Forty nations signed the convention, which establishes cooperative means for handling drug trafficking, money laundering, and forfeiture.

Extradition, the removal of a person from one country to another for trial or punishment, is governed by treaty and usually requires formal processing through diplomatic channels. The United States lacks extradition treaties with about one-third of the nations of the world. Procedures for extradition are complex, vary from country to country, and are subject to a number of defenses. Additionally, in the event the fugitive is at large during the time-consuming negotiations for extradition, it becomes necessary to request a provisional arrest warrant in order to secure the suspect until rendition (capture or surrender) is accomplished. Occasionally, efforts are made to circumvent obstacles to extradition by unilateral actions, such as ruses to lure the fugitive to the prosecuting country or arranging for the deportation of the suspect either to the United States or to a country from which extradition is more feasible. However, some federal courts have recently decided they lacked the jurisdiction to try individuals abducted from Mexico by U.S. authorities in violation of the extradition treaty in force between the United States and Mexico.

In conclusion, a wide range of statutes now grant U.S. courts jurisdiction over illegal activities that take place outside U.S. borders and territories. United States courts can try these cases only when the defendant is physically present in the courtroom. In the event the defendant must be brought to trial in the United States from another country, the international law-enforcement community must seek mutually acceptable means for securing the rendition of the defendant to the forum of prosecution.

Austin A. Andersen

Bibliography

Andersen, Austin A. "The Admissibility of Evidence Located in Searches by Private Persons." *FBI Law Enforcement Bulletin* (April 1989): 25–29; and (May 1989): 26–31.

———. "Foreign Searches and the Fourth Amendment." *FBI Law Enforcement Bulletin* (February 1990): 23–29.

———. "The Federal Grand Jury: Exceptions to the Rule of Secrecy." *FBI Law Enforcement Bulletin* (August 1990): 26–31; (September 1990): 27–32.

"Exporting United States Drug Law: An Example of the International Legal Ramifications of the 'War on Drugs.'" *B.Y.U. Law Review* (1992): 165–90.

"International Scope of Fourth Amendment Protections: *United States v. Verdugo-Urquidez* [110 S.Ct. 1056]." *Louisiana Law Review* 52 (November 1991): 455–77.

Kester, John G. "Some Myths of United States Extradition Law." *Georgia Law Review* 76 (April 1988): 1441–93.

Watson, Geoffrey R. "Offenders Abroad: The Case for Nationality-Based Criminal Jurisdiction." *Yale Journal of International Law* 17 (Winter 1992): 41–84.

Zagaris, Bruce, and Elizabeth Kingma. "Asset Forfeiture International and Foreign Law: An Emerging Regime." *Emory International Law Review* 5 (Fall 1991): 445–513.

U

Undercover Operations

There are two types of police undercover work: person surveillance and place surveillance. Person surveillance involves following a specific targeted individual to ascertain his or her behavior, lifestyle, daily movements, etc., and can be divided into two types: intimate and nonintimate surveillance. Intimate surveillance occurs when the police officer participates in a pretense of having a special relationship—like lover, lawyer, confessor, reporter, or doctor—with a target. In the context of the real relationship being simulated, information is arguably protected by the intimate communication privilege when divulged. Nonintimate surveillance entails a pretense of relationships of a business, social, or casual nature, or in general of a relationship to which the confidential communication privilege does not extend.

Observation of a location where criminal activity is anticipated or where evidence of criminal activity is sought is place surveillance and can be divided into two types: public and private place surveillance. The difference between them can be roughly sketched by using the criterion of whether an officer requires a warrant to gain access to the location, in case the owner does not welcome the officer. Private place surveillance does simply refer to private property, since some privately owned establishments are utilized as public places.

Legal Ramifications

Nothing in legislation or common law stops the police from either deceptively entering into long-term living arrangements with a suspect or from becoming romantically involved with a suspect, hoping to find evidence of illegal behavior. Not all undercover operations are the same; some are more intrusive than others. Those sorts of less invasive operations require less of a justification than those that are more invasive. Most people strolling through or living in certain areas would gain a sense of security by thinking that the police patrol these areas, even in an undercover capacity. These same people would feel much less assurance if they suspected that some of the people they interact with on a daily basis were really undercover police monitoring their behavior. Additionally, people would feel profoundly violated if they thought that the police had unencumbered access to the private places and intimate domains of their lives. This is especially so if the access is gained by trickery, for potential covert involvement tends to undermine trust in all relationships.

The reason undercover operations are so controversial has to do with the moral and constitutional rights to privacy. American law protects the privacy of persons, places, and relationships from certain kinds of state intrusion. These privacy protections are rebuttable provided that a threshold of suspicion is surpassed. Undercover operations as currently regulated (or rather as currently unregulated) stipulate neither a threshold of suspicion nor an independent judgment as to the appropriateness or the need for police to gain access to a citizen's privacy. It appears, therefore, that respect for a citizen's privacy falls out of balance once undercover operations that do not meet the standard of probable cause are permitted. Too often police show the least sensitivity to constitutional rights when compared with other criminal-justice professionals.

Several considerations further complicate the privacy picture. First of all, most of the restrictions that protect the privacy of persons, places, and relationships apply to law-enforcement agents, and not, to the same degree, to private citizens, even if these citizens act in an effort to assist them. For instance, employers may search through the desk of an employee, and school officials through the lockers or possessions of a student, without a warrant and without the standard of probable cause being met, even though here the standard of reasonable basis of suspicion does apply.

Second, the restrictions placed on law-enforcement agents that serve to protect the privacy rights of individuals can be voluntarily waived by citizens giving their permission to the agents to enter their private realm. When the permission is granted on the basis of a deliberate, carefully orchestrated deception with respect to who it is that is gaining access to this private realm, questions arise as to the "voluntariness" of the search. So if the police wish to look in a suspect's basement, officers can dress themselves as employees from the electric or gas company and claim that there is some hazard they want to deal with. The search the disguised officers carry on while in the basement is treated as voluntary. Similarly, if the police want to peer into someone's fenced-in backyard to see if plants that can be used to make illegal drugs are being cultivated, but do not have enough evidence to obtain a search warrant, they may pose as telephone repair workers and request permission to enter the yard to check wires.

Third, restrictions that apply to some law-enforcement agents do not apply to others. For instance, agents seeking to enforce administrative law do not face the same thresholds as do agents seeking to enforce the criminal law, even though what the first agents discover in their administrative capacity might prove incriminating.

Court Rulings
In those cases where the police, through deception, gain admittance to a private dwelling or to the inner dimensions of people's lives, the courts have refused to see this deception as a violation of the constitutional requirement or of the balance of values that the requirement reflects. In *United States v. Baldwin* (621 F.2d 251 [1963]), the Supreme Court found that police do not "require prior judicial approval in the form of a warrant before utilizing an undercover agent" and that the Fourth Amendment "does not protect wrongdoers from misplaced

confidence in their associates." In *Hoffa v. United States* (385 U.S. 293 [1966]), the Court found that the Fourth Amendment "does not protect a wrongdoer's misplaced belief that a person to whom he voluntarily confides his wrongdoing will not reveal it." And in *Lopez v. United States* (373 U.S. 427 [1960]), "the risk of being overheard by an eavesdropper or betrayed by an informer or deceived as to the identity of one with whom one deals is probably inherent in the conditions of human society. It is the kind of risk we necessarily assume whenever we speak."

What defenders of this policy have not articulated is an explanation of why it is permissible for the police to do by stealth what they are not permitted to do by force. It would seem that any argument that grounds the legitimacy of gaining access by trickery would also work for gaining access by force. Similarly, it would seem that any arguments to limit the state using force to achieve a certain end would also be effective reasoning in limiting the state from using deception to achieve the same end. Furthermore, although it is true that nothing in the Constitution prevents a citizen from voluntarily inviting the police into his or her home or from voluntarily offering private papers to the police for their inspection, when these invitations and offers are extended under conditions of deception, they are not "voluntary." In no other domain of law or morality would agreement based on such critical misjudgment be treated as voluntary. Even in criminal law, confessions after indictment that were extracted through trickery are treated as inadmissible because involuntary.

Another problem with undercover work when not citizen approved is lack of accountability. If nothing incriminating is found, the suspected person is typically not aware that he or she has been subjected to a police search. No one but the policing agency itself is situated to monitor the percentage of undercover operations that hit upon something incriminating. A just recommendation would require policing agencies to keep records of the undercover operations they initiate and subject these operations to regular external review as a way of maintaining accountability without prior judicial approval.

Further Recommendations
Undercover policies that combine sensitivity to investigative practices the police find essential

used by doctors and lawyers, and (2) pragmatically they believe they have a sound reputation so they use subtle, soft-sell tactics on the national level while allowing local lodges to be militant."

The International Union of Police Associations

The International Union of Police Associations (IUPA) traces its inception to the International Conference of Police Associations (ICPA). ICPA was officially disbanded on December 4, 1978, splitting over the issue of full affiliation with organized labor. The IUPA represents that segment of the ICPA remaining with the AFL–CIO.

Some of the major affiliates of IUPA include Houston (TX) Local 109, Toledo (OH) Local 10, Omaha (NE) Local 101, Tacoma (WA) Local 6, Shreveport (LA) Local 75, Fort Wayne (IN) Local 15, Las Vegas (NV) Local 23, Springfield (OH) Local 25, Duluth (MN) Local 3, Anaheim (CA) Local 80, Wayne County (MI) Local 502, Milwaukee (WI) Local 21, Long Beach (CA) Local 42, Alexandria (LA) Local 883, and several statewide associations, the largest being the California Organization of Police and Sheriffs (COPS) (*Law Officer*, April–May 1980; *AFL–CIO News*, August 14, 1982; *Police Labor Monthly*, September 1985).

IUPA literature states that only full-time sworn police officers who are members of an organized local, county, or state retirement system are eligible to belong. They accept no individual members, only bona fide police associations. IUPA guarantees local autonomy while acting as a union of police associations.

National Association of Police Organizations

The delegates to the ICPA Convention that opposed affiliation with organized labor formed a steering committee to organize another national police organization. Robert Skully, cochairman of the steering committee and vice president of the Detroit Police Officers Association, described the new organization in these terms: "Our intention is to become what the ICPA was supposed to be. We have nothing against the major unions. We support them, their goals, their achievements. But we feel nobody can represent police officers like police officers."

The National Association of Police Organizations (NAPO) was formed to replace the old ICPA. NAPO literature sells the organization as a national lobby group for police offic-

ers. It reports more than one hundred thousand members. They charge a fee of $1.50 per member/per year which is used to pay for a private law firm in Washington, D.C., to lobby for the organization. They consciously and deliberately maintain no office, no staff, and no services to offer affiliates.

The third annual convention—August 23–28, 1981—voted to support a legislative program to remove the bar by state government to collective bargaining by public employees (*PORAC News*, November 1981). NAPO's legislative counsel stated that "much of what NAPO is able to do is to prevent laws that adversely affect law enforcement from being passed." It is exclusively an affiliation for the purpose of monitoring and affecting federal legislation.

NAPO literature reports that the organization is composed of autonomous independent police associations in locations including San Diego, Detroit, San Jose, Los Angeles County, Suffolk County (NY), Dallas, and several statewide associations such as the Peace Officers Association of Michigan (POAM) and New Jersey State PBA. It appears to be a safe haven for large independent groups that wish to maintain a national organization for legislative and communicative purposes only.

International Brotherhood of Police Officers

The International Brotherhood of Police Officers (IBPO) was founded in 1964 by police officers in Rhode Island and affiliated with the National Association of Government Employees (NAGE) in 1969 as a separate division. Juris and Feuille (1973) report that IBPO had about two thousand members when it affiliated with NAGE. Reliable membership figures are not available since NAGE reports IBPO's membership figures in with its nonpolice members.

The per capita fee is approximately $12.00 per month—as compared for instance with the FOP's $2.50 per *year*. According to Bergsman (1976:3) IBPO is a police union that assists its locals in collective bargaining. IBPO literature describes their membership benefits as full-service legal protection in job-related criminal and civil cases, a $10,000 accidental death and dismemberment insurance policy, professional negotiators, national representatives for grievances, and lobbying representation in Washington, D.C. The national headquarters is located in Boston, but the union maintains fully staffed offices in Washington, D.C., Hollywood and

Orlando (FL), Burbank (CA), Cranston (RI), and Springfield (MA).

IBPO's membership has been primarily concentrated in the New England states; however, affiliations during the late 1970s broadened their territory (*Police Chronicle*, August 1981, August 1982). Various issues of *Police Chronicle* report IBPO locals in such places as Springfield, Cambridge, Worcester, and Middlesex County (MA); Pueblo, Arvada, and Greeley (CO); Chesapeake, Hampton, Newport News, and Norfolk (VA); Cranston (RI); Lewiston (ME); Manchester (NH); Orlando and Hollywood (FL); Lincoln and Lancaster County (NE); Evanston (WY); Missoula (MT); and Boise (ID).

A significant blow came in late 1981 when IBPO Local 442, representing 3,300 Washington, D.C., police officers and sergeants, was challenged by FOP to a representation election. *Police Magazine* (September 1979) reports that the battle over exclusive recognition of District of Columbia police officers was a hectic one. The police were initially represented by a social organization called the Police Association of D.C., until it was ousted by IBPO in 1974. In May 1977 the association defeated IBPO, but was beaten by IBPO again in March 1978. The FOP won the 1982 certification election. More recently, the IBPO has regained some lost ground by organizing Atlanta officers.

NAGE/IBPO affiliated in 1982 with the Service Employees International Union (SEIU)—itself an AFL–CIO affiliate. This created an interesting situation since the IUPA was already chartered by the AFL–CIO. There were some initial rumblings of potential mergers; however, the competing career lines of the union officers of the two organizations soon ended any thought of a police "super-union" affiliated with the AFL–CIO.

NAGE/IBPO will continue to operate with strength in New England. Since IBPO has a sound per capita income, large professional staff, and a substantial benefit package, it will at least maintain their regional base.

International Brotherhood of Teamsters
The most controversial labor union representing police officers is the International Brotherhood of Teamsters (IBT), which is the largest union in the United States (Stieber, 1973:5). The Teamsters' alleged links to organized crime and internal corruption problems caused the AFL–CIO to expel them in 1958.

Police officers joining the Teamsters, whether in a police-only local or as part of a large local, are a small fraction of the union's total membership and therefore would have very little voice in the union's affairs. The per capita fee is quite high. *The FOP Journal* (January 1981) reported that the Anchorage, Alaska, police dropped out of Teamsters Local 959 to form an independent police union after Teamster dues were increased to $1.46 per hour.

The Teamsters have been able to recruit police officers and sheriff's deputies in many parts of the country. The *Arizona Law Officer* (September 1980) stated that the Teamsters had locals for the Sioux Falls (SD) police, Flint (MI) deputies, Des Moines (IA) police, Albany (NY) sheriff's supervisors, and Boston (MA) highway and park officers. According to Frank (1978:22), the Teamsters have been strongest in Michigan, Minnesota, Wisconsin, Iowa, and Alaska. The Teamsters are reported to have recruited police in Florida, Louisiana, Virginia, California, Illinois, and most recently in Oklahoma (Frank, 1978:22; *Arizona Law Officer*, September 1980; *FOP Journal* January 1981; *Police Labor Monthly*, 1987).

The Teamsters suffered a severe setback after the fifteen-day police strike in New Orleans that ended on March 4, 1979 (*Police Magazine*, May 1979). The Teamsters organized the Police Association of New Orleans (PANO), which had dropped out of the Service Employees International Union (SEIU, AFL–CIO) after SEIU could not negotiate a contract with the city. Teamster Local 253 was just as unsuccessful as SEIU because the mayor refused to negotiate with the 800-member local, but instead chose to talk to the 300-member FOP lodge. The resulting strike caused the city to recognize PANO, but talks collapsed over the unit designation (46). The furor over cancellation of Mardi Gras turned public opinion against the union and resulted in no contract, 200 disciplinary actions, fines of $600,000, and disbanding of the Teamster local.

The Teamsters Union will probably continue to organize scattered groups of police officers. Police officers who are having trouble negotiating contracts or resolving grievances will continue to seek out the Teamsters to frighten police administrators and elected officials. Although the Teamsters have failed to recruit any large municipal departments, they have come close enough on several occasions and are not easily discouraged.

American Federation of State, County, and Municipal Employees

The American Federation of State, County, and Municipal Employees (AFSCME, AFL–CIO) is the largest public sector union in the AFL–CIO (Bornstein, 1978:28–29). Various sources estimate AFSCME's police membership at 10,000 to 15,000 members (Bopp, 1971:337; Bornstein, 1978:28–29; Spero, 1973:29). Since the AFL–CIO chartered IUPA, there has been very little activity by AFSCME in police organizing. There does not appear to be any evidence that AFSCME has increased its police membership in the last few years, but there does seem to be evidence that they are slowly losing police members to rival independent unions.

Major State Associations

In addition to "national" police labor organizations, there are at least five major state associations that must be taken into account in any synopsis of the current status of the police labor movement. Numerous state/regional police associations exist. However, in six states—California, Florida, New Jersey, New York, Texas, and Wisconsin—independent state associations dominate the labor scene among all but the largest cities.

In California, the Peace Officers Research Association of California (PORAC) is the largest and most influential police labor organization. PORAC probably possesses the most sophisticated service delivery system for its locals of any police labor organization. In Florida, the Florida Police Benevolent Association (PBA) continues to gain strength. Although almost every national union possesses at least one local in Florida, the PBA has survived innumerable certification challenges—and usually comes out on top. In 1985 the Florida PBA chartered several locals in Georgia and plans to continue the Combined Law Enforcement Associations of Texas (CLEAT). CLEAT claims almost all major municipal associations as affiliated locals. In New Jersey, New York, and Wisconsin, the New Jersey PBA, the Police Conference of New York, and the Wisconsin Professional Police Association, respectively, represent the bulk of smaller associations, while the major cities are either independent and/or affiliated with national organizations (Newark—FOP; New York City—independent; Milwaukee—IUPA).

Summary

Although police officers belong to just about every AFL–CIO affiliate, independent union, and police-employee organization in the United States, the largest units of police lie primarily within FOP, NAPO, NAGE/IBPO, IUPA, IBT, AFSCME, and several large statewide/regional independent police associations. In fact, independent state organizations such as the Peace Officers Research Association of California (PORAC), the Combine Law Enforcement Associations of Texas (CLEAT), and the Police Conference of New York are gaining strength. Why have police officers fragmented into so many different types of employee organizations while firefighters have but one international union (International Association of Firefighters), and the majority of teachers belong primarily to either of two organizations (National Education Association or American Federation of Teachers)?

It seems that police officers cannot agree on what type of organization best serves their interests, i.e., fraternal or militant; what type of organizational structure the group should have, i.e., democratic or benevolent dictatorial; what degree of service and benefits should be provided by the parent organization, i.e., decentralized or centralized; and, what type of per capita fee should be paid to the parent organization, i.e., high per capita/centralized services or low per capita/local services.

It does seem evident that several historical events may have changed the police labor movement and thus prevented the police from ever having one national voice. First, the Boston police strike of 1919 retarded the police labor movement until the 1960s. The AFL was prepared in 1919 to organize policemen in the same manner as they were organizing federal workers, firemen, and teachers, and the evidence indicated that policemen were hard pressed enough to unionize. Policemen at the time probably fit the axiom of union organizers that said, "A group will organize when indignation and hope are greater than apathy and fear" (Blackburn 1971: 44).

The same indicators were present in 1969, when IBPO president John Cassese tried to get AFL–CIO approval for a national police union charter. However, several police-employee organizations had developed since 1919, and they refused to join the effort. Had FOP and ICPA agreed to merge with Cassese's IBPO, the mood of police officers during the turbulent 1960s and 1970s would have probably been right for one national police union. Although it appears that such an opportunity has passed, the issue may appear again in the future.

Larry T. Hoover
Ronald G. DeLord

Bibliography

Bergsman, Ilene. "Police Unions." *Management Information Service Report* 8 (March 1976):1–19.

Blackburn, Jack, and Gloria Busman. *Understanding Unions in the Public Sector.* Berkeley, CA: Institute of Industrial Relations, University of California, 1971.

Bopp, William J. *The Police Rebellion.* Springfield, IL: Charles C. Thomas, 1971.

Bornstein, Tim. "Police Unions: Dispelling of the Ghost of 1919." *Police Magazine* (September 1978):25–29.

Burpo, John H. *The Police Labor Movement: Problems and Perspectives.* Springfield, IL: Charles C. Thomas, 1971.

Critical Issues in Police Labor Relations. Gaithersburg, MD: International Association of Chiefs of Police, 1974.

Frank, Allan Dobbs. "The Wages of Frustration: 'When All Else Fails, Call the Teamsters.'" *Police Magazine* (September 1978): 21–24, 30–34.

Gammage, Allen Z., and Stanley L. Sachs. *Police Unions.* Springfield, IL: Charles C. Thomas, 1972.

Juris, Hervey A., and Peter Feuille. *Police Employee Organizations.* Evanston, IL: Center for Urban Studies, Northwestern University, 1973.

———. *Police Unionism: Power and Impact in Public Sector Bargaining.* Lexington, MA: D.C. Heath, 1973.

Law Officer. (April–May 1980).

Levi, Margaret. *Bureaucratic Insurgency: The Case of Police Unions.* Lexington, MA: D.C. Heath, 1977.

Maddox, Charles. *Collective Bargaining in Law Enforcement.* Springfield, IL: Charles C. Thomas, 1975.

Salerno, Charles A. "Overview of Police Labor Relations." In *Collective Bargaining in the Public Sector.* Eds. Richard M. Ayres and Thomas L. Wheelen. Gaithersburg, MD: International Association of Chiefs of Police, 1977.

Spero, Sterling D., and John M. Carpzzola. *The Urban Community and Its Unionized Bureaucracies: Pressure Politics in Local Government Labor Relations.* New York: Dunellen, 1973.

Stieber, Jack. *Public Employee Unionism: Structure, Growth, Police.* Washington, DC: Brookings Institution, 1973.

United States Marshals

The offices of United States Marshal and Deputy United States Marshal were created by the Judiciary Act of 1789, the same law that erected the federal judicial system. The Judiciary Act provided for one U.S. marshal for each judicial district. Each marshal was empowered to hire as many deputy marshals as he felt necessary, including the deputation of able-bodied citizens for special situations, such as posses. Originally, President George Washington nominated and the Senate confirmed thirteen U.S. marshals, one for each of the eleven states and one each for the districts of Kentucky (a territory in 1789) and Maine (a part of Massachusetts until 1820). As the nation expanded across the continent and acquired new territories, more judicial districts were added. As of 1986 there were ninety-four districts, each with its own presidentially appointed U.S. marshal, and a total of 1,900 deputy marshals.

The duties of the marshals were loosely based on the marshals of the colonial admiralty courts established by England in its American possessions in 1697. As defined by the Judiciary Act of 1789, the marshals administered the federal courts, acting primarily as the disbursement officers. More important, the marshals were empowered to execute "all lawful precepts issued under the authority of the United States." These two duties, particularly the latter, have remained essentially unchanged over the past 200 years, though, of course, the specific work of the marshals has changed considerably in response to changing circumstances and laws. For example, marshals currently pursue federal fugitives, but they no longer catch fugitive slaves, a responsibility they had during the 1850s. Although marshals still pay the fees and expenses of witnesses and jurors, as well as write all the checks for U.S. attorneys, they no longer lease courtroom space or purchase fuel to heat it. They no longer pay the salaries of the federal attorneys, court clerks, and bailiffs; nor do they, as Marshal David M. Randolph of Virginia did in 1792, buy curtains for their courts.

Yet the marshals continue, as they have since 1789, to protect the operation of the federal court and its participants, to produce its prisoners and witnesses, and to enforce its orders. For most of this nation's history, the marshals, working in close cooperation with U.S. attorneys, provided the only nationwide law-enforcement authority available to the federal government. Until well into the twentieth century, the marshals executed all arrest warrants, regardless of which agency conducted the initial investigation.

As the federal government's principal law-enforcement agency, the marshals of the first half of the nineteenth century enforced the laws applicable to counterfeiting, neutrality violations, the African slave trade, robbing the mails, and murder on the high seas or on federal property. When new territories were established, marshals were appointed to provided a federal presence. In the Indian Territory (present-day Oklahoma) and in the territory of Alaska, the marshals were essentially the only law-enforcement authority. More than one hundred deputy marshals were killed enforcing the law in the Indian Territory between 1872 and 1896. It was during this period after the Civil War that the marshals earned their place in American folklore as lawmen.

Until 1853 U.S. marshals worked under the general supervision of the secretary of state, who established guidelines for the office, issued specific instructions, and coordinated their activities. This supervision was not particularly strict. For most of the time and for most of what marshals did, they were left on their own, cooperating closely with their district judges and attorneys.

Beginning in 1853, marshals increasingly came under the control of the attorney general, a process that was completed in 1861 by congressional statute. The marshals remained decentralized, with each marshal reporting directly to the attorney general. In the late 1950s, the justice department established the Executive Office of U.S. Marshals to handle administrative responsibilities. In 1962 James J.P. McShane was appointed the first (and only) chief marshal, with limited powers of supervision over the other marshals. The domestic turmoil of the 1960s, particularly the problems the marshals confronted enforcing the civil rights court decisions, pointed out the need for more centralized control. Thus in 1969 the U.S. Marshals Service was created, an office of director

was established, and the process of bringing the disparate districts under central control was begun. Despite this move toward a nationally cohesive law-enforcement agency, today's U.S. marshals retain considerable power within their districts, acting as local managers within a national organization to ensure that the duties assigned the Marshals Service are conducted efficiently and effectively.

As federal law-enforcement officers, marshals retain the broadest authority and jurisdiction. Their congressionally defined duty to execute "all lawful precepts issued under the authority of the United States" allows them to respond to orders from the federal courts, the president and attorney general, and Congress. During the 1960s deputy marshals effectively desegregated the nation's schools and colleagues under numerous court orders. In 1973, acting under orders of the attorney general, the Marshals Service besieged members of the American Indian Movement who had occupied the small hamlet of Wounded Knee, South Dakota, during the longest civil disturbance since the Civil War. Congressional precepts issued to marshals have included such different activities as taking the national census from 1790 through 1870, controlling enemy aliens in time of war, and supervising congressional elections from 1879 to 1894.

Today's U.S. Marshals Service carries out a wide variety of responsibilities. United States marshals provide the physical security for federal courthouses. Whenever necessary, deputy marshals protect federal judges and attorneys who have been threatened with bodily harm. In fiscal year 1985, for example, 240 federal judges received threats. The Marshals Service also operates the Witness Protection Program to protect witnesses, even to the extent of giving them new identities, in exchange for their testimony against organized crime. Since 1970, 4,845 witnesses have entered the program.

As they have had for 200 years, U.S. marshals have custody of all federal prisoners from the time of arrest until the prisoner's acquittal or delivery to prison. These federal prisoners are housed under contract in local jails, escorted to and from court by marshals. More than 83,000 federal prisoners pass through the court system each year, requiring more than 64,000 prisoner movements across the country via the National Prisoner Transportation System of jet aircraft, buses, and vans. It is a complex transportation network, further complicated by the need to provide tight security over the prisoners.

The Marshals Service also has the responsibility for the arrest of federal fugitives, a traditional duty that was briefly transferred to the Federal Bureau of Investigation but was turned back to the marshals in 1979. There are an estimated 300,000 state and federal fugitives at large in the United States. To combat this immense problem, the Marshals Service expends considerable effort daily to capture them, averaging about 11,000 arrests nationwide each year. Periodically, Fugitive Investigative Strike Team (FIST) operations are established in close cooperation with state and local law-enforcement agencies. The purpose of each FIST operation is to provide intense fugitive hunts in specific locations for specific periods of time. Since 1981 nine FIST operations have taken place, resulting in the arrest of 14,770 felons.

The marshals' traditional responsibility to seize property under court order was expanded under the Comprehensive Crime Control Act of 1984. This act gave the marshals responsibility to seize all assets accruing to criminals as a result of illegal, drug-related activities. In less than two years, more than $325 million worth of assets were seized. These assets, which range from gold and bauxite mines to racehorses and fighting cocks, are managed by the Marshals Service until the courts decide their ultimate disposal.

For 200 years, the U.S. marshals have acted as the hub of the federal judicial system, administering its finances, handling its prisoners, serving its processes, protecting its functions and personnel, enforcing its orders, and working with other law-enforcement agencies to assure the supremacy of the law in this country. Although best known for their part in settling the Wild West, marshals continue to play an essential role in the operation of justice. The marshals have, over the last two centuries, evolved from a collection of independent, largely inexperienced, and poorly trained amateurs into a centralized, cohesive law-enforcement agency, populated with highly trained, professional personnel dedicated to law enforcement. In an age of specialization, U.S. marshals and their deputies remain the last of the generalists, fully capable of carrying out an incredibly complex array of duties.

Stanley E. Morris

Bibliography

At present, no general history or study of the U.S. Marshals Service has been written. The best single-volume study pertaining to the marshals and their duties in the West during the 1800s is Larry Balls's *The U.S. Marshals of New Mexico & Arizona Territories, 1846–1912*. Albuquerque: University of New Mexico Press, 1978. Another useful though older source is Homer Cummings's *Federal Justice*. New York: Macmillan, 1937.

Information on this entry is based on primary documents at the National Archives, Judicial, Fiscal, and Social Branch, Record Group 60 (Records of the Department of Justice).

The U.S. Marshals Service has prepared a brief history entitled "The United States Marshals Service: Past and Present.," published in 1992 and available through the Government Printing Office or in Government Documents collections.

U.S. Secret Service

The U.S. Secret Service is composed of two uniformed forces: the U.S. Secret Service Uniformed Division and the Treasury Police Force. The Service has field offices located throughout the continental United States, Alaska, Hawaii, Puerto Rico, and a liaison office in Paris, France. Its more than 1,900 special agents rotate periodically between investigative and protective assignments. Numerous specialists also contribute their expertise to the Service: security specialists, electronics engineers, communications technicians, research psychologists, armorers, computer experts, intelligence analysts, polygraph examiners, forensic experts, and other professionals with unique training.

Secret Service Uniformed Division

The first formal attempt at providing security at the White House occurred during the Civil War. The "Bucktail Brigade" (members of the 150th Regiment of the Pennsylvania Volunteers) and four officers from the Metropolitan Washington Police Force were assigned to protect White House property. On September 14, 1922, President Warren G. Harding created the White House military aide's office. In 1930 President Hoover decided that White House police officers and Secret Service agents at the White House could better coordinate their efforts if they were under centralized control.

Thus the White House Police became a part of the U.S. Secret Service.

Treasury Police Force

Established in 1789, the Treasury Police Force is one of the oldest organizations of its kind in America. It became part of the Secret Service in 1937. In the beginning, officers accompanied money shipments from the Bureau of Engraving and Printing, guarded currency in the treasury vault, and ensured the security of those doing business in the Treasury Building's Cash Room. These activities changed substantially over the years and the responsibilities of the Treasury Police kept pace. Now officers maintain security twenty-four hours a day at the main Treasury Building and the Treasury Annex. They also guard the Office of the Secretary of the Treasury and assist with the investigation of crimes committed within the Treasury buildings.

Investigative Mission

The Secret Service was the first general law-enforcement agency of the federal government. At the close of the Civil War, between one-third and one-half of all U.S. paper currency in circulation was counterfeit. To combat this threat to the nation's economy, on July 5, 1865, the Secret Service was created as a division under the Department of the Treasury. Within less than a decade counterfeiting was sharply reduced. In addition to bogus money cases the agency investigated many diverse illegal activities. Among these were the Teapot Dome oil scandals, the Ku Klux Klan, government land frauds in the West, and counterespionage during the Spanish-American War and World War I. As other federal law-enforcement agencies came into being, the investigative jurisdiction of the Secret Service was limited to Treasury-related crimes. Today it is still charged with the investigation of counterfeit U.S. currency and all other obligations and securities of the United States (forgery of U.S. checks, bonds, etc.). In 1984 Congress passed legislation that expanded the agency's jurisdiction further to include fraud related to false identification documents and devices, fraud involving credit and debit cards, and computer fraud. At the direction of the secretary of the treasury, the Secret Service is also authorized to investigate fraud associated with the electronic funds-transfer system of the U.S. Treasury.

Protective Mission

When President William McKinley was assassinated in Buffalo, New York, in 1901, he was the third American president killed in thirty-six years. The public and Congress finally demanded that protection be provided for U.S. presidents. As a result Congress directed the Secret Service to protect the new president, Theodore Roosevelt. However, it was 1906 before legislation was passed making presidential protection a permanent Secret Service responsibility. Since that time the agency's guardian duties have increased dramatically. At present the Secret Service protects the president and vice president and their families; former presidents, their spouses, widows, and minor children; major candidates for the offices of president and vice president and their spouses; visiting heads of foreign states or foreign governments; and other individuals at the direction of the president.

Importance of the Service

The counterfeiting of money might seem a minor offense when daily American citizens endure robbery, burglary, rape, and possibly murder. But while these individual crimes are shocking, even in totality they do not enslave an entire people. As dramatic as this sounds, counterfeit notes can achieve just that. On the eve of World War II, Adolf Hitler and his Third Reich cabinet devised a plan to use paper weapons to destroy their enemies. They would copy world currencies and then flood whichever country they wanted to with bad money, causing economic panic. Moreover, they would purchase goods and materials needed for the war effort and pay off spies with counterfeit. At that time in Germany, the clever engravers available were Jewish artisans. Unlike their less fortunate counterparts in other work camps, these highly skilled "counterfeiters" (forced laborers) lived well and produced bundles of bogus currency. A veteran of the U.S. Secret Service, Captain George J. McNally, working with Scotland Yard, followed the production of German counterfeit. In one seizure of bad notes alone, they confiscated about $100 million worth. In 1945, with American troops bearing down on the money plant, the Germans madly rushed around destroying the evidence. Just how much counterfeit money was made during the war can only be guessed at—perhaps half a billion dollars. But whatever the amount it had fueled Hitler's war machine for half a decade of misery and mayhem.

In their book, *The United States Secret Service*, Walter S. Bowen and Harry E. Neal elaborate on this theme:

Counterfeit money as a weapon of war is not new, though the Nazi operation was undoubtedly the biggest of its kind. Napoleon Bonaparte once established a counterfeiting plant in Paris to turn out fake Russian money which he used to buy supplies for his Russian invasion. During the American Revolution the British dumped tons of phony Continental currency into the American economy, destroying all public faith in that money.

Public confidence in a national currency is essential to the economic welfare of any country.

Bibliography

Baker, La Fayette C. *The United States Secret Service in the Late War*. Hartford, CT: Park, 1989.

Baughman, Urbanus E. *Secret Service Chief*. New York: Harper, 1962.

Bowen, Walter S., and Harry E. Neal. *The United States Secret Service*. Philadelphia: Chilton, 1960.

McCarthy, Dennis V., and Philip W. Smith. *Presenting the President: The Inside Story of a Secret Service Agent*. New York: Morrow, 1985.

V

Lewis Joseph Valentine

Lewis Joseph Valentine (1882–1946), police commissioner of New York City, was born in Brooklyn, New York, of Irish descent. His father owned a small fruit store, and both parents, devout Catholics, taught him to love the church. He thought of becoming a priest one day, but due to family need dropped out of high school to work as an errand boy for Abraham and Straus department store. Right away he impressed management with his energy, and at age nineteen was placed in charge of the store's delivery depot at Greenport, Long Island. Not completely happy there and aware of his father's uncertain earning power, he noticed that many of his Irish chums had already joined either the police or fire department. The notion of knuckling down to the job of a "smoke-eater" appealed to him, so he took both entrance exams to better his chances of escaping the business world. Passing them easily he waited for the first opening, which happened to be for a probationary patrolman at $800 a year. He jumped at the opportunity and at age twenty-one began patrolling Manhattan and Flatbush. Never to don a fireman's hat, he quickly adapted to pounding the pavement as one face among many in the "mighty semi-military machine"—the New York Police Department.

Soon Valentine earned the reputation for being an honest cop. A praiseworthy appellation, but one that did not advance his career. Political control of the department persisted and he was seen as an obstruction rather than as a paragon. It took him ten years to make the rank of sergeant. Given new authority, he caused further irritation by ferreting out grafters from among his fellow officers. He could not be "fixed," which practically sanctified him in those days of easy fixes. Once again, his constant campaigning to clean up the streets and the police department hindered his rise to the top. Then a like-minded police commissioner was appointed, George V. McLaughlin, and for the moment honesty in service returned. McLaughlin recognized Valentine's unusual dedication to the force and made him first a captain, then a deputy inspector. At that point in his career, twenty-three years with the NYPD had elapsed. Under McLaughlin his primary assignment was to rid the city of gambling, which he undertook with a vengeance. Not only did he go after organized gambling, but he even invaded the inner sanctum of political clubhouses to make arrests. Two years later, however, his good fortune reversed. Another new police commissioner, Grover Whalen, demoted and removed him from the thick of action in Manhattan. Exiled to a quiet precinct where he could not bother Tammany gamblers, he languished until a New York State investigating committee subpoenaed him. Corruption in city government, embodied in Mayor James Walker and his Tammany associates, was the focus of this 1931 inquiry. Valentine told all he knew in such a startling manner that his testimony in part brought about the downfall of those guilty. He left the court a hero.

With Walker out, Fiorello La Guardia promised sweeping reform and was promptly elected mayor. He named John F. O'Ryan as his police commissioner and Valentine as chief inspector. Newspaper reporters asked Valentine how he felt about his promotion, knowing full well that he had been snubbed in the past: "Regardless of what has happened before, I bear no rancor against anyone. . . . Anything that pertains to transfers, assignments, promotions or to any so-called shakeup that may occur is a matter for the police commissioner to decide."

Fate smiled a second time when La Guardia and O'Ryan battled over policy and procedure. During the taxi strike of 1934, O'Ryan wanted to beat back the violent strikers, but La Guardia directed him to have his officers lay down their clubs to discourage retaliation. That and other differences brought on O'Ryan's resignation. The next day La Guardia appointed the one man he had unswerving confidence in, Lewis J. Valentine. Thirty-one years of exemplary service had finally been rewarded.

Police Commissioner Valentine encouraged his men to deal harshly with known criminals. A well-publicized event underlined his penchant when a patrolman friend of his was shot while on duty. Having arrived at police headquarters from the dying man's bedside, Valentine burst in on a lineup and seeing a cocksure dandy, arrested in connection with another murder, exploded with indignation. To his assembled officers he said:

> When you meet such men, draw quickly and shoot accurately. . . . Blood should be smeared all over that velvet collar. . . . You men will be supported by me no matter what you do, if what you do is justified. . . . We want to be careful not to kill innocent people, and we don't want to use brutality on others because of different political faiths, but with the criminals, racketeers, and gangsters, the sky is the limit.

His private talk intended to vent rage and to galvanize reluctant officers leaked out and was picked up by every major newspaper. When given an opportunity to retract his statements he announced to the New York press, "What I said yesterday I repeat today." The public cringed, believing that Valentine's police, and by association all police, would feel free to batter anyone and everyone. Then came a flood of responses from other police chiefs, mostly condemnatory. No sooner had Valentine won public trust with his appointment to the office of commissioner than he was under fire for extremist behavior. Fate appeared to ready him for yet another fall from grace.

But the tempest blew over and he stayed in office for a record eleven years. Discounting the bad press, he received kudos for his handling of the November 1934 election. The night before, he initiated a roundup of known criminals and posted guards at the polling places, with a warning that disorders would not be tolerated. The election proved to be the most upright in the city's recent history. Traffic deaths had been high in congested New York until he increased the number and visibility of road signs, plastered traffic-safety posters everywhere, and gave personal talks to community groups. To regenerate New York's 18,000-man police force, *Time Magazine* reported that Valentine "fired some three hundred men, officially rebuked three thousand, fined eight thousand," and was "even harder on the crooks." Mayor La Guardia had directed Valentine to clean up the city and that he did. Crime statistics in comparison with those when Tammany dictated to police showed a sharp reduction. New Yorkers sighed relief while the newspapers renewed their attacks on the commissioner because he disallowed reporters admittance to emergency scenes. Later he decided to curtail all press conferences, considering them a nuisance, and the press vilified him anew. Since he would no longer issue prepared statements, his "verbatim quotations" were collected from any source to make a headline. The press was at its ugliest when it ran an ongoing series about the police "suicide wave." Several officers had taken their own lives and it was implied that Commissioner Valentine had pushed them to it. Valentine broke his silence to deny the allegations but could not dispel the yellow journalism. His only recourse was to endure it.

In 1945 at age sixty-three he resigned as police commissioner. A new, but related, career awaited him. The weekly radio show *Gangbusters*, a dramatization of true crime investigations, was to shake with authority when his voice boomed over the air waves. As narrator-commentator for the acclaimed program, he convinced the public that law enforcement was brawnier than ever before. In 1946 General Douglas MacArthur asked him for his expert opinion on how to reorganize Japan's criminal-justice system. Occupation of that country after World War II was for the purpose of democratizing it and to remove any vestiges of a police state. Valentine went to Japan and soon presented MacArthur with a 283-page report. Among his many sound recommendations was one eye-catcher, that Japanese police candidates be sent to the United States for training. His boundless pride shone through.

Valentine served on the editorial board of *True Police Cases*, a new magazine, and was a tireless civic worker. He accepted the non-salaried position of chief investigator for New York State's Election Frauds Bureau and he devised a plan for National Crime Prevention Week. After his first wife, Elizabeth J. Donohue, died in 1910, he remarried to her sister, Theresa A. Donohue. They had all grown up together in the same neighborhood and he had always liked both of them. The tough and honest cop, forty-two years a policeman, fifteen months past retirement, died from liver disease. Theresa and his family of four married daughters and nine grandchildren attended his funeral at the Church of Our Lady of Guadalupe in Brooklyn.

Bibliography

Current Biography (1946): 609–11.
"Gang Buster." *Time Magazine* 46(12) (September 17, 1945): 72–73.
Limpus, Lowell M. *Honest Cop: Lewis J. Valentine.* New York: E.P. Dutton, 1939.
New York Times 31 (December 17, 1946): 31:1.

Vice Investigation

The major categories of vice or victimless crime are prostitution, gambling, pornography, and narcotics. The state charges police with enforcing all laws and investigating every crime. However, with so-called victimless crimes the police get much less support than normal from all concerned. Opinion polls show the majority of the public condones victimless crimes in part. This selective aspect confounds law enforcement and to a point directs it. Victimless crimes are those in which no one complains to the police. Personal morality is the arbiter. In another sense it can be said there is no such thing as victimless crime; the very term is an oxymoron. A crime is a crime, even though the victim does not recognize or acknowledge the fact.

Views on what constitutes vice and victimless crimes continue to change. The classic example is smoking marijuana. In the 1960s arrests for possession of "weed" were a common occurrence. The "establishment" punished "hippies" for defying authority. Prison sentences for holding—not dealing—as little as a joint or two were extreme. Since then society has become more tolerant and speaks of marijuana as a recreational drug much like alcohol. Still, marijuana has not been decriminalized.

Federal agents continue to destroy fields of the illegally grown plant and intercept shipments whether from domestic or foreign sources. The prevailing wisdom is still that smoking marijuana leads to use of more life-altering drugs like cocaine and heroin. Nevertheless, smoking marijuana appears to be a victimless crime, at least in part of the public's mind, and should be allowed. Conversely, the public believes use of strongly addictive drugs such as cocaine and heroin do produce victims, because the addict usually supports his or her habit by theft and is a burden on society. The drug legalization debate gets more complicated. Some advocates would legalize marijuana only; others would include hallucinogens; still others would sell depressants and stimulants over the counter; and total advocates would permit any and all drug use as a personal freedom. In 1989 the House Select Committee on Narcotics Abuse and Control held a hearing on drug legalization. The hearing evolved not from a public demand for legalization but from mounting frustration on the part of law enforcement over controlling the drug crisis. To no one's surprise, the hearing denounced legalization whether control was possible.

Changes of attitude about what constitutes vice come from policy-makers no less than the public. The conservative 1980s bred abnormal intolerance. The political climate of the decade dictated that homosexuality and abortion were despicable vices. Police already had the reputation for exhibiting indifference to the welfare of gays. If bigots wanted to have fun and beat up gays, police were not likely to interfere. Now well into the 1990s, gay power has become a potent force to change homophobic attitudes. Gays hold political office and proudly state their sexual preference, as do other gay people in all walks of life. Openly accepting gays in the military became a tenable topic for debate in 1993. Gay-bashing and harassment of gays is no longer acceptable behavior by the public or the police. Yet, homosexuality is still repugnant to many people who find it not only a crime against nature but a crime that yields many victims. Toilet snipes—gays who frequent public restrooms to entice minors into having sex—are deviants police must deal with. AIDS will always be known as the gay disease because promiscuous gays spread AIDS to the general population. Reports of gay teachers molesting children appear all too often in the media and never fail to shock listeners. So homosexuality engenders two opposing views: Gays are people with equal rights and gays by their very nature are wicked.

The second purported vice of the 1980s, abortion, according to pro-life activists, produced an imposing number of victims. The activists said more babies have been murdered in America by legalized abortion than in all U.S. wars combined. Furious at such a death toll, the activists rose up everywhere to go beyond rhetoric and take action. Their criminal activities, i.e., disrupting abortion clinic business, harassing medical staff, and bombing the clinics, were allowed to continue virtually unchecked. Law enforcement took its cue from the state, both doing little to protect the legal rights of pro-abortionists.

A final example of metamorphosed vice is gambling. While homosexuality and abortion incensed some Americans during the 1980s and into the 1990s, gambling did the opposite. Economically strapped states told voters that legalized gambling would provide income needed for education, highways, and other social goods. The public, ready to free gambling from its puritanical shackles, agreed with government. Lotteries and riverboat casinos appeared rapidly and enjoyed frenzied patronage. Also more evident, as a public service newspapers and television gave the odds on sporting events for making bets. By the year 2000 gambling in many forms may well be legal in the United States, whereas once it was a high priority for law-enforcement interdiction. A 1959 police text, *Plainclothesman*, carried the subtitle *A Handbook of Vice and Gambling Investigation*. Its chapters on "Horse and Sports Gambling," "The Numbers Game," and "Gambling Places, Games, and Apparatus" appear archaic. Today's texts usually make three brief statements about gambling: First, gambling statutes are unpopular, therefore difficult to enforce; second, gambling kickbacks are a major source of police corruption; and third, police department policies toward gambling are sketchy and unclear.

Statistics

Victimless crimes not only raise questions about definition and degree but also back law enforcement into a corner. How energetic should the effort be to halt vice? And which vices? And with what success? Prostitution, gambling, pornography, and narcotics are "not" among the FBI index crimes. Instead, data on victimless crimes fall under the heading of Persons Arrested. In 1991 total arrests in the United States for prostitution and commercialized vice reached 98,900; for gambling offenses, 16,600; and for drug abuse violations, 1,010,000. Pornography is buried somewhere in the "all other offenses" total of 3,240,000 (FBI, *Uniform Crime Reports*, 1992). For such "nonindex" crimes the 1991 arrest figures are sizable and indicate active law-enforcement response.

Narcotics

Of the four vice categories narcotics investigation is easily the most crucial. The current drug market is more widespread and profitable than ever. Even the most liberal observer would be wrong to repeat the victimless crime argument: If the fools want to take drugs and die, let them. The amount of money that drug dealing generates is so large that drug-related crime and murder are commonplace and cannot be accurately estimated. In a recent New York City bust police raiders found close to a million dollars in cash spilling off the apartment bed of an average dealer. Petty street dealers often have several thousand dollars in their pockets when arrested. Ambushes and drive-by shootings in which dealers and innocent bystanders die occur regularly. Drug-related crimes make up most of the yearly crime statistics. In *The War on Drugs* (1986), author James Inciardi concluded, "It would appear that the efficient control of drug-related crime is well beyond the scope of contemporary policing." Inciardi arrived at his conclusion after interviewing 573 drug users in Miami who admitted committing approximately 215,000 crimes—of which fewer than 1 percent resulted in arrest.

Federal law enforcment did not fare much better in the 1980s' war on drugs. Around Miami federal agents stopped every size of sailing vessel that might carry drugs into the country. The Miami waters are extremely busy, so the agents, in addition to making some notable confiscations, irritated pleasure-seekers and impounded vessels needlessly. The agents also intercepted airplanes flying in drugs and drug air-drops in the Everglades. Each successful bust made headline news—staggering amounts of drugs were seized. Yet the imported drug market grew by leaps and bounds. Other importation points along the serpentine United States–Mexican border proved no less challenging to federal agents. In June of 1993 Mexican police hunting the killers of a Roman Catholic cardinal discovered a 1,500-foot tunnel connecting

Mexico and California. The lighted, air-conditioned, and concrete-reinforced tunnel stretched from beneath a Tijuana industrial area near the international airport to the Otay Mesa border-crossing and beyond. The tunnel needed only to burrow another few hundred feet to open in an industrial zone in south San Diego. Three years before, authorities had closed another narco-tunnel in Douglas, Arizona, a 270-foot passage-way connecting a luxury home in Mexico and a U.S. warehouse. The Douglas tunnel operated for at least six months before being shut down. With the discovery of the second tunnel, the DEA, police, and the public wondered how many more drug moles permeated the border. Similar to Inciardi's study of the Miami drug scene, the federal effort appeared likewise stymied. Before leaving office, President George Bush admitted the war on drugs had been more of an expensive skirmish. President Bush advocated a different war in the future, a domestic one to slow the appetite for drugs rather than a bootless attempt to seal off all U.S. borders.

To give a better idea of the magnitude of the drug enforcement problem, Operation Gunsmoke need only be looked at. In 1992 deputy U.S. marshals teamed up with local law-enforcement officers from more than seventy agencies in fourteen major cities and a number of smaller communities across the United States. During the ten-week period of Operation Gunsmoke 3,313 arrests were made and almost $2 million in cash and property seized. Of those captured, 365 were armed at the time of arrest, and 730 guns and other weapons were confiscated. The numbers were impressive, if not startling to the general public, and showcased what law enforcement could do given the go-ahead. But in the end Operation Gunsmoke amounted to mere tokenism in the war on drugs. Even if Operation Gunsmoke had continued year-long and quadrupled the number of arrested and seized assets, the drug market still would have prospered.

Head of the Drug Enforcement Administration John C. Lawn reviewed DEA's efforts in 1989. Lawn identified the two Colombian cartels, the Medellin and Cali, as controlling "all significant aspects of worldwide cocaine production, transportation, and wholesale distribution." DEA's strategy to combat the cartels involved foreign and domestic collection of intelligence, development of informants, physical and electronic surveillance, asset inventory, and undercover operations—all standard investigative techniques used throughout law enforcement. To get a better picture of heroin supply and demand, the DEA commenced two studies. The first study sought to pinpoint geographic locations of heroin production through chemical analysis, while the second study attempted to count the number of heroin addicts in the United States. The DEA learned from the first study that Southeast Asia—Chinese and Thai producers—supplied the most heroin. That knowledge brought about the formation of an Asian task force in New York City to target Chinese traffickers, resulting in the quick arrest of 116 members. By 1989 the FBI had identified 450 major U.S. drug trafficking organizations out of a suspected much higher number. The DEA could not investigate all 450 organizations so it chose a different course of action. Lawn explained:

> We [the DEA] target our resources on key figures engaged in smuggling drugs into the United States from source countries. We have found that these international organizations are not necessarily aligned as well defined groups. In fact, because of the international scope of their operations, various groups sometimes make temporary alliances altering any semblance of a formal structure. Because of this, we place the greatest emphasis on identifying the leaders who direct the activities of these international drug organizations (Committee on Government Operations, 1989).

Jamaican drug gangs (posses) were also a concern of DEA in 1989. Thirty or more gangs had been distributing marijuana for at least ten years. That changed to distribution of cocaine and crack cocaine for greater profitability. Because the posses are gangs, all manner of drug-related violence accompanied distribution. DEA agents in Kingston worked with Jamaican authorities to single out the major players directing the gangs. Nonetheless, the posses increased distribution undaunted.

For all levels of law enforcement drug arrests and prosecutions are exceedingly difficult, owing to the absence of complaining victims and witnesses. Even with this limitation, the police make more arrests than prosecutors can prosecute, courts can adjudicate, and prisons can hold. Drug dealers adapt to law-enforcement efforts and usually rebound stronger than before. Police response then centers on reducing gang violence associated with drug trafficking to prevent organized crime groups from emerging. Police must control street-level drug dealing and reclaim urban neighborhoods thus afflicted. Police must segregate drug users, send them to rehabilitation programs, and teach children never to experiment with drugs. And last, police and criminal-justice institutions must maintain their integrity, i.e., not succumb to frustration, cynicism, or corruption when fighting such an immense social problem as drug abuse.

More specifically, police engage in what is called "expressive law enforcement." This means a war on drugs much like the federal effort. All drug-enforcement activities are stepped up to increase the number of narcotics arrests. Dealers are forced to move so frequently that buyers cannot find them. The streets are swept clean of drug trafficking, at least for the time being. In some neighborhoods citizens team with police; in other neighborhoods fear of retaliation and distrust of police override any thought of team-building.

Another strategy is for police to concentrate on infiltrating the drug gang/syndicate to topple the leader. Rather than a temporary display of strength on the streets, police move more slowly to sever the brain behind the organization. Drug gangs present another problem. No matter their youth, the gangs cannot be contained as they once were when members strutted more than committed murder. Police now treat drug gangs as organized criminals and handle them the same way. Persons arrested who also test positive for drug use face additional legal charges and penalties. Many police advocate mandatory urinalysis for arrestees, intensive probation, and prescriptive treatment for addicts. At present, these measures are not applied uniformly nationwide.

Prostitution
Prostitution is seen much in the same light as smoking marijuana. In a free society a person should be able to enjoy any pleasure as long as it causes no one harm. As the "oldest profession," prostitution has not been legislated out of existence, nor will it ever be. The thirty-six legal brothels in Nevada accommodate some 600,000 "dates" per year. Elsewhere in the United States police contain prostitution depending on citizen outcry, local politics, and its association with other vices. Rough estimates suggest that 500,000 prostitutes ply their trade

in the United States, and one in six American men visited a prostitute during 1987–1991. Undercover vice officers work somewhat differently today than in past years. Now they target Johns as well as Jills to cut back demand and shame the customer. In Oregon policewomen dressed as prostitutes enticed curb-crawlers whose cars were then confiscated. For a while in New York and Houston photographs of Johns were released to the media, and if their "mugs" were not shown, their names came through loud and clear. The public embarrassment was so extreme that victims of the victimless crime threatened to fill the air with lawsuits. In the good old days Johns crept away silently.

Authorities who permit prostitution—if it does not become a public nuisance—check health cards to prevent AIDS. In recent monitoring efforts, organized prostitutes were found to be cleaner overall since AIDS because of insistence on condom use. Those prostitutes who spread AIDS shared infected needles heedless of the danger. Now some advocates argue it is safer to visit a prostitute than to take chances in the singles' world. With new confidence in prostitute hygiene, business is reported better than before the AIDS epidemic. On average city police departments designate one in ten officers to work prostitution. In Los Angeles analysts estimate enforcement costs close to $100 million a year. Los Angeles's policy has been to push prostitutes out of the city by making it hard for them to work. Once across boundaries they become someone else's problem but still make forays back into LA whenever they please. Asian prostitution has expanded in LA and other major cities, and dwindling street trade resurfaces in escort services and massage parlors. Usually half the female population in city jails is made up of prostitutes.

As with drugs some people ask, Should prostitution be legalized? The one in ten officers assigned to vice could be redeployed to fight victim crime. Los Angeles and other cities could save millions of dollars spent on prostitution enforcement that amounts to ceremonial expulsion and return; and city health departments could register/inspect prostitutes while tax departments could rely on new income. With legalization the state and prostitutes would benefit. Sociologist Ronald Weitzer chronicled the COYOTE movement in San Francisco that lasted seventeen years beginning in the early 1970s. A prostitutes' rights organization, COYOTE stood for "Call Off Your Tired Old Ethics." Former prostitute Margo St. James led the group with affiliations nationwide. COYOTE's purpose was to raise consciousness for the plight of prostitutes, to improve their lives, to legitimize the profession, and to gain some measure of political power. Between legal battles and hookers' conventions, COYOTE paralleled (or mocked) the feminist movement. Weitzer said COYOTE failed because most of the public considered legalizing prostitution an "immoral crusade," unlike the gay and abortion rights movements that only some of the public denounced as immoral.

Criminologist Frank Morn studied prostitution, police, and city culture in a setting much smaller than Los Angeles, New York, or Houston. For his study he chose Bloomington, Illinois, 1900–1960, the years the Line flourished. A red-light district, the Line got its name because it was near the railroad tracks. The Line brothels were popular with farmers and other merchants whose commerce brought them to Bloomington. Morn's main interest was in chronicling the Line's demise as a "symbolic crusade," similar to what happened in other Bloomingtons across the country. The American Social Hygiene Association (ASHA), founded in 1914, fought venereal disease and prostitution by reporting quasi-scientific findings. The ASHA's highest award was to confer an "A" rating on a city or town, signifying that it was physically and morally clean. Bloomington finally got an "A" around 1955 and with it the designation "All American City." Boosterism was only one reason for the Line's demise. Change from a blue-collar to a white-collar economy was another. With the change, blatant prostitution—the kind enjoyed along the Line— had to be made a lot less visible. Racism and a concerted effort to clean up slums also combined to destroy the Line. Morn describes in detail the relationship of the various mayors and police chiefs. For half a century the Bloomington mayors condoned the Line as a "sporting" place in a segregated "sin" district. The police chiefs either agreed or disagreed. Each mayor won out through political machinations and some sensible thinking. With a sin district prostitution did not spread into respectable quarters, nor did the extra rowdiness associated with whoring overstep its bounds. Bloomington police were instructed to restrict prostitution to the Line, to warn people of the risks involved in entering the Line, and to leave customers alone after fair warning. As in larger cities, Bloomington police succumbed to corruption in allowing the Line to make every night Saturday night. What Morn discovered with his research was that the Progressive Era did effectively do away with sin districts in small as well as large municipalities. However, it took several decades for organizations like ASHA to accomplish the task and perhaps the effort was counterproductive. Prostitution did not disappear, and sin districts were much easier to police than today's shifting vice scene.

Pornography
In the history of undercover police work pornography was one of the first targets pursued, mainly because it was a simple matter to investigate. United States postal authorities ordered pornography through the mail, and once received, arrested the sender, who invariably pleaded First Amendment rights. As with prostitution, law enforcement attempted to stifle supply and demand. Today, entrapment may be resorted to. In a celebrated case aired on the television program *60 Minutes*, federal authorities kept sending catalogs of pornographic materials to a man living in a rural area. The man, Mr. Jacobson, had little or no access to adult bookstores so could be tempted into a mail purchase. After a number of catalog mailings that continued over a year Mr. Jacobson finally ordered an item. Upon returning home one day federal agents stood at his door with an arrest warrant. Bewildered, Mr. Jacobson admitted out of curiosity he had selected an item by title but did not know what was in it. When told he had purchased "child" porn, he again avowed ignorance. *60 Minutes* left the clear impression that Mr. Jacobson had been victimized by the 1980s war on crime and overzealous law enforcement (see *Jacobson v. United States*, 112 S.Ct. 1535 [1992]).

Anthony Comstock (1844–1915) made a name for himself as the foremost antivice crusader. He sponsored an 1873 Act of Congress that barred "obscene, lewd, lascivious, indecent, filthy, or vile" materials from circulating via the U.S. mail. In Comstock's day *obscene et al.* could be made to cover anything thought improper. Then, pornography's definition was too broad. Today, an exact definition is still elusive. The Meese Commission that issued a lengthy study on pornography in the mid-1980s (1,972 pages) defined pornography by listing hundreds of titles of materials confiscated by the federal government. While this showed variety and volume, the listings did not give a clear picture of pornographic content other than the fact that federal arbiters pronounced the materials obscene. Such listings confuse the public who now rent or buy x-rated videos without a second thought. When blue films could be seen only in sleazy movie houses populated by "degenerates," patronage was small. Home VCRs have freed people from the embarrassment of stepping foot in seedy establishments. Saturday night in the suburbs can include a porno film, and sex therapists recommend porno for couples in need of instruction or an aphrodisiac. Given that porno is now more socially acceptable, law enforcement should arrive at a better definition. Logically, those materials that depict adults having sex short of sadmasochism—the kind of materials readily available for home consumption—should be deemed permissible.

Police investigate pornography differently from the postal authorities by being more proactive. Police distribute porn where they know it will be received. They may act as suppliers or buyers to catch the trade on both ends. Police also create potential activity by working outside known criminal areas. Recalling the man caught by his own curiosity in the *60 Minutes* report, this tactic treads the fine line of entrapment. If a vice officer arrests a customer who wants to buy pornographic materials no different from those rented in video stores, it will be hard to make the charge stick. The community standard is another variable that police and other authorities "think" they understand well. In lieu of an exact definition of pornography what the community considers obscene becomes the rule. The problem here is the community does not know what to think about pornography, or has no experience with it, or has never been asked to decide the question, or has been told by antiporn forces what to think. A research team (Linz et al., 1991) reported some interesting findings in the *Public Opinion Quarterly*. They went to Mecklenburg County in North Carolina and arranged for a cross section of residents to view sexually explicit films and magazines or a control film. The residents filled out a questionnaire before and after viewing the materials. The results were these: The majority felt the films and magazines did not appeal to prurient interests, nor would they be offensive to the community. Smaller group results showed that personal feelings about prurience would not be reflected by the community. And the most important finding, the residents

thought the materials less prurient and more acceptable after viewing than before when they were quick to judgment. The Mecklenburg study had a purpose beyond establishing viewing norms. The results were used in a criminal case involving pornography to give the court a more informed look at community standards.

Consequences to Police

Gary T. Marx in *Undercover: Police Surveillance in America* (1988) tells a number of disheartening stories about police caught in the vice game. Undercover work takes many months and even years of patient infiltration and building trust before securing rewards. During that time vice officers have to transform themselves into plausible offenders and adopt the criminal subculture. Marx relates the story of a California officer who rode with the Hell's Angels for a year and a half. The officer produced a number of arrests and netted high-level drug dealers before getting out. His superiors praised him for an exemplary job but the officer paid a high price. He had become a drug addict, an alcoholic, and a brawler. His family had left him and he could not fit back into routine police assignments. He quit the police force, robbed several banks, and served a prison term. Even though his case was an extreme one, vice officers commonly experience some of the same problems in casting off the subculture.

Adoption of a criminal lifestyle is a serious problem, but police corruption overshadows it by far. Sociologist John Dombrink (1988) states:

> For virtually the entire existence of the urban American police force, situations involving vice and its control have presented opportunities for corruption and posed a challenge to police administrators who hoped to limit their officers' misconduct without alienating the officers' loyalties.

Dombrink traces the 1980s' wave of police corruption in Miami, Philadelphia, New York City, Boston, and San Francisco. He found that one hundred of 1,060 Miami police officers had been or were under investigation for corruption as of 1986. In Philadelphia residents complained that police underenforced vice laws, implying that police were on the take to keep it that way. A new police commissioner for New York City, Patrick Murphy, was chosen specifically for his intense dislike of corruption. Segments of the NYPD had grown so corrupt that

Commissioner Murphy continually reassigned officers to avoid old habits. In Boston where police are official agents of the liquor licensing board with power to inspect bars and restaurants, paying police for protection was routine and kickbacks lucrative. Corruption in San Francisco involved ethical lapses. Because of the youthfulness of its force some officers engaged in immoral behavior, e.g., hiring a prostitute for a party; other officers brutalized minorities in an ethnically sensitive city; and gay-bashing was taken for granted.

Rather than try to supply solutions for corruption, Dombrink restated the dilemmas involved. They are:

- Decriminalize vice—if so, what of the risk that worse crime will follow?
- Centralize vice patrol responsibility—Are decentralized operations too hard to supervise?
- Specialist versus generalist—Do officers who work only vice do a better job of control than regular officers who encounter vice as part of their daily routine?
- Autonomy versus supervision—Should vice officers be allowed to "call their own shots" or submit to strict management of their actions?

Dombrink concluded about the 1980s: "The events of the past decade have further confounded the ambivalence surrounding the policing of vice. New situations, new cohort attitudes, new policing demands, and more decriminalization have muddied the waters in the vice enforcement area."

Bibliography

Attorney General's Commission on Pornography. *Final Report*. Washington, DC: U.S. Department of Justice, 1986.

Committee on Government Operations. House of Representatives. *Federal Strategies to Investigate and Prosecute Major Narcotics Traffickers*. Washington, DC: Government Printing Office, 1989.

Dombrink, John. "The Touchables: Vice and Police Corruption in the 1980's." *Law and Contemporary Problems* 51 (Winter 1988): 201–32.

Egen, Capt. Frederick W. *Plainclothesman: A Handbook fo Vice and Gambling Investigation*. New York: Arco, 1959.

Giacopassi, D.J., and J.R. Sparger. "Cognitive Dissonance in Vice Enforcement." *American Journal of Police* 10 (1991): 39–51.

Greek, C., and M. Wright. "Law Enforcement and Antipornography Laws." *American Journal of Police* 7 (Spring 1988): 29–51.

Inciardi, James A. *The War on Drugs*. Palo Alto, CA: Mayfield, 1986.

Klecak, F.E. "Organization and Facilities of an Investigative Unit Within a Law Enforcement Agency." In *Criminal and Civil Investigation Handbook*. Eds. Joseph J. Grau and Ben Jacobson. New York: McGraw-Hill, 1981.

Linz, Daniel, et al. "Estimating Community Standards: The Use of Social Science Evidence in an Obscenity Prosecution." *Public Opinion Quarterly* 55 (1991): 80–112.

Marx, Gary T. *Undercover: Police Surveillance in America*. Berkeley: University of California Press, 1988.

Morn, Frank. "Prostitution, Police and City Culture in a Small Midwestern City: A History, 1900-1960." *Journal of Crime and Justice* 13 (1990): 149–74.

Noble, H.B. "Sweeping the Streets: A Return to the Old Morality Puts New Pressure on City Police." *Police Magazine* 2 (March 1979): 54–62.

Select Committee on Narcotics Abuse and Control. *Legalization of Illicit Drugs: Impact and Feasibility*. Washington, DC: Government Printing Office, 1989.

"Street Cleaning." *The Economist* 320 (September 7, 1991): 28–29.

Thibault, Edward A., et al. *Proactive Police Management*. 2d ed. Englewood Cliffs, NJ: Prentice-Hall, 1990.

Weitzer, Ronald. "Prostitutes' Rights in the United States: The Failure of a Movement." *Sociological Quarterly* 32 (1991): 23–41.

Wilson, G.P., et al. "State Intervention and Victimless Crimes: A Study of Police Attitudes." *Journal of Police Science and Administration* 13 (March 1985): 22–29.

Video Technology

The use of videotaping by law-enforcement personnel has steadily increased due to technological improvements and price decreases in equipment. But more important, judicial approval of videotaping has made it more acceptable in the courtroom—as hard-and-fast evidence it is practically incontrovertible. For example, when police tape drunk-driver coordination testing, convictions result in almost 100 percent of the cases—mainly because most drunk drivers plead guilty after their tape has been reviewed by a defense attorney. Videotaping is also used for surveillance, recording of confessions, traffic-control studies, public relations, recording of crime scenes, and, of course, for training.

Drunk-Driving Enforcement

Many police departments receive state and federal grants for the direct purchase of video equipment to aid them in enforcing drunk-driving laws. Most magistrates require that an officer have proper training in the use of the equipment. Training requirements are similar to those for breathalyzer testing, i.e., the officer must be able to demonstrate an ability to set up and employ the equipment. The officer need not be familiar with the electronics of the equipment or technical data beyond that of a layperson, but he or she must be able to verify in court that the recording made is an accurate one. Most courts also require that a clock and calendar be present in the camera's viewfinder during taping. As a matter of procedure, standard forms are read to the defendant on camera stating that he or she has been arrested for driving while intoxicated, that he or she is being videotaped, and that an attorney will be permitted to view the tape at a later time. It is also imperative that the camera never stop until the taping is finished. Otherwise, the defense attorney will question the validity of the tape, since the officer must have a justifiable reason for stopping taping (such as mechanical difficulty or failure).

Surveillance

At one time film was the only medium that was capable of recording moving images. This was costly and difficult for the untrained operator to use. Audio recording in sync with the film was virtually impossible without additional expensive equipment. Today's video camcorders can record in light intensity of seven lux and this is improving constantly. Audio recording is possible in undercover situations with the use of wireless microphones that transmit directly to the recorder. With a camcorder nothing could be easier for the surveillance officer; the image seen in the viewfinder is exactly what is recorded.

Confessions

Previously, police detectives were thought to "rough up" a suspect to secure a confession.

Whether true or not, whatever happened took place behind closed doors and later allegations of police brutality were difficult to prove or disprove. Now, videotaping a confession or the entire proceedings in lieu of an admission of guilt, shows the suspect's physical condition before questioning. The suspect's answers, body language, degree of cooperation, and other tell-tale signs are made evident. Also clearly captured on tape are the interrogator's method and manner. Videotaping a confession protects both the suspect and the police department in a court of law. As stated earlier, it is imperative to have a clock in view of the camera when the recording is being made. Passing time must be sequential to avoid any charges of tape manipulation or blackout.

Traffic Control

Many police departments conduct traffic surveys in which an officer stationed at a traffic post studies traffic flow and patterns. A video recorder and camera, properly placed and protected, frees the officer for other duties. Unassisted, videotaping continues for up to eight hours. Then the officer retrieves the tape, returns to headquarters, and examines it for pertinent information. This exchange of officer for machine is a powerful management tool. Another innovation entails placement of a video camera on the dashboard of a patrol vehicle to provide a full view of the roadway. The patrol officer activates the tape to record a traffic violation and stop. Using a wireless microphone, the officer can preserve his or her conversation with the motorist for presentation in court.

Public Relations

Videotapes made for the public address such perennial subjects as bicycle safety, crime prevention, and substance abuse. The public reacts favorably to this type of communication because on view are familiar settings, faces, and police in helping situations. Many citizens do not know how to handle themselves given a drastic change in their daily routine. An emergency or a crime reduces them to inadequacy or tears. In such situations, an instructional videotape can help dispel some of the fear.

Crime Scene

Police find that a video camera easily traces a perpetrator from the point of entry to the point of exit. Likewise, during a "walk-through" important evidence can be treated in a series of close-ups. Both practices supplant notebook jottings, reliance on memory alone, and flawed re-creation in court when attempting to describe a crime scene. So far there has been only one major problem with videotaping—the use of color equipment to tape a bloody crime. As with color photography, blood and gore shock the senses of the jurors, and sometimes graphic images are not permitted as evidence. Police remedy this problem by exhibiting the tape with all color turned off on the playback set.

Training

Covering virtually any subject, departmental training tapes are inexpensively made to supplement police education. Since many states mandate in-house training for police officers, videotaping is one way to get the job done. Tapes on firearms safety, shooting techniques, and liability avoidance are examples of suitable videotape production. Tapes of short duration are used for roll-call training in areas such as handcuffing techniques or searching of prisoners.

Still new to police departments, video technology has shown itself to be an innovation of lasting importance. It is well to remember that at one time radar was considered a luxury but now it is a necessity; so it will be with the video recorder. Law enforcement requires equipment that will increase its efficiency in apprehending suspects and in convicting them. Video technology does just that by putting an officer, in person or in absentia, "behind the camera" to record indelible and veracious images.

Joseph Missonellie

Bibliography

Missonellie, Joseph. "The Drunk Driver, Video Tape and More Convictions. "*Law and Order* 30(11) (November 1982): 32–35.
———. "Exploring the Television Frontier." *Law and Order* 31(5) (May 1983): 62–66.
Missonellie, Joseph, and James S. D'Angelo. *Television and Law Enforcement.* Springfield, IL: Charles C. Thomas, 1984.
———. "Using Video Equipment in Law Enforcement Work." *Law and Order* 22(4) (April 1974): 62–65, 80–82.

August Vollmer

August Vollmer (1876–1955), father of modern professional policing in the United States, was born in New Orleans, Louisiana. Orphaned as a child, he was educated in Germany before returning to the United States and settling in the San Francisco Bay area. After service in the Philippines during the Spanish-American War, which included two highly publicized acts of heroism, he was elected marshal of Berkeley, California, in 1905. From that point on his career never waned. In 1907 he was elected president of the California Police Chiefs Association; from 1909 to 1932 he served as chief of police for Berkeley; in 1922 he accepted the presidency of the International Association of Chiefs of Police; and from 1932 until his death he was an educator, a professor of police administration at the University of California. In between he reorganized the San Diego Police Department (1915), the Los Angeles Police Department (1923–1925), the Detroit Police Department (1925), the Havana (Cuba) Police (1926), the police agencies of Chicago and Kansas City (1929), the Minneapolis Police Department (1930), the Santa Barbara Police Department (1936), the police of Syracuse, New York (1943), of Dallas (1944), and of Portland, Oregon (1947). Moreover, in 1931 the Wickersham Commission retained him, and his *Report on Police* contributed in no small part to the successful campaign to repeal the Eighteenth Amendment (Prohibition) and the Volstead Act.

Vollmer was an innovator in an extremely conservative profession. He was an early advocate of college education for police officers and other unheard-of measures, such as probation for first offenders and the decriminalization of victimless crimes. He considered crime prevention a priority for police and opposed capital punishment. He instituted an in-service training program of such rigor and effectiveness that it was copied by numerous police agencies in the United States and other countries. In 1921 Vollmer introduced the first "lie detector" to be put to practical police use and for many years was the sole police executive to endorse its use as an investigative tool. Polygraph pioneers Clarence D. Lee, John Larson, and Leonarde Keeler acknowledged their debt to him for employing and defending the new device. As early as 1922 he inaugurated a single fingerprint classification system and a simple but effective method of classifying handwriting specimens. He also initiated the modus operandi approach to criminal investigation. In the 1920s and early 1930s, the Berkeley police laboratory became the model and training ground for police laboratory technicians throughout the country.

V

Vollmer's dedication to stringent recruitment standards, high levels of integrity, and freedom from political interference were unpopular with his contemporaries. But the Berkeley Police Department soon became the darling of progressive journalists and academics. In succeeding decades Berkeley police officers such as O.W. Wilson, V.A. Leonard, John P. Kenney, and many others, were recruited for high-ranking positions in other police agencies and were appointed to head up the many police-science curricula that burgeoned on America's university campuses in the 1940s and 1950s. Second only to J. Edgar Hoover in public relations expertise, Vollmer insisted on complete cooperation with the news media. He seemed always to be promoting the police through contributions to both professional and popular journals, lectures to college classes and to a variety of business and professional clubs, and presentations describing Berkeley police initiatives and programs. He never tired of delineating the future of policing.

Unlike J. Edgar Hoover, Vollmer was at home with academic criminologists and he respected them. He conducted a voluminous correspondence with such leaders of American criminology as Edwin Sutherland, Sheldon Glueck, Paul Tappan, Thorsten Sellin, and Martin Neumeyer. As founder and president of the organization now known as the American Society of Criminology (which presents annually the August Vollmer Award to a distinguished criminologist), he extended his influence considerably. A faithful student of scientific management and public administration, he ceaselessly reeducated himself.

Vollmer authored or coauthored a number of books, all now out-of-print but many of which are still footnoted in the contemporary police literature. Clearly stated in his writings is his plea for centralization and consolidation of police units and services. To this day his cherished wish for integrated policing is still elusive. On the national level centralization of criminal identification files and crime statistics has been realized, but the consolidation of many local police units into larger, more responsive law-enforcement agencies has not come to pass. In 1955, weary and almost blind, Vollmer shot himself in the right temple to end his life.

The Bancroft Library of the University of California, Berkeley, is the repository of the Vollmer Collection and of the oral history *August Vollmer: Pioneer in Professionalism*. Included in the collection are Vollmer's private correspondence, his files from the Berkeley Police Department days, his unpublished manuscripts, and taped interviews with Vollmer colleagues and protégés, such as O.W. Wilson, John D. Holstrom, V.A. Leonard, Willard E. Schmidt, Thomas P. Hunter, William F. Dean, Gene B. Woods, Milton Chernin, Austin MacCormick, Spencer D. Parratt, and Donal E.J. MacNamara.

Donal E.J. MacNamara

Bibliography

Carte, Gene E., and Elaine H. Carte. *Police Reform in the United States: The Era of August Vollmer*. Berkeley: University of California Press, 1975.

Deutsch, Albert. *The Trouble with Cops*. New York: Crown, 1955.

Kenney, John P. *The California Police*. Springfield, IL: Charles C. Thomas, 1964.

Leonard, V.A. *Police of the 20th Century*. Brooklyn, NY: Foundation Press, 1968.

MacNamara, Donal E.J. "August Vollmer: The Vision of Police Professionalism." In *Pioneers in Policing*. Ed. P.J. Stead. Montclair, NJ: Patterson Smith, 1977.

Parker, Alfred E. *Crime Fighter: August Vollmer*. New York: Macmillan, 1961.

———. *The Berkeley Police Story*. Springfield, IL: Charles C. Thomas, 1972.

U.S. National Commission on Law Observance and Enforcement (Wickersham Commission). *Report No. 14: Police*. Prepared under the direction of Vollmer. 1931. Reprint. Montclair, NJ: Patterson Smith, 1968.

Vollmer, August. *The Criminal*. Brooklyn, NY: Foundation Press, 1949.

———. *The Police and Modern Society*. 1936. Reprint. Montclair, NJ: Patterson Smith, 1971.

Vollmer, August, and Alfred E. Parker. *Crime and the State Police*. Berkeley: University of California Press, 1935.

———. *Crime, Crooks and Cops*. New York: Funk and Wagnall Press, 1937.

W.P.A. Writers Project. *Berkeley: The First 75 Years*. Berkeley, CA: Gillick Press, 1941.

W

Western Peace Officer

The image of the western peace officer remains a pervasive influence on public organizations, attitudes, and functions in the United States. While unsupported by fact, the consistent portrayal of the American frontier as a land of unrestrained violence, crime, and disorder has led to the popular myth of the fast-drawing, straight-shooting lawman bringing justice to the "Wild West."

In the popular mind, the legend of the town-taming marshal continues as a framework for the crime-fighting officer of the present. This, in turn, contributes to a host of contemporary issues and controversies. In truth, no evidence exists to support the view of America's frontier as a place distinguished by extreme degrees of crime. Police, court, and prison records of the time reveal no particular excess of violent or deviant behavior. Urban centers of nineteenth-century America probably experienced far higher rates of crime than the sparsely populated West.

Pioneers closely followed historic systems of law enforcement derived from England. Two major categories developed: governmental and private. But a variety of titles, duties, authorities, and personalities appeared to complicate any analysis of function. Officers routinely performed overlapping tasks, carried several commissions, and changed agency associations. Furthermore, the distinction between public and private authority remained quite confused both by statute and public perception.

In the absence of civil service, retirement plans, supervisory functions, training programs, and detailed records, law enforcement was quite different from today. But similarities far outweighed distinctions. Then, as now, officers had to adhere to the procedures of criminal justice while responding to public and political influences.

Structure of Law Enforcement

Community police agencies formed the primary level of law enforcement. Towns typically established the office of marshal upon their incorporation, if not before. With the growth of populations, deputies were appointed and eventually police forces created. The creation of large departments in eastern cities such as New York, Boston, and Philadelphia provided western centers with models for organization and structure. After the Civil War, uniforms and issued firearms became common among urban police agencies throughout the United States. Western cities such as San Francisco, Denver, and San Antonio maintained large structured forces organized and operating much as those of today decades prior to the twentieth century. Corruption and overt political control were, however, typical and major problems. Scandals in urban police agencies led in several cases to direct intervention by state legislatures.

A few frontier lawmen were transformed, within their lifetime, into figures of mystic stature. James Butler "Wild Bill" Hickok and Wyatt Earp never represented the typical western police officer in anything other than romanticized, fictional presentation. But together with such lesser-known figures as Dallas Studenmire and Ben Thompson, they served as the foundation for the false legend of the gunfighter-marshal. Local police officers spent their time checking doors, arresting drunks, and looking for lost children. They seldom used firearms and rarely encountered the fabled outlaws of the West.

Local officers were usually selected on the basis of personal knowledge of mayors, judges, and police chiefs. They often maintained their appointments through political involvement. In many instances they earned reputations as lazy, indifferent, corrupt, inefficient, and violent. Sheriffs, their deputies, and local constables provided counties with formal law enforcement. These officers were, of course, derived directly from patterns found in eastern states and may be traced through history to their centuries-old Anglo-Saxon and Norman origins.

The county sheriff emerged as a law-enforcement officer of great prominence in the American West. In the decades prior to the creation of state police agencies, and with town officers severely restricted in scope of jurisdiction, the county became a key basis for police authority. Sheriffs exercised power over vast areas. Many counties in the West were originally larger than some states in the East. Deputies might operate alone, several days travel away from the seat of local government. As a consequence, the county peace officer fulfilled an incredibly diverse assortment of responsibilities, usually with no preparation and minimal guidance.

County sheriffs had a variety of governmental functions to perform. They often collected diverse taxes, served civil papers and court orders, received bonds, appraised and sold property, summoned juries, licensed dogs, and inspected livestock. Furthermore, sheriffs often inflicted punishments determined by legal process. This could mean flogging prisoners or even performing executions. But in practice, the critical duty usually concerned operations of the county jail. The sheriff's responsibility to maintain prisoners provided opportunity for personal profit, for it typically led to fees paid without regard to conditions. As a consequence, many jails in the West were deplorable, with brutality and escape common events.

One New Mexico sheriff achieved rare distinction in the capture and eventual killing of one of America's truly legendary outlaws. In 1881 Patrick Floyd "Pat" Garrett shot "Billy the Kid" (William H. Bonney), thus becoming the most famous lawman of his time.

Vigilantism

Occasional instances of mass violence and widespread social disorder posed insurmountable problems for local lawmen. Dramatic confrontations between farmers and ranchers— sheep and cattle raisers—and feuding political factions could completely destroy the normal routines of frontier life.

Among the most notable examples of severe conflict were rather common disputes between labor and management in mining areas. Two extreme examples occurred at Bisbee, Arizona, and Ludlow Colorado, both shortly before World War I.

At the extreme, these demonstrations of unrest led to popular frontier forms of criminal justice commonly associated with vigilantism. Originally called "regulators," these private citizens sometimes performed all functions of law enforcement, from investigation to execution. Often operating with formal recognition and approval from officials, the vigilantes sometimes served as the only practical means of preserving order and maintaining justice. At the other extreme, they sometimes devolved into mobs intent only upon abuse and lynching of suspects and those deemed subversive.

Private Police Forces

Private police forces operated throughout the West, performing a multitude of functions, proper and improper, for special interests. Foremost among the companies providing law enforcement for hire was the Pinkerton Detective Agency, founded in Chicago in 1850. Within the next two generations this organization became international in scope and served as the nearest practical equivalent of a national police force. It maintained centralized files and a large force of professional detectives and pioneered many techniques of investigation.

The Pinkerton agency also acquired a reputation for bribery, unethical conduct, and excessive force. One notable example of the latter occurred in 1875, when detectives caused a murderous explosion in the Missouri home of Frank and Jesse James, thus helping the outlaw brothers to attain the stature of national heroes.

Another notable private organization was David Cook's Rocky Mountain Detective Association, headquartered for several decades in Denver. It demonstrated the value of cooperation and communication among police agencies throughout the central portion of the United States. Private companies in the West also developed their own powerful security forces, which were soon emulated by associations desiring to create their own specialized security units. Wells-Fargo, originally an express company, led the way to powerful, self-contained police forces. Its teams of guards and detectives were responsible for the security of stage and train shipments of vast treasures in gold and silver, from the Sierras to the Rockies.

The railroad police, however, may best exemplify the development of quasi-official law enforcement throughout the American West. Often with full authority as state peace officers, while privately employed, detectives for the Santa Fe, Missouri Pacific, and other lines began a tradition that continues to the present.

Perhaps the most colorful units of all those found within the railroad police of the nation was that formed by the Union Pacific to combat the legendary "Wild Bunch" in Wyoming. Special trains kept waiting could rush select teams of hard men and fast horses to the site of a robbery. These operations helped drive Butch Cassidy and the Sundance Kid from the country soon after the turn of the century.

Large ranches maintained their own law-enforcement officers, often with commissions obtained from local authorities. Other settlers formed fraternal orders such as the Anti-Horse Thief Association on the Great Plains. By 1873 groups of ranch owners began employing stock detectives to combat cattle theft. The "range inspectors" of Texas and Wyoming soon became extremely important figures, curtailing the efforts of rustlers on western ranch lands. They continue to perform the same functions today.

Rangers to Highway Patrol

Although town, country, and private officers usually worked reasonably well together, the need for another level of police authority slowly emerged. It was based, in many cases, upon the West's most famous law-enforcement organization, the Texas Rangers.

Even before the revolution against Mexico, English-speaking settlers in East Texas had organized small paramilitary units to scout Indian tribes to the west. They were called "rangers" and received formal recognition with independence and eventual statehood. Before the Civil War and again following Reconstruction, these soldiers and lawmen gradually evolved from Indian fighters to state police officers. The Texas Rangers clearly served as models for several similar forces in the West. California, Arizona, Colorado, Nevada, and New Mexico each experimented with such units prior to World War I.

During the 1920s and 1930s nearly all western states created highway patrols, using a variety of titles, to deal with the problems and opportunities created by the sudden popularity of automobiles and rapid expansion of highway networks. The California Highway Patrol, formed in 1929, then emerged as the largest and probably most influential of contemporary state police forces.

American Indian Police System

Of all the wide variety of western peace officers, the most unique was that of the American Indians. Tribes such as the Cheyenne, Cherokee, and Choctaw had long possessed their own law-enforcement units, but these forces had no formal recognition or support from federal authorities. In 1878 Congress finally appropriated funds for an Indian police system. Individual agents had, of course, been relying upon their own appointed officers for some time. These men sometimes functioned as scouts for the military, well exemplified by the San Carlos Apache detachment, which enabled the capture of the feared Geronimo.

Within a generation hundreds of Indian police officers appeared throughout the West. These gradually formed the complex mosaic of law enforcement now affecting tribal lands throughout the United States. Presently, jurisdiction extends from powerful independent forces, such as that of the Navajo, to investigators employed by the Bureau of Indian Affairs. And while some states and local governments have extended authority over reservations, other areas remain firmly under control of enduring tribal governments. Their powers reach back to formal treaties with the United States itself.

U.S. Marshals

Federal police agencies have long played major roles throughout the West. At times the military has performed obvious law-enforcement functions, but the federal agents most closely associated with police work were the U.S. marshals.

Establishment of a national judicial system in 1789 led directly to recognition of the need for officers working directly for the federal courts. Congress apparently turned to the precedent of English admiralty law creating the position of marshal for each judicial district. Later, with creation of vast federal territories in the West, these officers assumed a wide range of police duties.

With few exceptions the actual marshals were businessmen who obtained their presidential appointments through politics. Their deputies, however, performed a multitude of essential functions in such giant developing territories as Nebraska, Utah, and New Mexico. Until 1896 these federal officers received no regular salaries. Their income depended entirely upon collection of specified fees and occasional rewards.

The federal marshals and their deputies gained greatest fame through operations in the Oklahoma and Indian territories between 1889 and 1907. William M. "Bill" Tilghman, Christian "Chris" Madsen, and Henry A. "Heck" Thomas achieved particular acclaim in the continuing struggle against outlaw gangs, such as those of Bill Doolin and the Dalton brothers.

As federal territories became states, the role of the marshal diminished to that of the present. But numerous other police agencies of the national government appeared to fulfill more specialized functions. Inspectors for the post office and the separate customs service were quite active at particular times and places, but their small numbers and limited jurisdictions permitted only supporting roles on the closing frontier.

Other Federal Law Enforcement Agencies
One federal agency destined to have a significant impact on the modern West was created in 1924. In an effort to combat new problems of illegal immigration, Congress authorized formation of a Border Patrol within the Bureau of Immigration. For more than twenty years this unit worked in tandem with a separate force of mounted customs guards. Between World Wars I and II they were the largest federal police agencies, with operations concentrated then, as now, on the Mexican border.

Meanwhile, the mosaic of national law enforcement continued to increase in complexity and scope. The Secret Service, Federal Bureau of Investigation, and National Park Rangers were only three additional organizations active in the West.

The Lingering Myth
The public knows the peace officer of past and present through fiction more than fact. Misconceptions and misperceptions of crime and law enforcement are, of course, neither new nor restricted to the frontier. But it appears that errors in concept are particularly evident in connection with the West. Novels, films, and television series have created a romantic image

of law enforcement with little basis in fact. Exploits of real peace officers have blended with the fictional, such as the now very well remembered Matt Dillon of television's *Gunsmoke* and Rooster Cogburn of the motion picture *True Grit*.

And the mythical image of the western peace officer continues to exert a significant hold upon the public's imagination. It also influences the attitudes of many contemporary police officers, who often remain largely unaware of their profession's heritage. In truth, the history of western law enforcement reveals the remarkably enduring characteristics of police work. Fundamental conditions, while greatly altered in superficial respects by technical developments such as the automobile, radio, and computer, remain the same. Ultimate issues such as public relations, political influence, social problems, legal authority, and funding endure as major concerns without significant change.

Major legislative or administrative alterations have been rare, and the daily realities of police service are very similar to those of a century ago. Drunks, domestic disputes, thefts, and vandalism were as common to a peace officer of yesterday as to one of today.

Minimum requirements based largely upon those popularized by California's influential Commission on Peace Officer Standards and Training are bringing modification throughout the modern West. But efforts to promote consolidation and mandatory education for administrators have met with little success.

The western peace officer of the present faces new difficulties posed by urban growth and the development of serious social problems. An often misunderstood heritage appears to offer little guidance in their possible solution. But the image of the western peace officer does offer a degree of hope. His courage, initiative, and independence provide a foundation for the protection of individual rights and freedom.

The durable reputation of the western peace officer may appear an anachronism in our contemporary culture, but it has prospered and endured for more than a century. There is no doubt that it will face future application and even reincarnation.

Isolated town marshals, Texas Rangers, Indian police officers, and railroad detectives are as much a part of the present as of the past.

They may have become fixtures in the American mind.

Frank R. Prassel

Bibliography

Bancroft, Hubert Howe. *Popular Tribunals*. San Francisco: History Company, 1887.

Gard, Wayne. *Frontier Justice*. Norman: University of Oklahoma Press, 1949.

Hagan, William T. *Indian Police and Judges*. New Haven, CT: Yale University Press, 1966.

Prassel, Frank R. *The Western Peace Officer*. Norman: University of Oklahoma Press, 1972.

White-Collar Crime

The term *white-collar crime* refers to a loosely defined category of illegal behavior that, most fundamentally, is differentiated from "street" or "traditional" forms of crime such as robbery, burglary, assault, and homicide. No criminal code offense is specifically labeled "white-collar crime"; rather the designation covers diverse kinds of lawbreaking, particularly regulatory delicts. Prototypical white-collar crimes are insider trading in stocks, antitrust conspiracies in restraint of trade, knowing maintenance of dangerous workplace health conditions, and fraud by physicians against medical benefit programs. The key criterion used to differentiate a white-collar offense from other crimes is that the act was done as part of the occupational role of the offender, a role commonly located in the world of business, politics, or the professions (Green, 1990).

The term *white-collar crime* was coined by Edwin H. Sutherland, a sociology professor at Indiana University, in his presidential address to the American Sociological Association in 1939 (Sutherland, 1940). Sutherland's monograph *White Collar Crime*, published ten years later, gained an international reputation equaled by few, if any, criminological treatises. Hermann Mannheim (1965:170) maintained that if there were a Nobel Prize for criminology, Sutherland undoubtedly would have earned it for this contribution. *White Collar Crime* is a hard-hitting, carefully documented exposé of lawbreaking by corporations and persons in the upper echelons of society. It belittles popular theories of criminal behavior, such as those that blame broken homes for delinquency, by pointing out that white-collar malefactors have enjoyed the best

kinds of education as well as the luxuries of privilege and wealth. They do not suffer from unresolved oedipal complexes or stressful toilet training. Nonetheless, they are without doubt violators of the criminal law.

It has been noted that regular crime has the tendency to unite a society. "Good" and "decent" people come together to condemn the common criminal. They reinforce their own commitment to conformity, besides learning that such acts can lead to ill-fame and prison sentences. White-collar offenses, on the other hand, threaten the integrity of a society because they call into question the legitimacy of the social order, and they undermine trust and the sense of justice. Besides, they visit much more harm and death upon citizens than street offenses. More money is embezzled by bank officers than is stolen by bank robbers; more persons are likely killed by unnecessary surgery than are slain by traditional kinds of murderers.

The Police and White-Collar Crime

Enforcement of the laws against white-collar crime is largely the work of specialized investigators employed by regulatory agencies. The most extensive enforcement effort is at the federal level, in places such as the Food and Drug Administration, the Internal Revenue Service, the Securities and Exchange Commission, and the Federal Trade Commission. New concerns have produced a proliferation of additional federal agencies, including the Office of Surface Mining, the Environmental Protection Agency, the Occupational Health and Safety Agency, as well as a variety of federal bureaucracies that monitor nuclear plants.

In addition, fueled by growing cynicism about the honesty of those holding power that followed the Watergate scandal and the Vietnam War, many federal agencies themselves now are monitored by inspector-generals, often former law-enforcement agents, whose job, in the words of former President Reagan, is to be "as mean as a junkyard watch dog."

State, Local and Private Enforcement

State responses to fraudulent business, professional, and political practices have been less pronounced than at the federal level, primarily because of the resources needed to mount successful investigations and prosecutions and because of the federal preemption of much of the field.

Many states during the past few decades established Economic Crime Units (ECUs) to deal with white-collar offenses. These units tend to focus on quick-and-easy cases, such as home improvement con games and auto insurance frauds, rather than on illegal acts of entrenched business organizations. Somers (1982:12), in a handbook for economic crime investigators, sets out four skills essential for the work: (1) accounting, (2) computer science, (3) advanced investigative ability, and (4) knowledge of the special laws concerning economic crimes.

Examining the work of the Connecticut ECU, Whitcomb et al. (1976) reported that six kinds of cases received major attention: (1) those that involve a large number of victims or a large amount of money, (2) those likely to have a major deterrent impact, (3) those with a strong likelihood of success based upon the evidence gathered, (4) those involving serious statutory violations, (5) those in which the fraud appears likely to recur with some regularity, and (6) those with a high likelihood of victim restitution.

State and local policing of white-collar crime often operates under severe restraints because of limited personnel and funds (Benson et al., 1988, 1990). Typical of such handicapped policing is work assigned to Hector Villa, district manager in El Paso for the Texas Water Commission, the state's primary environmental enforcement agency. Villa has to police more than 8,800 square miles, including the 100 miles of the Rio Grande between Mexico and the United States. He attempts to intercept illegal hazardous waste shipments that are being transported across the border from the United States for dumping in Mexico as well as to impede similar traffic moving northward. Under Mexican law and international agreement, hazardous waste generated from material imported from the United States must be sent back into the United States for disposal. Getting rid of such waste legitimately can cost as much as $1,000 per barrel for some substances; law-evaders dump the hazardous material into sewers, landfills, and onto desert land (Tomsho, 1992).

Studies have indicated that citizens in the United States have become as concerned about white-collar offenses as they are about street crime. Cullen et al. (1982), for instance, found from a survey that the offense of knowingly selling contaminated food was rated as more serious than aggravated assault, forcible rape, or selling secret documents to a foreign government. Similarly, causing the death of an employee by neglecting to repair machinery was deemed to be more serious than both child abuse and kidnapping for ransom. Another survey found that a sample of American police chiefs viewed white-collar offenses much as the public ranked them, while investigators for federal agencies saw them as even more heinous then either the chiefs or the citizen group (Pontell et al., 1983).

On the local level, there is a need to establish a sensitivity to white-collar offenses among patrol officers. Some ECUs have generated reporting forms for use whenever communication or squad car officers encounter what appear to be white-collar offenses. Britnall (1978) notes a Los Angeles case in which a patrol officer observed an unusually large number of fights between the owners and the customers at an auto repair shop, and suspected that the owner was engaged in fraudulent activities. Los Angeles has a special detective squad to handle such incident reports, but in most jurisdictions, Britnall points out, officers typically file a report of a suspected fraud only once because they learn that nothing will come of it.

On the other hand, a British study has pointed out that many police officers subscribe to an ideal of egalitarianism: Interview subjects often told Reiner (1978:219) that they would relish taking action against a member of the upper class if the chance arose. "Nothing would give me greater pleasure than being able to arrest the Lord Mayor," one constable maintained.

Besides state and local police, there are also a large number of private investigators specifically engaged in ferreting out white-collar offenses committed against the companies that employ them. This work arena has been said to be "one of the fastest growing professional fields in the 1990s," and many sworn police officers, who tend to retire at relatively young ages, make a second career in private security work (Mannix et al., 1991:97). Private enforcement officers are known under a variety of names, such as fraud examiners, fraud auditors, and forensic accountants. The National Association of Certified Fraud Examiners, founded in 1988 and headquartered in Austin, Texas, now has 7,000 members and offers training courses nationwide on how to deal with offenses such as embezzlement, loan frauds, false claims, mail and wire fraud, money laundering,

bribery and kickbacks, and contract and procurement frauds.

The Federal Response

The growing focus of law enforcement on
white-collar crime was highlighted by the decision of the Federal Bureau of Investigation early
in the 1980s to downgrade efforts to solve offenses such as bank robbery and the interstate
transportation of vehicles (Dyer Act offenses) in
order to concentrate more intensively on frauds,
corruption, and violations of federal statutes
designed to control the behavior of the more
"respectable" elements of society. The FBI had
been stung by charges that it was "soft on establishment crime" and that its idea of white-
collar crime was "welfare cheating and other
examples of individual. . . small-scale frauds
against government" (Wilson, 1980:8–9). The
enforcement rankings established by the Department of Justice now give preeminence to
acts such as "crimes against the government by
public officials, including federal, state, and
local corruption," and "crimes against consumers, including defrauding of consumers, antitrust violations, energy pricing violations and
related illegalities" (U.S. Department of Justice,
1980).

Fruits of the FBI priority realignment were
particularly noticeable in the agency's "Abscam"
sting, in which two agents dressed as Arab businessmen tempted politicians with cash offers for
help in securing casino licenses. The sting led to
the conviction of a number of local officials,
several congressmen, and one U.S. senator.
Thereafter, the FBI launched "Greylord Operation," which uncovered corruption in the court
system in Cook County, Illinois, and resulted in
the indictment of some ninety judges, lawyers,
and court officials. An FBI sting in South Carolina—this one called "Operation Lost Trust"
but dubbed "Bubbagate" locally—caught ten
legislators taking bribes, while "Azcam," a
similar operation in Arizona, produced indictments of seventeen persons, including seven
state legislators (Sykes and Cullen, 1992: 269).

Regulatory Policing Styles

Studies of regulatory agency investigators find
distinctive differences between their performance and that of law-enforcement officers
who work street crime details. Regulatory inspectors, particularly if they have scientific
training (and many former police officers take
special courses when they enter regulatory

work), come to think of themselves more as
technical experts than as police officers. This
enforcement style becomes much the same as a
patrol officer who views his or her job as social
service for the accused rather than as crime
control. Assumption of the friendly "technical
expert" role permits an investigator to build
mutually satisfying relationships with business
organizations. Arguably, these companies will
inform the investigator of difficulties rather
than try to cover them up, thereby allowing
rapid remedy and improving public protection.
As Richardson et al. (1982:96–97) report regarding this enforcement style: "The majority
of officers of all ranks believed that control
could not be achieved without the cooperation
of industry and they ardently supported a
cooperative/accommodative approach to enforcement in preference to a policy of confrontation."

On the basis of a survey of the literature on
enforcement styles, Frank (1984:237) reported
that with few exceptions "studies. . . reveal a
preponderance of persuasion-oriented agencies." The "enforced compliance style" of regulatory control (Shover et al., 1986), however, is
employed almost universally against violators
who have been labeled "amoral calculators"
(Kagan and Scholz, 1983:67–68), and when, as
two Australian writers put it, "the public has
noticed blood on the floor and expects action
to symbolize the need for the law to be obeyed."
Prosecution, they observe, "is something for
the benefit of outsiders" (Braithwaite and
Grabosky, 1985:53).

Rule-oriented inspectors, in contrast to
those who prefer persuasion, routinely issue
citations for every violation they observe. They
minimize negotiation strategies, such as consultation and bargaining. Most research indicates
that this extreme enforcement compliance style,
though it shows short-term gains in compliance,
suffers in the long term because the businesses
never develop a commitment to conformity. "A
network of rules and regulations, backed by
threats of litigation, breed distrust, destruction
of documents, and an attitude that 'I won't do
anything more than I am absolutely required to
do,'" Stone maintains (1975:104). It is also argued that investigators, unlike street police, require tactical flexibility, given the complicated
array of situations with which they have to deal.
Most regulated businesses can be found guilty
of one or another kind of violation if an inspector elects to be hard-nosed about his role; in-

spectors, it is argued, must use their power carefully, in carrot-and-stick fashion, to best achieve their aims (Shover et al., 1986).

Investigators typically keep a keen watch on the mood and ethos of the prosecuting agency. District and federal attorneys tend to be reluctant to take on complicated white-collar crimes. For one thing, the cases demand technical knowledge that may take a good deal of time to master. They are also likely to be time-consuming and to lack the glamour of big drug cases or dramatic crimes of violence. In addition, defendants often have considerable funds and can pay for sophisticated defense attorneys. These attorneys can draw out hearings, smother the court with motions, and command resources, such as expert witnesses, that will overwhelm an inexperienced and limited-budget public prosecutor (Jesilow et al., 1993).

Wilson (1981:173) emphasizes that for economic crimes, compared to street crimes, "there is absolute necessity for integrating the prosecutor into the investigative effort from the very beginning. This is probably the single most important aspect of investigating a complex economic crime." The prosecutor, Wilson points out, must continually analyze the facts, alter his prosecutive theory if necessary, and redirect the investigator's efforts. As two other writers note:

> Economic crime investigations tend to be lengthy, to be revealed to the targets before indictment, and to involve numerous noncustodial contacts between the government and those who are being investigated. Consequently, defense counsel appear in behalf of targets much sooner than in the ordinary case. This makes the investigative stage of the criminal proceedings particularly crucial. (Wilson and Matz, 1977:713)

White-collar crime enforcement often requires cooperation among a number of police agencies, many of whom bring to the task jealousies about turf infringement, a desire for publicity, and a need to be in charge. To carry out collaborative work, Wilson (1981) notes, requires a great amount of diplomacy; he believes it essential that "recognition be given in proportion to each agency's contribution." Case studies of interagency investigative work on white-collar crime include Vaughan's (1983) study of the Revco pharmacy chain's violation of Ohio's

Medicaid law, and Pontell and Calavita's (1993) study of the tracking down of crooks involved in the savings and loan banking scandals.

A special problem associated with police work directed against white-collar crime is the need to take a proactive rather than a reactive stance. ECUs, for instance, at first typically used proactive tactics to discover offenses, but as they began to become known and generate citizen complaints, they allocated virtually all their resources to responding to such complaints. Constant proactive efforts are necessary, however, because most of the victimization is never known to those who are deprived or hurt; they usually do not realize that foul air in a factory is poisoning their lungs, insider trader is robbing them of portfolio earnings, that illegal overcharges are eating into their budget, and that falsified tests of pharmaceutical products are undermining their health. It has been argued in this regard that the use of "covert facilitation" (that is, undercover work like the Abscam sting operation) is essential for satisfactory enforcement of the laws against white-collar crime (Braithwaite, Fisse, and Geis, 1987).

As Stotland and Edelhertz have noted (1989), work investigating white-collar crime can offer more attractive law-enforcement assignments since white-collar offenders often are deterred by arrest and convictions, unlike the revolving door futility of much police work against street felons. White-collar policing, they also point out, can provide an intellectual challenge otherwise often absent in police work.

A proposal for the establishment of a National Academy of White Collar Crime has been advanced by Douglas (1978). Among other tasks, the academy would prepare investigators to cope with crime "planned in the boardrooms and over lunch at the club." Law-enforcement officials are also beginning to demand tougher sentences for economic offenders. As former Attorney General Richard L. Thornburgh put the matter: "We must insure that courts are collar-blind as well as color-blind."

Gilbert Geis

Bibliography

Benson, Michael L., et al. "District Attorneys and Corporate Crime: Surveying the Prosecutorial Gatekeepers." *Criminology* 26 (1988): 505–18.

———. "Local Prosecutors and Corporate Crime." *Crime and Delinquency* 36 (1990): 356–72.

as chief eventually cost him his job. He enforced the vice laws too vigorously, thus cramping the style of Wichita racketeers, so he had to go. Two city commissioners, in league with the vice lords, rode him hard, conjuring up every possible charge against him. In a letter to August Vollmer, Wilson disclosed what the city commissioners planned to do to him if he stayed:

1. Have my salary slashed.
2. Have the commission order the discontinuance of certain police activities, such as the maintenance of records.
3. The appointment of a disloyal subordinate officer as assistant chief, with complete control over police personnel.
4. Appointment of the same men as director of public safety and over police and fire.
5. An investigation of the department with a view of raising sufficient stench to justify ordering my suspension and leaving me simmering on the pan without salary until I was tired out.

He acquiesced and on May 15, 1939, left Wichita on leave of absence, his formal resignation to follow later.

Wilson was not left to wander long. The Public Administration Service in Chicago hired him to survey municipal police departments and to write papers on police administration. To his dismay he discovered that in Peoria, Illinois; Hartford, Connecticut; Huntington, West Virginia; and San Antonio, Texas, the police bent to political will as much as in Wichita. While he was on the road with his surveys, plans were underway to attract him to teach at his alma mater, UC Berkeley. Once again August Vollmer was his guiding light, convincing the president of the university that O.W. Wilson knew more about police administration than anyone else available. On July 24, 1939, Wilson accepted a tenured position as full professor with a reduced teaching load, time for consultative work, and the freedom to reshape the academic program. Moreover, the university allowed him to continue his work for the Public Administration Service. In January 1943 World War II interrupted his busy schedule and tested his abilities all the more. He entered the United States Army as a lieutenant colonel in the corps of military police, serving as chief public safety officer in Italy and England. The war over, he was discharged in November 1946, having earned the

rank of colonel, the Bronze Star, and the Legion of Merit. He did not return home right away but remained in Germany as the chief public safety officer in charge of denazification activities in the United States zone. Enforcing the regulations to the letter of the law was his trademark. He liked military life and leaned toward reenlisting, but by the next year he was back at Berkeley teaching police administration.

Wilson's second career at Berkeley had its ups and downs. From 1950 to 1960 he served as dean of the School of Criminology, during which time he successfully fought off efforts to relegate police studies to a minor academic status. Instead, he raised the program to an unprecedented level and made the school one of the foremost in the nation. He did this in spite of having to parry attacks from his fellow professors because he did not hold the Ph.D. degree, and from students because he was a poor lecturer. Always terse in his public and written comments, he was more a man of action than one of words. Wilson escaped the petty in-fighting at Berkeley whenever he visited various police departments to conduct reorganization surveys. Like August Vollmer before him, he crisscrossed the United States and beyond, sizing up local police conditions and recommending qualified colleagues to fill vacant positions. Known far and wide for his acuity as a police consultant, he was to put into practice every bit of his knowledge in the coming years.

In 1960 Chicago mayor Richard J. Daley named Wilson chairman of a five-man committee to choose a new police commissioner for the Windy City. The heat was on after city newspapers revealed that several policemen had aided and abetted a burglary ring. More than one hundred persons were considered for the office with the surprising result that O.W. Wilson, interrogator of the contenders, was finally selected. He took the job, but only after securing a promise that the police force would be free from political control. He then resigned his deanship at UC Berkeley, the university honoring him with the title of professor emeritus. The immediate changes he made in the Chicago Police Department were unpopular to say the least. He cut the number of police districts from thirty-eight to twenty-one, thus severing ties of favoritism between some police and criminal parties in certain neighborhoods. He established the Internal Investigation Division, whose main purpose was to uncover police corruption. He more than doubled the number of civilian employees to handle clerical duties, thereby releasing about one thousand regular policemen for patrol duty. He installed a $2 million modern police radio clock and doubled the size of the patrol car fleet. Other of his adjustments were equally hard to live with at first, but in the end greatly strengthened the department.

Wilson continued to do the unexpected. When the Reverend Martin Luther King, Jr., came to Chicago in 1966, having announced beforehand that he would lay bare housing discrimination in one of white America's mighty cities, he was invited to police headquarters to talk. Of all things, the two strong-willed men discussed police protection for King and his people, not police harassment. Later King acknowledged that Wilson had treated him more than fairly, unlike southern police. Also in that year one of the worst crimes of the century occurred in Chicago. Eight student nurses were murdered at a residence maintained by the South Chicago Community Hospital. Wilson's police were swift off the mark and the next day arrested a twenty-four-year-old itinerant seaman named Richard Franklin Speck, whose left arm bore the tattoo, "Born to Raise Hell." Wilson fingered the right man, but because he insisted that only Speck could have done the deed some legal authorities criticized him for "hanging the suspect" without a fair trial. Ironically, just a few months earlier in an article written for *Family Week*, he had said: "One of the problems that we, as police, face is when sympathy for the unfortunate merges into favoritism for the criminal. . . . In this country, tolerance for wrongdoers has turned into a fad. What we need is some intolerance toward criminal behavior."

On his sixty-seventh birthday he retired from the Chicago police force, stating in a letter to Mayor Daley, "It is my belief that the programs initiated slightly more than seven years ago for the reorganization of the police department are fully established." As befitted him, he was overly modest in assessing his accomplishments in Chicago, a city notorious for its haphazard law enforcement. But for all of his striking success he did display some faults. His biographer, William J. Bopp, explains:

> O.W. Wilson never questioned the idea
> that officers must be coerced, controlled,
> directed, and threatened before they
> would exert an effort to achieve the
> department's objectives. He instituted
> no job enrichment programs, no partici-
> patory management techniques. . . .
> He ruled by fiat, instead of persuading
> his officers of the rightness of reform. . . .
> It may well be that policemen will not
> act democratically in the community
> until they are treated democratically in
> police headquarters. Wilson was not a
> democratic leader.

Wilson wrote a number of books, articles, and pamphlets during his checkered career, all of which added substantially to the police literature. He saw his best-known book, *Police Administration* (McGraw-Hill, 1950, 1963), through a third edition, with Roy C. McLaren as coauthor; it appeared the year of his death (1972). Married twice he fathered three children. A stroke ended his life, his last years having been spent in Poway, California, an idyllic retreat far from the ingratitude of Wichita and the hustle of Chicago.

Bibliography

Bopp, William L. "O.W." O.W. Wilson and the Search for a Police Profession. Port Washington, NY: Kennikat Press, 1977.

Current Biography (1966): 452–54.

New York Times (March 3, 1960); 20:4; (June 15, 1966): 27:2; (October 19, 1972): 50:5.

Y

Youth Gangs: Definition

Although there is some disagreement concerning the characteristics of youth gangs, a general consensus among academicians and practitioners exists at the structural level. In essence, the term *youth gang* refers to a group or clique of young people (roughly between the ages of fourteen and twenty-one) who engage in acts of violence and criminal activity. Despite the common assumption that antisocial behavior is the primary mechanism which binds these young people together, in most instances, this does not seem to be the case. In fact, while not denying criminal gain as a critical component underlying gang formation and its outward effects, failure to equally examine other critical factors has led to an oversimplification of the gang problem.

From a functionalist perspective, youth gangs act as surrogate institutions in areas where family, school, and legitimate employment are almost nonexistent or not functioning properly. The lack of informal sanctions coupled with the inability or unwillingness of the youth's parent(s) to properly socialize the child often contribute to the need to seek alternative means for gaining that which he or she is unable to secure through "normal" acceptable channels.

For many youth who join gangs, the yearning for a sense of belonging, characteristic of the adolescent years, is often satisfied. Although initially persuaded and/or lured by the lucrative prospect of finding a niche in an often hostile or uncaring environment, such individuals soon learn that becoming a gang member entails a great deal more.

An extensive socialization process occurs during the indoctrination into gang membership. While members are ideally afforded the protection and excitement often accompanying such membership, a high price is often paid for such affiliation. The use of clear and deliberate designations (i.e., names, signs, symbols, dress, and location—"colors" or "turf"), which act to distinguish one gang from another, enables outward hostilities to be played out between opposing factions. Unfortunately, such hostilities more often than not translate into violence—violence that penetrates the world of gang members and innocent bystanders alike.

Youth gangs are not a new phenomenon. In fact, such gangs were first identified in England in the seventeenth century and the United States in the eighteenth century. However, the recent concern over the youth gang problem is due to unique characteristics that differ significantly from those of gangs of earlier times. While some commonalities exist between what were identified as the first youth gangs and contemporary gangs, it is their differences that prove most disturbing.

Within the last two decades, the gang problem has grown considerably. Currently, it is estimated that gang activity is developing in almost all states and territories of the United States, as well as in other countries. In fact, despite earlier accounts, youth gangs are not just a big city phenomenon but have penetrated mid-size and small cities as well as the suburbs, areas thought to be safe havens from inner-city problems.

It is not solely the prevalence of youth gangs that has led to such concern in recent times. Rather, it is the upsurge in gang violence and atrocities on a widespread scale that is drawing considerable attention and scrutiny. This scrutiny includes federal agencies—such as the FBI, DEA, and the Bureau of Alcohol, Tobacco and Firearms—as gangs have expanded.

Several factors have contributed to the level and extent of violence utilized by gang members. Oftentimes, gangs have easy access to sophisticated weaponry and once secured do not hesitate to use it in retaliatory or vindictive acts against rival gang members or to further their criminal transactions. In addition, better organization, greater mobility, larger membership, and the increase in the drug trafficking by gangs have played a critical role. These aspects of gang activity have simply compounded the problem, creating an ever-increasing atmosphere of fear and intimidation for communities where gangs literally run the streets.

It is important to note that the gang problem is by no means equally dispersed from community to community or from city to city. There is a tendency for gangs to form in areas with high degrees of social disorganization and where poverty runs rampant. These variables are further exacerbated by the growth of criminal opportunities, institutionalized racism, the insecurities of the working and middle class who are "threatened by newcomers," and the sudden and rapid movement of a minority population into a given community. While these factors may underlie gang formation in general, the specific factors vary as to the exact type of gang problem that develops within a given community.

Oftentimes, gang formation is ethnically and/or racially based. A large percentage of inner-city ghettos are occupied by African-American as well as Hispanic populations. In such areas, harsh conditions coupled with an often hostile environment are factors that are extremely conducive to the formation of gangs.

In addition, newcomers who are often forced to settle in such areas are frequently met with anger and hostility by permanent residents. In an attempt to protect themselves, often from physical attacks, the formation of gangs for defensive purposes enables them to stave off such attacks. However, over time, such gangs, like preexisting, well-established gangs, begin to take on a more offensive role. Such a transformation, although not inevitable, seems to characterize the evolutionary process of newcomer gang formation.

Although youth gangs are generally comprised of ethnic and/or racial minorities, this phenomenon is not restricted to such populations. In fact, the economic, social, and/or cultural hardships faced by families in areas defined as blue-collar or, in some instances, middle-class, are factors that have led to the formation of gangs. These predominantly white, formerly stable, communities have in recent times turned out a generation of youth whose own lives are filled with instability and anger. Gang formation is often the result of such outward hostilities, in that it (the gang) acts as an outlet for the alleviation of internal as well as external pressures.

Despite an illusion of national organization (i.e., the "Crips" and the "Bloods"), gangs are relatively localized. Typically, they are not hierarchical in nature and tend to be very loosely organized. Consequently, communication and collaboration between what are deemed "affiliates" in other cities and/or states are generally incidental rather than being a product of a plan.

Summary
In recent times, what is defined as the gang problem appears to be on the agenda of many federal, state, and local law-enforcement agencies. As a national initiative, the FBI, ATF, and DEA, in particular, are beginning to look at gangs as organized crime. And in an attempt to counteract or impede gang formation and/or membership, there is a recent movement toward the prosecution of gang members as part of continuing criminal enterprises. Such measures have led to stiffer and more punitive sentencing for gang members who engage in gang-related acts of violence.

For further information see the *National Youth Gang Suppression Intervention Program*, Chicago, Illinois: School of Social Service Administration, University of Chicago. Also contact the National Youth Gang Information Center, U.S. Department of Justice, Alexandria, Virginia.

David L. Carter
Andra J. Katz

Youth Gangs: Dimensions
As the youth gang problem has increased in visibility in most urban areas in the United States, the police have sought to develop some organizational response that might slow the emergence of gangs and provide an institutional structure for appropriate and quick response to immediate problems. To assess the evolution of police developmental activities, the Criminal

Justice Research and Training Center at the University of Texas at Arlington undertook a national survey of all police departments serving populations of at least 50,000. This survey was initiated in late spring 1992 and was completed in the summer of 1992.

Numerous questions in the survey sought to gauge the reaction of police to the gang problem. Questionnaires were mailed to 545 police departments, with the survey addressed to the chief of police. In most cases, the questionnaire was routed to and completed by a supervisor in the gang unit or a similar unit where such existed. A very good response of 213 usable questionnaires was received, representing a 39 percent response rate. Table 1 provides a description of the municipal population size represented by the responding departments.

Table 2 indicates the sworn officer strength of departments responding to the survey. Almost 80 percent of the departments employ over 100 officers. Table 3 reveals the departmental assignment of officers to some type of specialized unit responsible for dealing with gangs or gang activity. Some 75 percent of respondents claimed that sworn male officers were assigned to gang unit type activities while only 20 percent revealed assignment of female officers to similar duties. Most departments do not utilize civilians and it is assumed that those cases responding positively to this question use civilian personnel in either clerical or data processing types of activities.

Twenty-three percent of responding departments indicated that they have officers assigned to gang duties that specialize "according to ethnic group or type of gang." When analyzed by size of department, the data reveal that

TABLE 1

Estimated Municipal Population of Responding Cities

Population Range	Number of Departments	Percent
50,000–74,999	58	27
75,000–99,999	33	16
100,000–249,999	78	37
250,000–499,999	23	11
500,000–999,999	11	5
1,000,000 or more	7	3
Unknown	2	1
Total	212	100

TABLE 2

Number of Sworn Officers in Responding Departments

Range	Number of Departments	Percent
1–99	44	21
100–149	38	18
150–224	42	20
225–400	40	19
401+	45	21
Unknown	4	2

TABLE 3

Number of Personnel Assigned to Gang Units or to Assignments to Handle Gang Activities

Percentage of Departments Responding to Survey

Range	Sworn Male	Sworn Female	Civilian Male	Civilian Female
0	25%	80%	93%	83%
1	13	12	4	11
2	11	3	1	4
3	10	2		
4–5	13	2		
6–10	14			
11–20	8	1	1	1
21–442	5	1	1	

TABLE 4

Officers in Gang Units That Specialize according to Ethnic Group or Type of Gang by Size of Department

	Number of Officers				
	1–99	100–149	150–224	225–400	400+
Yes	21%	21%	19%	20%	39%
No	80%	71%	74%	75%	58%

the highest percentage for such specialization occurs in cities with 400 officers or more (see Table 4).

The responding departments for the most part indicated "an emerging gang problem" at the time of the survey. The identification of the situation as a "chronic gang problem" was related almost directly to city size as revealed by

TABLE 5

Type of Gang Problem Reported by Responding Police Departments

| | Number of Officers | | | | |
	1–99	100–149	150–224	225–400	400+
No gang problem	11%	13%	10%	15%	9%
Difficult to tell	9%	5%	10%	18%	4%
Emerging gang problem	71%	66%	41%	45%	49%
Chronic gang problem	9%	16%	36%	23%	36%

Table 5 which shows the percentages based on number of officers.

Since the implementation of school resource officer programs has been a popular response for police departments and for the school systems, several questions regarding the types of programs used were included in the survey. Some 39 percent of the responding departments indicated that they have a permanent school resource officer program while 42 percent revealed that officers are assigned to such duties on a rotating or part-time basis (see Table 6).

Also, as shown in Table 7, almost half the responding departments stated that they have some type of "gang intervention" program in effect. Some 39 percent of the agencies responded that there are other agencies within the city that also conduct gang intervention efforts.

These agencies vary widely in type of mission and program from private organizations to public social service agencies.

A major emphasis of this survey was to determine what criteria were used for selection of gang unit officers. Table 8 indicates that most departments do not require a rank higher than "patrol officer." Only 12 percent listed corporal or higher as a required rank for assignment. Over three-fourths of the departments listed no educational requirement for gang unit assignments. These departments probably use the basic requirement for entry as a patrol officer and do not stipulate a more extensive educational mandate for these specialized assignments. Years in service revealed that approximately one-half of the departments have some requirement on this factor. This is presumedly due to the feeling that officers need some expe-

TABLE 6

School Resource Officer (SRO) Programs in Responding Cities

Permanent School Resource Officer	39%
SRO on a Rotating Basis	28%
SRO on a Part-Time Basis	14%
No SRO Programs	17%

TABLE 7

Gang Intervention Programs

Question	Percent Yes
Does the department have gang intervention programs?	41%
Are there gang intervention programs conducted by other agencies in the city?	39%

TABLE 8

Requirements for Selecting Officers for Assignment to Duties and/or Units Dealing with Gangs

Rank Required		Education Required		Years in Service Required		Years in Grade Required
None Stated	47%	None Stated	77%	None Stated	53%	82%
Officer	40	High School	17	One	9	5
Detective	9	2 Years College	5	Two	18	8
Sergeant	3	4 Year Degree	1	Three	15	4
Corporal	1	Departmental Training Program	1	Four	2	1
				Five	3	1

rience as a patrol officer before receiving such specialized assignments. Years in grade, on the other hand, was not considered an important criterion and only 19 percent indicated that there is some length of time in grade necessary.

Questions concerning the types of tests and other requirements revealed that firearms proficiency is the most often cited criterion while residency in the city is least often required (see Table 9). Pre-assignment training is stipulated by only 17 percent of the departments. As indicated in response to other questions, most departments rely primarily on "on-the-job training" and other specialized programs after assignment.

TABLE 9

Selection Requirements for Assignment to Gang Unit

	Yes	No	No Response
Firearms proficiency test	31%	50%	19%
Pre-assignment training	17	64	19
Physical fitness test	13	68	19
Psychological testing	12	68	19
Residence in the city	8	73	18

Table 10 lists the various factors that could be considered important in the selection of officers for assignment to gang unit duties. Interestingly, the general criteria of common sense, emotional stability, interest in assignment, and self-confidence scored highest. All of these factors would generally be considered difficult if not impossible to measure and their value could be determined only through subjective assessment.

On the other end of the scale, the amount of formal education, age, race, sex, nationality, and previous military service was rated quite low. It had been expected that race and nationality might be more important given the fact that most gangs are based primarily on ethnic origin. Likewise, it was expected that age would be more important, with younger officers receiving preference over older officers, who might have some difficulty in relating to teenage gang members.

Table 11 reveals the types of assignments that gang unit officers might receive in the course of their overall police work. Activities

TABLE 10

Importance of Various Factors in Selecting Officers for Working with Gangs Related by Mean Values on Five Point Scale

Factor	Mean Value	Standard Deviation
Common sense	4.66	.57
Emotional stability	4.58	.57
Expressed interest in assignment	4.57	.67
Self confidence	4.43	.62
Performance as a patrol officer	4.41	.68
Open-mindedness	4.40	.69
Interviewing skills	4.37	.66
Oral communication skills	4.35	.76
Compatibility with Unit personnel	4.24	.84
Ability to judge human nature	4.18	.85
Adaptability to changing schedules	4.11	.99
Attention to detail	4.08	.77
Writing skills	4.03	.70
Disciplinary record	3.91	.92
Physical fitness	3.36	.86
Physical agility	3.30	.86
Previous work with juveniles	3.26	1.02
Marital stability	3.22	1.19
Length of departmental tenure	2.89	.82
Foreign language capability	2.78	1.30
Amount of formal education	2.72	1.02
Age	2.10	.94
Race or ethnic origin	1.97	1.16
Sex	1.72	1.06
Nationality	1.71	.98
Previous military experience	1.57	.82

associated with information collection, surveillance, conducting raids, and providing lectures on gangs were noted by high percentages of departments. A range of routine police duties was checked by many departments as assignments in which gang unit officers might "sometimes be used."

Ranking at the lower end of the scale, high percentages of departments indicated that gang unit officers are "never used" for investigating traffic accidents, handling routine calls for service, apprehending truants, and serving as school resource officers.

Finally, Table 12 lists the methods used by police agencies for gathering information on gangs and gang members. Normal departmen-

TABLE 11

Types of Assignments Given to Gang Unit
Officers Ranked by Percentage in
"Often Used" Category

	Never Used	Sometimes Used	Often Used
Collecting information on gang activities	1	9	72
Intelligence gathering	1	13	69
Interviewing gang members	3	19	61
Writing reports on gang event or activities	4	21	57
Surveillance of gang members	7	26	49
Filing cases with prosecuting attorney	7	29	48
Conducting raids on gangs involved in illegal activities	17	28	36
Providing antigang lectures in schools	13	34	35
Directed patrolling of high crime areas	18	31	33
Conducting routine patrol activities	24	30	30
Handling emergency calls when needed	8	47	27
Working at special events involving young persons	12	45	26
Patrolling of public rallies	19	45	19
Working in schools at athletic events	24	41	18
Handling routine calls for service	40	25	17
Serving as school liaison or school resource officer	33	32	16
Apprehending truants	39	37	7
Investigating traffic accidents and writing accident reports	66	10	7

tal information gathering processes along with interviews with gang members were noted by large percentages of departments. Reports from federal and state agencies and provision of information by schools and private organizations were considered to be sources that are "sometimes used" but that scored lower on the "often used" column.

Interestingly, infiltration of police officers into gangs or related groups was noted as "never used" by three-fourths of the departments. Use of paid informants and use of information from private organizations were also noted as "never used" by slightly over one in four departments.

Conclusion

This survey representing responses from over 200 police departments has revealed a range of information about the United States law-enforcement response to the growing gang prob-

TABLE 12

Methods Used for Gathering Information on
Gangs Ranked by "Often Used" Category

	Never Used	Sometimes Used	Often Used
Internal contacts with patrol officers and detectives	1	22	64
Internal departmental records and computerized files	4	22	62
Review of offense reports	2	25	60
Interviews with gang members	5	26	56
Obtain information from other local police agencies	1	35	51
Surveillance activities	6	37	44
Use of unpaid informants	2	44	42
Obtain information from other criminal justice agencies	3	43	42
Obtain information from other governmental agencies	3	47	37
Provision of information by schools	2	50	35
Reports from state agencies	11	63	14
Use of paid informants	28	46	13
Reports from federal agencies	16	62	9
Obtain information from private organizations	27	51	9
Infiltration of police officers into gangs or related groups	75	11	2

lem. In addition to the descriptive information about the departmental programs noted above, police respondents were asked to provide some general opinions about the gang problem in the United States and the types of programs that should be supported.

Officers strongly supported the idea that parents should be made aware of gang problems, that local schools should implement strong antigang programs, that each school should have a school resource officer, and that local governments should maintain a strong antigang unit in the police department. Likewise they felt that gangs are a major problem in the United States today and that they will dramatically increase as a problem in the next five years.

Overall, respondents did not consider the gang problem to be "only a local government problem," and they had mixed feelings about whether gang development is primarily a "social and economic problem that cannot be controlled by police." Respondents did feel slightly more strongly that the police departments should attempt to deal with the "underlying causes of gang development," and that the state and federal governments should increase their funding of antigang efforts at the local level.

James W. Stevens

Youth Gangs: Direction

Gangs and the response to gangs by the criminal-justice system and other segments of the community are two sides of the same coin. Frederic Thrasher (1927:26, 46), who studied 1,313 gangs in Chicago in the early 1900s, offered, in his definition of what constituted a gang, that gangs are "formed spontaneously" but become "integrated through conflict." For Thrasher, a pregang group does not "become a gang . . . until it begins to excite disapproval and opposition, and thus it acquires a more definite group-consciousness."

Though gangs are organizations, what we know about them has come from studying individual gang members or community reactions. Hence, studies of gangs have historically included both interviews and observational studies of limited samples of gang members from specific geographic areas, or analyses of official records compiled through the institutionalized processes of response. Although there has sometimes been antipathy between the two kinds of researchers, the findings of both are necessary for the widest possible understanding of gang phenomena. Participant observation and interviews are more likely to capture the totality of behavior engaged in by some gang members on a day-to-day basis. Analysis of official records, while limited to the fraction of gang activity that is criminal in nature, makes it possible to make comparisons and study variations in gang crime and official reaction to it across different communities and points in time. The importance of such comparisons is substantiated by the conclusions of all researchers that gangs vary greatly over both space and time.

What Are Gangs?

As in most social science research, individual researchers lay out their definition of what constitutes a "gang" in the context of their particular study. When we speak of problems in gang definition, most of us do not mean problems among definitions by researchers. Perhaps, in response to researchers' calls for more consistent definitions of what is a gang by law-enforcement practitioners, many jurisdictions have developed operational definitions of what constitutes a gang. In fact, a recent report (Institute for Law and Justice, forthcoming) notes that fourteen states now have state-level definitions of what constitutes a gang. The kinds of analysis problems to which this process of multiple operational definitions can lead are reflected in a study by Maxson and Klein (1990), which showed that if the Chicago definition of a gang-related crime were applied to the gang-related homicides for Los Angeles, Los Angeles would have half as many homicides.

Another factor in defining gangs is that for most of us, gangs are associated with some preconceived images. This is the result of the degree to which news and the entertainment media have seized on the gang as a subject for eliciting interest and emotion. *West Side Story*, a relatively contemporary retelling of the Romeo and Juliet myth, required gangs as conflict-based, more or less close-knit, social entities, as its central plot vehicle. The most common images that we have of gangs include violent male teenagers from lower socioeconomic backgrounds carrying out their activities in the setting of the nation's largest cities. Research has shown that none of these images is completely accurate.

Much of the activity in which gangs engage is neither violent nor criminal (Hagedorn,

1988; Miller, 1966; Spergel, 1964). Instead of maturing out of gangs by getting married or finding a job as was observed in the past, many young adults, unable to find jobs in a depressed inner-city economy, continue their gang affiliation well into adulthood. Some level of involvement of females in gangs has been observed for decades. Though fewer females are involved in gangs than are males, Campbell (1990) has suggested that female gang involvement has become increasingly independent of male involvement, with females becoming more dependent on other female gang members for status within the gang than on male gang members. Even the image of gangs as a lower-class phenomenon has been challenged. Some researchers (Myerhoff and Myerhoff, 1964) have noted the presence of delinquent groups of middle-class youths, who fail to be labeled as gangs only as a result of their access to middle-class resources.

Perhaps no image of gang activity has been more completely revised in recent years than the idea that gang crime is a large city phenomenon. In the seventy-nine largest U.S. cities, only three of their police departments report no officially recognized gang crime problem in 1992. All of the other seventy-six (96 percent) of the largest cities report either a gang or "gang-like" crime problem. (Gang-like problems include "crews" in Washington, D.C., "posses" in Raleigh, North Carolina; and "drug organizations" in Baltimore, Maryland. Studies had already revealed the presence of gang problems in smaller cities (Spergel, 1990), but analysis of a 1992 survey of law-enforcement agencies (Curry et al., 1994) showed that there was no relationship between the size of city and the probability of a reported presence of gang crime problems.

What Is the Magnitude of Gang Crime Problems?

Estimates of the size of national-level gang crime problems have increased. Walter Miller (1975) estimated that there were between 760 to 2,700 gangs and 28,500 to 81,500 gang members in six large U.S. cities. By 1982, Miller estimated 97,940 gang members in 2,285 gangs in 286 cities. For 35 jurisdictions, Spergel and Curry (1990) report 1,439 gangs and 120,636 gang members. Based only on official records for 88 law enforcement jurisdictions, a West Virginia University study (Curry et al., 1994) reported 4,881 gangs, 249,324 gang members, and 46,359 gang-related crimes for 1991.

How Are Females Involved in Gangs?

As noted above, the involvement of females in gangs has become of increased interest to researchers. Miller (1975) hypothesized three kinds of gangs in which females were involved: mixed-sex gangs with both male and female members, female gangs that are auxiliaries to male gangs, and independent female gangs. While research on female gang members (Campbell, 1990; Moore, 1991) has observed all three kinds of involvement, it has been generally agreed that the rarest is the independent female gang.

Since Miller, many researchers have followed his "10-percent" rule in describing female gang involvement. Simply stated, the 10-percent rule suggests that 10 percent of gang members are female and 10 percent of gang-related crimes are committed by females. The West Virginia study showed there to be 9,092 female gang members reported in official records by police over sixty-one different law-enforcement jurisdictions in 1991. Though this figure in comparison to the nearly one-quarter million gang members represented in official statistics is far below 10 percent, the study found that a number of law-enforcement agencies do not count females involved in gangs in the same way that males are counted as a matter of policy. In a few jurisdictions, females are counted only as "associate members," and in others, not at all. One police department that did not count females as gang members still attributed two gang-related homicides to females. As for the "rare" independent female gang, ninety-nine were reported across thirty-nine jurisdictions in 1992.

A comparison of the types of crimes attributed to females in official records with those of males revealed some marked differences. As a percentage of all crimes attributed to females, homicides and property offenses were significantly greater than the percentage of comparable crimes for males. Of gang-related crimes attributed to females, 4.5 percent were homicides; the comparable percent for males was 2.3 percent; of female gang-related crimes, 42.5 percent were petty offenses; for male gang-related crimes, only 14.8 percent were identified as property crimes. For gang-related crimes attributed to males, the largest percentage (48.5 percent) are identified as non-fatal violent offenses. The comparable statistic for female gang-related crimes was only 27.3 percent.

What Are the Social Correlates of Gang Involvement?

Curry and Spergel (1992) identified an incremental scale of self-reported behaviors that they associated with increasing gang involvement. These behaviors ranged from wearing gang colors, hanging out where gang members hang out, and having gang members as friends to engaging in deviant behavior with gang members, flashing gang signs, and getting involved in gang-related conflict. The researchers observed that both the patterns and social correlates of gang involvement differed for populations of African-American and Latino youths. For Latino youths, gang involvement and delinquency were associated with age, measures of self-esteem, and educational aspiration. For African-American youths, levels of gang involvement and delinquency were a function of levels of contact with gang members in school and in the community. The single variable that explained the greatest portion of variation in gang involvement and delinquency among African-American youths was the presence of a gang member in a youth's family. For both populations of youths, gang involvement was structurally a precursor of delinquency, but delinquency could not be identified as a precursor of gang involvement.

What Are Major Responses to Gangs?

Strategies of responding to gang-related crime problems have not changed much over the twentieth-century history of community reaction. Spergel and Curry (1990, 1993) group gang response strategies into five overarching categories: (1) suppression, (2) community organization, (3) opportunities provision, (4) social services, and (5) organizational change. The most common response for the heavily involved gang youth has almost always been suppression. Suppression includes all activities required to incarcerate gang members, which encompasses methods of member identification, agency coordination, and special processing of arrestees in terms of prosecution, trial, and sentencing. Community organization includes all efforts to promote the organization of legitimate forces within a community as a resistance to the organization of gangs. Opportunities provision is a strategy that operates under the long-standing assumption that gang involvement is not as appealing to individual youths as the alternative potential for employment and marriage. Social services provision operates under the assumption that gang members with counseling, role-modeling, attitude changes, and skills in conflict resolution will create their own opportunities to lead conventional lives. Organizational change incorporates increases in available resources or adjustments in institutional structures.

Based on an analysis of data gathered by the 1988 Office of Juvenile Justice and Delinquency Prevention/University of Chicago national survey of gang problems (Spergel and Curry, 1990), suppression was most often the strategy identified as primary by respondents regardless of what were perceived to be the causes of gang crime problems. However, community organization and opportunities provision as primary strategies were the only ones statistically associated with perceived effectiveness of community-level gang response programs.

Policy Recommendations

Though limited in quantity, research on gang-related crime is rich in findings. From these findings a number of policy recommendations can be offered.

1. Additional research on both gang activity and community reactions to gang activity is required.
2. Strategies of response and research on gangs should not be based on narrow definitions of what constitutes a gang developed within the parameters of a single locale and time.
3. Strategies of response developed on the basis of research on one gender or ethnicity should not be frivolously applied to gang involvement of another gender or ethnicity.
4. On the basis of Recommendation 3, strategies of gang response are best controlled by the people who reside in the communities concerned.
5. Strategies of community organization combined with strategies of opportunity provision offer the greatest potential for immediate improvements in the level of gang-related crime problems.

G. David Curry

Bibliography

Campbell, A. *The Girls in the Gang.* 2d ed. Cambridge, MA: Basil Blackwood, [1984] 1990.

Curry, G.D., and I.A. Spergel. "Gang Involvement and Delinquency among Hispanic and African-American Adolescent Males." *Journal of Research on Crime and Delinquency* 29(3) (December 1992): 273–91.

Curry, G.D., R.A. Ball, and R.J. Fox. "Criminal Justice Reaction to Gang Violence." In *Violence and Law*. Eds. M. Costanzo and S. Oskamp. Newbury Park, CA: Sage, 1994.

Hagedorn, J.M. *People and Folks: Gangs, Crime and the Underclass in a Rustbelt City*. Chicago: Lake View Press, 1988.

Institute for Law and Justice. *Gang Prosecution Legislative Review*. Washington, DC: National Institute of Justice, U.S. Department of Justice, 1994.

Maxson, C.L., and M.W. Klein. "Street Gang Violence: Twice as Great or Half as Great?" In *Gangs in America*. Ed. C.R. Huff. Newbury Park, CA: Sage, 1990.

Miller, W.B. "Violent Crimes in City Gangs. *Annals of the American Academy of Political and Social Science* 364 (1966): 97–112.

———. *Violence by Youth Gangs and Youth Groups as a Crime Problem in Major American Cities*. Washington, DC: Government Printing Office, 1975.

———. *Crime by Youth Gangs and Groups in the United States*. Washington, DC.: National Institute of Juvenile Justice and Delinquency Prevention, U.S. Department of Justice, 1982.

Moore, J.W. *Going Down to the Barrio: Homeboys and Homegirls in Change*. Philadelphia: Temple University Press, 1991.

Myerhoff, H. L., and B.G. Myerhoff. "Field Observations of Middle Class Gangs." *Social Forces* 42 (1964): 328–36.

Spergel, I.A. *Racketville, Slumtown, Haulburg*. Chicago: University of Chicago Press, 1964.

———. "Youth Gangs: Continuity and Change." In *Crime and Justice: An Annual Review of Research*. Eds. N. Morris and M. Tonry. Chicago: University of Chicago Press, 1990.

Spergel, I.A., and G.D. Curry. "Strategies and Perceived Agency Effectiveness in Dealing with the Youth Gang Problem." In *Gangs in America*. Ed. R.C. Huff. Newbury Park, CA: Sage, 1990.

———. "The National Youth Gang Survey: A Research and Development Process." In *Gang Intervention Handbook*. Eds. A. Goldstein and C.R. Huff. Champaign-Urbana: Research Press, 1993.

Thrasher, F.M. *The Gang*. Chicago: University of Chicago Press, 1927.

the Criminal Law System in Detroit. Chicago: American Bar Association, 1967.

McNutt, George W. *My Twenty-Three Years Experience as a Detective*. Kansas City: Empire, 1923.

McWatters, George S. *Detectives of Europe and America, or Life in the Secret Service: A Selection of Celebrated Cases, A Revelation of Struggles and Triumphs of Renowned Detectives*. Hartford: J.B. Burr, 1878.

Maltby, William J. *Captain Jeff; or, Frontier Life in Texas with the Texas Rangers; Some Unwritten History and Facts in the Thrilling Experience of Frontier Life*. Colorado, TX: Whipkey, 1906.

Mann, Henry, ed. *Our Police: History of Pittsburgh Police Force, Under the Town and City*. Pittsburgh, PA: City of Pittsburgh, 1889.

Marx, Gary T. *Undercover: Police Surveillance in America*. Berkeley and Los Angeles: University of California Press, 1988.

Mayo, Katherine. *The Standard-Bearers: True Stories of the Heroes of Law and Order*. Boston: Houghton Mifflin, 1918.

———. *Justice to All: The History of the Pennsylvania State Police*. Boston, Houghton Mifflin, 1920.

Miller, Joseph. *The Arizona Rangers*. New York: Hastings House, 1972.

Miller, Wilbur R. *Cops and Bobbies: Police Authority in New York and London, 1830–1870*. Chicago: University of Chicago Press, 1976.

Millspaugh, Arthur. *Crime Control by the National Government*. Washington, DC: Brookings, 1937.

Monroe, David G. *State and Provincial Police*. Evanston, IL: International Association of Chiefs of Police and Northwestern University Traffic Institute, 1941.

Moss, Stewart P. *Moss' Chicago Police Manual*. Chicago: T.H. Flood, 1923.

Mosse, George L., ed. *Police Forces in History*. Sage Readers in 20th Century History, vol. 2. London: Sage Publications, 1975.

Muller, Alix J. *History of the Police and Fire Departments of the Twin Cities*. Minneapolis: Minneapolis, St. Paul, American Land and Title Registration Association, 1899.

Murphy, Patrick V. *Commissioner: A View from the Top of American Law Enforcement*. New York: Simon & Schuster, 1977.

National Commission on Law Observance and Enforcement. *Wickersham Commission Reports*. 1931. Reprint. 14 vols. Montclair, NJ: Patterson Smith, 1968.

National Police Commission. *Official Proceedings of the National Police Convention*. 1871. Reprint. New York: Arno Press, 1971.

Ness, Eliot, and Oscar Fraley. *The Untouchables*. New York: Messner, 1957.

New Haven Police Mutual Aid Association. *History of the Department of Police Services of New Haven from 1639 to 1899*. New Haven: Police Mutual Aid Association, 1899.

New York State Police: The First Fifty Years, 1917–1967. Albany: New York State Police, 1967.

Niederhoffer, Arthur, and Abraham S. Blumberg. *Behind the Shield: The Police in Urban Society*. Garden City, NY: Anchor Books, 1969.

———. *The Ambivalent Force: Perspectives on the Police*. New York: Dryden Press, 1976.

Older, Fremont. *My Own Story*. New York: Macmillan, 1926.

Ottenberg, Miriam. *The Federal Investigators*. Englewood Cliffs, NJ: Prentice-Hall, 1962.

Paddock, William H. *History of the Police Service of Albany, from 1609 to 1902*. Albany, NY: Police Beneficiary Association, 1902.

Parker, Alfred E. *August Vollmer: Crime Fighter*. New York: Macmillan, 1961.

———. *The Berkeley Police Story*. Springfield, IL: Charles C. Thomas, 1972.

Peck, William F. *History of the Police Dept. of Rochester, New York, from the Earliest Times to May 1, 1903*. Rochester, NY: Police Benevolent Association, 1903.

Police in America. *Boston Police Debates: Selected Arguments*. 1863, 1869. Reprint. New York: Arno Press, 1971.

Police in America. *The Boston Police Strike: Two Reports*. 1920. Reprint. New York: Arno Press, 1971.

Police in America. Chamber of Commerce of the State of New York. *Committee on* the Police Problem. *Papers and Proceedings*. 1905. Reprint. New York: Arno Press, 1971.

Police in America. *Control of the Baltimore Police. Collected Reports.* 1860–1866. Reprint. New York: Arno Press, 1971.

Police in America. New York City Board of Aldermen. Special Committee to Investigate the Police Dept. *Police in New York City: An Investigation.* 1912–1913. Reprint. New York: Arno Press, 1971.

Police in America. Pennsylvania Federation of Labor. *The American Cossack: Pennsylvania State Federation of Labor.* Reprint. New York: Arno Press, 1971.

Police in America. U.S. Commission on Civil Rights. *Police and the Blacks: U.S. Civil Rights Commission Hearings.* 1961. Reprint. New York: Arno Press, 1971.

Police in America. U.S. Congress, Senate. Committee on Education and Labor. *Documents Relating to Intelligence Bureau or Red Squad of Los Angeles Police Department.* 1940. Reprint. New York: Arno Press, 1971.

Police in America. U.S. Congress, Senate. Committee on Education and Labor. *Private Police Systems.* 1939. Reprint. New York: Arno Press, 1971.

Police in America. U.S. Congress, Senate. Commitee on the District of Columbia. *Crime and Law Enforcement in the District of Columbia: Hearings and Report.* 1952. Reprint. New York: Arno Press, 1971.

Police in America. *Urban Police: Selected Surveys.* 1926–1946. Reprint. New York: Arno Press, 1971.

Post, Melville D. *The Man Hunters.* New York: J.H. Sears, 1926.

Powers, Edwin. *Crime and Punishment in Early Massachusetts.* Boston: Beacon Press, 1966.

Powers, Robert B. *Law Enforcement, Race Relations, 1930–1960: An Interview.* Berkeley: University of California, Bancroft Library, 1971.

Purvis, Melvin. *American Agent.* New York: Garden City, 1938.

———. *The Violent Years.* New York: Hillman, 1960.

Radano, Gene. *Stories Cops Only Tell Each Other.* New York: Stein & Day, 1974.

Raine, William M. *Famous Sheriffs and Western Outlaws.* Garden City, New York: Doubleday, 1929.

———. *Guns of the Frontier: The Story of How Law Came to the West.* Boston: Houghton Mifflin, 1940.

———. *Forty-Five Caliber Law: The Way of Life of the Frontier Peace Officer.* Evanston, IL: Row Peterson, 1941.

Reed, Lear B. *Human Wolves, Seventeen Years of War on Crime, in Which Is Told the Dramatic Story of the Rebuilding of Kansas City's Police Department.* Kansas City: Brown-White Lowell, 1941.

Regoli, Robert M. *Police in America.* Washington, DC: University Press of America, 1977.

Reiss, Albert J., Jr. *The Police and the Public.* New Haven: Yale University Press, 1971.

Reith, Charles. *The Blind Eye of History: A Study of the Origin of the Present Police Era.* London: Faber and Faber, 1952.

Report and Proceedings of the Senate Committee Appointed to Investigate the Police Department of the City of New York. (Lexow Committee) 5 vols. Albany: J.B. Lyons, 1895.

Repetto, Thomas A. *The Blue Parade.* New York: Free Press, 1978.

Reynolds, Quentin. *Headquarters.* New York: Harper, 1955.

Richardson, James F. *The New York Police: Colonial Times to 1901.* New York: Oxford University Press, 1970.

———. *Urban Police in the United States: A Brief History.* Port Washington, NY: Kennikat, 1974.

Robinson, C.D. *Legal Rights, Duties, and Liabilities of Criminal Justice Personnel: History and Analysis.* Springfield, IL: Charles C. Thomas, 1992.

Robinson, Louis N. *History and Organization of Criminal Statistics in the United States.* 1911. Reprint, Montclair, NJ: Patterson Smith, 1969.

Roe, George M. *Our Police: A History of the Cincinnatti Police Force, from the Earliest Period until the Present Day.* 1890. Reprint. New York: AMS Press, 1976.

Rubinstein, Jonathan. *City Police.* New York: Farrar, Strauss & Giroux, 1973.

Russell, Francis. *A City in Terror: 1919, the Boston Police Strike.* New York: Viking Press, 1975.

Sabbag, Robert. *Too Tough to Die: Down and Dangerous with the U.S. Marshals.* New York: Simon & Schuster, 1992.

Savage, Edward H. *Police Records and Recollections. Or, Boston, by Daylight and Gaslight for Two Hundred and Forty Years.* 1873. Reprint. Montclair, NJ: Patterson Smith, 1970.

Schmeckebier, Lawrence F. *Customs Service: Its History, Activities, and Organization.* 1924. Reprint. New York: AMS Press, 1974.

Schwartz, Richard, and Jerome Skolnick. *Society and Legal Order.* New York: Basic Books, 1970.

Schweppe, Emma. *The Fireman's and Patrolman's Unions in the City of New York.* New York: King's Crown Press, 1948.

Semmes, Raphael. *Crime and Punishment in Early Maryland.* Montclair, NJ: Patterson Smith, 1970.

Shalloo, Jeremiah P. *Private Police; with Special Reference to Pennsylvania.* Philadelphia: American Academy of Political and Social Science, 1933.

Shaw, Alonzo B. *Trials in Shadow Land: "Space" Stories of a Detective.* Columbus, OH: Hann, 1910.

Sherman, Lawrence. *Policing Domestic Violence.* New York: Free Press, 1992.

Shirley, Glenn. *Law West of Fort Smith: A History of Frontier Justice in the Indian Territory, 1834–1896.* Lincoln: University of Nebraska Press, 1969.

Siringo, Charles A. *A Cowboy Detective: A True Story of Twenty-Two Years with a World Famous Detective Agency.* New York: Ogilvie, 1912.

Skehan, James J. *Modern Police Work Including Detective Duty: A Book for Police Officers of All Ranks.* 2d rev. ed. New York: Francis M. Bausino, 1951.

Skolnick, Jerome H. *Justice Without Trial: Law Enforcement in Democratic Society.* New York: John Wiley and Sons, 1966.

Skolnick, Jerome H., and David H. Bayley. *The New Blue Line: Police Innovation in Six American Cities.* New York: Free Press, 1988.

Slovak, Jeffrey S. *Styles of Urban Policing: Organization, Environment, and Police Styles in Selected American Cities.* New York: New York University Press, 1988.

Smith, Bruce. *Chicago Police Problems.* Chicago: University of Chicago Press, 1931.

———. *The Baltimore Police Survey.* New York: Institute of Public Administration, 1941.

———. *The New Rochelle Police Survey.* New York: Institute of Public Administration, 1941.

———. *The State Police.* 1925. Reprint. Montclair, NJ: Patterson Smith, 1969.

Sparrow, Malcolm K., et al. *Beyond 911: A New Era for Policing.* New York: Basic Books, 1990.

Sprogle, Howard O. *The Philadelphia Police, Past and Present.* 1887. Reprint. New York: Arno Press, 1971.

Stead, Philip J. *Pioneers in Policing.* Montclair, NJ: Patterson Smith, 1977.

Thorwald, Jurgen. *The Century of the Detective.* New York: Harcourt, 1965.

———. *Crime and Science: The New Frontier in Criminology.* New York: Harcourt, 1967.

Tilghman, Zoe. *Marshall of the Last Frontier.* Glendale, CA: A.H. Clark, 1964.

Tillard, John N. *Memories of a Track-Sore Copper.* Altoona, PA: Times Tribune, 1927.

Tonry, Michael, and Norval Morris, eds. *Modern Policing.* Vol. 15. Chicago: University of Chicago Press, 1992.

Turner, William W. *The Police Establishment.* New York: Putnam, 1968.

U.S. Marshals Service. *Marshal: The Story of the U.S. Marshals Service.* New York: Dialogue Systems, 1991.

U.S. National Advisory Commission on Criminal Justice Standards and Goals. *Police.* Washington, DC: Government Printing Office, 1973.

U.S. President's Commission on Law Enforcement and Administration of Justice. *The Police and the Community: The Dynamics of Their Relationship in a Changing Society.* 2 vols. Washington, DC: Government Printing Office, 1967.

———. *Task Force Report: Science and Technology.* Washington, DC: Government Printing Office, 1967.

Valentine, Lewis J. *Night Stick: The Autobiography of Lewis J. Valentine, Former Police Commissioner of New York.* New York: Dial Press, 1947.

Vollmer, August. *Crime, Crooks and Cops.* New York: Funk & Wagnalls, 1937.

———. *Police in Modern Society.* 1936. Reprint. Washington, DC: Consortium Press, 1969.

Vollmer, August, and Alfred E. Parker. *Crime and the State Police.* Berkeley: University of California Press, 1935.

Walker, Samuel. *A Critical History of Police Reform: The Emergence of Professionalism*. Lexington, MA: Heath, 1977.

———. *The Police in America: An Introduction*. New York: McGraw-Hill, 1983.

Walling, George W. *Recollections of a New York Chief of Police*. 1890. Reprint. Montclair, NJ: Patterson Smith, 1972.

Watters, Pat, and Stephen Gillers, eds. *Investigating the FBI*. Garden City, NY: Doubleday, 1973.

Weaver, Thomas S. *Historical Sketch of the Police Service of Hartford from 1636 to 1801, from Authoritative Sources*. Hartford, CT: Hartford Police Mutual Aid Association, 1901.

Webb, Walter P. *Texas Rangers*. Austin: University of Texas Press, 1965.

Wegener, W. Fred, and Harry W. More. *Behavioral Police Management*. New York: Macmillan, 1992.

Whitaker, John C. *History of the Police Department of Dayton, Ohio*. Dayton, OH: Dayton Police Department, 1907.

White, Leslie T. *Me, Detective*. New York: Harcourt Brace, 1936.

Whitehead, Don. *The FBI Story*. New York: Random House, 1956.

Whitlock, Brand. *On the Enforcement of Law in Cities*. 1913. Reprint. Montclair, NJ: Patterson Smith, 1969.

Wiebe, Robert H. *The Search for Order: 1877–1920*. New York: Hill and Wang, 1967.

Wilkie, Donald W. *American Secret Service Agent*. New York: F.A. Stokes, 1934.

Willemse, Cornelius W. *A Cop Remembers*. New York: F.P. Dutton, 1933.

Wilson, Frank J., and Beth Day. *Special Agent*. New York: Holt, Rinehart, and Winston, 1965.

Wilson, James Q. *Varieties of Police Behavior: The Management of Law and Order in Eight Communities*. Cambridge, MA: Harvard University Press, 1968.

Wilson, Orlando W., and Roy C. McLaren. *Police Administration*. 4th ed. New York: McGraw-Hill, 1977.

Woodiwiss, Michael. *Crime, Crusades, and Corruption: Prohibitions in the United States, 1900–1987*. Totowa, NJ: Barnes & Noble Books, 1988.

Woods, Arthur. *Crime Prevention*. Princeton: Princeton University Press, 1918.

———. *Policemen and Public*. New Haven, CT: Yale University Press, 1919.

Woodward, P.N. *Secret Service of the Post Office Department*. 1876. Reprint. Swengel, PA: Reiner, 1976.

Dissertations

Anderson, Celestine E. "The Invention of the 'Professional' Municipal Police: The Case of Cincinnati, 1788–1900." Ph.D. diss., University of Cincinnati, 1979.

Bacon, Selden D. "The Early Development of American Municipal Police: A Study of the Evolution of Formal Controls in a Changing Society." 2 vols. Ph.D. diss., Yale University, 1939.

Belgum, Donald T. "The Anatomy of State Police Power, 1900–1938." Ph.D. diss., University of Minnesota, 1972.

Berney, Donald W. "Law and Order Politics: A History and Role Analysis of Police Officer Organizations." Ph.D. diss., University of Washington, 1971.

Cei, Louis B. "Law Enforcement in Richmond: A History of Police Community Relations, 1737–1974." Ph.D. diss., Florida State University, 1975.

Furtek, Joanne. "A Social History of Crime and Law Enforcement in the United States and Western Europe, 1630–1980." Ph.D. diss., Carnegie-Mellon University, 1984.

Goodbody, William L. "The Thin Blue Line for Social Service: An Analysis of the History, Problems, and Innovations of N.Y.C.P.D. Police Human Relations Training." Ph.D. diss., Boston College, 1992.

Greenberg, Douglas. "Crime and Law Enforcement in the Colony of New York, 1691–1776." Ph.D. diss., Cornell University, 1976.

Haring, Sidney, L. "The Buffalo Police, 1872–1915: Industrialization, Social Unrest, and the Development of the Police Institution." Ph.D. diss., University of Wisconsin at Madison, 1976.

Johnson, David R. "The Search for an Urban Discipline: Police Reform as a Response to Crime in American Cities, 1800–1875." Ph.D. diss., University of Chicago, 1972.

Johnson, Harold G. "The History of Mandatory Police Training in Illinois, Since

1955, and Recommendations for the Future." Ph.D. diss., Saint Louis University, 1983.

Jones, Marshall E. "A History of the Massachusetts State Police Force as a Changing Social Organization." Ph.D. diss., Harvard University, 1936.

Jordan, Kevin E. "Ideology and the Coming of Professionalism: American Urban Police in the 1920's and 1930's." Ph.D. diss., University of New Jersey, 1972.

Ketcham, George A. "Municipal Police Reform: A Comparative Study of Law Enforcement in Cincinnati, Chicago, New Orleans, New York, and St. Louis, 1844–1877." Ph.D. diss., University of Missouri at Columbia, 1967.

Lane, Roger. "The Police of Boston, 1822–1885." Ph.D. diss., Harvard University, 1963.

Leonard, Vivian A. "A Theory of Police Organization and Administration." Ph.D. diss., Ohio State University, 1949.

Levett, Allan E. "Centralization of City Police in the Nineteenth Century United States." Ph.D. diss., University of Michigan, 1975.

Levine, Jerald E. "Police, Parties, and Polity: The Bureaucratization, Unionization, and Professionalization of the New York City Police, 1870–1917." Ph.D. diss., University of Wisconsin, 1971.

Maniha, John K. "The Mobility of Elites in a Bureaucratizing Organization: The St. Louis Police Department, 1861–1961." Ph.D. diss., University of Michigan, 1970.

Marchiafava, Louis I. "Institutional and Legal Aspects of the Growth of Professional Urban Police Service: The Houston Experience, 1878–1948." Ph.D. diss., Rice University, 1976.

Miller, Frederic C. "History, Organization and Methods of the Police." Ph.D. diss., University of Minnesota, 1908.

Myers, Howard B. "The Policing of Labor Disputes in Chicago: A Case Study." Ph.D. diss., University of Chicago, 1929.

Reichard, Maximilian I. "The Origins of Urban Police: Freedom and Order in Antebellum St. Louis." Ph.D. diss., Washington University, 1975.

Reppeto, Thomas A. "Changing the System: Models of Municipal Police Organization." Ph.D. diss., Harvard University, 1970.

Richardson, James F. "The History of Police Protection in New York City, 1800–1870." Ph.D. diss., New York University, 1961.

Rider, Eugene F. "The Denver Police Department: An Administrative, Organizational, and Operational History, 1858–1905." Ph.D. diss., University of Denver, 1971.

Rousey, Dennis C. "The New Orleans Police, 1805–1889: A Social History." Ph.D. diss., Cornell University, 1978.

Swart, Stanley L. "The Development of State-Level Police Activity in Ohio, 1820–1928." Ph.D. diss., Northwestern University, 1974.

Tracy, Charles F. "The Police of Portland, 1840–1870." Ph.D. diss., University of California at Berkeley, 1978.

Zenk, Gordon K. "Project Search: A Political History of the Development of a National Computerized Criminal History System." Ph.D. diss., University of California at Santa Barbara, 1976.

Articles

American Bar Association. "Committee on Lawless Enforcement of Law. Report." *American Journal of Police Science* 1(6) (December 1930): 574–93.

Baker, Newman F. "One Hundred Questions and Answers on Traffic Law Enforcement." *Journal of Criminal Law and Criminology* 30 (November 1939): 546–67.

Bellman, Arthur. "Police Service Rating Scale." *Journal of Criminal Law and Criminology* 26 (May 1935): 74–114.

Bishop, L.V., and R.A. Harvie. "Law and Order in Beaverhead County, Montana, 1895–1916." *Journal of Police Science and Administration* 8(2) (1980): 173–82.

Bittner, Egon. "The Rise and Fall of the Thin Blue Line." *Reviews in American History* 6(3) (1978): 421–28.

Bopp, William J. "A Summary of American Police Administration in the Twentieth Century." *Police Journal* 57(3) (1984): 208–15.

Burdick, Charles K. "Meaning of Police Power." *North American Review* 214 (August 1921): 158–65.

Burns, R. Vernon. "History of the New York

Police Department." *Police Journal* 18(6) (July 1931): 16–17, 21.

Cameron, Diane M. "Historical Perspective on Urban Police." *Journal of Urban History* 5(1) (1978): 125–32.

Carr-Saunders, Alexander M. "Court System: The Police Courts." *Political Quarterly* 5 (January 1934): 83–91.

Columbus, E.G. "Automatic Data Processing: A Practical Police Tool." 9 parts in *Police Chief* 34 nos. 1–9 (January–September 1967).

Crawley, Frederick J. "Observations on American Police Systems." *Journal of Criminal Law and Criminology* 20 (August 1929): 167–78.

Cross, William T. "Jails, Lockups and Police Stations." *Journal of the American Institute of Criminal Law and Criminology* 7 (September 1916): 379–92.

Darwin, Maud. "Policewomen: Their Work in America." *Nineteenth Century* 75 (June 1914): 1371–77.

DuBois, Philip H., and Robert I. Watson. "Selection of Patrolmen." *Journal of Applied Psychology* 34 (April 1950): 90–95.

Fairlie, John A. "Police Administration." *Political Science Quarterly* 16 (March 1901): 1–23.

Gladis, Stephen D. "Promises Kept and a Promising Future: The FBI National Academy's First 50 Years." *FBI Law Enforcement Bulletin* 54(7) (1985): 2–9.

Grimshaw, Allen D. "Actions of Police and the Military in American Race Riots." *Phylon* 24 (Fall 1963): 271–89.

Hahn, Harlan, ed. "Police and Society." *American Behavioral Scientist* 13(5, 6) (May–August 1970): entire issues.

Hamilton, Lander C. "A Brief History of Police: Collected Essays on the Police Function." *Police* 13 (November–December 1968): 69–75.

Hatton, Augustus R. "Control of Police." *National Conference for Good City Government, Proceedings* (1909): 157–71.

Kuykendall, Jack. "The Municipal Police Detective: An Historical Analysis." *Criminology* 24 (February 1986): 175–201.

Lambourne, G.T.C. "A Brief History of Fingerprints." *Journal of Forensic Sciences Society* 17(2–3) (1977): 95–98.

Lee, Edward L. "An Overview of American Police History." *Police Chief* 38 (October 1971): 51–52, 257–59.

MacNamara, Donal E.J. "American Police Administration at Mid-Century." *Public Administration Review* 10(3) (1950): 181–89.

Mallonee, L. Dee. "Police Regulations—Essentials of Unconstitutionality." *American Law Review* 51 (March 1917): 187–202.

Martin, Edward M. "Experiment in New Methods of Selecting Policemen." *National Municipal Review* 12 (November 1923): 671–81.

Matthews, Franklin. "Characters of the American Police." *World's Work* 2 (October 1901): 1314–19.

Monkkonen, Eric H. "From Cop History to Social History: The Significance of the Police in American History." *Journal of Social History* 15(4) (1982): 575–91.

Moore, Mark H., and George L. Kelling. " 'To Serve and Protect': Learning from Police History." *Public Interest* 70 (1983): 49–65.

Moss, Frank. "Police Corruption and the Nation." *North American Review* 173 (October 1901): 470–80.

Murphy, Patrick V. "The Development of the Urban Police." *Current History* 70 (1976): 245–48, 272.

Nielson, R.C. "Equal Time for Unequal History. Police Training in Black American History." *Police Chief* 41(8) (1974): 59–61.

O'Brien, Daniel L. "Half-Century Mark for the Illinois State Police: 50-Year Chronicle of Progress." *Police Chief* 39 (June 1972): 62–70, 72.

Parratt, Spencer D. "Critique of the Bellman Police Service Rating Scale." *Journal of Criminal Law and Criminology* 27 (March 1937): 895–905. (See *Bellman* entry.)

———. "Scale to Measure Effectiveness of Police Functioning." *Journal of Criminal Law and Criminology* 28 (January 1938): 739–56.

Pigeon, Helen D. "Women's Era in the Police Department." *American Academy of Political and Social Science, Annals* 143 (May 1929): 249–54.

"Police and Street Mileage Statistics of 167 American Cities." *American City* 32 (June 1925): 633–34.

"Police Education and Training." *Police*

Chief 37 (August 1970): entire issue.

"Police Problems in Cities." *National Conference for Good City Government, Proceedings* (1909): 53–63.

"Police Statistics of 204 Cities." *American City* 14 (January 1916): 14+.

Puttkammer, Ernst W. "Organization of a State Police." *Journal of Criminal Law and Criminology* 26 (January 1936): 727–40.

Rapport, Victor A. "Unified State-Wide Police Force." *Journal of Criminal Law and Criminology* 30 (January 1940): 706–11.

Ray, Perley, O. "Metropolitan and State Police." *Journal of the American Institute of Criminal Law and Criminology* 11 (November 1920): 453–67.

Richardson, James F. "Police History: The Search for Legitimacy." *Journal of Urban History* 6(2) (1980): 231–46.

Rigler, Erik. "Frontier Justice in the Days Before NCIC." *FBI Law Enforcement Bulletin* 54 (July 1985): 17–22.

"Salaries of Policemen and Firemen: A Quarter Century Review." *Monthly Labor Review* 70 (June 1950): 633–34.

Sellin, Thorsten, ed. "The Police and the Crime Problem." *American Academy of Political and Social Science, Annals* 146 (November 1929): entire issue.

Sherman, Lawrence W. "Sociology and the Social Reform of the American Police, 1950–1973." *Journal of Police Science and Administration* 2 (September 1974): 255–62.

Smith, Bruce. "Politics and Law Enforcement." *American Academy of Political and Social Science* 169 (September 1933): 67–74.

———. "Enforcement of the Criminal Law," *American Academy of Political and Social Science* 217 (September 1941): 12–18.

———. "Great Years of American Police Development." *Journal of Criminal Law and Criminology* 34 (July 1943): 127–34.

———, ed. "New Goals in Police Management." *American Academy of Political and Social Science, Annals* 291 (January 1954): 1–158.

Smith, Bruce, et al. "What the Depression Has Done to Police Service." *Public Management* 16 (March 1934): 67–72.

Stinson, Steven A. "The Federal Bureau of Investigation: Its History, Organization, Functions and Publications." *Government Publications Review* 6(3) (1979): 213–40.

Van Winkle, Mina C. "Standardization of the Aims and Methods of the Work of Police-women." *National Conference of Social Work, Proceedings* (1920): 151–54.

Vollmer, August. "Practical Methods for Selecting Policemen." *Journal of the American Institute of Criminal Law and Criminology* 11 (February 1921): 571–81.

———. "Aims and Ideals of the Police." *Journal of the American Institute of Criminal Law and Criminology* 13 (August 1922): 251–57.

———. "Prevention and Detection of Crime as Viewed by a Police Officer." *American Academy of Political and Social Science, Annals* 125 (May 1926): 148–53.

———. "Police Progress in the Past Twenty-Five Years." *Journal of Criminal Law and Criminology* 24 (May 1933): 161–75.

Vollmer, August, and Albert Schneider. "School for Police as Planned at Berkeley." *Journal of the American Institute of Criminal Law and Criminology* 7 (March 1917): 877–98.

Walbrook, Henry M. "Women Police and Their Work." *Nineteenth Century and After* 85 (February 1919): 377–82.

Walton, Frank E. "Selective Distribution of Police Patrol Force: History, Current Practices, Recommendations." *Journal of Criminal Law* 49 (July–August 1958): 165–71; 49 (November–December 1958): 379–90.

Watts, Eugene J. "Police in Atlanta, 1890–1905." *Journal of Southern History* 39 (May 1973): 165–82.

Wells, Alice. "Policewomen Movement, Present Status and Future Needs." *Conference of Charities and Corrections, National Proceedings* (1916): 547–54.

Westley, William A. "Violence and the Police." *American Journal of Sociology* 59 (July 1953): 34–41.

Wickersham, George W. "Recent Extensions of the State Police Power." *American Law Review* 54 (November 1920): 801–31.

Wilson, Orlando W. "Picking and Training Police and Traffic Officers." *American City* 42 (May 1930): 114–18.

General Index

Accidental death, 3–4
Accidents, traffic. *See* Traffic services
Administration, 9–14, 32–33, 210, 381–383, 406–409, 478–480, 537, 599, 612, 637, 731–734. *See also* Organizational structure
Affirmative action, 509, 512
Age and crime, 14–21
Age Discrimination in Employment Act, 511
AIDS, 806
Air Force Office of Special Investigations, 426
Air Force Security Police, 425
Albert, Prince of Monaco, 389
Alcoholism, 737. *See also* Stress
Allan, Emilie Anderson, contributor, "Age and Crime," 14–21, and "Gender and Crime," 334–341
Alpert, Geoffrey P., contributor, "Multi-Ethnic Communities: Interactive Model," 436–440, and "Police Pursuit," 599–609
American Academy of Forensic Sciences, 324
American Bar Association Project on Standards for Criminal Justice (1972), 245
American Federation of Police, 598
American Federation of State, County and Municipal Employees, 795
American Indian Police, 815
The American Jury, 126
American Social Hygiene Association, 807
American Society of Criminology, 812
Americans with Disabilities Act, 511, 523–524, 675
Andersen, Austin A., contributor, "Transnational Crimes," 783–786
Anderson, Malcolm, contributor, "International Police Cooperation, 386–394
Anomie, 626
Anson, Richard H. and Nancy C. Anson, contributors, "Stress," 735–740
Anthropometry, 40
Anti-Defamation League, 349–350, 353
Armor, soft body, 310
Armstrong, David A., contributor, "Firearms: History," 307–311
Army Criminal Investigation Command, 426

Arrest, 4, 15–20, 21–26, 154–155, 163, 188, 207–208, 226–229, 246, 299–301, 334, 338–339, 397–399, 403, 507, 568, 688, 696, 704–710, 750–752
Arson investigation, 26–28
Artificial intelligence, 28–34
Assaults in jail, 399–403
Assaults on police officers, 34–37
Assessment centers, 37–39, 514–515
Asset forfeiture, 174, 243, 430, 692–694, 703, 784–785, 798
Attitude toward police (ATP), 67–75
Augustus, John, 657
Austin, Stephen F., 771–772
Authoritarianism, 481–483, 670–671, 749
Automated fingerprint identification system, 110, 171–172
Automatic vehicle location system, 113
Ayers, Richard M., contributor, "Operational Costs," 478–480

Baby boom, 19
Bailey, F. Lee, 125
Baker, J. Stannard, 469
Baldwin, Lola, 628
Baltimore County Police Department, 108
Baltimore Police Department, 443
Barnard, Chester, 541
Barr, Attorney General William P., 173–174
Batons, types of, 466–467
Bayley, David H., contributor, "Community-Oriented Policing: International," 98–103
Becker, Donald C., contributor, "Private Security," 650–656
Belknap, Joanne, contributor, "Domestic Violence," 223–231
Belli, Melvin, 125
Beretta pistol, 309
Berkeley Police Department. *See* Vollmer, August
Bertillon, Alphonse, 40
Bertillon system, 40–41, 322, 411
Bieck, William H., contributor, "Crime Analysis," 127–138

Birmingham Seven, 45

Blak, Richard A., contributor, "Critical Incidents," 183–185

Blankenship, Michael B., contributor, "Political Control of Police," 637–639

Blood sample, 315

Bloss, William P., contributor, "Police Misconduct: The Rodney King Incident," 582–588

Blue flu, 744

Blue lies, 552–553

Blumberg, Mark, contributor, "Deadly Force: Fleeing-Felon Doctrine," 197–200

Bobbies, 465, 662

Bonaparte, Attorney General Charles, 278

Bonnie and Clyde, 773

Booking process, 24

Bordner, Diane C., contributor, "Campus Police," 50–52

Boston Police Department, 189–190, 308

Boston Police Strike of 1919, 189–190, 745, 746

Bouquard, Thomas J., contributor, "Arson Investigation," 26–28

Bouza, Anthony, 227, 541, 543, contributor, "Drug Enforcement," 236–241, and "Inspection," 381–383

Bow Street Runners, 371, 555

Bracey, Dorothy, contributor, "Police Corruption," 545–549

Brandl, Steven G., contributor, "Criminal Investigation: Outcomes," 162–173

Bray, Dr. Douglas, 37

Brink, Washington P., 651

British Crime Surveys, 44

British police acts, 41–42

British policing, 41–48, 473, 487. *See also* London Metropolitan Police; Peel, Sir Robert

Brockway, Zebulon, 658

Brodrick, Commissioner Vincent, 81

Brown, Chief Lee P., 379–380, 454

Brown, Michael F., contributor, "Criminal Informants," 157–160

Brussel, Dr. James, 476

Buckley, Joseph B., III, contributor, "Interrogation," 394–396

Budgeting. *See* Police budgeting

Bufe, Noel C., contributor, "Traffic Services," 776–782

Bulletins, police department, 129, 134–135

Bullets, types of, 466–467

Burbank (Chicago) plan, 122

Burkoff, John M., contributor, "Exclusionary Rules," 262–267

Burnout, 595, 717–720, 738

Burns, William John, biography of, 48–49

Burrows, James W., contributor, "Property Crime Program," 663–666

Bush, President George, 8, 173–174, 238, 805

"buy-bust-flip" technique, 159, 441

Byrnes, Thomas, 205

Caldwell, Harry M., contributor, "Search and Seizure," 704–711

California Commission on Peace Officer Standards and Training, 719–720

California Highway Patrol, 522, 603, 815

Call box, 499–500

Campus police, 50–52, 723–724

Canine unit, 52–55, 502

Capital punishment, 7, 55–58, 65, 174, 197; police attitude toward, 56–57

Carfield, William E., contributor, "Horse-Mounted Police," 371–373

Carter, David L., contributor, "Youth Gangs: Definition," 827–828

Case attrition, 166

Case management, 58–60

Case-processing costs, 61–63

Central Florida Environmental Protection Forum, 261

Central Intelligence Agency, 37

Chaiken, Jan and Marcia Chaiken, contributors, "Multijurisdictional Drug Law Enforcement," 440–444

Chain of custody, 139, 142, 314

Chapman, Samuel, contributor, "Accidental Death/ Murder of Police Officers," 3–8, "Assaults on Police Officers," 34–37, and "Canine Unit," 52–55

Chicago Crime Commission (1919), 280

Chicago Police Department, 520, 825–826

Child abuse investigation, 63–67, 756

Christopher Commission (1991), 77, 582–588

Cincinnati Police Department, 308

Citation programs, 398

Citizen advisory councils, 435

Citizen attitudes and complaints, 67–80, 434, 592, 587, 614–619

Civil Rights Act of 1964, 38, 213–214, 271–272, 508–509, 512

Civil Rights Act of 1991, 520–521, 523

Civil Rights, section 1983, 571–574, 584

Civil service, 11

Civil unrest, 186–189

Civilian review, 73, 80–83, 682

Civilianization, 620

Classical approach to police administration, 12–13

Clearance rates, 28, 163, 205, 246, 316

Cleveland Police Department, 327

Cobb, Gail, 7

Code of ethics, 83–94, 547, 549–553, 622

Code of silence, 94, 622

Colby, Peter W., contributor, "Contract Police," 120–122

Colden, Dr. Cadwallader, 318

Collective bargaining, 510, 523, 745

Color of law, 572

Colorado State Patrol, 479

Colquhoun, Patrick, 291, 293

Colt revolver, 307

Colt, Samuel, 307

Index of Legal Cases